Birnbaum's United States for Business Travelers

A BIRNBAUM TRAVEL GUIDE

Alexandra Mayes Birnbaum
EDITORIAL CONSULTANT

Lois Spritzer
Editorial Director

Laura L. Brengelman
Managing Editor

Mary Callahan
Senior Editor

David Appell
Patricia Canole
Gene Gold
Jill Kadetsky
Susan McClung
Associate Editors

HarperPerennial
A Division of HarperCollinsPublishers

To Stephen, who merely made all this possible.

BIRNBAUM'S UNITED STATES FOR BUSINESS TRAVELERS 95. Copyright © 1995 by HarperCollins Publishers. All rights reserved. Printed in the United States of America. No part of this book may be used or reproduced in any manner whatsoever without written permission except in the case of brief quotations embodied in critical articles and reviews. For information address Harper-Collins*Publishers*, 10 East 53rd Street, New York, NY 10022.

FIRST EDITION

ISSN 0749-2561 (Birnbaum Travel Guides)
ISSN 0883-251X (United States for Business Travelers)
ISBN 0-06-278175-8 (pbk.)

95 96 97 ❖/CW 5 4 3 2 1

Cover design © Drenttel Doyle Partners

BIRNBAUM TRAVEL GUIDES

Bahamas, and Turks & Caicos
Berlin
Bermuda
Boston
Canada
Cancun, Cozumel & Isla Mujeres
Caribbean
Chicago
Country Inns and Back Roads
Disneyland
Eastern Europe
Europe
Europe for Business Travelers
France
Germany
Great Britain
Hawaii
Ireland
Italy
London
Los Angeles
Mexico
Miami & Ft. Lauderdale
Montreal & Quebec City
New Orleans
New York
Paris
Portugal
Rome
San Francisco
Santa Fe & Taos
South America
Spain
United States
United States for Business Travelers
Walt Disney World
Walt Disney World for Kids, By Kids
Washington, DC

Contributing Editors

Lawrence Baker
Margaret E. Beasley
Gene Bourg
Bob Butler
Anne Christopherson
Dan Christopherson
James Cortese
Scott Craven
Teresa Day
Brenda Fine
Robert Franklin
Connie Goddard
Richard Harris
David Hartley
Rosemary Peters Hinkle
Martin Hintz
Bob Hoover
Elliot S. Krane
Wendy Lefkon
Melanie Menagh
Stephen Mills
Elise Nakhnikian
Anita Peltonen
Patti Covello Pietschmann
Grace Renshaw
June Naylor Rodriguez
William Schemmel
Patricia Schultz
Allan Seiden
Laurie S. Senz
Susan C. Shipman
Tracy A. Smith
Molly Arost Staub
Janet Steinberg
Rick Sylvain
Warren Thompson
Peter Tietjen
Ginny Turner
Tom Weiner
Loralee Wenger
Leslie Westbrook
Don Woodward
Christine Zust

Maps

Mark Carlson
Susan Carlson
B. Andrew Mudryk
Paul J. Pugliese
Mark Stein Studios

Contents

Foreword...vii

Atlanta...3
Baltimore...24
Boston...40
Charleston, South Carolina...89
Chicago...102
Cincinnati...150
Cleveland...162
Dallas...176
Denver...198
Detroit...211
Ft. Lauderdale...227
Ft. Worth...253
Hartford...268
Honolulu...281
Houston...317
Indianapolis...332
Kansas City, Missouri...345
Las Vegas...357
Los Angeles...379
Louisville...425
Memphis...437

Miami–Miami Beach...449
Milwaukee...483
Minneapolis–St. Paul...496
Nashville...514
New Haven...528
New Orleans...539
New York City...586
Orlando...667
Philadelphia...685
Phoenix...707
Pittsburgh...727
Portland, Oregon...741
St. Louis...757
Salt Lake City...775
San Antonio...787
San Diego...805
San Francisco...831
Santa Fe...871
Savannah...896
Seattle...909
Washington, DC...925

Index...965

Foreword

If there's one curse common to all business travelers, it's got to be that oft-heard comment of non-traveling associates that goes, "Oh, you've got such a great job; you get to see all of the country/continent/world." Envy seeps through every syllable; the only problem is that this perception is almost entirely false.

Anyone who has ever been on the road for business—whether the territory covered domestic or international destinations—knows that jet planes long ago eliminated what little romance ever existed in connection with on-the-job travel. Schedules are more hectic and compressed, so it's hardly unusual to hear about a busy executive taking advantage of the differences between time zones by leaving New York at 5 o'clock in the afternoon for an 8 PM dinner in Los Angeles, then catching the "Red Eye" back to New York to be at a mid-Manhattan desk by 9 AM the next day. It may sound romantic in the telling, but it's more often the case that travelers arrive feeling stiff and exhausted—as though they've been shipped home in a plain white envelope.

Even for a business traveler who actually gets to spend the night in an unfamiliar city, the thought of really looking around is seldom even considered. Reliable local information is usually notable by its absence, and while the busy business traveler carries a briefcase full of important papers, these documents rarely include any information whatever about local life and environment. There's nothing about an especially evocative downtown restaurant, or an offbeat nearby theater, or a perfect site from which to view a unique panorama of the cityscape. More often, the business traveler moves from airport to taxi to meeting to hotel, feet seldom touching the ground, and the only non-commercial human contact is an occasional monosyllabic exchange with a room-service waiter.

Contemporary business travel schedules are understandably tight, but there's often a bit of spare time for working out, taking a peek at a local landmark, or savoring a regional delicacy. It makes all the difference between having actually *been* to a city or merely having passed through. Not knowing a city can make awesome endeavors out of otherwise minor chores. Sending a package across town can suddenly seem the equivalent of scaling Everest, while getting a page translated into (or out of) a foreign language borders on the impossible.

The purpose of this special guide for the business traveler is, therefore, to eliminate such frustrations, as well as to give an often harried and harassed stranger a satisfying glimpse of what various cities have to offer—beyond boardrooms and sales calls. We have organized our material into the most manageable size and format, eliminating superfluous data in favor of succinct descriptions of what we think is best and really worth seeing and doing.

Let me point out that every good travel guide is a living enterprise; that is, no part of this text is in any way cast in bronze. In each annual revision, we refine, expand, and further hone all our material to serve your needs even better. To this end, no contribution is of greater value to us than your reaction to what we have written as well as information reflecting your experiences while trying our suggestions.

We sincerely hope to hear from you, and ask that you address your letters to 10 E. 53rd St., New York, NY 10022.

Alexandra Mayes Birnbaum

ALEXANDRA MAYES BIRNBAUM, editorial consultant to the *Birnbaum Travel Guides*, worked with her late husband, Stephen Birnbaum, as co-editor of the series. She has been a world traveler since childhood and is known for her travel reports on radio on what's hot and what's not.

Birnbaum's United States for Business Travelers 95

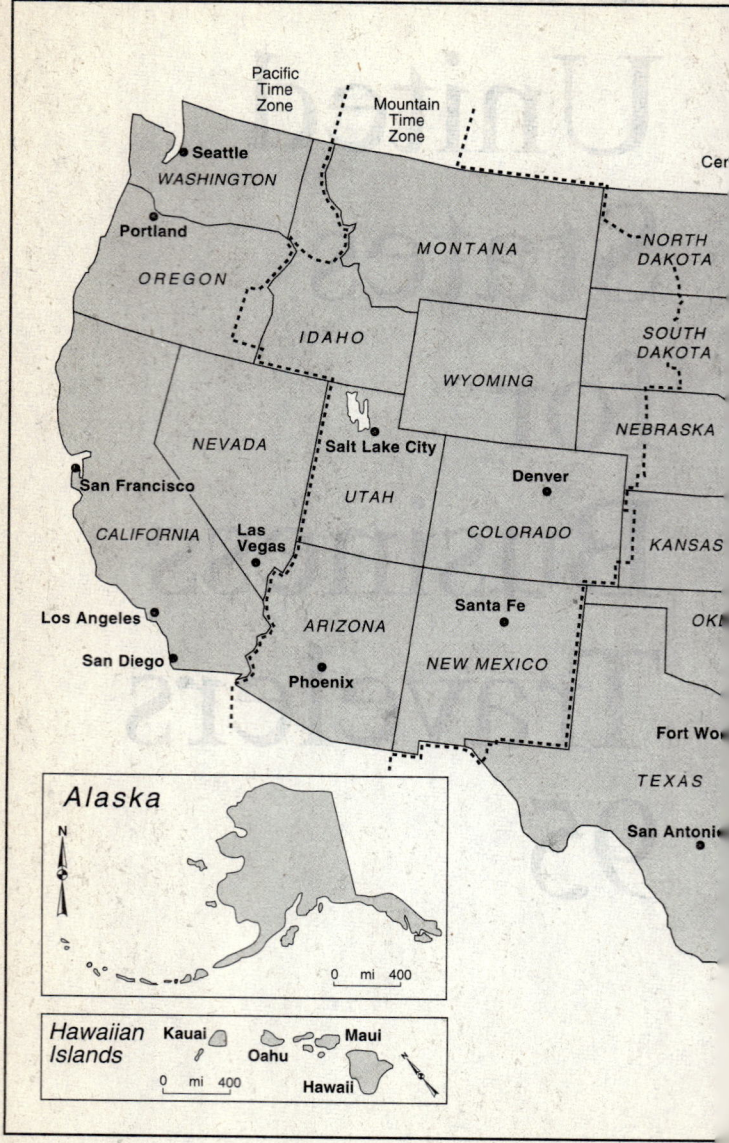

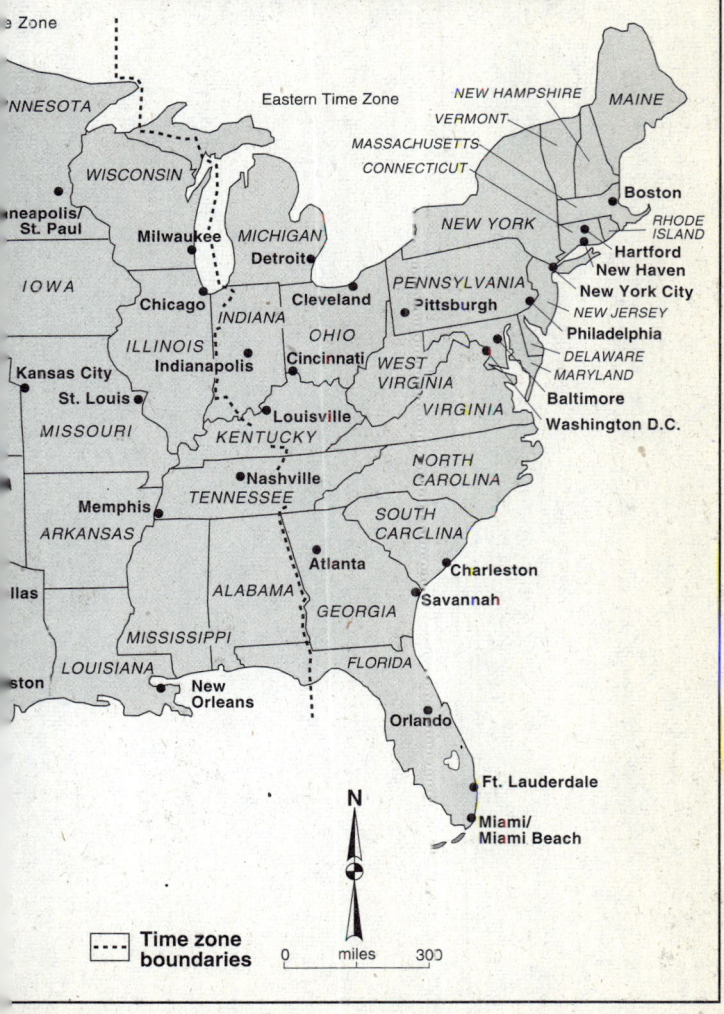

Atlanta

At-a-Glance

SEEING THE CITY

The view from the revolving *Sun Dial* restaurant on the 73rd floor of the *Westin Peachtree Plaza* hotel (see *Checking In*) is spectacular. On a clear day, your eye sweeps from the planes arriving and taking off at *Hartsfield International Airport* to the Blue Ridge Mountains. The *Sun Dial* can be reached only by an 80-second ride in one of the two glass elevators that skim up and down the outside of the building. You will have to order something to spend any time there; reservations advised. Peachtree St. at International Blvd. (phone: 589-7506).

SPECIAL PLACES

You can walk around downtown Atlanta without much difficulty, but be warned, the streets aren't laid out in an orderly grid. They roughly follow the paths of extinct rail lines, because the early streets ran parallel to the old tracks. As a result, visitors become confused as much by the erratic, tangled web pattern as by the fact that at least half the street names seem to include the words "Peachtree," "Circle," or "Hills." To add to the confusion, there are a number of streets whose names change at least once as you travel their length. The good news is that *MARTA*, the public transportation system, is excellent, especially if you are downtown or near Peachtree Street (see *Getting Around*).

DOWNTOWN

PEACHTREE CENTER Designed by celebrated local architect John Portman, this contemporary complex is the heart of modern Atlanta. Included here are several office towers; the *Atlanta Merchandise Mart* and *Apparel Mart;* and the *Marriott Marquis, Hyatt Regency,* and *Westin Peachtree Plaza* hotels, all linked by aerial skyways and landscaped plazas. The three-story *Peachtree Center Gallery* offers a variety of shopping, dining, and entertainment options. *MARTA's Peachtree Center* rapid-rail station is also part of the complex.

WOODRUFF PARK A few blocks south of *Peachtree Center,* this park is a gift from Atlanta's best-known benefactor, the late Coca-Cola millionaire Robert W. Woodruff, whose generosity has done more to change the face of the city than cosmetic surgery has done for Hollywood. (*Emory University*'s medical school is another beneficiary of his largesse.) At lunch, crowds of office workers, street people, wandering preachers, and Hare Krishnas swarm into the park. Grab a hot dog or a plate of shrimp fried rice at *Tokyo Shapiro's* (across from the park at 62 Peachtree St.) and settle down on the grass. At the junction of Auburn Ave. and Peachtree, Edgewood, and Pryor Sts.

APEX MUSEUM (AFRICAN-AMERICAN PANORAMIC EXPERIENCE MUSEUM) An excellent introduction to the neighboring Martin Luther King Jr. National

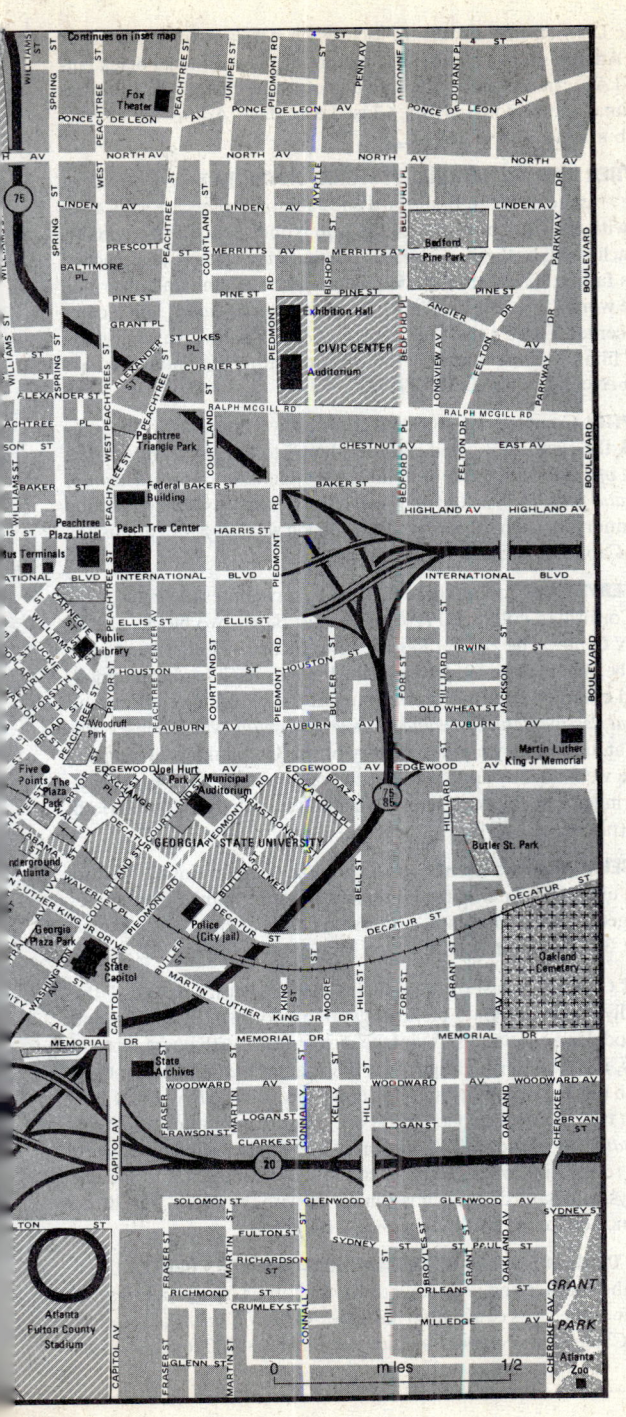

Historic District, this institution focuses on African-American art as well as Atlanta's black history. Permanent displays on local black culture and African arts and crafts are augmented by changing exhibitions by national and regional artists. Closed Mondays. Admission charge. 135 Auburn Ave. (phone: 521-2739).

MARTIN LUTHER KING JR. NATIONAL HISTORIC DISTRICT On five blocks of Auburn Avenue between Boulevard and Jackson Streets are sites associated with the life and times of the late Nobel Peace Prize winner. These include his birthplace; *Ebenezer Baptist Church,* where he preached with his father; his tomb, guarded by an eternal flame and inscribed with the words "Free At Last"; the *Interfaith Peace Chapel;* and a community center. There's also the *Center for Social Change,* which displays papers, films, and memorabilia that document his life and work (449 Auburn Ave. NE; phone: 331-3919).

GEORGIA CAPITOL Completed in 1889 and crowned by a dome of North Georgia gold, the classically styled capitol is home to the governor's office, the *Hall of Fame* with busts of notable Georgians, and the *Museum of Science and Industry.* Visitors may watch the *Georgia Assembly* in action from January through March; guided tours on weekdays. No admission charge. Capitol Sq. (phone: 656-2844).

FEDERAL RESERVE BANK To see where Federal Reserve notes are made, walk to the Corinthian-columned *Federal Reserve Bank,* two blocks east of the *CNN Center.* The *Federal Reserve* system's *Sixth District* headquarters has been here since 1914, though the building itself has been remodeled and enlarged over the years. Tours of the bank's operations and its *Federal Reserve Bank of Atlanta Monetary Museum,* which houses artifacts related to money and the history of the US banking system, are available weekdays by appointment; the museum itself is open weekdays during normal banking hours. No admission charge. 104 Marietta St. NW (phone: 521-8747).

SCITREK MUSEUM Atlanta's science and technology museum invites visitors to make electricity and learn the secrets of more than 100 machines and gadgets. Closed Mondays. Admission charge. *Civic Center Exhibition Hall,* 395 Piedmont Ave. at Ralph McGill Blvd. (phone: 522-5500).

FOX THEATER One of the last of the opulent 1920s "picture palaces," the beautifully restored theater blends Egyptian, Moorish, Byzantine, and Hollywood design elements. A vintage movie series, with newsreels and cartoons, is a summer highlight, but the theater's calendar mostly is filled with touring Broadway musicals and concerts. The *Fox* seats 4,518, making it the country's second-largest operating theater after New York City's *Radio City Music Hall.* A portion of every ticket sold goes toward ongoing restoration costs. Tours of the hall are conducted Mondays, Thursdays, and Saturdays. Admission varies with the event. Peachtree St. at Ponce de Leon Ave. (phone: 881-2100).

CNN CENTER, OMNI COLISEUM, GEORGIA WORLD CONGRESS CENTER Clustered at the southern edge of downtown, the three large structures are the center of the city's convention industry. At *CNN Center,* visitors may tour the Cable News Network studios (phone: 827-2300 for tour information), watch CNN newscasts, and then enjoy a glass of ale at cheery *Reggie's British Pub*. The deluxe *Omni at CNN Center* hotel (see *Checking In*) at the center's south end connects to the *Georgia World Congress Center* (phone: 223-4000), Atlanta's major convention complex. The adjacent *Omni Coliseum* (phone: 681-2100) is the scene of basketball games, rodeos, circuses, and other events.

CARTER PRESIDENTIAL CENTER Four connected circular buildings, set on 30 acres of trees, lakes, and Japanese gardens 2 miles east of downtown, contain memorabilia of Jimmy Carter's *White House* years. The complex includes the *Jimmy Carter Library and Museum*. Highlights include a re-creation of the Oval Office, elaborate state gifts to the Carters and other first families, and multimedia presentations on the presidency, human rights, and the environment. A gift shop and an attractive restaurant overlook the gardens. Open daily. Admission charge. N. Highland and Cleburne Aves. (phone: 420-5100).

ROAD TO TARA MUSEUM Just about everybody who visits Atlanta looks for Scarlett O'Hara's legendary white-columned mansion. Alas, *Tara* never existed, except in Margaret Mitchell's imagination and on David O. Selznick's movie sets. However, one of the world's largest collections of *Gone With the Wind* book and movie memorabilia is attractively displayed at this new museum in the *Georgian Terrace* hotel (659 Peachtree St.; phone: 897-1939). Items include scripts, props, costumes, and photos. Open daily. Admission charge. Memorabilia related to the book are also displayed in the *Margaret Mitchell Room* of the *Atlanta Public Library* (Peachtree and Forsyth Sts.; phone: 730-1700). But those in search of *Tara* will soon find what they've been looking for: The mansion is one of the scheduled attractions at *Gone With the Wind Country*, a theme park set to open in time for the 1996 *Summer Olympics*.

UNDERGROUND ATLANTA The city's most eclectic shopping and amusement area, a $145-million complex done in turn-of-the-century style, takes up six city blocks and houses 100 stores, 22 bars, restaurants, and nightclubs, and 20 fast-food establishments. The *Olympic Experience* has audiovisuals, gifts, and clothing related to the upcoming 1996 *Summer Games*. There are also displays on the 100-year history of the modern *Games*. Open daily. Martin Luther King Jr. Dr. and Peachtree St. (phone: 523-2311).

ATLANTA HERITAGE ROW Part of the *Underground* complex, this museum celebrates Atlanta's colorful past. Exhibits and films highlight the city's founding as a railroad center in the 1830s, its emergence from the ashes of the Civil War, Dr. Martin Luther King Jr. and the civil rights movement, and the city's successful bid for the 1996 *Summer Olympics*. Open daily. Admission charge. 55 Upper Alabama St. (phone: 584-7879).

WORLD OF COCA-COLA PAVILION A tribute to one of the world's favorite soft drinks, this three-story facility next to *Underground Atlanta* displays the most innovative outdoor neon sign ever created for the company—an 11-ton extravaganza that hangs 18 feet above the entrance. The pavilion contains more than 1,000 exhibits that chronicle the history of the Coca-Cola Company. A replica of a 1930s vintage soda fountain, complete with a "soda jerk," is part of the exhibit, and multimedia and interactive exhibits transport visitors into a Coke-filled future. Closed *Easter, Thanksgiving, Christmas Eve, Christmas,* and *New Year's Day.* No admission charge for children under six. Martin Luther King Jr. Dr. and Central Ave. (phone: 676-5151).

ENVIRONS

THE WREN'S NEST This Victorian cottage got its charming name from its owner, Joel Chandler Harris, best known as the creator of the *Uncle Remus* stories (starring Brer Fox and Brer Rabbit). The house has original furnishings and lots of memorabilia from the storyteller's life. Closed Mondays and major holidays. Admission charge. 1050 Ralph David Abernathy Blvd. (phone: 753-7735).

CHATTAHOOCHEE NATURE CENTER A seven-acre nature preserve on the peaceful banks of the Chattahoochee River 20 miles north of downtown, it has animal exhibits and classes for children and adults. Open daily. Admission charge. 9135 Willeo Rd., Roswell (phone: 992-2055).

PIEDMONT PARK Three miles north of downtown is a spacious green place for swimming, tennis, jogging, picnics, and people watching. The *Atlanta Arts Festival* is held here in early May, and the *Atlanta Symphony* presents outdoor concerts in summer. On the grounds, the 60-acre *Atlanta Botanical Garden* has greenhouses, a Japanese garden, rose gardens, a *Fragrance Garden* for the blind, and the *Dorothy Chapman Fuqua Conservatory,* with hundreds of tropical, desert, and endangered plants. Admission charge for the botanical garden, which is closed Mondays. Piedmont Ave. between 10th and 14th Sts. (phone: 876-5858).

ZOO ATLANTA An ambitious revitalization program has turned the once-depressing local zoo into an outstanding animal sanctuary with elephant shows, sea lion feedings, and a petting zoo. The highlight is the five-acre *Ford African Rain Forest,* where several families of gorillas and orangutans live in surroundings strikingly similar to their natural habitats. The star is silverback Willie B. Open daily. Admission charge. *Grant Park,* 800 Cherokee Ave., 3 miles from downtown (phone: 624-5600).

CYCLORAMA The dramatic circular painting of the Civil War Battle of Atlanta (50 feet high and 400 feet in circumference) has been beautifully restored and enhanced by new sound and lighting effects. Admission charge. Open daily. *Grant Park,* 800 Cherokee Ave., 3 miles from downtown (phone: 658-7625).

FERNBANK SCIENCE CENTER Often overlooked by those without children in tow, the center has the Southeast's third-largest planetarium, an observatory, and a nature trail leading through 70 acres of unspoiled forest. A see-and-touch museum, an electronic microscope laboratory, a meteorological laboratory, and an experimental garden also on the premises make this a fascinating place to spend an afternoon. Open daily. Admission charge. 156 Heaton Park Dr. NE, Decatur (phone: 378-4311).

FERNBANK MUSEUM OF NATURAL HISTORY The largest natural history museum south of the *Smithsonian,* this $45-million complex features hands-on exhibits and interactive displays, as well as an IMAX theater that shows films on a screen three stories high. Open daily. Admission charge. Located directly behind the *Fernbank Science Center.* 767 Clifton Rd., Decatur (phone: 378-0127).

HIGH MUSEUM OF ART The building is an architectural masterpiece, with an exterior of dazzling white enamel tiles and a central atrium flooded with natural light. It houses collections of American, European, and African art and a fine assemblage of decorative arts. 1280 Peachtree St. (phone: 892-4444). The *High*'s downtown branch, in the *Georgia-Pacific Center,* has changing exhibitions of regional, national, and international art. Closed Mondays and major holidays. Admission charge. 133 Peachtree St. (phone: 577-6940).

ROBERT W. WOODRUFF ARTS CENTER Named for the Coca-Cola patriarch and arts benefactor, the center is home to the *Atlanta Symphony Orchestra,* the *Alliance Theater,* the *Atlanta Children's Theater,* and the *Atlanta College of Art.* 1280 Peachtree St. NE (phone: 892-3600).

HERNDON HOME This Beaux Arts mansion was built in 1915 by Alonzo Herndon, former slave and founder of the Atlanta Life Insurance Company, the nation's largest owned by an African-American. The rooms, decorated with original furnishings, showcase his life and accomplishments. Closed Sundays and Mondays. No admission charge. 587 University Pl. (phone: 581-9813).

ATLANTA HISTORY CENTER To reach this 18-acre complex, go north along Peachtree Road to West Paces Ferry Road. Turn left and look for Andrews Drive. The center's showpiece is *Swan House,* built in 1928 and designed by well-known Atlanta architect Philip Shutze in the Anglo-Palladian style, a popular Italian Renaissance mode. It is handsomely furnished in 18th-century antiques, many of which belonged to the former owners, prominent Atlantans Mr. and Mrs. Edward Inman. The *Museum of Atlanta History,* which is part of the complex, uses interactive, hands-on exhibits to show the city's colorful history. The *McElreath Memorial Hall,* which also houses an extensive collection on Atlanta's history, is here, too. The *Tullie Smith House* is an authentic 1830s "plantation plain" Georgia farmhouse reconstructed on the property with all its attached buildings. Nearby are the Inmans' coach house, now a pleasant restaurant, gift shop, and art gallery; the *Dubois Civil War Collection,* with 5,000 artifacts; and a marked nature trail. Open daily. Admission charge. 3101 Andrews Dr. NW (phone: 814-4000).

SIX FLAGS OVER GEORGIA This huge theme park, which climbs a 260-acre forested hillside on the western edge of the city, is divided into six sections loosely based on the six governments whose flags have flown over Georgia—Spanish, French, British, Georgian, Confederate, and American. The US section, for instance, has elements of 1950s Americana in its design. There are paths for strolling, benches for sitting and inhaling the sweet southern air, and plenty of soda and hot dogs—plus more than 100 rides, including the *Mind Bender* and the *Great American Scream Machine,* one of the world's fastest, tallest, and longest roller coasters. In addition, there's a triple-loop coaster, a whitewater raft trip, and the terrifying 10-story *Free Fall.* Featured in a 2,500-seat amphitheater is the *Batman Stunt Show*, which showcases top stunt pros as well as Broadway-style musicals and topnotch magicians. Closed December through late March; closed weekdays late March through late May and September through November. Admission charge. Twelve miles west of Atlanta on I-20 (phone: 739-3400).

STONE MOUNTAIN PARK There's something for everybody here: a cable car ride to the top, an old steam train, hiking trails, a lake for riverboating or canoeing, an 18-hole golf course, an antebellum plantation—and the southern equivalent of *Mt. Rushmore*. Confederate heroes Jefferson Davis, Robert E. Lee, and Stonewall Jackson have been drilled into the sheer face of a giant mass of exposed granite. The enormous bas-relief (which took 50 years to complete) was begun—but not finished—by Gutzon Borglum, who also carved *Mt. Rushmore*. Facilities include campgrounds, restaurants, and motels. Open daily. Admission charge. Sixteen miles northeast of Atlanta on Rte. 78 (phone: 498-5690).

WHITE WATER PARK A relaxing relief from Atlanta's steamy summers, this attractive, well-maintained oasis offers a variety of cooling experiences, headed by an enormous wave pool and water slides designed for the adventurous as well as the timid. A children's area has numerous activities. There are lockers, showers, snack bars, and a picnic area. Closed October through April. Admission charge. At 250 N. Cobb Pkwy. (US 41), Marietta (phone: 424-9283).

KENNESAW MOUNTAIN NATIONAL BATTLEFIELD PARK The mountain and 2,800-acre park were the scene of one of the most important engagements in the Battle of Atlanta campaign. Attractions include a Civil War museum and defense lines. Open daily. No admission charge. Off I-75, 25 miles from downtown, near Marietta (phone: 427-4686). Also in the vicinity is the *Big Shanty Museum* in Kennesaw. Its locomotive *General* was involved in a famous Civil War spy chase. Open daily. Admission charge (phone: 427-2117).

EXTRA SPECIAL

Just 35 miles northeast of Atlanta is a resort area called Lake Lanier Islands. Centered around a manmade lake with 540 miles of shoreline, the 1,200 acres of hills and woods offer facilities for tennis, horseback riding, and camping, plus an excellent golf course (see *Golf*). There are sailboats and houseboats for rent, and Stouffer's *Pine Isle Resort* hotel (9000 Holiday Rd.; phone: 945-8921) is on the grounds. Open year round. On I-85 (phone: 932-7200).

Sources and Resources

TOURIST INFORMATION

For general information, brochures, and maps, contact the *Georgia Tourist Division* (PO Box 1776, Atlanta, GA 30301; phone: 656-3590) or the *Atlanta Convention and Visitors Bureau* (235 Peachtree St. NE, Suite 1414; phone: 521-6600), both closed weekends. Exhibitions on Georgia tourism and industry are at the *World Congress Center* (Marietta and Magnolia Sts. NW; phone: 656-7600). A covered pedestrian bridge links the center to the *Omni at CNN Center* hotel. Foreign visitors information is available during the week from the *Georgia Council for International Visitors* (999 Peachtree St.; phone: 873-6170). Contact the Georgia state tourism hotline (phone: 656-3590; 800-VISIT-GA) for maps, calendars of events, health updates, and travel advisories.

LOCAL COVERAGE *Atlanta Constitution,* morning daily; *Atlanta Journal,* evening daily; and *Atlanta* magazine, monthly. *Georgia Off the Beaten Path* (Globe Pequot Press, 1993; $8.95) offers an insider's look at attractions, dining, nightlife, and shopping in Atlanta and elsewhere in Georgia.

TELEVISION STATIONS WSB Channel 2–ABC; WAGA Channel 5–CBS; and WXIA Channel 11–NBC.

> **NOTE**
>
> CNN (Cable News Network), a major competitor in the network news race, has its headquarters at 1 CNN Center (phone: 827-1500).

RADIO STATIONS AM: WGST 640 (news/talk) and WSB 750 (contemporary music). FM: WABE 90 (public radio, classical music/news); WCLK 91.9 (jazz); and WVEE 103.3 (urban contemporary).

TELEPHONE The area code for Atlanta is 404.

SALES TAX State and city sales tax is 6%; the hotel tax is 13%.

CLIMATE Atlanta's temperatures vary from moderate winters to comfortable springs and falls to hot and humid summers. Winter is generally mild, but temperatures occasionally drop to near freezing, with sleet and light snow. May, September, October, and November tend to be the sunniest months. While Atlanta isn't exactly what you'd call dry, the average humidity hovers at 60%, which isn't intolerable either.

GETTING AROUND

AIRPORT Atlanta is served by *Hartsfield International Airport,* one of the world's largest and busiest. The airport's two terminals (North and South) are connected by a speedy, frequent, and efficient subway system. Except during rush hours, it's about a 20-minute drive between the airport and downtown. (Changing downtown traffic patterns make it easier to get *to* the airport in the morning and *from* the airport in late afternoon.) *Atlanta Airport Shuttle* vans provide transportation to downtown hotels and suburban areas such as *Emory University* and Lenox Square. The same company has bus service between the airport and suburban Roswell (phone: 766-5312 for van service; 768-7600 for bus service). Travelers without much luggage can take *MARTA (Metropolitan Atlanta Rapid Transit Authority)* trains from the airport to downtown in about 12 minutes for $1.25 one way (phone: 848-4711).

BUS *MARTA* is the backbone of Atlanta's public transportation system. Bus routes interlace the city, with frequent stops at downtown locations. The fare is $1.25; exact change or a token is required. A rapid-rail system runs 12 miles east-west and 12 miles north-south, connecting at the *Five Points* station downtown. Each station has been designed by a different architect and is decorated with murals, photos, and collages. *MARTA* maintains information booths at the intersection of Peachtree and West Peachtree, near the *Hyatt Regency* hotel and at Broad and Walton NE (phone: 848-4711).

CAR RENTAL All major national firms are represented.

TAXI Atlanta isn't known for efficient taxi service. Many are unclean and mechanically suspect, and their drivers are often unfamiliar with local geography. *Yellow Cab* (phone: 521-0200) and *Ealy Taxi* (phone: 223-6000) are among the more reliable.

LOCAL SERVICES

AUDIOVISUAL EQUIPMENT *Corporate Audio-Visual Services* (580 Dutch Valley Rd.; phone: 881-8234); *Southern Business Communications* (3175 Corners North Ct., Norcross; phone: 449-4088).

BUSINESS SERVICES *Peachtree Suite Word Processing* (phone: 688-2939); *Presenting Atlanta* (phone: 231-0200), convention services and consultants; *Team Concept* (1925 Century Blvd. NE; phone: 325-9754); *Tourgals* (phone: 262-7660), convention arrangements.

DRY CLEANER/TAILOR *Kim's One-Hour Valet* (201 Mitchell St.; phone: 688-8262).

LIMOUSINE *Atlanta Limousine Service* (2778 Hargrove Rd.; phone: 432-9200).

MECHANICS *Don Davis Gulf Service* (359 W. Ponce de Leon Ave., Decatur; phone: 378-6751); *Joe Winkler's Gulf Station* (2794 Clairmont Rd. NE; phone: 636-2940).

MEDICAL EMERGENCY *Piedmont Hospital* (1968 Peachtree Rd., NE; phone: 605-3297).

MESSENGER SERVICES *Central Delivery Service* (phone: 892-1350); *Flash Courier Service* (phone: 873-5052).

MONEY TRANSFERS *American Express MoneyGram* (phone: 800-926-9400 for information; 800-866-8800 for money transfers); *Western Union Financial Services* (phone: 800-325-6000 or 800-325-4176).

NATIONAL/INTERNATIONAL COURIER *DHL Worldwide Express* (phone: 349-9555); *FedEx* (phone: 321-7566).

PHARMACY *Big "B" Drugs* (Ponce de Leon Ave. NE at N. Highland; phone: 876-0381), located about 3 miles from downtown, open 24 hours.

PHOTOCOPIES *Center Office Supply & Printing* (233 Peachtree St.; phone: 681-3889); *Kinko's* (Peachtree and Fifth Sts.; phone: 876-4752).

POST OFFICE Downtown (240 Peachtree St.; phone: 522-1196).

PROFESSIONAL PHOTOGRAPHER *Richard and Mary Magruder Photography* (2156 Snapfinger Rd., Decatur; phone: 289-8985).

SECRETARY/STENOGRAPHER *Norrell Services* (phone: 897-1282).

TELECONFERENCE FACILITIES The *Hyatt Regency* and the *Westin Peachtree Plaza* hotels have facilities (see *Checking In,* below).

TRANSLATOR *Berlitz* (phone: 261-5062); *International Language School Service* (phone: 252-3829).

WESTERN UNION/TELEX Many offices are located around the city (phone: 800-325-6000 to find the location nearest you).

SPECIAL EVENTS

The best time to visit Atlanta is during the spring *Dogwood Festival* (phone: 952-9151), the second week in April, when the city explodes in color and celebration. During the summer months, the *Atlanta Symphony Orchestra* plays outdoors in *Piedmont Park* on Sunday evenings. Also in *Piedmont Park,* the *Arts Festival of Atlanta* takes place in September, as does the *Atlanta Greek Festival,* a potpourri of Greek costumes, movies, gifts, art, dances, and food (*Greek Orthodox Cathedral of the Annunciation,* 2500 Clairmont Rd. NE; phone: 633-5870).

MUSEUMS

In addition to those described in *Special Places,* there is another museum of note.

MICHAEL C. CARLOS MUSEUM Greek and Roman coins, amphorae, and an Egyptian mummy; art from the American Southwest to Southeast Asia, China, and Japan; and exhibits from major international museums are displayed in this recently expanded art and archaeology museum on the *Emory University* campus. Open daily. Donations accepted. N. Decatur and Oxford Rds. (phone: 727-4282).

SHOPPING

Atlanta offers a taste of Fifth Avenue, Rodeo Drive, and the rainbow's end. Huge department stores, malls, galleries, food and flea markets, and antiques centers offer tempting merchandise. Upscale shopping abounds in the affluent Buckhead neighborhood, along Peachtree Road, and about 6 to 8 miles north of downtown, where local branches of *Gucci, Tiffany, Neiman Marcus, Saks Fifth Avenue,* and *Lord & Taylor* are the venerable institutions for Southern spending. In *Underground Atlanta*'s festival-style downtown complex, scores of shops and vending carts feature apparel, gifts, food, and wine. The reborn in-town neighborhood of Virginia/Highlands is a place to shop for antiques; high fashion; African, Latin, and Irish imports; and other offbeat items. Shops are interspersed by trendy and ethnic restaurants and bars.

Lenox Square Atlanta's splashiest mall, where *Neiman Marcus, Macy's, Alfred Dunhill Tobacco Shop, Benetton, Burberry's,* and numerous California, European, and New York specialty shops reside. There are plenty of restaurants and bars as well. Peachtree and Lenox Rds. (phone: 233-6767).

Phipps Plaza Anchored by *Saks* and *Lord & Taylor,* this glamorous mall is filled with high-fashion shops and excellent restaurants. Across from Lenox Sq., 3500 Peachtree Rd. (phone: 262-0992).

Your DeKalb Farmer's Market This indoor market, which extends over three blocks, overflows with exotic fruits, seafood, herbs, spices, breads, and other delicacies from around the world. Patrons and clerks jointly form a mini–*United Nations.* 3000 E. Ponce de Leon Ave., Decatur (phone: 377-6400).

SPORTS AND FITNESS

A major league city, Atlanta is the home of the *Braves* and the nest of the *Falcons* and *Hawks.*

BASEBALL The Atlanta *Braves,* winners of the *National League* pennant in 1991 and 1992, play at *Atlanta–Fulton County Stadium* (521 Capitol Ave. SW; phone: 522-7630).

BASKETBALL The Atlanta *Hawks'* home games are played at the *Omni Coliseum* (100 Techwood Dr. NW; phone: 827-DUNK).

BICYCLING Bikes may be rented at *Skate Escape* (1086 Piedmont Ave. NE, across from *Piedmont Park;* phone: 892-1292).

FISHING There's good fishing at Lake Allatoona, Lake Lanier, and Lake Jackson. Fishing permits (necessary) can be purchased at *K-Mart, Wal-Mart,* and at hunting and fishing supply stores.

FITNESS CENTERS The *YMCA* (phone: 588-9622) has modern health centers throughout the metro area. Facilities are available to members of any "Y" nationwide.

FOOTBALL The Atlanta *Falcons* host their opponents at the new *Georgia Dome* (1 Georgia Dome Dr.; phone: 223-8000).

GOLF Atlanta is not a city automatically associated with golf; however, an outstanding course is just half an hour away.

A TOP TEE-OFF SPOT

Lake Lanier Islands *Golf Digest* has ranked this course near Atlanta one of the top 5 resort golf courses in the country. Short but difficult, this par 72 measures 6,254 yards. Thirteen holes are on the water, and there are no parallel fairways. Located at *Lake Lanier Islands Hotel & Golf Club* (7000 Holiday Rd., Lake Lanier Islands; phone: 945-8787; 800-768-LAKE).

In town, the best public courses are those at *Stone Mountain Park* (phone: 498-5690) and *Bobby Jones Golf Course* (384 Woodward Way; phone: 355-1009).

JOGGING From downtown, run along Peachtree Street or Piedmont Road to *Piedmont Park,* about 1½ miles, and enter at 10th or 14th Street; roads in the park are closed to traffic. You also can run just past 14th Street to the Ansley Park and Sherwood Forest areas of Atlanta and along the wide residential streets. For more information, call *Atlanta Track Club* (phone: 231-9064).

TENNIS The best clay courts are at the *Bitsy Grant Tennis Center* (2125 Northside Dr. NW; phone: 351-2774). *Lanier Islands* and *Stone Mountain* have good outdoor tennis courts, too. There are excellent public courts at the *Blackburn Tennis Center* (3501 Ashford-Dunwoody Rd.; phone: 451-1061) and at the *DeKalb Tennis Center* (off Clairmont Rd., in suburban Decatur; phone: 325-2520).

WHITEWATER RAFTING Burt Reynolds (with some help from poet and novelist James Dickey) made North Georgia whitewater infamous in the movie *Deliverance*. For an urban alternative, rent a raft at *Atlanta Rent-a-Raft* (1377 Powers Ferry Rd.; phone: 952-2824) during the summer.

THEATER

For complete performance schedules, check the publications listed in *Local Coverage* above. Among the best-known theatrical companies are the *Alliance Theater* and *Studio Theater* at the *Woodruff Arts Center* (Peachtree and 15th Sts.; phone: 892-2414); and *Theatrical Outfit* (Peachtree and 10th Sts.; phone: 872-0665). *Seven Stages Theater* (1105 Euclid Ave.; phone: 522-0911) offers topical, offbeat plays. The *Center for Puppetry Arts* (1404 Spring St.; phone: 873-3089) has performances and exhibitions. The nationally honored *Atlanta Ballet* (phone: 892-3303) has a repertoire of classical and contemporary works. *Agatha's A Taste of Mystery* (693 Peachtree St.; phone: 875-1610) is a dinner-theater where intrigue and suspense are served after your meal.

MUSIC

The *Atlanta Symphony Orchestra* (phone: 892-3600) plays virtually year-round at the *Woodruff Arts Center* and gives a variety of indoor and outdoor concerts. Chamber music groups include the *Atlanta Virtuosi* (phone: 938-8611) and *Atlanta Chamber Players* (phone: 651-1228).

NIGHTCLUBS AND NIGHTLIFE

Atlanta's nightlife covers the spectrum, with most places open nightly until 3 or 4 AM. There's excellent jazz at *Dante's Down the Hatch* (*Underground Atlanta;* phone: 577-1800; and 3380 Peachtree St.; phone: 266-1600). Blues heads the menu at *Blues Harbor* (2293 Peachtree Rd.; phone: 605-0661). Big-name comedians are featured at *The Punch Line* (280 Hildebrand Dr.; phone: 252-LAFF). *Blind Willie's* (830 N. Highland Ave.; phone: 873-2583) highlights New Orleans blues and food; *County Cork Pub* (5600 Roswell Rd.; phone: 303-1976) has Irish singers. British ales, darts, and a sing-along piano draw big crowds to *Churchill Arms* (3223 Cains Hill Pl., Buckhead; phone: 233-5633). *Reggie's British Pub* (*CNN Center;* phone: 525-1437) is another jolly good spot for ale, steak-and-kidney pie, and darts. Jazz is featured at *Otto's* (265 E. Paces Ferry Rd., Buckhead; phone: 233-1133). The best places to meet and mingle are *Peachtree Café* (268 E. Paces Ferry Rd.; phone: 233-4402), *Rupert's* (3330 Piedmont Rd. NE; phone: 266-9834), and *Velvetia Euro/High-Techno Club* (89 Park Pl.; phone: 681-9936). The most convivial old-fashioned neighborhood bars are *Manuel's Tavern* (602 N.

Highland Ave.; phone: 525-3447) and *P.J. Haley's Club* (1799 Briarcliff Rd.; phone: 874-3116). *Café Intermezzo* (1845 Peachtree Rd. NE; phone: 355-0411; and 4505 Ashford-Dunwoody Rd. NE; phone: 396-1344) is *the* place for after-theater espresso and decadent desserts. The *Cotton Club* (1021 Peachtree St.; phone: 874-2523) is a high-energy forum for the latest pop, rock, blues, and jazz.

Best in Town

CHECKING IN

Atlanta visitors can pick and choose from among one of the broadest accommodations assortments in the country. The largest selections are in the downtown convention district; the uptown Buckhead commercial area, near *Hartsfield International Airport;* and in commercial areas such as I-285/*Perimeter Mall* in northern DeKalb County and the *Cumberland Mall/Galleria* area of Cobb County. Remember to book early from fall through spring, when major conventions may have everything virtually locked up. Expect to pay $150 or more (sometimes a lot more) per night for a double room in hotels we've classified as very expensive; from $110 to $150 at those listed as expensive; and between $80 and $110 at those categorized as moderate; there are no exceptional inexpensive hotels in the city. But it is possible to stay very inexpensively in bed and breakfast establishments. For information and reservations, contact *Bed & Breakfast Atlanta* (1801 Piedmont Ave. NE, Suite 208, Atlanta 30324; phone: 875-0525). Unless otherwise noted, hotel rooms have air conditioning, private baths, TV sets, and telephones. All hotels are in the 404 area code unless otherwise indicated.

VERY EXPENSIVE

Hyatt Regency This John Portman–designed hotel sparked the interior atrium craze in the mid-1960s. Each of the 1,358 rooms in the main building has a balcony as well as a window overlooking the atrium. The adjoining tower has 200 additional rooms. The revolving rooftop restaurant, *Polaris,* is reached via a glass elevator. Facilities include a pool and a health club. Business services include a concierge, 37 meeting rooms, secretarial services, A/V equipment, photocopiers, computers, and express checkout. 265 Peachtree Rd. NE (phone: 577-1234; 800-233-1234; fax: 588-4137).

Nikko Atlanta Asian elegance and luxury are highly visible in this 440-room, Japanese-owned hotel. One of its restaurants serves French and Mediterranean dishes, while the other proffers Japanese fare. Facilities include a health club and a pool, and there is 24-hour room service, a concierge, a conference center, secretarial services, A/V equipment, computers, and express checkout. 3300 Peachtree Rd. (phone: 365-8100; 800-645-5687; fax: 233-5686).

Occidental Grand Hotel Atlanta This luxury establishment has a decidedly European feel. The 246 rooms and suites are lavishly decorated and appointed, and a valet and a concierge are available. Recreational facilities include a health club, steamroom, sauna, Jacuzzi, and indoor lap pool; there are two restaurants (including the elegant *Florencia*), a bar, and a lounge. Business amenities include 7,000 square feet of meeting space, A/V equipment, photocopiers, translation services, and foreign currency exchange. 75 14th St. (phone: 881-9898; 800-952-0702; fax: 873-4692).

Omni at CNN Center Attached to the *CNN Center* mega-structure, it has a surprisingly dignified atmosphere. Many of the 500 rooms, furnished with discreet European charm, have balconies overlooking all or part of the 14-story, five-and-one-half-acre *Omni* atrium. There is a restaurant, and business services include a concierge desk, 18 meeting rooms, secretarial services, A/V equipment photocopiers, computers, and express checkout. Marietta St. and Techwood Dr. (phone: 659-0000; 800-843-6664; fax: 659-1621).

Ritz-Carlton, Atlanta With its European decor and elegant extras, this luxury property, with 472 rooms, is especially attractive to those whose business takes them to the nearby downtown financial district and the *Georgia World Congress Center*. The hotel's dining room is one of the city's leading restaurants (see *Eating Out*). Business amenities include 24-hour room service, a concierge, 15 meeting rooms, secretarial services, A/V equipment, photocopiers, computers, and express checkout. 181 Peachtree St. NE (phone: 659-0400; 800-241-3333; fax: 688-0400).

Ritz-Carlton, Buckhead In the heart of the city's most upscale shopping, dining, and nightlife neighborhood, this is probably Atlanta's most fashionable stopping place. The plush dining room (see *Eating Out*) and lounges are *the* places to see and be seen. Its 574 rooms and suites are handsomely appointed, and facilities include an indoor pool and a health club. Among the business amenities are 24-hour room service, a concierge, 26 meeting rooms, secretarial services, A/V equipment, photocopiers, computers, and express checkout. 3434 Peachtree Rd. NW (phone: 237-2700; 800-241-3333; fax: 239-0078).

Stouffer Waverly In the heart of a suburban shopping and office complex, this deluxe, 545-room property has first class dining and entertainment, as well as two pools, a Jacuzzi, a health club, and a ballroom. Amenities include 24-hour room service, a concierge, 24 meeting rooms, secretarial services, A/V equipment, photocopiers, and express checkout. 2450 Galleria Pkwy. NW (phone: 953-4500; 800-468-3571; fax: 955-5445).

Swissôtel Atlanta Elegant, efficient hotel-keeping and Biedermeier-style furnishings classify this 358-room property as top-drawer. Its dining rooms prepare international and American dishes. Amenities include 24-hour room service, a concierge, 15 meeting rooms, a ballroom, secretarial services, A/V equipment, photocopiers, computers, and express checkout. 3391 Peachtree Rd. (phone: 365-0065; 800-253-1397; fax: 365-8787).

Westin Peachtree Plaza This 73-story silo-shaped landmark has 1,068 guestrooms and a lobby featuring attractive seating areas, cafés, and lounges. Atop the cylindrical structure is the *Sun Dial* restaurant and lounge, our choice for the best bird's-eye view of the city, though better food can be found in the hotel's *Savannah Fish Company* (see *Eating Out*).

Business amenities include 24-hour room service, a concierge, translation services, 41 meeting rooms, A/V equipment, computers, and express checkout. 210 Peachtree St. (phone: 659-1400; 800-228-3000; fax: 589-7586).

EXPENSIVE

Ansley Inn Formerly a 1907 mansion, this place has been attractively restored as a small hotel emphasizing personal service and attention to guests' comfort. Each of the 15 rooms features a Jacuzzi, antique-style furniture, Oriental carpets, and four-poster beds, creating an elegant atmosphere. There is no restaurant, but a complimentary continental breakfast is served. Other amenities include a concierge and a meeting room. The addition of 16 rooms, a pool, and formal gardens is scheduled for later this year. 253 15th St. NE (phone: 872-9000; 800-446-5416; fax: 892-2318).

MODERATE

Comfort Inn Downtown This 260-room property has attractive facilities, along with a restaurant, lounge, and pool. Amenities include small meeting rooms and photocopiers. 101 International Blvd. (phone: 524-5555; 800-228-5150; fax: 221-0702).

Days Inn The Atlanta-based chain offers basic, clean accommodations at very reasonable rates. Most have a pool, playground, and family restaurant; some have kitchenettes. Of the 10 Atlanta locations, the high-rise inn downtown (a block from the *Westin Peachtree Plaza* at 300 Spring St.; phone: 523-1144) may be the best value in the city. Call 800-325-2525 for information on the others.

Ramada Dunwoody Convenient to the northeast metro area's business district, this 391-room motor hotel has two outdoor pools, as well as tennis courts, a restaurant, and a lounge. Amenities include 12 meeting rooms, A/V equipment, and photocopiers. I-285 at Chamblee-Dunwoody Rd. exit (phone: 394-5000; 800-228-2828; fax: 394-5000, ext. 7698).

EATING OUT

Atlanta's hundreds of restaurants, cafés, and trendy grills and bistros specialize in everything from traditional Southern cooking to American regional dishes and an astonishing variety of international cuisines. Expect to pay between $80 and $100 for dinner for two at restaurants in the expensive category; from $45 to $80 at those rated moderate; and between $20 and $45 at inexpensive places. Prices do not include wine, drinks, tax, or tips. Unless otherwise noted, restaurants are open for lunch and dinner. All restaurants are in the 404 area code unless otherwise indicated.

EXPENSIVE

Bone's *The* place for prime beef and fresh seafood in clubby, convivial surroundings, it's very popular among executives and savvy out-of-towners. Open daily; dinner only on weekends. Reservations advised. Major credit cards accepted. 3130 Piedmont Rd. (phone: 237-2663).

Ciboulette The excellent presentations of French fare and the casual but smart atmosphere of this bistro have received quite a bit of favorable attention. Creations from chef/owner Jean Banchet's open kitchen might include *feuillette* of snails and asparagus, grilled veal medallions with wild mushroom and rosemary sauce, or lamb *en croûte. Note:* The restaurant's no-reservations policy means diners may have to wait as long as an hour. Open for dinner only; closed Mondays. Major credit cards accepted. 1529 Piedmont Ave. NE (phone: 874-7600).

La Grotta An elegant northern Italian dining room, where delicious veal, pasta, and seafood dishes are matched by some of Atlanta's most professional service. Open for dinner only; closed Sundays. Reservations advised. Major credit cards accepted. 2637 Peachtree Rd. NE (phone: 231-1368).

Hedgerose Heights Inn Pheasant, veal, beef, seafood, and fowl are served with either French, Swiss, or German flair, and complemented by a fine wine list and very good service. Open for dinner only; closed Sundays and Mondays. Reservations advised. Major credit cards accepted. 490 E. Paces Ferry Rd. (phone: 233-7673).

Nikolai's Roof With decor and atmosphere suggesting czarist opulence, the *Atlanta Hilton*'s rooftop restaurant was originally intended to heighten the establishment's prestige, not to make lots of money—which is why it seats only 67 diners and has just two dinner seatings. Waiters in Cossack attire recite the five-course menu from memory. The food is French, but then the old Russian courts were also shamelessly Francophilic. Open daily for dinner only. Reservations essential. Major credit cards accepted. Courtland and Harris NE (phone: 659-2000).

103 West A creative array of richly sauced dishes and superior wines is complemented by Victorian floral prints, potted palms, and marble-topped tables. The result is a memorable dining experience. Open for dinner only; closed Sundays. Reservations advised. Major credit cards accepted. 103 W. Paces Ferry Rd. (phone: 233-5993).

Pano's & Paul's This classy spot is hidden in a shopping center. Continental and American food is served, but the kitchen promises it will prepare anything if requested far enough in advance. Open for dinner only; closed Sundays. Reservations advised. Major credit cards accepted. *West Paces Shopping Center,* 1232 W. Paces Ferry Rd. (phone: 261-3662).

Patio by the River Enviably situated on the banks of the Chattahoochee River, this establishment marries a pretty setting of Regency antiques and lace napery to expert French cooking. Grilled salmon with shallot brown butter sauce and triple-cut lamb chops are standouts. Open daily; dinner only on Saturdays. Reservations advised. Major credit cards accepted. 4199 Paces Ferry Rd. NW (phone: 432-2808).

Pricci This busy place manages to create a romantic air with the help of warm lighting and touches of Venetian glass. The menu features such Italian specialties as fried risotto croquettes, grilled salmon over polenta with spinach, and fried calamari rings. The tuna steaks are also excellent, as is the cappuccino *crème brûlée.* Closed Mondays. Reservations advised.

Major credit cards accepted. 500 Pharr Rd. NE, Buckhead (phone: 237-2941).

Ritz-Carlton, Atlanta Among the best restaurants in town, this hotel dining room offers fine continental fare, including boneless chicken breast, fettuccine Alfredo, and steaks; the soufflés are also excellent. The decor is sumptuous and elegant, with mahogany accents and fine china and silver. Open daily; dinner only on weekends. Reservations necessary. Major credit cards accepted. 181 Peachtree St. (phone: 659-0400).

Ritz-Carlton, Buckhead Dinner here is a carefully orchestrated affair, with menus composed by Chef Guenter Seeger. The food is creative and memorable—melon soup with lobster and mint, tuna tartare with radish coulis, and for dessert, marinated strawberries in parchment with coconut sorbet. Closed Sundays. Reservations advised. Major credit cards accepted. 3340 Peachtree Rd. NE (phone: 237-2700).

Savannah Fish Company Fish and shellfish, flown in fresh from the Gulf of Mexico, the Pacific, and the North Atlantic, are the hallmark of this cozy restaurant in the *Westin Peachtree Plaza* hotel. Open daily. Reservations advised for lunch only. Major credit cards accepted. Peachtree St. and International Blvd. (phone: 589-7456).

MODERATE

Asiana Garden Bona fide Korean and Japanese cooking attracts area Asians and appreciative Occidentals to this attractive, always bustling dining room in north Atlanta's "Little Asia." Open daily. No reservations. Major credit cards accepted. In the *New Asia Square* shopping center, which also has Vietnamese, Hong Kong, and Taiwanese eateries and Asian shops and services. 5150 Buford Hwy., Doraville (phone: 452-1677).

Azalea The trendy fare served here imaginatively fuses dishes from Italy, Thailand, China, and California to produce some unorthodox but delicious alliances. Open daily for dinner only. No reservations. Major credit cards accepted. 3167 Peachtree Rd. (phone: 237-9939).

Buckhead Diner Gleaming stainless steel, neon, and leather are the signatures of this sleek chic 1990s eatery that has become a haven for the city's movers and shakers and hip out-of-towners. The menu is a trendy array of pasta, salads, seafood, and meat. Valet parking. Open daily. No reservations. Major credit cards accepted. 3073 Piedmont Rd. (phone: 262-3336).

Camille's Perpetually packed, this very New Yorkish Italian café serves big platters of pasta, seafood, veal, and chicken dishes. In warm weather, take a sidewalk table and watch the crowd go by. Open daily for dinner only. No reservations. Major credit cards accepted. 1186 N. Highland Ave. (phone: 872-7203).

Dante's Down the Hatch This late-night place with a faithful coterie is where jazz lovers come to hear *Paul Mitchell's Trio* and assorted combos. The fondue/wine/cheese menu is appealing, as is owner Dante Stephenson, who's usually available to recommend a vintage from his wine list. Open daily for dinner only. Reservations advised. Major credit cards accepted. Two locations: 3380 Peachtree Rd. (phone: 266-1600) and *Underground Atlanta* (phone: 577-1800).

Honto Fanciers of Asian cooking are lured by such Hong Kong–style seafood dishes as Dungeness crab with ginger and scallions, mussels in black bean sauce, and salt-and-pepper squid. Open daily. No reservations. Major credit cards accepted. 3295 Chamblee-Dunwoody Rd. (phone: 458-8088).

Indigo Coastal Grill This spiffy, laid-back little neighborhood café specializes in fresh seafood, conch chowder, and Key lime pie. Open daily for dinner only. No reservations. Major credit cards accepted. 1397 N. Highland Ave. (phone: 876-0676).

Lombardi's A wide range of Italian dishes and a great wine list are offered in a cheerful, low-key setting in *Underground Atlanta*'s best full-service restaurant. Open daily; dinner only on weekends. Reservations unnecessary. Major credit cards accepted. On the upper level (phone: 522-6568).

Marra's Seafood Grill A neighborhood favorite for almost a dozen years, the elegant two-level dining rooms feature Asian and Latin-inspired appetizers, grilled seafood, steak *au poivre,* and innovative pasta. Open daily for dinner only. Reservations advised for large parties. Major credit cards accepted. 1782 Cheshire Bridge Rd. (phone: 874-7347).

The Peasant Group Some of Atlanta's favorite dining places are the locally owned *Peasant* restaurants, which feature innovative American/continental meals served in a stylish, relaxed atmosphere. The group includes: the *Pleasant Peasant* (555 Peachtree St.; phone: 874-3223); the *Country Place* (Colony Sq., Peachtree and 14th Sts.; phone: 881-0144); *Dailey's* (17 International Blvd., downtown; phone: 681-3303); *Wirfield's* (1 Galleria Pkwy., Smyrna; phone: 955-5300); *Buck's* (*Underground Atlanta;* phone: 525-2825; and 116 E. Ponce de Leon Ave., Decatur; phone: 373-7797); the *Peasant Uptown* (*Phipps Plaza,* Peachtree and Lenox Rds.; phone: 261-6341); and the *Public House* (605 S. Atlanta St., Roswell; phone: 992-4646) Check each location for its operating days. No reservations. Major credit cards accepted.

Skeeter's Mesquite Grill This Texas steakhouse comes complete with country-and-western on the jukebox and faded denim on the patrons. Though the emphasis is on steaks, the grilled Cajun redfish is pretty tasty. Open daily. No reservations. Major credit cards accepted. Three locations: 2892 N. Druid Hills Rd. (phone: 636-3817); 2700 Town Center Dr., Kennesaw (phone: 499-0676); and 3505 Satellite Blvd., Duluth (phone: 476-3131).

A Taste of New Orleans Delectable creole and Cajun dishes are done with French Quarter flair in a casually sophisticated atmosphere. Open daily for dinner only. No reservations. Major credit cards accepted. 389 W. Peachtree St. (phone: 874-5535).

INEXPENSIVE

The Colonnade This is the best place in town for Southern home cooking and traditional American steaks, chops, and seafood. Pluses include a very friendly staff and a great bar. Open daily. No reservations or credit cards accepted. 1879 Cheshire Bridge Rd. (phone: 874-5642).

Hard Rock Café This branch of the famous chain serves burgers and other American fare with a generous helping of rock memorabilia, including Madonna's bustier from her "Blond Ambition" tour and the suit George Harrison wore when the *Beatles* performed on *The Ed Sullivan Show*. There are also items from local bands that made it big, such as *REM* and the *B-52s*. Open daily. No reservations or credit cards accepted. 215 Peachtree St. (phone: 688-7625).

Harold's Barbecue This quintessential Southern barbecue shack is a local legend for its grilled pork and beef sandwiches and hearty Brunswick stew. Closed Sundays. No reservations or credit cards accepted. 171 McDonough Blvd. (phone: 627-9268).

Huey's An upbeat café with an outdoor terrace, this popular late-night retreat features New Orleans gumbo, po' boys, coffee, and beignets (deep-fried doughnuts). Open daily. No reservations. Major credit cards accepted. 1816 Peachtree Rd. (phone: 873-2037).

King & I Exotic Thai dishes have made this place popular with adventurous Atlantans. Open daily. No reservations. Major credit cards accepted. Ansley Sq. at Piedmont Ave. and Monroe Dr. (phone: 892-7743).

Mirror of Korea The menu offers zesty soup, grilled meat, seafood, and sushi, all accompanied by kimchee, that fiery Korean staple. Open daily. No reservations. Major credit cards accepted. 1047 Ponce de Leon Ave. at N. Highland Ave. (phone: 874-6243).

Partners Morningside Café In a small room decorated with artwork, an upwardly mobile crowd dines on seafood and pasta. Open daily for dinner only. No reservations. Major credit cards accepted. 1399 Highland Ave. (phone: 876-8104).

Rio Bravo These cantinas, with campy Old Mexico decor, serve very good Tex-Mex victuals. Open daily. No reservations. Major credit cards accepted. Six locations: 240 Peachtree St. (phone: 524-9224) and 5565 New Northside Dr. (phone: 952-3241) in Atlanta; 3172 Roswell Rd. (phone: 262-7431) in N. Atlanta; 1570 Holcomb Bridge Rd. (phone: 642-0838) in Roswell; 440 Barrett Pkwy (phone: 429-0602) in Kennesaw; and Pleasant Hill Rd. (phone: 623-1096) in Duluth.

Sundown Café Chef Eddie Hernandez elevates Southwestern and Mexican cooking to great heights. Don't miss the shrimp cakes in *chipotle* (cactus-based) sauce. Closed Sundays; dinner only Thursdays through Saturdays. No reservations. Major credit cards accepted. 2165 Cheshire Bridge Rd. (phone: 321-1118).

Touch of India The city's best prepared tandoori dishes and curries. Open daily. No reservations. Major credit cards accepted. Two locations: 962

Peachtree St., near 10th St. (phone: 876-7777), and 2065 Piedmont Rd. (phone: 876-7775).

Varsity It's a scene right out of *American Graffiti*—a drive-in with singing car hops, an air of bedlam, and a menu of such all-American favorites as hot dogs, hamburgers, and sandwiches. Open daily. No reservations or credit cards accepted. 61 North Ave. NW (phone: 881-1706).

Baltimore

At-a-Glance

SEEING THE CITY

Baltimore offers its finest panoramic view from the *Top of the World,* an observation deck/museum devoted to changing displays about the city in the World Trade Center at the *Inner Harbor* (Pratt St., between South and Gay Sts.); admission charge. Downstream lies *Fort McHenry,* where the successful American repulsion of British forces in 1814 inspired Francis Scott Key to compose "The Star-Spangled Banner." To the northwest, the buildings and plazas of Charles Center stand out against the surrounding cityscape. To the east lie Little Italy, Fell's Point, and Canton.

SPECIAL PLACES

As most notable sights in Baltimore are concentrated in a few nicely designed areas, the best way to see the city is by walking. Buses and taxis, which serve the entire city, are convenient, but parking in the lots downtown is neither difficult nor expensive.

INNER HARBOR AND ENVIRONS

HARBORPLACE The dazzling kingpin in Baltimore's renaissance. A plethora of shops, restaurants, and market stalls—about 135 in all—fill its two glass-enclosed pavilions. On the first floor of the *Light Street Pavilion* is a marketplace where vendors hawk all manner of comestibles, while the upper level is chockablock with small eateries serving everything from hot dogs to knishes. And whether you want a crab mallet or a collector's comic book, chances are it's in the *Sam Smith Market* (also on the second floor), where merchants sell a raft of unusual wares from their pushcarts and kiosks. The *Pratt Street Pavilion* has its share of restaurants, boutiques, and specialty stores. Pratt and Light Sts. (phone: 332-4191).

NATIONAL AQUARIUM The aquarium has an impressive series of audiovisual displays on marine life, with a total of 5,000 specimens on seven different levels. The *Aquatic Educational Resource Center* features Atlantic bottle-nosed dolphins, along with educational presentations and audio-visual displays. "People movers" carry visitors between levels, which house shark and sting ray pools, puffins living in a reproduction of their natural habitat, the largest coral reef in the US, and a replica of Maine's coast with a display of shellfish and other shoreline creatures which can be handled. Finally, visitors can wander through a tropical rain forest. Open daily. Admission charge. Pier 3, *Inner Harbor* (phone: 576-3810).

FORT MCHENRY NATIONAL MONUMENT AND HISTORIC SHRINE In 1814, a young Maryland lawyer watched American forces successfully resist heavy British mortar bombardment and was so inspired by the sight of the Stars and Stripes still fluttering against the morning sky that he wrote

"The Star-Spangled Banner." Visitors can see the fort, the old powder magazine, the officers' quarters, the enlisted men's barracks, and then walk along Francis Scott Key's famed ramparts overlooking the harbor. During the summer on weekend afternoons, drills and military ceremonies modeled after those of 1814 are performed by uniformed soldiers and sailors. Closed *Christmas* and *New Year's Day*. Admission charge. South of *Inner Harbor,* at the end of East Fort Ave. (phone 962-4299).

USS CONSTELLATION The *US Navy*'s oldest warship still afloat (it was built in 1797), the *Constellation* (named by George Washington) defeated the French frigate *L'Insurgente* in America's first important victory at sea and served until after World War II. The city built a berth for the ship's permanent display in 1971, and plans for developing the *Inner Harbor* focused on the *Constellation*. A visitors' center provides an introduction to the ship through films and "living history" presentations. Open daily. Admission charge. Pier 1, *Inner Harbor* (phone: 539-1797).

MARYLAND SCIENCE CENTER AND PLANETARIUM Featured here are hundreds of hands-on activities, live demonstrations, and interactive displays ranging from a simulated space station control center to displays on sight, sound, magnetism, light, and mechanics. There is a 390-seat IMAX movie theater with a five-story screen capable of producing such vivid sensations of movement that viewers feel as if they are part of the action. Closed *Thanksgiving* and *Christmas*. Admission charge. At the southwest corner of the *Inner Harbor* (phone: 685-5225).

CHARLES CENTER AND DOWNTOWN

CHARLES CENTER Built during the past two decades, Charles Center is a 33-acre plot of office buildings, luxury apartment towers, overhead walkways, fountains, and plazas. It's bordered by Lombard Street on the south, Saratoga Street on the north, Hopkins Place and Liberty Street on the west, and Charles Street on the east. (One of the city's oldest and grandest thoroughfares, Charles Street has been revitalized in recent years with shops and restaurants to encourage new business.) Within the complex is *One Charles Center,* a 24-story tower of bronze-covered glass designed by Mies van der Rohe. Star performers, such as Jessica Tandy, Jason Robards, Lauren Bacall, and the late Rudolf Nureyev have performed at its *Morris Mechanic Theatre*. Charles and Baltimore Sts. Hopkins Plaza (between Hopkins Pl., Charles St., Baltimore St., and Lombard St.) is the scene for many events, including performances by jazz ensembles and chamber groups. Center Plaza (north of Fayette St. between Liberty and Charles Sts.) features a 33-foot bronze sculpture in the shape of a flame, designed by Francesco Somaini and presented to the city by the Gas and Electric Company. Pedestrian ramps link Charles Center to the *Convention Center* (1 West Pratt St.; phone: 659-7000; 800-899-9940) and to the *Baltimore Arena* (201 W. Baltimore St.; phone: 347-2010), which hosts professional soccer, circuses, ice hockey games, and rock concerts.

EDGAR ALLAN POE HOME AND GRAVE Poe lived here in the 1830s; he visited Baltimore again in 1849 long enough to die and be buried. His grave is

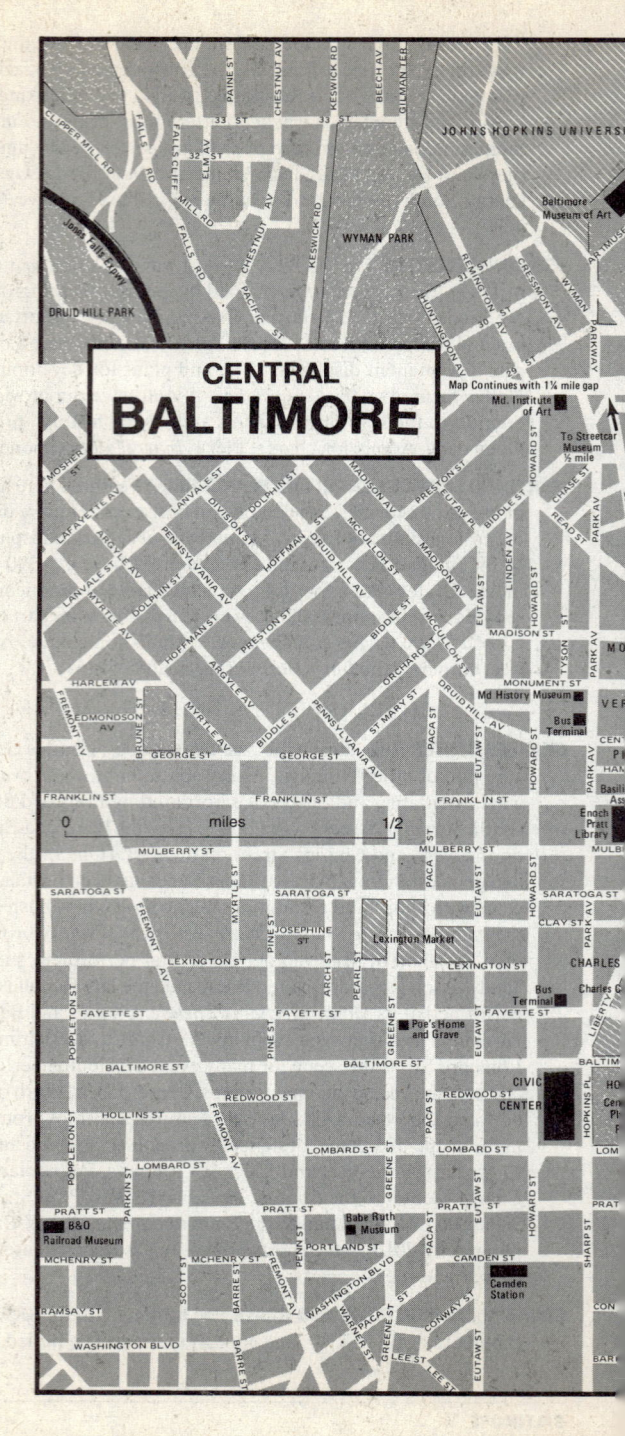

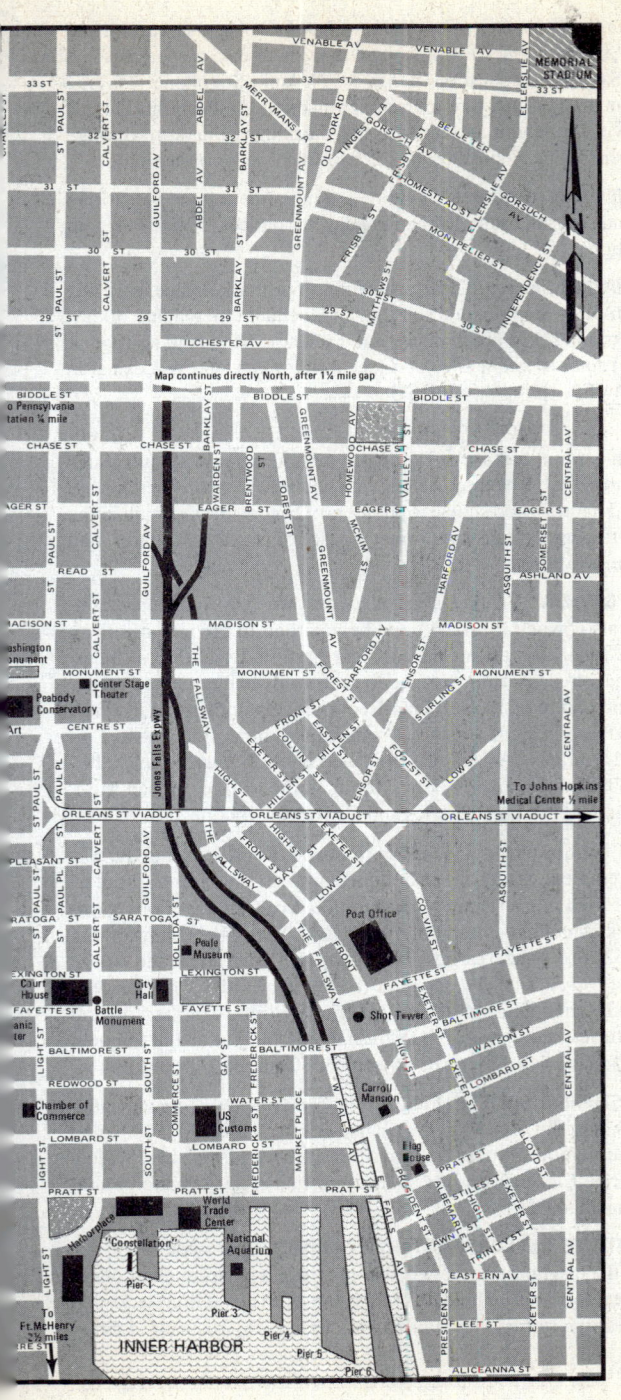

nearby, in the *Westminster Presbyterian Church Cemetery* at Fayette and Greene Streets. Home visiting hours are noon to 3:45 PM Wednesdays through Saturdays. Admission charge. 203 N. Amity St. (phone: 396-7932 for information). Graveyard tours are given on the first and third Friday evenings of the month and on Saturday mornings from April through November (phone: 706-2070; 706-7228 for recorded information).

CITY HALL Still in use, the domed building is a monument to mid-Victorian design and craftsmanship. 100 N. Holliday St. (phone: 837-5424 for tour information).

LEXINGTON MARKET Since 1782 this colorful indoor marketplace, covering two city blocks, has provided stalls for independent merchants. Today, 150 kiosks and shops are in operation. Lunch on Maryland seafood at its best at *John W. Faidley Seafood* (see *Eating Out*). 400 W. Lexington and Eutaw Sts. (phone: 685-6169).

MOUNT VERNON PLACE

This 19th-century bastion of Baltimore aristocracy now houses much of the 20th century's counterculture, with boutiques, plant stores, restaurants, and natural food shops. Reminders of bygone days remain in the lovely 19th-century merchant prince housefronts, stately squares, and cultural institutions.

WALTERS ART GALLERY This extensive collection, owned by the Walters family (who also owned railroads) and bequeathed to the city, offers an impressive span of art from ancient Near Eastern, Byzantine, and classical archaeological artifacts to medieval European illuminated manuscripts and painted panels, Italian Renaissance paintings, and French Impressionist works. The gallery's collection of Indian, Japanese, Chinese, and Southeast Asian art is displayed in *Hackerman House,* a historic 1850s mansion overlooking Mount Vernon Place. Closed Mondays. Admission charge. Charles and Centre Sts. (phone: 547-9000).

ANTIQUE ROW The 800 block of Howard Street and the area around the corner on West Read Street are an antiques-browser's paradise. About 65 shops here sell items ranging from antique furniture to various forms of artwork. Among the best are *Amos Judd & Son* (841 N. Howard St.; phone: 462-2000), which carries paintings by European artists and bronze sculpture; *Dubey's Art and Antiques* (807 N. Howard St.; phone: 383-2881), with Oriental, English, and American furniture of the 17th and 18th centuries; and *Imperial Half Bushel* (831 N. Howard St.; phone: 462-1192), featuring American silver pieces from the 19th century.

MARYLAND HISTORICAL SOCIETY Home of Francis Scott Key's original handwritten manuscript of the "Star-Spangled Banner," it features 18th- and 19th-century clothing, furniture, and silver. Its library is rich in genealogical material. Closed Mondays. Admission charge. 201 W. Monument St. (phone: 685-3750).

PEABODY INSTITUTE AND CONSERVATORY OF MUSIC Worth a visit simply for a look at the magnificently designed library. Amid pillars and balconies, this 19th-century interior holds 300,000 volumes on tiered iron stacks that spiral upward six stories. Free student concerts are held frequently. Library open daily. No admission charge. Mount Vernon Pl. at Monument and N. Charles Sts. (phone: 659-8163; 659-8124 for concert information).

WASHINGTON MONUMENT The very first Washington Monument, designed by Robert Mills, it was completed in 1829 and recently restored. Visitors can climb the 228 steps to the top, where a statue of Washington rests. Closed Mondays and Tuesdays. Donation suggested. Mount Vernon Pl. (phone: 396-3100, ext. 5540).

BALTIMORE CONSERVATORY Seasonal displays highlight this collection of 3,000 species of tropical plants and flowers. Closed Mondays through Wednesdays. No admission charge. Gwynns Falls Pkwy. and McCulloh St. (phone: 396-0180).

BALTIMORE ZOO More than 1,200 species of mammals, reptiles, and birds live here. A children's zoo and the new *African Watering Hole* are very popular. Closed *Christmas*. Admission charge. *Druid Hill Park* (phone: 396-7102 or 366-5466).

NORTH

BALTIMORE MUSEUM OF ART This museum is strong on 20th-century art, thanks to the *Cone Collection*—paintings, prints, and sculptures by Matisse, Picasso, and other Postimpressionists donated by the two wealthy Cone sisters of Baltimore. It also has period rooms that highlight the architectural and artistic development of Maryland from the 1700s through furniture and decorative art objects; the *Wurtzburger Collection* of African, Native American, pre-Columbian, and Oceanic art; a vast print collection; fine 19th- and 20th-century American paintings and sculpture; the spectacular outdoor *Levi* and *Wurtzburger Sculpture Gardens;* a stunning wing with galleries for changing exhibitions and a café overlooking the garden; and the *Jacobs Wing* of Old Masters paintings. Closed Mondays and Tuesdays. No admission charge on Thursdays. Art Museum Dr. near N. Charles and 31st Sts. (phone: 396-7100).

EXTRA SPECIAL

Just 30 miles south of Baltimore on Route 2 (Ritchie Hwy.) lies Annapolis, Maryland's capital, where the charm of the first peacetime capital of the US is still preserved. Around town are lovely 18th-century buildings, including the old *State House* (State Circle; phone: 974-3400), still in use today; the *Hammond-Harwood House* (19 Maryland Ave.; 269-1714), a Georgian home designed by William Buckland; and the campus of *St. John's College,* which appears much as it did to its most famous alumnus, Francis Scott Key. Also interesting is the *US Naval Academy,* which offers guided walking tours (phone: 267-3363). The remains of John Paul Jones lie in the crypt of the chapel. In town, the harbor is flanked by boutiques and restaurants, and sailing vessels can be seen coming and going.

Sources and Resources

TOURIST INFORMATION

The *Baltimore Area Convention and Visitors Association* offers useful tourist information, such as directions, maps, and brochures, as well as a listing of daily events. It's located at 300 West Pratt Street (closed Sundays) and at a kiosk at the *Inner Harbor* that is open daily during the summer (phone: 837-4636; 800-282-6632). Contact the *Maryland Tourism Office* (217 E. Redwood St., Baltimore, MD 21202; phone: 333-6611) for maps, calendars of events, health updates, and travel advisories.

LOCAL COVERAGE The *Baltimore Sun,* published twice daily and on Sundays, lists upcoming events. The weekly *City Paper,* which is free, offers a refreshing alternative and great classifieds. *Baltimore* is a monthly magazine with features on city life, restaurant listings, and calendars of events. All are available at newsstands. *Baltimore Scene* magazine and *Guest Informant in Baltimore* are comprehensive tourist publications, available for free in hotels and from the *Baltimore Area Visitors Center.*

TELEVISION STATIONS WMAR Channel 2–NBC; WBAL Channel 11–CBS; WJZ Channel 13–ABC; WMPB Channel 67–PBS; and WBFF Channel 45–Fox.

RADIO STATIONS AM: WBAL 1090 (news/talk); WFBR 1300 (pop music); and WWIN 1400 (urban contemporary). FM: WJHU 88.1 (classical/jazz); WYST 92.3 (adult contemporary/light rock); and WLIF 101.9 (easy listening/news).

TELEPHONE All telephone numbers are in the 410 area code unless otherwise indicated.

SALES TAX The state sales tax is 5%.

CLIMATE Baltimore weather is fickle, neither the rigorous clime of the North nor the mildness of the South. Unpredictable rainfall makes umbrellas advisable, particularly in the summer and early fall. In the summer, the weather can be hot and muggy, though the Chesapeake Bay exerts a modifying influence and brings relief with nighttime breezes. The winter is cold with moderate snowfall. Spring is windy and pleasant.

GETTING AROUND

AIRPORT *Baltimore/Washington, DC International Airport (BWI)* is usually a 20-minute ride from downtown Baltimore via the Baltimore-Washington Expressway. *Maryland Rail Commuter (MARC)* train service (phone: 800-325-7245) is available from the airport to the city's *Penn Station;* a shuttle bus transfers passengers from the air terminal to the airport train station. Trains run from 6:58 AM to 10:32 PM. *BWI Ground Transportation* offers van shuttle service between the airport and major downtown hotels every half hour from 6 AM to 11 PM (phone: 859-7545).

BUS The *Mass Transit Administration,* an inter-connecting system of buses, subway, and the *Light Rail,* covers the entire metropolitan area. Bus route information and maps are available at the *MTA*'s main office (300 W. Lexington St.; phone: 539-5000; 800-543-9809; 539-3497, for the hearing-impaired). The basic fare is $1.25, which increases depending on trip distance. Free transfers may be made between buses, subway trains, and the *Light Rail*.

CAR RENTAL All the major national firms are represented.

CRUISES For those intrigued by the thought of a cruise along Chesapeake Bay, one of the country's most scenic waterways, there are many charter boat companies in the area. *Chesapeake Marine Tours* (Box 3350, Annapolis, MD 21403; phone: 268-7600) has a variety of cruises; its day-long trip starts at Annapolis on the west side of the bay and sails to St. Michaels on the eastern shore, where passengers can delve into Chesapeake's maritime history, have lunch, and meander about. The *Chesapeake Flyer* (21053 Sharp St., PO Box 178, Rock Hall, MD 21661; phone: 639-7241) cruises between Baltimore, Annapolis, St. Michaels, Chestertown, and Rock Hall from April through November. *Harbor Cruises* (phone: 727-3113), the *Spirit of Baltimore* (phone: 752-7447), and *Maryland Tours* (phone: 745-9216) also offer cruises, and the *Water Taxi* (phone: 547-0090) allows passengers unlimited on/off privileges all day at all the waterfront attractions on its route.

LIGHT RAIL AND SUBWAY The *Light Rail* runs from Glen Burnie in the south of the city to Timonium in the north. The local station is at *Camden Yards* near the *Inner Harbor*. It operates from 6 AM to 11 PM weekdays, from 6 AM to 11 PM Saturdays, and from 11 AM to 7 PM Sundays; the base fare is $1.25. The subway system, called the *Metro Rail*, offers limited access to much of the downtown area. Trains operate from 5 AM to midnight on weekdays and from 8 AM to midnight on Saturdays. Base fare is $1.25. There is an additional charge for trips into the outer zones (phone: 539-5000). Free parking and bus shuttle service is available from the outlying stations.

TAXI Cabs may be hailed on the street but are usually called by phone. Major companies are *Yellow Cab/Sun* (phone: 685-1212), *Diamond* (phone: 947-3333), and *BWI Airport Cab* (phone: 859-1103).

TOURS Guided tours are available from *Baltimore Rent-a-Tour* (phone: 653-2998). *Baltimore Trolley Tours* (phone: 752-2015) has 17 boarding locations for all-day touring on weekends.

LOCAL SERVICES

AUDIOVISUAL EQUIPMENT *Audio Visual Service* (phone: 467-3620); *Avcom* (phone: 752-7838).

BABY-SITTING *Elizabeth Cooney Personnel Agency* (phone: 323-1700).

BUSINESS SERVICES *Able Temporaries* (2 N. Charles St.; phone: 685-8189).

DRY CLEANER/TAILOR *Apex Cleaners* (215 E. Baltimore St.; phone: 752-3979), shoe repair also.

LIMOUSINE *Chesapeake Limousine* (phone: 366-3000); *Maryland Limousine Service* (phone: 850-4100).

MECHANIC *Plotkin's* (600 W. Franklin St.; phone: 728-5533).

MEDICAL EMERGENCY *University Hospital* (22 Greene St.; phone: 328-6722).

MESSENGER SERVICES *Carl Messenger Service* (phone: 761-1234); *Central Delivery Service* (phone: 792-9098).

MONEY TRANSFERS *American Express MoneyGram* (phone: 800-926-9400 for information; 800-866-8800 for money transfers); *Western Union Financial Services* (phone: 800-325-6000 or 800-325-4176).

NATIONAL/INTERNATIONAL COURIER *DHL Worldwide Express* (phone: 636-5454); *FedEx* (phone: 792-8200; 800-238-5355).

PHARMACY *Rite-Aid* (17 W. Baltimore St.; phone: 539-0838), open daily 8 AM to 6 PM.

PHOTOCOPIES *Copy Cat Instant Press* (211 E. Baltimore St.; phone: 837-6411); *Day Speedy Printing* (106 E. Lombard St.; phone: 539-8500).

POST OFFICE Central office (900 E. Fayette St.; phone: 347-4422).

WESTERN UNION/TELEX Many offices are located around the city (phone: 800-325-6000 to find the location nearest you).

SPECIAL EVENTS

Though the city boasts a rich, year-round calendar of events, one is an odds-on favorite.

AND THEY'RE OFF!

The Preakness One of America's oldest horse races, it's the middle jewel of thoroughbred racing's Triple Crown. The race is run the third Saturday in May for more than $500,000 on the $1\frac{3}{16}$-mile dirt track at the *Pimlico Race Course*. The race started in 1873 and attracts the nation's best three-year-old thoroughbreds—not to mention crowds of over 90,000. *Preakness Festival Week,* held the week before, features outdoor concerts, exhibitions, and performances. For more information, contact the *Maryland Jockey Club, Pimlico Race Course,* Belvedere and Park Heights Aves. (phone: 542-9400; 800-638-3811).

From the last week of April through mid-May, the *Maryland House and Garden Pilgrimage* lavishly demonstrates Baltimoreans' pride in their own backyards. This statewide event for garden lovers is a series of self-guided tours through a group of outstanding homes and gardens. For details, contact the *Pilgrimage* offices (1105A Providence Rd., Baltimore, MD 21286; phone: 821-6933). Numerous ethnic fairs take place in warm weather and are held at a variety of locations (see newspapers for listings). The *Harborlights Music Festival* is held every summer, usually June through August, at Baltimore's 3,338-seat *Pier 6 Pavilion* (Pier 6 at Pratt St.; phone: 625-1400). Many concerts—from symphony to pop—are given.

MUSEUMS

In addition to those described in *Special Places,* Baltimore has several other museums of note.

BABE RUTH BIRTHPLACE Cooperstown may have the fame, but baseball buffs will find everything authentic here, from photos of the Babe to taped interviews and *Orioles* memorabilia. Open daily. Admission charge. 216 Emory St. (phone: 727-1539).

BALTIMORE CITY LIFE MUSEUMS Baltimore has organized its small museums into an integrated collection; each museum represents a facet of the city's culture and history. At the *Peale Museum* (225 Holliday St.; phone: 396-1149), enjoy the collection of the Peale family, featuring works by Early American portrait painters (including some Baltimoreans), as well as several changing exhibits. Get acquainted with Baltimore's most famous literary son at the *H. L. Mencken House* on Union Square (1524 Hollins St.; phone: 396-7997). A number of other museums line Lombard Street, which is known as *Museum Row*. These include *Carroll Mansion* (800 Lombard St.), the elegant townhouse of a signer of the Declaration of Independence; the *Center of Urban Archaeology* (802 E. Lombard St.), where you can dig into the city's past; the *1840 House* (50 Albemarle St., corner of E. Lombard), which offers a visit to a 19th-century middle class family through a dramatic living history presentation; and the *Courtyard Exhibition Center* (44-48 Albemarle St.), which provides a sense of the city's diverse character. All are closed Mondays. Admission charge (phone: 396-3524 for information).

BALTIMORE MARITIME MUSEUM The submarine USS *Torsk*, the *US Coast Guard* cutter *Taney*, and the lightship *Chesapeake* are open for tours daily in summer; closed Mondays through Thursdays in winter. Admission charge. Pier 3, *Inner Harbor* (phone: 396-3453).

BALTIMORE PUBLIC WORKS MUSEUM A representation of what goes on beneath the street is one of several exhibits on the history of public works. Also included is a children's activity center. Closed Mondays and Tuesdays. Admission charge. 751 Eastern Ave. (phone: 396-5565).

BALTIMORE STREETCAR MUSEUM Home of the nation's first electric streetcar, this museum features a mile-and-a-quarter ride on a vintage streetcar, an exploration of the original carhouse, and exhibits of antique vehicles. Open Sundays; also Saturdays from June through October. No admission charge, but there is a fee for the streetcar ride. 1901 Falls Rd. (phone: 547-0264).

B&O RAILROAD MUSEUM The most extensive collection of railroad memorabilia in the US and the second largest in the world. It includes the nation's first passenger and freight station as well as related exhibits. Closed major holidays. Admission charge. 901 W. Pratt St. (phone: 237-2387).

CLOISTERS CHILDREN'S MUSEUM Youngsters will be fascinated by all the hands-on, participatory displays and activities at this museum, including a mock grocery store and a computer exhibit. Closed Mondays. Admission charge. 10440 Falls Rd. (phone: 823-2551). *Note:* At press time, the museum was planning to move to *The Brokerage* (34 Market Pl.) this spring.

LACROSSE HALL OF FAME MUSEUM Baltimore is the cradle of lacrosse, and displayed here are memorabilia and records relating to all levels of play. Closed weekends July through February; closed Sundays March through June, when it is open Saturdays. Admission charge. On *Johns Hopkins University*'s Homewood Campus, 113 W. University Pkwy. (phone: 235-6882).

STAR-SPANGLED BANNER FLAG HOUSE Once the home of Mary Pickersgill, who hand-sewed the flag that flew over *Fort McHenry*, it is furnished with 18th-century antiques. Closed Sundays. Admission charge. 844 E. Pratt St. (phone: 837-1793).

SPORTS AND FITNESS

BASEBALL The *Orioles* play their home games at *Camden Yards*, a 48,000-seat stadium near the harbor. Tickets for good seats may be hard to get (phone: 685-9800).

BICYCLING A brochure and map describing bicycle routes through the countryside are available from the *Maryland State Highway Administration*'s Bicycle Hotline (phone: 800-252-8776). Bicycles can be rented from *Cross-Country Cycling Center* (11612 Reisterstown Rd., Reisterstown; phone: 833-4444) or *Race Pace* (8450 Baltimore National Pike, Ellicott City; phone: 461-7878).

BOATING *Middle Branch Park* is the site of the *Baltimore Rowing and Resource Center* (phone: 396-3838), a unique facility that includes boat storage and a fishing pier.

FITNESS CENTER The *Downtown Athletic Club* (210 E. Centre St.; phone: 332-0906) opens its pool and equipment to visitors.

FOOTBALL Baltimore's new *Canadian Football League* team plays at *Memorial Stadium* (1000 E. 33 St. at Ellerslie Ave.; phone: 554-1010).

GOLF The best public course is the 18-hole *Pine Ridge*, 3 miles north on Dulaney Valley Road (exit 27 on the Baltimore Beltway; phone: 252-1408). There are others at *Forest Park* (Hillside and Forest Park Aves.; phone: 448-4653) and *Carroll Park* (Monroe and Washington Blvds.; phone: 685-8344).

HORSE RACING The season runs from late March through early June, and August through early October. The high point is the *Preakness*, which, along with the *Kentucky Derby* and the *Belmont Stakes*, makes up the Triple Crown (see *Special Events*). At the *Pimlico Race Course* (Belvedere and Park Heights Aves.; phone: 542-9400; 800-638-3811).

LACROSSE The *Johns Hopkins Blue Jays* (*Homewood Field*, Charles St. and University Pkwy.; phone: 516-7490) are among the best of the college teams in the country. Seats usually are available.

SOCCER Watch the *Baltimore Spirit* indoors from October through April at the *Baltimore Arena* (201 W. Baltimore; phone: 625-2320).

STEEPLECHASE Point-to-point races (with timber barrier jumps) are run in the valleys north of the city (Western Run, Worthington, Long Green) on Saturday afternoons during April.

TENNIS The *Greenspring Racquet Club* (10803 Falls Rd.; phone: 821-5683) is a large indoor facility; non-members may use courts for a fee.

THEATER

For complete listings, see the publications listed in *Local Coverage*. Baltimore's theatrical offerings range from Broadway tryouts or road shows at the *Morris Mechanic Theatre* (Charles Center; phone: 625-1400) to resident productions at *Center Stage,* the state theater of Maryland (700 N. Calvert St.; phone: 332-0033), to the *Vagabond Players,* the oldest continuously operated "little theater" in the US (806 S. Broadway; phone: 563-9135), and experimental works at the *Theatre Project* (45 W. Preston St.; phone: 752-8558). There also are eight dinner-theaters that present Broadway shows. Try *Burn Brae Dinner Theatre* (3811 Blackburn Rd., Burtonsville; phone: 792-0290) or *F. Scott Black's Harborlights Dinner Theater* (100 E. Chesapeake Ave., Towson; phone: 321-6595).

MUSIC

The highly regarded *Baltimore Symphony Orchestra* performs throughout the year at the *Joseph Meyerhoff Symphony Hall* (1212 Cathedral St.; phone: 783-8100). *The Baltimore Opera* performs in the *Lyric Opera House* (140 W. Mt. Royal Ave.; phone: 727-6000). The *Baltimore Museum of Art* (Art Museum Dr.; phone: 396-7100) also hosts dance and music programs. Other concerts are presented by well-known visiting artists; check the newspapers.

NIGHTCLUBS AND NIGHTLIFE

The city's oldest comedy club, the *Charm City Comedy Club* (102 Water St.; phone: 576-8558) presents stand-up comics from New York and LA, including those from top late-night TV shows. *Buddies Pub* (313 N. Charles St.; phone: 332-4200) has a jazz quartet Thursday through Saturday nights. *Bertha's* (734 S. Broadway; phone: 327-5795) features jazz Mondays through Saturdays. *Eight by Ten* (10 E. Cross St.; phone: 625-2000) offers rhythm and blues, jazz, and alternative music.

Best in Town

CHECKING IN

There is an increasing number of luxury hotels and several less costly ones downtown. Expect to pay $140 or more per night for a couble room at hotels we list as very expensive, $100 to $140 at expensive places, and $65 to $100 at moderate hotels; there are no exceptional inexpensive hotels in the city. Note that there is free parking at many of the hotel chains downtown. For hotel reservations, contact the *Maryland Reservation Center* (phone: 800-654-9303) or *The Traveller in Maryland* (phone: 269-6232). For bed and breakfast accommodations, contact *Amanda's Bed and Breakfast and Reservation Service* (1428 Park Ave.; phone: 225-0001). Unless otherwise noted, hotel rooms have air conditioning, private baths, TV sets, and telephones. All hotels are in the 410 area code unless otherwise indicated.

VERY EXPENSIVE

Harbor Court The modest exterior of this brick hotel facing the *Inner Harbor* belies the elegance that can be found inside. Exquisitely decorated with marble floors, reproductions of 18th-century furnishings, and Chinese art, it is Baltimore's most luxurious property. Most of the 203 rooms and suites have views of the harbor or downtown; amenities include two-line telephones, 24-hour room service, and a concierge. There are two restaurants, one of which is the excellent *Hampton's* (see *Eating Out*), and the other a coffee shop; in addition, there is a complete fitness center, a rooftop croquet court, and a beauty salon. Other features include a full business center, eight meeting rooms, and a ballroom. 550 Light St. (phone: 234-0550; 800-824-0076; fax: 659-5925).

Hyatt Regency, Baltimore A glossy waterfront hostelry with 487 rooms, 29,200 square feet of meeting space, and a skywalk connecting it to *Harborplace* and the *Baltimore Convention Center*. It's also only a short walk to the *National Aquarium* and the *Maryland Science Center*. Recreational facilities include tennis courts, a fitness center, a jogging track, and an outdoor pool. There's a coffee shop (with a waterfall) for snacks, a dining room in a park-like setting, and a formal restaurant on the rooftop level. Room service is available until 12:30 AM, and a concierge desk, a business center, and express checkout are among the business amenities. 300 Light St., *Inner Harbor* (phone: 528-1234; 800-233-1234; fax: 685-3362).

Stouffer Harborplace A contemporary, elegant high-rise with 622 rooms, on the *Inner Harbor* at *Harborplace*. It is convenient to the aquarium, science center, and other attractions. *Windows* restaurant looks out over the harbor and features local seafood and continental dishes; there are also two lounges (one with a piano bar). Room service is available 24 hours a day. Business amenities include a concierge desk, 20 meeting rooms, and secretarial services. There's also express checkout. 202 E. Pratt St. (phone: 547-1200; 800-325-5000 or 800-HOTELS-1; fax: 539-5780).

EXPENSIVE

Admiral Fell Inn A historic bed and breakfast establishment with 50 rooms of various shapes and sizes carved out of four buildings. All rooms are named for famous city residents; most feature four-poster beds. There's a small restaurant and an English-style pub. Continental breakfast is complimentary. There's a free van to town and a summer ferry to *Inner Harbor*. A meeting room is available. Fell's Point, 888 S. Broadway (phone: 522-7377; 800-292-4667; fax: 522-0707).

Baltimore Marriott Inner Harbor Within walking distance of *Harborplace* downtown, this 525-room property is ideal for business travelers and, due to its convenient location, also a good bet for tourists. It has a restaurant and a lounge with entertainment. Room service is available until 11 PM, and a concierge desk, 20 meeting rooms, and secretarial services round out the list of conveniences. Pratt and Eutaw Sts. (phone: 962-0202; 800-228-9290; fax: 962-0202).

Latham The same people who restored Washington, DC's *Hay-Adams* hotel have brought similar distinctive qualities to this 104-room property (formerly the *Peabody Court*) in Baltimore's historic Mount Vernon Square. The European-style hotel offers fine service, old-fashioned decor, and a superb restaurant, the *Citronelle* (see *Eating Out*). Room service is available until midnight, and there are eight meeting rooms, a concierge, and secretarial services. Mount Vernon Pl. (phone: 727-7101; 800-528-4261; fax: 789-3312).

Mr. Mole Bed and Breakfast A truly lovely bed and breakfast establishment set in a late 19th-century home, it is named after a character from the story *The Wind in the Willows*. Inside is an elegant world of crystal chandeliers, touches of Italian marble, and period antiques; the five rooms and suites are equally sumptuous. There is no restaurant, but a Dutch-style buffet breakfast is served in the breakfast room. The inn is located in a historic uptown residential neighborhood with its own private security patrol. It also provides garages with automatic door openers for its guests. No smoking allowed. 1601 Bolton St. (phone: 728-1179).

MODERATE

Biltmore Suites This 1880s Victorian mansion is now a 24-suite hotel. Spacious rooms have high ceilings and antique furnishings, and connecting doors facilitate a variety of room arrangements. Guests can enjoy a generous European breakfast and an early evening wine and lager tasting; there is no restaurant. A meeting room and free limousine service to the downtown area are available. 205 W. Madison St. (phone: 728-6550; fax: 728-5829).

Days Inn Inner Harbor A property that is a favorite for its location near the city's most popular attractions, it has 250 rooms and a restaurant; guests may use a nearby fitness center that has a pool and exercise equipment. Business amenities include four meeting rooms that can accommodate up to 150 people, A/V services, a fax machine, and a photocopier. 100 Hopkins Pl. (phone: 576-1000; 800-325-2525; fax: 576-9437).

Holiday Inn Inner Harbor Its convenient location one block from the *Inner Harbor* is unusual for such a moderately priced hotel. Don't be put off by the rather unappealing exterior; inside, things brighten up considerably. There are 375 guestrooms and 13,000 square feet of adaptable meeting space that can accommodate up to 500. *McKenna's* is a large restaurant and lounge, and other amenities include an indoor pool and a fitness center. 301 W. Lombard St. (phone: 685-3500; 800-HOLIDAY; fax: 727-6169).

Tremont Four blocks south of Mount Vernon Square (and *not* to be confused with the nearby *Tremont Plaza*), the 60-room hostelry caters to celebrities and executives wanting the privacy and amenities of an all-suite hotel. There is a restaurant, and another attractive feature is guest privileges at the nearby *Downtown Athletic Club*. Room service is available until 10 PM, and there are three meeting rooms. 8 E. Pleasant St. (phone: 576-1200; 800-873-6668; fax: 685-4215).

EATING OUT

Dedicated eaters find happiness in Baltimore. From its regional specialties, seafood in the rough and crab cakes, to the authentic dishes of its Little Italy, there are restaurants to suit most palates and pocketbooks. Our selections range in price from $60 to $80 for a dinner for two in the expensive category, $30 to $60 in the moderate category, and $30 or less in the inexpensive category. Prices do not include drinks, wine, tax, or tips. Unless otherwise noted, restaurants serve lunch and dinner. All restaurants are in the 410 area code unless otherwise indicated.

EXPENSIVE

Citronelle Even if the food were mediocre, a meal here would be enjoyable simply for the lovely view overlooking Mount Vernon's cultural institutions. Fortunately, the menu is superb. Award-winning chef Michel Richard brings his style of California French cuisine to Baltimore via such specialties as tuna tournedos and chicken in a *porcini* mushroom crust. Open daily for dinner only. Reservations necessary. Major credit cards accepted. *Latham Hotel,* Mount Vernon Pl. (phone: 727-7101).

Hampton's The premier restaurant at the *Harbor Court* hotel is also one of the best in the city. Elegance is the watchword here, with fresh flowers, fine napery, china, silverware, and glowing candlelight; the menu is just as special. Oysters stuffed with crabmeat, smoked salmon and trout, and rack of lamb are just a few of the beautifully prepared and presented dishes. There's also a champagne brunch on Sundays. Jacket and tie required for men. Open for dinner only; closed Mondays. Reservations essential. Major credit cards accepted. 550 Light St. (phone: 234-0550).

Prime Rib A hangout for figures in the city's political and entertainment worlds. Its prime ribs are great, but no more so than the crab imperial. Jackets required for men. Open daily for dinner only. Reservations advised. Major credit cards accepted. Calvert and Chase Sts., in *Horizon House* (phone: 539-1804).

Tio Pepe The Spanish food here has rated highly among locals year after year, which means it's usually crowded; you might have to order another pitcher of sangria before your table is available. Open daily. Reservations (and jackets for men) necessary for dinner. Major credit cards accepted. 10 E. Franklin St. (phone: 539-4675).

MODERATE

Chiapparelli's This restaurant in Little Italy is popular for its casual atmosphere and prompt service. Homemade ravioli stuffed with ricotta and spinach is a specialty. Open daily. Reservations necessary on weekends. Major credit cards accepted. 237 S. High St. (phone: 837-0309).

Maison Marconi Here, the artistry is on the plate rather than in the decor. The specialty is filet of sole prepared in a variety of delicious ways. Closed Sundays and Mondays. Reservations advised. Major credit cards accepted. 106 W. Saratoga St. (phone: 727-9522).

Olde Obrycki's Crab House Roll back your sleeves, put on your bib, grab a mallet, and get ready to battle steamed crabs. The warm family atmosphere adds to the enjoyment of seafood feasts. Closed December through May; closed Mondays; dinner only on weekends. Reservations advised. Major credit cards accepted. 1729 E. Pratt St., Fell's Point. (phone: 732-6399).

Orchid Baltimore's first French and Oriental restaurant offers an award-winning menu of fresh meat, seafood, and crisp vegetables, in a marriage that combines the best of both worlds—creamy French sauces and fresh Oriental seasonings. Closed Mondays. Reservations necessary. Major credit cards accepted. Downtown near all attractions, 419 N. Charles St. (phone: 837-0080).

INEXPENSIVE

John W. Faidley Seafood One of the world's largest raw oyster bars; in the past 100 years, it has established itself as the place for oysters, crabs, and clams brought in fresh daily from the bay. The downtown lunch crowd regards a visit to its branch in *Lexington Market*—a vast assemblage of butchers and merchants—as the ultimate adventure. Closed Sundays. Major credit cards accepted. Paca at Lexington St. (phone: 727-4898).

HARBORPLACE

In addition to 33 food stalls, where visitors can find everything from Buffalo wings to chocolate-covered strawberries, the following restaurants have good food, harbor views, and moderate prices. In the *Light Street Pavilion* are *The American Café*, with a light American menu (phone: 962-8800); *City Lights*, featuring seafood and homemade desserts (phone: 244-8811); *Phillips Harborplace*, with Chesapeake Bay seafood and a piano bar (phone: 685-6600); and *Wayne's Barbeque*, with homemade soups (the crab soup is particularly good), salads, and desserts in addition to barbecued ribs and chicken (phone: 539-3810). In the *Pratt Street Pavilion* are *Taverna Athena*, with authentic Greek food (phone: 547-8900), and *Bamboo House*, for Chinese food (phone: 625-1191).

Boston

At-a-Glance

SEEING THE CITY

There are two unparalleled posts from which to view Boston: the *John Hancock Tower*'s 60th-floor *Observatory* (Copley Sq.; phone: 247-1977) and the 50th-floor *Prudential Center Skywalk* (800 Boylston St.; phone: 236-3318). The recently renovated *Observatory* offers a spectacular panorama that even includes the mountains of southern New Hampshire (weather permitting). It also has telescopes, recorded commentaries, a topographical model of Boston in 1775 (this is a must—we promise you'll be surprised), and a seven-minute film of a helicopter flight over the city. The *Skywalk* also offers an excellent 360° view. Both are open daily and charge admission.

Boston also has several fabulous rooms with views where you can relax with a drink and watch the sun set over the city. The most elegant is the *Bay Tower Room* on the 33rd floor of the 60 State Street tower, near *Faneuil Hall*. Though it is a private club and a favorite of the working lunch crowd, the elegant restaurant and piano bar on the top floor are open to the general public after 4:30 PM. The menu features creative American cooking; the baked stuffed lobster is especially succulent. A jacket is required for men. Enjoy free hors d'oeuvres, live music on weekends, and a dizzying view of the city's waterfront through three-story-high windows (phone: 723-1666). For a 360° view, visit the revolving restaurant on top of the *Hyatt Regency Cambridge* (see *Checking In*) or the *Top of the Hub* restaurant (phone: 536-1775; open daily) on the 52nd floor of the *Prudential* tower, two floors above the *Skywalk*.

SPECIAL PLACES

Boston is best seen on foot; the city is compact, and driving, even for residents, is often hair-raising.

DOWNTOWN

The confusing crisscross of narrow streets that gives Boston its charm is no more evident than in the city's cradle, the downtown area, which now consists of *Faneuil Hall, Government Center,* and the financial, retail, and waterfront districts.

BOSTON COMMON This pastoral green, established in 1634, is the nation's oldest park. The earliest Bostonians brought their cows and horses here to graze. Today, you'll find their descendants engaging in free-form pastimes that range from playing music to playing baseball. We suggest starting your tour of the city here—but don't walk alone at night, as the *Common* is often inadequately patrolled. The lovely *Public Garden* is adjacent to the *Common*, across Charles Street. For information about activities on the *Common*, call 536-4100. You can park at *Motor Mart* on Stuart Street or at the *57 Park Plaza* hotel.

FREEDOM TRAIL The city has made it both easy and fun to track down the important sites from its colonial and Revolutionary past. Just follow the red brick (or red paint) line set into the sidewalks, which leads through downtown Boston and the North End, then crosses the river into Charlestown. The trail may be followed only on foot; it takes about two hours to walk its length without stops or side trips. To begin, take the *Green* or *Red Line* to Park Street and walk down Tremont Street to the *Visitors' Information Center* on the *Common*, which has maps.

PARK STREET CHURCH Built in 1809, the church witnessed William Lloyd Garrison's famous first anti-slavery address in 1829 and heard the first singing of "My country, 'tis of thee" three years later. It's open Tuesdays through Saturdays in July and August; otherwise by appointment. 1 Park St. (phone: 523-3383).

OLD GRANARY BURYING GROUND In this 1660 cemetery, next door to the *Park Street Church*, are the graves of such Revolutionary notables as John Hancock, Samuel Adams, Paul Revere, and the victims of the Boston Massacre, as well as the parents of Benjamin Franklin. Open daily (phone: 635-4505, ext. 6516).

DOWNTOWN CROSSING A great meeting place. Winter meets Summer Street, the *Red Line* meets the *Orange Line*, and the display windows of the two giants of Boston retailing, *Filene's* and *Jordan Marsh*, face each other across a brick, pedestrians-only street. On Saturdays, when the shoppers, vendors, and street performers are out in force, this intersection resembles Mecca at the end of *Ramadan*, which may be why a good proportion of the world's lesser-known religions are represented here, looking for new members or donations. Business is brisk for the vending carts, which sell everything from T-shirts to llama-skin luggage. At the intersection of Winter and Washington Streets.

KING'S CHAPEL AND BURYING GROUND Founded as the Massachusetts Bay Colony's first Anglican church in 1686, *King's Chapel* was the place of worship for British officers and the royal governor. Since the colonists had fled England to escape the Anglican Church, the church's founding was taken as an insult. The ornate *Governor's Pew*, the church's centerpiece, was removed from the church in 1826, only to be restored a century later after it was clear that the colony had rid itself of British elitism. The cemetery next door, established in 1631, is the city's oldest and contains the graves and tombstones of many revered old Bostonians, including John Winthrop, the first Governor of the Massachusetts Bay Colony; William Dawes, who was Paul Revere's companion on his famous ride; and Mary Chilton, the first woman Pilgrim from the Plymouth Colony to go to Boston. The church hosts free chamber music and other concerts on Tuesdays just after noon. Open Mondays through Saturdays mid-June through *Labor Day;* Mondays, Fridays, and Saturdays mid-March through mid-June and *Labor Day* through October; Saturdays only the rest of the year. Tremont St. at School St. (phone: 227-2155).

OLD SOUTH MEETING HOUSE Though this well-preserved church was built in 1729 to serve Boston's Puritan congregation, its greatest hour was secular. When dissent began to rumble in the colonies before the Revo-

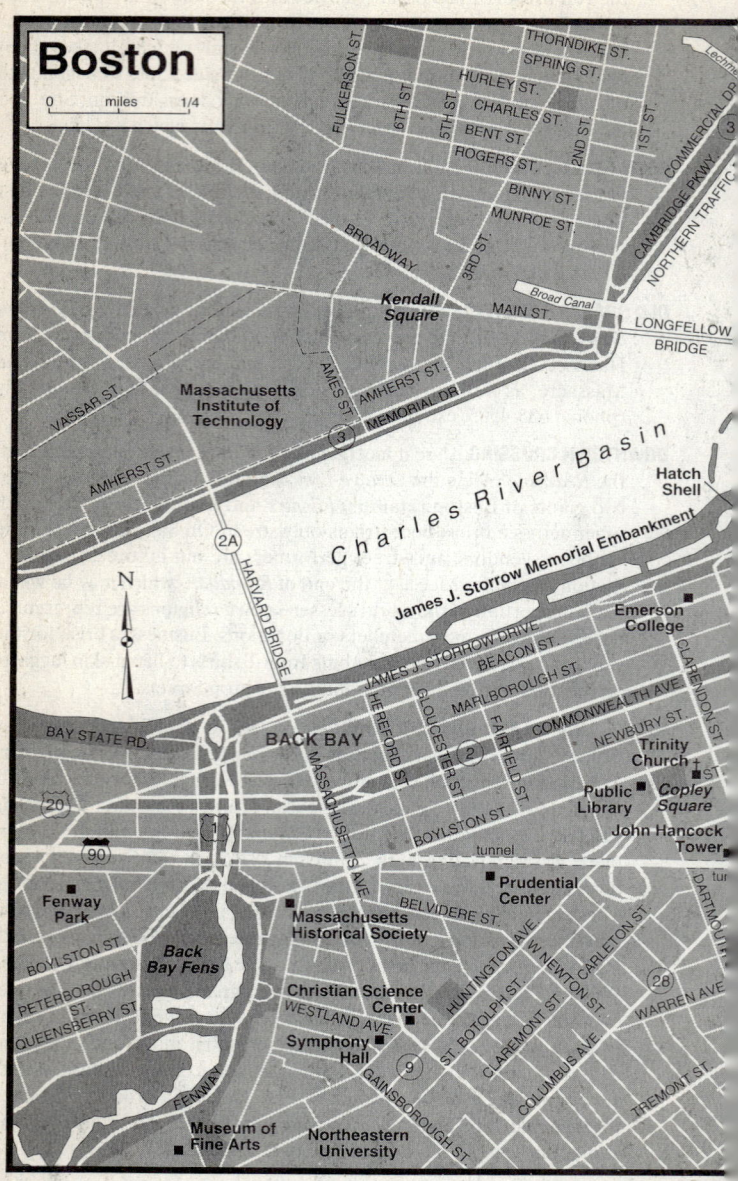

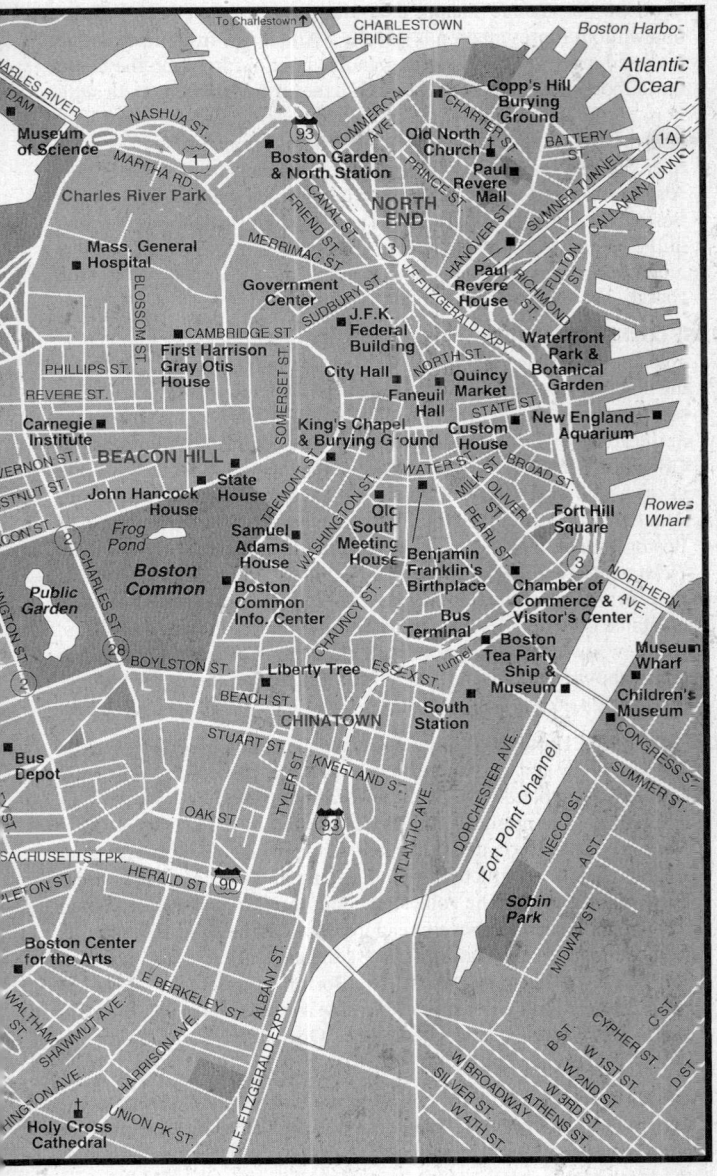

lution, it was here that patriots flocked to debate the issues of the day. It was here that, after failing to persuade the royal governor to send back to England three ships that were filled with dutiable tea and moored in the harbor, Samuel Adams announced, in December 1773, "Taxation without representation is tyranny." And it was from here that an incensed mob, some disguised as Indians, set out to dump the tea in the harbor and write a crucial chapter in the birth of this nation. In addition, Ben Franklin, who was born across the street, was baptized here when he was only hours old. An award-winning permanent audio exhibit re-creates the Tea Party and other exciting moments from Boston's past. Also on display are rare colonial artifacts and a scale model of early Boston. Costumed players reenact a town meeting on Saturday evenings in the summer, and from October through April, there's a Thursday lunchtime lecture series on American history. Open daily; admission charge. 310 Washington St. (phone: 482-6439).

GLOBE CORNER BOOKSTORE Formerly the *Old Corner Bookstore,* this venerable landmark was long the hub of Boston's literary scene. The building that first stood on this site belonged to the family of Anne Hutchinson, a religious dissident whose unorthodox beliefs became so popular in the 1630s that she was banished from the colony by an intimidated Governor Winthrop (he later conceded that he was about the only one in town who didn't like her opinions). The present building was constructed in 1718 after the Hutchinson home was destroyed in the Great Boston Fire of 1711. For years, it was the office of eminent publishers *Ticknor and Fields,* where editor Jamie Fields attracted such names as Emerson, Hawthorne, Holmes, Longfellow, Lowell, and Thoreau to his stable of writers. Fields's office was a center of literary discussion. It is now a working bookstore with abundant travel titles, as well as books about New England and by New England authors. 1 School St. (phone: 523-6658).

OLD STATE HOUSE Boston's 18th-century seat of government served both the English colony and the American state of Massachusetts until the *State House* was completed in 1798. Now dwarfed by modern towers of law and finance, the present building was erected in 1713. The *Old State House* served as the council chambers of the royal governors sent from England. As the conflict between England and the colonies became more pointed, so did the goings-on about the *Old State House.* When edicts and proclamations were read from the east balcony, the colonists would adjourn to local taverns to work themselves into a fury and then return, emboldened, to protest. The Boston Massacre was staged in front of the building's east side. It's now a museum, tracing Boston's history from early to contemporary times. Open daily. Admission charge. 206 Washington St. (phone: 720-3290).

CITY HALL The focal point of the *Government Center* plaza, Boston's looming, concrete *City Hall* (1968), designed by Kallman, McKinnell & Knowles, is considered a landmark of modern architecture, although the local populace loves to revile it. *City Hall* sits in the middle of an eight-acre plaza that is often the scene of civic celebrations and politicking. Congress St. (phone: 725-4000).

FANEUIL HALL MARKETPLACE The market takes its official name from adjacent *Faneuil* (pronounced *Fan-*yool) *Hall,* a historic meeting house. It is also known as *Quincy Market,* which is the name of the main market building. When it opened in 1826, this was the site of the city's meat and produce markets (11 of the original tenants still do business here). Redesigned between 1976 and 1978 by Benjamin Thompson and the Rouse Company, the market has become a much-copied prototype of urban renewal. Now a lively gathering place, it has performers and street vendors outside and eateries, trinket shops, and boutiques inside. Over a million people a month visit its stalls, restaurants, and shops. Open daily. Off I-93 between Clinton and Chatham Streets (phone: 338-2323).

WATERFRONT

There's much to do and see along Boston's waterfront. Walk along *Waterfront Park,* with its invigorating views of the harbor; browse in the many new shops set in the renovated wharf buildings; or take a sightseeing tour by water from Long Wharf (see *Getting Around,* below). Also here is the *Aquarium* (see below). Just over the Congress Street Bridge, past the *Boston Tea Party Ship and Museum* and into the commercial district of South Boston—some call it Wallpaper Row—are the wildly popular *Computer Museum* and *Children's Museum.* They are located on the park-like *Museum Wharf,* home of the enormous red-and-white H. P. Hood Milk Bottle, a vintage 1930s highway lunch stand that is 40 feet high.

NEW ENGLAND AQUARIUM One of the world's top collections of marine life—more than 2,000 species in all—it houses exhibits re-creating a tide pool, northern waters, and tropical marine environments. Of particular note is the four-story saltwater tank, girded by a spiral viewing ramp from which visitors can view the resident sharks, sea turtles, moray eels, and wide variety of fish. Divers regularly feed the underwater multitudes so they don't dine on each other. Penguins cavort in their own habitat, and seals and dolphins perform aboard the floating pavilion *Discovery,* next door to the main building. Films are shown in the auditorium, and there's an interesting gift shop. Open daily. Admission charge except for children under three and on Thursdays after 3 PM. Central Wharf, Waterfront (phone: 973-5200).

BOSTON TEA PARTY SHIP AND MUSEUM Board the *Brig Beaver II,* a full-size working replica of one of the three original ships at the Boston Tea Party, and throw a little tea into Boston Harbor. The adjacent museum houses documents relevant to the period as well as films and related exhibits. Open daily March through mid-December. Admission charge. Congress Street Bridge at Fort Point Channel (phone: 338-1773).

CHILDREN'S MUSEUM Formerly an old woolens warehouse, this kid-pleasing place has a number of hands-on exhibits, including *Grandmother's Attic,* a petting zoo, and an assembly line that teaches children how a factory operates. Open Tuesdays through Sundays; closed Mondays except during school holiday weeks and between July 1 and *Labor Day.* Admission charge. 300 Congress St., *Museum Wharf* (phone: 426-8855).

COMPUTER MUSEUM The first and only one of its kind in the US, this museum harbors several floors of gadgetry, interactive exhibits, and educational programs that trace the history and the future of what is probably the 20th century's greatest contribution to technology. A veritable circus of computerized equipment performs dazzling feats: coloring a map of the US at your verbal command, providing your piano playing with the appropriate orchestral accompaniment, even altering the contours of your face on screen. A walk-through computer allows a visitor to examine a computer's components from the inside bit by bit (or is that byte by byte?). Open daily in July and August; closed Mondays the rest of the year. Admission charge; free for children under four. Half price on Saturdays before noon. Within sight of the *Boston Tea Party Ship* at 300 Congress St., *Museum Wharf* (phone: 426-2800 or 423-6758).

BEACON HILL

Here is the heart of old Boston, including the *State House* and Mt. Vernon Street, with its stately old townhouses that were (and still are) the pride of the first families of Boston. The cobblestone Acorn Street, parallel to Mt. Vernon and Chestnut Streets, is the most photographed street in town.

BLACK HERITAGE TRAIL This 1.6-mile walking tour explores the history of Boston's black community throughout the 18th and 19th centuries. Free guided tours, led by *National Park Service* rangers, pass 14 sites of historic importance on Beacon Hill, including the *African Meeting House,* the oldest black church in the country, and the homes of well-known abolitionists. (The tour also may be self-guided; pick up the brochure from the *National Park Service Visitor Center* at 15 State St. or 46 Joy St.) Guided tours begin in front of the *State House* at the corner of Beacon and Park Streets, at the *Robert Gould Shaw Memorial.* The memorial honors the first US black regiment, which served under Shaw during the Civil War. Tours are conducted daily from *Memorial Day* through *Labor Day;* by appointment at other times of the year. Registration is not required, but it's advisable to call ahead (phone: 742-5415).

STATE HOUSE Designed by Charles Bulfinch, the gold-domed *State House* dates from 1795. Oliver Wendell Holmes (the author and doctor, not his son, the justice) remarked that the "Boston State House is the hub of the solar system," a remark that spawned the city's nickname, "the Hub." The original *State House* building is the ornate, red brick structure with white marble trim and a great golden dome. The various wings-come-lately are uninspired afterthoughts by comparison. If you squint just right you can block them out of view and see the building as James Monroe did in 1817. The president was so impressed that he put Bulfinch in charge of the reconstruction of the nation's *Capitol* in Washington, DC, where the architect repeated the rotunda and dome motif. Some final notes about the dome: Its original whitewashed shingles were replaced with copper in 1802 by a Grand Master of the Masons, a fellow by the name of Paul Revere. Gold leaf was added to the dome in 1866, though it was painted gray during World War II to hide the building from possible Axis bomb attacks. Enter through the side door of the right wing (the main door is hardly ever used). Pick up informational pamphlets or join a guided tour in *Doric Hall,* which features busts, statues, memorials, and paintings of famous Americans. Also worth a visit are *Memorial Hall* (also known as the *Hall of Flags*), the *Chamber of the House of Representatives,* the *Senate Chamber,* the *Senate Reception Room,* and a library (phone: 727-2590). Closed weekends. No admission charge. On Beacon St. facing the entrance to the *Common* (phone: 727-3676).

BOSTON ATHENAEUM One of the oldest libraries in the country, founded in 1807, is now housed here. This five-story National Historic Landmark building (the first three floors date from 1847–49; the top two from 1913–15) is a temple to civility. From its marble, mahogany, and ornate table lamps to its endless sea of volumes, the *Athenaeum* has the feel of a study in a colonial mansion, sumptuous yet studious. Once an art gallery whose exhibits were the foundation of the collection that became the *Museum of Fine Arts,* the *Athenaeum* still has a permanent collection of American and European works and displays the works of local artists and artisans in its second-floor gallery. In addition, it contains more than 600,000 titles, including the *King's Chapel Library* collection, sent in 1698 by England's William III; works from the *John Quincy Adams Library;* and part of George Washington's personal library. Look for a book written by Oliver Wendell Holmes, a former member of the *Athenaeum,* that has been edited in spots with a pen. The author, it is said, made a couple of later-than-last-minute corrections while leafing through the volume on a visit to the library. Asked why a visitor to the city should come here, a library administrator said it all: "Because it's just so darned Bostonian." Guided tours of the library are given Tuesday and Thursday afternoons (reservations necessary). At other times, the library is open only to members, scholars, and qualified researchers. There's no admission charge. 10½ Beacon St. (phone: 227-0270).

MT. VERNON STREET Henry James once called it the "only respectable street in America." This Beacon Hill street, which runs from behind the *State House* to Charles Street and beyond, is lined with homes that have rich historical associations—and owners. Look for the famous brass knockers, the charming carriage houses, and the intimate backyard gardens. A few blocks down is Louisburg Square, a rectangle of terribly proper houses facing a tiny park that was once home to Louisa May Alcott and Jenny Lind. The most history-intensive part of this area is between Louisburg Square and Joy Street, where you will find the *Nichols House Museum,* the only Beacon Hill home open to the public. Open Mondays, Wednesdays, and Saturdays from 1 to 5 PM in summer; hours vary during other seasons. Admission charge. 55 Mt. Vernon St. (phone: 227-6993).

CHARLES STREET Beacon Hill's one true commercial street stretches from Beacon Street to Cambridge Street. The street began as a seawall; before the Back Bay was filled in, Charles Street marked Beacon Hill's western shoreline, where tides rose nearly 15 feet. Along with lower Chestnut Street, Charles Street today forms Beacon Hill's "Antiques Row" and is home to a number of restaurants, shops, and pubs. The street's most interesting building, the *Charles Street Meeting House,* was built in 1807 as a Baptist church (it has since been converted into retail space). George Grant, the first black graduate of *Harvard* and the inventor of the wooden golf tee, lived at 108 Charles Street.

NORTH END

The *Paul Revere House* and *Old North Church* are both snugly tucked away among the narrow red brick streets of the North End, a colorful, Italian-American community with a lively street life and some excellent little restaurants (see *Eating Out*). To experience *la dolce vita,* stop at the *Caffè Dello Sport* (308 Hanover St.; phone: 523-5063) for cannoli, cappuccino, and good people watching.

PAUL REVERE HOUSE Home to the legendary Revolutionary War hero, this is the oldest wooden house in Boston. Revere moved here in 1770 with his wife, mother, and five children. He had eleven more children with his second wife, which is why his house was the only one on the block that didn't have to quarter British soldiers. On the night of April 18, 1775, after getting the nod from Joseph Warren in Boston that British troops were moving (British troops had already mustered in North Square), Revere quietly slipped into his house to change into his boots. From here he was rowed by friends across the Charles River, within sight of a British gunship. Borrowing a horse from Deacon John Larkin in Charlestown, the silversmith-cum-patriot galloped off on the ride that earned him a permanent place in American history. William Dawes and Samuel Prescott also rode forth with the news (as did many other area patriots). Although Revere completed his mission, which was to bring word to the town of Lexington, he decided to ride on to Concord; on the way he was captured by the British, questioned, then released. The exhibits inside the house, which include Revere's saddlebags, revolver, portraits, and the account of the ride in his own words, are sure to clear up some misconceptions about the man and his famous ride. Closed Mondays January through March; open daily except major holidays the rest of the year. Admission charge. 19 North Sq. (phone: 523-2338 or 523-1676).

OLD NORTH CHURCH Affectionately known as "Old North," this structure, built in 1723, is officially named *Christ Church.* On the night of April 18, 1775, sexton Robert Newman hung two lanterns outside to warn Bostonians that the British were coming by sea. His action and Paul Revere's famous ride were later immortalized by Henry Wadsworth Longfellow's poem. (The line you will want to remember is: "One if by land, two if by sea.") The church's original clock still ticks in the back, and services are still held every Sunday. Open daily. 193 Salem St. (phone: 523-6676).

BLACKSTONE BLOCK On the other side of the expressway, near *City Hall,* the city's first commercial district was named after Boston's first settler, William Blaxton (or Blackstone). Though most of the original 17th-century dwellings are gone, several from the 18th century remain, including the *Union Oyster House* restaurant (41 Union St.; phone: 227-2750) and the *Ebenezer Hancock House* (10 Marshall St.). Ebenezer's brother, John Hancock, actually owned the building; Ebenezer lived there from 1764 to 1785. As paymaster of the colonial troops, Ebenezer kept in the basement the two million silver crowns sent by France to help pay the Revolutionary troops (a deal artfully crafted by Benjamin Franklin). The *Boston Stone,* a millstone brought from England by a painter in the 1600s, is set in the foundation of a shop on Marshall Street. Originally used to grind colored powder into paint, it became to Boston what its counterpart, the London stone, was to that city— the official point from which all distances from Boston were measured. In back of the block is Blackstone Street, a malodorous little thoroughfare that should be avoided except on Fridays and Saturdays, when it is the site of *Haymarket,* the city's colorful outdoor produce market. Just north of *Faneuil Hall.*

BACK BAY

Arlington is the first of an alphabetically ordered series of streets created when the Back Bay was filled in during the mid-1800s. Broad streets and avenues were laid out in an orderly fashion, and along them wealthy Bostonians built palatial homes, churches, and public institutions. This area is a joy to walk and gives a better feeling of Victorian Boston than any other part of the city.

PUBLIC GARDEN A gem among city parks and a Boston treasure since 1861, the garden has fountains, formal gardens, and a variety of native and European trees that are labeled for identification. Abundant flowers grow along the garden's many footpaths and in plots near the Arlington Street entrance. The carefully tended beds are changed with the seasons—the spring tulips are particular favorites among locals and visitors alike. The flowers are not the only providers of color here: From the dark suits of the financiers en route between office and home to the brilliant hues of the tie-dyed T-shirts worn and sold here in summer, the *Public Garden* attracts an array of humanity that represents all of Boston. Treat yourself to a ride on the fabled, pedal-driven Swan Boats, which leisurely cruise the pond, past the geese and ducks on the lagoon. Rides are offered daily, from mid-April to mid-September except on extremely windy or rainy days. There's a fee for rides; group rates are available. Whether boating or walking, you may want to bring bread scraps for the resident ducks. In the winter, hardy locals tour the lagoon on ice skates. Adjacent to *Boston Common,* bordered by Beacon, Charles, Boylston, and Arlington Streets (phone: 522-1966).

COMMONWEALTH AVENUE Intended to replicate the broad boulevards of 19th-century Paris, with their stately, mansard-roofed homes, Commonwealth Avenue ("Comm. Ave." to the locals) has fulfilled its early promise. Stroll down the shady mall, with its statues of famous Bostonians. In April, the magnolias are magnificent. On the corner of Clarendon Street stands the *First Baptist Church,* a splendid Romanesque structure designed by H. H. Richardson and completed in 1872. Open Tuesdays through Fridays, 11 AM to 2 PM, or by prior arrangement. No admission charge. 110 Commonwealth Ave. (phone: 267-3148).

ESPLANADE This strip of parkland runs between Storrow Drive and the Charles River in the vicinity of Back Bay. Formerly just a 2-mile walkway, it was expanded into a park with money donated by Mrs. James

Storrow, widow of a wealthy Boston banker. A plush, clean, and relatively safe stretch of parkland, it is a convenient place for runners, bikers, roller skaters, and the rest of the Back Bay cardiovascular crowd—not to mention sunbathers. Several footbridges lead to the *Esplanade* from the Back Bay, over Storrow Drive, where Bostonians display their maniacal driving habits.

COPLEY SQUARE Seagoing vessels used to drop anchor in Copley Square; now it harbors Richardson's magnificent 19th-century *Trinity Church,* where there are free organ recitals every Friday at noon (phone: 536-0944). A perfect reflection of the church can be seen in the blue glass façade of the *John Hancock Tower,* a mirrored marvel designed by I. M. Pei that contains more than 13 acres of glass. When the building opened in 1975, the glass windows began popping out, much to the alarm of pedestrians who had to traverse the streets below. Just as all the glass was finally replaced, employees in the upper floors complained of a terrifying sway when the wind blew. The building underwent a massive shoring up, but the saga continued when the construction of the tower was found to have done serious structural damage to the beloved *Trinity Church.* Nonetheless, the *Tower's* 60th floor *Observatory* offers spectacular views of the city and beyond (see *Seeing the City*). Across Dartmouth Street from the square is the main branch of the *Boston Public Library,* the oldest municipally supported library in the country (it was founded in 1852). Completed in 1895, the building is considered one of the first outstanding examples of the Renaissance Beaux Arts style in the US. The huge bronze doors just inside the outer doors were created by Daniel Chester French, sculptor of the *Lincoln Memorial.* But the oldest section is under renovation (scheduled to continue until the end of the century), so visitors must enter through the blocky new addition, designed by Philip Johnson and built in 1972. Step inside the Copley Square entrance for a quiet moment in the library's lovely central courtyard. Closed Sundays (phone: 536-5400). Also on Dartmouth Street (on the other side of Huntington Ave.) is *Copley Place* (phone: 375-4400), a complex of hotels, fashionable shops (*Neiman Marcus, Tiffany, Godiva Chocolatiers,* and the like), restaurants, an 11-screen movie theater (phone: 266-1300), and an indoor waterfall.

NEWBURY STREET This is where fashionable Bostonians shop. There are many art galleries and boutiques, as well as a variety of restaurants and several outdoor cafés. Is all begins, sedately enough, where Arlington Street borders the *Public Garden* and the *Ritz* and the *Giorgio Armani* store hold sway. (Just one block away from the *Ritz,* at the end of Boylston Street, is the *Heritage on the Garden* complex, which has high-end, international stores, such as *Escada, Hermès,* and *Waterford-Wedgwood.* Here's where you also find *Biba,* one of Boston's trendiest restaurants, and *The Spa* at the *Heritage,* the perfect antidote to a hard day of shopping.) But continue down Newbury Street to Massachusetts Avenue and the boutiques gradually give way, ending in the mammoth *Tower Records* and the outrageous *Allston Beat.*

NEW ENGLAND HISTORIC GENEALOGICAL SOCIETY Since Bostonians are extremely curious about their lineage, it is fitting that one of the country's most exhaustive collections of family history is located here The collection, which covers primarily the 17th through 19th centuries, includes 17th-century diaries and journals documenting the lives of New Englanders, and some documentation on other parts of the US and Canada. Closed Sundays and Mondays. There's no admission fee to look around; there is a small fee for using the society's research facilities. 101 Newbury St. (phone: 536-5740).

INSTITUTE OF CONTEMPORARY ART Exciting contemporary artwork by local artists as well as touring exhibitions in several media can be seen at the *ICA,* one of Boston's most important showplaces. An interesting film series is shown in the gallery, which was converted from a 19th-century police station. Open Wednesdays through Sundays. Admission charge. 955 Boylston St. (phone: 266-5151/2).

KENMORE SQUARE Formerly a fashionable area, this square is now notorious for traffic jams and college students (*Fenway Park* and *Boston University* are nearby). A cherished Boston landmark, the *Citgo* sign, has evaded demolition several times and it looks as if it is here to stay. Except when it was turned off during the energy-conservation drive of the late 1970s, it has splashed Kenmore Square with blue, white, and red lights for decades.

THE FENWAY

Some of the city's finest medical, educational, and cultural institutions are located in this former marshland in southwest Boston. The *Museum of Fine Arts* and the *Isabella Stewart Gardner Museum* are located on *The Fens,* as are *Simmons College, Emmanuel College,* and branches of *Northeastern University. Symphony Hall,* home of the *Boston Symphony Orchestra* and the *Boston Pops Orchestra,* is here as well, and the *New England Conservatory of Music* and *Harvard Medical School* (located in the world-renowned Longwood Medical Area) are nearby.

THE FENS PARK Landscape designer Frederick Law Olmsted crafted this serene park out of mud flats, while preserving some of the area's original environment. In this 12-acre park are footbridges, statuary, reed-bound pools, rows of magnolias, a rose garden, community gardens, and a running path, all surrounded by the still-marshy Fens.

MUSEUM OF FINE ARTS This is one of the world's great art museums, with comprehensive exhibits from every major period and in every conceivable medium. Noteworthy are the collection of Impressionist paintings (with more Monets than anywhere outside Paris); the decorative arts and sculpture from the colonial period to the present; an outstanding assemblage of Egyptian art; the greatest collection of Asiatic art under one roof; an exhaustive gathering of American art, including numerous works by Homer, Copley, Sargent, and Hopper; and an impressive classical collection with artifacts from the 6th, 5th, and 4th centuries BC, and the early Roman Imperial period. The wares of silversmiths on display at the *MFA* will prove that the patriot Paul Revere had many valuable talents on top of riding fast on a horse and disturbing the peace. The main building was built in 1909; the airy West Wing, designed by renowned architect I. M. Pei, was added in 1981. It houses additional exhibition space, as well as a cafeteria, restaurant, café, and museum shop; special shows are often mounted here. Outside is the *Tenshin Garden,* which features New England flora and Japanese landscape design. Closed Mondays, open late Wednesdays (certain wings also open late Thursdays and Fridays). Admission charge except Wednesdays from 4 to 6 PM. Directly in back of *The Fens,* 465 Huntington Ave. (phone: 267-9300).

ISABELLA STEWART GARDNER MUSEUM This marble Venetian palazzo houses one of the world's magnificent private art collections. Isabella Stewart came to Boston in 1860 to marry John Lowell Gardner, a wealthy Brahmin industrialist. While she was a friend of some of the most famous folks of the era—art critic Bernard Berenson advised her on her collection, and artist John Singer Sargent painted her portrait—her flashy dress and spirited manner quickly made her suspect in the eyes of most proper Bostonians. The art Gardner collected during her worldwide travels is housed in a 15th-century–style Italianate mansion, built between 1899 and 1903, that remains furnished as it was during her lifetime. As a result, objects with as much sentimental as aesthetic value are exhibited next to several Rembrandts, Titian's *Rape of Europa,* a number of Tintorettos, Manets, Botticellis, Whistlers, and one Corot. (Because the art is arranged haphazardly and the museum signs and labels are not particularly detailed, it's a good idea to purchase the museum guide, sold at the main entrance.) When your feet are tired, you can take lunch or tea at a pleasant café on the premises. Every Sunday and Tuesday afternoon, except during the summer, the museum hosts classical concerts. Closed Mondays. No admission charge for children under 12. 280 The Fenway (phone: 566-1401; 734-1359 for concert information).

SOUTH END

Though it contains few recognizable tourist attractions, this reclaimed wetland is interesting for its beautiful architecture and its ethnic diversity.

THE FIRST CHURCH OF CHRIST, SCIENTIST, IN BOSTON (CHRISTIAN SCIENCE CHURCH WORLD HEADQUARTERS) The world headquarters of the religion founded in the 19th century by the American religious reformer Mary Baker Eddy, this 15-acre complex houses several interesting attractions. Mrs. Eddy's original granite *First Church of Christ, Scientist,* built in 1894, is visible, although enveloped by an overpowering Byzantine and Renaissance edifice erected in 1906. The rectangular reflecting pool, tucked between two modern buildings designed by I. M. Pei, is good for a quiet walk and a view of the Boston skyline. Most interesting is the *Mapparium,* a 30-foot stained glass globe built in 1935 (and reflecting the world as it was in 1935, with only 70 countries), through which you walk on a glass bridge that is also an echo chamber. The *Mapparium* is located in the *Christian Science Publishing Society Building,* the editorial home of the *Christian Science Monitor,* a newspaper with a truly global focus. The *Mapparium* is closed Sundays and Mondays June through mid-October and Saturdays through Mondays mid-October through May. Tours of the complex are available. Massachusetts and Huntington Avenues (phone: 450-3790).

SOUTHWEST CORRIDOR This pleasant, well-manicured footpath stretches from the Back Bay station on the *Orange Line* (just behind *Neiman Marcus*) to Massachusetts Avenue and beyond, affording a leisurely sampling of South End architecture, good people watching, and a view of Boston's skyline.

UNION PARK A residential block of Victorian townhouses that were among the first built during the mid-19th-century development of the South End, this is many Bostonians' favorite spot in the Hub. There are fountains, foliage, and a strip of greenery dividing the two rows of houses that give this pocket of civility a quiet, lazy feel. It is studded with magnolias during the summer months.

CHARLESTOWN

The Puritans first settled here in 1629 in their quest for a "city upon a hill." Charlestown's Breed's Hill was thought to be just fine, until a scarcity of safe drinking water forced the settlers to cultivate the marshy peninsula to the south that became Boston. The Battle of Bunker Hill was fought here, and Monument Hill and Winthrop Square are laced with excellent examples of 18th- and 19th-century architecture. City Square is where Paul Revere began his famed midnight ride. Nearby are the *Charlestown Navy Yard* and the USS *Constitution*.

BUNKER HILL MONUMENT This 221-foot granite obelisk was built in the 1800s to mark the site of the first major battle of the Revolutionary War. On June 17, 1775, on this hill overlooking the Boston Harbor, the British won the Battle of Bunker Hill—but hundreds of their soldiers were killed or wounded. Climb the 294 steps to the top of the monument (there's no elevator), or visit the information center below, which has exhibits and dioramas on the battle and the monument. Open daily; no admission charge. On Breed's Hill, in the center of town off Monument Square (phone: 242-5641).

USS *CONSTITUTION* This is the famous "Old Ironsides," the oldest commissioned ship in the *US Navy* and proud victor in 40 sea battles. An adjacent shoreside museum (phone: 426-1812) displays related memorabilia and a slide show. City Square bus stop. Open daily. Admission charge for museum; none for the *Constitution*. *Charlestown Navy Yard*, Charlestown (phone: 242-5670).

BUNKER HILL PAVILION Witness a vivid multimedia reenactment of the Battle of Bunker Hill on 14 screens, with seven sound channels. Open daily, with shows every half hour from April through December. Admission charge. Adjacent to USS *Constitution* (phone: 241-7575).

CAMBRIDGE

HARVARD SQUARE Just across the Charles River from Boston, Cambridge has always had an ambience all its own. Catering to the academic and professional communities, the square is a lively, "upscale" combination of the trendy and the traditional. It has the greatest concentration of bookstores in the country, many of which are open until late into the evening; movie options that range from vintage films to the latest from Hollywood and abroad; and the ever-present street musicians. When hunger pangs strike, everything from muffins to nouvelle cuisine awaits—with an authentic Italian ice to top it off. Take the *Red Line* toward Alewife and get off at the Harvard Square stop.

HARVARD YARD This tree-filled enclave is the focal point of the oldest (1636) and most prestigious university in the country (the *Law School* is nearby, the *Business School* just across the river, and the *Medical School* a bus ride away in Boston). Notice especially *Massachusetts Hall* (1720; *Harvard*'s oldest building), Charles Bulfinch's *University Hall,* and, in the adjoining quadrangle, *Widener Library* and H. H. Richardson's *Sever Hall.* Campus tours are given year-round; check at the information office in *Holyoke Center* (phone: 495-1573).

WEEKS MEMORIAL BRIDGE This graceful footbridge was built to link *Harvard*'s Cambridge campus with the school's *Graduate School of Business Administration,* on the Boston side. It offers a splendid view of the white, crimson, and gold *Harvard* steeples and the *Harvard* crew team's practices on the Charles River.

HARVARD UNIVERSITY ART MUSEUMS *Harvard*'s impressive collection of paintings, drawings, prints, sculpture, and silver is housed in three fine museums. The *Arthur Sackler Museum* (485 Broadway) houses ancient Roman, Egyptian, and Islamic antiquities, as well as traveling exhibitions, in a 1985 post-modern building designed by James Stirling. Nearby is the neo-Georgian building of the *Fogg Museum* (32 Quincy St.), which features European and American art from the Middle Ages to the present. Connected to the *Fogg* is the *Busch-Reisinger Museum,* the only museum in the US that specializes in the art of Germanic language-speaking countries. All three are closed Mondays and charge admission (phone: 495-9400).

HARVARD UNIVERSITY MUSEUMS On a short block parallel to Oxford Street is this complex housing the *Comparative Zoology, Peabody, Mineralogical and Geological,* and *Botanical Museums.* The *Peabody* houses extensive anthropological and archaeological collections, with an emphasis on South American Indians, as well as a fine gift shop. The *Botanical* houses a famous collection of glass flowers handmade for *Harvard* between 1887 and 1936 by Leopold and Rudolph Blaschka, a German father and son, and renowned for their scientific accuracy as well as their beauty. Renowned *Harvard* professor Stephen Jay Gould often lectures at *Comparative Zoology,* a natural history museum, and the *Mineralogical and Geological* museum displays rocks of all kinds. Reservations must be made for either group (phone: 495-2341) or individual (phone: 495-3045) tours for any of the museums. Open daily. Admission charge except on Saturdays from 9 to 11 AM. 26 Oxford St. (phone: 495-2341).

RADCLIFFE YARD One of the Seven Sister colleges, *Radcliffe* has evolved from its historical role as "*Harvard*'s Annex" to its current position, with its undergraduates fully integrated with *Harvard*'s. *Radcliffe* offers alternative programs for women at the graduate level and those interested in career changes. Its *Schlesinger Library* has one of the country's top collections on the history of women in America, as well as an important culinary collection. Closed weekends. No admission charge. 3 James St. (phone: 495-8647).

OLD BURYING GROUND This historic cemetery, also known as *God's Acre,* is on Garden Street just past *Christ Church.* The graves date back to 1635, and a number of Revolutionary War heroes and *Harvard* presidents are buried here. On the Garden Street fence, there's a mileage marker dating to 1754.

BRATTLE STREET This elegant Cambridge street was known in the 1770s as "Tory Row" because seven mansions owned by supporters of King George were located here (a couple still stand today). William Brattle, a Loyalist who fled Boston in 1774, lived at 42 Brattle, an 18th-century gambrel-roofed Colonial home that later became the home of Margaret Fuller, an early feminist. The building is now the headquarters of the *Cambridge Center for Adult Education* (phone: 547-6789). The yellow clapboard *Pratt House* at No. 56 is where Dexter Pratt, Longfellow's "Village Blacksmith," lived and plied his trade. It now houses the tiny *Blacksmith House Café and Bakery* (phone: 354-3036). Though the "spreading chestnut tree" that Longfellow referred to is long gone, a plaque on the corner of Brattle and Story Streets preserves its memory. Longfellow lived just down the street from 1837 until his death in 1882. That house (105 Brattle St.; phone: 876-4491), built in 1759, served as the headquarters for General Washington during the British siege of Boston. Concerts are now held there in summer, and guided tours are available. It's open daily; there's an admission charge.

MASSACHUSETTS INSTITUTE OF TECHNOLOGY The foremost scientific and technological school in the country, *MIT* opened its doors in Boston in 1865 and moved across the river to its present Cambridge campus in 1916. In addition to its world-famous laboratories and graduate schools in engineering and science, its professional schools include the *Sloan School of Management,* the *Joint Center for Urban Studies* (with *Harvard*), and the *School of Architecture.* Architect I. M. Pei is an alumnus; next to his *Green Building* for the earth sciences stands Calder's stabile *The Big Sail,* one of a superb collection of outdoor sculptures on the campus. Also worth noting are Eero Saarinen's chapel and his *Kresge Auditorium,* just across from the main entrance on Massachusetts Avenue. The main *MIT Museum* (265 Massachusetts Ave.; phone: 253-4429 or 253-4444) contains permanent collections and changing exhibits of contemporary art and technology. Closed Mondays; admission charge. The *Compton Gallery* (77 Massachusetts Ave.; phone: 258-9118) features changing technical exhibitions. Closed weekends; no admission charge. The *Wiesner Building* (20 Ames St.; phone: 253-4680) is another I. M. Pei landmark, worth a visit for its arresting interior and the often provocative changing exhibitions The *List Visual Arts Center* is located in this building. Open daily; no admission charge (phone: 253-4680). *MIT* campus tours are given year-round on weekdays at 10 AM and 2 PM. *Red Line,* Kendall Square/MIT stop, or No. 1 Dudley bus, headed toward Harvard Square 77 Massachusetts Ave. (phone: 253-4795).

MT. AUBURN CEMETERY The first garden cemetery in the United States. this rural retreat in the midst of Cambridge is bliss to the senses. Founded in 1831, *Mt. Auburn*'s 170 beautifully landscaped acres include hills, ponds, more than 3,500 magnificent trees (including 575 varieties), and an observation tower. An hour's stroll here might be the pinnacle of a sightseeing day—especially for bird watchers. Among the many famous people buried here are Mary Baker Eddy, Henry Wadsworth Longfellow, Julia Ward Howe, Oliver Wendell Holmes, and Winslow Homer. Open daily during daylight; tower open in fair weather from early spring to late fall. Stop for a map at the north entrance. 580 Mt. Auburn St. (phone: 547-7105).

OTHER SPECIAL PLACES

CHINATOWN This neighborhood has one of the largest Chinese-American populations in the country. Tucked between the "Combat Zone" (the city's rapidly shrinking enclave of pornography shops, clubs, and theaters), the leather merchants' district, and the Southeast Expressway, Chinatown is a pocket of faithfully preserved Chinese culture. There are frequent festivals in celebration of Chinese holidays, including a big bash for *Chinese New Year* (see *Special Events*). This is an interesting place for strolling, although most visitors are attracted by Chinatown's many restaurants, which garner most of the city's late-night business. Try *Ho Yuen Ting* (13A Hudson St.; phone: 426-2316) or *Chau Chow* (52 Beach St.; phone: 426-6266) for excellent Cantonese food served with minimal fuss and minimalist decor. The latter stays open until 4 AM on weekends. The best approach to the neighborhood is through the Chinese arch at the head of Beach Street, where it meets Atlantic Avenue.

JOHN F. KENNEDY LIBRARY Designed by architect I. M. Pei, this presidential library sits on the edge of a point of land projecting into Dorchester Bay, with a magnificent view of the Boston skyline and out to sea. There's an exhibit of documents, photographs, films, and memorabilia that may conjure up a bit of nostalgia even if you voted for Nixon. JFK's famed rocking chair is here, as are the desk at which he presided over nearly three years as president and the documents of the Kennedy administration. The museum also houses a section devoted to Robert F. Kennedy and, by special arrangement, the papers of Ernest Hemingway, which occupy an entire floor. Open daily except major holidays. Admission charge for adults; children under 16 free. By car, take the Southeast Expressway south to the JFK Library/UMass exit. Or take the *MBTA Red Line* (Ashmont train to the JFK/UMass stop; a shuttle bus will take you the rest of the way). Off Morrissey Blvd. next to the *University of Massachusetts* campus, in Dorchester. (phone: 929-4567).

COMMONWEALTH MUSEUM Next door to the *John F. Kennedy Library,* this museum has audiovisual presentations on the history of the people, places, and politics of Massachusetts. The state archives are also stored here; several are always on a rotating display. Closed Sundays. No admission charge. 220 Morrissey Blvd. (phone: 727-9268).

MUSEUM OF SCIENCE AND THE CHARLES HAYDEN PLANETARIUM Sitting astride the Charles River Dam and overlooking its boat locks is a cluster of modern buildings that make up one of Boston's greatest educational institutions. The *Museum of Science* includes over 400 interactive exhibits covering every aspect of science from medicine to geology to space exploration. Old favorites include the "Transparent Woman," whose internal organs light up as their functions are explained; the lightning exhibition, where lightning—and a resulting clap of thunder—are created before your very eyes; and the *Charles Hayden Planetarium*. The planetarium features a $2-million Zeiss planetarium projector and a multi-image program on cosmic discoveries, as well as laser light shows with computer animation and brilliant laser graphics. At the museum's *Omni Theater,* a 70-foot domed screen envelops the viewer in the ultimate film experience. The museum has a wonderful gift shop and a couple of cafeterias. Take the *MBTA Green Line* to *Science Park.* Closed Mondays. Admission charge for the museum; additional charge for the *Omni Theater;* advance reservations are advised for the *Omni Theater. Science Park,* on O'Brien Hwy. at the eastern end of Storrow Dr. (phone: 723-2500).

ARNOLD ARBORETUM Contained in these 265 acres of beautifully landscaped woodland and park are over 14,000 trees, shrubs, and vines, most of them labeled by their assiduous *Harvard* caretakers. The visitors' center shop has a large selection of books on botany and horticulture. Open daily, sunrise to sunset. No admission charge. By car, the main gate and visitors' center are 100 yards south of the rotary junction of Routes 1 and 203. Or take the *E* train (*Green Line*), the Arborway bus No. 39 from the Copley Square stop, or the *Orange Line,* Forest Hills stop. Six miles southwest of downtown Boston on The Arborway, Jamaica Plain (phone: 524-1717/8).

FRANKLIN PARK ZOO The highlight of this facility is an exciting rain forest exhibit in which jungle animals prowl in areas resembling their natural habitats. In the middle of the huge, climate-controlled, hangar-like structure is the gorilla area, where six mountain gorillas frolic over the rocky terrain and where birds fly free (sort of) under the soaring roof. Other animals—dwarf forest buffalos, crocodiles, a dwarf hippo, storks, and even scorpions—roam in a separate space; the zoo also boasts four waterfalls and the largest collection of tropical plants in New England. Other sections include *Bird's World, Hooves and Horns,* and a *Children's Zoo.* Open daily; admission charge except on Tuesdays after noon. Take Route 1 (VFW Parkway) to Route 203 East, or take Bus No. 16 from the Forest Hills stop on the *Orange Line* or the Andrew stop on the *Red Line.* Rte. 203, *Franklin Park,* Dorchester (phone: 442-4896 or 442-2002).

FREDERICK LAW OLMSTED NATIONAL HISTORIC SITE This house was occupied by Olmsted, the premier 19th-century landscape designer, and his two sons after the death of his wife. Best known as the designer of New York City's *Central Park,* Olmsted also designed Boston's 8-mile *Emerald Necklace* of green spaces, which ties the city to the suburbs. Tours are conducted of the house and of the grounds, which illustrate the principles of Olmsted's designs, and archives on the site include plans, drawings, and photographs of his work. Open Fridays through Sundays from 10 AM to 4:30 PM. No admission charge. 99 Warren St., Brookline (phone: 566-1689).

EXTRA SPECIAL

About 18 miles north of Boston on Route 107 is the town of Salem. It was the capital of the Massachusetts Bay Colony from 1626 to 1630, and again, briefly, in 1774, when the British closed Boston Harbor after the Boston Tea Party. However, Salem earned a bitter name in American history as the scene of the witch trials, in which a group of more than 100 villagers were accused of witchcraft. The hysterical allegations resulted in the deaths of 25 of the accused. Salem is also the site of Nathaniel Hawthorne's *House of the Seven Gables* (54 Turner St.; phone: 508-744-0991). Open daily. Admission charge. Hawthorne worked in the *Salem Custom House* and wrote his masterpiece, *The Scarlet Letter*, at 14 Mall Street. Like Boston, Salem has a history trail winding through its streets and port. Visit the *Salem Maritime National Historic Site* (174 Derby St.; phone: 508-744-4323 or 508-745-1470), run by the *National Park Service,* for information, maps, and a variety of seasonal tours. It's open daily.

Stop at the *Witch Museum* (19½ Washington Sq. N.; phone: 508-744-1692). It's closed *Thanksgiving, Christmas,* and *New Year's Day;* there's an admission charge. The *Witch House* (310½ Essex St.; phone: 508-744-0180), site of some of the interrogations, radiates a spooky feeling when you pass it at night. It's open daily, mid-March through December 1; there's an admission charge. Get in the mood for this tour by reading Arthur Miller's play *The Crucible.*

The *Peabody Museum* (E. India Sq.; phone: 508-745-1876) has fascinating scrimshaw carvings and nautical regalia from the early days of shipping and from far-off ports. It's closed *Thanksgiving, Christmas,* and *New Year's Day;* there's an admission charge. *Pier Transit Cruises* offers harbor tours that leave from *Salem Willows Pier* (phone: 508-744-6311 or 800-696-6311).

Sources and Resources

TOURIST INFORMATION

For tourist information, maps, and brochures, visit the visitors' information center at *Boston Common*. It's open daily. The *Boston Convention and Tourist Bureau* (*Prudential Center*; phone: 536-4100) has multilingual maps and brochures and is open daily. The *Massachusetts Office of Travel and Tourism* (100 Cambridge St.; phone: 727-3201) also can provide maps, calendars of events, health updates, travel advisories, and other tourist information; it's open weekdays. Another good source is the *Boston National Historical Park Downtown Visitor Center* (15 State St.; phone: 242-5642), located across from the *Old State House,* which has maps, brochures, books, and a slide show on the historic sites of Boston. In addition, park rangers here answer questions, offer advice, and lead walking tours. It's open daily.

The 24-hour Visitor's Channel of the Panorama Television Network, Channel 12 on local hotel television sets, provides weather updates every 15 minutes as well as travel advisories, traffic information, and half-hour bulletins on attractions within Boston and day trips outside the city.

LOCAL COVERAGE *Boston Globe,* morning daily; *Boston Herald,* morning daily; *Christian Science Monitor,* weekday mornings; *Boston Phoenix,* weekly; *The Tab,* weekly; *Boston* magazine, monthly; *Bostonia* magazine, quarterly.

A comprehensive guidebook is *In and Out of Boston (With or Without Children),* by Bernice Chesler (Globe Pequot Press; $15.95). Also good is *Historic Walks in Old Boston,* by John Harris (Globe Pequot Press; $12.95). For restaurant listings, see the *1995 Zagat Boston Restaurant Survey* (Zagat Survey, NY; $9.95), or *Robert Nadeau's Guide to Boston Restaurants* by Mark Zanger (World Food Press; $3.95). We also immodestly suggest you pick up a copy of *Birnbaum's Boston 95* (HarperCollins; $12), as well as *Boston ACCESS* (HarperCollins; $18).

TELEVISION STATIONS WBZ Channel 4–NBC; WCVB Channel 5–ABC; WHDH Channel 7–CBS; WGBH Channel 2–PBS; WXNE Channel 25–Fox; WSBK Channel 38; WLVI Channel 56.

RADIO STATIONS AM: WRKO 680 (talk); WHDH 850 (adult contemporary); WBZ 1030 (pop); WEEI 590 (sports). FM: WBUR 90.9 (classical/National Public Radio); WROR 93.5 (pop); WJIB 98 (pop); WFNX 101.7 (contemporary/new wave); WBCN 104.1 (rock/pop).

TELEPHONE The area code for Boston is 617. All numbers listed here are in the 617 area code unless otherwise indicated. *Note:* Some areas surrounding Boston are served by the 508 area code.

SALES TAX The city sales tax is 5%; there also is a 9.7% hotel tax.

CLIMATE Autumn may be the best time to see Boston. Days are generally clear and brisk, with temperatures in the 50s and 60s. At night it can drop into the 40s, with chilly winds. Winter can be formidable, with icy winds, snow, and sleet. If you intend to drive, make sure your car is properly equipped. Spring is brief and cool, and temperatures are usually in the 50s and low 60s. In summer, the mercury climbs into the 80s and 90s (sometimes even higher) and it is often humid, although nights can be breezy and cooler.

GETTING AROUND

AIRPORT Just 3 miles from the center of the city, *Logan International Airport* handles both international and domestic traffic. The ride from the airport to downtown usually takes from 10 to 30 minutes (or longer), depending on time of day and traffic. *City Transportation* (phone: 321-2282) runs minibuses from *Logan* to Back Bay hotels from 7:15 AM to 9:15 PM daily. *Peter Pan Trailways* (phone: 800-343-9999 or 426-7838) provides bus service between the airport and the company's bus station at 555 Atlantic Avenue daily from noon to 7:10 PM.

The most practical means of getting to *Logan* from virtually anywhere in the Boston area—if you aren't carrying much luggage—is by the *MBTA (Massachusetts Bay Transit Authority) Blue Line* trains, which cost 85¢ and run every 10 to 12 minutes (every 15 minutes on Sundays) from 5:30 AM to about 12:45 AM. There are free shuttle buses from airport terminals to the *Blue Line* airport stop, from which the trip to *Government Center Station* at City Hall Plaza takes under half an hour. A water shuttle operated by the *Massachusetts Port Authority* also connects Rowes Wharf (400 Atlantic Ave.) with *Logan* (for information, call 800-23-LOGAN). The trip takes about seven minutes.

BUS, TROLLEY, AND TRAIN The *MBTA* operates a network of trolleys and subways (referred to by locals as "the *T*") with four major lines, the *Red, Blue, Green,* and *Orange*. The *MBTA* also runs the city's bus system. *MBTA* service is fairly frequent during the day, less frequent at night, and nonexistent after about 12:30 AM. *MBTA* stations are marked with large, white circular signs bearing a giant "T." For schedules, directions, timetables, maps, and help in planning travel routes, call the *Travel Information Center* at 722-3200 or 800-392-6100 between 6 AM and 11:30 PM on weekdays and until 9 PM on weekends.

Compared to the mass transit systems in most major American cities, Boston is still a bargain: 60¢ for buses and 85¢ for the *T*. Exact change is required for the buses. Three-day visitors' passes are $9, and seven-day passes are $18. They entitle holders to free rides on all *MBTA* conveyances—trolleys, subways, trains, and buses—and to $50 worth of discounts on entertainment, restaurants, and other attractions around the city.

The *T* is the cheapest and often the fastest way to travel between downtown and the airport. Take the *Blue Line* to the airport stop; from there, a free *MBTA* shuttle bus will take you to your terminal. Warning: Don't try this at rush hour with several suitcases. *MBTA* commuter trains are an excellent way of getting to Boston's suburbs. From *South Station* (Atlantic Ave. at Summer St.; no phone), a gorgeous and sprawling train station inside an ornate 19th-century façade, there are commuter trains to points south and west of Boston, including Framingham, Stoughton, and Providence, Rhode Island. *South Station* is also Boston's link with *Amtrak* (phone: 482-3660), which makes frequent runs to Providence, Rhode Island, Connecticut, and New York City. *North Station* (on Causeway St., just behind the *Boston Garden;* no phone) is the point of departure for commuter trains north and west, including Concord, Gardner, Lowell, Ipswich, and other points on the North Shore.

CAR RENTAL All major national firms are represented.

SIGHTSEEING CRUISES *Bay State Cruise Company* (phone: 723-7800) provides service from *Memorial Day* through *Columbus Day* (and sometimes on warm weekends during the winter) out of two locations, Long Wharf and Commonwealth Pier. Boats take passengers on day trips to Georges Island (the site of *Fort Warren,* which was used as a Civil War prison) and the Inner Harbor; to Nantasket Beach and the Outer Harbor; on whale watching trips; and across Cape Cod Bay to Provincetown.

Boston Harbor Cruises (phone: 227-4320) runs whale watches from May through September, and harbor cruises of historical sites from April through mid-October, departing from Long Wharf. It also runs the *Navy Yard* water shuttle to Charlestown year-round. For $1, this is a great way to get from the *Aquarium* to the *Charlestown Navy Yard.*

Massport (phone: 800-235-6426) runs a water shuttle from Rowes Wharf to *Logan Airport* (a seven-minute ride) year-round except Saturdays and holidays.

SIGHTSEEING TOURS Boston's various trolley sightseeing tours have gained a reputation for colorful—albeit not always accurate—information. The major ones are *Old Town Trolley Tours* (phone: 269-7010), fully narrated tours of more than 100 historic Boston sites; *Boston Trolley* (phone: TRO-LLEY; fax: 269-8018), which has a number of boarding and reboarding stops at major Boston hotels; and *Brush Hills Tours/Gray Line Boston* and *Beantown Trolley* (phone: 236-2148; fax: 236-5570). *Sleuth & Company* (phone: 542-2525; fax: 542-3831) offers evening trolley tours built around crimes and misdeeds from the city's past; the tours are narrated by performers who act out the parts of various miscreants. You also can see the city from 500 feet in the air, with *The Boston Helicopter Company* (151 Tremont St.; phone: 800-55-PILOT in Massachusetts; 274-1230 elsewhere in the US; fax: 274-1237), which departs daily from the *Civil Air Terminal* at Hanscom Field in Bedford.

TAXI You can hail a taxi on the street, pick one up at a taxi stand downtown, or call *Boston Cab* (phone: 536-5010); *Independent Taxi Operators Association* (phone: 426-8700); *Town Taxi* (phone: 536-5000); *Checker Taxi* (phone: 536-7000); *Yellow Cab* (Cambridge; phone: 547-3000); or *Ambassador/Brattle Taxi* (Cambridge; phone: 492-1100).

COMPUTER GUIDES

Interactive video machines placed on various street corners assist visitors trying to get their bearings. Enter the name of a particular spot in the area or ask for a selection of shops and restaurants, and the machine will display detailed information. Other computer terminals located at *Logan Airport* provide information on cultural and tourist events throughout New England.

LOCAL SERVICES

For information about local services not listed here, call the *Boston Chamber of Commerce* (phone: 227-4500).

AUDIOVISUAL EQUIPMENT *Massachusetts Audio Visual Equipment Co.* (phone: 646-5410).

BABY-SITTING For Boston proper, call *Child Care Choices of Boston* (178 Tremont St.; phone: 357-6020, ext. 17) between 10 AM and 1 PM. For surrounding communities, call *Child Care Resource Center* (552 Massachusetts Ave., Cambridge; phone: 547-9861) or *Parents in a Pinch* (45 Bartlett Crescent, Brookline; phone: 739-5437).

BUSINESS SERVICES *Bette James & Associates* (678 Massachusetts Ave., Cambridge; phone: 661-2622) offers word processing, desktop publishing, mailing, packing and shipping, faxing, and photocopying services. *Headquarters Business Centers* (*HQ;* 100 Federal St.; phone: 342-7000) provides word processing, telex and fax services, and conference rooms; *Meeting House Offices* (121 Mt. Vernon St.; phone: 367-7171) offers office space and word processing and photocopying services. *OfficePlus* (8 *Faneuil Hall Marketplace;* phone: 367-8335) rents office space and provides access to a wide range of office services.

DRY CLEANER/TAILOR *Sarni Original Dry Cleaners* has a dozen locations. Try the one at 122 Milk St. (phone 338-9133).

LIMOUSINE *Carey of Boston* (phone: 623-8700); *Classic Limo* (phone: 266-3980); *Waites Transportation, Inc.* (phone: 567-5867 or 567-0420).

MECHANIC Ray Magliozzi (one of the amusing hosts of National Public Radio's "Car Talk"), at the *Good News Garage* (between Central Sq. and MIT at 75 Hamilton St., Cambridge; phone: 354-5383), will repair anything. But fame has its price—namely, $45 an hour.

MEDICAL EMERGENCY *Massachusetts General Hospital* (55 Fruit St., off Cambridge St.; phone: 726-2000).

MESSENGER SERVICES *Beacon Hill Courier Service* (phone: 742-1358); *Boston Cab Association,* 24-hour service (phone: 536-5010); *Central Delivery Service,* 24-hour service (phone: 395-3213); *Town Taxi,* 24-hour service (phone: 536-5000).

PHOTOCOPIES *Copy Cop* has many locations, including 815 Boylston St. (phone: 267-9267) and 85 Franklin St. (phone: 451-0233).

POST OFFICE The main post office, *Fort Point Station* (25 Dorchester Ave.; phone: 654-5327), provides window service 24 hours a day. Another office, at *John W. McCormack Station* (90 Devonshire St.; phone: 654-5684), is open weekdays from 7:30 AM to 5 PM.

PROFESSIONAL PHOTOGRAPHER *Atlantic Photo Service* (669 Boylston St.; phone: 267-7480); *Fay Foto Service* (45 Electric Ave.; phone: 267-2000).

SECRETARY *A-Plus Secretarial Office,* 4 Brattle St., Cambridge (phone: 491-2200).

TELECONFERENCE FACILITIES The *Charles; Colonnade; Hyatt Regency, Cambridge;* the *Marriott* hotels in Cambridge, at *Copley Place* and on Long Wharf; the *Meridien; Omni Parker House*; and the *Royal Sonesta* (see *Checking In*).

TRANSLATOR *Berlitz* (437 Boylston St.; phone: 266-6858); *Boston Language Institute* (636 Beacon St.; phone: 262-3500).

TRAVELER'S CHECKS *American Express* has several offices providing traveler's checks and travel agency services, including those at 1 Court St., Boston (phone: 723-8400); 44 Brattle St., Cambridge (phone: 661-0005); and 55 Boylston St., Chestnut Hill, Newton (phone: 964-0622). *Thomas Cook Currency Services* has offices at 160 Franklin St., Boston (phone: 426-0016); 800 Boylston St., Boston (phone: 247-3121); and 39 JFK St., Cambridge (phone: 868-6605).

WESTERN UNION/TELEX Telegrams (phone: 800-325-6000 to find the location nearest you).

SPECIAL EVENTS

The *Chinese New Year* is celebrated annually on every street in Chinatown in January or February, depending on the Chinese calendar. The one-day event, from noon to 6 PM, features a dragon and lion dance, firecrackers, and lots of food. Don't miss the *International Cultural Festival* at the *Ritz-Carlton* (see *Grand Hotels*) from the first week in January through the third week in March, featuring cuisine by various chefs and political and cultural lectures; each week a different country is highlighted. *St. Patrick's Day* and *Evacuation Day* (when the British fled Boston) are both celebrated in South Boston on March 17. *Patriots Day*, featuring a number of parades, reenactments of Revolutionary skirmishes, and other events, is observed in and around Boston (in Concord, Lexington, and so on) on the third Monday in April and the weekend before. The *Boston Marathon*, the oldest and most celebrated marathon in the US, is also held that Monday, with the front-runners usually crossing the finish line in Copley Square around 2 PM. The *Big Apple Circus*, sponsored by the *Children's Museum* (phone: 426-8855), comes to town from early April through mid-May, giving two performances daily. *Lilac Sunday*, the annual viewing of over 300 varieties of lilacs at the *Arnold Arboretum* (phone: 524-1717), is held on the third Sunday in May. The *Cambridge International Fair*, a celebration of summer and the arts with theater, dance, music, and food, is held in Central Square in early June (phone: 349-4380). June is also the month of colorful neighborhood street fairs, with the *Back Bay Street Fair* and the *Bay Village Fair* on the first Saturday, and the *St. Botolph Street Fair* in the South End on the third Saturday. The *Boston Globe Jazz Festival* (phone: 929-2651), a week-long series of jazz performances and free midday concerts, is held each year in mid-June, kicking off in the plaza of the *Charles* hotel in Cambridge and concluding at the *Hatch Shell* on the *Esplanade*. Boston is filled with color and pageantry during the annual *Fourth of July* celebrations. On *July 4*, the waterfront comes alive with *Harborfest*, a series of events on land and water: The Declaration of Independence is read from the balcony of the *Old State House* at 10 AM; the annual turnaround of the USS *Constitution*, "Old Ironsides," commences at 10:30 AM; and the *Boston Pops* holds its beloved annual holiday concert at the *Hatch Shell* in the evening, which features a sing-along of all-American favorites and culminates with its rousing rendition of the *1812 Overture* underneath a dazzling display of fireworks (phone: 800-858-0200). North End *Italian Festas*, a series of saint's day celebrations, always begin and end with religious services and processions, and feature a lot of food, games, dancing, and general festivity in between. They are held on nearly every weekend throughout July and August. The oldest American professional tennis championship, the nine-day *US Pro Tennis Championships at Longwood,* begins the third week of July and features many tennis greats (phone: 731-4500). Rowers from around the world and from a variety of American colleges compete in the annual *Head of the Charles Regatta*—which starts on the Charles near the Boston University Bridge and goes upstream to *Harvard* and beyond—on the last Sunday in October. In even-numbered years, the *Harvard-Yale Football Game* is held in Cambridge (phone: 495-2207). Boston's best *Christmas* tradition, the presentation of the *Handel & Haydn Society*'s *Messiah,* is on five evenings in early December (phone: 266-3605). At the *Tea Party Reenactment* (Congress St. Bridge; phone: 338-1773), uniformed participants throw chests of tea off the *Tea Party Ship* on the Sunday closest to December 16. The *First Night Celebration,* a series of musical, culinary, theater, and film events that draws more than 500,000 people to Boston's Back Bay and downtown, is held on *New Year's Eve* (phone: 524-1399).

MUSEUMS

In addition to those described in *Special Places,* other fine museums worth visiting include the following:

BOSTON CENTER FOR THE ARTS Multi-use arts complex in a city block of historic buildings. Open Wednesdays through Sundays from noon to 4 PM. No admission charge. 539 Tremont St. (phone: 426-5000 or 426-7700).

CARPENTER CENTER FOR THE VISUAL ARTS Part of *Harvard University,* this is Le Corbusier's only building in the US. Rotating exhibitions and film series are presented throughout the school year. The center is open daily; the *Sert Gallery* on the third floor is open Tuesday through Sunday afternoons. No admission charge. 24 Quincy St., Cambridge (phone: 495-3251).

FIRST HARRISON GRAY OTIS HOUSE The house was designed in the late 18th century by Charles Bulfinch for Otis, a lawyer, congressman, and Boston mayor. It is now the headquarters of the *Society for the Preservation of New England Antiquities.* Guided tours are available Tuesdays through Saturdays. Admission charge. 141 Cambridge St. (phone: 227-3956).

GIBSON HOUSE A Victorian-era home. Open Wednesdays through Sundays May through October, and on weekends only from November through April. Admission charge. 137 Beacon St. (phone: 267-6338).

MUSEUM OF AFRO-AMERICAN HISTORY The museum's changing exhibits focus on both historical and contemporary issues and personalities. It's located in the *African Meeting House,* the oldest black church in the country, which was built by free black labor in 1806. Closed weekends. No admission charge. 46 Joy St. (phone: 742-1854).

MUSEUM OF THE ANCIENT AND HONORABLE ARTILLERY COMPANY OF MASSACHUSETTS Chartered in 1638 to protect the early settlers, the *Ancient and Honorable* is America's oldest military outfit. On display are firearms, artifacts, flags, cannons, uniforms, and other memorabilia. Closed weekends. No admission charge. *Faneuil Hall,* third floor (phone: 227-1638).

MUSEUM OF THE CONCORD ANTIQUARIAN SOCIETY Here are 15 period rooms with contents dating from the 17th to the 19th centuries. Open Tuesdays through Sundays from April through December; daily from January through March. Admission charge. 200 Lexington Rd., Concord (phone: 508-369-9609).

MUSEUM OF OUR NATIONAL HERITAGE A museum and library of American history, it often hosts traveling exhibits of folk art and other artifacts. Open daily. No admission charge. 33 Marrett Rd., Lexington (phone: 861-6559).

RALPH WALDO EMERSON MEMORIAL HOUSE The former home of the essayist, philosopher, and poet. Open Thursdays through Sundays, mid-April through October; closed the rest of the year. Admission charge. 28 Cambridge Tpke., Concord (phone: 508-369-2236).

SPORTS MUSEUM Features memorabilia, photographs, equipment, temporary exhibits, interactive video presentations, and other artifacts of New England's rich sports history. Open daily. Admission charge. In the *Cambridgeside Galleria,* Memorial Dr., Cambridge (phone: 787-7678).

SHOPPING

Boston is a browser's paradise, with plenty of elegant and one-of-a-kind stores in a small area. Newbury Street is the place to go if your tastes run to art galleries, designer clothing, fine jewelry, expensive antiques, and outdoor cafés. Even if your preferences are more eclectic than elegant, don't rule out this pretty, European-looking venue. For atmosphere, walk the length of Charles Street, just across the *Public Garden* from the *Ritz*. The winding, gaslit street contains antiques shops, art and print galleries, and several intimate cafés. Newbury and Charles Streets are also a paradise for antiques aficionados. Just two blocks south of Newbury Street is *Copley Place,* a glitzy shopping mall near Copley Square (see *Special Places*). And finally, the *Downtown Crossing* area has the city's two best-known department stores—*Jordan Marsh* and *Filene's*—surrounded by blocks of so-so shops. Below is a list of some of the city's best emporia.

Allston Beat Blue jeans, leather, and metal, much loved by teens and collegians. 348 Newbury St. (phone: 421-9555).

Autre Fois The focus here is on French country furniture, although there is also furniture from Italy and England, plus a variety of decorative accessories. 125 Newbury St. (phone: 424-8823).

Avenue Victor Hugo Offers a wide range of used books and magazines. 339 Newbury St. (phone: 266-7746).

Betsey Johnson The wild, 1960s-inspired fashions of this New York designer enliven this street. 201 Newbury St. (phone: 236-7072).

Body Sculpture An unpretentious-looking little place that sells some of the city's most creative jewelry—gorgeous, hand-crafted stuff. Be sure to ask to see everything, since some of the most interesting designs are in drawers. 127 Newbury St. (phone: 262-2200).

Brattle Book Shop This Dickensian-style bookstore, located near the *Boston Common*, is an antiquarian book lover's Elysian Fields. More than 350,000 used, out of print, and rare books populate the three-story building, with original manuscripts and authors' autographs for sale. Closed Sundays. 9 West St. (phone: 542-0210 or 800-447-9595).

Le Chapeau A delightful little store that carries hats, caps, boaters, beanies, and other assorted headgear. *Copley Place* (phone: 236-0232).

Chocolate by Design Wander in to see the offbeat designs at this company, which will shape chocolate for you in almost any way you can imagine. 134 Newbury St. (phone: 424-1115).

Cuoio Shoes This little shop (pronounced *kwao*) has some of the most unusual and elegant women's shoes around. 115 Newbury St. (phone: 859-0636).

DeLuca's Market When almost every food emporium has become either part of a chain or homogenized to anonymity, here's a friendly, family-run food market devoted to high quality and personal service. 11 Charles St. (phone: 523-4343) and 239 Newbury St., Back Bay (phone: 262-5990).

Escada Elegant, colorful clothing by German designer Margaretha Ley. 308 Boylston St., at *Heritage on the Garden* (phone: 437-1200).

Essence The master perfumer here custom-makes scents to match your skin's special needs and your olfactory preferences. He also mixes up great imitations of well-known fragrances. 223 Newbury St. (phone: 859-8009).

FAO Schwarz This huge children's funhouse is almost as large as the New York City flagship. The centerpiece is the singing, two-story clock with moving figurines, a singing giraffe, and a bear tea party on top. If you're lost, ask Spanky, the talking bear, for help. 440 Boylston St. (phone: 262-5900).

Filene's A fine department store with a full line of clothing, accessories, and housewares. It is located above the famous *Filene's Basement*, but the two stores now have different owners. *Downtown Crossing*, 426 Washington St. (phone: 357-2100).

Filene's Basement Here you'll find the best bargains in town, with marked-down fashions and housewares from every state in the union and nearly every country in the world. *Downtown Crossing*. 426 Washington St. (phone: 542-2011).

Firestone and Parsons An elegant jewelry store in the *Ritz*, this establishment carries what may be the city's finest estate gems. Newbury and Arlington Sts. (phone: 266-1858).

George Gravert Orderly and uncluttered, this establishment specializes in 18th- and 19-century continental antiques. They offer a good selection of French country furniture and decorative accessories, as well as some 19th-century garden statuary. 122 Charles St. (phone: 227-1593).

Giorgio Armani This understated emporium is a fitting venue for this Italian designer's understated and elegant clothing for men and women. 22 Newbury St. (phone: 267-3200).

The Gods Buddhas, pharaohs, flying dragons, icons, madonnas, and all manner of other religious relics are packed into this fascinating little shop. 253 Newbury St. (phone: 859-3034).

Hermès Elegant and expensive French apparel and accessories for Boston's Brahmins. 22 Arlington St., at *Heritage on the Garden* (phone: 482-8707).

HMV There is a vast selection of CDs here, with an unbeatable World Music section. For other types of music, however, it may be worth going elsewhere, as prices veer to the high side. 1 Brattle St., Cambridge (phone: 868-9696).

Joan & David The well-known shoe designers have a boutique stocked with their beautiful, unique shoes and a small line of their clothing. *Copley Place* (phone: 536-0600).

Jordan Marsh New England's largest department store, this 19th-century landmark carries clothing, including most of the top designer labels, accessories, and housewares. There's a bargain basement, but it is not as highly esteemed as *Filene's Basement* across the street. 450 Washington St. (phone: 357-3000).

Joseph Abboud Native Bostonian Abboud went to New York, went national with his line of classic, earthy menswear, and returned to build this lovely, three-story boutique. 37 Newbury St. (phone: 266-4200).

Kakas Furriers An elegant fur and leather store near the *Public Garden* where older fashionable Bostonians like to shop. 93 Newbury St. (phone: 536-1858).

Louis, Boston Trendy, elegant menswear designed to make a statement. Also in the graceful old building is a floor of women's clothing, *Café Louis*, a continental bistro, and a hair salon called *The Cutting Room*. 234 Berkeley St., Back Bay (phone: 262-6100).

Marika's Antiques Loaded with tapestries, paintings, vases, and furniture from the US, Europe, and the Orient, this shop specializes in jewelry. 130 Charles St. (phone: 523-4520).

Newbury Comics All kinds of comic books, from classic to counterculture. 332 Newbury St. (phone: 236-4930) and seven other locations.

Nostalgia Factory A huge collection of original vintage ads, collectible prints, posters, and postcards is for sale here; there are also monthly exhibitions of such specialities as elections memorabilia and sheet music. 336 Newbury St. (phone: 236-8754).

Oilily Rainbows look dull next to the brightly colored children's clothing in this Dutch company's Boston store. 31 Newbury St. (phone: 247-9299).

Out of Town News A periodical lover's dream, staffed by folks who know when and where every journal under the sun is published, from a Des Moines

Sunday paper to a magazine from Cairo. Harvard Sq. (phone: 354-7777).

Priscilla: The Bride's Shop This exclusive bridal shop has been making gowns for society brides for decades. 137 Newbury St. (phone: 267-9070).

Rose Garden Head to this florist for the city's best roses at the best prices. A dozen cost from $10 to $25, depending on season and stem length. 110 Newbury St. (phone: 859-9800).

Rosie's Bakery and Dessert Shop A brightly lit storefront bakery in Cambridge's Inman Square, it's known for its prize-winning brownie, an indescribably rich concoction delicately named a "Chocolate Orgasm," and the best poppyseed cake you'll find anywhere. A great place to order cakes for special occasions, too, should you find yourself in Boston with something to celebrate. 243 Hampshire St., Cambridge (phone: 491-9488).

Shreve, Crump & Low One of Boston's oldest and finest jewelry stores, it also stocks crystal, clocks, silver, and a fine collection of American and English antiques from the 18th and 19th centuries. 330 Boylston St. (phone: 267-9100).

Society of Arts and Crafts Talented craftspeople have always gravitated to New England, and for the past 95 years, the *Society* has been carrying their works of furniture, jewelry, housewares, and clothing. 175 Newbury St. (phone: 266-1810) and 101 Arch St. (phone: 345-0033).

Strutters Fans of vintage clothing and accessories should check out the high-quality goods here. 257 Newbury St. (phone: 247-7744).

Sweet Enchantments Kids love walking over the bridge and through the fake forest in this unique candy store, especially since each tree knot is filled with a sweet surprise. 229 Newbury St. (phone: 236-2282).

Tiffany & Co. The prestigious house for jewelry and more. *Copley Place* (phone: 353-0222).

Toscanini's Ice cream heaven. Rumor has it that Bostonians eat more ice cream per capita than the residents of any other city, and this is one of their favorite places to get it—in a blizzard or in balmy weather, it's packed. The ice cream is made on the premises and features exotic foreign flavors such as Italian *nocciòla* (hazelnut) and *gianduia* (chocolate cream), and Indian cardamom-pistachio, mango, and saffron. 899 Main St., Central Sq., Cambridge (phone: 491-5877), and also in the *MIT Student Center* (phone: 494-1640).

Tower Records CDs, tapes, and LPs are housed in this dazzling three-story space at 360 Newbury St., on the corner of Massachusetts Ave. (phone: 247-5900). A second *Tower* store is near *Harvard* at 95 Mt. Auburn St. (phone: 876-3377).

Victorian Bouquet Ltd. More than just another flower shop, it has spectacular flower arrangements and a cordial, thoughtful staff. 53A Charles St. (phone: 367-6648).

Vose Galleries The specialty here is 18th-, 19th-, and early 20th-century American paintings. 238 Newbury St. (phone: 536-6176).

Waterford-Wedgwood This classy store features a full line of the classic brands of Irish crystal and English china. 288 Boylston St. (phone: 482-8886).

Waterstone's Booksellers Housed in an ornate old theater building, with about 150,000 titles, this is one of the largest bookstores in the city. 181 Newbury St. (phone: 859-7300).

Wenham Cross Country-style antiques, including hand-painted furniture, wooden toys, and hooked rugs, are for sale here. 179 Newbury St. (phone: 236-0409).

Women's Educational and Industrial Union Since 1877, the *WEIU* has been providing training and support for working women. Despite its age, the gift shop has a modern collection of housewares, children's clothes and toys, and knickknacks. There is an extensive needlework and crafts section, too. 356 Boylston St. (phone: 536-5651).

Wordsworth Bookstore A bookworm and gift-giver's paradise packed with every hard- and softcover book you can imagine, all discounted 10%-30%. 30 Brattle St., Cambridge, near Harvard Sq. (phone: 354-5201).

SPORTS AND FITNESS

No doubt about it, Boston is one of the all-time great professional sports towns.

BASEBALL The *Red Sox* play at *Fenway Park* (4 Yawkey Way; phone: 267-1700). *Green Line,* Kenmore stop.

BASKETBALL Beginning this fall, the *Celtics* play their home games at the *Shawmut Center* (150 Causeway St.; phone: 931-2000). *Green* or *Orange Line, North Station* stop.

BICYCLING A map of local bike trails is available from the *Department of Public Works* (*Transportation Building,* 10 Park Plaza; phone: 973-8000). A good place to rent a mountain or touring bicycle is the *Community Bike Shop* (490 Tremont St.; phone: 542-8623), which offers 12-speed Nishiki and Jakara bikes. (You'll need identification.) Bicycle tours in and beyond the city are conducted by *American Youth Hostels* (phone: 731-5430), the *Charles River Wheelmen* (phone: 625-0610), and the *Appalachian Mountain Club* (phone: 523-0636), among others.

BILLIARDS Some know it or its variations as pool or even snooker. Whatever the nomenclature, it is making a glorious comeback in Boston. The city's best-known place for billiards is *Jillian's Billiard Club* (145 Ipswich St.; phone: 437-0300), a staid pool hall near *Fenway Park* that is furnished like an English gentleman's library. Some think the *Boston Billiard Club* (126 Brookline Ave.; phone: 536-7665) is even classier. Both offer cocktail service, snacks, billiards, pool, snooker, darts, and backgammon.

FISHING *Boston Harbor Fishing* (619 E. Broadway, South Boston; phone: 268-2244) offers fishing charters, clambakes, and evening cruises; *Yankee Fishing Fleet* (75 Essex Ave., Gloucester; phone: 508-283-0313 or

800-942-5464) runs charters from April through November; *Boston Sail* (Long Wharf; phone: 742-3316) organizes deep-sea fishing excursions; and *Captain's Fishing Parties and Boat Livery* (Plum Island Pier, Newburyport; phone: 508-465-7733) features half- and full-day charters.

FITNESS CENTERS Try *Fitcorp Fitness and Physical Therapy Center* (133 Federal St.; phone: 542-1010), which has a track and workout equipment; *Wellbridge Center* (1079 Commonwealth Ave., Brighton; phone: 254-1711; and 695 Atlantic Ave., Boston; phone: 439-9600), which has workout equipment, a pool, and a steam room and sauna; or *Le Pli* at the *Charles* (5 Bennett St., Charles Sq., Cambridge; phone: 547-4081), which has workout equipment, a sauna, a pool, and steamrooms. Many Boston hotels have fitness centers for guests. The *Boston Athletic Club* (653 Summer St.; phone: 269-4300) offers daily memberships to those with a local hotel room key. The *Greater Boston YMCA* (316 Huntington Ave.; phone: 536-7800) operates branches at nine locations around the city; different branches have different equipment. All are open to nonmembers for a fee.

FOOTBALL Football (*New England Patriots*) and some soccer matches are played at *Foxboro Stadium* (Rte. 1, Foxboro; phone: 508-543-0350).

GOLF There's a city course in *Hyde Park*, where the *Parks and Recreation Department* offers golf instruction. Contact *George Wright Pro Shop* (420 West St., *Hyde Park;* phone: 361-8313 or 361-9679); you also can play or take lessons at the *Fresh Pond Golf Club* (691 Huron Ave., Cambridge; phone: 354-9130).

HOCKEY Beginning this fall, the *Bruins* hockey team faces off at the *Shawmut Center* (150 Causeway St.; phone: 931-2000 for tickets), which replaces the *Boston Garden. Green* or *Orange Line, North Station* stop.

JOGGING Run along the banks of the Charles River on Memorial Drive (in Cambridge) or along Storrow Drive (in Boston). Many bridges over the river make loops of varying lengths possible.

RACING Greyhounds race at *Wonderland Park,* Revere (on the *Blue Line;* phone: 284-1300).

SAILING Befitting its history as a port city, Boston offers several options for visitors interested in skippering their own skiffs on the Charles or serving as crew members on larger vessels in the harbor and beyond.

TAKING TO THE WATERS

Harvey Gamage Launched in 1973, this 95-foot schooner is one of the most technologically advanced of all the windjammers. The two showers aboard are cold, but only a few windjammers have any at all. The ship is also unusual in welcoming children of any age among its 30 passengers. Special rates are available for senior citizens. Cruises take in the New England coast in summer, the Virgin Islands during the winter. Sailing instruction is provided. Booked by *Dirigo*, which also represents other vessels, such as the ketch *Angelique* (with a deck lounge equipped with a piano and a fireplace), the *Nathaniel Bowditch* (bring your own beer for a lobster and clam cookout), and tall ships. Information: *Dirigo Cruises, 39 Waterside La., Clinton, CT 06413* (phone: 203-669-7068 or 800-845-5520).

Those who want to go it alone can rent boats at the *Boston Sailing Center* (Lewis Wharf; phone: 227-4198), *Boston by Sail* (66 Long Wharf; phone: 742-3313), and *Community Boating Inc.* (21 Embankment Rd.; phone: 523-1038).

SKIING There's cross-country skiing at *Weston Ski Track* on *Leo J. Martin Golf Course* (Park Rd., Weston; phone: 894-4903). *Lincoln Guide Service* (152 Lincoln Rd., Lincoln; phone: 259-9204) and *Pro-Motion* (111 South St., Bedford; phone: 275-1113) offer lessons daily. Within a two-hour drive of the city are a number of small downhill skiing areas: *Blue Hills Ski Area* in Canton (phone: 828-5070); *Boston Hill* in North Andover (phone: 508-683-2734); *Wachusett Mountain Ski Area* in Princeton (phone: 508-464-2300); and *Nashoba Valley Ski Area* in Westford (phone: 692-3033).

TENNIS There are courts at the *Charles River Park Tennis Club* (35 Lomasney Way; phone: 742-8922). The *Metropolitan District Commission (MDC)* also operates a number of well-maintained tennis courts throughout the city. All are available on a first-come, first-served basis except the *Charlesbank Courts,* which include two unlit courts on the bank of the Charles River and two lighted courts on the southwestern section of *Boston Common.* These require a permit, which may be picked up a few days in advance; for more information, contact *MDC Lee Memorial Pool* (20 Somerset St.; phone: 354-9523). *Hyde Park*, another cluster of *MDC* courts, has six tennis courts, four of which are lighted. Unlit courts are open until dusk, lighted courts until 11 PM. For further details, contact the *MDC* (phone: 727-8865).

Only members and their guests may play at the *Longwood Cricket Club,* but, as the home of the *US Pro Tennis Championships at Longwood,* this is Boston's primary site of competitive tennis. The championship, which takes place for approximately nine days in the latter half of July, draws some of the top names in tennis. Information: *Longwood Cricket Club, 564 Hammond St., Brookline, MA 02167* (phone: 731-2900; 731-4500 for tickets to the *US Pro* matches).

THEATER

Catch a Broadway show before it gets to Broadway. Trial runs often take place at the *Shubert Theater* (265 Tremont St.; phone: 426-4520), the *Colonial Theatre* (106 Boylston St.; phone: 426-9366), the *Wilbur Theater* (246 Tremont St.; phone: 423-4008), and the *Wang Center for the Performing Arts* (270 Tremont St.; phone: 482-9393). Or check out the *Charles Playhouse* (74 Warrenton St.; phone: 426-6912), a much smaller and often livelier place that hosts interesting contemporary plays. Currently in an open-ended run here is the long-running hit play *Shear Madness,* a participatory thriller in which the audience is invited to guess whodunit. The *New Theater* (755 Boylston St.; phone: 247-

7388) features new works with provocative themes. The *Lyric Stage* (140 Clarendon St.; phone: 437-7172) performs first-time, experimental works—often satiric and political—with aplomb. The *American Repertory Theater* (64 Brattle St., Cambridge; phone: 547-8300), one of the East Coast's premier repertory companies, is based at *Harvard*'s *Loeb Drama Center* and performs both classic and new plays during the school year. In addition, there are dozens of smaller theater groups, including several affiliated with colleges, such as the *Huntington Theatre Company* (264 Huntington Ave., Back Bay; phone: 266-3913 or 266-0800) at *Boston University*. The *Boston Ballet Company* gives performances at the *Wang Center* (see above; call 695-6950 for ballet information). Tickets for theatrical and musical events can be purchased through the *Out of Town Ticket Agency* (on the mezzanine level of the *Red Line*'s *Harvard Square Station;* phone: 492-1900); *TicketMaster* (phone: 244-8400 for *TicketMaster* locations; 931-2000 to order tickets by phone); or, on the day of the play, from *Bostix* (*Faneuil Hall Marketplace;* phone: 723-5181). For information on performance schedules, check the local publications listed above.

CINEMA

Boston features an array of movie theaters that screen everything from first-run action/suspense movies to zillionth-run classics and foreign films. The *Boston Globe*'s Thursday "Calendar" section is an invaluable source for current attractions and reviews. For a complete listing of times and locations of films showing in the area, call 333-FILM.

Several theaters specialize in showing eclectic, hard-to-find films. Two of the best are *Nickelodeon Cinemas* (606 Commonwealth Ave.; phone: 424-1500), which features foreign films and other first-run movies not intended to be blockbusters; and the beloved *Coolidge Corner Cinema* (290 Harvard St., Brookline; phone: 734-2500), which has been saved from the wrecking ball on several occasions and continues to feature foreign, classic, and avant-garde treasures.

In Cambridge, the *Brattle* (40 Brattle St.; phone: 876-6837) features oldies and the avant-garde; and *Harvard Square* (10 Church St.; phone: 864-4580) often screens non-mainstream movies. The *Harvard Film Archive* at the university (24 Quincy St.; phone: 495-4700) also shows classics and foreign films. In a struggle to compete with multiplex cinemas, the grand old *Somerville Theater* (55 Davis Sq., Somerville; phone 625-5700) hosts first-run foreign and repertory films, classic Disney animation festivals, and performances by local musicians.

MUSIC

Almost every evening, Bostonians can choose from among several classical and contemporary musical performances, ranging from the most delicate chamber music to the most ferocious alternative rock. The *Boston Symphony Orchestra,* usually under the baton of director Seiji Ozawa, performs at *Symphony Hall* (301 Massachusetts Ave.; phone: 266-1492) September through April; in summer, it's at the *Tanglewood Music Festival* in Lenox, Massachusetts. Selected members of the *Boston Symphony* make up the *Boston Pops Orchestra,* which performs less weighty orchestrations of popular music. In addition to performing at

Symphony Hall (see above) from April through July, the *Boston Pops* gives free outdoor concerts in the *Hatch Shell* on the *Charles River Esplanade* in June and July. Both the *Handel & Haydn Society* (300 Massachusetts Ave.; phone: 266-3605) and *Boston Baroque* in Cambridge (phone: 641-1310) perform historically correct music on period instruments. The *Boston Lyric Opera* performs a full season of classical operas at the *Emerson Majestic Theater* (219 Tremont St.; phone: 248-8660). Several colleges and universities also offer classical concerts: *Harvard*'s *Sanders Theater* (Kirkland and Quincy Sts., Cambridge; phone: 495-5595); *MIT*'s *Kresge Auditorium,* in a peculiar building on the West Campus that has a curved roof resting on only three points (77 Massachusetts Ave., Cambridge; phone: 253-2826); and the *Boston University Concert Hall* (855 Commonwealth Ave.; phone: 353-3345).

Soothing piano music can be found in the *Plaza* bar of the *Copley Plaza* hotel and energetic sing-alongs at *Diamond Jim's Piano Bar* at the *Lenox* hotel (see *Checking In* for both hotels). The premier jazz club in the area is the super-elegant *Regattabar* in Cambridge's *Charles* hotel (see *Checking In*), which showcases both local and national talent. Top-name blues and pop musicians play here, too. For more jazz, try the classy, two-level *Nightstage* (823 Main St., Cambridge; phone: 497-8200); the bustling, intimate *Ryles* (Inman Sq., Cambridge; phone: 876-9330); or the mixed bag, from avant-garde to be-bop, at *Scullers Jazz Lounge* in the *Guest Quarters Suite* (see *Checking In*), which showcases both national and local talent.

The *Paradise* (967 Commonwealth Ave.; phone: 254-2053) is an intimate room that regularly books top-name rock musicians. The *Rathskeller,* a.k.a. "The Rat" (528 Commonwealth Ave.; phone: 536-2750), is a head-banging Boston institution (many would contend its patrons belong in institutions) that relishes its role as the scourge of Kenmore Square. Here you'll find an endless stream of such bands as *The Queers* or *Slaughter Shack,* as well as nearby *Boston University*'s "existential" crowd. For some of the finest Irish music this side of Dublin, go to the *Purple Shamrock* (1 Union St.; phone: 227-2060); the *Black Rose* (160 State St.; phone: 742-2286); or the *Green Briar* (304 Washington St., Brighton; phone: 789-4100) on Monday nights. The *Tam O' Shanter* (1648 Beacon St., Brookline; phone: 277-0982) is an excellent venue for folk, blues, and the occasional jazz performance, as is the *Plough and Stars* (912 Massachusetts Ave., Cambridge; phone: 492-9653), where they pack them in cheek-to-jowl and serve some of the finest ales in the city. For folk music in a coffeehouse atmosphere, visit *Passim* (47 Palmer St., Cambridge; phone: 492-7679); for bluegrass, drop in at *Harpers Ferry* (158 Brighton Ave.; phone: 254-9734). The *Western Front* (343 Western Ave., Cambridge; phone: 492-7772) is Boston's focal point for reggae music. Once you step in the door, you'll think you're in Kingston, Jamaica.

NIGHTCLUBS AND NIGHTLIFE

A sophisticated and well-heeled crowd gathers nightly in the elegant *Plaza* bar at the *Copley Plaza* hotel (see *Checking In*) or at the *Palm Court* at *Cricket's* (101 Faneuil Hall Marketplace; phone: 720-5570). If dancing disco is your passion, try the sumptuous *Roxy* (279 Tremont St.;

phone: 338-7699). *The Last Hurrah,* downstairs at the *Omni Parker House* (see *Checking In*), also has live jazz bands on weekends, with no cover charge. Thursday through Saturday nights, there's dancing to pop music at *Club Nicole,* a spot in the *Back Bay Hilton* (see *Checking In*) reminiscent of the old *Stork Club* in New York. Among the trendiest clubs are *Avalon* (15 Lansdowne St.; phone: 262-2424); *Alley Cat* (1 Boylston Pl.; phone: 457-6200); *Venus de Milo* (7 Lansdowne St.; phone: 421-9595); *Zanzibar* (1 Boylston Pl., off Boylston St.; phone: 351-7000); and the *Harbor Club* (145 Northern Ave.; phone: 426-8600). A rather disheartening sight is the *Bull & Finch* pub (84 Beacon St.; phone: 227-9605) of television's "Cheers" fame, which still draws crowds of tourists despite an expansion from the basement to the first floor and a general lack of atmosphere. Only the façade of this tourist trap was used for the show; the interior is filled with kitsch.

COMEDY CLUBS Sometimes it seems that nearly everybody in Boston is a comedian—or wants to be. Those who have decided to turn professional can be found at one of the area's many comedy clubs. Big-name comics can be found at *Nick's Comedy Club* (100 Warrenton St.; phone: 482-0930). Other laugh joints include *Duck Soup* at *Faneuil Hall Rotunda* (phone: 248-9700), the city's largest comedy club; *Dick Doherty's Comedy Club* at *Remington's Eating & Drinking Exchange* (124 Boylston St.; phone: 337-6920); and the *Comedy Connection* at the *Charles Playhouse* (76 Warrenton St.; phone: 426-6339).

Best in Town

CHECKING IN

Boston has some gracious old hotels with the history and charm you'd expect to find in this dignified New England capital. But Boston experienced a hotel building boom in the 1980s, and there are now many modern places as well, offering standard contemporary accoutrements. Expect to pay $150 or more per night for a double room (including private bath, air conditioning, TV set, and phone, unless otherwise indicated) at those places noted as expensive; between $100 and $150 for those in the moderate category; and less than $100 in places listed as inexpensive. Many of these hotels offer special weekend packages for relatively low rates. Reservations always are required, so write or call well in advance. All telephone numbers are in the 617 area code unless otherwise indicated.

For B&B accommodations in the Boston area, write to the *Massachusetts Division of Tourism* (100 Cambridge St., 13th Floor, Boston, MA 02202) for its *Spirit of Massachusetts Bed & Breakfast Guide* or contact *Bed & Breakfast Associates of Bay Colony* (PO Box 166, *Babson Park,* Boston, MA 02157; phone: 449-5302); *Greater Boston Hospitality* (Box 1142, Brookline, MA 02146; phone: 277-5430); *Bed and Breakfast Cambridge & Greater Boston* (Box 665, Cambridge, MA 02140; phone: 576-1492); *Host Homes of Boston* (Box 117, Boston MA 02168; phone: 244-1308); *New England Bed and Breakfast, Inc.* (1753 Massachusetts Ave., Cambridge, MA 02138; phone: 498-9819); or *Bed & Breakfast*

Agency of Boston (47 Commercial Wharf, Boston, MA 02110; phone: 720-3540).

EXPENSIVE

Boston Harbor This distinctive, 16-story property, one of Boston's best hostelries, offers the most dramatic entry to the Hub. From *Logan Airport,* visitors are whisked by water taxi across Boston Harbor to dock within an anchor's throw of the hotel at Rowes Wharf, with its enormous eight-story golden arch that opens onto Atlantic Avenue and downtown Boston. The shopping district, the North End, and the *Faneuil Hall Marketplace* are all within walking distance. The property's 230 spacious guestrooms (some with balconies) have views of either the city or the harbor. *Foster's Rotunda,* a copper-domed observatory atop the arch, boasts mesmerizing views. Amenities include a spa, saunas, and a 60-foot indoor pool. There's also the glass-enclosed *Harborview Lounge,* a casual, outdoor café (in summer), and the elegant *Rowes Wharf* bar and restaurant, specializing in seafood prepared in unusual ways. Other conveniences include a full-service business center with desktop publishing capabilities, 24-hour room service, a concierge, secretarial services, seven meeting rooms, A/V equipment, photocopiers, and express checkout. 70 Rowes Wharf (phone: 439-7000 or 800-752-7077; fax: 330-9450).

Bostonian Understated and small (152 rooms), this beautifully appointed hotel is across from *Faneuil Hall Marketplace* and just two blocks from the North End and the revitalized waterfront. Its glass-enclosed, rooftop *Seasons* restaurant, which serves fine continental fare, discreetly overlooks the colorful bustle below. Other amenities include 24-hour room service, a concierge, secretarial services, two meeting rooms, A/V equipment, photocopiers, computers, and express checkout. North and Blackstone Sts. at *Faneuil Hall Marketplace* (phone: 523-3600; 800-343-0922; fax: 523-2454).

Copley Plaza This historic bowfront property, part of Copley Square's triangle of turn-of-the-century elegance, is on everybody's short list of Boston hotels. Although it has 373 splendid guestrooms, its public areas are what make this hotel truly great. Corporate Boston fills the seats of the *Plaza* bar, which has been compared to a British officers' club in India. Adjacent to the bar is the airy tea court, which is painted in the precise Victorian technique of photographic realism, creating the illusion that you're outdoors. There are two restaurants: The elegant *Plaza* (see *Eating Out*) has a French menu, and *Copley's* serves excellent American/New England fare in richly decorated Victorian-style rooms. The multilingual staff is refined and helpful. Other amenities include 24-hour room service, a concierge, 12 meeting rooms, secretarial services, A/V equipment, photocopiers, computers, and express checkout. 138 St. James Ave., Copley Sq. (phone: 267-5300; 800-223-7434; fax: 267-7668).

Eliot This all-suite Back Bay establishment was built in 1925 (a $4.3 million renovation was completed in the early 1990s) as the nearby *Harvard Club* guest facilities. The elegant lobby and all the rooms shine in a classic European manner; each of the 93 suites has a marble bath, antique furnishings, French doors between rooms, and a private pantry. Guestrooms away from bustling Commonwealth Avenue are quieter. Dual-line room telephones include modems, and writing desks are larger than usual. Amenities include continental breakfast, mini-bars, and concierge service. Business amenities include photocopiers and secretarial services. The popular bar of the same name next door is not part of the hotel. 370 Commonwealth Ave. (phone: 267-1607; 800-44-ELIOT; fax: 536-9114).

Four Seasons Service is this refurbished hotel's strong suit—which is not to say that the place is lacking in ambience. On the contrary: The 288 guestrooms, each with a bar and two to three phones, resemble a gracious Beacon Hill residence, with cherry furniture, floral prints, and marble vanities. This is one of only two Boston hotels that overlook the *Public Garden;* half the guestrooms enjoy leafy (or snow-swept) garden views. The hotel's formal restaurant, *Aujourd'hui* (see *Eating Out*), features an American-continental menu. The more informal *Bristol Lounge* offers live entertainment most nights and a Viennese dessert buffet Friday and Saturday nights. The location is convenient as well as attractive: Most of the city's popular sites are within walking distance. The full-service health club includes a pool, sauna, and whirlpool baths. Children get their own bathrobes, board games, Nintendo, milk and cookies, and food for the *Public Garden* ducks. Other amenities include 24-hour room service, a concierge, complimentary limousine service to downtown, eight meeting rooms, secretarial services, A/V equipment, photocopiers, computers, and express checkout. 200 Boylston St. (phone: 338-4400; 800-332-3442; fax: 423-0154).

Guest Quarters Suite A distinctive property on the Charles River, it has 10 conventional guestrooms and 310 luxurious suites. There's a restaurant, and complimentary breakfast is served on weekends. Its *Scullers Jazz Lounge* is one of the city's premier jazz venues, and there's a health club with a pool, a whirlpool bath, a sauna, and exercise machines. Other amenities include room service until 11 PM, a concierge, seven meeting rooms, secretarial services, A/V equipment, photocopiers, computers, and express checkout. 400 Soldiers Field Rd., at the Cambridge/Allston exit of I-90, the Massachusetts Turnpike (phone: 783-0090; 800-424-2900; fax: 783-0897).

Hyatt Regency, Cambridge Surrounding the atrium and glass-walled elevators are 469 rooms. The revolving rooftop restaurant offers a spectacular view of Boston, especially at sunset. The health club includes an indoor pool, a sauna, a whirlpool bath, and a steamroom. Other amenities include 24-hour room service, a concierge, meeting rooms, secretarial services, A/V equipment, photocopiers, and express checkout. On the Charles River, near *MIT* and *Harvard* (not easily accessible by public transportation). 575 Memorial Dr., Cambridge (phone: 492-1234; 800-233-1234; fax: 491-6906).

Lafayette Although the ambitious *Lafayette Place* complex has sunk to dismal lows, the hotel within maintains classic European standards of elegance and service. The 497 beautifully appointed rooms are grouped around four atriums. As befits a member of the Swissôtel group, one dining room is called the *Café Suisse;* for dinner, the *Lobby Lounge* serves informal American fare. A lap pool, a sun terrace, and saunas are also available. Other amenities include 24-hour room service, a concierge, 16 meeting rooms, secretarial services, A/V equipment, photocopiers, computers, and express checkout. 1 Ave. de Lafayette (phone: 451-2600; 800-621-9200; fax: 451-2198).

Lenox Built in 1900 and modeled after New York City's *Waldorf-Astoria,* this property has 222 guestrooms with high ceilings and rocking chairs (the corner rooms have fireplaces). Each is decorated in either French provincial, colonial, or Oriental style. The lobby is handsomely decorated in blue with gold trim and a fireplace—always blazing in the winter—that evokes the feel of a country inn. *Diamond Jim's Piano Bar* features sing-alongs starring musically talented waiters and waitresses. There also are two restaurants—the casual *Lenox Pub* and the more formal *Lenox Grill.* Other amenities include room service until midnight, a concierge, meeting rooms for up to 200, A/V equipment, photocopiers, and express checkout. 710 Boylston St. (phone: 536-5300).

Marriott, Long Wharf A striking five-story atrium is the centerpiece of this big downtown property (412 rooms) at the foot of State Street. The *Harbor Terrace Sea Grille* requires a jacket and tie; the more casual *Rachel's Lounge* provides taped contemporary music for dancing nightly. A ballroom, indoor-outdoor pool, and health club offer diversions. Other amenities include room service until midnight, a concierge, five meeting rooms, A/V equipment, photocopiers, and computers. 296 State St. (phone: 227-0800; 800-228-9290; fax: 227-2867).

Meridien The stylish French-owned hotel chain has created a small and delightful Gallic world in this splendid 1922 Renaissance Revival structure in downtown's Post Office Square. The 326 guestrooms, each with a small sitting area with a writing desk, are decorated in 150 different styles, from fin de siècle to modern. The elegant *Julien* restaurant offers a classical Gallic-inspired menu (see *Eating Out*)—the creation of consulting chef Marc Haeberlin of the three-Michelin-star *L'Auberge de L'Ill* in Alsace. Also on the premises is *Café Fleuri,* a French bistro housed in a leafy six-story atrium. The hotel hosts a delectable all-you-can-eat buffet of chocolate desserts on Saturday afternoons; Sunday brunch is wonderful here as well. *La Terrasse,* an informal outdoor café, serves breakfast, lunch, and cocktails. There's also a health club, an indoor pool, lobby shops, 24-hour room service, and a concierge. Business services include 11 meeting rooms, express checkout, and a full-service business center with A/V equipment, photocopiers, and computers. 250 Franklin St., Post Office Sq. (phone: 451-1900; 800-543-4300; fax: 423-2844).

Omni Parker House When it opened in 1855, the elegant *Parker House* became a Boston institution almost immediately; it was here that Charles Dickens would dwell during his heavily publicized Boston visits. The 540 rooms are richly decorated with dark wood and tapestries, and the building, located on the historic Freedom Trail, is within walking distance of the *King's Chapel,* the *Park Street Church,* Beacon Hill, *Boston Common,* and the *Faneuil Hall Marketplace.* Boston cream pie and Parker

House rolls were born at *Parker's,* the hotel's main restaurant (which still features both on its contemporary continental menu). The restaurant was once the meeting place of the *Saturday Club,* a 19th-century literary association whose membership list included such luminaries as Longfellow, Emerson, and Oliver Wendell Holmes. Other amenities include room service until midnight, a concierge, 14 meeting rooms, secretarial services, A/V equipment, photocopiers, computers, and express checkout. 60 School St. (phone: 227-8600; 800-THE-OMNI; fax: 742-5729).

Park Plaza Just south of the *Public Garden,* between Back Bay and the theater district, this venerable establishment has a large and bustling lobby and spacious rooms. *Legal Sea Foods,* with good seafood (see *Eating Out*), and *Café Rouge,* with respectable American dishes, are here. Other amenities include 24-hour room service, a concierge, meeting rooms for up to 2,000, A/V equipment, photocopiers, and express checkout. One Park Plaza at Arlington St. (phone: 426-2000; 800-225-2008; fax: 426-5545).

Ritz-Carlton This grande dame of Boston hotels has reigned since 1927. Strategically located near most of Newbury and Boylston Streets' smart shops, it overlooks the *Public Garden,* with the windows on the north side of the building offering views of the magnolia-lined Commonwealth Avenue mall. All 278 guestrooms are traditionally furnished and decorated with 17th- to 19th-century paintings. The rooms in the hotel's older section are the fanciest. Afternoon tea in the upstairs lounge is a Boston institution. The large and lovely *Ritz* dining room serves excellent continental fare (see *Eating Out*), and the serene *Ritz* bar makes the best martini in town; both look out over the garden. Legions of staff members do their best to serve you. Other amenities include 24-hour room service, a concierge, 13 meeting rooms, secretarial services, A/V equipment, photocopiers, and express checkout. 15 Arlington St. (phone: 536-5700; 800-241-3333; fax: 536-1335).

Westin, Copley Place This opulent 36-story, 804-room property is one of two hotels in burgeoning *Copley Place.* Its *Turner Fisheries* restaurant serves award-winning clam chowder in a town renowned for its chowder. There's also a fully outfitted health club with a pool, saunas, and masseuse. Other amenities include 24-hour room service, a concierge, 23 meeting rooms, secretarial services, A/V equipment, photocopiers, computers, and express checkout. 10 Huntington Ave. (phone: 262-9600; 800-228-3000; fax: 451-2750).

MODERATE

Newbury A brick and brownstone townhouse that has been converted into an urban bed and breakfast establishment. Its location—in the heart of Back Bay, on a street of boutiques, cafés, and galleries—is perfect for city-philes who prefer country living. The 15 rooms are decorated in a simple, 19th-century style. A continental breakfast is served in the parlor and on the streetside patio in the summertime. 261 Newbury St. (phone: 437-7666).

267 Commonwealth A stay in this nine-room urban inn in the middle of Boston's Back Bay can be a memorable experience. Built in an 1880 townhouse, it was restored several years back (by Bob Vila, former host of the "This Old House" series on public television). The suites all feature kitchens, working fireplaces, and gorgeous woodwork. The helpful staff provides guests with a variety of personal services, from dry cleaning to tour arrangements. Even if you don't stay here, you may want to incorporate this place into your tour of the Victorian buildings of the Back Bay. No credit cards accepted. 267 Commonwealth Ave. (phone: 267-6776).

INEXPENSIVE

Chandler Inn Modest and comfortable, and conveniently located between Copley and Park Squares, near *Copley Place,* it has 56 rooms and provides a complimentary continental breakfast in the lobby. 26 Chandler St. at Berkeley St. (phone: 482-3450; 800-842-3450).

Howard Johnson's Fenway A perfect location for *Fenway Park,* the *Museum of Fine Arts,* the *Isabella Stewart Gardner Museum,* and *Prudential Center.* There is a restaurant, lounge, outdoor pool, valet service, bellhops, and a multilingual staff. 1271 Boylston St. (phone: 267-8300; fax: 267-8300, ext. 151).

Midtown In Back Bay, across the street from the *Christian Science World Headquarters* and near the *Prudential Center,* this low-rise property, flanked by ritzier lodgings on either side, is a darling of tour groups. All rooms feature cable TV. 220 Huntington Ave. (phone: 262-1000; 800-343-1177; fax: 262-8739).

EATING OUT

Boston doesn't have a reputation as a culinary capital, but the 1980s brought a wealth of sophisticated restaurants—both expensive and moderately priced—opened by talented young chefs, many of whom actively sought to develop a new New England–style cuisine. Bostonians' appetites and culinary standards rose to the occasion, and the city now supports a vital restaurant community. Visitors have their pick of many wonderful dining spots. Expect to pay $100 or more for two at one of the places we've noted as expensive; between $50 and $100 at those rated moderate; and $50 or under at those listed as inexpensive. Prices do not include drinks, wine, or tips. All telephone numbers are in the 617 area code unless otherwise indicated. Unless otherwise noted, restaurants are open daily for lunch and dinner and accept most major credit cards. Where they are accepted, *reservations are advised.*

EXPENSIVE

Anago Bistro An understated, tranquil space enlivened by bouquets of fresh flowers, it serves some of the city's best continental fare from a menu that changes constantly. Specialties include crab and scallop casserole, braised venison, maple barbecued chicken, and wild mushroom stew. Closed Sundays and Mondays. Reservations advised. Major credit cards accepted. 798 Main St., Kendall Sq., Cambridge (phone: 492-9500 or 876-8444).

Armani Express This upscale dining emporium offers dishes as finely tailored as the suits in the adjacent *Armani* boutique: Try chef Roberto Saracino's *pansoti* (triangular ravioli) *al funghi porcini* sautéed in a butter and sage sauce, or any of the consistently wonderful seasoned rice dishes such as the *risotto al pescatore,* with seafood and a light tomato broth. There is a trattoria downstairs, with a busy oak bar, and the refined, Italianate upstairs dining room was designed by Armani himself. Major credit cards accepted. Reservations advised. 214 Newbury St. (phone: 437-0909).

Aujourd'hui The lovely, second-story centerpiece of the *Four Seasons,* this hotel dining room has few peers for ambience, food, or wine. The American-cum-continental menu, which changes seasonally, features appetizing "alternative cuisine" specials, the creation of chef Jamie Mammano, that are both good and good for you. Excellent service. Open daily for all three meals. Reservations advised. Major credit cards accepted. 200 Boylston St. (phone: 451-1392).

Bay Tower Room Featuring a breathtaking view of Boston Harbor from 33 stories up, this restfully elegant dining room is the perfect setting for special-occasion suppers and banquets. The American and continental specialties change seasonally. Piano music is featured during early evening hours, with a live combo taking over later on Fridays and Saturdays. Open Mondays through Saturdays for dinner only; open on Sundays for private functions. Reservations necessary. Major credit cards accepted. 60 State St. (phone: 723-1666).

Biba Facing the *Public Garden,* this dramatic two-level restaurant and bar is the creation of Lydia Shire, one of Boston's most admired and interesting chefs. The inventive, six-part menu affords amazing choices for varying appetites and changing seasons. The sweetbreads are heavenly, and the wine list is remarkable in both range and price. Open daily, 11:30 AM to 9:30 or 10:30 PM (no lunch on Saturdays; snack menu available at bar). Reservations necessary. Major credit cards accepted. 272 Boylston St. (phone: 426-7878).

Le Bocage Some of the most consistently delectable French food available in New England is served in this elegant establishment, located in a suburb west of Boston. Both Gallic regional and classic entrées grace the menu, which changes to suit the season. A bright, efficient staff and a fine wine cellar add to the pleasurable dining. Closed Sundays. Reservations advised. Major credit cards accepted. 72 Bigelow Ave., Watertown (phone: 923-1210).

Café Budapest Decorated in the lavish Eastern European tradition, it is renowned for fine continental and Hungarian cooking. This is a wonderful place to linger over superb strudel and some of the best coffee anywhere. Reservations advised. Major credit cards accepted. 90 Exeter St. (phone: 266-1979).

Davide Though on the edge of the North End, it's far from the typical neighborhood red-checked tablecloth and red sauce place. Specialties include rack of lamb *valdostana,* a lightly breaded veal chop stuffed with prosciutto and fontina cheese, and pasta, which is hand-rolled by Davide himself. Closed at lunchtime on weekends. Reservations advised. Major credit cards accepted. 326 Commercial Ave. (phone: 227-5745).

Davio's This northern Italian eatery has developed into a local chain. Regional and continental entrées are consistently well prepared, highlighted by veal chops, homemade pasta, and "upscale" pizza combinations. Good wines, good service, elegant surroundings. Reservations advised. Major credit cards accepted. Three locations: 269 Newbury St. (phone: 262-4810); 204 Washington St. in Brookline Village (phone: 738-4810); and in the *Royal Sonesta,* 5 Cambridge Pkwy., Cambridge (phone: 661-4810).

L'Espalier When money is no object, Bostonians visit this contemporary French restaurant. Among devotees' favorites are the salad of Maine lobster with corn fritters, tempura soft-shelled crab, grilled Atlantic salmon, morels and minted peas, and maple cheesecake. The fixed price menu offers many choices for a three-course meal. Chef Frank McClelland now features simpler dishes and larger portions, but he has not tampered with the impressive 150-item wine list. This eatery resides in a beautiful Back Bay townhouse with three elegant, intimate dining rooms. Closed Sundays. Reservations advised. Major credit cards accepted. 30 Gloucester St. (phone: 262-3023).

Hampshire House Thoroughly evocative of 19th-century Boston is this former mansion turned tavern, restaurant—and tourist trap. The *Oak Room Lounge* is a paneled, clubby café-bar with moose heads on the wall and a fire blazing in the winter. It offers a simple continental menu and a range of lighter fare. In the eminently Victorian dining room overlooking the *Public Garden,* more elegant American offerings, such as New York strip steaks and chicken Divan, are served. The *Bull & Finch* pub was the inspiration for (but not the actual setting of) the television series "Cheers" (see *Nightclubs and Nightlife*). Reservations necessary. Major credit cards accepted. 84 Beacon St. (phone: 227-9600).

Jasper's Chef Jasper White has an inventive touch and a national (and well-deserved) reputation, manifested skillfully in his unique creations. The varied (and often changing) menu includes such offerings as an elegant version of a New England boiled dinner with johnnycakes and caviar, pan-roasted lobster with chervil, and a mixed grill of marinated quail and duck sausage. White also makes his own pasta and serves it with flair. Open Tuesdays through Saturdays for dinner only; last seatings at 9:45 PM. Reservations advised. Major credit cards accepted. 240 Commercial St. (phone: 523-1126).

Julien The grandeur of the decor, with its high ceilings, gilded walls, and graceful Queen Anne chairs, creates a wonderful dining atmosphere. Situated in the old Members Court of the former *Federal Reserve Bank Building* (now the *Meridien* hotel), this dining spot produces Alsatian-inspired creations such as homemade terrine of foie gras, a ragout of sea scallops and sea urchins, and breast of squab with cabbage and truffles, under the attentive eye of consulting chef Marc Haeberlin, whose *L'Auberge de L'Ill* in Alsace has earned three Michelin stars. Reservations advised. Major credit cards accepted. 250 Franklin St. (phone: 451-1900).

Locke-Ober Café A splendid, albeit somewhat stuffy, tradition in one of Boston's classic dining places. Though it was once an exclusive male bastion, today both sexes can eat in the handsome *Men's Grill,* with its glowing mahogany bar lined with massive silver tureens, its stained glass, snowy linen, and indefatigable gray-haired waiters. The food is identical in the less distinguished upstairs room—heavy on continental dishes and seafood; try the lobster bisque or the chicken Richmond under glass. Jacket and tie required for men. Open daily. Reservations advised. Major credit cards accepted. 3 Winter Pl. (phone: 542-1340).

Maison Robert Among the finest French restaurants in the city, with first-rate food, drink, ambience, and service. Owner-chef Lucien Robert, one of the founding fathers of Boston's culinary revolution, has taught many of the city's chefs and continues to prepare unusual sauces for his fish, fowl, and meat dishes. Two dining areas, *Ben's Café* downstairs (on the patio in summer) and the elegant *Bonhomme Richard* upstairs, are open for lunch and dinner. Closed Sundays. Reservations necessary. Major credit cards accepted. 45 School St., in the *Old City Hall* (phone: 227-3370).

Marais The latest hot spot in Boston's theater district, it resembles an intimate Paris bistro from the 1920s, with dark wood furniture, yellow walls, and authentic posters from the period. The menu features a wide array of Mediterranean dishes. Open for dinner only. Closed Sundays. Reservations advised. Major credit cards accepted. 116 Boylston St. (phone: 482-7799).

Mr. Leung's Linen napery, artful flower arrangements, lavish service, and a subdued, elegant setting dispel the myth that Chinese restaurants have to mean Formica tables and noisy dining. The flavors of the dishes are as subtle as the decor. Specialties include Peking duck and lobster with ginger and scallions. Closed for lunch on weekends. Reservations advised. Major credit cards accepted. 545 Boylston St. (phone: 236-4040).

Plaza The space and decor are the height of Victorian splendor, the menu is classic continental, and the service is exquisitely correct. A great place to go when you want to impress someone. Open for dinner Tuesdays through Saturdays. Reservations advised. Major credit cards accepted. *Copley Plaza Hotel,* 138 St. James St. (phone: 267-5300, ext. 1048).

Ritz-Carlton Large, lovely, and serenely elegant, this is one of only two places in town where you can enjoy a view of the *Public Garden* while dining with old-fashioned formality. The cuisine is continental, very good, and served by an expert staff. Men must wear jackets and ties at dinner. Reservations advised. Major credit cards accepted. *Ritz-Carlton Hotel,* 15 Arlington St. (phone: 536-5700).

St. Cloud One of the first culinary outposts in the now-trendy South End, it's still one of the best. The menu changes monthly, but you'll always find dishes such as rack of lamb with grilled vegetables and roasted salmon served with artichoke risotto. They serve the city's best hamburgers, too: A recent incarnation was accompanied by avocado salsa and a Maine crab fritter. A light, café-style menu is also available. Reservations advised. Major credit cards accepted. 557 Tremont St. (phone: 353-0202).

Upstairs at the Pudding Set in the old upstairs dining room of *Harvard's* famous *Hasty Pudding Club* (the walls are lined with original, hand-painted show bills from the club's productions of years past), this elegant place is truly Old Ivy, but the food is decidedly contemporary—and first-rate. Subtle northern Italian fare is featured. The veal scaloppine is excellent. Order from the à la carte menu, or choose the prix fixe tasting menu, which allows you to choose one dish from each of the four courses offered. The outdoor terrace, situated in the herb garden, offers a savory dining experience on warm summer nights. *Harvard* singing groups frequently perform at Sunday brunch. Reservations advised. Major credit cards accepted. 10 Holyoke St., Cambridge (phone: 864-1933).

MODERATE

Art Zone Among the city's trendiest dining spots, it features delicious barbecued meat, served in a funky former warehouse. The tables are especially interesting—dioramas under glass, they were created by local artists especially for this place, and each one is different. Reservations advised. Major credit cards accepted. 150 Kneeland St. (phone: 695-0087).

The Blue Room Despite the name, the latest inspiration of local restaurateurs Chris Schlesinger and Stan Frankenheimer feels as warm and cozy as a red brick oven, thanks to the open kitchen, glowing grills, and exposed brick walls. The house specialties are grilled and roasted meat and seafood, such as rabbit mole, black-and-blue T-bone steaks, Persian spiced duck, and peanut-crusted tuna steaks. Their pupu platter—an assortment of exotic salads, pickles, and noodles—is a real treat. Closed at lunchtime on weekends. Reservations necessary. Major credit cards accepted. 1 Kendall Sq. (phone: 494-9034).

Broadway Deli The Boston–New York "deli wars" have found a savory, satisfying harmony in this bright, bustling little eatery in the theater district. From corned beef and chopped liver to authentic egg creams and ultra-rich cheesecake, all the required deli delights are available at tables and for takeout. No reservations. Major credit cards accepted. 275 Tremont St. (phone: 426-1344).

Café Lampara The Italian-cuisine cousin to *Skipjack's* (see below) in terms of the creativity of the menu, this is the place to get excellent and unusual pizza and pasta. The café's popular roasted half chicken, however, is the item many favor. Reservations advised. Major credit cards accepted. 916 Commonwealth Ave. (phone: 566-0300).

Cajun Yankee The original gathering place of the New England crawdaddy crowd, this down-home, creole spot is perpetually packed. All the Cajun staples are here—blackened fish, jambalaya, sweet potato pie—in spicy, pungent abundance, and the beverages are correspondingly "down South." Closed Sundays and Mondays. Reservations advised. Major credit cards accepted. 1193 Cambridge St., Inman Sq., Cambridge (phone: 576-1971).

Changsho The food served in the recently relocated home of this Cambridge institution is still the best Chinese cooking you'll find outside New York's Chinatown. The restaurant has moved from its tiny, crowded storefront into a strikingly elegant—and much larger—space a block away. No reservations. Major credit cards accepted. 1712 Massachusetts Ave., Cambridge (phone: 547-6565).

Chart House In the oldest building on Boston's waterfront, its interior is a strikingly handsome arrangement of lofty spaces, natural wood, exposed red brick, and comfortable captain's chairs. The menu consists of abundant portions of steaks and seafood, with all the salad you can eat included in the reasonable prices. The award-winning clam chowder is superb. Reservations advised on weekend nights. Major credit cards accepted. 60 Long Wharf (phone: 227-1576).

Dali Garlic braids hanging from the ceiling, white plaster walls daubed with kitschy swirls, and waiters in red jackets and black cummerbunds are not the only things that make this *tapas* bar not far from *Harvard* seem authentic: The kitchen turns out Spanish specialties seldom seen outside Iberia. From the marinated olives served with drinks to the changing list of *tapas* (hors d'oeuvres) and entrées such as *pescado al sal* (whole snapper baked in a salt crust) or *conejo escabechado* (rabbit braised in red wine with juniper berries), dining here is a delicious adventure. There's usually a wait for a table, but if you're not in a hurry, order a pitcher of sangria and have another dish of olives. Closed Sundays. No reservations. Major credit cards accepted. 415 Washington St., Somerville (phone: 661-3254).

David's This new restaurant, which took over the space previously occupied by the popular *Bnu* trattoria, is busy establishing its own dedicated following. Its decor reflects the restaurant's theater district location, as does its pre- and post-theater dinner service. The menu is heavily influenced by the flavors of the Mediterranean, with an imaginative pasta selection and entrées such as lamb kebabs with couscous and minted chutney. In fine weather, there is limited outdoor seating as well. Closed Sundays. Reservations advised. Major credit cards accepted. 123 Stuart St. (phone: 367-8405).

Dover Sea Grille This understated, relaxed, beautifully appointed seafood restaurant and lounge in Brookline is just a clamshell's throw from both *Fenway Park* and the *Harvard Medical School*. Marvelous grilled entrées, especially salmon and swordfish, are specialties, as are bountiful salads and superb desserts. A lighter café menu is also served. "Early Catch" specials are available weeknights from 5:30 to 6:30 PM. Reservations advised. Major credit cards accepted. 1223 Beacon St. (phone: 566-7000).

Durgin-Park Though famed for generous servings of roast beef, pot roast, prime ribs, oyster stew, Boston baked beans, and Indian pudding, the kitchen now is way below par. However, its long, communal tables are still crowded with convivial diners attended by sharp-witted waitresses who like to give patrons a rough time (it's partly an act). No reservations. No credit cards accepted. 340 *Faneuil Hall Marketplace* (phone: 227-2038).

Icarus For some reason, this respected restaurant is never crowded, making it a great place for a quiet, intimate meal. The room resembles a Brahmin's drawing room with dark wood, green walls, and oversize sculptures. The contemporary American food is always imaginative and well prepared. The menu, which is predominantly seafood, changes every six weeks. On Sunday nights, the wine café offers *tapa*-size portions and wine by the glass. Open daily for dinner; there is also brunch on Sundays. Reservations advised. Major credit cards accepted. 3 Appleton St. (phone: 426-1790).

Jimmy's Harborside Located about a whale's tail from the Fish Pier, this is an incredibly popular seafood spot with a solid reputation. Every seat in the main dining room has an excellent view of Boston Harbor. The traditional seafood menu has been expanded to include some Italian dishes, veal, and tenderloin. The wine list is replete with fine American wines. Don't mistake *Jimmy's* for *Jimbo's*, a less engaging place across the street. Reservations advised. Most major credit cards accepted. 242 Northern Ave. (phone: 423-1000).

Legal Sea Foods If you don't mind waiting in line, you'll find fresh and well-prepared seafood. No reservations. Major credit cards accepted. Several locations: *Park Plaza Hotel*, corner of Columbus Ave. and Arlington St. (phone: 426-4444); in the *Chestnut Hill Shopping Mall*, 43 Boylston St. (phone: 277-7300); 5 Cambridge Center, Kendall Sq., Cambridge (phone: 864-3400); and *Copley Place* (phone: 266-7775).

Mirabelle Beautifully adorned with murals and warms woods, this place is the pride of catering wizard Stephen Elmont. Chefs are adept at many cuisines. Open daily for breakfast, lunch, and dinner. Reservations advised. Major credit cards accepted. 85 Newbury St. (phone: 859-4848).

Olives Superb Tuscany-influenced Italian food is served here in a soothing dove-colored dining room with comfortable banquettes. Try the grilled lobster with white bean *raviolone* and artichoke sauce or the *tortelli* of butternut squash with brown butter and sage. Open Tuesdays through Saturdays. Reservations advised for groups of six or more. MasterCard and Visa accepted. 67 Main St., Charlestown (phone: 242-1999).

Paolo This sophisticated place is piles of pasta above every other Hanover Street eatery, offering elegant northern Italian fare in intimate subterranean rooms. You can choose from unusually shaped homemade pasta—the lasagna is a delicate roulade—and delicious meat dishes, such as a veal chop with wild mushrooms in cognac. Ray Santisi and other local pianists make the most of the 1917 Steinway grand. Open for dinner Tuesdays through Sundays. Reservations advised. Major credit cards accepted. 216 Hanover St. (phone: 227-5550).

Rebecca's In this comfortable, modern place, the walls are decorated with hand-painted flowers and accented by exposed brick and works by local artists. The menu, described as "new American," borrows from French, Greek, Indian, and Italian cuisines. No reservations. Major credit cards accepted. 21 Charles St. (phone: 742-9747).

Rocco's The decor in this theater district dining place is as dramatic as the neighborhood's atmosphere, with stage-scale curtains, murals on the ceiling, and two-story picture windows overlooking the street. The menu offers an eclectic choice of Italian fare. Closed Sunday dinner. Reservations advised. Major credit cards accepted. 5 S. Charles St. (phone: 723-6800).

Skipjack's With a dazzling aquarium-like decor, this mariner's delight features an extensive array of innovative seafood dishes (it claims to serve the widest variety of seafood in New England). Snapper Veracruz, ginger calamari, grilled cilantro shrimp, and blackened redfish are just a few of the outstanding choices. For dieters, a spa menu offers 10 items of 400 calories or less. The wine list is extensive and carefully assembled, and the Sunday jazz brunch is a treat. Reservations advised. Major credit cards accepted. Several locations: 500 Boylston St., Copley Sq., Back Bay (phone: 536-3500); 2 Brookline Pl., Brookline (phone: 232-8887); 5 Bennett St., Charles Sq. (phone: 876-9900).

Sonsie Owner Patrick Lyons has made a splash with his new restaurant on this busy shopping thoroughfare by offering a menu as inviting as the atmosphere. Doors open into the café in front, and just beyond is a salon filled daily with international newspapers and overstuffed Parisian 1930s chairs. Then there is the dining room, with spacious booths (total dining room capacity is 90), Oriental rugs, and bird's-eye maple paneling; the paintings on the walls were commissioned for the restaurant. Some of the menu choices are grilled pork loin, salmon cooked in sake, and pizza with lime guacamole chicken and jack cheese. Open for breakfast, lunch, and dinner. Reservations strongly advised. Major credit cards accepted. 327 Newbury St. (phone: 351-2500).

Toscano Authentic northern Italian food is served in this elegant room with brick walls and red tiles. The menu changes daily, but you'll always find excellent risotto, homemade pasta, and fresh truffles in season. Closed Sunday lunch. Reservations necessary. American Express accepted. 41 Charles St. (phone: 723-4090).

West Street Grill Off the beaten track, between the *Common* and *Lafayette Place,* this trendy meeting place is the historic home of the Peabody family. Here Nathaniel Hawthorne married Sophia, and Elizabeth opened the bookstore that became the meeting place for such literati as Emerson and Thoreau. Today, it has been renovated to accommodate a striking restaurant (formerly *Cornucopia*) and bar. The menu changes seasonally, but always relies heavily on pasta and grilled dishes. Closed Sundays; dinner only Thursdays through Saturdays. Reservations advised. Major credit cards accepted. 15 West St. (phone: 423-0300).

Ye Olde Union Oyster House It's the real thing: Boston's oldest restaurant. Daniel Webster himself used to guzzle oysters at the wonderful mahogany bar, where skilled shuckers still pry them open before your eyes. Full seafood lunches and dinners are served upstairs, amid well-worn colonial ambience. (One booth is dedicated to John F. Kennedy, once a frequent diner.) Don't miss the seafood chowder. Reservations advised. Major credit cards accepted. 41 Union St. (phone: 227-2750).

INEXPENSIVE

Addis Red Sea Boston's best Ethiopian restaurant (it doesn't have a lot of competition). Patrons sit on tiny, handwoven benches and (the fulfillment of everybody's secret dream) eat only with fingers without social demerit. You just scoop up piles of *watts* (stew) with *injera*, the spongy Ethiopian pancake. Portions are large, the music and ambience are quietly mesmerizing, and the Ethiopian red wine is a delight. Open daily for dinner and for lunch on weekends. Reservations advised. Major credit cards accepted. 544 Tremont St. (phone: 426-8727).

The Barking Crab At the city's only urban clam shack, customers sit at picnic tables under a tent, look out over a none-too-scenic channel of water, and order fresh seafood—fried clams, grilled fish, and boiled lobsters—from a take-out window. Don't miss the homemade clam chowder (New England, natch) and coleslaw. It's rustic, but that doesn't stop legions of suited businesspeople from the nearby financial district from stopping in for a summertime lunch. Closed October through April; closed Monday dinnertime during the first two weeks of May; open until 1 AM nightly the rest of the season. No reservations. No credit cards accepted. 88 Sleeper St. (phone: 426-2722).

Boca Grande If Tex-Mex is what you crave, this eatery is one of the best food values in Boston. Black bean tostadas, generous handmade tamales, and burritos are the favored fare. Reservations unnecessary. Major credit cards accepted. Two locations: 1728 Massachusetts Ave. (phone: 354-5550) and 149 First St., Cambridge (phone: 354-7400).

Casa Romero Though most people don't link Boston with Mexican food, there are indeed a couple of good Mexican eateries. The food here is authentic—marinated tenderloin of pork, *enchiladas verdes*, garlic soup, and *mole poblano*. The tile tables and wrought iron give this place enough of a Latin American feel to let you forget for a moment that when Bostonians think of south of the border, they're thinking Rhode Island. Open daily for dinner. Reservations advised. Major credit cards accepted. 30 Gloucester St. (phone: 536-4341).

La Groceria Northern Italian cooking in an old house with several dining rooms, each with a distinct character (the intimate top floor is recommended). The pasta is homemade, as are the cheesecake and cannoli. The veal dishes and antipasto, hot and cold, are excellent. Extensive wine list. Open daily for dinner. Reservations advised for large parties. Major credit cards accepted. 853 Main St., Cambridge (phone: 547-9258 or 876-4162).

Jae's Café The food is Korean in inspiration and healthy in preparation. You can find *yukhai* (Korean raw beef), pan-fried dumplings stuffed with shrimp, and several light, mild curries. Every dish has lots of fresh vegetables and little oil. There's also a sushi bar downstairs. Reservations advised. Major credit cards accepted. 520 Columbus Ave. (phone: 421-9405).

No-Name Restaurant The name was not a conscious decision. Beginning as a ramshackle joint that counted only the local fishermen as its clientele, this has become a Boston institution serving the freshest seafood in the city (though the folks at *Jimmy's* might dispute this point) to tourists, businesspeople, and the ancient mariners who still frequent the place. With a view of the harbor, this nameless place is also frill-less: Expect Formica tables, paper napkins, and plastic cups. But that's its charm. Though the waitresses are a tad surly, they will fetch some of the finest fried seafood, boiled lobster, and broiled scallops on record. No reservations. No credit cards accepted. 15½ Fish Pier, just off Northern Ave. (phone: 338-7539).

Rubin's Kosher Delicatessen One of only a few kosher restaurants in the Boston area. Its chopped liver, potato *latkes* (pancakes), and lean pastrami (hot or cold) are the genuine articles. Closed Saturdays, and on Fridays after 2 PM. Reservations unnecessary. Major credit cards accepted. 500 Harvard St., Brookline (phone: 566-8761).

S&M New York Deli This large, bright, and bustling delicatessen is filled with the financial district crowd at lunchtime. The food is authentically New York–style, and the sandwiches (try the Reuben) rival the Big Apple's best. There are about 10 stools along a front counter and 20 tables in the back, or take your order out and have a picnic on *Boston Common,* a short walk up Beacon Street. Closed Sundays. No reservations. No credit cards accepted. 12 Beacon St. (phone: 523-8776).

NORTH END RESTAURANTS

This Old World, predominantly Italian district boasts dozens of restaurants crowded into a few square blocks, ranging in quality and price. For cozy, homemade meals, try *Mother Anna's* (211 Hanover St.; phone: 523-8496; reservations only on weekdays; American Express accepted). For great seafood Italian-style, try the *Daily Catch,* which specializes in calamari (squid) dishes, cooked in an open kitchen (323 Hanover St.; phone: 523-8567; reservations advised; major credit cards accepted). Similar in spirit but less well known is *Giacomo's* (355 Hanover St.; phone: 523-9026; no reservations; American Express accepted). Many locals swear by the crunchy, crusty pizza at *Circle Pizza* (361 Hanover St.; phone: 523-8787; reservations accepted for large groups only; no credit cards accepted). Don't leave the North End without experiencing *la dolce vita*—that's short for how sweet life seems when you're sitting at a sidewalk café, sipping espresso, savoring a cannoli or gelati, watching the world go by. The best espresso and sweets are at *Caffè Dello Sport* (307 Hanover St.; phone: 523-5063) and *Caffè Roma* (241 Hanover St.; phone: 723-1760). Neither accepts reservations or credit cards.

Charleston, South Carolina

At-a-Glance

SEEING THE CITY

Charleston is set in that sea-level area of southeastern South Carolina known as the Low Country. There are no hills from which to get a good view of the city. Charleston has been nicknamed "the Holy City" because of its many churches; the best view of it is from the ground looking up, especially at night, when floodlights illuminate the church spires.

SPECIAL PLACES

The Old City is approximately 7 square miles, and even a five-day visit could be spent walking without covering the same street twice. An evening stroll is most popular with residents.

FORT SUMTER The fort where the first shots of the Civil War were fired in 1861 sits on a small manmade island at the entrance to Charleston's harbor. *Fort Sumter* withstood federal attacks between 1863 and early 1865. To the Union, it represented treachery; to the Confederates, it meant courageous resistance to oppression. The fort can be reached only by boat. *Fort Sumter Tours* leave *City Marina* (17 Lockwood Blvd.) daily at 2:30 PM in winter, three times daily in summer. One tour leaves *Patriot's Point* daily at 2:30 PM; three times daily in summer. Admission charge (phone: 722-1691).

CHARLES TOWNE LANDING Charleston was called Charles Towne in 1670 by the first permanent English settlers. Now a state park, *Charles Towne Landing* has restored houses, a full-scale replica of a 17th-century trading vessel, an open-air pavilion with archaeological artifacts, and a forest with indigenous animals. There are plenty of picnic tables, bike trails, and tram tours, too. The recently reopened interpretive center offers several displays, including maps and Indian artifacts. Open daily. Admission charge. 1500 Old Towne Rd. (phone: 852-4200).

MAGNOLIA PLANTATION AND GARDENS Listed in the *National Register of Historic Places, Magnolia Plantation* has been the home of the Drayton family since the 1670s. World-famous for its abundance of colors and scents, *Magnolia Gardens'* 30 acres abound with 900 different varieties of camellias, 250 varieties of azaleas, and dozens of exquisite plants, shrubs, and flowers. In addition to the boat tours, a small zoo, and a ranch exhibiting a breed of miniature horse, *Magnolia Gardens* offers canoeing, bird watching, and bike trails through its 400-acre wildlife refuge. Another attraction here is the *Audubon Swamp Garden,* a separate, very secluded 60-acre cypress swamp. Closed *Christmas.* Admission charge. Ten miles northwest of downtown on Rte. 61 (phone: 571-1266).

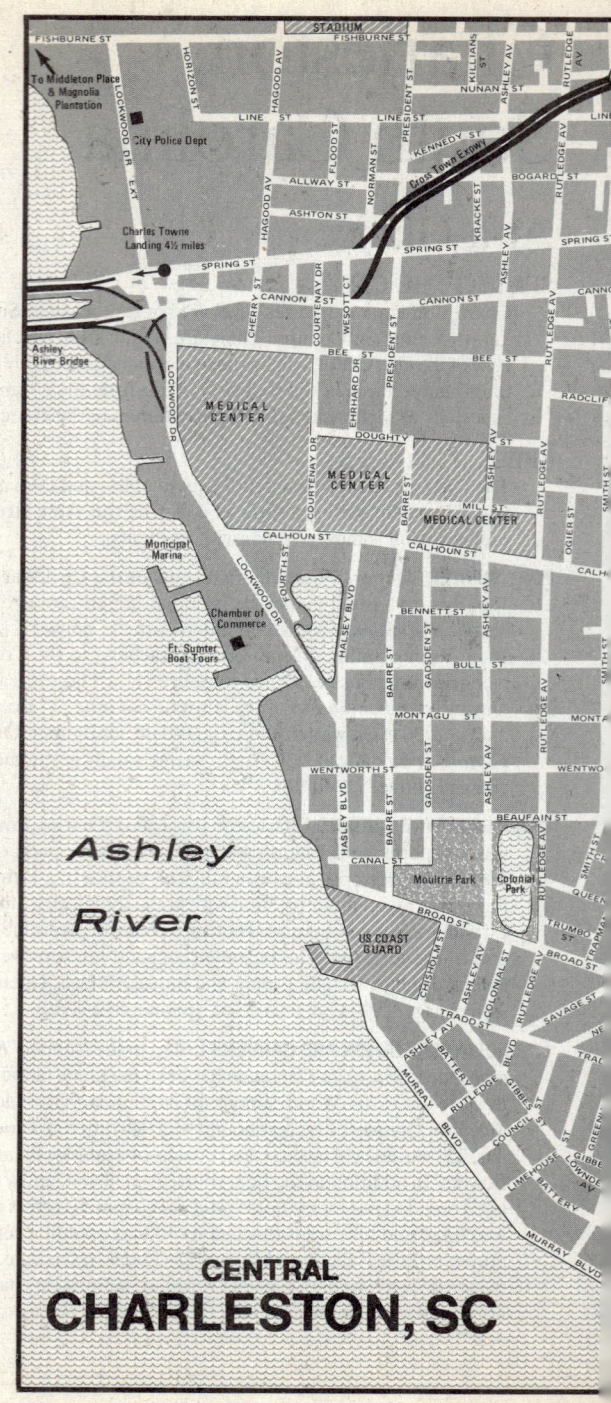

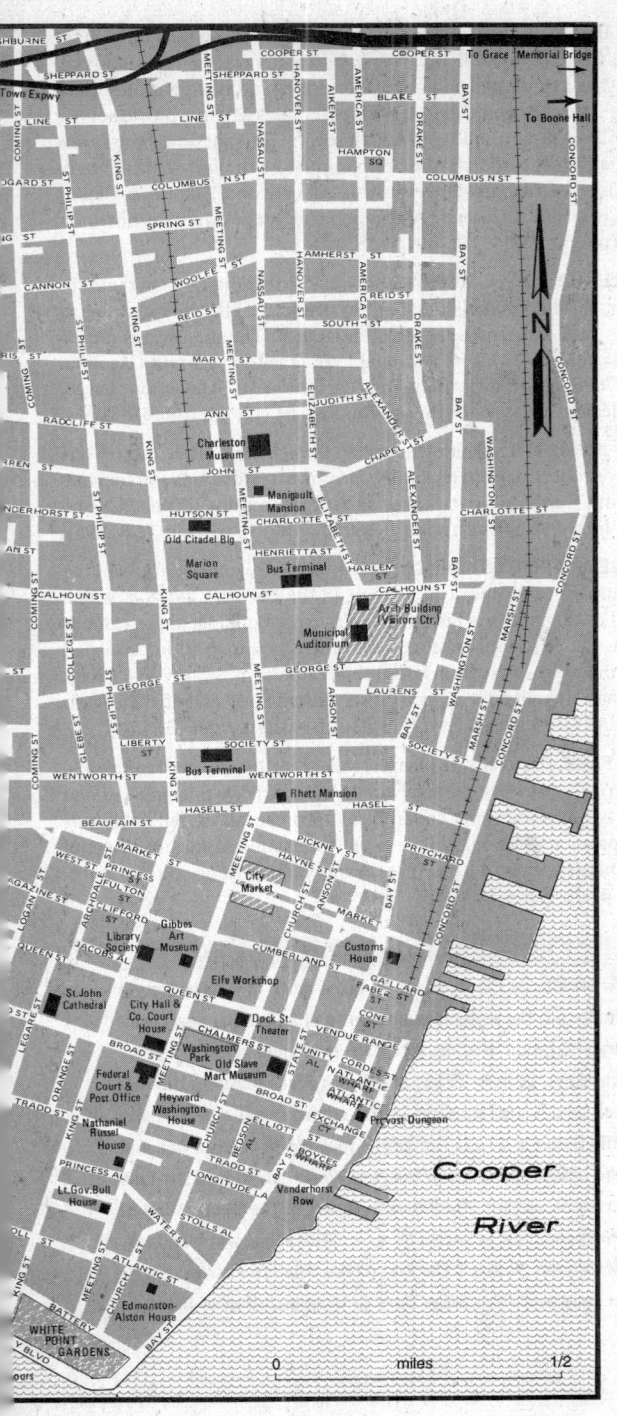

BOONE HALL If you ever imagined yourself as one of those romantic characters in *Gone With the Wind, Boone Hall* is the place to live out your dream. This lovely 738-acre estate, formerly a cotton plantation settled by Major John Boone in 1681, closely resembles MGM's movie set (or is it the other way around?). Although several original slave houses are here, true history buffs may be disappointed by the fact that the main building has been extensively reconstructed—not once, but twice. Closed *Thanksgiving* and *Christmas*. Admission charge. Seven miles north on Rte. 17 (phone: 884-4371).

DRAYTON HALL The only pre-Revolutionary mansion remaining on the Ashley River, this national historic landmark is one of the finest surviving examples of Georgian Palladian architecture. The mansion is unfurnished, but its tower offers a special look at colonial South Carolina. Closed *Thanksgiving, Christmas,* and *New Year's Day*. Admission charge. Nine miles northwest of downtown on Rte. 61 (phone: 766-0188).

CHARLESTON MUSEUM This oldest municipal museum in the country has impressive collections of arts, crafts, furniture, textiles, and implements from South Carolina's early days, as well as occasional films. Closed major holidays. Admission charge. 360 Meeting St. (phone: 722-2996).

OLD EXCHANGE AND PROVOST DUNGEON During the Revolutionary War, the British imprisoned American patriots in the *Provost Dungeon,* which dates to 1780 and is in the historic *Old Exchange* building; today, exhibits show how the prisoners were treated during their detention. Attached to the *Provost* are excavations from the Half Moon Battery (ca. 1690), the original city wall built by the British. Closed Sundays and major holidays. Admission charge. East Bay St. at Broad (phone: 727-2165).

WATERFRONT PARK A real crowd-pleaser, this beautiful city park in the historic district features swinging benches and a striking pineapple-shape fountain with a pool where children cavort on hot days. Tall palmettos line the promenade along the Cooper River, and harbor breezes cool the air. On the corner of Concorde St. and Vendue Range on the southeast side of the downtown area.

EXTRA SPECIAL

At *Middleton Place,* about 15 miles north of Charleston via Route 61, the self-sustaining world of a Carolina Low Country plantation is re-created daily by people in 18th-century costume. Built in 1755, *Middleton Place* features the oldest landscaped gardens in the country, laid out by Henry Middleton in 1741. The 1,000-year-old Middleton Oak and the oldest camellias in the New World flourish on the lush grounds. Arthur Middleton, a signer of the Declaration of Independence, is buried here. A national historic landmark, *Middleton House* is the site of the *Spoleto Festival Finale* in June and *Plantation Days* (a dramatization of life on a plantation) in November. Open daily. Admission charge (phone: 556-6020).

Sources and Resources

TOURIST INFORMATION

The *Charleston Convention and Visitors Bureau* (375 Meeting St.; Charleston, SC 29401; phone: 853-8000) offers advice and brochures on tours, hotels, and restaurants. The staff will assist you in making reservations. It's open daily. A 25-minute multimedia show on the city's heritage, *Forever Charleston,* is shown frequently at the bureau; admission charge (phone: 723-5225). In the historic district, the *Preservation Society of Charleston* (147 King St. at Queen St.; phone: 723-4381) also offers information and tours, as well as a gift shop. It's closed Sundays.

For information on events and performance schedules, call the *Charleston Convention and Visitors Bureau* or the *Charleston County Parks and Recreation Commission* (phone: 762-2172). Contact the South Carolina state tourism hotline (phone: 803-734-0122) for maps, calendars of events, health updates, and travel advisories.

LOCAL COVERAGE *Charleston News & Courier,* morning daily; *Evening Post,* evening daily; *Charleston* magazine, a monthly.

TELEVISION STATIONS WCBD Channel 2–ABC; WCIV Channel 4–NBC; WCSC Channel 5–CBS; and WITV Channel 7–PBS.

RADIO STATIONS AM: WTMA 1250 (country music). FM: WSCI 89.3 (classical/jazz); WAVF 96.1 (rock 'n' roll); and WXLY 102 (classic rock).

TELEPHONE The area code for Charleston is 803.

SALES TAX The sales tax in Charleston is 6%.

CLIMATE Charleston's average temperature is 65F. Winters are mild, summers hot. March and April, when everything is abloom, are the best spring months to visit. In fall, October and November are ideal.

GETTING AROUND

AIRPORT *Charleston International Airport* is a 20-minute drive from downtown. *LowCountry Limousine* (phone: 767-7117) provides van service from the airport to the downtown hotels.

BUS The *South Carolina Electric and Gas Company* (665 Meeting St.; phone: 747-0922) operates the city bus system; the fare is 75¢. The *Downtown Area Shuttle* (*DASH*; phone: 724-7420)) operates from 8 AM to 9 PM. The fare is 75¢, or $1 for an all-day pass.

CAR RENTAL Major national agencies are represented at the airport.

TAXI Cabs are inexpensive and a better bet than buses; they must be ordered by phone. Call *Yellow Cab* (phone: 577-6565).

TOURS Guided bus or van tours are available from *Adventure Sightseeing* (phone: 762-0088) and *Gray Line Bus Tours* (phone: 722-4444). To see the city from the harbor, take a *Gray Line* water tour, departing at 2 PM daily (more often in summer) from the *City Marina* (17 Lockwood Blvd.; phone: 722-1112). It's also possible to rent a tape cassette from the gift shop at the *Mills House* hotel (see *Checking In*) for a walking or driving tour. Narrated tours in horse-drawn carriages are provided by *Charleston Carriage Co.* (phone: 577-0042), *Palmetto Carriage Tours* (phone: 723-8145), and *Old South Carriage Co.* (phone: 723-9712). Walking tours are conducted by *Charleston Tea Party* (phone: 577-5896) and *Civil War Walking Tours* (phone: 722-7033). Or take a bicycle tour with a map and a bike from *The Bicycle Shop* (phone: 722-8168).

LOCAL SERVICES

For information about local services, call the *Chamber of Commerce* (phone: 577-2510).

BUSINESS SERVICES For any work involving office automation, call *Norell Temporary Services* (phone: 554-4933).

MECHANICS *Lewis & Hesse Auto Repair* (1480 Savannah Hwy.; phone: 766-9011); *University Exxon* (Rutledge and Calhoun Sts.; phone: 577-7736).

MEDICAL EMERGENCY *Charleston Memorial Hospital* (326 Calhoun St.; phone: 577-0600).

MESSENGER SERVICES *Bullet Deliveries of Charleston* (phone: 763-4129); *Yellow Cab* (phone: 577-6565).

MONEY TRANSFERS *American Express MoneyGram* (phone: 800-926-9400 for information; 800-866-8800 for money transfers); *Western Union Financial Services* (phone: 800-325-6000 or 800-325-4176).

NATIONAL/INTERNATIONAL COURIER *DHL Worldwide Express* (phone: 800-227-6177); *FedEx* (phone: 767-0275; 800-238-5355).

PHARMACY *Eckerd* (466 Savannah Hwy.; phone: 766-5593), open daily, 8 AM to midnight.

PHOTOCOPIES *American Speedy Printing Center* (1660 Sam Rittenberg Blvd.; phone: 571-7556); *Kinko's* (King and Calhoun Sts.; phone: 723-5130), open 24 hours.

POST OFFICE Branches at Central, Broad, and Meeting Sts. (phone: 724-4333).

PROFESSIONAL PHOTOGRAPHER *Alterman Studios* (phone: 577-0647); *Larry Workman Photography* (phone: 723-3667).

SECRETARY/STENOGRAPHER See *Business Services,* above.

TRANSLATOR *Interpreter's Guide* available from the *Chamber of Commerce* (phone: 577-2510).

WESTERN UNION/TELEX Many offices are located around the city (phone: 800-325-6000 to find the location nearest you).

SPECIAL EVENTS

The *Southeastern Wildlife Exhibition* draws over 40,000 visitors to its conservation and wildlife artwork exhibits during the second week of February, at 15 different locations downtown (phone: 723-1748 for information). During the *Festival of Houses and Gardens,* from mid-March to mid-April, more than 100 private homes and gardens are open to the public (phone: 723-1623 for information; 722-3405 for reservations). The annual *Spoleto Festival USA,* 12 days of chamber music, dance, jazz, opera, and theater, begins in late May (phone: 722-2764 for schedule information). An array of local events, many free, make up *Piccolo Spoleto,* which coincides with the main festival (phone: 724-7305). The *Preservation Society* conducts *Candlelight Tours of Homes and Gardens* in September and October (phone: 722-4630).

MUSEUMS

In addition to those described in *Special Places,* some other notable museums include the following:

GIBBES MUSEUM OF ART A fine collection by 18th- and 19th-century American painters, local and regional art, and portrait miniatures. Closed Sunday and Monday mornings. Admission charge. 135 Meeting St. (phone: 722-2706).

PATRIOTS POINT MARITIME MUSEUM This US naval history museum features the aircraft carrier USS *Yorktown,* among other ships. Open daily. Admission charge except for children under 6. On Highway 17N, just across the Cooper River (phone: 884-2727).

HISTORIC HOUSES

Except where noted, the houses listed below are open daily except holidays. All charge admission.

AIKEN-RHETT MANSION (1817) Closed Mondays and Tuesdays. 48 Elizabeth St. (phone: 723-1159).

CALHOUN MANSION (1876) Closed January and Mondays through Wednesdays. 16 Meeting St. (phone: 722-8205).

EDMONSTON-ALSTON HOUSE (1828) 21 E. Battery St. (phone: 722-7171).

HEYWARD-WASHINGTON HOUSE (1770) 87 Church St. (phone: 722-0354).

JOSEPH MANIGAULT HOUSE (1803) 350 Meeting St. (phone: 723-2926).

NATHANIEL RUSSELL HOUSE (1808) 51 Meeting St. (phone: 722-3405).

SHOPPING

Charleston's historic district offers the best and most varied places to shop in the city, ranging from stores carrying "Prehistoric Charleston" T-shirts to boutiques with high-fashion European-designed clothing to antiques shops. The *Public Market,* with its main entrance on Meeting Street at Market Street, is a prime focus of attention. Open-air stalls feature works by local artisans, including sweetgrass baskets, a local tradition that harks back several generations. Other items sold here are hand-packaged red rice, a traditional Low Country side dish made with tomato sauce and spices, as well as the more prosaic T-shirts and paperweights. Flanking the *Public Market* along Market Street are gift shops that carry art prints of Charleston and home accessories.

Almost directly across from the market is *Charleston Place,* an upscale mall anchored by the *Omni* hotel and including such shops as *Godiva Chocolates, Victoria's Secret,* and several designer boutiques. Nearby is *Christian Michi* (220 King St.; phone: 723-0575), a boutique whose high-fashion clothing and eclectic home furnishings have attracted such celebrity clients as Melanie Griffith and Carly Simon.

Also in the historic district, the *Historic Charleston Foundation Museum Shop* (108 Meeting St.; phone: 724-8484) sells books, furniture, jewelry, and other souvenirs and offers a permanent exhibit on preservation. *Historic Charleston Reproductions* (105 Broad St.; phone: 723-8292) sells licensed reproductions of furniture and jewelry.

The three-block stretch of King Street north of Queen Street is the city's antiques area. The following are just a few of the assorted shops here: *Geo. C. Birlant & Co.* (191 King St.; phone: 722-3842), the largest in the city, features 18th- and 19th-century American and English furniture, dishes, glassware, and clocks; *American Sterling Galleries* (195 King St.; phone: 723-7197) sells antique silver, flatware, and holloware (teapots, creamers, and the like); and *Livingston Antiques* (163 King St.; phone: 723-9697) imports turn-of-the-century English porcelain and furniture, as well as old books. In addition to its King Street location, there is also a branch at 2137 Savannah Highway (phone: 556-6162). It's fun to poke around, but you probably won't be able to negotiate many bargains: The shopkeepers know what their wares are worth.

SPORTS AND FITNESS

BICYCLING Many parks have bike trails. Bikes may be rented from the *Bicycle Shop* (283 Meeting St.; phone: 722-8168).

FISHING The best fishing is in the estuarine creeks that teem with bass, sheepshead, flounder, and trout (in fall and winter). In summer and fall, the creeks are full of crabs. Fishing for crabs and oysters as well as creek fishing are especially good on Capers, Dewees, Bulls, Kiawah, and Seabrook Islands. There are some public oyster beds closer to Charleston. For really good surf fishing, try Capers and Dewees Islands. For fishing and hunting regulations, write to the *South Carolina Wildlife Resources Department* (PO Box 167, Columbia, SC 29202).

FITNESS CENTERS *Roper Health and Fitness Center* (910 Hwy. 17 Bypass, Mt. Pleasant; phone: 884-2120) has Nautilus and free-weight equipment, aerobics classes, racquetball courts, and a pool, and is open to non-members for a fee.

GOLF There are public courses at *Patriots Point Links* (Hwy. 17, Mt. Pleasant; phone: 881-0042) and the *Shadowmoss Plantation Golf and Country Club* (20 Dunvegan Dr.; phone: 556-8251). Kiawah and Seabrook Islands have fine golf courses, but one of the most popular golfing areas in the country, Myrtle Beach, is only 98 miles north of Charleston on Route 17. This year-round resort town has 28 golf courses, many of them first rate. Even better is Hilton Head Island, 167 miles south of Charleston, with more than 20 golf courses, including *Harbour Town Golf Links* at *Sea Pines Plantation.* Hilton Head's accommodations are classier and more comfortable than those in the Myrtle Beach area.

Daufuskie Island, reached by ferry from Hilton Head, is another first-rate golfing destination.

JOGGING Run around Colonial Lake, on Ashley Avenue. Or, for a nice 5-mile loop, run from Lockwood Drive to Battery, up East Bay Street, turn left onto Broad Street, right onto Meeting Street, and left onto Calhoun, which intersects with Lockwood.

SAILING Both crewed and bareboat sailboat charters, as well as sport fishing excursions, are available through *Bohicket Yacht Charters* (20 miles from Charleston, between Kiawah and Seabrook Islands; phone: 768-7294).

SWIMMING Near the city, Sullivan's Island and the Isle of Palms have fairly nice beaches, crowded in summer. North of Charleston, Capers and Dewees Islands have more secluded beaches, probably because they're only accessible by boat. Both are state wildlife refuges.

TENNIS The courts at the resorts on Kiawah and Seabrook Islands are open to the public but can be expensive, and resort guests have priority. Try *Shadowmoss Plantation Golf & Country Club* (20 Dunvegan Dr.; phone: 556-8251) for inexpensive public courts.

THEATER

Built in 1736, the 463-seat *Dock Street Theater* (on the corner of Church and Queen Sts.; phone: 723-5648) is the oldest in the country. It stages frequent performances of original drama, Shakespeare, Broadway, and 18th-century classics. Call in advance for up-to-date information and performance times. Tours of the theater are conducted sporadically during the week; admission charge. The *Robert Ivey Ballet* (1910 Savannah Hwy.; phone: 556-1343) presents major performances in the spring and fall at the *College of Charleston*'s *Simons Center for the Performing Arts* and at other venues around the city and state.

MUSIC

For *Community Concert Association* and *Symphony Orchestra* schedules, call the visitors' bureau (see *Tourist Information*). The *Spoleto Festival USA*, 12 days of chamber music, dance, jazz, opera, and theater, begins every year in late May (see *Special Events*).

NIGHTCLUBS AND NIGHTLIFE

The *Jukebox* (4 Vendue Range; phone: 723-3431) offers music from the 1960s and 1970s in the early evenings and changes to Top 40 later. The *Back Market Café* (61 State St.; phone: 720-2114) presents rock bands on weekends. For a quieter atmosphere, try the *Best Friend Bar* in the *Mills House* hotel (see *Checking In*). *Myskyn's Tavern* (5 Faber St.; phone: 577-5595) hosts rock, reggae, and jazz groups. *East Bay Trading Company* (corner of E. Bay and Queen Sts.; phone: 722-0722) is filled with fun antiques and an unusual bar; next door is *Fanigan's* (159 E. Bay St.; phone: 722-6916), a favorite spot for businesspeople. *Café 99* (99 Market St.; phone: 577-4499) features an outdoor patio, raw bar, and live entertainment. The best nightspot north of town is the *Windjammer* (1008 Ocean Blvd.; phone: 886-8596), a beer-and-billiards beach bar on the Isle of Palms with live music on weekends.

Best in Town

CHECKING IN

Expect to pay $150 or more per night for a double room at hotels we list as very expensive, $100 to $150 at expensive places, and $75 to $100 at those categorized as moderate; there are no exceptional inexpensive hotels in the city. For bed and breakfast accommodations, contact *Historic Charleston Bed & Breakfast* (43 Legare St., Charleston, SC 29401; phone: 722-6606). Unless otherwise noted, hotel rooms have air conditioning, private baths, TV sets, and telephones. All hotels are in the 803 area code unless otherwise indicated.

VERY EXPENSIVE

John Rutledge House Inn The former home of a signer of the Constitution, this property has been meticulously restored, right down to the intricately carved mantels. Its 19 rooms and three suites boast lovely parquet floors and antique reproductions. Relax in the ballroom with complimentary sherry. There is no restaurant, but amenities include breakfast served in the courtyard or delivered to your room with a morning newspaper, and turn-down service. 116 Broad St. (phone: 723-7999; 800-476-9741; fax: 720-2615).

Omni Charleston Place This glitzy hotel is the centerpiece of *Charleston Place,* an impressive arcade of stylish shops and restaurants in the historic district. It has 440 rooms, plus an indoor pool, a spa, and fitness facilities. The *Palmetto Café* features fine continental dining, and *Louis' Bar & Grill* is open for dinner. Amenities include 24-hour room service, a concierge, a meeting room, secretarial services, photocopiers, and express checkout. 130 Market St. (phone: 722-4900; 800-THE-OMNI; fax: 722-0728).

EXPENSIVE

Battery Carriage House On the Battery facing the harbor, this sophisticated eight-room inn provides guests with four-poster beds, continental breakfast in bed, and turn-down service. There's no restaurant, but you can sip complimentary wine in the hospitality room or in the wisteria-draped, walled garden. 20 S. Battery (phone: 727-3100 between 10 AM and 5 PM).

Hawthorne Suites at the Market An elegant property in the heart of the historic district. One of its many beauties is the entranceway, an 1874 portico. Its 164 one- and two-bedroom suites, furnished with antique reproductions, also have kitchens. Other niceties are the heated pool, concierge service, fitness facilities, and breakfast delivered to your room. There's no restaurant. Business amenities include two meeting rooms, secretarial services, and express checkout. 181 Church St. (phone: 577-2644; 800-527-1133; fax: 577-2697).

Lodge Alley Inn Quiet and tasteful, this hostelry is in Charleston's best shopping and sightseeing area. It has 34 rooms, each with a fireplace, as well as 37 one- and two-bedroom suites and a penthouse. The *French Quarter* restaurant serves country French fare, and the *Charleston Tea Party*

Lounge is a lovely place to sip an aperitif. Amenities include room service (available only for breakfast) and a meeting room. 195 E. Bay (phone: 722-1611; 800-845-1004; fax: 722-1611, ext. 7777).

Maison Du Pré At the northern end of the historic district, three 19th-century single houses and two carriage houses have been fashioned into a warm, elegant inn. All 12 rooms and three suites have Oriental rugs, antique armoires, and marble-and-tile bathrooms. There's no restaurant, but a continental breakfast and afternoon tea are included in the rate. 317 E. Bay St. (phone: 723-8691; 800-844-4667; fax: 723-3722).

Mills House A topnotch 214-room property operated by Holiday Inn, it is a Charleston classic. Its antebellum decor reflects its 19th-century history, and, fittingly, it's in the center of the historic district. The *Barbados Room* specializes in tableside preparation of continental food; you'll definitely want to make reservations for the famous Sunday buffet. Amenities include room service until 10 PM, a concierge, a meeting room, secretarial services, and photocopiers. 115 Meeting St. (phone: 577-2400; 800-874-9600; fax: 722-2112).

Two Meeting Street Inn A real "find" in Charleston, built in 1891 and much like a European pension, it has been a guesthouse for more than 60 years. Nine spacious rooms and a wide second-floor verandah overlook *White Point Gardens* and the harbor. It's furnished with family antiques, silver, and Oriental rugs. 2 Meeting St. (phone: 723-7322).

MODERATE

Best Western King Charles Inn In the center of the historic district, it reflects old Charleston in the decor of its 90 rooms. There's free parking, a pool, and a dining room for breakfast only. 237 Meeting St. (phone: 723-7451; 800-528-1234; fax: 723-2041).

Days Inn Meeting St. The best deal in the historic district: 124 rooms, a restaurant, and a pool. Free parking. 155 Meeting St. (phone: 722-8411; 800-325-2525; fax: 723-5361).

Hampton Inn Historic District Right next to the visitors' bureau (with its easy access to the Historic District by shuttle), this property in a former warehouse offers 166 rooms and five suites decorated with antique reproductions, and an attractive garden courtyard. There's no restaurant. Amenities include an outdoor pool, complimentary newspapers, and continental breakfast. 345 Meeting St. (phone: 723-4000; 800-HAMPTON; fax: 722-3725).

EATING OUT

A large number of good restaurants have sprung up in Charleston over the past several years—so many, in fact, that a visitor would have to stay here a long time to sample them all. Expect to pay $100 or more for dinner for two at places listed as very expensive; $70 to $100 at those categorized as expensive; $30 to $70 at places listed as moderate; and less than $30 at inexpensive eateries. Prices do not include drinks, wine tax, or tips. Unless otherwise noted, restaurants are open for lunch and dinner. All restaurants are in the 803 area code unless otherwise indicated.

VERY EXPENSIVE

Restaurant Million One of Charleston's dining gems, this nouvelle French establishment is housed in a beautifully restored old tavern. Two prix fixe menus offer such sumptuous dishes as smoked salmon ravioli and squab prepared with herbs. There's à la carte dining as well. Open for dinner only; closed Sundays. Reservations necessary. Major credit cards accepted. 2 Unity Alley (phone: 577-7472).

Robert's of Charleston Located in the *Planter's Inn* in the market area, this is one of the city's top dining spots. A prix fixe dinner of mouth-watering beef tenderloin includes wine and gratuity, and for a relaxing dining experience, a pianist and vocalist are featured each evening. Open for dinner only; closed Mondays through Wednesdays. Reservations necessary. Major credit cards accepted. 112 N. Market St. (phone: 577-7565).

EXPENSIVE

Anson's Decorated with antique beveled-glass doors and ironwork, this eatery combines elegance with a friendly, casual ambience. Seafood is the specialty—cashew-crusted grouper is a particular favorite—but steaks are also offered. Open daily for dinner only. Reservations advised. Major credit cards accepted. 12 Anson St. (phone: 577-0551).

Carolina's A varied menu featuring game, beef, and pasta dishes is served in a contemporary-style dining room. Smoked Carolina quail is a popular entrée, as is the filet of beef served with crabmeat. Open daily for dinner only. Reservations advised. Major credit cards accepted. 10 Exchange St. (phone: 724-3800).

Louis' Charleston Grill Owner-chef Louis Osteen's cooking has been lauded since he opened this place five years ago. The menu offers a range of Low Country entrées, focusing on fresh seafood. A jazz combo lends a festive air. Open daily for dinner only. Reservations advised. Major credit cards accepted. 224 King St. (phone: 577-4522).

Magnolia's Formerly the city's *Customs House,* it's now a popular restaurant decorated with huge oil paintings of magnolias and other elegant touches. The menu features Tex-Mex and Cajun dishes prepared with Low Country flair, such as grilled salmon served over grits with dill and shallot butter. Open daily. Reservations advised. Major credit cards accepted. 185 E. Bay St. (phone: 577-7771).

MODERATE

Celia's Porta Via As cozy as a visit to an Italian relative, this small place offers seafood dishes and homemade pasta; its fresh-baked bread draws raves. Closed Sundays; dinner only on Saturdays. Reservations advised. Major credit cards accepted. 49 Archdale St. (phone: 722-9003).

82 Queen Nestled in a lovely 18th-century townhouse with a garden court, this spot specializes in seafood and boasts three bars; the *Wine Bar* makes a nice spot for a pre- or post-dinner glass of wine. One of its noteworthy seasonal specials is sautéed veal in sun-dried-tomato butter. Open daily. Reservations advised. Major credit cards accepted. 82 Queen St. (phone: 723-7591).

Garibaldi's This small café serves Italian home cooking with big-city service. A wide range of pasta dishes is offered daily, as are regular specials, including veal and seafood. Open daily for dinner only. Reservations advised. Major credit cards accepted. 49 S. Market St. (phone: 723-7153).

Marianne The regular dinner menu is French and excellent: beef, veal, seafood, and lamb, plus a good wine list. A late supper also is available, with appetizers, soup, steaks, and omelettes. Open daily for dinner only. Reservations advised. Major credit cards accepted. 235 Meeting St. (phone: 722-7196).

Pinckney's Café and Espresso A mom-and-pop café whose seafood gumbo is highly touted by the artists and musicians who make up a good part of the clientele. Closed Sundays and Mondays. Reservations accepted for groups of six or more. No credit cards accepted. 18 Pinckney St. (phone: 577-0961).

Poogan's Porch Fresh seafood and Low Country fare in an old Charleston house, with floral wallpaper and ceiling fans. Grilled alligator is a popular appetizer. Open daily. Reservations necessary. Major credit cards accepted. 72 Queen St. (phone: 577-2337).

Primerose House Set in a renovated 1317 mansion, this place offers an innovative menu that's hard to pin down, although Carolina, Cajun, and creole influences are evident. Entrées change nightly, but they usually include two or three seafood dishes, pasta, and some classic continental choices. Open daily. Dinner only on Saturdays; brunch only on Sundays. Reservations advised. Major credit cards accepted. 332 E. Bay St. (phone: 723-2954).

Slightly North of Broad A maverick Southern kitchen that features seafood, Low Country, and some international dishes—in two sizes to encourage sampling. Ambience is casual. Closed Sundays. No reservations. Major credit cards accepted. 192 E. Bay St. (phone: 723-3424).

INEXPENSIVE

Gaulart & Maliclet A local hangout, this tiny bistro serves simple French fare emphasizing fresh ingredients—seafood, a variety of healthful salads, and sandwiches on baguettes and croissants are some of the items on the menu. Closed Sundays; lunch only on Mondays. No reservations. Major credit cards accepted. 98 Broad St. (phone: 577-9797).

Martha Lou's Kitchen This small eatery serves Southern soul food: fried chicken, pork chops, white rice, collard greens, and the like. For the price, the food is unbeatable. Closed Sundays. No reservations. No credit cards accepted. 1068 Morrison Dr. (phone: 577-9583).

Shem Creek Bar and Grill Grilled seafood, chicken, and prime ribs, in a casual atmosphere overlooking the creek. Open daily with late-night offerings from 10:30 PM to 2 AM. Reservations unnecessary. Major credit cards accepted. 508 Mill St (phone: 884-8102).

Chicago

At-a-Glance

SEEING THE CITY

The 110-story *Sears Tower* (Wacker and Adams Sts.; phone: 875-9696) maintains a *Skydeck* on the 103rd floor (check out the Calder *Universe* sculpture and see the ground-floor audiovisual show about Chicago before heading skyward). It's open daily; admission charge. For a view from the north, visit the *John Hancock Building*; the fifth-tallest building in the world, it's fondly nicknamed "Big John." On the 95th floor are a bar and restaurant (closed Saturday lunch; 875 Michigan Ave.; phone: 787-9596). Observation deck open daily; admission charge (phone: 751-3681).

SPECIAL PLACES

A sophisticated public transport system makes it easy to negotiate Chicago's streets. You can explore the Loop, the lakefront, and suburbs by El train, subway, and bus (see *Getting Around*). In addition, Chicago's grid plan and street numbering system even make it easy for newcomers to find their way around. State Street is the north-south axis, Madison Street the east-west axis: 1200 North on any street is at Division Street; 800 West is at Halsted Street.

THE LOOP

The Loop generally refers to Chicago's central business district, which is circled by the elevated train known as the "El."

ARCHICENTER The *Exhibition Gallery* has changing shows that span a wide range of architectural topics. Run by the *Chicago Architecture Foundation,* the *ArchiCenter* also offers a variety of tours. Guided walking tours of the Loop (and other neighborhoods) are conducted daily May through November, Fridays through Mondays the rest of the year. The "Chicago Highlights" bus tour is offered Saturdays year-round. There's a charge for the tours. Santa Fe Bldg., 224 S. Michigan (phone: 922-3432).

ART INSTITUTE OF CHICAGO El Greco's *Assumption of the Virgin,* Seurat's *Sunday Afternoon on the Island of La Grande Jatte—1884,* and Grant Wood's *American Gothic* are among the works in this museum's outstanding collections, which also include excellent Impressionist and Postimpressionist works, Japanese prints, Chinese sculpture and bronzes, European and American prints and drawings, decorative arts and sculpture, and more housed in the impressive *Rice Building.* The *American Galleries* are wonderfully conceived to show off the development of US culture; the Chagall stained glass windows and the *Trading Room,* from the old *Chicago Stock Exchange Building,* are not to be missed. The photography department is one of the most sophisticated facilities of its kind in the world. The renovated *Galleries of Modern Art 1900–1950* display outstanding examples of European and American art, including Edward Hopper's *Nighthawks*, Vincent van Gogh's *Bedroom at Arles,* and Toulouse-Lautrec's *Ballet Dancers,* as well as one of the major Surrealist collections in the world. Open daily. Admission charge except on Tuesdays. Michigan Ave. at Adams St. (phone: 443-3600 or 443-3500 for recorded information).

AUDITORIUM THEATER Brilliant Chicago architect Louis Sullivan died penniless, but this 104-year-old landmark, one of his most important works, still stands. Hand-painted murals and gold leaf abound here, and the interior—which houses a 2,412- to 3,661-seat theater (depending on the production), a hotel, and an office center—features 55 million pieces of mosaic tile. There's not a bad seat in the house. During World War II this theater was turned into a bowling alley, but a major fund-raising effort in the mid-1960s brought about a restoration. Now used for a variety of cultural functions, from stage plays to pop concerts, the theater's recent offerings have included such blockbusters as *The Phantom of the Opera* and *Les Misérables.* Tours are offered for groups of 10 or more, but individuals can join, if space is available. There's a charge for the tours. 50 E. Congress Pkwy. (phone: 922-4046 or 559-1212 for performance information).

CHICAGO BOARD OF TRADE The largest grain exchange in the world, this Art Deco treasure was built in 1930 and, half a century later, gained a new trading floor to accommodate expanding markets. Stand in the visitors' gallery and watch traders gesticulating on the floor, runners in colored jackets delivering orders, and an electronic record of all the trades displayed overhead. Free tours and a 15-minute movie run throughout the morning. Closed afternoons and weekends. No admission charge. 141 W. Jackson Blvd. at LaSalle St. (phone: 435-3590).

CHICAGO CULTURAL CENTER This 1897 Italian Renaissance–style building originally served as the *Chicago Public Library.* Its impressive interior, including green and white marble, elaborate mosaics, and a Louis Tiffany stained glass dome, is a fitting backdrop for a continuous schedule of dance performances, concerts, art exhibits, photography shows, lectures, and films. The city presents more than 500 free programs and exhibits at the *Center* annually. The *Museum of Broadcast Communications* is also housed here (see below). Open daily. No admission charge. 78 E. Washington St. (phone: 346-3278 for recorded message; 744-6630 for general information).

CHICAGO MERCANTILE EXCHANGE AND INTERNATIONAL MONETARY MARKET The spectacle is much the same as at the *Board of Trade,* only here you can sit down. Opened in 1898 as the Butter and Egg Board, today more than 4,000 traders and staff crowd the trading floor daily. Visitors can watch the auction from a fourth floor gallery. Each commodity has its own opening and closing time. Free tours are available and must be scheduled in advance. Closed weekends. No admission charge. 30 S. Wacker Dr. (phone: 930-8249).

CHICAGO THEATER Restored to its 1920s splendor, this stage offers pop music concerts, contemporary dramas, and musicals against a Baroque backdrop of marble and crystal chandeliers. Even if you aren't going for the

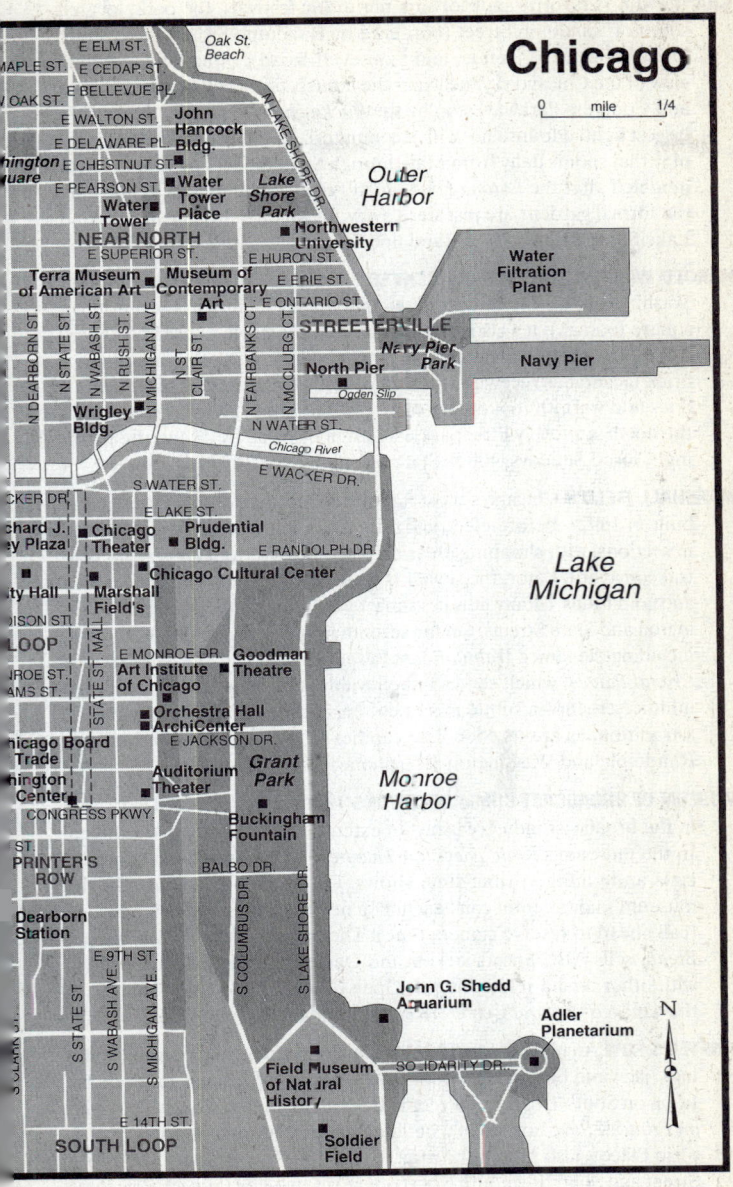

show, stop by for a look at its interior. 175 N. State St. (phone: 443-1130).

GRANT PARK A favorite spot for summer music festivals, the park, located south of Randolph Street (bordered by Randolph Street, Lake Shore Drive, Michigan Avenue, and Roosevelt Road), offers an incredible view of the Chicago skyline. Near the intersection of Columbus Avenue and Congress Parkway, stop by the *Buckingham Fountain,* the world's largest lighted fountain—with a computerized 135-foot-high water display that spouts daily from May through September. The fountain was modeled after the *Latona Fountain* at *Versailles,* but it is twice the size; the formal gardens are just steps away. Between S. Michigan Ave. and Lake Shore Dr., south of Randolph St. (phone: 294-2307).

HAROLD WASHINGTON LIBRARY CENTER Named for the city's late Mayor Washington, it's the largest municipal library facility in the world (in square footage); it's also expansive and comfortable to use and chock-full of an amazing array of contemporary art. The ornamental rose-brick façade has received its share of criticism as well as praise, but it does add warmth to a dreary corner of the Loop. Across the street to the north is a lovely little park, its design inspired by a Magritte painting. Closed Sundays. 400 S. State St. (phone: 747-4999).

MARSHALL FIELD'S Chicago's most famous department store. When it was built in 1892—before electric lighting was common—it was designed in sections, with shopping areas on balconies overlooking a skylit central courtyard. Later, the skylights were covered, one with a vivid blue and gold Louis Tiffany mosaic visible by entering on the corner of Washington and State Streets. On the seventh floor is a marvelous food court, including the famed *Walnut Room* (a special treat at *Christmas*) and the *Crystal Palace,* which serves unbelievable ice cream sundaes (Frango mint ice cream—a subtle mix of coffee, chocolate, malt, and mint—is a tradition, as are its chocolate candies). Open daily. Wabash, State, Randolph, and Washington Sts. (phone: 335-7700).

MUSEUM OF BROADCAST COMMUNICATIONS This facility traces the city's role in the broadcast industry using an extensive tape library and exhibits. In the museum's *Kraft Television Theatre,* you can watch old commercials and vintage prime-time shows. On weekends, visitors to the museum's news center can "anchor" a newscast, then watch it on video (call ahead to reserve camera time). The museum's shop, *Commercial Break,* sells ABC Sports jackets and David Letterman T-shirts, along with other media-related items. Open daily. No admission charge. In the *Chicago Cultural Center,* 78 E. Washington St. (phone: 629-6000).

PRINTER'S ROW Architecture buffs will find a haven among the restored buildings, jazz and blues clubs, bookstores, and galleries just south of the Loop on South Dearborn Street and South Plymouth Court. The *Hyatt on Printer's Row,* housed in a building on the National Register of Historic Places, also graces the area. Every June along South Dearborn Street and South Plymouth Court, there is a two-day *Printer's Row Book Fair* with exhibits dedicated to all aspects of printing and publishing. While in the neighborhood, stop for a drink or an elegant dinner at the

Printer's Row restaurant (see *Eating Out*), or have a snack at the *Upfront* (161 W. Harrison St.; phone: 554-1991)—everything you always wanted in a sports bar and more, including a ticket service for local sporting events. Also a jazz spot, the spacious wood-floored *Upfront* has pool tables and dart boards, all housed in the elegant *Patten Building*.

NAVY DEVELOPMENT/SKYLINE STAGE THEATER At the beginning of this century, the *Navy Pier* was the place where Chicago families boarded boats for a summer outing. Long neglected, the pier is enjoying a renaissance, this time as a multipurpose development that includes the new, 1,500-seat *Skyline Stage Theater*, site of stage shows and concerts plus ballet performances and children's theater. Among the other additions to the complex—scheduled for completion this March—are the *Family Pavilion*, with shops and restaurants, a 15-story Ferris wheel, and a carousel. For theater tickets, phone *Ticketmaster* at 559-1212; for information on the pier, dial 791-PIER.

SEARS TOWER At 1,454 feet and 110 stories, it's the world's tallest building; it also boasts the world's fastest elevator (it travels more than 20 miles per hour and takes only 55 seconds to get to the 103rd floor). Some 16,500 people use the building each day. The tower, which consists of nine staggered square tubes, was completed in 1974. The arched glass entryway was added in 1985 and generated another of Chicago's seemingly endless architectural controversies. Some thought the plaza too stark without the addition; others, particularly architectural purists, thought it glitzed up a building that made a strong enough statement on its own. Check out the Calder *Universe* sculpture and see the ground-floor audiovisual show about Chicago before heading for the *Skydeck* on the 103rd floor. The *Skydeck* is open daily; admission charge. 233 S. Wacker Dr., between Adams St. and Jackson Blvd. (phone: 875-9696, *Skydeck*).

NEAR SOUTH SIDE

ADLER PLANETARIUM Exhibitions here include everything from surveying and navigating instruments to modern space exploration devices, plus a real moon rock and an antique instrument collection that is considered the best in the Western Hemisphere and one of the top three in the world. You can see it all before or after the sky show, which is the reason that most people come. There are new shows every six months, one for adults and one for children five years old and younger. Open daily. Admission charge for the sky shows only. 1300 S. Lake Shore Dr. on Museum Point (phone: 322-0304).

FIELD MUSEUM OF NATURAL HISTORY Not only do the outstanding collections of more than 19 million artifacts and specimens on more than nine acres make this one of the largest public museums in the US, but through ongoing fieldwork and basic research, the museum has become an international center for scientific study and public learning. The museum's public exhibitions have shifted over the years from conventional displays to a strategy of introductory exhibits, major thematic exhibits, and resource centers. One of its most famous attractions is the pair of fighting elephants in the *Main Hall*. Other must-sees include the hands-on

Place for Wonder, where youngsters can touch a fish skeleton from the dinosaur age and try on ethnic masks; the *Plants of the World Hall,* with reproductions of about 500 plants from around the globe; the full-scale model of a Pawnee earth lodge, where there are daily programs on Indian life; and a full-size, three-level ancient Egyptian tomb. The *Hall of Chinese Jade* and the display of Japanese lacquerware are also outstanding. Closed *Thanksgiving, Christmas,* and *New Year's Day.* Admission charge except on Thursdays. S. Lake Shore Dr. at Roosevelt Rd. (phone: 922-9410).

PRAIRIE AVENUE HISTORIC DISTRICT This area of 19th-century mansions, along Prairie Avenue, between 18th and Cullerton Streets, is where Chicago's wealthy citizens once lived. The buildings that remain have been restored to their former elegance, and other historic buildings have been moved here. Standouts are the *Glessner House* (1800 S. Prairie Ave.), built by architect H. H. Richardson in 1886, and the *Henry B. Clark House,* the city's oldest building, built in 1836. The *Chicago Architecture Foundation* (phone: 922-3432) runs tours of the homes every Wednesday, Friday, Saturday, and Sunday.

JOHN G. SHEDD AQUARIUM The largest aquarium in the world, it has more than 200 fish tanks and a collection of over 7,000 specimens: sturgeon from Russia, Bahamian angelfish, Australian lungfish, and a coral reef where divers feed the fish several times a day. The *Oceanarium* re-creates a Pacific Northwest coastal exhibit with whales, seals, dolphins, and otters. Closed *Christmas* and *New Year's Day.* Admission charge. Museum Point at 1200 S. Lake Shore Dr. (phone: 939-2426; 939-2438 for the *Oceanarium*).

NORTH MICHIGAN AVENUE

CHICAGO CHILDREN'S MUSEUM This hands-on museum for youngsters has an observation deck for viewing the city's skyline and a kid-size perspective of the city. Children can learn about architecture, try out a fully equipped mini-kitchen, and climb, ride, and fly—all at the same time—in a "Fantasy Vehicle." There is one room filled with nothing but Lego building blocks. Closed Mondays. Admission charge. 435 E. Illinois St., North Pier (phone: 527-1000).

MUSEUM OF CONTEMPORARY ART Lively changing exhibitions—retrospectives of contemporary artists as well as surveys of 20th-century art movements and avant-garde phenomena—are featured here. The museum also mounts shows by Chicago artists and sponsors symposia and other special events. Closed Mondays. Admission charge except on Tuesdays. 237 E. Ontario St. (phone: 280-5161).

PEACE MUSEUM The only one of its kind in the US, it features exhibits and special programs at a variety of sites throughout the city on issues related to war, peace, and nonviolence. Closed Sundays and Mondays. Admission charge. 350 W. Ontario St. (phone: 440-1860).

TERRA MUSEUM OF AMERICAN ART The permanent collection here reads like a *Who's Who in American Art* over the past two centuries, including works by Mary Cassatt, Winslow Homer, John Singer Sargent, William

Merritt Chase, Samuel F. B. Morse, Edward Hopper, and Andrew Wyeth. Morse, inventor of the Morse code, painted the *Gallery of the Louvre,* a huge canvas re-creating dozens of paintings from the *Louvre.* One of the few museums in the country dedicated solely to American art and artists, it also has visiting exhibits. Closed Mondays. Admission charge. 666 N. Michigan Ave. (phone: 664-3939).

WATER TOWER AND WATER TOWER PUMPING STATION Now landmarks, these distinctive matching castle-like structures are the only survivors of the Great Fire of 1871. The *Water Tower* (N. Michigan Ave. and Pearson St.), which masks a 135-foot-tall standpipe, now houses the *Chicago Office of Tourism* (see *Tourist Information,* below). Across Michigan Avenue is the *Water Tower Pumping Station* (803 N. Michigan Ave.), which now is the home of *Here's Chicago,* a multimedia show about the city. The show is presented daily except holidays; there's an admission charge (phone: 467-7114).

WATER TOWER PLACE This incredible, vertical shopping mall gets busier and better every year. Asymmetrical glass-enclosed elevators shoot up through a seven-story atrium, past shops selling dresses, books, and gift items, plus restaurants and a movie theater. Branches of *Marshall Field's, FAO Schwarz,* and *Lord & Taylor* are here, along with the lovely *Ritz-Carlton* hotel, reaching 20 stories above its 12th-floor lobby in the tower. The hotel's skylit *Greenhouse* is great for tea or cocktails after a hard day of shopping. N. Michigan Ave. at Pearson St.

NORTH SIDE

BIOGRAPH THEATRE A legend, although not as a theater; it was here in 1934 that the Lady in Red (Anna Sage) turned bank robber John Dillinger over to the federal agents who then shot him, ending a massive manhunt for the FBI's "Public Enemy No. 1." Today the theater shows foreign and contemporary films. 2433 N. Lincoln Ave. (phone: 348-4123).

CHICAGO ACADEMY OF SCIENCES This museum features particularly lively exhibitions about the natural history of the Great Lakes area; the reconstruction of a 300-million-year-old forest that once stood near the present site, complete with gigantic insects and carnivorous dragonflies, is especially interesting. A "walk-through" cave and canyon are other highlights. Closed *Christmas.* Admission charge except on Mondays. In *Lincoln Park* at 2001 N. Clark St. (phone: 549-0606).

CHICAGO HISTORICAL SOCIETY Pioneer crafts demonstrations and a slide show about the Chicago Fire make this one of the city's most fascinating museums. New galleries focus on Chicago's beginnings and explore 19th-century American life through furniture and decorative objects. Closed *Thanksgiving, Christmas,* and *New Year's Day.* Admission charge except on Mondays. N. Clark St. and North Ave. (phone: 642-4600).

GRACELAND CEMETERY Buried here are hotel barons, steel magnates, architects Louis Sullivan and Daniel Burnham—enshrined in tombs and miniature temples, and overlooking islands, lakes, hills, and other scenic views. The ranks of Chicago's rich and famous interred here also include George Pullman, inventor of the sleeper railcar, Cyrus McCormick, who invented the harvester, and merchant Marshall Field. The *Getty Tomb,* designed by Sullivan, is a must stop. On most Sundays in August, September, and October, the *Chicago Architecture Foundation* sponsors two-hour tours of the cemetery. There's a charge for the tour. Call the foundation in advance for details (phone: 922-3432). N. Clark St. and Irving Park Rd.

LILL STREET With more than 40 professional potters working in dozens of studios, this is the largest ceramics center in the Midwest. Visitors can watch the artisans or buy some of their work. *Lill Street* potters offer classes, including a one-day family clay workshop. 1021 W. Lill St. (phone: 477-6185).

LINCOLN PARK CONSERVATORY This botanical delight features changing floral displays and a magnificent permanent collection that includes orchids, a 50-foot African fiddle-leaf rubber tree with giant leaves, fig trees, and more ferns than you can shake a stick at. Closed *Christmas.* No admission charge. In *Lincoln Park,* Stockton Dr. at Fullerton Ave. (phone: 294-4770).

LINCOLN PARK ZOO The best thing about this zoo is that it has the largest group of great apes in captivity, all happily coexisting in a *Great Ape House.* There's also a *Lion House,* a *Bird House,* and the standard houses of monkey, tiger, bear, and bison, plus the zoo's popular farm. Next door, a building restored to its early 20th-century charm now houses the *Café Brauer* (phone: 294-4660), with a fine view of the park and the Chicago skyline, as well as an office for bike and skate rentals, a small cafeteria, and the *Ice Cream Shoppe,* which dishes out old-fashioned ice cream creations. Open daily. No admission charge. 2200 Cannon Dr., *Lincoln Park* (phone: 294-4660).

SOUTH SIDE

MUSEUM OF SCIENCE AND INDUSTRY Chicago's most popular attraction has computers to question, buttons to push, rides to ride, and much more. There are some 2,000 exhibitions in 75 major halls examining the principles of science and technology (as well as other subjects). High points: Colleen Moore's fairy castle of a dollhouse, and the Sears circus exhibit, full of dioramas of circus scenes, piped-in circus music, and a dynamic short film (the kind you want to sit through twice in a row). The working coal mine, the walk-through human heart, and the German *U-505* submarine are every bit as much fun as they always have been. And there also are exhibits on chemistry, physics, geology, the brain, the post office, anesthesiology, and the life sciences, as well as a *Business Hall of Fame* and an exciting section on computers. The *Henry Crown Space Center* features the *Omnimax Theater* and space exhibitions. (Be warned, it's a madhouse on weekends.) Closed *Christmas.* Admission charge except Thursdays. S. Lake Shore Dr. at E. 57th St. (phone: 684-1414).

ORIENTAL INSTITUTE MUSEUM This collection of art, archaeological artifacts, and textiles from the ancient Near East boasts a colossal statue of Tutankhamen and a winged bull with a human head from Assyria. Run by the *University of Chicago,* the museum offers guided tours and free films on Sunday afternoons. Closed Mondays. No admission charge. 1155 E. 58th St. (phone: 702-9521).

PULLMAN COMMUNITY Founded by George Pullman in 1880 as the nation's first company town, this early example of comprehensive urban planning is now a city, state, and national landmark. Walking tours conducted on the first Sunday of the month from May through October tell the story in detail; at other times, find the *Greenstone Church* and other important sites on maps available at the *Florence* hotel, a Pullman-era structure that serves as a visitors' center of sorts (and provides lunch on weekdays, breakfast and lunch on Saturdays, and brunch on Sundays). A number of the privately owned row houses are open for special tours held annually on the second weekend in October. West of the Dan Ryan Expwy. between 111th and 115th Sts. (phone: 785-8181).

UNIVERSITY OF CHICAGO Guided walking tours of this illustrious university, founded in 1892 by John D. Rockefeller, include a stop at the *Robie House* (5757 S. Woodlawn Ave.), a fine example of the Prairie School of architecture, designed by Frank Lloyd Wright (as was its furniture) in 1909. The campus also has a marker commemorating the site of the world's first controlled atomic test in 1942 and *Rockefeller Chapel;* anecdotes about the chapel invariably involve famous statesmen, politicians, and celebrities. Free campus tours are conducted Mondays through Saturdays at 10 AM; call in advance for the meeting place. Also on campus is the *Smart Museum of Art,* a permanent collection that spans 5,000 years of Western and Asian art. The campus is in Hyde Park, a neighborhood bounded by Cottage Grove Ave., 55th St., Dorchester Ave., and 61st St. (phone: 702-8374).

WEST SIDE

GARFIELD PARK CONSERVATORY Here are four and a half acres under glass. The *Palm House* alone is 250 feet long, 85 feet wide, and 65 feet high; it looks like the tropics. There's a *Fernery* luxuriant with greenery, mosses, and pools of water lilies. The *Cactus House* has 85 genera, 400 species. At *Christmas,* poinsettias bloom; in February, azaleas and camellias; at *Easter,* lilies and bulb plants; and in November, mums. Open daily. No admission charge. 300 N. Central Park Blvd. (phone: 533-1281).

HALSTED STREET If you have time to get to know only one Chicago street, make it Halsted; locals claim that you could live your entire life perfectly well without ever leaving here. Spanning 20 miles of metropolitan Chicago—from 3766 North to 12961 South and on through West Pullman and Calumet—it boasts hundreds of restaurants, bars, and nightclubs; 30 churches; 50 liquor stores; and offbeat shops you won't find on Michigan Avenue. West of the Loop on Halsted Street is Chicago's Greektown area with restaurants such as the *Neon Greek Village* (310 S. Halsted St.; phone: 648-9800), offering great Greek food—and even belly dancing. Theaters also line some blocks of Halsted Street, as do jazz and blues bars.

HULL HOUSE Social welfare pioneer Jane Addams founded *Hull House* as a community service organization working for political reform and to improve garbage collection, to end sweatshops, and to protect abused children. Only two of the original *Hull House* buildings still exist, nestled into the modernist *University of Illinois* campus, with exhibits commemorating Addams, who was a peace activist, a humanitarian, and the first North American woman to win the Nobel Peace Prize. There are also exhibits commemorating her associates and the neighborhood they served. Closed Saturdays. No admission charge. 800 S. Halsted St. (phone: 413-5353).

MEXICAN FINE ARTS MUSEUM The first Mexican museum in the Midwest, and the largest in the country, pays tribute to the wide and varied Mexican culture with exhibits, theatrical performances, and workshops. The museum's gift shop specializes in Mexican folk art and multilingual publications. Closed Mondays. No admission charge. 1852 W. 19th St. (phone: 738-1503).

OUTSKIRTS

BROOKFIELD ZOO Some 200 acres divided by moats and natural-looking barriers make this one of the most modern zoos in the country. There is an indoor rain forest, special woods for wolves, a bison prairie, a replica of the Sahara, and a dolphin show. *Tropic World* features South American, Asian, and African birds, primates, and other animals. Open daily. Admission charge except on Tuesdays and Thursdays. 1st Ave. at 31st St. in Brookfield, 15 miles west of the Loop. Take Rte. 290 or I-55 to the 1st Ave. exit (phone: 242-2630 or 708-485-0263).

CHICAGO BOTANIC GARDEN This 300-acre collection of plants, trees, and shrubs from around the world is open year-round—except *Christmas Day*. Its special attractions include a three-island Japanese garden, a rose garden, 10 greenhouses, and a mile-long nature trail. There also is a tram tour of the gardens, an exhibit hall, a library, the *Museum of Floral Arts,* a gift shop, and a café. Admission charge to park your car, only. Half a mile east of the Edens Expwy. at Lake-Cook Rd. in Glencoe (phone: 708-835-5440).

FOX RIVER CASINOS Gambling has come to the Chicago area, if not yet to the city itself: A couple of cities along the Fox River on the Chicago area's western edge have welcomed the arrival of floating casinos—boats that cruise the river for two and a half hours once a group of gamblers is onboard. Sailings are scheduled throughout the day and night. In Aurora, *Hollywood Casino,* which offers slots, blackjack, craps, and poker, is open daily, all day (one of its restaurants offers breakfast). There's an admission charge and reservations are necessary for the casino on weekends. The casino is docked in Aurora, 35 miles southwest of the Loop on I-88, along New York Street at the Fox River (phone: 708-801-7000). In the waters off Joliet, the *Empress River Casino* also offers the usual games of chance and numerous places to eat. Its sessions last two hours and departures are throughout the day. The casino is open daily; there's an admission charge. Reservations are necessary on weekend evenings. To get there, take I-55 south of Joliet to the Chanahon exit; the casino is docked along Empress Drive (phone: 815-744-9400).

FRANK LLOYD WRIGHT HOME AND STUDIO In Oak Park, approximately 10 miles west of the city, this home and studio, designed by the master himself, was the birthplace of the so-called Prairie School of architecture and is a fine example of that style. At the center of the home is a fireplace around which the rest of the rooms are spread. Wright, who was self-taught, also designed the furniture—perhaps in his two-story, octagon-shaped, cantilevered drafting room. Open daily. Admission charge. Guided tours are required. 951 Chicago Ave., Oak Park (phone: 708-848-1500). This is also the headquarters of the *Oak Park Tour Center*, which operates architectural tours of the town, which is home to several other Wright buildings (see *Oak Park*, below).

LIZZADRO MUSEUM OF LAPIDARY ART Located 45 minutes from Chicago, its collection of Oriental jade carvings is one of the most extensive in the US. About 150 exhibits show off cameos, gemstones, minerals, and fossils. Closed Mondays. Admission charge except on Fridays. 220 Cottage Hill Rd., Elmhurst (phone: 708-833-1616).

MORTON ARBORETUM Sterling Morton ran a salt company ("when it rains, it pours"), but he was more fond of trees than salt (his birthday, April 26, is now recognized as Arbor Day), and therefore his niece established an arboretum in his name. A 1,500-acre living museum of roads and trails through an extraordinary array of flora—4,000 species at a recent count—its highlights include a Japanese garden, a prairie fragrance garden, a pinetum of conifers, dwarf shrubs, and every other kind of green that can be coaxed to grow in Illinois's harsh climate and clay soil. Open daily. Admission charge. Located about 25 miles west of downtown, easily accessible on I-88, where it intersects with Rte. 53 (phone: 708-719-2466).

OAK PARK Twenty-five buildings in this suburb, most of them remarkably contemporary looking, show the development of Frank Lloyd Wright's Prairie style of architecture. In addition to the architect's residence/workshop (see above), Wright's *Unity Temple* (875 Lake St., Oak Park; phone: 708-848-6225) is open to the public. There are daily tours (except on holidays); admission charge. The homes of Edgar Rice Burroughs and Ernest Hemingway (see *Museums*) are here, too, along with numerous gingerbread and turreted Queen Anne mansions. The *Oak Park Tour Center*, based in the *Frank Lloyd Wright Home and Studio*, operates most area walking tours as well as a visitors' center, where you can see photo exhibitions and take in an orientation program. At the *Wright Plus Festival*, the third Saturday in May, many private homes are open to the public. For more information, call the *Oak Park Visitor Center* (158 Forest St.; phone: 708-848-1500).

O'HARE INTERNATIONAL AIRPORT Opened in 1955, the world's busiest airport was named for Congressional Medal of Honor recipient Edward O'Hare, a navy pilot killed at the Battle of Midway. Nearly 57 million travelers pass through here annually. There are free 90-minute tours of the terminals and taxi-ways daily; for tour information, call the *Chicago Department of Aviation* (phone: 686-2300).

RAVINIA PARK In name, this park is a tribute to the little streams that wend their way through steep cliffs to Lake Michigan. In reputation, it's the place where musical talent, such as the *Chicago Symphony Orchestra* and *Peter, Paul & Mary,* is drawn from around the world for open-air concerts in the summer. Locals relish an evening on the 36-acre lawn, to which they bring their own picnics, wine, and candles for one of Chicago's most sybaritic yet spiritual celebrations. There is also a variety of restaurants where visitors can carry out all that's needed for a memorable picnic under the stars or dine in style before taking their seats in the covered pavilion. Open June through *Labor Day.* Admission charge to the park; additional charge for pavilion seats. Reservations advised for pavilion seats. Located on Green Bay and Lake-Cook Roads in Highland Park, it's about an hour's drive from the city. Take Edens Expwy., then Rte 41, north to the Ravinia exit; better yet, take the 40-minute ride on *Metra's* Northwestern line, which has a stop right in the park (phone: 728-4642).

SIX FLAGS GREAT AMERICA An extravagant roller coaster and a double-tiered carousel are the highlights of this theme park featuring more than 130 rides, shows, and attractions. Musical shows are performed throughout the season, and there's a giant participatory play area for kids, complete with merry-go-rounds and rides. It also is home to the world's largest IMAX movie theater. Open weekends only in May and September; open daily *Memorial Day* through *Labor Day.* Admission charge. Located one hour and fifteen minutes from Chicago, it is off I-94 at Rte. 132 in Gurnee (phone: 708-249-1776).

EXTRA SPECIAL

You don't have to go very far from downtown to reach the North Shore suburbs. Take Sheridan Road north through the lovely old suburbs of Evanston and Winnetka, or follow US 41 or I-94 north. US 41 goes through Lake Forest, an exquisite residential area, and Lake Bluff, site of the *Great Lakes Naval Station*. Along the way, there are several excellent restaurants, especially *Carlos'* (429 Temple Ave., Highland Park; phone: 708-432-0770) and *Froggy's* (306 Green Bay Rd., Highwood; phone: 708-433-7080). In the working class town of Waukegan, *Mathon's* seafood restaurant has been delighting seafood addicts since before World War II (from Sheridan Rd. turn east on Mathon St., then one block south to Clayton St.; phone: 708-662-3610; closed Mondays). A few miles north on Sheridan Road is the *Illinois Beach State Park*, with a nature refuge offering miles and miles of unspoiled beach (Sheridan and Wadsworth Rds., Zion; phone: 708-662-4811). Heading inland from Waukegan on Route 120 leads directly to lake country. Although the area is not a state park, there are many lakes in the region after Route 120 becomes Route 134. Three large lakes near the Wisconsin border—Fox, Pistakee, and Grass—offer water sports, fishing, golf, and tennis. Right on the Wisconsin border, the 4,900-acre *Chain O'Lakes State Park* has campsites and boat rentals. Pick up Wilson Road north at Long Lake, which is on Route 134, then take Route 132 past Fox Lake. This leads to US 12, which runs to Spring Grove and the state park (phone: 708-587-5512).

Sources and Resources

TOURIST INFORMATION

The *Chicago Visitor Information Center*, in the historic *Water Tower* (N. Michigan Ave. and Pearson St., Chicago, IL 60611; phone: 567-8500), distributes a downtown map that pinpoints major attractions and hotels. You may also get information from the *Chicago Office of Tourism* (310 S. Michigan Ave.; phone: 744-2400). For more information on Illinois, contact the state hotline (phone: 800-223-0121). The *Mayor's Office of Special Events* provides information on listings of special events (phone: 744-3315).

LOCAL COVERAGE Chicago newspapers are the *Sun-Times* and the *Tribune;* both are morning dailies. Other local publications include the *Reader,* a weekly newspaper that has the most complete listing of events and reliable event reviews, and *Chicago* magazine, a monthly whose section of restaurant reviews is the most up-to-date local source on where and what to eat. Also useful are the following *Chicago Transit Authority* brochures, available at El and subway stations: the *Chicago Street Directory,* which locates streets by their distance from State Street or Madison Street; the *CTA Route Map* of bus, subway, and El routes; and the *CTA Downtown Transit Map.*

For self-guided walking tours see Ira J. Bach's architecturally oriented *Chicago on Foot* (Chicago Review; $16.95). For information on ethnic areas, we recommend *Chicago, City of Neighborhoods* by Dominic A. Pacyga and Ellen Skerrett (Loyola University; $22.95). Also, pick up copies of our own *Birnbaum's Chicago 95* (HarperCollins; $12), as well as *Chicago ACCESS* (HarperCollins; $18).

TELEVISION STATIONS WBBM Channel 2–CBS; WMAQ Channel 5–NBC; WLS Channel 7–ABC; WGN Channel 9–superstation; WTTW Channel 11–PBS; WFLD Channel 32–Fox.

RADIO STATIONS AM: WMAQ 670 (news); WGN 720 (talk/sports); WBBM 780 (news); WLUP 1000 (rock). FM: WBEZ 91.5 (public radio for Chicago); WNUA 95.5 (smooth jazz); WBBM 96.3 (talk/news); WLUP 97.9 (rock); WFMT 98.7 (classical); WKQX 101.1 (classic rock); WGCI 107.5 (pop/rap).

Chicago also has four 24-hour Spanish language stations: WOJO 105.1 FM and AM stations WIND 560, WOPA 1200, and WTAQ 1300.

TELEPHONE The area code for Chicago is 312. The area code for all of Chicago's suburbs is 708. Unless otherwise indicated, the telephone numbers in this chapter are in the 312 area code.

SALES TAX City sales tax is 9%, and there is a 14.9% hotel tax.

CLIMATE They don't call it the Windy City for nothing. Fierce winter winds can knock you down, and wind-chill factors occasionally measure 60F below zero! The optimal visiting season is autumn, when temperatures are in the 50s and 60s F; second-best is spring. Summers are muggy, but the temperatures usually don't get higher than the mid-80s.

GETTING AROUND

AIRPORTS *O'Hare International Airport* is about 20 miles northwest of the Loop and, depending on traffic, a 30- to 60-minute ride by cab. *Continental Air Transport* (phone: 454-7800) has van service to the airport from 24 city locations (including all the major hotels). The trip takes almost an hour, and vans run approximately every 30 minutes. Ask your hotel concierge for *Continental*'s return schedule; some hotels require that reservations be made in advance. *Chicago Transit Authority* (phone: 836-7000) *O'Hare Line* trains run from several downtown locations on Dearborn Street to *O'Hare's* main terminal in approximately 45 minutes.

Midway Airport, which handles an increasing volume of domestic traffic, is nine miles south of the Loop. A taxi ride to *Midway* from the Loop will take 20 to 30 minutes. The No. 62 *Archer Express* bus (heading south) can be picked up from any stop along State Street in the Loop; transfer at Cicero Avenue to the No. 54B bus and get off at 58th and Cicero Streets, a short walk from the airport. This ride takes about 60 to 75 minutes, depending on whether you're traveling during peak or off-peak hours. During morning and afternoon rush hours on weekdays, the No. 99M bus runs directly between the Loop and *Midway Airport*. It can be boarded on State Street. *Continental Air Transport* (phone: 454-7800) also provides van service to the airport from all major hotels, but reservations must be made in advance. The run to the airport takes 30 to 45 minutes, and the cost is $9.50. A direct *O'Hare Line* train to *Midway* was being instituted as we went to press; for information about fare and schedules, call 836-7000.

BUS, SUBWAY, AND EL *Chicago Transit Authority* operates bus, subway, and El services (phone: 836-7000). The basic fare is $1.50 (there are discounts for off-hour trips and for seniors). Packs of 10 tokens are available at most currency exchanges and cost only $12.50.

CAR RENTAL All the major national firms are represented.

TAXI Cabs can be hailed in the street or picked up at stands in front of the major hotels. You also can call one of Chicago's taxi services: *American United* (phone: 248-7600); *Flash Cab* (phone: 561-1444); or *Yellow and Checker Cabs* (phone: TAXI-CAB).

TOURS For an aerial view of Chicago, there are helicopter tours, including sunset flights, run by *Head West Sky Operations* (at *Waukegan Regional*

Airport; phone: 708-546-3333). For a river view, *Wendella Sightseeing Boats* (phone: 337-1446), *Mercury Cruise Line* (phone: 332-1353), and the *Odyssey Cruises* (phone: 708-990-0800) offer boat trips on the Chicago River and Lake Michigan daily from mid-April through mid-October. A charter craft, *Engine Company #41,* runs sightseeing excursions on a 92-foot fireboat; call the *Chicago Fire Boat Cruise Company* (phone: 579-1988). The *Spirit of Chicago,* at *Navy Pier* (455 E. Illinois St.; phone: 836-7899), has dining, dancing, and moonlight cruises, as well as narrated tours. Other sightseeing cruise lines include *A Admiral's Sight-Seeing Cruise Line* (641-7245), *Chicago from the Lake* (phone: 527-2002), and *Shoreline Sightseeing* (phone: 222-9328).

At street level, try the *Chicago Architecture Foundation*'s bus tour of important architectural sites (phone: 922-3432). The *Historic Pullman Foundation* offers tours of the landmark district where the *Pullman Railroad* built offices and housing for its workers in the 19th century. Several private firms offer bus tours around Chicago; call *American Sightseeing Tours* (phone: 427-3100), the *Chicago Gray Line* (phone: 427-3107), and the *Chicago Motor Coach Company* (phone: 922-8919). There's also a do-it-yourself tour by public bus. The No. 151 bus route starts in the Loop, goes through *Lincoln Park,* past the *Historical Society,* and into New Town. When you've had your fill, get off and catch the same bus going in the opposite direction. *Untouchable Tours* (phone: 881-1195) offers a two-hour bus ride through neighborhoods once frequented by Chicago's notorious gangsters. Tours depart from the *Water Tower Pumping Station* (in winter, tours are held only on Wednesdays and weekends). *Chicago Supernatural Tours* (708-499-0300) offers tours of lurid and legendary sites, including haunted houses, sites of notorious murders, and gangster hideouts.

If a horse and buggy ride strikes your fancy, contact *J. C. Cutters,* which has a carriage stand at the corner of Superior Street and Michigan Avenue (phone: 664-6014); or *Antique Coach and Carriage* (236 W. Division St.; phone: 735-9400). For a guided tour that highlights Chicago's literary and cultural history, call Leah Axelrod's *My Kind of Tour* (Box 924, Highland Park, IL 60035; phone: 708-432-7003).

The *Chicago Architecture Foundation (CAF)* conducts about 50 different architectural tours of the city. The *CAF* Saturday bus tours depart from 224 South Michigan Avenue (phone: 922-3432). The four-hour tours may be booked in advance, although walk-in visitors are accepted if space is available. There are also boat tours of the Chicago River from May through October. Days and times vary and some weekday tours are included, so it is best to call for a schedule (phone: 527-1977). The 90-minute tours leave from North Pier (phone: 922-TOUR for recorded information).

TRAIN *Metra* (phone: 322-6900) offers commuter service between the city and its suburbs. Trains depart from the *North Western Station* (500 W. Madison St.) to the north and northwest suburbs; from *Union Station* (210 S. Canal St.) to the west and southwest suburbs; and from the *Randolph Street Station* (151 E. Randolph St.) and the *LaSalle Street Station* for the south suburbs (phone: 322-6777). *Amtrak* (phone: 800-872-7245) departs from *Union Station.*

LOCAL SERVICES

AUDIOVISUAL EQUIPMENT *Audio Visual Systems* (phone: 733-3370).

BABY-SITTING Check at your hotel or contact the following: *American Child Care* (505 N. Lake Shore Dr., Suite 203; phone: 644-7300), with licensed and insured baby-sitters who care for children in hotel suites or accompany youngsters over the age of 12 to museums and parks; or *Nanny's Sitting Service* (103 Fern St., Island Lake; phone: 708-526-2853), which charges hourly for child care in the northern suburbs.

BARBERS *Frank's Barber Shop* (in the *Monadnock Building* at the corner of Van Buren and Federal Sts.; phone: 922-0904) and *Truefitt & Hill* (900 N. Michigan Ave., Sixth Floor; phone: 337-2525).

BUSINESS SERVICES *A. S. A. P. Word Processing* (phone: 558-9333); *Business Center* (in the *O'Hare Hilton;* phone: 686-0400) for desk space and typewriters, conference rooms, and photocopying; *Headquarters Business Centers* (*HQ;* phone: 214-3500) for word processing, telexing, faxing, and conference rooms; *International Office Centers* (203 N. LaSalle St., Suite 2100; phone: 346-2030).

DRY CLEANERS/TAYLORS *Downtown Cleaners* (331 S. LaSalle St.; phone: 939-3718; and 407 S. Peoria St.; phone: 733-8174); *King Cleaners & Tailors* (16 E. Delaware Pl.; phone: 337-3896); *Pronto One-Hour Cleaners* (1700 W. Madison St.; phone: 666-8943); *Sewing Express Cleaners & Alterations* (803 W. Randolph St.; phone: 226-3110). Most hotels offer dry cleaning service, too.

EYEGLASS REPAIR/REPLACEMENT *American Vision Center* (10 N. Michigan Ave.; phone: 346-0222; and 540 N. Michigan Ave.; phone: 644-0885); *Eyelines* (300 W. Washington Blvd.; phone: 236-6460); *LensCrafters* (205 N. Michigan Ave.; phone: 819-0205); *Pearle Vision Center* (134 N. LaSalle St.; phone: 372-3204; and 350 N. Michigan Ave.; phone: 726-8255).

LIMOUSINES *Airport Express Limousine Service* (phone: 227-1000) is available 24 hours.

MECHANICS/ROAD SERVICE *B's Brothers Automotive and Towing* (2901 N. Clybourn Ave.; phone: 787-2266); *Wells Automotive Service* (1317 N. Wells; phone: 944-9388).

MEDICAL EMERGENCY *Northwestern Memorial Hospital* (233 E. Superior St. at Fairbanks Ct.; phone: 908-5222).

MESSENGER SERVICES *Cannonball Messenger Service* (phone: 829-1234); *Chicago Messenger Service* (phone: 666-6800).

PHOTOCOPIES/FACSIMILES *Aims Copy Services* (69 W. Washington Blvd.; phone: 332-2604) and *Modern Impressions* (123 W. Madison St.; phone: 368-8445). In addition, *Kinko's* has many sites in the city, some of which are open 24 hours. Check the phone book for exact locations.

PHOTOFINISHING *Fromex One-Hour Photo System* (188 W. Washington Blvd.; phone: 853-0067); *Magna One-Hour Photo* (540 N. Michigan Ave.; phone: 527-0776).

POST OFFICE Main branch (433 W. Van Buren St.; phone: 765-3585).

PROFESSIONAL PHOTOGRAPHERS *Photo Ideas* (phone: 666-3100); *Stuart-Rodgers-Reilly Photographers* (phone: 787-8696).

SECRETARIES/STENOGRAPHERS *International Office Center* (phone: 346-2030). Many hotels have business centers as well.

SHOE REPAIR *Bee Hive Shoe Works* (1 N. Dearborn St.; phone: 236-4837; 11 N. Wells St.; phone: 263-4888; 320 N. Michigan Ave.; phone: 419-8444; and 79 E. Madison St.; phone: 419-1660); and *Sam the Shoe Doctor* (162 W. Van Buren Blvd.; phone: 939-9571; 132 S. Franklin St.; phone: 332-9390; 101 W. Adams St.; phone: 332-8528; and *Sears Tower*, lower level at Franklin St.; phone: 876-9001).

SHOESHINE *Frank's Barber Shop* and *Truefitt & Hill* (see *Barbers*, above).

TRANSLATORS *Berlitz* (phone: 782-7773); *Chicago-European Language Center* (phone: 276-6683); *Joan Masters & Sons* (phone: 787-3009).

WESTERN UNION/TELEX Many locations around the city (phone: 800-325-6000).

SPECIAL EVENTS

Chicago is a city of year-round festivals, and every season brings a variety of shows and celebrations, many with a special ethnic or cultural focus. If no information number is given for a particular event, call the city's *Department of Special Events* (phone: 744-3315) for up-to-the-minute details.

The first ethnic celebration of the year is *Chinese New Year* in late January or early February, when all Chinatown turns out for its dragon parade, fireworks, and other festivities.

February brings the *Chicago Folk Festival*, sponsored by the *University of Chicago* and featuring folk music, arts, crafts, and food (phone: 702-9793). February is also *Black History Month*, which is celebrated with special exhibits at the *DuSable Museum* and other cultural institutions.

In March, the entire city plunges wholeheartedly into *St. Patrick's Day*, even dyeing the river green for the occasion. The official *St. Patrick's Day Parade*, which runs along Dearborn Avenue from Wacker Drive to Van Buren Boulevard, is held on March 17 (phone: 263-6612). On the Saturday closest to March 17, there is the separate *South Side Irish St. Patrick's Day Parade* (phone: 238-1969).

April brings the *Easter Flower Shows*, held at both the *Lincoln Park Conservatory* and the *Garfield Park Conservatory* (phone: 294-4770). In heavily Mexican Pilsen, *Easter* is observed with a reenactment of Christ's walk to Golgotha on *Good Friday*. In May, the same neighborhood holds a *Cinco de Mayo* (fifth of May) festival celebrating Mexico's successful (if only temporary) repulsion of invading French forces in 1862. Downtown on the first weekend of May, three international art expositions attract dealers from around the world; and the *International Theater Festival*, also in May, draws top international and domestic productions.

In June, the festival season gets into full swing with the two-day *Gospel Festival*, followed a week later by the *Chicago Blues Festival*, both in *Grant Park* (phone: 744-3315). June also brings the *Old Town Art Fair,* which fills block after block of charming Lincoln Park residential streets with artists and craftspeople selling their wares. On *Father's Day,* it's time for the *Printer's Row Book Fair,* when hundreds of new and used book dealers line the streets of the South Loop.

The week-long *Taste of Chicago* begins in June and ends on July 3 with an immense fireworks display. Restaurateurs fill several acres of *Grant Park* with booths offering samples of their wares, and popular radio stations broadcast the nearly continuous music performed on stages up and down the main thoroughfare. The *Chicago Country Music Festival* adds to the festivities, which end with a rousing *Fourth of July* celebration, when the *Grant Park Symphony* performs the "1812 Overture" accompanied by a dazzling fireworks display.

Another event during *Fourth of July* weekend is the *Motorola Western Open Golf Tournament* (phone: 708-724-4600) at Cog Hill in suburban Lemont. Mid-July brings the *Air and Water Show,* which features a display of precision flying; the best place to watch it is North Avenue Beach.

In August, lovely old Oz Park (so named because *Wizard of Oz* writer Frank Baum lived there) gives a party that's geared toward children. Other August events are the *Gold Coast Art Fair,* now held in the River North gallery district; the *Venetian Night* parade of colorfully lighted boats through Monroe Street Harbor; the *Bud Billiken Day Parade,* a noisy and joyful celebration of the city's African-American community, held on the South Side (phone: 225-2400); and the *Midwest Buddhist Temple Ginza Holiday,* held in Old Town. On the turf course at *Arlington International Racecourse,* the world's top thoroughbreds compete in the prestigious and colorful *Arlington Million* (phone: 708-255-4300).

Highlights of *Labor Day* weekend include the *Chicago Jazz Festival;* performers at the four-day event have included Ray Charles, Miles Davis, and Ella Fitzgerald (phone: 744-3370). Later in September, "*Viva! Chicago,*" a two-day celebration of Latin music, attracts lovers of salsa, merengue, mambo, and samba to *Grant Park* (phone: 744-3315). There's also a celebration modeled after the German *Oktoberfest,* sponsored by the *Berghoff* restaurant (phone: 427-3170) and held on Adams Street from State Street to Dearborn Avenue. During the last weekend of the month, the *Latino Film Festival* runs for 10 days at theaters around the city. Call for locations and film listings (phone: 431-1330 or 935-5744).

October features the last of the year's major parades, on *Columbus Day* in the Loop. This is also the month when the city hosts a two-week *International Film Festival,* an annual tradition since 1965. Various theaters on the North Side screen the long list of films (phone: 644-3400).

November marks the start of the *Michigan Avenue Holiday Lights Festival* (from the Saturday before *Thanksgiving* through December 31); processions of horse-drawn carriages and fireworks add to the festivities along the Magnificent Mile, which glows with holiday lights. During the holiday season, State Street windows get dressed up and the *Goodman Theatre* (phone: 443-3800) presents its now-classic *Christmas*

Carol. And, finally, December brings the *Nutcracker* ballet to the *Arie Crown Theater* at *McCormick Place* (phone: 791-6000).

MUSEUMS

In addition to those described in *Special Places,* other museums of interest include the following:

BALZEKAS MUSEUM OF LITHUANIAN CULTURE This unique museum has dolls, textiles, folk art, antique weapons, and a hands-on children's museum. Open daily. Admission charge. 6500 S. Pulaski Rd. (phone: 582-6500).

DUSABLE MUSEUM OF AFRICAN-AMERICAN HISTORY Chicago more than likely is the country's only major city whose first permanent resident was of African descent. Set in the South Side's *Washington Park,* the museum is named after Jean-Baptiste Point duSable, a fur trader from Haiti who settled on the banks of the Chicago River in 1789.

Among the museum's major features are a 10-foot-high carved mahogany mural depicting highlights of African-American history; there also is a large display of African artifacts. Among the changing exhibits are depictions of life in the Caribbean. Open daily. Admission charge. 57th St. at S. Cottage Grove (phone 947-0600).

ERNEST HEMINGWAY MUSEUM Located in suburban Oak Park where the author was born and raised, the museum mounts major exhibitions on Hemingway's life and times and work. Closed Mondays, Tuesdays, Thursdays, and Fridays. Admission charge. 200 N. Oak Park Ave. (phone: 708-848-2222).

MUSEUM OF HOLOGRAPHY More than 150 three-dimensional images created by lasers are displayed. Closed Mondays and Tuesdays. Admission charge. 1134 W. Washington Blvd. (phone: 226-1007).

POLISH MUSEUM OF AMERICA Offers 350 paintings by Polish and Polish-American artists, costumes, and a 30,000-volume library. Closed *Christmas Eve* and *Christmas Day.* No admission charge. 984 N. Milwaukee Ave. (phone: 384-3352).

SPERTUS MUSEUM OF JUDAICA A collection that spans 3,500 years of Jewish history, plus special temporary exhibitions. Closed Saturdays, Jewish holidays, and some federal holidays. Admission charge. 618 S. Michigan Ave. (phone: 922-9012).

SWEDISH-AMERICAN MUSEUM Historic documents plus works of famous Swedish artists, including Carl Larson and Anders Zorn; at *Christmas,* there is a traditional Swedish *Festival of Lights* complete with candles, *Christmas* decorations, and songs. Closed Mondays. Admission charge except for children under 12. 5211 N. Clark St. (phone: 728-8111).

UKRAINIAN NATIONAL MUSEUM A large collection of folk art, including Ukrainian ceramics, *Easter* eggs, and costumes. Closed Mondays through Wednesdays. Admission charge. 2453 W. Chicago Ave. (phone: 276-6565).

In addition, great sculpture and art can be seen in the plazas of downtown skyscrapers: Harry Bertoia's spellbinding *Sounding Sculpture,* at the *Standard Oil Building* (200 E. Randolph St.); *Flamingo,* a stabile by Alexander Calder, at Federal Center Plaza (Adams and Dearborn Sts.); Calder's gaily colored mobile *Universe,* in the *Sears Tower* lobby (Wacker Dr. and Adams St.); sculptor Claes Oldenburg's 101-foot-high baseball bat, *Batcolumn* (600 W. Madison St.); Marc Chagall's *Four Seasons* mosaic, at First National Plaza (Monroe and Dearborn); and *Chicago's Picasso* (its formal title because no one could agree on a name), a giant sculpture on the Richard J. Daley Plaza (Washington and Clark Sts.).

And don't miss Chicago's roof art. There are four wind-powered sculptures, each weighing more than a ton, atop the city's *Sporting Club* (211 N. Stetson Dr. near the *Fairmont* hotel). *Children of the Sun,* by Japanese artist Shingu, is made of stainless-steel pipe and punched metal.

> **MUSIC TO MUNCH BY**
>
> **If you're at Richard J. Daley Plaza (on Washington and Clark Sts.) at lunchtime, you might catch a free concert. There are noon music and dance performances under the giant *Chicago's Picasso* sculpture two or three days a week from June through September, weather permitting (phone: FINE-ART, i.e., 346-3278, for schedule information).**

SHOPPING

Some of Chicago's best sights are indoors, along the aisles of the city's many shops and department stores. While Los Angeles boasts Rodeo Drive and New York has Fifth Avenue, in Chicago the chic shopping district is known as the Magnificent Mile, the blocks along North Michigan Avenue between the Chicago River and Oak Street. Along the Magnificent Mile is *900 North Michigan Avenue,* an enclosed mall of elegant stores; a block away is *Water Tower Place,* another elegant indoor shopping center; and *Chicago Place,* an eight-level enclave of upscale shops, is at 700 North Michigan Avenue. Oak Street, just west of Michigan Avenue, is lined with international designer shops. State Street in the Loop is the setting for *Marshall Field's. T. J. Maxx, Filene's Basement,* and *Toys R Us* are also on this famed shopping street.

North Pier Chicago, a renovated multi-use building that was formerly a shipping terminal, has three floors filled with dozens of unusual shops and restaurants as well as museums and gamerooms. Locals looking for fine jewelry at good prices head for the *Mallers Building* (5 N. Wabash St.), which features 16 floors of retail and wholesale jewelry stores. And Hyde Park, a neighborhood near the *University of Chicago,* is the place for bookworms.

Avid shoppers also trek to the River North district's boutiques (north of the river, west of LaSalle St.); the Armitage/Halsted/Sheffield shops; the stores along Clark Street (in the Fullerton area); and the *Century Mall* (Diversey Pkwy./Clark St.), which was once a movie theater. The *Merchandise Mart,* between Orleans and Wells Streets and the Chicago River, has stores from many of the national chains. Here are some of our favorite Windy City shops.

Accent Chicago Every item in stock has "Chicago" imprinted on it—and we mean everything. *Water Tower Place*, Level 7 (phone: 944-1354); *Sears Tower* (phone: 933-0499); and the *Chicago Hilton and Towers* (phone: 360-0115).

Archicenter Although this is actually the museum/office for the *Chicago Architecture Foundation*, it has one of the most complete gift shops for those seeking architecture-theme souvenirs. Its book collection is especially impressive. *Santa Fe Bldg.*, 224 S. Michigan Ave. (phone: 922-3431/2).

Avventura Some of the showiest men's shoes anywhere, plus more traditional footwear, ties, and belts. It's worth a trip here just to see the giant black cowboy boots with the red bull on front and No. 23 on back, custom designed for Michael Jordan. *Water Tower Place*, Level 4 (phone: 337-3700).

Bloomingdale's The Midwest flagship store for this legendary New York retailer has six floors of merchandise plus four spas and two restaurants. The Art Deco touches are a plus. *900 North Michigan Avenue* (phone: 440-4460).

Bogner A branch of the German retailer specializing in high-end skiwear, cashmere, and leather goods. 56 E. Oak St. (phone: 664-6466).

Bottega Veneta Fine Italian leather items, carefully crafted and tastefully displayed. Everything from luggage to desk accessories, plus a small selection of women's shoes and scarves. 107 E. Oak St. (phone: 664-3220).

Branca Elegant home furnishings, from picture frames to linen; many items are uniquely hand-painted by the owner. 65 W. Illinois St. (phone: 822-0751).

C. D. Peacock This landmark, founded the same year as Chicago, in 1837, has purveyed silver, crystal, jewelry, and fine china to Chicagoans ever since. With chandeliers, fine cabinetry, and bronze peacock doors, it's known for its service (and for its expert repair shop). In *Northbrook Court* on Lake-Cook Rd., Northbrook (phone: 708-564-8030).

Carson Pirie Scott and Company You can't get any more Chicago than this department store, whose Windy City tradition stretches back more than 130 years. Even if you aren't in a spending mood, stop by to see the elegant building designed at the turn of the century by architect Louis Sullivan (note the distinctive iron ornamentation on the northwest corner). 1 S. State St. (phone: 641-7000).

Cartier The Midwest outpost of the fine French jeweler. 630 N. Michigan Ave. (phone: 266-7440).

Chanel Classic clothes and accessories from this world-famous name. 940 N. Michigan Ave. (phone: 787-5500)

Chiasso Euro-design (largely Italian and contemporary) in fine home furnishings and gifts. *Chicago Place*, 700 N. Michigan Ave. (phone: 642-2808); 231 S. LaSalle St. (phone: 357-0437); and 303 W. Madison St. (phone: 419-1121).

City of Chicago The place for memorabilia and souvenirs, this store carries everything from tote bags to a Chicago manhole cover to the ever-popular Chicago street signs. Pick up one in stock or special order a custom-made sign. 435 E. Illinois St. (phone: 467-1111).

Crate & Barrel Ten Chicago area stores that purvey everything for the home, from pie plates to pine furniture. The flagship store is a knockout at 646 N. Michigan Ave. (phone: 787-5900).

Elements The last word in designer housewares and jewelry by international artisans. 738 N. Wells St. (phone: 642-6574).

Famous Fido's Just about everything for dogs and cats, including the "Famous Fido's Doggie Deli" with a dining area and carryout of all-natural dog food, pet treats, and cakes. 1533 W. Devon Ave. (phone: 973-3436).

Fannie May Chicago's favorite chocolates for more than seven decades are sold in more than 100 shops around the city. Best-known outlets: *Water Tower Place* (phone: 664-0420) and *North Pier* (phone: 527-9372).

FAO Schwarz Kiddie heaven, with dolls, stuffed animals, and video games galore. Grownups don't have a bad time here, either. *Water Tower Place*, Level 2 (phone: 787-8894) and 840 N. Michigan Ave. (phone: 587-5000).

Feline Inn A celebration of cats, packed with everything you can imagine—from clothes to coat hangers—with felines emblazoned on each item. 1445 N. Wells St. (phone: 943-2230).

Flashback Retro collectibles from television shows of the 1960s and 1970s, including "Lost in Space" and "Rocky and Bullwinkle" lunch boxes, "I Dream of Jeannie" dolls, and the poster that made Farrah Fawcett an overnight pinup girl. 3450 N. Clark St. (phone: 929-5060).

Gianni Versace This Italian designer's two-story boutique is stocked with his latest European fashions. 101 E. Oak St. (phone: 337-1111).

Giorgio Armani The noted Milanese designer offers his beautifully tailored *haute* threads to fashion-savvy devotees of both sexes. This is the only source of Armani *couture* collections between the coasts. 113 E. Oak St. (phone: 751-2244).

Godiva Chocolatier For those with a taste for sumptuous sweets. If chocolate is not your fatal attraction, try the rich cappuccino and espresso at this shop in *Water Tower Place*, Level 3 (phone: 280-1133).

The Goldsmith Custom-designed jewelry, plus a great selection of antique gems—and a repair service. *Water Tower Place*, Level 2 (phone: 751-1986).

Gucci The fine Italian leather emporium, with merchandise ranging from men's and women's sportswear and shoes to key rings. *900 North Michigan Avenue* (phone: 664-5504).

Hammacher Schlemmer Everything imaginable in elegant and unique gifts, from heated pet beds to a personalized Wurlitzer to a wide variety of kitchen and electronic gadgets. 618 N. Michigan Ave. (phone: 664-9292).

Illinois Artisans Shop A wide array of items made by the state's top craftspeople. *Thompson Building*, 100 W. Randolph St. (phone: 814-5321).

Isis Unusual fashions for women, all in one-size-fits-all, including hand-painted items, fringed jackets, and parachute-silk skirts. 38 E. Oak St. (phone: 664-7076).

Krivoy Named for her grandmother, Cynthia Hadesman's shop offers dresses, skirts, and hats whose styles run the gamut from contemporary to antique. 1145 W. Webster Ave. (phone: 248-1466).

Mallers Building This 21-story office building has 16 floors of retail and wholesale jewelers. Here shoppers can buy diamonds, get a watch repaired, sell silver and gold, and have a favorite piece engraved. Stop on the third floor to visit a genuine old-time deli with great cheese blintzes and potato pancakes. 5 N. Wabash St.

Marshall Field's This Chicago landmark offers everything from rare books and Frango mints to wardrobe coordinators and foreign language translators (111 N. State St.; phone: 781-1000). A second downtown location is at *Water Tower Place* (phone: 781-1234). See also *Special Places*.

Museum Shop of the Art Institute of Chicago Mobiles, stained glass, books, note cards, calendars, and a variety of high-quality gifts, including faithful reproductions of works in the museum's collection, are sold. An extensive stock of jewelry is especially worth inspecting. On *Valentine's Day*, a calligrapher is on hand to personalize cards. N. Michigan Ave. at Adams St. (phone: 443-3534).

NBC Store The *NBC Tower* houses a shop that carries NBC memorabilia, plus T-shirts emblazoned with the names of your favorite TV shows. 455 N. Columbus Dr. (phone: 836-5555).

Nicole Miller Novelty print silk scarves and ties, plus eveningwear for men and women. 62 E. Oak St. (phone: 664-3532).

Nike Town The latest in shoes and sportswear in a visually dramatic setting, surely worth a visit if not a purchase. 669 N. Michigan Ave. (phone: 642-6363).

North Beach Leather Trendy leather fashions for men and women; repair service, too. *Water Tower Place*, Level 3 (phone: 280-9292).

Nuts on Clark Nuts, coffee, wine, exotic teas, fruit, and chocolate are featured at this 30,000-square-foot store, just two blocks north of *Wrigley Field*. 3830 N. Clark (phone: 549-6622).

Pavo Real Boutique Sweaters from Peru and Bolivia plus handmade jewelry crafted by local and international artists. *900 North Michigan Avenue* (phone: 944-1390).

Sonia Rykiel Knits, knits, and more knits are featured in this designer's boutique—everything from dressy sportswear to activewear with a Gallic touch. There's a small line of children's wear, too. 106 E. Oak St. (phone: 951-0800).

Sony Gallery of Consumer Electronics For sampling and buying the latest in electronic marvels for business and entertainment. 633 N. Michigan Ave. (phone: 943-3334).

Sugar Magnolia African-print skirts, funky children's clothes, and silk-screened ties. 34 E. Oak St. (phone: 944-0885).

Tiffany & Co. The Midwest branch of the place where the late Audrey Hepburn breakfasted. 715 N. Michigan Ave. (phone: 944-7500).

Ultimo Men's designer fashions; plus women's apparel, shoes, and jewelry. 114 E. Oak St. (phone: 787-0906).

A Unique Presence Exceptional crafts and gifts in a year-round art fair atmosphere. Unusual items from more than 175 North American artists. 2121 N. Clybourn Ave. (phone: 929-4292).

Waterstone's One of the two US branches of the famous British bookseller specializing in literature, art and travel books, history, and biography. 840 N. Michigan Ave. (phone: 587-8080).

Women & Children First The only truly feminist bookstore in the city offers regular book signings and special events linked to feminism in literature. 5233 N. Clark St. (phone: 769-9299).

> **NOTE**
>
> **If you don't want to traipse but still want to take advantage of Chicago's chic stores, call any of the city's major department stores for personal shoppers. The personal shoppers at *Neiman Marcus* even make house (or hotel) calls. *Bloomingdale's* has separate personal shopper services for men and women.**

SPORTS AND FITNESS

There's plenty of major-league action in town year-round.

BASEBALL The *White Sox* play at *Comiskey Park* (35th and Shields, off the Dan Ryan Expwy.; phone: 924-1000). Seating 43,500 spectators, this state-of-the-art park is equipped with efficient escalators and elevators, plus numerous services and concessions for the fans. The *Cubs* play at *Wrigley Field* (Addison and Clark Sts.; phone: 404-2827), now also at night.

BASKETBALL The 1993 *NBA* champion *Bulls,* only the third team in history to win three consecutive *NBA* titles, play at the new *United Center* (1800 W. Madison; phone: 733-5300).

BICYCLING Chicago has a glorious bike path along the shore of Lake Michigan, running from the Loop to the North Side—about six miles. You can rent bikes in summer from *Village Cycle Center,* 1337 N. Wells St. (phone: 751-2488). For more information about cycling, contact the *Chicagoland Bicycle Federation* (phone: 427-3325).

BOCCE Remember how good Marlon Brando looked playing this Italian bowling game in *The Godfather*? Nearly 400 members of the *Highland Bocce Club* gather at *Highwood Bocce Court* (440 Bank La.; phone: 708-432-9804), beneath an Italian deli and the train tracks, to play in good weather. There also are *bocce* courts at three city parks: *McGuane*

(290 S. Poplar Ave.), *Riis* (6110 W. Fullerton Ave.), and *Smith* (2526 W. Grand Ave.).

BOWLING Turn back the clock 35 years and try *Southport Lanes* (3325 N. Southport Ave.; phone: 472-1601), where boys still set pins for the four alleys. Some Chicagoans rate this as the best of its kind. For 24-hour-a-day bowling, try *Waveland* (3700 N. Western Ave.; phone: 472-5900).

CRICKET Games sponsored by the *United Cricket Conference* (phone: 684-6530) are played Sundays at noon from mid-May through mid-September in *Washington Park* (55th St. and King Dr.; phone: 684-6530).

FISHING In summer, people flock to the rocks and piers along the shore, casting lines for a variety of fresh fish. In April, the smelt run draws hundreds to the shore with their nets. The rocks around *Northwestern University at Evanston* are especially popular.

FITNESS CENTERS *Combined Fitness Centre* (1235 N. LaSalle St.; phone: 787-8400) admits non-members for a fee.

FOOTBALL The *NFL Bears* (phone: 294-2200) play at *Soldier Field* (Lake Shore Dr. south of Roosevelt Rd.; phone: 708-295-6600).

GOLF Chicago has 18 public golf courses, some along the lakeshore. The most accessible municipal course is *Marowitz,* traditionally known as *Waveland,* a nine-hole course in *Lincoln Park* (3700 N. Waveland Ave). The *Chicago Park District* offers golf instruction (phone: 753-8670).

HIKING The *Forest Preserve District* for Cook and Du Page Counties offers numerous places to hike (phone: 708-366-9420). The *Sierra Club* (53 W. Jackson Blvd.; phone: 431-0158) also organizes outings.

HOCKEY The *NHL Blackhawks* play in the new *United Center* (1800 W. Madison St.; phone: 733-5300).

HORSE RACING Thoroughbreds race at four tracks in the Chicago area: *Arlington Park* (Euclid Ave. and Wilke Rd., Arlington Heights; phone: 708-255-4300); *Hawthorne* (3501 S. Laramie, Cicero; phone: 708-780-3700); *Maywood Park* (North and 5th Aves., Maywood; phone: 708-626-4816); and *Sportsman's Park* (3301 S. Laramie, Cicero; phone: 708-652-2812).

ICE SKATING Once temperatures dip below 45F, ice skating begins at Daley Bicentennial Plaza (337 E. Randolph St.; phone: 294-4790) and Block 37 in the Loop (State and Washington Sts.; phone: 744-2893). There also is ice skating year-round at the indoor rink at *McFetridge Sports Center* (3843 N. California Ave.; phone: 478-0211). Skate rentals are available at all three.

JOGGING There's a jogging path along the entire lakeshore from *Jackson Park* north to *Lincoln Park,* accessible via numerous pedestrian walkways.

POLO Matches are held in the summer at the *Oak Brook Polo Club* (3500 Midwest Ave., Oak Brook; phone 708-990-POLO).

SAILING Lake Michigan offers superb sailing, but as experienced sailors can tell you, the lake is deceptive. Storms with winds of up to 40 knots can blow in suddenly. Check with the Coast Guard before going out (phone: 708-251-0185).

SKIING There are more than 50 ski clubs in the Chicago area. For information, contact the *Chicago Metro Ski Council* (PO Box 7926, Chicago, IL 60680; phone: 346-1268).

SOCCER Montrose, with four fields, is *the* soccer place. Walk up the 32-foot Cricket Hill for a bird's-eye view of the games. The *International Soccer League* plays on Sundays; the less popular, though equally enthusiastic, *Central American Soccer League* plays Saturdays. Weekend games start in the summer and run through October.

SWIMMING Beaches line the shore of Lake Michigan. Those just to the north of the Loop off Lake Shore Drive are the most popular and often the most crowded. *Oak Street Beach* (at the top of Michigan Avenue) and *North Beach* (1600 North Ave.) afford swimming with skyscrapers as a backdrop; admission is free. If you go farther north, you'll find fewer people. The most accessible public beach outside the city is in north suburban Wilmette. There's an admission charge.

TENNIS The city has 708 outdoor municipal courts, including two downtown facilities. The better of the two (by far) consists of 12 well-lit clay courts at Daley Bicentennial Plaza, in the northern end of *Grant Park* (337 E. Randolph St.) near several residential high-rises. The courts are open daily. Reservations are necessary; there's a court fee (phone: 294-4790).

TOBOGGANING The *Cook County Forest Preserve District* operates 14 slides at five locations daily when the weather allows. Equipment rentals are available (phone: 708-366-9420).

THEATERS

For schedules and tickets, call the *League of Chicago Theatres' Hot Tix Hotline* (phone: 977-1755), or visit a *Hot Tix* booth (108 N. State St.; in Evanston, at the Sherman Ave. municipal parking garage between Church and Davis Sts.; in Oak Park, at 158 Forest Ave.; in Arlington Heights, at the *Metra* train station at 19 E. Northwest Hwy.; and at many *Rose Records* stores throughout the Chicago area). Full-price, advance-sale tickets are available by phone or at a *Hot Tix* booth. Half-price day-of-sale tickets are sold for cash only at the booths on Mondays through Saturdays (Wednesdays through Saturdays at Evanston, Arlington Heights, and Oak Park locations); half-price Sunday tickets are sold at the booths the day before. *Ticketmaster's Chicago Arts Line* (phone: 902-1500) takes phone orders for full-price, advance-sale tickets for an additional surcharge—which varies depending on the specific show.

Chicago's thriving theater scene breaks down into two camps: eclectic showcases for homegrown talent, and Broadway-caliber commercial houses. Listed below are two of our favorite Chicago venues.

CENTER STAGE

Goodman Theatre The second-oldest regional theater in the country, the *Goodman* mounts frequent productions of works by living writers, brings classics up to date in eye-opening ways, and stages that colorful favorite, *A Christmas Carol,* at the end of the year. There are actually two theaters housed here: the *Studio,* which seats 135, and the *Mainstage,* which seats 683. Between the two theaters, eight to 10 plays are produced annually; because the productions are usually well received (and have long runs), the season extends throughout the year. 200 S. Columbus Dr. (phone: 443-3800).

Organic Theater Dedicated to producing world premiere theater, from the science fiction trilogy *Warp!* to the pirate epic *Bloody Bess,* award-winning *Adventures of Huckleberry Finn,* baseball comedy *Bleacher Bums, Do the White Thing, E/R Emergency Room* (which ran for four years), and the recent adaptation of Clive Barker's horror tale *In the Flesh,* the *Organic* has explored the full range of theatrical expression. David Mamet's *Sexual Perversity in Chicago* started out here, too. Every Saturday morning brings the *Cookie Crumb Club* a participatory sing-along for young audiences and their grown-up friends. Closed Mondays. 3519 N. Clark St. (phone: 327-5588).

Steppenwolf Theatre Chicago's acclaimed pipeline to both Hollywood and Broadway, this homegrown company launched the careers of John Malkovich and Emmy-winner Laurie Metcalf (of "Roseanne" fame). Garry Marshall and Steve Martin have developed original plays for the cutting-edge *Steppenwolf* troupe. The company's production of *The Grapes of Wrath* won it a Tony, and its New York production of *The Song of Jacob Zulu* (which featured the South African group *Ladysmith Black Mambazo*) earned raves. In addition to its excellent ensemble, *Steppenwolf* boasts one of the city's finest (and newest) theaters. Each year the company produces five or six mainstage shows and a smattering of smaller workshop performances. 1650 N. Halsted St. (phone 335-1650).

Other Chicago theatrical troupes include the *Victory Gardens Theater* (2261 N. Lincoln Ave.; phone: 371-3000), dedicated to staging plays by such local playwrights as James Sherman (*Beau Jest*) and John Logan (*Hauptmann*); the funky *Remains Theatre* (phone: 549-7725), known for its talented artists as well as its laid-back attitude; the *Pegasus Players* (1145 W. Wilson Ave.; phone: 271-2638), renowned for their productions of Stephen Sondheim musicals; *Shakespeare Repertory* (1016 N. Dearborn St.; phone: 642-2273), which focuses exclusively on the Bard's works; and *City Lit Theater Company* (3914 N. Clark St.; phone: 271-1100), which specializes in adapting works of literature for the stage. Several local troupes share space in the *Theatre Building* (1225 W. Belmont Ave.; phone: 327-5252); it's worth a quick call to find out what's playing there.

The main commercial theaters are the *Auditorium Theater* (50 E. Congress Pkwy.; phone: 922-4046; 922-2110 for performance information), where both *The Phantom of the Opera* and *Les Misérables* played for years; the *Shubert* (22 W. Monroe St.; phone: 977-1700); the *Apollo Theater Center* (2540 N. Lincoln Ave.; phone: 935-6100); the *Briar Street Theatre* (3133 N. Halsted St.; phone: 348-4000); and the *Wellington Theater* (750 W. Wellington St.; phone: 975-7171). The *Mayfair Theatre* at the *Blackstone* hotel (636 S. Michigan Ave.; phone: 786-9120) presents *Shear Madness,* a comedic mystery involving audience participation, nightly except Tuesdays.

Dinner-theaters include the *Drury Lane South* (2500 W. 95th, Evergreen Park; phone: 779-4000); *Marriott's Lincolnshire Theatre* (10 Marriott Dr., Lincolnshire; phone: 708-634-0200); *Pheasant Run* (*Pheasant Run Lodge,* Rte. 64, St. Charles; phone: 708-584-6300); and the *Candlelight Playhouse,* the nation's first dinner-theater (5620 S. Harlem Ave. in Summit; phone: 708-496-3000).

Chicago's arts and theater community in recent years has given more attention to poets with innovative forums called "Poetry Slams." In the best beat tradition, Chicago's top performance poets listen, read, and compete at the nationally recognized *Uptown Poetry Slam,* held Sundays at the *Green Mill* cocktail lounge (4802 N. Broadway; phone: 878-5552). The *West Side Poetry Slam* is geared toward a more gentele audience, which is encouraged to participate on Tuesdays at *Fitzgerald's* (6615 W. Roosevelt Rd. in Berwyn; phone: 708-788-2118).

Fans of classic, foreign, or art films will find them at *Facets Multimedia* (1517 W. Fullerton Ave.; phone: 281-4114); the *Film Center of the Art Institute* (Columbus Dr. at Jackson Blvd.; phone: 443-3737); and *Fine Arts Theater* (418 S. Michigan Ave.; phone: 939-3700). For a golden-age film experience, try the *Music Box,* with its mammoth screen, sky ceiling with winking stars and moving clouds, dramatic lobby—and great popcorn. Films shown here are Hollywood standards, foreign fare, and some independents (3733 N. Southport Ave.; phone: 871-6604). The *Biograph,* where John Dillinger was gunned down, also still shows films (2433 N. Lincoln Ave.; phone: 348-4123).

MUSIC

Good music (and lots of it) abounds all over the city. The world-renowned *Chicago Symphony Orchestra,* under the baton of Daniel Barenboim, can be heard from late September until early June at *Orchestra Hall,* a National Landmark building (220 S. Michigan Ave.; phone: 435-6666). The orchestra also plays at the *Ravinia Festival* outside the city in Highland Park from late June through *Labor Day* (1575 Oakwood Ave. at Lake-Cook and Green Bay Rds.; phone: 708-433-8800). Don't miss the *Grant Park Symphony,* which plays four times weekly in the summer under the stars along Lake Michigan. Concerts are free; audiences usually pack picnic dinners and sit out on the lawn. Another favorite is the *Chicago Sinfonietta,* a professional orchestra that performs classical, romantic, and contemporary music at *Orchestra Hall* on the campus of *Rosary College* (7900 W. Division St. in River Forest; phone: 708-366-1062).

Some of the hottest tickets in town from September through February are for performances of the *Lyric Opera of Chicago*, which stages classics and new productions at the *Civic Opera House* (20 N. Wacker Dr.; phone: 332-2244). *Chamber Music Chicago* (phone: 242-6237) presents classical and avant-garde music concerts at venues throughout the city. From February through May, you can hear the *Chicago Opera Theater* (2936 N. Southport Ave.; phone: 663-0555), which performs operas in English.

As for dance, *Ballet Chicago* presents classical ballet; the *Hubbard Street Dance Company* and the *Joel Hall Dance Company* are known for jazz; modern dance is the forte of the *Joseph Holmes Dance Company*; and the *Chicago Repertory Dance Ensemble* stages classical and modern dance. Each spring the *Civic Theater* (20 N. Wacker Dr.; phone: 346-0270) presents a series of dance performances featuring local troupes and internationally renowned companies, such as the *American Ballet Theater*. The *Dance Center of Columbia College* (4730 N. Sheridan; phone: 271-7928) offers contemporary, modern, and avant-garde dance performances throughout the year. For the current schedule of dance events, call the *Chicago Dance Coalition*'s 24-hour information line (phone: 419-8383).

NIGHTCLUBS AND NIGHTLIFE

Don't leave the Windy City without taking in some of its fine blues, jazz, reggae, and folk music. Or try an offbeat bar, a neighborhood sports pub, or a comedy club in one of the few Midwest cities where nightlife lasts until dawn.

Chicago's blues tradition is revered, and some of the country's finest blues performers can be found in a handful of clubs around the city. *Blue Chicago* (937 N. State St.; phone: 642-6261) books a lot of notable female performers, as does its sister bar, *Blue Chicago on Clark* (536 N. Clark St.; phone: 661-0100). Crowded *B.L.U.E.S.* (2519 N. Halsted St.; phone: 528-1012) is built around solid blues acts and a lively environment; its roomier relative, *B.L.U.E.S. Etcetera* (1124 W. Belmont Ave.; phone: 525-8989), books major acts like Bo Diddley and Albert King. At *Buddy Guy's Legends,* in the former home of Chess Records (754 S. Ave.; phone: 427-0333), bluesman Guy holds court over new and veteran performers. But Chicago's standout blues club is *Kingston Mines* (2548 N. Halsted St.; phone: 477-4646), where local blues musicians—and celebrities—go after other clubs have closed. Blues enthusiasts may also want to venture to the South Side's haven, the *Checkerboard Lounge* (423 E. 43rd St.; phone 624-3240), or to the West Side to check out *Rosa's* (3420 W. Armitage Ave.; phone: 342-0452), Chicago's friendliest blues bar.

As strong as the city's blues legacy is its love of jazz. At *Andy's Lounge,* (11 E. Hubbard St.; phone: 642-6805) patrons dressed in anything from T-shirts to pin-stripes enjoy jazz at lunchtime (live music starts at noon) and after work (sets start at 5 PM). The *Cotton Club* (1710 S. Michigan Ave.; phone: 341-9787) is decorated with photos of the stars of the original Harlem club. Joe Segal's *Jazz Showcase* at the *Blackstone* hotel (636 S. Michigan Ave.; phone: 427-4846) draws such top jazz performers as McCoy Tyner and Dorothy Donegan. The *Green*

Mill cocktail lounge (4802 N. Broadway; phone: 878-5552) looks like the Al Capone haunt it once was, with an ornate interior and live jazz six nights a week. As its name suggests, the *Gold Star Sardine Bar* (680 N. Lake Shore Dr.; phone: 664-4215) is ultra-tiny, but attracts big names—Liza, Tony, and Frank have all stopped by to give unannounced performances.

Jazz also reigns supreme at *Pops for Champagne* (2934 N. Sheffield Ave.; phone: 472-1000), an upscale jazz club with a formal French garden and a choice of champagnes to sip while you relax and listen. The crowd from *Pops* pops across the street for more jazz and acoustic rock at *Oz* (2917 N. Sheffield; phone: 975-8100). *Toulouse* (49 W. Division St.; phone: 944-2606) has an intimate piano bar, and *Yvette* (1206 N. State St.; phone: 280-1700) features enthusiastic twin piano duets, while its sister establishment *Yvette Wintergarden* (311 S. Wacker Dr.; phone: 408-1242) offers combos for dancing. The elegant *Inta's* (308 W. Erie St.; phone: 664-6880) is the perfect spot for dancing to jazz orchestras, enjoying an evening snack, or savoring a fine cigar in the club's smoking lounge.

North Clark Street is to reggae what North Halsted Street is to blues. A Caribbean pub-crawl might begin at the *Wild Hare* (3530 N. Clark; phone: 327-4273). Cross the street to find *Exedus II* (3477 N. Clark St.; phone 348-3998). Local and international reggae bands perform at both bars seven nights a week.

The *Old Town School of Folk Music* (909 W. Armitage Ave.; phone: 525-7793) is Chicago's premier folk music venue and also sponsors frequent concerts by musicians from South America, Africa, and Europe. The *Abbey Pub* (3420 E. Grace St.; phone: 478-4408) is the place for traditional Irish music, and at *No Exit* (6970 N. Glenwood St.; phone: 743-3355), folk musicians perform while the crowd sips java and plays chess (6970 N. Glenwood; phone: 743-3355).

Chicago's lively dance spots range from the mega-clubs (huge playhouses with separate rooms for dancing, live music, games and pool, or conversing) housed in warehouses west of the Loop to little neighborhood bars. The most chic of the big clubs is *Shelter* (564 W. Fulton St.; phone: 648-5500); if you go, dress to kill and be prepared to deal with difficult doormen. *Ka-Boom!* (747 N. Green St.; phone: 243-8600) has a two-level dance floor and a kooky cabaret lounge with giant teacup-shape booths. A giant dance floor dominates *Crobar* (1543 N. Kingsbury; phone: 587-1313), the newest mega-club in town.

Smaller but equally lively dance clubs abound. The *Lizard Lounge* (1824 W. Augusta Blvd.; phone: 489-0379) is an eclectic little spot known for its funk and K-tel kitsch nights. The DJs at the *Artful Dodger* (1734 W. Wabansia Ave.; phone: 227-6859) spin everything from 1960s British rock to world beat to high-energy dance tracks. *Red Dog* (1958 W. North Ave.; phone: 278-1009) is a spacious second-story dance club that overlooks the funkiest intersection in artsy Wicker Park. *Neo* (2350 N. Clark St.; phone: 528-2622) offers a different theme each night. *Berlin* (954 W. Belmont Ave.; phone: 348-4975) draws an especially flamboyant crowd.

More informal pubs and taverns include *Sheffield's Wine and Beer Garden* (3258 N. Sheffield Ave.; phone: 281-4989), which has an extensive selection of exotic and imported and domestic micro-brewed beers; the fireplace in the back café and pool room keeps things cozy in wintertime. Also try *John Barleycorn Memorial Pub* (658 W. Belden; phone: 348-8899) where classical music soothes patrons trying any of 30 imported beers against a backdrop of prints of famous paintings and sculptures; in the summer, it has the city's most attractive outdoor beer garden. *Lucky's* (213 W. Institute Pl.; phone: 751-7777) is the trendy hangout of the young and beautiful, most of whom show up in something expensive and black. Sports bars are also plentiful: In the shadow of Wrigley Field, *Hi-Tops* (3551 N. Sheffield Ave.; phone: 348-0009) is the largest in town. There's also *Justin's* (3358 N. Southport Ave.; phone: 929-4844), with two satellite dishes and six TV sets; and *McGee's* (950 W. Webster; phone: 871-4272) where the folks behind the bar say you can request any game you want on the projection TV set in the back room.

Though the video sing-along craze started in Japan, *karaoke* (which means "empty orchestra") has caught on here in the Midwest. The most popular *karaoke* bars in Chicago are *Who's Next* (711 N. State St.; phone: 943-8780) and *Kerrigan's* (2310 W. Lawrence Ave.; phone: 334-0620).

Two-steppers and line-dancing fans can strut their spurs at several country-and-western clubs about town. The clubs offer free lessons at least one night a week. *Bub City* (901 W. Weed St.; phone: 266-1200) and *Whiskey River* (1997 N. Clybourn Ave.; phone: 528-3400) are the premiere country-and-western dance bars in the city; *Cadillac Ranch* (1175 W. Lake St., Bartlett; phone: 708-830-7200) is another fun place.

COMIC RELIEF

Chicago has been a comedy center since the 1959 founding of the *Second City* comedy club, whose graduates include Joan Rivers, David Steinberg, the Belushi brothers, and much of the cast of *Saturday Night Live*. *Second City* and its spin-off, *Second City E.T.C.*, are located at 1608 and 1616 North Wells Street, respectively (phone: 337-3992). Meanwhile, the *Comedy Womb* is a star-making club above the *Pines* restaurant (8030 W. Ogden St. in Lyons; phone: 708-422-0030), and *Zanies* (1548 N. Wells; phone: 337-4027) plays the best of the locals as well as such national talent as Richard Lewis. The *Improv* (504 N. Wells St.; phone: 782-6387), with 400 seats, and the *Funny Firm* (318 W. Grand Ave.; phone: 321-9500) feature national acts as well as up-and-coming talent. Said to be giving *Second City* stiff competition is the *Annoyance Theater* (3153 N. Broadway; phone: 929-6200), a group of loonies who put on such bizarre productions as *Manson: The Musical* and *Coed Prison Sluts* at their makeshift theater.

Best in Town

CHECKING IN

There are quite a number of interesting hotels in Chicago, varying in style from the intimate clubbiness of the *Tremont* and the *Talbott* to the supermodern elegance of the *Ritz-Carlton* and *Le Meridien*. Unless otherwise noted, all listed here have at least one restaurant; the choice of eating places normally increases with the price of a room and the size of the hotel. Big hotels have shops, meeting places, and nightly entertainment. All hotels have air conditioning, private baths, TV sets, and telephones unless otherwise indicated. Rates in Chicago are higher than in most other Midwestern cities: Expect to pay $180 to $250 per night for a double room in expensive hotels; $100 to $165 in those classified as moderate; and from $50 to $90 in those listed as inexpensive. If money is no object, ask for a room with a view. North Michigan Avenue hotels are close to the Gold Coast, *Lincoln Park*, and *Water Tower Place*; Loop locations (about 10 minutes away by taxi) are convenient to businesses and the fine old downtown department stores.

For B&B accommodations, contact *Bed and Breakfast Chicago* (PO Box 14088, Chicago, IL 60614; phone: 951-0085). They also rent homes and apartments while their owners are away. Units are available in the downtown, Near North, Lakeshore, Lincoln Park, and nearby neighborhoods at prices starting at $55 per person per night.

The city government, in conjunction with dozens of hotels, offers special winter rates from September through March. The *Chicago Office of Tourism* (phone: 744-2400) can provide a list of hotels with reduced rates or special packages for visitors during the winter (or off-season). There are also many hotels in the suburbs, most located near office complexes and major highway interchanges. The major chains have hotels at or near *O'Hare Airport* and along the TriState Tollway; a few are listed below. Rates tend to be lower outside the city limits. All telephone numbers are in the 312 area code unless otherwise indicated.

EXPENSIVE

Chicago Hilton and Towers This elegantly renovated 30-story hotel features 1,543 rooms, the most lavish of which is the two-story Conrad Hilton Suite for $4,000 a night. Restored to their 1927 grandeur are the Great Hall and the Versailles-inspired Grand Ballroom. Facilities include an extensive fitness center and a computerized business center. Large groups of enthusiastic conventioneers can make it difficult to feel comfortable without a name tag. Check out *Kitty O'Shea's Pub* for good, simple fare. There's a 140,000-square-foot convention center and a self-parking garage. Amenities include 24-hour room service, a concierge, 46 meeting rooms, secretarial services, A/V equipment, photocopiers, computers, and express checkout. 720 S. Michigan Ave. (phone: 922-4400; 800-HILTONS; fax: 922-5240).

Claridge With 174 rooms and six suites (three with wood-burning fireplaces), this reasonably priced hotel is 10 minutes from the Gold Coast and steps away from Astor Street's elegance and Division Street's bars. Health club facilities are available nearby, and *My Neighborhood* restaurant serves Italian, Spanish, and continental fare. Photocopying services are also available. 1244 N. Dearborn St. (phone: 787-4980; fax: 266-0978).

Drake A 535-room institution, with a graciousness not often found in hotels these days. The *Cape Cod Room* is a favorite seafood eatery, and the *Oak Terrace* has a fine view of the Gold Coast. The hotel has 24-hour room service, a concierge, 19 meeting rooms, secretarial services, A/V equipment, photocopiers, computers, and express checkout. Near North Side. 140 E. Walton St. (phone: 787-2200; 800-HILTONS; fax: 787-1431).

Fairmont Opulent and sophisticated, its 700 rooms and suites overlook the city skyline and Lake Michigan. Located in *Illinois Center* between the Chicago River and *Grant Park*, it features such appointments as marble bathrooms equipped with TV sets, telephones, and lighted dressing tables. There's also a bank of 12 meeting rooms with teleconference facilities and a spectacular penthouse boardroom with a panoramic view of the lake. Amenities include 24-hour room service, a concierge, A/V equipment, photocopiers, computers, and express checkout. 200 N. Columbus Dr. (phone: 565-8000; fax: 856-9020).

Four Seasons One of the city's most luxurious hotels occupies 19 floors of a stunning high-rise that also is home to the local branch of *Bloomingdale's* and numerous other classy emporia. There are 343 rooms (more than a third boast separate sitting rooms), an opulent Presidential Suite, and 16 residential apartments in this member of what is arguably the best-managed hotel group in the world. *Seasons* restaurant serves exquisitely prepared nouvelle American dishes (see *Eating Out*). Guest facilities include two-line telephones, lighted makeup mirrors, a spa, a sauna, and an indoor pool. Other amenities are 24-hour room service, a concierge, 12 meeting rooms, secretarial services, A/V equipment, photocopiers, computers, and express checkout. This is a luxury hotel worthy of the adjective. 120 E. Delaware Pl. (phone: 280-8800; 800-332-3442; fax: 280-9184).

Hyatt on Printer's Row A National Historical Register building in the Printer's Row District (formerly the *Morton*), it has an elegant green-and-black lobby, 161 rooms and suites, lounges, meeting areas, an exercise room and gym, plus the first-rate *Prairie* restaurant (see *Eating Out*). Other amenities include a concierge, complimentary morning newspaper, and photocopiers. 500 S. Dearborn St. (phone: 986-1234; 800-233-1234).

Hyatt Regency Chicago With 2,000 rooms in two ultramodern towers, this leading convention hotel is conveniently located between the Loop and North Michigan Avenue, just south of the Chicago River. There's fine dining at *Truffles,* and the *Big Bar* has the city's most extensive selection of brandies. Amenities include 24-hour room service, a concierge, 102 meeting rooms, secretarial services, A/V equipment, photocopiers, computers, and express checkout. 151 E. Wacker Dr. (phone: 565-1234; 800-233-1234; fax: 565-2966).

Hyatt Regency O'Hare Ideal for a comfortable overnight stop between planes. There are 1,100 rooms, a health club, a plant-filled, multistory atrium lobby, and a rotating rooftop restaurant. Amenities include 24-hour room service, a concierge, 48 meeting rooms, secretarial services, A/V equipment, photocopiers, computers, and express checkout. 9300 W. Bryn Mawr Ave.; South River Rd. exit off Kennedy Expwy. (phone: 708-696-1234; 800-233-1234; fax: 708-696-1418).

Hyatt Regency Suites In the heart of downtown, this 347-suite link in the Hyatt chain has luxury amenities offered in an apartment-like setting. Its *Jaxx* restaurant offers superb English breakfasts with a seventh-story view of Michigan Avenue. 676 N. Michigan Ave. and Huron St. (phone: 337-1234; 800-233-1234).

Inter-Continental A recent restoration enhanced the sophisticated Biedermeier-style rooms and suites that distinguished the old *Medinah Athletic Club*. Built during the crash of 1929, the club has been transformed into a 337-room hotel overlooking Michigan Avenue. Butlers serve afternoon tea in a lobby sitting room. There is a concierge desk, as well as 11 meeting rooms, a junior Olympic pool, secretarial services, A/V equipment, photocopiers, computers, and express checkout. A sister hotel, the moderately priced, 517-room *Forum* next door, shares many of its facilities. 505 N. Michigan Ave. (phone: 944-4100; 800-327-0200; fax: 944-3050).

Le Meridien Chicago There are 247 rooms, 35 suites, and six penthouse suites in this elegant hotel. Its *Brasserie Bellevue* restaurant offers unusual interpretations of traditional dishes. Rooms have CD players, VCRs, and remote-control TV sets. Health club facilities are available nearby. 21 E. Bellevue Pl. (phone: 266-2100; 800-543-4300).

Nikko Chicago This elegant, 425-room hotel overlooking the Chicago River was built by Nikko Hotels International, Japan's largest hotel chain. Japanese touches abound—landscaped indoor gardens, native artwork, even Japanese suites with tatami sleeping rooms. Its *Celebrity Café* overlooks the Chicago River and offers American food; the *Benkay* is a fine Japanese restaurant. A three-floor amenity area includes a two-story executive lounge, a business center with computer terminals, a business library, and a health club. Other pluses are 24-hour room service, a concierge, six meeting rooms, secretarial services, A/V equipment, photocopiers, computers, and express checkout. 320 N. Dearborn St. (phone: 744-1900; 800-NIKKO-US; fax: 527-2650).

Omni Ambassador East Listed as a historic American hotel by the National Trust for Historic Preservation, this lovely old property hasn't lost an ounce of charm. It still houses the famous *Pump Room* restaurant (see *Eating Out*), a Chicago institution whose entryway is lined with photos of famous guests, who always dined in Booth No. 1. Convenient location in the Gold Coast area, close to *Lincoln Park*, Rush Street, and the Magnificent Mile of Michigan Avenue. Amenities include 24-hour room service, a concierge, nine meeting rooms, secretarial services, A/V equipment, photocopiers, computers, and express checkout. 1301 N. State Pkwy. (phone: 787-7200; 800-THE-OMNI; fax: 787-4760).

Park Hyatt Small, with 255 elegant rooms and suites, and as convivial as it is convenient to North Michigan Avenue and the historic *Water Tower*. Its excellent *La Tour* restaurant looks out on the *Water Tower* and is the place for power breakfasts and other elegant meals; its lounge is comfortable for coffee or cocktails. The hotel offers 24-hour room service, a concierge, four meeting rooms, secretarial services, A/V equipment, photocopiers, computers, and express checkout. 800 N. Michigan Ave. (phone: 280-2222; 800-233-1234; fax: 280-1963).

Radisson Plaza Ambassador West This historic hotel on the Gold Coast was built in 1924; its 216 rooms were renovated in 1989. Staying here offers a taste of living in Chicago's most elegant neighborhood; down the street and around the corner are blocks of turn-of-the-century homes; you're also steps away from the nightlife on Division Street and a brisk walk from North Michigan Avenue. Amenities include a restaurant, a concierge, a gift shop, a photocopier, room service, and parking (for an additional fee). Some rooms are equipped with fax machines. Weekend packages are available year-round and include a horse-drawn carriage ride. 1300 N. State Pkwy. (phone: 787-7900; 800-333-3333; fax: 787-2067).

Ritz-Carlton Contemporary and chic, this beautifully appointed 432-room luxury establishment, a member of the fine Four Seasons chain, rises 20 stories above its 12th-floor lobby; the beautifully proportioned fountain is a signature centerpiece. Housed in the spectacular *Water Tower Place* complex, it has all the accoutrements of elegance, including a fine health club and skylit indoor swimming pool. Its *Café* offers first-rate continental fare in a lush setting, just off the lobby. Amenities include 24-hour room service, a concierge, six meeting rooms, secretarial services, A/V equipment, photocopiers, computers, and express checkout. Near North Side. 160 E. Pearson St. (phone: 266-1000; 800-241-3333; fax: 266-1194).

Swissôtel Spectacular views of the Chicago River and Lake Michigan are the pride of this property, along with 625 spacious guestrooms (among the largest in the country at 450 square feet) complete with marble bathrooms. Despite the hotel's distinctly European flavor (more than 20% of the staff and close to half the guests are European), *Land of Plenty,* its signature dining room, emphasizes American cooking. Amenities include 34 function and conference rooms, a 60-seat theater, and a business center with a stock market quotation board, newswire, and business library. 323 E. Wacker Dr. at Illinois Ctr. (phone: 565-0565; 800-65-GRAND).

Tremont The paneled lobby, with its elaborate moldings and chandeliers, is more like a private sitting room than a public foyer. The 139 rooms offer traditional elegance. The hotel also is the home of *Cricket's,* one of Chicago's best restaurants (see *Eating Out*). Amenities include 24-hour room service, a concierge, four meeting rooms, secretarial services, A/V equipment, photocopiers, computers, and express checkout. 100 E. Chestnut St. (phone: 751-1900; 800-621-8133; fax: 280-1304).

MODERATE

Allerton Close to museums and shopping on Michigan Avenue and 10 minutes from the Loop, this 380-room property is an economical but quite pleasant choice—and a steal in this location. There's a new restaurant, called *The Avenue,* which offers moderately priced American dishes. Amenities include 10 meeting rooms, secretarial services, A/V equipment, and photocopiers. 701 N. Michigan Ave. (phone: 440-1500; fax: 440-1819).

Bismarck There are 525 rooms and some nice suites. Amenities include 19 meeting rooms, secretarial services, A/V equipment, photocopiers, and express checkout. The *Chalet* is open for lunch and dinner. 171 W. Randolph St. at LaSalle St. (phone: 236-0123; fax: 236-3177).

Executive House Offers 415 rooms and 60 suites, all with wonderful city views. Conference and meeting rooms are available; the *LaSalle* restaurant offers fine continental cooking; and guests can use nearby health club facilities. Catering to members of the international business community, it offers a special telephone system that allows access to dialing and travel instructions in various foreign languages. Valet parking is available. 71 E. Wacker Dr. (phone: 346-7100; 800-621-4005).

Holiday Inn City Centre Architecturally more interesting than you might expect, this 500-room establishment has many amenities—swimming pools and a health club, indoor tennis courts, racquetball, and free parking—making it almost a bargain. There's also a concierge desk, 11 meeting rooms, A/V equipment, photocopiers, and express checkout. 300 E. Ohio (phone: 787-6100; 800-HOLIDAY; fax: 787-6259).

Holiday Inn O'Hare Convenient to the airport and the many offices nearby, it has 507 rooms and offers weekend packages. The hotel's "Holidome" has indoor and outdoor pools, a health club, saunas, a tanning salon, and a gameroom. Other amenities include free parking, three restaurants, two bars, and a business center. 5440 River Rd., Rosemont (phone: 708-671-6350; 800-HOLIDAY).

Marriott Downtown This convention hotel dates from the 1960s, but its 1,172 rooms were extensively renovated a couple of years ago. Located right on Michigan Avenue, it's within walking distance of the *Water Tower, North Pier,* and both of the city's major gallery districts, and not far from the Loop. Its spacious lobby includes a cocktail area and piano bar where guests can watch each other come and go; its three restaurants offer a choice of seafood, Italian fare, and steaks. It also boasts two lounges, 24-hour room service, an extensive health club and pool, a business center with computers and a photocopier, and shopping. Parking is available for a fee. 540 N. Michigan Ave. (phone: 836-0100; 800-228-9290; fax: 836-6139).

INEXPENSIVE

Best Western Grant Park Near the funky art life of the south Loop, this modest 172-room property is also within walking distance of the downtown museums, shopping, and offices. It has a Mexican restaurant, and room service is available. There's also a fitness center and an outdoor pool. 1100 S. Michigan Ave. (phone: 922-2900; 800-528-1234).

Days Inn Lake Shore Drive Convenient to North Michigan Avenue and Lake Shore Drive, this 33-story, 578-room hotel offers marvelous views, an outdoor pool, standard business services, on-premises parking, and all laundry services, plus a revolving banquet hall on the top floor. Its *Gold Star Sardine Bar* is one of the city's popular after-hours spots, offering cabaret singers nightly. 644 N. Lake Shore Dr. (phone: 943-9200).

HoJo Inn This 70-room motel is in the River North gallery district, a formerly seedy neighborhood that has become quite fashionable. Its coffee shop is popular with neighboring office workers, and there's free parking—right in front of each room. 720 N. LaSalle St. (phone: 664-8100).

Quality Inn Downtown Located just west of the Loop in the midst of Greektown's lively nightlife and restaurant scene, it's also right next to the Kennedy Expressway. There are 406 rooms, plus a restaurant, a lounge, and an outdoor pool. Parking and room service are available. 1 S. Halsted St. ([phone: 829-5000).

EATING OUT

The city's restaurant business is booming, and some of the finest cooking in America can be found here. Expect to pay from $70 or more for a meal for two at those restaurants we've described as expensive; between $50 and $70 at places in the moderate category; and less than $40 at our inexpensive choices. Prices do not include drinks and wine, tips, or taxes. Unless otherwise noted, all restaurants are open for lunch and dinner, and all telephone numbers are in the 312 area code.

EXPENSIVE

Ambria Everything about this place charms, from the comfortable setting to the menu's sophisticated variations on nouvelle cuisine. Dinner might begin with a salad of sliced duck, pine nuts, and fresh pears with red currant dressing, or a tropical lobster salad. Desserts are simply remarkable. There's also a *dégustation* dinner for four or more with samplings of many dishes. Closed Sundays. Reservations necessary. Major credit cards accepted. 2300 N. Lincoln Park W. (phone: 472-5959).

Arun's One of the city's most elegant Thai dining spots, it offers such daily specials as quilted shrimp with fried rice cracker and curry sauce, prawns with garlic-lime sauce, and catfish curry. End the meal with fragrant layered rice custard and Thai iced coffee. Open for dinner only; closed Mondays. Reservations advised. Major credit cards accepted. 4156 N. Kedzie Ave. (phone: 539-1909).

Bice The people watching here may be even more of a draw than the food; in summer, diners can sit outdoors and observe Chicago street life as it passes by. The menu features fancy preparations of Italian dishes, and the three-level dining room is decorated in a contemporary style, with dark wood paneling and tablecloths of imported Italian linen. Closed Sunday lunch. Reservations advised. Major credit cards accepted. 158 E. Ontario St. (phone: 664-1474).

Cape Cod Room An institution, this seafood spot serves reliable fresh pompano, lobster, and other finny fare. Closed *Christmas*. Reservations advised. Major credit cards accepted. *Drake Hotel,* 140 E. Walton St. (phone: 787-2200).

Charlie Trotter's The menu changes daily in this adventuresome, two-room nouvelle cuisine restaurant, home of some of the city's most imaginative dishes. Appetizers range from caviar-topped sea scallops to sweetbreads with *pancetta,* radicchio, shredded potato, sweet peppers, and sharp cilantro butter presented in a crisp potato shell. Entrées are equally varied: tender venison and smoked quail with hazelnuts. Service is excellent; the wine list is extensive. Closed Sundays and Mondays. Reservations necessary; there's a six-month wait for its most popular table: in the kitchen where you can watch the master chef at work. Major credit cards accepted. 816 W. Armitage Ave. (phone: 248-6228).

Cricket's Styled after the *"21" Club* in New York, be prepared for red-checkered tablecloths, bare floors, low ceilings, walls festooned with corporate memorabilia, and a menu that includes chicken hash Mornay and various daily specials. A very good choice for Sunday brunch, and popular for people watching any time. Open daily. Reservations necessary. Major credit cards accepted. *Tremont Hotel,* 100 E. Chestnut St. (phone: 280-2100).

Everest Room An elegant French restaurant, it has a commanding view from atop the *Chicago Stock Exchange Building* in Chicago's financial center. The cornucopia of original dishes reflect the chef's Alsatian roots. Try roast filet of sea bass wrapped in crisp shredded potatoes, black squid risotto, salmon soufflé, oxtail terrine with horseradish sauce, or venison with elderberries. Closed Sundays and Mondays. Reservations necessary. Major credit cards accepted. 440 S. LaSalle St. (phone: 663-8920).

Le Français For years, Jean Banchet made this one of America's finest French restaurants. Today the kitchen is in the hands of Roland and Mary Beth Liccioni, and the still-excellent fare has a somewhat lighter touch. Standouts include rack of lamb served with tiny fresh vegetables and couscous, stuffed Dover sole, Lyonnaise sausage served *en croûte* with port wine sauce, and crayfish bisque. The pastries are superb. Closed Sundays. Reservations necessary. Major credit cards accepted. 269 S. Milwaukee Ave., Wheeling; take Kennedy Expwy. to Rte. 294 north, Willow exit (phone: 708-541-7470).

Frontera Grill and Topolobampo A pair of upscale Mexican dining rooms. *Frontera* specializes in tempting appetizer platters of guacamole, deep-fried chicken taquitos, and ceviche. *Topolobampo* offers, among other treats, roast pork loin with red-chili apricot sauce and pumpkin purée. Closed Sundays and Mondays. Reservations advised. Major credit cards accepted. 445 N. Clark St. (phone: 661-1434).

Gene and Georgetti In an old, wood-frame building near the *Merchandise Mart,* hearty sirloin, T-bone steaks, and animated conversation mingle. This eatery also dishes up popular Italian dishes and huge salads. Closed Sundays and Mondays. Reservations unnecessary. Major credit cards accepted. 500 N. Franklin St. (phone: 527-3718).

Gordon When owner Gordon Sinclair's culinary imagination ignites, the results are superlative. On any given night, you're likely to find artichoke fritters with béarnaise sauce, beef tenderloin with sweet potatoes, or goat cheese fondue with caraway seeds and walnut vinaigrette. Top off the meal with a great dessert like the warm chocolate torte. Open daily. Reservations advised. Major credit cards accepted. 500 N. Clark St. (phone: 467-9780).

Jackie's In this intimate 50-seat neighborhood spot serving some of the finest nouvelle cooking in the city, French food with Oriental highlights is featured: Consider delicate orange-honey-glazed squab served with Chinese vermicelli and cabbage garnished with cashews and cloud-ear mushrooms. Closed Sundays and Mondays. Reservations necessary. Major credit cards accepted. 2478 N. Lincoln Ave. (phone: 880-0003).

Jimmy's Place Opera fans can experience the glory of Verdi, Puccini, and Mozart while dining on medallions of veal, spicy shrimp ragout in sesame crêpes, and veal sweetbreads atop grilled, smoked leeks. Closed Sundays. Reservations advised. Major credit cards accepted. 3420 N. Elston Ave. (phone: 539-2999).

Le Mikado The ultimate in subtle urban style; the menu features a classy array of Eurasian dishes, including cold noodle dishes, oysters tempura, and green tea ice cream. The decor has a dramatic Oriental flavor. Open daily for dinner only. Reservations advised. Major credit cards accepted. 21 W. Goethe St. (phone: 280-8611).

Morton's of Chicago Another fine steak-and-potatoes establishment whose loyal fans gulp down everything from kosher hot dogs to chicken in the pot to fabulous cheesecake. Open daily. Reservations advised. Major credit cards accepted. 1050 N. State St. (phone: 266-4820). There are more moderately priced versions in suburban Westchester (1 Westbrook Corporate Center; phone: 708-562-7000), and in Rosemont (9525 W. Bryn Mawr Ave.; phone: 708-678-5155).

Nick's Fishmarket The number of choices on the menu is bewildering, but it's tough to make a wrong decision here. The cold appetizer assortment of shellfish is always a good bet, and try the pan-fried whole baby salmon or an abalone dish as an entrée. First National Plaza location closed Sundays. Reservations necessary. Major credit cards accepted. First National Plaza, Monroe St. (phone: 621-0200); and 10275 Higgins Rd., Rosemont (phone: 708-298-8200).

Palm Owned by the same people who run the well-known New York restaurants called *Palm* and *Palm, Too*, this eatery has a similar decor of sawdust-covered floors and walls hung with drawings of regular patrons. Also like its East Coast counterparts, the kitchen here specializes in producing great steaks and lobsters. Closed Sundays. Reservations necessary. Major credit cards accepted. 181 E. Lake Shore Dr. (phone: 944-0135).

Le Perroquet Recently reopened by innovative Michael Foley of *Printer's Row* (see below), this sumptuous spot is as elegant as before, with grilled seafood, creative presentations of game birds, and heavenly desserts prepared in the famed Foley style (although he is not the chef here). Closed Sundays. Reservations advised. Major credit cards accepted. 70 E. Walton St. (phone: 944-7990).

Prairie Quite possibly where the term "Midwestern cooking" was coined, this intimate spot offers fine regional fare. The decor is elegant and uncluttered à la Frank Lloyd Wright, and the open kitchen is a fine place to pick up new cooking techniques as you watch your food being prepared. Whitefish smothered with onions, crisp bacon, puréed squash, and smoked whitefish caviar is just one of the thoughtfully prepared entrées, and those willing to chance an extra pound should try the warm carrot raisin cake with bourbon glaze and sugarplums. Closed Sundays. Reservations advised. Major credit cards accepted. 500 S. Dearborn St. (phone: 663-1143).

Pump Room A winning formula of fine food, diligent service, and lovely decor have made this a legend among Chicago restaurants. Continental dishes are the mainstays, but there are some nouvelle cuisine specialties; both are complemented by the restaurant's good wine list. Open daily. Reservations necessary. Major credit cards accepted. *Omni Ambassador East Hotel,* 1301 N. State Pkwy. (phone: 266-0360).

Seasons This opulent, urbane room features some of the most inventive nouvelle preparations in the city, all with an American accent. Try the quail with game-sausage stuffing or the venison. Open daily. Reservations necessary. Major credit cards accepted. *Four Seasons Hotel,* 120 E. Delaware Pl. (phone: 280-8800).

Spiaggia Expertly prepared northern Italian food—including unique pasta dishes, veal, and a grilled fish of the day—served in a beautiful setting at the top of Michigan Avenue. Next door, the *Spiaggia Café* serves pizza, salads, pasta, and other Italian favorites in a more casual setting (open daily; no reservations). Restaurant closed for Sunday lunch. Reservations advised. Major credit cards accepted. 980 N. Michigan Ave. (phone: 280-2750 or 280-2764).

Yoshi's Café French technique and Japanese mastery combine to produce a menu featuring such inventive dishes as striped sea bass stuffed with herbs and served with lobster cream sauce, sautéed veal medallions on homemade buckwheat pasta, and tuna tartare on a bed of guacamole. Open for dinner only; closed Mondays. Reservations advised. Major credit cards accepted. 3257 N. Halsted St. (phone: 248-6160).

MODERATE

Art Institute Restaurant in the Park Even many long-time Chicagoans think this elegant spot overlooking *Grant Park* is for members only: not so. Designed by the late Norman DeHaan, the stylish yet comfortable dining room offers first rate service and a continental menu with magnificent desserts. Open for lunch only; closed Sundays. Reservations advised. Major credit cards accepted. Columbus Dr. between Monroe St. and Jackson Blvd. (phone: 443-3543).

Bella Vista This vast place was once a bank, and the restaurant's owners (who are also responsible for *Bacino's* popular pizza places) took full advantage of the space with lush trompe l'oeil murals on all the walls; the tableware picks up both the color and floral motifs of the murals. The menu is contemporary Italian; diners can walk through the glassed-in wine rooms. Reservations advised. Major credit cards accepted. Somewhat out of the way, but convenient to *Wrigley Field* and *Lincoln Park;* also a block away from an elevated stop on the Howard Line. 1001 W. Belmont Ave. (phone: 404-0111).

Bistro 110 Everything about this place really clicks: an energetic ambience mixed with inventive yet casual cooking. The food—most notably items prepared in the wood-burning oven—is everything bistro fare should be. Meals begin with a lovely roasted garlic served with a crusty baguette. Especially popular entrées are cassoulet, oven-roasted chicken, and steak *au poivre*. Their Sunday brunch features live jazz. Open daily. Reservations advised. Major credit cards accepted. 110 E. Pearson St. (phone: 266-3110).

Blackhawk Lodge Many years ago, co-owner Doug Roth's father ran the *Blackhawk Inn,* a stylish and hearty favorite in the Loop. Now Roth *fils* has teamed with first-generation restaurateur Larry Levy to create a version of a Wisconsin summer camp for grown-ups. The concept works at this lively and popular place. The contemporary American fare, which is heavy on light foods like fish and salads, may have been inspired by summers at the lake, but is far more interesting. Crowds move out to the screened-in porch in the summer. Open daily. Reservations advised. Major credit cards accepted. 41 E. Superior St. (phone: 280-4080).

Blue Mesa Southwestern cooking is one of this city's latest dining crazes, and Santa Fe style reigns in this comfortable room with whitewashed adobe and bleached pine. Lovers of wonderfully pulpy guacamole and steaks smothered in green chilies and onions will be quite content. Reservations necessary for parties of eight or more. Open daily. Major credit cards accepted. 1729 N. Halsted St. (phone: 944-5990).

Bub City A rollicking, mammoth, down-home Texas eating house, featuring shrimp and crab barbecue and "Big Easy" (read, New Orleans) bayou music to wash it all down. This is one loud, entertaining joint. Wear denim. Open daily. Reservations advised. Major credit cards accepted. There's lots of parking near this out-of-the-way spot where Halsted Street and North Avenue meet. 901 W. Weed St. (phone: 266-1200).

Bukhara This Indian place claims its recipes go back 1,000 years. The focus is on marinated fresh seafood, poultry, beef, and lamb roasted in tandoors (hollow clay ovens). Try the tandoori chicken in pomegranate juice or the shish kebab with cumin-flavored lamb. Finish with a pudding of dates, almonds, and milk. Open daily. Reservations advised. Major credit cards accepted. 2 E. Ontario St. (phone: 943-0188).

Café Ba-ba-Reeba! Everything about this place is festive and upbeat. The emphasis on *tapas* (Spanish appetizers) gives diners an opportunity to sample lots of dishes, although entrée-size options are also available. Selections change, but the menu usually includes such specialties as octopus in vinaigrette, grilled sausage, paella, and flan for dessert. Closed for lunch Mondays and in January and February. Reservations unnecessary. Major credit cards accepted. 2024 N. Halsted St. (phone: 935-5000).

Carson's Probably the best spareribs in the city. Salads with a creamy, anchovy-flavored dressing and tangy au gratin potatoes are the other lures. Don't dress up because bibs (supplied) are essential. Open daily. No reservations, so expect to wait. Major credit cards accepted. 612 N. Wells St. (phone: 280-9200); 5970 N. Ridge Rd. (phone: 271-4000); 400 E. Roosevelt Rd., Lombard (708-627-4300); and 8617 Niles Center Rd., Skokie, for carryout only (phone: 708-675-6800).

The Eccentric This is Oprah Winfrey's baby, and it lives up to its name: lots of wild colors; paintings by local artists; an amalgam of French, English, American, and Italian cooking styles; and such dishes as cold fruit soup with chili peppers. Don't pass up Oprah's lumpy mashed potatoes with horseradish. Open daily. Reservations advised. Major credit cards accepted. 159 W. Erie St. (phone: 787-8390).

Emilio's Iberian and inventive, from the man who introduced *tapas* (Spanish appetizers) to Chicago at *Café Ba-ba-Reeba!* Open daily. Reservations unnecessary. Major credit cards accepted. 4100 W. Roosevelt Rd., Hillside (phone: 708-547-7177).

Geja's Café This restaurant has good food—from fondue to seafood—and a romantic atmosphere, with flamenco and classical guitar played every night of the week. There's a superb wine list. Reservations advised. Major credit cards accepted. 340 W. Armitage Ave. (phone: 281-9101).

Hat Dance Kicky, as the name suggests: Aztec decor, Mexican food with a Japanese accent. Closed at lunch weekends. Reservations advised. Major credit cards accepted. 325 W. Huron St. (phone: 649-0066).

Hatsuhana Delicious sushi and sashimi; tables as well as counter seating is available. Open daily. Reservations advised. Major credit cards accepted. 160 E. Ontario St. (phone: 280-8287).

Italian Village Visitors to Chicago may wonder why there are so few restaurants in the Loop; likely because executives go to private clubs and office workers do fast food or company cafeterias. But the *Italian Village* offers three, right in the middle of the downtown area. Downstairs is the clubby and casual *La Cantina;* on the second floor is a country restaurant called the *Village Room;* both are reasonably priced and offer a standard selection of Italian fare. Main floor *Vivere* is a recent addition, offering far more sophisticated, and pricey, regional Italian dishes in a dramatic setting. *La Cantina* and the *Village Room* are closed Sunday lunch; *Vivere* is closed Saturday lunch and Sundays. Reservations advised. Major credit cards accepted. 71 W. Monroe St. (phone: 332-7005, *La Cantina* and *Village Room;* 332-4040, *Vivere*).

Maggiano's A Chicago hot spot, it packs them in nightly. The menu features hearty Italian fare served on heaping platters meant to be shared. Breads from the *Corner Bakery* (right next door) are not to be missed. Open daily for lunch and dinner. Reservations advised. Major credit cards accepted. 516 N. Clark St. (phone: 644-7700).

Printer's Row Chef Michael Foley awakens sluggish palates with his delicious fare. Choose to dine in either the snug wine library, an intimate room lined with bookcases (including Michael's cookbooks); a cozy room decorated with a hunting motif; or the main dining area. The roast pheasant with *jus au naturel* and five kinds of onions and the grilled salmon with basil cream sauce and sun-dried-tomato pasta are true standouts. Chocoholics should dive into the chocolate terrine studded with fresh raspberries or the white and dark chocolate cheesecake with amaretto sauce. Closed Sundays. Reservations advised. Major credit cards accepted. 550 S. Dearborn St. (phone: 461-0780).

Santorini's The elegant decor draws the elite of Chicago's Greek community; the menu, featuring lamb chops wrapped in phyllo and several seafood dishes, is equally classy. Open daily. Reservations advised. Major credit cards accepted. 138 S. Halsted St. (phone: 829-8820).

Scoozi A cavernous former garage that's been turned into a smashing gathering place with evocative period decor. Besides the chef's daily specials, the unusually large menu includes provincial Italian specialties such as a three-foot-long pizza served on a wooden plank (calorie counters, fear not; they do come smaller); osso buco (braised veal shanks); and pheasant that is smoked on the premises and served with a choice of soft, baked, or sautéed polenta (the Italian version of grits). Closed at lunch weekends. Reservations advised. Major credit cards accepted. 410 W. Huron St. (phone: 943-5900).

Shaw's Crab House This is a mammoth, immensely popular pre–World War II–style seafood house. Don't miss the stone or soft-shell crabs if they're in season. The pecan pie may be Chicago's best. Open daily. Reservations advised. Major credit cards accepted. 21 E. Hubbard St. (phone: 527-2722). *Shaw's Blue Crab Lounge* (660 Lake Cook Rd., Deerfield; phone: 708-948-1020) is a similar, but more casual, enterprise under the same ownership.

St. Germain Bakery-Café If this lively bistro makes you wonder whether you are on the Gold Coast or the Left Bank, no wonder; that's the intention. Particularly popular for Sunday brunching, it specializes in breads and croissants. The ambience is terrific. There are pastries, pâtés, and cheese to go as well. Open daily. Reservations advised for Sunday brunch only. Major credit cards accepted. 1210 N. State Pkwy. (phone: 266-9900).

Szechwan House The hot-and-sour soup and the crispy duck are just as appetizing as the chef's more unusual dishes—snails in spicy sauce and deep-fried ground shrimp wrapped in seaweed. Open daily. Reservations advised. Major credit cards accepted. 600 N. Michigan Ave. (phone: 642-3900).

Tucci Milan Offering elegantly prepared Italian dishes, it's very popular at lunch with the advertising set. The vast array of antipasti (try the goat cheese or eggplant) leads to entreés such as meatless lasagna, rosemary-seasoned chicken cooked on a spit, and thin-crust pizza. Closed Sunday lunch. Reservations advised. Major credit cards accepted. 6 W. Hubbard St. (phone: 222-0044).

Tuscany A newcomer drawing crowds to Little Italy west of the Loop, this stylish Northern Italian trattoria offers innovative pasta dishes and an extensive wine list. Rack of lamb, rotisserie chicken, and risotto are specialties. Open daily. Reservations advised. Major credit cards accepted. 1014 W. Taylor St. (phone: 829-1990).

INEXPENSIVE

Ann Sather's There actually are three, but the original (on West Belmont Ave.) may be the world's only Swedish restaurant housed in a former funeral home. The menu varies from time-honored Swedish dishes to hearty American fare: pork sausage patties and rich country gravy, and beefsteak and eggs with cinnamon rolls. Brunch is particularly good. Open daily. Reservations unnecessary. MasterCard and Visa accepted. 929 W. Belmont Ave. (phone: 348-2378); 5207 N. Clark St. (phone: 271-6677); and 1329 E. 57th St., Hyde Park (phone: 947-9323).

Army & Lou's This hangout for Chicago aldermen serves the best soul food in the city. Try the greens and neck bones, the Northern beans with ham hocks, the smothered chicken and corn bread dressing, or better yet, the "Taste of Soul," which includes everything from chicken to catfish to chitlins and more ham hocks. Closed Tuesdays. Reservations unnecessary. Major credit cards accepted. 422 E. 75th St. (phone: 483-3100).

Beau Thai One of Lincoln Park's fine collection of Southeast Asian eateries. Specialties include *pad thai,* a warm noodle dish; duck Beau Thai, cooked with cashews and vegetables; and sweet, creamy cold Thai coffee for dessert. Closed Mondays. Reservations accepted on weekends only. Major credit cards accepted. 2527 N. Clark St. (phone: 348-6938).

Berghoff Another Chicago tradition—and one sometimes thinks it's the only local restaurant visitors have ever heard of. Although the service is rushed, the meals are bountiful and the selection wide-ranging: ragout, Wiener schnitzel, steaks, and seafood. Closed Sundays. Reservations accepted for five or more. Major credit cards accepted. 17 W. Adams St. (phone: 427-3170).

Billy Goat Tavern Every newspaper town has to have a bar where reporters and editors congregate for inexpensive drinks and greasy fries. For Chicagoans, this home of juicy thick burgers is the place. The walls of the underground bar are decorated with clippings from some of the city's journalistic legends; and though its decor won't win any awards, it's a lively lunchtime spot with newspaper people, local sports fans, and tourists. It's worth a stop for a taste of gritty old Chicago. Open daily. No reservations. No credit cards accepted. 430 N. Michigan Ave. (phone: 222-1525).

Ed Debevic's The creation of Rich Melman, king of Chicago restaurateurs, this is a 1950s diner that has crowds lining up outside. Burgers, chili, malts, fries, and a rollicking *American Graffiti* atmosphere. Wear crinolines and chew bubble gum—just like the waitresses! Open daily. No reservations. No credit cards accepted. 640 N. Wells St. (phone: 664-1707).

Greek Islands You can find thoughtfully prepared dishes such as gyros, squid, lamb, and fresh broiled red snapper at this simple eatery. The decor is pleasant, with blue-and-white-checkered cloths, and it's particularly popular with faculty at the nearby *University of Illinois*. Open daily. Reservations unnecessary. Major credit cards accepted. 200 S. Halsted St. (phone: 782-9855).

Hard Rock Café Yes, Chicago has one, too. The walls of this hip hamburger emporium are covered with an assortment of rock music artifacts and declarations of world peace. Chili and grilled burgers lead the menu. Wash it all down with a fruit and honey "health shake." At the very least, it's the place to pick up an essential addition to any trendy T-shirt collection. Open daily. No reservations. Major credit cards accepted. 63 W. Ontario St. (phone: 943-2252).

Helmand Come here for savory Afghan baby pumpkin and lamb Kabuli in an exotic, attractive setting. Top off the meal with cheese-like *burfee* or baklava baked with ground pistachios. The service is as good as the food. Open for dinner only, closed Sundays. Reservations advised. Major credit cards accepted 3201 N. Halsted St. (phone: 935-2447).

Ina's Kitchen Ever since Ina Pinckey opened this cozy spot in Lincoln Park two years ago, there have been lines out the door. Breakfast is served until 3 PM, when the kitchen closes. Lunch is added to the menu at 11:30 AM. Specials include a noodle and vegetable frittata, corn and blackbean scrapple, whole-wheat oatmeal pancakes, and a full range of pastries. Open for breakfast and lunch only. No reservations. No credit cards. 934 W. Webster Ave. (phone: 525-1116).

Lou Mitchell's For those who consider the idea of awakening before noon a barbaric proposal, make an exception and head for this outstanding breakfast spot. Freshly squeezed orange juice is followed by perfectly prepared pancakes, omelettes served in the pan, biscuits baked that morning, and fantastic coffee. Formica tabletops, eccentric waitresses, and a low-key clientele complete the picture. Lunch is served here, too, but breakfast has made this place a landmark on the city's restaurant scene. The doors open at 5:30 AM Closed Sundays. No reservations. Major credit cards accepted. 563 W. Jackson Blvd. (phone: 939-3111).

Parthenon This eatery, a Greektown institution for more than two decades, offers good food in comfortable surroundings. The extensive menu runs from chicken shish kebabs to Greek sausage to baked lamb's head. Juicy gyros and wine-marinated octopus are among the bite-size appetizers; for dessert, try the moist almond-honey cake. Open daily. Reservations advised for groups of six or more. Major credit cards accepted. 314 S. Halsted St. (phone: 726-2407).

Pasteur This attractive corner storefront is among the best of some two dozen Vietnamese restaurants in the city. Recommended entrées are whole fried red snapper topped with sweet-salty sauce with scallions and lime or the charming nest of crispy fried egg noodles filled with seafood and vegetables. Closed Monday lunch. Reservations advised on weekends. Major credit cards accepted. 4759 N Sheridan Rd. (phone: 271-6673).

Three Happiness Get a group together and head out early to avoid a wait at Chinatown's favorite dim sum spot. It's big, crowded, noisy, and dirty, but you'll feast for about $10 per person. Skip the regular menu; wait for the carts laden with steamed dumplings and buns, deep-fried pastries, plates of cold meat, scrumptious sweets, and other exotic fare that comprises the traditional Cantonese tea lunch. Open daily. No reservations. Major credit cards accepted. 2130 S. Wentworth Ave. (phone: 791-1228).

Tulpe This Lithuanian haven with only eight tables exemplifies the best in neighborhood restaurants, offering hearty, honest cooking at low prices in unpretentious surroundings. Among the specials are meat-filled dumplings, juicy pork chops, roast chicken, and homemade sausage. The staff is cheerful and friendly. During warm weather, there is outdoor dining on weekends. No liquor is served. Open daily for breakfast, lunch, and early dinner (until 8 PM). No reservations. No credit cards accepted. 2447 W. 69th St. (phone: 925-1123).

Wishbone A fun spot that serves up some terrific down-home Southern cooking. Chicken is the thing here: Grilled until juicy, Southern-fried, or Louisiana-blackened in a salad. Don't miss dessert, either: marble cheesecake, pecan pie served plain or oozing chocolate, and custard like Mom used to make. Open for breakfast, lunch, and dinner; closed Saturday lunch and Sunday lunch and dinner. No reservations. Credit cards accepted at Washington Street location only. 1001 W. Washington St. (phone: 850-2663) and 1800 W. Grand Ave. (phone: 829-3597).

HOT DOG! (AND PIZZA, TOO)

If all of the above fails to appeal to your culinary sensibilities, *Michael's* (1946 N. Clark St.; phone: 787-DOGS) is a terrific alternative. It's also just the spot for those with the I-can't-get-a-good-hot-dog blues. The special here is the "chardog," a half pound of spicy beef on a soft bun with onions, tomatoes, cucumbers, pickles, mustard, relish, and perhaps the kitchen sink. (If you're not in the mood for a hot dog, *Michael's* also offers an incredible salad bar, stuffed baked potatoes, grilled sandwiches, and world-famous cheddar fries.)

Hamburger and hot dog fans would be remiss to miss *Gold Coast Dogs* (2100 N. Clark St.; phone: 327-8887; 418 N. State St.; phone: 527-1222; and 325 S. Franklin St.; phone: 939-2624), where they can sample a real Chicago hot dog (it comes with fresh onions and peppers, not soggy sauerkraut). For funky 1950s fare, *Byron's* (850 W. North Ave.; phone: 266-3355) will take you back to the days of the drive-in, as will *Portillo* in the suburbs (806 W. Dundee Rd., Arlington Heights; phone: 708-870-0870; 611 E. Golf Rd. Schaumburg; phone: 708-884-9020; and 950 S. Barrington Rd., Streamwood; phone: 708-213-6656).

Finally, a visit to this city's eating establishments wouldn't be complete without a taste of Chicago's famous deep-dish pizza—layer upon layer of toppings baked in a deep pan. The pioneer of this pizza fit for Goliath is *Pizzeria Uno* (29 E. Ohio St.; phone: 321-1000), a place whose food more than makes up for its lack of atmosphere. Also in the area is *Pizzeria Due* (619 N. Wabash Ave.; phone: 943-2400), under the same ownership and serving the same hearty fare. *Gino's East* (160 E. Superior St.; phone: 943-1124) uses cornmeal crusts to vary the flavor. Other places to try this local delicacy are *Giordano's of Lincoln Park* (1840 N. Clark St.; phone: 944-6100); *Bacino's* (75 E. Wacker Dr.; phone: 263-0070; and 2204 N. Lincoln; phone: 472-7400); and *Edwardo's Natural Pizza* (1321 E. 57th St.; phone: 241-7960; and 9300 Skokie Blvd., Skokie; phone: 708-674-0008). The latter also serves another local favorite, stuffed pizza—a thick, gooey, pie-like creation. All of the above eateries are open daily; reservations are unnecessary and major credit cards are accepted.

Cincinnati

At-a-Glance

SEEING THE CITY
For the best view of Cincinnati, go to the top of the *Carew Tower*. You may see the original seven hills on which the town is said to have been built. No admission charge for children under six. Fifth and Vine Sts. (phone: 579-9735).

SPECIAL PLACES
Pedestrians can traverse the city above the traffic via a Skywalk system that is totally covered. In many areas, it is enclosed and climate-controlled.

CINCINNATI ART MUSEUM This outstanding collection of paintings, sculpture, prints, and decorative arts fills more than 80 galleries and exhibition rooms (with an exceptionally fine section on ancient Persia). Ancient musical instruments, costumes, and textiles also are on view. Closed Mondays, *Thanksgiving, Christmas,* and *New Year's Day.* No admission charge on Saturdays or for children under 18. *Eden Park* (phone: 721-5204).

MUSEUM CENTER AT UNION TERMINAL This collective center, whose façade resembles a 1930s radio set, is the home of the *Cincinnati Historical Society Museum and Library,* the *Cincinnati Museum of Natural History,* and an Omnimax movie theater. The center and theater are open daily, with evening movies Tuesdays through Saturdays. Admission charge. 1301 Western Ave., Ezzard Charles Dr. exit off I-75 (phone: 287-7000; 800-733-2077).

TAFT MUSEUM During his presidency, William Howard Taft was entertained in this house, the home of his older half brother. Once nicknamed "the Little White House," it is now a museum with Chinese porcelain and portraits and landscapes by Rembrandt, Turner, Gainsborough, and Corot. Open daily. Admission charge. 316 Pike (phone: 241-0343).

CONTEMPORARY ARTS CENTER "What is art?" is a puzzler as old as the Cincinnati hills, and the *Contemporary Arts Center* keeps residents wondering. Not only are there constantly changing modern painting and sculpture exhibits, but the center's multimedia shows dazzle the mind, the eye, and the mind's eye. Closed *Easter, Thanksgiving, Christmas,* and *New Year's Day.* No admission charge Sundays and Mondays. 115 E. Fifth St. (phone: 721-0390).

CINCINNATI FIRE MUSEUM All kinds of old fire engines and paraphernalia in a 1907 firehouse listed on the *National Register of Historic Places.* Closed Mondays and holidays. No admission charge for children under two. 315 W. Court St. (phone: 621-5553).

CINCINNATI ZOO The second-oldest zoo in the nation, known for its expertise in the propagation of rare and endangered species. It has more than

6,000 animals; the most popular exhibits are the rare white Bengal tigers, the *Bird of Prey Flight Cage,* the *Outdoor Gorilla Exhibit,* the *Children's Zoo,* the *Insectarium,* and the *Cat House.* Open daily. Admission charge. 3400 Vine St. (phone: 281-4700).

KROHN CONSERVATORY One of the largest public greenhouses in the world, it contains 1,500 labeled specimens of tropical plants and seasonal flowers. Displays change six times a year. Open daily, with extended hours during the *Christmas* and *Easter* seasons. No admission charge for residents. *Eden Park* (phone: 421-4086).

EXTRA SPECIAL

Just 25 miles north of Cincinnati is *Paramount's Kings Island,* one of the best amusement parks in the US. A family entertainment center with live stage entertainment, shopping, dining, and rides for kids of all ages. Eight roller coasters are featured: the *Beast,* the longest wooden roller coaster in the world; *King Cobra,* a stand-up coaster; the *Racer,* with cars running forward and backward; *Vortex,* a steel coaster that turns riders upside down six times; *Adventure Express,* a runaway mine train coaster; *Top Gun,* a suspended coaster; and *The Beastie* and *Scooby Zoom,* two children's coasters. *WaterWorks* features 16 aquatic attractions including thrilling body and tube slides. Lodging and camping are available near the park. 6300 Kings Island Dr. (phone: 398-5600).

Six miles north of Kings Island in Lebanon, Ohio, is the *Golden Lamb Inn,* the state's oldest operating inn, now also a Shaker museum and a first-rate restaurant (phone: 621-8373 or 932-5065). While in Lebanon, visit the *Warren County Historical Society Museum* (105 S. Broadway; phone: 932-1817), which also has a major Shaker collection.

Sources and Resources

TOURIST INFORMATION

For maps and brochures, write or visit the *Greater Cincinnati Convention and Visitors Bureau* (300 W. Sixth St., Cincinnati, OH 45202; phone: 621-2142; 800-344-3445). It also can provide self-guided walking tour maps. Contact the Ohio state tourism hotline (phone: 800-BUCKEYE) for maps, calendars of events, health updates, and travel advisories.

LOCAL COVERAGE The *Cincinnati Enquirer,* mornings and Sundays; the *Cincinnati Post,* an afternoon daily. The best guide to events and places of interest is *Cincinnati* magazine, a monthly, available at newsstands; particularly useful is the magazine's annual restaurant guide, available from the *Chamber of Commerce.*

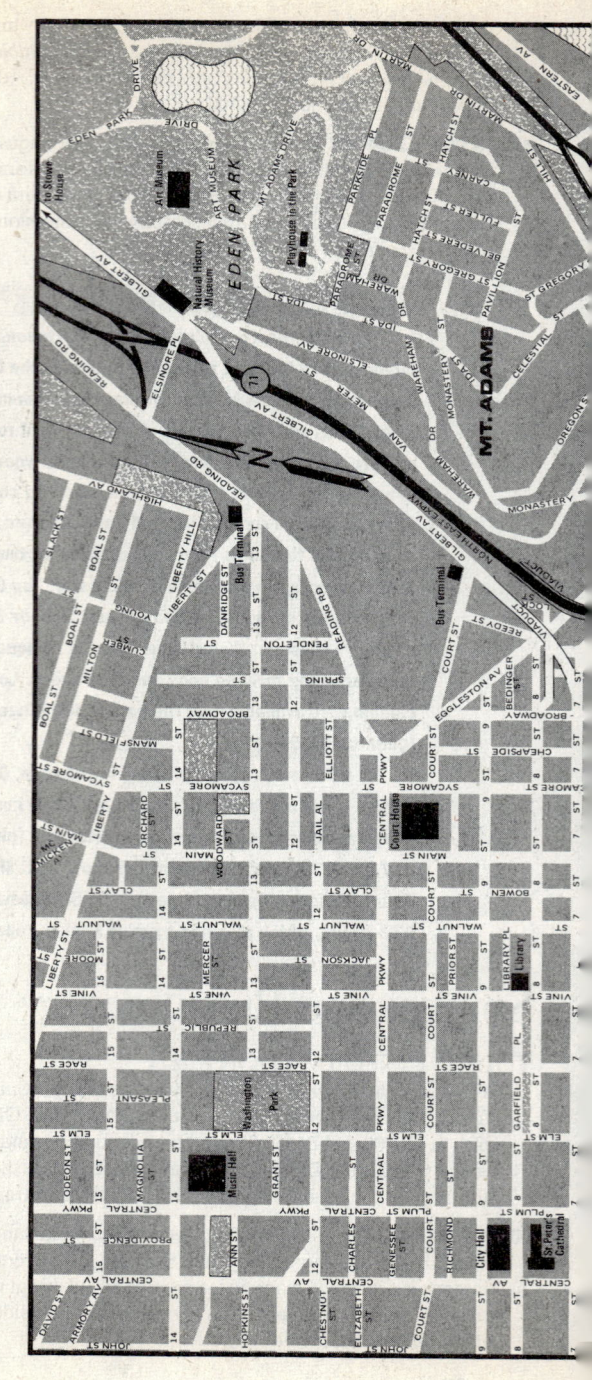

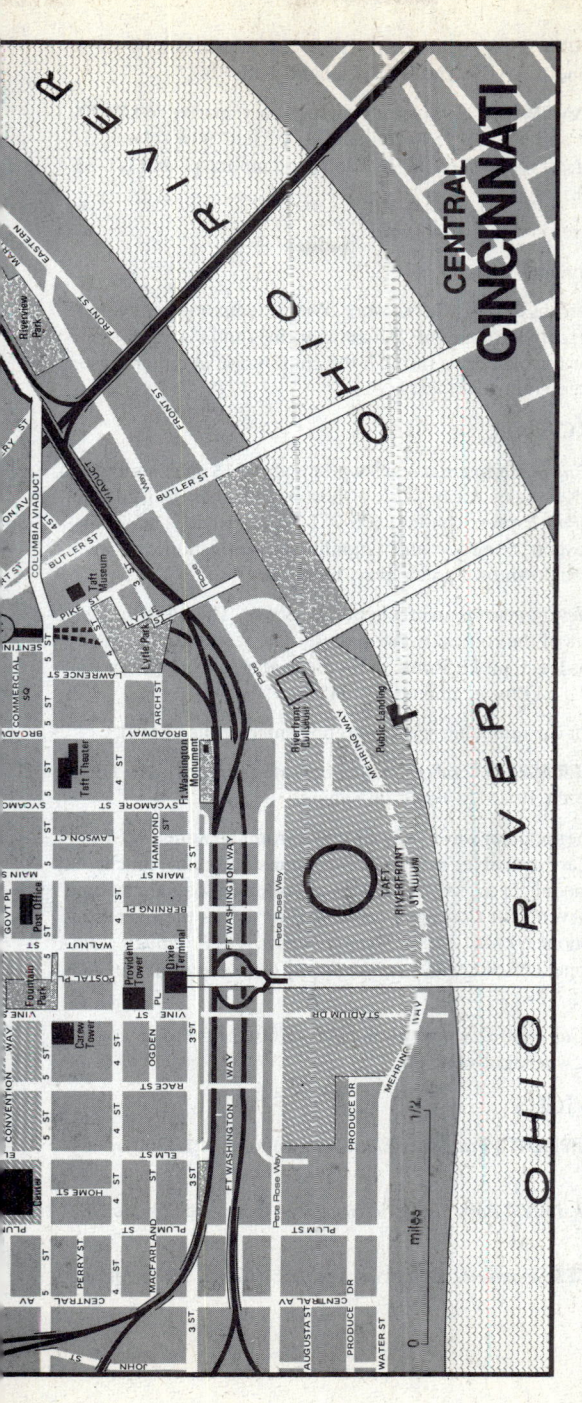

TELEVISION STATIONS WLWT Channel 5–NBC; WCPO Channel 9–CBS; WKRC Channel 12–ABC; and WCET Channel 48–PBS.

RADIO STATIONS AM: WKRC 550 (adult contemporary/sports); WLW 700 (sports/talk); and WCKY 1530 (talk). FM: WGUC 90.9 (classical); WWEZ 92.5 (soft rock); WRRM 98 (adult contemporary); and WUBE 105 (country).

TELEPHONE The area code for Cincinnati is 513.

SALES TAX The city sales tax is 5½%.

CLIMATE Cincinnati has four distinct seasons. Winter temperatures average 31F; summer temperatures, 76F. Blossomy springs and blazing falls are pleasanter for travel; a drive through the countryside in either season is a joy, but keep rain gear handy.

GETTING AROUND

AIRPORT *Greater Cincinnati International Airport* is about 13 miles southwest of the city in Kentucky. A trip to the airport by cab takes from 20 to 30 minutes. *Jet Port Express* (phone: 606-767-3702) provides bus transportation between the airport and major hotels. Buses shuttle between the airport and downtown hotels every half hour.

BUS *Queen City Metro* operates an excellent bus service. The bus stop signs carry numbers of the routes that stop there. The fare, which varies by destination, is less than $1. Route maps are available from *Queen City Metro* (122 West Fifth St.; phone: 621-4455).

CAR RENTAL Major car rental agencies are represented at the airport.

HORSE-DRAWN CARRIAGES Several companies operate carriages in the Fountain Square area. Board at Fountain Square.

RIVERBOAT Another popular way to see the city is from the water. *BB Riverboats* vessels are available for one- to two-hour sightseeing; luncheon, dinner, and moonlight cruises; or day-long adventures. Boats are moored at Madison Avenue at *Covington Landing* (just across the river from Cincinnati; phone 606-261-8500). Also try *Barleycorn's Riverboats* (Ludlow, KY; phone: 606-581-0300) or *The Star of Cincinnati* (phone: 723-0100).

TAXI Call *Yellow Cab* (860 Dellway; phone: 241-2100), or go to any of the major hotels, where cabs line up.

LOCAL SERVICES

AUDIOVISUAL EQUIPMENT *Visual Aids Electronics* (phone: 421-1300 or 684-0800).

BABY-SITTING *Jack and Jill Baby Sitting Service* (5234 Rose Ave.; phone: 731-5261).

BUSINESS SERVICES *Secretarial Office Services, Inc.* (*Carew Tower;* phone: 381-2277).

COMPUTER RENTAL *Peter Paul Office Equipment* (phone: 721-0865), one-week minimum; *Scot Business Machines* (phone: 421-9030), daily, weekly, or monthly.

DRY CLEANER/TAILOR *Teasdale Fentor Cleaners* (236 E. Sixth St.; phone: 241-4074).

LIMOUSINE *Adams Superior Limousine Service* (phone: 761-7734); *Washington Limousine Service* (phone: 221-0074).

MECHANIC *Certified Car Care* (412 Liberty St., between Central Ave. and John St.; phone: 721-2886).

MEDICAL EMERGENCY *Jewish Hospital Medical Center* (417 Vine St., across from the *Westin* hotel; phone: 241-3322), weekdays 8 AM to 6 PM.

MESSENGER SERVICES *Cincinnati Express* (phone: 721-1900).

MONEY TRANSFERS *American Express MoneyGram* (phone: 800-926-9400 for information; 800-866-8800 for money transfers); *Western Union Financial Services* (phone: 800-325-6000 or 800-325-4176).

NATIONAL/INTERNATIONAL COURIER *DHL Worldwide Express* (phone: 800-225-5345); *FedEx* (phone: 530-5660), closed Sundays.

PHARMACY *Walgreens* (121 E. Fifth St.; phone: 721-0840), open weekdays from 7 AM to 6 PM, Saturdays from 9 AM to 5 PM.

PHOTOCOPIES *Quik Graphics* (615 Main St.; phone: 241-5100).

POST OFFICE Downtown (Fifth and Walnut Sts.; phone: 684-5664).

PROFESSIONAL PHOTOGRAPHER *Corporate Photo Group* (phone: 241-8273); *Mayhew & Peper Photographers* (phone: 421-0111).

TRANSLATOR *Berlitz* (phone: 381-4650); *Inlingua* (phone: 721-8782).

WESTERN UNION/TELEX Many offices are located around the city (phone: 800-325-6000 to find the location nearest you).

SPECIAL EVENTS

Ever since 1873, Cincinnati has celebrated its annual *May Festival:* This series of concerts, often featuring opera superstars, is the oldest continuing choral festival in the Western Hemisphere. It is held at the *Music Hall* (1241 Elm St.; phone: 721-8222) during the last two weekends in May. The *Jack Nicklaus Sports Center* at *Kings Island* (6042 Fairway Dr., Mason) hosts the *Senior PGA Tour Classic* in July (phone: 398-5742) and the annual *ATP Tournament* in August (phone: 651-2872). In mid-September, Cincinnati celebrates its German heritage with an *Oktoberfest,* similar to the famous Munich festival, in and around Fountain Square.

SPORTS AND FITNESS

Cincinnati is one of the country's most enthusiastic baseball cities, and it favors football as well.

BASEBALL The *Reds* play at *Riverfront Stadium* (201 E. Pete Rose Way; phone: 421-REDS).

BASKETBALL The *University of Cincinnati Bearcats* play in *Shoemaker Hall* on campus in Clifton (phone: 556-2287), and the *Xavier University Musketeers* play at the *Cincinnati Gardens* (2250 Seymour Ave.; phone: 745-3411).

BICYCLING There is a 6.2-mile (10-km) bike trail at *Airport Playfield, Lunken Airport* (Wilmer Ave.; phone: 321-6500). In summer months, call to see if rental bikes are available.

FISHING There's moderately good fishing at Lake Isabella, Winton Woods (the largest of the county lakes), and in the Ohio River. Serious Cincinnati sportfishers drive four hours to Lake Cumberland and Kentucky Lake in southern Kentucky.

FITNESS CENTER The *YMCA* (1105 Elm St.; phone: 241-5348) provides a pool, sauna, equipment, and a track, as well as an outdoor jogging map; it is open to non-members for a fee.

FOOTBALL The *NFL Bengals* play at *Riverfront Stadium* (201 E. Pete Rose Way; phone: 621-3550).

GOLF For spectators and golfers, the *Jack Nicklaus Sports Center* (6042 Fairway Dr., Mason; phone: 398-5200) is among the best. Also consider the *Glenview* and *Neumann* city courses or county links in *Winton Woods* and *Sharon Woods* parks.

HORSE RACING Enthusiasts should check out the action at the *River Downs* (6301 Kellogg Ave.; phone: 232-8000) and *Turfway* racecourses (7500 Turfway Rd., Florence, KY; phone: 606-371-0200; 800-733-0200).

JOGGING For a 6-mile jaunt, follow tree-lined Central Parkway to Ludlow Street and come back; or run back and forth across the Ohio River Suspension Bridge, designed by Brooklyn Bridge builder John A. Roebling. The *Cincinnati Recreation Commission* publishes a free brochure, *Healthline Fitness Course,* available at the convention and visitors bureau.

SWIMMING A good public pool is *Sunlite Pool* at Coney Island just before *River Downs* (on Rte. 50; phone: 232-8230); call ahead. There are lake beaches at nearby Hueston Woods in Butler County and Caesar's Creek in Warren County.

THEATER
We start with our favorite place in Cincinnati for live theater.

CENTER STAGE

Cincinnati Playhouse in the Park World premieres of plays by new American playwrights, classics, rarely presented works, musicals, and comedies are the staples on the two stages of this much-praised regional professional theater, which operates year-round. Its lavish production of Dickens's *A Christmas Carol* is an annual yuletide tradition. (The two theaters are wheelchair accessible and have a sound-enhancement system, large-print *Playbills,* and signed and audio-described performances.) Mt. Adams Circle, *Eden Park* (phone: 421-3888; 800-582-3208 in Ohio).

The city's other major theater, the *Taft* (Fifth and Sycamore; phone: 721-0411) features touring companies, and has spring, fall, and winter seasons. The *University of Cincinnati* produces plays during the spring, summer, and fall on its *Showboat Majestic* (moored downtown; phone: 241-6550).

MUSIC

The internationally famous *Cincinnati Symphony Orchestra*, founded in 1895, has a September to May season at the *Music Hall* (1241 Elm St.; phone: 381-3300); its summer home is the *Riverbend Music Center* (6295 Kellogg Ave.; phone: 381-3300 or 232-6220). The *College Conservatory of Music* is one of the nation's oldest and most prominent professional music schools; it offers frequent concerts and recitals on the *University of Cincinnati* campus (Corbett Drive; phone: 556-4183). The *Cincinnati Opera* (phone: 241-ARIA), the second-oldest opera company in the US, performs at the downtown *Music Hall*, as does the *Cincinnati Ballet* (phone: 621-5219; 749-4949 for ticket information), whose *Music Hall* performances of *The Nutcracker* each December are part of Cincinnati's holiday tradition.

NIGHTCLUBS AND NIGHTLIFE

Cincinnati is pretty much a couples' town. The most popular nightspots are *Caddy's* (phone: 721-3636) and *Flanagan's Landing* (phone: 421-4055); both are on West Pete Rose Way. Just across the Ohio River, on the Kentucky riverfront, are *Covington Landing Entertainment Complex*, with a variety of nightclubs, bars, and eateries (phone: 606-291-9992); *Barleycorn's Yacht Club* (phone: 606-292-2978); and the *Waterfront* (phone: 606-581-1414). Cincinnati hotel bars that swing into the wee hours include *Joe's Bar (Terrace)*, *Fifth and Vine Street Bar (Westin)*, *Champs (Hyatt)*, *Palm Court (Netherland)*, the *Cricket (Cincinnatian)*, and the bar atop the *Regal Cincinnatian* (see *Checking In*). There also are numerous nightspots at the top of Mt. Adams.

Best in Town

CHECKING IN

Cincinnati's accommodations rival those of any other comparably sized US city. Expect to pay between $100 and $195 per night for a double room at any hotel listed as expensive, and $70 to $100 at moderate places; there are no exceptional inexpensive hotels in the city. For bed and breakfast accommodations, contact *Ohio Valley Bed and Breakfast* (11557 Taylor Mill Rd., Independence, KY 41051; phone: 606-356-7848). Unless otherwise noted, hotel rooms have air conditioning, private baths, TV sets, and telephones. All hotels are in the 513 area code unless otherwise indicated.

EXPENSIVE

Cincinnatian This restored 112-year-old landmark provides European-style elegance that has made it the city's premier hotel. There are 146 well-appointed rooms, some with balconies overlooking an eight-story atrium. Its elegant *Palace* restaurant (see *Eating Out*) serves American regional food. Amenities include a full health and fitness center, 24-hour room service, a concierge, four meeting rooms, secretarial services, A/V equipment, photocopiers, computers, and express checkout. One block from Fountain Sq. at 601 Vine St. (phone: 381-3000; 800-942-9000; fax: 651-0256).

Hyatt Regency It has 485 rooms, 12 suites, and a health club, including a pool. *Champs Italian Chop House* (see *Eating Out*) features Italian specialties, seafood dishes, and steaks; *Findlay's* has more casual dining and breakfast buffet on Sundays. Amenities include room service until midnight, a concierge, 18 meeting rooms, A/V equipment, photocopiers, and express checkout. There's also valet parking. 151 W. Fifth St. (phone: 579-1234; 800-233-1234; fax: 579-0107).

Omni Netherland Plaza One of the city's finest, it's connected by the Skywalk to the *Convention Center*, with lots of meeting space of its own (18 meeting rooms; capacity for 1,200), and the *Tower Place Shopping Mall*. In addition to its 610 rooms, there are 11 suites. Dining can be either formal at *Orchids at the Palm Court* (see *Eating Out*) or a bit more casual at the *Café at the Palm Court*. Amenities include a fully equipped health club with an indoor pool, 24-hour room service, a concierge, A/V equipment, photocopiers, computers, and express checkout. 35 W. Fifth St. (phone: 421-9100; 800-THE-OMNI; fax: 421-4291).

Westin Overlooking Fountain Square, this 17-story downtown property has 448 rooms and 18 suites. The *Fifth Street Market* offers casual dining. There's also a pool, fitness center, whirlpool, and sauna. Additional amenities include 24-hour room service, a concierge, express checkout, 17 meeting rooms, and a business center offering secretarial services, A/V equipment, photocopiers, and computers. Fountain Sq. (phone: 621-7700; 800-228-3000; fax: 852-5670).

MODERATE

Embassy Suites Northeast Cincinnati's finest suburban hotel is located 12 miles from downtown and 8 miles from *Kings Island*. Each of the 235 two-room suites has a wet bar, refrigerator, and microwave. There is also a restaurant and lounge. Amenities include complimentary breakfast and cocktail hour, room service until 10 PM, nine meeting rooms, secretarial services, A/V equipment, and express checkout. 4554 Lake Forest Dr., Blue Ash (phone: 733-8900; 800-EMBASSY; fax: 733-3720).

Kings Island Inn A favorite of golfers, since it's near the Jack Nicklaus course, this Alpine chalet–style hostelry offers good accommodations in an attractive setting. In addition to its 288 rooms, it has indoor and outdoor pools, a playground, tennis courts, a gameroom, a cocktail lounge with entertainment, a dining room, and bus service to *Kings Island* theme park. There are also two conference centers, as well as room service from 7 AM to 2 PM and 5 PM to 10 PM Mondays through Saturdays, a concierge desk during the summer, photocopiers, and express checkout. 5691 Kings Island Dr., Mason (phone: 398-0115; 800-727-3050; fax: 398-1095).

Regal Cincinnatian Business travelers and conventioneers stay at this very modern, 887-room downtown place (formerly the *Clarion*) with a heated outdoor pool, health club, sauna, lounge, restaurant, barber, and valet parking. Diners can get a panoramic view from its restaurant. Amenities include room service until 2 AM, a concierge, 14 meeting rooms, secretarial services, A/V equipment, photocopiers, computers, and express checkout. Connected by the Skywalk to the *Convention Center*. 141 W. Sixth St. (phone: 352-2100; 800-876-2100; fax: 352-2148).

EATING OUT

Cincinnati's most notable gastronomic eccentricity is its chili, which usually is served over spaghetti, to which may be added cheese ("three-way"), cheese and raw onions ("four-way"), or cheese, raw onions, and beans ("five-way"). Many of the city's finest restaurants are found in its hotels. At restaurants listed as expensive, expect to pay at least $50 to $75 for dinner for two; between $25 and $50 at those places designated as moderate; and under $25 at places listed as inexpensive. Prices do not include drinks, wine, tax, or tips. Unless otherwise noted, restaurants are open for lunch and dinner. All restaurants are in the 513 area code unless otherwise indicated

EXPENSIVE

Maisonette It may be in an unlikely spot but it's one of the best French restaurants in the country. Its food has consistently won major awards, and the service is friendly and warm. Closed Sundays; dinner only on Saturdays and Mondays. Reservations necessary. Major credit cards accepted. 114 E. Sixth St. (phone: 721-2260).

Morton's of Chicago Award-winning steaks are the specialty of this elegant, club-like restaurant. Its intimate mahogany bar is one of Cincinnati's in spots. Oriental rugs and mahogany walls decorate the stunning boardroom. Open daily except major holidays; dinner only on weekends. Reservations advised. Major credit cards accepted. *Tower Place Shopping Mall*, at Fourth and Race Sts. (phone: 241-4104).

Orchids at the Palm Court Diners can feast on well-prepared, sophisticated Midwestern fare, including grilled steaks presented with a variety of exquisite sauces in a splendidly restored Art Deco setting. Open daily. Reservations advised. Major credit cards accepted. *Omni Netherland Plaza*, 35 W. Fifth St. (phone: 421-9100).

Palace This highly acclaimed restaurant in the *Cincinnatian* epitomizes elegance. The menu changes each season, but it often features exquisite versions of rack of lamb, veal steaks, and seafood dishes. Open daily. Reservations advised. Major credit cards accepted. 601 Vine St. (phone: 381-3000).

Restaurant at the Phoenix In what was once an exclusive turn-of-the-century men's club, there is elegant dining in the *President's Dining Room* (the former library) or the less formal *Chef's Dining Room* (adjoining the glass-walled kitchen). An excellent contemporary American menu and an award-winning wine list are offered. Open for dinner only; closed Sundays and Mondays. Reservations advised. Major credit cards accepted. 812 Race St. (phone: 721-2255).

Waterfront Afloat directly across the Ohio River from downtown, it offers a spectacular skyline view along with its gustatory specialties—fresh grilled seafood, a raw bar, and steaks. Upstairs, the casual *Sports Rock Café* mingles good food with music, dancing, and televised sports. Open daily for dinner only; café open for lunch on weekends. Reservations advised. Major credit cards accepted. 14 Pete Rose Pier, Covington, KY (phone: 606-581-1414).

MODERATE

Champs Italian Chop House Regional Italian specialties, steaks, and fresh seafood dishes are the mainstays of the menu. An unusual attraction here is the exposed kitchen, so diners can watch their food being prepared. Closed Sundays. Reservations advised. Major credit cards accepted. *Hyatt Regency Hotel,* 151 W. Fifth St. (phone: 579-1234).

Forest View Gardens Waiters and waitresses sing your favorite show tunes and serve tasty German and American food in a garden setting. The *Dining Room/Showplace* is open for dinner only; closed Mondays through Wednesdays. Reservations necessary. Its *Edelweiss Room* is open for lunch on weekdays and for dinner Tuesdays through Sundays; reservations advised for parties of six or more. A special luncheon show on the third Thursday of the month; reservations advised. Major credit cards accepted. 4508 N. Bend Rd., a 15-minute drive from downtown (phone: 661-6434).

Mallorca This authentic Spanish restaurant serves gargantuan portions of ambitious dishes, including *paella valenciana,* clams in green sauce, and broiled Spanish sausage. There are also seafood dishes, veal, and marinated baby goat. Open daily. Reservations advised. Major credit cards accepted. 124 E. Sixth St. (phone: 723-9506).

Mike Fink An authentic riverboat, moored on the Kentucky side of the Ohio River, it is famous for its raw bar, in addition to traditional tableside service. Open daily; breakfast served on Sundays. Reservations advised. Major credit cards accepted. At the foot of Greenup St., Covington, KY (phone: 606-261-4212).

Montgomery Inn at the Boathouse The latest jewel in the crown of Ted Gregory, Cincinnati's restaurant king. The barbecued loin back ribs and chicken are laudable, and the wonderful view attracts celebrities. The sampler platter of appetizers is a must. Open daily. Reservations advised. Major credit cards accepted. 925 Eastern Ave., adjacent to Sawyer Point (phone: 721-7427).

La Normandie Grill Adjacent to the *Maisonette,* this steakhouse is renowned for its chops and fresh seafood. Casual conviviality is its hallmark. Closed Sundays and major holidays; dinner only on Saturdays. Reservations advised. Major credit cards accepted. 118 E. Sixth St. (phone: 721-2761).

Pigalls Café This fine restaurant is located in a downtown landmark building near the *Convention Center*. The atmosphere is casual and the bar is lively. Don't miss the goat cheese pizza with spinach, artichoke hearts, and olive-walnut pesto. Closed Sundays. Reservations advised. Major credit cards accepted. 127 West Fourth St. (phone: 651-2233).

Precinct Located in a turn-of-the-century police precinct house, five minutes from downtown, this award-winning place is a good choice for an evening of dining and chatting with friends over what some say are the best steaks in town. Other selections include veal, pasta, and fresh seafood. Open daily for dinner only. Reservations advised. Major credit cards accepted. 311 Delta Ave. at Columbia Pkwy. (phone: 321-5454).

Primavista Reputed to be the city's finest Italian restaurant, this establishment offers beef, chicken, veal, seafood, and pasta specialties complemented by a splendid view of the Cincinnati skyline and the Ohio River. Open for dinner only; closed most major holidays. Reservations advised. Major credit cards accepted. 810 Matson Pl. (phone: 251-6467).

Terrace Garden Located a block from Fountain Square atop the *Terrace* hotel, this eatery offers outstanding American and continental fare, along with a stunning view of downtown. The fresh salmon, chicken, and steaks are fine dinner entrées, and the Sunday breakfast buffet is especially good. Open daily. Reservations advised for groups of more than eight. Major credit cards accepted. 15 W. Sixth St. (phone: 381-4000).

INEXPENSIVE

Barleycorn's Yacht Club This riverfront dining spot across from the stadium has a wonderful view of the Cincinnati skyline. The fare is casual—the Buffalo chicken wings are favorites. Open daily. Reservations unnecessary. Major credit cards accepted. 201 Riverboat Row, Newport, KY (phone: 606-292-2978).

Rookwood Pottery Atop Mt. Adams, in the original kilns of the historic Rookwood Pottery building, patrons devour gigantic burgers and overindulge at the do-it-yourself ice cream sundae bar. Open daily. Reservations unnecessary. Major credit cards accepted. 1077 Celestial St. (phone: 721-5456).

WHAT'S HOT

Sensational, soul-satisfying chili, rich with meat, kidney beans, tomato sauce, and spices, has been a mainstay of the Cincinnati diet ever since immigrant Greek restaurant owners started cooking a batch in case they ran out of other fare. Now there are innumerable chains devoted exclusively to this hearty dish, including *Skyline Chili* (4180 Thunderbird La.; phone: 874-1188) and *Goldstar Chili* (5204 Beechmont Ave.; phone: 231-4541). The secret behind the unique taste may never be revealed, for chili makers everywhere guard their recipes, but rumor has it that chocolate is the latest ingredient.

Cleveland

At-a-Glance

SEEING THE CITY

Stouffer's Top of the Town restaurant (100 Erieview Plaza; phone: 771-1600) offers a panoramic view of Cleveland, the downtown, the nearby *Galleria,* and Lake Erie with its recreation and shipping activity. The *Terminal Tower*'s 42nd-floor observation deck (Public Sq.; phone: 621-7981) is open weekends. Admission charge.

SPECIAL PLACES

Many of Cleveland's most interesting sights are served by public transportation, but stroll around the city anyway, particularly in the University Circle area, the cultural heart of Cleveland, and in the lovely suburbs of Shaker Heights and Chagrin Falls.

DOWNTOWN

PUBLIC SQUARE In the heart of the business area, this is a good place to get one's bearings. Statues pay tribute to the city's founder Moses Cleaveland and to populist reform mayor Tom Johnson; and the *Soldiers and Sailors Monument* commemorates Cleveland's Civil War dead. Dominating the square are the world headquarters of BP America and the 52-story *Terminal Tower* built by the Van Sweringen brothers on the eve of the stock market crash that leveled their vast empire. *Terminal Tower* is the nucleus of the *Tower City Center,* which connects to the *Ritz-Carlton* and *Stouffer Tower City Plaza* hotels. Bounded by Euclid Ave., Superior Ave., and Ontario St.

THE ARCADE This 19th-century marketplace is a multitiered structure topped by a stunning block-long skylight of steel and glass. Bookstores, boutiques, eateries, and galleries line the arcade. At lunchtime, local musicians offer free classical, pop, and jazz concerts. 401 Euclid Ave. (phone: 621-8500).

UNIVERSITY CIRCLE AREA

CLEVELAND MUSEUM OF ART A major American museum, and one of the few that is still free to the public, this private institution boasts an enviable collection of more than 30,000 works of art representing all periods and cultures—ancient Egypt, Greece, and Rome; the Near and Far East; India; Europe; America; Africa; and the pre-Columbian Americas. Galleries are organized chronologically, with decorative arts pieces displayed alongside paintings and sculpture of the same period and place. The Asian collection is one of the finest in the Western world, and the museum has particularly fine medieval, European painting, and decorative arts collections. In recent years, the museum has been developing its collection of contemporary art and photography. Throughout the year there are frequent concerts and films, with gallery talks every afternoon except Mondays. The original 1916 building overlooks a garden and lagoon; a 1970 wing, designed by Marcel Breuer, houses special exhibition galleries, the musical arts department, and the education department (one of the largest professionally staffed education departments in the country). The *Museum Café* connects to an outdoor sculpture garden. A number of Cleveland's other cultural institutions face the museum across a grassy oval. Closed Mondays. 11150 East Blvd. at University Circle (phone: 421-7340).

WESTERN RESERVE HISTORICAL SOCIETY The largest collection of Shaker memorabilia in the world is here, including inventions such as the clothespin, the ladder-back chair, and farming implements and furnishings. There are also an extensive genealogical collection, exhibitions on Indians and pioneers, and a gift shop. At the same location is the *Crawford Auto-Aviation Museum,* with 200 antique autos and old airplanes; displays trace the evolution of the automobile and describe Cleveland's prominence as an early car manufacturing center. Visit the museum's restoration shop. Closed Mondays. Admission charge. 10825 East Blvd. (phone: 721-5722).

CLEVELAND MUSEUM OF NATURAL HISTORY Exhibitions of armored fish and sharks found preserved in Ohio shales, a 70-foot mounted dinosaur, skeletons of mastodon and mammoth, and *Lucy,* the most complete fossil of one of the ancestors of *Homo sapiens,* are all here. The museum also has a planetarium and observatory. Open daily. Admission charge. Wade Oval Dr. at University Circle (phone: 231-4600).

CLEVELAND PLAY HOUSE More than 75 years old and designed by renowned architect Philip Johnson, this is reputed to be one of the finest theaters in the nation, with productions that range from Shakespearean tragedies to contemporary plays, including Broadway tryouts. No tours are offered. 8500 Euclid Ave. (phone: 795-7000).

CLEVELAND CENTER FOR CONTEMPORARY ART The major works of American-born, internationally acclaimed artists such as Roy Lichtenstein, Jasper Johns, Red Grooms, and Andy Warhol are exhibited in this stunning gallery. A spiral staircase leads up to a balcony where you can get a bird's-eye view of the open space with its pristine white walls and hardwood floors. Closed Mondays. No admission charge. 8501 Carnegie Ave. (phone: 421-8671).

KARAMU HOUSE Founded in 1915, America's first interracial cultural center has hosted many of the country's finest African-American performers. Productions have included *Dreamgirls, Ain't Misbehavin',* and *Black Nativity,* a version of the *Christmas* tale by Langston Hughes that has become an annual yuletide tradition in Cleveland. 2355 E. 89th St. (phone: 795-7070).

CLEVELAND HEALTH EDUCATION MUSEUM A first of its kind, with exhibitions on the workings of the human body and health maintenance. See everything from a walk-through model of a human eye to *Juno,* the transparent woman, and the inspiring *Wonder of New Life* display. Open daily. Admission charge. 8911 Euclid Ave. (phone: 231-5010).

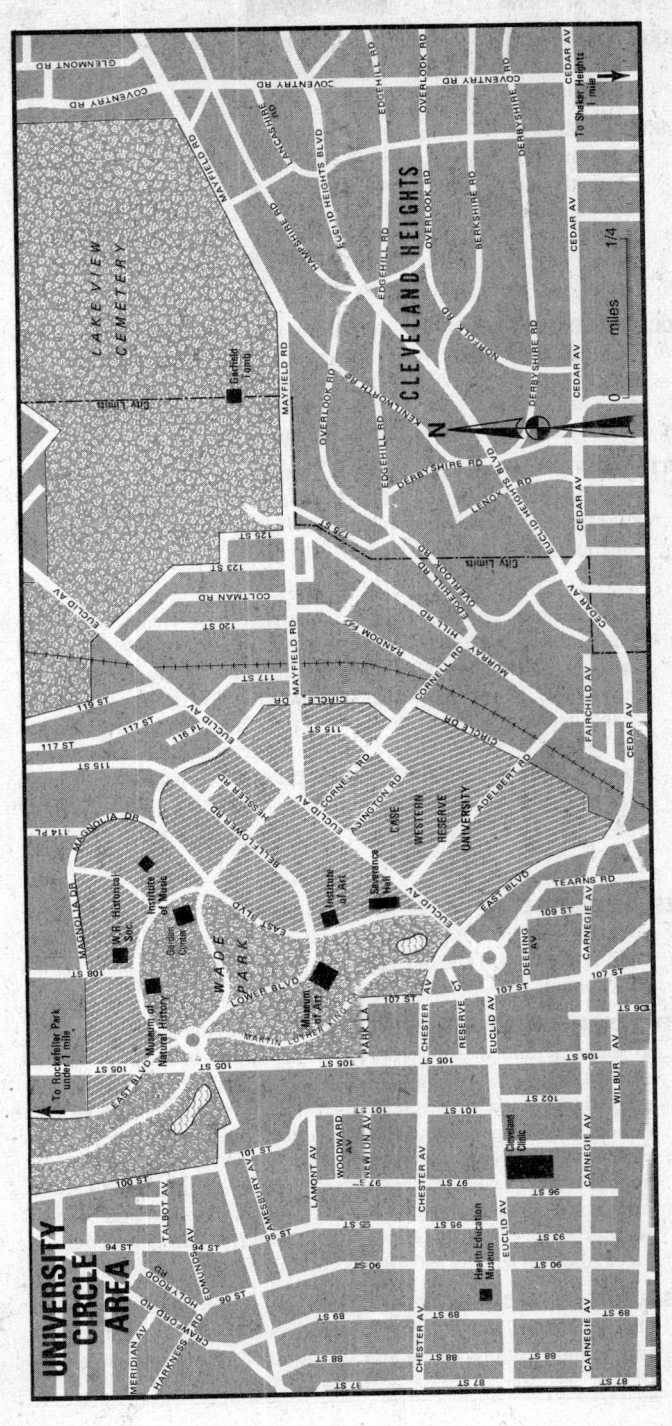

CLEVELAND CHILDREN'S MUSEUM Permanent and temporary exhibits explore science and nature. Closed Tuesdays. Admission charge. At 10730 Euclid Ave. (phone: 791-KIDS).

LAKE VIEW CEMETERY The plantings are beautiful, the view fine, and the company illustrious. Among the natives buried here are President Garfield (you can't miss the monument); Mark Hanna, a shipping magnate and US senator; John Hay, secretary of state under McKinley; and John D. Rockefeller, founder of the fortune. The *Garfield Monument* offers a great view of downtown. Closed December through May. 12316 Euclid Ave. (phone: 421-2665).

ROCKEFELLER PARK This 296-acre park features the *Cultural Gardens* (between East Blvd. and Martin Luther King Jr. Dr.), a series of gardens with sculptures representing the 20 nationalities that settled the city. The *City Greenhouse* has a *Japanese Garden*, tropical plants, and a *Talking Garden* (with audio descriptions). 750 E. 88th St. (phone: 664-3103).

LITTLE ITALY This ethnic neighborhood, just around the corner from University Circle, is filled with artists' galleries and studios, especially along Murray Hill Road. Gallery walks are held here regularly. For fresh, hot doughnuts, visit *Presti's* (1211 Mayfield Rd.).

SHAKER HEIGHTS

One of the most affluent suburbs in America, Shaker Heights was developed in the early 1900s by brothers O. P. and M. J. Van Sweringen and now houses Cleveland's elite in lovely old homes on wide, winding, tree-lined streets. The area was originally Shaker Lakes, the rural commune established by the 19th-century religious sect that left American industrial life for a religious regime featuring strict celibacy. Today, all that remains of the Shakers are the *Shaker Historical Museum* (16740 South Park; phone: 921-1201), and the *Shaker Cemetery* (Lee Rd. at Chagrin Blvd.).

WEST SIDE

WEST SIDE MARKET One of the largest Old World indoor markets in the country, it offers fresh produce, meat, and baked goods year-round. Closed Tuesdays, Thursdays, and Sundays. 1979 W. 25th St. at Lorain Ave. (phone: 664-3386).

CLEVELAND METROPARKS ZOO AND THE RAINFOREST Among the oldest zoos in America (and, at 165 acres, one of the largest in the Midwest), its exhibits include *Birds of the World,* an indoor/outdoor aviary with feathered friends from the seven continents; *Northern Trek,* with Bactrian camels, white-lipped deer, and other animals from the northern plains of Asia; and a greenhouse with 300 different plant species. The $30-million *RainForest* features more than 600 species of animals and insects from seven continents and simulates a tropical thunderstorm every 20 minutes or so. Closed *Christmas* and *New Year's Day.* No admission charge for children under two. 3900 Brookside Park Dr. (phone: 661-6500).

NASA LEWIS RESEARCH CENTER The NASA complex and its visitors' center offer exhibitions, lectures, and films on aeronautics, energy, space travel, and communications. There also are tours of a propulsion systems laboratory and a supersonic wind tunnel. Open daily. No admission charge. 21000 Brookpark Rd. (phone: 267-1187).

> ### EXTRA SPECIAL
>
> *The Pro Football Hall of Fame* (2121 George Halas Dr. NW; phone: 456-8207; 456-7762 for recorded information) is in Canton, 53 miles south of Cleveland on I-77. Inside are mementos of the game and its players, as well as a research library. Open daily. Admission charge. On the way, you may want to stop at *Hale Farm Village* (2686 Oak Hill Rd., Bath; phone: 575-9137 in Cleveland; 666-3711 in Akron), where you'll find homesteads, crafts shops, and a working farm typical of those of the Western Reserve between 1825 and 1850. Closed Mondays. Admission charge.
>
> You also can stop in Akron for a tour of the *Stan Hywet Hall and Gardens* (714 N. Portage Path; phone: 836-5533), an excellent example of Tudor Revival architecture with 70 acres of gardens. Closed Mondays. Admission charge for house tour. Also check out the *Akron Art Museum* (70 E. Market St.; phone: 376-9185), a gem of a collection featuring contemporary exhibitions from video art to sculpture. Closed Mondays. No admission charge.
>
> In Kirtland, a town about 30 miles east of Cleveland, is *Holden Arboretum* (9500 Sperry Rd.; phone: 946-4400), one of the largest of its kind in the country. Closed Mondays. Admission charge. Another attraction here is *Lake Farmpark* (8800 Euclid-Chardon Rd.; phone: 256-2122), a working farm with agricultural exhibits and activities, a restaurant, and a gift shop. Open daily. Admission charge.

Sources and Resources

TOURIST INFORMATION

The *Convention and Visitors Bureau of Greater Cleveland* (3100 Tower City Center, Cleveland, OH 44113; phone: 621-4110; 621-8860 for events), which is closed weekends, is best for brochures, maps, and other information. For information on entertainment and dining, call the Cleveland Activity Line (phone: 899-1555). For the latest information on events around the city, call the visitor information hotline (phone: 800-321-1004). Contact the Ohio state tourism hotline (phone: 800-BUCKEYE) for maps, calendars of events, health updates, and travel advisories.

LOCAL COVERAGE *Cleveland Plain Dealer*, morning daily; *Northern Ohio LIVE*, monthly; and *Cleveland* magazine, monthly. All are available at newsstands.

TELEVISION STATIONS WKYC Channel 3–NBC; WEWS Channel 5–ABC; WJW Channel 8–CBS; WVIZ Channel 25–PBS; and WOIO Channel 19–Fox.

RADIO STATIONS AM: WWWE 1100 (talk/sports) and WERE 1360 (talk). FM: WCLV 95.5 (classical) and WMMS 100.7 (rock).

TELEPHONE The area code for Cleveland is 216.

SALES TAX The city sales tax is 7%.

CLIMATE Cleveland has cold and snowy winters followed by brief springs and humid summers. Fall is generally the most pleasant season, with mild, sunny weather that often extends through November.

GETTING AROUND

AIRPORT *Cleveland Hopkins International Airport* is a 20- to 30-minute drive from downtown. The *Regional Transit Authority*'s *Airport Rapid Transit* train runs from the airport to downtown's *Terminal Tower* in the same amount of time; the fare is $1.50.

BUS *Regional Transit Authority (RTA)* serves both downtown and the outlying areas. The fare is $1.25 for local buses; $1.50 for express buses. Complete route and tourist information is available from the downtown office. 615 W. Superior Ave. (phone: 621-9500).

CAR RENTAL Cleveland is served by the major national firms.

TAXI Cabs can be hailed in the street in the downtown area around Public Square or ordered on the phone. *Yellow Cab* (phone: 623-1500) and *AmeriCab* (phone: 881-1111) are the major operators.

TOURS From April through December, *Trolley Tours* (phone: 771-4484) takes visitors on city excursions daily in buses that resemble trolley cars; reservations are necessary. The *Goodtime III* boat tour (phone: 861-5110) is the best introduction to "the Flats"—the industrial valley along the river basin where Rockefeller and shipping magnates Sam Mather and Mark Hanna made their fortunes. The 1,000-passenger boat departs daily from May through October from the *East Ninth Street Pier* and goes down the Cuyahoga as far as the steel mills.

TRAIN *Rapid Transit* trains (fare, $1.50) serve the city's east and west sides.

LOCAL SERVICES

AUDIOVISUAL EQUIPMENT *Hughie's Audio Visual Center* (phone: 241-7731); *Presentation Techniques* (phone: 328-9009).

BABY-SITTING *Ba-B-Sit Service Enterprises* (592 Cahoon Rd.; phone: 871-9595).

BUSINESS SERVICES *Kelly Services* (1111 Superior Ave.; phone: 771-2800).

DRY CLEANER/TAILOR *Avon Cleaners* (1830 Superior Ave.; phone: 771-3636).

LIMOUSINE *American Academy Limousine Service* (phone: 221-9330).

MECHANIC *Park Auto Repair Co.* (2163 Hamilton Ave.; phone: 241-7390).

MEDICAL EMERGENCY *St. Vincent Charity Hospital* (2351 E. 22nd St.; phone: 363-2536).

MESSENGER SERVICES *Bonnie Speed Delivery* (phone: 696-6033); *Star Delivery Service* (phone: 241-2410).

MONEY TRANSFERS *American Express MoneyGram* (phone: 800-926-9400 for information; 800-866-8800 for money transfers); *Western Union Financial Services* (phone: 800-325-6000 or 800-325-4176).

NATIONAL/INTERNATIONAL COURIER *DHL Worldwide Express* (phone: 800-225-5345); *FedEx* (phone: 800-238-5355).

PHARMACY *Revco* (1400 E. Ninth St.; phone: 621-0132), open 7 AM to 11 PM.

PHOTOCOPIES *Original Copy Centers* (3333 Chester Ave.; phone: 881-3500); *Rapid Printing & Copy Center* (426 Superior Ave.; phone: 621-9777), after hours by arrangement.

POST OFFICE Central office (2400 Orange Ave.; phone: 443-4059; 443-4096 for information after 5 PM and on weekends); also a branch office (1200 Huron Rd.; phone: 861-2978).

PROFESSIONAL PHOTOGRAPHER *Shuba & Associates* (phone: 351-5080).

SECRETARY/STENOGRAPHER *Secretariat Inc.* (phone: 234-4913), word processing.

TELECONFERENCE FACILITIES *Marriott West* (see *Checking In,* below).

TRANSLATOR *Berlitz* (phone: 861-0950); *Language Bank of Cleveland* (phone: 781-4560).

WESTERN UNION/TELEX Many offices are located around the city (phone: 800-325-6000 to find the location nearest you).

SPECIAL EVENTS

Cleveland swings into high gear with the onset of spring. The *Cleveland Performance Art Festival* is held in March, and the *Tri-C Jazz Fest* and the *Cleveland International Film Festival* in April. Among the events in June are the *Boston Mills Art Festival;* the *Ohio Derby* horse race at *Thistledown Park* in Warrensville Heights (phone: 662-8600); *Parade the Circle* (phone: 791-3900), a festival celebrating the performing arts institutions in University Circle; and *Square to Square* (phone: 621-3300), a weekend of family entertainment, including dance and music performances, face painting, and contests, held on Euclid Ave. between Public and Playhouse squares. The *Budweiser Grand Prix, Annual Rib Burn-Off,* and *Riverfest* on the river are held in July. August sees the *Feast of the Assumption* in Little Italy, and fall festivities include the *Cleveland Air Show* and *Oktoberfest.* Annual *Holiday Lighting* takes place the day after *Thanksgiving* on Public Square.

MUSEUMS

In addition to those described in *Special Places* is the *Rock and Roll Hall of Fame and Museum* (phone: 781-ROCK), scheduled to open this year at *North Coast Harbor.* In Kent, 45 miles southeast of Cleveland, is the *Kent State University Fashion Museum* (Rockwell Hall, Main St.; phone:

672-3450), one of the finest collections of haute couture clothing in the country. Closed Mondays. Admission charge.

SHOPPING

You can buy anything you want in Cleveland because somewhere, someone is selling it. Besides the revitalized downtown shopping district, with its upscale *Galleria* and dazzling *Tower City Center,* there's Coventry Road in Cleveland Heights, which resembles New York's Greenwich Village, and *Beachwood Place,* a posh shopping mall in the suburb of Beachwood.

SPORTS AND FITNESS

BASEBALL The *American League Indians* play at the new *Jacobs Field* (2401 Ontario St.; phone: 420-4200) from April through early October.

BASKETBALL The *NBA Cavaliers* play at their new home, the *Arena at Gateway* (1 Center Court; phone: 420-2000) from mid-October through early April.

BICYCLING Rent from *U-Rent-Um of America* (15400 Brookpark Rd.; phone: 676-6776) or *Easy Rider Bicycle Shop* (3974 E. 131st St.; phone: 752-1555). The *Cuyahoga Falls Reservation* nearby has good biking trails.

FITNESS CENTERS The *13th Street Sports Club* (1901 E. 13th St.; phone: 696-1365) has exercise equipment and a track. It is open to guests of area hotels for a fee. The *Athletic Club* (1375 E. Ninth St.; phone: 621-0770) has a track, a pool, and exercise equipment. It is open to guests of the Sheraton and other hotels (check with your hotel).

FOOTBALL The *Browns* play pro ball at *Cleveland Municipal Stadium* (1085 W. Third St.; phone: 696-3800); the *Thunderbolts* play arena football, an indoor version of the game, at the *Arena at Gateway* (1 Center Court; phone: 351-2658).

GOLF *Punderson State Park* (Rtes. 44 and 87; phone: 564-5465) has the best public 18-hole golf course.

HIKING The *Cleveland Metroparks* circle the city, offering 19,000 acres with trails for the ambitious hiker. Also, the *Cuyahoga Valley National Recreation Area* links Cleveland and Akron with 22 miles of paths and walkways (phone: 526-5256).

HOCKEY The *International Hockey League Lumberjacks* play at the *Arena at Gateway* (1 Center Court; phone: 696-0909).

JOGGING Run along Euclid Avenue to Public Square and on to the Flats; stop in at *Koening Sporting Goods* at the *Galleria* (phone: 575-9900). Run at *Cleveland State University* (Euclid and E. 24th St.).

SOCCER The *National Professional Soccer League* Cleveland *Crunch* play at the *Cleveland State University Convocation Centre* (2000 Prospect Ave.; phone: 349-2090).

TENNIS The best public courts are at *Cain Park* (Superior Rd. at Lee Rd., Cleveland Heights; phone: 371-3000).

THEATER

For current offerings and performance times, check the publications listed in *Local Coverage* above. Cleveland has a variety of theatrical offerings, some locally produced, others traveling shows, including some pre-Broadway tryouts. Best bets for shows: *Cleveland Play House* (see *Special Places*); *Karamu House* (2355 E. 89th St.; phone: 795-7070) for multicultural performing arts; *Great Lakes Theater Festival, Ohio Theatre* (1501 Euclid Ave.; phone: 241-5490) for traditional drama from Shakespeare to Arthur Miller; *Eldred Theatre* (2070 Adelbert Rd.; phone: 368-6262) for an eclectic selection of 20th-century drama. *Cleveland Public Theatre* (6415 Detroit Ave.; phone: 631-2727) offers avant-garde performances. For big-name entertainment, try the *Playhouse Square Center* (1511 Euclid Ave.; phone: 241-6000). Also, the *Cleveland Ballet* (1 Playhouse Sq.; phone: 621-2260) is a must for dance lovers.

MUSIC

The *Cleveland Orchestra* performs with noted soloists and guest conductors from October through mid-May in *Severance Hall* (11001 Euclid Ave. at East Blvd.; phone: 231-1111). From June through early September, it plays at *Blossom Music Center* (1145 W. Steels Corner Rd., Cuyahoga Falls; phone: 566-9330), as do pop and rock bands and visiting orchestras.

NIGHTCLUBS AND NIGHTLIFE

Favorites are *Peabody's* (2140 S. Taylor Rd.; phone: 321-4072) for folk or blues; *Club Isabella* (2025 Abington Rd.; phone: 229-1177) for jazz; and the *Smart Bar* (1575 Merwin Ave.; phone: 522-1575), a trendy tavern with tasty teas and fruit juices in addition to alcoholic beverages. At *Mirage on the Water* (2510 Elm St.; phone: 348-1135), view the stars through a 20-foot retractable roof; or try *Trilogy Night Club* (2325 Elm St.; phone: 241-1444) for futuristic music in a restored warehouse. For comedy, try the *Improv*, in the *Powerhouse in the Flats* entertainment complex (2000 Sycamore St.; phone: 696-4677), or the *Hilarities Comedy Hall* (1230 W. Sixth St.; 781-7733), which offers local and national talent. Dueling pianos bring something different to the bar of *Howl at the Moon* (*Powerhouse in the Flats* complex, 2000 Sycamore St.; phone: 861-4695). Reggae fans should try the *Splash Nite Club* (1545 Merwin Ave.; phone: 589-9797), which has live bands and dancing.

Best in Town

CHECKING IN

Cleveland has a number of attractive and reasonably priced accommodations. Its newest hotel, the 207-room *Wyndham*, is scheduled to open this year. As an alternative to the major hotels, a company called *Private Lodgings* (PO Box 18590, Cleveland, OH 44118; phone: 321-3213) finds accommodations in private residences in a variety of price ranges. Expect to pay $150 or more per night for a double room at the hotels listed in the very expensive category; $110 to $150 at those listed as expensive; $60 to $110 at those categorized as moderate; and less than $60 at the inexpensive places. Unless otherwise noted, hotel rooms have air conditioning, private baths, TV sets, and telephones. All hotels are in the 216 area code unless otherwise indicated.

VERY EXPENSIVE

Omni International An elegant property 10 minutes from downtown, it has 330 guestrooms and 14 suites. All of the beautifully appointed rooms have large work desks, and the suites feature Jacuzzis and sitting areas with wet bars. *Classics* (see *Eating Out*) offers fine dining in a formal setting, and *Le Bistro* and *Le Café* serve more casual fare. Business services include foreign language interpreters, meeting rooms accommodating up to 500, a concierge, complimentary shuttle service to downtown and University Circle, photocopiers, A/V equipment, fax machines, and express checkout. 2065 E. 96th St. (phone: 791-1900; 800-THE-OMNI; fax: 231-3329).

Ritz-Carlton Conveniently located in the *Tower City Center* complex, it has 208 rooms and 19 suites with panoramic views of the city. The *Restaurant* offers elegant dining overlooking the riverfront, and high tea is served every afternoon in the lounge. There are banquet facilities, a ballroom, and a fitness center with pool, sauna, steamroom, and spa. Twice-daily maid service, 24-hour room service, a concierge, six meeting rooms, secretarial services, A/V equipment, photocopiers, and express checkout are some of the features. 1515 W. Third St. (phone: 623-1300; 800-241-3333; fax: 623-1492).

Stouffer Tower City Plaza This member of the *National Trust for Historic Preservation*'s Historic Hotels of America has 493 rooms and luxury suites, as well as three restaurants, one of which, *Sans Souci,* offers exquisitely prepared Mediterranean food. Special feature: a 10-story atrium complete with waterfall and swimming pool. Other amenities include 24-hour room service, a concierge, 10 meeting rooms, A/V equipment, photocopiers, computers, and express checkout. 24 Public Sq. (phone: 696-5600; 800-325-5000 or 800-HOTELS-1; fax: 696-3102).

EXPENSIVE

Marriott Society Center This 25-story hotel has 402 comfortably appointed rooms, a restaurant, a bar that serves light meals, a fitness center, and a gift shop. There are four meeting rooms and a ballroom, fax machines, teleconferencing services, A/V equipment, secretarial services, photocopiers, computers, and express checkout. 1360 W. Mall Dr. (phone: 696-9200; 800-228-9290; fax: 696-0966).

Marriott West Near the airport, Cleveland's best motor inn has 374 rooms, an indoor pool, a therapy pool, a sauna, miniature golf, a putting green, volleyball, and badminton. There is also the *Wintergarden* dining room, *Duke's* restaurant, a lounge with entertainment, and a coffee shop. Other amenities include a concierge desk, 13 meeting rooms, A/V equipment, photocopiers, a free airport bus, and express checkout. 4277 W. 150th St. (phone: 252-5333; 800-228-9290; fax: 251-1508).

MODERATE

Glidden House This stately mansion on University Circle, a short walk from the city's cultural center, has been transformed into an elegant bed and breakfast inn with 52 rooms and eight suites. Business facilities include three meeting rooms, secretarial services, and photocopiers. 1901 Ford Dr. (phone: 231-8900; fax: 231-2130).

Radisson Plaza The only all-suite downtown hotel, its 252 units have kitchens and work areas. There's also a pool, a restaurant, and a fitness center. Business facilities include four meeting rooms, A/V equipment, a fax machine, a photocopier, concierge services, and express checkout. 1701 E. 12th St. (phone: 523-8000; 800-333-3333; fax: 523-1698).

INEXPENSIVE

Alcazar A European-style property nestled in the trendy Cedar Hill area, 4 miles east of downtown. There are 110 rooms and 180 suites. Features include a full-service restaurant, heated garage, beauty salon, and laundromat. Surrey and Derbyshire Rds., Cleveland Heights (phone: 321-5400).

EATING OUT

Restaurants reflect the huge ethnic diversity of the city. Expect to pay $60 or more for dinner for two at places listed as expensive, $30 to $60 at those categorized as moderate, and less than $30 at inexpensive places. Prices do not include drinks, wine, tax, or tips. Unless otherwise noted, restaurants are open for lunch and dinner. All restaurants are in the 216 area code unless otherwise indicated.

EXPENSIVE

Classics This award-winning restaurant in the *Omni* hotel is known for its rack of lamb *persille* and steak Diane (both prepared at your table) and its special desserts. The inviting, intimate atmosphere, with live jazz and classical music playing in the background, perfectly complements the sophisticated fare. Closed Sundays; dinner only on Saturdays. Reservations advised. Major credit cards accepted. E. 96th St. and Carnegie Ave. (phone: 791-1300).

Giovanni's Pasta is prepared in delectable ways, and the veal and sweetbreads are equally satisfying. The decor is quite elegant, so dress accordingly. Closed Sundays. Reservations necessary. Major credit cards accepted. 2550 Chagrin Blvd., Beachwood (phone: 831-8625).

Hyde Park Grille This is the place for hearty meat eaters. Choose from steaks, filet mignon with king crab and béarnaise sauce, or an elegant chateaubriand for two, all served with delicately deep-fried onion crisps. Dark green upholstery and dark paneling complete the clubhouse atmosphere. There's jazz on weekends. Open daily. Reservations advised. Major credit cards accepted. 1825 Coventry Rd., Cleveland Heights (phone: 321-6444).

Johnny's Bar This tavern's trendiness belies its location—an old residential neighborhood. The menu features veal and shrimp with linguine, bell pepper pasta with shrimp, veal steaks, and filet mignon. Closed Sundays; dinner only on Saturdays. Reservations advised. Major credit cards accepted. 3164 Fulton Rd. (phone: 281-0055).

Parker's Flavorful French fare is prepared from fresh, organically grown ingredients. Specialties include medallions of pork, Belgian Blue beef, and free-range chicken. A delicate lemon soufflé is the house specialty dessert. Closed Sundays; prix fixe dinner only on Saturdays. Reservations necessary. Major credit cards accepted. 2801 Bridge Ave. in Ohio City (phone: 771-7130).

Sammy's Wooden beams and brick walls make this 116-year-old converted warehouse a real gem. The adventurous offerings include chicken in phyllo with vegetables, and rack of lamb with pistachio nut coating and black currant sauce. For dessert, there is *boule de neige,* a rum and chocolate espresso cake with whipped cream. This eatery also has one of the best raw seafood bars in the city and live jazz nightly. Closed Sundays. Reservations advised. Major credit cards accepted. 1400 W. 10th St. (phone: 523-5560).

Z Contemporary Cuisine Delectable West Coast–inspired fare, emphasizing grilled meat and fish. A house specialty is grilled chicken breast and skinny fried potatoes. Salads, pasta, and rich desserts are also worthwhile. Closed Sundays. Reservations necessary. Major credit cards accepted. 28601 Chagrin Blvd., Woodmere Village (phone: 591-1545).

MODERATE

Café Brio Fresh California-style fare blends perfectly with an open, airy decor. Make a meal of the raw bar and appetizers or enjoy an excellent Caesar salad, Southwestern pizza, grilled chicken breast, or the house specialty, linguine with pesto and pine nuts. There is also a nice selection of international wines. Open daily. Reservations advised. Major credit cards accepted. 5433 Mayfield Rd., Lyndhurst (phone: 473-1670).

Great Lakes Brewing Company A block from the *West Side Market,* this eatery is popular for lunch. As befits a brewery, beer is the main attraction, with a golden Dortmunder-style lager and a darker, porter-style ale among the award-winning selections. Homemade soups, walleye, perch, and other fish dishes give you something to go with the brews. Open daily. Reservations advised for dinner. Major credit cards accepted. 2516 Market Ave. (phone: 771-4404).

López y González Hearty portions of Mexican favorites—*tacos al carbón,* for example—are washed down with Mexican beer or oversize margaritas. Mesquite-smoked game hen, tequila chicken, and fresh fish round out the menu. Closed Sundays. Reservations advised. Major credit cards accepted. 2066 Lee Rd., Cleveland Heights (phone: 371-7611).

Pearl of the Orient Chinese food is carefully presented here. Worth noting are the house specialties: Peking duck and hot and sour soup. Open daily. Reservations necessary. Major credit cards accepted. 21021 Van Aken Blvd., Shaker Heights (phone: 751-8181).

That Place on Bellflower Set in a charming century-old carriage house, this is the fleur-de-lis of the city's French restaurants. Specialties are veal Oscar, *escalope* of veal, and fresh salmon renaissance (a combination of chopped salmon, onions, and spinach in pastry). In the summer, dining is alfresco. Closed Mondays; dinner only on Sundays. Reservations advised. Major credit cards accepted. 11401 Bellflower Rd., at University Circle (phone: 231-4469).

INEXPENSIVE

Balaton The atmosphere isn't much—bright lights and paper placemats—but the Hungarian food is the real thing. No alcoholic beverages are served. Closed Sundays and Mondays. No reservations or credit cards accepted. 12523 Buckeye Rd. (phone: 921-9691).

Ruthie and Moe's A refurbished 1920s railroad dining car is the unusual setting for this friendly, comfortable eatery dishing up down-home cooking. Homemade matzoh ball soup, chicken gumbo, and daily specials make this a hot spot both for business lunches and family outings. The Thai chicken salad is also popular. Closed Saturdays and Sundays. No reservations. MasterCard and Visa accepted. 4002 Prospect Ave. (phone: 431-8063).

Tommy's Hearty soups, salads, creative sandwiches, and tasty spinach pies are the vegetarian fare here, all served fast and hot. The decor is simple. Open daily. No reservations or credit cards accepted. 1820 Coventry Rd., Cleveland Heights (phone: 321-7757).

Dallas

At-a-Glance

SEEING THE CITY

For the best view of Dallas, go to the top of *Reunion Tower* (300 Reunion Blvd.; phone: 651-1234 or 741-3663), alongside the huge mirror-faced *Hyatt Regency* hotel, also a Dallas landmark. The tower has a revolving cocktail lounge, restaurant, and observation deck. Admission charge.

SPECIAL PLACES

Although attractions in Dallas are spread out, most of the museums are clustered at *Fair Park*.

FAIR PARK

Three miles east of downtown Dallas, *Fair Park* is the site of 24 attractions, including seven museums of science, history, and technology; the *Cotton Bowl Stadium*, site of the *New Year's Day* college football game; and *Fair Park Coliseum* (1300 Robert B. Cullum Blvd., two blocks south of I-30). Some 150 events take place throughout the park annually, but the biggest of them is the *State Fair of Texas* (phone: 565-9931; 800-375-1839), which lasts for three incredibly jammed weeks in October. Grand Ave. (phone: 426-3400; 890-2911 for a 24-hour information line).

MUSEUM OF NATURAL HISTORY In order to attract the *Texas Centennial Exposition* to Dallas in 1936, the city fathers built a group of museums at *Fair Park*. The *Museum of Natural History*, a neoclassical, cream limestone building, contains a variety of fauna and flora from the Southwest's 600-million-year history. There are some interesting zoological and botanical exhibitions, too. Open daily. Admission charge. *Fair Park*, 3535 Grand Ave. (phone: 421-DINO).

MIDWAY AND THE TEXAS HALL OF STATE As you walk along the *Midway*, you will find it hard to imagine the frenetic carnival activity for which it is known. But during the *State Fair* or occasional special events, you'll probably be swept into the frenzy, stopping only long enough to try your luck at a shooting gallery or pitch 'n' toss. There is an assortment of scream-inducing rides, as well as great food stands—Greek, barbecue, and Mexican. At one end of the *Midway*, the *Texas Hall of State* (phone: 421-4500) has paintings devoted to Texas heroes. It was built in 1936 for the *Texas Centennial*. Open daily. No admission charge. *Fair Park* (phone: 670-8400).

AGE OF STEAM MUSEUM With steam engines and other railroad memorabilia, this museum is sure to bring a lump to the throat of anyone who ever loved an old train. Closed Mondays through Wednesdays. Admission charge. *Fair Park*, Washington and Parry Sts. (phone: 428-0101).

SCIENCE PLACE Permanent exhibits on science and technology geared to all age groups include *Body Tech*, an interactive display about human life and health; an exhibit of live bees busily at work; and electricity demonstrations. There are traveling exhibits as well. An on-site planetarium has a variety of shows, classes, and demonstrations designed to explore the mystery of the stars. Open daily. Admission charge. *Fair Park*, 1318 Second Ave. (phone: 428-7200).

MUSEUM OF AFRICAN-AMERICAN LIFE AND CULTURE This new 38,000-square-foot heritage repository is the only one of its kind in the Southwest, dedicated exclusively to the study, preservation, and showcasing of exhibits and artifacts of the African-American people. Closed Mondays. No admission charge. *Fair Park,* 3536 Grand Ave. (phone: 565-9026).

DOWNTOWN

Here among the tall skyscrapers of the central business district are the *Kennedy Memorial,* the Arts District, *Thanks-Giving Square Park* (Pacific, Bryan, and Ervay Sts.), and an intriguing 3-mile network of underground walkways and skybridges lined with shops and restaurants.

TEXAS SCHOOL BOOK DEPOSITORY AND THE SIXTH FLOOR Known to millions as the place from which Lee Harvey Oswald allegedly fired, the *Texas School Book Depository* is the most-photographed site in Texas. Open daily except major holidays. Admission charge; there is an additional charge for a 35-minute audio tour (phone: 633-6659; 653-6657 for groups). The *Sixth Floor* (located on the sixth floor of the Depository), a project of the *Dallas County Historical Foundation,* is a permanent exhibition which examines the life, death, and legacy of John F. Kennedy. Historic photographs, artifacts, interpretive displays, videos, and award-winning films evoke powerful feelings of an unforgettable chapter in American history. Open daily. Admission charge. 411 Elm St.; entrance on Houston St. between Elm and Pacific Sts. (phone: 653-6666).

JOHN F. KENNEDY MEMORIAL Near the spot where Kennedy was assassinated, this monument consists of four unconnected, 30-foot-high walls defining an area for meditation that is open to the sky and marked only by a center stone slab. Main and Market Sts.

UNION STATION This renovated 1916 rail station, which currently houses a grand hall and banquet rooms, a snack bar, and a visitors' center, is such a treat that travelers passing through town on *Amtrak* trains sometimes disembark just to view it. 400 S. Houston (phone: 746-6600).

MORTON H. MEYERSON SYMPHONY CENTER Designed by I. M. Pei, who was also the architect for Dallas's cantilevered *City Hall,* the center is a major facility for music and other performing arts. A computer was used in designing the unusual structural shapes and supports, which were intended to "uplift" audiences. Flora and Pearl Sts. (phone: 692-0203).

DALLAS MUSEUM OF ART The keystone of Dallas's downtown Arts District houses a permanent collection of pre-Columbian art, African sculpture, and 19th-century modern and contemporary works. The *Sculpture Garden,* featuring works by Henry Moore and Ellsworth Kelly, is an urban oasis, replete with cascades and shade trees. The *Reves Collection,* hung in a reconstructed Italian villa, and the *Bybee Collection*

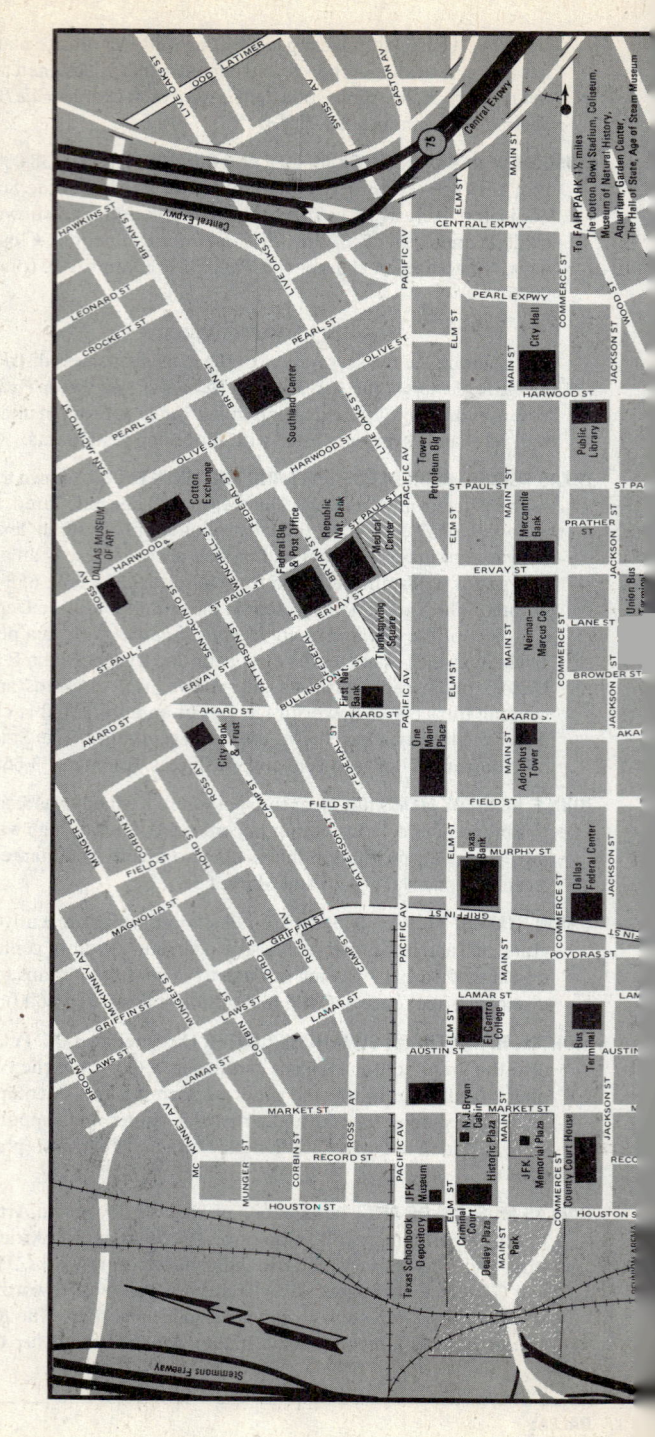

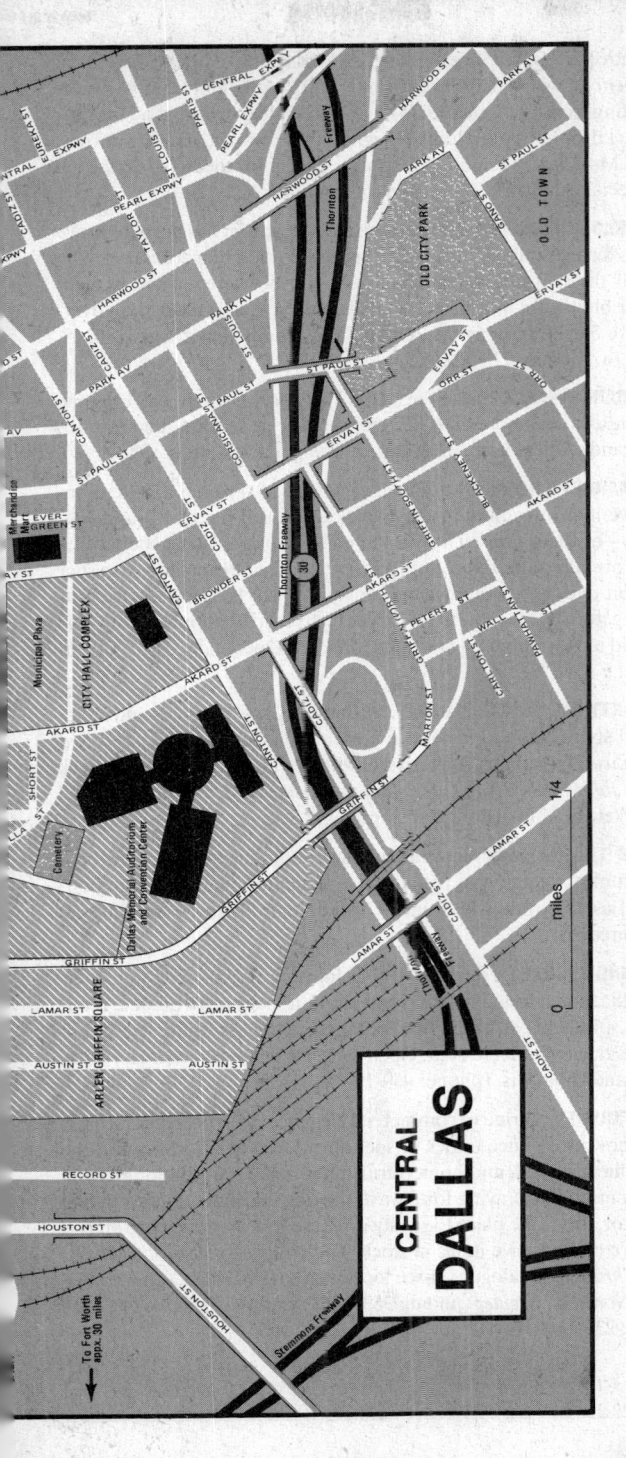

(furniture) are worth investigating. Also inside is the new *Museum of the Americas,* with 4,000 works from North, South, and Central America, dating from pre-Columbian days. The Dallas skyline is an impressive backdrop to the building designed by Edward Larrabee Barnes. Closed Mondays. No admission charge, except for the *Reves Collection* and special exhibits. 1717 N. Harwood (phone: 922-1200).

DALLAS WORLD AQUARIUM This revolutionary aquarium has garnered rave reviews for its exhibits, including a representation of a coral reef. You can walk through a triangular-shape tunnel tank where sea horses, giant clams, ribbon eels, and sharks swim around you, and there is a terrarium with blackfoot penguins. Open daily. Admission charge. 1801 N. Griffin St. (phone: 720-2224).

WEST END MARKETPLACE In the West End Historical District, this onetime warehouse boasts more than 125 shops, pushcart vendors, and refreshment stands. Open daily. Market St. at Munger Ave. (phone: 954-4350).

FARMERS' MARKET This is down-home, earthy Texas. From 6 AM on, farmers drive into town in their trusty pickups to sell the fruit—and vegetables—of their labor. The market consists of a tin-roof shelter and dozens of stalls staffed by colorful characters. The vegetables are fresher and a bit cheaper than anywhere else in town; the flowers are outstanding, too. In May, there's a flower festival, in September a fall harvest, and in November an arts and crafts fair. Open daily. 1010 S. Pearl (phone: 670-5879).

DALLAS COUNTY HISTORICAL PLAZA A fascinating range of history and architectural styles is found in several buildings in this area. The *Old Red Courthouse* is a Romanesque marvel with leering gargoyles; also check out the *John Neely Bryan Cabin* and the *Kennedy Memorial.* Bordered by Market, Elm, Houston, and Commerce Sts.

DEEP ELLUM This former industrial neighborhood has been transformed into a funky collection of restaurants, nightclubs, galleries, and boutiques. East of downtown, bounded by the Central Expwy. and Elm and Commerce Sts.

THANKS-GIVING SQUARE Designed by Philip Johnson and funded by an interfaith educational foundation, this meditation space has a garden, fountains, a spiral chapel, and a horizontal stained glass window. Melodious bells ring to mark the hour. Open daily. No admission charge. Pacific, Bryan, and Ervay Sts. (phone: 969-1977).

NEIMAN MARCUS The shrine of commercial elegance, this specialty store has been known to induce orgies of spending. Designer clothing and the finest china, crystal, and home furnishings make it a standout. If you have an insatiable craving for a wave-making machine or a biorhythm calculator, this is the place to satisfy it. These toys, however, are among the more conservative items in stock. The really exotic stuff is offered in the *Christmas* catalogue. Three locations: 1618 Main St. (phone: 741-6911); *NorthPark Center* (phone: 363-8311); and the *Prestonwood Mall* (phone: 233-1100).

ELSEWHERE

Outside the central business district lie many other attractions that make Dallas a place of never-ending excitement, from the battlefield of the Dallas *Cowboys* to the re-created natural environments of the *Dallas Zoo*.

DALLAS ARBORETUM Sixty-six acres on the eastern shore of White Rock Lake are dedicated to horticultural displays, education, and research. Just minutes from downtown are fragrant gardens, rolling green lawns, and tall shade trees. Admission charge. 8525 Garland Rd. (phone: 327-8263).

INFOMART This copy of London's 19th-century *Crystal Palace* exposition hall is one of the city's most distinctive architectural works. It's also a computer marketplace, so you can go shopping after admiring the façade. 1950 Stemmons Fwy. (phone: 746-3500).

MEADOWS MUSEUM Within *Southern Methodist University*'s School of Fine Arts is a prestigious assembly of Spanish paintings, drawings, and prints dating from the 16th century to the present. Closed Wednesdays. No admission charge. On campus, Bishop at Binkley (phone: 768-2516).

FRONTIERS OF FLIGHT MUSEUM This aviation museum at *Love Field Airport* highlights the history of flight in Dallas from *Fair Park*'s turn-of-the-century barnstormers to *Dallas/Ft. Worth*'s current position as one of the nation's leading airports. Closed Mondays. Admission charge. Located just above the main terminal lobby. Mockingbird La., *Love Field* (phone: 350-1651).

BIBLICAL ARTS CENTER Paintings by the Old Masters, contemporary spiritual works, and archaeological artifacts are used to help people understand the places, people, and events portrayed in the Bible. Closed Mondays. No admission charge. 7500 Park La. (phone: 691-4661).

MEMORIAL CENTER FOR HOLOCAUST STUDIES An outstanding exhibit of photographs, artifacts, documentary films, and videos tells the tragic story of the Holocaust, including tales of local survivors. There's a memorial room and a library as well. Closed Saturdays. No admission charge. 7900 Northaven St. (phone: 750-4654).

SWISS AVENUE HISTORIC DISTRICT Opulent mansions grace this grand boulevard, the most prestigious address in town almost a century ago. The buildings that are in the best shape are in the Wilson Block Historic District, within the 2800 and 2900 blocks of Swiss Avenue.

WAGON WHEEL RANCH Close to the airport, this is a family fun place offering horse rentals and group night rides as well as barbecues, country entertainment, and hayrides on 300 acres of wooded trails and picnic areas. Riding lessons, Western or English style, are offered. Reservations necessary. Northwest of Dallas in Grapevine (phone: 817-481-8284).

DALLAS ZOO About 1,400 mammals, reptiles, and birds live comfortably within this 70-acre zoo. The *Wilds of Africa* section provides several species of African animals with 25 acres that simulate their natural habitat. A monorail carries visitors along the treetops high over the *Wilds of Africa* for a prime view of the animals in their environment. Open daily. Admission charge. *Marsalis Park*, 621 E. Clarendon Dr. (phone: 946-5154).

SAMUELL FARM Here, you can get a taste of life on a 340-acre, turn-of-the-century farm—complete with livestock. There's also fishing, horseback riding, hayrides, and hiking. Closed Sundays in winter. Admission charge. 100 E. Hwy. 80 in Mesquite (phone: 670-8262).

STUDIOS AT LAS COLINAS As the film industry in Texas booms, so does the production business at this state-of-the-art movie and television complex. For a behind-the-scenes look at the complex where films such as *RoboCop, Trip to Bountiful,* and *JFK* were made, take a guided tour, which includes the *National Museum of Communications*. Closed Sundays through Tuesdays. Admission charge. 6301 N. O'Connor Rd. at Royal Ln., Irving (phone: 869-3456).

TEXAS STADIUM *Cowboys* fans go crazy here. This 64,000-seat stadium packs 'em in during home games. It's constructed to give you the sense of being in a theater or auditorium rather than a stadium, but critics point out that with the dome partially open, part of the field is always in shadow. Tours of the *Cowboys'* locker room, players' tunnel, pressbox, and some private suites are offered daily for a fee; reservations necessary. Hwy. 183 at Loop 12 in Irving (phone: 438-7676).

SOUTHFORK RANCH The Ewing family ranch, as seen on TV's "Dallas," has had an uneasy existence since the show was canceled. It closed after going bankrupt in 1991, but it has reopened after a $1-million renovation. A tram tour offers an overview of the property, including longhorn cattle and horses, and there are several restaurants, a visitors' center, and a gift shop. Future plans call for the addition of a western store, a museum about the history of television, and concerts and other special events. Open daily. Admission charge. Follow US Hwy. 75 north from Dallas about 35 miles to Parker Rd., Plano, then continue east 5½ miles to Farm Rd. 2551 (phone: 442-7800).

ARLINGTON

SIX FLAGS OVER TEXAS Located midway between Dallas and Ft. Worth, this family entertainment center covers 205 acres and offers over 100 rides, shows, and attractions. The $5-million *Looney Tunes Land* is a special children's area featuring the park's celebrity host, Bugs Bunny, and his Warner Brothers cartoon friends. The musical revue in the *Southern Palace Music Hall* and the country-style show in the *Crazy Horse Saloon* help to draw nearly three million visitors here each year. Summers are hot—but nearly everything that can be air conditioned is. Open weekends spring and fall; daily June through August. No admission charge for children under two. I-30 at Hwy. 360 (phone: 817-640-8900).

THE BALLPARK AT ARLINGTON The former *Arlington Stadium* is gone, replaced by a facility designed to evoke the feel of baseball's past. Built of Texas pink granite and red brick, with tiered balconies, it is decorated with icons of the Texas *Rangers*—both the police officers and the baseball players. The complex also features a hall of fame, an amphitheater, Little League fields, picnic grounds, numerous stores, and several restaurants. Nolan Ryan Expwy., at I-30 and Pennant Dr., Arlington (phone: 817-273-5100).

WET 'N' WILD This Texas-size recreation park attracts huge crowds on blistering summer weekends (weekdays are a bit less jammed). Water slides, inner-tube chutes, body-surfing pools, and children's play areas provide heat relief for all ages. Closed November through April and weekdays, May and September. Admission charge. Two locations: across I-30 from *The Ballpark at Arlington* at 1800 E. Lamar Blvd. (phone: 817-265-3013) and 12715 LBJ Expwy., near the intersection of I-635 and Northwest Hwy. in Garland (phone: 271-5637).

EXTRA SPECIAL

Before the advent of its skyscrapers and highways, Dallas was a simpler place where architecture combined Victorian grace with the less refined Prairie influence. One of the few places still able to convey a sense of those earlier, unhurried days is *Old City Park,* an oasis of greenery and history close to downtown. Restored Victorian houses, a railroad depot, pioneer log cabins, and other historically significant structures have been moved in from various locales in North Texas and are open for exploration. Closed Mondays. Admission charge. Gano and St. Paul (phone: 421-5141).

Safari buffs should consider taking a side trip to the *Fossil Rim Wildlife Center* (phone: 897-3147 for information) in the town of Glen Rose, about a one-and-a-half-hour drive south from the *Dallas/Ft. Worth Airport.* The center is a 2,900-acre safari camp where you can watch wildebeest, water buck, and the endangered oryx and addax. Nearly 30 other species are in residence here, including giraffes, zebras, gazelles, gemsbok, and kudus.

Sources and Resources

TOURIST INFORMATION

For brochures, maps, and general information, contact the *Dallas Convention and Visitors Bureau* (1201 Elm St., Suite 2000, Dallas, TX 75270; phone: 746-6677), which is closed weekends. There are three *Dallas Visitor Information Centers,* all open daily: at *West End MarketPlace* (603 Munger; phone: 880-0405); 1303 Commerce St. (phone: 746-6665); and *NorthPark Center* (phone: 368-5164). Call the Special Events Info-Line (phone: 746-6679) for daily information on Dallas events. Contact the

Texas state tourism hotline (phone: 800-8888-TEX) for maps, calendars of events, health updates, and travel advisories.

LOCAL COVERAGE *Dallas Morning News,* daily (see *Guide,* a section in Friday's paper, for entertainment information); and *Dallas Observer,* weekly. The Dallas restaurant guide in *Texas Monthly* magazine is useful for food listings.

TELEVISION STATIONS KDFW Channel 4–CBS; KXAS Channel 5–NBC; WFAA Channel 8–ABC; and KERA Channel 13–PBS.

RADIO STATIONS AM: WBAP 820 (full service); KRLD 1080 (news); KVIL 1150 (contemporary); and KLIF 570 (talk). FM: KERA 90.1 (eclectic); KSCS 96.3 (country); WRR 101.1 (classical); KDMX 102.9 (light rock); and KVIL 103.7 (contemporary).

TELEPHONE The area code for Dallas is 214.

SALES TAX There is an 8% sales tax on most goods and services, including dining. Hotel room tax is 13%.

CLIMATE Summers are blisteringly hot and humid, with temperatures sometimes climbing to over 100F. Sudden thunderstorms punctuate the dry, blazing heat. From October through December, the weather is mild, although it can be in the 70s one day and in the 30s the next. From January through March, there are occasional sharp cold snaps and high winds (and once in a great while, some ice and snow), and between March and June you can expect rain and dust storms. (For local weather, call 787-1111. For temperature—and time—call 844-4444.)

GETTING AROUND

AIRPORT *Dallas/Ft. Worth Airport (D/FW),* one of the country's largest, is in Ft. Worth, approximately 20 miles from downtown Dallas. In light traffic, the drive into the city takes about a half hour. The inner-city *Love Field Airport* serves Texas and surrounding states. Most major hotels offer shuttle service. Companies providing transportation to area hotels include *SuperShuttle* (phone: 817-329-2000 in Ft. Worth) and *Shuttlejack* (phone: 484-7577).

BUS *Dallas Area Rapid Transit (DART)* (phone: 828-6841) operates the bus service (fare: 75¢).

CAR RENTAL A car is necessary in Dallas; all major national firms are represented.

MCKINNEY AVENUE TROLLEY Serving downtown, the Arts District (including the *Dallas Museum of Art* and the *Morton H. Meyerson Symphony Center*), and the McKinney strip, the trolley makes stops along the 2.8-mile route on McKinney Avenue and St. Paul Street. The fare is $1.50; a one-day pass costs $2; a three-day pass costs $5. The trolley runs daily (phone: 855-0006).

TAXI There are taxi stands at most major hotels, but the best way to get one is to call *Yellow Checker Cab* (phone: 565-9132).

TOURS *Gray Line*'s "All About Dallas" tour covers downtown Dallas. Motorcoach pickups are available at major downtown hotels (phone: 824-2424).

LOCAL SERVICES

AUDIOVISUAL EQUIPMENT *Ford Audio-Video Systems* (phone: 241-9966).

BABY-SITTING *Babysitters of Dallas* (2703 Fondren; phone: 692-1354).

BUSINESS SERVICES *Kelly Services* (500 N. Akard, and several other locations; phone: 740-3666).

CELLULAR PHONE RENTAL *Fonz by the Day* (phone: 484-4044); *Road and Show Cellular* (phone: 934-1212).

LIMOUSINE *Dallas Limousine Service* (phone: 484-5770).

MECHANICS *Exxon Car Care* (Hillcrest and Arapaho; phone: 233-7034), for American cars; *Fischer's Foreign Car Service* (4770 Memphis; phone: 630-2807), for foreign cars. In emergencies, *AAA Emergency Road Service* (phone: 528-7481, *AAA* members only); and *Dallas Vehicle Recovery* (phone: 247-2477).

MEDICAL EMERGENCY *Baylor University Medical Center* (3500 Gaston Ave.; phone: 820-0111).

MESSENGER SERVICES *Big D Messenger Service* (phone: 744-4726).

MONEY TRANSFERS *American Express MoneyGram* (phone: 800-926-9400 for information; 800-866-8800 for money transfers); *Western Union Financial Services* (phone: 800-325-6000 or 800-325-4176).

NATIONAL/INTERNATIONAL COURIER *DHL Worldwide Express* (phone: 800-225-5345); *FedEx* (phone: 358-5271), several locations.

PHARMACY *Eckerd* (phone: 272-0411), at five locations, open 24 hours daily.

PHOTOCOPIES *Quik Print* (phone: 741-1425), 14 locations with pickup and delivery; also offers fax service.

POST OFFICE Downtown (400 N. Ervay St.; phone: 953-3045).

PROFESSIONAL PHOTOGRAPHER *John Haynesworth* (86½ Highland Park Village; phone: 559-3700); *Bob Mader* (500 Crescent Ct.; phone: 871-5511).

SECRETARY/STENOGRAPHER *A-AAA Answering Secretary* (phone: 890-4200).

TELECONFERENCE FACILITIES *Adolphus, Hyatt Regency, Plaza of the Americas* (see *Checking In*), and the *Summit* (phone: 243-3363).

TRANSLATOR *Berlitz* (phone: 380-0404).

WESTERN UNION/TELEX Many offices are located around the city (phone: 800-325-6000 to find the location nearest you).

SPECIAL EVENTS

College football teams face off in the *Cotton Bowl* on *New Year's Day* (phone: 638-BOWL). The *Scarborough Faire* (phone: 214-937-6130) is a six-weekend, 16th-century olde-English fair held in nearby Waxahachie during April and May with 400 entertainers and plenty of food and drink; the *Byron Nelson Golf Classic* (phone: 717-1200) occurs in mid-May; and *Artfest* (phone: 361-2011) is held at *Fair Park* during *Memorial Day* weekend. The *Shakespeare Festival of Dallas* (phone: 559-2778) takes place during the last week in June through July. *Dallas Summer Musicals* are held from June through August at *Fair Park Music Hall* (phone: 373-8000 or 691-7200). The *State Fair of Texas* (phone: 565-9931; 800-375-1839) is held for three weeks in October in *Fair Park*.

SHOPPING

Despite stereotypes of Texan attire, from the 10-gallon hat on downward, cosmopolitan chic decidedly has replaced cowboy dandy, and shopping in Dallas has emerged as a tony pastime. Cowboy boots, however, are fashionable everywhere, and there may not be a better selection anywhere than in Dallas. Would-be Texans should stop at *Cavender's Boot City* (5539 LBJ Freeway; phone: 239-1375), with 30 stores in Texas, billed as the world's largest boot dealer, specializing in handmade Lucchese boots, jeans, and other Western wear. Also try *Boot Town* (5909 Belt Line Rd. at Preston Rd.; phone: 385-3052), with shelves piled high with discounted boots by Acme, Tony Lama, Justin, Mocona, and Lucchese.

The city can be split into four shopping districts—downtown, uptown, Park Cities, and North Dallas. NorthPark, with *NorthPark Center,* Dallas's top mall, whose 150-odd stores include *Lord & Taylor, Neiman Marcus,* and *J. Crew,* is also a major shopping destination.

DOWNTOWN

Dallas Museum of Art Costume jewelry, gold earrings encrusted with semi-precious stones, and clay ornaments are enticing, as is the vast collection of art books, posters, and children's books. 1717 N. Harwood (phone: 922-1271).

Neiman Marcus Top-drawer goods have long been de rigueur at this venerable flagship store (see *Special Places*). 1618 Main St. (phone: 741-6911).

Taylor's Bookstore The city's leading bookstore chain has an exceptional selection of best sellers and reference books on a variety of topics—from astrology to computers. *Renaissance Tower,* 201 Field St. (phone: 744-5500) and seven other locations in the city.

Wild Bill's Official Western Wear Those who crave Western gear can try on a pair of Roy Rogers fringed leather gloves or a Texas belt buckle. Less orthodox, but guaranteed to garner notice, are the snakeskin tennis shoes. In the *West End MarketPlace* (phone: 954-1050).

UPTOWN

Adams-Middleton Gallery Renowned for its fine collections of paintings and sculpture. 3000 Maple (phone: 871-7080).

Afterimage Gallery Local photographers and artists display and sell their works here. At the *Quadrangle,* 2828 Routh St. (phone: 871-9140).

Aldredge Book Store Treasured tomes from as recent as last year to as far back as the 16th century attract lovers of old bindings, marbleized endpapers, and silk bookmarks. Out of print and second-hand books are also available. 2909 Maple (phone: 871-3333).

Gerald Peters Gallery The work of noted contemporary artists, including sculptures, oil paintings, and drawings, is displayed and sold here. In addition, there are often special exhibits. 2913 Fairmount (phone: 969-9410).

Lady Primrose's English Countryside Devotees of English antiques will find an amazing selection from the remotest corners of Great Britain. 2200 Cedar Springs, in the *Crescent* hotel complex (phone: 871-8333).

La Mariposa Mexican and South American clothing is all the rage here. Also notable is the collection of folk art. 2817 Routh St. (phone: 871-9103).

Militaria This military arts gallery offers such items as a Royal Irish Rifleman's uniform, modern toy soldiers, historical statuettes, and books from all over the world. 2615 Fairmount (phone: 871-1565).

Stanley Korshak European designer men's and women's clothing, including Giorgio Armani, is available here. 2200 Cedar Springs, in the *Crescent* hotel complex (phone: 871-3600).

PARK CITIES

Anteks Southwestern, Texan, and Western home accessories—with emphasis on ranch antiques and reproductions—are packed into this store. Even such unusual items as antler candelabras and hand-crafted and -painted headboards can be found here. 5814 Lovers La. (phone: 528-5567).

Collector's Covey The bronze wildlife sculptures, decoys, and limited edition animal and bird prints here are very appealing. 15 *Highland Park Village* (phone: 521-7880).

La Crème Coffee and Tea The delicious scent of hand-blended coffees fill the air. Unusual teas also are available, as are a variety of coffee makers, teapots, and mugs. 4448 Lovers La. (phone: 369-4188).

Highland Park Village Built in 1931 and purported to be America's oldest shopping center, it is Dallas's equivalent of Rodeo Drive. Among its more famous boutiques are *Ann Taylor, Chanel, Godiva Chocolatier, Hermès, Polo/Ralph Lauren, Victor Costa,* and *William Noble Jewels.* Mockingbird and Preston Sts. (phone: 521-0050).

NORTH DALLAS

The Galleria This enormous, four-level, skylit mall boasts lots of stylish shops, including *Saks Fifth Avenue, Tiffany & Co.,* and *Marshall Field.* Best of all, valet parking is available at the *Westin* hotel on the mall's west side. *Gerlo Scherer* features the chic fashion of German designer Jil Sander, who specializes in silk and cashmere suits for women. Handsome stationery, sleek desk accessories, and fine writing implements are sold at *William Ernest Brown,* and *Optica* has a great selection of eyewear, including frames from Porsche, Ferre, and Paloma Picasso. 13350 Dallas Pkwy. (phone: 702-7100).

Olla Podrida This classic, albeit unusual Dallas landmark, originally an artisans' showplace, is packed with wonderful boutiques. *The Bunker* has military paraphernalia, while *The Clockworks* has watches and antique timepieces. *De Falco Winemaker* offers a good selection of international wine, as well as homemade varieties. *Earthen Vessels and Treasures* features oddities of Southwestern art, while *The Patchworks* proffers unusual women's clothing. For the small of stature and age, *Through The Looking Glass* presents ornate dollhouses and other miniatures. Lovers of stained glass and hand-blown art should visit the *Kitrell Glassworks*. 12215 Coit Rd. (phone: 934-3603).

SPORTS AND FITNESS

Dallas has enough professional sports to satisfy just about everyone.

BASEBALL The *American League* Texas *Rangers* play at the recently built *Ballpark at Arlington* (Nolan Ryan Expwy. at I-30 and Pennant Dr., Arlington; phone: 817-273-5100).

BASKETBALL Dallas's *NBA* team, the *Mavericks,* plays at *Reunion Arena* (777 Sports St.; phone: 939-2712).

BICYCLING Dallas has some pretty trails in the White Rock Lake–East Dallas area and at Bachman Lake, off Northwest Highway near *Love Field*. For maps of the trails, call the *City Parks Department* (phone: 670-4272).

FITNESS CENTERS The *Downtown YMCA* (601 N. Akard at Ross, across from the *Fairmont;* phone: 954-0500) has an indoor and an outdoor pool, tracks, squash and racquetball courts, exercise equipment, and a sauna. Facilities are open to non-members for a fee. *Dr. Kenneth Cooper's Aerobics Center* (12230 Preston Rd.; phone: 386-0306) has a guest lodge available for those who wish to stay overnight.

FOOTBALL The *NFL Cowboys,* 1994 *Super Bowl* champions, play at *Texas Stadium* (Hwy. 183 at Loop 12, Irving; phone: 579-5000). The *Cotton Bowl* is held every *New Year's Day* at *Fair Park* (phone: 638-BOWL). The Dallas *Texans* of the *Arena Football League* take the field at *Reunion Arena* (777 Sports St.; phone: 517-4000 or 424-9660).

GOLF There are several municipal courses in Dallas, including the new 18-hole course at *Buffalo Creek Golf Club* (Lake Ray Hubbard; phone: 771-4003). *Tennison Memorial* (3501 Samuell; phone: 670-1402) is best known as the home of Lee Trevino. Many hotels also have courses. The *Dallas Convention and Visitors Bureau* (see *Tourist Information* above) has a complete listing.

HOCKEY The Dallas *Stars* of the *NHL* (formerly the Minnesota *North Stars*) play at *Reunion Arena* (777 Sports St.; phone: 467-8277).

ICE SKATING Ice Capades Chalets runs two skating rinks: in the *Galleria Mall* (13350 Dallas Pkwy.; phone: 702-7100) and in the *Prestonwood Mall* (530 Belt Line Rd.; phone: 980-8988). *America's Ice Gardens* also has a huge rink (700 N. Pearle St.; phone: 922-9800).

JOGGING For a 6-mile stint, head north on Akard, right onto Cedar Springs, then take Turtle Creek Boulevard, left onto Avondale, left onto Oak Lawn, left onto Irving, back to Turtle Creek, and retrace your steps home. Or take a bus (40 Bachman Bank or 43 Park Forest) to Bachman Lake for a 3-mile course, or to White Rock Lake (60 White Rock North on Commerce or East St.) for a 10-mile course.

RODEO Professional cowhands compete at the *Mesquite Championship Rodeo* (LBJ Fwy. and Military Pkwy. Exit in Mesquite; phone: 285-8777) on Friday and Saturday evenings, April through September.

SOCCER The *Continental Indoor Soccer League (CISL) Sidekicks* play at *Reunion Arena* (777 Sports St.; phone: 653-0200 or 939-2712).

TENNIS Tennis is a year-round sport here, and it's terrifically popular. Of the more than 200 municipal courts, the best are at *Samuell Grand Park* (6200 Grand Ave.; phone: 821-3811) and at *Fretz Park* (Hillcrest and Belt Line; phone: 670-6622).

THEATER

The city has a number of fine regional theater companies. For a complete up-to-date listing on performance schedules, see the publications listed in *Local Coverage*. The following is our favorite place in Dallas for live theater.

CENTER STAGE

Dallas Theater Center Conventional dramas and plays by contemporary authors, many of them premieres, alternate here between the *Kalita Humphreys Theater* and the *Arts District Theater*, the latter a flexible, open performance space. Preston Jones's *A Texas Trilogy* got its start here. Besides the six works presented each season on both stages, the center also produces the *Big D Festival of the Unexpected,* a celebration of new plays in development. Two locations: 3636 Turtle Creek Blvd. (phone: 922-0427) and 2401 Flora St. (phone: 526-8857).

Other major Dallas theaters are *Theatre Three* (2800 Routh; phone: 871-3300) and the beautiful *Majestic Theatre* (1925 Elm; phone: 880-0137). Several "underground" theater companies perform in the Deep Ellum area.

MUSIC

Dallas's $100-million *Morton H. Meyerson Symphony Center* (see *Special Places*) is home to the *Dallas Symphony Orchestra* (phone: 692-0203), which performs in the center's 2,066-seat *Eugene McDermott Concert Hall* (2301 Flora St.; phone: 670-3600). For information on opera, call the *Dallas Opera* (phone: 443-1000), which performs at *Fair Park Music Hall* (First and Parry Sts.). Big-name rock and pop stars (such as Eric Clapton and Bruce Springsteen) play at *Fair Park*'s *Starplex* (1818 First St.; phone: 421-1111); for information about other pop-rock concerts, call *Rainbow-Ticketmaster* (phone: 787-2000).

NIGHTCLUBS AND NIGHTLIFE

Dallas crowds are so notoriously fickle that before this guidebook is printed everyone may have boogied on down the road to another hangout. But regardless of what's hot and what's not, there's never far to go. Nightlife in Dallas finds four major centers. One is Greenville Avenue, a north-south artery chockablock with restaurants and nightclubs on the east side. *Poor David's* (1924 Greenville; phone: 821-9891) in Lower Greenville features every style of music, from reggae to jazz, and *Studebakers* (*NorthPark Center;* phone: 696-2475) in Upper Greenville, with a 1950s theme, is one of the area's popular discos. There's country-and-western dancing at *Borrowed Money* (9100 N. Central; phone: 361-9996) in Upper Greenville, and *Terilli's* (2815 Greenville; phone: 827-3993) in Lower Greenville is a great jazz spot.

A second center is the West End Historical District, a downtown area of renovated warehouses (one, *Dallas Alley,* contains eight clubs; phone: 988-WEST). *Dick's Last Resort* (1701 N. Market; phone: 747-0001) features live Dixieland jazz. McKinney Avenue is the third major nightlife center. It runs south to downtown and features some of the best restaurants, along with the tourists' favorite, *Hard Rock Café* (2601 McKinney; phone: 855-0007).

For something more avant-garde, head down to the fourth area, Deep Ellum/Near Ellum, a bohemian district where many blues musicians performed in the 1930s. At *Club Dada* (2720 Elm; phone: 744-3232), poetry, classical guitar, rockabilly, and Middle Eastern jazz can be heard. *2826* (2826 Elm; phone: 741-2826) is a jumping joint with alternative dance music. *Club Clearview* (2806 Elm; phone: 283-5358) is the place for a variety of bands. Near *Fair Park,* where some of the uprooted artists moved, is *Bar of Soap* (3615 Parry; phone: 823-6617), a bar/laundromat with live music. Away from those four regions, try *Strictly Tabu* (4111 Lomo Alto; phone: 528-5200), another good choice for jazz lovers, and *The Monopoly* (609 N. Harwood; phone: 953-0007) for salsa and Tejano, a Hispanic and Tex-Mex form of music.

Best in Town

CHECKING IN

As the third-most popular convention city in the country, Dallas has many comfortable accommodations. Some hotels cater almost exclusively to conventions, so it may be difficult to book as an individual. It will save a lot of trouble if you inquire ahead of time. For something different and a little less expensive, try *Bed & Breakfast Texas Style,* a service that offers lodging in private homes. Contact Ruth Wilson (4224 W. Redbird La., Dallas 75237; phone: 298-5433 or 298-8586) for information. Dallas also has international youth hostel beds available at the *Anchor* motel (10230 Harry Hines Blvd.; phone: 438-6061). At the hotels below, expect to spend $130 or more per night for a double room at those places we describe as very expensive; $105 to $130 at those listed as expensive; between $60 and $105 at those in the moderate category; and less than $60 at inexpensive places. Unless otherwise noted, hotel rooms have air conditioning, private baths, TV sets, and telephones. All hotels are in the 214 area code unless otherwise indicated.

VERY EXPENSIVE

Crescent Court Designed by award-winning architect Philip Johnson, this impressive 190-room, 28-suite Rosewood Group property offers high style and excellent service. The soaring Great Hall lobby links an 18-story office tower (with the hottest private club in town) to an elegant courtyard of shops and galleries with a five-story fountain. The spacious, airy rooms were designed for style as well as comfort. There is a lobby lounge, the *Conservatory* for formal dining, and the *Beau Nash* for more casual fare (see *Eating Out* for both). Among the many amenities are a concierge, 24-hour room service, baby-sitting, a pool, and a spa. In addition to extensive conference facilities and five meeting rooms, other pluses are A/V equipment, photocopiers, and free shuttle service to downtown. 400 Crescent Ct. (phone: 871-3200; 800-654-6541; fax: 871-3272).

Mansion on Turtle Creek Dallas's most elegant address is a member of the prestigious Relais & Châteaux group. Custom-made furnishings, opulent bathrooms, attentive service (including a concierge, twice-daily maid service, and complimentary limousine transport), and the superb *Mansion* restaurant (see *Eating Out*) make this the best of the city's deluxe hotels. Twenty-four-hour room service is available. Five meeting rooms, secretarial services, A/V equipment, photocopiers, computers, a concierge desk, and express checkout are pluses. 2821 Turtle Creek Blvd. (phone: 559-2100; 800-442-3408 in Texas; 800-527-5432 elsewhere in the US; fax: 528-4187).

St. Germain A converted 1906 mansion provides the setting for this luxurious seven-suite inn. Exquisite French antiques, canopied beds, and fireplaces give the rooms an understated elegance, and there's also a lovely courtyard and a fine eponymous restaurant (see *Eating Out*). Amenities include room service, a butler, a concierge, a multilingual staff, and access to a nearby health spa. The dining room, library, and parlor are available for meetings. 2516 Maple Ave. (phone: 871-2516; fax: 871-0740).

EXPENSIVE

Adolphus Built in 1912, this elder giant among Dallas hotels is listed on the *National Register of Historic Places*. The decor is turn-of-the-century elegant; rooms are large and individually appointed. Its *French Room* (see *Eating Out*) is one of the city's classiest restaurants, and the *Walt Garrison Rodeo Bar* is a posh watering hole. There's also 24-hour room service. Business amenities include 16 meeting rooms, concierge and secretarial services, A/V equipment, photocopiers, computers, and express checkout. 1321 Commerce (phone: 742-8200; 800-441-0574 in Texas; 800-221-9083 elsewhere in the US; fax: 747-3532).

Courtyard by Marriott Spacious rooms (with king-size beds) surround pleasant courtyards, each of which has an indoor or outdoor pool. Business amenities include secretarial services, two meeting rooms, and express checkout. There are seven locations in the Dallas area, including two right in the city (which are more expensive). Call 800-321-2211 for central reservations.

Fairmont This Dallas favorite has a Texas pink granite façade and an elegant entrance and porte cochère. All 550 rooms have been redone, and the restaurants are fine (see the *Pyramid* in *Eating Out*). Room service responds around the clock. Among the business amenities are 24 meeting rooms, concierge and secretarial services, A/V equipment, photocopiers, computers, and express checkout. In the Arts District, within walking distance of the West End, at 1717 N. Akard St. (phone: 720-2020; 800-527-4727; fax: 720-5269).

Four Seasons Numerous awards for its conference facilities have been bestowed on this 315-room property. Other amenities on its 400 acres include a spa and sports club, two 18-hole golf courses, four restaurants, a tennis stadium, racquetball, squash, and tennis courts, a jogging track, two pools, and 24-hour room service. Near the airport at 4150 N. MacArthur Blvd., Irving (phone: 717-0700; 800-332-3442; fax: 717-2550).

Grand Kempinski This 529-room hotel with a resort ambience is an attraction in itself. There is 24-hour room service, a concierge floor, tennis and racquetball courts, a spa, indoor and outdoor pools, and fine restaurants. Business facilities include secretarial services, A/V equipment, photocopiers, and express checkout. 15201 Dallas Pkwy. (phone: 386-6000; 800-426-3135; fax: 991-6937).

Hyatt Regency One of Dallas's most popular hotels, it has a silver-burnished exterior that mirrors the downtown skyline, 947 rooms and suites, a rooftop restaurant, and a health club. Room service is on call 24 hours a day. Fifteen meeting rooms are available, as well as concierge and secretarial services, A/V equipment, photocopiers, and express checkout. 300 Reunion Blvd. (phone: 651-1234; 800-233-1234; fax: 742-8126).

Loews Anatole The red brick exterior doesn't look much like a Dallas hotel, but many residents find it a welcome change from the monolithic rectangles of sparkling tinted glass. It has 1,620 rooms and 145 suites, 16 restaurants and lounges, 13 shops, tennis and racquetball courts, and the *Verandah Club Spa*. Around-the-clock room service is available. Other amenities include 26 meeting rooms, a concierge desk, secretarial services, A/V equipment, photocopiers, computers, and express checkout. 2201 Stemmons Fwy. (phone: 748-1200; 800-235-6397; fax: 761-7520).

Melrose A small, luxury place dating from the 1920s, its 185 rooms give it the feel of a country estate. A cozy, English-style lounge and an Art Deco restaurant, the *Landmark*, add to its appeal. Six meeting rooms, A/V equipment, photocopiers, and express checkout are available. 3015 Oak Lawn Ave. (phone: 521-5151; 800-635-7673; fax: 521-9306).

Omni Mandalay at Las Colinas This 27-story enclave dedicated to luxury is in Las Colinas, a business center west of Dallas. Convenient to both the *Dallas/Ft. Worth Airport* and downtown, it has a fine restaurant, *Enjolie*, a health club, and a heated pool. Among the amenities are 24-hour room service, 19 meeting rooms, a concierge desk, A/V equipment, photocopiers, and express checkout. 221 E. Las Colinas Blvd., Irving (phone: 556-0800; 800-843-6664; fax: 556-0729).

Plaza of the Americas Part of the Forte chain, its management has hired the best help available—from the staff at the coffee shop to the chef at the *650 North* restaurant, which features nouvelle cuisine and a well-stocked wine cellar. In the adjacent shopping mall are 16 restaurants, 25 shops, and an ice-skating rink. Room service is available around the clock. Business facilities include nine meeting rooms, secretarial and concierge services, A/V equipment, photocopiers, computers, and express check-out. 650 N. Pearl Expy. at Bryan St. (phone: 979-9000; 800-225-3050; fax: 953-1931).

Westin Galleria With 440 balconied rooms, this elegant hostelry opens onto the *Galleria*. Amenities include a pool, a jogging track, saunas, exercise facilities, and three restaurants, including *Huntington's,* which serves first-rate continental fare (see *Eating Out*). Convenient to North Dallas business districts, the hotel offers 24-hour room service and such business pluses as 16 meeting rooms, concierge and secretarial services, A/V equipment, photocopiers, computers, and express checkout 13340 Dallas Pkwy. (phone: 934-9494; 800-228-3000; fax: 450-2979).

INEXPENSIVE

Amerisuites These bright, modern rooms with large kitchenettes are perfect for families. City bus transportation is within two blocks, and complimentary airport transport is provided. There is a meeting room as well as secretarial services, photocopiers, and computers. 3950 Airport Fwy., Irving (phone: 790-1950; 800-255-1755; fax: 790-4750).

La Quinta Motor Inns If you're looking for a clean, inconspicuous place to sleep, try any of this chain's 14 motels throughout the area, including the airport. They provide nonsmoking rooms and free local calls. Each has a 24-hour adjacent restaurant. Other pluses include meeting rooms, with a capacity of 30 to 40 (depending on the location), a concierge desk, secretarial services, photocopiers, and express checkout. Call 800-531-5900 for central reservations.

EATING OUT

Restaurant dining in Dallas has become as sophisticated as that in any major American city over the last decade, with an emphasis on Southwest cooking. Expect to spend $60 or more for dinner for two in those places we've listed as expensive; between $30 and $60 at those categorized as moderate; and less than $30 at inexpensive places. Prices do not include wine, drinks, tax, or tips. (Parts of Dallas are "dry," but alcoholic beverages generally are available with an inexpensive club membership.) Unless otherwise noted, restaurants serve lunch and dinner. All restaurants are in the 214 area code unless otherwise indicated.

EXPENSIVE

Baby Routh The casual, chic little sister of the defunct *Routh Street Café* serves excellent Southwestern fare, including catfish, barbecued salmon, and hummus with olive bread. Open daily. Reservations advised. Major credit cards accepted. 2708 Routh St. (phone: 871-2345).

Café Pacific An interesting variety of dishes is served in an attractive setting. The lobster and scallop ceviche and polenta grain with crabmeat are especially good, and this dining spot offers one of the most extensive and reasonably priced wine lists in town. Closed Sundays. Reservations advised. Major credit cards accepted. 24 *Highland Park Village* (phone: 526-1170).

City Café This chic eatery features a distinctive "nouvelle American" menu with such tidbits as warm cabbage salad with bacon, Caesar salad, grilled sweetbreads, and triple chocolate sour cream cake. Open daily. Reservations advised. Major credit cards accepted. 5757 W. Lovers La. (phone: 351-2233).

Conservatory A refined, elegant introduction to New American productions, which tend to be artistic and imaginatively seasoned. Outstanding dishes include grilled shrimp in basil and grilled halibut served with smoked salmon. Open daily; dinner only on weekends. Reservations advised. Major credit cards accepted. In the *Crescent Court Hotel,* with its entrance at 2215 Cedar Springs (phone: 871-3242).

Del Frisco's There's no better place in Dallas for steaks. This crowded, club-like eatery offers generous portions of every cut of beef imaginable, along with elegantly cut onion rings. The menu also features a good spinach soufflé. Closed Sundays. Reservations advised. Major credit cards accepted. 5251 Spring Valley Rd. (phone: 490-9000).

East Wind This upscale Vietnamese eatery in the trendy Deep Ellum section of the city offers near-perfect concoctions, including asparagus soup with crabmeat, grilled catfish with lemongrass, and beef dishes with cilantro. Open daily. Reservations advised. Major credit cards accepted. 2711 Elm St. (phone: 745-5554).

French Room With its rich Louis XIV decor, this is known as the most lavish dining room in the city. The menu combines American and French fare, such as roasted yellowfin tuna *au poivre* and New Zealand venison with wild mushroom soufflé. Closed Sundays. Reservations advised. Major credit cards accepted. In the *Adolphus Hotel,* 1321 Commerce (phone: 742-8200).

Huntington's This fine restaurant in the *Westin Galleria* presents sumptuous food in an elegant setting. The menu features such American fare as lobster tacos and pan-seared salmon. Closed Sundays. Reservations advised. Major credit cards accepted. 13340 Dallas Pkwy. (phone: 851-2882).

Mansion Though a hotel dining spot, the atmosphere is that of a handsome private mansion. Quiet elegance, Southwestern fare (including baked potato enchiladas and rack of lamb served atop cheese potatoes), polished service, and a VIP crowd make dining here a memorable experience. Open daily. Reservations necessary. Major credit cards accepted. In the *Mansion on Turtle Creek,* 2821 Turtle Creek Blvd. (phone: 526-2121).

Old Warsaw One of the oldest restaurants in Dallas, it features such continental selections as Dover sole, chateaubriand, and roast quail. Various pâtés also are offered. Open daily for dinner only. Reservations necessary. Major credit cards accepted. 2610 Maple (phone: 528-0032).

Pyramid This dining room in the *Fairmont* hotel serves a four-course *table d'hôte* that has won high praise. Closed Sundays. Reservations necessary. Major credit cards accepted. 1717 N. Akard St. (phone: 720-5249).

Riviera The South of France inspired this gem with a distinct—but not overwhelming—continental atmosphere. Its first-rate menu, featuring roasted-tomato soup with crabmeat and mixed grill of sausage, lamb, and veal, has made it one of the city's best places. Open daily for dinner only. Reservations advised. Major credit cards accepted. 7709 Inwood (phone: 351-0094).

St. Germain The exquisite dining room at the eponymous hotel has brought genteel, refined dining back in style, thanks to nice touches such as Waterford crystal, Limoges china, and white-gloved waiters. The food is as attractive and elegant as the atmosphere: The prix fixe meals may feature pan-roasted snapper with prawns in red curry, warm crab custard, or oysters *velouté*. Open only Fridays and Saturdays for dinner (private dinners at other times may be arranged). Reservations necessary. Major credit cards accepted. 2516 Maple Ave. (phone: 871-2516).

311 Lombardi's Formerly *Lombardi's,* this sophisticated Italian trattoria serves risotto with seafood, grilled chicken with gnocchi and garlic, and *focaccia*. Live jazz. Open daily. Reservations advised. Major credit cards accepted. 311 Market at Ross (phone: 747-0322).

MODERATE

Beau Nash The atmosphere in this small dining room in the *Crescent Court* hotel is stylish but casual; standout dishes include chili with peppery cheese biscuits, calamari, pizza, and grilled fresh fish. Open daily. Reservations unnecessary. Major credit cards accepted. 400 Crescent Ct. (phone: 871-3240).

Café Madrid Anyone craving excellent *tapas* will find them at this charming, popular European outpost. Menu delights include potato omelette in saffron sauce, fried calamari, mussels in vinaigrette, grilled pork tenderloin, and paella (offered only on weekends). Closed Sundays. Reservations advised. MasterCard and Visa accepted. 4501 Travis (phone: 528-1731).

Deep Ellum Café With an atmosphere that evokes New York's SoHo, this casual, comfortable place is located in Deep Ellum, a onetime hot spot for jazz. The menu is broad, encompassing everything from Vietnamese salads to chicken with dill dumplings, to superb chicken-fried steaks and spinach ravioli. Open daily. Reservations advised. Major credit cards accepted. 2706 Elm St. (phone: 741-9012).

Dick's Last Resort For a boisterous evening of another kind, this *West End MarketPlace* eatery serves up Cajun-influenced food in tin buckets, 74 varieties of beer, and lively music. Open daily. Reservations unnecessary. Major credit cards accepted. 1701 N. Market, Suite 110 (phone: 747-0001).

Hard Rock Café The Supreme Court of rock 'n' roll, this restaurant occupies a renovated Baptist church where the walls are hung with such memorabilia as Jimi Hendrix's lead guitar and another that Elvis once strummed. Try the baked potato soup or the grilled *fajitas*—portions are generous. Open daily. Reservations unnecessary. Major credit cards accepted. 2601 McKinney Ave. (phone: 855-0007).

Joey Tomato's Atlantic City This Italian dining spot boasts spaghetti dishes prepared eight different ways, as well as great *focaccia,* steaks, and seafood. The big, shiny tomato over the front door makes this place hard to miss. Open daily. Reservations unnecessary. Major credit cards accepted. 3232 McKinney Ave. (phone: 754-0380).

Kathleen's Art Café This hip hangout—with its own bakery next door—begins the day with unforgettable blue corn pancakes, homemade pastries, and eggs scrambled with tortillas and salsa or poached atop *tomatillo* enchiladas. Wait till lunch or dinner for eggplant-garlic-feta pizza or angel hair pasta with shrimp. The contemporary art on the walls is for sale. Open daily. Reservations advised. MasterCard and Visa accepted. 4424 Lovers La. (phone: 691-2355).

Mario's Chiquita This isn't an Americanized Tex-Mex joint—the food is really Mexican. The *carne asada* Tampico-style is a filet, broiled over a hickory fire, then served with green peppers, onions, and soft tacos topped with ranchero sauce. Far and away one of the finest Mexican eateries north of the border. Open daily. No reservations. Major credit cards accepted. Two locations: 4514 Travis Walk, Suite 105 (phone: 521-0721) and 221 W. Parker Rd., Plano (phone: 423-2977).

Matt's No Place The power of Matt Martinez's culinary reputation is uncontested: he packs this restaurant nightly without ever hanging a sign out front. The exceptional fare includes huge shrimp grilled with bacon, onions, and peppers; grilled quail; New York strip steaks; homemade bread; divine salads; and cheesecake with praline sauce. Open for dinner only; closed Sundays. Reservations necessary. Major credit cards accepted. 6310 La Vista (phone: 823-9007).

Mia's A casual, family-run place well known for Tex-Mex specialties, particularly *chiles rellenos.* Closed Sundays. Reservations unnecessary. MasterCard and Visa accepted. 4322 Lemmon (phone: 526-1020).

On the Border Drop by for a taste of Tex-Mex, particularly the *fajitas,* served sizzling on a hot platter. Outdoor tables placed on a good people watching corner supplement those in the spacious (and sometimes boisterous) dining rooms. Open daily; brunch on Sundays. Reservations unnecessary. Major credit cards accepted. 3300 Knox St. (phone: 528-5900).

Patrizio A fashionable Italian trattoria, it serves pizza with eggplant or shrimp, pasta dishes, chicken with Southwestern pesto, and smoked salmon, as well as delicious *tiramisù.* Open daily. Reservations advised. Major credit cards accepted. 25 *Highland Park Village* (phone: 522-7878).

Ranchman's Café About an hour's drive north of Dallas is the town of Ponder (pop. 208) and one of the best little hometown cafés in Texas. Its old wooden screen doors open into a room with longhorns and stirrups on the walls and an authentic country-and-western jukebox. Specialties are chicken-fried or T-bone steaks, French fries, and possibly the best pecan pie in the country, along with other home-baked fruit pies. Bring your own alcohol. Open daily. Reservations unnecessary (but you have to call before you come if you want a baked potato). No credit cards accepted. Bailey St., Ponder (phone: 817-479-2221).

St. Martin's A well-chosen, reasonably priced wine list coupled with imaginatively prepared seafood make this intimate place a favorite with those who like to linger over a meal. Open daily. Reservations advised. Major credit cards accepted. 3020 Greenville Ave. (phone: 826-0940).

INEXPENSIVE

Peggy Sue's BBQ Across from *Southern Methodist University* and decorated with memorabilia from the 1950s, this café offers great oak-smoked beef and barbecued chicken. Don't pass up the fried pies for dessert—chocolate, apricot, and peach are the best. Open daily. No reservations. Major credit cards accepted. 6600 Snider Plaza (phone: 987-9188).

Snuffer's There's no match for this cozy bar's oversized burgers or for its messy cheese fries, which are best with jalapeños and ranch dressing. More virtuous diners can have soft tacos, quesadillas, and chicken Caesar salads—but everyone goes for the strawberry margaritas. The rock music from the jukebox can be a bit loud, but the food is well worth the din. Open daily. No reservations. Major credit cards accepted. 3526 Greenville Ave. (phone: 826-6850).

Sonny Bryan's Few would argue that this place serves the best barbecue in Dallas, although some might object to the crowds and small, drab interior where school desks serve as tables. Open daily for lunch only. No reservations or credit cards accepted. 2202 Inwood Rd. (phone: 357-7120).

Denver

At-a-Glance

SEEING THE CITY

The best view of Denver is from the top of the *Capitol* rotunda (between E. 14th and E. Colfax Aves.; phone: 866-2604), with the Rockies to the west, the Great Plains stretching to the east, and Denver itself sprawled below. On the 13th step of the *Capitol* is an inscription noting that you are exactly 1 mile above sea level. The view is also spectacular from the *Museum of Natural History* in *City Park* (phone: 322-7009).

SPECIAL PLACES

It's a pleasure to walk around Denver. The downtown section has a number of Victorian mansions as well as the city's public institutions and commercial buildings.

US MINT Appropriately enough for a city that made its fortune in gold, Denver still has more of it than anyplace else in the country (except *Fort Knox*). On the outside, the *Mint* is a relatively unimpressive white sandstone Federal building with Doric arches over the windows. Inside, you can see money being stamped and printed and view the display of gold bullion—only a fraction of the total stored here. Most impressive is the room full of money just waiting to be counted. Twenty-minute guided tours are given on weekdays. Closed weekends. No admission charge. Delaware St. between Colfax and 14th; tour entrance on Cherokee St. (phone: 844-3582).

DENVER ART MUSEUM Besides having an overall collection that covers the period from 1100 to the present, this museum has top collections of pre-Columbian art and artifacts, Spanish colonial art, and Asian art. The museum has added modern, contemporary, African, and Oceanic galleries as well. Be sure to visit the American Indian collection on the second floor—it has superlative costumes, basketry, rugs, and totem poles. Some display halls completely re-create another time and place. Stop for lunch or a snack at the terrace restaurant. Closed Mondays. No admission charge on Saturdays or for children under six. 100 W. 14th Ave. and Bannock St. (phone: 640-2793 or 640-2295).

DENVER PUBLIC LIBRARY This seven-story building houses a vast collection of books, photographs, and documents related to the history of the West. There is also a splendid children's collection as well as exhibitions on Western life. Rare book lovers will be delighted with the library's special collections. Open daily. 1357 Broadway (phone: 640-8800).

COLORADO STATE HISTORY MUSEUM This popular attraction features exhibits on people who've contributed to Colorado history, period costumes from the early frontier days, and Indian relics. Many of these authentic costumes were donated by members of old Denver families. Life-size dioramas show how gold miners, pioneers, and Mesa Verde cliff dwellers used to live. Open daily. No admission charge for children under six. 1400 Broadway (phone: 866-3682).

CAPITOL The rotunda looks like the dome of the *US Capitol,* coated with $50,900 worth of Colorado gold leaf; the impressive marble staircases rate a look even if you don't want to climb them. There are 30-minute tours. Closed Saturdays and Sundays (September through May). No admission charge. Between E. 14th Ave. and Colfax, at Sherman Ave. (phone: 866-2604).

MOLLY BROWN HOUSE When gold miner Johnny Brown and his wife, Molly, moved into their Capitol Hill mansion, Denver society snubbed them as nouveau riche. Ironically, their former house has become a leading attraction. She is particularly remembered for taking charge of a lifeboat when the *Titanic* sank, commanding the men to row while she held her chinchilla cape over a group of children to keep them warm—which is how she came to be known as the "unsinkable Molly Brown." Closed Mondays (September through May). No admission charge for children under six. 1340 Pennsylvania St. (phone: 832-4092).

LARIMER STREET Walk along the *16th Street Mall* to Larimer, Denver's most interesting shopping street, and pass the *Daniels and Fisher Tower,* a 1920s landmark said to be a copy of the campanile in Venice. It used to be the tallest building in town, but it has been overshadowed by more modern edifices. Larimer Street is lined with fascinating art galleries, curio shops, silversmiths, and cafés. Most interesting is *Larimer Square* (between 14th and 15th Sts.), where various restaurants, crafts shops, and microbrewery taverns have been restored to reflect the flavor of Denver's past.

CITY PARK This 640-acre park has two lakes, spreading lawns, the *Denver Zoo* (phone: 331-4110), and the *Museum of Natural History* (phone: 322-7009). Known for its exhibitions of animals in natural settings, the museum was the first in the country to use curved backgrounds with reproductions of mountain flowers, shrubs, and smaller animals to give a feeling of nature. There are displays of fossils, minerals, gold coins, and birds; and the *Hall of Life* attempts to unravel the mysteries of the human machine. It's open daily; there's an admission charge. The museum also houses the popular *Gates Planetarium* (phone: 370-6351) and the *IMAX Theatre* (phone: 370-6300). Both are open daily and charge admission. The *Denver Zoo,* which has designed a number of natural mountain environments for its animals, is open daily; there's no admission charge for children under six.

HYLAND HILLS WATER WORLD Colorado is not the place for an ocean vacation, but this is one spot where you can body-surf a mile above sea level. There are 25 exciting rides, two ocean-wave pools, and a special area for small children. Closed between *Labor Day* and *Memorial Day.* Admission charge. 1850 W. 89th Ave. (phone: 427-7873).

CHILDREN'S MUSEUM A kid-size basketball court, a miniature grocery store, and a real television studio will enthrall youngsters, as will the miniature ski mountain, where kids can try out Colorado trails. Open daily.

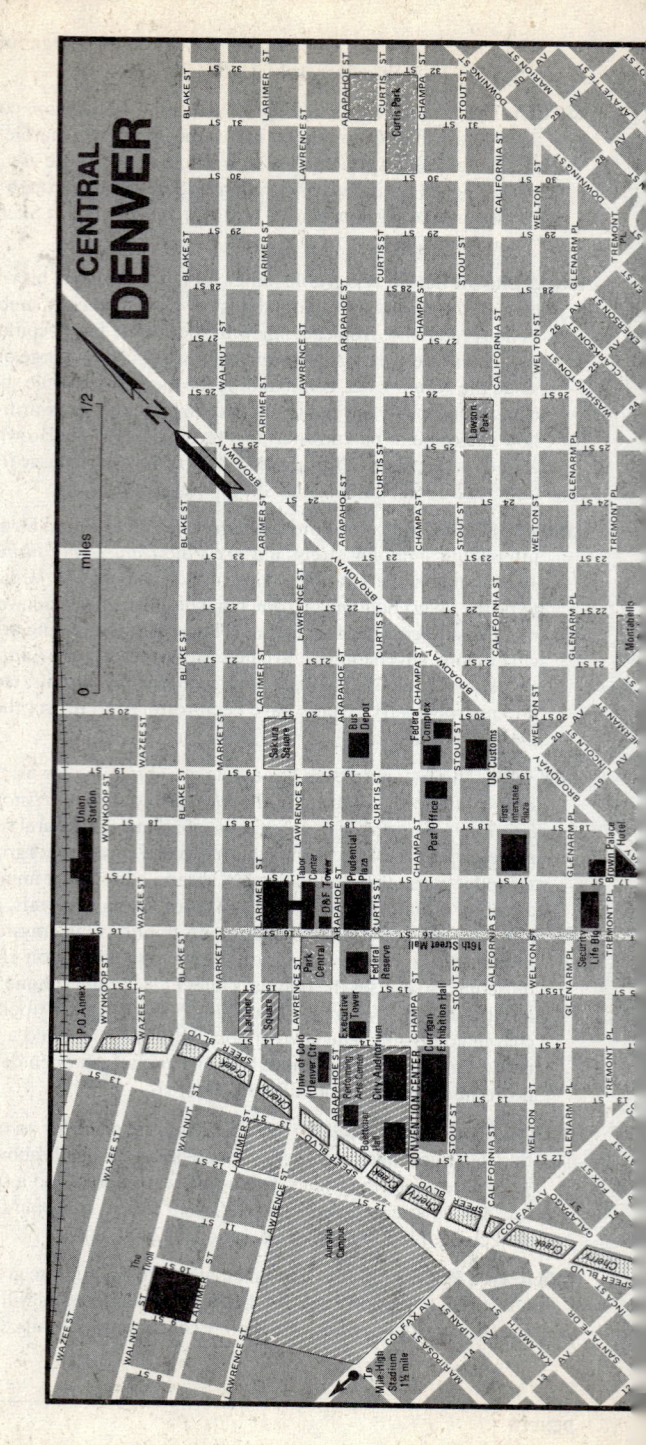

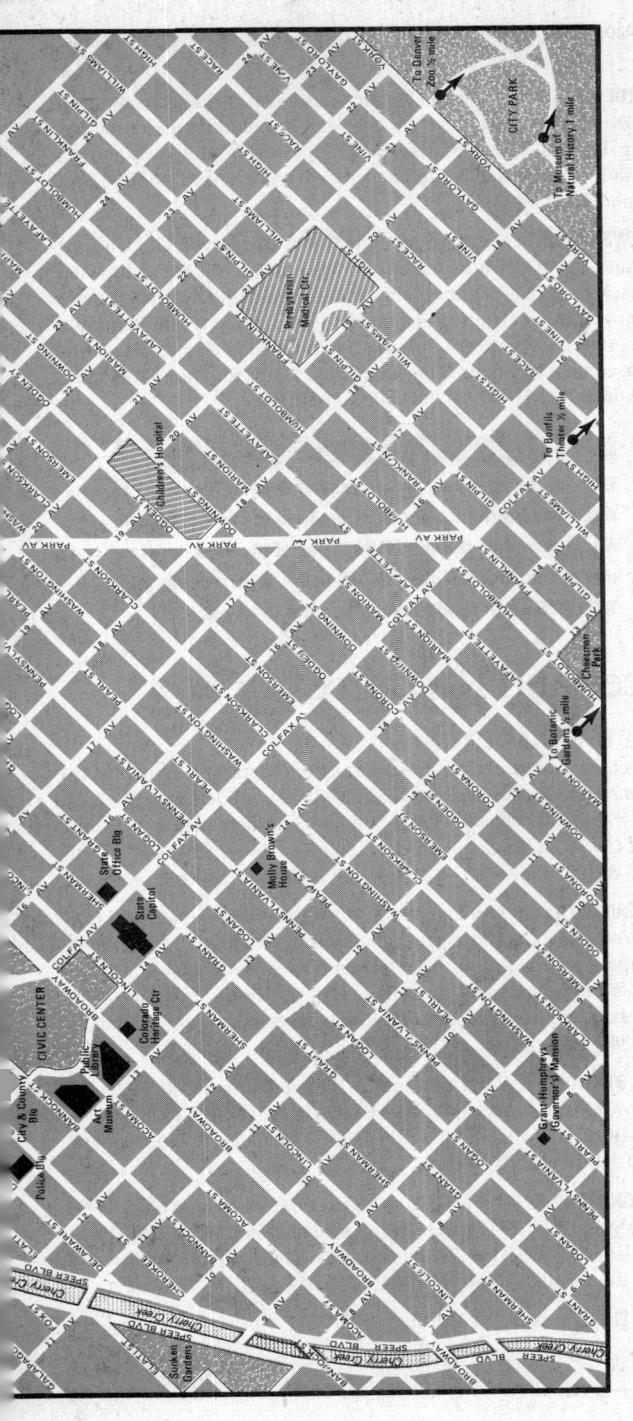

Admission charge. 2121 Crescent Dr., off I-25 at 23rd Ave. (phone: 433-7444).

ELITCH GARDENS One of America's oldest amusement parks, it has retained its charm over the years. The park is clean, the gardens are attractive, and the rides will have the kids asking for more. Grounds-only and all-rides admissions available. Closed October through April. 4621 W. 38th Ave. (phone: 455-4771).

COORS BREWERY For beer enthusiasts, the Coors Brewery in Golden (just 20 minutes from downtown Denver) will explain the entire brewing process. Visitors can see thousands of six-packs flash by every minute and enjoy an ice-cold mug of—what else?—Coors beer. The 30-minute tour is offered daily except Sundays. No admission charge. For information, contact Coors Brewing Company, Guest Relations/Tours, BC 200, Golden, CO 80401 (phone: 303-277-BEER).

EXTRA SPECIAL

With all the gorgeous places around Denver, it's unfair to single out any particular one. If you have to choose, though, *Rocky Mountain National Park* is one of the most spectacular scenic areas of the US—it makes a perfect day trip. Take I-25 north for 50 miles, then Rte. 34 west.

Sources and Resources

TOURIST INFORMATION

For brochures, maps, and general information, contact the *Denver Metro Convention and Visitors Bureau* (225 W. Colfax Ave., Denver, CO 80202; phone: 892-1112), which is closed Sundays. For information on skiing, contact *Colorado Ski Country USA* (1560 Broadway, Suite 1440, Denver, CO 80202; phone: 837-0793), which is closed weekends.

LOCAL COVERAGE *Denver Post* and *Rocky Mountain News,* dailies; and *Colorado Homes & Lifestyles* magazine, monthly. *Westword,* a free weekly newspaper, is the best guide to the Denver area; it's available at newsstands and in grocery and convenience stores. Friday editions of the *Denver Post* and *Rocky Mountain News* have complete entertainment and activity guides.

TELEVISION STATIONS KWGN Channel 2–Independent; KCNC Channel 4–NBC; KRMA Channel 6–PBS; KMGH Channel 7–CBS; KUSA Channel 9–ABC; KBDI Channel 12–PBS; KTVD Channel 20–Independent; and KDVR Channel 31–Fox.

RADIO STATIONS AM: KHOW 630 (talk); KOA 850 (talk/sports); KYGO 950 (country); and KDEN 1340 (children's programming). FM: KCFR 90.1 (NPR/classical); KHIH 94.7 (jazz/new age); KRFX 103.5 (classic rock); KXKL 105.1 (oldies); and KAZY 106.7 (rock).

TELEPHONE The area code for Denver is 303.

SALES TAX The sales tax is 7.2%; the hotel tax is 11.9%.

CLIMATE Because of its altitude, Denver is pretty dry; the city gets an average of only 15 inches of rain a year. Even when the temperature hits the 90s in summer (it hits 100F every five years!), it's not intolerable. Nights cool to the 70s. In winter, the days are often sunny and in the 40s or 50s, but it does snow occasionally.

GETTING AROUND

AIRPORT *Denver International Airport* is about a 45-minute drive from downtown. *Regional Transportation District (RTD)* buses (phone: 299-6000) travel from the airport to downtown for $6 one way or $9 round trip.

BUS *RTD* runs buses throughout the Denver area. The fare is 50¢ or $1 depending on time of day. For information, contact the *Downtown Information Center,* 626 16th St. (phone: 299-6000).

CAR RENTAL All major national firms are represented.

TAXI Taxis cannot be hailed in the streets. Call *Yellow Cab* (phone: 777-7777), *Zone Cab* (phone: 861-2323), or *Metro Taxi* (phone: 333-3333). There are cab stands at the airport, bus station, *Union Station,* and at major hotels.

LOCAL SERVICES

AUDIOVISUAL EQUIPMENT *Colorado Visual Aids* (phone: 778-1111).

BABY-SITTING *Rent a Mom* (360 S. Monroe; phone: 322-1399).

BUSINESS SERVICES *Record Executive Services* (7730 E. Belleview; phone: 771-8686).

DRY CLEANER/TAILOR *Colorado Lace* (200 E. Seventh Ave.; phone: 837-1338; and other downtown locations).

LIMOUSINE *Colorado Limousine* (phone: 832-7155).

MECHANIC *Goodyear Auto Center* (14th St. and Tremont Pl.; phone: 573-1502).

MEDICAL EMERGENCY *Denver General Hospital Emergency Service* (Eighth and Cherokee Sts.; phone: 436-6070).

MESSENGER SERVICES *Express Messenger* (phone: 936-0200); *Speedy Messenger* (phone: 292-6000).

MONEY TRANSFERS *American Express MoneyGram* (phone: 800-926-9400 for information; 800-866-8800 for money transfers); *Western Union Financial Services* (phone: 800-325-6000 or 800-325-4176).

NATIONAL/INTERNATIONAL COURIER *FedEx* (phone: 892-7981).

PHARMACY *Walgreens* (801 16th St. and Stout; phone: 571-5314), open daily 7 AM to 6:30 PM.

PHOTOCOPIES *Sir Speedy* (1438 Tremont Pl. and other downtown locations; phone: 534-2529).

POST OFFICE Terminal Annex, open daily 24 hours (1595 Wynkoop St.; phone: 297-6800).

PROFESSIONAL PHOTOGRAPHER *CoMedia* (phone: 832-2299).

TELECONFERENCE FACILITIES *Brown Palace*; *Hyatt Regency Denver* (see *Checking In,* below).

TRANSLATOR *Berlitz* (phone: 399-8686); *Rocky Mountain Translations* (phone: 449-6954).

WESTERN UNION/TELEX Many offices are located around the city (phone: 800-325-6000 to find the location nearest you).

SPECIAL EVENTS

The *National Western Stock Show and Rodeo* in January lasts two weeks and attracts cowfolk from all over. The *Denver Art Museum*'s annual exhibition of Western art runs from January through March. *Easter* Sunrise Service at *Red Rocks Natural Amphitheater* attracts thousands. In July and August, the *University of Colorado at Boulder* presents its annual *Shakespeare Festival.* And *Larimer Square* is the site of the *Oktoberfest,* held (oddly enough) in September.

MUSEUMS

In addition to those listed in *Special Places,* there are several other museums of note in Denver.

BLACK AMERICAN WEST MUSEUM AND HERITAGE CENTER Exhibits chronicle African-American cowboys, miners, and soldiers, and other black pioneers of the Wild West. Closed Saturdays through Tuesdays. Admission charge. 3091 California St. (phone: 292-2566).

BUFFALO BILL MUSEUM Especially interesting for children, this museum is full of memorabilia relating to the life of Buffalo Bill, the quintessential frontiersman, who is buried on the grounds. Closed Mondays. Admission charge. Lookout Mountain (phone: 526-0747).

COLORADO RAILROAD MUSEUM For railroad buffs, there are 50 historic cars exhibited outside as well as railroad artifacts and a model railroad inside. Open daily. Admission charge. 17155 W. 44th Ave. (phone: 279-4591).

KIDSPORT This center, affiliated with the *Children's Museum,* moved from *Stapleton Airport* to the new *Denver International Airport.* There are exhibits on travel, the dynamics of flight, diet and fitness, as well as a climbing wall where youngsters move horizontally by gripping exposed pegs in a simulation of mountain climbing. Open daily. Admission charge. *Denver International Airport* (phone: 333-6507).

MUSEUM OF WESTERN ART Paintings by Georgia O'Keeffe, Thomas Moran, and Alfred Bierstadt, and bronze sculptures by Frederic Remington are featured here. Closed Sundays and Mondays. Admission charge. 1727 Tremont (phone: 296-1880).

SHOPPING

Denver is rapidly becoming a shoppers' paradise and soon may rival Dallas as a regional retail center. *Neiman Marcus, Lord & Taylor,* and

Saks Fifth Avenue all reside at the *Cherry Creek Mall* (on Cherry Creek Drive in east central Denver). Several old favorites are going strong, too, such as downtown's spectacular *Tabor Center* (16th and Lawrence Sts.), home to *Brooks Brothers, Sharper Image,* and others; and *Cherry Creek North* (north of First Ave., just across from the mall), featuring dozens of quaint shops, boutiques, restaurants, and one of the world's truly great bookstores—*The Tattered Cover* (2955 E. First Ave.; phone: 322-7727), with over 400,000 titles. Along Larimer Street, *Cry Baby Ranch* (1422 Larimer St.; phone: 623-3979) features Western relics, reproductions, and books with a slant toward the unusual; the *Squash Blossom Gallery* (1428 Larimer St.; phone: 572-7979) focuses on folk art, crafts (some from Mexico), and jewelry; and *MAX* (1411 Larimer St.; phone: 623-2888) is a boutique selling high-fashion women's clothing by Norma Kamali, Philippe Adec, and Liza Bruce, as well as the latest jewelry.

SPORTS AND FITNESS

BASEBALL The *National League* Colorado *Rockies* play at *Mile High Stadium* (1700 Federal Blvd.; phone: 856-0428); the team will hold its home games here until its new stadium, *Coors Field,* is completed.

BASKETBALL The *NBA Nuggets* play at *McNichols Sports Arena* (1635 Clay St.; phone: 893-3865).

BICYCLING Bicycle tours can be arranged by *Two Wheel Tours* (2949 E. Cresthill; phone: 798-4601).

FISHING There's good fishing at Dillon Reservoir, 70 miles west of Denver on I-70, and Cherry Creek Reservoir, just 8 miles southeast of the city on I-225. The South Platte River near Deckers, a town 28 miles southwest of Denver, is a good place for fly fishing.

FITNESS CENTERS *Indian Springs Resort* (302 Soda Creek Rd., one block south of Miner St., in Idaho Springs; phone: 623-2050) has relaxing, hot mineral baths. The *International Athletic Club* (1630 Welton; phone: 623-2100) welcomes guests from several downtown hotels; it offers exercise classes, tracks, racquetball and squash courts, a sauna, and massage.

FOOTBALL The *NFL Broncos* play at *Mile High Stadium* (1700 Federal Blvd.; phone: 433-7466).

GOLF Among the area's public golf courses, the best are *Kennedy* (10500 E. Hampden Ave.; phone: 751-0311), *Park Hill* (3500 Colorado Blvd.; phone: 333-5411), and *Wellshire* (3333 S. Colorado Blvd.; phone: 757-1352).

HOCKEY The *University of Denver Pioneers* play at the *DU Arena* (E. Jewell Ave. and S. Gaylord Way; phone: 871-2336).

JOGGING Follow the Highline Canal trail; or run in *Washington Park,* which is 4½ miles from downtown, or in *City Park,* 2 miles from downtown.

RACING Horse racing takes place from May through September at *Arapahoe Park* (26000 E. Quincy St.; phone: 690-2400). Greyhounds race at

Mile High Kennel Club (6200 Dahlia Rd.; phone: 288-1591) from June through August. No one under 21 is admitted.

SKIING Colorado ski country is famous all over the world. The slopes closest to the city are in *Loveland Basin* (60 miles west on I-70; phone: 571-5580). *Keystone and Arapahoe Basin* (phone: 468-2316), *Breckenridge* (phone: 453-5000), and *Copper Mountain* (phone: 968-2882) are all from 15 to 25 miles farther on I-70. To reach *Winter Park* (phone: 892-0961) drive west on I-70, then north on Rte. 40, or take the *Ski Train* (phone: 296-4754) to *Winter Park* from Denver's *Union Station*, weekends from late December through early April. The renowned *Vail* resort (phone: 476-1000) is 100 miles west of Denver on I-70, and equally acclaimed *Aspen* and *Snowmass* (phone for both: 925-1220) are about 190 miles southwest of the city (on I-70 and Hwy. 82). *Crested Butte* (237 miles southwest; phone: 349-2333) and *Steamboat Springs* (163 miles northwest; phone: 879-0740) are also popular.

TENNIS The best public courts are at *Gates Tennis Center* (100 S. Adams St.; phone: 355-4461).

THEATER

For complete up-to-the-minute listings on theatrical and musical events, see the publications listed in *Local Coverage* above. The *University of Colorado at Boulder*—about 20 miles northwest of Denver—hosts a *Shakespeare Festival* every summer (see *Special Events*). The *Denver Center for the Performing Arts* (14th and Curtis Sts.; phone: 893-4000) presents Broadway productions as well as those of local companies. The *Country Dinner Playhouse* (6875 S. Clinton in Englewood, just south of Denver; phone: 799-1410), a dinner-theater, presents light offerings and musicals throughout the year.

MUSIC

Two outdoor amphitheaters feature summer concerts: *Red Rocks,* which provides a spectacular mountain setting (12 miles west of Denver off I-70; phone: 575-2637), and *Fiddler's Green* (12 miles south of downtown, off I-25 in the Denver Tech Center; phone: 770-2222). Most large indoor concerts are held at *McNichols Arena* (1635 Clay St.; phone: 640-7333). The *Colorado Symphony* performs classical and pop concerts November through May at *Boettcher Hall* (14th and Arapahoe Sts.; phone: 595-4388). During summer lunch hours, street musicians give concerts in the financial district, on the plazas outside the Norwest Bank Center and the First Interstate Bank of Denver.

NIGHTCLUBS AND NIGHTLIFE

Jazz venues are *El Chapultepec* (1962 Market St.; phone: 295-9126) and *Jazzworks* (1634 18th St.; phone: 297-2111), downstairs from the *Wynkoop Brewing Company* (phone: 297-2700), where national acts alternate with local musicians from week to week. Comedy is king at *Comedy Works* (1226 15th St.; phone: 595-3637). Singles and rockers have an almost limitless array of choices; among the best are *Panama Reds* (2797 S. Parker Rd., Aurora; phone: 695-1750) and *1082* (1082 Broadway; phone: 831-1082).

Best in Town

CHECKING IN

Denver's plentiful hotel facilities often provide great lodging values compared to those in other major US cities. Expect to pay between $100 and $195 per night for a double room at those places listed as expensive; between $60 and $100 at those in the moderate category; and less than $60 at inexpensive places. Unless otherwise noted, hotels have air conditioning, private baths, TV sets, and telephones. All hotels are in the 303 area code unless otherwise indicated.

EXPENSIVE

Brown Palace Built in the 1890s, this 231-room hotel was one of the first to have a multistory atrium lobby with balconies on every floor. Throughout the years, it has retained a rather faded glamour. There are three restaurants, and business amenities include 13 meeting rooms, secretarial services, and A/V equipment. 17th St. and Tremont Pl. (phone: 297-3111; fax: 293-9204).

Hyatt Regency Denver In the middle of downtown, this 26-story, 540-room property boasts superior restaurants, a rooftop complex with a pool, a tennis court, and a jogging track, and lavish room amenities. Thirteen meeting rooms, secretarial services, A/V equipment, and photocopiers are available. 1750 Welton St. (phone: 295-1200; 800-233-1234; fax: 292-2472).

Loews Giorgio This elegant hotel, the only Colorado member of the Loews chain, boasts 200 rooms and an Italian motif. From the imported Italian marble and original artwork in the public areas to the romantic guestrooms, this is one of Denver's best. The library, bar, and *Tuscany* restaurant are quiet and relaxed, and guests may use the nearby *Cherry Creek Sporting Club*. Business amenities include seven meeting rooms and photocopiers. About eight blocks from the *Cherry Creek* shopping area. S. Colorado Blvd. and E. Mississippi Ave. (phone: 782-9300; 800-223-0888; fax: 758-6542).

Oxford A short stroll from the *Tabor Center*, Writer Square, and historic *Larimer Square*, this 82-room hotel is a bit of history itself, having opened in 1891. With a restaurant and bar, it is a Denver showplace. 17th St. and Wazee (phone: 628-5400; 800-228-5838; fax: 628-5413).

Radisson Denver Downtown Designed by I. M. Pei, this property is the largest downtown hotel, with 740 rooms, *Finnegan's* pub, *Windows* restaurant, and a lounge. There is also a rooftop pool, a health club, a business center, 27 meeting rooms, and A/V equipment. 16th St. and Court Pl. (phone: 893-3333; 800-333-3333; fax: 892-0521).

Sheraton DTC The Denver Tech Center's largest hotel and one of the city's better values, with 623 rooms, racquetball courts, a 24-hour deli, and *Compari's* Italian restaurant. Business facilities include 24 meeting rooms, secretarial services, A/V equipment, and photocopiers. There is also a commercial airport shuttle. 4900 DTC Pkwy. (phone: 779-1100; 800-325-3535; fax: 721-0752).

Westin Tabor Center The centerpiece of the *Tabor Center,* this 420-room complex is in Denver's *16th Street Mall.* Its *Augusta* restaurant (see *Eating Out*) is among the best of a number of excellent downtown dining spots. There is also a pool, a sauna, racquetball courts, and a fitness center. 16th and Lawrence Sts. (phone: 572-9100; 800-228-3000; fax: 572-7288).

MODERATE

Castle Marne An 1889 Victorian mansion has been turned into a lovely bed and breakfast inn with elaborately carved masonry. Its nine rooms are simply furnished (no TV sets or air conditioning), but the ambience is quaint and elegant. Conveniently located three blocks from *City Park,* but the neighborhood isn't the best for walking around at night. Breakfast and afternoon tea are included in the rate. 1572 Race St. (phone: 331-0621; 800-92-MARNE).

Marriott Courtyard A "few frills" entry on the Denver lodging scene that's not to be overlooked. If you can forgo a bellhop and room service, you can secure a Marriott-style room and access to a restaurant for a lot less. Two-room suites are only about $20 more than a standard room. I-25 and Arapahoe Rd. (phone: 721-0300; 800-321-2211; fax: 721-0037).

Merritt House Less than 10 minutes from downtown by car, this Victorian house offers 10 comfortable rooms and the atmosphere of a country inn. There's a pleasant dining room (full breakfast is complimentary). 941 17th Ave. (phone: 861-5230; fax: 832-5317).

Queen Anne Inn Denver's best-known bed and breakfast spot is just four blocks from the downtown *16th Street Mall.* This restored 1879 Victorian home is a 14-room treasure: Each room has a unique decor. The surrounding historic neighborhood is reemerging after years of decline. No smokers or children under 15. 2147 Tremont Pl. (phone: 296-6666; 800-432-4667).

INEXPENSIVE

Comfort Inn–Downtown Originally part of the *Brown Palace,* this 230-room structure was converted into a separate establishment for budget-conscious travelers. Complimentary breakfast and access to a health club are provided. 17th St. and Tremont Pl. (phone: 296-0400).

EATING OUT

Denver seems to be a magnet for great chefs and adventurous restaurateurs. Beef is king, but there are enough places featuring nouvelle cuisine, Southwestern fare, and pizza to keep everyone happy. Expect to pay $60 or more for dinner for two at restaurants listed as expensive, $40 to $60 at places in the moderate category, and $40 or less at those listed as inexpensive. Prices do not include wine, drinks, tax, or tips. Unless otherwise noted, restaurants are open for lunch and dinner. All restaurants are in the 303 area code unless otherwise indicated.

EXPENSIVE

Augusta A spectacular view of Denver's skyline accompanies superb American dishes such as rack of lamb, spit-roasted duck, and grilled silver salmon. The atmosphere is elegant, the service excellent. Closed Sundays; dinner only on Saturdays. Reservations advised. Major credit cards accepted. In the *Westin Tabor Center,* 16th and Lawrence Sts. (phone: 572-9100).

Buckhorn Exchange Established in 1893 by a former scout for Buffalo Bill Cody, this restaurant is on the *National Register of Historic Places.* A city institution, it is festooned with hunting trophies, and its game dishes—elk, buffalo, and quail, among others—continue to make history. For those who aren't "game," generous beef cuts and other standard fare are available. Don't pass up the navy bean soup or homemade apple pie with ice cream and hard cinnamon sauce. Open daily; dinner only on weekends. Reservations advised. Major credit cards accepted. Near downtown, 1000 Osage (phone: 534-9505).

The Fort Near the foothills southwest of Denver, it gives you a taste of Denver's pioneer spirit. Frontier recipes have been adapted to modern tastes, including elk, Buffalo Boodie Sausage, and Rocky Mountain Oysters (bull's testicles). Try a combination to get a sampling. The restaurant is a replica of Colorado's famous *Bent's Fort.* In warm weather, make sure you get a seat on the patio: the scenery is fantastic. Open daily for dinner only. Reservations necessary. Major credit cards accepted. US 285 at Colorado Hwy. 8 (phone: 697-4771).

Tante Louise The atmosphere of this decades-old Denver dining tradition is intimate, evoking a French country *auberge,* replete with hardwood floors, candlelit tables, and glowing fireplaces. The food is equal to the Gallic ambience but adds an accent of Colorado with local products, such as rack of lamb and veal loin. Closed Sundays; lunch served Fridays only. Reservations necessary. Major credit cards accepted. 4900 E. Colfax Ave. (phone: 355-4488).

MODERATE

La Coupole The only French bistro downtown, this dining spot is riding a crest of local popularity. Gallic influences prevail, from the Belle Epoque decor to its traditional bistro fare. Try the homemade pork sausage in red wine sauce or the salmon *galette.* Open daily. Reservations advised. Major credit cards accepted. 2191 Arapahoe St. (phone: 297-2288).

Denver Buffalo Company Dinner at this combination restaurant, deli, and art gallery is dedicated to the buffalo and originates at the restaurant's own 14,000-acre buffalo ranch about 35 miles southeast of Denver. Buffalo prime ribs, roasted in their own juices, and buffalo short ribs are among the most popular offerings. Sample the buffalo chili. Non-buffalo entrées also are available. Open daily; dinner only on Sundays. Reservations advised. Major credit cards accepted. 1109 Lincoln St. (phone: 832-0880).

Fresh Fish Company What's in a name? Everything. The seafood here is so fresh you might think they pulled the swordfish from the Colorado River. In fact, the fish is flown in daily from all over, so the menu items include Maine lobster, Florida stone crab, Canadian walleye, and Hawaiian *ahi.* The food is cooked over imported Mexican mesquite wood. The health- and weight-conscious can choose "Healthmark" entrées, which are low in fat, cholesterol, and sodium. Open daily; dinner only on Saturdays. Reservations accepted for five or more. Major credit cards accepted. 7800 E. Hampden Ave. (phone: 740-9556).

La Loma Here is diverse and authentic Mexican fare, from enchiladas and tacos to the more ambitious *camarones* (large Gulf shrimp sautéed in seasoned butter) and *fajitas*. Try the fried ice cream. The service may sometimes be a bit inattentive, but it's always cheerful and pleasant. Open daily. Reservations advised for parties of six or more. Major credit cards accepted. 2527 W. 26th Ave. (phone: 433-8307).

INEXPENSIVE

Bonnie Brae Tavern In a city where most pizza seems to come from a "hut" or a "domino," this is one pizza place Denverites like to boast about. Founded in 1934, its setting is rustic and there's usually a wait for a table, but no one seems to mind. Closed Mondays. No reservations. Major credit cards accepted. 740 S. University Blvd. (phone: 777-2262).

My Brother's Bar Denver's best hamburger is here, just a few blocks north of downtown (try the jalapeño burger). Don't look for a sign out front—there's never been one. Closed Sundays. Reservations advised for six or more. MasterCard and Visa accepted. 2376 15th St. (phone: 455-9991).

Wynkoop Brewing Company This is the first pub in Colorado where beer is brewed on the premises and served directly from aging tanks. The menu features American fare made with fresh ingredients and organically grown produce. Sausages (also made here), fresh-baked breads and pastries, and gorgonzola ale soup are good choices. Open daily. Reservations unnecessary. Major credit cards accepted. 1634 18th St. (phone: 297-2700).

Detroit

At-a-Glance

SEEING THE CITY

The best view of the city is from the top of the 73-story *Westin* hotel. Part of the *Renaissance Center*, it is one of the city's most dramatic creations. Views are from the hotel's top three floors, called the *Summit*, with a revolving restaurant, cocktail lounge, and observation deck (see *Checking In* for details). Ever-changing views are possible from the *Detroit People Mover* (see *Getting Around*). From Windsor, Ontario, there are great skyline views of Detroit, particularly from rooms in the *Windsor Hilton* (see *Checking In*) and *Compri* hotels, and from *Dieppe Gardens,* a riverside park at the foot of Ouellette Avenue, Windsor's main street.

SPECIAL PLACES

We've divided the city into Civic Center, Cultural Center, and Other Special Places. Civic Center is a good place to begin sightseeing.

CIVIC CENTER

RENAISSANCE CENTER Detroit's very own Oz, this city-within-the-city dominates Detroit's skyline. Dining, entertainment, boutiques, and more have made *RenCen* tick since it opened in 1977. The huge complex is connected by a maze of walkways, atriums, gardens—even an indoor lake. With seven circular buildings to stroll around, first-timers always get lost. Group tours are available (phone: 591-3611). Jefferson Ave. between Randolph and Beaubien Sts.

MILLENDER CENTER Tethered to *RenCen* by an arcing skywalk over Jefferson Avenue, *Millender* is a smaller version of the complex without the dizzying confusion. Both the *Millender Center* and the abutting *Omni* hotel boast quality shops and restaurants.

PHILIP A. HART PLAZA Detroit's riverfront playground was designed by the international sculptor Isamu Noguchi. What it lacks in grass, this paved esplanade makes up for in action. The $30-million *Dodge Fountain* spouts 30 computer-controlled water displays. It's also the home of Detroit's summer riverfront festivals of food and entertainment. The Detroit River runs alongside, with Windsor, Ontario, on the far bank.

THE FIST Robert Graham's downtown sculpture of the fist and forearm of legendary Detroit boxer Joe Louis earns a split decision. Supporters say it celebrates Detroit's fighting spirit, while others feel that a city with a high crime rate hardly needs a four-ton fist in its midst. At Woodward and Jefferson Aves.

WASHINGTON BOULEVARD TROLLEY A charming, antique trolley car (the conductor wears 1890s regalia) travels south from *Grand Circus Park* along Washington Boulevard and east to *RenCen*. It runs past *St. Aloysius*

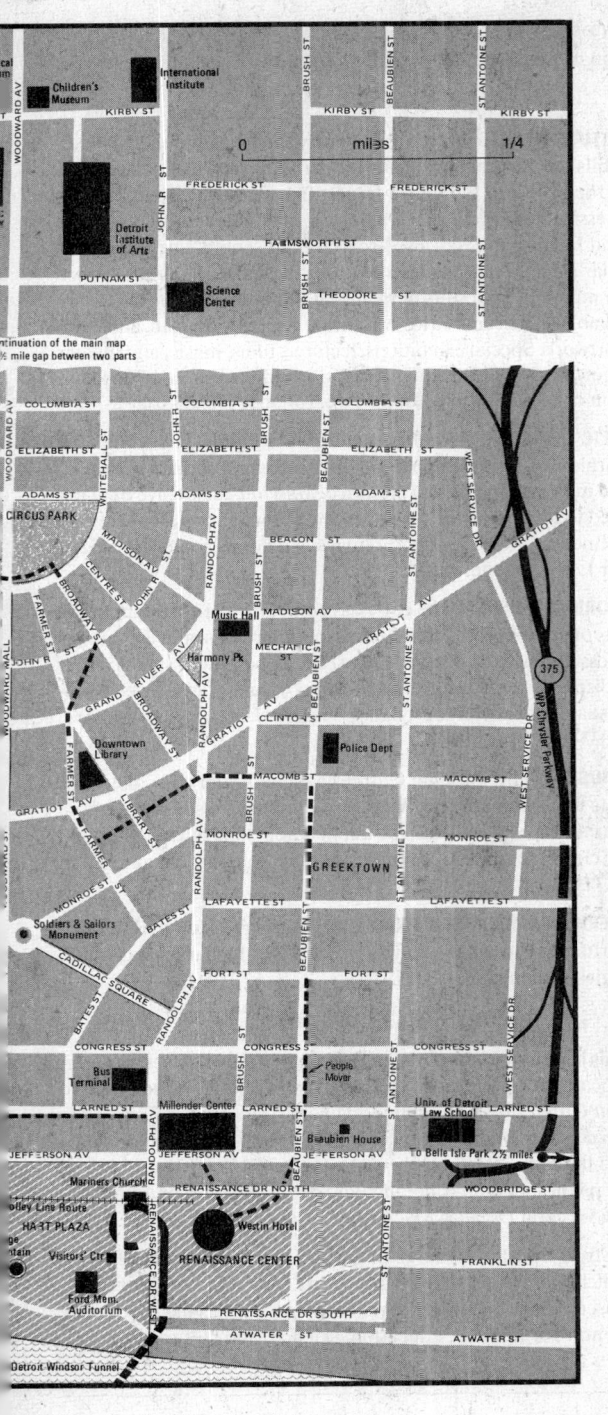

Church, *Cobo Center* (*Cobo Arena* and *Cobo Hall*), and the *Mariner's Church* on its way to the *Renaissance Center*.

CULTURAL CENTER

DETROIT INSTITUTE OF ARTS One of this country's most comprehensive collections fills the 130 galleries here. Italian art is only one of the areas in which the institute (the fourth-largest fine arts museum in the US) has impressive holdings; French painting and decorative arts and the Dutch and Flemish masters also are well represented. Diego Rivera's spectacular *Detroit Industry* frescoes cover the walls of a central court. Egyptian mummies and suits of medieval armor are on display, as are pre-Columbian, African, Native American, Asian, American, and 20th-century artwork. Special exhibitions, lectures, films, music, and theater performances are held frequently. Closed Mondays and Tuesdays. Admission charge. 5200 Woodward Ave. (phone: 833-7900).

DETROIT PUBLIC LIBRARY This Italian Renaissance building of white Vermont marble has not only books but also paintings, stained glass windows, and mosaics. The *Burton Historical Museum,* an archive of material related to Detroit history, is one of the library's special collections. Closed Sundays, Mondays, and holidays. No admission charge. 5201 Woodward Ave. (phone: 833-1000).

DETROIT HISTORICAL MUSEUM The early days of Detroit are brought to life by models of early streets and railroads, period rooms, and exhibitions of horseless carriages and automobiles. In the basement stands a permanent display of actual storefronts from bygone eras. Closed Mondays, Tuesdays, and holidays. Donation suggested. 5401 Woodward Ave. (phone: 833-1805).

CHILDREN'S MUSEUM This museum features a planetarium and collections of puppets and small animals. Kids love the life-size sculpture of the horse near the entrance—it's made out of automobile bumpers. Closed Sundays; closed Saturdays, June through September. No admission charge. 67 E. Kirby Ave. (phone: 494-1210).

MUSEUM OF AFRICAN-AMERICAN HISTORY Black heritage is explored through art and artifacts. Closed Mondays and Tuesdays. Donation suggested. 301 Douglass (phone: 833-9800).

OTHER SPECIAL PLACES

BELLE ISLE This beautiful island in the middle of the Detroit River was originally allocated for pasture by M. Cadillac himself. Now the home of the *Detroit Grand Prix,* the 2-mile-long park has a children's zoo; the *Dossin Great Lakes Museum* (phone: 267-6440) with its displays of model ships; and the *Belle Isle Aquarium* (phone: 267-7159). It's also a good place for picnics, biking, canoeing, and jogging. South of Jefferson, across the General Douglas MacArthur Bridge (phone: 267-7121).

CRANBROOK Stroll through 49 acres of gardens surrounding an English manor, catch a laser light show, visit a nature center, or browse through an art museum or science exhibition. It's all part of this internationally known center for the arts, education, science, and culture. A maple sugar festival, concerts, and other special events make *Cranbrook* a compelling place, worth the 25-mile drive north from Detroit. Lone Pine Rd., Bloomfield Hills (phone: 810-645-3000).

GREENFIELD VILLAGE AND HENRY FORD MUSEUM Legend has it that when Henry Ford couldn't find a copy of McGuffey's *Reader*, he feared such examples of Americana would disappear entirely unless he founded a museum. The result of his efforts is a collection of dozens of antique automobiles and thousands of 19th- and 20th-century machines. Next-door *Greenfield Village* boasts many historically interesting houses. McGuffey's school is reconstructed here, along with Thomas Edison's Menlo Park laboratory. An English shepherd's cottage and Noah Webster's house are also here. Open daily. Separate admissions for *Greenfield Village* and *Henry Ford Museum;* combination tickets available. South of Michigan Ave. between Oakwood Blvd. and Southfield Fwy., Dearborn (phone: 271-1620).

EASTERN MARKET A carnival of sights, smells, and sounds, this has been a farmers' market since 1892. Saturdays are great fun, watching shoppers haggle with merchants selling the freshest produce, meat, fish, poultry, and cheeses. Closed Sundays through Fridays. Russell at Fisher Fwy. (phone: 833-1560).

FOX THEATRE Part theater, part fantasyland, this $8-million restoration of C. Howard Crane's 1928 movie palace has brought name acts back to the great stage and suburbanites back downtown. The gilded lobby is striking, with red-eyed griffins and faux marble columns. The golden elephant above the proscenium and the stained glass chandelier that hangs above 4,800 seats are from the original theater. 2211 Woodward Ave. (phone: 396-7600).

GREEKTOWN This downtown enclave of restaurants serving authentic Greek fare, quaint shops, bakeries, and *Old St. Mary's Church* makes for an interesting stroll. *Trappers Alley* is a five-level mall full of restaurants and specialty shops. Monroe St. between Beaubien and St. Antoine.

MOTOWN MUSEUM This brick and stucco building, called *Hitsville, USA,* turned out more gold than *Fort Knox*—pop music gold, that is. Motown memories abound here, including Berry Gordy Jr.'s original studio, where the *Supremes,* Stevie Wonder, the *Temptations,* the *Four Tops,* and others recorded. Michael Jackson is the museum's biggest benefactor. Open daily. Admission charge. 2648 W. Grand Blvd. (phone: 875-2264).

PLANT TOURS Watch luxury Fords being built at the *Wixom Assembly Plant* in Wixom, a suburb west of Detroit. Tours are given on Fridays; call ahead for reservations (phone: 344-5358). Also with advance notice, you can take the Thursday tour of the high-tech *Auto Alliance* (Mazdas and Fords) plant in Flat Rock, south of the city (phone: 782-7128). Tours of Windsor's *Hiram Walker Canadian Club Distillery* (with free tastings) are held at 2 PM weekdays during summers only (phone: 965-6611 for reservations).

ROYAL OAK This town midway between Detroit and Pontiac has been reborn with attractions such as the *Detroit Zoological Park* (see below), restau-

rants, coffeehouses, sidewalk cafés, bistros, boutiques, an art theater—
and unbounded energy. At all hours, in any weather, Royal Oak teems
with people out on the streets (in everything from tuxedos to tank tops).

Detroit Zoological Park The first zoo in the US to use barless dwellings
is home to hundreds of species of animals in a setting of lakes and flower
gardens. Open daily in summer; closed Mondays and Tuesdays in winter. No admission charge for children under two. In Royal Oak at Woodward and I-696 (phone: 810-398-0903).

BIRMINGHAM Detroit's hip, village-like northern suburb is the place to hang
out, shop, drink, and be seen. The area is filled with parks, trendy stores
and eateries, a theater, and the ritzy homes of social climbers. Fifteen
miles north of downtown Detroit, where Woodward forks at Hunter.

EXTRA SPECIAL

Canada lies across the river, only a mile from Detroit. In just a few minutes, you can enter a different country, and you don't even need a passport if you're a US citizen—be prepared to show your birth certificate, though. Don't expect any drastic change from Detroit. Windsor, Ontario, is another automobile-producing city, with Canadian GM, Chrysler, and Ford plants. Still, there's Vegas-style gaming at the casino on Riverside Drive, and Windsor is a good place to buy English woolens, glassware, and china. From Detroit, you can reach Windsor by bus or taxi through the Detroit-Windsor Tunnel or over the Ambassador Bridge.

Sources and Resources

TOURIST INFORMATION

The *Metropolitan Detroit Convention and Visitors Bureau* (Tower 100 *RenCen*, Detroit, MI 48243; phone: 567-1170; 800-DETROIT) maintains a 24-hour "What's Line" directory of events and distributes free brochures and maps. Closed weekends. Call the state tourism hotline (phone: 800-543-2937) for maps, calendars of events, and travel advisories.

LOCAL COVERAGE *Detroit Free Press,* morning weekdays; *Detroit News,* morning and afternoon weekdays, combined papers weekends; and *Royal Oak Tribune* and *Oakland Press* (Pontiac, both afternoon). *Key* (free) and *Travel Host* magazines are available at hotels. *Detroit Monthly* is the popular city magazine. *Detroit Visitor's Guide* (free from the *Metropolitan Detroit Convention and Visitors Bureau*) is the best guide to the area. For about-town happenings and attractions, pick up a free *Detroit Monitor* or the more avant-garde *Metro Times* at newsstands.

TELEVISION STATIONS WJBK Channel 2–CBS; WDIV Channel 4–NBC; WXYZ Channel 7–ABC; WXON Channel 20; WKBD Channel 50–FOX; WTVS Channel 56–PBS; and WGPR Channel 62.

RADIO STATIONS AM: WJR 760 (news/talk); WWJ 950 (news); WXYT 1270 (talk); and CKWW 580 (big band). FM: WLTI 93.1 (adult contemporary); WJLB 97.9 (urban contemporary); WDET 101.9 (news and a wide variety of music); WOMC 104.3 (oldies); WQRS 105.1 (classical music); WJZZ 105.9 (jazz); and WGPR 107.5 (urban contemporary).

TELEPHONE The area code for Detroit is 313; 810 for suburban Oakland and Macomb counties. Unless otherwise indicated, phone numbers are in the 313 area code.

SALES TAX The city sales tax is 4%; hotel tax ranges from 2% to 8%, depending on the size and location of the establishment.

CLIMATE Seasons usually procrastinate in Detroit. You might miss spring if you blink, and summer doesn't really peak until July. Autumn can last a day. The local joke is that if you don't like the weather, wait a few minutes. Temperatures range into the 70s and 80s F in summer. Sub-freezing temperatures are often the rule in January and February.

GETTING AROUND

AIRPORT *Detroit Metropolitan Wayne County Airport* handles the city's air traffic and is about a 30-minute drive from downtown. *Commuter Transportation* (phone: 941-3252; 800-351-5466) provides bus transport to the downtown area from the airport's north, south, and international terminals. You also can opt for a chauffeur-driven Lincoln or Cadillac from *Metro Cars, Inc.* (phone: 946-5700; 800-456-1701). *Kirby Tours* (phone: 278-2224; 800-521-0711) offers shuttle service between *Metro Airport* and city hotels.

CAR RENTAL All the major national firms are represented.

PEOPLE MOVER Downtown, an elevated, 2.9-mile cement ribbon carries pedestrians in automated, weatherproof cars. The complete 13-station loop takes 14 minutes and costs 50¢ (phone: 962-7245).

RIVER CRUISES Restaurants/bars that are tugboats, sidewheelers, or otherwise waterbound are anchored in the Detroit River between Detroit and Windsor. During the summer, *Diamond Jack's River Tours* (phone: 843-7676) operates two-hour narrated boat trips along the Detroit River Wednesdays through Sundays from Hart Plaza and *St. Aubin Park*.

TAXI Cabs can be hailed in the street or picked up at the stands in front of hotels. Some of the cabs are licensed to cross over to Canada. If you prefer to call for a cab, we suggest *Checker* (phone: 963-7000).

TOURS *Detroit Upbeat* (phone: 341-6808) and *Kirby Tours* (phone: 278-2224; 800-521-0711) offer tours of Detroit, Ann Arbor, and southeast Michigan.

LOCAL SERVICES

AUDIOVISUAL EQUIPMENT *Allied Audio Visual* (phone: 568-0855); *Gavco* (phone: 567-2155).

BUSINESS SERVICES *Kinko's* (phone: 800-743-2679), which is open 24 hours, and *National Reproductions Corp.* (*NRC*; at *Renaissance Center*; phone:

259-5066) provide photocopying services; *Silver's* (151 W. Fort; phone: 963-0000), sells stationery and office supplies.

DRY CLEANER/TAILOR *Renaissance Dry Cleaners* (*Renaissance Center;* phone: 568-8566).

LIMOUSINE *Detroit Limousine Service* (phone: 810-471-0980).

MECHANIC *Downtown Auto Service* (1200 Cass Ave.; phone: 963-2744).

MEDICAL EMERGENCY *New Detroit Receiving Hospital* (4201 St. Antoine St.; phone: 745-3000).

MESSENGER SERVICES *Pony Express* (phone: 965-7420).

MONEY TRANSFERS *American Express MoneyGram* (phone: 800-926-9400 for information; 800-866-8800 for money transfers); *Western Union Financial Services* (phone: 800-325-6000 or 800-325-4176).

NATIONAL/INTERNATIONAL COURIER *DHL Worldwide Express* (phone: 942-6500); *FedEx* (phone: 961-8771).

PHARMACY *Perry Drugs* (1124 Griswold St.; phone: 964-5020), open weekdays, 7 AM to 6 PM; Saturdays, 8 AM to 6 PM.

PHOTOCOPIES *Duffy's Printing & Copying* (*Renaissance Center,* Tower 200, Sixth Floor; phone: 259-1833); *National Reproductions Corp.* (*NRC;* 433 E. Larned St.; phone: 961-5252, and *Renaissance Center;* phone: 259-5066), pickup and delivery.

POST OFFICE Central (1401 W. Fort St.; phone: 226-8672), 24-hour, self-service lobby; *Renaissance Center* branch (Tower 200; phone: 259-4477).

PROFESSIONAL PHOTOGRAPHER *Ashley Photography* (phone: 645-5164); *Image Concepts* (phone: 459-4707); *Larry Peplin* (phone: 882-7057).

SECRETARY/STENOGRAPHER *CDI* (phone: 259-7516); *Employer's Temporary Services* (phone: 372-7700).

TELECONFERENCE FACILITIES At the *Hyatt Regency Dearborn* (see *Checking In*) and *Pontchartrain* hotels.

TRANSLATOR *Berlitz* (phone: 810-874-2777).

WESTERN UNION/TELEX Many offices are located around the city (phone: 800-325-6000 to find the location nearest you).

OTHER *Eagle Aviation* (phone: 676-8880), helicopter service to downtown and to the *Hyatt Regency Dearborn*; *Fox Studios* (phone: 526-2220), videotaping.

SPECIAL EVENTS

The *Detroit Grand Prix* (phone: 393-7749) sends Indy-type cars thundering around Belle Isle every June. This is also the month when hydroplanes race off Belle Isle during the annual *Thunderfest Gold Cup*. The friendship between Windsor and Detroit is celebrated in the *International Freedom Festival* (phone: 259-5400), a series of events during *Fourth of July* week, highlighted by spectacular fireworks over the river. The *Montreux-Detroit Jazz Festival* (phone: 259-5400) has become quite an annual event the week surrounding *Labor Day* weekend. Concerts are held in Hart Plaza, *Chene Park,* a riverside amphitheater, and at many other locations. The *Michigan Thanksgiving Day Parade* (phone: 923-7400), a Detroit tradition since 1926, still marches on every "Turkey Day."

MUSEUMS

In addition to those described in *Special Places,* Detroit has several other museums of note.

Four of the majestic homes created by Detroit's automotive wealth are part of the Auto Barons Tour. Henry Ford's *Fairlane* mansion (Dearborn; phone: 593-5590); his son Edsel's home (where Henry II grew up), the *Edsel and Eleanor Ford House* (Grosse Pointe Shores; phone: 884-4222); the ornate riverfront entertainment estate of Lawrence P. Fisher, now the *Bhaktivedanta Cultural Center* (phone: 331-6740); and *Meadow Brook Hall* in Rochester (phone: 810-370-3140), which cost Matilda Dodge Wilson $4 million to complete in 1929.

SPORTS AND FITNESS

Detroit wouldn't be Detroit without its top major league teams.

BASEBALL Home base for the *American League Tigers* is *Tiger Stadium* (Michigan at Trumbull; phone: 962-4000).

BASKETBALL The *NBA Pistons* shoot hoops at the *Palace of Auburn Hills* (2 Championship Dr.; phone: 810-377-0100).

FISHING Fishing is pretty good in the Detroit River, especially around Belle Isle. Of the area's hundreds of lakes, we recommend Orchard Lake or Lake St. Clair.

FITNESS CENTERS *Power House Gym* (2580 N. Squirrel Rd., Auburn Hills; phone: 810-377-3383) is a full-service health club open to non-members for a fee.

FOOTBALL The *NFL Lions* play in the covered, 80,000-seat *Silverdome* (M-59 at Opdyke, Pontiac; phone: 810-335-4151).

GOLF Two of the better public courses are *Kensington Metropark* (2240 W. Buno Rd., Milford; phone: 810-635-1561) and *Pine Knob* (5580 Waldon, Clarkston; phone: 810-625-4430).

HOCKEY *NHL Red Wings* action is on the ice at *Joe Louis Arena* (Civic Center Dr.; phone: 396-7600).

HORSE RACING Thoroughbreds race at *Ladbroke DRC* (28001 Schoolcraft, Livonia; phone: 525-7300); *Hazel Park Harness Raceway* (1650 E. Ten Mile, Hazel Park; phone: 810-398-1000); *Northville Downs* (301 S. Center St., Northville; phone: 810-349-1000); and *Windsor Raceway,* fall and winter harness racing (Hwy. 18, Windsor, Ont.; phone: 961-9545 in Detroit).

JOGGING The ideal spot is *Belle Isle Park.* To get there, run 2½ miles east along Jefferson and a half mile over the arched bridge; or take the Jefferson bus, then jog around the island's perimeter. An annual rite of fall is the *Detroit Free Press Mazda International Marathon* (phone: 222-6676) in Windsor and Detroit.

ROLLER SKATING You can skate in *Belle Isle Park* or in the *Silverdome* (phone: 810-646-7655).

TENNIS The city operates several public courts. The best are at *Palmer Park* and Belle Isle. Call *Parks and Recreation* (phone: 224-1100) for schedule information.

THEATER

Detroit's active theatrical life provides plenty of choices. There may be a Broadway-bound hit breaking in at the *Fisher Theatre* (Second at Grand Blvd.; phone: 872-1000). The *Birmingham Theatre* (211 S. Woodward, Birmingham; phone: 810-644-3533) features drama and comedy, as does the *Meadow Brook Theatre* on the *Oakland University* campus (University Dr. east of I-75, Rochester Hills; phone: 810-377-3300). Its season runs from September to May. The restored *Gem Theatre* (58 Columbia St.; phone: 963-9800) presents musicals and revues. Other good venues are the *Hilberry Classic Theatre* (4743 Cass; phone: 577-2972) for literary classics and the *Attic Theatre* (7339 Third Ave.; phone: 875-8284) for off-Broadway productions.

MUSIC

Just about any kind of music thrives in Detroit—symphonic, jazz, and soul. Detroit is the birthplace of Motown, the sound epitomized by the music of Stevie Wonder, the *Supremes,* and the *Temptations.* Today rockers like Bob Seger call Detroit home. Rock and soul concerts are played at the *Palace of Auburn Hills* (2 Championship Dr.; phone: 810-377-8200); *Cobo Arena* (Jefferson at Washington Blvd.; phone: 396-7600); *Joe Louis Arena* (Civic Center Dr.; phone: 396-7600); *Pontiac Silverdome* (M-59 at Opdyke, Pontiac; phone: 910-456-1600); *Masonic Temple Theatre* (500 Temple; phone: 832-2232); *Royal Oak Music Theatre* (318 W. 4th St.; phone: 810-546-7610); and the *Fox Theatre* (2211 Woodward; phone: 396-7600). The *Detroit Symphony*'s concert season runs from September to May at historic *Orchestra Hall* (3711 Woodward; phone: 833-3700), which also offers other classical, dance, and jazz concerts. *Meadow Brook Music Festival* (*Oakland University* campus; phone: 810-377-2010) offers summer symphonies and pop and jazz artists. Top-name entertainers perform at the outdoor *Pine Knob Music Theater* (Sashabaw Rd., north of I-75, Clarkston; phone: 810-377-8200). *Music Hall Center for the Performing Arts* (350 Madison Ave.; phone: 963-7680) hosts traveling dance and music concerts. Another restored vintage theater—the *Grand Circus Theatre* (1526 Broadway; phone: 874-SING)—is the home of the *Michigan Opera Theater.*

NIGHTCLUBS AND NIGHTLIFE

Dance to big band sounds at *Lido's on the Lake* (24026 E. Jefferson, St. Clair Shores; phone: 810-773-7770). *Midtown Café* (139 S. Woodward, Birmingham; phone: 810-642-1133) and *Norman's* (245 S. Eton, Birmingham; phone: 810-963-2098), a former 1931 train station, are the places where singles mingle. At the *Soup Kitchen Saloon* (1585 Franklin; phone: 259-1374), there's blues from Wednesdays through Sundays. Windsor's *Top Hat* (73 University; phone: 963-3742 in Detroit) has lounge acts. *The Rhinoceros* (265 Riopelle; phone: 259-2208) is the city's hippest piano bar. *Sudy's* (4758 Greenfield, Dearborn; phone: 846-5377) does the blues nightly; live jazz reigns at *Club Penta* (Fisher Bldg., W. Grand Blvd. at Second; phone: 872-3760); and the *State Theatre* (2115 Woodward; phone: 961-5450) is an arena set in an old Detroit movie house that features old films, reggae, and Saturday night dancing. *Mark Ridley's Comedy Castle* (E. Fourth at Troy, Royal Oak; phone: 810-542-9900) presents national acts with local openers, and open-mike night on Mondays; bigger-name yuckmeisters such as Paula Poundstone and Tim Allen (of TV's "Home Improvement") perform at *Chaplin's* (34244 Groesbeck, Fraser; phone: 810-792-1902); The *Second City—Detroit* (2301 Woodward; phone: 965-2222) stages satirical revues exploring social and political issues.

In nearby Pontiac, night owls can choose between the *Ultimate Sports Bar and Grill* (40 W. Pike; phone: 810-253-1300) with its boxing-ring dance floor, and *Industry* (15 S. Saginaw; phone: 810-334-1999), a club with factory-style decor.

Best in Town

CHECKING IN

Expect to pay between $90 and $130 per night for a double room at establishments in the expensive category; from $65 to $90 at those listed as moderate. Inexpensive lodging (less than $65) is available at chain hotels such as *Days Inn, Budgetel, Red Roof Inn,* and *Knights Inn*. For bed and breakfast accommodations, contact *Blanche House Inn* (506 Parkview; phone: 593-3366). *Direct Connect* (phone: 800-DETROIT) lists area hotels and can connect you with them. Unless otherwise noted, hotel rooms have air conditioning, private baths, TV sets, and telephones. All hotels are in the 313 area code unless otherwise indicated.

EXPENSIVE

Atheneum Formerly a warehouse, this all-suite hotel sits on the fringe of Greektown. Each of the 175 suites has a living room, bedroom, and spacious marble bath; ask for one with a view of the city skyline. Amenities include room service until midnight and a concierge; there is no restaurant, but the hotel is only a short stroll away from Greektown's many excellent eateries. Business features include eight meeting rooms, A/V equipment, fax machines, photocopiers, computers, and express checkout. 1000 Brush (phone: 962-2323; 800-772-2323; fax: 962-2424).

Hyatt Regency Dearborn Its 776 spacious, airy rooms overlook the landscaped park of the Ford World Headquarters in Dearborn. Nearby are *Fairlane Town Center Shopping Mall, Greenfield Village, Henry Ford Museum,* and a *University of Michigan* campus. Amenities include a restaurant, room service until midnight, and a concierge. Also available are 30 meeting rooms, secretarial services, A/V equipment, photocopiers, and express checkout. Michigan Ave. and Southfield Fwy., Dearborn (phone: 593-1234; 800-233-1234; fax: 593-3366).

Omni International Abutting the *Millender Center,* this 25-story hostelry with 258 spacious and imaginatively appointed rooms also has an exercise room, health club, restaurant, and lounge. Business services include room service until midnight, a concierge, eight meeting rooms, secretarial services, A/V equipment, photocopiers, computers, and express checkout. 333 E. Jefferson, at the junction of *RenCen* and the Detroit-Windsor Tunnel (phone: 222-7700; 800-843-6664; fax: 222-8517).

Radisson Plaza A 385-room property, it has an indoor pool and health club. *Boquet's* restaurant and *Tango's* bar are popular. Amenities include 24-hour room service, a concierge, 18 meeting rooms, secretarial services, photocopiers, computers, and express checkout. *Prudential Town Center,* Southfield (phone: 810-827-4000; 800-333-3333; fax: 810-827-1364).

Ritz-Carlton Dearborn From the outside, it looks like a French château; inside, its 18th- and 19th-century art and antiques create a warm, elegant atmosphere. Traditional decor defines the 308 guestrooms. Fine dining is available at *The Restaurant;* the *Grill and Bar* is a good steaks-and-chops place. There's also an exercise room and an indoor pool. Amenities include 24-hour room service, a concierge, seven meeting rooms, secretarial services, A/V equipment, photocopiers, computers, and express checkout. 300 Town Center Dr., across from Ford's headquarters, Dearborn (phone: 441-2000; 800-241-3333; fax: 441-2051).

Townsend George Washington may not have slept here, but Paul McCartney, Michael Jackson, and Madonna have. This surprisingly traditional building offers 87 rooms (including executive and two-room suites). The elegant marble baths have brass fixtures, and there's morning newspaper delivery and afternoon tea. Everything from beef to seafood is served at the *Rugby Grille.* Guests have privileges at a local health club (transportation provided). Amenities include 24-hour room service, a concierge, six meeting rooms, secretarial services, A/V equipment, photocopiers, and computers. 100 Townsend St., Birmingham (phone: 810-642-7900; 800-548-4172; fax: 810-645-9061).

Troy Marriott Located in Troy, a booming northern suburb, this hotel has 350 rooms, including four suites, which radiate from a skylight atrium. It is convenient to the *Pontiac Silverdome. Stacy's Sea Grille* serves up delicious seafood. Business amenities include room service until midnight, a concierge, 16 meeting rooms, secretarial services, A/V equipment, photocopiers, and express checkout. 200 W. Big Beaver, east of I-75, Troy (phone: 810-680-9797; 800-777-4096; fax: 810-680-9774).

Westin Renaissance Center This 1,400-room, 73-story round building has a number of dramatic public areas: The lobby takes up the first eight stories, with fountains, trees, aerial walkways, shops, and lounges. There are three levels of revolving bars and restaurants at the top of the building; downstairs, there's casual dining at the *River Bistro.* Amenities include 24-hour room service, a concierge, 27 meeting rooms, and express checkout. At the east end of Hart Plaza, on Jefferson at St. Antoine (phone: 568-8000; 800-228-3000; fax: 568-8146).

MODERATE

Botsford Inn Originally an 1836 stagecoach stop, it has 75 spacious, antiques-filled rooms and serves hearty American fare in the *Coach Room.* Amenities include a concierge desk, three meeting rooms, secretarial services, A/V equipment, photocopiers, and express checkout. 28000 Grand River Ave. at Eight Mile, Farmington Hills (phone: 810-474-4800; fax: 810-474-7669).

Dearborn Inn A few hundred yards down the road from the *Henry Ford Museum* and only 20 minutes from downtown stands this Georgian-style mansion; it was built by Henry Ford in 1931 and later expanded with reproductions of five historic colonial homes and two motel-style wings. The charm and beauty of a bygone era have been re-created in the 222 rooms and suites. Guests can choose from among three dining rooms offering tasty American fare, and for those who wish to put history aside in favor of activity, there are tennis courts. Other amenities include valet, laundry, airport limousine, and baby-sitting service. Room service is available until midnight, and there are concierge and secretarial services, 12 meeting rooms, A/V equipment, and express checkout. 20301 Oakwood Blvd., Dearborn (phone: 271-2700; 800-221-7236; fax: 271-7464).

Embassy Suites "Rooms to roam" is the concept. Each of the 240 suites consists of a bedroom and parlor. Guests receive complimentary full breakfast and cocktails, and there's a pool, sauna, and whirlpool bath. Ideally situated if your interest is in the Southfield area. Amenities include room service until midnight, nine meeting rooms, A/V equipment, photocopiers, and express checkout. 27754 Franklin Rd., Southfield (phone: 810-350-2000; 800-EMBASSY; fax: 810-350-2000, ext. 7033).

Hilton Suites Auburn Hills Each of this hotel's 224 suites boasts a VCR, a wet bar, a refrigerator, and a microwave oven. It's conveniently located near the *Palace of Auburn Hills,* the *Pontiac Silverdome,* and Pontiac's *Phoenix Center.* There's an indoor pool, Jacuzzis, a sauna, a billiards room, and an exercise room. Other amenities include room service between 5:30 AM and 10 PM daily, A/V equipment, computers, teleconferencing facilities, and a business center. 2300 Featherstone, at I-75 and M-59 (phone: 810-334-2222; 800-HILTONS; fax: 810-334-2922).

Mayflower Bed & Breakfast This family-owned, 73-room inn offers guests a full, complimentary breakfast. Amenities include a concierge desk, four meeting rooms, and photocopiers. On the town square in quaint Plymouth. 827 Ann Arbor Trail (phone: 453-1620; fax: 453-0193).

Windsor Hilton Just across the Detroit River, this hotel commands a sparkling view of Detroit's skyline from each of its 307 rooms. There are two executive floors with concierge service and mini-bars in every room. Amenities include a restaurant, 24-hour room service, a concierge, 20 meeting rooms, secretarial services, A/V equipment, photocopiers, and express checkout. 277 Riverside Dr. W. (phone: 519-973-5555; 962-3834 in Detroit; 800-463-6655; fax: 519-973-1600).

Wyndham Garden In a nearby suburb, this hotel has 151 rooms (including 31 suites) in a building with elegant touches of marble and brass; there's also a lovely garden. Amenities include a restaurant, a pool, a sauna, a Jacuzzi, and use of an adjacent health club. There's room service until 11:30 PM; among the business features are four meeting rooms, A/V equipment, photocopiers, and express checkout. 42100 Crescent Blvd., Novi (phone: 810-344-8800; 800-822-4200; fax: 810-344-8535).

EATING OUT

Detroit has a number of moderately priced restaurants serving everything from steaks, crêpes, and pheasant to natural foods and Coney Island hot dogs. The nationalities represented include French, Middle Eastern, and Alsatian. Expect to pay $45 or more for dinner for two at the restaurants listed here as expensive; between $25 and $45 at places categorized as moderate; and less than $25 at those described as inexpensive. Prices do not include drinks, wine, tax, or tips. Unless otherwise noted, restaurants are open for lunch and dinner. All restaurants are in the 313 area code unless otherwise indicated.

EXPENSIVE

Joe Muer's Some people say this place serves the best seafood west of the Atlantic; others say it's even better. Be prepared to wait, though (a waiter will bring you a drink while you're standing in line). Closed Sundays and holidays. No reservations. Major credit cards accepted. 2000 Gratiot (phone: 567-1088).

Opus One The finely tuned menu features breast of duck; roulades of salmon; sea bass in a subtle champagne sauce; salads that are arranged, not tossed; and inventive soups, led by a crayfish bisque. The decor is classical, with tapestry-covered banquettes, varying shades of white, and etched glass. Open daily. Reservations advised. Major credit cards accepted. 565 E. Larned, Bricktown (phone: 961-7766).

Rattlesnake Club No, it is not on the menu. This lively, contemporary room, with wide river-view windows, features highly acclaimed and ever-changing appetizers and sinful desserts. Main courses tend toward such unusual dishes as pickerel with spiced crust and green papaya, or pork with leeks, apples, and cider. Save room for the chocolate ice cream rolled in cocoa powder. Atmosphere can best be described as "theatrical." Open daily. Reservations advised. Major credit cards accepted. 300 Stroh River Pl., foot of Joseph Campau St. (phone: 567-4400).

Too Chez Amid Pucci-like patterns, pictureless frames over the fireplace, and lamps made of magnum champagne bottles, diners are treated to a multi-ethnic menu. Try the assertively spiced orzo, a barley-like pasta cooked to a Thai spiciness in a purée of jalapeño peppers (if you can eat the whole thing, you don't have to pay for it!). Closed Sundays. Reservations advised. Major credit cards accepted. 27000 E. Sheraton, Novi (phone: 348-5555).

Whitney Located in an opulent midtown mansion, circa 1894, this is the place for fish and seafood. The menu is replete with Michigan trout, Florida Keys shrimp, Maryland crabmeat, grilled or poached Maine lobster, California mussels, and farm-raised game. Save room for the chocolate taco: a raspberry mousse–filled walnut *tuile* (a super-thin cookie) topped with kiwi and grated white chocolate, and surrounded by raspberry, lemon, and lime purée. Open daily. Reservations advised. Major credit cards accepted. 4421 Woodward at Canfield (phone: 832-5700).

MODERATE

Avenue Diner Homemade ketchup and potato chips aren't the only surprises under chef Ed Janor's toque. Others include seafood sliders, white bean chili and "Thanksgiving on a Bun," combining sliced turkey with a side of cranberry relish. Tinfoil-shiny with bright neon and Art Deco lamps, this diner is updated with upholstered booths and seats facing an open kitchen—the better to watch the preparation of the dry-aged Black Angus beef or the fish flown in from Florida. Open daily. No reservations. Major credit cards accepted. 4616 Woodward Ave., Royal Oak (phone: 810-549-2000).

Centro Ristorante This former Detroit home has been converted into a low-key restaurant decorated with Italian touches. The menu features pasta, sturdy-crust pizza, and veal dishes. An excellent appetizer is *focaccia*, a doughy bread dipped in olive oil and an intense tomato sauce. Closed Sundays when the *Fisher Theatre* across the street is dark. Reservations advised. Major credit cards accepted. 670 Lothrop (phone: 872-5110).

Charley's Crab The seafood menu and the ragtime piano player are real crowd pleasers. Open daily. Reservations advised. Major credit cards accepted. 5498 Crooks Rd. at I-75, Troy (phone: 879-2060).

La Cuisine The chef at this tiny French bistro whips up heavenly three-mustard kidneys and tasty fish soup from his kitchen in the middle of the room. Closed Sundays and Mondays. Reservations necessary. Major credit cards accepted. 417 Pelissier, Windsor, Ontario (phone: 519-253-6432).

Durango Grill Gussied up with Westerns on TVs, a denim-draped waitstaff, and tables stamped with cattle brands, Durango is cowboy-comfortable. So is the all-day menu, which includes buffalo burgers, chili, hickory-smoked beef brisket, and chicken-fried steak. Open daily. No reservations. Major credit cards accepted. 222 Sherman Dr., Royal Oak (810-544-2887).

Fishbone's Rhythm Kitchen Café In a renovated warehouse in Greektown, Cajun-style food is served in an atmosphere reminiscent of New Orleans's French Quarter. As Dixieland music plays in the background, diners can feast on peel-and-eat shrimp, spicy chicken wings, ribs, and bayou caviar (deep-fried crawfish). Open daily. Reservations advised. Major credit cards accepted. 400 Monroe (phone: 965-4600).

Traffic Jam and Snug A relaxed, roadhouse-in-the-city coziness, along with such eclectic goodies as chili meat loaf, four-cheese linguine, and acorn squash stuffed with wild rice and nuts, give "TJ's" its unique appeal. Try the "Carlotta Chocolatta" ice cream cheesecake, just one of the decadent desserts baked on the premises. Closed Sundays. Reservations unnecessary. MasterCard and Visa accepted. Canfield and Second, near *Wayne State University* (phone: 831-9470).

Très Vite A bright, modern, urban café where the people watching is eclipsed only by snappy, contemporary cooking that features imported Italian pasta with interesting sauces and thin-crusted pizza topped with four different cheeses. Closed Sundays when the adjacent *Fox Theatre* is dark. Reservations advised. Major credit cards accepted. 2203 Woodward in the *Fox Theatre* building (phone: 964-4144).

INEXPENSIVE

Chimayo A café decorated with Southwestern flair—desert colors, brightly painted ceramics, and hanging strings of chili peppers. The menu continues the theme, with roasted pepper soup, New York strip steaks with coffee mustard sauce, and sautéed mahimahi in black bean and shrimp sauce. For dessert, try a banana taco with chocolate shavings and passion fruit. Closed Mondays. Reservations advised. Major credit cards accepted. 1 N. Saginaw at Pike St., Pontiac (phone: 810-338-7337).

New Hellas The hub of Detroit's one-block Greek community is as Hellenic as they come, with moussaka, calamari (squid), and baklava. Open daily until 3 AM. No reservations. Major credit cards accepted. 583 Monroe (phone: 961-5544).

Xochimilco In a near-downtown neighborhood called Mexican Town, this is the Big Enchilada: good, affordable Mexican food, potent margaritas, endearingly cheesy decor. Open daily. Reservations unnecessary. Major credit cards accepted. 3409 Bagley (phone: 843-0179).

Ft. Lauderdale

At-a-Glance

SEEING THE CITY

The most commanding view of this area is available from the *Pier Top Lounge* of the 17-story *Pier 66 Crowne Plaza* hotel (see *Checking In*). As the lounge makes one complete revolution every 66 minutes, it affords sweeping vistas of the Atlantic Ocean and its beaches to the east; Port Everglades and *Ft. Lauderdale International Airport* to the south; the city's many canals, sprawling suburbs, and the Everglades to the west; and more canals and the Intracoastal Waterway to the north.

SPECIAL PLACES

The best way to get around Ft. Lauderdale is by car. It's a sprawling city, and there's a lot to see in all directions.

DOWNTOWN AREA

PORT EVERGLADES Because it has the deepest water of any port between Norfolk, Virginia, and New Orleans, Port Everglades is a natural magnet for cargo ships and the marine outfitting business, as well as for luxury cruise ships. In fact, it's the world's second-largest cruise port, after Miami. Thanks to the remodeling of former warehouses and new construction, the port today presents an attractive face. There's a restaurant, *Burt & Jack's*, co-owned by Burt Reynolds (see *Eating Out*). And, while there are no organized tours, visitors are free to roam around the port (except in the secured areas). At times, naval vessels in port are open for free tours. State Rd. 84, east of US 1 (phone: 523-3404).

Business travelers and vacationers often combine an area visit with a cruise. A few ships make Port Everglades their home port, offering several options for day cruises. Cruise lines that sail from Port Everglades on a variety of itineraries include *Celebrity Cruises* (phone: 800-437-3111); *Costa Cruises* (phone: 358-7330; 800-462-6782); *Crystal Cruises* (phone: 800-446-6612); *Cunard Line* (phone: 800-221-4770); *Discovery Cruises* (phone: 525-7800; 800-937-4477); *Holland America Line* (phone: 800-426-0327); *P & O Cruises* (phone: 415-382-9086); *Premier's Big Red Boat* (phone: 800-473-3262); *Princess Cruises* (phone: 800-421-0522); *Seabourn Cruise Line* (phone: 800-351-9595); *SeaEscape* (phone: 800-432-0900); and *Sun Line* (phone: 800-468-6400).

MUSEUM OF DISCOVERY AND SCIENCE One lure of Ft. Lauderdale's 85,000-square-foot museum is its five-story IMAX screen, which is housed in a 300-seat theater. Others include walk-through simulated Florida ecological habitats, two simulated space rides, a laser game, a human gyroscope, and a children's display in which a giant bubble forms around young museum-goers. There are lots of fun hands-on exhibits for everyone and Saturday classes for children. A cafeteria and museum store are on the premises. Extended hours on Saturdays; closed Sunday mornings. Admission charge (additional charge for the theater, which offers

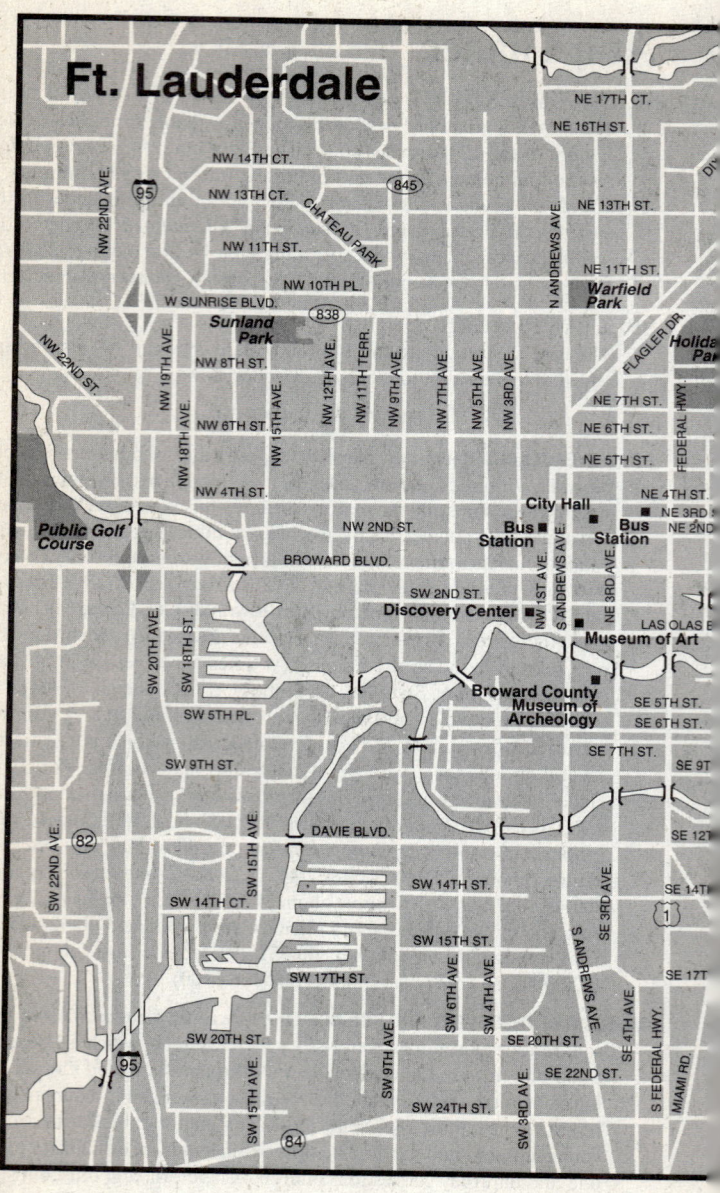

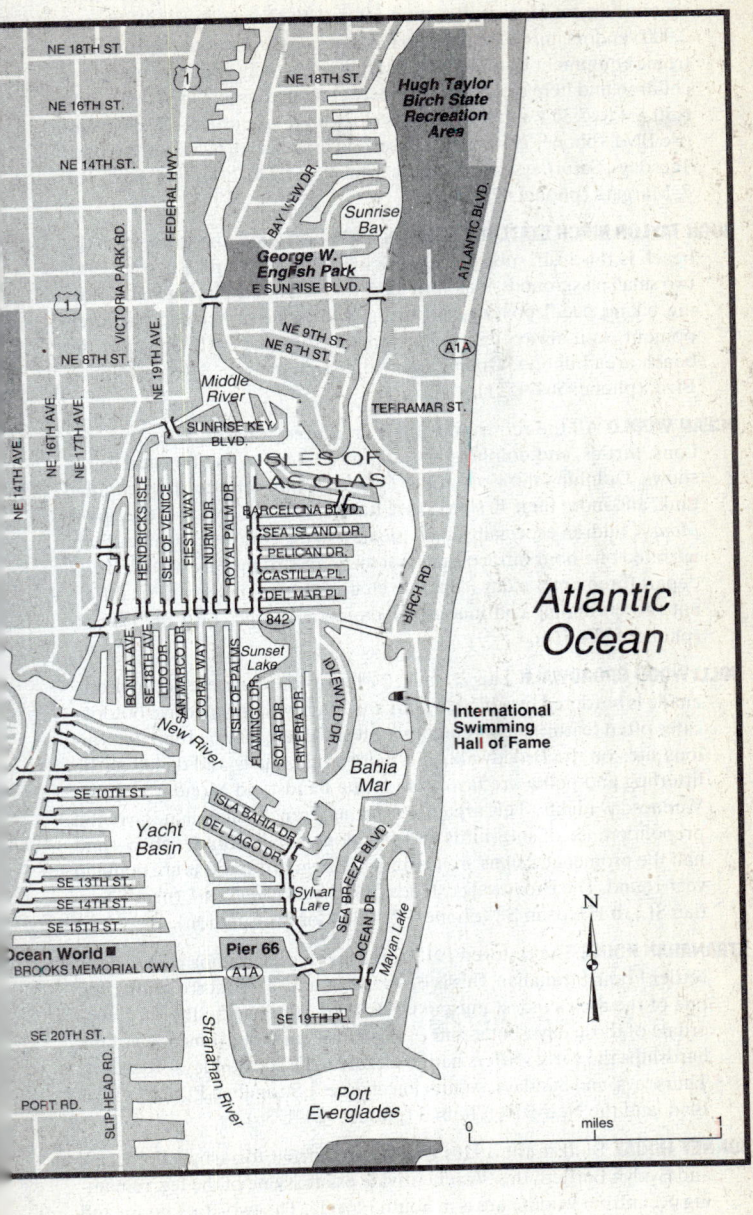

up to 11 shows daily). 401 SW Second St., across from the *Broward Center for the Performing Arts* (phone: 467-MODS or 463-IMAX).

SWAP SHOP The largest flea market in the South, it claims to be Florida's second-largest tourist attraction after *Walt Disney World*. With over 2,000 vendors, this is *the* place to find bargains on everything from electronic equipment to tomatoes. There's also a daily circus to amuse the children and help clear the mind between purchases. Open daily from 6:30 AM to 7:30 PM; outdoor stalls close an hour earlier. 3291 W. Sunrise Blvd. (phone: 791-SWAP). A second branch with 625 booths is open Tuesdays, Saturdays, and Sundays from 4:30 AM to 2 PM. 1000 State Rd. 7, Margate (phone: 971-SWAP).

HUGH TAYLOR BIRCH STATE RECREATION AREA Just across the street from the beach is this lush, subtropical park, with 180 acres, nature trails, and two small playgrounds, making it ideal for picnicking, playing ball, canoeing, biking, paddleboating, and hiking. The park is protected from development, so it always will remain a beautiful spot in the midst of the beach area hubbub. Open daily. Admission charge. 3109 E. Sunrise Blvd. (phone: 564-4521).

OCEAN WORLD All the requisite aquatic creatures—sharks, alligators, sea lions, turtles, and dolphins—are featured here in exhibits and water shows. Dolphins show off in the *Dolphinarium*, a three-story circular tank, and more than 40 sharks, sea turtles, and fish reside in the *Shark Moat*. Children especially enjoy the new living coral reef exhibit. Fully narrated one-hour intracoastal boat tours aboard the *Miss Ocean World* depart three times a day (separate charge). Open daily, with six different shows running continuously. Admission charge. 1701 SE 17th St. (phone: 525-6611).

HOLLYWOOD BROADWALK This 2¼-mile, 24-foot-wide, concrete ocean promenade is bordered by a bicycle path and lined with inexpensive outdoor cafés often featuring contemporary music. Bikes may be rented at various sites on the Broadwalk, and there's free music and dancing (the jitterbug and polka are favorites) at the bandstand Monday through Wednesday nights. This area has a strong French-Canadian flavor—a preponderance of snowbirds and vacationers hail from Quebec—and half the promenade signs are in French. Lifeguard stations are manned year-round. The Broadwalk extends from *North Beach Park* (near Sheridan St.) to Harrison St. (phone: 921-3404 for information).

STRANAHAN HOUSE The restored 1913 home and Indian trading post of early settler Frank Stranahan, this is Broward County's oldest structure (and one of the area's oldest museums). It's hard to imagine the Ft. Lauderdale of those days, but a tour of this house provides some idea of the hardships the early settlers had to endure. Closed Mondays, Tuesdays, Thursdays, and Sundays. Admission charge. 1 Stranahan Pl. at Las Olas Blvd. and the New River Tunnel (phone: 524-4736).

BONNET HOUSE Built in the 1920s as a family retreat for artists Frederick and Evelyn Bartlett, this 36-acre private estate is one of the few remaining oceanfront wildlife areas in South Florida. The two-story house and grounds have been preserved and are on the *National Registry of His-*

toric Places. Tours are offered Tuesdays through Fridays and Sundays, May through November. Admission charge. 900 N. Birch Rd. (phone: 563-5393).

INTERNATIONAL SWIMMING HALL OF FAME Many of the world's top swimming and diving competitions are held here, but the Olympic-size pools are open to the public when there's no meet scheduled, and swimming lessons are offered year-round. The adjoining museum houses unusual aquatic memorabilia from more than 100 countries. Open daily. Admission charge. 1 Hall of Fame Dr., off Seabreeze Blvd. (phone: 462-6536).

GREATER FT LAUDERDALE

EVERGLADES HOLIDAY PARK Take a narrated airboat ride through this small park, and you'll see some of the most beautiful birds Mother Nature has ever created (you might even spot an American bald eagle) as well as alligators nesting in the gold-colored sawgrass. (Your tour guide will give you a healthy respect for the power of alligator jaws, even those of the seemingly cute young ones.) Special tours offer insights into the lives of Seminole Indians. If you're feeling adventurous, rent a boat or an RV for a closer experience with nature. There's also a campground here. Open daily 24 hours; airboat rides conducted daily. No admission charge to the park, but a fee is charged for airboat rides. 21940 Griffin Rd. (phone: 434-8111).

FLAMINGO GARDENS This 60-acre botanical garden has a flamingo exhibit (of course), a tropical plant house, a museum about the Everglades, orange groves, alligators, crocodiles, and river otters. A guided tram tour takes visitors through the groves, wetlands, and an indigenous hardwood hammock (a raised area of dense vegetation). A screened-in aviary re-creates several native settings for those who can't get out to the Everglades; throughout the groves are free-flying local birds, including cormorants and ospreys. There's also a snack bar, a gift shop, and a produce stall for purchasing and shipping citrus fruit. Open daily. Admission charge. 3750 Flamingo Rd., Davie (phone: 473-2955).

LOXAHATCHEE EVERGLADES TOURS Visitors to northern Broward County can participate in an easy airboat trip through the Everglades without traveling great distances to the south. Ramps afford easy access to disabled passengers. Skim over the "river of grass," spotting alligators and their babies in nests, plus myriad wild fowl. There's a small (and sparsely stocked) snack shop at the park. Open daily. No admission charge to the park, but there's a fee for airboat rides. From Rte. 441 take Lox Rd. (between Hillsboro Blvd. and Palmetto Park Rd.), then drive 6 miles west to the Everglades (phone: 407-482-0313; 800-683-5873).

SAWGRASS MILLS MALL This 2.2 million-square-foot discount shopping complex, billed as the world's largest outlet mall, boasts such stores as *Saks Fifth Avenue*, *Brandsmart*, *Sears*, *Marshall's*, and *Spiegel*—and 200 specialty shops. Among the temptations are an *Ann Taylor* clearance center and a *Joan & David* shoe outlet. Although some stores offer valid savings of 20% to 60%, this mall is for savvy shoppers: It's important to know what things sell for elsewhere. Several restaurants, two food courts, and an 18-screen movie theater complete the picture. Open daily. 12801 W. Sunrise Blvd., Sunrise (phone: 846-2350; 800-FL-MILLS).

BUTTERFLY WORLD Visitors can walk among the multicolored creatures fluttering freely in this three-acre, re-created jungle habitat. The butterflies are seen in all their stages of life, from larvae and pupae to cocoon and full-grown adult. Certain species are attracted to light-colored clothing and particular scents; if you've spent a hot morning in traffic or sightseeing, you may find yourself converted into a temporary perch. There are butterflies from all over the world and a spectacular museum of mounted insects. Closed *Thanksgiving* and *Christmas Day*. Admission charge. 3600 W. Sample Rd., Coconut Creek (phone: 977-4400).

JOHN U. LLOYD BEACH STATE RECREATION AREA Many Ft. Lauderdale residents consider this to be *the* place for picnicking, swimming, fishing, canoeing, and other recreation. There are 244 acres of beach, dunes, mangrove swamp, and hammock. Park rangers lead nature walks during winter months. Open daily. Admission charge. 6503 N. Ocean Dr., Dania (phone: 923-2833).

TOPEEKEEGEE YUGNEE PARK Locally called "T-Y Park" due to its difficult-to-pronounce Indian name, this is one of the area's more popular places for families. Visitors can enjoy all kinds of activities—swimming, boating, canoeing, picnicking, barbecuing, hiking, biking, and water sliding. Open daily. Admission charge on weekends and holidays. 3300 N. Park Rd., just off I-95, Hollywood (phone: 985-1980).

SEMINOLE INDIAN RESERVATION The *Native Village* includes a museum, a gift shop, demonstrations of alligator wrestling, and snake and turtle shows. The museum gives an interesting glimpse into this little-known Native American group, which never signed a treaty with the United States. Although bingo games for profit are not legal elsewhere in Florida, they're allowed here; winners have pocketed as much as $110,000 for a single game. There's an admission charge for the village and another for the bingo hall, which includes four bingo cards. Both are open daily. The village is at 3551 N. State Rd. 7, Hollywood (phone: 961-4519); the bingo hall is at 4150 N. State Rd. 7, Hollywood (phone: 961-3220).

GOODYEAR BLIMP Though tourists may not go for a ride in the *Stars & Stripes* (it's only for corporate clients), they can see the 192-foot-long blimp up close at its hangar at various times from November through May (call in advance for a schedule). No admission charge. 1500 NE Fifth Ave., Pompano Beach (phone: 946-8300).

GRAND PRIX RACE-A-RAMA A 1990s-style amusement park that's fun for the whole family (and a lifesaver on a rainy day), with a 24-hour video arcade, three miniature golf courses, batting cages, boat tag, bumper carts, bumper boats, and miniature basketball. Open daily; extended hours on weekends. Admission charge for individual games and amusements. 1500 NW First St., Dania (phone: 921-1411).

> **EXTRA SPECIAL**
>
> To experience fully the subtropical beauty and laid-back ambience that is Ft. Lauderdale, drive east on Las Olas Boulevard past its chic boutiques and palm-lined streets. Continue through the Isles of Las Olas area, which is laced with canals and filled with fancy homes nestled among royal palm trees. Large, luxurious boats are docked outside many of the homes. Look up and you may spot some of the red and blue parrots that nest here; some people believe they're native to the area; others say that they were visitors who liked the neighborhood and stayed. Proceed on past the sailboat cove, where towering masts salute the blue sky, and cruise over the small bridge to Route A1A, along the Atlantic Ocean. Drive north, and around 4 PM, stop at one of the hotel patio bars facing the ocean for a cocktail with the "end-of-the-day" beach people. In an hour or so, the beach will become nearly deserted, yet the ocean will be filled with boats returning to safe harbor, their multicolored sails bright against the dark water, and cruise and cargo ships steaming out to distant corners of the world. Take off your shoes, walk along the sand at the water's edge—and let the images soak in.

Sources and Resources

TOURIST INFORMATION

The *Greater Ft. Lauderdale Convention and Visitors Bureau* is in an easily accessible high-rise downtown (200 E. Las Olas Blvd.; Ft. Lauderdale, FL 33301; phone: 765-4466; 800-356-1662). Stop in or call for information on accommodations, activities, attractions, sports, dining, shopping, touring, and special events (closed weekends). Or call in advance for a free, information-filled book (phone: 800-22SUNNY, ext. 711). There is also a 24-hour hotline that provides local travel directions in English, Spanish, French, and German (phone: 527-5600; cellular phone: #333). The Broward County arts and entertainment hotline (phone: 357-5700) is updated weekly and provides recorded schedules of events and additional sources of information about visitor attractions. Contact the Florida state hotline (phone: 904-487-1462) for maps, calendars of events, and travel advisories.

LOCAL COVERAGE The *Fort Lauderdale Sun-Sentinel,* a morning daily, carries the following week's events in its "Showtime" section on Fridays; the free weekly alternative newspaper *XS* and the monthly *Promenade* and *South Florida* magazines list nightlife happenings, cultural events, and restaurants.

We also immodestly recommend our own *Birnbaum's Miami & Ft. Lauderdale 95* (HarperCollins, $12).

TELEVISION STATIONS WPBS Channel 2–public television; WTVJ Channel 4–NBC; WCIX Channel 6–CBS; WSVN Channel 7–Fox; and WPLG Channel 10–ABC.

RADIO STATIONS AM: WEAT 850 (easy listening) and WINZ 940 (news/talk). FM: WTMI 93.1 (classical music); WZTA 94.9 (classic rock); WFLC 97.3 (soft rock); WKIS 99.9 (country); WLYF 101.5 (easy listening); WSHE 103.5 (album rock); and WJQY 106.7 (easy listening).

TELEPHONE The area code for Ft. Lauderdale is 305.

SALES TAX The city sales tax is 6%; there is also a 3% Broward County hotel tax.

CLIMATE Summers tend to be humid, sometimes oppressively so, with frequent short rainfalls; winters are usually mild and dry with occasional chilly days from late December through February. Spring and fall are sunny and dry with daily temperatures averaging 75F. Swimming is possible almost every day.

GETTING AROUND

AIRPORT *Ft. Lauderdale/Hollywood International Airport* is a 10- to 15-minute drive from downtown. *Broward County Transit*'s No. 1 bus runs between the airport (pickup at terminals: Delta Dash pull-in area in terminal 1 and next to terminal 3, both Lower Level) and the downtown bus terminal (NW 1st St. and 1st Ave.). *Grayline Airport Service* (phone: 527-8690) offers car service between the airport and anywhere in Broward County. For trips to the airport, reservations must be made at least 24 hours in advance.

BOAT TOURS Dubbed the "Venice of America," Ft. Lauderdale is best seen by boat. The *Jungle Queen* (at the *Bahia Mar Yachting Center*, Rte. A1A; phone: 462-5596) offers three-hour sightseeing tours twice daily; it also takes riders down to Miami twice weekly for shopping sprees. The *Paddlewheel Queen* (docked next to *Charley's Crab* at 3000 NE 32nd Ave.; phone: 564-7659) runs a variety of sightseeing cruises up and down the Intracoastal Waterway, with dinner sails that include music and dancing Wednesdays through Saturdays. The *Carrie-B* (docked behind *Woolley's* supermarket on Las Olas Blvd. and SE Fifth Ave.; phone: 768-9920) runs daily one-and-a-half-hour trips on the New River down to Port Everglades. Large families and small business groups can charter the 92-foot *Sir Winston* (formally the *Wrecking Krew;* on the New River dock; phone: 462-7411), which transports groups along the waterways past millionaires' homes.

The *Ft. Lauderdale Historical Society* (phone: 463-4431) offers two-hour guided water taxi tours of the historic New River and the Intracoastal Waterway, passing by the mansions and yachts of the area's more well-heeled residents. Two-hour glass-bottom boat tours are conducted on *Pro Diver II*, sailing from the *Bahia Mar Yachting Center* (phone: 467-6030) daily except Mondays.

In addition to the tours, *Water Taxi* boats run from the 17th Street Causeway to the *Boca Raton Resort & Club* on demand daily from 10 AM until the wee hours, covering 80 landings. Vessels are also available for charter.

BUS *Broward County Transit* serves most of the area. Fares are 85¢; 10¢ for transfers (exact change is required). Weekly passes cost $8 and are available at most hotels. For information, call 357-8400.

CAR RENTAL Ft. Lauderdale is served by all the major national firms, one of which has its corporate headquarters in the city: *Alamo* (110 SE Sixth St.; phone: 522-0000; 800-327-9400). There are also several regional agencies; check the yellow pages.

HOT-AIR BALLOON *Rohr Balloons* (6000 NW 28th Way; phone: 491-1774; 371-9410 from Dade County) literally gives passengers a bird's-eye view of Ft. Lauderdale. The balloons fly twice daily; reservations are required.

TAXI While you can hail a cab on the street, it's best to pick one up at a major hotel or restaurant or to call for one. The major cab company is *Checker/Yellow Cab* (phone: 565-5400). For information on cabs that accommodate wheelchairs, call 565-2800.

TRAM TOURS Another wonderful way to sightsee is aboard the open-air *South Florida Trolley Tour*, which winds its way through both the new and older sections of Ft. Lauderdale. Passengers can get on and off any of the three daily tours, or stay put for the entire one-and-a-half-hour tour. There's a trolley booth on Route A1A, a half-block south of Las Olas Boulevard (419 S. Ocean Blvd.; phone: 768-0700), where you can get tickets for the tram tours and other events as well. In winter, separate tours also are offered to the *Swap Shop* and *Sawgrass Mills Mall* (see *Special Places*). *Trolley World Tours* picks up cruise ship passengers at the pier in Port Everglades, offering shopping excursions and a two-and-a-half-hour city tour in conjunction with *Ellerworld Travel* (phone: 463-8550).

TRI-RAIL A double-decker train runs from West Palm Beach south through Ft. Lauderdale to Miami, and connects with Miami's *Metrorail/Metromover* and county and shuttle bus lines to deliver visitors to most of each city's major attractions. The train also travels to the airport in Broward (with a short shuttle bus ride), as well as to the airports in Dade and Palm Beach counties. Extra trains are scheduled for games at Miami's *Joe Robbie* and *Orange Bowl* stadiums, special events, and shopping trips to the *Swap Shop* and *Bayside Marketplace* in Miami. At times, special sightseeing package tours are available. This is a convenient way to see a large part of South Florida and its attractions. The trains are accessible to the disabled. For information, call 728-8445, 800-TRI-RAIL, or 800-874-7245.

WALKING TOURS The *Ft. Lauderdale Historical Society* (see *Boat Tours*) conducts three-hour walking tours of the historical district (between October and May), where participants learn about the Seminole Wars and early 19th-century farms and trading posts along the then-inhospitable New River. Individual tours are also offered by history professor Dr. Paul S. George (phone: 858-6021).

LOCAL SERVICES

AUDIOVISUAL EQUIPMENT *Central Audio Visual* (1212 S. Andrews Ave.; phone: 522-3796).

BABY-SITTING *Lul-A-Bye Sitters Registry* (PO Box 24945, Oakland Park; phone: 565-1222).

BUSINESS SERVICES *Uniforce Services* (2987 W. Commercial Blvd.; phone: 485-TEMP) offers temporary services.

DENTAL EMERGENCY Dr. Robert Dolgow (5441 N. University Dr.; phone: 741-4500). The *American Dental Association* also maintains a 24-hour referral service (phone: 944-5668).

DRY CLEANERS/TAILORS *Fashion Cleaners* (2427 W. Broward Blvd.; phone: 583-8225); *Lauderdale-by-the-Sea Cleaners* (4329 N. Ocean Dr., Lauderdale-by-the-Sea; phone: 776-0055).

EQUIPMENT RENTAL *Kinko's* (1555 S. Federal Hwy., Ft. Lauderdale; phone: 467-1007; and 3775 Hollywood Blvd., Hollywood; phone: 985-0411) provides typewriters and computers for hourly rentals. *A & J Business Machines* (phone: 563-0438) rents typewriters; there's a one-week minimum.

LIMOUSINES *Absolute Limousine* (phone: 800-765-7433); *Airport Express* (phone: 527-8690); *Club Limousine Service* (phone: 522-0277).

LOCKSMITH Locked your keys in the car? *A Lock & Safe* (phone: 763-7479) offers 24-hour service.

MECHANICS *Ocean Chevron* (3001 N. Ocean Blvd.; phone: 561-3120) for American and foreign makes.

MEDICAL EMERGENCY *Holy Cross Hospital* (4725 N. Federal Hwy.; phone: 771-8000); *North Beach Hospital* (2835 N. Ocean Blvd.; phone: 568-1000).

MESSENGER SERVICES *All Florida Messenger & Delivery* (6822 NW 20th Ave.; phone: 973-3278) and *Sunshine State Messenger Service* (6775 NW 15th Ave.; phone: 975-8100) are both open 24 hours.

PHOTOCOPIES *Copyright* (969 W. Commercial Blvd.; phone: 491-2679; and 1135 S. Federal Hwy.; phone: 779-2649) and *Kinko's* (see *Equipment Rental*) for standard and color copies.

POST OFFICE There are two offices: the main branch (1900 W. Oakland Park Blvd.; phone: 735-3596 or 527-2077) and a downtown branch (330 SW Second St.; phone: 761-1172).

PROFESSIONAL PHOTOGRAPHERS *University Studios* (phone: 772-6644); *Woodbury & Associates* (phone: 977-9000).

SECRETARIES/STENOGRAPHERS *Uniforce Services* (see *Business Services*).

TELECONFERENCE FACILITIES *Marriott Harbor Beach Resort* and *Ft. Lauderdale Marina Marriott* hotels (see *Checking In*).

TRANSLATORS *Berlitz* (2455 E. Sunrise Blvd.; phone: 563-6303; 800-523-7548) and *Master Translating Services* (1881 NE 26th St., Wilton Manors; phone: 563-2899).

WESTERN UNION/TELEX There are many offices located around town (phone: 800-325-6000).

SPECIAL EVENTS

The *Las Olas Art Festival*, hosted by the *Museum of Art*, takes place in January and February. The festival attracts 300 artists, whose work is displayed in a juried show at *Bubier Park;* many of the artists don't exhibit elsewhere (phone: 472-3755). The *Seminole Indian Tribal Fair* at *Flamingo Gardens,* usually held during the first two weeks in February, is a showcase of Indian crafts, entertainment, and food (phone: 584-0400 for information). Out in Davie, cowboys kick up their heels at the March *Orange Blossom Festival and Rodeo* (phone: 581-0790). The *Honda Golf Classic,* one of the biggest *PGA* tournaments, is held in early March at the *Weston Hills Country Club;* it attracts the *PGA*'s top players (phone: 384-6000). Also in March, the *Florida Derby Festival* hits town; activities include a beauty pageant, the *Derby Ball,* and parades, culminating in a thoroughbred race with a purse of about $500,000 (phone: 454-7000). The other big March event is the annual *Sun-Sentinel New River Jazz Festival,* which brings three days of jazz to the *Broward Center for the Performing Arts,* with free outdoor concerts along the New River's Riverwalk (phone: 468-2687). In April, seafood is king at the *Ft. Lauderdale Seafood Festival* at *Bubier Park,* where over 30 leading restaurants offer visitors samples of their house specialties (phone: 463-4431). About two weeks later, Pompano Beach holds its own gala *Pompano Beach Seafood Festival & Art Show* right on the beach at the end of East Atlantic Boulevard (phone: 941-2940). In May, anglers test their skills during the *Pompano Beach Fishing Rodeo,* where more than $250,000 in cash is awarded for the largest catches (phone: 942-4513). On *July 4* there's the *Sun-Sentinel SandBlast,* where contestants create sand sculptures on the beach for prizes; kids' sand-sculpting lessons and fireworks add to the fun (phone: 761-5363).

September brings the *Las Olas Labor Day Art Fair,* which turns the entire boulevard into a pedestrian mall lined with art exhibits, street performers, and food booths (phone: 472-3755). *Oktoberfest* falls (naturally) in October and features lots of German food, drink, and music (in *Bubier Park;* phone: 761-5363). The *Ft. Lauderdale Boat Show,* held in October at the *Bahia Mar Yachting Center,* is the world's largest in-water display of all types and sizes of watercraft (phone: 763-3661). In November, the *Promenade in the Park* features arts and crafts, food, and entertainment at *Holiday Park* (phone: 764-5973). Also held in November are the *Greater Ft. Lauderdale Film Festival,* with screenings of more than 50 independent films (phone: 563-0500), and the *Broward County Fair* in Hallandale (phone: 923-FAIR). The year's activities are capped by the December-long *Winterfest;* highlights include the Ft. Lauderdale and Pompano Beach boat parades, with about 100 boats festooned with colored lights and *Christmas* decorations plying the Intracoastal Waterway (phone: 767-0686), and a *Light-up Lauderdale* laser show downtown on *New Year's Eve* (phone: 767-0686).

MUSEUMS

In addition to those described in *Special Places*, other museums include the following:

FT. LAUDERDALE HISTORICAL SOCIETY Located in the historic district, the society headquarters hosts exhibits on topics of local historic interest such as "South Florida's Mediterranean Revival Architecture." The society also conducts tours of downtown Ft. Lauderdale. Closed Sunday mornings and Mondays. Admission charge. 219 SW Second Ave. (phone: 463-4431).

MUSEUM OF ART Housed in a 63,800-square-foot building designed by Edward Larabee Barnes, the museum features 19th- and 20th-century European and American art, as well as West African, pre-Columbian, and American Indian works. There are more than 2,000 paintings and 5,000 prints in the collection. Traveling exhibits are housed in three galleries, and there's a sculpture garden and auditorium. Open extended hours on Tuesdays; closed Sunday mornings and Mondays. Admission charge. 1 E. Las Olas Blvd. (phone: 525-5500).

YOUNG AT ART CHILDREN'S MUSEUM Primarily a hands-on museum, where young artists can develop their skills. Closed Sunday mornings and Mondays. Admission charge, except for children under two. 801 S. University Dr., Plantation (phone: 424-0085).

SHOPPING

For a break from the beach (believe it or not, people do need that once in a while), visit one of the many shopping malls and stores in the Ft. Lauderdale area. The following places are in Ft. Lauderdale unless otherwise noted.

Broward Mall One of the South's largest shopping malls, with 130 specialty shops, this ultramodern mart's main stores are *Burdine's, Sears, Mervyn's,* and *JC Penney.* Broward Blvd. and University Dr., Plantation (phone: 473-8100).

Fashion Row Known as "Shmatte Row" (after the Yiddish word for garments or rags), it offers discounts, discounts, and more discounts. One section of dress and handbag shops is located off Hallandale Beach Boulevard on Northeast First Avenue (dubbed "Fashion Row" on street signs); the other is on Northeast Second Avenue between Northeast Third and Northeast Fourth Streets. This area also has stores offering lower prices on home furnishings and accessories. Stop at *Barnett's* (100 E. Hallandale Beach Blvd., Hallandale; phone: 456-0566), or try the *Dansk Factory Outlet* (27 W. Hallandale Beach Blvd., Hallandale; phone: 454-3900) for discounts on seconds and overstocks of fine Danish housewares. Most Fashion Row shops are open daily from December through March; closed Sundays the rest of the year.

Festival Flea Market At this 400,000-square-foot indoor flea-market-type mall in western Ft. Lauderdale, 650 vendors offer brand-new merchandise as well as antiques and collectibles. There are also eight movie theaters, an amusement arcade, and an international food court. Many items are discounted. Closed Mondays from after *Thanksgiving* through

April 30, with extended hours on Fridays; closed Mondays and Tuesdays the rest of the year. 2900 W. Sample Rd., Coconut Creek (phone: 979-4555).

Galleria High-fashion clothes and home furnishings are sold at this three-story mall, featuring *Neiman Marcus, Saks Fifth Avenue, Lord & Taylor, Burdine's,* and numerous smaller stores. Valet parking available. 2414 E. Sunrise Blvd. (phone: 564-1015).

Lord & Taylor Clearance Center Here you'll find clothing discounted 50% initially, with further reductions for special sales. 7067 W. Broward Blvd., Plantation (phone: 581-8205).

Maus & Hoffman Upscale men's clothing is offered at this shop. Closed Sundays. 800 E. Las Olas Blvd. (phone: 463-1472).

Sawgrass Mills Mall This gigantic, alligator-shape, 2.2 million-square-foot shopping center is billed as the world's largest outlet mall. 12801 W. Sunrise Blvd., Sunrise (phone: 846-2350; 800-FL-MILLS). For more information, see *Special Places*.

Sophy Curson High-fashion women's clothing is the specialty here. Open only from late October through May; closed Sundays. 1508 Las Olas Blvd. (phone: 462-7770).

Swap Shop Indoor and outdoor booths beckon at this massive flea market—the largest in the South and a true bargain-hunter's heaven. 3291 W. Sunrise Blvd. (phone: 791-SWAP). A second branch has 625 stores. 1000 State Rd. 7, Margate (phone: 971-SWAP). For more information, see *Special Places*.

Zola Keller Upscale fashions for women. Closed Sundays. 818 Las Olas Blvd. (phone: 462-3222).

SPORTS AND FITNESS

BASEBALL Fans can watch spring training and pre-season games during February and March. The New York *Yankees* play at *Yankee Stadium* (5301 NW 12th Ave.; phone: 776-1921). The stadium also hosts the *Mickey Mantle Week of Dreams* (phone: 606-474-7771) and *Whitey Ford Fantasy Baseball Camp* (phone: 201-943-0599); the former is held in May and October, the latter in November. At both camps, Mantle, Ford, Hank Bauer, Mike Ferraro, and other former diamond biggies teach the over-thirtysomething crowd how to hit home runs.

FISHING There are lots of charter boat fishing operators at *Bahia Mar Yacht Basin,* across A1A from the beach (801 Seabreeze Blvd.; phone: 523-5400) and at *Pier 66 Aquatic Center* at *Pier 66* (2301 SE 17th St. Cswy.; phone: 768-9500). Landlubbers fish 24 hours a day from the 1,080-foot *Pompano Beach Fishing Pier* (two blocks north of East Atlantic Blvd.; phone: 943-1488), and *Anglin's Fishing Pier* (2 Commercial Blvd.; phone: 491-9403) for an admission charge

FITNESS CENTERS *Nautilus Fitness Center* (1624 N. Federal Hwy.; phone: 566-2222), with certified instructors, offers all the standard Nautilus exercise equipment, plus saunas. It's open to the public for a fee.

GOLF There are more than 76 golf courses in the area. Among those open to the public are *American Golfers Club* (3850 N. Federal Hwy.; phone: 564-8760); *Bonaventure* (200 Racquet Club Rd.; phone: 389-2124); *Palm-Aire* (2601 Palm-Aire Dr. N., Pompano Beach; phone: 972-3300); *Rolling Hills* (3501 W. Rolling Hills Cir., Davie; phone: 475-0400); *Grand Palms* (110 Grand Palm Dr., Pembroke Pines; phone: 437-3334); *Weston Hills* (2603 Country Club Way; phone: 384-9422); and *Jacaranda* (9200 W. Broward Blvd., Plantation; phone: 472-5836). For additional information, call the *Broward County Parks and Recreation Department* (phone: 357-8100).

HORSE AND DOG RACING There's thoroughbred horse racing at *Gulfstream Park* (Hallandale Beach Blvd. and US 1, Hallandale; phone: 454-7000) daily except Wednesdays from mid-January through March, and harness racing at *Pompano Harness Track* (1800 SW Third St., Pompano Beach; phone: 972-2000) from October through August. You can "go to the dogs" at *Hollywood Greyhound Track* (831 N. Federal Hwy., Hallandale; phone: 454-9400) from December through April. Call for racing dates.

HORSEBACK RIDING Most people don't envision southern Florida as the Wild, Wild West, but horse country is within closer range than you would imagine. In southwestern Ft. Lauderdale, in Davie, many stables offer trail rides and horse rentals. Among the larger ones are *Bar-B Ranch* (4601 SW 128th Ave., Davie; phone: 434-6175), which offers horse rentals, and *Myrland Stables* (5550 SW 73rd Ave., Davie; phone: 587-2285), which has supervised rides. Both are open daily. On Saturdays and Sundays, Broward County also operates stables at *Tradewinds Park* (3600 W. Sample Rd., Coconut Creek; phone: 968-3880).

JAI ALAI This Basque import is the area's most fast-paced sport, with pari-mutuel betting adding spice. The season is year-round, except for 10 days in April and May. The action takes place at *Dania Jai-Alai* (301 E. Dania Beach Blvd., Dania; phone: 927-2841 or 920-1511 for reservations); it's closed Sundays and Mondays.

NATURE HIKES The *Broward County Parks and Recreation Department* sponsors a different nature walk each Friday and Saturday, October through May. Call for a schedule (phone: 357-8100 or 536-PARK).

PARASAILING Soar like a bird over Ft. Lauderdale with *Watersports Unlimited* (301 Seabreeze Blvd.; phone: 467-1316 or 941-4044) or *Sunrise Watersports* (2025 E. Sunrise Blvd.; phone: 462-8962).

RODEO Cowboys compete in bronco riding, calf roping, and other activities at the *Rodeo Arena* in Davie, just behind the *Davie Town Hall* (6591 SW 45th St.; phone: 797-1166 or 437-8800). There's an admission charge.

SAILING After the sunshine, the water is one of South Florida's greatest draws. The US Corps of Engineers has eliminated most of the shoal areas and maintains navigational aids. Private and public marinas provide virtually every type of boat for rent. For large charters, power-, or sailboats, see *Fishing* in this section. Jet skis and mini–cigarette boats may be rented from *Sunrise Watersports* (2025 E. Sunrise Blvd.; phone: 462-8962).

SCUBA DIVING Stretching north from the Keys past Ft. Lauderdale, Florida's natural coral reef has suffered an environmental impact: Broken reef in some places, and pollution in others threaten to reduce both living spaces for sea life and an interest in scuba diving. But diving is making a strong comeback in this part of Florida.

BEST DEPTHS

Ft. Lauderdale Reef There are more than 80 different dive sites along the 23-mile-long Broward County shoreline, ranging from some only 15 feet deep (about 100 yards offshore) to the Tenneco Platforms 115 feet down. Several wrecks, including the famous German freighter *Mercedes,* have served to increase reef life and also make for some challenging dives. The area's dive operations offer a variety of all-inclusive packages for certified divers, as well as half-day dive trips, specialty classes, and "Discover Scuba" introductory courses (also known as "resort" courses). For more information, contact *Pro Dive* (*Bahia Mar Yachting Center,* 801 Seabreeze Blvd.; phone: 761-3413 or 800-772-DIVE) or the visitors' bureau.

Dozens of dive shops such as *Ocean Diving Schools* (750 E. Sample Rd., Pompano; phone: 943-3337) and *Pro Dive* (*Bahia Mar Yachting Center,* 801 Seabreeze Blvd.; phone: 761-3413 or 800-772-DIVE outside Florida) feature scheduled dives two or three times a day. Many operators also offer package deals with hotels.

SNORKELING The 60-foot glass-bottom boat *Pro Diver II* offers snorkeling trips Tuesdays through Sundays from the *Bahia Mar Yachting Center* (801 Seabreeze Blvd.; phone: 761-3413 or 800-772-DIVE).

SPAS With its ideal climate and prodigious natural beauty, Florida makes the perfect setting for spas; and Ft. Lauderdale has plenty of them. But for sheer physical pampering, one is by far the best.

A SYBARITIC SPA

Bonaventure A haven for world-weary celebrities, this resort spa provides just about any personal service that the mind can envision. Guests can head straight for the pool, then flex their muscles on the rowing machine, take a challenging aerobics class, and collapse with an aromatherapy massage. There are programs that analyze your percentage of superfluous body fat, determine a sound nutrition program for you, or develop a fitness schedule for your particular needs. 250 Racquet Club Rd. (phone: 389-3300; for reservations, 800-327-8090).

SWIMMING The most crowded beach is along "The Strip," from Sunrise Boulevard to Bahia Mar. The Galt Ocean Mile is quieter, with an older crowd. Perhaps the quietest strand is the stretch between Galt Ocean

Mile and NE 22nd Street, and if you search you may find small pockets of peace in *John U. Lloyd Beach State Recreation Area* (see *Special Places*) or *North Beach Park* (Sheridan Rd. and Rte. A1A, Hollywood; phone: 926-2444). Deerfield Beach, from the border of Broward and Palm Beach counties south to SE 10th Street, is a favorite of locals. This beach area has some of the best shower facilities around, and its huge boulders in the water create intriguing coves that invite exploration.

TENNIS Most major hotels have tennis courts; some of the best are found at the *Bonaventure* resort (see *Spas,* above). There also are numerous courts open to the public. Among them are *Holiday Park Tennis Center* (701 NE 12th Ave.; phone: 761-5378); *Dillon Tennis Courts* (4091 NE Fifth Ave., Oakland Park; phone: 561-6180); *Pompano Beach Tennis Center* (900 NE 18th Ave.; phone: 786-4115); and *George W. English Park* (110 Bayview Dr.; phone: 566-0622). For more information, contact the *Broward County Parks and Recreation Division* (phone: 357-8100).

THEATER

The area's major theaters are the *Parker Playhouse* (707 NE Eighth St.; phone: 764-0700), which features name actors in touring companies of Broadway productions, and *Sunrise Musical Theater* (5555 NW 95th Ave.; phone: 741-7300), which offers touring Broadway musicals and individual performers in concert. Opened in 1991, the $50-million regional *Broward Center for the Performing Arts* (201 SW Fifth Ave.; phone: 522-5334 or 462-0222 for tickets) stages opera, theatrical, ballet, and philharmonic productions. Theatrical and cultural events also are staged at the *War Memorial Auditorium* (800 NE Eighth St.; phone: 761-5381) and *Bailey Hall* at *Broward Community College* (3501 SW Davie Rd., Davie; phone: 475-6880), which also presents children's productions. Local youngsters also perform in the *Ft. Lauderdale Children's Theatre* (640 N. Andrews Ave.; phone: 763-6901). The playwright Vinnette Carroll, who wrote *Your Arms Too Short to Box with God,* opened the *Vinnette Carroll Theater* (503 SE Sixth St.; phone: 462-2424), a multicultural theater in a converted church. For current offerings, check the newspapers.

MUSIC

The *Philharmonic Orchestra of Florida* usually plays at the *Broward Center for the Performing Arts* (address above; phone: 561-2997 or 800-226-1812 for *Philharmonic* tickets). The center is also the site for performances by the *Sinfonia Virtuosi* (phone: 561-5882) and the *Opera Guild* (phone: 728-9700) during winter months; the latter often features visiting artists from New York and from the *Greater Miami Opera Company*. Student and guest chamber music, jazz, opera, and symphonic performances are staged throughout the year at *Broward Community College* (phone: 475-6884).

NIGHTCLUBS AND NIGHTLIFE

Most hotels and larger motels offer music and/or comedy acts nightly. Just for laughs, reserve seats at *The Comic Strip* (1432 N. Federal Hwy.; phone: 565-8887), which showcases New York and Los Angeles comics. The *Musician's Exchange Café* (729 W. Sunrise Blvd.; phone: 764-1912) is the place to go for jazz, blues, and rock. For dance and disco, the young and wild go to *Baja Beach Club* (3200 N. Federal Hwy.; phone: 561-2432). *Confetti's* (2660 E. Commercial Blvd.; phone: 776-4080) gets the mid-20s crowd; *Yesterdays* (3001 E. Oakland Park; phone: 561-4400), the mid-30s crowd; and the *Pier Top Lounge* at the *Pier 66 Crowne Plaza* hotel attracts romantic couples of all ages (see *Checking In*). At *Squeeze* (2 S. New River Dr.; phone: 522-2151), there's dancing to progressive and alternative music. Night owls do a second shift at *Flix* (2669 N. Federal Hwy., Pompano Beach; phone: 781-2002), which doesn't get crowded until 1 AM. Jazz lovers flock to *O'Hara's Pub* (722 E. Las Olas Blvd.; phone: 524-1764); cowpokes and country-and-western wanna-be's to *Do Da's American Country Saloon* (700 S. State Rd. 7, Plantation; phone: 792-6200); and the blues and beer group to *Cheers* (941 E. Cypress Creek Rd.; phone: 771-6337). The hottest gay club remains *The Copa* (624 SE 28th St.; phone: 463-1507). While patrons rarely dance on tables (hey, this isn't South Beach), Ft. Lauderdale's hottest supper club is *Mario's East* (1313 E. Las Olas Blvd.; phone: 523-4990). Those nostalgic for the folk music of the 1960s and 1970s will find it at *Coconut's* (429 Seabreeze Blvd.; phone: 467-6788). Female impersonators put on a fabulous show at *Cabaret* (120 SW Third Ave.; phone: 467-3456). And if you just want to sit at a sidewalk café, watch the waves and the people, and listen to good jazz, *Mistral* (see *Eating Out*) has just the thing every Friday and Saturday.

Best in Town

CHECKING IN

Ft. Lauderdale's busiest period is winter, when reservations should be made as far in advance as possible. In addition to the major hotels listed here, Ft. Lauderdale has hundreds of smaller chains (check the phone book for their toll-free 800 numbers) and family-operated hotels and motels. During high season, a double room listed in the very expensive range could run $200 to $300 per night; a room in the expensive range will cost $155 to $190; in the moderate category, $110 to $150; and in the inexpensive range, $75 to $100. In the summer, occupancy (and room) rates drop. Note that a 3% county tourist development tax and a 6% state sales tax are added to all hotel bills. Unless noted otherwise, hotel rooms have air conditioning, private baths, TV sets, and telephones. All hotels are in Ft. Lauderdale and telephone numbers are in the 305 area code unless otherwise indicated.

For an unforgettable Ft. Lauderdale vacation experience, we begin with our favorite, followed by our recommendations of cost and quality choices of hotels, listed by price category.

A REGAL RESORT

Boca Raton Resort and Club Just 30 minutes north of Ft. Lauderdale is this elegant (and pricey) country-club-styled resort. Old World elegance permeates the *Cloister*, the original

1926 hotel building. Richly decorated contemporary rooms are found in the 27-story *Tower*, and soft pastels dominate the spacious beachfront *Beach Club* rooms. The club's site on a spit of land between the Intracoastal Waterway and the Atlantic guarantees a watery vista from all but the *Cloister* rooms. Lanais are available for lounging, and there's direct access to the beach on the Atlantic side. Guests also can use the two large pools, 34 tennis courts, two championship golf courses, three fitness centers, and myriad other amenities of the sprawling 963-room resort, including nine restaurants and lounges, meeting space, and a concierge level. 501 E. Camino Real, Boca Raton (phone: 407-395-3000; 800-327-0101; fax: 407-391-3183).

VERY EXPENSIVE

Bonaventure Although it's a long drive to the beach, this resort is hardly short on outdoor activities. Set in a lush 1,250-acre residential complex amid waterfalls, lakes, and manicured grounds are two championship 18-hole golf courses (see *Golf*); a racquet club with 24 tennis courts (see *Tennis*), five racquetball courts, and a squash court; five swimming pools; and a spa that offers a full range of health and nutrition programs in separate facilities for men and women (see *A Sybaritic Spa*, above). There are 504 rooms and suites, four restaurants, and two lounges. On weekends, the resort runs supervised activities programs for children ages three to 12. Business facilities include room service until 2 AM, meeting rooms for up to 1,200, a concierge, secretarial services, A/V equipment, photocopiers, and computers. 250 Racquet Club Rd. (phone: 389-3300; 800-327-8090; fax: 984-6157).

Ft. Lauderdale Marina Marriott There are great views north and south from this property's 14-story tower and two low-rise sections. Most of the 580 rooms have balconies, and all have in-room safes and two telephones. There's a free-form pool, with an adjacent bar, a marina with slips for up to 35 yachts, four tennis courts, a health club, a sauna, an outdoor Jacuzzi, a gift shop, restaurants, lounges, and a free shuttle to the beach. Business facilities include 24-hour room service, meeting rooms for up to 2,000, a concierge, secretarial services, A/V equipment, photocopiers, computers, and express checkout. On the Intracoastal Waterway at the 17th Street Causeway, 1881 SE 17th St. (phone: 463-4000; 800-228-9290; fax: 527-6705).

Marriott Harbor Beach Resort Ft. Lauderdale's premier resort offers 16 acres of beachfront elegance. Guests think they're in a posh Caribbean retreat, what with five restaurants (including the outstanding *Sheffield's;* see *Eating Out*), two lounges, a pool bar, five tennis courts, and exercise facilities. There's also a tropically landscaped free-form pool with a waterfall and 50 cabañas. The 589 rooms are undersized for the price; the 35 suites, however, are super. Free transportation to the *Bonaventure Country Club* is provided for golfers. This place is popular with families due to the year-round "Beach Buddies" supervised camp program for children ages five to 12. Business facilities include 24-hour room service, meeting rooms for up to 3,500, a concierge, secretarial services, A/V equipment, photocopiers, computers, and express checkout. 3030 Holiday Dr. (phone: 525-4000; 800-222-6543; fax: 766-6152).

EXPENSIVE

Crown Sterling Suites Formerly *Embassy Suites,* the chain's largest property in Florida offers 359 suites at prices equivalent to a deluxe hotel room. On the premises are a restaurant and lounge, a pool, a sauna, and a Jacuzzi. Lots of freebies are included in the room rate—daily full American breakfasts, happy hour cocktails, beach shuttle service, parking, and airport transportation. Saluted by *Consumer Reports* magazine, the rooms are attractive and feature sleep sofas in the living rooms, wet bars with mini-fridges, dining tables, and kitchenettes with microwave ovens and coffee makers. Two children under the age of 12 may stay for free in their parents' room. Business facilities include meeting rooms for up to 440, a concierge, A/V equipment, photocopiers, and express checkout. 1100 SE 17th St. Causeway (phone: 527-2700; 800-854-6146; fax: 760-7202).

Guest Quarters Next to the *Galleria* shopping mall and situated on the Intracoastal Waterway, its 230 modern suites are good values, with fully equipped kitchens, cable TV, 24-hour room service, and sleep sofas in the living rooms. Facilities include a pool, Jacuzzi, small exercise room, restaurant, lounge, and gameroom. The beach is within walking distance and airport transfers are complimentary. Also accessible by water taxi. Business facilities include 24-hour room service, meeting rooms, a concierge, secretarial services, A/V equipment, photocopiers, computers, and express checkout. 2670 E. Sunrise Blvd. (phone: 565-3800; 800-424-2900; fax: 561-0387).

Pier 66 Crowne Plaza Set on the Intracoastal Waterway with 338 rooms and suites in a 17-floor tower and two low-rise sections, this resort was recently renovated, giving it a sleek, contemporary look and restoring it to its former position as one of Ft. Lauderdale's most prestigious hotels. On 22 acres, the property offers a full-service 142-slip marina, plus six restaurants and lounges, including the famous *Pier Top Lounge,* which offers a 360-degree view of Ft. Lauderdale. Guests keep busy at the aquatics center, tennis courts, three pools, and the full-service *Spa LXVI.* Shopping is nearby, and there's a free water shuttle to the beach. Business facilities include 24-hour room service, meeting rooms, a concierge, secretarial services, A/V equipment, photocopiers, computers, and express checkout. 2301 SE 17th St. Causeway (phone: 525-6666; 800-327-3796 or 800-HOLIDAY; fax: 728-3595).

Westin Cypress Creek The Westin group's first foray into Florida, this 14-story, 293-room, luxury property overlooks a five-acre lagoon that's spectacularly lighted at *Christmastime.* It features a health club, a large outdoor pool, and a lakeside pavilion; tennis and golf are a five-minute drive away. There are two restaurants—one for fine dining, a second for casual food—and a bar complex. Free parking is available. Business facilities include 24-hour room service, meeting rooms for up to 600, a concierge, secretarial services, A/V equipment, photocopiers, computers, and express checkout. 400 Corporate Dr., in the Radice Corporate Center (phone: 772-1331; 800-228-3000; fax: 491-9087).

MODERATE

Bahia Mar This nautically oriented hotel and marina, at the *Bahia Mar Yachting Center* at the southern end of "The Strip," has 298 rooms, two restaurants (the *Schooner's Lounge* and the *Deli*), a free-form pool, a dive shop, glass-bottom boats for rent, four lighted tennis courts, and several boutiques. There are 350 slips for fishing boats and pleasure yachts, and the country's largest in-water boat show takes place here (see *Special Events*). Be sure to request a refurbished room, decked out in tropical hothouse colors. Business facilities include meeting rooms for up to 1,200, a concierge, secretarial services, A/V equipment, photocopiers, and express checkout. 801 Seabreeze Blvd. (phone: 764-2233; 800-327-8154; fax: 523-5424).

Palm-Aire Home of Ft. Lauderdale's original spa, this resort is part of a residential complex of over 1,500 acres. The 191 rooms were undergoing a face-lift at press time, but are still somewhat tired looking. Guests have the use of six tennis courts, one executive and two championship 18-hole golf courses (see *Golf*), three pools, a half-mile ParCours running track, two racquetball courts, a squash court, two restaurants, and a lounge. Special packages may be booked at their pricey spa, where health and beauty programs prevail. Business facilities include room service, meeting rooms, a concierge, secretarial services, A/V equipment, photocopiers, computers, and express checkout. 2601 Palm-Aire Dr. N., Pompano Beach (phone: 972-3300; 800-272-5624; fax: 968-2744).

Ramada Beach All 220 rooms at this beachfront property have balconies, some overlooking the Atlantic Ocean. (Be sure to request one of the lovely renovated rooms, as the others are disappointing.) The *Ocean Café* offers a mostly continental menu, and the lounge features live music and dancing on weekends. Other features include a heated pool, a tiki bar for hors d'oeuvres and cocktails, and sailboat rentals. Business facilities include room service, meeting rooms, a concierge, secretarial services, A/V equipment, photocopiers, computers, and express checkout. 4060 Galt Ocean Dr. (phone: 565-6611; 800-678-9022; fax: 564-7730).

Sheraton Yankee Clipper "Moored" on the beach, the oldest building at this landmark resort looks like—what else?—a clipper ship. The four-building complex (some buildings are across the street and connected to the beach by an overpass) boasts 504 refurbished rooms, all with two double beds. There are three heated swimming pools, a restaurant, a beachside bar, two lounges that offer entertainment, and an exercise room with weights and workout machines. Business facilities include meeting rooms for up to 200, a concierge, A/V equipment, and express checkout. 1140 Seabreeze Blvd. (phone: 524-5551; 800-325-3535; fax: 524-0777).

INEXPENSIVE

Bahia Cabana Small, unpretentious, and very Floridian, this very informal place is nestled within the *Bahia Mar Yachting Center*. There are 116 rooms and apartments with kitchenettes located in five buildings (request the one most recently renovated), three swimming pools, a Jacuzzi, saunas, an indoor sports bar, and an outdoor patio bar/restaurant overlooking the marina. While the standard rooms are reasonably priced, this hostelry is usually noisy, with a lot of young guests. 3001 Harbor Dr. (phone: 524-1555; 800-BEACHES or 800-922-3008 in Florida; fax: 764-5951).

A Little Inn by the Sea Former New York City theater set designer Chuck Murawski owns this 30-room bed and breakfast hostelry on the beach. It's pleasant, homey, and down-to-earth, with a bilingual staff. Children under 10 stay for free in their parents' room. 4546 El Mar Dr., Lauderdale-by-the-Sea (phone: 772-2450; fax: 938-9354).

Riverside Offering 110 rooms and suites, this European-style hostelry has a convenient downtown location as well as a sedate ambience and a cozy lobby with a fireplace. Built in 1936, it is one of the city's oldest structures. There's a restaurant, an intimate restaurant/lounge decorated with etched glass, and a swimming pool set amid tropical landscaping on the New River. Note that just a handful of rooms fall into the inexpensive category, and these have only one double bed. Business facilities include meeting rooms for up to 190, a concierge, secretarial services, A/V equipment, photocopiers, and express checkout. 620 E. Las Olas Blvd. (phone: 467-0671; 800-325-3280; fax: 462-2148).

EATING OUT

There are nearly 2,500 restaurants in Broward County. Many of these are well known and most get quite crowded during the winter season—in fact, a recent magazine survey ranked Ft. Lauderdale's restaurants second only to New York City's as the country's busiest—so it's always a good idea to make reservations. Casual dress is accepted at most restaurants, though a few of the more expensive ones prefer that men wear jackets. Restaurants serve lunch and dinner unless otherwise indicated. Expect to pay $80 or more for dinner for two in a restaurant listed in the very expensive category; $55 to $75 in the expensive category; $30 to $50 in the moderate category; and $25 or less in the inexpensive category. Prices do not include wine, drinks, taxes or tips. All restaurants are in Ft. Lauderdale and all telephone numbers are in the 305 area code unless otherwise indicated.

VERY EXPENSIVE

Darrel & Oliver's Café Maxx The decor is simple, leaving the focus on the food. The dishes created here are on the cutting edge of "new" American cooking; many of the recipes have appeared in well-known food magazines. Each course is a carefully created visual masterpiece: Oysters are dipped in ground pistachios, fried, placed in their shells atop a bed of corn and tomato salsa, and surrounded by a mound of red and green curly lettuce, *enoki* mushrooms, lemongrass, and a nasturtium blossom. The Peking pork with a honey-sesame glaze and the white chocolate mousse pie with raspberry sauce and a white chocolate truffle are two other examples of the chef's melting-pot inventiveness. Open daily for dinner. Reservations necessary. Major credit cards accepted. 2601 E. Atlantic Blvd., Pompano Beach (phone: 782-0606).

Burt & Jack's Owned by actor Burt Reynolds and partner Jack Jackson, this beautiful Spanish-style villa offers first-rate lobsters and steaks. Reserve a window table so you can watch the cruise and cargo ships pass by. Open for dinner only; closed Mondays. Reservations necessary; jackets required for men. Major credit cards accepted. Berth 23, Port Everglades (phone: 522-5225).

Plum Room One of South Florida's more romantic, intimate dining rooms, this spot features beautifully presented continental food as a harpist plays in the background. There are classic dishes, including sole Véronique and beef Wellington, as well as such exotica as ostrich and elk. Don't miss the cream of mushroom soup, made with shiitake, *enoki*, and white mushrooms. There's also an extensive wine list. Open daily for dinner. Reservations necessary. Major credit cards accepted. 3001 E. Oakland Park Blvd. (phone: 563-4168).

Sheffield's Located in the *Marriott Harbor Beach Resort* hotel, this posh dining room offers superb gravlax, lobster bisque, chateaubriand, and chicken *forestière* with a mountain of wild mushrooms. Dinner ends with arguably the best *tiramisù* on the coast. Open daily for dinner October through May; closed Mondays and Tuesdays the rest of the year. Reservations necessary. Major credit cards accepted. 3030 Holiday Dr. (phone: 525-4000).

La Vielle Maison Attentive service and classic French fare are the hallmarks in this historic home 20 minutes from Ft. Lauderdale. Combined with courtyards, flowing fountains, gaslights, a profusion of fresh flowers, and Old World antiques, they have made this award-winning restaurant the top romantic retreat in South Florida. Outstanding entrées include incomparable venison, sweetbreads with cumin, and poached grouper with mustard and red wine *beurre blanc*. The flawless *crêpe soufflé au citron* should not be missed. Both prix fixe and à la carte menus are available. Open daily for dinner. Reservations necessary. Major credit cards accepted. 770 E. Palmetto Park Rd., Boca Raton (phone: 421-7370 or 407-391-6701).

EXPENSIVE

Armadillo Café Large portions of nouveau Southwestern fare are served in this smoke-free eatery chock-full of cacti, cowboy hats, and steer horns. The tequila-grilled shrimp and roasted corn cakes with *chipotle* butter and tomato salsa are fabulous. Other favorites include smoked duck quesadillas, Armadillo filet (butterflied beef tenderloin marinated in a special sauce and grilled), and yellowtail snapper seared with roast peppers and garlic. Delicacies such as fresh rattlesnake, buffalo, and venison occasionally are offered. There are also chocolate cinnamon fritters (for dessert), chili beer (with a fresh chili in it), and excellent wines by the glass. Open daily for dinner; closed major holidays. Reservations necessary. Major credit cards accepted. 4630 SW 64th Ave., Davie (phone: 791-4866).

By Word of Mouth This European café–style spot is expensive, but a true treat for gastronomes. The owner has not advertised since opening the restaurant 12 years ago, but folks flock here to order the abundant salads, hand-size Portobello mushrooms stuffed with brie, duckling soaked in apricot brandy, wild mushroom lasagna, outrageous lobster tarragon pie, and star-quality desserts (our favorite is "brownie decadence," followed closely by white chocolate cheese cake with Key lime curd). The menu changes daily. Closed Sundays; no dinner on Mondays and Tuesdays, no lunch on Saturdays. Reservations advised. Major credit cards accepted. 3200 NE 12th Ave. (phone: 564-3663).

Charley's Crab One of the best of Chuck Muer's seven South Florida restaurants, it has a wonderful location on the Intracoastal Waterway, with dining inside and out. Specialties include an excellent Martha's Vineyard salad, a wide range of fresh fish prepared almost every way imaginable, and a terrific apple tart with homemade cinnamon ice cream. This spot can be reached by water taxi. Open daily; brunch served on Sundays. Reservations advised. Major credit cards accepted. 3000 NE 32nd Ave. (phone: 561-4800).

Chart House This branch of the chain offers the standard steaks and seafood with unlimited salad and fantastic mud pie for dessert. Its downtown Ft. Lauderdale location is a knockout. Housed in two homes (ca. 1904) on the New River, it has window tables that offer a passing show of pleasure craft and working vessels. After dining, stroll along the 2 miles of the lushly landscaped *Riverwalk* to the *Broward Center for the Performing Arts,* or take a water taxi back to your hotel. Open daily for dinner. Reservations advised. Major credit cards accepted. 301 SW Third Ave. (phone: 523-0177).

La Coquille One of Ft. Lauderdale's best-kept secrets, this family-run establishment entrances diners with meals that look—and taste—good enough to grace the cover of *Bon Appétit* magazine. The ambience is country French and the fare Provençal, and bilingual French waiters serve with warmth and humor. Menu highlights include tender and succulent lamb, shrimp grilled to perfection, and salmon with just the right amount of champagne sauce and leeks. The four-course, prix fixe dinner for two includes a bottle of French wine, allowing couples to celebrate in style without seriously damaging their wallets. Splurge on the Grand Marnier or chocolate soufflés, the latter served with fresh raspberry sauce. Open Fridays for lunch; daily for dinner; closed August and Mondays from May through October. Reservations advised. Major credit cards accepted. 1619 E. Sunrise Blvd. at 16th Ter. (phone: 467-3030).

Go Fish The owners of the landmark restaurant *Casa Vecchia* converted their well-known establishment (a waterfront mansion built in the 1930s by the Pond's cold cream family) into a whimsically romantic Caribbean oasis, complete with the lilting music of a steel band on weekends. All the fruits of the sea appear on the innovative menu—from oven-baked bluepoint oysters with lemon chive hollandaise sauce to guava-glazed dorado fish to two-pound broiled Maine lobster. The Caribbean surf and turf is a hands-down winner, with spicy Jamaican jerk pork, tender Florida lobster, jumbo garlic shrimp, fried plantains, and a wonderful sweet-potato mash. If you can, reserve a table in the *Garden Room,* overlooking the Intracoastal Waterway, with a fish-ornament–adorned ficus tree centerpiece beneath a glass skylight. This spot can be reached by water taxi. Open daily for dinner except *Labor Day* and *Memorial Day.* Reservations advised. Major credit cards accepted. 209 N. Birch Rd. (phone: 463-7575).

Mai-Kai This place is a Ft. Lauderdale landmark, with its huge entranceway torches flanking a rattling plank-bridge entrance. Choose from the main dining room, where you can watch the nightly Polynesian show; smaller, lavishly decorated dining rooms; or outdoor seating by a waterfall. The gardens are lush, with authentic South Seas statuary, and the drinks exotic. The food is even better than the ambience, with Polynesian, American, and Cantonese dishes (a specialty is Peking duck). The *Molokai Bar* is filled with old-time nautical memorabilia. The Polynesian show (cover charge) is professional and highly entertaining. Open daily for dinner. Reservations advised. Major credit cards accepted. 3599 N. Federal Hwy. (phone: 563-3272).

Martha's Located on the Intracoastal Waterway, this eatery has a split personality—the glitzy downstairs serves dress-up types, while the second-floor deck is less formal, more tropical in flavor. The same courteous service and outstanding menu apply to both. Steaks, chops, and seafood are well prepared; fresh Florida snapper is offered eight different ways. Chicken gorgonzola with walnuts is also first-rate. Boat dockage available. Open daily; brunch served Sundays. Reservations necessary Saturday nights, advised otherwise. Major credit cards accepted. 6024 N. Ocean Dr., Hollywood (phone: 923-5444).

Silverado Café A bit of the Napa Valley has been transplanted to the *University Park Plaza* shopping center, where good cooking and California wines prevail. Dine amid Victorian decor or in a small room designed to look like the gondola of a hot-air balloon. Appetizers include an outstanding black bean soup and lobster ravioli; fresh grilled fish and cashew chicken *à l'orange* are tops for main courses. Closed Sunday lunch and Mondays. Reservations advised. Major credit cards accepted. 3528 S. University Dr., Davie (phone: 474-9992).

MODERATE

Bimini Boatyard There's Bahamian decor and a view of the marina here—plus good food at reasonable prices and lots of singles action at the bar on Fridays. Specialties include conch fritters, pasta, grilled swordfish with black bean sauce, and jerk ribs—along with wonderful Bimini bread. Open daily. Reservations accepted only for parties of eight or more. Major credit cards accepted. 1555 SE 17th St. (phone: 525-7400).

Brasserie Max Noted restaurateur Dennis Max created this affordable spot (though he no longer owns it) where the young and young at heart eat in a casual atmosphere. Creative pizza and pasta dishes are favorites, but the restaurant hits its peak with oak-grilled specialties such as Caribbean pork chops served with homemade applesauce. Open daily; brunch served Sundays. Reservations advised. Major credit cards accepted. In *The Fashion Mall,* 321 N. University Dr., Plantation (phone: 424-8000).

Brazilian Tropicana Brazilian specialties are dished out here, along with a knock-out show replete with soaring headdresses and skimpy outfits (on the men as well as the women!). Favorite dishes include *mariscada en molho verde* (clams, shrimp, scallops, mussels, and lobster in a garlic and white wine sauce), the all-you-can-eat *rodizio* (skewers of homemade sausage, chicken pork loin, and sirloin steak presented and sliced at your table), and shrimp casserole. Open daily for dinner; shows presented Thursdays through Sundays (cover charge). Reservations necessary. Major credit cards accepted. 410 N. Federal Hwy., Pompano Beach (phone: 781-1113).

Gibby's An enormous eatery offering good value in a pretty setting—several dining rooms aglow with twinkling lights. A humongous salad is included with basic steaks, fish dishes, and veal parmesan. Among the country's busiest restaurants, it serves about 1,500 dinners nightly in season. In summer, the lobster specials are unbeatable. Closed weekday lunch. Reservations advised. Major credit cards accepted. 2900 NE 12th Ter. (phone: 565-2929).

L'Ile de France This bistro serves outstanding French fare. The ever-changing menu may include chicken breast stuffed with goat cheese and sundried tomatoes or honey-smoked duck with sun-dried fruit relish. Come Thursday nights for the bouillabaisse. Leave room for the white chocolate mousse cake with praline *ganache* filling and molasses sauce. Open for dinner only; closed Mondays. Reservations advised. Major credit cards accepted. 3025 N. Ocean Blvd. (phone: 565-9006).

Mario's East On weekends, be prepared to wait at this noisy, ultramodern eatery, where cheerful waiters often dance down the sleek parquet-floored aisles and a female singer belts out pop songs. The consistently excellent fare is traditional Italian, with an amazingly large selection of pasta, veal, chicken, and fresh seafood dishes as well as individual pizzas. The garlicky steamed clams and broccoli appetizers and the veal Marsala, homemade ravioli, and scungilli marinara receive rave reviews. There's a small dance floor and a popular bar. If you prefer a quieter meal, sit on the outdoor terrace or come early. Closed Saturday lunch; brunch served Sundays. Reservations accepted only for parties of eight or more. American Express accepted. 1313 E. Las Olas Blvd. (phone: 523-4990).

Sea Watch One of the few South Florida dining spots set on the Atlantic Ocean beach, this woodsy eatery has been here for almost 21 years. The fare is mostly fresh fish, including those famous stone crabs; oysters Rockefeller and Gulf garlic shrimp are also favorites. Open daily. Reservations accepted only for parties of five or more. Major credit cards accepted. 6002 N. Ocean Blvd. (phone: 781-2200).

Victoria Park Set on a quiet side street, this tiny (only 11 tables) gem, built to resemble a house in St. Barts, produces outstanding French cookery with Caribbean overtones. The pork loin seasoned with Jamaican spices and sliced to resemble a castle is only excelled by the grilled duck breast with ginger cherry sauce. A prix-fixe three-course meal, with pesto ravioli and soft-shell crab for appetizers, is an excellent value, and is served Sundays through Thursdays. This spot can be reached by water taxi. Open daily for dinner. Reservations advised. Major credit cards accepted. 900 NE 20th Ave. (phone: 764-6868).

INEXPENSIVE

Brother's This popular place offers bagels and lox and corned beef on rye, as well as roasted chicken dinners and the like, to droves of locals. Save room for the seven-layer cake. Open daily for breakfast, lunch, and dinner. No reservations. Major credit cards accepted. 1325 S. Powerline Rd., Pompano Beach (phone: 968-5881).

Carlos & Pepe's The clientele at this popular hangout is eager and hungry; the setting is crowded but pleasant (light wood, green plants, and tile tables); and the menu is lighthearted Mexican (*fajitas, chimichangas,* and *chiles rellenos*). Open daily. No reservations. Major credit cards accepted. 1302 SE 17th St. (phone: 467-7192).

Ernie's Bar-B-Que A local institution for almost 40 years, its ribs, chicken, pork, and beef are prepared in a special barbecue sauce that's famous throughout the area. For something different, try the fiery conch chowder. The decor has a rustic Key West style. Open daily. Reservations unnecessary. Major credit cards accepted. 1843 S. Federal Hwy. (phone: 523-8636).

Flamingo Diner Besides hamburgers and salads, the nostalgic may indulge in the *Flamingo*'s old-fashioned meat loaf, cabbage soup, or black cow (root beer with ice cream). Open daily. No reservations. Major credit cards accepted. 7750 Peters Rd., Plantation (phone: 424-7464).

Mistral This trendy sidewalk café on Ft. Lauderdale's "Strip" also boasts breeze-cooled indoor dining amid Mediterranean decor. People watching is an art form here. Repeat diners come more for the ambience than the food, which tends to be spotty and overly seasoned, but the black bean dip is wonderfully addictive, and the *tapas* platter (with blackened fish, stuffed mussels, crawfish, and chick-pea dip) is excellent. Jazz bands play every Friday and Saturday night. Open daily. Reservations accepted only for parties of six or more. Major credit cards accepted. 201 A1A (phone: 463-4900).

Shooter's Right at the edge of the Intracoastal Waterway, this is a great luncheon spot for watching the boats breeze by. The Friday night happy hour features a band, and hordes of locals stop in to see, be seen, and end the week with a few friends. Menu choices range from grilled tuna sandwiches to Mexican pizza to California-style salads. Casual, fun, and always hopping, this place has become a Florida institution. Open daily. No reservations. Major credit cards accepted. 3033 NE 32nd Ave., off A1A (phone: 566-2855).

Ft. Worth

At-a-Glance

SEEING THE CITY

Panoramic views of Ft. Worth turn up serendipitously over a hill or around a corner, but the best one is from the esplanade at the east entrance of the *Amon Carter Museum*. Get some homemade ice cream from the *Back Porch* (across Camp Bowie Blvd.), and then enjoy the spectacular view of downtown from the rolling lawn of the nearby *Kimbell Art Museum*.

SPECIAL PLACES

One of the nicest things about Ft. Worth is that sightseeing is easy, with most attractions divided into the Stockyards District, the Cultural District, and the Downtown District. The major museums are within walking distance of one another; the Stockyards area is best seen on foot; and the botanical gardens and zoo are just down the street from each other.

STOCKYARDS DISTRICT

FT. WORTH STOCKYARDS Wear your jeans to prowl around the north side of Cowtown. If any area best embodies the city's promotional slogan, " The way you want Texas to be," the Ft. Worth Stockyards is it. Disaster struck the Stockyards many times during the first half of this century, but the district of saloons, hotels, and western outfitters that grew up in the area thrived until the packing industry's demise. In the 1960s and early 1970s, the area deteriorated into a near-slum, but after years of neglect, this isolated enclave of history is in the throes of a renaissance, its integrity preserved with National Historic District status. Today, residents and tourists come to soak up its authentic western flavor.

To get to the Stockyards, take Main Street north from downtown 2½ miles to the corner of North Main and Exchange Avenue. Park your car anywhere you can; everything is within walking distance. The Stockyards area includes the restored *Cowtown Coliseum*, which hosts live rodeo performances every Saturday night from April through September and other events October through March (phone: 625-1025; 626-2228 for rodeo tickets). Any Monday at 10 AM, you can sit in on a cattle auction at the *Coliseum* or people watch at the *Coliseum*'s *Cattlecar Café* (phone: 624-2241), a tiny place where real Texas traders and other livestock folk lean back and put their boots up while waiting for the café's home cooking. Also in the Stockyards area is the *Livestock Exchange Building*, with several fine art galleries, and dozens of stores where you can pick up a Stetson, a pair of lizard-skin boots, or a bridle for your bronco. *M.L. Leddy's* (2455 N. Main St.; phone: 624-3149) offers leather boots made from ostrich, kangaroo, and sea turtle. The new *Stockyards Station Market* (140 E. Exchange Ave.; phone: 625-9715)

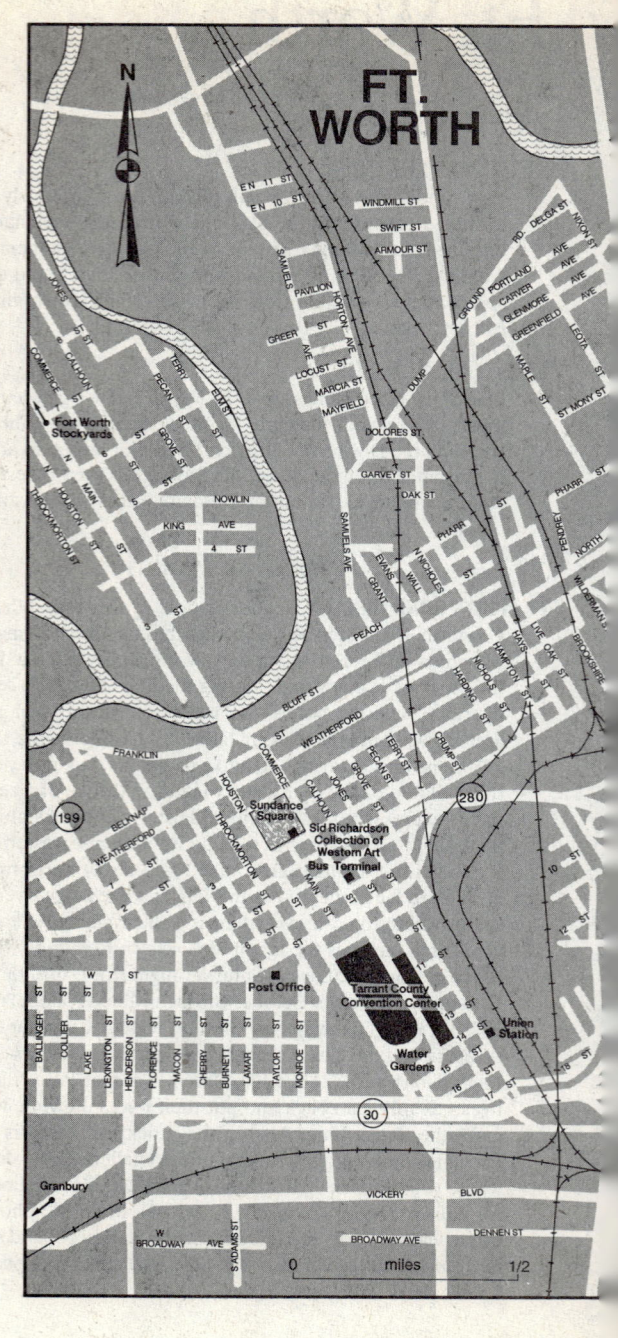

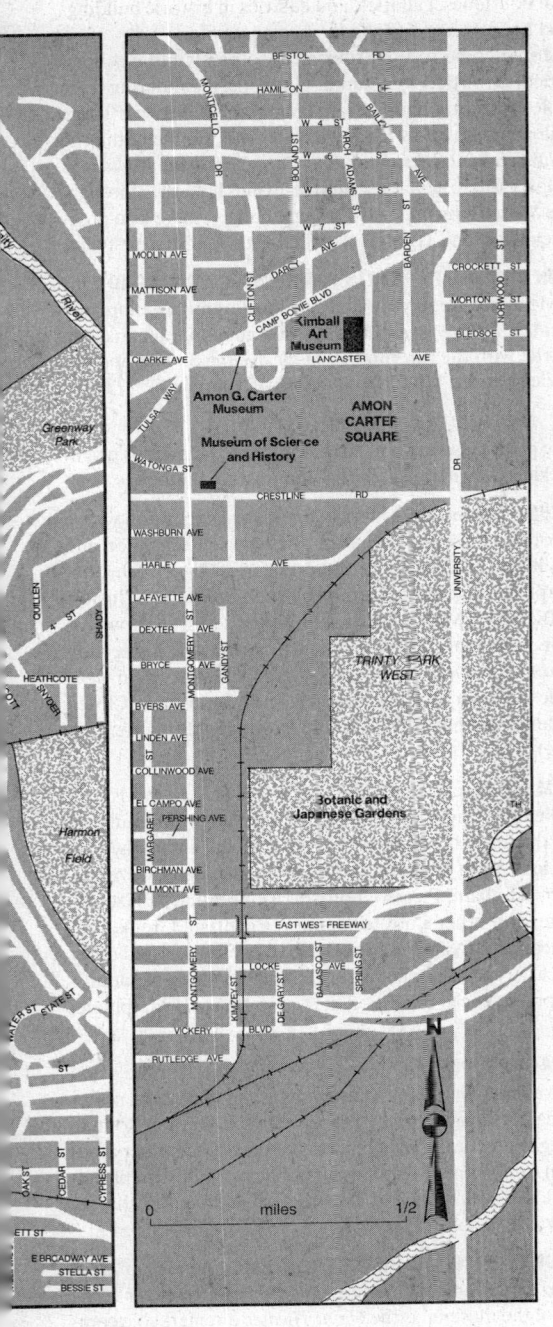

houses dozens of boutiques, galleries, and eateries in historic buildings where 83 million head of hog and sheep were once sold.

But most people come to the Stockyards to party: On weekend nights, the district is crowded with denim-clad folks meandering from one watering hole or country-and-western dance hall to the next. There are about two dozen nightspots from which to choose, including the century-old *White Elephant Saloon* and *Billy Bob's Texas* (see *Nightclubs and Nightlife*, below). There are also several festivities held here throughout the year (see *Special Events*). And if you get hungry, there's no problem finding a meal—as long as you're satisfied with Tex-Mex or steaks.

STOCKYARDS STATION AND THE FT. WORTH AND WESTERN RAILROAD This 19th-century–style depot greets visitors riding the Tarantula Company's restored *Ft. Worth and Western* cars. The steam excursion train links the Stockyards District with the downtown *Eighth Avenue Station* and the historic Southside District. 140 E. Exchange Ave. (phone: 625-7245).

CULTURAL DISTRICT

In addition to the great museums and attractions listed below, this neighborhood is chockablock with art galleries and upscale boutiques.

AMON CARTER MUSEUM Chronicling America's westward expansion with a huge collection of paintings and sculpture by Frederic Remington and Charles Russell, it also exhibits American art from 1800 to 1950: 19th-century landscapes and genre paintings by such artists as Winslow Homer, Albert Bierstadt, Mary Cassatt, and Thomas Moran, as well as 20th-century works by Georgia O'Keeffe and Stuart Davis. A selection of the 300,000-item American photography collection also is on view. A theater provides a center for films, lectures, and symposiums. Closed Mondays. No admission charge. 3501 Camp Bowie Blvd. (phone: 738-1933).

KIMBELL ART MUSEUM Architect Louis Kahn's last work (1973), this is considered one of the most important and beautiful small art museums in the country. It is the result of a bequest by Kay Kimbell, and today contains an incredible array of works by Caravaggio, Mantegna, Cézanne, Duccio, El Greco, Holbein, Picasso, Poussin, Rembrandt, Velázquez, Watteau, Matisse, and others, not to mention Egyptian, Greek, pre-Columbian, African, and Asian art. Special loan exhibitions and other public programs are regularly scheduled. Closed Mondays. No admission charge except for special exhibits. 3333 Camp Bowie Blvd. (phone: 332-8451).

MODERN ART MUSEUM OF FT. WORTH Opened in 1892, it was the state's first art museum. The collection of 20th-century paintings, drawings, sculpture, and prints features major works by Picasso, Louis, Warhol, Rothko, Stella, de Kooning, Rauschenberg, Motherwell, Pollock, and other modern masters. Loan exhibitions and numerous public programs are prominent features. Closed Mondays and Tuesdays. No admission charge. 1309 Montgomery St. (phone: 738-9215).

FT. WORTH MUSEUM OF SCIENCE AND HISTORY It includes the *Hall of Medical Science, Dino Dig, Man and His Possessions,* and *Computer Technology.* Also part of the museum is the *Omni Theater,* a remarkable computerized 70mm multi-image projection and sound system. The museum is closed Mondays; the *Omni Theater* is open daily. Admission charge. 1501 Montgomery (phone: 732-1631).

CATTLEMAN'S MUSEUM Life-size displays complete with talking figures make an unusual introduction to the history of ranching. Particular emphasis is on the historic and contemporary battles of ranchers and lawmen against cattle rustlers; the museum presents a complete picture of the life of a cattleman. Closed weekends. No admission charge. 1301 W. Seventh St. (phone: 332-7064).

FT. WORTH ZOO Part of *Forest Park*, with picnic tables and a small amusement park, it contains America's largest herpetarium, a lovely rain forest with rare and exotic birds, and an outstanding collection of 4,500 mammals. Exotic new exhibits include contemporary-style habitats for primates, big cats, and bears. Also popular is an exhibit called *Texas!*, with native flora and fauna such as longhorns, buffalo, and wild boars, as well as a barnyard area of domestic animals and a blacksmithy. Adjacent to the zoo is the longest miniature train ride in the country, a leisurely and scenic 5-mile trip covering the length of several parks. Open daily. Admission charge. 2727 Zoological Park Dr., off University Dr. (phone: 871-7050).

LOG CABIN VILLAGE Seven cabins from the 1850s have been restored and furnished with period antiques. Costumed "villagers" demonstrate typical pioneer crafts—weaving, quilting, etc. Open daily. Admission charge. 2100 Log Cabin Village La. near the zoo (phone: 926-5881).

BOTANIC AND JAPANESE GARDENS The *Botanic Gardens* encompass several acres for exploring and studying hundreds of different plant species and varieties of roses. Within are the *Japanese Gardens,* tranquil arrangements of trees and shrubs, bridges, pools, waterfalls, and tea houses. A café serves light meals. Open daily. Admission charge for *Japanese Gardens* only. 3220 Botanic Garden Dr., off University Dr. (phone: 871-7686).

THISTLE HILL Built in 1903, this elegant old house is the last one remaining from the days when the cattle barons built their mansions along Pennsylvania Avenue. Closed Saturdays. Admission charge. 1509 Pennsylvania Ave. (phone: 336-1212).

DOWNTOWN DISTRICT

SUNDANCE SQUARE This charming square is formed by Commerce, Houston, Second, and Fourth Streets and is bordered by an interesting collection of boutiques, craft shops, restaurants, and art galleries. Main Street, which bisects the square, is notable for its red brick sidewalks, period streetlamps, and turn-of-the-century buildings. Don't miss the wonderful Chisholm Trail mural at Third and Main Streets. Several restaurants, fashionable shops, and an 11-theater movie complex indicate the area's growth. The well-known *Sid Richardson Collection of Western Art* (309 Main St.; phone: 332-6554) features 60 original paintings by Western artists Frederic Remington and Charles Russell. *Fire Station No. 1* (201-203 Commerce; phone: 732-1631) houses a museum showcasing the city's history with the exhibition "150 Years of Ft. Worth." Open daily. No admission charge.

CARAVAN OF DREAMS This innovative performing arts center occupies a Victorian-cum-Western building in the heart of Sundance Square. There's a cabaret-style nightclub featuring live performances of jazz, rock, and blues by such big names as Lyle Lovett and Wynton Marsalis. A wide variety of productions is performed at *Stage West,* and there's a rooftop grotto bar with a neon-lit cactus garden. 312 Houston St. (phone: 877-3000).

WATER GARDENS Renowned New York architect Philip Johnson designed this outdoor water park, where some 19,000 gallons of water pour over pebbled concrete sculptures every minute. South of the *Convention Center* between Commerce and Houston Sts.

OLD TYME POSTIQUE The downtown post office has opened this permanent exhibit of memorabilia, information, and merchandise (for sale) for philatelists. The 1930s building has an interior of marble, bronze, and gold leaf. Closed weekends. No admission charge. Lancaster and Houston Sts. (phone: 336-3018).

TARRANT COUNTY COURTHOUSE This masterpiece of pink Texas granite and marble, built in 1895 at a cost of $450,000 (a lot of money back then), resembles the beautiful, Renaissance-style *State Capitol* in Austin. Closed weekends. No admission charge. 100 E. Weatherford St. (phone: 884-1111).

EXTRA SPECIAL

Granbury, an easy 30-minute-drive southwest of Ft. Worth on Highway 377, is a charming little town filled with historic buildings. A limestone courthouse dominates a town square ringed with crafts shops, ice cream parlors, and restaurants, all in 19th-century structures. In fact, Granbury has so many Old West buildings that the town is entered in the *National Register of Historic Places.* Surrounding Granbury is a manmade lake of the same name with beautiful camping and picnicking facilities; the *Convention and Visitors Bureau* (phone: 573-5548; 800-950-2212) has further information. For a country-style buffet, try the *Nutt House* restaurant (121 E. Bridge St.; phone: 563-9362; closed Mondays). "Country-style" means you go through a line, cafeteria-style, pick up some grits, fried or baked chicken, catfish, meat loaf, famous hot-water corn bread, and buttermilk pie, then sit down at a long table.

You might want to spend a day at *Texas Lil's,* a Western dude ranch about 30 minutes north of town. An all-inclusive ticket covers a full day's worth of activities, including an hour-long horseback ride on a 3-mile scenic trail, an all-you-can-eat barbecue, a hayride, swimming, hiking, and fishing. There's also a petting zoo. Closed Mondays. Reservations necessary. Admission charge. Off Hwy. 407, in Justin (phone: 430-0192).

Arlington, about 20 minutes east of Ft. Worth, has several attractions, including *Six Flags Over Texas, Wet 'n' Wild,* and the new *Ballpark at Arlington,* home of the Texas Rangers baseball team (for more information, see *Dallas,* above).

Sources and Resources

TOURIST INFORMATION

For brochures, maps, and general information, contact the *Ft. Worth Convention and Visitors Bureau* (415 Throckmorton St., Ft. Worth, TX 76102; phone: 336-8791; 800-433-5747), which is closed weekends. They may also be picked up at the *Sid Richardson Collection of Western Art* (309 Main St., Sundance Sq.; phone: 332-6554); the *Ft. Worth Museum of Science and History* (1501 Montgomery; phone: 732-1631); as well as at the *Visitors' Information Center* (123 E. Exchange in the Stockyards District; phone: 624-4741), which is closed Sundays. For information on special events, call 800-433-5747. Contact the Texas state tourism hotline (800-8888-TEX) for maps, calendars of events, health updates, and travel advisories.

LOCAL COVERAGE The *Fort Worth Star-Telegram* is published mornings, evenings, and Sundays. See Friday's issue for *Star Time,* an insert with entertainment and restaurant listings. *Texas Monthly* magazine publishes reviews of Ft. Worth's best restaurants.

TELEVISION STATIONS KDFW Channel 4–CBS; KXAS Channel 5–NBC; WFAA Channel 8–ABC; and KERA Channel 13–PBS.

RADIO STATIONS AM: KLIF 570 (talk); KKDA 730 (soul); KRLD 1080 (talk/news); and KAAM 1310 (adult contemporary). FM: KSCS 96.3 (country); KEGL 97.1 (Top 40); KLUV 98.7 (oldies); WRR 101.1 (classical); and KVIL 103.7 (adult contemporary).

TELEPHONE The area code for Ft. Worth is 817.

SALES TAX There is a 7.75% sales tax on all purchases except food. Hotel room tax is 13%.

CLIMATE Officially, Ft. Worth's average daily temperature during the spring is 65F; summer, 84F; fall, 66F; and winter, 47F. But don't be fooled by averages: Plan on summer scorchers and some pretty nippy winter days, sometimes (though rarely) with a touch of ice and snow.

GETTING AROUND

AIRPORT *Dallas/Ft. Worth Airport (D/FW),* one of the country's largest, is on the northeast edge of Ft. Worth, a 20- to 25-minute drive from downtown. Bus transportation between *D/FW,* the downtown hotels, and the downtown terminal is provided by the city-owned *Airporter Bus Service and Park & Ride Terminal* (100 Weatherford St.; phone: 334-0092); fare is $7. The *Supershuttle* (phone: 329-2000) also provides airport transportation; reservations are required.

BUS The public transportation system, simply known as the *T,* provides bus service throughout Ft. Worth; travel in the downtown area is free (pick up a pass when you board the bus). A $3 VisiTour pass allows you to travel throughout the city. To check on routes and schedules, call 871-6200.

CAR RENTAL The major national agencies are represented.

TAXI The best way to get a cab is to phone for one. Try *Yellow Cab* (phone: 534-5555).

TOURS For guided tours, call *Dan Dipert Tours* (phone: 543-3700) year-round for groups of eight or more. There are also horse-drawn carriage tours of the downtown area year-round, if you'd rather let a Clydesdale show you the sights (phone: 336-0400). Tours of the Stockyards depart from the Stockyards visitors' center (130 E. Exchange Ave.; phone: 625-9715) once daily during the week and more often on weekends. The *Ft. Worth Convention and Visitors Bureau* suggests two walking tours, the *Western Heritage Trail* and the *Museum and Garden Tour.* Maps are available at their office (see *Tourist Information,* above).

LOCAL SERVICES

AUDIOVISUAL EQUIPMENT *AV Presentations* (phone: 589-2159).

BABY-SITTING *Luv-N-Care* (4451 Boatclub Rd.; phone: 237-5683).

BUSINESS SERVICES *Kelly Services* (801 Cherry St., Suite 2365; phone: 332-7807).

COMPUTER AND COPIER RENTAL *University Computers* (3409 W. Seventh St.; phone: 870-2921).

DRY CLEANER/TAILOR *Gunn's Quality Cleaners* (1001 W. Magnolia; phone: 927-8859); *Tom James Custom Apparel* (1401 Ballinger St.; phone: 335-2186); *Twin Kell Cleaners* (4011 Camp Bowie Blvd.; phone: 738-9975).

LIMOUSINE *Candleridge* (phone: 294-8747); *Ft. Worth Limousine* (phone: 870-9783).

MECHANICS *Pep Boys* (4621 E. Lancaster; phone: 534-2227), for American cars; *Automotive Center of Texas* (2609 White Settlement Rd.; phone: 336-8189), for all makes.

MEDICAL EMERGENCY *Harris Methodist Ft. Worth* (1301 Pennsylvania; phone: 882-3333); *Harris Methodist HEB* (1600 Hospital Pkwy.; phone: 685-4611).

MESSENGER SERVICES *Express 60 Minutes Delivery* (1 Summit Ave.; phone: 336-5333); *One-Hour Delivery Service* (1800 Ft. Worth Center; phone: 877-1233).

MONEY TRANSFERS *American Express MoneyGram* (phone: 800-926-9400 for information; 800-866-8800 for money transfers); *Western Union Financial Services* (phone: 800-325-6000 or 800-325-4176).

NATIONAL/INTERNATIONAL COURIER *DHL Worldwide Express* (phone: 800-225-5345); *FedEx* (phone: 800-238-5355).

PHARMACY *Eckerd* (2414 Jacksboro Hwy., in the *Town & Country Shopping Center;* phone: 626-8255), open 24 hours.

PHOTOCOPIES *Alphagraphics* (301 Commerce St., Suite 220; phone: 335-2679).

POST OFFICE (251 W. Lancaster Ave.; phone: 332-3260).

PROFESSIONAL PHOTOGRAPHER *Gittings Portraiture* (6100 Camp Bowie Blvd., balcony level; phone: 732-2501).

TELECONFERENCE FACILITIES *Clarion, Hyatt Regency D/FW, Radisson Plaza, Worthington* (see *Checking In*).

TRANSLATOR *Berlitz* (phone: 214-380-0404 in Dallas).

WESTERN UNION/TELEX Many offices are located around the city (phone: 800-325-6000 to find the location nearest you).

SPECIAL EVENTS

Any child who spent any time at all in the Ft. Worth Independent School District can attest that the highlight of the year comes during the 17 days in late January and early February when the *Southwestern Exposition and Livestock Show and Rodeo* comes to town. Schoolchildren have one day designated as *Stock Show Day* and receive free tickets, but the world's oldest indoor rodeo, midway, and stock show are fun for anyone. For more information, contact the *Southwestern Exposition*, PO Box 150, Ft. Worth, TX 76101 (phone: 877-2400 or 877-2420). *Cowtown Goes Green* is a *St. Patrick's Day* celebration held in the Stockyards District; events include a parade, a pub crawl, and a liar's contest. Ft. Worth's restored Main Street becomes a marketplace of food, arts and crafts, and entertainment during the *Main Street Ft. Worth Arts Festival* in April. Other special events are *Mayfest*, a celebration with food, music, and games on the banks of the Trinity River the first weekend in May; the *Chisholm Trail Roundup* (phone: 625-7005), a fair with street dances, chili cook-offs, and gunfights in the Stockyards area the second weekend in June; the *Shakespeare in the Park* series at the *Trinity Park Playhouse* in late June, when spectators bring picnic suppers and enjoy the free performances; *Pioneer Days*, a three-day western wingding held in September in the Stockyards; *Oktoberfest*, the first weekend in October; and the *National Cutting Horse Futurity*, one of the country's premier Western events, with some of the highest monetary awards outside a racetrack; it's held the first week in December at *Will Rogers Coliseum* (phone: 244-6188).

SPORTS AND FITNESS

BASEBALL The *American League* Texas Rangers play at the new *Ballpark at Arlington* (1700 Copeland Rd., Arlington; phone: 817-273-5100).

BICYCLING The *Department of Parks* (4200 South Frwy.; phone: 871-8700) provides maps of scenic biking trails that circle *Forest Park* and *Trinity Park*.

FITNESS CENTERS The coed *YMCA* (512 Lamar; phone: 332-3281) provides a pool, a track, aerobics courses, weight training, and basketball, racquetball, hardball, and volleyball courts. Another fitness center is *Bally's President's* (6833 Green Oaks Rd.; phone: 738-8910). Both are open to non-members for a fee.

GOLF There are 11 country clubs and nine municipal courses in Ft. Worth. The *Colonial National Invitation* is held in May at the *Colonial Country Club* (3735 Country Club Circle; phone: 927-4278).

HORSE RACING *Trinity Meadows* (15 miles west of the city in *Willow Park*, Exit 418 off I-20; phone: 441-9240) was one of the first tracks to open after the state legislature approved pari-mutuel betting in 1987. The season runs from early March until late November.

JOGGING Maps of the jogging trails around *Forest Park* and *Trinity Park* are available from the *Department of Parks* (4200 South Fwy.; phone: 871-8700). The Trinity trail winds 8.2 miles through three city parks.

TENNIS The *Mary Potishman Lard Tennis Center* at *Texas Christian University* (3609 Bellaire; phone: 921-7960) offers 22 outdoor and five indoor courts to the public. The *McLeland Tennis Center* (1600 W. Seminary Dr.; phone: 921-5134) has 14 outdoor courts, two indoor courts, and one practice court, all lighted. Instruction available.

THEATER

Casa Mañana ("the house of tomorrow") is probably Ft. Worth's best-known playhouse (3101 W. Lancaster at University Dr.; phone: 332-2272). A theater-in-the-round, it mounts a variety of dramatic productions. Others include the *Fort Worth Theatre* (3505 Lancaster; phone: 738-6509), which offers family entertainment as well as avant-garde productions; *Stage West* (3500 S. University; phone: 784-9378), where current and classic comedy and drama are performed; and the outdoor *Hip Pocket Theater* (1620 Las Vegas Trail N.; phone: 927-2833). The *Jubilee Theater* (506 Main; phone: 338-4411) offers a cross-section of African-American theater on Fridays and Saturdays. The *Ft. Worth Ballet* performs at the *Ft. Worth/Tarrant County Convention Center* (1111 Houston; phone: 763-0207). The city makes much of the fact that it sustains a major ballet company, something that rival city Dallas has not been able to do.

MUSIC

The *Ft. Worth Opera* (phone: 731-0833) and the *Ft. Worth Symphony Orchestra* (phone: 926-8831) both perform at the *Ft. Worth/Tarrant County Convention Center* (1111 Houston St.). Ft. Worth's Grammy-winning *Texas Boys Choir* (phone: 924-1482) gives concerts in a variety of places. The *Schola Cantorum of Texas* (phone: 737-5788) is a 50-member chorus that also performs in different venues. For more information, call the *Ft. Worth Convention and Visitors Bureau* (see *Tourist Information* above).

NIGHTCLUBS AND NIGHTLIFE

The *White Elephant Saloon* (106 E. Exchange; phone: 624-1887) is a popular watering hole that features "buffalo sweat" margaritas and country music; it's in the historic Stockyards area. *Billy Bob's Texas* (2520 Rodeo Plaza; phone: 624-7117) is a huge honky-tonk place with 42 bars, an arena for bull riding, and live entertainment Friday and Saturday evenings. Also worth visiting in the Stockyards is the *Longhorn Saloon* (121 W. Exchange; phone: 624-4242), a huge bar and the place to hear live country bands. *Caravan of Dreams* (312 Houston; phone: 877-3000), an avant-garde performing arts center, has a jazz and blues nightclub and a theater. It is the preeminent jazz club in the region, and its *Rooftop Garden and Grotto Bar* is the city's most unusual. The *Hop* (2905 W. Berry; phone: 921-0075) has a mixed bag of jazz, rock, and good food, and *J & J Blues Bar* (937 Woodward; phone: 870-2337) offers the best in regional blues.

Best in Town

CHECKING IN

While Ft. Worth has no shortage of traditional hotels, another alternative, *Bed and Breakfast Texas-Style,* offers lodging and either continental or Texas-style breakfasts in private homes in the city's most desirable neighborhoods. Contact Ruth Wilson, 4224 W. Red Bird La., Dallas, TX 75237 (phone: 214-298-5433). Expect to pay $100 or more per night for a double room at the hotels listed as expensive, and $50 to $100 at those categorized as moderate; there are no exceptional inexpensive hotels in the city. Unless otherwise noted, hotel rooms have air conditioning, private baths, TV sets, and telephones. All hotels are in the 817 area code unless otherwise indicated.

EXPENSIVE

Hyatt Regency D/FW Big, convenient, and busy, this attractive property in the airport complex is a good place to stay if you're planning to divide your time between Dallas and Ft. Worth—or to visit the amusement parks between the two cities. It has 1,400 rooms, four restaurants, 10 racquetball courts, seven tennis courts (four outdoor lighted, three indoor), an outdoor pool, and access to a nearby club with 36 holes of golf. Ask about summer family rates. There are 80 meeting rooms from which to choose for business functions, and other amenities include concierge and secretarial services, A/V equipment, photocopiers, and computers. Express checkout is a boon. *D/FW Airport* (phone: 214-453-1234; 800-233-1234; fax: 214-615-6826).

Marriott Solana The newest hotel in the airport area is this small, pretty complex. It offers 198 well-appointed guestrooms, an outdoor pool, a large health and fitness club, and golf privileges at the nearby *Fossil Creek Club. Cielo,* its restaurant, serves a variety of Mediterranean fare. Other amenities include a concierge, nine meeting rooms accommodating up to 500, and full business services. *Hwy. 114 at Kirkwood Blvd., Westlake* (phone: 430-3848; 800-228-9290; fax: 430-4870).

Radisson Plaza This circa 1921 Texas hotel has retained more original Western flavor than any other in the city. There are 516 guestrooms, including 30 suites, as well as two restaurants, two cocktail lounges, an outdoor pool, a sun deck, a fitness center, and a concierge floor. Business amenities include meeting rooms for up to 1,800, an exhibition hall, A/V equipment, photocopiers, and express checkout. Facing the *Convention Center*, 815 Main St. (phone: 870-2100; 800-333-3333; fax: 335-3408).

Stockyards Dating to cowboy boomtown days, this place with 44 rooms and eight suites is popular with tourists since the *White Elephant Saloon*, numerous restaurants, and other attractions are within walking distance. Much is made of the time Bonnie and Clyde put up here. Check out the saddles that serve as barstools in the *Booger Red Saloon*. Three meeting rooms, A/V equipment, photocopiers, secretarial services, and express checkout are available. 109 E. Exchange (phone: 625-6427; 800-423-8471 outside Texas; fax: 624-2571).

Worthington This lovely European-style hostelry is across the street from Sundance Square. There are 507 rooms (including 70 luxury suites), two outdoor tennis courts, indoor pools, athletic club, several ballrooms, and the fine *Reflections* restaurant (see *Eating Out*). Business services include meeting rooms, A/V equipment, computers, secretarial services, and a concierge desk. Express checkout is another plus. 200 Main St. (phone: 870-1000; 800-772-5977 from Texas; 800-433-5677 from elsewhere in the US; fax: 332-5679).

MODERATE

Clarion Hotel and Conference Center Formerly the *Plaza Ft. Worth*, it's smack in the middle of a historic center alongside the Chisholm Trail, with a small historic cemetery *in* the parking lot. The 197-room hotel is decorated in light, bright colors and has a spacious lobby. Concierge and secretarial services, as well as A/V equipment, photocopiers, computers, and eight meeting rooms round out the amenities. 2000 Beach St. (phone: 534-4801; 800-233-1441; fax: 534-3761).

Miss Molly's Those who clamor for the flavor of the Old West should check out this eight-room hostelry, previously a bordello. Each room is cleverly decorated and named according to decor (the "Cowboy Room," the "Cattleman's Room"). You can get bountiful bites at the *Star Café*. 109½ W. Exchange (phone: 626-1522).

EATING OUT

In a city once called Cowtown, you'd naturally expect good beef, but natives pride themselves more on ferreting out superior Tex-Mex fare and chicken-fried steaks. You also can find some better-than-average continental fare and an assortment of ethnic eats. Expect to spend more than $50 for dinner for two at expensive restaurants; $30 to $50 at those listed as moderate; and less than $30 at inexpensive places. Prices do not include drinks, wine, tax, or tips. Unless otherwise noted, restaurants are open for lunch and dinner. All restaurants are in the 817 area code unless otherwise indicated.

EXPENSIVE

Balcony Dressy and romantic, it overlooks Camp Bowie Boulevard and serves traditional continental cooking. Broiled lamb chops and veal are the specialties. Closed Sundays. Reservations advised. Major credit cards accepted. 6100 Camp Bowie (phone: 731-3719).

Cacharel Set atop a high-rise, it's appealingly decorated in shades of pale pink and gray, and serves elegant New American fare. Outstanding menu choices include sautéed sea scallops and wild rice cakes with a saffron and Pernod sauce, crabmeat salad, and grilled salmon. The chocolate–Grand Marnier soufflé is unforgettable. Closed Sundays. Reservations advised. Major credit cards accepted. 2221 E. Lamar Blvd., Arlington (phone: 640-9981).

Café Matthew The soft lighting and rich, muted fabrics make this a dreamy, semi-formal place to indulge in Southwestern cooking. Creamy onion soup, grilled shrimp with black bean salsa, strip steaks stuffed with gorgonzola and chilies, and enterprising salads made with goat cheese and smoked mozzarella combine to create a great dining experience. The espresso is especially good. Closed Sundays. Reservations advised. Major credit cards accepted. 8251 Bedford-Euless Rd., North Richland Hills (phone: 577-3463).

Le Chardonnay A light and airy French bistro with several small dining rooms and a delightful red-brick patio, this place serves imaginative dishes, including sautéed frogs' legs with a creamy *ancho* chili sauce and ginger-laced puffed pastry, fresh grilled salmon with tarragon butter, and roast lamb or veal stuffed with fresh herbs. The extensive wine list presents an array of fine choices. Open daily. Reservations advised. Major credit cards accepted. 2443 Forest Park (phone: 926-5622).

La Piazza Italian dishes are elegantly presented in a warm, intimate room decorated with watercolors and fresh flowers. Munch on the fresh-baked bread served with herbed oil, then move on to mozzarella-basil-tomato salad, red snapper, or veal medallions in wine sauce. Jacket and tie required. Closed Sundays. Reservations advised. Major credit cards accepted. 3431 W. Seventh St. (phone: 334-0000).

Reflections An outstanding example of what a hotel restaurant should be. The Art Deco surroundings provide a counterpoint to elegant presentations of coho salmon and game birds, as well as decadent desserts. Closed Sundays. Reservations advised. Major credit cards accepted. In the *Worthington Hotel*, 200 Main St. (phone: 870-1000).

Saint-Emilion Creatively prepared meat, fish, and fowl are featured at this country French bistro. Two- and four-course prix fixe meals are offered for dinner; there's also an extensive wine selection. Open daily. Reservations advised. Major credit cards accepted. 3617 W. Seventh (phone: 737-2781).

MODERATE

Cattlemen's Steak House The portraits of blue-ribbon beef that grace the walls in this Stockyards stronghold are a little-needed reminder of each T-bone's heritage. Many of the cowboy customers are urban, but look carefully, since old-timers still like to splurge here. Open daily; dinner only on Sundays. No reservations on Saturdays. Major credit cards accepted. 2458 N. Main (phone: 624-3945).

Hedary's Everything is fresh and flavorful at this Lebanese eatery, where customers may watch their dinners being prepared. Try the chicken with lemon, veal sausages, grilled lamb chops, and fresh pita bread. Closed Mondays. No reservations. Major credit cards accepted. 3308 Fairfield in *Ridglea Center* (phone: 731-6961).

Lucile's This piano bar-café occupies a historic building and serves outstanding American favorites, such as wood-burning oven pizza, New York strip steaks, homemade ravioli, Maryland crab cakes, fried green tomatoes, and Maine lobster. The roasted chicken with feta is memorable. Weekend breakfasts are known for scones, beignets, and excellent café au lait. Open daily; breakfast served on weekends. Reservations advised. Major credit cards accepted. 4700 Camp Bowie (phone: 738-4761).

Sardine's This cabaret-like trattoria is more spacious than you might think, given its name. The Old World Italian atmosphere is dark, warm, and cozy, with live jazz music on weekends; the pasta dishes and meat specials are tasty. The warm seafood antipasto is a good choice. Open daily for dinner only. Reservations advised on weekends. Major credit cards accepted. 3410 Camp Bowie (phone: 332-9937).

Szechuan If you hanker for Chinese food in Cowtown, this is the place—heaping portions, helpful service, and an extensive menu. The house specialties are heartily recommended. Open daily. Reservations advised. Major credit cards accepted. 5712 Locke (phone: 738-7300).

INEXPENSIVE

Angelo's Hearty barbecue with the finest of trimmings is all this Ft. Worth institution offers. But what more could one ask for than an icy beer and a paper plate heaped with tangy ribs (served after 4:30 PM only) or barbecued beef plus a scoop of potato salad, coleslaw, a pickle, and bread. Closed Sundays. No reservations or credit cards accepted. 2533 White Settlement (phone: 332-0357).

Benito's The best place in Ft. Worth to sample a variety of Mexican dishes. The standard Tex-Mex combos are available, but the more authentic Mexican fare—homemade tamales and *chiles rellenos*—hasn't been tamed for American taste buds. The restaurant stays open until 3 AM Fridays and Saturdays. Open daily. No reservations. Major credit cards accepted. 1450 W. Magnolia (phone: 332-8633).

Carshon's Split-pea soup, corned beef on rye, and butterscotch pie aren't exactly the stuff of Ft. Worth's fame, but this kosher deli is touted statewide. Closed Mondays. No reservations or credit cards accepted. 3133 Cleburne Rd. (phone: 923-1907).

Joe T. Garcia's This famous North Ft. Worth dive serves Tex-Mex food family-style to crowds that are willing to line up out front for more than an hour on weekends. The wait may be eased (and the food improved) by a couple of delicious frozen margaritas, and in warm weather, you can eat outside on the patio. Open daily. Reservations advised only for groups of 20 or more. No credit cards accepted. 2201 N. Commerce (phone: 626-4356).

Kincaid's For decades, this corner grocery has been a popular local spot to grab a big, juicy hamburger. There are some picnic tables for diners who don't want to eat standing up at the counter. Closed Sundays. No reservations or credit cards accepted. 4901 Camp Bowie (phone: 732-2881).

Massey's No theory of evolution has been more often debated here than the origin of its chicken-fried steaks. They're a delight—tender beef and a crunchy crust topped with thick creamy gravy. Open daily. No reservations. Major credit cards accepted. 1805 Eighth Ave. (phone: 924-8242).

Paris Coffee Shop Home-style cooking like grits 'n' gravy, homemade soup, and corn bread muffins are definitely de rigueur here. The clanging of dishes and table chatter provide the background music. Open for breakfast and lunch only; closed Sundays. No reservations. Major credit cards accepted. 700 W. Magnolia Ave. (phone: 335-2041).

Hartford

At-a-Glance

SEEING THE CITY

The top of *Travelers' Tower,* 527 feet above the madding crowd in the Travelers' Insurance Company building, offers the best view of the city. There are 72 steps to climb before reaching the top. Closed November through April; open weekdays only the rest of the year. No admission charge, but call in advance. 700 Main St. (phone: 277-2431).

SPECIAL PLACES

Walking through Hartford can be highly enjoyable, especially since the city combines classical and contemporary architectural styles. Capitol Hill is a good place to begin.

CONNECTICUT STATE CAPITOL Described as High Victorian Gothic, the *Capitol,* built in 1879, houses the state legislature. Guided tours are given on weekday mornings year-round and on Saturdays from April through October. 210 Capitol Ave. (phone: 240-0222).

RAYMOND E. BALDWIN MUSEUM OF CONNECTICUT HISTORY Three and a half centuries of Connecticut's heritage are packed into this museum with exhibitions tracing the growth of major manufacturers in the state. Most notable is the collection of Colt firearms. Closed weekends and holidays. 231 Capitol Ave. (phone: 566-3056).

BUSHNELL PARK In the heart of downtown Hartford, *Bushnell Park* is an arboretum for rare and native trees as well as the home of a delightful 1914 carousel. Frederick Law Olmsted, who designed New York City's *Central Park,* also worked on *Bushnell.* Concerts are often held here during the summer. Carousel closed October through March, weekdays during April and September, and Mondays from May through August. Bounded by Asylum, Elm, Ford, Wells, and Jewell Sts. (phone: 246-7739).

BUTLER-McCOOK HOMESTEAD Within strolling distance of downtown is the oldest private home in the city, built in 1792. It has an extensive collection of 18th-century furnishings and vintage American paintings, and a fascinating collection of Japanese armor and other curios. Closed mid-October through mid-May and Mondays, Wednesdays, Fridays, and Saturdays from mid-May through mid-October. Admission charge. 396 Main St. (phone: 522-1806).

CENTER CHURCH In 1807, this was the Meeting House of the original founders of the city. Now a church with stained glass by Tiffany, it is called the *Center Church* because of its location in the middle of town. Outside the church is the *Ancient Burying Ground* (1640–1803), a restored cemetery where the city's founders now rest. The church is open for services on Sundays and by appointment only other times. *Burying Ground* open daily. *First Church of Christ* on Main St. (phone: 249-5631).

HARTFORD CIVIC CENTER This "city within a city" has about 50 shops, 13 restaurants, and the 388-room *Sheraton-Hartford* hotel (see *Checking In*), plus 79,000 feet of exhibition space for the *Boat Show,* the *Auto Show,* and other large events. The Hartford *Whalers* hockey team plays in a 16,200-seat arena, which hosts other sporting events and concerts in the off-season. 1 Civic Center Plaza (phone: 727-8080 for concert ticket information; 728-6637 or 800-WHALERS for *Whalers'* tickets).

PRATT STREET Located right next to the *Civic Center,* this street has been restored to its former glory as a stylish shopping area. Numerous boutiques and restaurants line the pedestrian-oriented brick thoroughfare.

OLD STATE HOUSE At one time an active meeting house for statesmen, this Federal building designed by Charles Bulfinch is now a privately owned museum which also has a souvenir and craft shop. The colonial furniture and other artifacts on display date to 1796, when the *Old State House* was built. There is also information here about local attractions and special events, as well as a cannon-firing and fife and drum ceremony carried out several times daily by authentically dressed "soldiers." The souvenir shop is closed Sundays. No admission charge. 800 Main St. (phone: 522-6766).

WADSWORTH ATHENEUM America's oldest continuously operating public art museum was founded in 1842 by philanthropist Daniel Wadsworth, and has grown to a five-building complex with more than 45,000 works of art: American and European fine and decorative arts, 20th-century paintings and sculpture, contemporary art, costumes, and textiles. The highlights of the collection include Hudson River School paintings; works of such European masters as Renoir, Picasso, Monet, Goya, Cézanne, and Miró; American furniture (the *Nutting Collection* of Pilgrim-era furniture is particularly noteworthy); Renaissance and Baroque paintings; the *J. Pierpont Morgan Collection* of European decorative arts; a number of Surrealist works from the 1920s and 1930s; and the Amistad Foundation's collection of African-American art. Stop for a bite at the *Museum Café* (see *Eating Out*). Closed Mondays. No admission charge on Thursdays and from 11 AM to 1 PM on Saturdays. 600 Main St. (phone: 247-9111).

ELIZABETH PARK Another of Hartford's "firsts" is this botanical wonderland, the first municipally owned rose garden in the country. More than 900 varieties of roses, as well as 14,000 other plants, are on view every summer, while the greenhouses stay open year-round. Open-air concerts are performed in summer. In winter, the park's pond is a popular place for ice skating. Prospect and Asylum Aves. (phone: 722-6514).

MARK TWAIN MEMORIAL AND HARRIET BEECHER STOWE HOUSE A 19th-century writers' community here on the former Nook Farm estate contained several authors' houses. Mark Twain lived in one of them, a three-story, riverboat-shaped house made of brick, stone, and wood. Harriet Beecher Stowe, the author of *Uncle Tom's Cabin,* lived in an only slightly less elaborate painted brick house next door. A two-hour tour takes you through both houses. Closed January through May and Mondays from mid-October through November. Admission charge. *Mark Twain*

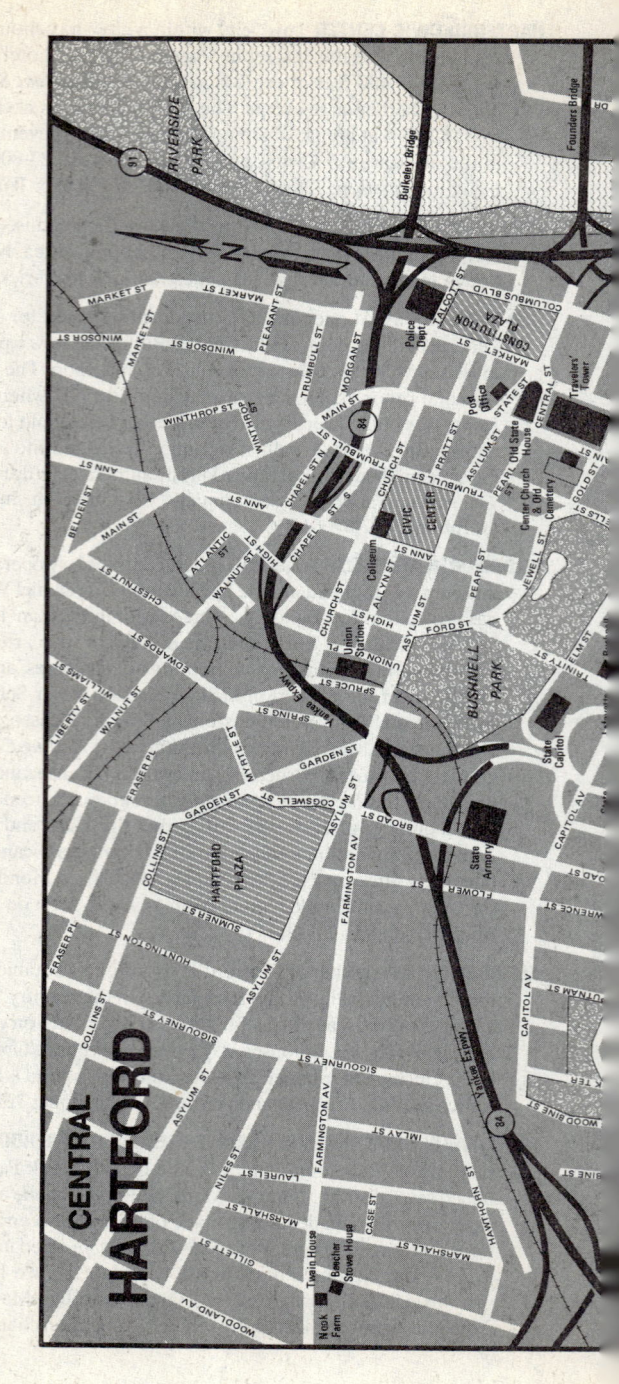

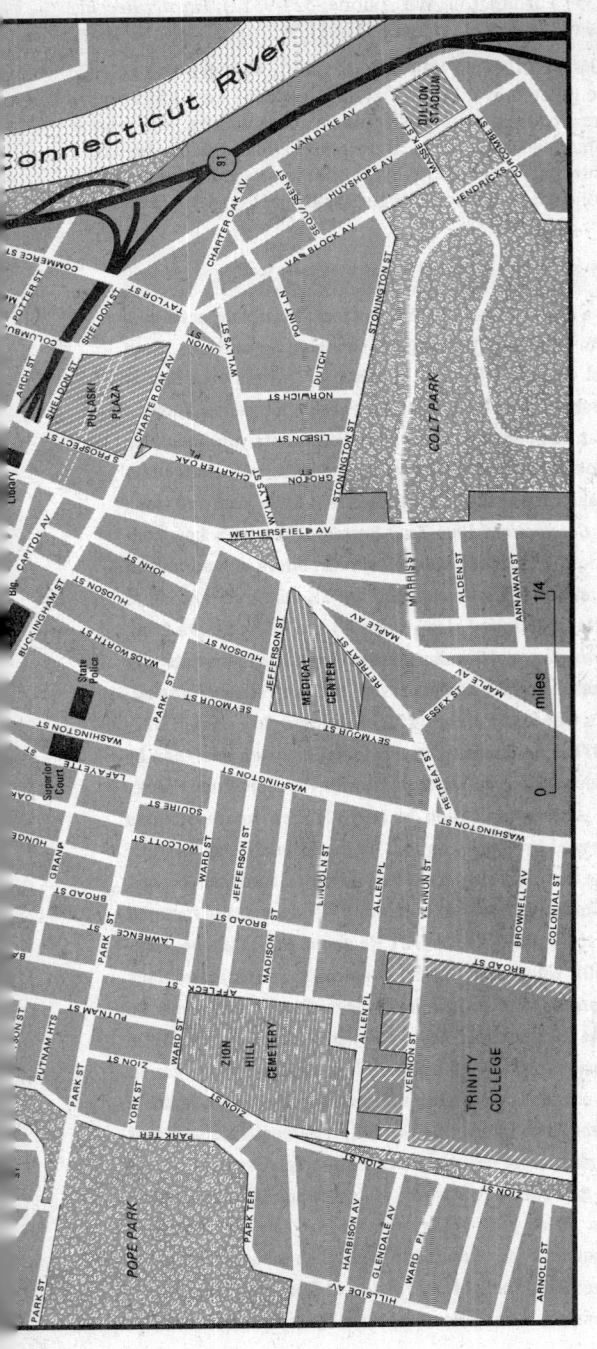

Memorial (351 Farmington Ave.; phone: 525-9317); *Harriet Beecher Stowe House* (77 Forest St.; phone: 525-9317).

SCIENCE MUSEUM OF CONNECTICUT Visitors to this progressive science museum are greeted by a life-size, walk-in replica of a 60-foot sperm whale. There are also traveling exhibitions, a tank with aquatic animals that can be handled, a mini-zoo, and a planetarium-auditorium where laser light shows are presented. Closed Mondays except in summer and on school holidays. Admission charge. 950 Trout Brook Dr., West Hartford (phone: 231-2824).

EXTRA SPECIAL

For a diverting day trip that can include outdoor activities, visits to historic houses, and shopping for antiques, head west on Route 44. This scenic road travels over thickly forested Avon Mountain to the Farmington Valley. There, a great number of outdoor activities awaits you, including canoeing, fishing, and exploring the hiking and cross-country ski trails in the *Talcott Mountain State Park* and along the *Connecticut Blue Trail System*. The area's key landmark, the 165-foot *Heublein Tower,* offers a panorama of five states to those who hike the 1½-mile trail starting at Route 185. Dotted along Route 44 and Route 10 are Avon, Farmington, and Simsbury—cozy New England hamlets with numerous crafts boutiques and antiques shops. Farmington's *Hill-Stead Museum* (35 Mountain Rd.; phone: 677-4787) is an imposing neo-colonial mansion designed by architect Stanford White and owner Theodore Pope Riddle. The superb collection of early French Impressionists amassed by Riddle, as well as the exquisite furnishings, make it worth a visit. It's closed Mondays; admission charge. In Simsbury, dine in 19th-century elegance at the restored *Simsbury 1820 House* (731 Hopmeadow St.; phone: 658-7658), which also has 34 guestrooms, each individually decorated with antique furnishings. Farther southwest on Route 202 is Litchfield, a charming village of huge white mansions set around a classic New England village green. Just outside Litchfield, 3½ miles south on Route 63, is *White Flower Farm* (phone: 567-8789), a perennial nursery that is a magnet for countless New England gardeners. Even for non-gardeners, it is worth a visit to see the display gardens, which peak in May and June; in July and August, a greenhouse full of magnificent English tuberous begonias shares the limelight with fields of flowering shrubs and perennials. Closed November through mid-April.

Sources and Resources

TOURIST INFORMATION

Brochures, maps, and general tourist advice are available from the *Greater Hartford Tourism District* (1 Civic Center Plaza, Hartford, CT 06103; phone: 800-793-4480; fax: 520-4493), the *Greater Hartford Convention and Visitors Bureau* (1 Civic Center Plaza, Hartford, CT 06103; phone: 728-6789; 800-446-7811), both closed weekends, and the tourist information booth at the Center Court of the *Hartford Civic Center* (phone: 275-6456), open daily.

LOCAL COVERAGE The *Hartford Courant* (the oldest American daily newspaper in continuous circulation), morning daily; *Connecticut Magazine*, monthly; the *Hartford Advocate*, a free alternative news and entertainment publication, weekly; and *Metropolitan Hartford*, a bi-monthly city magazine, featuring events, restaurant, and entertainment listings.

TELEVISION STATIONS WFSB Channel 3–CBS; WTNH Channel 8–ABC; CPTV Channel 24–PBS; WVIT Channel 30–NBC; and WTIC Channel 61–Fox.

RADIO STATIONS AM: WTIC 1080 (news) and WPOP 1410 (news). FM: WPKT 90.5 (public radio); WWYZ 92.5 (country); WTIC 96 (rock); WDRC 102.9 (solid gold); and WIOF 104 (adult contemporary).

TELEPHONE The area code for Hartford is 203.

SALES TAX The city sales tax is 6%; hotel room tax is 12%.

CLIMATE Hartford's humidity is sometimes a problem in the summer, when temperatures reach the 80s and 90s F; winters are intermittently snowy, generally in the 20s and 30s; spring and fall are delightful.

GETTING AROUND

AIRPORT *Bradley International Airport* is about 12 miles from downtown Hartford. The drive usually takes 20 to 30 minutes. *The Airport Connection* (phone: 627-3400) and *Peter Pan* (phone: 247-5329) provide bus service between the airport, *Union Station*, and area hotels.

BUS The state-owned *Connecticut Transit Company* (100 Leibert Rd.; phone: 525-9181) operates the municipal bus service. The basic 85¢ fare increases with distance traveled.

CAR RENTAL All major national firms are represented at the airport as well as downtown.

CRUISES The *Lady Fenwick*, a reproduction of an 1850 steam-powered yacht, takes passengers along the scenic Connecticut River. Organized by *Charter Oak Cruises* (phone: 526-4954), excursions run three times daily from *Memorial Day* through *Labor Day*, and then weekends only through October.

TAXI Recently, it has become fairly easy to hail a cab in the street. Other options are to pick one up at *Union Station* and the *Goodwin* and *Sheraton* hotels, or call *Yellow Cab* (phone: 666-6666).

LOCAL SERVICES

AUDIOVISUAL EQUIPMENT *Audio Visual Equipment Resources* (phone: 258-4194).

BABY-SITTING *Send One Sitter* (phone: 296-4321).

BUSINESS SERVICES *Headquarters Business Centers* (*HQ;* at 1 Corporate Center; phone: 249-7000; and at *CityPlace;* phone: 275-6500).

DRY CLEANER/TAILOR *M-Z Cleaners* (*CityPlace,* 14 Haynes St.; phone: 527-8511).

LIMOUSINE *Connecticut Limousine* (phone: 800-472-LIMO).

MECHANIC *Maple Automotive, Inc.* (880 Wethersfield; phone: 296-8071).

MEDICAL EMERGENCY *Hartford Hospital* (80 Seymour St.; phone: 524-2525).

MESSENGER SERVICES *Corporate Couriers Inc.* (94 Connecticut Blvd.; phone: 282-7840).

MONEY TRANSFERS *American Express MoneyGram* (phone: 800-926-9400 for information; 800-866-8800 for money transfers); *Western Union Financial Services* (phone: 800-325-6000 or 800-325-4176).

NATIONAL/INTERNATIONAL COURIER *DHL Worldwide Express* (phone: 653-5558); *FedEx* (phone: 800-238-5355).

PHARMACY *Arthur* drugstores (190 Farmington Ave. and Sigourney St.; phone: 527-1164, and at the *Civic Center;* phone: 549-7278); *Rite-Aid* (45 Pratt Ave.; phone: 728-9918).

PHOTOCOPIES *Alphagraphics* (97 Pratt St.; phone: 247-5715); *Kinko's,* (253 Asylum St.; phone: 527-4488 and 544 Farmington Ave.; phone: 233-8245), open 24 hours; *PIP* (21 High St.; phone: 278-1561).

POST OFFICE Central office (Statehouse Square; phone: 249-9446).

PROFESSIONAL PHOTOGRAPHER *AD Photography & Design* (phone: 536-3149); *Capital Studios* (phone: 525-1175).

TELECONFERENCE FACILITIES *Holiday Inn Hartford Downtown* (see *Checking In,* below).

TRANSLATOR *Accent* (phone: 236-2817); *Inlingua* (phone: 236-2351).

WESTERN UNION/TELEX Many offices are located around the city (phone: 800-325-6000 to find the location nearest you).

SPECIAL EVENTS

A Taste of Hartford, New England's largest food festival, is held at Constitution Plaza in June. It's a giant block party with music, dancing, and menu samples from over 60 restaurants. Hartford's *July 4th River Festival* features concerts, sporting events, and fireworks displays along the Connecticut River. *Kidrific* is a two-day event held the weekend after *Labor Day;* specially designed for children and their parents, it features a petting zoo, rides, and games. The *Festival of Lights,* with thousands of tiny white lights illuminating Constitution Plaza, is held every year from the day after *Thanksgiving* until January 6. Santa Claus always starts things off by making a dramatic appearance on top of the Fleet Bank Building in a helicopter and descending in a window-washer's gondola that looks surprisingly like a sleigh.

MUSEUMS

A directory describing several dozen Hartford art galleries is available at the Center Court of the *Hartford Civic Center*. Another good source of information is *Real Art Ways* (56 Arbor St.; phone: 232-1006), a prominent avant-garde arts organization. In addition to those described in *Special Places*, three other museums are worthy of note.

CONNECTICUT HISTORICAL SOCIETY Here is an important collection of American antiques and artifacts. Closed Mondays, Saturdays in summer, and major holidays. Admission charge. 1 Elizabeth St. (phone: 236-5621).

MUSEUM OF AMERICAN POLITICAL LIFE An extensive collection of American political memorabilia (second only to the one at the *Smithsonian*) is handsomely displayed at the *University of Hartford*. Closed Mondays. No admission charge. 200 Bloomfield Ave., West Hartford (phone: 768-4100).

THE WATKINSON LIBRARY This library contains a major collection of rare books, including several Audubon folios and the writings of Samuel Clemens (Mark Twain). Closed weekends. No admission charge. On the campus of *Trinity College* (phone: 297-2268).

SPORTS AND FITNESS

BASKETBALL The *Huskies* (phone: 486-2724), the nationally ranked basketball team of the *University of Connecticut*, play their home games in the *Hartford Civic Center* (1 Civic Center Plaza) as do the Hartford *Hellcats* (phone: 947-6200; 800-230-CATS), an *NBA* farm team.

FISHING For the best fishing, try Wethersfield Cove, south of Hartford in Wethersfield.

FITNESS CENTERS The *YMCA* (160 Jewell; phone: 522-4183) has a pool, squash and racquetball courts, a track, and a masseur. The *YWCA* (135 Broad St.; phone: 525-1163) has a pool, sauna, and weight room. Both are available to non-members for a fee.

GOLF There are 24 golf courses in the Hartford area. The best public courses in the city are located in *Keney Park* and *Goodwin Park*. PGA tour pros compete in the *Canon Greater Hartford Open Golf Tournament* in late June at the *Tournament Players Club* in Cromwell (phone: 635-5000).

HOCKEY The *NHL Whalers* play at the *Hartford Civic Center* (1 Civic Center Plaza; phone: 728-3366; 800-WHALERS).

JAI ALAI This lightning fast combination of hardball and lacrosse is played year-round at *Hartford Jai Alai* (89 Weston St.; phone: 525-8611).

JOGGING The perimeter of *Bushnell Park*, across from the *YMCA*, is seven-eighths of a mile; other running courses include *Goodwin Park*, 1½ miles from downtown, with a 2-mile perimeter; and *Elizabeth Park*, 2 miles from downtown, with a 2½-mile perimeter.

SKIING There's excellent cross-country skiing at the *Metropolitan District Commission* reservoir in West Hartford. Downhill enthusiasts like *Mt. Southington* (25 minutes west on I-84), *Powder Ridge Ski Area* (20 minutes south on I-91), *Ski Sundown* (35 minutes west on Rte. 44), and *Mt. Tom* (45 minutes north on I-91).

SWIMMING The Connecticut River is acceptable for boating, but the currents and tides are dangerous for swimming, even though it may look tempting on a hot day. Hartford residents recommend swimming at the *YWCA* or the *YMCA* (See *Fitness Centers*)—both charge a fee.

TENNIS The best public courts are at *Elizabeth Park* (Prospect and Asylum Aves.); there are indoor courts at *In-town Tennis* (360 Broad St.; phone: 246-7448).

THEATER

Hartford has no shortage of fine theater. For complete performance schedules, check the newspapers listed in *Local Coverage*. The following is our favorite place in Hartford for live theater.

CENTER STAGE

Hartford Stage Company This innovative Tony Award–winning organization presents an assortment of six plays during its season (October through June) in productions that are noteworthy for their style, verve, and aesthetic vision; the focus is on presenting new works and rediscovering—and reinterpreting—the classics. 50 Church St. (phone: 527-5151).

In addition, the 2,800-seat *Bushnell Memorial Hall* (166 Capitol Ave.; phone: 246-6807) features performances by the *Hartford Ballet* (phone: 525-9396) and the *Connecticut Opera* (phone: 527-0713), as well as touring Broadway productions. *TheatreWorks* (233 Pearl St.; phone: 527-7838) offers modern, avant-garde drama, while *The Producing Guild* (at the *Wallace Stevens Theater,* 690 Asylum Ave.; phone: 528-2143) presents both on- and off-Broadway productions.

MUSIC

Concerts, operas, and symphonies are performed at *Bushnell Memorial Hall* (166 Capitol Ave.; phone: 246-6807) and the renowned *Goodspeed Opera House* (East Haddam, 30 minutes south on Rte. 9; phone: 873-8668). The *Hartford Civic Center* (1 Civic Center Plaza; phone: 727-8010) features rock concerts. The *Charter Oak Cultural Center* (21 Charter Oak Ave.; phone: 249-1207) has an eclectic mix of zydeco, blues, gospel, and jazz music. The *Hartford Symphony Orchestra* (phone: 244-2999) performs January through May at *Bushnell Memorial Hall.*

NIGHTCLUBS AND NIGHTLIFE

Hartford's nightclubs center around Union Place. At *Mad Murphy's* (22 Union Pl.; phone: 549-1722), a deejay plays oldies but goodies, with live music on weekends. Try *Challenges* (201 Ann St.; phone: 278-9051), a sports bar with large-screen TV, darts, billiards, and a dance floor with deejay. *Spencers* (Capitol and Main Sts.; phone: 247-0400) is a block-long fun park for adults with live and deejay music, a sports bar, and a café. Just across from the *Civic Center, The Russian Lady* (191 Ann St.; phone: 525-3003) rocks with live music Thursdays through Saturdays; the rest of the week the club features dancing to top 40 dance hits. *Bourbon Street North* (70 Union Pl.; phone: 525-1014) is a popular hangout featuring live and recorded alternative music and dancing Thursdays through Sundays. The *880 Club* (880 Maple Ave.; phone: 956-2428) has live jazz most nights, as does the *Blue Star Café* (26 Trumbull St.; phone: 527-4557), which also features blues. The *Last Laugh Club* features comedy at *Brown Thomson & Co.* (942 Main St.; phone: 525-1600) on Friday and Saturday nights.

Best in Town

CHECKING IN

The quality of Hartford's lodgings has taken a quantum leap forward as a result of the millions spent on renovations of downtown hotels. For bed and breakfast listings and referrals, contact *Nutmeg Bed & Breakfast* (PO Box 1117, West Hartford, CT 06127; phone: 236-6698). Expect to pay $90 or more per night for a double room at places listed as expensive, and $60 to $90 at those in the moderate category; there are no exceptional inexpensive hotels in the city. Unless otherwise noted, hotel rooms have air conditioning, private baths, TV sets, and telephones. All hotels are in the 203 area code unless otherwise indicated.

EXPENSIVE

Avon Old Farms Only 15 minutes from downtown, this gracious, elegant hotel offers all the benefits of a country setting, along with one dining place on the premises and a fine restaurant, *Avon Old Farms Inn* (see *Eating Out*), just across the street. Many of the 162 spacious rooms have grand views. Located on 20 acres of manicured grounds, it is near a public golf course and a health club. There is an outdoor pool as well as an exercise room and sauna, and hiking trails behind the hotel. Business facilities include seven meeting rooms for up to 200, A/V equipment, computers, and photocopiers. Rtes. 10 and 44, Box 961, Avon (phone: 677-1651; 800-836-4000; fax: 677-0364).

Goodwin This 124-room luxury establishment, formerly the home of J. P. Morgan, has individual, quirkily shaped rooms with dormer windows, unexpected corners, and lots of space. Genuine antiques and turn-of-the-century reproductions, such as sleigh beds and period-style wallpaper, are combined with contemporary furnishings to produce a quiet elegance. Formal dining is offered at *Pierpont's* restaurant, sandwiches and lighter meals at the *America's Cup* lounge. Room service can be ordered around the clock. Business facilities include eight meeting rooms with a 125-person capacity, a concierge desk, A/V equipment, adapters for computers, secretarial services, photocopiers, and express checkout. Some rooms have computer-compatible phone lines. Conveniently located across from the *Civic Center.* 1 Haynes St. (phone: 246-7500; 800-922-5006; fax: 247-4576).

Sheraton-Hartford Connected to the *Civic Center,* this 388-room, recently renovated property offers a wider range of indoor sports than any other Hartford hotel. There is an indoor heated pool, and the health club has a whirlpool, a sauna, and exercise and recreation rooms. In-room movies are available, and *93 Church St.,* a casual eatery, serves continental fare. There's a concierge desk; A/V equipment, photocopiers, and computers are available. Meeting rooms accommodate up to 800, and there is express checkout. Trumbull St. at the *Civic Center* (phone: 728-5151; 800-325-3535; fax: 240-7247).

MODERATE

Holiday Inn Hartford Downtown On the fringe of downtown, this 340-room high rise has easy access to I-84 and I-91. The *Rover Lounge* offers cocktails and hors d'oeuvres, and *O'Neill's* is a casual restaurant serving American food. A popular choice among corporate travelers, the hotel has an outdoor pool, a health club with Nautilus equipment, concierge services, and 13 meeting rooms for up to 500 as well as an executive floor with special amenities. Other conveniences are secretarial services, A/V equipment, and a business center. 50 Morgan St. (phone: 549-2400; 800-HOLIDAY; fax: 527-2746).

Ramada Inn, Capitol Hill The 96 cheery if standard rooms at this chain establishment are enhanced by a spectacular view across *Bushnell Park* to the *State Capitol* (be sure to ask for a room on the park side) as well as by *Sharkey's* restaurant. Steps away from downtown and restaurants and clubs on Union Street. 440 Asylum St. (phone: 246-6591; 800-2RAMADA).

EATING OUT

The variety of ethnic food available in the city has increased dramatically in the past few years. Expect to pay between $50 and $100 for dinner for two at restaurants designated as expensive; between $25 and $50 at those we've listed as moderate; and less than $25 at inexpensive places. Prices do not include drinks, wine, tax, or tips. Unless otherwise noted, restaurants are open for lunch and dinner. All restaurants are in the 203 area code unless otherwise indicated.

EXPENSIVE

Avon Old Farms Inn Once a colonial-era blacksmith shop, this inn has been serving meals since 1757, which makes it one of the oldest restaurants in the nation. It is across the street from the *Avon Old Farms* hotel. In the *Old Forge Room,* you can sit among antique smithy tools, and linger over veal, beef, and seafood specialties. A spectacular brunch is offered on Sundays. Open daily. Reservations advised. Major credit cards accepted. Rtes. 10 and 44, Avon, about a 15-minute drive from downtown Hartford (phone: 677-2818).

Capitol Fish House Known as one of the best seafood restaurants in the state, this place offers a staggering variety of fish dishes (although the menu does have a few meat and chicken items). The daily specials are a particularly good deal. Closed Sundays; dinner only on Saturdays. Reservations advised. Major credit cards accepted. 391 Main St. (phone: 724-3370).

Carbone's Northern Italian dishes are featured at this family-owned South End fixture that has been around for more than 45 years. Closed Sundays. Reservations advised. Major credit cards accepted. 588 Franklin Ave. (phone: 296-9646).

Gaetano's On the mezzanine of the *Civic Center*, but away from its major bustle, this downtown sister of *Carbone's* is a businessperson's favorite. Insist on a window seat overlooking Trumbull Street. The chef chooses fresh local and imported produce in his rich, haute Italian creations. The adjacent *Gaetano's Café* offers simpler, less pricey fare. Open daily; dinner only on Sundays. Reservations advised. Major credit cards accepted. 1 Civic Center Plaza (phone: 249-1629).

Max on Main Although this restaurant is fashioned as a bistro, the subtly chic, well-heeled clientele indicates it's much more than that. The menu bears this out, with oysters on the half shell, fine champagnes by the glass, and exceptional Mediterranean and New American entrées. Awash in subtle sea tones, the atmosphere is soothing, while the open-to-view grill adds an air of vigor. Open daily; dinner only on weekends. Reservations necessary. Major credit cards accepted. 205 Main St. (phone: 522-2530).

Peppercorn's Grill Near the *Wadsworth Atheneum*, this sprightly, modern spot, with neon mobiles aloft, features pasta specialties, pizza, and northern Italian dishes. Closed Sundays; dinner only on Saturdays. Reservations advised, particularly on Saturdays. Major credit cards accepted. 357 Main St. (phone: 547-1714).

MODERATE

Bangkok Cuisine Excellent Thai fare is served here in intimate surroundings. Try chicken *satay*, *Goong-Tod* (marinated shrimp wrapped in a pastry shell and fried), and spicy squid salad. Open daily. Reservations advised. Major credit cards accepted. 2477 Albany Ave., W. Hartford (phone: 236-8142).

Brown Thomson & Co. In the *Richardson Building* complex, this antiques-filled restaurant popular with a young crowd offers the most extensive menu in town—125 separate items. Sandwiches, Mexican food, and delicacies such as fried ice cream are included. A comedy club operates in the back room on Saturday nights. Open daily; lunch only on Sundays. Reservations unnecessary. Major credit cards accepted. 942 Main St. (phone: 525-1600).

Congress Rotisserie The long, sleek bar, black-and-white décor, and stylish clientele all indicate that this is one of Hartford's favorite eating establishments. Diners can watch chefs prepare their selections on the huge rotisserie. The menu features American fare as well as a number of vegetarian dinner salads and pasta dishes. Open daily. Reservations necessary. Major credit cards accepted. Three locations: 7 Maple Ave.

(phone: 560-1965); 276 Farmington Ave. (phone: 278-7711); and 333 N. Main, West Hartford (phone: 231-7454).

Costa del Sol Spanish food is the draw at this inviting spot on the south side of town. Specialties include *tapas* and paella, and there's a fair selection of Spanish wines. The decor is simple, with a burgundy and white color scheme and candlelight. Visit the outdoor patio in summer. Closed Mondays; dinner only on weekends. Reservations advised. Major credit cards accepted. 901 Wethersfield (phone: 296-1714).

Hot Tomato's This casual watering hole has taken over one wing of *Union Station,* offering a pleasant respite to travelers. The American menu lists somewhat predictable selections—burgers, pastas, fish—but they are surprisingly well prepared. There's a fun, noisy crowd at the bar. Closed Mondays; dinner only on weekends. Reservations unnecessary. Major credit cards accepted. One Union Pl. (phone: 549-5100).

Hubbard's This old Hartford favorite has casual fare, with pizza, pasta, and burgers heading the menu. There's an active social scene centered at the bar. Open daily. Reservations unnecessary. Major credit cards accepted. 26 Trumbull St. (phone: 560-3311).

Museum Café at the Wadsworth Atheneum Decorated with paintings from the museum's collection and overlooking a sculpture garden, this pleasant spot offers an eclectic blend of international flavors in its soups, salads, sandwiches, pasta, and game. Open for lunch only; closed Mondays. Reservations unnecessary. Major credit cards accepted. 600 Main St. (phone: 728-5989).

Shishkebab House of Afghanistan Genuine Afghan food is served here in spacious, tiled, plant-filled rooms. Kebabs are the main attraction—the chicken is excellent, and shrimp and swordfish kebabs are popular. *Bowlani* (a lightly fried crêpe filled with potatoes and scallions) is also recommended, and the unusual desserts are worth a try. Closed Sundays. Reservations advised. Major credit cards accepted. 360 Franklin Ave. (phone: 296-0301).

INEXPENSIVE

Truc Orient Express Hartford heads here for Vietnamese food served in a pleasant dining room with comfy rattan chairs and a glassed-in room out front. The food is excellent, with the subtle to spicy-strong flavors of Indochina. Try the "Happy Pancake" with chicken or shrimp. Closed Sundays; dinner only on Mondays. Reservations unnecessary. Major credit cards accepted. 735 Wethersfield (phone: 296-2818).

Honolulu

At-a-Glance

SEEING THE CITY

For an eye-popping view of the shoreline, take the outdoor glass elevator to the top of the *Ilikai* hotel (1777 Ala Moana Blvd.; phone: 949-3811). There are equally spectacular views from the *Hanohano Room* atop the *Sheraton Waikiki* (2255 Kalakaua Ave.; phone: 922-4422) and from *Nicholas Nickolas,* atop the *Ala Moana* hotel (410 Atkinson Dr.; phone: 955-4811). For another good perspective, visit the 10th-floor observatory in the *Aloha Tower,* with a panorama that stretches from the airport to Diamond Head (at the bottom of *Fort Street Mall;* phone: 537-9260). The popular *Tantalus Lookout* provides a sweeping perspective that takes in much of Honolulu, Waikiki, Diamond Head, and Manoa Valley. The lookout from Punchbowl Crater offers another panoramic perspective of the city, all the way from downtown Honolulu to Waikiki.

SPECIAL PLACES

Although it is now considerably overbuilt, Waikiki is nonetheless an interesting place to wander. We suggest getting to know your neighborhood first with a 4-mile walking tour.

WAIKIKI

DIAMOND HEAD Guarding the southeasternmost boundary of Waikiki, this 760-foot volcanic crater is a world-famous landmark. You can climb around the slopes of Diamond Head along the tricky trail that begins at a gate off Makalei Place. It is also possible to drive into the crater through a tunnel to a state park inside, where there is a half-hour-long hike to the summit along a trail that passes World War II bunkers. Open daily. For information, call the *Division of State Parks* at 587-0300.

KAPIOLANI PARK This 220-acre park, named for the wife of Kalakaua, the last King of Hawaii, has plenty to keep you busy. Just off Monsarrat Avenue, the *Kodak Hula Show* (phone: 833-1661) is performed at 10 AM Tuesdays through Thursdays. Get there early if you want a good seat. Drift along toward the scent of the *Kapiolani Flower Garden* on the corner of Paki and Monsarrat. Other attractions in the park include the *Waikiki Aquarium, Honolulu Zoo,* tennis courts, beaches, jogging trails, and the *Shell,* featuring entertainment under the stars. Kalakaua Avenue, named after the good king, begins here. Pronounced Ka-la-*cow*-wah, it is the principal thoroughfare of Waikiki.

WAIKIKI BEACH Just outside the park, alongside Kalakaua Avenue, begins the famous, 2½-mile-long curve of Waikiki Beach, one of the most famous beaches and surfing spots in the world. The two- to five-foot waves that are standard along the shoreline for much of the year are perfect for novices and amateurs. (On the few summer days when they reach 15 feet, Waikiki's waves should be avoided by all but experts.) Several hotels

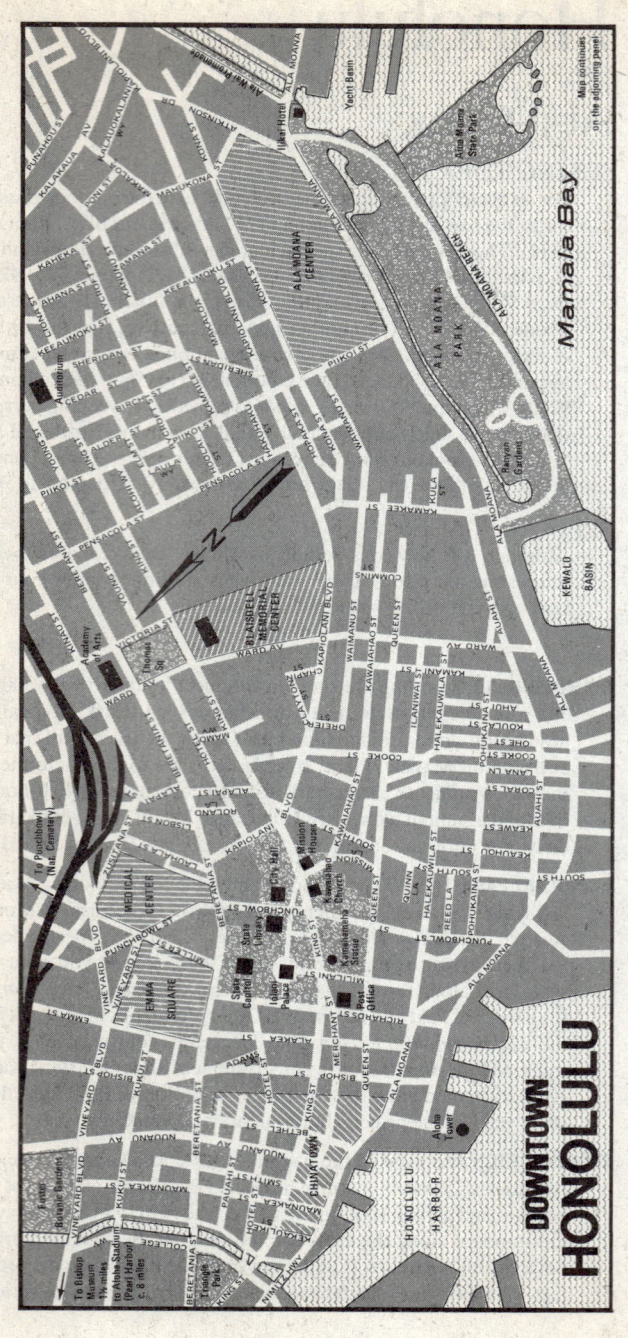

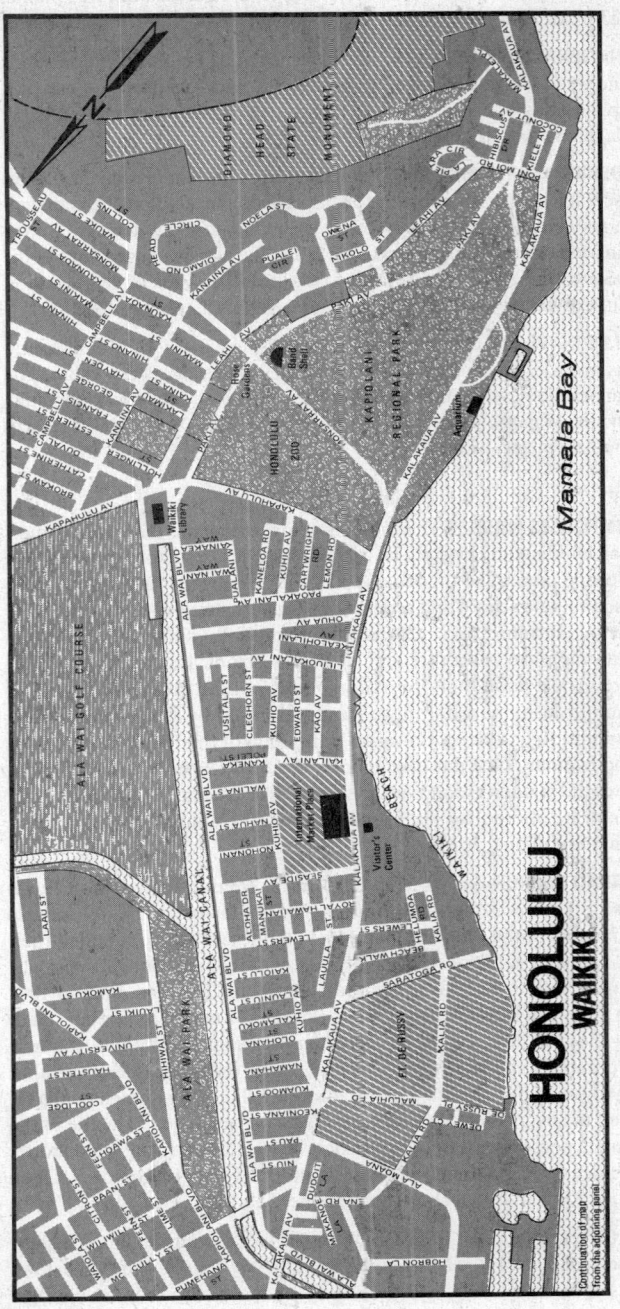

along Waikiki—for example, the *Outrigger* (2335 Kalakaua Ave.; phone: 923-0711; ask for Beach Services)—provide instruction and surfboards.

INTERNATIONAL MARKET PLACE A great place to poke around outdoor stalls underneath a giant banyan tree festooned with lanterns. You can pick up all kinds of exotic junk and treasures you can't live without. 2330 Kalakaua Ave. (phone: 923-9871).

FORT DERUSSY ARMY MUSEUM Weapons used by ancient Hawaiians, Japanese soldiers, and US troops are on display here. In addition, there are uniforms worn by US and enemy forces. The most fascinating items are Hawaiian weapons made from shark's teeth and the newspaper accounts of the US involvement in World War II following the invasion of Pearl Harbor. Closed Mondays. No admission charge. Kalia Rd. (phone: 438-2821).

TANTALUS DRIVE The country road that spirals up 2,013-foot Mount Tantalus provides some of the most beautiful urban scenery anywhere. The panoramic views include Waikiki, Diamond Head, downtown Honolulu, and the Waianae Mountains. A state park provides one of several places to relax, picnic, or hike.

DOWNTOWN

MISSION HOUSES MUSEUM This museum complex contains the earliest American buildings in Hawaii. The three frame houses, shipped around Cape Horn in pieces and then reassembled in 1821 by the first missionaries, used to be a school and a minister's home, as well as a mission. They contain furniture and artifacts more reminiscent of New England than Hawaii, as well as a rare archive of the islands' history. The *Printing House* next door, built from coral blocks in 1831, contains a replica of the old-fashioned Rampage handpress used by the printer, Elisha Loomis, to produce a Hawaiian translation of the Bible, schoolbooks, and hymnals. One day each month, the *Living History* program populates the mission grounds with volunteers dressed in 19th-century garb. Tours are offered Tuesdays through Sundays. Admission charge. 553 S. King St. (phone: 531-0481).

KAWAIAHAO CHURCH Across from the *Mission Houses, Kawaiahao Church* also is known as the *Westminster Abbey* of Hawaii, and indeed, those remnants of the old Hawaiian royal families who have retained their Congregational faith occasionally do use the church for baptisms, marriages, and funerals. It's the oldest church in Honolulu, built in 1842 on the site of Hawaii's first mission, which was a thatch-roofed hut standing close to an ancient and sacred *hao* (spring). Tall *kahilis* (feather-decorated staffs symbolic of royalty) placed on either side of the altar testify to its distinguished past. It was here that King Kamehameha III used the expression *Ua mau ke ea o ka aina i ka pono* ("The life of the land is perpetuated in righteousness"), which now is the state motto. Services are conducted in English and Hawaiian on Sundays. Open daily. King and Punchbowl Sts. (phone: 522-1333).

CHINATOWN Located on the easternmost fringe of downtown, this neighborhood spills across the Nuuanu Stream into *Aala Triangle Park*. Chinatown has open-air meat, fish, and vegetable markets; herb shops selling age-old medications; and elderly people who still dress in traditional costume. This also is the "sin' quarter of Honolulu, where sleazy sex shows sit beside family-style chop suey houses. A gentrification program is under way, however, bringing new shops and galleries into renovated turn-of-the-century buildings. A walking tour of Chinatown with an optional lunch (a real bargain) takes place on Tuesday mornings, starting from the *Chinese Chamber of Commerce* (42 N. King St.; phone: 533-3181).

ALOHA TOWER/FESTIVAL MARKETPLACE Overlooking Honolulu Harbor, the recently restored *Aloha Tower* (ca. 1927) is now the centerpiece of a harborside redevelopment that includes shops, restaurants, a museum, cruise boat piers, and a lookout. Adjacent to the *Hawaii Maritime Museum,* and within a short walk of Chinatown, it is part of an ongoing plan designed to open the coast with a series of parks and promenades linking Waikiki and downtown Honolulu.

MAUNAKEA MARKETPLACE At the core of the neighborhood, the marketplace serves as a commercial centerpiece for Chinatown's on-going renewal. The use of Chinese architectural detail is particularly beautiful. The central courtyard is filled with vendors, shops, restaurants, and food stalls which offer a variety of Asian tastes. Maunakea and Pauahi Sts.

HAWAII MARITIME MUSEUM Pier 7 is the home of the four-masted *Falls of Clyde* and the outrigger voyaging canoe *Hokulea,* returned from its three transpacific voyages along Polynesian migration routes. There also are displays related to Hawaii's maritime history, plus a library and photo archive. Open daily. Admission charge. Pier 7, near *Aloha Tower* (phone: 536-6373).

IOLANI PALACE With elaborate surroundings, *Iolani Palace* sits in state, receiving tribute from admirers. Highly revered by historians and sentimentalists alike, the palace was the residence of monarch and songwriter Queen Liliuokalani. (In fact, she wrote some of her famous songs, including *Aloha Oe,* while imprisoned here in 1895.) *Iolani* was built by her brother, King Kalakaua, between 1878 and 1882. In 1883, he placed a crown on his own head in what is now *Coronation Bandstand,* where, every Friday at noon, the *Royal Hawaiian Band* gives free, informal concerts. Palace tours are given every 15 minutes, Wednesdays through Saturdays. Admission charge; children under five years old are not admitted. King and Richards Sts. (phone: 538-1471 for information; 522-0832 for reservations).

STATE CAPITOL Built in 1969, the capitol takes its inspiration from the natural history of the islands. All of its features—columns, reflecting pools, courtyard—reflect aspects of Hawaii's environment. Outside the capitol stands a beautiful bronze statue of Queen Liliuokalani and the controversial modern statue of Father Damien, founder of the leprosy settlement at Kalaupapa on the island of Molokai. Open daily. No admission charge. 415 S. Beretania St. (phone: 586-2211).

OTHER SPECIAL PLACES

ALA MOANA CENTER Among the largest shopping centers in the world, it was built in 1959 and has undergone several renovations and expansions.

The Pacific's major retail outlet, it attracts 56 million customers a year. The open-air mall often features performances of island music and dance on its outdoor stage, and includes several large department stores—*Liberty House, Shirokiya, Sears*—as well as many European designer boutiques, mainland specialty stores including *Tiffany's* and *Cartier*, and such local favorites as the *Coral Grotto* and *Honolulu Book Shop*. Don't miss the *Makai Market Food Court*, 20 stalls dispensing Chinese, Japanese, Korean, Italian, Mexican, Hawaiian, and American fare. Open daily. 1450 Ala Moana Blvd., opposite *Ala Moana Park* (phone: 946-2811).

USS ARIZONA MEMORIAL More than a million people a year (a surprising number are Japanese) come to honor the American sailors who perished on the USS *Arizona*, sunk when the Japanese bombed Pearl Harbor in 1941. The only boat tour of the memorial leaves the visitors' center daily except *Thanksgiving, Christmas,* and *New Year's Day*. The *National Park Service* operates a large museum, with exhibitions and films. *Paradise Cruises* (phone: 536-3641) departs from Kewalo Basin (hotel transfers are included) for the morning tour that passes the memorial but does not stop. *Pearl Harbor Day* (December 7) is commemorated with a service at the memorial. The *USS Bowfin/Pacific Submarine Museum* (11 Arizona Memorial Pl.; phone: 423-1341) is adjacent to the visitors' center. Open daily. Admission charge.

BISHOP MUSEUM AND PLANETARIUM Near Likelike (pronounced *Lee-kay-lee*-kay) Highway, in the working class neighborhood called Kalihi, this prestigious museum houses the greatest collection of Hawaiiana in the world. Founded in 1899, it is the center for much of the anthropological research done throughout the Pacific. In addition to excellent displays, the museum has daily performances of Hawaiian music and dance. Shows are also featured at the adjacent planetarium. Open daily. Admission charge. 1525 Bernice St. (phone: 848-4129).

FOSTER BOTANIC GARDENS Often overlooked by tourists, this cool, tranquil retreat in the middle of the city is a museum of growing things. The No. 4 bus from Waikiki will bring you close to the garden at Nuuanu and Vineyard. Open daily. Admission charge. 180 N. Vineyard Blvd. (phone: 522-7065).

HONOLULU ACADEMY OF ARTS Across Thomas Square from *Blaisdell Center*, this museum has Oriental art and some European and American works. Interesting items include a Japanese ink and color handscroll dating to 1250, John Singleton Copley's *Portrait of Nathaniel Allen*, and Segna di Bonaventura's *Madonna and Child*. Lunch and dinner served in the museum garden. Reservations necessary. Closed Mondays. Admission charge. 900 S. Beretania St. (phone: 532-8700).

PACIFIC AEROSPACE MUSEUM This $1.75-million, high-tech museum—dedicated to aviation and aerospace achievement in the Pacific—traces the history of Pacific exploration: from the celestial navigation of the ancient Polynesians to the study of space now underway at nine international observatories atop 14,000-foot Mauna Kea on the Big Island of Hawaii. There are flight simulators, a *NASA* space shuttle flight deck, recorded voices of famous aviators, and a mission control exhibit that simulates space launches. At the *Great Skyquest Theater,* a three-room, three-dimensional multimedia production, original artifacts, models, art, and music are used to re-create the glory days of such aviators as Amelia Earhart, Charles Kingford-Smith, and US Navy Commander John Rodgers. Open daily. Admission charge. Central Waiting Lobby, *Honolulu International Airport* (phone: 839-0777).

QUEEN EMMA'S SUMMER PALACE This royal retreat in the cool highlands of Nuuanu Valley was the summer home of Kamehameha IV and Queen Emma, given to them by the queen's aunt and uncle. Built between 1847 and 1850, the simple building has Doric columns and a roof that overhangs a broad lanai (verandah). It was rescued from wreckers by the *Daughters of Hawaii,* and the civic group has operated it as a museum since 1915. Both furnishings and personal memorabilia are on display, including a Gothic-design cabinet, a gift of Queen Victoria's consort, Prince Albert; a stereopticon presented to Queen Emma by Napoleon III; and the christening robe made for the royal couple's only child, Prince Edward Albert, who died at age four. Open daily. Admission charge. 2913 Pali Hwy. (phone: 595-3167).

ROYAL MAUSOLEUM Considered the most sacred burial ground in the islands, this three-acre site serves as the resting place for the monarchs King Kamehameha II through V, Queen Emma, King Kalakaua, and Queen Liliuokalani. (Not buried here are King Kamehameha I, who died on the Big Island and whose remains were never found, and King Lunalilo, who requested a private burial crypt adjacent to *Kawaiahao Church.*) The Gothic-style rock and limestock mausoleum initially was planned by Kamehameha IV and Queen Emma following the death of their son in 1862. Construction, however, did not start until after the king died in 1863. Upon the completion in 1865 of the permanent mausoleum overlooking the beautiful Nuuanu Valley, the remains of the monarchs formerly interred in the *Iolani Palace* were transferred here. Open weekdays. No admission charge. 2261 Nuuanu Ave. (phone: 536-7602).

NATIONAL MEMORIAL CEMETERY OF THE PACIFIC Also known as Punchbowl Crater, this is the *Arlington National Cemetery* of the Pacific. In prehistoric times it was the site of human sacrifices. Now, more than 26,000 servicemen lie buried among its 112 peaceful acres overlooking downtown Honolulu. Commercial bus and van tours visit Punchbowl, but if you're on your own, you'll need a car or taxi. A lookout from the crater's rim offers panoramic city views. Take Puowaina Drive to its end.

POLYNESIAN CULTURAL CENTER The closest thing Hawaii has to *Disneyland,* this 42-acre "living" theme park, run by the Mormon Church in conjunction with the Hawaii branch of *Brigham Young University,* features replicas of villages and displays from the cultures of old Hawaii, the Marquesas, Samoa, Tonga, Fiji, Tahiti, and New Zealand. Although it is 45 miles from Waikiki, each year the park attracts more than 800,000 people who pay from $25 to $87 to walk, ride on trams, float on canoes on artificial streams through historic villages, have dinner, and watch a show in which "natives" (actually *Brigham Young* students) wearing traditional costume sing and dance. A shuttle bus rounds up parkgoers outside Waikiki hotels each morning and whisks them over to Laie, on the north side of Oahu, and back (phone: 293-3000). Also see *Reconstructed Villages* in DIVERSIONS.

WAIMEA FALLS PARK & VALLEY This 1,800-acre canyon is home to *Waimea Falls Park,* an arboretum, and a botanical garden. The valley includes a lovely falls, as well as a rock-girt swimming pool, botanical gardens, and 7½ miles of hiking and mountain bike trails. It is without a doubt Oahu's most attractive tourist development. The ancient Hawaiian games and sports that are demonstrated on the lower meadow do not intrude on the visitor who wants to walk casually among the exotic plants and trees. Excavated house sites and fishing shrines from Polynesian times remain much the same as when they were found. Although many of the plants have been introduced from other parts of the tropics, one of the main functions of *Waimea Falls Arboretum* is to preserve and propagate Hawaii's endangered native flora. For people taking *TheBus* No. 52 marked Wahiawa/Kaneohe from Honolulu, there is a 15-minute walk to the *Falls Visitor Center* from the Kamehameha Highway stop. (For information about Honolulu's municipal busline, *TheBus,* see *Getting Around* below.) The delightful hike runs through the lower part of the canyon along Kamananui Stream. Open daily. Admission charge (free admission for children under age six). When the moon is full, escorted walks of the park grounds are conducted free of charge. 59-864 Kamehameha Hwy. (phone: 638-8511).

SEA LIFE PARK Porpoises, whales, and penguins ham it up here several times a day in the entertainment part of what is otherwise a serious marine life research project at *Whalers Cove.* A major attraction is the Hawaiian Reef Exhibit, a 300,000-gallon tank, three fathoms deep and 70 feet across, in which a Pacific reef is re-created with the exotic plants and animals found in the real thing. Open daily. Admission charge. Off Kalanianaole Hwy. at Makapuu Point (phone: 259-7933).

CONTEMPORARY MUSEUM Situated on the Tantalus hillside, with a beautiful view of the city, it features contemporary sculpture, paintings, graphics, and more, most of it in well-displayed, changing exhibitions. There's a major permanent display of the works of David Hockney. In addition, satellite galleries are located in the news building of the Honolulu Newspaper Agency on Kapiolani Boulevard, and at the *Alana Waikiki* hotel on Ala Moana Boulevard. Closed Mondays. Donations requested. 2411 Makiki Heights Dr. (phone: 526-1322).

EXTRA SPECIAL

Honolulu is the great jumping-off point for island-hopping expeditions. Kauai, the oldest island, is known for golf at the *Princeville* and *Poipu* resort courses, sunny Poipu Beach, and the spectacular beauty of Waimea Canyon and the Na Pali Coast. Maui offers valleys, waterfalls, beaches, and the crater of the dormant Haleakala Volcano. The small *Kapalua/West Maui Airport* offers direct flights to Lahaina, Kaanapali, Kahana, Napili, and Kapalua resorts. Hawaii, also called the Big Island, is the home of Mauna Loa and Kilauea, two of the world's most active volcanoes, as well as Hawaii's premier archaeological sites, including *Puuhonua O'Honaunau* and *Puukohola Heiau*. On Lanai, only 17 miles long, the main draws are two resort hotels and a sense of away-from-it-all isolation. Molokai, 37 miles long, a relatively untouched ranchers' island, offers tourists the opportunity to see a rural side of Hawaii, or visit the isolated lepers' settlement at *Kalaupapa,* now administered as a National Historic Park. There is also a resort at Kaluakoi and several small condos and hotels along the east coast for those who wish to stay awhile. For information about flights to these islands from Honolulu, see *Getting Around* below.

Sources and Resources

TOURIST INFORMATION

For information, maps, and brochures, contact the *Hawaii Visitors Bureau* (2270 Kalakaua Ave., Room 801, Honolulu, HI 96815; phone: 923-1811). The office is open weekdays only. Call the Hawaii state hotline (phone: 808-923-1811) for maps, calendars of events, health updates, and travel advisories.

LOCAL COVERAGE *Honolulu Advertiser,* morning daily; *Honolulu Star-Bulletin,* evening daily; *Honolulu* magazine, monthly. *This Week, Spotlight Hawaii, Oahu Destinations, Here in Hawaii,* and *Guide to Oahu* are the best of the numerous free publications aimed at visitors, and they are available in most hotel lobbies. They sometimes contain discount coupons as well as information about attractions, lodgings, and restaurants. We also immodestly suggest you pick up a copy of *Birnbaum's Hawaii 95* (Harper-Collins, $18).

TELEVISION STATIONS KHON Channel 2–NBC; KITV Channel 4–ABC; KGMB Channel 9–CBS; KHET Channel 11–PBS; and KHNL Channel 13–FOX.

RADIO STATIONS AM: KSSK 59 (oldies and contemporary); KHVH 99 (news). FM: KHPR 88.1 (classical); KUMU 94.7 (easy listening); KQMQ 93.1 (soft rock); KPOI 97.5 (rock); KHNR 65 (CNN headline news); and KINE 105.1 (contemporary Hawaiian).

TELEPHONE The area code for Honolulu is 808. For all inter-island calls, exclude the area code and dial 1 before the number.

SALES TAX There is a 4% sales tax and a 6% hotel tax in Honolulu.

CLIMATE In ancient times, the Hawaiians had no word for weather. They did, however, have words for two seasons—winter and summer. Winter, which runs from about October through April, means daytime highs reaching the mid-70s and low 80s F, dropping into the low 60s at night. There can be several short rains in a day. You can count on 11 hours of daylight. Summer temperatures hover around the mid- to upper 80s; rains are less frequent, and you get about 13 hours of daylight, more vacation for your money.

GETTING AROUND

AIRPORT *Honolulu International Airport* is about a 20- to 25-minute drive from Waikiki (in moderate traffic), slightly less from the downtown area. *Airport Motorcoach* (phone: 926-4747) provides van shuttle service for $6 from the airport to Waikiki. Vans leave every 20 minutes. Reserve at least 24 hours ahead for the return trip. *Hawaiian Air* (phone: 537-1155) and *Aloha Island Air* (phone: 484-1111; 800-227-4900) both fly to Maui, Kauai, and the Big Island, with scheduled jet service throughout the day. Flights range from 20 to 35 minutes. In addition, *Hawaiian* offers jet service to Molokai. Commuter carrier *IslandAir* (phone: 484-2222) offers 18-passenger prop service to Lanai and Molokai, as well as service to Maui and Kauai. *Mahalo Airlines* (phone: 833-5555) serves Maui and Kauai. At press time, plans had been announced for Big Island service as well. Departures on *Aloha, Hawaiian, IslandAir,* and *Mahalo* are from the main inter-island terminal.

BUS *TheBus,* as the municipal transit line is called, is the least expensive way to get around Honolulu. Whether you go one stop or 80 miles around the island, it costs 85¢, which you must pay with exact change. You can get a map of bus routes at your hotel, at *Ala Moana Center,* or from the *Honolulu Department of Transport, Mass Transit Lines (MTL;* 811 Middle St.; phone: 848-5555).

CAR RENTAL All of the major car rental companies have offices at the airport and in Waikiki. In addition, *Classic* (phone: 951-8331) features a fleet of vintage 1950s and 1960s autos, while *Ferrari Rentals* (phone: 942-8725) goes high-brow. Most of these firms serve four or five islands, and multi-island rates are offered.

HELICOPTER TOURS *Papillon Hawaii Pacific* (phone: 836-1566) offers a series of aerial tours from *Honolulu International Airport. Cherry Helicopter* (phone: 833-4339) departs from the *Turtle Bay* resort on the North Shore. *Rainbow Pacific Helicopters* (phone: 834-1111) offers Honolulu's least expensive helicopter charters.

MOPED/MOTORCYCLE They're a breezy way to see the island or just to cruise around Waikiki and the southeast. Be careful: Pickup truck drivers on the Waianae Coast tend to look askance at riders of these motorized "toys," and driving them on newly wet surfaces can be tricky if you're not completely accustomed to them. *Aloha Funway Rentals* (408 Lewers; phone: 926-2277) is the best-known motorcycle/moped rental outfit in Honolulu.

TAXI Although taxis sometimes can be hailed on the street, most are on call. To be sure of getting a cab, call for one. Some reliable companies are *SIDA* (phone: 836-0011); *Charley's* (phone: 955-2211 or 531-2333); and *Aloha State Taxi* (phone: 847-3566).

TROLLEY *Waikiki Trolley* (phone: 599-2561) has launched a fleet of motorized, open-air reproductions of the horse-drawn trolleys that operated at the turn of the century. Today, they provide tour and point-to-point service between Waikiki and such shopping and cultural attractions as the *Bishop Museum and Planetarium,* Dole Cannery Square (the cannery itself is closed, but there's a children's museum and shops in the square), *Ala Moana Center, Ward Warehouse,* Chinatown, and the *Aloha Tower.* The narrated trolley tour operates daily; all-day passes cost $15.

LOCAL SERVICES

BABY-SITTING *Aloha Baby-Sitting* (phone: 732-2029) or check with the hotel concierge or activity desk.

BUSINESS SERVICES *Una May Young* (5304 Apo Dr.; phone: 373-3180).

DRY CLEANER/TAILOR *Hakuyosha* (730 Sheriden St.; phone: 955-6116).

LIMOUSINE *Cloud Nine Limousine* (phone: 524-7999); *Executive Limousine* (phone: 941-1999).

MECHANIC *Toguchi Chevron Service Station* (825 N. Vineyard Blvd.; phone: 845-6422).

MEDICAL EMERGENCY *Queen's Hospital* (Discovery Bay (phone: 943-1111), open until 10 PM..

MESSENGER SERVICES *ADDS Messenger Service* (phone: 545-2067, 545-2174, or 947-4228); *Courier Express* (phone: 955-0079).

NATIONAL/INTERNATIONAL COURIER *DHL Worldwide Express* (phone: 836-0441); *FedEx* (phone: 395-3339).

PHARMACY *Long's* drugstore (phone: 941-4433); *Outrigger* (2335 Kalakaua Ave.; phone: 923-0711); *Pillbox* (1133 11th Ave.; phone: 737-1777), open daily until 11 PM.

PHOTOCOPIES *Ditto's* (1500 Kapiolani Blvd.; phone: 944-8500 or 2570 S. Beretania St.; phone: 943-0005), open 24 hours; fax service also; *Island Instant Printers* (2270 Kalakaua Ave.; phone: 922-1225); *Second Image* (2600 S. King St.; phone: 955-7498).

POST OFFICE Several locations downtown (335 Merchant St. at Richards St.; phone: 541-1962); in Waikiki (330 Saratoga Rd.; phone: 831-3434); and at substations in the *Royal Hawaiian Shopping Center* (phone: 926-3710), the *Hilton Hawaiian Village* (phone: 949-4321), and at the airport (phone: 423-3930).

PROFESSIONAL PHOTOGRAPHER *Creative Focus* (phone: 734-4677); *Marc Schecter* (phone: 537-9464).

SECRETARY/STENOGRAPHER *Kelly Services* (phone: 536-9343).

TELECONFERENCE FACILITIES *Kahala Hilton* (see *Checking In,* below).

TRANSLATOR *Academia Language School* (phone: 946-5599); *A-1 Kanner Language Systems* (phone: 415-365-3046).

WESTERN UNION/TELEX Many offices located around the city (phone: 800-325-6000).

WORD PROCESSING/TYPEWRITER RENTAL *Alexander Brothers* (phone: 837-7828), hourly in-office use or two-week minimum rentals; *Computer House* (phone: 422-7253), rentals and repairs; *Pacific Business Machines* (phone: 946-5059), one- and two-week minimums, depending on equipment.

OTHER *Lyn's Video Rental* (phone: 941-1253).

SPECIAL EVENTS

Festivities are held year-round. In late January and early February, the *Chinese New Year* is celebrated in Chinatown. On *Lei Day* (May 1), a queen is crowned at the *Waikiki Band Shell* in *Kapiolani Park*, where there is also a lei-making contest and at sunset, a hula show. The week-long *Festival of the Pacific*, highlighting the songs, dances, arts and crafts, and competitive sports of more than 40 Pacific Rim nations, is held in early June. The most spectacular annual parade in the islands is held on *King Kamehameha Day*, the Saturday closest to the king's birthday (June 11), when his statue (opposite the Judiciary Building in downtown Honolulu) is draped with 40-foot leis. In July, the *Prince Lot Hula Festival* is held in a lovely outdoor setting at *Moanalua Gardens*. September's *Aloha Week* is Honolulu's biggest celebration. It features canoe races, luaus, balls, athletic events, parades, and more. The *Triple Crown of Surfing* competition is held on the North Shore in November and December. December 7 is *Pearl Harbor Day*, commemorated by a service at the USS *Arizona* Memorial. Late in November or early December, the *Hawaii International Film Festival* presents a week of free movies. And *First Night*, the city's New Year's Eve celebration, takes place on the streets of downtown, with musical entertainment and general high spirits.

MUSEUMS

In addition to those described in *Special Places*, there are two other museums of note.

DAMIEN MUSEUM AND ARCHIVES This museum is dedicated to Father Damien de Veuster, the Belgian priest who worked with the lepers at Kalaupapa on Molokai for 16 years, contracting leprosy himself before he died. On display are his mementos and personal papers. Closed Sundays. No admission charge. 130 Ohua Ave. (phone: 923-2690)

HAWAII CHILDREN'S MUSEUM This $1.5-million "hands-on, minds-on" exploratorium is geared to children between the ages of three and 13. See what insects look like magnified on the optech bioscanner, send a fax to grandma, build a dome out of bubbles, meet Einstein the dog inside the giant toy box, or make a video visit to a faraway city. Closed Mondays. Admission charge. 650 Iwilei Rd., in Dole Cannery Sq. (phone: 522-0040).

SHOPPING

If you can drag yourself away from the beach long enough, you'll discover that Honolulu is a tropical shopping heaven—not so much for bargains, but for the incredible diversity of wares that stream into this Pacific capital from Asia, Europe, and the US mainland, as well as from the other South Pacific and Hawaiian islands. With some exceptions, the Honolulu shopping scene is centered around its malls; some have an architectural or commercial theme, usually Asian or Hawaiian, and a few are outdoors. The emphasis is on designer goods; alohawear and other resort clothing; vacation sundries such as lotions, beach towels, and mats; and Polynesian handicrafts. Mixed in are boutiques that carry such famous international names as *Chanel* and *Gucci*, and high-fashion sportswear. Most shopping malls are open daily from 10 AM to 9 PM; Sundays until 5 PM, but Waikiki malls have longer hours, 9 AM to 11 PM daily.

SHOPPING CENTERS

Ala Moana Center This is among the largest malls in the world (see *Special Places*). Ala Moana Blvd. opposite *Ala Moana Park* (phone: 946-2811).

Hyatt Regency Waikiki The first three floors of the *Hyatt* complex are dominated by more than 50 shops. 2424 Kalakaua Ave. (phone: 923-1234).

International Market Place This outdoor market is a bustling, noisy bazaar of shops and booths (see *Special Places*). 2330 Kalakaua Ave. (phone: 923-9871).

Kahala Mall This 86-shop mall, a smaller and less crowded alternative to *Ala Moana*, is located in an exclusive neighborhood east of Waikiki. There's also an eight-plex movie theater. 4211 Waialae Ave. (phone: 732-7736).

Kilohana Square Located about 1 mile from Waikiki's eastern border, this small complex includes Western and Asian antiques shops, art galleries, and specialty stores. 1016 Kapahulu Ave.

King's Village This pastel complex of quaint townhouse-style buildings and cobblestone walkways, located behind and across the street from the *Hyatt Regency Waikiki* hotel, offers more than 40 shops, including a branch of *Burberry's of London*. It is designed to resemble urban Honolulu in the days of the 19th-century monarchs, complete with a changing-of-the-guard ceremony daily at 6 PM—although the *Rose and Crown Pub* (phone: 923-5833), with its horse brasses, etched-glass mirrors, and timber beams, manages to be a fair replica of an English country pub. 131 Kaiulani Ave.

Rainbow Bazaar Some 30 boutiques sell ethnic handicrafts, jewelry, resortwear, and objets d'art. *Hilton Hawaiian Village* (phone: 949-4321).

Royal Hawaiian Shopping Center This ultramodern, four-story, three-block-long arcade of boutiques and restaurants, which covers six-and-a-half acres, appeals primarily to tourists, but it is definitely worth exploring. Here, European and American boutiques, including *Cartier, Van Cleef & Arpels, Hermès, Chanel,* and *Coach*, stand side by side with shops selling Chinese art, beach and sportswear, jewelry, candy, and cookies, as well as restaurants and the ubiquitous souvenir shops. 2201 Kalakaua Ave. (phone: 922-0588).

Waikiki Shopping Plaza The merchandise in this complex has to compete with a five-story water display that is part fountain and part Plexiglas sculpture. There are a few shops of interest as well as some fine restaurants on the upper floors. 2270 Kalakaua Ave. (phone: 923-1191).

Ward Center On Ala Moana Boulevard, across the street from *Ward Warehouse* and from *Ala Moana Beach Park,* this low-key mall has a selection of upscale shops and art galleries as well as some popular eateries.

Ward Warehouse A two-story complex of 70 boutiques and restaurants opposite the Kewalo Boat Basin. Ala Moana Blvd.

SPECIALTY AND DISCOUNT SHOPS

WAIKIKI

Alfred Dunhill The who-can-afford-it prices of this shop, located in the Moana wing of the *Moana Surfrider* hotel, are as awesome as the jewelry, leather goods, and accessories that carry the Dunhill imprint (phone: 971-2020).

Betty Imports Real bargains can be found here on all kinds of costume jewelry and imported bric-a-brac, often at prices 30% to 50% lower than at other shops. Fifth floor of the *Waikiki Shopping Plaza* (phone: 922-3010).

Center Art Gallery Although the store has signed prints by Chagall, Dalí, and some other prolific printmakers, its specialty is canvases by celebrities such as Elke Sommer and Red Skelton. If you would like an original painting of Woody Woodpecker commanding an outrigger canoe by his creator, Walter Lantz, hurry on over. *Royal Hawaiian Shopping Center* (phone: 926-2727).

Chanel Here is every Chanel item you can imagine at prices that maybe you hadn't. Accessories, perfumes, jewelry, and more. *Ala Moana Center* (phone: 942-5555); and *Royal Hawaiian Shopping Center* (phone: 923-0255).

Cotton Cargo This shop offers a refreshing change from alohawear, featuring 100% cotton fashions for women. The clothes have style; most are imported from India, Bali, Turkey, Greece, and Central America. *Hyatt Regency Waikiki Center* (phone: 923-5811).

Down Under Honolulu One of the best sources for men's swimwear in Hawaii, it stocks designer labels as well as merchandise designed in-house. Everything from nearly revealing to very revealing is here, plus a fine selection of generic shorts and T-shirts. 2139 Kuhio Ave. (phone: 922-9229).

Endangered Species Endangered animals are safely "captured" in art forms—from sculpture to dolls, coffee mugs to T-shirts. 2335 Kalakaua Ave. (phone: 922-6293).

Helen & Suzanne For the best selection of glitzy costume jewelry in Hawaii. The main shop is in the promenade at the *Royal Hawaiian* (phone: 923-7727), with a smaller shop in the lobby.

Little Hawaiian Craftshop This place has one of Hawaii's best collections of carved wood objects and museum-quality reproductions of Hawaiian sculpture. It's also known for handicrafts made from nuts, gourds, bones, fossil ivory, and seaweed, as well as jewelry, ornaments, and "conversation pieces" made from cowrie shells. *Royal Hawaiian Shopping Center* (phone: 926-2662).

McInerny Galleria This is one of the best places in town for designer clothing for men, women, and children. Some of the labels include Giorgio Armani and Ferragamo. *Royal Hawaiian Shopping Center* (phone: 971-4200).

Sawada Golf Fill all your golf needs at this large duffer's depot. *Waikiki Shopping Plaza* (phone: 923-0144).

Van Brugge House Designer labels from Australia are found here, as well as a cache of that country's pink, champagne, and cognac colored diamonds. *Royal Hawaiian Shopping Center* (phone: 971-6678).

Wyland Gallery The paintings, sculptures, and multimedia artwork here all share a marine theme created by owner-artist Wyland. *Hyatt Regency Waikiki* (phone: 923-3133).

Yokohama-Okadaya An international gift shop, it has a fine collection of designer leather goods. *Royal Hawaiian Shopping Center* (phone: 922-5731); *Waikiki Shopping Plaza* (phone: 922-5731).

DIAMOND HEAD

As Time Goes By Antique jewelry, paintings, and silver are showcased at this antiques shop. *Kilohana Square*, 1016 Kapahulu Ave. (phone: 732-1174).

Apropos The women's clothes available here exhibit European flair. *Kahala Mall* (phone: 735-1611).

Carriage House The mix at this store is European, Oriental, and American antiques. *Kilohana Square* (phone: 737-2622).

Juma Colorful clothing for men and women is highlighted by the eye-popping designs of Jams, Baik Baik, and other style-conscious lines. *Kahala Mall* (phone: 739-5305).

Max Davis High-quality Oriental antiques are available here. *Kilohana Square* (phone: 735-2341).

Needlepoint, Etc. This shop sells kits and patterns with tropical flowers and other Hawaii motifs. *Kilohana Square* (phone: 737-3944).

Quilts Hawaii Collectible Hawaiian quilts come in traditional as well as contemporary designs. 2338 S. King St. (phone: 942-3195).

Vue Hawaii The artwork, clothing, and koa wood items here are created locally. *Kilohana Square* (phone: 735-8774).

MIDTOWN

Artlines Browse through artistic collectibles from all over the globe. *Ala Moana Shopping Center* (phone: 941-1445).

Chocolates for Breakfast The women's clothing sold here is often elegant, sometimes daring, and occasionally counter-chic, but always sophisticated. For the pure of heart there are muslins that *look* innocent enough. *Ala Moana Shopping Center* (phone: 947-3434).

Crack Seed Center Preserved seeds and fruits, including dried cherries, plums, ginger, and lemon peel, are featured. *Ala Moana Shopping Center* (phone: 949-7200).

Honolulu Book Shop This store is one of the largest and most comprehensive of its kind in Hawaii. *Ala Moana Shopping Center* (phone: 941-2274).

Iida's The specialty here is things Japanese, from bronze statues to porcelains to back-massage rollers. It's fun to see what's being offered. *Ala Moana Shopping Center* (phone: 973-0320).

Images International/Otsuka Gallerie The photographs of Japan's Hisashi Otsuka are worth seeing, even if the price tags are high. *Ala Moana Shopping Center* (phone: 926-5081).

Liberty House At Hawaii's leading department store, which is represented in hotels on all the major islands, the emphasis is on men's, women's, and children's fashions—not quite designer creations, but not simply alohawear, either. The *Ala Moana* branch also has housewares, toys, and books. The staff is, on the whole, extremely helpful. *Ala Moana Shopping Center* (phone: 941-2345).

Nohea Gallery The superior Hawaiian arts and crafts shown here include prints, drawings, woven goods, chimes, ceramics, pottery, and scrimshaw with nautical etchings. *Ward Warehouse* (phone: 599-7927).

North Beach Leather From coats to dresses, pants to accessories, everything here is made of leather—with high-fashion design and price tags to match. *Ala Moana Shopping Center* (phone: 949-6719).

Pocketbook Man With what is perhaps Hawaii's most complete selection of luggage and handbags, this shop offers some very elegant choices. *Ala Moana Shopping Center* (phone: 949-3535).

Pomegranates in the Sun The name's a bit far-fetched, but the selection of hand-painted and ethnic clothing for men and women is intriguing. *Ward Warehouse* (phone: 531-1108).

Products of Hawaii Hawaiian perfume, Hawaiian *tiki* carvings, Hawaiian *lau hala* mats, Hawaiian-designed greeting cards are sold here—as advertised. It's a good spot to do all your souvenir shopping at one time. *Ala Moana Shopping Center* (phone: 949-6866).

Royal Hawaiian Heritage This is the place to visit if you've become enamored of the black and gold Hawaiian-style jewelry that graces many local women. Across from the *Ala Moana Center* at 1430 Kona St. (phone: 973-4343).

Royal Hawaiian Mint Numismatists will enjoy watching Hawaiian coins being minted in bronze, gold and silver, then buying them. The process is fascinating and the designs are beautiful, with many royal themes from Hawaii's 19th-century past. 1421 Kalakaua Ave. (phone: 949-6468).

Tahiti Imports Polynesian fashions for women, a lot of them quite classy in their brief way, are sold here. The *pareu,* in simple and elegant designs, can be turned into intriguing cover-ups and skirts. *Ala Moana Shopping Center* (phone: 941-4539).

Willowdale Gallery Here are antiques, most hailing from Europe. *Ward Center* (phone: 536-2080).

DOWNTOWN

Aala Lei Shop A wide selection of leis and flower arrangements can be found at good prices. 79A N. Beretania St. (phone: 521-5766).

Bushido Specializing in antique Japanese armaments, Korean ceramics, and other Orientalia, this is one of the more interesting antiques shops on Maunakea. 936 Maunakea St. (phone: 536-5693).

Gallery Mirado Lovely Japanese prints and a variety of antiques, including porcelains, netsuke, and bronze sculpture, make for interesting browsing and buying. 938 Maunakea St. (phone: 521-3999).

Honolulu Chocolate Company Chocoholics beware, your taste buds will confirm the initial impulse to surrender to temptation. The prices are steep, but worth it. Restaurant Row (phone: 528-4033), *Ward Center* (phone: 531-2997), and Manoa Valley (phone: 988-4999).

Jenny's Lei Shop One of a number of downtown shops that specialize in the traditional Hawaiian art of lei making, this outlet has a larger and better-priced selection than that found in Waikiki. 65 N. Beretania St. (phone: 521-1595).

Lai Fong This long-established store features Oriental collectibles and bric-a-brac. 1118 Nuuanu Ave. (phone: 537-3497).

Mellow's Fans of antique jewelry will relish shopping here. 841 Bishop St. (phone: 533-6313).

Pegge Hopper Gallery The work of its namesake artist is featured at this gallery. 1164 Nuuanu Ave. (phone: 524-1160).

Penthouse Some real bargains can be found at this reduced-price merchandise outlet for *Liberty House*. 1 N. King St. (phone: 945-5151).

Ramsey Galleries and Café Changing exhibits of high-quality watercolors, pen-and-ink drawings, ceramicware, and other art forms are shown here. Linger for a little live music (Friday evenings and Saturday afternoons) and sustenance at the café. 1128 Smith St. (phone: 537-ARTS).

Robin Buntyn The fine antiques featured here focus on Japanese prints, netsuke, lacquerware, jade, and ivory. 900A Maunakea St. (phone: 523-5913).

SPORTS AND FITNESS

Hawaii is one of the world's great centers for water sports. Surfing, canoeing, kayaking, and swimming contests are held often. *Aloha Stadium* (phone: 486-9300) is the site of the *Hula Bowl* college football game each January. Basketball and boxing events are held at the *Neal S. Blaisdell Center* (777 Ward Ave.; phone: 521-2911).

BICYCLING *Aloha Funways* (408 Lewars St.; phone: 926-2277) has good-quality rentals.

FISHING Fishing enthusiasts from all over the world flock to Hawaiian waters. Fishing boats can be chartered or are available on a half- and full-day share boat basis from *Coreene C's Sport Fishing Charters* (phone: 226-8421) or *Island Charters* (phone: 536-1555). Most boats leave from Kewalo Basin, at the end of Ward Avenue, on Ala Moana Boulevard.

FITNESS CENTERS The *YMCA* (401 Atkinson Dr.; phone: 941-3344) has a pool, racquetball court, sauna, exercise machines, and weights. For a treat, set up an appointment with the massage (shiatsu) specialist at the *Sheraton Moana Surfrider* (2365 Kalakaua Ave.; phone: 922-3111). The *Ilikai* hotel (phone: 949-3811) and the *Outrigger Waikiki* (phone: 923-0711) both offer nice, small workout facilities.

GLIDING *Hawaii Glider Rides* (phone: 677-3404) has three-seat sailplanes departing about every 20 minutes daily at the north shore's *Dillingham Air Field*.

GOLF There are numerous public courses on Oahu, many providing gorgeous scenery as well as challenging golfing. Several more are in the planning stages.

A TOP TEE-OFF SPOT

Ko Olina Just 30 minutes from downtown Honolulu, this five-year-old course is one of the best in Hawaii, according to *Golf Digest*. The par 72, 6,867-yard layout is designed to complement 16 spectacular water features—including cascading waterfalls, rock gardens, lakes, and quiet pools. Golf pros are available to give lessons and supervise tee times. There's an enormous practice range for driving balls and practicing chip shots, as well as a putting area. Reservations are accepted up to one week in advance. Proper golf attire is mandatory. 92-1220 Aliinui Dr., Ewa Beach (phone: 676-5300; fax: 676-5100).

Other courses include *Ala Wai*, the closest to Waikiki (phone: 296-4653); *Pali*, in Kaneohe (phone: 296-7254); *Hawaii Prince* (phone: 944-4567) in Ewa; *Sheraton West* course (phone: 695-9544) and *Makaha Valley Country Club* (phone: 695-9578), both in Makaha; and *Turtle Bay Hilton* (phone: 293-8574), near Kahuku on the North Shore. In late January or early February, the nationally televised four-day *Hawaiian Open International Golf Tournament* is played at the *Waialae Country Club* in the Kahala District.

JOGGING Run along Kalakaua Avenue to *Kapiolani Park,* where a group meets at the bandstand at 7:30 AM every Sunday from March through December for a short lecture and a run. The distance around the park is 1.8 miles; to tack on more mileage, continue along Kalakaua to Diamond Head Road and circle the base of Diamond Head. The road turns into Monsarrat Avenue, which leads back to Kalakaua (4½ miles altogether). Or take Diamond Head Road as far as Kahala Avenue, one of the island's most beautiful runs. Also popular is the 2-mile perimeter of *Ala Moana Beach Park*.

- **KAYAKING** *Go Bananas* (732 Kapahulu Ave.; phone: 737-9514) offers rentals on single and double kayaks. *Twogood* rents one- or two-passenger kayaks per day and offers escorted early morning coastal trips from Kailua Mondays, Wednesdays, and Fridays. 171-B Hamakua Dr., Kailua (phone: 262-5656).

- **SKIN DIVING** *Dan's Dive Shop* (660 Ala Moana Blvd.; phone: 536-6181) rents diving gear, offers instructions for beginners, and has brush-up courses for those with some experience. On the North Shore, call *Underwater Hawaii* (at the *Turtle Bay Hilton*, 57091 Kam Hwy., Kahuku, HI 96731; phone: 293-8811) for lessons, or *Surf and Sea* in Haleiwa (phone: 637-9887) for rentals. Snorkelers can take an inexpensive day trip to Hanauma Bay with *Hanauma Bay Snorkeling Tours* (phone: 944-8828).

- **SURFING** The quest for the perfect wave attracts surfers from all over the world. Some hotels along Waikiki Beach have surfing instructors and concessions that rent equipment. The most famous surfing beaches are Sunset, Ehukai, and Waimea, on the north side of the island. Major international competitions are held here in late November through mid-December.

- **SWIMMING** With Waikiki Beach generally very crowded, an alternative is to head to nearby Ala Moana or Diamond Head beach parks, or to beaches on the other side of the island. Equally spectacular settings include Sandy Beach and Makapuu, where just about everyone body-surfs; Waimanalo and Kailua, where swimming and windsurfing are popular; and on up the coast to Kahana and the legendary surfing beaches of the North Shore. Many beaches are dangerous for swimming; stick to those with lifeguards.

- **TENNIS** There are public courts at 40 places around Oahu. Try *Ala Moana Tennis Center* (phone: 522-7031), *Diamond Head Tennis Center* (phone: 971-7150), *Kapiolani Tennis Courts* (no phone), or *Honolulu Tennis Club* (phone: 944-9696). The *Ilikai* hotel has six courts (one lighted for night play), the *Hawaiian Regent* has one court, the *Pacific Beach* has two courts, while the *Kahala Hilton* offers six courts at the *Maunalua Bay Club*.

- **WINDSURFING** *Naish Hawaii* (phone: 261-3539 or 262-6068) features rentals and lessons on Windward Oahu, off Kailua.

THEATER

You can get tickets at the door for most plays and musicals in Honolulu. The main theaters are *Blaisdell Center Concert Hall* (Ward and King Sts.; phone: 537-6191), *Diamond Head Theater* (Makapuu and Aloha Aves.; phone: 734-0274); and *Hawaii Performing Arts Company*'s *Manoa Theatre* (2833 E. Manoa Rd.; phone: 988-6131). Also check for under-the-stars performances at the *Waikiki Shell* (phone: 521-2911).

MUSIC

The *Honolulu Symphony* plays at the *Blaisdell Center Concert Hall* (phone: 537-6191). Rock musicians appear at the *Blaisdell Center Arena* (phone: 521-2911) or sometimes at *Aloha Stadium* (phone: 486-9300) or the *Waikiki Shell* (phone: 521-2911).

NIGHTCLUBS AND NIGHTLIFE

With a large tourist industry to support it and a Hawaiian musical tradition to provide the raw material, the Waikiki area swings from 8 PM until 1 AM, with some clubs open until 4 AM, most nights of the week. For information on hotels listed, see *Checking In* (below).

The smooth-crooning Danny Kaleikini headlines a Hawaiian-Polynesian variety show at the *Kahala Hilton's Maile Terrace*. Don't miss illusionist John Hirokawa at the *Hilton Hawaiian Village;* his mix of magic and Polynesian revue is one of Waikiki's most entertaining shows. The *Society of Seven* offers a Las Vegas–style revue that's become a Waikiki classic at the *Outrigger Waikiki*. The *Brothers Cazimero,* the most popular and enduring of Hawaii's musical entertainers, frequently perform at the *Royal Hawaiian's Monarch Room*. Popular discos include *Annabelle's* (atop the *Ilikai* hotel); *Rumours* (at the *Ala Moana*); *Wave Waikiki* (1877 Kalakaua Ave.; phone: 941-0424); *Moose McGillycuddy* (310 Lewers St.; phone: 923-0751; and 1035 University Ave.; phone: 944-5525); *Maharaja* (at the *Waikiki Trade Center,* 2255 Kuhio Ave.; phone: 922-3030); and *Hula's* (2103 Kuhio Ave.; phone: 923-0669), with a crowd ranging from punk to gay. At *Studebaker's* (500 Ala Moana Blvd.; phone: 526-9888) in Restaurant Row on the outskirts of downtown Honolulu, crowds line up to enjoy music of the 1950s and 1960s with let-it-all-hang-out dancing by waiters and waitresses as well as patrons. The *Comedy Club* at the *Ilikai* (phone: 949-3811) has several shows nightly. Local comic Frank Delima performs a consistently funny show at the *Polynesian Palace* (phone: 923-7469), where crooner Don Ho is also featured. *Legends* (phone: 971-1400) at the *Royal Hawaiian Shopping Center* features lip-synch entertainment by Michael Jackson, Madonna, and other such celebrity look-alikes.

Best in Town

CHECKING IN

Honolulu hotels vary in personality, so check carefully before picking one. Remember, it's not just a place to sleep; it also will serve as your tropical headquarters during your visit. Expect to pay $250 or more per night for a double room at those places we've listed as very expensive; $160 to $250 at those rated expensive; between $70 and $160 at those categorized as moderate; and less than $70 at places listed as inexpensive. For B&B accommodations, contact *Bed & Breakfast Hawaii* (Box 449, Kapaa, HI 96746; phone: 822-7771; 800-733-1632), *Pacific Hawaii Bed & Breakfast* (19 Kai Nani Rd., Kailua, HI 96734; phone: 262-6026; 800-999-6026), *Bed and Breakfast Honolulu Statewide* (3242 Kaohinani Dr., Honolulu, HI 96817; phone: 595-7533), or *Hawaii's Best Bed and Breakfast* (Box 563, Kamuela, HI 96743; phone: 885-4550; 800-262-9912). Unless noted otherwise, all hotel rooms and condominium units have air conditioning, private baths, TV sets, and telephones. Many have private lanais. Most hotels and condominiums feature on-site pool facilities. All phone numbers are in the 808 area code unless otherwise indicated.

Below is our favorite Honolulu haven, followed by our recommendations of cost and quality choices of hotels and condominiums, listed by price category.

A HEAVENLY HOTEL

Halekulani Many generations of Waikiki visitors who have noted the truth in this venerable hostelry's name, which means "house befitting heaven," return yearly to this oasis of tranquillity and refinement in the heart of Waikiki, adjacent to the beach. The design incorporates the restored two-story main building of the original hotel into a complex of multilevel structures with a total of 456 rooms surrounding tranquil courtyards and gardens. The *House Without a Key* restaurant, immortalized in one of Earl Derr Biggers's Charlie Chan novels, has been rebuilt on the same spot, and the old bungalow rooms have been replaced by large, luxurious, expansively balconied rooms facing the Pacific. All three restaurants (including the excellent *La Mer* and *Orchids;* see *Eating Out* for both) overlook the ocean and Diamond Head, and the famous century-old *kiawe* tree continues to preside. The striking tiled orchid design accenting the large oceanside pool has come to be a symbol for the hotel itself. Room service is available around the clock. Among the business conveniences are six meeting rooms, a concierge, secretarial services, A/V equipment, photocopiers, computers, and express check-out. 2199 Kalia Rd. (phone: 923-2311; 800-367-2343; fax: 926-8004).

VERY EXPENSIVE

Aston Waikiki Beachside Small and sumptuous, this place is perfect for those who appreciate lovely surroundings. Inside, European and Oriental period pieces add to the ambience, while the service is impeccable. A minor drawback is that some of the 79 guestrooms are small, albeit appealingly appointed. In-room VCRs and French toiletries are just some of the extras. Although there are no restaurants on the premises, it's merely a five-minute walk to the *Hyatt Regency Waikiki* and other resort complexes in the area. Conveniently located across from the beach. Amenities include a concierge desk and photocopiers. 2452 Kalakaua Ave. (phone: 931-2100; 800-92-ASTON; fax: 931-2129).

Hawaii Prince Attention to detail, panoramic views of the neighboring *Ala Wai Yacht Tower,* and fine fare offered at this 521-room hotel's five restaurants (including the *Prince Court;* see *Eating Out*) justify the top-of-the-scale rates. Guests are also offered complimentary shuttle service to the hotel's golf course in Ewa (about 45 minutes away), as well as to a nearby health spa, downtown, and Waikiki. It is a short walk from either Ala Moana Beach or Waikiki Beach. There is a concierge,

24-hour room service, and six meeting rooms. Also available are secretarial services, A/V equipment, photocopiers, and express checkout. 100 Holomoana St. (phone: 956-1111; 800-321-6284; fax: 946-0811).

Hilton Hawaiian Village With nearly 2,600 rooms on 22 acres, it is Hawaii's largest hotel, Waikiki's most self-contained resort, and the western terminus of Waikiki Beach. Offered here are several executive floors, which include a concierge, complimentary breakfast, cocktails, and *pupus*. It also has a shopping center, post office, and a catamaran for day and night cruises. The *Rainbow Tower*, famed for its 30-story rainbow mosaic, and the *Tapa Tower*, with 250 corner suites, have the best views, while the *Alii Tower* contains the hotel's most elegant accommodations and features a private pool and concierge services. The village has lots of great features—pools, beachfront setting, fine dining, luaus, showroom entertainment—but lacks serenity. Tropically landscaped grounds surround a stream and pool which lead to a palm-lined beach. "Aloha Friday," a weekly celebration dedicated to King Kalakaua, features crafts displays, hula dancing, and a luau-style dinner, capped off by fireworks after dark. There are 32 meeting rooms, plus secretarial services, A/V equipment, photocopiers, computers, and express checkout. 2005 Kalia Rd. (phone: 949-4321; 800-HILTONS; fax: 947-7914).

Kahala Hilton This is one of Hilton International's prime showpieces, with a property-wide renovation set for completion by the end of this year. Queen Elizabeth II spent a couple of nights here, and King Juan Carlos of Spain came for part of his honeymoon with Queen Sofia. The main structure of this lavish, 369-room hostelry is 12 stories high and overlooks a glorious (though manmade) 800-foot beach. Additional beachside bungalows and a two-story wing watch over a large lagoon in which dolphins and turtles cavort. Rooms in the main building have charming semicircular lanais decorated with bougainvillea. Guests are greeted with chilled pineapple, and an orchid is placed on each pillow in the evening. Besides ocean and pool swimming, the hotel provides kayaks and snorkeling equipment and can arrange deep-sea fishing and scuba diving; and there are several fine restaurants (see *Eating Out*). Business amenities include three meeting rooms, secretarial services, A/V equipment, photocopiers, and computers. A concierge, 24-hour room service, and express checkout are also available. 5000 Kahala Ave., Kahala (phone: 734-2211; 800-367-2525; fax: 737-2478).

EXPENSIVE

Aston Waikiki Shores Next to the *Fort DeRussy Army Museum*, this apartment hotel has an unobstructed view across the museum grounds. From each lanai there is a panorama of both ocean and mountains. Some apartments have been refurbished; others are a little worse for wear. Linen, cooking utensils, and dishes are provided. There are full kitchens and daily maid service. Cost and location combine to make this one of the best buys on the beach, especially for families. 2161 Kalia Rd. (phone: 926-4733; 800-922-7866; fax: 922-2902).

Colony Surf Located right on the beach, it is one of the most delightful places to stay in Honolulu. The 50 apartments are decorated in the plush, off-white tones often associated with seaside living. There are no lanais, but floor-to-ceiling windows offer glorious views. Kitchens are modern and fully equipped, and daily maid service and laundry facilities are available. The small, elegant lobby leads to *Michel's* restaurant (see *Eating Out*). Another 50 studios with lanais and kitchenettes are available in the adjacent *Colony East* hotel (owned and operated by the same company); they lack the flair and views of the main building. 2895 Kalakaua Ave. (phone: 923-5751; 800-252-7873; fax: 922-8433).

Diamond Head Beach This 14-story structure on the beach is one of the more attractive places in terms of price and location in Honolulu, although views are rather limited. The 56 units range from hotel rooms to one-bedroom suites. Rooms are smallish but quite comfortable. There are no shops, pools, or tour desks on site, but they are available in the nearby *New Otani* (see below). Services include a concierge desk and photocopiers. 2947 Kalakaua Ave. (phone: 922-1928; 800-367-2317; fax: 924-8980).

Hyatt Regency Waikiki The hotel's two octagonal towers are a visual landmark among the concrete blocks along Kalakaua Avenue. The Great Hall, with its outdoor tropical garden, three-story waterfall, and massive hanging sculpture, is a sightseeing spot in its own right. Each of its 1,230 rooms is handsomely furnished; the artwork that graces the walls is worthy of note. Suites feature some exceptional Japanese and European antiques. Guests in the Regency Club (on floors 37 through 40) have their own complimentary bar and a concierge. The pool deck is one of the most attractive in Honolulu, and the bars, cafés, and restaurants—including *Ciao Mein*, *Musashi* (see *Eating Out* for both), and *Harry's Bar*—are among the best in Waikiki. The service here is exemplary. Amenities include 24-hour room service, eight meeting rooms, A/V equipment, photocopiers, and express checkout. 2424 Kalakaua Ave. (phone: 923-1234; 800-233-1234; fax: 923-7839; telex: 7238278).

Ilikai Located at the western edge of Waikiki, this 800-room property has spruced up its spacious guestrooms (some with kitchenettes; many with lovely marina views) and public areas. The hotel has Waikiki's best tennis facilities, with six courts and a staff of pros available. The open area at the lobby level has pools, terraces, and fountains. The beach, Duke Kahanamoku Lagoon, and the yacht marina are just a short walk away. Among the business conveniences are 12 meeting rooms, a concierge desk, secretarial services, A/V equipment, photocopiers, and express checkout. 1777 Ala Moana Blvd. (phone: 949-3811; 800-367-8434; fax: 947-4523).

Manoa Valley Inn This may be Honolulu's most complete bed and breakfast facility; with eight bedrooms in a beautifully restored turn-of-the-century Manoa Valley home and separate cottages, it is highly recommended. Rates include an ample continental breakfast, afternoon *pupus*, and sunset cocktails. Bus connections to *Ala Moana Center*, and from there to all other parts of Oahu, are available. About 2 miles from Waikiki, at 2001 Vancouver Dr. (phone: 947-6019; 800-634-5115; fax: 946-6168).

New Otani Kaimana Beach The location is the thing at this 124-room property: on the Diamond Head side of *Kapiolani Park*, just a few minutes away from Waikiki by foot or bus. The beach is right outside, and beautiful reefs are within easy snorkeling distance. The *Hau Tree Lanai* restaurant overlooks the beach and *Miyako* serves *shabu shabu*–style cooking (see *Eating Out* for both). Oceanside rooms have stunning views. Families and women traveling alone find this a friendly, safe haven. There's a concierge desk, as well as secretarial services, two meeting rooms, A/V equipment, photocopiers, and express checkout. 2863 Kalakaua Ave. (phone: 923-1555; 800-356-8264; fax: 922-9404).

Outrigger Reef With 885 rooms, this totally updated beachfront hotel in Waikiki is popular with young couples and singles traveling in pairs; it's right on the beach, with most of the rooms facing either Diamond Head or across *Fort DeRussy Beach Park* to the ocean, although only upper floors offer unobstructed views. Other draws are the three enjoyable restaurants with pleasant settings and reasonable prices. Four meeting rooms, secretarial services, A/V equipment, photocopiers, computers, and express checkout are among the business amenities. 2169 Kalia Rd. (phone: 923-3111; 800-462-6262; fax: 924-4957).

Pacific Beach Standing on the site of the summer home of Queen Liliuokalani, this 365-room property is famous for its 280,000-gallon indoor oceanarium, which can be viewed from its bars and restaurants. Along with the pool, there are two tennis courts and a Jacuzzi. Other pluses are seven meeting rooms, a concierge, secretarial services, A/V equipment, photocopiers, computers, and express checkout. A good value. 2490 Kalakaua Ave. (phone: 922-1233; 800-367-6060; fax: 922-0129).

Royal Hawaiian "The Pink Lady," as this flamingo-colored, six-story Spanish-Moorish landmark is known, is one of the two grand old hotels in Waikiki (the *Moana* is the other). The pink color scheme runs throughout the hotel, including the 526 guestrooms. Once away from the busy lobby, which attracts spectators as well as guests, this remains the most charming hotel in Waikiki. There are five meeting rooms, secretarial services, A/V equipment, photocopiers, and express checkout. 2259 Kalakaua Ave. (phone: 923-7311; 800-325-3535; fax: 924-7098).

Sheraton Moana Surfrider This beautifully restored, 793-room Victorian hostelry has stood at the edge of the Waikiki surf since 1901. A $55-million renovation five years ago brought back the glow of its early days, with brass headboards, antique lamps, and Victorian armoires adorning many of the rooms. These touches, and in many cases a ceiling fan, help to obscure the more modern iconography of Waikiki outside. Ask for a room in the old building, as the Surfrider wing is more contemporary. Amenities include 24-hour room service, seven meeting rooms, a concierge, secretarial services, A/V equipment, photocopiers, computers, and express checkout. 2365 Kalakaua Ave. (phone: 922-3111; 800-325-3535; fax: 923-0308).

Sheraton Waikiki With 1,852 rooms, this establishment is the second-largest in Waikiki (second to the *Hilton Hawaiian Village*). Lanais on the Pacific side loom over the ocean as precipitously as a cliff. It's a splendid sensation if you don't suffer from vertigo, and the sunsets can be memorable. The lobby and rooms are pleasantly decorated in subtle tans with casual tropical touches. There is never a dearth of taxis; the hotel is a pick-up point for every major tour operator, *TheBus* stops nearby, and there is just about every kind of restaurant you could crave, except a truly first class one. Ten meeting rooms, secretarial services, A/V equipment, photocopiers, computers, and AP wire service round out the business amenities. There's also a concierge desk and express checkout. 2255 Kalakaua Ave. (phone: 922-4422; 800-325-3535; fax: 923-8785).

Waikiki Banyan One of the largest condos in Waikiki, it's a short walk to the beach, zoo, and the *Ala Wai* golf course. The living rooms are handsomely decorated and have attractive breakfast counters that separate them from the kitchen. The building features 313 spacious units, a sauna, a large recreation area with tennis courts, laundry facilities on each floor, and daily maid service. From the top floor on the Diamond Head side you can see beyond the crater to Maunalua Bay. 201 Ohua Ave. (phone: 922-0555; 800-366-7765; fax: 922-0906).

Waikiki Joy Upscale and contemporary, this small hostelry (93 rooms) has a pleasant marble entry and lounge. Avoid the lower-level studios, as they can be a bit noisy; the suites on the upper floors are quieter and larger. A complimentary continental breakfast is served in the lobby each morning, and there is a restaurant serving continental fare. There's a concierge desk, and room service is available during meal times. Secretarial services, A/V equipment, photocopiers, and express checkout are pluses. 320 Lewers St. (phone: 923-2300; 800-733-5569; fax: 924-4010).

Waikiki Lanais With its 160 attractively furnished one- and two-bedroom apartments on one of Waikiki's quieter streets, this well-maintained condominium features a mix of vacation rentals and full-time residences that adds to its appeal, as does its location near the beach and the commercial heart of Waikiki. 2452 Tusitala St. (phone: 923-0994; 800-367-7042).

MODERATE

Alana Waikiki This boutique hotel provides a comfortable Waikiki base for travelers. Both public areas and the 313 rooms are elegantly styled, with plenty of marble, stylish furnishings and artwork, including a fine collection of Picasso ceramics. In addition, guests enjoy two good restaurants, including *Harlequin's* (see *Eating Out*). Business services are also available. Located several blocks from the *Hilton Hawaiian Village* and the western end of Waikiki Beach. 1956 Ala Moana Blvd. (phone: 941-7275; 800-367-6070; fax: 949-0996).

Coconut Plaza Overlooking the Ala Wai Canal, this small hostelry three blocks from Waikiki Beach offers 80 nicely furnished guestrooms (some with mountain views), a friendly staff, and complimentary continental breakfast. Other amenities include exercise equipment and a restaurant. A particularly good value. 450 Lewers St. (phone: 923-8828; 800-882-9696; fax: 923-3473).

Island Colony Another high-rise with 740 units looking out on the Koolau Mountains and the canal, it is decorated with bleached-wood furniture, white walls, and beige carpets. It also has a restaurant, sauna, and hydro-massage facilities, as well as a Jacuzzi. Daily maid service. 445 Seaside Ave. (phone: 923-2345; 800-92-ASTON; fax: 922-0991).

Outrigger Edgewater This smallish place (185 rooms) looks more like a seaside apartment house than a hotel and exudes a quiet, calm air. For those who find the hurly-burly of large establishments either intimidating or just plain exhausting, this is the ideal spot at an ideal price. An added attraction is the *Trattoria*, a well-regarded Italian restaurant (see *Eating Out*). A concierge and express checkout are pluses. 2168 Kalia Rd. (phone: 922-6424; 800-462-6262; fax: 800-622-4852).

Outrigger Prince Kuhio Quietly set on Kuhio Avenue, just one block from the beach, it feels like a more intimate residence despite its 620 rooms on 37 floors. Rooms are nicely decorated, each with its own wet bar and marble bathroom. The lobby is a graceful and airy place where complimentary coffee is poured from a silver samovar every morning. Rooms high on the Diamond Head side have stunning views of the crater. The top three floors are part of the exclusive *Kuhio Club* (where guests can take advantage of a concierge and other special services). There's a concierge desk, as well as seven meeting rooms, secretarial services, A/V equipment, photocopiers, computers, and express checkout. 2500 Kuhio Ave. (phone: 922-0811; 800-462-6262; fax: 800-622-4852).

Outrigger Reef Lanais A small gem, with 110 rooms (some with kitchenettes) that look out over the expanse of *Fort DeRussy* and the beach. It's a stylish, well-priced alternative to the big hotels that predominate in Waikiki. One block from the beach and convenient to shops and restaurants. 225 Saratoga Ave. (phone: 923-3881; 800-462-6262; fax: 800-622-4852).

Outrigger Waikiki Village Brightly decorated with an emphasis on greens and blues, this 439-room member of the Outrigger chain is popular with young couples visiting Hawaii for the first time. The poolside area is surprisingly busy, considering that the ocean is two blocks away. Perhaps what attracts so many is its underwater viewing area. Some rooms have kitchenettes. Photocopiers are available for guests' use. 240 Lewers St. (phone: 923-3881; 800-462-6262; fax: 800-622-4852).

Royal Garden at Waikiki Elegance is the word here, with plush furnishings, frescoed ceilings, chandeliers, and marble providing a sense of European style. The 230 rooms are spacious and nicely furnished, with spectacular views of the beach. On-site facilities include the excellent *Cascada* restaurant (see *Eating Out*), two pools, and a fitness center. Guests enjoy the complimentary shuttle to various Waikiki locations. Executive level floors receive concierge service. 440 Olohana St. (phone: 943-0202; 800-367-5666; fax: 946-8777).

Royal Islander This is another stopping place where smallness is an advantage: The front desk personnel usually manage to remember guests' names. The 100 recently renovated rooms are on the small side, though not oppressively so, and each has a lanai, refrigerator, and coffee maker on request. Street noise may prove bothersome. The property is now managed by the Outrigger chain and located opposite the *Reef* hotel, which is on the beach. 2164 Kalia Rd. (phone: 922-1961; 800-462-6262; fax: 800-622-4852).

Waikikian This low-rise hotel emanates the scale and mood of a Waikiki from the 1950s. Rooms are decorated with Hawaiian motifs, ceiling fans, exposed timber ceilings, and wooden lanais, all contributing to a South Seas atmosphere. Some units also have kitchenettes. An adjacent six-story building offers more conventional accommodations. The beach, on Duke Kahanamoku Lagoon, and a particularly attractive palm-fringed poolside area with a popular outdoor café called the *Tahitian Lanai* (see *Eating Out*), are just two of the amenities. Room service is available, and there is a concierge desk as well as photocopiers. 1811 Ala Moana Blvd. (phone: 949-5331; 800-922-7866; fax: 946-2843).

INEXPENSIVE

Hawaiiana This 95-room, low-rise property, a short walk from the beach, has provided a comfortable, friendly base for a Waikiki stay since it opened in 1955. All rooms are air conditioned and have kitchenettes, daily maid service, and a complimentary washer/dryer. Guests enjoy a hula show on Wednesdays and Sundays. Continental breakfast is included. 260 Beach Walk (phone: 923-3811; 800-367-5122; fax: 926-5728).

Royal Grove An apartment hotel with personality, like the *Royal Hawaiian* it is painted pink. There are 76 very comfortable, cheerful studios as well as 11 one-bedroom units. Although the ocean, a block and a half away, is visible from some of the lanais, many people prefer to look out on the pool and tropical gardens. Most rooms have air conditioning and kitchenettes. On the grounds are a sushi bar, a Korean barbecue eatery, and a health food store. There is maid service but no room service. 151 Uluniu Ave. (phone: 923-7691; fax: 922-7508).

Waikiki Surf Truly one of the "finds" of Honolulu, this 228-room hotel in a semi-residential part of Waikiki is friendly, clean, quiet, and delightfully inexpensive. Some rooms have kitchenettes. Perhaps best of all the hotel has two companions—the 102-room *Waikiki Surf East* (422 Royal Hawaiian Ave.) and the 110-room *Waikiki Surf West* (412 Lewers St.)—all owned and run by the Outrigger group. The original *Waikiki Surf* is at 2200 Kuhio Ave. (phone for all three properties: 923-7571; 800-462-6262; fax: 800-622-4852).

EATING OUT

Honolulu now has an emerging regional cuisine that blends the best foods and spices of Asia and the Pacific with European styles and sauces. Today, many restaurants delight visitors with dishes that use local fish and tropical fruits and vegetables in imaginative ways (although finding authentic Hawaiian fare in Honolulu takes some doing). With Hawaii's proximity to Asia, restaurants serving authentic Pacific Rim specialties abound, as do traditional continental restaurants. Expect to pay $100 or more for dinner for two at those places we've described as very expensive; between $60 and $100 at those listed as expensive; between $35 and $60 at moderate places; and under $35 at those rated as inexpensive. Prices don't include drinks, wine, tax, or tip. Unless otherwise indicated, all restaurants are open for lunch and dinner. All telephone numbers are in the 808 area code unless otherwise indicated.

VERY EXPENSIVE

Café Sistina A quality menu is the major attraction at this high-energy establishment, but a re-creation of a section of the Sistine Chapel above the bar adds to the appeal of the contemporary decor. Plentiful portions of hearty northern Italian fare are served, with numerous antipasti and pasta dishes to tempt and surprise the palate. Open daily. Reservations advised. Major credit cards accepted. 1314 S. King St. (phone: 526-0071).

Hajibaba's A bit out of the way in tony, residential Kahala (10 minutes by car from Waikiki), this Moroccan restaurant offers oversize portions of delicious eat-more-than-you-should specialties, such as lamb couscous and *pastilla* lemon chicken. Seating is on cushions, decor appropriately Moroccan (the owners are the real thing, so this isn't simply a "theme" dining experience), and most evenings there are two shows that feature the talents of belly dancers accompanied by Moroccan music. Open daily for dinner. Reservations necessary. Major credit cards accepted. 4614 Kilauea Ave., Kahala (phone: 735-5522).

John Dominis Spectacularly located on a promontory overlooking the Kewalo Basin and the Pacific, this dramatic eatery has floor-to-ceiling windows to showcase the extraordinary views. At a central island inside the dining room, a chef shucks oysters, steams clams, and makes broth. This is the ideal place to sample island seafood: *Ono* (wahoo), *onaga* (red snapper), and *opakapaka* (white snapper) are all available in season. The cioppino (fish stew) and fresh fish cooked in tomatoes, herbs, and spices are unbeatable. Open daily for dinner. Reservations necessary. Major credit cards accepted. 43 Ahui St. (phone: 523-0955).

La Mer The distinctive menu suits one of Hawaii's most refined restaurants. Try the grilled filet with steamed asparagus and orange sauce or the roast duck with cherries marmalade and port wine sauce. The service is excellent and the decor an appealing blend of Oriental styles. Open daily for dinner. Reservations necessary. Major credit cards accepted. At the *Halekulani Hotel,* 2199 Kalia Rd. (phone: 923-2311).

Maile The *maile* leaf, often seen dipped in gold and worn as jewelry, is to Hawaii what the laurel was to Rome, a symbol of victory and good fortune. Here, the name is fitting for one of Honolulu's most charming restaurants. Guests descend through a minor jungle of anthuriums, yellow heliconia, and orchids into this dining room beneath the lobby of the *Kahala Hilton,* where kimono-clad waitresses provide expert, unobtrusive service. Among the items on the award-winning menu are native specialties that receive opulent treatment, including roast duckling Waialae topped with lychee nuts, bananas, oranges, and spiced peaches. Live dance music begins at 9 PM. Open daily for dinner; brunch is served Sundays on the *Maile Terrace.* Reservations necessary. Major credit cards accepted. In the *Kahala Hilton,* 5000 Kahala Ave. (phone: 734-2211).

Michel's At most beachfront restaurants in Honolulu, the cooking takes a back seat to the view. Not here. The dining room is elegant and subdued. Although there are occasionally deft local touches, such as prosciutto served with papaya, the dishes tend to be classic. Even the *opakapaka* is served with champagne sauce and grapes. Open daily. Reservations necessary. Major credit cards accepted. In the *Colony Surf Hotel*, 2895 Kalakaua Ave. (phone: 923-6552).

Prince Court Two indisputable facts about this dining establishment are its simple, yet elegant, decor and its polite, unobtrusive staff. A third is the superb menu, whose specialties range from *kiawe* (mesquite) grilled capon to pan sautéed tenderloin of veal with porcini mushrooms to blackened blue *ahi* (tuna) to Hawaiian bouillabaisse. Open daily for breakfast, lunch, and dinner; the Sunday brunch is a knockout. Reservations advised. Major credit cards accepted. In the *Hawaii Prince Hotel*, 100 Holomoana St. (phone: 956-1111).

Roy's Master chef Roy Yamaguchi has created an eclectic Eurasian menu that has made this one of Honolulu's most popular eateries. The lively ambience, with the kitchen on display, the casually elegant dining room, the prompt service, and specialties such as Mongolian loin of Niihau lamb with island vinaigrette and cabernet sauce, and smoked Peking-style duck with candied pecans and a *lilikoi* (passion-fruit) ginger sauce, are first-rate reasons to come here. Open daily for dinner; Sunday brunch. Reservations necessary. Major credit cards accepted. 6600 Kalanianaole Hwy., Hawaii-Kai (phone: 396-7697).

The Secret One of the top dining rooms in Honolulu, it has consistently won prizes for its cooking. Guests dine in a setting of high-backed rattan chairs with red velvet cushions, background piano, a carp pool, and a fountain. Among the house specialties are medallions of veal with essence of truffle, and lamp chops with *ohelo* sauce. For dessert there are Polynesian fruits with kirsch, followed by Irish coffee. Oenophiles can select a rare vintage or two from the vast 6,000-bottle wine room. Open daily for dinner. Reservations advised. Major credit cards accepted. In the *Hawaiian Regent Hotel*, 2552 Kalakaua Ave. (phone: 922-6611).

EXPENSIVE

Andrew's The steamed clams in herbs and spices and the veal dishes are particularly noteworthy at one of Honolulu's less touted Italian restaurants. A good choice for a relaxed evening in pleasant surroundings. Open daily for dinner. Reservations advised. Major credit cards accepted. *Ward Center*, 1200 Ala Moana Blvd. (phone: 523-8677).

Bali by the Sea Contemporary elegance, enhanced by a mix of cool whites and Mediterranean pastels, sets the scene for seaside dining. The food is excellent, with appetizers like *coquille* of shrimp and scallops with ginger sauce, enticing entrées such as Kaiwi Channel *opakapaka* with fresh basil, and an irresistible dessert tray. Open daily for dinner. Reservations advised. Major credit cards accepted. Valet parking is available. *Hilton Hawaiian Village Rainbow Tower*, 2005 Kalia Rd. (phone: 949-4321).

Bon Appetit Perhaps Honolulu's best French dining spot, it has the look of an elegant bistro in the French provinces. In addition, it features Hawaii's only tapas bar. The menu is imaginative and includes an unusual scallop mousse, bouillabaisse, snails baked in wild mushroom and garlic sauce, and fine French country specialties. The wine list is extensive. The three- and four-course dinners are especially well priced. Closed Sundays. Reservations advised. Major credit cards accepted. In the *Discovery Bay* complex at 1778 Ala Moana Blvd. (phone: 942-3837).

Cascada Set facing a garden and a waterfall that provide a calming ambience, the innovative menu features a mix of continental and "Pacific Rim" specialties, including poached *opakapaka* and oysters, Marseilles bouillabaisse, and papillote of *onaga*. Service is excellent and attentive without being obtrusive; tables set with linen, china, and crystal add to the sense of elegance and quality. Open daily for breakfast, lunch, and dinner. Reservations necessary. Major credit cards accepted. At the *Royal Garden at Waikiki,* 400 Olohana St. (phone: 943-0202).

Ciao Mein This pleasantly casual restaurant offers an unlikely mix of Italian and Chinese cuisines. The masterful results from either menu are superb. Appetizers include savory sesame asparagus and black mushrooms in oyster sauce, and *antipasto misto* (buffalo mozzarella, copa ham, fried spring rolls, kalamata olives, roasted onions, and sun-dried tomato croutons). Entrées include roast duck served with carrots and cucumber, broiled prawns with Italian tomato butter sauce, salmon baked in parchment in a sea salt crust, and cake noodles topped with lobster and chicken. Open daily for dinner. Buffet brunch on Sundays. Reservations advised. Major credit cards accepted. *Hyatt Regency Waikiki,* 2424 Kalakaua Ave. (phone: 923-1234).

Coasters Nestled in a harborside setting at the back of the *Hawaii Maritime Center,* this place serves excellent fare, with appetizers such as a seafood sampler and stuffed mushrooms, plus a full range of seafood, veal, and steak entrées. Open daily for dinner; no lunch on Sundays. Major credit cards accepted. Reservations advised. At Pier 7 (phone: 524-2233).

Golden Dragon This is possibly Hawaii's most elegant Chinese restaurant, and the food happily lives up to the surroundings. One specialty, Imperial Beggar's chicken, is wrapped in lotus leaves with spices, then cooked for six hours inside a sealed clay pot to retain natural juices and flavor. Another specialty is the Peking roast duck, and be sure to leave room for the celestial desserts. Thanks to the exquisite decorative flourishes, dining indoors is as appealing as alfresco. Valet parking is available. Open daily for dinner. Reservations advised. Major credit cards accepted. *Hilton Hawaiian Village Rainbow Tower,* 2005 Kalia Rd. (phone: 949-4321).

Harlequin's Chef Kelly Degala has created a "Pacific Rim" menu with specialties including herb-crusted *opakapaka* with grilled Kahuku prawn-avocado sushi, and roast tenderloin of pork with celery root purée. The setting is intimate and quiet, the decor enhanced by Picasso's harlequin art, and the service attentive and friendly. Open daily for dinner. Reservations suggested. Major credit cards accepted. At the *Alana Waikiki Hotel,* 1956 Ala Moana Blvd. (phone: 941-7275).

Hau Tree Lanai One of the best alfresco locales in Waikiki, this restaurant takes its name from the ancient tree beneath which it offers beachside patio seating. Soft-shell crabs, New York strip steaks, and Cajun sashimi are some of the dinner offerings. Open daily for breakfast, lunch, and dinner. Reservations advised. Major credit cards accepted. In the *New Otani Kaimana Beach Hotel,* 2863 Kalakaua Ave. (phone: 923-1555).

Hy's Steak House Entering this place is like walking into a magnificent Victorian private library, full of velvet chairs and etched glass. But the difference is the gleaming brass broiler inside a glassed-in gazebo, where steaks and chops are prepared with loving care. Although chicken and seafood are available, the main attraction is steak, which is superb. Open daily for dinner. Reservations advised. Major credit cards accepted. 2440 Kuhio Ave. (phone: 922-5555).

Matteo's Low lighting, pleasant decor, and high-backed banquettes all combine to make this a place for quiet dining. The service is good, as is the food. The calamari, chicken, and veal dishes are highly recommended. Open daily for dinner; the bar is open until 1:30 AM. Reservations advised. Major credit cards accepted. In the *Marine Surf Hotel,* 364 Seaside Ave. (phone: 922-5551).

Miyako *Shabu-shabu*–style cooking (meat, vegetables, and seafood prepared in boiling water at the table) is emphasized here. Seating is either in the main dining room with its rooftop, oceanside views, or in small tatami rooms where guests sit on mats on the floor. Two days' advance notice will procure the special *kaiseki* dinner, a set menu of seven, eight, or nine courses, all using the freshest produce and seafood available. Open daily for dinner. Reservations advised. Major credit cards accepted. *New Otani Kaimana Beach Hotel,* 2863 Kalakaua Ave. (phone: 923-1555).

Musashi This very elegant Japanese restaurant in the *Hyatt Regency Waikiki* features *teppanyaki* grill, cooked-in-broth *shabu-shabu* dishes, and cooked-in-sauce sukiyaki dishes, all prepared tableside. There's also an excellent sushi bar. The appealing decor includes rock gardens and pools. Open daily for dinner. Reservations advised. Major credit cards accepted. 2424 Kalakaua Ave. (phone: 923-1234).

Nicholas Nickolas Fine dining amid soft lights and elegance is featured at this place, plus magnificent views from its location atop the 40-floor *Ala Moana* hotel. The extensive menu focuses on both American and continental dishes, ranging from veal to lamb, with pasta, soup, salads, as well as catch-of-the-day entrées. Open daily for dinner, with live entertainment nightly. Reservations necessary. 410 Atkinson Dr. (phone: 955-4466).

Nick's Fishmarket This is one of the best fish restaurants in Honolulu. With a contemporary, casual ambience, guests enjoy live Maine lobsters in addition to other fresh fish including *opakapaka, mahimahi,* and *ulua.* The combination seafood Louis salad is enormous and beautifully prepared. Open daily for dinner. Reservations necessary. Major credit cards accepted. In the *Waikiki Gateway Hotel,* 2070 Kalakaua Ave. (phone: 955-6333).

Orchids Sliding French doors that open onto a green lawn and expansive views of Diamond Head and the sea create a perfect backdrop for fine dining which features fresh island seafood and Asian specialties. Breakfast is a highlight, as is the Sunday brunch, although lunch and dinner are also first-rate. Open daily. Reservations advised. Major credit cards accepted. *Halekulani Hotel*, 2199 Kalia Rd. (phone: 923-2311).

3660 on the Rise In residential Kaimuki, this well-acclaimed restaurant sports stylish, contemporary decor, with a nouvelle "Pacific Rim" menu to match the chic look. Specialities worth a try include *ahi katsu* (deep-fried seared tuna wrapped in spinach), linguine with Polynesian-style chicken, and *pulehu* lamb chops with tomato mint chutney. Open for lunch Tuesdays through Fridays, dinner Tuesdays through Sundays. Reservations necessary. Major credit cards accepted. 3660 Waialae Ave. (phone: 737-1177).

Touch of East The decor is eclectic, as is the menu. Subtle blends of Oriental spices combine to create such dishes as chicken salad with ginger honey sauce, and crabmeat crêpe with a delicate red and green tomato sauce. Open daily; the sushi bar is open until midnight on weekends. There's *karaoke* performed nightly. Reservations necessary. Major credit cards accepted. Restaurant Row (phone: 521-5144).

Uraku Owner-chef Yoshino Saito presents a refined Eurasian menu with numerous pasta specialties. Favorites such as *ahi* (tuna) tartare, smoked rack of lamb, and catch of the day combined with capers, black olives, tomatoes, and parsley make decisions difficult. Open for dinner. Reservations necessary. Major credit cards accepted. 1341 Kapiolani Blvd. (phone: 951-5111).

MODERATE

Café Brio The menu combines the flair of innovative dishes with the elegance of classic fare such as grilled fish with green tomatillo-mango chutney, and sautéed fish with ginger, fennel, and pears. Also try the seafood pasta. Open weekdays for lunch; Mondays through Saturdays for dinner. Reservations advised. Major credit cards accepted. 2576 Woodlawn Dr. (phone: 988-5555).

Café Che Pasta Homemade pasta is only part of a menu that includes fresh grilled fish, calamari, and other nouvelle-style dishes. Open Tuesdays through Fridays. Reservations advised. Major credit cards accepted. 1001 Bishop Sq. (phone: 524-0004).

Caffèlatte Alfresco seating and the feel of a contemporary bistro complement top-notch northern Italian cuisine. The Milanese owner-chef, Roberto Magni, provides a warm ambience and a menu to match. Don't miss the *ravioli burro e salvia* (stuffed pasta with butter and sage), which is memorably delicious, as are many of the other pasta specialities. Dinner nightly. Reservations suggested. MasterCard and Visa accepted. 330 Saratoga Rd. (phone: 924-1414).

El Charro Avitia The Mexican specialties at this restaurant are surprisingly well prepared and presented in large portions. South of the border decor makes you feel like you're in Mexico. Try the shrimp and scallop *fajitas,* or the lamb marinated in beer with mint and citrus. Open daily. Reservations advised. Major credit cards accepted. 14 Oneawa St. (phone: 263-3943).

China House The cavernous dining room of this Honolulu favorite is often full. If shark fin or bird's nest soup is your thing, try it here. Four varieties of the former and three of the latter are served. The dim sum is famous throughout the island, and is served from 9 AM to 9 PM. Open daily. Reservations advised. Major credit cards accepted. At the top of the ramp from Kapiolani Blvd. adjacent to the *Ala Moana Center* (phone: 949-6622).

Compadres Delicious Mexican food, a comfortable setting, and good prices make this a popular spot. Open daily. Reservations advised. Major credit cards accepted. *Ward Center* (phone: 523-1307).

Detlef's A tasty menu of continental and German specialties is offered at this new eatery. Chef Detlef Grelert (formerly of the *Kahala Hilton*) features pan-fried rainbow trout, Hungarian goulash, Wiener schnitzel, and scallops and prawns sautéed with dill sauce. Open for dinner only; closed Mondays. Reservations advised. Major credit cards accepted. 2700 S. King St. (phone: 949-8839).

Il Fresco High-tech design and tables set with crystal and linen fit its chic location. A varied menu features blackened *ahi* (tuna) and pasta. Open weekdays for lunch; daily for dinner. Reservations advised. Major credit cards accepted. *Ward Center* (enter on Auahi St.; phone: 523-5191).

Hala Terrace Sit in the shade at this lovely lunchtime spot and watch the Pacific across one of the most beautiful beaches on Oahu. Meals here are on the light side, so order vichyssoise or a spring salad as a starter. Elegant sandwiches are the main item on the menu, and there are daily specials such as delicious Kahuku prawns. Open daily; don't miss the delicious Sunday brunch. Reservations advised. Major credit cards accepted. *Kahala Hilton*, 5000 Kahala Ave., Kahala (phone: 734-2211).

Hard Rock Café The Honolulu branch of this trendy international chain attracts a young crowd. Food is good, crowds are standard day or night, and the eardrum-splitting noise level doesn't allow comfortable conversation. But, then, that's part of the appeal. Guitars of famous rockers are integral to the decor, as are other rock 'n' roll memorabilia, and patrons come as much to buy T-shirts and other signature souvenirs as to eat or drink. Open daily. No reservations. Major credit cards accepted. 1837 Kapiolani Blvd. (phone: 955-7383)

Horatio's The nautical decor is most appropriate in this tavern overlooking the Kewalo Boat Basin. Among the house specialties are island seafood and Nebraska beef. Freshly baked Russian rye bread accompanies each entrée. Open daily. Reservations advised Fridays and Saturdays. Major credit cards accepted. *Ward Warehouse,* 1050 Ala Moana Blvd. (phone: 521-5002).

Kirin This bustling Hong Kong–style restaurant serves traditional Cantonese and Mandarin fare, including steaming platters of shrimp, crab, and lobster. Don't miss the minced pork with sesame buns and sesame rice balls in *azuki* bean soup. Open daily. Reservations advised. Major credit cards accepted. 2518 S. Beretania St. (phone: 942-1888).

Legend Seafood Nowhere in Oahu will you find such an array of delicacies of the ancient Hunan, Szechuan, and Mandarin cuisines as in this lovely dining room. The decor is intricate and elaborate, influenced no doubt by styles in Hong Kong during the days of Queen Victoria. There are over 100 items from which to choose. Lobster with supreme sauce is outstanding. Beware—many of the dishes are indeed very hot! Also popular are the 80 dim sum dishes that highlight the lunch menu. Open daily; reservations for dinner only. Major credit cards accepted. Conveniently located in the *Chinese Cultural Plaza,* 100 S. Beretania St. (phone: 532-1868).

Mezzanine "Designer" pizza, topped with everything from goat cheese to cilantro, is the staple here. Less adventurous folks can try the rack of lamb grilled over local *kiawe* wood, as well as numerous pasta and fish dishes. There's indoor and alfresco seating, as well as nightly entertainment. Open daily; no lunch on weekends. Reservations advised. Major credit cards accepted. In the *Waikiki Terrace Hotel,* 2045 Kalakaua Ave. (phone: 955-6000).

Monterey Bay Canners The Waikiki branch of this restaurant, in the *Outrigger Waikiki* hotel, offers a limited number of alfresco tables that take full advantage of the beachfront location. The best bet on the menu is one of the catch-of-the-day specials, which are reasonably priced and delicious. Open daily. Reservations advised for dinner. Major credit cards accepted. 2335 Kalakaua Ave. (phone: 922-5761).

Murphy's Bar and Grill A pleasant eatery in the revitalized Merchant Square area and a good choice for people who are tired of exotic restaurant grub. From quesadillas to salads and pasta, the menu offers many tasty specials. Live sports events are beamed in courtesy of a satellite dish. Open for lunch, with *pupus* served until 7 PM; closed Sundays. Lunch reservations advised. 2 Merchant St. (phone: 531-0422).

Orson's Downstairs is a coffee shop called the *Chowder House,* which serves fresh salads as well as seafood; upstairs, a dining room decorated with beautifully stained wood offers more fine seafood. Open daily. Reservations advised. Major credit cards accepted. *Ward Warehouse,* 1050 Ala Moana Blvd. (phone: 521-5681).

Parc Café The food is delicious and the prices reasonable. Pasta, catch of the day, chicken, and prime ribs are the usual fare. The Sunday brunch is first-rate; the lunch and dinner buffets are impressive. Open daily for lunch and dinner. Reservations advised. Major credit cards accepted. In the *Waikiki Parc Hotel,* 2233 Helumoa Rd. (phone: 921-7272).

Phillip Paolo's Just a five-minute drive from Waikiki and set in an eclectically decorated private home, this establishment receives high praise for its fine Italian fare. Daily specials complement such standard features as *fettuccine Vigario* (pasta with mushrooms and spinach in a light basil cream sauce) and shrimp parmigiano. Open daily for dinner. Reservations necessary. Major credit cards accepted. 2312 Beretania St. (phone: 946-1163).

Salerno This is like a neighborhood restaurant in New York's Little Italy, where generous amounts of delicious food are served (order a half portion if you're not very hungry). Open daily; dinner only on weekends. Reservations advised. Major credit cards accepted. Just over the McCully Bridge from Waikiki. 1960 Kapiolani Blvd., second floor (phone: 942-5273).

Siam Inn There has been high praise for this Thai restaurant located in the heart of Waikiki, where imported spices and fresh local produce and seafood are combined to advantage. Normally fiery Thai dishes are prepared with Western tastebuds in mind. Open daily. Reservations unnecessary. Major credit cards accepted. 407 Seaside (phone: 926-8802).

Singha Thai This spot serves authentic Thai appetizers, soups, curries, seafood, and noodle and rice dishes, prepared by chef Chai Chaowasaree. Before he came to Honolulu, Chaowasaree owned an award-winning restaurant in Bangkok. Thai dancers and musicians perform Sunday, Monday, and Tuesday evenings. Open daily; no lunch on Sundays. Reservations advised. Major credit cards accepted. 1910 Ala Moana Blvd., across from the *Hilton Hawaiian Village* (phone: 941-2898).

Sunset Grill The style is California-casual; the food is cooked over *kiawe* wood to provide a distinctive flavor. Specialties include chicken, veal, lamb, and fish with rotisserie, oven, and grill preparations. Open daily; breakfast on Sundays only. Reservations advised. Major credit cards accepted. Restaurant Row (phone: 521-4409).

Trattoria The chef doesn't overload the menu with tomato paste, and many dishes are cooked *al burro*—delicately, in butter—instead of doused in olive oil. The lasagna in this charmingly decorated restaurant is well worth tasting, as are the *cotoletta di vitello alla parmigiana* (veal cutlet parmesan) and *pollo alla romana* (Roman-style chicken). The cannelloni Milanese is definitely a "don't miss." Open daily for dinner. Reservations necessary. Major credit cards accepted. *Outrigger Edgewater Hotel*, 2168 Kalia Rd. (phone: 923-8415).

Yanagi Sushi Two Tokyo-style sushi bars serve a sushi lover's abundance of specials. The atmosphere is upbeat, the decor simple but appealing, and the sushi first-rate. Open daily. Reservations necessary. Major credit cards accepted. 762 Kapiolani Blvd. (phone: 537-1525).

INEXPENSIVE

Ba-Le Sandwich Shop Started in Chinatown as a lively hole-in-the-wall eatery, this Vietnamese-run operation now has 10 branches. The menu includes Honolulu's best croissants and espresso, as well as sandwiches, fresh fruit, and some hot entrées. Open daily. No reservations. No credit cards accepted. 150 N. King St. (phone: 531-0704).

Caffè Guccini The warm welcome at this low-key café is followed by fine pasta, rich cappuccino, and tempting desserts. Guests may bring their own wine or beer, but there's also a full bar. Open daily for dinner. Reservations unnecessary. MasterCard and Visa accepted. 2139 Kuhio Ave. (phone: 922-5287).

Chiang Mai Tasty, home-cooked northern Thai food is served in this tiny flower-filled restaurant by a large family from the town of Chiang Mai. Open daily; no lunch on weekends. Reservations advised. Major credit cards accepted. 2239 S. King St. (phone: 941-1151).

Eggs 'n' Things Breakfast hounds will well appreciate this casual eatery, where an extensive breakfast menu is available daily. Portions are hearty, with eggs in all forms as well as French toast, waffles, pancakes, and crêpes. No reservations. No credit cards accepted. 1911B Kalakaua Ave. (phone: 949-0820).

King Tsin Known for its spicy Chinese fare, this eatery serves up very tasty hot and sour soup. The crackling chicken is chopstick-lickin' good, as is the Hunan pork sautéed with broccoli. Open daily. Reservations advised. Major credit cards accepted. 1110 McCully St. (phone: 946-3273).

La Mariana This little-known South Seas–style waterfront hangout is too salty to be a yacht club, even though many of those who eat here are sailors anchored in Keehi Lagoon. All the seafood is just-caught fresh; try the fish and chips made with local mahimahi. Open daily. No reservations. Major credit cards accepted. 50 Sand Island Access Rd. (phone: 848-2800).

Ono Hawaiian Foods In Hawaiian *ono* means delicious, and for years the search for good Hawaiian food in Honolulu has ended here. Try the chicken long rice soup (slender noodles and chicken in a clear broth) or *kalua* pig (shredded roast pork). Closed Sundays. No reservations. No credit cards accepted. 726 Kapahulu Ave. (phone: 737-2275).

Sea Fortune Located in the heart of Chinatown, this very popular Cantonese-style eatery has a diverse menu that includes a variety of seafood specialties, with shrimp dishes particularly well prepared. Reservations for dinner only. Major credit cards accepted. N. King St. (phone: 536-3822).

Tahitian Lanai Dine by the sea under thatch-roofed shacks, and on a steamy Honolulu night, when ukuleles plink in the bar, there's no greater fun this side of Bora Bora. Seafood is recommended here, and Sunday brunch features eggs Benedict and Portuguese sausage. Open daily. Reservations advised. Major credit cards accepted. *The Waikikian Hotel,* 1811 Ala Moana Blvd. (phone: 946-6541).

Wo Fat At the ripe old age of 103, this is the granddaddy of Chinese restaurants in Honolulu. Hong Kong chicken, beef in oyster sauce, and *Wo Fat* noodles draw people here from all over the island for lunch and dinner. Open daily. Reservations advised. Major credit cards accepted. 115 N. Hotel St. (phone: 537-6260).

Woodlands A little Chinese eatery run by an ex–Hong Kong wigmaker, who also happens to make what nearly everyone in Honolulu agrees are the city's greatest potstickers (dumplings filled with meat or seafood). Closed Tuesdays. Reservations advised. Major credit cards accepted. 1289 S. King St. (phone: 526-2239).

Houston

At-a-Glance

SEEING THE CITY

The revolving *Spindletop* restaurant atop the *Hyatt Regency* hotel (1200 Louisiana; phone: 654-1234) turns on the Houston panorama. To the south stands downtown, to the north an industrial area and the Ship Channel, to the east industrial sprawl, and to the west Houston's residential neighborhoods. Open daily.

Stationary, but splendid for a view of the downtown skyline, is *Sam Houston Park* (1100 Bagby St.). Dominating the cityscape are the futuristic *Pennzoil Towers*, designed by Philip Johnson, and the city's other big oil headquarters, Shell and Tenneco.

SPECIAL PLACES

Several of the city's attractions are concentrated in a few areas, so you can park and walk; otherwise, you'll be driving from place to place.

MUSEUM OF NATURAL SCIENCE Each of the 13 halls pertains to a different natural science, including two subjects near and dear to the wallets of Houstonians—oil and space. Learn how oil is formed, see a model of an offshore oil rig, or manipulate a working model of a fault—turn a wheel and create an earthquake. The space exhibit includes artifacts from the *Mercury, Gemini*, and *Apollo* projects. In the *Museum of Medical Science*, you can listen to the rhythm of your heartbeat or test your lung capacity. The *Burke Baker Planetarium* features astronomy programs and daily laser shows. The museum and the planetarium are open daily. Admission charge; credit cards are accepted, but there is a $2 service fee. The *Wortham IMAX Theatre* features an 80-foot-wide, six-story-high screen. Shows start precisely on the hour with no late seating. Open daily. Admission charge. 1 Hermann Circle Dr., in *Hermann Park* (phone: 639-4600).

HOUSTON ZOOLOGICAL GARDENS One of the best zoos around, this has some rarely seen animals in unusual settings: vampire bats, flying squirrels, and bush babies in a red-light district where time is reversed and you can see the bats feeding on blood at 2:30 in the afternoon. The *Tropical Bird House* has more than 200 exotic birds in a rain forest. But our favorite is the *Gorilla House,* where the royal couple of the jungle swing in primordial splendor complete with waterfalls, vines, moats, and skylighting. There's also a children's zoo where kids can make contact with creatures from four regions of the world. Open daily; children's zoo is closed Mondays. Admission charge except on city holidays. 1513 N. MacGregor in *Hermann Park* (phone: 525-3300).

CHILDREN'S MUSEUM This Robert Venturi–designed museum for kids four months to 14 years old is a hands-on experience and learning center. Children give impromptu performances in a closed-circuit TV station, complete with costumes and sets; go under the hood of a car to learn

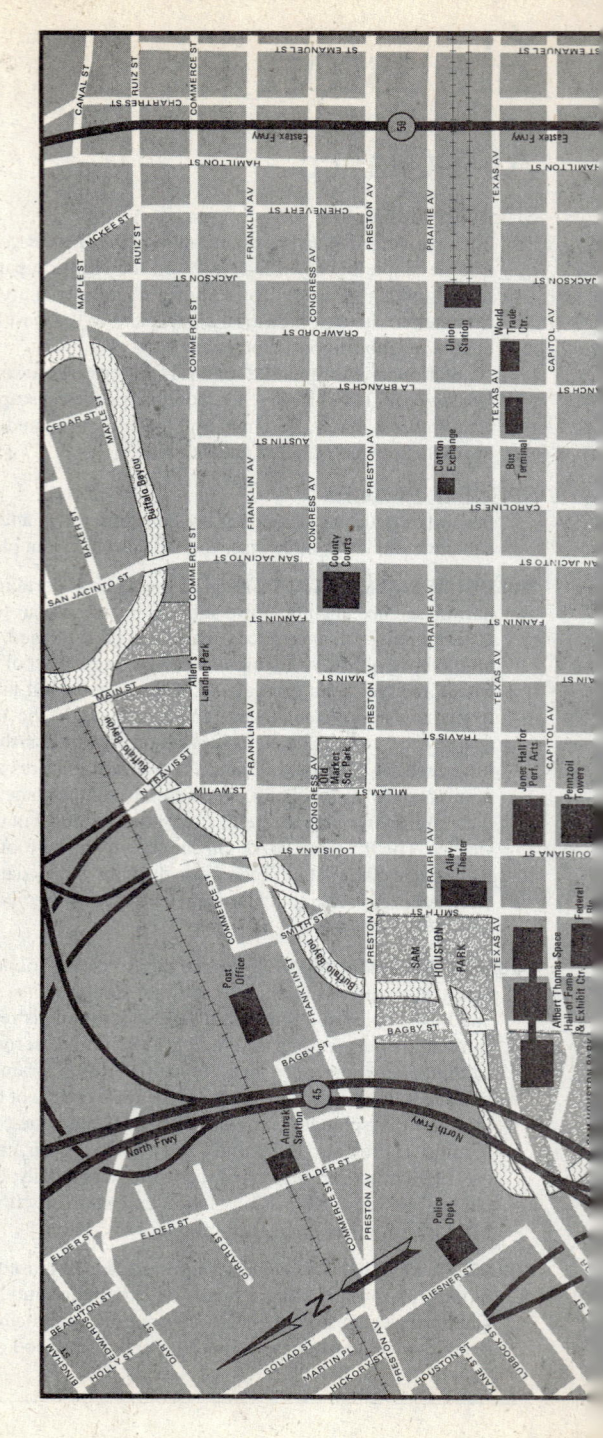

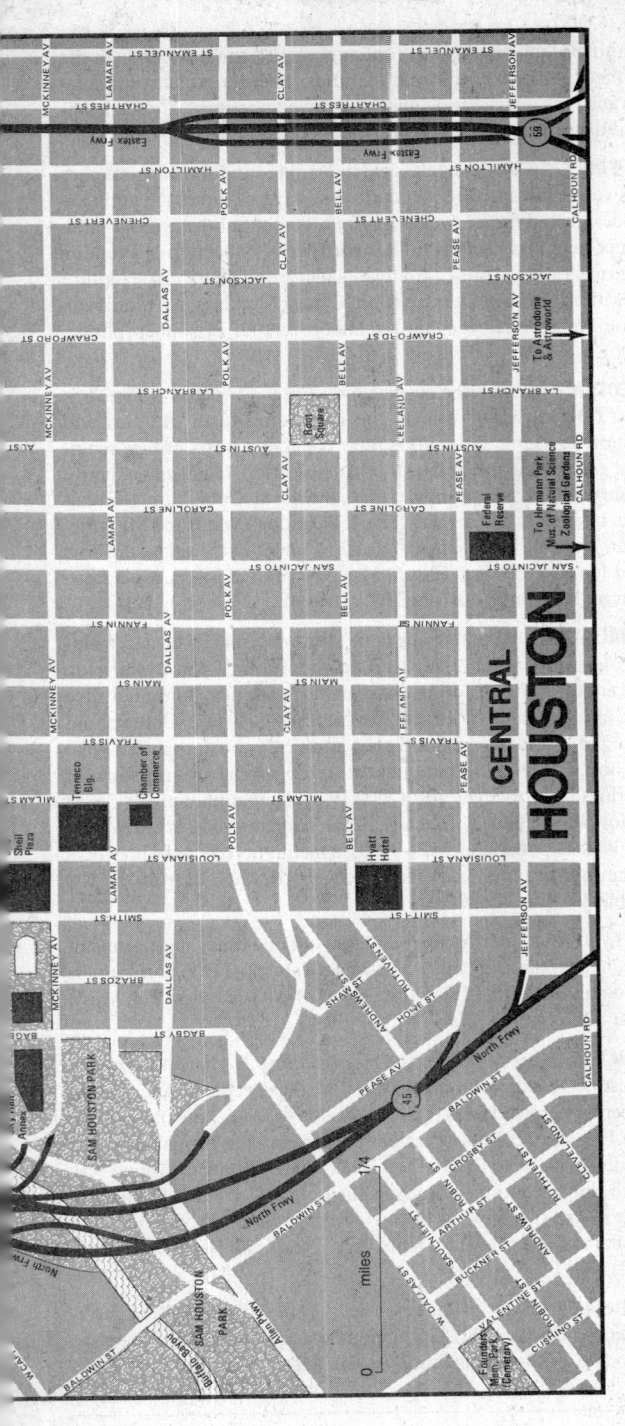

about auto mechanics; play in a contemporary Spanish dwelling; or dig for artifacts in an Orcoquisac Indian hut. There are environmental exhibits and outside play areas, including a wading stream. Closed Mondays. Admission charge. 1500 Binz (phone: 522-1138).

MUSEUM OF FINE ARTS With neoclassical beginnings and finishing touches by Mies van der Rohe, this structure could house almost anything—and it does, including the *Ima Hogg Collection* of Southwestern Indian art with pottery and kachina dolls, an extensive collection of Frederic Remington's works, a pre-Columbian gallery, and a modern sculpture garden with Alexander Calder's *Crab*. Closed Mondays. No admission charge on Thursdays or for children under six. 1001 Bissonnet (phone: 639-7300).

MENIL COLLECTION Though often overshadowed by the *Museum of Fine Arts*, this first-rate museum reflects the discerning taste of John and Dominique de Menil and houses their collection of paintings, sculpture, and antiquities, amassed over a 40-year period. Included are native masks, shrunken heads, and Byzantine, medieval, Cubist, and Surrealist works by such artists as Max Ernst, Salvador Dalí, René Magritte, Dorothea Tanning, and local sculptor Jim Love. The displays are well designed for easy viewing. Closed Mondays and Tuesdays. No admission charge. 1515 Sul Ross (phone: 525-9400).

INTERNATIONAL STRIP On the main drag of Montrose, one of the city's oldest and most bohemian residential neighborhoods, you can browse through antiques shops, foreign bazaars, art galleries, boutiques, flea markets, and offbeat book shops. The art festivals held in October and April are the largest in the South. Sidewalk cafés, restaurants, a wine tasting shop, a tree house bar, and exotic nightspots are just some of the offerings. *A Moveable Feast* (2202 W. Alabama; phone: 528-3585) is great for health food sandwiches. In the neighborhood is the *Rothko Chapel* (3900 Yupon; phone: 524-9839), a meditation chapel with works by Russian-born painter Mark Rothko. The Strip extends from the 100 to 1800 block of Westheimer.

RIVER OAKS If you're wondering where all that old oil money went, some of it is here, in the palatial mansions and huge estates of Houston's super-rich, who still have it and flaunt it. River Oaks Blvd. between Westheimer and the *Country Club*.

SAM HOUSTON PARK This project of the *Harris County Heritage Society* features a restored country church, homes, and shops, depicting the lifestyle of 19th-century Houstonians. The *Kellum-Noble House*, the oldest brick house in Houston, contains pioneer equipment and furnishings, and the *Nichols-Rice–Cherry House* is a Greek Revival home furnished with American Empire antiques. Tours begin at the office (1100 Bagby St.), but you can explore on your own as well. Open daily. No admission charge, but there is a charge for tours. Allen Pkwy. and Bagby St. (phone: 655-1912).

ASTRODOME Besides serving as home for the *Astros, Oilers,* and the *University of Houston Cougars*, this $36-million domed stadium, big enough to accommodate an 18-story building or 66,000 spectators, is one of Texas's most popular attractions. Guided tours are offered. Open daily. Admission charge. 4¾ miles southwest at I-610 and 8400 Kirby Dr. (phone: 799-9544 or 799-9595).

ASTROWORLD This park is big, clean, as glossy as the Space City itself, and rife with rides and attractions (over 100 of them) for the entire family, including a replica of the famous Coney Island *Cyclone*—one of the most exciting roller coasters ever built—a stomach-churning shuttle loop coaster; a wild river-rapids ride; *Sky Screamer;* and the *Ultra Twister,* a unique coaster that dives 92 feet and rotates backward and forward 360 degrees. One of the best times to visit the park is during its Fright Nights just before *Halloween,* when the park offers spook houses and magic shows. Next door is *Waterworld,* a 15-acre aquatic recreation park. Closed September through May and weekdays during spring and fall. Admission charge. 9001 Kirby Dr., across from the *Astrodome* (phone: 799-1234).

SAN JACINTO BATTLEGROUND The 570-foot-tall *San Jacinto Monument*—the world's largest masonry structure—marks the spot where General Sam Houston and his forces defeated the Mexican Army of Santa Anna in 1836 to win Texas's independence. From atop the monument, the view includes the Gulf Coast as well as the Houston skyline. The monument lobby contains the *San Jacinto Museum of History* (phone: 479-2421) with exhibits tracing regional history from Native American civilization to statehood. The museum is open daily; no admission charge. The 460-acre state park is 21 miles east of downtown Houston on Texas Hwy. 134, off Texas Hwy. 225 in La Porte. Next to the battleground, the *Battleship Texas,* forever moored in the Ship Channel, is unique in being a veteran of two world wars. Decommissioned in 1948 and given to the state, it is now a museum (phone: 479-2411) with wartime artifacts and detailed exhibits on its history. Closed Mondays and Tuesdays. Admission charge.

PORT OF HOUSTON From an observation platform atop Wharf 9, see the turning basin area of this country's third largest port. To inspect some of the elaborate developments in industrial shipping, take an excursion along the Ship Channel aboard the MV *Sam Houston* (make reservations months in advance). No trips on Mondays or holidays. No admission charge. Gate 8, off Clinton Dr. (phone: 225-4044).

ANHEUSER-BUSCH BREWERY Nine different malt-and-barley beverages are brewed here, and the 45-minute guided tour takes visitors through the process from grains to suds. Also included is the history of the famous American company, from its beginnings in 1861 when Adolphus Busch married Lilly Anheuser in St. Louis and turned her father's weak company into the great American success story. Tours offered daily except Sundays. No admission charge. 775 Gellhorn (phone: 670-1696).

SPACE CENTER HOUSTON AT LYNDON B. JOHNSON SPACE CENTER You may never fly to the moon, but this very popular attraction will give you a taste of what it's like. The $70-million Disney-esque complex is at the *Johnson Space Center.* Visitors begin in *Space Center Plaza,* where there are exhibits, video presentations, *NASA* updates, and lectures by astronauts, scientists, and engineers. During missions, a large video screen allows viewing of live launches and landings. *Starship Gallery* starts with the film *On Human Destiny* and displays space flight artifacts, even a genuine moon rock you can touch. Visitors can walk through *Skylab* and explore a re-creation of the shuttle mid-deck and flight deck. Tram tours of the *Johnson Space Center* guide you through Mission Control and show you how astronauts train for their missions. *To Be an Astronaut,* a film detailing the selection and preparation of astronauts, is shown several times a day on a screen that is five stories tall and 80 feet wide; and *The Feel of Space* lets you attempt to land the shuttle through computer simulation, try the Manned Maneuvering Unit jet pack trainer, and wear a space helmet; you'll also learn how such everyday tasks as eating, sleeping, and showering are accomplished in space. The crowds are often formidably huge. Open daily. Admission charge. 20 miles southeast via I-45 in Clear Lake at 1601 NASA Rd. 1 (phone: 244-2105; 800-972-0369; fax: 283-7724).

> **EXTRA SPECIAL**
>
> Just 51 miles south of Houston along I-45 is Galveston Island, a leading Gulf Coast resort area. *Stewart Beach* is the principal public beach, and there's good swimming, surfing, sailing, water skiing, and deep-sea fishing (reservations taken at boats on Piers 18 and 19 of the *Galveston Yacht Basin*). Seafood restaurants, art galleries, and restored turn-of-the-century homes are in the former vacation destination of the oil magnates clustered around Strand Boulevard.

Sources and Resources

TOURIST INFORMATION

The *Greater Houston Convention and Visitors Bureau* (801 Congress St., Houston, TX 77002; phone: 227-4422) is the best source for brochures, maps, and general information; it's closed weekends. Many banks also provide free visitor information kits, as does the *Chamber of Commerce* (1100 Milam; phone: 651-1313), also closed weekends. Contact the Texas state tourism hotline (phone: 800-8888-TEX) for maps, calendars of events, health updates, and travel advisories.

LOCAL COVERAGE The *Post* and the *Chronicle,* both daily newspapers, are available at newsstands. The *Houston Press* is a respected alternative weekly. The revised edition of *Texas Monthly's Guide to Houston* by Felicia Coates and Harriet Howle (Gulf Publishing Co.; $7.95) is a comprehensive guide. *Texas Monthly,* the monthly magazine, has extensive and timely dining information.

TELEVISION STATIONS KPRC Channel 2–NBC; KUHT Channel 8–PBS; KHOU Channel 11–CBS; and KTRK Channel 13–ABC.

RADIO STATIONS AM: KILT 610 (all news/weather) and KPRC 950 (news/talk). FM: KTSU 90.9 (jazz/urban contemporary); KRTS 92.1 (classical); KLTR 93.7 (adult contemporary music); and KUHF 88.7 (National Public Radio).

TELEPHONE The area code for Houston is 713.

SALES TAX The sales tax is 8.25%.

CLIMATE In the summer, Houston is hot and humid. Winds from the Gulf of Mexico create warm summer nights, and keep the winters and the rest of the year relatively warm. But ice and (more rarely) snow sometimes shut down the city in winter.

GETTING AROUND

AIRPORT The city's main airports are *Houston Intercontinental* and *William P. Hobby Airport*. Those familiar with Houston traffic allow at least 45 minutes to reach either one from downtown (note that it is not unusual for rain, fog, or the nightly rush hour to double this time). *Airport Express* (phone: 523-8888) operates a shuttle service from *Intercontinental* to its three downtown terminals. Buses leave every half hour, and tickets may be purchased at stands outside each terminal.

BUS *Metropolitan Transit Authority of Harris County* serves downtown and the suburbs, but the system can be confusing. The fare is 85¢. Minibuses run in the downtown shopping area. For route information contact the main office (401 Louisiana; phone: 635-4000).

CAR RENTAL A car is a necessity in Houston. Mass transit is unreliable and not always accessible. Try to avoid being caught in Houston's rush hour, when traffic is impossibly snarled. All the major national rental firms serve the city.

HOT-AIR BALLOON The *Rainbow's End Balloon Port* (7826 Fairview; phone: 466-1927) sends 'em up weekend mornings at dawn when the winds are calm. You can take a ride and watch the balloonists rise to the occasion. If you don't want to get up that early, balloon rides are offered later in the day as well.

TAXI Cabs can be ordered on the phone, picked up in front of hotels and terminals, or—with some difficulty—hailed in the street. Major companies are *United Taxicab* (phone: 699-0000) and *Yellow Cab* (phone: 236-1111). Be warned, however, that taxi rates are rather high.

LOCAL SERVICES

AUDIOVISUAL EQUIPMENT *Photo & Sound Co.* (phone: 956-9566).

BUSINESS SERVICES *Abby Executive Suites* (6776 Southwest Fwy.; phone: 789-7800).

DRY CLEANER/TAILOR *One Hour Martinizing* (Chimney Rock at Westheimer; phone: 781-0057).

LIMOUSINE *Action Limousine Service* (phone: 781-5466); *Houston Executive Limousines* (phone: 928-5511).

MECHANICS *Lightsey's Auto & Diesel Repair* (7000 Synott; phone: 498-3535), for American cars; *Freeman's Auto Service* (3540 Oak Forest; phone: 681-9484), for foreign cars.

MEDICAL EMERGENCY *Ben Taub General Hospital* (1502 Taub Loop; phone: 793-2600).

MESSENGER SERVICES *Astro City Courier* (phone: 827-8233).

MONEY TRANSFERS *American Express MoneyGram* (phone: 800-926-9400 for information; 800-866-8800 for money transfers); *Western Union Financial Services* (phone: 800-325-6000 or 800-325-4176).

NATIONAL/INTERNATIONAL COURIER *DHL Worldwide Express* (phone: 443-8500); *FedEx* (phone: 800-238-5355).

PHARMACY *Eckerd* (6011 Kirby; phone: 522-3983), open 24 hours.

PHOTOCOPIES *Kinko's* (1430 San Jacinto; phone: 654-8161), pickup and delivery; coin-operated photocopiers also are available at many pharmacies and groceries.

POST OFFICE Main branch (401 Franklin St.; phone: 226-3069).

PROFESSIONAL PHOTOGRAPHER *Dan Ford Connolly* (phone: 367-7156); *Memory Makers Video* (phone: 495-5136).

SECRETARY/STENOGRAPHER *Kelly Services* (phone: 972-1151).

TELECONFERENCE FACILITIES Omni Houston (see *Checking In*, below).

TRANSLATOR *Berlitz* (phone: 529-3665); *Omni Intercommunications* (phone: 781-2188).

WESTERN UNION/TELEX Many offices are located around the city (phone: 800-325-6000 to find the location nearest you).

SPECIAL EVENTS

Check the publications noted above in *Local Coverage* for exact dates. During April and October, local and regional artists show their work in the *Westheimer Colony Art Show* (phone: 521-0133), an outdoor arts and crafts festival on Westheimer Road. Most area hotels are filled for the four-day *Offshore Technology Conference,* the world's biggest oil industry show, in late April and early May. But one of the country's major rodeo and livestock shows is held here as well, and it's the event of the year.

A ROLLICKING RODEO

Houston Livestock Show and Rodeo This event, which runs for two weeks beginning in mid-February, features a Texas-size rodeo, complete with musical concert, held in the *Astrodome;* and the world's largest livestock show, which fills up the *Astrohall* and *Astroarena* with horses, sheep, chickens, pigs, and cattle for display and for sale at auction. It isn't unusual to see a grand champion steer sell for a quarter-million dollars. For tickets and information, write to PO Box 20070, Houston, TX 77225 or call 791-9000.

MUSEUMS

In addition to those described in *Special Places,* there are two other notable Houston museums.

BAYOU BEND This museum displays an outstanding collection of Americana. Open daily. Admission charge. 1 Westcott St. (phone: 520-2600).

CONTEMPORARY ARTS MUSEUM Exhibits include a wide variety of works by regional as well as international artists. Traveling exhibitions are featured along with films and lectures. Closed Mondays. Admission charge. 5216 Montrose at Bissonnet (phone: 526-3129).

SHOPPING

The stunning, glass-domed *Galleria Center* is still the most popular local shopping spot, where anything from the best shoeshine in town (a one-chair operation in *Cole's* hair salon on the lower level) to high-priced items at *Tiffany's* and *Neiman Marcus* can be found. Those shopping for real Texan Western wear go to nearby *Stelzig's of Texas* (3123 Post Oak Blvd.; phone: 629-7779), the oldest family-owned store of its kind in Houston, and *Cavender's Boot City* (9525-B Westheimer St.; phone: 952-7102) for a large selection of cowboy boots at reasonable prices. Custom-designed footwear in exotic leathers can be had at *Wheeler Boot Co.* (4115 Willowbend; phone: 665-0224); the store's clients have included Robert Duvall and the pope. The suburban malls near such areas as Baybrook, Deer Park, Greenspoint, Memorial City, Seabrook, and Westbrook contain major chain stores including *Sears, Montgomery Ward, JC Penney,* and *Macy's.*

SPORTS AND FITNESS

Tickets to all professional games can be picked up at *Houston Ticket Company,* in the *Galleria* area at 2707 Chimney Rock (phone: 877-1555).

BASEBALL The *National League Astros* play at the *Astrodome* (I-610 and Kirby Dr.; phone: 799-9555) from April through October.

BASKETBALL The 1994 *NBA* champion *Rockets* play from November through April at the *Summit* (10 Greenway Plaza; phone: 627-2115).

BICYCLING You can rent bikes at *Memorial Park Bicycle Rentals* (5427 Blossom; phone: 864-9335). There's a good bike trail running from the Sabine Street Bridge (just east of *Allen's Landing*) along Buffalo Bayou to Shepherd, and back along the *Memorial* side of the Bayou. The *City of Houston Parks and Recreation Department* (2999 S. Wayside ; phone: 845-1000) offers a list of other bike routes.

FISHING Best for fishing is Galveston, where you can wet a line in the Gulf of Mexico off piers or from deep-sea charters that leave from Piers 18 and 19 of the *Galveston Yacht Basin.*

FITNESS CENTER The *YMCA* (1600 Louisiana; phone: 659-8501) has a pool, indoor and outdoor tracks, exercise classes, and handball and racquetball courts. Facilities are open to non-members for a fee.

FOOTBALL The *NFL Oilers* play at the *Astrodome* (I-610 and Kirby Dr.; phone: 797-1000).

GOLF The best public 18-hole course for the duffer is in *Hermann Park* (6201 Golf Course Dr.; phone: 526-0077). The most challenging municipal 18-hole course is in *Brock Park* (8201 John Ralston Rd., off Old Beaumont Hwy.; phone: 458-1350).

JOGGING Most running is done along a 3-mile loop in *Memorial Park,* 4 miles from downtown and reached on foot from Buffalo Bayou or by taking the No. 16 Memorial or the No. 17 Tanglewood bus. Other possibilities are *Hermann Park* and the well-used trails along Ellen Parkway.

RODEO In nearby Simonton, 45 minutes west of the city, the *Roundup Rodeo* (Westheimer Rd.; phone: 346-1534) offers real live rodeo followed by country-and-western dancing every Saturday night. There's also the *Houston Livestock Show and Rodeo* in February (see *Special Events*).

SWIMMING There are 42 municipal pools in Houston, open from June through *Labor Day.* The *Stude Park* pool (1031 Stude St.; phone: 861-0322) is conveniently located downtown.

TENNIS The municipally run *Memorial Tennis Center* (1500 Memorial Loop Dr.; phone: 861-3765) has 18 Laykold courts, showers, lockers, a tennis shop, and a practice court. There are free courts in most of the city parks.

THEATER

Houston has a wide variety of productions and theater companies; our favorite venue is listed below. For current offerings, check the daily and weekly publications listed under *Local Coverage* above.

CENTER STAGE

Alley Theatre This 48-year-old company produces new plays and musical theater works, unconventional productions of classic and/or neglected texts from the past, and contemporary plays using the talents of the theater's resident company of actors. The shows are presented on a large thrust-stage theater and a smaller arena theater, which are in a stunning concrete and glass structure downtown. Among the country's oldest resident professional theater companies, the *Alley* tours both nationally and internationally. 615 Texas Ave. (phone: 228-8421; 800-259-ALLE).

In addition, the *Miller Outdoor Theater* (100 Concert Dr. in *Hermann Park;* phone: 520-3290) offers free pop concerts during the summer. *Theater Under the Stars* musical extravaganzas are held at the *Miller* or the *Music Hall* (810 Bagby; ticket office is at 4235 San Felipe St.;

phone 622-8887). Area colleges and universities also produce plays and musicals. The *Houston Ballet,* one of the nation's top companies, performs year-round at the *Gus S. Wortham Theater Center* (501 Texas Ave.; phone: 237-1439 for general information; 227-2787 for tickets).

MUSIC

Jones Hall for the Performing Arts (615 Louisiana; phone: 227-2787) is the home of the nationally acclaimed *Houston Symphony Orchestra* and offers concerts and performances throughout the year by internationally renowned guest artists and companies. The *Houston Grand Opera* performs at the *Gus S. Wortham Theater Center* (501 Texas Ave.; phone: 237-1439 for general information; 546-0246 for tickets) from September through May. All give free performances at the *Miller Outdoor Theater* in *Hermann Park* in the summer. Big rock and occasional country-and-western concerts are held at the *Summit* (10 Greenway Plaza; phone: 961-9003) throughout the year.

NIGHTCLUBS AND NIGHTLIFE

Depending on what you want, you can unwind or recharge at one or more of Houston's nightspots. Current favorites are *The Rose on Richmond* (6367 Richmond; phone: 978-5913) or *Wild West* (10086 Long Point; phone: 465-7121) for progressive country music, Texas-style, and local color; *Paradox at Bell Park* (1010 Banks St. at Montrose; phone: 526-4565) for jazz and blues; *Al Marks Melody Lane Ballroom* (3027 Crossview; phone: 785-5301) for ballroom dancing; and *Yucatan Liquor Stand* (6353 Richmond Ave.; phone: 789-6055) for rock. *Laffstop* (1952-A W. Grey St.; phone: 524-2333) has a triple bill of comedians on national tour.

Best in Town

CHECKING IN

Even though hotels were overbuilt during the 1970s boom and some are having problems filling their available inventory, rates have not gone down. There are, however, several moderate to inexpensive motel chains scattered about Houston, including *Motel 6, Ramada, Best Western, La Quinta, Days Inn,* and *TraveLodge.* Expect to pay $150 or more a night for a double room at hotels we list as expensive, $90 to $150 at those rated moderate, and $60 to $90 at those in the inexpensive category. Unless otherwise noted, hotels have air conditioning, private baths, TV sets, and telephones. All hotels are in the 713 area code unless otherwise indicated.

EXPENSIVE

La Colombe d'Or This converted mansion, next to *St. Thomas University* in the heart of Houston's Montrose area, is known for its haute French restaurant of the same name (see *Eating Out*). A member of the prestigious Relais & Châteaux group, it features five antiques-filled suites with private dining rooms, and also has a penthouse for $575 a night. There is a walnut-paneled bar; public areas with original artwork on display; and an obliging concierge desk. Among the business conveniences are secretarial services, A/V equipment, photocopiers, one meeting room, and express checkout. 3410 Montrose Blvd. (phone: 524-7999; fax; 524-8923).

Omni Houston In the *Riverway* complex, it overlooks a scenic bayou area populated by swans and features an interesting sculpture garden. Amenities include two restaurants, a lounge, a health club, four tennis courts, and a garage. Twenty-four-hour room service is available. A concierge desk, meeting rooms for up to 600, secretarial services, A/V equipment, photocopiers, and express checkout all can be found here. In *Riverway* at Post Oak La. and Woodway Dr. (phone: 871-8181; 800-THE-OMNI; fax: 871-8116).

Ritz-Carlton Considered the top of the line in Houston, this establishment offers all the attention and amenities normally found in a top European hotel. There is a restaurant and grill, a bar, a lounge, a heated pool, access to a health club, and 24-hour room service. Business conveniences include meeting rooms for up to 300, a concierge desk, secretarial services, A/V equipment, photocopiers, and express checkout. 1919 Briar Oaks La. (phone: 840-7600; 800-241-3333; fax: 840-0616).

Westin Oaks and Westin Galleria Smack in the middle of the luxurious *Galleria Mall*, the ideal spot for a shopping spree, the 406-room *Oaks* (5011 Westheimer Rd.; phone: 960-8100; fax: 960-6554) is the older (but no less grand) facility of the two. Really big spenders can splurge on its Crown Suite, a penthouse with two fireplaces and a banquet table for 14—all for only $1,300 a night. Other features include a heated pool, cafés, entertainment and dancing, and access to ice skating, a running track, and indoor tennis. Also available is 24-hour room service, meeting facilities for up to 2,000, a concierge desk, secretarial services, A/V equipment, photocopiers, and express checkout. At the other end of the mall is the 500-room *Galleria* (5060 W. Alabama; phone: 960-8100; fax: 960-6553), which is every bit as fine. The toll-free reservations number for both properties is 800-228-3000.

Wyndham Warwick Located in the museum district, this Texas institution features marble floors, 17th- and 18th-century French oak and ash paneling, and a 17th-century Aubusson tapestry. There are 307 wonderfully appointed guestrooms, and a 13,000-square-foot conference facility. Additional amenities include room service until 11 PM, a concierge, limited secretarial services, A/V equipment, photocopiers, and express checkout. 5701 Main St. (phone: 526-1991; 800-822-4200; fax: 639-4545).

MODERATE

Allen Park Inn Just outside the downtown area, this picturesque, antiques-filled property is a favorite of film crews shooting in Houston—although be warned that its neighborhood is pretty rough. There's a 24-hour restaurant, a bar, and health club facilities, plus meeting rooms for up to 150, A/V equipment, secretarial services, and photocopiers. 2121 Allen Pkwy. (phone: 521-9321; 800-231-6310; fax: 521-9321).

INEXPENSIVE

Rodeway Inn-Southwest Freeway This well-sited property offers 81 modest rooms. The express checkout desk will speed you on your way. 3135 Southwest Fwy. (phone: 526-1071; 800-228-2000; fax: 526-8668).

EATING OUT

Besides fine regional cooking—chili parlors and Mexican restaurants abound—Houston offers a great variety of foods, with the total number of eateries steadily growing. Dining out here is a relative bargain—even the most expensive restaurants cost significantly less than in other similarly sized cities. Expect to spend $75 or more for dinner for two at restaurants in the expensive category, $35 to $75 at those rated moderate, and $35 or less at those listed as inexpensive. Prices do not include drinks, wine, tax, or tips. Unless otherwise noted, restaurants serve lunch and dinner. All restaurants are in the 713 area code unless otherwise indicated.

EXPENSIVE

Anthony's This popular restaurant in a superb new location offers an innovative menu selection, which typically includes grilled portobello mushrooms, risotto packed with seafood in sherry-lobster sauce, roasted red snapper, and a huge osso buco. Open daily; dinner only on weekends. Reservations advised. Major credit cards accepted. 4007 Westheimer (phone: 525-1922).

Brennan's A bit of New Orleans's Vieux Carré in Houston, this place is one of the city's most popular dining spots. Patio tables and a lovely pillared dining room are the setting for fine Louisiana-style and creole specialties. Open daily, with wonderful brunches on weekends. Reservations necessary. Major credit cards accepted. 3300 Smith (phone: 522-9711).

Café Annie Another outstanding Houston establishment, this local favorite specializes in original presentations of Southwestern-style dishes. Meat, game, and seafood are grilled over mesquite; good choices are rack of lamb with toasted sesame seeds in a thick chili sauce, chicken breast with avocado salsa and garlic cream, and black bean terrine with goat cheese and tomato and corn salsas. It's a bit noisy, and the service is somewhat disorganized, but this is a friendly, lively spot. Closed Sundays; dinner only on Saturdays. Reservations necessary. Major credit cards accepted. 1728 Post Oak Blvd. (phone: 840-1111).

Chez Georges Cozy with charming service and atmosphere, this is *the* place in Houston for fine French country dining. Menu highlights include silky salmon pâté with avocado and mustard sauce; sole and scallops *en brochette;* and profiteroles *au chocolat*. Closed Sundays and Mondays. Reservations advised. Major credit cards accepted. 11920-J Westheimer (phone: 497-1122).

La Colombe d'Or Located in the hotel of the same name, many say this place serves the best French food in Texas. Chef Fabrice Beaudoin, one of four Relais Gourmand chefs in the country, prepares at least four specialties daily, such as roasted red snapper, grilled tuna, and prime ribs, duck, or rabbit. The "Oil Barrel" lunch special is often served; its cost fluctuates with the price of oil that day. Jacket required. Open daily; dinner only on weekends. Reservations advised. Major credit cards accepted. *La Colombe d'Or Hotel,* 3410 Montrose Blvd. (phone: 524-7999).

Great Caruso Singers belt out Broadway show tunes while diners enjoy Italian and continental cooking in a European opera house setting. The food is fine, the service superb, and the show (at no extra charge) is an added treat. Dinner only; closed Mondays. Reservations necessary. Major credit cards accepted. 10001 Westheimer (phone: 780-4900).

Quilted Toque Set in a loft, this restaurant is austerely decorated with wooden saddle frames and antique farm tools; the food is trendy and nouvelle: imaginative preparations of seafood and meat with influences from California, the Southwest, Europe, Asia, and Africa. Open daily. Reservations advised. Major credit cards accepted. 3939 Montrose Blvd. (phone: 942-9233).

Ruth's Chris Steak House This is a true Texas establishment—redolent with the aroma of beef. Decorated with oil company paraphernalia and flashing the latest Dow Jones reports, it's much appreciated for its prime cuts: filet, porterhouse, and strip steaks. Open daily for dinner only. Reservations advised. Major credit cards accepted. 6213 Richmond (phone: 789-2333).

Tony's Owner Tony Vallone is on hand most of the time to oversee this stronghold of elegance in an otherwise purposely informal city. Punctilious service by waiters in black tie, understated wood-paneled decor, and fresh flowers provide the backdrop for excellent continental food. The pâtés, risotto, game, and sauces are impeccable. Jacket and tie required. Closed Sundays; dinner only on Saturdays. Reservations necessary. Major credit cards accepted. 1801 Post Oak Blvd. (phone: 622-6778).

MODERATE

Cadillac Bar This is a Houston favorite for fine Mexican food. Try the *queso flameado con chorizo* (melted white cheese with sausage) with tender tortillas for starters. Ask about house specialties, which include such exotic dishes as mesquite-smoked kid. Open daily. Reservations advised. Major credit cards accepted. 1802 Shepherd at I-10 (phone: 862-2020).

Ninfa's A must for Mexican fare, this place seems to be on every local's list, so you may have to wait. But it's worth it, particularly for the *tacos al carbón* (tortillas wrapped around barbecued pork or beef) and *chilpanzingas* (ham and cheese wrapped in pastry, fried, and topped with sour cream). There are 14 locations now, but the downtown site is still the best. Open daily. Reservations advised. Major credit cards accepted. 2704 Navigation (phone: 228-1175).

Nit Noi Extremely popular with the *Rice University* area crowds, this little jewel is representative of Houston's outstanding Asian food selection. Menu favorites are the Thai egg rolls stuffed with cream cheese and grated veggies; soft spring rolls packed with tofu, rice noodles, and cilantro; and for dessert, sticky rice with mango. Open daily; dinner only on Sundays. No reservations. Major credit cards accepted. 2462 Bolsover (phone: 524-8114).

Pappasito's Possibly the only thing more wonderful than this wildly popular cantina's charbroiled swordfish with Mexican spices is the sparkling service—or the spine-tingling margaritas. The roll-your-own *fajites* also deserve notice. Open daily. Reservations advised. Major credit cards accepted. Several locations, but the most central is 6445 Richmond at Hillcroft (phone: 784-5253).

INEXPENSIVE

Goode Company Barbecue Without any doubt, this down-home eatery is the best place in Houston to eat smoked beef, chicken, links, and ribs, along with divine but fattening fixin's and great fresh breads, particularly the jalapeño-cheese. Leave room for pecan pie, too. Open daily. No reservations. Major credit cards accepted. 5109 Kirby at US Hwy. 59 (phone: 522-2530).

Goode Company Seafood Excellent, fresh Texas seafood, most of it from just 50 miles away, dominates the menu. Among the highlights are oysters, frogs' legs, crawfish, homemade gumbo, and mesquite-grilled rainbow trout and swordfish. Open daily. No reservations. Major credit cards accepted. 2621 Westpark (phone 23-7154).

Harlow's Hollywood Café Open daily until 4 AM, this is the place to go after all the other nightspots have closed. Urban cowboys and New Wave dudes rub shoulders with the opera set everything from deli sandwiches to Mexican dishes to Greek food and pre-dawn breakfast is on the menu. Parking is hard to find, and you'll probably have to stand in line if you're not among the first to arrive, but it's worth it for people watching. No reservations. Major credit cards accepted. 3102 Hillcroft (phone: 780-9500).

Rio Ranch Robert Del Grande, the wizard of Southwestern cuisine at venerable *Café Annie's,* brings what *Texas Monthly* food critics call "Haute on the range" chow to an affordable table. Try pork loin in pumpkinseed mole; quail in a creative chili sauce; or spicy shrimp salsa. The interior is neo-Texana, with stone walls, iron-work detail, and rodeo-print linen. Open daily; breakfast from 6:30 AM as well. Reservations advised. Major credit cards accepted. 9999 Westheimer (phone: 952-5000).

Indianapolis

At-a-Glance

SEEING THE CITY

Indianapolis has some breathtaking vantage points. The highest is in *Crown Hill Cemetery* (3402 Boulevard Pl.; phone: 925-8231), at the grave of author James Whitcomb Riley. (John Dillinger and Benjamin Harrison also are buried at *Crown Hill,* a National Historic Site.) The view from *Teller's Cage,* the restaurant at the top of the *NBD Tower* (1 Indiana Sq.; phone: 266-5211), also is exceptional. Another stunning view can be taken in from the 28th floor of the *City—County Building Observatory* (200 E. Washington St. between Delaware and Alabama Sts.; phone: 327-4345).

The 13-by-13-foot model of the city at the *Indianapolis City Center* (201 S. Capitol Ave.; phone: 237-5200; 800-468-INDY), a visitor and community information center, can help you get your bearings. To find out where a museum or monument is located, press a button on a panel, and the site will light up on the model.

SPECIAL PLACES

Indianapolis is an easy place to get around. Washington Street is the north-south dividing line; Meridian Street is the east-west dividing line. Numbered streets always run east and west, and the number of the street represents the number of blocks north of Washington Street. Many of the city's great places are spread out north of Washington Street.

UNION STATION One of the state's most popular attractions is the historic *Union Station.* During the mid-1980s, the once-decrepit railroad terminal was transformed into a festival marketplace like *Faneuil Hall Marketplace* in Boston and *South Street Seaport* in New York. Across from the *Indiana Convention Center & RCA Dome,* the three-block structure features nearly 75 shops, restaurants, and nightclubs. Attached to *Union Station* is the *Holiday Inn Crowne Plaza* (see *Checking In*).

EITELJORG MUSEUM OF AMERICAN INDIANS AND WESTERN ART The $14-million adobe-style building, on the grounds of *White River State Park,* is a work of art in itself, and the collection, considered one of the finest of its kind in the country, features works by Frederic Remington, Georgia O'Keeffe, and Ernest L. Blumenschein. Closed Mondays. Admission charge. 500 W. Washington (phone: 636-9378).

INDIANA STATE MUSEUM This entertaining museum relates the natural and cultural history of the state. Open daily. No admission charge. 202 N. Alabama, at Ohio (phone: 232-1637).

SCOTTISH RITE CATHEDRAL This vast Tudor Gothic structure has a 54-bell carillon, two organs, and an interior that looks like 3-D lace turned into wood. Free tours are given on weekdays. 650 N. Meridian (phone: 262-3100).

JAMES WHITCOMB RILEY HOME Indiana's underrated poet laureate lived in this comfortable house between 1892 and 1916. The whole Lockerbie Street neighborhood has been restored to look as it might have then, and is considered one of the finest Victorian preservations in the country. Closed Mondays. Admission charge. 528 Lockerbie (phone: 631-5885).

BENJAMIN HARRISON MEMORIAL HOME This 16-room Victorian-Italianate mansion, built in 1875 for the 23rd president, has many of the original furnishings. Open daily. Admission charge. 1230 N. Delaware (phone: 631-1898).

INDIANAPOLIS MOTOR SPEEDWAY Minibuses take visitors around the 2½-mile oval where the 500-mile race is held every year on the Sunday before *Memorial Day*. You also can visit the *IMS Hall of Fame Museum,* where race cars from the early days to the present are on display. Open daily. Admission charge. 4790 W. 16th St. (phone: 241-2500).

INDIANAPOLIS MUSEUM OF ART By any standard, this is a truly remarkable museum. The *Mary F. Hulman Pavilion* houses the *Eiteljorg Collection of African Art,* and the *Krannert Pavilion* contains American, Oriental, primitive, and 18th- and 19th-century European art. The adjacent *Clowes Pavilion* is full of medieval and Renaissance art, plus some watercolors by Turner; there's also a skylit, plant-filled courtyard. In the gardens are modern sculptures, including Robert Indiana's *LOVE,* and a wonderful, geometrical fountain. The grounds originally were the riverview estate of the Lilly family, whose mansion now contains a collection of English, French, and Italian 18th-century art. The 154 beautifully landscaped acres also feature a greenhouse, botanical gardens, and a large children's playhouse that has been converted into a restaurant. Open daily. Admission charge for special exhibits. 1200 W. 38th St. (phone: 923-1331).

CHILDREN'S MUSEUM At the largest children's museum in the world, kids and adults can explore the galaxies in the planetarium, ride a turn-of-the-century carousel, spelunk in a simulated limestone cave, and see a real mummy and the largest collection of toy trains on public display. Also featured are antique fire engines, a furnished Hoosier log cabin, folk art toys from around the world, and hands-on displays exploring the natural and physical sciences. Special programs are held regularly. Closed Mondays from *Labor Day* through *Memorial Day*. Admission charge. 3000 N. Meridian (phone: 924-5431).

INDIANAPOLIS ZOO More than 2,000 animals live in simulated natural habitats at this 64-acre, world class zoo. The *Deserts Conservatory* features free-roaming lizards and birds, and whale and dolphin shows take place in one of the world's largest totally enclosed whale and dolphin pavilions. Rides on ponies, camels, and elephants are also available. Open daily. Admission charge. 1200 W. Washington St. (phone: 630-2001).

ZIONSVILLE The streets of this restored mid-19th-century village are now full of ritzy shops. It's a good spot to spend a long afternoon. 86th St. north on Zionsville Rd. Contact the *Greater Zionsville Chamber of Commerce* (phone: 873-3836) for information.

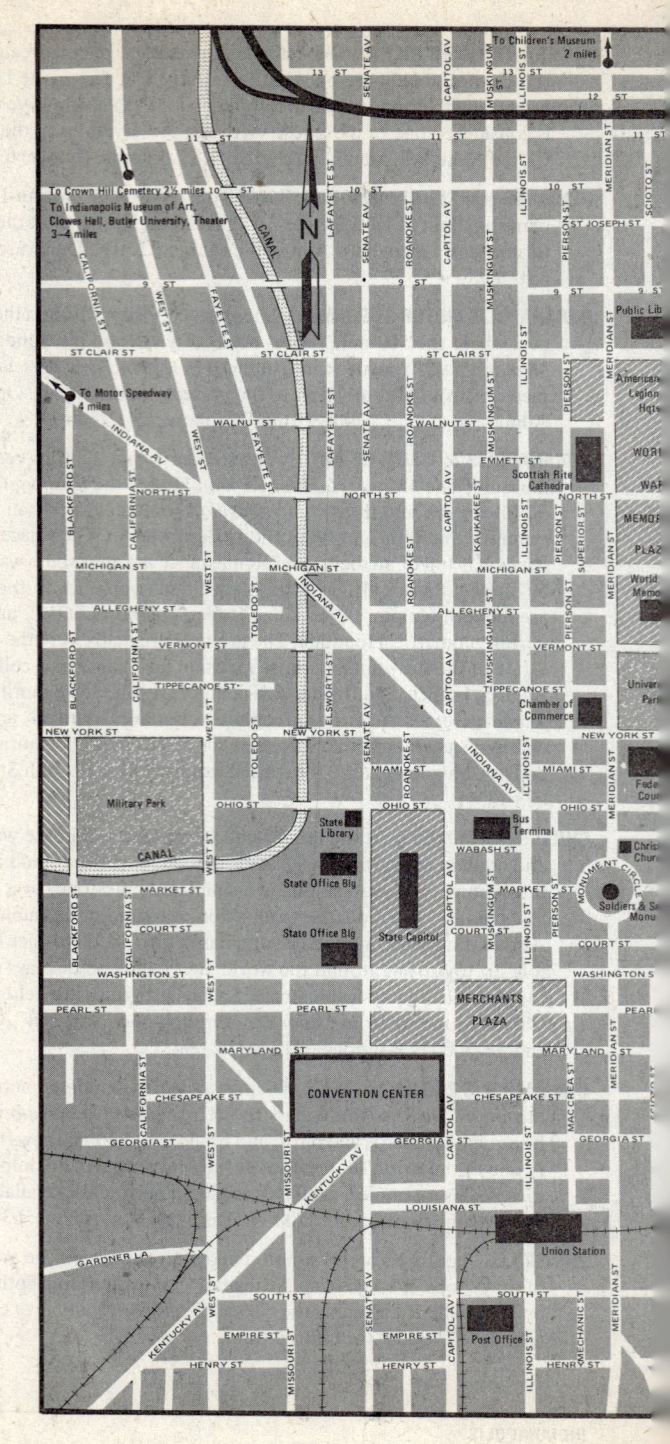

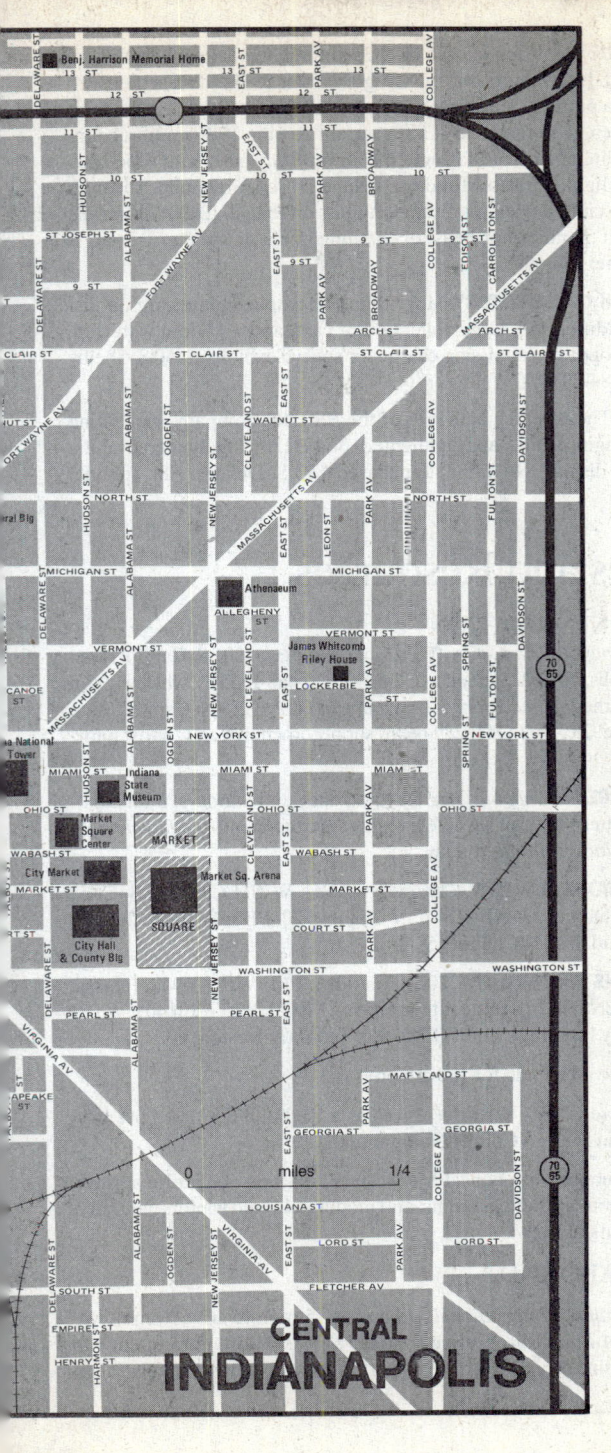

CONNER PRAIRIE Step back in time to 1836 and see the daily life of the era re-created. Interpreters portray villagers in this 25-building settlement: a doctor, a potter, a blacksmith, and an innkeeper talk as they perform their duties. Also featured is a restaurant serving 19th-century country-style dinners, an old-fashioned *Fourth of July* bash, and *Christmas* by candlelight. Closed Mondays; village closed November through March; restaurant open year-round. Admission charge. 13400 Allisonville Rd., about 30 miles northeast of Monument Circle via Rte. 37 and I-465 (phone: 776-6000).

GARFIELD PARK CONSERVATORY More than 500 tropical plants are on display in addition to a large collection of cacti and a 15-foot waterfall. Closed Mondays. Admission charge for special exhibits. 2450 S. Shelby (phone: 784-3044).

LILLY CENTER The research activities of the Eli Lilly Company—including genetic engineering—are highlighted. Some Lilly family memorabilia also is on display. No admission charge. 893 S. Delaware St. (phone: 276-3514).

Sources and Resources

TOURIST INFORMATION

The *Indianapolis City Center* (Pan American Plaza, 201 S. Capitol Ave., Indianapolis, IN 46225; phone: 237-5200; 800-468-INDY), which is open daily, and the *Indiana Tourism Development Division* (1 N. Capitol, Suite 700; phone: 232-8860; 800-289-6646) supply brochures and tourist information.

LOCAL COVERAGE *Indianapolis Star*, morning daily and Sundays; *Indianapolis News*, afternoon daily; *NUVO*, weekly entertainment; and *Indianapolis Small Business Journal*, weekly.

TELEVISION STATIONS WRTV Channel 6–ABC; WISH Channel 8–CBS; WTHR Channel 13–NBC; WFYI Channel 20–PBS; WTTV Channel 4–local; and WXIN Channel 59–Fox.

RADIO STATIONS AM: WIBC 1070 (news/talk). FM: WFBQ 94.7 (classic rock); WENS 97.1 (adult contemporary); WZPL 99.5 (Top 40); WTPI 107.9 (easy listening); and WFMS 95.5 (country-western).

TELEPHONE The area code for Indianapolis is 317.

SALES TAX There is a 5% sales tax as well as a 5% hotel tax, and a 6% beverage tax in Marion County (Indianapolis).

CLIMATE Indianapolis has typical Midwestern weather—beautiful springs, steamy summers, mild autumns, and moderately cold winters with varying amounts of snow.

GETTING AROUND

AIRPORT *Indianapolis International Airport* is a 15-minute drive from downtown. *AAA Limousine Service* (phone: 247-7301) offers frequent van and limousine service from the airport to most downtown hotels. *Metro*

Transit's No. 9 West Washington Street bus (see below) travels between the airport and downtown; for the return trip, catch the bus on Washington between Illinois and Maryland Streets.

BUS Service has improved in recent years; for schedules and fare information, call *Metro Transit* (phone: 635-3344). The fare is 75¢ off-peak, $1 rush hours; exact change is required.

CAR RENTAL You can get around by public transportation, but a car is more convenient. All the major national companies are represented.

TAXI Call *Yellow Cab* (phone: 487-7777).

LOCAL SERVICES

AUDIOVISUAL EQUIPMENT *Markey's Ideal Pictures* (2909 S. Meridian; phone: 783-1155).

BABY-SITTING Most hotels can help you arrange for sitters. Failing that, contact *Kinder Care,* with several locations in the city (phone: 578-4234, main office).

BUSINESS SERVICES *Integra Management and Business Services, Inc.* (22 E. Washington St.; phone: 634-1545); *Manpower* (251 N. Delaware; phone: 635-1001).

DRY CLEANER/TAILOR *Karstadt-Reed Cleaners* (1449 N. Illinois St.; phone: 634-5333); *Tuchman Cleaners* (Lockerbie Market Place, downtown; phone: 635-5810).

LIMOUSINE *Indy Connection Limousine* (phone: 241-7100); *VIP Limousine Service* (phone: 635-2308).

MECHANICS *Chuck's Amoco* (5061 E. Washington St.; phone: 357-5209); *Emergency Road Service* (phone: 923-3311); *Approved Auto Repair Service* (phone: 924-5687), affiliated with *AAA Motor Club*, gives locations and phone numbers of reputable shops.

MEDICAL EMERGENCY *Methodist Occupational Health Center* (1919 N. Capitol Ave.; phone: 926-4471); *Methodist Hospital* (1701 N. Senate Blvd.; phone: 929-8355).

MESSENGER SERVICES *Special Dispatch* (355 W. Merrill; phone: 638-0608); *Zipp Express* (3340 S. Shelby; phone: 782-9665).

MONEY TRANSFERS *American Express MoneyGram* (phone: 800-926-9400 for information; 800-866-8800 for money transfers); *Western Union Financial Services* (phone: 800-325-6000 or 800-325-4176).

NATIONAL/INTERNATIONAL COURIER *FedEx* (phone: 800-238-5355).

PHARMACY *Hook's* (1744 N. Illinois St.; phone: 923-1491; and a downtown branch at 175 N. Illinois St.; phone: 636-6664), open 24 hours; *Osco* (310 N. New Jersey St.; phone: 639-4539).

PHOTOCOPIES *Insty-Prints* (114 N. Delaware St.; phone: 635-2282); *Quik Print* (34 N. Delaware St.; phone: 637-8282).

POST OFFICE Central office (125 W. South St.; phone: 464-6000).

PROFESSIONAL PHOTOGRAPHER *B & L Photographers* (2105 N. Meridian St.; phone: 924-1615); *Banayote Photography* (333 E. Ohio, Suite 120; phone: 267-8962); *Cassell Productions* (2950 E. 55th Pl.; phone: 251-1201).

TELECONFERENCE FACILITIES *University Place Executive Conference Center and Hotel* (850 W. Michigan St.; phone: 269-9000).

TRANSLATOR *International Bureau of Translations, Inc.* (3254 N. Washington Blvd.; phone: 923-8670); *Prolingua* (50 E. 91st St., Suite 209; phone: 571-9197).

WESTERN UNION/TELEX Many offices are located around the city (phone: 800-325-6000 to find the location nearest you).

SPECIAL EVENTS

The *Indianapolis 500-Mile Race* is held at the *Indianapolis Motor Speedway* the Sunday before *Memorial Day;* myriad activities surrounding the *Indy 500* take place in May as part of the *500 Festival,* including the nation's largest mini-marathon (in 1994 more than 14,000 runners participated in the 13.1-mile race) and only interactive parade (the spectators take part). On the Saturday nearest the summer solstice in June, thousands crowd Monument Circle downtown for the *Mid-Summer Fest,* a music fair. During July, *Indiana Black Expo,* the nation's largest exposition of African-American culture, history, and enterprise, takes place at the *Indiana Convention Center* and throughout the city. August brings the exuberant *Indiana State Fair;* the *Indiana Avenue Jazz Festival,* featuring jazz, blues, and an array of food vendors; and *Circlefest,* the city's largest festival of food and live entertainment. The same month, Indianapolis hosts the *RCA Championships,* a men's hardcourt tournament in a modern tennis stadium, and the *Brickyard 400,* a *NASCAR* race at *Indianapolis Motor Speedway.* The *National Hot Rod Association* drag races are held at *Indianapolis Raceway Park* every Labor Day weekend. September also brings the city's largest art fair, *Penrod. Celebration of Lights* is a month of *Christmas* festivities in the heart of the city.

SPORTS AND FITNESS

BASEBALL The Indianapolis *Indians* of the *AAA American Association,* the Cincinnati *Reds'* top farm team, play in *Bush Stadium* (1501 W. 16th St.; phone: 269-3545).

BASKETBALL The *NBA* Indiana *Pacers* play in *Market Square Arena* (300 E. Market; phone: 639-2112).

BICYCLING The *Major Taylor Velodrome* (3649 Cold Spring Rd.; phone: 327-8356) has a smooth, 28-degree banked track open year-round (except when sporting events are in progress), depending on the weather. Helmet and bicycle rentals are available for a nominal fee.

FISHING There's good fishing at Eagle Creek Reservoir (7840 W. 56th St.; phone: 327-7130). Farther out of town are Geist and Morse Reservoirs and, about two hours south, the much larger Monroe Reservoir, near Bloomington.

FITNESS CENTERS The *National Institute for Fitness and Sport* (250 N. University Blvd.; phone: 274-3603) and *Bally's Scandinavian Health and Racquet Club* (8831 Commerce Crossing; phone: 844-1515) welcome exercise devotees. The pool at the *YMCA* (860 W. 10th; phone: 634-2478) is available to non-members.

FOOTBALL The Indianapolis *Colts* of the *NFL* play in the *RCA Dome* (200 S. Capitol; phone: 262-3389).

GOLF The 27-hole golf course at *Eagle Creek Park* (8802 W. 56th St.) has been rated one of the top public courses in the country. There are 11 other municipal public courses around the city. For information on all of them, call the *Parks and Recreation Department* (phone: 924-9151). The *Brickyard Crossing* course (4400 W. 16th St.; phone: 244-4694) at the *Indianapolis Motor Speedway* has 14 holes outside the track and four inside.

HOCKEY The *Ice*, a farm team of the *NHL* Chicago *Blackhawks,* plays at the *Pepsi Coliseum* (*State Fairgrounds;* phone: 239-5151 for tickets).

ICE SKATING The *Indiana/World Ice Skating Academy and Research Center* (Pan American Plaza, near *Union Station*; phone: 237-5565) offers indoor skating and skate rental to the public except during competitions. You can skate October through April at *Ellenberger City Park* (5301 E. St. Clair; phone: 353-1600) and *Perry City Park* (541 E. Stop 11 Rd.; phone: 888-0070); October through March at the *Pepsi Coliseum* (*State Fairgrounds;* phone: 927-7536); and year-round at the *Carmel Skadium* (1040 Third SW; phone: 844-8888).

JOGGING Take advantage of the walkways around Canal Walk and the *Indiana Statehouse,* at Capitol and Washington Streets, in the early morning and evening. Joggers also use *Military* and *University Parks* and the *World War Memorial* area downtown. Another possibility is the combined campus of *Indiana University–Purdue University, Indianapolis* (*IUPUI*; 1100 W. Michigan). The *Indiana University Track & Field Stadium* (901 W. New York St.; phone: 274-3518) has a nine-lane, 400-meter rubber track that's considered one of the world's fastest. It's open to the public for a fee. Still other joggers use the *IUPUI* campus to the half-mile River Promenade, a pedestrian walkway at *White River State Park*.

SWIMMING The *Indiana University Natatorium* (901 W. New York St.; phone: 274-3518), one of the premier aquatic facilities in the world, has two 50-meter pools that are open to the public for a fee.

TENNIS One of the most popular spots is the *Indianapolis Tennis Center* (815 W. New York St.; phone: 636-7719). Most high school courts are open to the public. Municipal courts can be found throughout the city. For specific locations, call 924-9151.

THEATER

The professional *Indiana Repertory Theatre* (140 W. Washington St.; phone: 635-5252), which has grown by leaps and bounds in the last few years, presents everything from musicals to Shakespeare. The *American Cabaret Theatre* offers European-style cabaret in a renovated ballroom at the historic Athenaeum Turners Building (401 E. Michigan; phone: 631-0334). Indianapolis also is home to the *Indianapolis Civic*

Theater (1200 W. 38th; phone: 923-4597), the oldest continuously active civic theater in the US, offering a varied lineup of plays and musicals. Community theater can be found at the *Christian Theological Seminary* (1000 W. 42nd; phone: 923-1516). For dinner-theater, *Beef & Boards* (9301 N. Michigan Rd. NW; phone: 872-9664) features stars of TV, Broadway, and Hollywood. *The Phoenix Theatre* (749 N. Park Ave.; phone: 635-7529) offers avant-garde and contemporary alternatives. The *Butler Ballet* performs primarily at *Clowes Hall* (4600 Sunset Ave. on *Butler University* campus; phone: 283-9231).

MUSIC

The *Circle Theatre* (45 Monument Pl.; phone: 639-4300) is where the *Indianapolis Symphony Orchestra* plays most of its concerts. The *Indianapolis Opera Company* performs at *Clowes Hall* (4600 Sunset Ave.; phone: 921-6444; 800-732-0804).

NIGHTCLUBS AND NIGHTLIFE

Like every other aspect of city life, nightlife in Indianapolis has grown. For dancing, there's *Ike & Jonesy's* (17 Jackson Pl.; phone: 632-4553). Sports fans catch the latest scores at the *Sports Bar* (231 S. Meridian St.; phone: 631-5838). Young singles patronize both locations of *TGI Friday's* (3502 E. 86th; phone: 844-3355; and in the *Courtyard by Marriott,* 501 W. Washington St.; phone: 685-8443). *Crackers Comedy Club* (8702 Keystone Crossing; phone: 846-2500) features nationally known comedians Tuesdays through Sundays; reservations necessary. Comedy is also king (or queen) at *Indianapolis Comedy Connection* (247 S. Meridian St., Second Floor; phone: 631-3536), reservations necessary; and at the *Broad Ripple Comedy Club* (6281 N. College; phone: 255-4211), reservations necessary. There are also some promising nightclubs in the rejuvenated *Union Station,* across from the *Convention Center. Ltl Ditty's* (*Union Station;* phone: 687-0068), a participatory piano bar with two baby grands, is especially popular. Blues are often featured at the *Slippery Noodle Inn* (372 S. Meridian St.; phone: 631-6968), Indiana's oldest—ca. 1850—bar. Jazz can be heard at the *Madame Walker Urban Life Center* (617 Indiana Ave.; phone: 236-2099) on Friday nights, at the *Chatterbox* (435 Massachusetts Ave.; phone: 636-0584), and at the *City Taproom* (28 S. Pennsylvania St.; phone: 637-1334). There's country-western–style line and circle dancing at *A Little Bit of Texas* (111 N. Lynnhurst; phone: 487-9065).

Best in Town

CHECKING IN

All the expected national chains are here—most of them immediately off I-465, which rings the city, or I-65, which runs diagonally through it. For a list of local bed and breakfast facilities, contact the *Indiana Tourism Development Division* (phone: 800-289-6646). Expect to pay $150 or more per night for a double room at hotels categorized as very expensive; from $90 to $150 at those listed as expensive; between $45 and $90 at those classified as moderate; and less than $45 at inexpensive places. Rates are usually higher during *Indianapolis 500* weekend and other major sporting events. Unless otherwise noted, hotels have air conditioning, private baths, TV sets, and telephones. All hotels are in the 317 area code unless otherwise indicated.

VERY EXPENSIVE

Omni Severin A blend of old and new across from *Union Station*, this renovated, historic 423-room establishment boasts a nine-foot fountain in its atrium lobby. (Don't confuse this hotel with its franchise, the *Omni North*, about 25 minutes from town.) There's a restaurant, indoor pool, and health club. Business amenities include room service until 11:30 PM, a concierge, 17 meeting rooms, secretarial services, A/V equipment, fax machines, photocopiers, and express checkout. 40 W. Jackson Pl. (phone: 634-6664; 800-THE-OMNI; fax: 687-3612).

Westin Now the largest hotel in the state (574 rooms), it is connected by a skywalk to the *Indiana Convention Center & RCA Dome*. Its restaurant, *Graffiti's*, features an open grill and buffet, and the lobby lounge has a cappuccino bar. The 39,000 square feet of meeting and banquet space can handle receptions for up to 1,500 people. Room service is available 24 hours, and there are secretarial services, A/V equipment, photocopiers, computers, a concierge desk, and express checkout. 50 S. Capitol Ave. (phone: 262-8100; 800-228-3000; fax: 231-3928).

EXPENSIVE

Canterbury A small, European-style hostelry, two blocks from *Union Station*, it offers 99 rooms and penthouse suites with skylights. Its romantic *Beaulieu* restaurant specializes in French fare. Among the hotel's business amenities are 24-hour room service, a concierge, five meeting rooms, secretarial services, A/V equipment, photocopiers, and computers. Morning limo service whisks guests to the airport. 123 S. Illinois St. (phone: 634-3000; fax: 685-2519).

Courtyard by Marriott This location is especially convenient—across from the *Eiteljorg Museum of American Indians and Western Art* and two blocks from the *Indiana Convention Center & RCA Dome*. It has 233 rooms and *TGI Friday's* restaurant. Facilities include six meeting rooms, a heated outdoor pool, and an exercise room. There is also room service until midnight, secretarial services, A/V equipment, fax machines, photocopiers, and express checkout. 501 W. Washington St. (phone: 635-4443; 800-321-2211; fax: 687-0029).

Holiday Inn Crowne Plaza at Union Station Built within the train shed of an existing 1888 railway depot, the hotel has retained a great deal of the original architecture. It also is conveniently connected to the *Union Station* marketplace. There are 276 rooms (including 26 that resemble authentic railway carriages), a restaurant, a heated pool, a Jacuzzi, a sauna, and an exercise room. Business amenities include 16 meeting rooms, a concierge area, A/V equipment, and photocopiers. 123 W. Louisiana St. (phone: 631-2221; 800-HOLIDAY; fax: 236-7474).

Radisson Plaza Connected to more than a hundred of the city's best shops and restaurants, this 550-room hotel is convenient as well as comfortable. Amenities include a pool, a Jacuzzi, and saunas as well as free access to a nearby health club. *Waterson's* restaurant is a pleasant dining spot. Room service orders are accepted until 1 AM; other conveniences include a concierge desk, 36 meeting rooms, secretarial services, A/V equipment, photocopiers, and express checkout. 8787 Keystone Crossing (phone: 846-2700; 800-333-3333; fax: 846-2700).

MODERATE

Indianapolis Motor Speedway Motel Next to the racetrack, this 108-room motel has many leisure-time pluses, including an 18-hole golf course (four holes of which are in the infield of the track) and an outdoor heated pool. The *Brickyard* restaurant overlooks the track and the golf course; the *Speedway Museum* is easily accessible. Business amenities include eight meeting rooms, photocopiers, and express checkout. 4400 W. 16th St. (phone: 241-2500; fax: 241-2133).

INEXPENSIVE

Days Inn South A pleasant swimming pool makes the typical low rates at this 104-room motel especially noteworthy. There is no restaurant. On US 31 south and I-465 (phone: 788-0811; 800-325-2525).

EATING OUT

Indianapolis has always had more than its share of steak-and-baked-potato places and very few ethnic eateries, but this situation is changing. In addition to the variety of foods available at the places listed below, the revamped *Union Station* (phone: 267-0701; 800-969-1888) features over 40 eateries with every imaginable type of fare. You'll pay $40 or more for dinner for two at restaurants listed as expensive, $25 to $40 at places categorized as moderate, and less than $25 at inexpensive places. Prices do not include drinks, wine, tax, or tips. Unless otherwise noted, all restaurants are open for lunch and dinner. All restaurants are in the 317 area code unless otherwise indicated.

EXPENSIVE

Adam's Rib and Seafood House Prime and barbecued ribs are the specialties, but fresh fish is flown in daily, and the appetizer menu always lists at least one exotic viand such as venison, alligator, or antelope. The salad bar is one of the best in town. Closed Sundays and Mondays; dinner only on Saturdays. Reservations advised. Major credit cards accepted. 40 S. Main, in Zionsville (phone: 873-3301).

Benvenuti Contemporary Italian food is served here in an elegant, yet warm and comfortable setting. The menu changes daily. Closed Sundays; dinner only on Fridays and Saturdays. Reservations advised. Major credit cards accepted. 36 S. Pennsylvania (phone: 633-4915).

Glass Chimney Some of the city's best continental fare appears on the carefully set tables of this consistently fine establishment in a charming old house. Open for dinner only; closed Sundays. Reservations necessary. Major credit cards accepted. 12901 N. Meridian (phone: 844-0921).

Illusions Magicians perform tableside at this unusual eatery that features seafood, steaks, poultry, fresh fish, and homemade pastries. Open for dinner only; closed Sundays. Reservations necessary. Major credit cards accepted. 969 Keystone Way (phone: 575-8312).

Jonathan's English country accents fill the four dining rooms of this tasteful place specializing in American cooking, including a fine New York strip steak, roast pork, and prime ribs. Darts, backgammon, and chess are played in the Old English-style pub. Open daily; Sunday brunch. Reservations advised. Major credit cards accepted. 96th and Keystone Ave. (phone: 844-1155).

New Orleans House Visit this relatively plain establishment with a very empty stomach. Unless you're ravenous, it's impossible to do justice to the extravagant all-you-can-eat seafood buffet. Allow plenty of time to consume your fill of oysters and clams on the half shell, chowders and creole dishes, crab legs and lobster. Open for dinner only; closed Sundays. Reservations necessary. Major credit cards accepted. 8845 Township Line Rd. (phone: 872-9670).

Peter's Made with local ingredients whenever possible, menu items include American and Midwestern dishes such as Indiana duckling, oven-roasted quail stuffed with corn bread, and sweet potato polenta. This elegant, contemporary restaurant also boasts an award-winning wine list. Open for dinner only; closed Sundays. Reservations advised. Major credit cards accepted. 8505 Keystone Crossing (phone: 465-1155).

St. Elmo's A local tradition since 1902 for steaks, chops, the hottest shrimp cocktails this side of Hades, and fine wines. Open daily for dinner only. Reservations advised. Major credit cards accepted. 127 S. Illinois (phone: 635-0636).

MODERATE

Broad Ripple Brew Pub As the name suggests, a specialty of this quaint pub is beer—six varieties are served from steel tanks visible through a glass wall. Scotch eggs (hard-boiled eggs that are wrapped in sausage, breaded, and deep-fried) and shepherd's pie are two popular selections. Closed Sundays. No reservations. Major credit cards accepted. 842 E. 65th St. (phone: 253-BREW).

Hollyhock Hill One of Indianapolis's several family-style spots, it serves steaks, fried chicken, and vegetables in generous portions. Closed Mondays; dinner only Tuesdays through Saturdays; lunch and dinner on Sundays. Reservations advised. Major credit cards accepted. 8110 N. College Ave. (phone: 251-2294)

Mark Pi's China Gate The Mandarin, Hunan, and Szechuan dishes on the menu are reasonably priced and prepared without MSG. Open daily. Reservations advised. Major credit cards accepted. 135 S. Illinois St. (phone: 631-6757).

Milano Inn The best place in town for Italian fare. The succulent specialties include fettuccine Alfredo, chicken marsala and *timballo* (lasagna with ground beef, sausage, three types of cheese, and homemade noodles).

Open daily; dinner only on Sundays. Reservations advised. Major credit cards accepted. 231 S. College Ave. (phone: 264-3585).

Parthenon Surrounded by the boutiques of *Broad Ripple Village,* this restaurant serves authentic Greek and Middle Eastern cooking. The *spanakopita,* a pastry filled with spinach and feta cheese, is especially good. On Friday and Saturday nights, a belly dancer entertains. Open daily. Reservations advised. Major credit cards accepted. 6319 Guilford Ave. (phone: 251-3138).

Shapiro's This is Indianapolis's best deli, and the food is served cafeteria-style. Open daily. No reservations or credit cards accepted. 808 S. Meridian (phone: 631-4041).

Snax The menu at this sleek, stylish eatery features nothing but appetizers—and not just the usual potato skins and cheese sticks. Grilled prawns wrapped in bacon, spicy calamari, and black bean cakes with salsa and sour cream are just a few of the unusual choices. Open for dinner only; closed Sundays and Mondays. No reservations. Major credit cards accepted. 2413 E. 65th St. (phone: 257-6291).

INEXPENSIVE

Essential Edibles This eclectic vegetarian restaurant is housed in the basement of a former church academy in the Lockerbie Square area. Hickory smoked tofu, pepper slaw sandwich, shepherd's pie in potato crust, and veggie burgers are among the unusual entrées. Closed Sundays and Mondays; dinner served on Fridays and Saturdays only. No reservations or credit cards accepted. 429 E. Vermont St. (phone: 266-8797).

Forbidden City The menu here is several pages long. Chinese fare is the specialty; excellently prepared Hunan, Szechuan, and Mandarin dishes are tastefully served in an elegant Oriental atmosphere. Open daily. Reservations advised. Major credit cards accepted. 2605 E. 65th St. at Keystone Ave. (phone: 257-7388).

MCL Cafeterias Ten locations in the city offer homemade fried chicken, vegetables, cinnamon rolls, and pies. Open daily. No reservations or credit cards accepted. (phone: 257-5425 for information on all locations.)

Paramount Music Palace A lively family pizza place and ice cream parlor that features "the mighty Wurlitzer theater pipe organ," which plays all kinds of music. The sing-alongs, ballroom dancing, and silent movies are also popular. Open daily. No reservations. Major credit cards accepted. I-465 at 7500 E. Washington St. (phone: 352-0144).

Kansas City, Missouri

At-a-Glance

SEEING THE CITY

One of the best views of Kansas City is from the *Observation Tower* on the 30th floor of *City Hall* (414 E. 12th St.; phone: 274-2000). It's open weekdays; there's no admission charge. Even more dramatic is the view from atop the *Liberty Memorial* (100 W. 26th St.; phone: 221-1918), the great limestone column at the south edge of the downtown area, from which you'll see massive *Union Station* (second in size only to New York's *Grand Central*), the downtown skyline, and *Crown Center*. It's closed Mondays; there's an admission charge.

SPECIAL PLACES

Kansas City's three major shopping complexes are self-contained units that can entertain visitors for a whole day.

CROWN CENTER This $300-million development is the brainchild of the late Joyce Hall, founder of Hallmark Cards. Start out from the lobby of the super-elegant *Westin Crown Center* hotel, dominated by a tropical rain forest and waterfall that winds its way down the limestone hillside on which the hotel was built. Then move on to the more than 80 stores that offer everything from fine art to frivolities. 2450 Grand (phone: 274-8444).

WESTPORT The cry of "Westward, ho!" used to echo across the field that is now the *Westport* shopping and entertainment district. Pioneers outfitted themselves here for the great journey west. Although times have changed, the tradition of seeking out supplies at *Westport* is implanted solidly in the consciousness of Kansas City residents. A lot of work has gone into restoring the old buildings, many of which date to the 1850s. Broadway at Westport Rd.

COUNTRY CLUB PLAZA A few blocks south of *Westport,* this plaza is a Midwestern *Disneyland*. Statues, fountains, and murals line the shaded walks of this spectacular Spanish- and Moorish-style shopping center with over 150 shops, restaurants, and nightclubs. West of 47th and Main Sts. (phone: 753-0100).

NELSON-ATKINS MUSEUM OF ART The comprehensive collections here cover eras ranging from the ancient Sumerian civilization (3000 BC) to modern times. Egyptian, Greek, Roman, and medieval sculpture and a reconstructed medieval cloister make this more than just a museum of Old Masters, although there are plenty of classics—Titian, Rembrandt, El Greco, Goya, van Gogh, and the Impressionists. Contemporary works include the largest number of Henry Moore works in the US and the

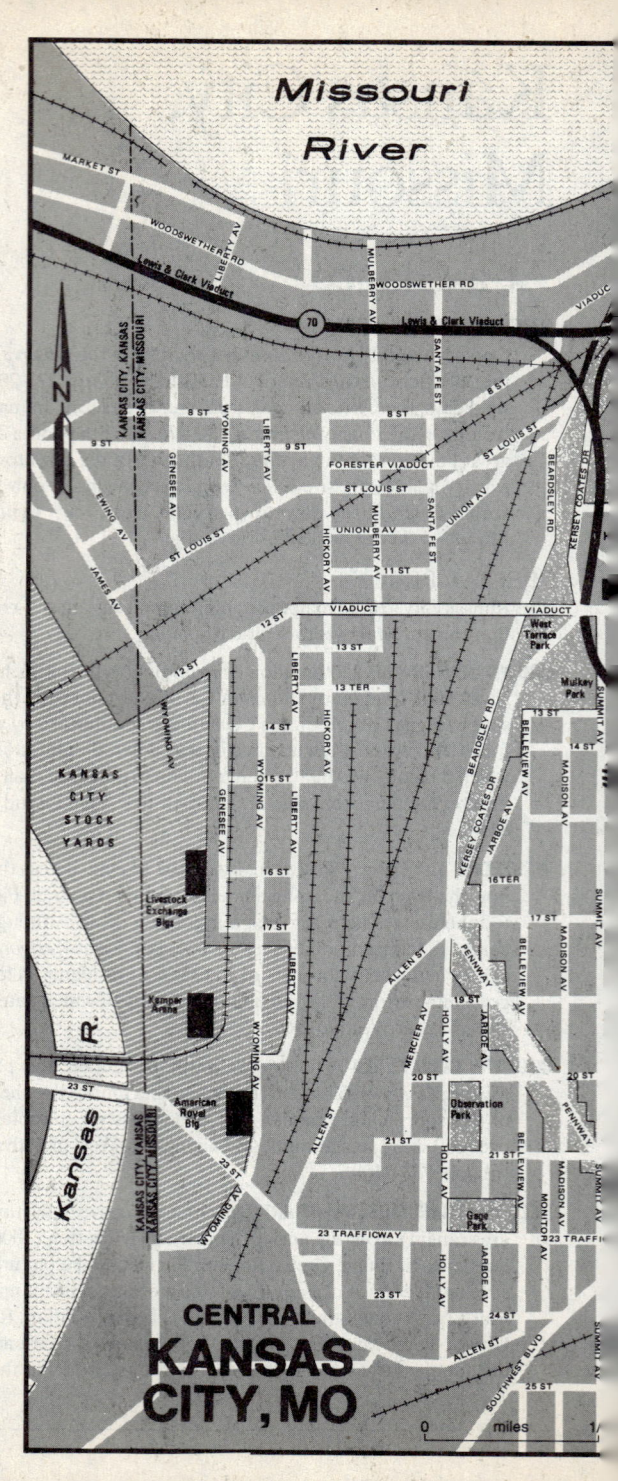

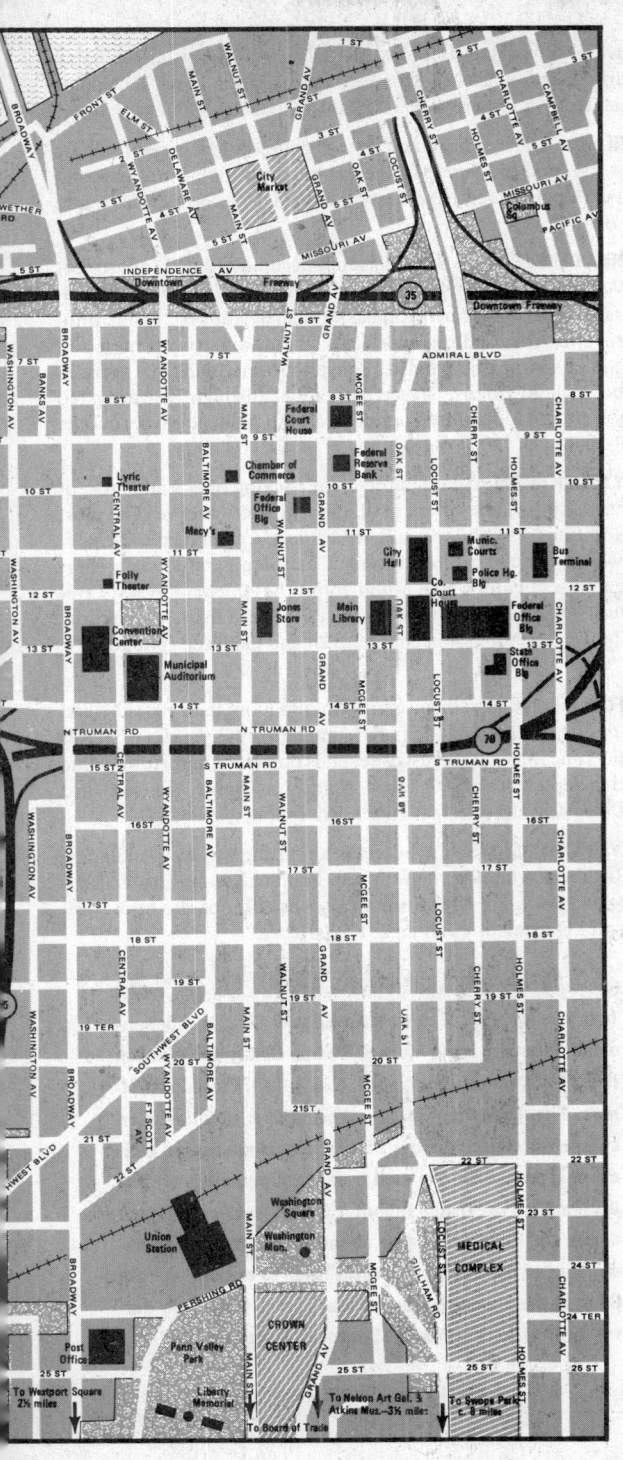

definitive Thomas Hart Benton collection. It also houses a notable Asian art collection. Closed Mondays and major holidays. No admission charge on Saturdays. 4525 Oak St. (phone: 561-4000).

SWOPE PARK This 1,772-acre park has two golf courses, a pool, picnic areas, a zoo, and the *Starlight Theater,* where popular musicals and concerts are performed in summer (see *Theater*). Swope Pkwy. and Meyer Blvd.

NCAA VISITORS' CENTER This sports museum occupies 12,000 square feet of the *National Collegiate Athletic Association (NCAA)* national headquarters in Overland Park, Kansas, a nearby suburb. It has photographs and video salutes to *NCAA* champions (both men and women) in 21 sports. There's also a souvenir shop with *NCAA* apparel, sports books, and videos. Closed November through February. No admission charge for children under five. 6201 College Blvd. (phone: 913-339-1906).

KANSAS CITY STOCKYARDS Although the great packing plants and most of the steers are long gone, there's still plenty of action here. The most recent addition is the *American Royal Visitors' Center* next to *Kemper Arena,* where you can explore Kansas City's equine and bovine heritage in a museum and watch a film about the *American Royal Livestock and Horse Show.* You may even get to see a livestock auction. Closed Mondays. Admission charge. 16th and Genesee (phone: 221-9800).

WORLDS OF FUN This 140-acre theme park contains more than 100 rides and *Oceans of Fun,* a huge aquatic park (summers only). *Worlds of Fun* is open daily June through August; weekends only from mid-April to late May and in September and October. Admission charge. On I-435, just north of the Missouri River, at Parvin Rd. (phone: 454-4545).

MISSOURI RIVER EXCURSIONS A river trip is a relaxing way to spend a few hours. Riverboat cruises leave from Kaw Point in Kansas City, Kansas, just a few blocks west of downtown. Cruises usually operate from April through mid-December. (phone: 281-5300).

EXTRA SPECIAL

Just 8 miles east of downtown Kansas City, in Independence, Missouri, is the *Harry S. Truman Library and Museum* (US 24 at Delaware St.; phone: 833-1400). Closed *Christmas, Thanksgiving,* and *New Year's Day.* No admission charge for children under 15 and school-sponsored educational groups. Up the road from the *Truman Library and Museum* is *Fort Osage* (about 15 miles east of Independence on US 24, in Sibley; phone: 795-8200), a reconstruction of the trading post established by explorer William Clark of the famous Lewis and Clark team. Open daily during daylight hours, March 15 through December 15.

Sources and Resources

TOURIST INFORMATION

The *Kansas City Convention and Visitors Bureau* has a 24-hour hotline (phone: 221-5242) for the latest information on city activities. It also provides brochures, maps, and a restaurant and hotel guide. The bureau, which is closed weekends, is in the City Center Square Building (Suite 2550, 1100 Main St., Kansas City, MO 64105; phone: 800-767-7700). There is also a visitor information center (in *River Market* at Fifth and Grand; phone: 842-4386), which is closed Sundays. Contact the Missouri state tourism hotline (800-877-1234) for maps, calendars of events, health updates, and travel advisories.

LOCAL COVERAGE *Kansas City Star*, daily; *K. C. Pitch* and *New Times*, weekly alternative newspapers.

TELEVISION STATIONS WDAF Channel 4–NBC; KCTV Channel 5–CBS; KMBC Channel 9–ABC; KCPT Channel 19–PBS; KSHB Channel 41; KSMO Channel 62; and KYFC, Channel 50.

RADIO STATIONS AM: WDAF 610 (country music); KCMO 810 (news/talk); and KMBZ 980 (news, talk, sports). FM: KCUR 89.3 (NPR, classic, jazz); KMXV 93.3 (adult contemporary); KLTH 99.7 (adult contemporary); KCFX 101.1 (classic rock, football coverage); KBEQ 104.3 (country); and KLZR 105.9 (alternative rock).

TELEPHONE The area code for Kansas City, Missouri, is 816.

SALES TAX The sales tax is 6.675%.

CLIMATE Kansas City's Midwestern climate is notorious. It's fine in the spring and fall, but the winters are rough (frequently the thermometer doesn't rise above freezing in January), and the summers are hot and humid. Rain is particularly likely in spring.

GETTING AROUND

AIRPORT *Kansas City International Airport* is usually a 30- to 40-minute drive from the city. The green *KCI Airport Express* buses run from the airport to the major downtown and *Plaza* area hotels every 30 minutes. Tickets can be purchased at Gate 63 in Terminal C (take the inter-airport red buses to this terminal). Return schedules vary; ask for a timetable at your hotel or call 243-5000.

BUS The Kansas City *Metro Bus* (phone: 221-0660) covers the downtown area, as well as the *Westport* and *Country Club Plaza* shopping and entertainment districts. The fare is 90¢.

CAR RENTAL The best way to see Kansas City is by car. Major rental firms are represented.

TAXI Call *Yellow Cab* (phone: 471-5000).

TROLLEY One of the best ways to see major sites is from the open-air trolleys that go from the *Plaza*, through *Westport* and *Crown Center* shopping centers, to downtown and back again. The trolleys (named Molly,

Dolly, Polly, and so on) stop at the special trolley signs between March and December. The chatty drivers will fill you in on sights along the way. *Kansas City Trolley Corp.* (phone: 221-3399).

LOCAL SERVICES

AUDIOVISUAL EQUIPMENT *Hoover's Audio-Visual* (phone: 221-7663); *Kansas City Audio-Visual* (phone: 931-8940).

BUSINESS SERVICES *AAA Secretarial Service* (3312 Broadway; phone: 531-4615).

DRY CLEANER/TAILOR *English Cleaners* (3747 Broadway; phone: 531-1848); *Royal Master Cleaners* (1501 Grand Ave.; phone: 842-3375).

LIMOUSINE *American Limousine Service* (phone: 471-6050); *Mid-America Limousine Service* (phone: 346-4848).

MECHANIC *Glenn Freely Auto Repair* (1922 Baltimore; phone: 421-2436).

MEDICAL EMERGENCY *St. Joseph's Health Center* (1000 Carondelet Dr.; phone: 943-2711); *St. Luke's Hospital* (4400 Wornall Rd.; phone: 932-2171).

MESSENGER SERVICES *Flexfeet Couriers* (phone: 756-3505); *Instant Delivery* (phone: 432-7979).

MONEY TRANSFERS *American Express MoneyGram* (phone: 800-926-9400 for information; 800-866-8800 for money transfers); *Western Union Financial Services* (phone: 800-325-6000 or 800-325-4176).

NATIONAL/INTERNATIONAL COURIER *Emery Worldwide* (phone: 800-443-6379); *FedEx* (phone: 661-0255).

PHARMACY *Osco* (40th and Main Sts.; phone: 561-9680), open daily 8 AM to 9 PM.

PHOTOCOPIES *Quik Print* (910 Walnut St.; phone: 421-3780); *Sir Speedy* (1101 Grand St.; phone: 421-7137), pickup and delivery.

POST OFFICE The central office is at 315 Pershing Rd. (phone: 374-9275).

PROFESSIONAL PHOTOGRAPHER *Jeff Brooks* (phone: 362-7667); *Swetnam & Associates* (phone: 421-6484); *Wilborn & Associates* (phone: 531-9000).

TELECONFERENCE FACILITIES *Ritz-Carlton* (see *Checking In*, below).

TRANSLATOR *Languages on Wing* (phone: 262-9464); *Transimplex Translators* (phone: 331-1863).

WESTERN UNION/TELEX Many offices are located around the city (phone: 800-325-6000 to find the location nearest you).

SPECIAL EVENTS

The *Renaissance Festival of Kansas City* runs for seven weekends each fall, beginning *Labor Day*. The *RenFest*, a popular re-creation of 16th-century life, features musicians, courtiers, knights, actors, acrobats, craftspeople, and lots of food and drink. It takes place on 40 wooded acres at the *Agricultural Hall of Fame* (Bonner Springs, just 20 minutes west of downtown on I-70; phone: 561-8005). The *American Royal Horse and Livestock Show* is held in November at *Kemper Arena* (1800 Genesee; phone: 221-9800).

MUSEUMS

In addition to those described in *Special Places*, Kansas City has a number of other noteworthy museums.

KANSAS CITY MUSEUM OF HISTORY AND SCIENCE In addition to a planetarium, there are several exhibits about the Native Americans who once lived in the region. Closed Mondays. Admission charge. 3218 Gladstone (phone: 483-8300), and a downtown branch at the Town Pavilion (1111 Main St.; phone: 472-9600).

LIBERTY MEMORIAL MUSEUM The country's only museum devoted to World War I features artillery pieces, uniforms, maps, posters, and a simulated trench. Closed Mondays and Tuesdays. No admission charge for children under 12. 100 West 26th St. (phone: 221-1918).

SHAWNEE METHODIST MISSION AND INDIAN MANUAL LABOR SCHOOL A school for Native American children in the 19th century, it now exhibits furniture and tools used during the period. Closed Mondays. No admission charge. Indian Mission, 53rd and Mission Rd., Fairway, KS (phone: 913-262-0867).

TOY AND MINIATURE MUSEUM OF KANSAS CITY A remarkable collection of toy trains, dolls, dollhouses, and exquisite miniatures is on display here. Closed Mondays and Tuesdays. Admission charge. 5235 Oak St. (phone: 333-2055).

SPORTS AND FITNESS

Kansas City has major league baseball and football teams.

BASEBALL The *American League Royals* take the field at *Ewing M. Kauffman Stadium* at the *Harry S. Truman Sports Complex* (I-70 at the Blue Ridge Cutoff; phone: 921-8000).

BASKETBALL The *Kangaroos* of the *University of Missouri–Kansas City* play home games in the *Municipal Auditorium* (14th and Wyandotte Sts.; phone: 276-2700).

BICYCLING Bikes can be rented in summer at *Shelter House One* in *Swope Park*, at the main entrance (Swope Pkwy. and Meyer Blvd.).

FITNESS CENTERS *Woodside Racquet Club* (2000 W. 47th Plaza; phone: 831-0034) offers pools, exercise equipment, and aerobics; *Town & Country Health Club*, on the fifth floor of the *Westin Crown Center* hotel (see *Checking In*), has a pool, steamroom, sauna, and coed whirlpool bath.

FOOTBALL The *NFL Chiefs* call *Arrowhead Stadium*, at the *Harry S. Truman Sports Complex*, home (I-70 at the Blue Ridge Cutoff; phone: 924-9400).

GOLF The best is at *River Oaks* (140 and US 71, in Grandview; phone: 966-8111).

HOCKEY The Kansas City *Blades* of the *International Hockey League* play at *Kemper Arena* (1800 Genesee; phone: 842-1063).

HORSEBACK RIDING In addition to guided trail rides, *Benjamin Ranch* (6401 E. 87th at I-435; phone: 761-5055) offers hayrides and barbecues.

JOGGING The best places to run are *Penn Valley Park,* at 25th to 33rd Sts. and Pershing Rd. near the *Westin Crown Center* hotel; *Jacob L. Loose Park* inner and outer loops, 1½ blocks south of the *Ritz-Carlton* hotel; and Ward Parkway, a large, lovely boulevard (pick it up at the *Ritz-Carlton* and run south). An excellent jogging and exercise trail is in *Mill Creek Park,* just east of the *Country Club Plaza.*

SOCCER The Kansas City *Attack,* a *National Professional Soccer League* team, plays its home games at *Kemper Arena* (1800 Genesee; phone: 474-2255).

TENNIS There are more than 200 public tennis courts in the Kansas City metro area. Most are free. *Swope Park* has good courts at the picnic area north of the *Starlight Theater.* For information, contact the parks department (871-5600).

THEATER

For the latest information on theater and musical events, call 968-4100. The city's *Theater League* (phone: 421-7500) presents touring companies of Broadway hits in the *Music Hall* (12th and Wyandotte Sts.) and produces its own shows at *Johnson County Community College.* Dramatic and musical productions are also booked into the *Municipal Auditorium* (200 W 13th St.; phone: 274-2900) and the *Folly Theatre* (12th and Central; phone: 474-4444). The *Missouri Repertory Theatre* performs both classic and contemporary drama at the *Spencer Theater* (on the *University of Missouri–Kansas City* campus; phone: 235-2700). The *Starlight Theater* (phone: 363-7827) in *Swope Park,* an under-the-stars amphitheater, features musical comedy and concerts with top-name stars from May to mid-September. The *Plaza Dinner Playhouse* (5028 Main; phone: 756-2266) offers musicals and comedies in the *Plaza* area; similar productions can be found at the *New Theater Restaurant* (92nd and Metcalf Sts., Overland Park, KS; phone: 913-649-7469). Closer to downtown is the *American Heartland Theater* (*Crown Center;* phone: 842-9999), with comedies and musicals on its main stage and the long-running mystery *Shear Madness* in a smaller theater. Fans of off-Broadway shows should check out the *Unicorn Theater* (3820 Main; phone: 531-7529). There are two fine children's theaters: *Theater for Young America* (*Mission Mall Shopping Center,* 4811 Johnson Dr., Mission; phone: 913-831-1400) and the *Coterie* (*Crown Center;* phone: 474-6552).

MUSIC

The *Kansas City Symphony* features internationally known conductors and soloists from November through May. Performances are held on Friday and Saturday nights and Sunday afternoons in the *Lyric Theater* (11th and Central; phone: 471-7344). There are two opera seasons, in April and October, at the *Lyric* (the operas are sung in English). For up-to-date data on concert happenings, call 968-4100 or check the newspaper. Another good guide to current musical offerings is the *Concert Connection* (phone: 276-2730), sponsored by the *UMKC Conservatory of Music.*

NIGHTCLUBS AND NIGHTLIFE

Kansas City's after-dark scene is now one of the liveliest in the Midwest. Because of its bistate location, however, liquor laws in Kansas City are a bit confusing. In Missouri, bars may remain open until 1 AM; clubs with cabaret licenses, until 3 AM. Bars are closed on Sundays, but hotels and restaurants may still serve liquor. The state of Kansas legalized the selling of liquor by the drink in the fall of 1986, and more counties are implementing this referendum each year. This means that in Kansas you may encounter taverns selling only 3.2 beer (lower alcohol content), restaurants with full-service bars, or private clubs requiring memberships.

Jazz thrives in Kansas City; call the *Municipal Jazz Commission* hotline (phone: 763-1052) for information. To find out who's playing at the clubs, check the arts section of the Sunday *Kansas City Star* or pick up a copy of the *K. C. Pitch* or *New Times,* free at most record stores (see *Local Coverage*). Numerous nightspots feature jazz from both local and national performers. In the downtown area, there's the *Tuba* (333 Southwest Blvd.; phone: 471-6510) and *The Phoenix Piano Bar and Grill* (302 W. Eighth St.; phone: 472-0001). In the midtown and *Plaza* areas, try the *City Light Jazz Club* (4749 Pennsylvania; phone: 444-6969), *The Point* (917 W. 44th St.; phone: 531-9800), *Starker's* (200 Nichols Rd.; phone: 753-3565), or *The Levee* (16 W. 43rd St.; phone: 561-2821). After midnight on Saturdays, stop in at the *Mutual Musicians Foundation* (1823 Highland St.; phone: 421-9297) to hear local musicians play all night long. Famous jazzmen stop in regularly at this spot, which also functions as a nonprofit foundation that provides a support network for local jazz musicians.

For country sounds, try the *Beaumont Club* (phone: 561-2668) in the Manor Square development in *Westport*. Blues and world music (reflecting a variety of international cultures) can be heard at the *Grand Emporium* (3832 Main; phone: 531-1504), and rock and pop are played to enthusiastic crowds in *Westport* at the *Lone Star* (4117 Mill St.; phone: 561-1881).

Singles action is liveliest at *Houlihan's Old Place* (4743 Pennsylvania; phone: 561-3141) and at the *Longbranch Saloon* (in nearby Seville Square, 500 Nichols Rd.; phone: 931-2755). The best bet for out-of-towners is to park in the *Country Club Plaza* or in *Westport* and barhop. There are dozens of clubs and bars—some with live entertainment—within easy walking distance of each other. *Westport* is very casual; the *Country Club Plaza* is a bit more formal, and some restaurant-bars require a coat and tie.

Best in Town

CHECKING IN

Expect to pay $100 or more per night for a double room at hotels categorized as expensive, and $80 to $100 in moderate places; there are no exceptional inexpensive hotels in the city. Unless otherwise noted, hotel rooms have air conditioning, private baths, TV sets, and telephones. All hotels are in the 816 area code unless otherwise indicated.

EXPENSIVE

Hyatt Regency Kansas City's fanciest hostelry has 731 rooms and 42 suites. Facilities include a health club, a pool, and tennis courts, plus a covered walkway to the *Crown Center* shops. There are three restaurants, most notably the *Peppercorn Duck Club,* with its diversified menu, and *Skies,* which offers a revolving view of the city. Also available are 15 meeting rooms (with A/V equipment and photocopiers available), a concierge desk, 24-hour room service, and express checkout. South of the downtown loop; McGee at Pershing Rd. (phone: 421-1234; 800-233-1234 or 800-228-9000; fax: 435-4190).

Raphael This charming, European-style place, which bills itself as "Kansas City's elegant 'little' hotel," has a lovely view of the tree-lined, Moorish *Country Club Plaza.* Its 123 spacious rooms and suites offer hospitality without smothering. There is a restaurant and lounge on the premises, and several excellent dining spots are within walking distance. Amenities include 24-hour room service and complimentary continental breakfast and newspapers each morning. Business facilities include A/V services and meeting space for small groups; computer hookups in the guestrooms are available on request. 325 Ward Pkwy. (phone: 756-3800; 800-821-5343; fax: 756-3800).

Ritz-Carlton This hotel has won awards for the quality of its service and amenities. Many of the 374 elegantly appointed rooms overlook *Country Club Plaza.* Facilities include the *Top of the Ritz* restaurant, marble baths, twice-daily maid service, a concierge desk, 22 meeting rooms, secretarial services, photocopiers, 24-hour room service, and express checkout. 401 Ward Pkwy. (phone: 756-1500; 800-241-3333; fax: 756-1635).

Sheraton Suites on the Country Club Plaza Formerly the *Marriott Kansas City Plaza,* this luxury property has 259 well-appointed suites with French doors separating the bedroom and parlor areas, and a restaurant; amenities include coffee makers and refrigerators. Among the business features are A/V equipment, photocopiers, meeting space for small groups, and express check-in and checkout. 770 W. 47th St. (phone: 931-4400; 800-325-3535; fax: 931-3352).

Westin Crown Center Built on a huge chunk of limestone known as Signboard Hill because of the commercial embellishments that once hung on it, this 730-room ultramodern property is part of the *Crown Center* complex. It integrates the hill's limestone face into the lobby, where there is a winding stream, five-story waterfall, and tropical rain forest. It has several restaurants, including *Trader Vic's* and *Benton's Steak & Chop House.* There's 24-hour room service, 27 meeting rooms, A/V equipment, photocopiers, computers, and express checkout. 1 Pershing Rd. in *Crown Center* (phone: 474-4400; 800-228-3000; fax: 391-4438).

MODERATE

Doubletree The once-sleepy community of Johnson County, Kansas, is now buzzing with business, thanks to the industrial growth along I-435 and I-35 southwest of downtown Kansas City, and this 356-room hotel is geared to the needs of visitors with business in that part of town. There is a restaurant. Business amenities include 14 meeting rooms, A/V equipment, photocopiers, computers, and express checkout. 10100 College Blvd. (phone: 913-451-6100; 800-441-1414; fax: 913-451-3873).

EATING OUT

Kansas City has great steaks and good French food. Its pride and joy, however, is barbecue. Visitors can select a relatively high-price haute cuisine restaurant or one with superb food at more moderate prices—although prices are reasonable everywhere. Expect to pay $60 or more for dinner for two at those places listed as expensive; $35 to $60 at those described as moderate; and less than $35 at inexpensive places. Prices do not include drinks, wine, tax, or tips. Unless otherwise noted, restaurants are open for lunch and dinner. All restaurants are in the 816 area code unless otherwise indicated.

EXPENSIVE

American This top-end choice, perched high above the *Westin Crown Center*, upholds the loftiest of standards. The atmosphere is down-to-earth and informal but the food is fabulous, with a wide variety of influences—from the Southwest to Asia. Appetizers include ravioli stuffed with puréed sweet potato and prosciutto, and grilled chicken livers; featured entrées are spiced venison, tuna steak in red bean sauce, and salmon wrapped in seaweed. Open daily. Reservations advised. Major credit cards accepted. 2450 Grand Ave. (phone: 426-1133).

Jasper's Decades worth of dining awards do not lie. Kansas City's most honored restaurant lives up to its reputation for exquisite, French-influenced northern Italian fare. Service hits the heights, though the tuxedoed waiters have a reputation for hovering. Closed Sundays. Reservations advised. Major credit cards accepted. 405 W. 75th St. (phone: 363-3003).

Plaza III—The Steakhouse This steakery rose from the remains of an establishment that had a far more diverse menu, but the specialization serves the diner well. Premium cuts are served in a setting that recaptures a half-real, half-imagined era of steakhouse opulence. Open daily. Reservations advised. Major credit cards accepted. 4749 Pennsylvania Ave. (phone: 753-0000).

Savoy Grill No K. C. restaurant has been around longer than this one, which opened in 1903 and has catered to celebrities as diverse as Teddy Roosevelt and W. C. Fields. Seafood has always been a specialty, particularly dishes such as lobster thermidor and shrimp de Jonghe. White-jacketed waiters, stained glass windows, and well-preserved murals complete the classic picture. Open daily. Reservations advised, especially for parties of four or more. Major credit cards accepted. 219 W. Ninth (phone: 842-3890).

Venue Works by local and national artists enliven the walls of this casually elegant eatery. The menu changes frequently but always features roasted and grilled fish, steaks, and several vegetable dishes using local produce. Grilled marinated salmon on a bed of sticky rice and sirloin tips sautéed in a veal sauce with mushrooms are good choices. Try the warm fig bar for dessert. On Friday evenings, live jazz, rock and roll, or country bands may inspire customers to take a turn on the dance floor. Open daily; breakfast on weekdays; brunch on weekends. Reservations advised. Major credit cards accepted. 4550 Main St. (phone: 561-3311).

MODERATE

Golden Ox This haven for dedicated steak lovers is located in the heart of the stockyards, near *Kemper Arena*. It offers good, solid American cooking and arguably the best steaks in town. Open daily. Reservations advised. Major credit cards accepted. 1600 Genesee (phone: 842-2866).

Princess Garden Chef Robert Chang's ever-growing Szechuan/Mandarin menu leaves the town's other Chinese restaurants scrambling to keep up. The entire Chang family gets into the act, providing consistently superb service. Open daily. Reservations advised. Major credit cards accepted. 8906 Wornall Rd. (phone: 444-3709).

INEXPENSIVE

Stroud's The decor at this popular eatery is early roadhouse (which is exactly how the place began). The chicken is fried in big black skillets and served with your choice of equally comforting side dishes, including mashed potatoes, pan gravy, and homemade cinnamon rolls. And the service is appropriately casual. Open daily. No reservations. Major credit cards accepted. 1015 E. 85th St. (phone: 333-2132).

A WORD ON BARBECUE

Kansas Citians are a peaceful lot, but you always can start a fight about who has the best ribs in town: There's no doubt that most natives would rather eat barbecue than anything else. Our advice is to check the phone book, snoop around, and ask locals what they prefer—and why. There's a wide choice, from *Gates & Sons* to *Richard's Famous Bar-B-Q*, *Hayward's Pit*, *Zarda's*, and a dozen more. Most are differentiated by their sauces, which range from sweet and thick to thin and peppery. There's surely a perfect rib to tickle your taste buds.

Las Vegas

At-a-Glance

SEEING THE CITY

The *Skye Room* restaurant in *Binion's Horseshoe* hotel (128 Fremont St.; phone: 382-1600) offers a panoramic view of Las Vegas. As you ascend in the glass elevator, the entire downtown glitters around you. As you reach the top, the expanse of desert appears, and your eye is drawn to the neon of the Strip and, to the west, the greenery of Mt. Charleston.

SPECIAL PLACES

Gambling is the name of the game in Las Vegas. Just about every type of game of chance known to man (and woman) is available here; from the ubiquitous one-armed bandits and basic games—blackjack, craps, roulette, Big Six (wheel of fortune), and poker—to pari-mutuel horse racing bets, bingo, and keno. There are also variations on the basic games, such as "double exposure" blackjack (where the player sees both of the dealer's cards). Poker has recently become permeated with Asian themes that mix the rules of different games. Pai Gow, Super Pan 9, Red Dog, and Caribbean Stud Poker take a little time to learn to play successfully, but all are very exciting once you catch on. House personnel can instruct you about the gaming rules, or you can consult the gaming guidebooks offered at the larger casinos. The legal age for gambling is 21.

Both high- and low-rollers can participate in the action; table limits range from $2 to $5,000, and you can pull on the one-armed bandits for as little as a penny. (By the way, it's considered the height of rudeness to forget to tip the dealer when you win big. Local protocol dictates that you toss a few largish chips his or her way. Never openly hand over cash; the dealer will not be able to accept the gratuity.)

The cultural aspects of the city are limited but expanding, and its history has been all but obliterated by its rapid growth. But the surrounding area is rich in outdoor diversions that can fill your days with a wide variety of non-casino pleasures, leaving the nights for the air conditioned paradise of green felt, dazzling neon, and flashy production numbers.

THE STRIP

If gambling is the game, the Strip (Las Vegas Blvd. S.) is the place. Shining brightly in the desert sun, this 3½-mile stretch of highway 2 miles south of downtown glows more intensely at night, ablaze with the glittering opulence of a seemingly never-ending stream of hotels. The *MGM Grand, Treasure Island,* and the Egyptian-theme *Luxor* are the latest and greatest entries on the hotel-casino scene (also see *Checking In* for information on these and many of the other Vegas hotels). From production spectaculars featuring superstars to 24-hour dining, it's all here and rolling around the clock. Here are a few highlights:

MGM GRAND HOTEL/CASINO AND THEME PARK This is a fantastical coupling of Hollywood icons with the excess of Las Vegas. The 5,005-room, 112-

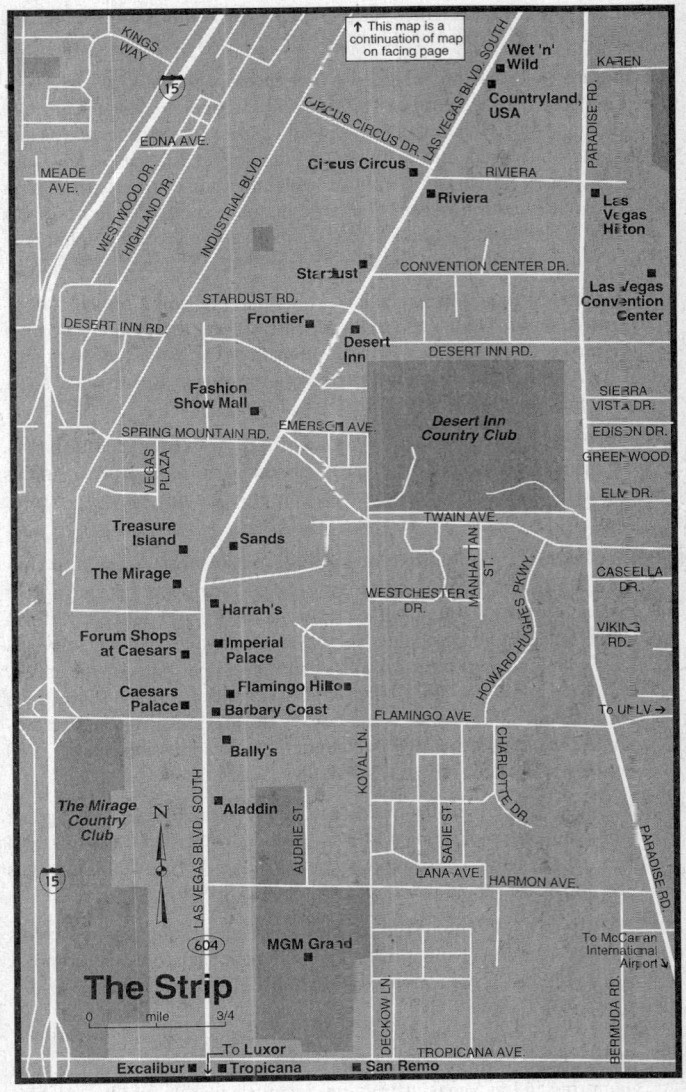

acre property (the world's largest hotel) has a Disneyesque atmosphere, with characters from *The Wizard of Oz* greeting you at the casino door, iridescent neon peacocks, and an 88-foot statue of Leo the Lion, the famed MGM trademark. There is also a huge entertainment complex with a theater, showroom, rides, and other attractions; it's called the Emerald City—an appropriate name, since you'll probably feel as though you've stepped into the Land of Oz. 3799 Las Vegas Blvd. S. (phone: 891-1111).

THE MIRAGE The brainchild of Steve Wynn, developer of the *Golden Nugget*, this 3,000-room property cost $725 million. Its opulent design features a gold-and-white Y-shaped edifice, Polynesian decor, caged animals (including the white tigers used by the hotel's feature act, *Siegfried & Roy*), cascading waterfalls, and a 60-foot volcano that erupts with a piña colada–scented spray every 15 minutes in the evenings. Natural habitats in the lobby display a rain forest and sharks, and there is a dolphin pool near the swimming pool. 3400 Las Vegas Blvd. S. (phone: 791-7111).

EXCALIBUR Though no longer the largest hotel in the world, it's still a wonder to behold. The façade looks like a castle out of a Hans Christian Andersen tale, complete with colorful turrets. Two dinner shows nightly offer Arthurian performances and royal feasting in Renaissance style. 3850 Las Vegas Blvd. S. (phone: 597-7777).

CAESARS PALACE Las Vegas's stab at ancient Rome, with Romanesque names for casinos and a toga-clad staff. Superstars perform here often, and its $40-million *Forum Shops* shopping center is the most lavish in town. 3570 Las Vegas Blvd. S. (phone: 731-7110).

CIRCUS CIRCUS This is the first Vegas hotel to cater to families with children. In its tent-shaped casino, trapeze and high-wire artists gambol high above the gambling, while clowns, acrobats, and dancers perform to the music of a brass band. The observation gallery at circus level is lined with food and carnival stands. Children are permitted in the gallery but not on the casino floor. There's also a carousel, a clown-shape pool, and a new five-acre amusement park with rides, theaters, and restaurants. The circus is open 11 AM to midnight. No admission charge. 2880 Las Vegas Blvd. S. (phone: 734-0410).

WET 'N' WILD A 26-acre, family-oriented water playground with a surf lagoon, water chutes, rapids, flumes, a 70-foot water drop called *Der Stuka*, and even pearl diving. Closed November through April. 2600 Las Vegas Blvd. S., next to the *Sahara* hotel (phone: 737-3819).

CONVENTION CENTER One of the reasons Las Vegas is among the world's major convention destinations is this million-square-foot steel complex next to the *Las Vegas Hilton*. 3150 Paradise Rd. (phone: 733-2323).

DOWNTOWN

GOLDEN NUGGET The most spectacular hotel downtown and one of the most glamorous in Las Vegas. Attractions include a marble-and-brass lobby, the biggest gold nugget in the world (weighing in at about 63 pounds), *Lillie Langtry's* and *Stefano's* restaurants for fine dining, and a 500-seat theater-ballroom. This is the only downtown property that does not use neon to decorate its exterior; instead, the outside of the building is encased in Italian marble. A must-see during any visit. 129 E. Fremont St. (phone: 385-7111).

THE OUTDOORS

HOOVER DAM AND LAKE MEAD Completed in 1936, this 726-foot-high structure, the Western Hemisphere's highest concrete dam, was selected by the *American Society of Civil Engineers* as one of the country's Seven Modern Wonders of Civil Engineering; when you take the 528-foot, 52-story elevator ride to the power plant, you'll probably agree. Daily tours. No admission charge for children under 15. Some 115 miles long, with 550 miles of shoreline when full, Lake Mead (behind the dam) is by volume one of the world's largest manmade reservoirs. Fishing (striped bass, crappie, and catfish), swimming, and boating are available year-round. The visitors' center for *Hoover Dam* (phone: 293-1081) and the *Alan Bible Visitors Center* (phone: 293-8906) for *Lake Mead National Recreation Area* are 30 minutes south of the city on Boulder Highway (US 95). For information on guided tours, call 293-8321 or 293-8367.

MT. CHARLESTON Just 35 minutes west of the city, the 12,000-foot mountain exhibits a wide variety of trees and wildlife. With plenty of fresh, cool mountain air, it's an excellent place for camping or hiking. During the winter months, snow covers the ground and temperatures often hover below freezing at the *Lee Canyon* ski slopes while vacationers swim in Las Vegas hotel pools just half an hour away. Take US 95 north to the Mt. Charleston exit, then follow the signs.

RED ROCK CANYON CONSERVATION AREA Featuring red and gold sandstone formations and spectacular views, *Red Rock* is becoming a popular rock climbing area. Just a few miles farther west, the *Spring Mountain State Park* has Old West buildings on a ranch that has belonged to such well-known capitalists as Howard Hughes and the Krupp family (the German armament folks). State rangers lead tours through the old buildings Fridays through Mondays. W. Charleston Blvd., 15 miles west of the city (phone: 363-1921).

EXTRA SPECIAL

Just two hours northwest of Las Vegas lies *Death Valley*, the hottest, driest, and lowest area in the US. It also is starkly beautiful, with a variety of colors and textures. Take US 95 north to Lathrop Wells, then head south on Route 373 to Death Valley Junction, then north on Route 190; follow the signs to the park (phone: 619-786-2331).

Sources and Resources

TOURIST INFORMATION

The *Las Vegas Chamber of Commerce* (711 E. Desert Inn Rd., Las Vegas, NV 89109; phone: 735-1616), closed weekends, and the *Las Vegas Convention and Visitors Authority* (3150 Paradise Rd., Las Vegas, NV 89109;

phone: 892-0711), open daily, are the best sources for brochures, maps, suggestions, and general tourist information. Contact the Nevada state tourism hotline (800-NEVADA-8) for maps, calendars of events, health updates, and travel advisories. The *Las Vegas Hotline* (phone: 900-446-9797) offers up-to-the-minute tips on events and hotels; the call costs $1.95 a minute.

LOCAL COVERAGE *Review Journal*, morning daily; *Las Vegas Sun*, afternoon daily. Weekly entertainment guides, such as *Showbiz*, are available at newsstands. *What's On*, a weekly entertainment guide available free at hotels and at the *Las Vegas Convention and Visitors Authority*, covers everything from theater to music to nightlife.

TELEVISION STATIONS KVBC Channel 3–NBC; KVVU Channel 5–Fox; KLAS Channel 8–CBS; KLVX Channel 10–PBS; and KTNV Channel 13–ABC.

RADIO STATIONS AM: KDWN 720 (talk); KORK 920 (big band); KNUU 970 (news); KFM 1410 (country); and KENO 1460 (sports). FM: KNPR 89.5 (National Public Radio); KILA 90.5 (Christian music); KUNV 91.5 (jazz); KOMP 92.3 (rock 'n' roll); KEYV 93.1 (country); KXTZ 95.5 (easy listening); KLUC 98.5 (top 40); and KKLZ 103.5 (classic rock).

TELEPHONE The area code for Las Vegas is 702.

SALES TAX There is a 7% tax on all purchases except groceries, and an 8% hotel tax.

CLIMATE Las Vegas summers are hot and dry. Average daytime temperature can reach 115F, but it usually cools down at night to a comfortable 80–85F. Winters are pleasant and mild (but cold at night); average daytime and nighttime temperatures are in the 50s and 30s, respectively. Outdoor activity takes place year-round.

GETTING AROUND

Although Las Vegas is not a large city, the summer heat makes walking difficult. If you are going any farther than a hundred yards or so, you'll probably do better on wheels.

AIRPORT *McCarran International Airport* is a 10- to 20-minute drive from the Strip; allow 20 to 25 minutes to get to the downtown area. *Gray Line* (phone: 739-5700) provides van service to Strip and downtown hotels. The service runs daily every 15 minutes. For return service, call 24 hours in advance for reservations. Plan to arrive at the airport at least an hour before flight time, since the distances between the main entrance and the check-in gates are long.

BUS The public bus system covers the entire city ($1.25 fare). A discount commuter ticket offers a real savings if you expect to use the buses frequently. Route information is available at 1550 Industrial Rd. (phone: 384-1234). Also, *Whittlesea* (phone: 384-6111) operates red and green trolleys that travel along the Strip.

CAR RENTAL The large national firms serve Las Vegas; other companies include *Abbey Rent-A-Car* (3769 Las Vegas Blvd. S.; phone: 736-4988) and *Allstate* (5175 Rent-A-Car Rd., just outside of the airport; phone: 736-6147).

TAXI Cabs can be hailed in the street, ordered on the phone, or picked up at taxi stands in front of hotels. Major companies are *Whittlesea Cab* (phone: 384-6111); *Yellow and Checker Cab* (phone: 873-2000); and *Desert Cab* (phone: 386-9102).

LOCAL SERVICES

AUDIOVISUAL EQUIPMENT *Las Vegas Video Sound Rentals* (phone: 362-4660); *Nevada Audio Visual Services* (phone: 876-6272).

BABY-SITTING *Sandy's Sitter Service* (953 E. Sahara; phone: 731-2086), 24-hour service.

BUSINESS SERVICES *Home Office* (phone: 873-5700) provides office space, photocopying, and typing services; *Manpower Temporary Services* (314 Las Vegas Blvd. N.; phone: 386-2626).

CHECK CASHING *A-Able Check Cashing* (3049 Las Vegas Blvd. S., across from the *Stardust* hotel; phone: 732-2541); *Strip Check Cashing Service* (3665 Las Vegas Blvd. S.; phone: 734-6900). Some hotel/casinos will cash checks for their guests as well.

COMPUTER RENTAL *Business Computer Rentals* (3560 Polaris Ave.; phone: 871-8009).

DRY CLEANER/TAILOR *Al Phillips, the Cleaner* (3659 S. Maryland Pkwy., in the *Maryland Square Shopping Center;* phone: 735-2805), open 24 hours.

LIMOUSINE *Bell Trans* (phone: 739-7990); *Lucky 7* (phone: 739-6177).

MECHANIC *Stiver's* (2300 Western; phone: 385-2407).

MEDICAL EMERGENCY *Sunrise Hospital & Medical Center* (3186 Maryland Pkwy.; phone 731-8000).

MESSENGER SERVICES *Armored Transport* (phone: 457-0856).

MONEY TRANSFERS *American Express MoneyGram* (phone: 800-926-9400 for information; 800-866-8800 for money transfers); *Western Union Financial Services* (phone: 800-325-6000 or 800-325-4176).

NATIONAL/INTERNATIONAL COURIER *DHL Worldwide Express* (phone: 798-4090); *FedEx* (phone: 800-238-5355).

PHARMACY *White Cross Drugs* (1700 Las Vegas Blvd. S.; phone: 382-1733), open 24 hours.

PHOTOCOPIES *Kinko's* (4440 S. Maryland Pkwy.; phone: 735-4402); *PDQ,* (3820 S. Valley View; phone: 876-3235).

POST OFFICE Main office (near the airport at 1001 E. Sunset Rd.; phone: 361-9212); downtown office (301 E. Stewart Ave.; phone: 385-8944); and another along the Strip (1001 Circus Circus Dr.; phone: 735-2525).

PROFESSIONAL PHOTOGRAPHER *Photo Finish* (phone: 732-1878); *Positive Images* (phone: 791-3287).

SECRETARY/STENOGRAPHER *Best Business Support Services* (phone: 737-3900).

TELECONFERENCE FACILITIES *Caesars Palace* and the *Las Vegas Hilton* offer facilities (see *Checking In,* below).

TRANSLATOR *Arriaga's Bilingual Services* (phone: 382-5497).

WESTERN UNION/TELEX Many offices are located around the city (phone: 800-325-6000 to find the location nearest you).

SPECIAL EVENTS

Las Vegas rings in the new year with huge *New Year's Eve* bashes at all the big hotels with shows featuring big-name performers such as Frank Sinatra, Liza Minnelli, and Shirley MacLaine. There are also fancy-dress balls with dinner and dancing. The *Las Vegas International Marathon and Half-Marathon* is held the first Saturday in February (phone: 876-3870). In late April, the *Sheraton Desert Inn* hosts the *Senior PGA Golf Tournament;* the *World Series of Poker* is played at *Binion's Horseshoe* (128 Fremont St.; phone: 382-1600) in April or May. During the *Helldorado Festival,* held in mid-May, the city celebrates its western heritage with rodeos, parades, and beauty contests. The *Jaycees State Fair* takes place in October at *Cashman Field* (850 Las Vegas Blvd. N.; phone: 457-8832) and has carnival acts, magic shows, rides, livestock, and craft exhibits.

A ROLLICKING RODEO

National Finals Rodeo In early December, the top 15 money-winners in seven events who have competed in the more than 640 *Professional Rodeo Cowboy Association*–sanctioned rodeos qualify for the *National Finals*—and from there they compete for the championships in the various divisions. At stake are over $2 million in prizes and the *National Finals Rodeo (NFR)* and world titles, and the competition is fierce. Most tickets for the 10 performances, held at the *Thomas and Mack Center* at the *University of Nevada at Las Vegas,* sell out well in advance (send for tickets at *least* 10 months early). For more information, contact *Las Vegas Events,* 2030 E. Flamingo Ave., Suite 200, Las Vegas, NV 89119 (phone: 731-2115).

MUSEUMS

Though it's not noted for its cultural draw, Las Vegas and its environs do contain a few museums and places of interest. Many of the hotels have commercial art exhibitions with works of well-known artists. *Herigstad's Gallery* (2290 E. Flamingo Rd.; phone: 733-7366) has art shows as well as works for sale. Closed Sundays. Also worth a visit are *Minotaur Fine Arts Ltd.* (*Fashion Show Mall;* phone: 737-1400) and the *Thomas Charles Gallery* (*Caesars Forum,* 3500 Las Vegas Blvd. S.; phone: 369-8000). Some other museums of note are listed below.

BOULDER CITY, HOOVER DAM MUSEUM This place was established to preserve the historical artifacts relating to the construction of *Hoover Dam* (also known as *Boulder Dam*) in the 1930s. There are exhibits chronicling the workers' lifestyle during the time the dam was being built. A movie detailing the process of building the dam is shown several times daily. Open daily. No admission charge. 444 Hotel Plaza, Boulder City (phone: 294-1988).

CLARK COUNTY HERITAGE MUSEUM Exhibits displayed in several buildings depict the early pioneer and mining history of southern Nevada. On the grounds—located between Las Vegas and Boulder City—is "Heritage Street," a row of houses from the 1920s, 1930s, and 1940s, complete with period furnishings, as well as a 1905 *Union Pacific* steam engine. Open daily. Admission charge. 1830 S. Boulder Hwy., Henderson (phone: 455-7955).

GUINNESS WORLD OF RECORDS MUSEUM A collection detailing many of the world records and feats found in the *Guinness Book of Records*. The museum is divided into six sections: *Sports World; Amazing Humans; Nature's Wonders; Music, Arts, and Entertainment; Amazing Animals;* and *Buildings and Structures*. Exhibits include a model of the world's tallest man (8 feet, 11 inches); displays on *Death Valley,* which holds the record for the highest temperature sustained over a long period of time (120F or more for 43 consecutive days); the *Grand Canyon* (the world's largest land gorge); and videos of some of the records being set. There's also a special display focusing on Las Vegas. Open daily. Admission charge. 2780 Las Vegas Blvd. S., next to the *Circus Circus* hotel (phone: 792-3766).

LAS VEGAS NATURAL HISTORY MUSEUM Exhibits feature animal life—from prehistoric to the present—including woodcarvings, wildlife paintings, artifacts, and more than 2,000 birds, fish, and mammals, preserved and mounted. Open daily. Admission charge. 900 Las Vegas Blvd. N. (phone: 384-3466).

LIBERACE MUSEUM Three buildings house the late, flamboyant entertainer's costumes, pianos, and vintage automobiles (including a Rolls-Royce covered with mirrors), along with other memorabilia. This is the third-most popular attraction in the state, after the casinos and *Hoover Dam*. Open daily. Admission charge (the proceeds go toward music scholarships). 1775 E. Tropicana Ave. (phone: 798-5595).

LIED DISCOVERY CHILDREN'S MUSEUM Youngsters can learn about science and the humanities from the hands-on displays on pollution, weather, computers and electronics, and hot-air balloons. Open daily. Admission charge. 833 Las Vegas Blvd. N., across from the *Natural History Museum* (phone: 382-5437).

MINERAL COLLECTION A display of gems and minerals from the area and around the world. Closed weekends. No admission charge. At the *University of Nevada at Las Vegas,* Geoscience Hall, Room 103 (phone: 895-3262).

NEVADA STATE MUSEUM AND HISTORICAL SOCIETY Four galleries contain dioramas depicting the history of southern Nevada, with emphasis on prehistoric humans. Native American culture and lifestyles over the past 13,000 years are shown, as are the area's characteristic plants and animals. Open daily. Admission charge. 700 Twin Lakes Dr., *Lorenzi Park* (phone: 486-5205).

SHOPPING

It doesn't get top billing in Las Vegas; visitors come here to spend their money at the casinos, not to search for the best bargains. However, there are several good shopping spots in the city. *Las Vegas Factory Stores* (9155 Las Vegas Blvd. S.; phone: 897-9090) is ideal for shoppers seeking designer merchandise at 20% to 60% below retail prices; the 70 shops here offer numerous well-known labels. For western-style clothing, try *Sam's Town Western Emporium* (5111 Boulder Hwy.; phone: 454-8017); you'll find a good selection of cowboy boots and hats, jewelry, belt buckles, and string ties.

There are also a couple of specialty shops focusing on—you guessed it—gambling. *Gambler's Book Club* (630 S. 11th St.; phone: 382-7555) deals primarily in new and used books about gambling history, rules of the games, and the influence of organized crime on its development. Many types of gaming souvenirs and memorabilia can be found at *Gambler's General Store* (800 S. Main St.; phone: 382-9903).

SPORTS AND FITNESS

Las Vegas offers a wide variety of sporting events and fine sports facilities.

BASEBALL The Las Vegas *Stars,* a farm club for the San Diego *Padres,* play from April through September at *Cashman Field* (850 Las Vegas Blvd. N.; phone: 386-7200).

BASKETBALL *The University of Nevada at Las Vegas* has fielded one of the finest (and most controversial) collegiate basketball teams in the nation for several years—the *Runnin' Rebels* were the 1990 *NCAA* Champions. They play from December through March in the *Thomas and Mack Center* (phone: 895-3900), an 18,000-seat arena on campus. Tickets usually are available, but for really good seats you'll need help from your hotel bell captain or casino pit boss.

BETTING If you want to bet on almost any athletic event taking place outside of Nevada, numerous race and sports bookmakers dot the city. The most lavish facilities on the Strip are in *Caesars Palace, The Mirage, Stardust, MGM Grand,* and *Las Vegas Hilton. Plaza's Book* (*Plaza Hotel*, 1 Main St.; phone: 386-2110) and *Binion's Horseshoe* (128 E. Fremont St.; phone: 382-1600) top the downtown locales for laying odds.

BOXING If punching is your bag, you're in luck; the major hotels promote many boxing matches. Bouts between professional contenders are held at *Caesars Palace, Las Vegas Hilton, MGM Grand,* and *The Mirage.*

FISHING You can wet a line all year round at Lake Mead, the manmade body of water created by *Hoover Dam.* Among the types of fish here are striped and largemouth bass, crappie, catfish, and bluegill. Licenses for three or 10 days can be purchased at any of the five marinas around the lake, and there are boats for rent, too (*Lake Mead Marina;* phone: 293-3484).

FITNESS CENTERS Most Las Vegas hotels have fitness centers. Among the best: The health club at *Caesars Palace* has exercise classes, a whirlpool bath, a steamroom, and exercise equipment; the *Aristocrat Health Spa* in the *Las Vegas Hilton* has a sauna, a whirlpool bath, and massage; the multimillion-dollar facility at the *Sheraton Desert Inn Country Club* offers full health services; *The Mirage* has men's and women's spa facilities, an exercise room, and aerobics studios; and the *Golden Nugget* hotel offers a swank spa and a coed gym with a sauna, a whirlpool bath, and exercise equipment.

FOOTBALL From September through November, the *University of Nevada at Las Vegas*'s *Rebels* play at the *Sam Boyd Silver Bowl* (7000 E. Russell Rd.; phone: 895-3900). Las Vegas's pro team, the *Posse,* is in the *Canadian Football League* and plays at the *Sam Boyd Silver Bowl* (phone: 242-4200).

GOLF Dozens of courses dot the desert landscape. The *Sahara Country Club* (1911 E. Desert Inn Rd.; phone: 796-0016) and the *Sheraton Desert Inn Country Club* (phone: 733-4444) are the best. For lower greens fees, try the public courses. Best bet is the *Las Vegas Golf Club* (Washington Ave. and Decatur Blvd.; phone: 646-3003), which offers a reasonable challenge and good greens. *The Mirage* has an 18-hole course on the former *Dunes* property that is open to non-guests. The city has more than 15 additional courses; for information, contact the *Nevada Commission on Tourism* (5151 S. Carson St., Carson City, NV 89710; phone: 702-882-1565; 800-NEVADA8).

JOGGING It's possible to run right along the Strip between Flamingo Road and Spring Mountain, where there are no cross streets to slow the pace (about one-half mile each way); stay on the *Caesars Palace* side. Another possibility is *Squires Park,* one-half mile from downtown; or drive to *Sunset Park,* 7 miles from downtown, or *Bob Baskin Park* (W. Oakey Blvd. at Rancho Dr.). The *University of Nevada at Las Vegas* has a jogging track, as do most of the city's high schools. Note that at the height of the summer, the heat can make running a dangerous sport, even in the morning; however, determined joggers may run inside at the air conditioned *Fashion Show Mall* before its stores open at 10 AM.

SKIING Believe it or not, Las Vegas is only an hour away from the slopes. *Lee Canyon,* a resort at Mt. Charleston, is about 45 miles northwest of the city. The 8,000-foot ski area, with natural and manmade snow, is good for downhill skiing. The season runs from December through February (phone: 593-9500 for snow conditions; 646-0008 for information on free bus).

TENNIS Almost all the Strip hotels have good tennis facilities open to the public. Call first.

THEATER

For current performances, check the publications listed above. Besides the entertainment at the Strip hotels, there are some old standbys, such as the *New West Stage Company* (phone: 657-5000), which presents its season at the *Charleston Heights Arts Center* (901 Brush St.; phone: 229-6383), and the *Actor's Repertory Theater,* which performs at the *Clark*

County Library (1401 E. Flamingo Rd.; phone: 647-7469); both present a range of contemporary and traditional drama. There also are a number of local theater groups, including the *Repertory Theater* at *Judy Bayley Theatre* (*University of Nevada at Las Vegas* campus; phone: 895-3801). The *Clark County Community College* and other local companies are featured in *Theatre Under the Stars,* outdoors at the *Spring Mountain Ranch* in the summer. Productions are usually major musicals; the sets make fine use of the environment and the acting is first rate. Tickets can be purchased at the ranch (18 miles west on Charleston Blvd.; phone: 875-4141). The *Nevada Dance Theatre* (phone: 732-3838) performs at the *Judy Bayley Theatre;* and the *Nevada Opera Theater* (phone: 737-6373) at *Artemus W. Ham Concert Hall,* both on the *UNLV* campus.

MUSIC

Symphony concerts, opera, and jazz are featured during the school year at *Artemus W. Ham Concert Hall* and the *Judy Bayley Theatre* on the *UNLV* campus. For tickets, call 895-3801. The *Las Vegas Chamber Orchestra,* under the baton of Rudolfo Fernandez, plays at the *Clark County Library* (1401 E. Flamingo Rd.; phone: 647-7469).

NIGHTCLUBS AND NIGHTLIFE

When it comes to nightlife, Las Vegas is king. The city never sleeps and can keep visitors entertained all night. The Strip hotels offer a wide variety of entertainment, with musical and comedy headliners such as Liza Minnelli, George Carlin, Frank Sinatra, and Julio Iglesias. There are nightly production spectaculars, with dancing girls, lavish costumes and sets, and all kinds of specialty acts. *Jubilee* at *Bally's* features a cast of more than 100 singers and dancers performing on one of the largest stages in the world. The *MGM Grand*'s multimillion-dollar, high-tech visual spectacular is the most extravagant. Other notables of this genre are *Siegfried & Roy* at *The Mirage,* featuring the famed illusionists performing magic on a grand and gaudy scale; *Splash* at the *Riviera,* with Esther Williams–style production numbers; the French cancan dancing of the *Folies Bergère* at the *Tropicana; City Lites* at the *Flamingo Hilton,* featuring both dance numbers and choreographed figure skating; and *Enter the Night* at the *Stardust,* with a gymnast/acrobat sharing the stage with some scantily clad showgirls. Smaller-scale productions can be seen at several hotels, including the *Sahara* and the *Rio Suite Hotel & Casino;* and *Starlight Express* is at the *Las Vegas Hilton.*

In the main showrooms of all the other hotels on the Strip, a constant parade of stars performs for audiences of 800 to 1,200 people. The *Tropicana* and *Flamingo Hilton* serve dinner at the early show. The *Excalibur* serves a Renaissance dinner, with two shows a night depicting the Arthurian legend. The early show of *Luxor*'s Egyptian-themed *The Winds of the Gods* includes dinner.

At many of the hotels, you can buy a ticket for a specific seat instead of making a general admission reservation and being seated by the maître d'. Hotel guests get first priority for many shows, so consider staying at the hotel that has the show you most want to see. Always call in the morning, or better still, go in person to buy tickets or make reservations. Most hotels do *not* take show reservations or sell tickets more than one day in advance. The ticket booths open at 10 in the morning and stay open till show time. If you've been gambling a good deal, ask the pit boss for assistance, and if you haven't, you might try tipping the bell captain and hope for the best. Bring along a sweater or jacket, as powerful air conditioners are at work everywhere. And though dress is casual during the day, you can opt to dress up more for the shows.

Often overlooked are the casino lounges, where lesser-known performers (many of whom—like Wayne Newton, Kenny Rogers, and Don Rickles—soon become better known) entertain for just the cost of your drinks. Comedy clubs are gaining in popularity as well; the best ones are at *Bally's,* the *Riviera,* and the *Tropicana.*

Favorite non-hotel nightspots are the *Shark Club* (75 E. Harmon Ave.; phone: 795-7525) and *L.J.'s Sports Bar* (4405 W. Flamingo Rd.; phone: 871-1424). Try the *Silver Dollar Saloon* (2501 E. Charleston Blvd.; phone: 382-6921), *Sam's Town Western Dance Hall* (5010 Boulder Hwy.; phone: 456-7777), or *Rockabilly's* (4660 Boulder Hwy.; phone: 458-0096) for live country-and-western music.

Las Vegas also presents the best-known striptease artists in the world. Tops (or topless, more likely) is the *Palomino Club* (1848 Las Vegas Blvd. N.; phone: 642-2984). Other choices are *Crazy Horse One and Two* (4034 Paradise Rd.; phone: 732-1116) and the *Can Can Room* (3155 Industrial Rd.; phone: 737-1161).

SEX TEASE CLUBS

Watch out for brothels masquerading as legitimate nightclubs (some places even advertise in the local yellow pages). Once you enter the club, a "waitress" will offer to perform certain favors if you purchase a $300 bottle of champagne (and we're not talking Dom Perignon). If you find yourself in this situation, keep in mind that although prostitution is legal in some areas of Nevada, it is *not* legal in Las Vegas; your best bet is to steer clear of these clubs.

Best in Town

CHECKING IN

In Vegas, the hotel's the thing. The Strip's 3½-mile stream of hotel-casinos and motels is nearly matched in number—though usually not in quality—by the downtown "Glitter Gulch" area. Competition is fierce among the major hotels, which keeps room costs modest; rates are lowest during the two weeks before *Christmas;* discounts can be as much as 60%, even at the most luxurious hotels. In general, expect to pay $75 or more per night for a double room at those places listed as expensive; $40 to $75 at those categorized as moderate; and $20 to $40 at inexpensive establishments. Unless otherwise noted, hotel rooms have air conditioning, private baths, TV sets, and telephones. All hotels are in the 702 area code unless otherwise indicated.

EXPENSIVE

Bally's More grandiose than ever, this 3,000-room hotel has six restaurants—among them *Al Dente* for Italian food and *Seasons* for continental (see *Eating Out* for both)—a 40-store shopping arcade, the *Ziegfeld Room* for lavish production numbers, and the *Celebrity Room* for top-name entertainment. The hotel also features two excellent buffets, the Sterling Brunch on Sundays and the Big Kitchen Buffet daily. Health spas, tennis courts, an Olympic-size pool, 24-hour room service, 42 meeting rooms, A/V equipment, photocopiers, and express checkout are some of the amenities. 3645 Las Vegas Blvd. S. (phone: 739-4111; 800-634-3434; fax: 739-4405).

Caesars Palace This is one of the places that immediately comes to mind when the subject of Las Vegas hotels is mentioned. Even the most basic of its 1,520 rooms are ornate, while the high roller suites are tributes to excess, with large classical statues to make you feel right at home—if you've just flown in from ancient Rome. The service is excellent, and the location—midway on the Strip—puts guests right in the middle of the action. It has big-name entertainment, bars, restaurants (including the fine *Palace Court;* see *Eating Out*), an Olympic-size pool, tennis, golf privileges, the *Forum Shops* arcade, and free parking. There are more than 128,000 square feet of meeting space, as well as A/V equipment and photocopiers, 24-hour room service, and express checkout. 3570 Las Vegas Blvd. S. (phone: 731-7110; 800-634-6661; fax: 731-6636).

Golden Nugget One of the glitzier of the downtown spots, it combines an overall turn-of-the-century look with mountains of marble, brass, and crystal in its casino, spa, and entertainment room. The 1,908 rooms are attractively decorated, and *Stefano's* and *Lillie Langtry's* feature fine dining. Amenities include 24-hour room service, a health spa, a concierge desk, 12 meeting rooms, A/V equipment, photocopiers, and express checkout. 129 E. Fremont St. (phone: 385-7111; 800-634-3454; fax: 386-8362).

Las Vegas Hilton This huge 3,174-room hostelry sits off the Strip next to the *Convention Center.* It offers entertainment, bars, a dozen restaurants including *Le Montrachet, Andiamo,* and *Benihana Village* (see *Eating Out* for all three), a 10-acre rooftop recreation center with a pool, tennis, a health club, putting greens and golf privileges, shops, and free parking. Crystal chandeliers and marble floors glisten in the hotel's refurbished lobby, and an extensive landscaping project was recently completed. Business facilities include 41 meeting rooms, A/V equipment, and photocopiers. Twenty-four-hour room service and express checkout make life easier. 3000 Paradise Rd. (phone: 732-5111; 800-732-7117; fax: 732-5805).

The Mirage This $725-million property has become the talk of the town. The lobby is decorated with lush plants, waterfalls, lagoons, and an aquarium stocked with exotic fish; and then there's that famous volcano—complete with flames and piña colada–scented smoke—erupting outside every 15 minutes after dark. There are 3,049 rooms with light-colored cane and rattan furnishings, bright, cheerful fabrics, and tropical flowers. Other amenities include nine restaurants, a spa and salon, shops, convention facilities, and 15 meeting rooms. The hotel's photocopiers and A/V equipment are at guests' disposal, and 24-hour room service and express checkout are available. 3400 Las Vegas Blvd. S. (phone: 791-7111; 800-627-6667; fax: 791-7414).

Sheraton Desert Inn This hotel's purchase by Howard Hughes in 1966 sparked the influx of investment that turned the fledgling gambling center into the resort complex it is today. More like a city than a hotel, there are five locations on 2,000 acres with 821 rooms and suites, each offering something unique. There's the *Wimbledon*, for example, a seven-story pyramid structure which practically sits on the golf course; Augusta Tower overlooks both the Strip and the mountains of Nevada. The rooms include amenities such as wet bars, refrigerators, private patios, and phones in the bathroom. The dining facilities are numerous and just as varied, including the exquisite *Monte Carlo Room* (see *Eating Out*). There are several bars, a health spa, golf courses, a pool, tennis courts, and many shops, including separate golf and tennis pro shops, plus six meeting rooms (with A/V equipment and photocopiers available), and a *Hertz* rental car counter, if you should feel the need (but why?) to leave. Around-the-clock room service and express checkout are available. 3145 Las Vegas Blvd. S. (phone: 733-4444; 800-634-6906; fax: 733-4774).

MODERATE

Aladdin The original Arabian theme has been replaced by a more modern look for its 1,100 rooms, four restaurants, and public areas. The *Sun Sun* restaurant features Asian fare, and *Fisherman's Port* has a Cajun/seafood menu. Other facilities include a showroom, pools, meeting rooms, shops, and tennis courts. 3667 Las Vegas Blvd. S. (phone: 736-0111; 800-634-3424; fax: 798-2787).

Excalibur The 4,032 rooms have a castle-like decor, with red and blue fabrics and wallpaper that resembles stonework; baths have oversize showers and tubs. There's a dinner theater, as well as six other restaurants. Room service is available until 11 PM. Other conveniences are photocopiers and express checkout. 3850 Las Vegas Blvd. S. (phone: 597-7777; 800-939-7777; fax: 597-7009).

Flamingo Hilton The glitz that is Vegas today all started when Benjamin "Bugsy" Siegel opened this hotel as the *Flamingo* in 1946. It now has 4,000 guestrooms, decorated in contemporary style. *City Lites,* one of the few dinner shows in the city, is performed nightly. There are nine restaurants, including the *Flamingo Room* (see *Eating Out*); other amenities include a fitness center, 14 meeting rooms, A/V equipment, and express checkout. 3555 Las Vegas Blvd. S. (phone: 733-3111; 800-732-2111; fax: 733-3499).

Luxor A $300-million, Egyptian-style extravaganza under the same ownership as *Circus Circus* (below), the structure resembles an ancient pyramid and sits on 47 acres. In addition to its 2,526 rooms, it offers seven restaurants, a lagoon-like pool and manmade beach, and—its most spectacular feature—a replica of the Nile River that flows between the hotel and casino, complete with barges to transport guests around the property. There's also a full-size model of King Tut's tomb. A concierge desk and 24-hour room service are other pluses. 3900 Las Vegas Blvd. S. (phone: 262-4000; 800-288-1000; fax: 262-4454).

MGM Grand Hotel/Casino and Theme Park The newest kid on the block of Strip properties is a billion-dollar fantasyland with 5,005 rooms (the largest on the planet). Hollywood meets Las Vegas with a flourish of lavishly designed features. The 30-story building sits on 112 acres and offers a casino (also the world's largest), eight restaurants (including the *Coyote Café*—see *Eating Out*), and a 15,000-square-foot complex with a theater, showroom, rides, and other attractions. Other amenities include a full health spa, three pools, five tennis courts, and 24-hour room service. 3799 Las Vegas Blvd. S. (phone: 891-1111; 800-829-1111).

Rio Suite Hotel & Casino An all-suite hotel near the Strip, the 860 rooms have floor-to-ceiling windows, separate dressing areas, refrigerators, and coffee makers (with complimentary coffee); some offer views overlooking *Caesars Palace* and the rest of the Strip. The pool has waterfalls and a "beach" made of real sand (purportedly from Rio de Janeiro), and there are volleyball courts. Other amenities include six restaurants, among them the first-rate *Antonio's* (see *Eating Out*), 24-hour room service, and express checkout. 3700 W. Flamingo Rd. (phone: 252-7777; 800-888-1808; fax: 252-0080).

Riviera One of the oldest hotels in the city, it has a 100,000-square-foot casino (the second largest in the world since the *MGM Grand* opened). Its 2,100 rooms and 177 suites are decorated in pastel colors and feature a variety of styles, from English Tudor to contemporary. There are five restaurants, a food court, and five showrooms; its *Splash* production is a popular nighttime attraction. Business amenities include 100,000 square feet of meeting space, a business center, 24-hour room service, and express checkout. 2901 Las Vegas Blvd. S. (phone: 734-5110; 800-634-6753; fax: 794-9230).

Sahara The first stop on the Strip is notable for its relatively tasteful decor and traditional style. The service at this large (2,100-room) property is personalized and generally excellent. There also is nightly entertainment, *La Terrazza* and the *House of Lords* restaurants, a bar, pools, a health club, 25 meeting rooms (A/V equipment and photocopiers are available), and shops. Express checkout and 24-hour room service are other pluses. 2535 Las Vegas Blvd. S. (phone: 737-2111; 800-634-6666; fax: 791-2027).

Sands This circular hotel made a name for itself in the 1960s as the hangout of "the Rat Pack"—Frank Sinatra, Dean Martin, Sammy Davis Jr., Peter Lawford, and Joey Bishop. Ask for a room facing the Strip if you want a good view of *The Mirage*'s volcano. The hotel has four restaurants, two pools, fitness facilities, beauty and barber shops, and gift shops. It also offers its own convention center, with 14 meeting rooms, and express checkout. 3355 Las Vegas Blvd. S. (phone: 733-5000; 800-634-6901; fax: 734-7324).

Stardust Once the largest resort on the Strip, this 2,461-unit property has been eclipsed by the rise of such gargantuan hotels as the *Excalibur* and the *MGM Grand*. The accommodations in the high-rise East Tower are the newest; there are also Southwestern-style villas. There's a landscaped pool, six restaurants, including *Tony Roma's* and *Ralph's Diner* (see *Eating Out* for both), and *Enter the Night*, a lavish production. Amenities include 24-hour room service, 15 meeting rooms, A/V equipment, photocopiers, and express checkout. 3000 Las Vegas Blvd. S. (phone: 732-6111; 800-634-6757; fax: 732-6296).

Treasure Island Steve Wynn, the man behind *The Mirage* and the *Golden Nugget*, has done it again with this $430-million, 2,900-room resort. Not only is it named after the famous Robert Louis Stevenson classic, the theme is further expressed with an hourly extravaganza in front of the hotel: pirates battling it out with the HMS *Britannia*. The casino and public areas are decorated in "early pirate," with treasure chests and skull and crossbones. Amenities include restaurants, a spa, a salon, a pool, and 18,000 square feet of meeting space. 3300 Las Vegas Blvd. S. (phone: 791-7111; 800-627-6667; fax: 894-7446).

Tropicana Self-billed as "The Island of Las Vegas," it has 1,908 well-appointed guestrooms and is conveniently located near the airport. Many of the suites have hot tubs and large-screen TV sets. The hotel's *Folies Bergère*, modeled after the original French production, with high-stepping can-can dancers, is the longest-running show in the city. There are also eight restaurants, a pool (with swim-up blackjack tables), 18 meeting rooms, and express checkout. 3801 Las Vegas Blvd. S. (phone: 739-2222; 800-634-4000; fax: 739-2323).

INEXPENSIVE

Circus Circus Dedicated to family entertainment (at family prices), with an amusement park and a full-scale circus, complete with sideshows, this 2,800-room hotel has plenty for children; for adults, there's *The Steak House* (see *Eating Out*), cafés, bars, a health club, and a sauna. Among the extras are photocopiers and express checkout. 2880 Las Vegas Blvd. S. (phone: 734-0410; 800-634-3450; fax: 734-2268).

EATING OUT

Probably the only sure bet in Vegas is the food. No matter where you go, there's plenty to eat, and the food is much better than standard hotel or nightclub fare. Though the offerings are basically American—steaks and seafood—there are also many good ethnic restaurants. Expect to pay $100 or more for dinner for two at restaurants in the very expensive category; $65 to $100 at places described as expensive; $40 to $65 at those listed as moderate; and less than $40 at those described as inexpensive. Prices do not include drinks, wine, tax, or tips. Unless otherwise noted, restaurants are open for lunch and dinner. All restaurants are in the 702 area code unless otherwise indicated.

VERY EXPENSIVE

Le Montrachet The best of the *Las Vegas Hilton*'s dining dozen. Try the medallions of veal or venison. The wine list is extensive and exceptional. Desserts are rich and very tempting. Open for dinner only; closed Tuesdays. Reservations necessary. Major credit cards accepted. 3000 Paradise Rd. (phone: 732-5111).

Palace Court This *Caesars Palace* restaurant is considered the ultimate in dining grace in Las Vegas. The menu is French, accompanied by wines from the hotel's distinguished wine cellar. The candelabra, vermeil flatware, and hand-blown crystal are the accoutrements of an unforgettable experience. (If asked in advance, the chef will prepare a meal according to your specifications—even if the items are not on the menu.) Open daily for dinner only. Reservations necessary. Major credit cards accepted. 3570 Las Vegas Blvd. S. (phone: 731-7110).

Piero's Northern Italian cooking with an emphasis on veal. The dishes change regularly, but favorites are *vitello del chef* (veal scaloppine sautéed in egg batter and topped with bell peppers and cheese) and *zuppa di pesce* (a seafood stew). A selection from the large wine cellar enhances the experience. The price is very high (about $160 for two), but it's well worth it. Open daily for dinner only. Reservations advised. Major credit cards accepted. 305 Convention Center Dr. (phone: 369-2305).

EXPENSIVE

Andiamo A highly regarded northern Italian restaurant in the *Las Vegas Hilton*. One of the menu's outstanding pasta dishes is *fettuccine all'aragosta e gamberi* (egg noodles with lobster and shrimp in a creamy white wine sauce). Open daily for dinner only. Reservations advised. Major credit cards accepted. 3000 Paradise Rd. (phone: 732-5664).

André's A French restaurant in an old home, it is very popular with the downtown crowd. Open daily for dinner only. Reservations necessary. Major credit cards accepted. 401 S. 6th St. (phone: 385-5016).

Benihana Village The unusual ambience here is as much of a draw as the traditional Japanese fare. This is actually a complex composed of *Hibachi* and the *Seafood Grille,* two eateries built around a re-creation of a small Japanese village. Open daily for dinner only. Reservations advised. Major credit cards accepted. *Las Vegas Hilton,* 3000 Paradise Rd. (phone: 732-5111).

Chin's This expanded version of the original restaurant now nestles in the glittering *Fashion Show Mall* on the Strip. Among the many specialties are *Chin's* beef and "crispy pudding." Open daily. Reservations advised. Major credit cards accepted. 3200 Las Vegas Blvd. S. (phone: 733-8899).

Coyote Café Just as he did so successfully at the *Coyote Café* in Santa Fe and *Red Sage* in Washington, DC, owner Mark Miller offers a unique menu of Southwestern, Mexican, and Native American cooking that ranges from warm to spicy to red hot. The restaurant and café feature signature dishes such as Southwestern painted soup (a combination of pumpkin and black bean), howlin' *chiles rellenos,* and pumpkin-seed crusted salmon, plus an imaginative dessert menu and impressive wine list. Open daily. Reservations advised. Major credit cards accepted. *MGM Grand Hotel,* 3799 Las Vegas Blvd. S. (phone: 891-7349).

Hugo's Cellar In the *Four Queens* hotel, this is one of the most respected dining rooms in the city. The romantic atmosphere is enhanced by its remote, quiet location (well away from the casino) and the fresh red roses presented to the ladies. The menu features many duck preparations; also recommended are medallions of lobster. Open daily for dinner only. Reservations advised. Major credit cards accepted. 202 Fremont St. (phone: 385-4011).

Michael's A gem in the Times Square section of the Strip. Among the offerings are shrimp served on frosted globes and double-dipped chocolate desserts. Outstanding service. Open daily for dinner only. Reservations necessary. Major credit cards accepted. *Barbary Coast Hotel,* 3595 Las Vegas Blvd. S. (phone: 737-7111).

Monte Carlo Room This dining room overlooks lush poolside vegetation. Hobo steaks (New York sirloin sliced thin and served with a sauce of Dijon mustard, shallots, cognac, and herbs) and quail in red wine are just two of the entrées. The pride of the *Sheraton Desert Inn,* it's pricey—but worth it. Open for dinner only; closed Tuesdays and Wednesdays. Reservations advised. Major credit cards accepted. 3145 Las Vegas Blvd. S. (phone: 733-4524).

Morton's of Chicago Carnivores will love the huge portions of beef offered at this steakhouse. Asking for a doggie bag here isn't just accepted; it's expected. The menu does offer lobster for those who don't enjoy red meat, but this definitely isn't the place for vegetarians. Open daily for dinner only. Reservations necessary. Major credit cards accepted. *Fashion Show Mall,* 3200 Las Vegas Blvd. S. (phone: 893-0703).

Palm The newest branch of the steakhouse group that began in New York, it carries on the tradition of serving first-rate beef, lobster, and veal. The crab cakes are great, too, and the Key lime pie and Jack Daniels chocolate cake finish the meal with a flourish. Open daily. Reservations advised. Major credit cards accepted. In the *Forum Shops* at *Caesars Palace,* 3500 Las Vegas Blvd. S. (phone: 732-7256).

Pamplemousse This charming, romantic little spot offers a taste of the French countryside (its name translates to "grapefruit") in the glitzy setting of Las Vegas. The menu items change based on what fresh ingredients are available, but they are likely to include innovative presentations of duck, chicken, and veal. Open for dinner only; closed Mondays. Reservations necessary. Major credit cards accepted. 400 E. Sahara Ave. (phone: 733-2066).

Seasons This dining room at *Bally's* has seasonal continental menus featuring everything from filet mignon to Maine lobster. The seafood is outstanding, particularly the Dover sole and mahimahi; other entrées include veal medallions and rabbit served with roasted pine nuts. Closed Tuesdays and Wednesdays. Reservations advised. Major credit cards accepted. 3645 Las Vegas Blvd. S. (phone: 739-4651).

Spago of Las Vegas Yet another addition to Wolfgang Puck's line of successful restaurants that began in Beverly Hills. In the elegant dining room, you can enjoy innovative pastas and salads, special dishes such as blackened sea bass with fettuccine in black bean sauce, and fabulous desserts. Puck's signature designer pizza is featured in the café "outside" on the sidewalk, where you can see passersby (and they can see you). Open daily. Reservations necessary for the dining room; no reservations for the café. Major credit cards accepted. In the *Forum Shops* at *Caesars Palace,* 3500 Las Vegas Blvd. S. (phone: 369-6300).

MODERATE

Al Dente Elegant, modern ambience and impeccable service make this hotel dining room, formerly *Caruso's,* an especially popular setting. Northern Italian veal and seafood dishes are the menu mainstays. Open for dinner only; closed Sundays and Mondays. Reservations advised. Major credit cards accepted. *Bally's Hotel,* 3645 Las Vegas Blvd. S. (phone: 739-4111).

Antonio's Flowers brighten the rooms of this hotel dining room featuring well-prepared Italian fare. The staff is friendly and attentive; among the dishes they might recommend are the osso buco and the veal marsala. A tempting appetizer is fresh-baked breadsticks dipped in olive oil. Open daily for dinner only. Reservations advised. Major credit cards accepted. *Rio Suite Hotel & Casino,* 3700 W. Flamingo Rd. (phone: 252-7777).

Battista's Hole in the Wall Plentiful pasta is accompanied by all the wine you can drink and an occasional Italian aria by Battista himself. Open daily for dinner only. Reservations unnecessary. Major credit cards accepted. 4041 Audrie, across from *Bally's* (phone: 732-1424).

Bertolini's Among the best Italian eateries in town, it offers heavenly versions of carpaccio, wild mushroom risotto, pasta, Caesar salad, and *tiramisù*. If you can, sit at an "outdoor" table—it's the perfect spot for people watching. Open daily. Reservations advised. Major credit cards accepted. In the *Forum Shops* at *Caesars Palace,* 3500 Las Vegas Blvd. S. (phone: 735-4663).

Bootlegger Nestled in a quiet area about 3 miles from the Strip, this cozy place specializes in southern Italian dishes. The homemade pasta is especially good; be sure to try the lasagna or the lobster *fra diavolo.* Closed Mondays; dinner only on weekends. Reservations advised. Major credit cards accepted. 5025 S. Eastern Ave. (phone: 736-4939).

California Pizza Kitchen Informal and friendly, this is a pizza place with a twist: Instead of pepperoni and anchovies, the pies here are topped with the likes of duck sausage, artichoke hearts, and baby shrimp. Though priced higher than the usual pizza, they're still relatively reasonable. Open daily. No reservations. Major credit cards accepted. *The Mirage Hotel,* 3400 Las Vegas Blvd. S. (phone: 791-7111); and the *Golden Nugget Hotel,* 129 E. Fremont St. (phone: 385-7111).

China First More elegant than the typical Chinese restaurant, this is one of the city's most popular eateries. One of the reasons is well-prepared dishes such as crystal shrimp (glazed and served with stir-fried vegetables). Open for dinner only; closed Mondays. Reservations advised. Major credit cards accepted. 1801 E. Tropicana Ave. (phone: 736-2828).

Cipriani An exhibition kitchen prepares an unusual, attractively presented Italian menu. Special dishes include salmon and ricotta, *porcini* lasagna, and chicken Saronno (sautéed with almonds and amaretto). Imaginative desserts, an extensive wine list, and excellent service are added bonuses. Open daily; dinner only on weekends. Reservations advised. Major credit cards accepted. 2790 E. Flamingo Rd. (phone: 369-6711).

Ferraro's This classic Roman-style dining room features columns, recessed lighting, and dramatic black carpet. Southern Italian cooking predominates, but there are some northern Italian dishes on the menu. Among the specialties are *panzerotti* (potato croquettes with roasted peppers, according to a family recipe), outstanding osso buco, imaginative pasta presentations, and Rosalba Ferraro's *tiramisù*. Open daily for dinner only. Reservations advised. Major credit cards accepted. 5900 W. Flamingo Rd. (phone: 364-5300).

Flamingo Room A large, attractive, Art Deco room in the *Flamingo Hilton Hotel*, it is dominated by a savory salad bar and overlooks the pool. The extensive menu features American dishes. Open daily. Reservations advised. Major credit cards accepted. 3555 Las Vegas Blvd. S. (phone: 733-3111).

Manfredi's Limelight This lively family-run establishment serves such specialties as veal scaloppine marsala with demi-glaze and sea bass poached with chablis, leeks, and cream. Open daily for dinner only. Reservations advised. Major credit cards accepted. 2340 E. Tropicana Ave. (phone: 739-1410).

Marrakech Authentic Moroccan fare, including couscous, lamb en brochette, and chicken baked with turmeric and served over rice, is featured here. Diners sit on cushions in an exotic setting, and there's belly dancing. Open daily for dinner only. Reservations advised. Major credit cards accepted. 3900 Paradise Rd. (phone: 737-5611).

Rafters This San Francisco–style restaurant offers some of the best seafood in town. Try the splendid bouillabaisse, which comes topped with a whole soft-shell crab. Open daily for dinner only. Reservations advised. Major credit cards accepted. 1350 E. Tropicana Ave. (phone: 739-9463).

Skye Room Perched on the 28th floor of *Binion's Horseshoe*, this restaurant's view of the city lights is a lovely counterpoint to its fine preparations of beef, veal, and seafood. Open daily for dinner only. Reservations advised. Major credit cards accepted. 128 Fremont St. (phone: 382-1600).

Steak House In the *Circus Circus* hotel, this is among the best places for steaks. Generous portions of sirloin are served in such a quiet, pleasant atmosphere, you could easily forget that the casinos are right nearby. Open daily for dinner only. Reservations advised. Major credit cards accepted. 2880 Las Vegas Blvd. S (phone: 794-3767).

Tillerman This pleasant place off the Strip serves fresh fish and seafood flown in daily—at reasonable prices. Open daily for dinner only. No reservations. Major credit cards accepted. 2245 E. Flamingo Rd. (phone: 731-4036).

Tony Roma's Among the best rib joints in the city, this informal eatery offers slabs of pork and beef coated with a spicy barbecue sauce. Try the onion rings on the side. Open daily for dinner only. Reservations unnecessary. Major credit cards accepted. *Stardust Hotel,* 3000 Las Vegas Blvd. S. (phone: 732-6111); the *Fremont Hotel,* 200 Fremont St. (phone: 385-3232); and 620 E. Sahara Ave. (phone: 733-9914).

INEXPENSIVE

Ralph's Diner Right out of *American Graffiti,* here's a diner that serves burgers, meat loaf, and chocolate malts. The employees sometimes interrupt their duties to sing 1950s hits with a vintage jukebox as backup. Open daily. No reservations. Major credit cards accepted. *Stardust Hotel,* 3000 Las Vegas Blvd. S. (phone: 732-6330).

BEST MUNCHES AND BRUNCHES

If all-you-can-eat sounds good to you, Las Vegas is the place to be. Most hotels have buffet breakfasts, lunches, and dinners where, for a few dollars, you can feast to your heart's (or stomach's) content on salads, fish, chicken, pasta, occasionally roast beef, and dessert. Best bets are the *Golden Nugget, Caesars Palace,* the *Riviera,* the *Sahara,* and *The Mirage.*

A really special treat is the Sunday Champagne Brunch at *Caesars Palace*—a feast for the eyes as well as the taste buds with its selections of fresh pastries, fresh melons, eggs, bacon, ham, sausage, and all the champagne you can drink. Some locals claim that the Sterling Brunch, served in the *Steakhouse* restaurant in *Bally's,* is the best in town. The food is presented in silver chafing dishes by white-gloved waiters, sushi and omelettes are made to order, and the dessert display is exquisite.

Los Angeles

In Los Angeles, the movie capital of the world, despite all adversity, almost everything has a happy ending—although last year had its share of skeptics. On January 17, 1994, Angelenos—the people of the city of Los Angeles—were rudely awakened by a devastating earthquake that measured 6.8 on the Richter scale and killed dozens of apartment dwellers and destroyed homes, buildings, freeways, and bridges as it snaked from its epicenter in Northridge, in the San Fernando Valley, southwest to the Santa Monica beaches. The most powerful in the city's history, this destructive tremor and consequent aftershocks caused billions of dollars in damage, not to mention the emotional toll on city residents still reeling from the fires, mudslides, and riots of recent years.

As the year progressed, however, souls slowly mended while freeways and other structures were repaired at breakneck speed. Of the handful of hotels, restaurants, and businesses that suffered damage, the vast majority were repaired and back in business within months. However, a few closed their doors forever. (At press time we checked on the status of those that had been affected and reported what we found, but you are advised to call ahead for updated information.) Transportation returned to normal surprisingly quickly, too, with roads like the collapsed San Diego Freeway reopened in April 1994, and most others speedily repaired. One large attraction ravaged by the quake, the Los Angeles Memorial Coliseum *(home of the* Raiders *and the* University of Southern California *football teams), was undergoing repairs that would cost nearly $40 million and was scheduled to reopen at press time (again—call for updates).*

Back in business once again, Los Angeles has fulfilled the dream of living happily ever after—and then some. Read on.

At-a-Glance

SEEING THE CITY

There are at least two great places to go for a fantastic view of Los Angeles. The most famous is Mulholland Drive, a twisting road that winds through the Hollywood Hills. Another is the top of Mount Olympus, in Laurel Canyon, north of Sunset Boulevard.

SPECIAL PLACES

OLD HOLLYWOOD:
MEMORIES AND EMPTY BUILDINGS

A walk along Hollywood Boulevard from Vine Street to Highland Avenue and beyond will delight anyone who loves the great movies that made Hollywood famous. The area is no longer the physical center of film production, however, and its glamour is, sadly, long gone. X-rated movies now seem to outnumber the kinds of films that made Hollywood world renowned. Hollywood Boulevard usually bustles with tourists

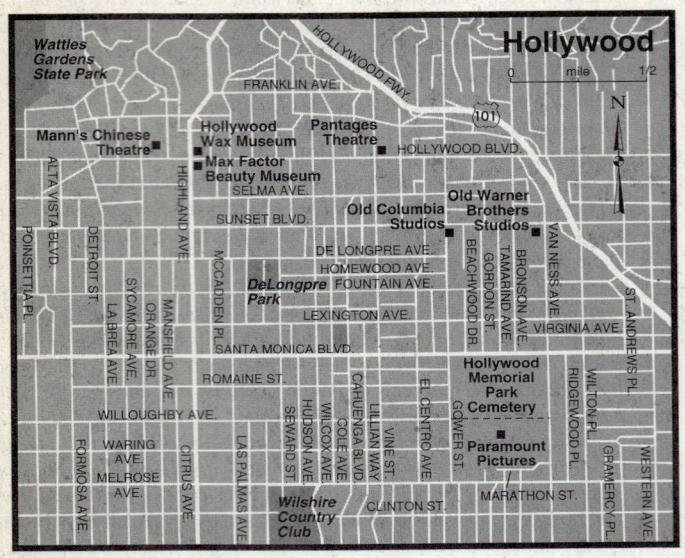
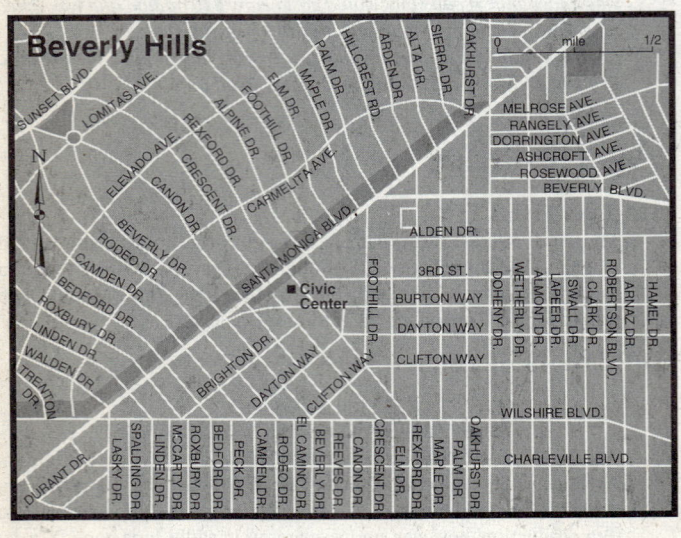

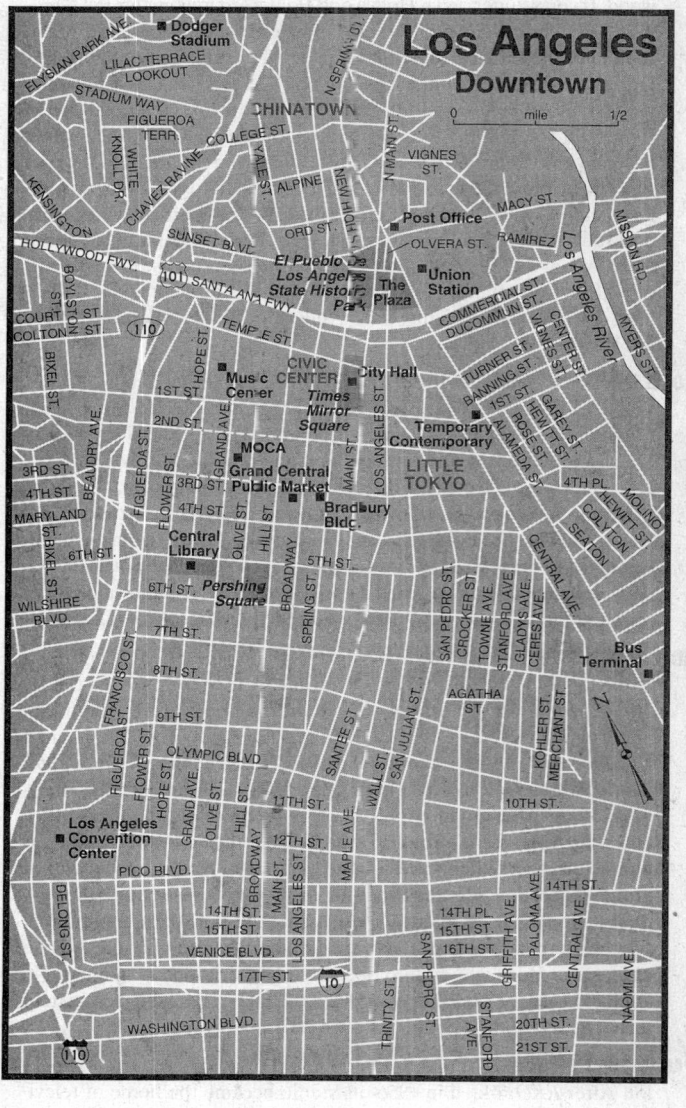

and a smattering of locals night and day. There is a lot to enjoy here, much of it at little or no cost.

MANN'S CHINESE THEATRE Known to movie fans around the world as *Grauman's Chinese Theatre,* this is probably the most visited site in Hollywood. If you wander down Hollywood Boulevard looking for the *Grauman's* sign, however, you'll never find it. Several years ago, Ted Mann took over the theater, added it to his movie chain, and replaced Syd Grauman's name with his. The *Chinese Theatre* forecourt is world-famous for its celebrity footprints and handprints immortalized in cement. If you join the crowd of visitors outside the box office, you'll probably find imprints of your favorite stars from the 1920s to the present. If you buy a ticket to get in, you'll be treated to one of the world's most impressive and elaborate movie palaces. The ornate carvings, high, decorative ceiling, traditionally plush seats, heavy curtains that whoosh closed when the film ends, and the enormous screen itself are all part of a Hollywood that no longer exists. The less opulent *Chinese Twin* next door also shows films. 6925 Hollywood Blvd. (phone: 213-464-8111).

HOLLYWOOD WAX MUSEUM If the *Chinese Theatre* makes you nostalgic for the faces belonging to celluloid souls, stop in at the *Hollywood Wax Museum.* Here images of many of the immortals of the film industry are captured both in and out of character—in wax. Marilyn Monroe, Jean Harlow, Paul Newman, Raquel Welch, Michael Jackson, Madonna, Sylvester Stallone as Rambo, and many more fill the star-studded display cases. There's also the *Academy Award Film Library,* a horror chamber, and a re-creation of the Last Supper. Open Sundays through Thursdays until midnight, Fridays and Saturdays to 2 AM. No admission charge for children under six. 6767 Hollywood Blvd. (phone: 213-462-8860).

HOLLYWOOD STUDIO MUSEUM If nostalgia is what you seek, you can find it at the largest single historic movie artifact in existence. Called the *De Mille Barn,* it was the production site of the first feature-length film made in Hollywood—Cecil B. De Mille's *The Squaw Man.* Designated a California Cultural Landmark in 1956, it was moved by *Paramount Studios* to the *Hollywood Bowl* parking lot and turned into the *Hollywood Studio Museum* in 1979. Inside are a replica of De Mille's office and stills from silent motion pictures. The outside of the building is interesting, too: When it was on the back lot of *Paramount Studios,* it often was used in Westerns and, for many years, was seen as the railroad station in the "Bonanza" TV series. In addition, there's a gift shop, filled with old autographs, books, and pictures. The museum is open weekends only in winter, also open Friday afternoons in summer. No admission charge for children under six. 2100 N. Highland, across from the *Hollywood Bowl* (phone: 213-874-2276).

PARAMOUNT PICTURES At one time, *RKO Studios* adjoined the *Paramount* lot. After *RKO* folded in 1956, its studio became the home of television's Desilu Productions, which in turn sold its property to next-door *Paramount.* Close to the Bronson Avenue intersection with Melrose is the famous *Paramount Gate,* the highly decorative studio entrance that many people will remember from the film *Sunset Boulevard.* The Gower

Street side of today's *Paramount* was the old front entrance to *RKO*. It once featured Art Deco doors and a marquee with distinctive Deco neon letters spelling out *RKO*. Today, it's simply an unimpressive back door to *Paramount,* painted in that dull, flat beige many studios use to protect their exterior walls. *Paramount* extends from Melrose Avenue on the south to Gower Street on the west, Van Ness Avenue on the east, and Willoughby Avenue on the north (phone: 213-956-5000).

GOWER STREET This was once the center for so many small film studios that it became known in the biz as "Gower Gulch." It was also nicknamed "Poverty Row," since so many of its independent producers were perpetually strapped for production money. Poverty Row's most famous studio was *Columbia Pictures,* which ultimately grew healthy enough to acquire most of the smaller parcels of studio real estate in the neighborhood. *Columbia's* old studios still stand at Gower Street and Sunset Boulevard, although *Columbia* moved out several years ago. (It found a new home in Burbank.)

WARNER BROTHERS During the late 1920s, when Warner's was introducing "talkies" to America, its pictures were filmed here. This also was the home of *Warner's* radio station at the time, KFWB. Today the old studio is the headquarters for KTLA-TV and KMPC radio. The stately Southern mansion that served as *Warner's* administration building still stands on Sunset Boulevard. Sunset Blvd. and Van Ness Ave.

MAX FACTOR BEAUTY MUSEUM The only museum in the world devoted to makeup is housed in the famous Max Factor Building, just off Hollywood Boulevard, where (since the 1930s) the stars came to have their faces painted, their hair styled, and to be fitted for wigs or toupees. There are exhibits of beauty techniques used in the early days of Hollywood, and some outlandish makeup tools invented by Max Factor. One of the most unusual displays is a collection of special head blocks of famous stars, used to create wigs and toupees without the actors and actresses having to spend hours being fitted and styled. There is also "The Scroll of Fame," one of the most extensive collections of movie star autographs around. Closed Sundays. No admission charge. Free parking. 1666 N. Highland Ave. (phone: 213-463-6668).

"HOLLYWOOD": ALIVE AND WELL

"Hollywood," meaning the film business, is no longer geographically in the district bearing that name. If your nostalgic walking tour of Old Hollywood has made you curious about modern production methods, we suggest a tour of one of the following Los Angeles studios.

UNIVERSAL STUDIOS HOLLYWOOD Only during a trip to *Universal Studios Hollywood* can one encounter a 30-foot, 6.5-ton King Kong, beam up to the starship *Enterprise,* and experience 15 minutes in the life of a "Miami Vice" cop. The combination movie studio tour and theme park has been attracting more than five million people a year. There is a guided tram tour past all the attractions on the grounds, which include some of the 34 sound stages and other production facilities; the house used in Alfred Hitchcock's *Psycho;* re-created sets from such movies as *All Quiet on the Western Front, Jaws,* and *The Sting;* a burning house; a collapsing bridge; a multimedia special-effects show; the parting of the Red Sea; the *Doomed Glacier Expedition,* where you get to plunge down an alpine avalanche; and an earthquake simulation called *The Big One.* If this isn't enough, there are other tricks and treats: *An American Tale,* a musical production; *The Riot Act,* a western stunt show; *Backdraft,* a vivid re-creation of the burning warehouse from the movie; and *Back to the Future,* which reveals how the special effects were created for that movie series. You also can travel through time on *Back to the Future: The Ride.* Fans of the late Lucille Ball will enjoy *Tribute to Lucy,* a dazzling display of memorabilia and highlights of the comedienne's TV and movie career. Meanwhile, Flintstone fans will flip over the new *Flintstone Show,* a fanciful extravaganza with comedic dictabirds, lava-spewing volcanoes, and characters like "Walter Concrete" and "Masadonna." Open daily. No admission charge for children under three. Hollywood Fwy. to Lankershim exit, Universal City (phone: 818-508-9600).

WARNER BROTHERS STUDIOS To take a look at a real production studio rather than the Universal extravaganza, try these studios in Burbank—home of Warner Brothers, as well as many independent production companies. Nothing on the tour is staged, so visitors watch whatever is happening on that particular day. Not only do you get to see some actual shooting whenever possible, you also witness behind-the-scenes action—scenery construction, sound recording, and prop selection. Since tours are limited to 12 people (children under 10 are not permitted), reservations are required a week in advance. Tours are at 10 AM and 2 PM; closed Sundays. Admission charge. 4000 Warner Blvd. (phone: 818-954-1744).

UNIVERSAL CITYWALK If the studio tours aren't enough to keep you entertained, stroll over to this $100-million shopping and entertainment extravaganza—a four-block stretch of retail shops, restaurants, theaters, and offices created by the folks at MCA Development Company, owners of Universal Studios. It's worth the trip if only for an affordable pizza at the *Wolfgang Puck Café* (phone: 818-985-9653), where the Italian pies cost a fraction of their higher priced cousins at *Spago,* or for the show at the *Wizardz Magic Theater* (phone: 818-506-0066), where the world's top magicians strut their illusionary stuff. You can even walk down a replica of Olvera Street and grab a bite of authentic Mexican fare at *Camacho's Cantina* (phone: 818-622-3333). Then enjoy a cup of coffee with a good book at *Upstart Crow,* a coffee bar/bookstore (phone: 818-763-1811). And if you're too nervous for a real roller coaster ride, you can get your thrills vicariously at *Cinemania: The Motion Simulation Theater* (phone: 818-752-3399), which lets you experience the sensation through visual effects. The complex also houses the *Museum of Neon Art* (see *Museums,* below), *Gladstone's 4 Fish* restaurant (phone: 818-622-3474), and a 14-classroom *UCLA Extension Center. CityWalk* is located in the center of Universal City and is accessible from the Universal off-ramps of the Hollywood (101) Fwy. via Lankershim, Cahuenga, or Barham Blvd. entrances; Universal Center Dr.

BEVERLY HILLS After a hard day on the lot, movie stars still living in Beverly Hills return to their mansions for a good night's sleep. Even during the sunshiny daylight hours, Beverly Hills's residential section is remarkably tranquil, with only a handful of people on the streets. Without a doubt the most affluent and elegant neighborhood in Southern California, Beverly Hills is a must-see. If you want to window-shop or purchase high-fashion clothing, stroll along Rodeo Drive between Santa Monica and Wilshire Boulevards. To guarantee that you won't make an impulsive (and expensive) purchase, go during the evening or on Sundays, when many stores are closed. *Gray Line* is one of several companies offering van and limousine tours of the area (phone: 213-856-5900). From June through *Labor Day*, an old-fashioned trolley, which departs from in front of the *Chanel* boutique on Rodeo Drive, tours Beverly Hills daily (phone: 310-271-8174).

DOWNTOWN LOS ANGELES

To see a Los Angeles that most people don't know about, take a walking tour downtown.

EL PUEBLO DE LOS ANGELES If you're wondering what LA looked like before shopping centers were created, go to *El Pueblo de Los Angeles*, where the city was born in 1781. Today the 44-acre Mexican-style site is a state historic park. At the center of the park is the Old Plaza, a wide historic square that is the scene of tours and monthly fiestas. The *Old Plaza Church*, which dates from 1822, has a curious financial history: It was partially paid for by the sale of seven barrels of brandy. The city's first firehouse is here—it is now the *Plaza Firehouse* museum (phone: 213-628-1274). The museum is closed Mondays. No admission charge. Colorful local anecdotes are retold during a narrated 45-minute walking tour of the Plaza, offered hourly Tuesday through Saturday mornings. For information, contact *El Pueblo de Los Angeles State Historic Park* on the Plaza (845 N. Alameda St.; phone: 213-628-1274).

OLVERA STREET The music from the Plaza fiestas spills over to this block-long pedestrian alley filled with colorful Mexican shops, restaurants, and stalls selling spicy food. The oldest house in Los Angeles is here—the 1818 adobe *Avila House* (E10 Olvera; phone: 213-628-1274). It is closed Mondays. No admission charge. The first brick house also is here, but now it's home to *La Golondrina* restaurant (W17 Olvera St.; phone: 213-628-4349). There is a *Visitors' Center* in the 1887 *Sepulveda House* (622 N. Main St.; phone: 213-628-1274). The center, which is closed Sundays, offers a free 18-minute film on the history of Los Angeles.

LOS ANGELES CIVIC CENTER AND MALL An unusually quiet, well-landscaped city mall, it features tropical plants, gently splashing fountains, and sculptures half hidden among the lush greenery. It's the first and only mall of shops and restaurants to be built on LA *City Hall* property. The covered bridge between *East City Hall* and *City Hall* features changing art exhibits. The mall is open daily. *City Hall* is between Main and Spring Sts. (phone: 213-485-2121).

THIRD AND BROADWAY Several places in this area are worth noting. First is the skylit, five-story indoor court of the *Bradbury Building*, now a registered historic landmark (closed weekends). You can ride an old hydraulic elevator to the top balcony and walk down a magnificent staircase guaranteed to evoke visions of bygone splendors. Across the corner from the *Bradbury Building* is the *Million Dollar Theater*—Syd Grauman's first—with a fascinating interior; it's currently a Spanish-language picture palace. Just south of the theater is the entrance to the *Grand Central Public Market,* a conglomeration of stalls selling food from all over the world amid the sounds and smells of a Mexican *mercado.*

LITTLE TOKYO This is the social, economic, cultural, and religious center of the largest Japanese-American community in the US. There are four specialty shopping centers here, as well as the *Japanese Cultural Center* and many fine restaurants. First and San Pedro Sts. (phone: 213-620-8861).

MUSIC CENTER The best time to visit the *Music Center* is during a concert or performance, but it's worth seeing anytime. This large cultural complex encompasses three performance halls (with another in the works). The *Ahmanson Theater* is the base of a branch of the *Center Theater Group;* it stages classical dramas, comedies, and international premieres with big-name stars. The *Mark Taper Forum,* a small, award-winning theater, houses the branch of the *Center Theater Group* that specializes in new works and experimental material. The glittering *Dorothy Chandler Pavilion,* a 3,200-seat auditorium best known as the site of the Academy Awards ceremonies, is the home of the *Los Angeles Philharmonic* and the *Los Angeles Master Chorale.* It's also the setting for most of the season of the *Los Angeles Opera Company.* The orchestra season runs from October through May; musical theater is presented generally in summer, when the orchestra moves to the *Hollywood Bowl.* If you take the free guided tour of the theaters, you will get a sneak preview of the *Walt Disney Concert Hall*—a mega-million-dollar, 2,380-seat, Frank Gehry–designed facility; scheduled to open in 1997, it will house the *Los Angeles Philharmonic.* Made possible by a $50-million grant from Lillian B. Disney in memory of her husband, the hall will contain four theaters, an outdoor park, and gardens. First St. and Grand Ave. (phone: 213-972-7483 for tour information; 213-972-7211 for general information).

NATURAL HISTORY MUSEUM With exhibits illustrating the cultural and technological changes of the 20th century, this museum has a wing devoted to American history, a dazzling hall of gems and minerals, the *Ralph W. Schreiber Hall of Birds,* a large taxidermy collection of North American and African mammals imaginatively posed in picturesque display cases, and ever-changing, traveling exhibitions. The *Ralph M. Parsons Discovery Center* is entertaining and educational. Learning is easy with hands-on exhibits that are as much fun for adults as they are for children. Closed Mondays. No admission charge on the first Tuesday of each month. 900 Exposition Blvd. (phone: 213-744-3466).

CHINATOWN LA's Chinatown has the usual assortment of restaurants, vegetable stores, and weird little shops selling ivory chess sets and acupuncture charts. The 900 block of N. Broadway.

MUSEUM OF CONTEMPORARY ART This is one museum in two buildings: the *MOCA* building at California Plaza, designed by Arata Isozaki (and a work of modern art in itself), and the *Temporary Contemporary,* a renovated warehouse about 10 blocks away, on Bunker Hill downtown. Both house artworks from the 1940s to the present. In addition, the Media and Performing Arts Program at *MOCA*'s *Ahmanson Auditorium* looks at performance—contemporary dance, theater, film, and video—as an art form. There's also a gift shop, as well as a pleasant café. Closed Mondays. Admission charge (except Thursdays from 5 to 8 PM). One ticket covers admission to both buildings on the same day. (*Note:* The *Temporary Contemporary* was closed for construction at press time; it is scheduled to reopen this year; call for details.) *MOCA:* 250 S. Grand Ave. at California Plaza (phone: 213-621-2766; 213-626-6222 for recorded information); *Temporary Contemporary:* 152 N. Central Ave.

MIDTOWN

FARMERS' MARKET Here you'll find just about everything within the reach of gastronomic imagination—both fresh produce and prepared dishes. There are more than 160 stalls of American, Mexican, Italian, and Chinese food and any number of exquisite bakeries and fruit and candy shops. If you don't like to eat standing up, there are tables set among the aisles of this indoor, covered market. It's a great place to be hungry. Open daily. 6333 W. Third St. at Fairfax (phone: 213-933-9211).

LA BREA TAR PITS These pools of sticky, bubbling asphalt, dating back some 40,000 years, are one of the world's most famous fossil sites. Once part of a Mexican land grant called Rancho La Brea, the pits are now part of *Hancock Park,* thanks to oil magnate Captain G. Allan Hancock, who deeded the property to the county in 1916. A natural phenomenon, tar pits develop when asphalt seeps to the earth's surface and forms pools, primarily during warm weather. For thousands of years, unsuspecting animals and at least one human—the 9,000-year-old La Brea Woman—became trapped in the pits, and their skeletons eventually fossilized. Scientists have recovered literally millions of animal and plant fossils from the La Brea site. For two months each summer, visitors can watch a pit excavation. Also in the park near the pits is the colorful *George C. Page Museum of La Brea Discoveries,* which has in excess of one million fossils from the Ice Age, as well as entire skeletons of prehistoric animals that were trapped in the tar pits. There are specimens of plants, reptiles, insects, birds, and mammals. One of the museum's more unusual exhibits is the open paleontological laboratory, where one may observe the cleaning and identification of fossils found in the pits. Also of interest are two films, the *La Brea Story,* which runs every half hour at the *La Brea Story Theater;* and *A Whoppingly Small Dinosaur,* which is shown continuously in the *Dinosaur Theater.* Also near the pits is the *Los Angeles Museum of Art* (see below). Closed Mondays. Admission charge (combination *Museum of Art* and *Page Museum* tickets are available). 5801 Wilshire Blvd. (phone: 213-936-2230).

LOS ANGELES MUSEUM OF ART With five buildings surrounding a spacious central court at the *La Brea Tar Pits* (see above), this is one of the top museums in the country and the largest in the West. The permanent collection features paintings, sculpture, graphic arts, photography, costumes, textiles, and decorative arts from a wide range of cultures and periods from prehistoric times to the present. The museum's holdings include American and European painting, sculpture, and decorative arts; 20th-century arts; pre-Columbian Mexican art; a unique assemblage of glass from Roman times to the 19th century; the renowned Gilbert collection of mosaics and monumental silver; and Indian and Islamic art. Major traveling loan exhibitions also are presented, along with lectures, films, concerts, and other educational events in the 600-seat *Leo S. Bing Theater*. The *Pavilion for Japanese Art* houses the internationally renowned *Shin'enkan Collection* of Japanese paintings, as well as Japanese ceramics, sculpture, lacquerware, screens, scrolls, and prints. Closed Mondays. Admission charge. 5905 Wilshire Blvd. (phone: 213-857-6000).

FARTHER AFIELD

GRIFFITH PARK AND THE LOS ANGELES ZOO The largest municipal park in the country, *Griffith* has three golf courses, a wilderness area and bird sanctuary, tennis courts, three miniature railroads, a carousel, pony rides, and picnic areas within its 4,043 acres. On top of all that, this is where you'll find the famous *Los Angeles Zoo*, home to more than 1,500 mammals, birds, and reptiles. Be sure to check out the *Tiger Fall*, an 18-foot waterfall in the wildcats' enclosure. The zoo is closed *Christmas Day*. No admission charge for children under two (5333 Zoo Dr.; phone: 213-666-4650). If you like railroads, you'll love *Travel Town*, a unique outdoor museum of old railroad engines, cars, railroad equipment, and fire trucks, also located in the park. The *Griffith Observatory* (2800 E. Observatory Rd.; phone: 213-664-1191) near Mt. Hollywood houses a 500-seat planetarium/theater, a twin-refracting telescope, and the *Hall of Science*. Most park facilities are open daily. Admission charge for planetarium shows. The park is in the Las Feliz district; call for details of how to reach it by car (phone: 213-665-5188).

SIX FLAGS MAGIC MOUNTAIN A 260-acre family theme park, featuring 100-plus rides, shows, and other attractions, this is the home of Bugs Bunny and his Looney Tunes friends in *Bugs Bunny World*. In addition to the mighty *Colossus* (a huge, wooden roller coaster) and the spine-tingling *Revolution* (a 360° vertical loop coaster), there's also the challenge of *Roaring Rapids* (a whitewater rafting experience), the *Z Force* mock starship ride, and a magic show run by the wily rabbit himself. *Ninja*, the West Coast's only suspended roller coaster, promises a delightfully terrifying trip. Other attractions include *Batman the Ride*, a 50-mile-per-hour, two-minute romp through Gotham City, complete with hair-raising spins, loops, and turns; the six-coaster *Psyclone,* a replica of Coney Island's *Cyclone;* and *Flashback,* a thrilling roller coaster that shoots through six 180° dives, fast switchbacks, and a startling 540° spiral. The *Viper* is one of the world's largest—and LA's scariest—multiple-looped roller coasters. The dolphin show and a children's village and petting zoo also are worthwhile. Open daily from *Memorial Day* through *Labor Day,* weekends only the rest of the year. No admission charge for children under three. Twenty-five minutes north of Hollywood on the Golden State Fwy., Magic Mountain exit in Valencia (phone: 818-367-2271 or 805-255-4101; 805-255-4111 or 818-367-5965 for recorded information).

PORTS O' CALL VILLAGE Some 60 specialty shops here feature merchandise from around the world. You can take a boat or helicopter tour of Los Angeles Harbor and dine in your choice of 25 restaurants and snack shops. Open daily. Berths 76–79 at the foot of the Harbor Fwy., San Pedro (phone: 310-831-0287).

REDONDO BEACH MARINA A delightful waterfront recreation showplace, the marina offers boat cruises and sport fishing. Open daily. 181 N. Harbor Dr., Redondo Beach. Take the Harbor Fwy. to the Torrance Blvd. exit and proceed west to the ocean (phone: 310-374-3481).

FOREST LAWN MEMORIAL PARK A major tourist attraction, this huge cemetery is the final resting place of Humphrey Bogart, Walt Disney, W. C. Fields, Clark Gable, and Bette Davis, among others; it advertises on huge billboards overlooking the freeways. The cemetery also contains a major collection of art treasures and marble sculptures including the largest religious painting in the world, Jan Styka's 195-by-45-foot *The Crucifixion*. And don't be surprised if you also find a real live bride and groom—some people like to get married here. Donations appreciated. 1712 S. Glendale Ave., Glendale (phone: 818-241-4151).

QUEEN MARY SEAPORT You can explore the 81,000-ton ship, now permanently docked in Long Beach, from stem to stern, either on your own or with one of the daily guided tours; you even can spend the night—some 365 converted staterooms now make up the *Queen Mary* hotel. When she was launched in 1936, the *Queen* was the ultimate transatlantic travel experience of its time. In 1971, after retiring from a long career on the high seas, she was "relaunched" in this picturesque harbor by the Disney Company. After Disney pulled out in late 1992, the behemoth boat closed down for several months before being bought and reopened by a local entrepreneur. Open daily. Admission charge. Long Beach Fwy. to *Queen Mary* exit (phone: 310-435-3511).

CATALINA ISLAND Here you can spend the day wandering around the flower-filled hills, swimming, sightseeing, playing golf, or riding horses. There are places to stay overnight, but be sure to reserve in advance during the summer. Boats operated by *Catalina Cruises* (phone: 213-253-9800) leave daily from *Catalina Landing* (320 Golden Shore Blvd., downtown Long Beach); the super-fast *Catalina Express* boats (phone: 310-519-1212 or 310-519-7957) depart from the *Queen Mary* terminal in Long Beach and from the *Catalina Terminal Building* (foot of Harbor Fwy., Berths 95 and 96, San Pedro); travel time: an hour from Long Beach, an hour and a half from San Pedro.

J. PAUL GETTY MUSEUM The home of Vincent van Gogh's masterpiece, *Irises*, this museum also houses an extensive collection of Greek and Roman antiquities; pre-20th-century Western European paintings, drawings, sculpture, illuminated manuscripts, and decorative arts; and 19th- and 20th-century American and European photographs. The museum building is patterned after a 1st-century Roman country villa that was buried at Herculaneum in AD 79 by the eruption of Mt. Vesuvius. Closed Mondays. No admission charge. Parking is by reservation only. 17985 Pacific Coast Hwy. (phone: 310-458-2003).

ORANGE COUNTY

DISNEYLAND The original dream of Walt Disney, celebrating its 40th anniversary this year, is as fantastic as you've probably heard, as magical as Tinker Bell's fairy dust, and perfect to the last detail. Thrill rides aren't the big deal. Instead, there are "adventures"—you get bombarded by cannonballs fired by *Pirates of the Caribbean,* visit a haunted mansion, explore the frontier, or fly through outer space. The special effects are truly astounding. During summer evenings, the *Main Street Electrical Parade*—floats and creatures outlined in thousands of tiny white lights—is supercalifragilisticexpialidocious, and the fireworks are stupendous. Ditto for *Fantasmic!,* a high-tech battle between the forces of good (led by Mickey Mouse) and several classic Disney villains; and *Fantasyland,* whose old-fashioned kiddie attractions have been treated to some $55 million of Disney's most magical special effects. Speaking of special effects, George Lucas designed a few for one of the park's most popular attractions, *Star Tours,* a flight simulator in which riders experience a *Star Wars*–type journey to the moon of Endor, home of the Ewoks. *Mickey's Toontown,* the park's latest addition to its many neighborhoods, is "home" to many of the Disney characters. And then there is *Splash Mountain,* the ultimate flume ride. Not to be overlooked is the techno-spectacular *Imagination,* where classic animated Disney films and live performers are staged in an after-dark show on *Tom Sawyer's Island.* Future plans include the addition of *WESTCOT Center*—inspired by Florida's *EPCOT*—that showcases foreign lands and theme pavilions. If you still can't get enough Disney, you can stay at the adjacent *Disneyland* hotel. *Birnbaum's Disneyland* (Hyperion; $10.95) can provide complete details about this still-expanding wonderland. Located 40 minutes from downtown LA, *Disneyland* is open daily. Admission charge. 1313 Harbor Blvd., Anaheim (phone: 714-999-4565).

MOVIELAND WAX MUSEUM About a 10-minute drive from *Disneyland,* this museum has more than 250 movie and television stars depicted in wax, molded into stances from their most famous roles. Newer arrivals include Bette Davis, Marlon Brando, and Clint Eastwood. The original props and sets from many films are here, too. At the *Chamber of Horrors,* 15 sets with wax figures re-create the special effects that made movies such as *Psycho* and *The Exorcist* famous. Open daily. Admission charge. 7711 Beach Blvd., Buena Park (phone: 714-522-1154).

MEDIEVAL TIMES An arena set in a castle-like structure is the site of evenings of 11th-century entertainment featuring colorfully attired knights on horseback competing in medieval games, jousting, and sword fighting. The show comes with dinner (whole roasted chicken, spareribs, and various other finger foods, since people in those days didn't use forks). Open daily. Admission charge. Across the street from the *Movieland Wax Museum,* 7662 Beach Blvd., Buena Park (phone: 714-521-4740; 800-899-6600).

KNOTT'S BERRY FARM The theme of this amusement park is the Old West. An old-fashioned stagecoach and an authentic steam coach take visitors around the grounds, which are divided into five sections (*Fiesta Village*, a *Roaring Twenties* area, a *Ghost Town*, an early-California-Spanish area, and *Camp Snoopy*, a children's park featuring the world's largest Snoopy, a 38-foot tall replica of the cartoon canine). Among the attractions are rides with such names as the *Whirlpool, Mountain Log Ride, Sky Jump, XK-1, Tumbler, Slammer*, and *Slingshot;* a mine train; *Montezooma's Revenge*, the multiple-looped *Boomerang* roller coaster; and the exciting *Kingdom of the Dinosaurs*. The *Pacific Pavilion* features delightful aquatic attractions, and you can play games in the largest arcade west of the Mississippi. Top country-and-western artists perform here frequently; there are also cancan dancers, marionettes, and a great ice show during the *Christmas* season. There's plenty of good eating right on the grounds: Stop in at *Mrs. Knott's Chicken Dinner Restaurant*, which is older than the park, or any of the stands selling Sicilian pizza, extra-juicy hot dogs, and barbecued ribs. Open daily. Admission charge. Located 10 minutes from *Disneyland* at 8039 Beach Blvd., Buena Park (phone: 714-827-1776; 714-220-5200 for recorded information).

EXTRA SPECIAL

For one of the most spectacular drives in California, follow the Pacific Coast Highway (Rte. 1) north about 95 miles from LA to Santa Barbara, a picturesque California mission town facing the Pacific, where bougainvillea bursting with purple and magenta blossoms adorn Mediterranean-style buildings of white adobe. A "red tile" walking tour zigzags through the historic district and runs along downtown State Street—a truly Spanish experience down to the last tile-enclosed trash bin and mailbox. The Spanish-Moorish courthouse is worth a visit for its opulent interior and the incomparable panorama from the tower. The city center owes its harmonious look to the strict architectural guidelines for reconstruction that were imposed after the devastating earthquake of 1925. Overnighters can opt for a hacienda-style hostelry, such as the *Four Seasons Biltmore* (1260 Channel Dr.; phone: 805-969-2261); Charlie Chaplin's favorite hotel, the *Montecito Inn* (1295 Coast Village Rd.; phone: 805-969-7854); an exclusive hideaway such as the *San Ysidro Ranch* (900 San Ysidro La., Montecito; phone: 805-969-5046; 800-368-6788), with its excellent French *Stonehouse* restaurant; the Victorian *Upham* hotel (1404 De la Vina; phone: 805-962-0058), which features *Louie's*, a highly regarded restaurant serving California fare; or one of many period bed and breakfast establishments. The *Cold Spring Tavern* (5995 Stagecoach Rd.; phone: 805-967-

0066), about 10 miles northwest of Santa Barbara on Route 154, goes back to the old stagecoach days. Chili is popular at lunch. At dinner, the menu tends more toward chicken, steaks, and game.

Sources and Resources

TOURIST INFORMATION

For free information, brochures, and maps, contact the *Los Angeles Visitors' and Convention Bureau* (633 W. Fifth St., Suite 6000, Los Angeles, CA 90071; phone: 213-624-7300). Closed Sundays. For all the latest information on events and happenings, call the *Visitors' and Convention Bureau Events Hotline* (phone: 213-689-8822); the service is available 24 hours a day in English, plus Spanish, French, Japanese, and German. Another information line, run by the *City of Los Angeles Cultural Affairs Department,* provides a recorded events listing covering the fine arts, museum exhibitions, and upcoming festivals (phone: 213-688-ARTS).

Contact the California state hotline (800-TO-CALIF) for maps, calendars of events, health updates, and travel advisories. Also, *West Hollywood Marketing Corporation* provides free brochures, maps, and information (phone: 310-274-7294).

LOCAL COVERAGE The *Los Angeles Times* and the *Daily News,* published in the San Fernando Valley, are daily morning newspapers. *Los Angeles* is a monthly magazine, and *LA Weekly* and *LA Reader* are free weekly newspapers with local listings of events about town.

For the best (albeit most expensive) maps of the Los Angeles area, as well as travel books, try *Thomas Bros. Maps & Books* (603 W. Seventh St.; phone: 213-627-4018). In addition to our *Birnbaum's Los Angeles 95* (HarperCollins; $12), another good guide is *Los Angeles ACCESS* (HarperCollins; $18). To really get a handle on this massive metropolis, pick up a copy of *50 Maps of LA* (H. M. Gousha; $9.95). This whimsical yet informative tome—a compilation of hot spots from artists, movie stars, and critics in map form—includes such gems as where Nancy Reagan gets her facials and a diagram of celebrity seating at *Laker* games. An even more unusual guide is *Permanent Californians: An Illustrated Guide to the Cemeteries of California,* by Judi Culbertson and Tom Randall (Chelsea Publishing Co.; $16.95), which describes the final resting places of many famous Californians and provides some interesting biographical notes.

TELEVISION STATIONS KCBS Channel 2–CBS; KNBC Channel 4–NBC; KABC Channel 7–ABC; KTTV Channel 11–Fox; and KCET Channel 28–PBS.

RADIO STATIONS AM: KLAC 570 (country); KABC 790 (talk); KFWB 980 (all news); and KNX 1070 (all news). FM: KCRW 89.9 (public); KUSC 91.5 (public); KCBS 93.1 (oldies); KXEZ 100.3 (adult contemporary); KRTH 101.1 (oldies); KBIG 104.3 (adult contemporary); and KNAC 105.5 (Top 40).

TELEPHONE The area code for central Los Angeles is 213. For Santa Monica, Inglewood, Beverly Hills, West Los Angeles, and Long Beach, the area code is 310. The 818 area code covers the San Fernando Valley and the upper half of the San Gabriel Valley. The 805 area code covers the Ventura–Santa Barbara area; the 714 area code, Orange County. All telephone numbers in this chapter include area codes.

SALES TAX The sales tax is 8.25%; there also is a 12.5% hotel tax.

CLIMATE Summers are hot and dry, with temperatures reaching the 90s during the day, but cool enough for sweaters after sundown. In winter, there are occasional rainy days and hot days, with an average temperature of 68F.

GETTING AROUND

It's always more convenient to have a car for exploring Los Angeles; however, there are buses, taxis, tour operators, and the *Metrolink* rail service.

AIRPORTS *Los Angeles International Airport* (known as *LAX;* phone: 310-646-5252 for general information) is the city's major airport and handles most international and domestic traffic. The drive downtown from *LAX* takes from a half hour to an hour, depending on traffic. The *Metropolitan Transit Authority (MTA)* provides bus service between *LAX* and downtown Los Angeles at Broadway and Sixth Street; the trip takes about an hour. Scheduled buses running to other parts of the city require one or more transfers; for information, call the *MTA* (phone: 310-273-0910 in the Beverly Hills/West LA area; 213-626-4455 in Hollywood/central LA; and 818-781-5890 in the San Fernando Valley). A more efficient alternative, however, is one of the private transport companies. *Supershuttle* (phone: 213-775-6600 or 310-782-6600) offers transportation by van from *LAX* to downtown hotels. At the airport, *Supershuttle* and several other companies can be summoned through the courtesy phones in the baggage claim area. For the return trip, call at least 24 hours ahead for a pickup at your hotel.

BUS For city bus route and schedule information, call the *MTA* (see above). The bus fare is $1.10. *DASH* minibuses (phone: 213-485-7201 for information), run by the *MTA,* travel through downtown's most scenic areas—from the *Civic Center* district to California Plaza, Broadway, or Pershing Square—24 hours a day, Mondays through Saturdays. The minibus fare is a mere 25¢.

CAR RENTAL All major firms are represented throughout Greater Los Angeles. Offering economical rates throughout the year is *Bob Leech's Auto Rental* (phone: 800-635-1240 or 310-673-2727), with free airport pickup and drop-off. *CEDI Exotic Car Rental* (phone: 800-537-0044 or 310-337-7827) and *LuxuryLine Rent-a-Car* (phone: 800-826-7805 or 310-659-5555) can snag you a Rolls-Royce, Mercedes, Porsche, BMW, Range Rover, or another suitably esoteric vehicle.

SUBWAY The city's underground rail system is still in the works, but part of the *Red Line* has been in operation since 1993. It runs between *Union Station* (Alameda St. at Sunset Blvd.) and *MacArthur Park* from 5 AM to 7 PM daily with stops at the *Civic Center* (First and Hill Sts.), Pershing Square (Fifth and Hill Sts.), Seventh Street, and *Westlake-MacArthur Park*. Tokens and tickets are available from vending machines at each station and cost $1.10 each.

TAXI Cabs *don't* cruise the streets in LA. Check at your hotel desk; different firms serve different areas. A few companies to try: *Bell Cab* (phone: 213-221-1112); *LA Taxi* (phone: 213-627-7000); and *United Independent Taxi* (phone: 213-653-5050).

TRAIN If all goes according to schedule, LA's first major rail system—linking *Los Angeles International Airport (LAX)* with downtown LA, Long Beach, and major attractions along the way—should be in full swing by the end of this year. Passengers arriving at *LAX* will be able to hop a free shuttle bus to *Union Station*. To reach downtown, they will then take the new *Green Line* to *Imperial/Wilmington* station, and transfer to the *Blue Line*. The *Green Line* will connect 13 communities between Norwalk and Redondo Beach. At press time the fare was slated to be $1.10, with tokens available in vending machines at the station. For information, contact the *MTA* (see *Airports*, above).

TOURS *Star Line/Gray Line* (541 Hollywood Blvd., Hollywood; phone: 213-856-5900) is one of many companies offering tours of downtown LA (including the *Music Center*, Chinatown, Little Tokyo, Olvera St., and more) and of the Hollywood–Beverly Hills area, as well as *Disneyland, Knott's Berry Farm,* and *Universal Studios Hollywood*. There are tours that offer more than the usual sights, including tasteful trips through Southern California wine country given by *Burbury Wine Tours* (2554 Lincoln Blvd., Marina del Rey; phone: 310-208-0980; 800-345-4265) and the ghoulish *Graveline Tours* (PO Box 931694, Hollywood, CA 90093; phone: 213-876-4286), which visits scenes of scandals, crimes, and misdemeanors in a renovated hearse.

LOCAL SERVICES

AUDIOVISUAL EQUIPMENT *Ametron Rents* (phone: 213-466-4321).

BABY-SITTING *Weston's Babysitters Guild* (phone: 213-658-8792); *Community Job Shop* (phone: 818-345-2950).

BUSINESS SERVICES *Century Secretarial Service* (2040 Ave. of the Stars, Suite 400, Century City; phone: 310-277-3329); *Headquarters Business Centers (HQ:* 2121 Ave. of the Stars; phone: 310-277-6660 or 310-551-6666), which offers word processing, conference rooms, and telex and fax machines; and *Word Shop* (phone: 213-381-3801) for word processing. Many hotels also offer business services (see *Checking In*).

DRY CLEANERS/TAILORS The *Cleaning Baron* (510 Washington Blvd.; phone: 310-823-8003), which offers free pickup and delivery service; *Top Hat Cleaners* (8122 Santa Monica Blvd., W. Hollywood; phone: 213-654-5595).

LIMOUSINE *Brentwood Limousine* (phone: 310-395-0932; 800-296-5466); *Carey Limousine* (phone: 310-275-4153 or 310-272-0081); *Classic Fleet Limousine Service* (phone: 213-753-4384).

MECHANIC *Bliss & Bothwell Auto Service* (2110 Kotner Ave.; phone: 310-444-9958).

MEDICAL EMERGENCY *California Medical Center* (1401 S. Hope St.; phone: 213-748-2411); *Cedars Sinai Medical Center* (8700 Beverly Blvd.; phone: 310-855-5000); *University of Southern California Medical Center* (1200 N. State St.; phone: 213-226-2622).

MESSENGER SERVICES *Jet Delivery Inc.* (phone: 213-749-0123). Many hotels also can make arrangements.

PHOTOCOPIES *Barbara's Place* (7925 Santa Monica Blvd., W. Hollywood; phone: 213-654-5902) is open around the clock Mondays through Thursdays, until 10 PM Fridays, and from 10 AM to 4 PM Saturdays; *Copy Print* (404 S. Figueroa Ave., in the Bonaventure hotel; phone: 213-620-6279) offers 24-hour service, pickup, and delivery.

POST OFFICE There are several branches throughout the city, including the main office (7101 S. Central Ave.; phone: 213-586-1723); the *World Way* post office near *LAX* (5800 Century Blvd.; phone: 310-337-8885); and an office in Beverly Hills (235 N. Maple Dr.; phone: 310-247-3400).

PROFESSIONAL PHOTOGRAPHERS *Atkinson Business Photography* (phone: 213-624-5950); *Wayne Seidel* (phone: 213-467-0552).

TELECONFERENCE FACILITIES Most of the city's luxury hotels have teleconferencing facilities (see *Checking In*).

TRANSLATORS *Berlitz* (3345 Wilshire Blvd.; phone: 213-380-1144).

WESTERN UNION/TELEX Many offices are located around the city (phone: 800-325-6000).

SPECIAL EVENTS

There are more special events than we could possibly list here. For complete listings, check the local publications listed above or call the *Los Angeles Visitors' and Convention Bureau* (see *Tourist Information*, above). Annual attractions include: the *Tournament of Roses Parade* and *Rose Bowl*, the traditional *New Year's Day* gridiron spectacle; *Los Angeles Open Golf Tournament*, Pacific Palisades, in February; *Los Angeles Marathon*, in March; *Long Beach Grand Prix Formula One Auto Racing*, in April; *Disneyland's Easter Parade*, *UCLA's Mardi Gras*, *Cinco de Mayo* celebrations throughout the area, the *California Strawberry Festival*, and *Manhattan Beach Art Festival*, in May; the *Playboy Jazz Festival*, at the *Hollywood Bowl*, in June; *Fourth of July* fireworks at *Anaheim Stadium* and the *Pasadena Rose Bowl*, as well as at the *Hollywood Bowl* and *Burton Chase Park* in Marina del Rey; *All-Star Shrine Football Game*, usually held in the *Pasadena Rose Bowl*, also in July; *International Surf Festival*, Redondo Beach, in late July or August; *SeaFest*, Long Beach, and *Festival of Arts and Pageant of the Masters*, Laguna Beach, in August; *Los Angeles County Fair*, Pomona, mid-September through early October; *Hollywood Christmas Parade* and the irreverent *DooDah Parade*, Pasadena, in November; and the *Christmas Boat Parade*, Marina del Rey, in December.

MUSEUMS

In addition to those described in *Special Places,* the following are other fine museums in LA:

ARMAND HAMMER MUSEUM OF ART Rembrandts, van Goghs, Cézannes, and Goyas are among the masterpieces that the late industrialist collected during his lifetime. Open daily. Admission charge. 10899 Wilshire Blvd. (phone: 310-443-7000).

GENE AUTRY WESTERN HERITAGE MUSEUM Featuring art and artifacts from the Wild West, this nonprofit collection, sponsored and run by the legendary Western singer–film star's Autry Foundation, spans the years from the late 17th century to the present. Fun for the whole family; many of the hands-on displays were created by the Walt Disney Imagineering design firm. Closed Mondays. Admission charge. 4700 Western Heritage Way, Hollywood (phone: 213-667-2000).

JAPANESE AMERICAN NATIONAL MUSEUM Dedicated to preserving the history of Japanese-Americans, this museum is housed in poignant and appropriate quarters. The building, erected in 1925 as a Buddhist temple, was used as a warehouse for the possessions of Japanese-Americans when they were herded into internment camps during World War II. The exhibits, which change quarterly, include photographs, moving images, letters, tools, clothing, works of art, and personal possessions that have been passed from generation to generation. Closed Mondays. Admission charge. 369 E. First St. (phone: 213-625-0414).

LOS ANGELES CHILDREN'S MUSEUM There are 18 hands-on exhibits and special workshops for children of all ages. Open daily. No admission charge for children under two. 310 N. Main St. (phone: 213-687-8800).

MUSEUM OF FLYING A collection of vintage flying machines is on display along with a simulator ride and a theater showing various films on topics related to air travel, such as old airplanes and the history of flight technology. Closed Mondays. Admission charge. 2772 Donald Douglas Loop N., Santa Monica (phone: 310-392-8822).

MUSEUM OF NEON ART Calling this "art" is debatable, but still you're bound to get a charge out of this whimsical collection of neon and electric signs, including sculpture and classic theater marquees. Closed Sundays and Mondays. Admission charge. 1000 Universal Center Dr., No. 154 *CityWalk* (phone: 213-617-0274).

MUSEUM OF SCIENCE AND INDUSTRY Science, mathematics, aerospace, energy, and health exhibits are featured. Open daily. Admission charge for the *IMAX* theater only (phone: 213-744-2014). 700 S. State, *Exposition Park* (phone: 213-744-7400).

NORTON SIMON MUSEUM OF ART The rich industrialist's multimillion-dollar collection includes five centuries of European art from the Renaissance to the 20th century. There's also Asian sculpture spanning a period of 2,000 years. Closed Mondays through Wednesdays. Admission charge. 411 W. Colorado Blvd., Pasadena (phone: 818-449-6840).

RICHARD NIXON LIBRARY & BIRTHPLACE Opened in 1990, it includes a 52,000-square-foot, Spanish-style library with exhibits chronicling the former president's life and career, as well as an art gallery with changing shows. Also on the property are the modest frame house in which Nixon was born in 1913 and his grave. Open daily. Admission charge. 18001 Yorba Linda Blvd., Yorba Linda (phone: 714-993-3393).

ROY ROGERS AND DALE EVANS MUSEUM An exact replica of a frontier fort features highlights of the lives of this famed Wild West celluloid couple, who trotted their way through dozens of motion pictures. There's a tribute to Roy's faithful steed Trigger and Dale's Buttermilk—the horses themselves are preserved and mounted on pedestals. Open daily. Admission charge. 15650 Seneca Rd., Victorville (phone: 619-243-4547).

SIMON WIESENTHAL CENTER BEIT HASHOAH MUSEUM OF TOLERANCE A $50-million, 165,000-square-foot museum and educational center, it was founded in 1993 to "challenge visitors to confront bigotry and racism and understand the Holocaust in both historical and contemporary contexts." Besides a permanent exhibition level, the center features a multimedia learning facility with 30 workstations from which visitors can access extensive historical data; an extensive archival collection; and the dramatic *Tower of Witness*, which showcases more than 2,000 photographs of victims of Auschwitz-Birkenau. The eight-level complex also features a theater, an auditorium, a memorial plaza, and a temporary exhibit area. Closed Saturdays. Admission charge. 9786 W. Pico Blvd. (phone: 310-553-8403 or 310-553-9036).

SOUTHWEST MUSEUM Devoted to the anthropology of the American Southwest, this museum contains some of the finest examples of Native American art and artifacts in the US. Periodically there are special displays dealing with Indian culture and lore. Closed Mondays. Admission charge. 234 Museum Dr., near *Dodger Stadium* (phone: 213-221-2163).

SHOPPING

No single street on this planet so typifies consumer excess as Rodeo Drive in Beverly Hills. Few mortals will be able to afford the prices, but window-shopping along this avenue for the affluent makes for as much fun as studying the boutiques along Paris's Rue du Faubourg-St.-Honoré, London's Bond Street, or New York's Fifth Avenue. In fact, many of the shop names are the same. Only a few are homegrown, such as *Fred Hayman* (see below). Don't miss *Two Rodeo,* a charming enclave of pricey shops and boutiques set on Italianate cobblestone lanes that surround a piazza, travertine fountains, and an elaborate staircase similar to the *Spanish Steps* in Rome. The retail newcomers who have settled here represent the crème-de-la-crème in high fashion and jewelry. Here is a list of the top emporia along and near Rodeo:

Barneys New York A five-level, 108,000-square-foot cathedral of cutting-edge fashion. Also on the premises is the *Chelsea Passage Gift Department,* offering marvelous collectibles from all over the world. 9570 Wilshire Blvd. (phone: 310-888-2200).

Bijan Where the rich and famous shop for men's clothing; by appointment only. 420 N. Rodeo Dr. (phone: 310-273-6544). *Bijan USA,* where no appointment is required, is at 431 N. Rodeo Dr. (phone: 310-285-1800).

Bulgari A long-established purveyor of fine jewelry, also known for exquisitely designed bangles and baubles. 201 N. Rodeo Dr. (phone: 310-858-9216).

Carroll & Co. Ivy League clothing for men. 466 N. Rodeo Dr. (phone: 310-273-9060).

Cartier Internationally renowned jewelers since 1847, with two locations on Rodeo. 370 N. Rodeo Dr. (phone: 310-275-4272) and 220 N. Rodeo Dr. (phone: 310-275-4855).

Chanel Boutique Clothes, scents, and accessories from the famous fashion house, which in 1993 moved to a new, greatly expanded facility. 400 N. Rodeo Dr. (phone: 310-278-5500).

Charles Jourdan Clothes, shoes, and accessories from the French firm. 201 N. Rodeo Dr., in the *Two Rodeo* complex (phone: 310-273-3507).

Dyansen Galleries Fine art. 339 N. Rodeo Dr. (phone: 310-275-0165).

Elliott Katt's Books on the Performing Arts Crammed with a tremendous selection of rare books pertaining to the performing arts, this amazingly informative shop is frequented by professionals in the movie and theater industries, who thumb through the vast casting and agency directories. Owner Katt stocks biographies of actors and directors, books on film, scores from famous Broadway musicals, as well as how-to books on everything from writing for television to getting a job in the music industry. 8568 Melrose Ave. (phone: 310-652-5178).

Frances Klein Antique and estate jewelry. 310 N. Rodeo Dr. (phone: 310-273-0155).

Fred Hayman A Beverly Hills shopping landmark, this supposed model for the title store of Judith Krantz's steamy novel *Scruples* sold its name and wildly successful fragrance to Avon. It's now home of the "273" and "Touch" fragrances, FHBH signature leather goods and evening bags, and collections from hot, young designers such as Eva Chun, Zang Toi, Christian Francis Roth, and C. D. Greene. There's a stand-up bar with complimentary drinks for shoppers. 273 N. Rodeo Dr. (phone: 310-271-3000).

Fred Joaillier Expensive jewelry, leather goods, and gifts. 401 N. Rodeo Dr. (phone: 310-278-3733).

Giorgio Armani Boutique The designer's coveted clothes for men and women. 436 N. Rodeo Dr. (phone: 310-271-5555).

Gucci Italian leather goods, jewelry, clothing, and accessories. 347 N. Rodeo Dr. (phone: 310-278-3451).

Krizia The Italian designer's boutique. 410 N. Rodeo Dr. (phone: 310-276-5411).

Louis Vuitton Famous French handbags, accessories, and luggage. 307 N. Rodeo Dr. (phone: 310-859-0457).

The Rodeo Collection A posh half-block mall; *Gianni Versace, Sonia Rykiel, Merletto, Fogal,* and *Furla* are among the designer boutiques. 421 N. Rodeo Dr. (phone: 310-858-7580).

Samuel French This West Coast outlet for the oldest play publishers in the world (since 1833) has an extensive collection of drama books, biographies of film directors and stars, and a tremendous selection of plays. 7623 Sunset Blvd. (phone: 310-876-0570).

Scriptorium This gallery sells the autographs of a wide variety of famous people—mostly historical figures such as Jimmy Carter, Abraham Lincoln, Lillian Gish, and Andy Warhol, although there are a few signatures of contemporary celebrities as well. Closed Mondays. 427 N. Canon Dr. (phone: 310-275-6060).

Superior Stamp & Coin Gold coins and rare stamps. 9478 W. Olympic Blvd. (phone: 310-203-9855).

Tiffany & Co. Fine jewelry in the famous blue boxes. 210 N. Rodeo Dr. (phone: 310-273-8880).

Yves Saint Laurent Boutique One of only two in the US (the other is in New York City), this Beverly Hills branch of the chic Paris boutique is a must-see (and looking is all most can afford). It is a sensational showcase for the French designer's fashions, jewelry, shoes, furs, fragrances, and cosmetics, framed by a theatrical limestone arch outside. A majestic staircase leads from the plush ground floor to a luminous mezzanine. Closed Sundays. 428 N. Rodeo Dr, (phone: 310-859-2389).

For specialty shopping with a more native character, browse in several burgeoning areas, such as the following:

MELROSE AVENUE This street runs an eastward gamut from upscale to funky to weird, with Gallery Row found roughly between Doheny Drive and Fairfax Avenue. *LA Impressions* (8318 Melrose Ave.; phone: 310-659-3336), open by appointment only, specializes in Mexican art. At *Gemini Gel* (8365 Melrose Ave.; phone: 213-651-0513), a superb creator and exhibitor of limited-edition prints, customers watch the printing process through upstairs gallery windows. For an offbeat souvenir, try *Wild Blue* (7220 Melrose Ave.; phone: 213-939-8434) where the ceramics and crockery seem to have a sense of humor. Antiques and gift shops, fashion boutiques, restaurants, and small theaters prosper all the way to La Brea Boulevard.

MONTANA AVENUE A cornucopia of small shops has sprung up between Seventh and 17th Streets along this Santa Monica thoroughfare, making it a window-shopper's delight. Among the pricey and super-specialized boutiques are *Lisa Norman* (1134 Montana Ave.; phone: 310-451-2026; also at 8595 Sunset Blvd.; phone: 310-854-4422), selling silk lingerie; *Where's My Conga!* (1615 Montana Ave.; phone: 310-451-1879) for funky, retro clothing; and *Private Stock* (1617A Montana Ave.; phone: 310-451-9431), which features unusual men's apparel. After making your selections, quench your thirst with a brew at *Father's Office* (1018 Montana Ave.; phone: 310-393-BEER) a fun, English-style (albeit *nonsmoking*) pub.

LA'S MALLS Lest anyone forgo the rather overwhelming experience of shopping in a mall, LA offers some of the finest, as well as some of the most eclectic, merchandise marts in the country. Among the largest shopping complexes are *Beverly Center* (8500 Beverly Blvd.; phone: 310-854-0070); *Century City Shopping Center* (10250 Santa Monica Blvd.; phone: 310-277-3898); *Del Amo Shopping Center* (Hawthorne Blvd. and Carson St.; phone: 310-542-8525); *Glendale Galleria* (100 W. Broadway; administrative offices: 2148 *Glendale Galleria;* phone: 818-240-9481); *South Coast Plaza* (3333 Bristol St.; phone: 714-435-2000); *One Colorado* (24 E. Union St., Pasadena; phone: 818-564-1066); *Sherman Oaks Galleria* (15301 Ventura Blvd.; phone: 818-884-7090); *Westside Pavilion* (10800 W. Pico Blvd.; phone: 310-474-5940); and *Woodland Hills Promenade* (6100 Topanga Canyon; phone: 818-884-7090).

VINTAGE SHOPPING

It doesn't get any hipper or more happening than *American Rag,* an Art Deco complex of five affiliated shops set along one city block on the east side of La Brea Avenue. The place showcases a mixed bag of high-ticket haute couture, outrageous accessories, and budget-friendly fashions, but even if you're not in a shopping mood, stroll through to see Margot Werts's riveting window displays with their lifelike mannequins. The shops sport a French countryside motif with high, vaulted ceilings and funky flooring. *American Rag* (150 S. La Brea Ave.; phone: 213-935-3154), the main store, proffers new and vintage fashions from designer jeans to outlandish leather jackets priced as high as $8,000; happily, most of the clothes are more affordable. *Maison et Café* (148 S. La Brea Ave.; phone: 213-935-3157), next door and accessible through an inside passageway, is a perky sidewalk café and curio shop rolled into one. Enjoy a cappuccino and baguette or browse among unique bric-a-brac and artifacts. For collectors, there are antique Pernod bottles and rare books, marvelous mosaic tile tables, and hand-picked European dinnerware. A short walk away is *Shoes* (144 S. La Brea Ave.; phone: 213-931-6903), a Moroccan-style bootery featuring everything from French and Italian sandals to sneakers. *Colours* (124 S. La Brea Ave.; phone: 213-931-6903), a super-hip bargain outlet, is popular with rock and rap stars; nothing here costs more than $30. Next door is *Youth* (136 S. La Brea Ave.; phone: 213-965-1404), a stylish kid's shop with unusual togs, accessories, and playthings.

SPORTS AND FITNESS

There is no question that Southern California is a paradise for sports lovers.

BASEBALL The Los Angeles *Dodgers* play at *Dodger Stadium* (1000 Elysian Park Ave.; phone: 213-224-1500); *Anaheim Stadium* (2000 State College Blvd., Anaheim; phone: 714-937-7200) is the home of the California *Angels*.

BASKETBALL The *NBA Lakers*' home court is at the *Great Western Forum* (3900 Manchester Blvd., Inglewood; phone: 310-419-3100 or 310-419-3182 for tickets). The *Clippers* play at the *LA Memorial Coliseum and Sports Arena* (3939 S. Figueroa; phone: 213-748-6131).

BICYCLING Biking is great around the Westwood *UCLA* campus, *Griffith Park* (see *Special Places*), and on the oceanside, where there is a 19-mile bike path between the cities of Torrance and Pacific Palisades.

FISHING Power and sailboats can be rented from *Rent-A-Sail* (13719 Fiji Way, Marina del Rey; phone: 310-822-1868). Fishermen catch halibut, bonito, and bass off the LA shores. Sport fishing boats leave daily from San Pedro, site of the LA port, about 20 minutes from downtown Los Angeles, and from the Redondo Beach Marina in Redondo Beach.

FITNESS CENTERS *Bally's Sports Connection* (8612 Santa Monica Blvd., W. Hollywood; 310-652-7440) caters to starlets, models, and movie industry types. This branch of a Southern California chain is equipped with Nautilus machines, weight rooms, steamrooms, saunas, a pool, and a Jacuzzi, and offers a full schedule of exercise classes. The shortest membership term is two weeks. *Sports Club LA* (1835 Sepulveda Blvd.; phone: 310-473-1447), a $22-million fitness center complete with state-of-the-art amenities, is where the city's "power" players work out; some regulars are Madonna, Debra Winger, and Brooke Shields. It is open to non-members for a fee. *Nautilus and Aerobics Plus*, on the ground floor of the International Tower Building (888 Figueroa St.; phone: 213-488-0095), offers aerobics classes and has a Jacuzzi and sauna. It also has branches all over the metropolitan area which are open to non-members for a fee. Many hotels have their own health clubs, too (see *Checking In*).

FOOTBALL Champions of the *Big 10* and *Pacific 10* college conferences meet in the *Pasadena Rose Bowl* (1001 Rose Bowl Dr.; phone: 818-577-3100) every *New Year's Day*. UCLA plays its home games at the *Pasadena Rose Bowl*, and *USC* takes the field at the *Coliseum* (3939 S. Figueroa; phone: 213-747-7111 or 213-748-6131). The *NFL Rams* play at *Anaheim Stadium* (see *Baseball*, above; phone: 213-625-1123 or 714-937-6767). The *NFL Raiders* kick off at the *Coliseum* (see above).

GOLF The *Industry Hills Golf Club* (1 Industry Hills Pkwy., City of Industry; phone: 818-810-HILL) boasts two 18-hole golf courses, designed by William Bell, with 160 sand bunkers, eight lakes, and miles of astoundingly long fairways. The club also has an ultramodern, lighted driving range and four practice putting greens.

HOCKEY The *Kings* make their home at the *Great Western Forum* (3900 Manchester Blvd., Inglewood; phone: 310-673-1300 or 310-480-3282 for tickets). And the *Mighty Ducks* push their pucks at *The Pond of Anaheim* (2695 Katella Ave.; phone: 714-704-2400 for tickets).

HORSE RACING If you like to spend your nights at the track, make tracks for *Los Alamitos*. There's harness, quarterhorse, and thoroughbred racing year-round. Take Freeway 605 south to Katella Avenue exit in Orange County (phone: 310-431-1361 or 714-995-1234). If you prefer daytime action, try *Hollywood Park* between mid-April and late July and from early November to *Christmas Eve* (near *Los Angeles International Airport* between Manchester and Century Blvds.; phone: 310-419-1500). from late December to mid-April and in October and November, There's also thoroughbred racing at *Santa Anita Park,* home of the *Breeder's Cup* (Huntington Dr. and Baldwin Ave., Arcadia; phone: 818-574-7223).

JOGGING Downtown, run around *Echo Park Lake* (a little less than a mile) during the day only; get there by going up Sunset and taking a right onto Glendale. In *Griffith Park*, run in the woodsy Ferndale area near the Vermont Avenue entrance; get to the park via the Golden State Freeway and watch for the sign to turn off (also see *Special Places*). In Westwood, *UCLA* has a hilly 4-mile perimeter course and a quarter-mile track. Four blocks from Century City, *Cheviot Hills Park* (at 2551 Motor Ave.) has a runners' course. And in Beverly Hills, jog in *Roxbury Park* (entrance at 471 S. Roxbury Dr. and Olympic) or along the 1½-mile stretch of Santa Monica Boulevard between Doheny and Wilshire. Jogging also is popular along the oceanside bike path between Marina del Rey and the Palos Verdes Peninsula, in Santa Monica's *Palisades Park* on Ocean Avenue, and along San Vicente Boulevard from Brentwood to Ocean Avenue.

SWIMMING AND SURFING For swimming, the best beaches are El Porto Beach in Manhattan Beach, Will Rogers State Beach in Pacific Palisades, and Zuma Beach, north of Malibu. For surfing, Malibu Surfrider Beach, Hermosa Beach, El Porto Beach, and Zuma Beach are tops.

TENNIS *Griffith Park*, featuring one of the top 25 municipal tennis facilities in the US according to *Tennis* magazine, boasts 12 outdoor courts, all with lights for night play (Riverside and Los Feliz; phone: 213-664-1191). Reservations can be made for a small fee. At the *Racquet Centre* (10933 Ventura Blvd., Studio City; phone: 818-760-2302), there are 20 lighted courts, a tennis shop, and a locker room and showers. The *Tennis Place* (5880 W. Third St.; phone: 213-931-1715), with a prime LA location, has 16 lighted, hard-surface courts; lessons and practice sessions with a ball machine are also available. Top-seeded players on the pro circuit generally show up for the *Volvo/Los Angeles Pro Tournament* held in July at *UCLA* (phone: 310-208-0730).

VOLLEYBALL If volleyball is your game, you won't have any trouble having a hands-on or a spectator's experience here. There are nets up on most beaches in Los Angeles County, and both amateur and professional tournaments take place year-round. At Manhattan and Hermosa Beaches, 26 professional competitions are held during March and September. For a schedule of the competitions, contact the *Association of Volleyball Professionals* (phone: 310-337-4842). Indoor volleyball is also popular and played regularly by local leagues at most of the area's 150 public parks. For more information, contact the *Southern California Volleyball Association* (phone: 310-320-9440) or the *Valley Municipal Sports Office* (phone: 818-989-8070).

THEATER

There is no shortage of stages in LA, despite the overshadowing presence of the film industry. We begin with one of our favorite venues.

CENTER STAGE

Mark Taper Forum One of the nation's most respected resident theaters, it offers many premieres and an occasional revival; the subject matter tends toward the timely, the currently problematic. The *Mark Taper* production of *Jelly's Last Jam* went on to win Broadway's Tony Awards for best actor, actress, and lighting design in a musical in 1991, and in 1993 and 1994 *Angels in America* (parts I and II) won in the best play, director, actor, and featured actor categories. Also under the *Taper* wing are the *Improvisational Theatre Project,* the intimate *Taper, Too* house, and the Sunday afternoon *Literary Cabaret.* 135 N. Grand Ave. (phone: 213-972-7211).

The *Center Theater Group* performs at the *Music Center*'s *Ahmanson Theater* and *Mark Taper Forum* (see *Special Places*). Also downtown is the *Los Angeles Theatre Center* (514 S. Spring St.; phone: 213-627-6500). The revived *State Theatre of California* is at the *Pasadena Playhouse* (39 S. El Molina Ave.; phone: 818-356-7529). Other Los Angeles theaters include the *Doolittle Theatre* (1615 N. Vine St., Hollywood; phone: 213-462-6666 or 213-972-0700); the *Shubert Theatre* (in the *ABC Entertainment Center,* 2020 Ave. of the Stars, Century City; phone: 310-201-1500; 800-233-3123 for information and credit card reservations); the *Odyssey Theatre Ensemble,* which performs in three small theaters (all at 2055 S. Sepulveda; phone: 310-477-2055); and the *Pantages Theatre* (6233 Hollywood Blvd.; phone: 310-410-1062). Tickets for all major events can be ordered over the telephone through *Ticketmaster* (phone: 213-480-3232).

MUSIC

All kinds of music can be heard in LA's concert halls and clubs. The *Los Angeles Philharmonic* plays at the *Dorothy Chandler Pavilion* at the *Music Center* (see *Special Places*). The *Hollywood Bowl* (2301 N. Highland Ave., Hollywood; phone: 213-850-2000) is a 17,630-seat hillside amphitheater that features famous guest entertainers and is the summer home of the *Philharmonic.* Leading popular performers in a wide range of musical styles play year-round at the *Universal Amphitheatre* (Hollywood Fwy. at Lankershim Blvd.; phone: 818-980-9421). The *Greek Theatre* (2700 N. Vermont Ave.; phone: 310-410-1062) is a 6,200-seat indoor theater with concerts by top names. The *Roxy Theatre* (9009 Sunset Blvd.; phone: 310-276-2222) is also good for concerts. For country music, check out the *Palomino Club* (6907 Lankershim Blvd., N. Hollywood; phone: 818-983-1321). Rock and jazz buffs should try the *Palace* (1735 N. Vine, near Hollywood and Vine; phone: 213-462-3000), where the rock theater–dance club downstairs often has live shows, as well as dancing. Upstairs, the *Palace Court* has live jazz on weekends. Other choices include the *Cinegrille*, an Art Deco cabaret with blues, jazz, and Broadway show performances at the *Radisson Hollywood Roosevelt* hotel (see *Checking In*); and *Kingston 12* (814 Bwy., Santa Monica; phone: 310-451-4423) for reggae.

NIGHTCLUBS AND NIGHTLIFE

Anything goes in LA, especially after dark. Swinging nightspots open and close quickly, since the restless search for what's "in" keeps people on the move. *Doug Weston's Troubadour Club* (9081 Santa Monica Blvd., W. Hollywood; phone: 310-276-6168) has introduced a number of top rock music acts. Another place that seems to be able to hold its own with live rock shows nightly is *Whisky A Go-Go* (8901 Sunset Blvd.; phone: 310-652-4202). *Roxbury* (8225 Sunset, W. Hollywood; phone: 213-656-1750) is popular with celebrities and the wannabe crowd. There are three levels for entertainment, a good restaurant, and an exclusive VIP room. Other hot nightspots include *Club Lingerie* (6507 Sunset Blvd., Hollywood; phone: 213-466-8557), a hip, happening rock club; *Hollywood Athletic Club* (6525 Sunset Blvd.; phone: 213-962-6600), with pool tables plus the latest rock groups; and *Café Largo* (432 Fairfax, Hollywood; phone: 213-852-1073), a modern cabaret with a mix of rock 'n' roll, folk, country, and oldies. In downtown LA, step out at the hip *Mayan* (1038 Hill St.; phone: 213-746-4287) or *Glam Sam* (333 S. Boylston; phone: 213-747-4849), owned by rocker Prince, where a well-heeled crowd gathers on weekend nights to dine and dance until 4 AM. If you want to mingle with LA's trendiest, try to make the scene at the *Olive* (119 S. Fairfax Ave.; phone: 213-939-2001); admission here depends on who you are, who you know, and how you're dressed. Since it's not often easy to get in the door at these hot spots, *LA NightHawks* (phone: 310-392-1500) has club-hopping tours conducted in stretch limousines that travel to your choice of 250 popular nighttime nooks. Prices vary depending on destinations and include cover charges and a bottle of French champagne.

For blues buffs there's *Mint* (6010 W. Pico Blvd.; phone: 213-937-9630), a neighborhood bar, and the *House of Blues* (across the street from *The Comedy Club* in W. Hollywood at 8439 W. Sunset Blvd.; phone: 310-652-0247), the 1,000-seat music club/restaurant opened last year by Dan Aykroyd and *Aerosmith*.

With Movietown's pool of talent, comedy clubs here are a better bet than elsewhere. Among the options: *Improvisation* (8162 Melrose Ave.; phone: 213-651-2583, and at 321 Santa Monica Blvd., Santa Monica; phone: 310-394-8664), the grandparent of them all; and the *Comedy Store* (8433 Sunset Blvd.; phone: 213-480-3232), another survivor. If you want to get into the act, head over to *All That Glitz* (1911 Sunset Blvd.; phone: 310-278-7712), where musical comedy comes with a twist—cast members "roast" certain folks in the audience. Comedy is king at the *Groundling Theater* (7307 Melrose Ave., W. Hollywood; phone: 213-934-9700), LA's answer to Chicago's *Second City* and the launching pad for *Saturday Night Live* funny man Phil Hartman.

Best in Town

CHECKING IN

Los Angeles is the city where mere mortals stand the best chance of checking in alongside a movie star, although, obviously, the privilege will cost you dearly. (Note: The Beverly Hills hotel, one of the most popular with members of the film industry, has temporarily closed while it undergoes a complete renovation; it's scheduled to reopen next year.) If you're looking for someplace simply to shower and sleep, you'll be happier at one of the smaller hotels or motels sprinkled throughout the area. Generally speaking, accommodations are less expensive in the San Fernando and San Gabriel Valleys than in Hollywood or downtown. Expect to pay $245 or more (sometimes *much* more) per night for a double room at hotels we've described as very expensive; between $140 and $240 at those places listed as expensive; between $80 and $140 at places in the moderate category; and less than $80 at places listed as inexpensive. (Be sure to ask about special commercial rates and weekend package deals.) For statewide information on bed and breakfast accommodations, contact *Eye Openers Bed & Breakfast* (PO Box 694, Altadena, CA 91001; phone: 213-684-4428 or 818-797-2055) or *California Houseguests International* (605 Lindley Ave., Suite 6, Tarzana, CA 91356; phone: 818-344-7878). Unless otherwise indicated, all hotels have air conditioning, private baths, TV sets, and telephones. Twenty-four-hour room service is the norm, unless otherwise noted. All telephone numbers below include area codes.

For an unforgettable experience in Los Angeles, we begin with our favorite, followed by our recommendations of cost and quality choices of accommodations, listed by price category.

A SPECIAL HAVEN

Bel-Air In the fashionable Bel-Air district of Los Angeles, this member of the prestigious Relais & Châteaux group has been a favorite hideaway of Gary Cooper, Howard Hughes, Grace Kelly, Sophia Loren, Marilyn Monroe, and other celebs since it opened during the 1920s. The hotel's perfectly appointed 92 rooms (39 of which are suites) are in one- and two-story mission-style buildings and bungalows scattered amid 11.5 exquisitely landscaped acres; privacy prevails. Executive chef Gary Clausen caters to the sophisticated tastes of patrons with "back to basics" culinary artistry: Meat is lightly marinated rather than doused in rich sauces, and herbs are grown on the premises. Meeting rooms accommodate up to 200; and other business amenities include secretarial assistance, photocopiers, and

A/V equipment. There's also a very gracious and helpful concierge desk. 701 Stone Canyon Rd. (phone: 310-472-1211; 800-648-4097 outside California; fax: 310-476-5890).

VERY EXPENSIVE

Bel Age This hotel with a European ambience offers 188 suites, gracefully decorated with hand-carved rosewood and pecan wood furniture. *La Brasserie* is the hotel's casual café; *Diaghilev,* its more formal dining room, serves Franco-Russe cuisine. Also on the premises is a heated rooftop pool. Meeting rooms can accommodate up to 500, and there's a concierge, secretarial services, A/V equipment, and photocopiers. 1020 N. San Vicente Blvd., W. Hollywood (phone: 310-854-1111; 800-424-4443; fax: 310-854-0926).

Century Plaza Extensively renovated last year, the 750-room hotel and the 322-room tower (which boasts spectacular views from spacious rooms and private balconies) are run separately but share many facilities. This is a favorite spot for conventiongoers; the hotel has a full-service business center. There are plenty of shops in which to browse and several fine restaurants on the premises, including the casual seafood bar and grill, *Waters Edge,* and the California-continental *La Chaumière*. Located in Century City, near the *ABC Entertainment Center,* it offers complimentary town car service for trips within a 5-mile radius. Meeting rooms accommodate up to 2,000, and additional business services include a concierge desk, secretarial services, A/V equipment, photocopiers, computers, and express checkout. 2025 Ave. of the Stars, Century City (phone: 310-277-2000; 800-228-3000; fax: 310-551-3355).

Checkers Kempinski Geared to the needs of the business traveler, this 188-room property in the center of Los Angeles's financial district has conference rooms, fax machines, A/V equipment, photocopiers, secretarial and courier services, and interpreters. To ease the stress of the work day, there's a guest library and a rooftop spa with a sauna, a steamroom, and exercise equipment. And for mixing business with pleasure, *Checkers* restaurant, open for "power" breakfasts and lunches, as well as dinners, serves sophisticated American fare. Complimentary limo service is available to downtown business locations, and guests may choose from six complimentary newspapers each day. Additional conveniences include modems for computers and fax outlets in all the rooms. There's also a concierge desk. 535 S. Grand Ave. (phone: 213-624-0000; 800-426-3135; fax: 213-626-9906).

Four Seasons Located in a residential area referred to as "Beverly Hills adjacent," this elegant place is reminiscent of a grand European manor house. The 285 rooms are large and luxuriously appointed, the decor pleasantly subdued, with an emphasis on comfort. On the fourth-floor rooftop terrace is a heated pool/spa area surrounded by palm trees, with a small exercise area nearby. The *Gardens* restaurant, bright, cheery, and casually elegant, is a delight for lunch, dinner, or a lavish Sunday buffet brunch; it's also known for its oversize club sandwiches. All the rooms have computer modems. Other conveniences include a concierge, meeting rooms for up to 500, secretarial services, A/V equipment, photocopiers, and express checkout. 300 S. Doheny Dr. (phone: 310-273-2222; 800-332-3442; fax: 310-859-3824).

J. W. Marriott On spacious grounds in Century City, this is Marriott's West Coast luxury flagship, designed in fashionable château style. The lobby is opulent yet intimate, with art objects and a resident live cockatoo. The hotel features 375 rooms, of which more than half are suites, and indoor and outdoor pools. Among the extra-special touches here are loofahs and natural sponges on tub edges. There's a concierge desk and express checkout. Meeting rooms can accommodate up to 300; and secretarial services, A/V equipment, photocopiers, and computers all are on call. 2151 Ave. of the Stars (phone: 310-277-2777; 800-228-9290; fax: 310-785-9240).

Peninsula Beverly Hills A world class hotel, this stylish property has 200 rooms, suites, and villas, but its intimate scale, residential location (complete with lavish gardens and winding gravel pathways), antique furnishings, and fine artworks give it the feel of a private palazzo. Suites are equipped with private fax machines, VCRs, and CD players. Another 16 rooms and suites are located in five villas, some of which offer private terraces and fireplaces. The wonderful rooftop deck has its own lush garden—it even boasts a manicured lawn and Moroccan–style cabañas. A health spa features a weight room, lap pool, whirlpool, steam/sauna sun deck, and masseuses. The business center offers secretarial services, A/V equipment, photocopiers, and computers. A 24-hour room attendant is on call on every floor. Express checkout is also available. *The Living Room,* a lobby lounge, serves traditional afternoon tea, and *The Belvedere* is a topnotch continental restaurant. 9882 Santa Monica Blvd., Beverly Hills (phone: 310-273-4888; 800-462-7899; fax: 310-788-2319).

Regent Beverly Wilshire Just walk out the front door into the middle of the elegant Beverly Hills shopping district. The mood of this Regent group hotel is more businesslike and subdued (i.e., authentically elegant), less Hollywood flash than at spots like the *Peninsula* (above). In the tower wing, all the rooms are done in different color schemes, furniture styles, and themes. The Wilshire Wing (our favorite) has 147 units, as well as three restaurants (the *Dining Room* is the best) and bars. There are 294 rooms in all, and the marble bathrooms are particularly plush. Meeting rooms hold up to 850. Other services include a concierge desk, secretarial assistance, photocopiers, A/V equipment, computers, and express checkout. 9500 Wilshire Blvd., Beverly Hills (phone: 310-275-5200; 800-545-4000; fax: 310-274-3709).

Ritz-Carlton Marina del Rey This Los Angeles outpost borders the world's largest pleasure-craft harbor. There are sailboats for rent and a shore promenade, as well as tennis courts, a pool and fitness center, and 306 rooms with traditional decor. The club-like *Grill* serves dinner; all meals are provided in *The Café,* which has both indoor and outdoor seating with marina views. Afternoon tea and after-dinner cordials are served in the handsome library and lounge. Transportation to and from *LAX* is complimentary. Business conveniences include meeting rooms accommodating up to 800, secretarial services, a concierge, A/V equipment, photocopiers, computers, and express checkout. 4375 Admiralty Way, Marina del Rey (phone: 310-823-1700; 800-241-3333; fax: 310-823-2403).

St. James's Club The first American link in this international hotel chain—with branches in London, Paris, and Antigua—its West Coast outpost is located smack-dab in the middle of the Sunset Strip, in the lovingly restored 1931 Art Deco *Sunset Tower* building. To rub shoulders with celebrities (Joan Collins, Quincy Jones, and David Bowie to name just a few), check into one of the 18 rooms and 44 suites or have dinner at the *St. James* restaurant (formerly the *Members Room*). For the business traveler, there are meeting rooms accommodating up to 200 people, secretarial services, A/V equipment, photocopiers, and express checkout. 8358 Sunset Blvd., W. Hollywood (phone: 213-654-7100; 800-225-2637; fax: 213-654-9287).

Sheraton Grande Pampering on a grand scale—this is the only hotel in town with personal butler service on every floor and other services beyond the call of duty. The 469 spacious rooms are tastefully decorated. There's a pool (but no health club), and each guest receives a complimentary membership to the *YMCA,* right across the street via a pedestrian bridge. Conference and entertainment space includes a ballroom, meeting rooms, teleconferencing, and, during the day, use of a four-cinema complex in the building. Meeting rooms can accommodate up to 600, and there are secretarial and concierge services, A/V equipment, photocopiers, computer modems in all the rooms, a video message system, and express video checkout. 333 S. Figueroa (phone: 213-617-1133; 800-325-3535; fax: 213-613-0291).

Westwood Marquis This is a favorite among businessfolk who appreciate quality. The attractive high-rise holds 258 suites, and the bustling college town of Westwood is all around. The *Garden Terrace Room* is popular for Sunday brunch, and the elegant *Dynasty Room* (see *Eating Out*) serves California-French food. The *UCLA* running track is less than a half-mile away. There's also a lovely pool surrounded by cabañas. Secretarial assistance is available, as are A/V equipment, photocopiers, computers, and express checkout. There's also a concierge desk. 930 Hilgard Ave., Westwood (phone: 310-208-8765; 800-421-2317; fax: 310-824-0355).

EXPENSIVE

Beverly Hilton It's not quite as convenient to downtown Beverly Hills as the *Regent Beverly Wilshire* (see above), but if you plan to spend a lot of time in the hotel, you'll be happy in this self-contained 579-room establishment. *Trader Vic's* is a consistently good restaurant, and *L'Escoffier,* under the exclusive direction of executive chef Michel Blanchet, now offers superb food along with entertainment and dancing (see *Eating Out*). Meeting rooms hold up to 1,200, and there are secretarial services, a concierge desk, A/V equipment, photocopiers, computers, and express checkout. Other pluses for business travelers: complimentary cellular phones, a public fax in the lobby, and two-line phones with data ports in all rooms. 9876 Wilshire Blvd., Beverly Hills (phone: 310-274-7777; 800-922-5432; fax: 310-285-1313).

Biltmore The grande dame of downtown hotels offers dramatic interiors that combine the classical architecture typical of European palaces with contemporary luxury (even more plush after an early 1990s renovation). There are 700 well-appointed rooms, an indoor pool, and a Jacuzzi. Other pluses include the fine French restaurant *Bernard's* and the *Grand Avenue* bar, with great jazz nightly. Business amenities include meeting rooms for up to 1,000, a concierge, secretarial services, photocopiers, A/V equipment, and express checkout. 506 S. Grand Ave. (phone: 213-624-1011; 800-245-8673; fax: 213-612-1545).

Inter-Continental Los Angeles Downtown's newest hotel, this massive 469-room establishment is geared to business travelers. There is a fully equipped business center; each room has fax, computer, and modem capabilities; and two Club Inter-Continental floors provide business conference and secretarial facilities. Two restaurants, a pool, and a health club are also on the premises. 251 S. Olive St. (phone: 213-617-3300; 800-327-0200; fax: 213-617-3399).

Loews Santa Monica Loews' first venture on the West Coast, this 349-room property provides 20th-century comfort in a 19th-century setting, recalling an era when the area flourished as a resort community. A five-story atrium affords spectacular Pacific views; there's also an extensive fitness center with a personal trainer, an indoor/outdoor pool, and a Jacuzzi. The beach is a few steps away. The decor features antique ironwork, cool Pacific colors, and marine themes in paintings and sculptures by local artists. There are two restaurants, the contemporary Italian *Riva* and the more casual *Coast Café*, and a lobby bar that also serves afternoon tea. Business services include five meeting rooms, secretarial services, a concierge, A/V equipment, photocopiers, and express video checkout. 1700 Ocean Ave., Santa Monica (phone: 310-458-6700; fax: 310-458-6721).

Le Mondrian This contemporary 188-room establishment on Sunset Strip pays homage to Piet Mondrian with its checkerboard exterior and its original paintings by the Dutch artist. The suites provide stunning city views, and the decor is upbeat and sophisticated—rock stars, models, and other Hollywood types are among the clientele. There's a pool, a fitness center, a beauty salon, and a restaurant featuring northern Italian cooking. The jazz lounge provides entertainment nightly. Business amenities include a state-of-the-art computer center, which also has drafting tables and video editing equipment, meeting rooms for up to 120, secretarial services, photocopiers, and A/V equipment. There is also a concierge desk. *Note:* At press time it was uncertain whether the hotel would still be operating under the same name and management this year. 8440 Sunset Blvd., W. Hollywood (phone: 213-650-8999; 800-255-5168; fax: 213-650-5215).

Nikko at Beverly Hills East meets West in this high-tech, Japanese-style hostelry. Busy executives will appreciate the full-service business center as well as the 304 guestrooms, each of which is equipped with a fax, computer hookup, voice mail, oversize desk, and a multi-line computer phone that also controls the lights, stereo, and TV set. Other features include a private bar, terry robes, and a Japanese soaking tub in each striking, black marble bathroom. The hotel also has a small swimming pool; a well-equipped fitness center; and the *Panagaea* restaurant, specializing in Pacific Rim fare. *Arnie Morton's of Chicago* is located next door (see *Eating Out*). 465 S. La Cienega Blvd. (phone: 310-247-0400; 800-NIKKO-US; fax: 310-247-0315).

Ritz-Carlton, Huntington Pasadena's Spanish-style landmark, razed after it was declared earthquake-unsafe, has risen like the proverbial phoenix, albeit Ritz-Carlton–style. Set on 23 acres, the 1920s building has been reconstructed, complete with its imposing Alamo Arch at the entrance, Japanese horseshoe gardens, six cottages, and leaded crystal chandeliers. Other features include the hotel chain's signature dark woods, art and antiques in 385 guestrooms, an Olympic-size pool, a Jacuzzi and fitness center, three tennis courts, three restaurants, and three lounges. Business facilities include meeting rooms that seat 1,000, a concierge, secretarial services, A/V equipment, photocopiers, computers, and express checkout. 1401 S. Oak Knoll Ave., Pasadena (phone: 818-568-3900; 800-241-3333; fax: 818-568-3159).

Sofitel Ma Maison The broad carved staircase, country French furniture, and gaily patterned wall-and-window treatments create a fittingly homey atmosphere in this 311-room, château-style property whose name includes the French words for "My House." The *Ma Maison* restaurant, airy and plant-filled, features expertly prepared French-California fare. For less formal dining, there's the bistro, *La Cajole,* an approximate re-creation of an old Parisian artists' hangout. Additional amenities include meeting rooms that can accommodate 440, secretarial services, a 24-hour concierge desk, A/V equipment, photocopiers, and express checkout. 8555 Beverly Blvd. (phone: 310-278-5444; 800-521-7772; fax: 310-657-2816).

Sunset Marquis If you're looking for a romantic hideaway, this Mediterranean-style paradise is just the ticket. Lush tropical gardens dotted with *koi* ponds and inhabited by exotic birds shelter guests from the outside world; the privacy is just what the many celebrities who stay here are looking for. The 118 luxury suites and villas are furnished with canopy beds, fireplaces, saunas, and Jacuzzis; each has its own butler to cater to guests' needs. Amenities include two restaurants, two pools, a swinging bar called *Whiskey,* a full health club with personal trainers available, a concierge, and full business services. 1200 N. Alta Loma Rd., W. Hollywood (phone: 310-657-1333; 800-858-9758; fax: 310-652-5300).

Westin Bonaventure This 1,474-room giant is a major downtown convention hotel that boasts an all-suite tower designed especially for the business traveler (extras for tower guests include free local calls and a complimentary breakfast). Its cylindrical, mirrored towers are an LA skyline landmark, and it is especially convenient for downtown activities. This city within a city has 20 restaurants and lounges. The rooms, however, do not live up to the promise of the lobby and public spaces. Business services include a concierge desk, meeting rooms that seat 3,000, secretarial services, A/V equipment, photocopiers, computers, and express checkout. 404 S. Figueroa St. (phone: 213-624-1000; fax: 213-612-4800).

Westin, LA Airport If it's Tuesday, this must be LA—a mile from the airport, this 750-room hotel (formerly the *Stouffer Concourse*) announces the day of the week on its elevators' carpets. With travelers often adjusting to time changes from faraway places like the Orient, this thoughtful touch could save the day. There is an outdoor swimming pool and a health club, the *Trattoria Grande*, and the *Charisma Café*. Twenty-one suites have private outdoor Jacuzzis. The meeting rooms seat up to 1,300. Additional amenities include a concierge desk, A/V equipment, photocopiers, and express checkout. 5400 W. Century Blvd., Los Angeles (phone: 310-216-5858; 800-228-3000; fax: 310-645-8053).

MODERATE

Barnabey's Possibly the best value in Southern California, with the charm of an English country inn and a convenient location less than 3 miles from the airport and within walking distance of Manhattan Beach. All rooms are furnished with antiques, and breakfast is included in the rate. Dine in *Barnabey's* restaurant and relax at *Rosie's Pub*. There's also complimentary 24-hour shuttle service to and from the airport, beach, and shopping. Room service is available until 10 PM. Meeting rooms seat 125, and A/V equipment and photocopiers are available for guests' use. Sepulveda Blvd. at Rosecrans Ave., Manhattan Beach (phone: 310-545-8466; 800-552-5285; fax: 310-545-8621).

Beverly Prescott Hotelier Bill Kimpton took over the former *Beverly Hillcrest* and transformed the place into another one of his snazzy boutique hotels. Perched on a hilltop—with private balconies overlooking Beverly Hills, Century City, Hollywood, and the Pacific Ocean—this 140-room hostelry has a palm-tree-lined, canopied entrance, a jewelry-box reception desk inlaid with onyx and mother of pearl, and gardens in its indoor/outdoor lobby. Each room has its own balcony; executive suites come with fax machines, computers, and printers. Other highlights include a health club, an outdoor pool with cabañas and food service, the newspaper delivered to your door, room service, and a great restaurant, *Rox*, run by Hans Rockenwagher. There's also a concierge; full secretarial services are available. 1224 S. Beverwil Dr., W. Los Angeles (phone: 310-277-2800; 800-421-3212; fax: 310-203-9537).

New Otani Within walking distance of the *Music Center*, it has 448 rooms featuring Japanese luxury and service in a lovely garden-like setting—a soothing respite from the madness of downtown LA. The suites have an authentic tatami room and futon bedding as well as deep bathtubs. *A Thousand Cranes* is its serene Japanese restaurant (see *Eating Out*). For more casual dining, the cheery *Azalea Restaurant & Bar* serves breakfast, lunch, and dinner. There's also a shopping arcade and a Japanese health club that offers shiatsu massage and acupuncture therapy. Business services include meeting rooms for up to 750, a concierge, secretarial services, A/V equipment, photocopiers, and express checkout. 120 S. Los Angeles St. (phone: 213-629-1200; 800-252-0197 within California; 800-421-8795 elsewhere in the US; fax: 213-622-0980).

Radisson Hollywood Roosevelt Once the social center of old Hollywood, this 322-room establishment has LA-Spanish charm and an essence of the not so distant past. Traces of Tinseltown still remain—photographs of movie celebrities grace the walls, the Hollywood sign is up the hill, and the star-studded Walk of Fame is right outside. A restaurant, as well as a pool, Jacuzzi, and weight room are on the premises. Room service is available from 6 AM to 11 PM. Business amenities include meeting rooms for up to 300 people, a concierge desk, A/V equipment, photocopiers, and express checkout. 7000 Hollywood Blvd., Hollywood (phone: 213-466-7000; 800-333-3333; fax: 213-462-8056).

INEXPENSIVE

Beverly Garland Holiday Inn Close to *Universal Studios,* this 258-room, California mission–style hotel offers pleasant rooms at very appealing rates (their weekend package features breakfast and free accommodations on Sunday night). Amenities include an outdoor pool, a sauna, a putting green, tennis, free parking, room service from 6 AM to 11 PM, and a restaurant. 4222 Vineland Ave., Studio City (phone: 818-980-8000; 800-HOLIDAY; fax: 818-766-5230).

Courtyard Marriott Formerly the *Chesterfield,* this is a charming find; the 133-room hotel provides guests with all the amenities of higher-priced hostelries such as a concierge, a fine restaurant, and afternoon tea. In the rooms, you'll find complimentary mineral water, bathrobes, hair dryers, and even potpourri sachets. 10320 W. Olympic Blvd., W. Los Angeles (phone: 310-556-2777; 800-321-2211; fax: 310-203-0563).

Safari Inn If you're planning to visit the studios in Burbank, this will be more convenient than Beverly Hills or downtown LA hotels. The spacious valley environment also provides more of a sense of being in the open. There are 85 rooms and 20 suites as well as a restaurant and room service. Meeting rooms can accommodate up to 50, and photocopiers are available for guests' use. 1911 W. Olive Ave., Burbank (phone: 818-845-8586; 800-STAHERE; fax: 818-845-0054).

EATING OUT

These days, Los Angeles may be the country's most exciting restaurant town. Only the purest of purists still look to *L'Escoffier.* Ethnic places abound in all price ranges, and imaginative chefs meld superb raw materials, international accents, and good nutrition into pots of culinary gold. Though popularity with the show-biz crowd is often inversely proportional to the quality of a kitchen and the maître d's treatment of non-celeb guests, good food and good manners are creeping back at the hot spots. Regrettably, dining in din is still in, even when the food is exquisite, but some new restaurants have rediscovered the joy of calm. Los Angeles has banned smoking in all restaurants in the city proper (alfresco dining places, bars, and nightclubs are exempt, however). For dinner for two, expect to pay $100 or more at those places we've listed as very expensive; $75 to $90 at places in the expensive category; $40 to $70 at moderate places; and less than $30 at restaurants described as inexpensive. Prices do not include drinks, wine, or tips. Note that all restaurants serve lunch and dinner, unless otherwise noted. All telephone numbers below include area codes.

VERY EXPENSIVE

Arnie Morton's of Chicago, the Steakhouse Direct from the Windy City comes this LA steakhouse franchise where beef is the name of the game. Although you can get a great lamb or veal chop, porterhouse, New York strip, and rib eye steaks are the raison d'être for eating here. Open daily. Reservations necessary. Major credit cards accepted. 435 S. La Cienega Blvd. (phone: 310-246-1501) and several other locations around LA.

Citrus Owner Michel Richard's French-Provençal-California fare uses delicate seasonings and creative touches to turn ordinary entrées into masterpieces. Among the highlights are grilled swordfish with lentils, pepper tuna steaks, roast veal, and rack of lamb. Don't miss the tasty fish specialties or his famous signature desserts. Closed Saturday lunch and Sundays. Reservations necessary. Major credit cards accepted. 6703 Melrose Ave. (phone: 213-857-0034).

Geoffrey's The wings of Eros beat here, and whether you fall in love with the views of the Pacific, the tasty food, or your dinner companion, it's nigh impossible not to find contentment here. Rich, roasted garlic soup topped with parmesan cheese, addictive rosemary muffins, and hearty braised veal ribs are the stars of the menu. The gallant service continues through the end of the meal, when ladies are offered a rose. Open daily. Reservations advised. Major credit cards accepted. 27400 Pacific Coast Hwy. (phone: 310-457-1519).

L'Orangerie One of LA's truly elegant French restaurants, this posh, flower-filled, special-occasion spot is among the most beautiful dining places in town. The delicacies served here include coddled eggs with caviar, rack of lamb, roasted squab, lobster fricassee, and scrumptious desserts. Still a favorite for special occasions for Hollywood's high and mighty. Closed weekends for lunch and Mondays. Reservations necessary. Major credit cards accepted. 903 N. La Cienega Blvd. (phone: 213-652-9770).

EXPENSIVE

Adriano's High atop the Hollywood hills is this picturesque restaurant decorated with a vaulted ceiling and a brass-trimmed sculpture surrounded by flowers. A favorite with celebrities, it offers tasty northern Italian fare, with perfect pasta and a superb Caesar salad. Open daily. Reservations advised. Major credit cards accepted. 2930 Beverly Glen Blvd. (phone: 310-475-9807).

Babylon Supermodel and actress Tia Carrere's interpretation of an Arabian-style restaurant draws celebs in limos (Tom Cruise, Cher, k. d. lang), some eager to feast on Middle Eastern dishes, others on filet mignon. Closed Sundays; open from 7 PM until the wee hours the rest of the week. Reservations necessary (dress trendy if you don't know any celebrities). Major credit cards accepted. 616 N. Robertson Blvd. (phone: 310-277-6200).

Bikini The young, the hip, and the beautiful squeeze into this stunning, Japanese-style eating emporium. The eclectic, health-conscious menu offers everything from East Indies enchiladas to dim sum dumplings. The high-tech Japanese decor spreads over two stories with a rooftop garden patio. Closed Saturday lunch and Sunday dinner. Reservations advised. Major credit cards accepted. 1413 Fifth St. (phone: 310-395-8611).

Café Four Oaks One of LA's loveliest cafés, this indoor/outdoor spot is unabashedly romantic. Indoors, there's a roaring fireplace. Outdoors, a fabulous garden with lush flora and bubbling fountains that make you feel you're no longer in the city. The food here is a visual treat and a pleasure to eat; especially appealing are the gorgeous salads (such as Belgian white and California red endive with walnuts), and the lightly sauced grilled fish selections (such as farm-raised catfish with a lobster-orange-ginger infusion). There are fabulous goodies for dessert and the service is friendly and unobtrusive. It's one of the prettiest places in LA for a leisurely Sunday brunch. Closed Mondays. Reservations suggested. Major credit cards accepted. 2181 N. Beverly Glen Blvd., Bel-Air (phone: 310-470-2265).

Campanile Named for the tower that crowns this 1928 Charlie Chaplin–built landmark, this stunning place is run by the husband and wife team of Mark Peel and Nancy Silverton, veterans of *Michael's* and *Spago*. Enter through a delightful, skylit café and walk through a long, cloister-like room with tables on one side and the kitchen on the other to get to the balcony-rimmed dining room in the rear. The food is California-Italian, with other Mediterranean influences. The tastes of Tuscany—like antipasto and poached mozzarella—abound; other specialties include all-American grilled prime ribs and sinfully delicious desserts. Open weekdays for all three meals, Saturdays for dinner only; closed Sundays. Reservations necessary (the farther in advance the better). Major credit cards accepted. 524 S. La Brea Ave. (phone: 213-938-1447).

Chasen's A somewhat stuffy LA institution for decades, this celebrity favorite has shed its former image for a more casual atmosphere. There's a new, more budget-friendly, prix fixe menu. Specialties include scampi maison, signature chili, and chicken pot pie. Frank Sinatra, Rosemary Clooney, and Jimmy Stewart are regular patrons. Closed Sunday lunch and Mondays. Reservations advised. American Express accepted. 9039 Beverly Blvd. (phone: 310-271-2168).

Chianti Tasty Italian and continental fare are served in a romantic, old-fashioned room with cozy banquettes and extremely professional service. Some favorites are veal piccata and angel hair pasta with shrimp and crabmeat. Open daily for dinner only. Reservations necessary. Major credit cards accepted. 7833 Melrose Ave., W. Hollywood (phone: 213-653-8333).

Chinois on Main It took the Austrian-born owner Wolfgang Puck (proprietor of *Spago*, see below) to combine Oriental and French cooking into a delicious melting pot of superb but unlikely orchestrations, such as goose liver with marinated pineapple and ginger-cinnamon sauce, barbecued squab with scallion noodles, and charcoal-grilled Szechuan beef in a cilantro-shallot sauce. Open daily for dinner, Wednesdays through Fridays for lunch. Reservations advised (but be warned—they're tough to get). Major credit cards accepted. 2709 Main St., Santa Monica (phone: 310-392-9025).

Cicada Former *L'Orangerie* chef Jean François Meteigner has created a menu to delight all palates in this charming, auberge-like dining room. The Norwegian smoked salmon melts in your mouth; other menu highlights are large, grilled Santa Barbara shrimp, *penne* with *porcini* mushrooms, and linguine with scallops. Plan on a leisurely evening of fine food and some serious "star-gazing." Closed Saturday lunch and Sundays. Reservations necessary. Major credit cards accepted. 8478 Melrose Ave., W. Hollywood (phone: 213-655-5559).

Le Dôme This Art Deco setting in the heart of the Sunset Strip is great for star watching, especially at lunch on Saturdays and after midnight at the magnificent bar. The food is French-continental; there's also an extensive wine list. Closed Saturday lunch and Sundays. Reservations necessary. Major credit cards accepted. 8720 Sunset Blvd. (phone: 310-659-6919).

Drago One of Santa Monica's trendy spots. Chef-owner Celestino Drago demonstrates his culinary talents with such stylish Sicilian dishes as cannellini beans and tuna and *tramezzino di polenta* with wild mushrooms. The cheesecake accompanied by an espresso ends the meal on just the right note. Closed at lunch on weekends. Reservations necessary. Major credit cards accepted. 2628 Wilshire Blvd., Santa Monica (phone: 310-828-1585).

Drai's Chanel-clad women and Armani-draped men drive up to Victor Drai's hot new bistro in Rolls Royces, Mercedes, and BMWs. They come for the fantastic creations of chef Claude Segal: impeccably prepared whitefish wrapped in phyllo, crabmeat-stuffed pasta, grilled Spencer steaks coated with rich cream, and his signature potatoes *boulangère*. For dessert, there's divine *crème brûlée* or an equally celestial chocolate hazelnut cake. Adding to the dining experience are Villeroy & Boch china with Christofle silver amid an elegantly whimsical setting of mismatched furnishings. Open daily for dinner only. Reservations necessary. Major credit cards accepted. 730 N. La Cienega Blvd. (phone: 310-358-8585).

Dynasty Room California-French food is served in a dining room that showcases original artwork and artifacts from China's T'ang Dynasty. The creative fare coupled with an eye-opening Sunday brunch are among the reasons it's remained one of the most popular dining spots in town. Baby abalone and pink-lip scallops on green beans with sauce *citronette* is just one of several winning combinations. Open daily for dinner. Reservations advised. Major credit cards accepted. In the *Westwood Marquis Hotel*, 930 Hilgard Ave., Westwood (phone: 310-208-8765).

L'Escoffier This once formal and somewhat snobby local landmark now boasts a brighter, more casual look and is under the direction of the celebrated culinary genius Michel Blanchet. The inviting room, high atop the *Hilton*, offers a spectacular view of Beverly Hills and an equally wonderful menu of such Blanchet specialties as tartlet of shrimp with asparagus, Maine lobster in lemon and vegetable broth on couscous, and *côte de boeuf* with grilled vegetables and choron sauce. For dessert, the chocolate and Grand Marnier soufflés are to die for. Open for dinner Tuesdays through Saturdays. Reservations necessary. Major credit cards accepted. In the *Beverly Hilton Hotel*, 9876 Wilshire Blvd., Beverly Hills (phone: 310-274-7777).

Georgia A dark, brooding supper club, it features hand-painted upholstered canvas walls, rich mahogany furnishings and a très chic celebrity clientele (the latter is not too surprising considering the owners: Debbie Allen, Eddie Murphy, Norm Nixon, Denzel Washington, and Connie Stevens). The food's terrific, too: "Southern comfort" dishes such as charred tomato okra stew, grits, catfish, and hushpuppies. Open for dinner only; closed Mondays. Reservations necessary. Major credit cards accepted. 7315 Melrose Ave. (phone: 213-933-8410).

Granita Wolfgang Puck's Malibu entry. Designed by his wife, Barbara Lazaroff, the restaurant has an aquarium theme: mosaics, shells, and a *koi* fishpond. Puck's designer pizza still ranks among the best, and the seafood is superb. But the star-struck staff tends to ignore anybody less famous than the local celebrities who flock from their nearby beachfront homes. Closed Monday and Tuesday lunch. Reservations necessary. Major credit cards accepted. 23725 W. Malibu Rd., Malibu (phone: 310-456-0488).

Ivy A favorite venue for lunchtime power deals, it is an anomaly—an old brick farmhouse on bustling Robertson Boulevard, bordering Beverly Hills. Its rustic decor is the perfect setting for the eclectic (with a Southern accent) American menu; it's also a great place for outdoor dining. Corn chowder with fresh tarragon, salad with mesquite-grilled chicken or shrimp, and twice-cooked Cajun prime ribs—first oven-seared and then grilled—are standouts on the changing menu. Then there are the desserts—the likes of which mama could only dream of making. Open daily. Reservations necessary (during evening hours, expect at least an hour's wait even with reservations). Major credit cards accepted. 113 N. Robertson Blvd. (phone: 310-274-8303).

Jimmy's Popular with the Beverly Hills set, this elegant dining place is unbeatable for a romantic dinner or a late-night supper. Try the peppered salmon on a bed of spinach or grilled veal chop with chanterelles. Leave room for the delicious chocolate truffle cake with espresso sauce; insulin shock aside, it's a knockout. Closed Saturday lunch and Sundays. Reservations advised. Major credit cards accepted. 201 Moreno Dr., Beverly Hills (phone: 310-879-2394).

Locanda del Lago A spunky Italian trattoria–style eatery set along Santa Monica's Third Street Promenade, it has oversize windows that afford a great view of the crowd strolling by. Favorite menu selections include wild mushroom polenta, grilled eggplant, *osso buco con risotto alla milanese,* and just about any pasta. Closed weekends for lunch. Reservations advised. 231 Arizona Ave., Santa Monica (phone: 310-451-3525).

Locanda Veneta A tiny trattoria offering some of the most sophisticated Italian food this side of Rome. Try the arugula, mushroom, and parmesan salad; the veal chop is nearly perfect, juicy and charred just so. For dessert, the *tiramisù* is a must. Closed Saturday lunch and Sundays. Major credit cards accepted. Reservations necessary. 8638 W. Third St. (phone: 310-274-1893).

Maple Drive The comfortable, upscale café-like restaurant features down-home meat loaf and the tastiest chili outside of Texas. Other menu options might include the roast turkey, bouillabaisse, and Caesar salad (made without eggs). And while you're spotting celebrities (such as co-owner Dudley Moore), enjoy the live entertainment nightly. Closed Saturday lunch and Sundays. Reservations necessary. Major credit cards accepted. 345 N. Maple Dr. (phone: 310-274-9800).

Michael's Now that prices have dropped closer to the level of LA's other high-priced restaurants, this pioneer eatery—where California nouvelle was first new—just may be accessible to a few more diners. The gorgeous garden and contemporary art add visual pleasure to the gustatory feats. Try the wild mushroom salad and the grilled Norwegian salmon filet with beurre blanc sauce and steamed vegetables. Closed Mondays, Saturday lunch, and Sunday dinner. Reservations advised. Major credit cards accepted. 1147 Third St., Santa Monica (phone: 310-451-0843).

Morton's Relocated last year in a spanking new building, set on the site where *Trumps* once reigned, *Morton's* is still the place of choice for tinseltown moguls, mavens, and anyone else seeking to dine on good food while basking in the social spotlight. The menu has undergone a few small changes, but still offers the standards that made *Morton's* famous—pasta, pizza, salads, and grilled dishes. Closed Sundays. Reservations necessary. Major credit cards accepted. 8764 Melrose Ave. (phone: 310-276-5205).

Orso Although the outside decor is extremely unassuming, this popular northern Italian trattoria more than compensates with its interior ambience and its charming patio framed by ficus trees and candlelit tables. Earthy country salads, pizza with all-but-transparent crusts, grilled meat, and delicious calf's liver are served on attractive Italian pottery plates. There is an extensive wine list as well. Well-known actors frequent this spot, and the bar becomes lively after theater hours. Open daily. Reservations advised. MasterCard and Visa accepted. 8706 W. Third St. (phone: 310-274-7144).

Pacific Dining Car Steaks—cut on the premises from aged, corn-fed beef—are the house specialty, although the menu also offers four types of fresh fish every day. The restaurant is set in a real dining car (plus an additional building) that's been at the same downtown location since 1921. This is a good place for early dinner or late supper when you have tickets for a show at the *Music Center.* Open daily, around the clock. Reservations necessary. Major credit cards accepted. 1310 W. Sixth St. (phone: 213-483-6000).

Patina Superchef Joachim Splichal has really pulled out all the stops with a whimsical menu that includes a corn *blini* "sandwich" filled with marinated salmon; a soufflé (how French) of grits (how American) with Herkimer cheddar and an apple-smoked bacon sauce; or New York duck liver with blueberry pancakes and blueberry sauce. Closed weekends for lunch. Reservations necessary. Major credit cards accepted. 5955 Melrose Ave., W. Hollywood (phone: 213-467-1108).

Pinot *Patina*'s sister bistro, housed in a charming yellow brick building, offers creative fare—also inspired by Splichal—that continues to wow the trendsetters and mega-stars (Warren Beatty for one) who flock here. Closed Sundays. Reservations necessary. Major credit cards accepted. 12969 Ventura Blvd., Studio City (phone: 818-990-0500).

Remi Evocative of a tony seaside Italian restaurant (even though it's three blocks from the sea), and named for Venetian gondoliers' oars, this eatery serves ambrosial Venetian fare in a casually elegant atmosphere. The rich wood, gleaming brass, and nautical theme provide an airy backdrop for enjoying such dishes as whole fish infused with herbs and the wonderful selection of grappas. The outdoor tables are ideal for people watching on Santa Monica's *Third Street Promenade*. Open daily. Reservations necessary. Major credit cards accepted. 1451 Third St. Promenade (phone: 310-393-6545).

Spago When you're hot, you're hot. Famed chef Wolfgang Puck (see *Chinois on Main* and *Granita*) turned pizza making into an art form. His are baked in wood-burning brick ovens and topped with shrimp, duck, sausage, and goat cheese. Celebrity diners also munch on Sonoma lamb, Washington oysters, North Pacific salmon, and grilled free-range chicken. Be sure to leave room for one of the incredible desserts. Open daily for dinner only. Since this still is one of the most popular spots in town, make reservations weeks in advance. Major credit cards accepted. 1114 Horn Ave., W. Hollywood (phone: 310-652-4025).

Tatou This lavish, 1930s-style supper club, where the dressed-to-the-nines clientele dine under a 25-foot-high, tented ceiling accented with a crystal chandelier, is patterned after the legendary *Coconut Grove* nightclub. Plush banquettes line the ornate walls, and center stage tables are shaded by faux palm trees. Live entertainment accompanies chef Desi Szonntagh's traditional, hearty American-French-Provençal fare. A sampling of menu items might include Maine lobster, Caesar salad, crispy roast duck with ginger and black currants, and herb-packed red snapper with oven-dried tomatoes. Desserts are a chocolate lover's paradise. After dinner, go upstairs and dance off those calories (the club is open weekdays until 2 AM, Fridays and Saturdays until 4 AM). Jackets are required for men. Closed Sundays. Reservations necessary. Major credit cards accepted. 233 N. Beverly Dr., Beverly Hills (phone: 310-274-9955).

Water Grill The only oyster bar in the downtown area is located in this handsome spot. Eight varieties of the mollusk are served along with a wide selection of fresh regional seafood: Atlantic soft-shell crabs with cranberries, northern pike with succotash, and California cioppino are just a hint of what you can experience. Closed weekends for lunch. Reservations advised. Major credit cards accepted. 523 W. Sixth St. (phone: 213-891-0900).

MODERATE

Benvenuto A tiny trattoria offering friendly service and exquisitely prepared Italian food. This cozy café is a popular hangout for celebs, artists, entertainers, and other assorted Hollywood types. Although chef Mustapha

Sadd's menu is the main attraction—designer pizza, fresh fish, pasta, baked rabbit, *tiramisù*—lingering over an espresso in the candlelit dining room or on the patio overlooking Santa Monica Boulevard while watching the celebrity parade pass by makes this place hard to leave. Closed weekends for lunch. No reservations. Major credit cards accepted. 8512 Santa Monica Blvd., W. Hollywood (phone: 310-659-8635).

Bistro Garden The very same Beverly Hills celebrities who have parked their Rolls-Royces up the street at the *Bistro* for years have made its sister restaurant the "in" spot. Lunch is especially chic, with such fare as baked sea scallops with a muscat-ginger sauce. The garden-like patio is *the* place to be seen, and it's quite a pretty place at that. Closed Sundays. Reservations necessary. Major credit cards accepted. 176 N. Canon Dr., Beverly Hills (phone: 310-550-3900).

Ca' Brea The clone of the higher-priced and equally popular *Locanda Veneta* (see above), the northern Italian fare is as good as it gets. Specialties include tortelloni filled with spinach and ricotta, and grilled lamb chops with a robust mustard sauce and truffles. Be sure to leave room for the *tiramisù*—it's worth every calorie. Closed Saturday lunch and Sundays. Reservations advised. Major credit cards accepted. 346 S. La Brea (phone: 213-938-2863).

Café La Bohème This whimsical West Hollywood eatery attracts a lively crowd that comes mostly for the ambience: The high-ceilinged Nouveau Baroque dining room is draped in faded velvet and adorned with gilded mirrors. The menu has something for everybody—pizza, pasta, salads topped with garlic-seared beef, and filet mignon with shiitake mushrooms. Open daily. Reservations advised. Major credit cards accepted. 8400 Santa Monica Blvd., W. Hollywood (phone: 213-848-2360).

Celestino The young Italian chef draws on his Sicilian roots and Tuscan training for a limited menu with innovative twists, such as the highly praised seafood baked in a paper bag. The restaurant is airy and unpretentious. The art exhibit changes periodically, as does the menu. Closed weekends for lunch. Late-night suppers are served Fridays and Saturdays until 1 AM, with jazz until 2 AM. Reservations advised. Major credit cards accepted. 236 S. Beverly Dr. (phone: 310-859-8601).

Chaya Venice The family responsible for the *Chaya* (Japanese for tea house) chain has been operating tea houses in Japan for three centuries now. Their latest venture blends Japanese and American fare with such dishes as Hawaiian-tuna spring rolls accompanied by a spicy salsa, charred rare tuna *niçoise,* and broiled sea eel with julienned vegetables. The decor is high-tech—an eclectic mix of chrome, copper, stone, and wood, reflecting the diversity of the menu. Open daily for dinner; closed Saturday lunch. Reservations necessary. Major credit cards accepted. 110 Navy St., Venice (phone: 310-396-1179).

Chez Mélange This South Bay eatery is true to its name, offering an international variety of victuals. There is a champagne bar, a wine bar with tastings on Tuesdays, and a dining room, all in a former coffee shop of a motor inn. Open daily for all three meals. Reservations advised. Major credit cards accepted. 1716 Pacific Coast Hwy., Redondo Beach (phone: 310-540-1222).

Il Cielo Set in a brick cottage, with several romantic dining rooms (a fireplace glows in the winter) and a heated patio, this place serves excellent northern Italian food. During quiet hours the staff treats guests as if they were at a family reunion. On a balmy evening, eating in the garden feels like dining in Tuscany. Closed Sundays. Reservations advised. Major credit cards accepted. 9018 Burton Way, Beverly Hills (phone: 310-276-9990).

David Slay's La Veranda Crowd-pleasing California-Italian fare served in generous portions is the staple of this charming and comfortable dining room. Chef-owner Slay features robust roasted garlic soup, roast veal loin, and salmon tartare with waffle-cut potatoes. Save room for one (or two or three) of the homemade pastries—our favorites are the tiny puffs filled with vanilla cream and caramel sauce. Closed weekends for lunch. Reservations advised. Major credit cards accepted. 225 S. Beverly Dr., Beverly Hills (310-274-7246).

Engine Co. No. 28 This converted firehouse re-creates an American grill of the 1940s, but serves what chef Naomi Serizawa calls old-fashioned comfort food with a health-conscious attitude. Popular dishes include seafood salad, turkey burgers on whole-wheat buns, a light "Firehouse" chili, and special pasta. Weekly specials feature recipes created by firehouse cooks from around the US. Open daily for dinner; weekdays only for breakfast and lunch. Reservations advised. Major credit cards accepted. 644 S. Figueroa St. (phone: 213-624-6996).

Epicentre Although some Angelenos fail to see the humor in the faux post-earthquake damage decor presented here, the place attracts a steady clientele. Gimmicky food names—"seismic entrées"—include quesadillas, crab cakes in corn chili sauce, curries, and homemade ice cream. Closed Saturday lunch, Sundays, and Monday dinner. Reservations advised. Major credit cards accepted. *Kawada Hotel,* 200 S. Hill St. (phone: 213-625-0000).

Gilliland's The owner is Irish but the fare is Californian—with Irish accents (such as soda bread on Sundays). Closed Saturday lunch. Reservations necessary on weekends. Major credit cards accepted. 2425 Main St. (phone: 310-392-3901).

Jackson's The decor is unpretentious, with wagon-wheel ceiling lights and a Western, ski-lodge feel; the mood is frisky; and both the home-style and more elaborate dishes are first-rate. Try the rabbit with polenta, roasted pork loin with crispy potato pancake, or crab- and leek-stuffed ravioli, with a fresh raspberry tart for dessert. Open daily. Reservations advised. Major credit cards accepted. 8908 Beverly Blvd. (phone: 310-550-8142).

Joss The austere decor makes this a high-style showcase for unfamiliar regional Chinese delicacies, such as glazed ginger venison with *quei hua* wine. The waiter shows off the whole perfectly crisped, golden brown Hong Kong Pin-Pei chicken before carving and preparing it in the style of Peking duck on a side table. Closed weekends for lunch. Reservations advised. Major credit cards accepted. 9255 Sunset Blvd. (phone: 310-276-1886).

Mandarin Northern Chinese cooking is presented in elegant surroundings instead of the usual plastic, pseudo-Oriental decor. Not on the menu, but well worth requesting as an appetizer, is the minced squab wrapped in lettuce leaves; also be sure to try the spicy prawns. Closed weekends for lunch. Reservations advised. Major credit cards accepted. 430 N. Camden Dr., Beverly Hills (phone: 213-272-0267).

Matsuhisa The Japanese fare with Peruvian accents (honest!) is described by its chef as "New Wave seafood." The most popular dishes are squid cut like pasta, with an asparagus topping, and seafood with soy, *wasabi,* and garlic. Closed weekends for lunch. Reservations necessary two to three days in advance. Major credit cards accepted. 129 N. La Cienega Blvd. (phone: 310-659-9639).

Mon Kee's Amazing seafood combinations are the draw at this bustling Chinese dining spot, which caters to downtown LA's business crowd as well as to tourists. "Live ' lobster, 15 squid dishes (try the crispy squid with special salt), and steamed or fried saltwater and freshwater fish are the mainstays of the seafood menu. For those not compelled by the above or the conch, clams, or oysters, there are dozens of traditional pork, poultry, beef, and vegetable dishes by which to be dazzled. Open daily. Reservations advised. Major credit cards accepted. 679 N. Spring St. (phone: 213-628-6717).

Musso & Frank Grill It really is a grill, operating in Hollywood since 1919, and apparently not redecorated once (not that its regulars—film people, journalists, the moiling LA middle class—want it to change one iota). The kind of place whose cachet is having none at all, it's fine if you like nostalgia and surly waiters. Traditional American food is served—try the short ribs, chicken pot pie, or macaroni and cheese. Closed Sundays. Reservations advised. Major credit cards accepted. 6667 Hollywood Blvd. (phone: 213-467-7788).

Pane Caldo Bistro An unpretentious Italian *ristorante* with a great view of the city's famed hills. What it lacks in fancy appointments, it more than makes up for with careful food preparation, generous portions, and reasonable prices. A complimentary appetizer and basket of *focaccia* arrive with the menu to ease the difficult task of choosing from among Tuscan specialties such as warm bell-pepper salad, risotto specials, tagliatelle with *porcini* mushrooms, spinach tortelloni with butter and sage, osso buco, and a selection of 14 kinds of individual pizza. Try the ultrarich *tiramisù* for dessert. Closed Sunday lunch. Reservations advised. Major credit cards accepted. 8840 Beverly Blvd. (phone: 310-274-0916).

Rockenwagner It's loud, even raucous, but the food's great at this Frank Gehry–designed, high-tech eatery. Set behind a glass façade, it features booths lighted by modern streetlamps and a huge German countryside mural. The creative menu features tasty appetizers such as garlic flan, goat cheese, and beet terrine with grilled radicchio; among the entrées is cilantro fettuccine with chicken, mild chilies, onion, and roasted jalapeño tomato sauce. Desserts highlights include caramelized pear

Napoleon, crisp warm apple pizza, and scrumptious signature cookies. Open weekdays for all three meals; brunch and dinner on weekends. Reservations advised. Major credit cards accepted. 2435 Main St., Santa Monica (phone: 310-339-6504).

Rustica Brothers James and John Beriker's romantic restaurant offers two lovely settings for dinner: a gracious garden room/patio with real fruit trees and an Italian fountain under a retractable roof, and the elegant yet cozy front room with a striking bar and pretty tables nestled among live plants. The excellent fare suits the setting; choose from wood-fired pizza, homemade pasta, charbroiled fish, and specialties such as roasted eggplant and potato mousse with black Kalamata olives. Closed Sundays. Reservations necessary. Major credit cards accepted. 435 N. Beverly Dr. (phone: 310-247-9331).

Siamese Princess This Oriental eatery, which predates the Thai proliferation, looks like an antiques shop. European furniture and collectibles vie for space with Siamese gift items and photos of British, Thai, and show-biz royalty. The food, billed as "Royal Thai" and beautifully presented, ranks high above run-of-the-mill. For example, slivers of orange peel turn rice noodles into a delicacy. Closed Saturday through Wednesday lunch. Reservations necessary. Major credit cards accepted. 8048 W. Third St. (phone: 213-653-2643).

A Thousand Cranes Besides having such a beautiful name, this Japanese spot is well versed in the traditional art of serving beautiful food. It has several tatami rooms and a Western dining room. Go for Sunday brunch, a spectacular Japanese buffet accompanied by live music. Open daily. Reservations advised. Major credit cards accepted. In the *New Otani Hotel,* 120 S. Los Angeles St. (phone: 213-629-1200).

INEXPENSIVE

California Pizza Kitchen *Spago* for the masses, it's Beverly Hills's favorite pizza place. Upscale fast food is served in a sleek black-, white-, and yellow-tiled environment—this is not your average neighborhood pizzeria. Nouvelle cuisine pizza specialties, served straight from a wood-fired oven, include such delights as Original BBQ Chicken Pizza, Thai Chicken Pizza, Tandoori Chicken Pizza, Peking Duck Pizza, BLT Pizza, and Tuna-Melt Pizza. The menu also offers fresh pasta with interesting sauces, and yummy desserts. Open mid-morning to late evening daily. Unlike *Spago,* there's no need for a reservation here—but there'll probably be a line. Major credit cards accepted. 207 S. Beverly Dr., Beverly Hills (phone: 213-272-7878) and several other locations around LA.

Chianti Cucina Sister to the far pricier *Chianti* next door (see above), this casual trattoria specializes in great-tasting pasta and pizza. Open daily. Reservations necessary. Major credit cards accepted. 7383 Melrose Ave. (phone: 213-653-8333).

Chin Chin Delicious dim sum and traditional Chinese food, cooked without MSG, account for its ongoing popularity as do its quick service and low prices. Takeout also is available. Open daily. Reservations unnecessary. Major credit cards accepted. Five locations: 8618 Sunset Blvd., Sunset

Plaza (phone: 213-652-1818); 11740 San Vicente Blvd., Brentwood (phone: 213-826-2525); 12215 Ventura Blvd., Studio City (phone: 213-985-9090); 16101 Ventura Blvd., Encino (phone: 818-783-1717); and 13455 Maxella Ave , Marina del Rey (phone: 213-823-9999).

DIVE! Yes, LA has another theme restaurant—this one, the brainchild of film director Steven Spielberg, is designed like a submarine and decorated with many of the appropriate sub parts and gadgets, with underwater sights and sounds appearing on a 210-square-foot video wall. The menu offers more than 20 types of hot, cold, and "nuclear spicy" submarine sandwiches, including ones filled with soft-shell crab, Tuscan steak, and three vegetarian choices. Also on the menu are wood-oven-roasted shrimp and chicken, ribs, main course salads, home fries, and unusual desserts. Inventive drinks are served at the bar, and a retail window sells *DIVE!* T-shirts and the like. Though it looks more like a Hollywood set than a restaurant, the food rates star billing. Open daily (after-theater meals, takeout, and delivery are available). No reservations. Major credit cards accepted. *Century City Shopping Center,* 10250 Santa Monica Blvd (phone: 310-203-0928).

Emporio Armani Express Café and Restaurant After busting your budget downstairs on Italian designer clothing, head for the balcony and the comfort of a glass of wine and a plate of ravioli *di zucca* (homemade pasta filled with pumpkin and mascarpone cheese) or risotto with artichoke hearts and duck prosciutto. There's also lighter fare, such as a salad of crisp greens tossed in lemon dressing over a bed of sliced oranges and fennel. Open daily for all three meals. Reservations unnecessary. Major credit cards accepted. 9533 Brighton Way (phone: 310-271-9440).

Gladstone's Malibu One of the best beachfront restaurants for casual dining, this funky fish house offers alfresco, picnic-style dining on wooden tables stationed on a floor rife with peanut shells and sawdust (or you can eat indoors, but you'll miss the fresh sea air). The menu offers a variety of seasonal seafood in soups, salads, and an assortment of appetizers and entrées. Bring a hearty appetite because portions are generous. Open daily for all three meals. Reservations unnecessary. Major credit cards accepted. 17300 Pacific Coast Hwy., Pacific Palisades (phone: 310-454-3474).

Hamayoshi One of the reasons Japanese diplomats request appointments to Los Angeles is this sushi bar for connoisseurs favoring flatfish of all kinds—a list unequaled almost anywhere. The place is small and simple, and customers sometimes have to wait outside for a spot. Free parking. Open daily for dinner; lunch weekdays. Reservations advised. Major credit cards accepted. 3350 W. 1st St. (phone: 213-384-2914).

Hugo's This charming, country-style café with attentive waiters and great coffee is the home of the "power breakfast" for studio heads and major stars (Julia Roberts, Bette Midler, and Geena Davis are regulars). Million-dollar deals are made over pumpkin pancakes, pasta *alla Mamma* (the house specialty: linguine, eggs, garlic, and Hugo's secret seasoning), and smoked salmon omelettes with tomatoes and sour cream. Get here early; window tables go fast. Lunch and dinner have a calmer atmosphere, but the food is equally first-rate: pasta carbonara, fresh fish, veal parmesan, and so forth. Open daily. No reservations. Major credit cards accepted. 8401 Santa Monica Blvd., W. Hollywood (phone: 213-654-3993).

Nosh of Beverly Hills Stop in for a quick, delicious bite of "authentic delicatessen" at this New York–style eatery, where the sizable portions would make any Jewish mother proud. It's all here—bagels and lox, chicken soup, and incredible cheesecake. Open daily. No reservations. Major credit cards accepted. 9689 Little Santa Monica Blvd., Beverly Hills (phone: 310-271-3730).

Old Town Bakery A real charmer. Chef-owner Amy Pressman's bakery-cum-restaurant caters to hefty appetites, offering giant country crêpes (filled with chicken, herb pesto, ratatouille, or ricotta), great rotisserie chicken tacos, crisp bow tie pasta, and home-style pan pizza. Leave room for delectable desserts—bittersweet chocolate terrine, orange poppyseed cake, and Amy's hand-spun ice cream. Open daily. No reservations. No credit cards accepted. 166 W. Colorado Blvd., Pasadena (phone: 818-792-7943).

Original Pantry The decor is early greasy spoon—the food, waiters, and prices ditto—yet long lines at lunch have forced the first expansion since its opening in the 1920s. A potful of raw vegetable sticks precedes big portions of basic food. If the mood for a big American breakfast strikes at 3 AM, one might even find a parking place outside. Open nonstop. Reservations unnecessary. No credit cards accepted. 877 S. Figueroa (phone: 213-972-9279).

Thunder Roadhouse The theme at this trendy bar/restaurant is motorcycles, with a decor that features antique bikes, iron sculptures, motorcycle memorabilia, and mementos of the Old West. The 30-foot brass and copper bar is thick with beer-drinkers after dark, while the restaurant dishes out just what you would expect: burgers, shakes, sandwiches, omelettes, Cajun catfish, grilled pork chops, and hot pecan or sweet potato pie for dessert. Open daily for all three meals. Reservations unnecessary. Major credit cards accepted. 8363 Sunset Blvd. (phone: 213-650-6011).

Whitney's A special little place where chef/owner Whitney Werner and wife, Cheryl Kunitake Werner, work their culinary wonders. Seafood lovers should sample the seared sea bass with tomatillo and black bean salsa or the peppered tuna with crispy wontons and *ponsu* sauce. If pasta's your passion, try the linguine with Norwegian smoked salmon or *arrabbiata penne* (fresh parsley and tomato sauce over quill-shape pasta) with Japanese eggplant smothered with warm goat cheese. Open daily. Reservations unnecessary. Major credit cards accepted. 1518 Montana Ave., Santa Monica (phone: 310-458-4114).

THE FINAL TOUCH

For dessert, try the luscious ice cream made by *Robin Rose* and sold in the *Robin Rose* shops in Venice (215 Rose Ave.; phone: 310-399-1774) and downtown in the Wells Fargo Center (333 S. Grand Ave.; phone: 310-687-8815).

Louisville

At-a-Glance

SEEING THE CITY

The *Spire* restaurant and cocktail lounge on the 19th floor of the *Hyatt Regency Louisville* (see *Checking In*) revolves to show views of downtown Louisville, the Ohio River, and, when it's not too hazy, southern Indiana across the river.

SPECIAL PLACES

The best way to get around Louisville is by car. You can hop a trolley or walk around downtown, but attractions like *Churchill Downs*, historic homes, and the lovely surrounding countryside require transportation. But first . . .

CHURCHILL DOWNS By far Louisville's most popular attraction, the *Kentucky Derby* draws close to 140,000 people to *Churchill Downs* on the first Saturday in May. Modeled after England's *Epsom Derby*, this first jewel of the Triple Crown has been run over the same course ever since its beginnings in 1875 (though the original 1½-mile distance was trimmed to 1¼ miles in 1896). It's a big deal for the horse owners because of the race's prestige, as well as its big purse (usually close to $1 million); for the horses because of the competition and the distance (which is considerable for a three-year-old so early in the season); and for the whole city. The twin-spired track is packed with fans sipping mint juleps, shedding a few tears at the sound of "My Old Kentucky Home," and, if they're lucky, catching a glimpse of some of the world's most expensive horseflesh. If you can stand the unabashed sentimentality, the crowds, and the expense (accommodations are offered at a substantial premium on *Derby* weekend), it's worth the trip—at least once.

Reserved seats for the race are hard to get (most box-holders renew their tickets annually), but all you need to join the general admission party in the infield is $20. (There are no seats here, so a blanket or lawn chair and sunscreen also would be nice.) In addition, a limited number of general admission tickets to the *Clubhouse Gardens* area are sold on the day of the race or by phone after March 1. As for a seat in the *Clubhouse* or *Grandstand*, every year the track gets more than 30,000 requests for the few tickets that become available. Seats are usually sold out by January, so send your written request early (right after the current year's race). Write *Churchill Downs*, Derby Ticket Office, 700 Central Ave., Louisville, KY 40208 (phone: 636-4400).

There are several *Kentucky Derby* tour package offerings which are probably the best bet for anyone hoping to get a seat for this prestigious event. Contact *Wagonlit Travel* (211 Holiday Manor, Louisville, KY 40222; phone: 800-866-9882); *Delta Queen Steamboat Co.* (30 Robin Street Wharf, New Orleans, LA 70130-1890; phone: 800-543-1949); or *Frontier Travel & Tours* (1923 N. Carson St., Suite 105, Carson City, NV 89701; phone: 800-248-4782).

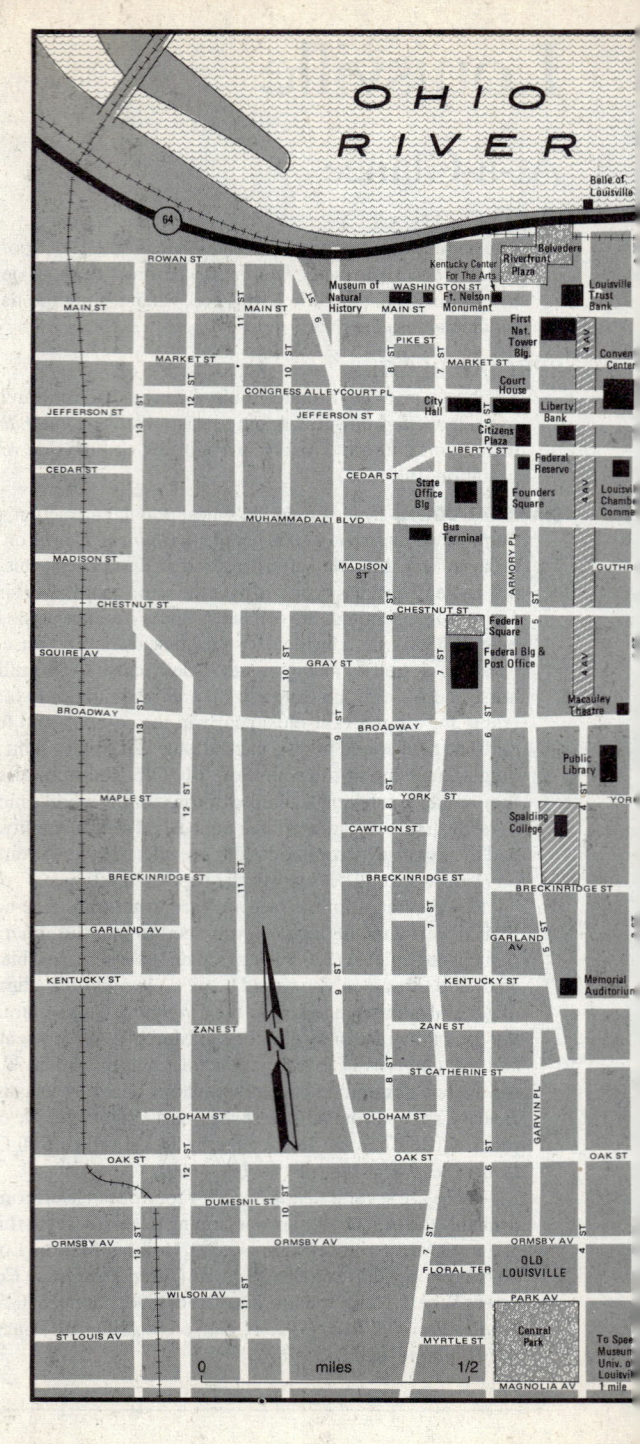

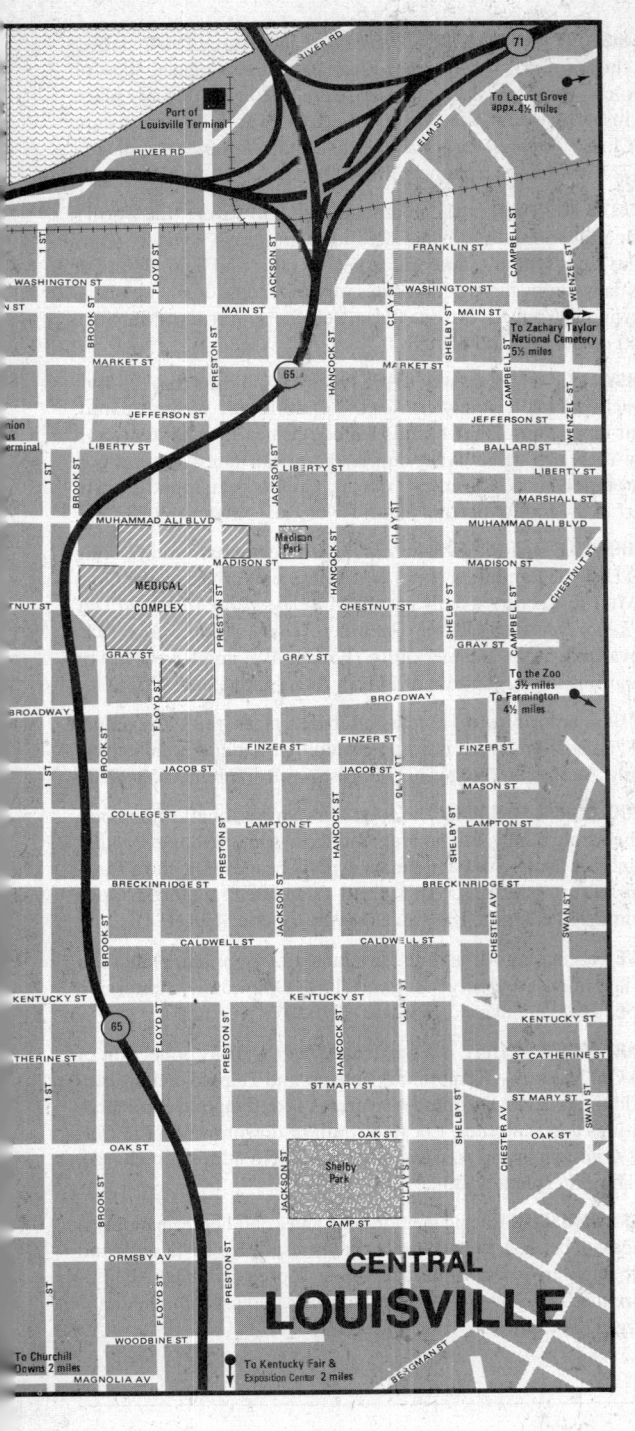

MUSEUM OF HISTORY AND SCIENCE *Space Hall,* a 360-degree IMAX movie theater, the *Mummy's Tomb,* and *Kidspace,* with hands-on activities for preschoolers, combine with temporary exhibits to give this airy place located in a renovated 19th-century riverfront warehouse consistent appeal. Closed *Thanksgiving, Christmas Eve,* and *Christmas.* Admission charge. 727 W. Main St. (phone: 561-6100).

LOUISVILLE FALLS FOUNTAIN In the middle of the Ohio River, "the world's largest floating fountain" creates 375-foot-high sprays, a watery fleur-de-lis (the city's symbol), and other special water and light effects. It operates daily, spring through fall (dates vary depending on the weather). Best viewing is from Riverfront Plaza/Belvedere, north of Main St., between Fourth Ave. and Sixth St.

STAR OF LOUISVILLE An elegant way to see the area is aboard this 130-foot luxury yacht, which leisurely cruises the Ohio River. Well-prepared, abundant lunch and dinner buffets include dishes such as snow crab and New York strip steaks. After dinner, diners can dance to a jazz-pop combo or taped music played by a deejay. Cruises year-round. Fourth St. Wharf at the foot of Second St. on River Rd. (phone: 589-7827).

BELLE OF LOUISVILLE Board a 19th-century–style steamboat (and floating National Historic Landmark) for a nostalgic, scenic cruise on the Ohio River. Afternoon cruises daily except Mondays from *Memorial Day* through *Labor Day* weekend, with Saturday evening dance cruises. Tickets are available at the steamer office (Fourth Ave. and River Rd.) or in the boarding line at the foot of Fourth Ave. (phone: 625-2355).

FARMINGTON Built according to Thomas Jefferson's plans, the 19th-century home of Judge John Speed is a fine example of Federal architecture. Open daily. Admission charge. 3033 Bardstown Rd. (phone: 452-9920).

LOUISVILLE ZOOLOGICAL GARDENS The zoo offers a pleasant afternoon outing for the whole family, but be prepared to do some walking. Popular exhibits include an up-close-and-personal polar bear exhibit and a *Herp-Aquarium,* with amphibians, reptiles, and a simulated rain forest. Open daily. Admission charge. 1100 Trevilian Way (phone: 459-2184).

LOCUST GROVE Fascinating for architecture fans, this Georgian plantation was the last home of George Rogers Clark. Open daily. Admission charge. 561 Blankenbaker La. (phone: 897-9845).

J. B. SPEED ART MUSEUM Here is a particularly noteworthy collection of works by Old Masters—Rembrandt, Rubens, and Tiepolo, among others. In addition, there is an impressive array of contemporary and modern paintings and sculpture. Located south of downtown on the *University of Louisville* campus. Closed Mondays. No admission charge. 2035 S. Third St. (phone: 636-2893).

KENTUCKY DERBY MUSEUM Racing memorabilia and a 360-degree panorama of the race can be seen; "hands-on" exhibits test *Derby* trivia skills and explore the mysteries of pari-mutuel betting. Closed *Oaks Day* (the Friday before the *Derby*), *Derby Day, Thanksgiving,* and *Christmas.* Admission charge. 704 Central Ave. (phone: 637-1111).

KENTUCKY KINGDOM More than 70 amusements are here at this family theme park on the grounds of the *Kentucky Fair & Exposition Center,* including three roller coasters; *The Quake,* a motion machine that'll get you shaking all over; an international *Grand Carousel;* and the *Hurricane Bay* water park. Open June through August; weekends only April, May, and September. Admission charge. Two miles south of central Louisville off I-264, Watterson Expy. (phone: 366-2231).

> ### EXTRA SPECIAL
>
> Kentucky history comes to life in Bardstown, about 40 miles south of Louisville. At *My Old Kentucky Home State Park* (501 E. Stephen Foster Ave.; phone: 348-3502), visitors can tour the Federal mansion that inspired Stephen Foster to write what is now the state song. The park is closed *Thanksgiving, Christmas* week, *New Year's Eve,* and *New Year's Day;* admission charge. An outdoor drama, *The Stephen Foster Story,* is presented from June through *Labor Day* weekend in the park. You can see how whiskey is made at *Maker's Mark Distillery* (3350 Burks Spring Rd.; phone: 865-2881). It's closed weekends January through February and Sundays the rest of the year. Tours are free. Traditional Kentucky food can be found at the *Old Talbott Tavern* (107 W. Stephen Foster Ave.; phone: 348-3494), whose patrons once included Abraham Lincoln and Andrew Jackson. To get to Bardstown, take I-65 south out of Louisville, exiting to Route 245.

Sources and Resources

TOURIST INFORMATION

The *Louisville Convention and Visitors Bureau* (400 S. First St., Louisville, KY 40402; phone: 582-3732; 800-633-3384 in Kentucky; 800-626-5646 from elsewhere in the US) provides maps and brochures and answers questions. There's also a visitors' information booth in the atrium of the *Louisville Galleria* (Fourth Ave. between Muhammad Ali Blvd. and Liberty St.; 583-4636) and one at *Standiford Field Airport* (phone: 367-4636). All information centers are open daily. Contact the Kentucky state tourism hotline (phone: 800-225-TRIP) for maps, calendars of events, health updates, and travel advisories.

LOCAL COVERAGE *Louisville Courier-Journal,* daily (Friday's *Weekend* section has highlights of the coming week's events); and *Louisville* magazine, a monthly that includes a calendar of events.

TELEVISION STATIONS WAVE Channel 3–NBC; WHAS Channel 11–ABC; WLKY Channel 32–CBS; WDRB Channel 41–Fox; and WKET Channel 68–PBS.

RADIO STATIONS AM: WHAS 840 (contemporary/sports/news); WAVG 970 (oldies/news/sports); and WLOU 1350 (black-oriented). FM: WFPL 89.3 (jazz/information); WUOL 90.5 (classical music); and WLRS 102.3 (rock).

TELEPHONE The area code for Louisville is 502.

SALES TAX There is a 6% state sales tax.

CLIMATE The general tendency is toward mild winters, brief but exquisite springs and falls, and long, humid, and polluted summers. But snow in April or a 60F day in December isn't unheard of.

GETTING AROUND

AIRPORT Louisville's *Standiford Field Airport* (5 miles south of downtown on Rte. 65; phone: 367-4636 for airport information) handles only domestic flights. Depending on the traffic, the drive to the airport can take anywhere from 10 to 30 minutes. The airport limousine service makes stops at a few downtown hotels, but most hotels in town offer courtesy vans to pick up registered guests. The city's *TARC* buses stop near the airport's main entrance and travel downtown; for the return trip, buses can be picked up along the southbound side of First Street.

BUS *TARC* bus system serves the downtown area adequately during the day but is limited in the suburbs and after dark downtown. The fare is 35¢ or 60¢, depending on the time of day. Route information is available at the *Transit Authority Office* (1000 W. Broadway; phone: 585-1234).

CAR RENTAL Most national firms are represented.

HORSE AND CARRIAGE This is a romantic way to see the city. Visitors can pick one up in front of the *Galt House* hotel at Sixth and Main Streets or make arrangements in advance to be dropped off or picked up at any downtown restaurant. The carriages operate evenings mid-March through December; contact *Louisville Horse Trams* (phone: 581-0100).

TAXI Cabs must be ordered by phone and are often slow to respond. The major company is *Yellow Cab* (phone: 636-5511).

TROLLEY The *Toonerville II* (phone: 585-1234) provides free service on Fourth Avenue between Broadway and Main Street. It doesn't operate on Sundays.

LOCAL SERVICES

AUDIOVISUAL EQUIPMENT *Audio Visuals of Louisville* (phone: 568-6030); *Videobred* (phone: 584-5787).

BABY-SITTING *Family Tree* (Starks Bldg., 455 Fourth Ave.; phone: 583-9618).

BUSINESS SERVICES *Private Secretary* (604 Embassy Square Blvd.; phone: 499-5588); *Secretaries Unlimited* (1303 Clear Springs Trace; phone: 425-8786).

COMPUTER RENTAL *Advance Business Machines* (phone: 636-5566); *Xerox Business Services* (phone: 429-4295).

DRY CLEANER/TAILOR *Meyers Dry Cleaning & Alterations* (516 W. Main St.; phone: 587-8733).

LIMOUSINE *Yellow Cab* (phone: 636-5517).

MECHANICS *Lee's Auto Service* (301 E. Breckinridge; phone: 583-6912); *Smith Imported Car Service* (1250 E. Broadway; phone: 583-4724).

MEDICAL EMERGENCY *Humana University Hospital* (530 S. Jackson St.; phone: 562-3015); *Jewish Hospital* (217 E. Chestnut St.; phone: 58-HEART), renowned for dealing with cardiac emergencies.

MESSENGER SERVICES *Yellow Cab* (phone: 636-5511); *Zip Express* (phone: 587-3487).

MONEY TRANSFERS *American Express MoneyGram* (phone: 800-926-9400 for information; 800-866-8800 for money transfers); *Western Union Financial Services* (phone: 800-325-6000 or 800-325-4176).

NATIONAL/INTERNATIONAL COURIER *DHL Worldwide Express* (phone: 451-4691); *FedEx* (phone: 800-238-5355).

PHARMACY *Walgreens* (573 S. Fourth St.; phone: 584-4342), open 8 AM to 7 PM Mondays through Saturdays.

PHOTOCOPIES *Copy Boy* (518 W. Main St.; phone: 582-2679); *Kinko's*, 24 hours (315 W. Market; phone: 584-0407).

POST OFFICE Main office (1420 Gardner Ln.; phone: 454-1632); downtown office (Seventh and York Sts.; phone: 587-8546).

PROFESSIONAL PHOTOGRAPHER *Earl Fansler Photographers* (phone: 587-6443); *Moseley Photography* (phone: 585-4042).

TRANSLATOR *EHK Company* (phone: 513-761-2611); *Languages Unlimited* (phone: 456-4414).

WESTERN UNION/TELEX Many offices are located around the city (phone: 800-325-6000 to find the location nearest you). There are offices in all *Kroger* supermarkets; downtown location at Second and Breckinridge Sts. (phone: 589-6040).

SPECIAL EVENTS

The *Humana Festival of New American Plays* takes place from February to late March or early April at the *Actors Theatre of Louisville* (see *Theater*). The week preceding the *Derby* in May, the *Kentucky Derby Festival* unfolds with a parade, music, hot-air balloons, and a race between the *Belle of Louisville* and *Delta Queen* steamboats. Many events are free (write to 137 W. Muhammad Ali Blvd., Louisville KY 40202; phone: 584-6383). The *Kentucky State Fair* is held in mid-August at the *Kentucky Fair & Exposition Center* (2 miles south of central Louisville off I-264, Watterson Expy.; phone: 367-5000).

SHOPPING

The downtown *Galleria* (Fourth Ave. between Liberty St. and Muhammad Ali Blvd.; phone: 584-7170) combines more than 60 stores and restaurants under a glass roof. Pottery collectors will want to stop at

Hadley Pottery (1570 Story Ave. in Butchertown; phone: 584-2171) and at *Louisville Stoneware* (731 Brent St. off E. Broadway; phone: 582-1900) for hand-crafted dishes and decorative items. Antiques shoppers should try *Joe Ley Antiques* (615 E. Market St.; phone: 583-4014 or 583-4017), the 50,000-square-foot *Louisville Antique Mall* (900 Goss Ave.; phone: 635-2852), or the shops along Bardstown Road in the Highlands neighborhood. For authentic, high-quality Kentucky crafts, stop at the *Berea College Crafts* shop (140 N. Fourth Ave. in the *Galt House* hotel; phone: 589-3707) or *Kentucky Art and Craft Gallery* (609 W. Main St.; phone: 589-0102).

SPORTS AND FITNESS

BASEBALL The minor league Louisville *Redbirds,* members of the *American Association,* play April through September at the *Kentucky Fair & Exposition Center* (off I-264, Watterson Expy.; phone: 367-9121).

BICYCLING Rent from *Highland Cycle* (1737 Bardstown Rd.; phone: 458-7832). Nearby *Cherokee Park* has good bike trails over hilly terrain.

COLLEGE SPORTS The *University of Louisville*'s basketball and football teams play at the *Kentucky Fair & Exhibition Center* (off I-264, Watterson Expy.; phone: 852-5151).

FITNESS CENTERS The *Louisville Athletic Club* (Fifth and Muhammad Ali Blvd., at the red awning; phone: 585-6399) has a lot to offer: exercise classes, a steamroom, a sauna, a whirlpool, and basketball, racquetball, and squash courts; there's a lounge and restaurant as well. The *YMCA* (Second and Chestnut; phone: 587-6700) has a pool, exercise room, gym, racquetball court, and indoor track. Both fitness centers are open to visitors who are guests of a Louisville hotel.

GOLF Two excellent public 18-hole courses are *Quail Chase* (7000 Cooper Chapel Rd.; phone: 239-2110) and *Seneca Park* (Taylorsville Rd. and Cannons La.; phone: 458-9298).

HOCKEY The minor league Louisville *Icehawks,* members of the *East Coast Hockey League,* play in *Broadbent Arena* at the *Kentucky Fair & Exposition Center* (off I-264, Watterson Expy; phone: 367-7797). The season runs from October through March.

HORSE RACING There's thoroughbred racing from late April through July and during November at *Churchill Downs* (700 Central Ave.; phone: 636-4400; for *Kentucky Derby* information, see *Special Places*). At other times, thoroughbred races at other Kentucky tracks are televised (with wagering) at *Sports Spectrum* (4520 Poplar Level Rd.; phone: 962-2200).

ICE SKATING The Ohio River rarely freezes over, but there is good outdoor skating from November through March at the *Belvedere Ice Rink* (Riverfront Plaza/Belvedere, north of Main St. between Fourth and Sixth; phone: 625-3689). Admission charge.

JOGGING For a 3-mile run, start at the *Hyatt Regency Louisville* on Fourth Avenue. Run north to Main Street, turn right onto Main Street, turn left at Second Street, and head across Clark Memorial Bridge; then retrace your steps.

TENNIS The best outdoor clay courts in the area are at the *Louisville Tennis Center* (Trevilian Way, across from the *Louisville Zoological Gardens*; phone: 239-6000), which is open April through November. Indoor courts are available at the *Louisville Indoor Racquet Club* (8609 Westport Rd.; phone: 426-2454).

THEATER

Considering its size, Louisville is a culturally rich city, offering one nationally recognized theater company and several other fine groups. For current offerings, check the papers listed in *Local Coverage*.

CENTER STAGE

Actors Theatre of Louisville In recent years, the two stages here have become bright spots on the American theater scene. The annual *Humana Festival of New American Plays,* initiated in 1977, has gained international critical attention and has sent graduates on to successful runs on both coasts: *Agnes of God, Extremities,* and the Pulitzer Prize–winning *Crimes of the Heart* premiered here. The 30 productions each season, both classics and innovative new works, are presented in a main auditorium and a smaller upstairs theater—both in a grand old columned building that has been designated a National Historic Landmark. 316-320 W. Main St. (phone: 584-1205).

In addition, *Stage One: Louisville Children's Theatre,* the *Louisville Ballet Company,* and touring repertory groups, including Broadway road shows, perform at the *Kentucky Center for the Arts* (5 Riverfront Plaza; phone: 584-7777; 800-775-7777)

MUSIC

The *Louisville Orchestra* and the *Kentucky Opera Association* perform at the *Kentucky Center for the Arts* (see *Theater*).

NIGHTCLUBS AND NIGHTLIFE

Current favorites include the *Phoenix Hill Tavern* (644 Baxter Ave.; phone: 589-4630), which features popular music on three stages, including a large rooftop beer garden. *Butchertown Pub* (1335 Story Ave.; phone: 583-2242) for a variety of "hot" bands, plus a lively, friendly atmosphere; and *Silo Microbrewery Complex* (630 Barret Ave.; phone: 585-4453) for blues and other live music plus locally brewed specialty beers. For elegant, quiet, after-dinner drinking, try the *Seelbach Bar* in the *Seelbach* hotel (see *Checking In*).

Best in Town

CHECKING IN

Louisville's accommodations range from standard large hotels to Victorian-style inns. The hotels listed as expensive charge $100 to $160 per night for a double room; moderate hotels charge from $70 to $100, and those in the inexpensive category charge from $50 to $70. (Less expensive weekend rates may be available in all categories.) For bed and breakfast accommodations, contact *Kentucky Homes Bed & Breakfast* (1507 S. Third St., Louisville, KY 40208; phone: 635-7341). Unless otherwise noted, hotel rooms have air conditioning, private baths, TV sets, and telephones. All hotels are in the 502 area code unless otherwise indicated.

EXPENSIVE

Brown Built in the 1920s, this extensively renovated, 294-room architectural landmark is a step into Louisville history. From the marble-floored lobby and archway-adorned mezzanine to the *Crystal Ballroom* and warm wood interior of the *English Grille,* it harks to a more gracious time. Amenities include two good restaurants (try a Hot Brown turkey sandwich, invented at the hotel), a cocktail lounge, and a fitness center. Its meeting rooms hold up to 1,400, and other business conveniences include a concierge desk, limited secretarial services, A/V equipment, and photocopiers. There is 24-hour room service and express checkout. Fourth and Broadway (phone: 583-1234; 800-866-7666; fax: 587-7006).

Hyatt Regency Louisville Contemporary atmosphere, spacious accommodations, and attentive service mark this 388-room hotel in the heart of the downtown business district. Features include an 18-story atrium, the revolving *Spire* restaurant, an indoor pool, a Jacuzzi, and outdoor tennis courts. Meeting rooms accommodate up to 1,200, and a concierge, limited secretarial services, A/V equipment, and photocopiers are available. Each room has its own fax machine. Express checkout will speed you along. 320 W. Jefferson (phone: 587-3434; 800-233-1234; fax: 581-0133).

Old Louisville Inn This elegant bed and breakfast establishment is set in a large Victorian mansion in Old Louisville, complete with 12-foot ceilings, leaded glass windows, and a lobby with massive columns. Most of the 11 guestrooms (including three suites) offer private baths and are tastefully furnished with antique furniture. Complimentary breakfast includes delicious popovers, blueberry muffins, and fresh fruit. Business amenities include meeting space for up to 20 people and catered luncheons. Not all rooms have TVs. Inexpensive and moderately priced rooms are available. 1359 S. Third St. (phone: 635-1574).

Seelbach Immortalized by F. Scott Fitzgerald in *The Great Gatsby,* this Beaux Arts showplace from the early 1900s offers the best of modern and period amenities. There are 321 elegantly furnished rooms and suites; fine food in the *Oak Room* (see *Eating Out*), a comfortable bar, and respectful service are standard features here. The hotel offers 24-hour room service, meeting rooms for up to 600, a concierge, A/V equipment, photocopiers, express checkout, and valet parking. Adjoining the *Galleria* shopping complex. 500 S. Fourth Ave. (phone: 585-3200; 800-333-3399; fax: 587-6564).

MODERATE

Executive Inn English manor decor sets the tone for this comfortable 465-unit motel adjacent to both the airport and the *Kentucky Fair & Expo-*

sition Center. Amenities include indoor and outdoor pools, a health club, and fine food. Secretarial services, A/V equipment, photocopiers, and meeting rooms for up to 400 are available. Watterson Expy. (phone: 367-6161; 800-626-2706; fax: 363-1880).

Galt House The 655-unit hotel, which adjoins the Riverfront Plaza/Belvedere, includes two cocktail lounges, a pool, on-site shops, and three restaurants, one of which, the *Flagship*, has a revolving section to make the most of the wonderful view of the Ohio River. Although there are limited secretarial services, other business services—A/V equipment, photocopiers, a concierge desk, and meeting rooms that seat up to 4,000—are available. 140 N. Fourth St. (phone: 589-5200; 800-626-1814; fax: 589-3444).

INEXPENSIVE

Lakeview This resort-style hotel features some unusual extras: an 11-acre lake with boating and fishing, and, next door, a "Wave-Tek ocean" (a huge pool with mechanically created waves). It has 356 rooms and suites, health club access, baby-sitting, and a restaurant and lounge. Business services include meeting rooms with a capacity for 750, limited secretarial services, A/V equipment, and photocopiers. Two miles north of downtown off I-65 at 505 Marriott Dr., Clarksville, Indiana (phone: 812-283-4411; 800-544-7075; fax: 812-288-8976).

EATING OUT

Our restaurant selections range in price from $55 to $90 for dinner for two at places in the expensive category, $30 to $55 at moderate restaurants, and less than $30 at inexpensive places. Prices do not include drinks, wine, tax, or tips. Unless otherwise noted, all restaurants are open for lunch and dinner. All restaurants are in the 502 area code unless otherwise indicated.

EXPENSIVE

Oak Room Antique furnishings combine with a continental menu and formal service to make dining here an elegant affair. Rack of lamb is a specialty; also try the seafood linguine or grilled swordfish. There's an excellent wine list and an elaborate Sunday brunch. Open daily. Reservations advised. Major credit cards accepted. *Seelbach Hotel,* 500 S. Fourth Ave. (phone: 585-3200).

Le Relais Located in the historic terminal building of *Bowman Field,* the city's general aviation airport, this charming restaurant takes French cuisine in Louisville to new heights. Try the veal chop with ginger-mustard-caper marinade. The Art Deco decor suggests a more elegant era, and you can dine formally inside (jackets required for men) or casually outside on the deck. Open daily. Reservations advised. Major credit cards accepted. Taylorsville Rd. (phone: 451-9020).

Vincenzo's Chef Agostino Gabriele and his brother Vincenzo make dining here an exciting experience. The menu is Italian/continental (try the fettuccine Mondello—tomato pasta in a rich clam sauce—or any of the veal dishes); the atmosphere is classic European and the attention is nonstop. Jacket and tie required for men. Closed Sundays. Reservations advised. Major credit cards accepted. 150 S. Fifth St. (phone: 580-1350).

MODERATE

Bristol An informal bar and grill in the heart of downtown. Continental entrées include trout meunière and steak *au poivre* seared in a cognac sauce; lighter fare, including a very popular burger, also is offered. Open daily. No reservations. Major credit cards accepted. *Kentucky Center for the Arts,* 5 Riverfront Plaza (phone: 583-3342).

Café Metro Urbane yet unpretentious, this eatery offers creative entrées such as grilled swordfish with soy sauce, ginger, and sesame seeds. Save room for dessert—try the Empress Carlotta (a rich chocolate cake with Kahlúa-flavored whipped cream and almonds) or Chocolate Seduction (a fudgy chocolate pie). Closed Sundays. Reservations advised. Major credit cards accepted. 1700 Bardstown Rd. (phone: 458-4830).

Hasenour's Prime rib and sauerbraten are house specialties, but the seafood and daily specials also are reliable in this venerable neighborhood restaurant. There's a wide variety in both food and price, and the drinks are among the most masterfully mixed in town. Open daily. Reservations advised. Major credit cards accepted. 1028 Barret Ave. (phone: 451-5210).

Jack Fry's Imaginative food (try the grilled Japanese salmon, black-eyed pea burrito, or grilled-chicken Caesar salad) in a neighborhood-pub atmosphere. Closed Sundays. Reservations advised. Major credit cards accepted. 1007 Bardstown Rd. (phone: 452-9244).

La Paloma Louisville chic with a Mediterranean accent, this place has garnered national acclaim with its airy, elegant, but casual atmosphere and its imaginative presentations of chicken, lamb, and seafood. Roasted Tuscan chicken served in a shallot port sauce, lamb kebabs, and a sinful Chocolate Caramel Bombe are among the decadent delights. Open daily. Reservations advised. Major credit cards accepted. 3612 Brownsboro Rd. (phone: 895-5493).

INEXPENSIVE

Ditto's Food & Drink An informal eatery serving scrumptious crab cakes and tasty pizza. Open daily. Reservations unnecessary. Major credit cards accepted. 1114 Bardstown Rd. (phone: 581-9129).

KT's This casual eat-and-meet restaurant is usually busy and boisterous, making it a great place to take children. Best are the light pasta dishes or prime ribs and "mansion-size" house salad. Open daily. No reservations. Major credit cards accepted. 2300 Lexington Rd. (phone: 458-8888).

Memphis

At-a-Glance

SEEING THE CITY
The best way to see Memphis is by drifting along the legendary Mississippi. Captain Jake Meanley's *Memphis Queen II* and *Island Queen* paddle wheelers travel along the river. The one-and-a-half-hour cruise leaves daily from *Memphis Downtown Harbor* (Monroe Ave. and Riverside Dr.; phone: 527-5694), March through mid-December. Daylong cruises and private charters are also available.

SPECIAL PLACES
A natural place to start a tour of Memphis is by the riverbanks. From there, you can wander through downtown—stopping at *Court Square,* a delightful little park with a statue of the goddess Phoebe atop the center fountain—and then wend your way out to the suburbs.

MUD ISLAND Legend has it that *Mud Island,* measuring 1 by 5 miles, was formed by mud deposits clinging to a gunboat sunk during the Civil War. Residents are sure it was a Union gunboat, because, they say, Confederate gunboats were unsinkable. Now the site of a $63-million tribute to the history and heritage of the Mississippi River, the island houses exhibits on the legends, music, and people of the river; a 5,000-seat outdoor amphitheater; a five-block scale model of the Mississippi; and restaurants, shops, a marina, and a picnic area. The *Mud Island Amphitheater* presents the best in local and national music, including rock, hillbilly, and rockabilly. Here also is the *Memphis Belle,* the famed World War II B-17 bomber featured in the movie of the same name. *Mud Island* has had some management problems of late, but it continues to operate. Accessible by monorail. Enter on Front St. between Poplar and Adams (phone: 576-6595).

THE PYRAMID Since Memphis was named after an Egyptian city, it's only right that it should have a pyramid. And it finally got one. This 321-foot structure by the riverfront is an entertainment complex with 85,000 square feet of space inside, part of which contains an arena that seats 22,500. It hosts large-scale concerts, ice shows, basketball games, and anything else that calls for plenty of space. It has become a true Memphis landmark. Located off Front St. (phone: 521-9675).

BEALE STREET Renovated buildings along this historic street, where the blues were born in the early 1900s, contain specialty shops, restaurants, bars, and offices. At the corner of Beale and Third is *W. C. Handy Park,* and at Beale and Main, Elvis Presley Plaza; both feature statues honoring these two musicians from Memphis. Don't miss W. C. Handy's home (Fourth and Beale; no phone), which is open during the summer, or *A. Schwabs* (at 163 Beale), an old dry goods store that stocks a little bit of everything from voodoo potions to 99¢ ties. Another popular attrac-

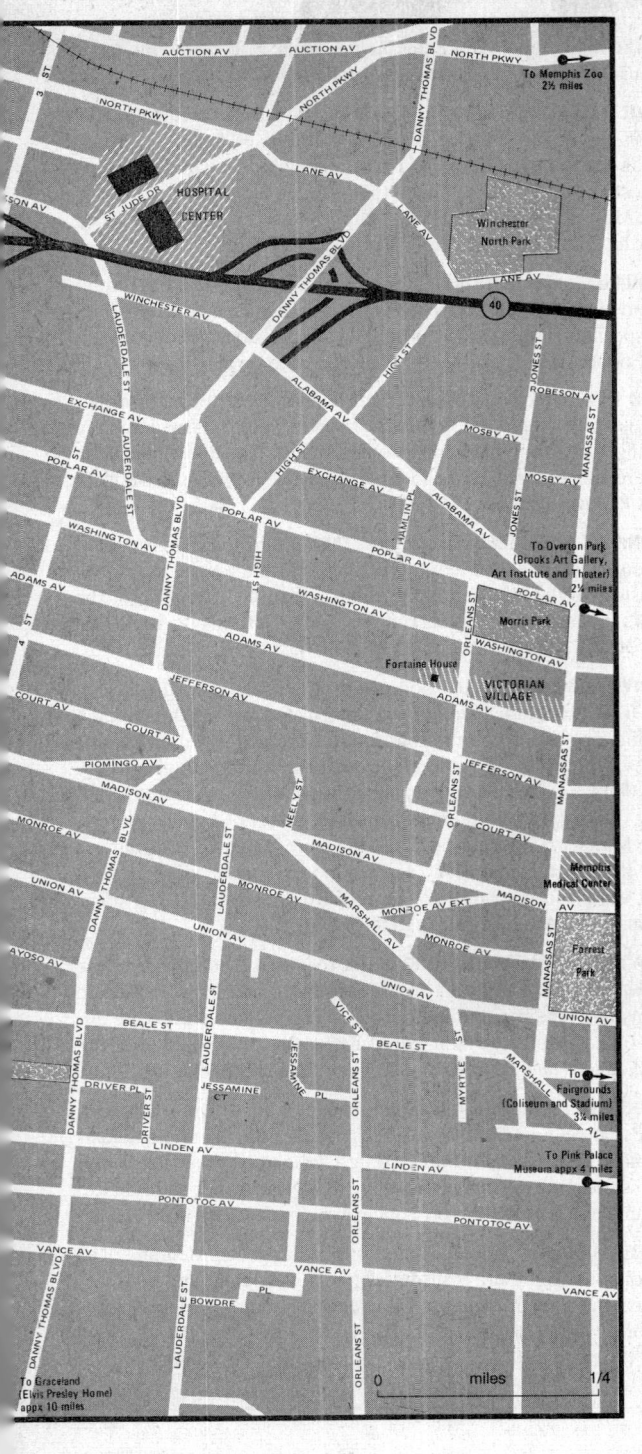

tion is the nightclub at 139 Beale named after B. B. King, the great Memphis-born blues guitarist (see *Nightclubs and Nightlife*).

VICTORIAN VILLAGE Homes and churches in this downtown area date from the 1830s and feature a variety of architectural styles, among them late Victorian, neoclassic, Greek Revival, French, and Italianate. Among the oldest are the *Fontaine House* (680 Adams St.; phone: 526-1469) and the *Mallory-Neely House* (652 Adams St.; phone: 523-1484). Open daily. Admission charge. 100 to 700 block of Adams St.

OVERTON SQUARE A 15-minute drive from downtown, the square has restaurants and bistros, nightclubs featuring jazz trios and rhythm and blues bands, specialty shops, an art gallery, and a professional theater. Madison at Cooper (phone: 274-0671 for information on activities).

LIBERTYLAND This theme park focuses on nostalgia and patriotism (its roller coaster is aptly named the *Revolution*). Open weekends beginning in the spring, daily from mid-June through August. No admission charge for children under three. At the *Fairgrounds,* a mile from Overton Square on East Parkway (phone: 274-1776).

MEMPHIS PINK PALACE MUSEUM AND PLANETARIUM The museum is built of pink Georgia marble, and features exhibitions on the natural and cultural history of the mid-South, including a restored *Piggly-Wiggly,* the country's first self-service grocery store. Closed Mondays. Admission charge. 3050 Central Ave. (phone: 320-6320).

NATIONAL CIVIL RIGHTS MUSEUM Located in the former *Lorraine* motel, where Dr. Martin Luther King Jr. was assassinated in 1968, this museum is the only one in the country that focuses exclusively on civil rights activities, both in this country and around the world. It houses more than 10,000 square feet of exhibits highlighting the bus boycott in Montgomery, Alabama, the landmark *Brown vs. Board of Education* case, and the March on Washington. The cell where King wrote his famous "Letter from Birmingham Jail" and the motel room he was staying in when he was killed are realistically reproduced. Closed Tuesdays. Admission charge. 450 Mulberry St. (phone: 521-9699).

CHUCALISSA ARCHAEOLOGICAL MUSEUM A reconstructed village where Choctaw Indians live and work. Grass huts and a ceremonial house and museum are on the site, and Indian tools, weapons, and pottery are displayed. Closed Mondays. Admission charge. Six miles south of downtown, adjoining *Fuller State Park* on Indian Village Dr. (phone: 785-3160).

MEMPHIS ZOO AND AQUARIUM A complete range of lions, tigers, monkeys, and birds can be found in this well-designed zoo. An aquarium adjoins the animal sections. Closed *Thanksgiving, Christmas Eve,* and *Christmas.* No admission charge Mondays from 3 to 4:30 PM in winter and 3:30 to 5 PM in summer. *Overton Park,* off Poplar Ave. (phone: 726-4787).

GRACELAND Elvis Presley's home is the most popular site in Memphis. The white-columned Southern mansion is open to the public, and Elvis fans can take a bus tour through the 14-acre estate and pay respects at the graves of Elvis and his mother, father, and grandmother. Don't forget to look closely at the *Musical Gate* at the foot of the winding circular driveway. It has a caricature of Elvis with guitar and a bevy of musical notes in ornamental iron. Elvis's plane, the *Lisa Marie,* also is on display. Closed Tuesdays, November through February, and *Thanksgiving, Christmas,* and *New Year's Day.* Admission charge. Make tour reservations in advance. 3764 Elvis Presley Blvd. in Whitehaven, South Memphis (phone: 332-3322; 800-238-2000).

SUN RECORDING STUDIO Elvis, Johnny Cash, Jerry Lee Lewis, Carl Perkins, and other musicians cut their first records here. Restored and operated by the Graceland Division of Elvis Presley Enterprises. Tours daily. Admission charge. 706 Union (phone: 521-0664).

MEMPHIS INTERNATIONAL MOTORSPORTS PARK Auto racing is the name of the game at this 600-acre, multimillion-dollar racing park. Races are held year-round. Admission charge. 5500 Taylor Forge Rd. (phone: 358-7223).

EXTRA SPECIAL

About two and a half hours away by car, *Shiloh National Military Park* (off US 64 in Shiloh; phone: 689-5275) lets visitors follow the sequence of the famous Civil War Battle of Shiloh, in 1862. It's closed *Christmas.* In Henning, about 35 miles north on US 51, is the boyhood home and burial place of late author Alex Haley (*Roots*); it's now a museum. Closed Mondays. Admission charge. (200 S. Church St., Henning; phone: 738-2240).

Sources and Resources

TOURIST INFORMATION

The *Memphis Visitor Information Center* (340 Beale St., Memphis, TN 38108; phone: 543-5333), which is open daily; the *Memphis Convention and Visitors Bureau* (47 Union St., Memphis, TN 38103; phone: 543-5300; fax: 901-543-5350) and the *Memphis Area Chamber of Commerce* (22 N. Front St.; phone: 575-3500), which are closed weekends, are all good places for general information. Contact the Tennessee state tourism hotline (phone: 615-741-2158) for maps, calendars of events, health updates, and travel advisories.

LOCAL COVERAGE *Memphis Commercial Appeal,* morning daily; *Memphis* magazine, monthly; and *Memphis Business Journal,* weekly. *Key* magazine and the *Convention and Visitors Guide* are the best sources for information about Memphis activities.

TELEVISION STATIONS WREG Channel 3–CBS; WMC Channel 5–NBC; WKNO Channel 10–PBS; WHBQ Channel 13–ABC; WLMT Channel 30–Independent; and WPTY Channel 24–Fox.

RADIO STATIONS AM: WHBQ 560 (sports); WREC 600 (news/sports/entertainment); WMC 790 (talk); and WDIA 1070 (rhythm & blues). FM: WKNO 91 (classical/news) and WEGR 103 (rock).

TELEPHONE The area code for Memphis is 901.

SALES TAX The combined city and state sales tax is 8¼%.

CLIMATE Memphis humidity is formidable. Even though temperatures seldom drop below the 30s F in winter, it's wet. The worst month is February, when it occasionally snows. July and August get dripping hot, as the temperature climbs into the 90s and 100s.

GETTING AROUND

AIRPORT *Memphis International Airport* is usually about a 30-minute drive from downtown and midtown. The *Airport Limousine Service* (phone: 922-8238) meets incoming flights and takes passengers to the city. When returning to the airport, call in advance for a pickup. Although public bus No. 32 stops at the terminal building, a transfer to bus No. 20 is required to get downtown. The fare is $1.10.

BUS Memphis buses generally run between 5 AM and 8 PM during the week, with limited service on weekends. The fare is $1.10. For information, contact the *Memphis Area Transit Authority* (1370 Levee Rd.; phone: 274-6282).

CAR RENTAL All the major national firms are represented.

TAXI There are taxi stands near the bus station and at the airport. It's best to call *Yellow Cab* (phone: 577-7777).

LOCAL SERVICES

AUDIOVISUAL EQUIPMENT *Memphis Communications Corp.* (1381 Madison Ave.; phone: 725-9271).

BABY-SITTING *Crosstown Christian Daycare and Elementary School* (1258 Harbert; phone: 725-4666) provides 24-hour, seven-day service for children 15 months and older.

BUSINESS SERVICES *American Resource Systems* (phone: 382-9595), for word processing, photocopying, desk space; *Answering Memphis* (88 Union Ave.; phone: 526-2102); *Diversified Services Agency* (phone: 794-5385); *Memphis Offices Inc.* (phone: 345-3900).

DRY CLEANER/TAILOR *Kraus Model Cleaners* (1023 Linden Circle; phone: 528-0400).

LIMOUSINE *Memphis Executive Limousine Service* (phone: 396-7733); *Yellow Cab* (phone: 577-7777).

MECHANIC *Ed Martin* (411 Monroe; phone: 527-8606); *OK Alignment & Brake* (3900 Jackson; phone: 382-4999).

MEDICAL EMERGENCY *Baptist Memorial Hospital* (899 Madison Ave.; phone: 227-2727).

MESSENGER SERVICES *American Courier Service* (phone: 360-9185); *Yellow Cab* (phone: 577-7780).

MONEY TRANSFERS *American Express MoneyGram* (phone: 800-926-9400 for information; 800-865-8800 for money transfers); *Western Union Financial Services* (phone: 800-325-6000 or 800-325-4176).

NATIONAL/INTERNATIONAL COURIER *DHL Worldwide Express* (phone: 795-9911); *FedEx* (phone: 345-5044); *Purolator Courier* (phone: 800-645-3333).

PHARMACY *Walgreens* (1801 Union; phone: 272-2006).

PHOTOCOPIES *Dawson's Printing Inc.* (347 S. Front St.; phone: 525-3311); *Gator Print* (118 Madison; phone: 523-2134).

POST OFFICE Main office (555 S. Third St. at Calhoun Ave.; phone: 521-2140).

PROFESSIONAL PHOTOGRAPHER *Frank Braden* (phone: 767-7897); *Brasher-Rucker Photography* (phone: 324-7447).

TELECONFERENCE FACILITIES *Comsat* (phone: 367-1444).

TRANSLATOR *Language Services* (417 Fieda Rd.; phone: 683-3575).

WESTERN UNION/TELEX Many offices are located around the city (phone: 800-325-6000 to find the location nearest you).

SPECIAL EVENTS

The *Kroger St. Jude International Indoor Tennis Tournament* takes place in February. The *Memphis in May International Festival* stretches from late April into early June. Highlights of the festival are the *International Children's Festival, International Cooking Contest* (barbecue), *Beale Street Musical Festival,* and a *Sunset Symphony* on the banks of the Mississippi. The *Great River Carnival,* held in early June, has parades, a midway, music, and a riverside pageant. The $300,000 *PGA–Federal Express St. Jude Classic Golf Tournament* is held in July and August at the *Southwind* golf course. *Elvis Tribute Week* is observed primarily at *Graceland* around August 17, the day the "King" died. In September one of the largest fairs in the country, the *Mid-South Fair,* takes place at the *Mid-South Fairgrounds.* December heralds college football's *Liberty Bowl* at the *Liberty Bowl Stadium.*

MUSEUMS

In addition to those described in *Special Places,* Memphis has several other museums of note.

CHILDREN'S MUSEUM OF MEMPHIS This discovery museum offers hands-on exhibits and activities for children. Closed Mondays. Admission charge. 2525 Central Ave. (phone: 458-2678).

DIXON GALLERY AND GARDENS French and American Impressionist art is on exhibit here. Closed Mondays. Admission charge. 4339 Park Ave. (phone: 761-5250).

MEMPHIS BROOKS MUSEUM OF ART The collection here encompasses both American and European art. Closed Mondays. Admission charge. *Overton Park* (phone: 722-3500).

WONDER OF WONDERS

Wonders: Memphis International Cultural Series is a continuing program that presents art and cultural displays of international significance at various venues throughout the city. Previous exhibitions have included "Splendors of the Ottoman Empire," "The Etruscans—Legacy of a Lost Civilization," and "Napoleon"; for information on current events and locations in the series, call 576-1231.

SPORTS AND FITNESS

BASEBALL The Memphis *Chicks* (short for Chickasaw Indians, who once lived in the area) are a *Southern League* farm club for the Kansas City *Royals.* They play at *Tim McCarver Stadium* (*Fairgrounds;* phone: 272-1687), named for the Memphis-born former catcher for the St. Louis *Cardinals,* who is now a sports announcer.

DOG RACING *Southland Greyhound Park* (1550 N. Ingram Blvd.; phone: 501-735-3670) is across the Mississippi in West Memphis, Arkansas. It's closed Sundays.

FISHING The lakes have bass, bream, crappies, and catfish. Sardis Lake is a good bet; *Meeman-Shelby Forest* is a 14,000-acre park with two large lakes.

FITNESS CENTER The *Peabody Athletic Club* (in the *Peabody* hotel, 149 Union Ave.; phone: 529-4161) offers aerobics classes and a sauna. It's open to non-guests for a fee.

GOLF The *PGA–Federal Express St. Jude Classic* is held in July and August (see *Special Events*). The best public golf course is the 18-hole *Galloway* (3815 Walnut Grove Rd.; phone: 685-7805).

HOCKEY The Memphis *RiverKings* play in the minor league *Central Hockey League* from November through March at *Mid-South Coliseum* (*Fairgrounds;* phone: 278-9009).

JOGGING Run in *Audubon Park* on Park Avenue, and *Overton Park* on Poplar Avenue.

SWIMMING Some of the lakes are polluted. The nearest good swimming pool is *Maywood* (8100 Maywood Dr.; phone: 601-895-2777), just across the state line in Olive Branch, Mississippi.

TENNIS The best year-round public courts are at *Audubon Tennis Center* (4145 Southern; phone: 685-7907).

THEATER

The *Orpheum Theater* (89 Beale St.; phone: 525-3000) offers touring Broadway shows and concerts, while contemporary drama is staged at the *Circuit Playhouse* (1705 Poplar Ave.; phone: 726-5521), the *Playhouse on the Square* (51 S. Cooper; phone: 726-4656), and *Theater Memphis* (630 Perkins Ext.; phone: 682-8323).

MUSIC

Big-name country and rock concerts are held at *The Pyramid* (off Front St.; phone: 521-9675), *Mid-South Coliseum* (*Fairgrounds;* phone: 274-3982), and *Dixon-Meyers Hall* at the *Cook Convention Center* (255 N. Main; phone: 576-1200). Headliners appear from May through September at the *Mud Island Amphitheater* (take the monorail to Front St. between Poplar and Adams; phone: 576-6595) and year-round at the *Orpheum Theater* (see *Theater*).

NIGHTCLUBS AND NIGHTLIFE

Memphis blues originated on Beale Street with W. C. Handy, and is performed nightly at *Rum Boogie* (182 Beale; phone: 528-0150) and at the *B. B. King Nightclub* (143 Beale St.; phone: 527-5464), where the great musician himself plays when he's in town. Other popular downtown nightspots include *Alfred's* (197 Beale; phone: 525-3711) and the *Anchor Bar* at *Captain Bilbo's* (see *Eating Out*), both in the *Beale Street Landing* shopping and restaurant complex (at the corner of Beale and Wagner). In midtown, the Overton Square area at Madison and Cooper, try the *Public Eye* (phone: 726-4040). Best bets elsewhere are *Silky Sullivan's* (2080 Madison; phone: 725-0650) and *Bad Bob's Vapors* country and rock (1743 Brooks Rd. E.; phone: 345-1761). Casinos—among them *Splash, Lady Luck,* and *Harrah's*—all within 10 miles of nearby Tunica, Mississippi, combine the romance of riverboat gambling and the excitement of Las Vegas. Buses run the 35 miles from Memphis (phone: 396-7229 for information).

Best in Town

CHECKING IN

There's an abundance of *Holiday Inns* (six, to be exact)—hardly surprising since the chain was founded in Memphis. Other chains, such as Ramada, TraveLodge, Hilton, and Sheraton, also are represented. Expect to pay more than $100 per night for a double room at hotels listed as expensive, and between $60 and $100 at those described as moderate. Unless otherwise noted, hotel rooms have air conditioning, private baths, TV sets, and telephones. All hotels are in the 901 area code unless otherwise indicated.

EXPENSIVE

Peabody In 1935, Mississippi author David Cohn wrote that "The Delta begins in the lobby of the *Peabody* and ends on Catfish Row in Vicksburg." Built in 1925, the 13-story, 400-room hotel reopened 15 years ago after a $20-million renovation. A focal point of the elegant Renaissance lobby is a marble fountain to which the *Peabody* ducks—trained mallards—march each day to take a swim. *Chez Philippe* is the hotel's fancy restaurant; *Dux,* its theme restaurant (see *Eating Out* for both). For music and dancing, there's the *Skyway,* a rooftop nightclub. The *Plantation Roof* affords splendid views of the river and city. The hotel's lower level has a pool, snack bar, health club, beauty shop, barber shop, and shoeshine parlor. Room service responds around the clock, and there's an obliging concierge desk. Business pluses include secretarial services, A/V equipment, photocopiers, computers, and express checkout. 149 Union Ave. (phone: 529-4000; 800-732-2659; fax: 529-9600).

MODERATE

Adams Mark Memphis This circular, 27-story, all-glass structure, known affectionately as "the glass silo," has changed hands a lot—from Hyatt to Omni and now to the Adams Mark hotel group. On the eastern outskirts of town, the 400-room property has a pool, café, and bar with nightly entertainment and dancing, as well as free parking and free cots and cribs. Children under 18 stay for free in their parents' rooms. Meeting rooms hold up to 1,350. Concierge and secretarial services are available, as well as A/V equipment and photocopiers. There's also express checkout. 939 Ridge Lake Blvd. (phone: 684-6664; 800-444-2326; fax: 762-7411).

Holiday Inn Crowne Plaza Focusing on the affluent business traveler and adjacent to the *Convention Center*, it offers 415 rooms, a pool, a health club, and a sauna. *Chervil's* is the ambitious restaurant, and there's a coffee shop and 24-hour room service. Business services include meeting rooms with a capacity up to 400, a concierge, A/V equipment, photocopiers, computers, and express checkout. 250 N. Main (phone: 527-7300; 800-HOLIDAY; fax: 527-7300).

EATING OUT

A visitor to Memphis can dine at fancy restaurants, feast on some of the best barbecue anywhere, or enjoy home-cooked meals. Expect to pay more than $40 for dinner for two at restaurants in the expensive category; $25 to $40 at places listed as moderate; and $25 or less at eateries described as inexpensive. Prices do not include drinks, wine, tax, or tips. Unless otherwise noted, restaurants are open for lunch and dinner. All restaurants are in the 901 area code unless otherwise indicated.

EXPENSIVE

Chez Philippe Decorated in an elegant, French Baroque style, this three-tiered dining room in the *Peabody* hotel is among the best in Memphis. Its sophisticated French menu features such specialties as roast tenderloin of lamb wrapped in goat cheese and served with a caramelized garlic sauce, filet of Dover sole and salmon, and veal medallions. A harpist plays on Friday and Saturday nights. Jacket required for men. Open for dinner only; closed Sundays. Reservations advised. Major credit cards accepted. 149 Union Ave. (phone: 529-4188).

Dux Another delightful place in the *Peabody* hotel, serving excellent seafood specialties. Open daily. Reservations advised. Major credit cards accepted. 149 Union Ave. (phone: 529-4199).

Folk's Folly This supreme steakhouse serves the largest bites of beef in Memphis. Of the Cajun-style vegetables, try the sautéed mushrooms or fried dill pickles. Open daily. Reservations advised. Major credit cards accepted. 551 S. Mendenhall (phone: 762-8200).

Justine's Often acclaimed as one of the nation's notable restaurants, and deservedly so. The French cooking is first-rate. Baking is done on the premises. A rather formal ambience prevails in this antebellum mansion, however. Jacket and tie are required. Closed Sundays. Reservations necessary. Major credit cards accepted. 919 Coward Pl. (phone: 527-3815).

MODERATE

Captain Bilbo's Have a drink at the bar and listen to nightly entertainment while viewing beautiful sunsets on the Mississippi River. And don't be surprised if an *Illinois Central Gulf Railroad* train rumbles past—the railroad track is only 22 feet away. Next, enjoy the excellent salad bar, seafood gumbo, steaks, and fish. Open daily. Reservations advised for groups of 12 or more. Major credit cards accepted. 263 Wagner (phone: 526-1966).

Grisanti's This northern Italian eatery features spicy food and a chance to swap insults with owner Big John Grisanti, a Memphis legend. The cannelloni, manicotti, and veal are recommended highly. Closed Sundays. Reservations advised for groups of 10 or more. Major credit cards accepted. 1489 Airways Blvd. (phone: 458-2648).

INEXPENSIVE

Pete and Sam's Pound for pound, the best all-around restaurant in town; serves dynamite Italian-American food. Order anything: The steaks are as good as the pizza. Open daily. Reservations advised. Major credit cards accepted. 3886 Park (phone: 458-0694).

Rendezvous In a basement in a back alley, this classic little place is chockfull of Memphis memorabilia. It's as much a museum as a restaurant, and it serves the best barbecued ribs, beef, and pork in town. Closed Sundays, Mondays, and holidays. No reservations. Major credit cards accepted. General Washburn Alley, off S. Second and behind the *Ramada Inn* (phone: 523-2746).

BEST BARBECUE BETS

Memphis is a major league barbecue town, so everyone has his or her own favorite spot. *Gridley's* (6430 Winchester Rd., phone: 794-5997; 6065 Macon Rd., phone: 388-7003; and 1355 Lynnfield Rd., phone: 681-9192); *Charlie Vergos's Rendezvous* (52 S. Second; phone: 523-2746); and *Corky's BBQ* (5259 Poplar Ave.; phone: 685-9744) not only serve up great ribs, they'll ship them to your home via Federal Express (but you have to buy $60 to $90 worth). Other good places are *John Wills Bar-Be-Q Pit* (5101 Sanderlin Dr.; phone: 761-5101); *Smokey Ridge Barbecue* (near the airport at 4085 American Way; phone: 795-7534); *Payne's*

(1762 Lamar; phone: 272-1523); *The Cozy Corner* (745 N. Parkway; phone: 527-9158); and *Willingham's World Champion Bar-B-Que* (6189 Heather Dr.; phone: 767-6759). If you don't mind driving 40 miles for maybe the best barbecue of all (for about $5), try *Bozo's* (in Mason, on Summer Ave. and Hwy. 70; phone: 294-3400).

Miami–Miami Beach

At-a-Glance

SEEING THE CITY

The *Rusty Pelican* (see *Eating Out*) and the *Bayside Seafood* restaurant (3501 Rickenbacker Causeway, Key Biscayne; phone: 361-0808) look across Biscayne Bay at the spectacular Miami skyline and have outdoor seating areas with good views. The *South Pointe Seafood House* (see *Eating Out*), on the southernmost tip of Miami Beach, affords spectacular views of Government Cut, the throughway for the dozens of cruise ships that dock at the Port of Miami.

SPECIAL PLACES

The best way to see Greater Miami is by car.

MIAMI BEACH

ART DECO DISTRICT New and restored buildings, hotels, and cafés with façades of bright pink, turquoise, and peach gleam in the sun in this Miami hot spot. The area's name is actually a bit of a misnomer—the fanciful structures here are a mixture of traditional Art Deco, Art Moderne (a French-influenced hybrid), and Spanish-Mediterranean Revival styles. In recent years, hundreds of buildings in the South Beach area from Ocean Drive to Lenox Court, and on Española Way from Drexel to Washington Avenues between 14th and 15th Streets, were rehabilitated and redecorated. The Spanish-Mediterranean Revival–style buildings, many containing funky shops and art galleries on the ground floors, have been painted in warm coral tones and adorned with gaily striped awnings; gaslight lamps lend a romantic glow.

BASS MUSEUM OF ART The museum building is listed on the *National Registry of Historic Places* for its classic Art Deco design; it is constructed of stone from the Florida Keys and features whimsical touches inspired by traditional Maya architecture. Inside, the small museum counts several gems in its permanent collection, among them works by Botticelli, Ghirlandajo, and Rubens. Changing exhibitions, lectures, concerts, readings, and a film series complete the picture. Closed Sunday mornings and Mondays. No admission charge for children under 12. 2121 Park Ave., off Collins Ave. (phone: 673-7533).

HOLOCAUST MEMORIAL This $3-million memorial park is dedicated to the survivors of the Holocaust in Europe during World War II. At the center of the park is the sculpture *Love and Anguish,* a 42-foot bronze outstretched hand that seems to grow from the ground, symbolic of the concentration camp victims' struggle for survival. A walk surrounding the reflecting pool features touching photographs etched into a granite wall by a special chemical process. Open daily. No admission charge. Meridian Ave. and Dade Blvd. (phone: 538-1663).

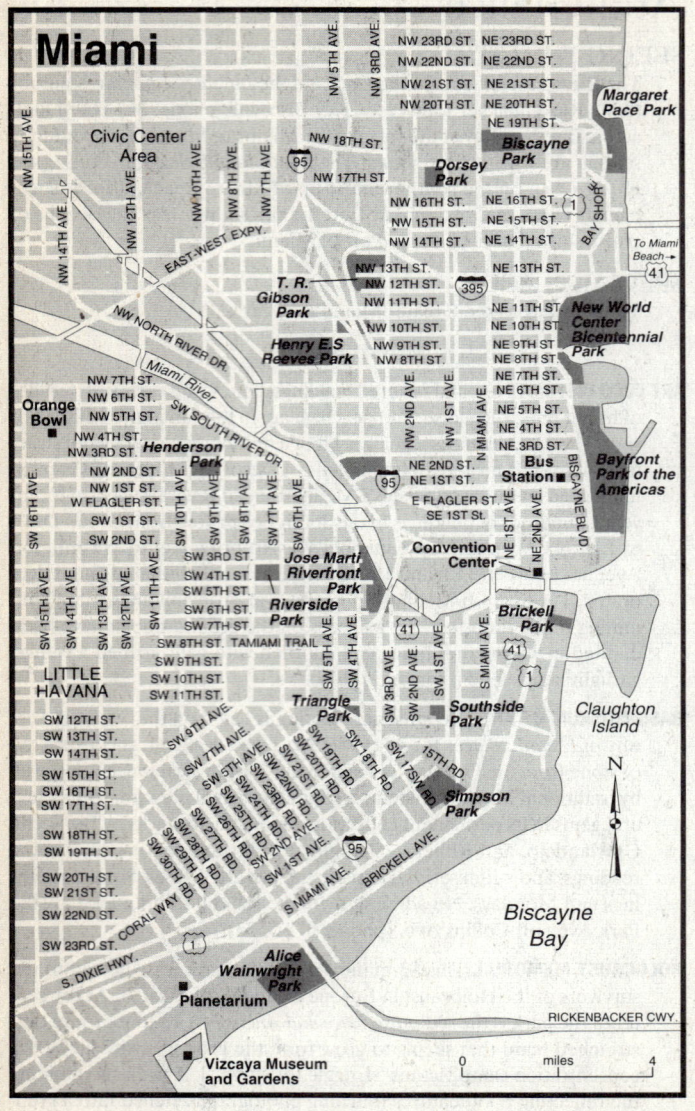

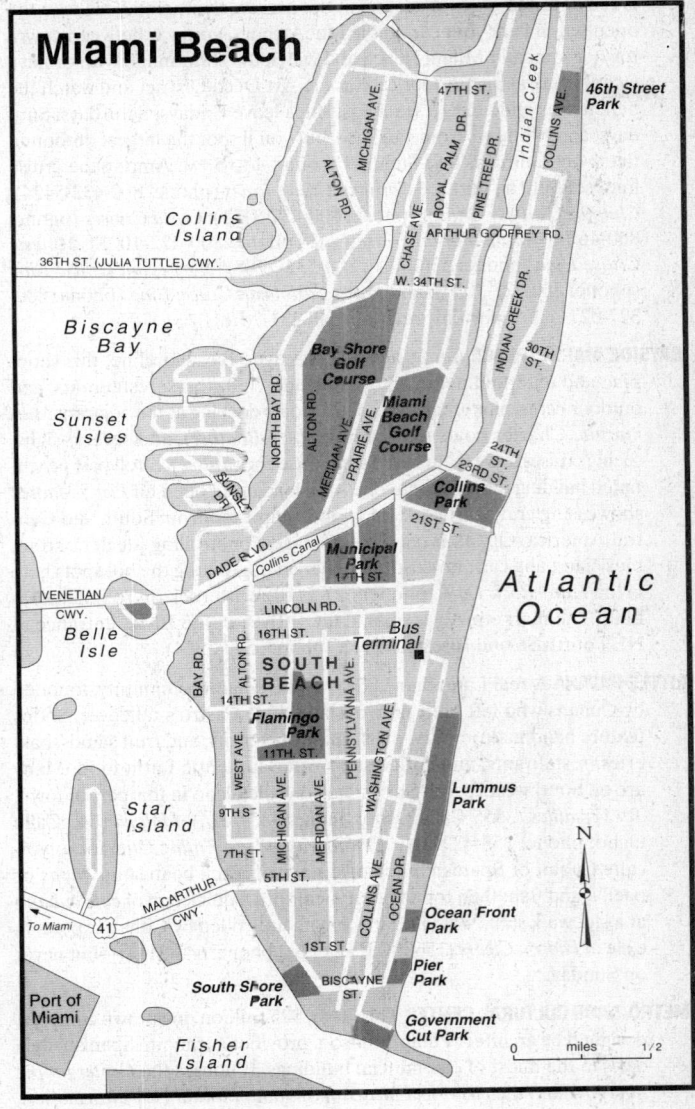

DOWNTOWN AREA

PORT OF MIAMI Every year about three million people depart from here on cruises, primarily to the Bahamas or the Caribbean, making Miami the world's busiest cruise port. Cruises aren't free, but watching the tourist-laden ocean liners turn around in the narrow channel that leads to the open sea is. Park your car on the MacArthur Causeway between downtown Miami and Miami Beach and watch the ships maneuver, or have a cool drink at an outdoor café in the Art Deco District and watch the behemoths glide out to sea. Most ships leave Fridays, Saturdays, Sundays, and Mondays from 4 to 7 PM, but you'll spot the largest outbound fleets on Saturdays and Sundays around 4 to 5 PM. Among the cruise lines serving the port are *Carnival Cruise Lines* (phone: 800-432-5424); *Chandris Fantasy Cruises* (phone: 800-437-3111); *Costa Cruises* (phone: 800-462-6782); *Dolphin Cruise Line* (phone: 800-222-1003); *Majesty Cruise Line* (phone: 536-0000; 800-532-7788); *Norwegian Cruise Line* (phone: 800-327-7030); and *Royal Caribbean Cruise Line* (phone: 800-327-0271). For port information, call 371-7678.

BAYSIDE MARKETPLACE On 16 acres of Biscayne Bay shoreline, this shopping and entertainment complex includes 150 stores, restaurants, and outdoor cafés, plus great views of the boats docking at the adjacent *Miamarina*. Charter boats may be hired (see *Boating*), and several sightseeing cruises leave from here (see *Sightseeing Cruises*). Stroll past peach-tinted buildings housing boutiques or the adjacent open-air *Pier 5 Market*, showcasing crafts, artwork, and goods imported from South and Central America. Open plazas serve as stages for strolling jugglers, street musicians, and cartoon-costumed characters. Among the hot spots here is the *Hard Rock Café* (phone: 377-3110), with rock 'n' roll memorabilia. The marketplace is open daily. 401 Biscayne Blvd., entrance at NE Fourth St. and Biscayne Blvd. (phone: 577-3344).

LITTLE HAVANA A real Latin flame burns in this Miami community, founded by Cubans who left their native island after Castro's takeover. Shops feature handmade jewelry, dolls, and works of art; and fruit stands, bakeries, restaurants, and coffee stalls offer authentic Latin food. Many are on Southwest Eighth Street, called Calle Ocho in this part of town. Try *Versailles* (3555 Calle Ocho; phone: 445-7614), *Málaga* (740 Calle Ocho; phone: 858-4224), or *Centro Vasco* (see *Eating Out*) for a typically Cuban or Spanish lunch or dinner of black bean soup, *tapas* or paella, and flan; then top off your meal with a quick cup of *café cubano* at a sidewalk stall. Watch cigars being hand-rolled by Cuban experts in exile at *Padrón Cigars* (1566 W. Flagler St.; phone: 643-2117)—but never on Sunday.

METRO-DADE CULTURAL CENTER This huge, $25-million downtown complex, designed by architect Philip Johnson, provides a tranquil Spanish-style oasis in the midst of commercial buildings. It houses the *Center for the Fine Arts* and the *Historical Museum of South Florida* (for information, see *Museums*). The *Miami-Dade Public Library* also is here (open extended hours on Thursdays; closed Sunday mornings; phone: 375-BOOK). The cultural center is at 101 W. Flagler St. (phone: 375-1700).

CORAL GABLES

FAIRCHILD TROPICAL GARDEN Founded by a tax attorney, this is one of the most lyrical tax shelters imaginable—83 acres of paradise dotted with lakes and lush with tropical and subtropical plants and trees. Something's always blooming here. In the wake of Hurricane Andrew, a one-acre hurricane exhibit plot has been left in its storm-tossed state, so that students and scientists can observe the natural patterns of regrowth. Other exhibits include the world's largest collection of palms, a rain forest, and a rare plant house. Complimentary tram rides and walking tours are available, complete with commentary. Visitors also may take a leisurely stroll around the 11 lakes; benches are provided for contemplation. Other features include a snack bar open on weekends from November through April, and a bookstore focusing on horticulture. Closed *Christmas Day*. Admission charge. 10901 Old Cutler Rd. (phone: 667-1651).

VENETIAN POOL Once a rock quarry that provided material for many of the stately stone homes in Coral Gables and now the only swimming pool listed in the *National Registry of Historic Places*, this 800,000-gallon free-form lagoon is fed by underground artesian wells. With its varying levels and waterfalls, coral caves, a palm-fringed island, bridges, and painted gaslight poles, it's a place for Esther Williams fantasies. In fact, movie stars such as Williams, the queen of water ballet, and Johnny "Tarzan" Weismuller once backstroked here. Visitors may swim in the pool (amenities include lockers and a café, and swimming, scuba, and snorkeling lessons are available), but it is extremely crowded during the summer, when kids from local camps come to splash around. Closed Mondays. Admission charge. 2701 DeSoto Blvd. (phone: 460-5356).

COCONUT GROVE

VIZCAYA MUSEUM This palatial estate is where James Deering, the International Harvester magnate, enjoyed the fruits of his personal harvest. Built in 1916, the 70-room Venetian palazzo, with 34 rooms open to the public, is furnished with European antiques, precious china, and artwork from the 15th to the 19th centuries. The Roman sculpture, 17th-century Italian marble tables, and a Chinese snuff-bottle collection are very special. The site of Miami's annual *Italian Renaissance Festival*, it is set on 10 acres of formal gardens, with fountains, grottoes, statuary, and wonderful plant life. Guided tours of the house are given daily. Closed *Christmas Day*. Admission charge. 3251 S. Miami Ave., just off US 1 (phone: 250-9133).

MUSEUM OF SCIENCE AND SPACE TRANSIT PLANETARIUM The coral reef and Everglades exhibitions here are enlightening, and there's a participatory science arcade, a wildlife center housing 180 live animals, and natural history collections with cases of fossils and butterflies. Kids love the hands-on exhibits and mini-shows on Florida natural life. The planetarium has several shows daily, and inspired visitors may search for the stars themselves with the *Weintraub Observatory*'s telescope atop the building. The observatory is open Friday and Saturday evenings only, weather permitting. The museum is closed *Thanksgiving* and *Christ-*

mas Day. Separate admission charges to the museum and planetarium; no admission charge to the observatory. 3280 S. Miami Ave. (phone: 854-4247, general information; 854-2222, planetarium).

KEY BISCAYNE

BILL BAGGS CAPE FLORIDA STATE RECREATION AREA This 604-acre state park was hit hard by Hurricane Andrew in 1992. At press time, however, the park was open (though short of shade trees), and the doves, ospreys, hawks, and other birds had returned. There's great fishing all along the seawall and snorkeling just off the beach (bring your own gear and bait); wide beaches stretch for 1¼ miles; open-air pavilions are being constructed for picnickers; and the *El Farito* concession sells sandwiches and rents four-wheel surrey bicycles. This is the site of Florida's first lighthouse, a 95-foot-tall structure built in 1825, and Stiltsville, a "town" of houses built in the sea on stilts, can be seen just off the southern tip of the park. Facilities here include restrooms, changing areas, and four short boardwalks. Open daily. Admission charge. 1200 Crandon Blvd. (phone: 361-5811).

MIAMI SEAQUARIUM Among the 10,000 sea creatures swimming around the tide pools, jungle islands, and huge reef tank (under a geodesic dome) at South Florida's largest tropical marine aquarium are killer whales, sharks, sea lions, and performing seals and dolphins. The biggest stars of the bunch are Lolita, a killer whale, and Flipper, named after the famous TV dolphin (many episodes of the TV series were filmed here). There are 15 shows daily, including one with Salty, star of the TV film *Salty the Sea Lion*. Snack stands and a café are on the premises. Open daily. Admission charge. 4400 Rickenbacker Causeway (phone: 361-5705).

SOUTH DADE COUNTY

METROZOO Miami's cageless zoo boasts over 250 different species of rare and exotic animals. Pathways lead through re-creations of Asia, the Eurasian steppes, the European forest, the African jungle, and the African plains—each filled with the area's indigenous animals including Bengal tigers, elephants, chimpanzees, silverback gorillas, and white tigers. An elevated, air conditioned monorail encircles the zoo every 45 minutes. Several snack stands are open daily, and an on-site restaurant is open on weekends. Open daily. Admission charge. 12400 SW 152nd St. (phone: 251-0401).

PARROT JUNGLE Here is more of the tropics—but this time, it's screaming, colorful, and talented. Not only do these parrots, macaws, and cockatoos fly, but they also ride bicycles, roller-skate, and solve math problems—all amid a jungle of huge cypress and live oaks. Don't miss the opportunity to pose for photos with brilliantly plumaged red, turquoise, and yellow parrots poised on your arms and head. Other daily wildlife shows feature snakes, bald eagles, and scorpions. There's also a monkey exhibit and a petting zoo with pigs, goats, and miniature deer. The coffee shop here is a great breakfast stop. Open daily. Admission charge. Two miles south of US 1 at 11000 SW 57th Ave. (Red Rd.) and Killian Dr. (phone: 666-7834).

MONKEY JUNGLE The monkeys run free, go swimming, swing from trees, and wander about while visitors watch from inside encaged walkways. There are also orangutans and gibbons. Naturally, some chimp stars perform (four daily shows rotate continuously). Open daily. Admission charge. 14805 SW 216th St. (phone: 235-1611).

ELSEWHERE

FRUIT AND SPICE PARK Some 20 tropical acres feature over 500 species of fruit, nut, and spice trees and plants. Guided tours by *Dade County Parks Department* naturalists include samplings of seasonal fruits, and you're free to eat anything that's fallen to the ground. This also is the site of the *National Arts Festival* each January and the *Tropical Agricultural Fiesta* each July. Tours are conducted Saturday and Sunday afternoons for a nominal charge. Closed *Thanksgiving, Christmas Day,* and *New Year's Day.* Admission charge. Thirty-five miles southwest of Miami, at 24801 SW 187th Ave., Homestead (phone: 247-5727).

CORAL CASTLE Hand-built by a man who was jilted the day before his wedding, this unusual home is testimony to lost love. More than 1,000 tons of coral rock were dug by hand and fashioned into a two-room tower and a walled-in, roofless courtyard divided into several sections containing outdoor furniture and solar-heated bathtubs. Open daily. Admission charge. 28655 US 1, Homestead (phone: 248-6344).

MICCOSUKEE INDIAN VILLAGE Just 25 miles west of Miami, descendants of Florida's original settlers are maintaining the lifestyle of their forebears. Among the attractions are alligator wrestling, crafts demonstrations, a small museum featuring the history of the tribe, and airboat rides (also see *Special Events,* below). Open daily. Admission charge. US 41 (Tamiami Trail) West (phone: 223-8380, weekdays; 223-8388, weekends).

A WORD ABOUT CRIME

In the wake of the much-publicized murders of several tourists in roadway robberies, South Florida has taken several steps to prevent crimes against visitors. Many hotels now offer guests free transportation from the airport and arrange for rental cars to be delivered to the hotels. For the benefit of people renting cars at the airport, easier-to-read signs have been posted on exit roadways pointing tourists directly to the beach and city areas, and more police are now stationed at rental car parking lots. In addition, rental agencies are prohibited from putting company bumper stickers and special license plates on rental cars (to eliminate the obvious signs that a car is being driven by a visitor). Other measures include establishing undercover police patrols and increasing the number of tourist information centers throughout the Miami area.

Nonetheless, travelers should be aware that criminals may deliberately bump a car from behind and then rob the driver when he or she gets out to check for damage. Another common crime is the "smash and grab," where a robber approaches a car at a traffic light, smashes the window, and then grabs for purses or jewelry. To avoid such crimes, drive alertly and always carry a map or clear directions to where you're going. If your car is bumped or you are told you have a flat tire, don't stop until you have reached a safe and well-lit location. If someone suspicious approaches your car at a red light, check for oncoming traffic, and then drive on quickly. Take taxis if you're going out late at night or to an unfamiliar area, and keep valuables in your hotel vault. Remember, it's always wise to err on the side of caution to ensure a safe vacation.

Sources and Resources

TOURIST INFORMATION

The Greater Miami Convention and Visitors Bureau (701 Brickell Ave., Suite 2700, Miami, FL 33131; phone: 539-3000; 800-283-2707; fax: 539-3113) is best for brochures, maps, and general tourist information. It's closed weekends. For information on fairs, art shows, and events in the area's parks, call the *Dade County Parks and Recreation Department*'s information line (phone: 857-6868). Call the *Florida State Hotline* (phone: 904-488-1234) for maps, calendars of events, health updates, and travel advisories. *Activity Line* (phone: 557-5600), a visitor information phone guide in six languages, offers updated schedules of events, plus dining, sports, and shopping tips.

LOCAL COVERAGE The *Miami Herald,* a morning daily, publishes its "Weekend" section, with a full schedule of upcoming events, on Fridays. *New Times,* an alternative weekly—Miami's answer to New York City's *Village Voice*—includes "The Wave," a listing of weekly happenings. Also of interest are *South Florida* magazine, a monthly, and *New Miami,* a monthly business magazine. Spanish publications include the dailies *El Nuevo Herald* and *El Diario las Américas,* and the monthly magazines *Miami Mensual* and *Selecta.* We also immodestly recommend our own *Birnbaum's Miami & Ft. Lauderdale 95* (Harper-Collins; $12).

TELEVISION STATIONS WPBT Channel 2–PBS; WTVJ Channel 4–NBC; WCIX Channel 6–CBS; and WPLG Channel 10–ABC.

RADIO STATIONS AM: WIOD 610 (news); WEAT 850 (easy listening); and WINZ 940 (news/talk). FM: WTMI 93.1 (classical music); WKIS 99.9 (country); WMXJ 102.7 (oldies); and WJQY 106.7 (easy listening).

TELEPHONE The area code for Miami is 305.

SALES TAX There is a 6% statewide sales tax. There's also a 12.5% Dade County hotel tax, although three municipalities have different rates: the hotel tax is 11.5% in Miami Beach, 9.5% in Bal Harbour, and 10.5% in Surfside. Local meals taxes are generally from 7.5% to 8.5%; in Bal Harbour, the rate is 9.5%.

CLIMATE Miami is warm all year, with average daily temperatures in the mid-80s F in summer and lots of sunshine. Summers can be prohibitively humid. Temperatures also can get cool indoors, where air conditioning prevails. The average daytime temperature in winter is in the upper 60s to mid 70s. However, winter evenings can get quite chilly, with the temperature sometimes plunging into the 40s.

GETTING AROUND

AIRPORT *Miami International Airport* is usually a 15-minute drive from downtown and about a half hour from Miami Beach, longer during rush periods (8:30 to 9:30 AM and 4:30 to 6:30 PM). The *Supershuttle* (phone: 871-2000) has van service from *Miami International Airport* to all hotels. Contact one of their representatives just outside the baggage claim area on the lower level and a van will come and pick you up in 15 minutes or less. Call *Supershuttle* 24 hours in advance when returning to the airport.

BUS *Metrobus* serves downtown Miami, Collins Avenue in Miami Beach, Coral Gables, and Coconut Grove fairly well, but service to other areas tends to be slow and complicated. Fares are $1.25 plus 25¢ for a transfer. For information on routes and schedules, call 638-6700.

CAR RENTAL Miami is served by all the large national firms. Intensive competition makes rates here among the least expensive in the country, but if you want to drive a convertible during peak season, be sure to reserve one well in advance.

METRORAIL/METROMOVER *Metrorail*, an elevated rail system, operates from the *Dadeland* shopping mall in the Kendall area to downtown Miami, and beyond to the *Civic Center* and Hialeah; fare, $1.25. The *Metromover* rail system is a recently expanded 4.3-mile downtown loop; the fare is 25¢, free for those transferring from the *Metrorail*. For information, call 638-6700.

TAXI You sometimes can hail a cab in the street, but it's better to order one on the phone or pick one up in front of any of the big hotels. Major cab companies are *Central Cab* (phone: 532-5555); *Metro Taxi* (phone: 888-8888); *Super Yellow Cab* (phone: 888-7777); and *Yellow Cab* (phone: 444-4444).

TOURS Miami is largely a waterfront city, and one good way to get to know it is by boat—excursions range from narrated tours of Millionaire's Row to romantic sunset cruises. Departing from the marina at *Bayside Marketplace* (see *Special Places*, above) are three popular cruises: The *Island Queen* (phone: 379-5119) offers daily hour-and-a-half tours; *Bayside Cruises* (phone: 822-2428) offers five cruises daily on the 49-passenger *Pauhana*, docked next to the *Hard Rock Café;* and the *Heritage of Miami* (phone: 442-9697), a dramatic tall ship, offers daily two-hour tours of

Biscayne Bay and is also available for charters. The *Lady Lucille* docks in front of the *Fontainebleau Hilton* hotel (4441 Collins Ave., Miami Beach; phone: 534-7000) and offers three sightseeing cruises daily.

Popular 90-minute narrated sightseeing trips are provided by *Old Town Trolley*, with on-and-off-again access for those wishing to spend time at different spots along the route. Tours leave every half hour, boarding at seven locations (phone: 374-TOUR).

Knowledgeable and folksy narrated walking, boat, and *Metromover* rail tours, sponsored by the *Historical Museum of Southern Florida*, are led by Dr. Paul S. George, a local history professor. Itineraries include Little Havana, the Art Deco District, Coconut Grove, Coral Gables, a Miami River boat tour, and a Stiltsville/Key Biscayne boat tour (phone: 858-6021 or 375-1625). *EcoTours Miami* (phone: 232-5398) offers natural history tours of the Everglades in five different languages.

For a different view of the city, *Miami Helicopter* (phone: 685-8223) offers flights over Miami Beach from *Opa-Locka Airport*. On the south side of MacArthur Causeway, between downtown Miami and Miami Beach, *Dade Helicopter Rides* offers 10-, 18-, and 25-minute tour flights; children under 12 must be accompanied by two adults (phone: 374-3737). *Chalk's International Airlines* offers half-hour seaplane flights on Saturday afternoons (phone: 371-8628; 800-4-CHALKS).

TRI-RAIL The 67-mile commuter railroad system began operating in 1989, connecting Dade, Broward, and Palm Beach counties with increasingly frequent daily routes. The fare is $3 ($5 round trip), with seniors, students, the disabled, and children ages 5 to 12 paying $1.50 ($2.50 round trip). Passengers board the double-decker trains at any of 15 stops, with free connecting passes to *Metrorail/Metromover* and to county and shuttle buses. The train provides access to major sights and, via connecting buses, to the *Miami, Ft. Lauderdale/Hollywood*, and *Palm Beach Airports*. Extra trains are scheduled for games at the *Joe Robbie* and *Orange Bowl Stadiums* and for special events. There are also guided tours to *Bayside Marketplace* and other attractions. The *Tri-Rail* system is accessible to disabled passengers (phone: 800-TRI-RAIL).

WATER TAXI The *North Dade Water Taxi* (phone: 545-5051) runs daily, stopping at major restaurants and other popular landings. The taxis operate on demand and must be summoned by phone between 11 AM and about 11:30 PM. Fare is $6; $14 for an all-day pass.

LOCAL SERVICES

AUDIOVISUAL EQUIPMENT *Spire Audio-Visual* (24 NW 36th St., Miami; phone: 576-5736).

BABY-SITTING *Lul-a-Bye Sitters Registry* (phone: 565-1222).

BUSINESS SERVICES *Uniforce Services* (14750 NW 77th Court, Miami Lakes; phone: 820-0531) is a firm specializing in providing temporary help.

CONVENTION FACILITIES *Miami Beach Convention Center* (1901 Convention Center Dr., Miami Beach; phone: 673-7311); *Miami Convention Center* (400 SE Second Ave., Miami; phone: 579-6341); and *Coconut Grove*

Convention Center (2700 S. Bayshore Dr., Coconut Grove; phone: 579-3310).

DENTAL EMERGENCY The *American Dental Association* (phone: 667-3647) maintains a 24-hour referral service.

DRY CLEANERS/TAILORS *La Salle Cleaners* (2341 LeJeune Rd., Coral Gables; phone: 444-7376); *Mark's* (1201 20th St., Miami Beach; phone: 538-6104).

EQUIPMENT RENTAL *A-1 Etron* (phone: 264-4652) and *Beach Typewriter* (phone: 538-6272) rent typewriters; there's a one-week minumum at both. *Kinko's* (1309 SW 107th Ave., Miami; phone: 220-8172; and 1246 S. Dixie Hwy., Coral Gables; phone: 662-6716) offers hourly rentals of typewriters and computers and is open 24 hours a day.

LIMOUSINES *All City Limousine* (phone: 865-0009); *Club Limousine* (11055 Biscayne Blvd., Miami; phone: 893-9850).

LOCKSMITH *Master Key* (phone: 638-8078) is a lifesaver if you've locked your keys in the car; open 24 hours daily.

MECHANICS *Dave's Car Clinic* (5800 Commerce La., South Miami; phone: 661-7711); *Martino* (7145 SW Eighth St., Miami; phone: 261-6071).

MEDICAL EMERGENCY *Jackson Memorial Hospital* (1611 NW 12th Ave., Miami; phone: 325-7429); *Mt. Sinai Medical Center* (4300 Alton Rd., Miami Beach; phone: 674-2200).

MESSENGER SERVICES *Crown Courier* (phone: 592-4000) and *Sunshine State Messenger Service* (phone: 944-6363) are both open 24 hours daily.

PHOTOCOPIES *Sir Speedy* (locations include 1659 James Ave., Miami Beach; phone: 531-5858) and *Kinko's* (see *Equipment Rental*).

POST OFFICE Three branches: the main office (2200 NW 72nd Ave., Miami; phone: 470-0243); a downtown office (500 NW Second Ave., Miami; phone: 371-2911); and a Miami Beach office (1300 Washington Ave., Miami Beach; phone: 531-3763).

PROFESSIONAL PHOTOGRAPHERS *Convention Photographers International* (1630 Cleveland Rd., Miami Beach; phone: 865-5628); *Pelham Photographic* (665 Mokena Dr., Miami Springs; phone: 885-2006).

SECRETARIES/STENOGRAPHERS *Secretarial Service* (2320 S. Dixie Hwy., Coconut Grove; phone: 856-8877) has English- and Spanish-speaking secretaries; also see *Business Services,* above.

TELECONFERENCE FACILITIES *Inter-Continental Miami* hotel (see *Checking In*) and *Omni International* hotel (1601 Biscayne Blvd., Miami; phone: 374-4399). Also see *Convention Facilities,* above.

TRANSLATORS *Berlitz* (phone: 371-3685; 800-523-7548) and *Professional Translating Services* (phone: 371-7887).

WESTERN UNION/TELEX Many offices are located around the city (phone: 223-8000; 800-325-4045).

OTHER *ABC Office Equipment* (phone: 891-5090); *Florida Tent Rental* (phone: 633-0199), tent pavilions for conferences or receptions, often set up at *Vizcaya Museum and Gardens; Pearl's and Jessie's Catering* (20160 W. Dixie Hwy., North Miami; phone: 937-1511); *US Passport Agency* (51 SW First Ave., Miami; phone: 536-5395), open weekdays except federal holidays.

SPECIAL EVENTS

Miami is the site of the annual *King Orange Jamboree Parade* (phone: 371-4600 for information), nationally televised from Biscayne Boulevard each *New Year's Eve* as a prelude to the *Orange Bowl* football classic, which is played in the evening on January 1 (phone: 371-4600 for information). The *King Mango Strut* parade, held a few days earlier, pokes fun at the lavish *Orange Bowl* festivities (phone: 444-7270). *New Year's Day* also boasts the *Carquest Auto Parts Bowl* (formerly the *Blockbuster Bowl*), a top-ranked collegiate football classic (phone: 564-5000). The *Kwanzaa Festival* is an African-American holiday celebrated on *New Year's Day* with food, music, and arts and crafts (phone: 936-5805). The annual *Art Miami Fair*, which showcases contemporary art, a good percentage of it Latin American, is held at the *Miami Beach Convention Center* in early January. This year, Miami is hosting the *Super Bowl*, to be played in January at the *Joe Robbie Stadium* (phone: 620-2578). Every January, an *Art Deco Weekend* takes place on Ocean Drive, in the heart of South Beach's historic Art Deco District (phone: 672-2014).

Miami Beach also hosts the *Festival of the Arts* each February (phone: 673-7733). The *Coconut Grove Art Festival* (phone: 447-0401) is also held in February, as is the *Miami Film Festival*, 10 days of national and international film premieres with visiting directors, producers, and stars (phone: 377-3456). Other February events include the *International Boat Show* (phone: 531-8410), the largest boat show in the world, which is held at the *Miami Beach Convention Center*, and the *Grand Prix of Miami*, which attracts top race drivers to the downtown "track" (Biscayne Blvd. between Flagler and NE Eighth Sts.; phone: 665-RACE or 379-5660).

In March, natives and visitors alike head for Calle Ocho (SW Eighth St.) in Little Havana for *Carnaval Miami* (phone: 644-8888), a nine-day festival featuring a 23-block-long street party, Latin foods, conga lines, salsa bands, and lots of people. In April, the *Greater Miami Billfish Tournament* attracts more than 500 anglers in pursuit of marlin and sailfish, vying for South Florida's richest fishing purse (phone: 365-0497). May ushers in the *Miami Home Show* at the *Miami Beach Convention Center* (phone: 666-5944). Coconut Grove is the site of the *Miami/Bahamas Goombay Festival* in June, celebrating the area's Bahamian heritage and considered the country's largest black heritage festival, with *junkanoo* groups (local citizens who form bands and play calypso and reggae music continuously on homemade instruments) and lots of conch chowder and fritters (phone: 372-9966).

July brings the *Tropical Agricultural Fiesta* at the *Fruit and Spice Park* (see *Special Places*) and the *Annual International Music and Crafts Festival* at the *Miccosukee Indian Village* in the Everglades (see *Special Places*). Chocoholics won't want to miss the *Chocolate Festival* in September at the *Fontainebleau Hilton* (phone: 535-3240 for details). For sailboat enthusiasts, the two-day *Columbus Day Regatta* in October attracts more than 600 entrants (phone: 448-7417). In November, the *Miami Book Fair International,* held at *Miami Dade Community College* (phone: 237-3258), welcomes authors, publishers, booksellers, and street vendors to one of the world's largest week-long celebrations of the printed word, considered the country's premier literary event by *The New York Times* and *Publisher's Weekly.* The Miccosukee tribe's annual *Arts Festival* in late December draws members from 40 tribes who perform songs and dances, and demonstrate other skills at the *Miccosukee Indian Village* (see *Special Places*).

MUSEUMS

In addition to those described in *Special Places,* other museums to see include the following.

AMERICAN POLICE HALL OF FAME AND MUSEUM A marble monument commemorates more than 3,400 slain officers. Exhibits include law enforcement vehicles and equipment, such as a guillotine and an electric chair. At a mock crime scene, visitors are encouraged to solve a murder. Open daily. Admission charge; free to police officers and families of slain officers. 3801 Biscayne Blvd., Miami (phone: 573-0070).

ART MUSEUM AT FLORIDA INTERNATIONAL UNIVERSITY The exhibits shown here include painting retrospectives, photography shows, and displays of university graduates' work. Open extended hours on Mondays; closed Saturday mornings and Sundays. No admission charge. University Park, SW 107th Ave. and Eighth St., Miami (phone: 348-2890).

CENTER FOR THE FINE ARTS Designed by Philip Johnson as part of the lovely complex at the *Metro-Dade Cultural Center,* it hosts major traveling exhibitions of works by artists such as Pablo Picasso and Jasper Johns. Signs are in English and Spanish. There is a small gift shop. Open extended hours on Thursdays; closed Sunday mornings and Mondays. Admission charge; voluntary contributions on Tuesdays. 101 W. Flagler St. at First Ave., Miami (phone: 375-1700).

CUBAN MUSEUM OF ARTS AND CULTURE Changing exhibitions here promote the cultural heritage of Miami's Cuban and other Hispanic communities. Closed Mondays and Tuesday through Sunday mornings. No admission charge, but donations are requested. 1300 SW 12th Ave., Miami (phone: 858-8006).

HISTORICAL MUSEUM OF SOUTH FLORIDA Located at the *Metro-Dade Cultural Center,* it boasts excellent exhibits on the histories of the various groups that have settled here. Numerous displays depict Native American life, the Spanish exploration period (there's a mock-up of a fort that kids can climb), and the ongoing contributions made by Cubans, African-Americans, and Jews. In addition, maritime history displays include artifacts from treasure fleets, and there's a full-size trolley car used in Miami in the 1920s. Signs and recorded messages are in both English and Spanish. There's a fine gift shop. Open extended hours on Thursdays; closed Sunday mornings. Admission charge. 101 W. Flagler St. at First Ave., Miami (phone: 375-1492).

LOWE ART MUSEUM The highlight here is the *Kress Collection of Renaissance and Baroque Art*, a permanent collection of period works; pre-Columbian, Asian, and African art; and furniture and paintings. There also are visiting exhibits. Closed Sunday mornings and Mondays. Admission charge. 1301 Stanford Dr., on the *University of Miami* campus in Coral Gables (phone: 284-3535).

MIAMI YOUTH MUSEUM Hands-on exhibits here include *Kidscape*, a miniature neighborhood with a dental office, a fire station, and a supermarket. Among the newer offerings are a "Metro-Dade Safe Neighborhood" exhibit and a newspaper exhibit called "Hot off the Press." Guided tours are in both English and Spanish. Closed holidays. Admission charge. *Bakery Centre*, 5701 Sunset Dr., South Miami (phone: 661-3046).

WOLFSONIAN MUSEUM Multimillionaire Mitchell Wolfson Jr.'s eclectic—and still growing—collection of over 60,000 objets d'art, rare books, and everyday items finally was catalogued; the result is a rare documentary of American and European cultural history from 1885 to 1945. Hours were changing at press time, so call ahead. Admission charge. 1001 Washington Ave., Miami Beach (phone: 531-1001).

SHOPPING

In addition to sparkling blue waters and powdery white beaches, Miami offers some sand-free sports—and the best of them is shopping. The places listed below carry a wide variety of items, and many have lovely restaurants and scenic views as well.

Aventura Mall One of South Florida's largest malls, with 200 shops and stores on two levels. Anchors are *Lord & Taylor*, *Macy's*, *JC Penney*, and *Sears*. A large food court offers a pause that refreshes. 19501 Biscayne Blvd., North Miami Beach (phone: 935-1110).

Bal Harbour Shops Lovely open-air shopping amid gardens and fountains. The 100 upscale stores include *Saks Fifth Avenue, Neiman Marcus, Martha, Cartier, Gucci, Brooks Brothers,* and *FAO Schwarz*. Good snack stops include *Ms. Grimble, American Way,* and *Coco's*. 9700 Collins Ave., Bal Harbour (phone: 866-0311).

Bayside Marketplace From the designers of Boston's *Quincy Market*, this shopping and entertainment complex overlooking the water has 150 shops and restaurants. There are also pushcarts where you can buy arts and crafts items from South America, Central America, and the Caribbean. Also see *Special Places*. 401 Biscayne Blvd., Miami (phone: 577-3344).

Books & Books Both locations, one in Coral Gables and the other in Miami Beach, offer frequent readings by authors such as Carlos Fuentes and Susan Sontag. The Coral Gables store also features a sizable selection of used and out of print books. 296 Aragon Ave., Coral Gables (phone: 442-4408), and 933 Lincoln Rd., Miami Beach (phone: 532-3222).

CocoWalk An exciting open-air, Mediterranean-style shopping complex in the heart of Coconut Grove, it boasts three dozen shops, several eateries, and entertainment for the young and young-at-heart. There's also

Café Tu Tu Tango (see *Eating Out*). Stores are closed holidays. 3015 Grand Ave., Coconut Grove (phone: 444-0777).

Dadeland Mall This large mall in the Kendall section of southwest Miami claims Florida's largest *Burdine's,* along with *Saks Fifth Avenue, Lord & Taylor,* and 200 other shops. 7535 N. Kendall Dr., Kendall (phone: 665-6226).

Elite Fine Art Latin American art by masters and emerging artists. Includes paintings, drawings, and sculpture by Brazilian artist Antonio Amaral, Cuban Mario Bencomo, and Panamanian Guillermo Trujillo, among others. Closed Sundays and Mondays. 3140 Ponce de León Blvd., Coral Gables (phone: 448-3800; 800-USA-ELITE outside Florida).

Epicure Market *The* place on the Beach for unusual grocery items and takeout goodies for sand or sea, including three types of smoked salmon, imported caviar, fresh-ground coffee, large cooked shrimp, and prepared meals. 1656 Alton Rd., Miami Beach (phone: 672-1861).

Falls Shopping Center More than 60 upscale stores and restaurants set among splashing waterfalls in the Kendall section of Miami. 8888 Howard Dr., Kendall (phone: 255-4570).

A Likely Story Children's books and imported educational toys, including easels, games, and specialized items. 5740 Sunset Dr., South Miami (phone: 667-3730).

Mayfair Shops in the Grove High-fashion shops such as *Polo/Ralph Lauren* and *Ann Taylor* are still found here, but now the mix is more mainstream. At press time, this mall was under renovation, with a 10-screen movie theater, a number of new boutiques and shops, and the trendy *Planet Hollywood* café scheduled to open. The mall is worth a visit if only to bask in the fabulous Alhambresque atmosphere. Grand Ave., Coconut Grove (phone: 448-1700).

Miami Duty-Free Travelers planning to leave the country, even for a short cruise, may buy items at duty-free prices right in Miami, in this clean, uncluttered shop. *MDF* will deliver your purchases to your plane or ship on the day of departure. Items include Givenchy and Calvin Klein scents, Cartier watches, liquor, Fendi purses, Wedgwood china, and leather goods. Salespeople speak seven languages. Prices are 20% to 40% below retail, and no Florida tax is levied. 125 NE Eighth St., Miami (phone: 358-9774).

Unicorn Village Market This large, immaculate shop associated with the *Unicorn Village* restaurant features enormous displays of organically grown produce, prepared Pritikin Diet items, and wines produced without pesticides or added sulfites. Prepared takeout also available. At *The Shops at the Waterways,* 3595 NE 207th St., North Miami Beach (phone: 933-8829).

Virginia Miller Galleries Features contemporary artwork by Latin Americans, including Carlos Loarca; European artists, including Karel Appel of the Netherlands; and US artists Larry Gerber, Tom Hopkins, and the late Alice Neel; plus Australian aboriginal paintings of the Turkey Creek art community. Closed Sundays. 169 Madeira Ave., Coral Gables (phone: 444-4493).

SPORTS AND FITNESS

BASEBALL The *University of Miami Hurricanes* play at *Mark Light Stadium* (on campus at 1 Hurricane Dr., corner of Ponce de León and San Amaro, Coral Gables; phone: 284-2655; 800-GO-CANES). The *National League*'s Florida *Marlins* play at *Joe Robbie Stadium* in North Miami (2269 NW 199th St.; phone: 620-2578 or 623-6100). Fans also can watch pre-season games of the Baltimore *Orioles,* whose spring training camp is in Miami; they often play the New York *Yankees,* who train in nearby Ft. Lauderdale at *Yankee Stadium* (5301 NW 12th Ave.; phone: 776-1921).

BASKETBALL The *Heat,* Miami's *NBA* entry, burns up the court at the *Miami Arena* (701 Arena Way, Miami; phone: 577-HEAT for tickets; 530-4400 for other information). The *Harlem Globetrotters* occasionally present their frantic antics here, too.

BICYCLING Cyclists have more than 100 miles of bicycle paths at their disposal in the Miami area. A self-guided bicycle tour of Key Biscayne originates in *Crandon Park.* The 3.5-mile path goes through the beach area, woods, and hammocks of trees and cane grass, ending at *Sundays on the Bay* restaurant. The *Dade County Parks and Recreation Department* has more information (phone: 857-6868). Another favorite spot for cyclists and runners is *Tropical Park.* The 2-mile path winds through a wooded area, along two lakes, and past sports facilities. Pick up a map at the park office (7900 40th Rd., Miami; phone: 553-3616; open weekdays) or the tennis center (same address and phone as the park office; open daily).

Bicycle rentals are available throughout the Greater Miami area. A few places to try: *Cycles on the Beach* (713 Fifth St., Miami Beach; phone: 673-2055); *Dade Cycle Shop* (3216 Grand Ave., Coconut Grove; phone: 443-6075); *Key Biscayne Rental* (260 Crandon Blvd., Key Biscayne; phone: 361-5555); *Miami Beach Bicycle Center* (923 W. 39th St., Miami Beach; phone: 531-4161); *Spokes Bicycle Shops* (3488 Main Hwy., Coconut Grove; phone: 529-1688; and 601 Fifth St., South Beach; phone: 672-2550).

BOATING Greater Miami is laced with navigable canals and has many private and public marinas with all kinds of boats for rent. Sailboats are available at *Dinner Key Marina* (3400 Pan American Dr., Coconut Grove; phone: 579-6980). Sailboats and powerboats, along with windsurfers and day sailers, are available from *Easy Sailing* (3400 Pan American Dr., Coconut Grove; phone: 858-4001); some rentals include free instruction. Sailboat rentals are available through *Sailboats Miami* (Rickenbacker Causeway; phone: 361-SAIL) and *Sailboats of Key Biscayne* (*Crandon Park Marina,* 4000 Crandon Blvd.; phone: 361-0328). The *Pauhana,* a 49-passenger catamaran, is available for charter or sunset tours (401 NE Fourth St. at *Bayside Marketplace,* Miami; phone: 888-3002 or 822-2428). *Club Nautico,* good for powerboat rentals, has docks in Miami (phone: 371-4252 or 372-9931); Miami Beach (phone: 673-2502);

Coconut Grove (phone: 858-6258); and North Miami Beach (phone: 945-3232). Bareboat charters also are available through *Haulover Marine Center* (15000 Collins Ave., Miami Beach; phone: 945-3934). For information on sport fishing charters, see also *Fishing*, below.

DOG RACING Greyhound racing is held at the *Biscayne Kennel Club* (320 NW 115th St., Miami; phone: 754-3484) and at the *Flagler Greyhound Track* (NW 37th Ave. and Seventh St., Miami; phone: 649-3000). Check the racing dates before heading to the track.

FISHING Surf and offshore saltwater fishing is available year-round. The boardwalks on the Rickenbacker, MacArthur, and Venetian causeways are popular fishing spots. The *Holiday Inn* Newport Pier (16701 Collins Ave., Miami; phone: 949-1300), is open 24 hours daily and provides equipment rental (admission charge). There's also plenty of freshwater action in canals and backwaters, including the Everglades and Florida Bay.

FITNESS CENTERS Staying in shape is no problem in Dade County. Try the *YMCA* (at the downtown World Trade Center; phone: 577-3091); visitors who are members of a *Y Away Plan* back home (more than 50 miles away) are welcome without charge. The *Downtown Athletic Club* (atop the Southeast Financial Center building; phone: 358-9988); *World Gym* (799 Galiano St., Coral Gables; phone: 445-5161); *Gold's Gym* (1617 SW 107th Ave., Miami; phone: 553-8878); and *Cross Training Fitness Centers* (2901 Florida Ave., Coconut Grove; phone: 442-2400) are also open to visitors for a fee.

FOOTBALL The *NFL Dolphins* are the team, and *Dolphin*-mania sweeps through the entire city during the pro football season, so for good seats call the *Joe Robbie Stadium* in North Miami in advance (2269 NW 199th St.; phone: 620-2578). The *University of Miami Hurricanes* play at *Orange Bowl Stadium* (1501 NW Third St.); for tickets, contact the *University of Miami* ticket office (1 Hurricane Dr., Coral Gables; phone: 284-2655), or go to the stadium.

GOLF Its almost constant sunshine, balmy breezes, and picturesque fairways make Greater Miami a golfer's dream—witness the preponderance of golf tournaments held here. Resorts and hotels without their own courses usually can provide access to other clubs.

TOP TEE-OFF SPOT

Doral Resort & Country Club At the moment, this 651-room resort is the grande golfing dame of the Miami–Miami Beach tourist axis. The *Doral*'s superb golf facilities (five 18-hole layouts, plus a par 3 executive course) thus far remain unsurpassed. The fabled championship *Blue Monster* is still one of the most formidable challenges in the state, and the *Gold* course offers little diminution in challenge. The pro is Rob Brand; the *Jim McLean Learning Center* is the pro workshop. 4400 NW 87th Ave., Miami (phone: 592-2000; 800-327-6334 or 800-22-DORAL; fax: 594-4682).

In addition, Miami has more first-rate courses open to the public than most places you can name. Among the better ones are *Kendale Lakes* (6401 Kendale Lakes Dr., Miami; phone: 382-3930); *Miami Springs* (650 Curtiss Pkwy., Miami Springs; phone: 888-2377); *Bayshore* (2301 Alton Rd., Miami Beach; phone: 532-3350); *Palmetto* (9300 SW 152nd St., Miami; phone: 238-2922); and *The Links at Key Biscayne* (6700 Crandon Blvd., Key Biscayne; phone: 361-9129). For more information about golfing in Miami, call *Tee Times,* a 24-hour reservation line (phone: 669-9500) or the parks and recreation departments of Dade County (phone: 857-6868), Miami Beach (phone: 673-7730), or Miami (phone: 575-5240).

The *Honda Golf Classic* is one of the major US events on the *PGA* circuit, played in March at the private *Weston Hills Country Club* in Coral Springs. You might spot such pros as Nick Faldo, Tom Watson, or Greg Norman attempting a birdie here (phone: 384-4600). The $1.4-million *Doral-Ryder Open* is held annually on the championship *Blue Monster* course at the *Doral Resort & Country Club* in Miami in late February or early March.

HOCKEY The *Panthers,* an NHL expansion team, currently play at the *Miami Arena* (721 NW 1st Ave.; phone: 768-1900).

HORSE RACING Betting is big in Miami. The *Hialeah Race Track* (2200 E. Fourth Ave., Hialeah; phone: 885-8000 or 800-442-5324), listed on the *National Registry of Historic Places,* is worth a visit just to see the beautiful grounds and clubhouse and the famous flock of pink flamingos. Call for racing times. There also is thoroughbred racing at *Calder Race Course* in North Miami, next to *Joe Robbie Stadium* (21001 NW 27th Ave.; phone: 625-1311 in Dade County; 523-4324 in Broward County). The country's only all-weather racetrack, it's open from May through January. The stadium's "Family Sundays" feature clowns, games, face painting, and a petting zoo. Dining is available in the *Citation Room, Flamingo Terrace,* and *Turf Club.*

JAI ALAI Almost year-round, there's jai alai (a Basque game resembling a combination of lacrosse, handball, and tennis) and betting action nightly at the *Miami Jai-Alai Fronton,* the country's largest (3500 NW 37th Ave., Miami; phone: 633-6400). You can buy tickets at the gate or reserve them in advance.

JET SKIING The latest craze in water fun, available at *Tony's Jet Ski Rentals* (3501 Rickenbacker Causeway, Key Biscayne; phone: 361-8280) and *Fun Watersports* (*Miami Airport Hilton and Marina*, 5101 Blue Lagoon Dr., Miami; phone: 261-7687).

JOGGING In Miami, run along South Bayshore Drive to *David Kennedy Park,* at 22nd Avenue, and jog the Vita Path; or jog in *Bayfront Park,* at Biscayne and Northeast Fourth Street. In Miami Beach, run on a wooden boardwalk that extends along the ocean from 21st to 51st Street, or run toward the parcourse on the southern tip of South Beach. The *Miami Mile,* a world class event fashioned after New York's *Fifth Avenue Mile* and San Francisco's *California Mile,* is off and running the third week of January. For more information, call 759-5990.

NATURE WALKS There are nature walks at *Fairchild Tropical Garden* and the *Fruit and Spice Park;* the *Dade County Parks and Recreation Department* (phone: 857-6868) offers frequent guided tours through natural hammocks, tree forests, bird rookeries, and even through water (a marine walk, nature lesson, and dousing are at Bear Cut, Key Biscayne).

SCUBA DIVING Diving opportunities abound along the coast, where the same three-banded basic reef system extends upward from the Florida Keys, past Miami and Ft. Lauderdale. Although it's broken up in spots, and some areas are polluted, plenty of opportunities exist for spotting elkhorn and brain coral—with bright red soft corals at deeper levels—and colorful tropical fish. The first reef is about 15 feet deep, the second about 40 feet deep, and the third is 60 to 100 feet deep. The practice of sinking freighters and other large objects in the sea to create artificial reefs lures oceans of finny friends at 100- and 200-foot depths (although some of these were disturbed by Hurricane Andrew). Miami boasts about 150 wrecks, and numerous dive shops operate in this area. Among them are *Diver's Paradise* (*Crandon Park Marina,* Key Biscayne; phone: 361-DIVE); *The Diving Locker* (223 Sunny Isles Blvd., Miami; phone: 947-6025); and *Team Divers* (1290 Fifth St., Miami Beach; phone: 673-0101; 800-543-7887). Also look in the yellow pages.

SKATING Roller-skate to a computerized light show—two million lights, synchronized to music—at *Hot Wheels Roller Skating Center* (12265 SW 112th St., Kendall; phone: 595-2958).

SKY DIVING *Skydive Miami* (*Homestead General Airport;* phone: SKYDIVE; 800-758-3483) will fly you up and let you sail down. The company also will provide—for a fee—video or still shots of your dive.

SPAS With its balmy climate and beautiful surroundings, Miami is an ideal spa setting; indeed, there are plenty of hotel facilities from which to choose. Listed below is our favorite.

A SYBARITIC SPA

Doral Saturnia Modeled after *Terme di Saturnia* in Italy, this is a palatial retreat for those who thrive on precise attention to detail, from impeccable room service to super-thick terry cloth towels. Gushing fountains and Roman arcades are the highlights of this Old World spa, which fuses the practices of American nutrition and high-energy fitness with European face and body treatments. The therapeutic waters of Italy's *Saturnia* are re-created, with imported extracts that contain mineral salts and plankton. The "cure" comes in many packages, from a day of massages and mud treatments to a week's "crash" cellulitis program. 8755 NW 36th St. (phone: 593-6030; 800-331-7768 or 800-22-DORAL).

SWIMMING Miami Beach and Key Biscayne offer some great places for swimming, all water sports, and another prime activity: sedentary sun worshiping. A 2-mile stretch of beach is open at *Crandon Park* (Rickenbacker Causeway to Key Biscayne; phone: 361-5421). Haulover Beach (A1A north of Bal Harbour; phone: 947-3525) is a long stretch of beautiful beach, good for surfing; the southern end is popular with families, while the northern end is Miami's unofficial clothing-optional beach. There are also a marina, sightseeing boats, charter fishing fleets, and restaurants. Miami Beach has several long stretches of public beach at various places, including South Beach (Fifth St. and Collins Ave.), a favorite of surfers; *Lummus Park* (South Beach on Ocean Ave.), with lots of shaded beaches; and North Shore Beach (71st St. and Collins Ave.), with landscaped dunes and an oceanfront walkway. There are also small public beaches at the east ends of streets near major hotels.

TENNIS Mild and sunny weather make South Florida ideal for year-round tennis, as attested to by illustrious residents Gabriella Sabatini and Steffi Graf.

CHOICE COURTS

Doral Resort & Country Club A veritable metropolis of a resort, this 2,400-acre establishment offers 15 well-kept clay and hard-surface tennis courts, backboards, ball machines, private lessons, and group clinics. The late Arthur Ashe was director of tennis; the program is currently managed by *Peter Burwash International Clinics*. 4400 NW 87th Ave., Miami (phone: 592-2000; 800-327-6334 or 800-22DORAL; fax: 594-4682).

In addition, most of Miami's major resort hotels have tennis courts for the use of their guests, and there are also public facilities throughout the county, including those at the *Abel Holtz Tennis Stadium* in Miami Beach's *Flamingo Park* (1200 12th St.; phone: 673-7761), with hard and clay courts; *Tamiami* (11201 SW 24th St., Miami; phone: 223-7076); *North Shore Center* (350 73rd St., Miami Beach; phone: 993-2022); and *Tropical Park* (7900 SW 40th St., Miami; phone: 553-3161). In addition, there are over 550 public courts in metropolitan Dade County (phone: 579-2676).

The 10-day *Lipton International Players Championships* is one of the world's largest tennis happenings, with such top players as Boris Becker and Ivan Lendl on hand in March. For information, contact the *International Tennis Center* (7300 Crandon Blvd., Key Biscayne, FL 33149; phone: 361-6161); for tickets, contact the *Tennis Center* (phone: 361-5252) or the tournament office (2 Alhambra Plaza, Coral Gables, FL 33134; phone: 446-2200).

WATER SKIING Those not staying at a beachfront resort can try the sport via *Fun Watersports* (*Miami Airport Hilton and Marina*, 5101 Blue Lagoon Dr., Miami; phone: 261-7687).

WINDSURFING Major beachfront hotels rent equipment, but the best spot is arguably Windsurfer Beach at Key Biscayne. Bring your own board or rent from *Sailboats Miami* (Rickenbacker Causeway; phone: 361-SAIL); also offered are two-hour lessons guaranteed to teach any novice.

THEATER

For current offerings, check the publications listed in *Tourist Information* in this chapter. The *Coconut Grove Playhouse* (3500 Main Hwy.; phone: 442-4000) imports New York stars for its season of classics that runs from October through May. The *Jackie Gleason Theater of the Performing Arts*, referred to locally as *TOPA* (1700 Washington Ave., Miami Beach; phone: 673-7300), offers touring plays and musicals, including some pre- and post-Broadway shows. The *Gusman Center for the Performing Arts* (174 E. Flagler St., Miami; phone: 372-0925) and the *Dade County Auditorium* (2901 W. Flagler St., Miami; phone: 854-1643) book theatrical and cultural events year-round.

MUSIC

Visiting orchestras and artists perform in Miami at the *Gusman Center for the Performing Arts* and at the *Dade County Auditorium*, or in Miami Beach at the *Theater of the Performing Arts* (see *Theater*, above, for details on all three). The *Greater Miami Opera Association* (1200 Coral Way, Miami; phone: 854-7890; 800-741-1010) stages a full complement of major productions during the winter season, as does the *New World Symphony* (541 Lincoln Rd., Miami Beach; phone: 673-3331). Luminaries including Gloria Estefan, Madonna, and Billy Joel often perform at the *Miami Arena* (701 Arena Way, Miami; phone: 530-4444) or the *Orange Bowl* (1501 NW Third St., Miami; phone: 371-3351).

DANCE

The *Miami City Ballet* (905 Lincoln Rd., Miami Beach; phone: 532-7713), headed by Edward Villella, is one of the country's best young companies, and performs a full season beginning each fall. Touring companies such as the *American Ballet Theatre* often visit in season, and there are numerous performances of *The Nutcracker* throughout the region around *Christmastime*.

NIGHTCLUBS AND NIGHTLIFE

For night owls interested in Miami's myriad after-dark destinations, there are several 24-hour recorded information lines, among them the *Jazz Hotline* (phone: 382-3938); *Blues Hotline* (phone: 666-MOJO); the *Salsa Hotline* (phone: 89-DANCE); the *PACE Free Concert Line* (phone: 948-9285); and the *Swing Dance Hotline* (phone: 944-9917).

The *Club Tropigala* show at the *Fontainebleau Hilton* (phone: 672-7469; see *Checking In*) may make customers think they're watching a lavish "flesh and feathers" production in pre-Castro Havana; *Les Violins* (1751 Biscayne Blvd., Miami; phone: 371-8668) also presents a flashy show with a Cuban twist. Shout *olé* to flamenco shows in Little Havana at *Málaga* (740 Calle Ocho; phone: 858-4224). Latin jazz and salsa bands enliven *Centro Vasco* (see *Eating Out*) late Friday nights. Las Vegas–style revues fill two stages at the *Holiday Inn Newport Pier* (16701 Collins Ave., Miami Beach; phone: 949-1300).

For live blues and a bit of history, stop in at *Tobacco Road* (626 S. Miami Ave., Miami; phone: 374-1198), Miami's oldest bar. If jazz is your bag, try *Greenstreet's* (2051 LeJeune Rd., Coral Gables; phone: 445-2131) or *MoJazz* (928 71st St., Miami; phone: 865-2636). Dancing hot spots are the *Alcazaba* in the *Hyatt Regency Coral Gables* (50 Alhambra Plaza, Coral Gables; phone: 441-1234), featuring Top 40, salsa, and merengue music on Wednesdays, Fridays, and Saturdays; the *English Pub* (320 Crandon Blvd., Key Biscayne; phone: 361-8877); and *Bash* (655 Washington Ave., South Beach; phone: 538-2274), which is owned by Mick Hucknall, the lead singer of the pop group *Simply Red*. The *Hungry Sailor* (3426 Main Hwy., Coconut Grove; phone: 444-9359) offers live reggae or rock 'n' roll nightly.

The south end of Miami Beach, known as South Beach or SoBe, is the current "in" spot for nightlife. Supper clubs to see and be seen in (after 10 PM) are *Cassis* (764 Washington Ave., Miami Beach; phone: 531-7700), on Tuesday nights; *Mezzanotte* (1200 Washington Ave., Miami Beach; phone: 673-4343), on Saturday nights; and *Bang* (1516 Washington Ave., Miami Beach; phone: 531-2361), on Sunday nights. Dress hot, and be prepared to dance on the tables—like everyone else. For hip-hop dancing, head to the *Island Club* (701 Washington Ave., Miami Beach; phone: 538-1213); *Van Dome* (1532 Washington Ave., Miami Beach; phone: 534-4288); or *Penrod's* (1 Ocean Dr., Miami Beach; phone: 538-1111). *Egoist* (455 Ocean Dr., Miami Beach; phone: 534-7436), a late-night dance bistro, features reggae on Sundays. South Beach clubs favored by gays include the *Paragon* (1235 Washington Ave., Miami Beach; phone: 534-1235) and the *Warsaw Ballroom* (1450 Collins Ave., Miami Beach; phone: 531-4555); Saturday is "straight" night at the latter. Just for laughs, hit the *Improv* (*CocoWalk*, 3015 Grand Ave., Coconut Grove; phone: 441-8200), where dinner is served at several shows nightly.

Best in Town

CHECKING IN

Winter is the busy season, and reservations should be made well in advance. In winter, a double room at hotels in the very expensive category will run $230 or more per night; in the expensive category, $160 to $210; in the moderate category, $110 to $160; and in the inexpensive category, $50 to $110. Besides the ones listed below, there are hundreds of other hotels in the Greater Miami area, including those run by such chains as Howard Johnson and Holiday Inn. Check the yellow pages, call the hotel chains' toll-free 800 numbers, or call the *Central Reservation Service for Greater Miami* (phone: 800-950-0232). In summer, most hotels cut their rates, some quite substantially, so shop around. For information about bed and breakfast accommodations, contact the *Greater Miami Convention and Visitors Bureau* (see *Tourist Information*, above). Unless we note otherwise, rooms in the hotels listed below have air conditioning, private baths, TV sets, and telephones. All telephone and fax numbers are in the 305 area code unless otherwise indicated.

For an unforgettable Miami vacation experience, we begin with our favorites, followed by our recommendations of cost and quality choices of hotels, listed by price category.

GRAND HOTELS

Doral Resort & Country Club It's virtually impossible to pick the centerpiece here: the world class golf (five championship courses and a par 3 practice course); the 15 tennis courts; or the essentially unlimited access (and free transportation) to its sister properties, the *Doral Ocean Beach* and the *Doral Saturnia International Spa* resorts (see *A Sybaritic Spa*, above, and *Checking In*, below). The club itself offers 595 rooms and 56 suites, an Olympic-size pool (heated in winter), three restaurants, three lounges, two Jacuzzis, and a fitness center. Add to that the facilities available at the other *Doral*s, and virtually no physical or spiritual need is left unattended. Business facilities include 24-hour room service, meeting rooms for up to 200, a concierge, secretarial services, A/V equipment, photocopiers, computers, and express checkout. 4400 NW 87th Ave., Miami (phone: 592-2000; 800-327-6334 or 800-22-DORAL; fax: 594-4682).

Turnberry Isle Set on a verdant, 300-acre island on the Intracoastal Waterway in North Miami, this complex of two hotels—both with a Mediterranean design but each with its own distinct personality—offers a total of 340 rooms and suites, all with spacious baths complete with sunken whirlpool tubs. The *Country Club* is a stunner. Its lobby/lounge is palatial, its guestrooms oversized and beautifully decorated, and even the meeting rooms are bright and airy, with French doors opening onto the golf course. The *Veranda* restaurant serves such innovative dishes as plantain-crusted salmon filet and fire-roasted ranch veal chops. At the *Yacht Club*, museum-quality ship models enhance the decor. Guests can charter *Miss Turnberry*—a 140-foot yacht that makes this her home berth—for $12,000 per day. The marina facilities are superb, and the roster of sports facilities includes five pools, a beach reachable by free shuttle, two Robert Trent Jones Sr. championship golf courses, and 24 tennis courts. There's an adjacent spa, beside which sits the *Marina* hotel, favored by such notables as Bill Cosby and Elton John for its no-lobby privacy. All 70 rooms were being upgraded at press time, part of a $2 million renovation project. The complex, linked by a complimentary shuttle, offers 11 restaurants and lounges, a private beach club, 24-hour room service, a concierge, meeting rooms for up to 1,000, A/V equipment, photocopiers, computers, and express checkout. 19999 W. Country Club Dr., Aventura, Turnberry Isle (phone: 932-6200; 800-327-7028; fax: 932-9096).

VERY EXPENSIVE

Alexander This elegant, yet surprisingly homey all-suite condominium hotel was once a luxury apartment building. A chandeliered portico, a grand lobby with a curving stairway and antiques from the Cornelius Vanderbilt mansion in New York, and 170 spacious, antiques-filled suites are all impressive; each suite boasts a fully equipped kitchen, a king-size bed, and a sleep sofa in the living room. *Dominique's* restaurant, with a main dining room overlooking the ocean, specializes in rack of lamb and *tarte tatin*. There's also a poolside grill and snack bar and a ballroom. The grounds include an acre of tropical gardens, two lagoon swimming pools—one with its own waterfall—and four soothing whirlpools. A private marina and golf and tennis facilities are nearby. Business facilities include room service from 7 AM until 11 PM, meeting rooms for up to 200, a concierge, secretarial services, A/V equipment, photocopiers, and computers. 5225 Collins Ave., Miami Beach (phone: 865-6500; 800-327-6121; fax: 864-8525).

Colonnade Still sporting its original façade, this 1920s hostelry has 157 luxury rooms and suites and a rooftop pool and Jacuzzi overlooking Coral Gables. The intimate lobby boasts dark paneling, overstuffed sofas, and Oriental rugs. The hotel's ballrooms often are the settings for lavish banquets. The *Aragon Café* is one of Miami's best hotel restaurants (see *Eating Out*). *Doc Dammers Bar & Grill* is an informal eatery with interesting early photos of the region and live music most nights. Business facilities include meeting rooms, secretarial services, A/V equipment, photocopiers, computers, and express checkout. A small health club, a concierge, and 24-hour room service complete the picture. 180 Aragon Ave., Coral Gables (phone: 441-2600; 800-533-1337; fax: 445-3929).

Doral Ocean Beach Relaxed elegance and a friendly staff are the hallmarks of this 420-room high-rise. The lobby gleams with European-style gold mosaics, marble, and a crystal chandelier. Other highlights include exclusive shops, an Olympic-size pool, water sports, two outdoor Jacuzzis, a disco, a lounge with live piano music, a fitness center, a video gameroom, two lighted tennis courts, and an FAA-licensed helipad. On the 18th floor is the heralded *Alfredo the Original of Rome* restaurant, and two other restaurants (one of them on the beach) offer both indoor and outdoor dining. Not to be overlooked is the stunning view of the water, the city, and the cruise ships. There's courtesy shuttle service to the *Doral Resort & Country Club* and the *Doral Saturnia* (see below); guests may use the facilities at these two locations at the normal guest rates. Business facilities include meeting rooms for up to 1,300, a concierge, secretarial services, A/V equipment, photocopiers, computers, and express checkout. 4833 Collins Ave., Miami Beach (phone: 532-3600; 800-22DORAL; fax: 532-2334).

Doral Saturnia International Spa This luxurious $40-million facility was modeled after the *Terme di Saturnia* in Tuscany. Each of its 48 plush suites has its own whirlpool bath, and there's everything needed by those in search of enhanced fitness, health, and stress management. The health-conscious Tuscan menu is served in the informal *Ristorante di Saturnia* or the luxurious *Villa Montepaldi*. All the facilities at the *Doral Ocean Beach* and the *Doral Resort & Country Club* are available to guests here (also see *A Sybaritic Spa*, above). Adjacent to the *Doral Country Club*, 8755 NW 36th St., Miami (phone: 593-6030; 800-331-7768 or 800-22DORAL; fax: 591-9266).

Grand Bay Run by the Aga Khan's CIGA chain, this 184-room property overlooking Biscayne Bay is Miami's most elite hotel. There are two restaurants, including the famed *Grand Café* (see *Eating Out*); two lounges; and an outdoor pool and hot tub. Attention to detail even extends to white gloves arriving with your morning newspaper so that the print won't stain your hands. There's 24-hour room service, and afternoon tea is served in the elegantly furnished lobby. Business services are available. The health club is open 24 hours daily, and the hotel provides limo service to the *Mayfair Health Club*. Business facilities include meeting rooms for up to 300, a concierge, secretarial services, A/V equipment, photocopiers, computers, and express checkout. 2669 S. Bayshore Dr., Coconut Grove (phone: 858-9600; 800-341-0809 from Florida; 800-327-2788 from elsewhere in the US; fax: 859-1532).

Mayfair House Located in the heart of Coconut Grove, this five-story, all-suite hotel is built around an open-air atrium. The first level houses the revitalized *Mayfair Mall* complex, and the lobby boasts two original Tiffany windows. Each of the 182 oversized suites is beautifully decorated and designed for the ultimate in comfort, featuring a terrace Jacuzzi, kimonos, a fully stocked mini-bar and mini-fridge, a state-of-the-art marble bathroom, a central stereo system, and a VCR. There are antique pianos in 52 of the suites. Dining and/or drinking options include the highly regarded *Mayfair Grill* (see *Eating Out*); the private *Ensign Bitters* lounge, for hotel guests and members only; the elegant lobby lounge; the bar at the intimate rooftop pool with a view of the bay; and more than 70 restaurants in the mall, just steps away. Guests have privileges at the exclusive *Cross Training* gym across the street. Business facilities include 24-hour room service, meeting rooms, a concierge, secretarial services, A/V equipment, photocopiers, computers, and express checkout. Value packages are offered year round. 3000 Florida Ave., Coconut Grove (phone: 441-0000; 800-341-0809 in Florida; 800-433-4555 elsewhere in the US; fax: 447-9173).

Sheraton Bal Harbour Located in the exclusive Bal Harbour area, this 614-room, 53-suite property sits within a lushly landscaped 10-acre garden leading directly to the ocean. Enticements include two outdoor pools, two tennis courts, a jogging path along the beach, a new health club with exercise equipment, volleyball, a Vita exercise course on the beach, water sports, and a gameroom. For sipping and supping, there are the *Bal Harbour Bar & Grille*, a steak and seafood restaurant with open-hearth kitchen; an oceanside snack and drink bar; three lounges; and a 24-hour deli. Directly across the street are the elegant *Bal Harbour Shops*. Business facilities include 24-hour room service, meeting rooms, a concierge, secretarial services, A/V equipment, photocopiers, computers, and express checkout. 9701 Collins Ave., Bal Harbour (phone: 865-7511; 800-325-3535; fax: 864-2601).

Sonesta Beach Key Biscayne Just minutes away from Miami's action lies this beachside high-rise. The sea-at-sunset color scheme extends from the fashionable lobby to the 300 deluxe rooms, which feature private balconies and stocked mini-fridges and bars. Parents rejoice in the complimentary program of daily supervised activities for children ages five to 13. Adults keep busy by exercising at the fitness center, playing tennis (there are nine courts), or relaxing on the beach or around the Olympic-size pool. Water sports include snorkeling, windsurfing, kayaking, and sailing. Bicycle rentals are available, and there's complimentary shuttle service to four popular shopping complexes. Dining options include the innovative *Purple Dolphin* (see *Eating Out*), a Chinese restaurant, a café/deli, and a beachside grill; there's also a disco and lounge. 350 Ocean Dr., Key Biscayne (phone: 361-2021; 800-SONESTA; fax: 361-3096).

EXPENSIVE

Biltmore Originally opened in 1926, this gracious edifice in the ornate, whimsical Mediterranean–Moorish Revival style was the creation of George Merrick, who built Coral Gables. Now affiliated with Westin hotels and listed on the *National Registry of Historic Places,* the 273-room property boasts gorgeous coffered and vaulted ceilings; hand-carved mahogany elevators; miles of travertine marble floors and columns; and original 1920s chandeliers. Al Capone lived for eight years in the bi-level, two-bedroom Everglades Suite. Rooms are spacious and boast sitting areas and 10-foot ceilings; some have balconies. There's a 17,000-square-foot J-shaped pool (arguably the country's largest hotel pool), an 18-hole Donald Ross–designed championship golf course, tennis on 10 lighted courts, and the extensive *Biltmore Club and Spa.* The hotel also has three restaurants, a spectacular Sunday brunch (see *Eating Out*), 24-hour room service, free airport transportation, and car rental at the hotel. Business facilities include meeting rooms for up to 450, a concierge, secretarial services, A/V equipment, photocopiers, computers, and express checkout. 1200 Anastasia Ave., Coral Gables (phone: 445-1926; 800-727-1926; fax: 448-9976).

Fontainebleau Hilton This Miami Beach grande dame, with 1,206 guestrooms on 20 acres of beachfront real estate, is still glamorous. The lagoon-like pool has a grotto bar inside a cave; there are also three whirlpool baths. The 12 restaurants and lounges include *Kamon,* a new Japanese steakhouse and sushi bar, and a kosher kitchen. There's also a fully equipped *Spa Pavilion* and seven night-lit tennis courts with a pro shop. Business facilities include 24-hour room service, meeting rooms for up to 3,000, a concierge, secretarial services, A/V equipment, photocopiers, computers, and express checkout. 4441 Collins Ave., Miami Beach (phone: 538-2000; 800-548-8886 in Florida; 800-HILTONS elsewhere in the US; fax: 673-5351).

Inter-Continental Miami Built in the grand old hotel tradition, this property is in the city center. The 644 rooms in the soaring 34-floor travertine triangle have marble baths and modern furnishings with Oriental accents. The lobby, with its 18-foot Henry Moore sculpture, is all beige and bone travertine marble, accented with green rattan furniture and area rugs.

There are two restaurants, including the highly regarded *Le Pavillon Grill,* and a lounge. An outdoor jogging trail takes advantage of the stunning views of Biscayne Bay, and there's a swimming pool. Three floors are reserved for nonsmokers. Stores include a duty-free shop. Business facilities include 24-hour room service, meeting rooms for up to 200, a concierge, secretarial services, A/V equipment, photocopiers, computers, and express checkout. 100 Chopin Plaza, Miami (phone: 577-1000; 800-327-3005; fax: 577-0384).

Marlin This Art Deco District hostelry combines 1930s architecture with 1990s amenities in 12 suites complete with kitchens and VCRs. The decor in the public rooms is "Jam-Deco"—classic Art Deco with hot Jamaican colors. The hotel was developed by Chris Blackwell, founder of Island Records, who included a recording studio on the premises, attracting lots of show-biz types. The *Shabeen* restaurant serves Jamaican food, and the bar specializes in exotic drinks. The beach is just across the street. 1200 Collins Ave., Miami Beach (phone: 673-8770; 800-688-7678; fax: 673-9609).

MODERATE

Cavalier Built back in 1936, this 41-room property is decked out in tangerine, turquoise, and pink African-inspired decor; many rooms have canopy beds. All rooms feature cable TV, VCRs, CD players, and in-closet safes. No restaurant on the premises, but there are plenty of eateries nearby. The beach is just across the street. 1320 Ocean Dr., Miami Beach (phone: 534-2135; 800-338-9076; fax: 531-5543).

Miami Airport Hilton Located on a lagoon at the airport (natch), the 500-room hostelry offers a pool, a Jacuzzi, a sauna, jet and water skiing (for a fee), and free use of three lighted tennis courts (they'll even lend you a racquet). There's also a concierge floor, a restaurant, a café/pool grill, a nightclub, and a bar. Ten floors are reserved for nonsmokers. Free parking and free transportation to the airport are available. Business facilities include meeting rooms for up to 1,000, a concierge, secretarial services, A/V equipment, photocopiers, computers, and express checkout. 5101 Blue Lagoon Dr., Miami (phone: 262-1000; 800-HILTONS; fax: 267-0038).

Place St. Michel Charming, cozy, and elegant describe this 27-room European-style bed and breakfast establishment built in 1926. In the heart of Coral Gables, it's favored by international architects who appreciate its Art Deco details and antique furnishings. On the premises is *Stuart's,* a jazz bar; *St. Michel,* an excellent dining spot; and a deli that's popular with the local lunch crowd. Continental breakfast is included; room service is available until 11 PM, and there's an obliging concierge desk. 162 Alcazar Ave., Coral Gables (phone: 444-1666; 800-247-8526; fax: 529-0074).

Sol Miami Beach Originally the *Cadillac* hotel, this 270-room, oceanfront property (ca. 1938) is now owned by the Spain-based Grupo Sol. The cool turquoise and blue Deco exterior belies its glitzy interior: plum and yellow, with lots of neon. There are two restaurants and two lounges. Some units have kitchenettes; all have cable TV. For action, there's a pool, volleyball and shuffleboard courts, and water sports. Business facilities include meeting rooms for up to 100. 3925 Collins Ave., Miami Beach (phone: 531-3534; 800-336-3542; fax: 531-1765).

INEXPENSIVE

Leslie Another vintage 1930s hotel in South Beach. The 43 recently renovated rooms are decorated in vivid island prints and feature cable TV, VCRs, and CD players. At press time, a lobby restaurant was under construction. Located across the street from the beach. 1244 Ocean Dr., Miami Beach (phone: 534-2135; 800-338-9076; fax: 531-5543).

Miami River Inn Claiming to be the oldest continuously operating inn south of St. Augustine, this charming bed and breakfast establishment on the Miami River was built in 1908. The 40 antiques-furnished rooms in four wooden buildings and the lushly planted pool and whirlpool area make guests feel they're in another place and time. Close to Little Havana and downtown Miami, this inn is protected by security gates at night. 118 SW South River Dr., entrance on SW Second St., Miami (phone: 325-0045; 800-468-3589; fax: 325-9227).

Paradise Inn Located one block from the beach in Surfside, this two-story motel with a Key lime façade trimmed in orange is a budgeter's delight, with 45 basic and clean rooms and another 45 efficiency units with kitchenettes. All feature remote control satellite TV and in-room safes. The quietest rooms face the inner courtyards. There's a pool, free parking, complimentary morning coffee, and laundry facilities. 8520 Harding Ave., Miami Beach (phone: 865-6216; fax: 865-9028).

Ritz Plaza This 1940s-style hostelry, with its much-photographed Art Deco squared finial, has a soaring lobby featuring the original four-color terrazzo floor and a front desk made of coral—one of the few such pieces extant. The 132 renovated rooms and suites contain such period details as the original cast-iron tubs (now modernized). Though a bit small and without any views, the standard rooms are great values. An Olympic-size pool overlooks the ocean, and water sports are also available. Meals are served in the elegant *Ritz Café* and on the terrace; *Harry's Bar*, which has lots of chrome and a jukebox playing 1950s music, offers a light menu. Business facilities include meeting rooms for up to 150, a concierge, A/V equipment, photocopiers, and computers. Near the *Convention Center*, 1701 Collins Ave., Miami Beach (phone: 534-3500; 800-522-6400; fax: 531-6928).

EATING OUT

Much of Miami's socializing centers around restaurant dining, so be prepared for long lines from December through April, when snowbirds swell the ranks of resident regulars. Residents always make reservations. Expect to pay $85 or more for a dinner for two at places in the very expensive category; $65 to $85 at a place in the expensive category; $40 to $65 at restaurants in the moderate range; and under $40 at an eatery in the inexpensive range. Prices do not include drinks, wine, taxes, or tips. Many establishments in the very expensive and expensive categories request that men wear jackets; it's wise to call ahead to inquire.

Unless otherwise noted, all restaurants serve lunch and dinner. All telephone numbers are in the 305 area code unless otherwise indicated.

VERY EXPENSIVE

Aragon Café The *Colonnade* hotel's outstanding dining room features Old World decor, with mahogany trim and crystal chandeliers. The menu includes a blue crab cake appetizer, an enormous veal chop, and exquisitely prepared Muscovy duck with polenta. A delicious sweet-potato mousse accompanies entrées, and the pistachio soufflé with chocolate chips on a bed of vanilla sauce is superb. (Dessert soufflés must be ordered at the beginning of dinner.) Service is impeccable. Open for dinner only; closed Sundays. Reservations advised. Major credit cards accepted. 180 Aragon Ave., Coral Gables (phone: 441-2600; 800-533-1337).

Café Chauveron Transplanted many years ago from New York City to Bay Harbor without the slightest disturbance to its famous mile-high soufflés, this is an elegant French dining place. Everything is beautifully prepared, from *coquille de fruits de mer au champagne* (shellfish in champagne) and pompano *en papillote* (local fish cooked in parchment paper) to the Grand Marnier soufflé with raspberry *coulis* and *crème fraîche*. Docking space is provided if you arrive by boat. Open daily for dinner, but closed from June through early October. Reservations advised. Major credit cards accepted. 9561 E. Bay Harbor Dr., Bay Harbor Island, Miami Beach (phone: 866-8779).

Chef Allen's Here is regional South Florida cooking in a setting of lacquered furniture and bright neon lights, using local produce and fish, such as yellowtail, tuna, and snapper. Specials on the daily changing menu include Florida bay scallop ceviche with cilantro, as well as many creative "spa cuisine" dishes. Award-winning chef/owner Allen Susser's white chocolate bombe is as rewarding to the eyes as it is to the taste buds. Open daily for dinner. Reservations advised. Major credit cards accepted. 19088 NE 29th Ave., North Miami Beach (phone: 935-2900).

Fish Market Far more elegant than its name implies, this is a topnotch seafood restaurant replete with a decor of marble and mirrors. You can order just about any kind of fish grilled, with a broad choice of sauces, but the kitchen also performs magic with specialties like colossal shrimp (succulent Central American crustaceans as large as baby lobster tails) and grilled snapper with buckwheat pasta. For dessert, try the pâté of tropical fruits and berries with passion-fruit sauce. Businesspeople love the "executive service" lunch, when a two-course meal is served in less than 30 minutes or there's no charge. Closed Sundays and Saturday lunch. Reservations advised. Major credit cards accepted. In the *Omni International Hotel*, 1601 Biscayne Blvd., Miami (phone: 374-4399).

Forge Once more famous for its 300,000-bottle wine collection and its elegance than for its dishes, this ornately decorated restaurant has ditched its stodgy steaks and chops for more imaginative, continental fare, including roast duck with black currant sauce and grilled salmon on a Mediterranean salad with citrus sauce. Open daily for dinner. Reservations necessary. Major credit cards accepted. 432 Arthur Godfrey Rd., Miami Beach (phone: 538-8533).

Grand Café This elegantly European bi-level dining room features attentive service and wonderful culinary creations. Recommended appetizers include the renowned black linguine with calamari and five-spice duck served with sesame soy mousseline. Incredible entrées range from marinated boneless rack of lamb, lightly smoked with oolong tea, to Indochina-spiced Florida jumbo shrimp served with a tropical papaya, tomato, and herb garlic sauce. Leave room for the chocolate *crème brûlée*. Open daily for breakfast, lunch, and dinner; brunch served Sundays. Reservations necessary for dinner, advised for other meals. Major credit cards accepted. In the *Grand Bay Hotel*, 2669 S. Bayshore Dr., Coconut Grove (phone: 858-9600).

Joe's Stone Crab Our hands-down favorite for the ultimate Miami dining experience, this place has been selling tons of the best stone crabs around since 1913, along with scrumptious home fries, delectable creamed spinach, and to-die-for Key lime pie. Diners who don't arrive early often have to wait hours to be seated and service can be rushed and sporadic, but devoted fans—like us—say it's well worth the wait and inconvenience. Besides the crabs, lobster and fresh fish also are served. Picnickers can buy lunch from the restaurant's take-out section and avoid the lunacy in the dining room. Closed Sunday lunch, Mondays, and from mid-May to mid-October. No reservations. Major credit cards accepted. 227 Biscayne St., Miami Beach (phone: 673-0365; 800-780-CRAB)

A Mano The Art Deco section along Ocean Drive boasts numerous restaurants, but this one rises far above the others. Award-winning chef Norman Van Aken specializes in "New World" cooking, which combines contemporary American techniques with local and Caribbean ingredients to create unique dishes. Outstanding examples are the tamarind-glazed grilled veal chop and fried crab cakes with Peruvian purple potato salad. Open for dinner only; closed Mondays. Reservations advised. Major credit cards accepted. In the *Betsy Ross* hotel, 1440 Ocean Dr., Miami Beach (phone: 531-6266).

Yuca This award-winning restaurant's name derives from both a Miami acronym for Young Upscale Cuban-Americans, as well as a starchy vegetable ("yucca" in English) that is a staple of Cuban cooking. The chef's visually spectacular creations offer nouvelle twists on Cuban standards, such as sweet plantains stuffed with dried cured beef and *salsa verde,* and excellent pan-seared yellowtail filet dusted with cumin and pumpkin seeds and served with *poblano* mashed potatoes. Chocoholics will adore the *tres leches de chocolate*, a milk-soaked cake layered with mousse and covered with chocolate meringue. (You can diet tomorrow.) A Latin band entertains at happy hour on Fridays and late evening Saturdays. Jackets are not required. Closed Sunday lunch. Reservations necessary. Major credit cards accepted. 177 Giralda Ave., Coral Gables (phone: 444-4448).

EXPENSIVE

Cassis Bistro A hip South Beach bistro with Art Nouveau chandeliers, high ceilings, and a long mahogany bar, this is *the* place to be on Tuesday nights when the beautiful, the rich, and the wanna-bes gather for dancing after 9 PM—but it's romantic and quiet on weekends. The menu is a mix of classic Provençal and South Florida cooking techniques; while the choices are limited, diners can select from such elegant dishes as roasted montrachet goat cheese, duckling in blackberry sauce, and red snapper *en papillote* with thyme. Open daily for dinner. Reservations necessary. Major credit cards accepted. 764 Washington Ave., Miami Beach (phone: 531-7700).

Mark's Place The modern interior—dramatized by vibrant contemporary Venetian glass sculptures—serves as an exciting backdrop for this Miami "in" spot. Chef Mark Militello whips up such imaginative dishes as grilled yellowtail snapper with Mediterranean salsa; West Indian pumpkin and hearts of palm salad; and salmon with couscous, fried onion strips, and nasturtiums. The rich desserts include a terrific pear tart. Closed for lunch on Saturdays and Sundays. Reservations necessary. Major credit cards accepted. 2286 NE 123 St., North Miami Beach (phone: 893-6888).

Mayfair Grill Mahogany, Tiffany windows, and etched glass set the tone at this dining spot in Coconut Grove's *Mayfair House* hotel. The menu, created by chef Guy Schnaars, formerly of *Mark's Place*, features Florida fare, marrying classic techniques and local ingredients. Specialties include grilled veal chops with wild mushroom risotto, grilled grouper with black beans and fried plantains, veal medallions with stone crab sauce, and grilled baby chicken with corn pancakes. Open daily for breakfast, lunch, and dinner; brunch is served on Sundays. Reservations necessary for dinner Thursdays through Sundays. Major credit cards accepted. 3000 Florida Ave., Coconut Grove (phone: 441-0000).

Nick's at the Miami Beach Marina Overlooking the sleek yachts docked in the *Miami Beach Marina* is Florida's largest restaurant. Owned by Nick Nickolas, who created Chicago's acclaimed *Nick's Fishmarket*, this haven for lobster lovers serves possibly the best and freshest seafood in Miami Beach—all within a Mediterranean seaside town setting. The menu is a mix of classic and creative dishes, ranging from succulent two-and-a-half-pound steamed Maine lobsters served with codcakes to "black and blue *ahi*," a seared yellowfin tuna appetizer served with a spicy soy mustard sauce. The service is first-rate. After dinner, guests may repair to the *Marina Bar* or the Art Deco-style *Ruby's Nightclub*, both on the premises. There's valet and free parking; also accessible by water taxi. Open daily; no lunch on weekends. Reservations advised. Major credit cards accepted. 300 Alton Rd., Miami Beach (phone: 673-3444).

Rusty Pelican For a dynamite view of downtown Miami across the bay, try the fare in this nautically decorated spot. Drinks are served on the waterside patio. Meals range from burgers and prime ribs of beef to seafood and tropical fruits. Open daily; brunch served on Sundays. Reservations advised. Major credit cards accepted. 3201 Rickenbacker Causeway, Key Biscayne (phone: 361-3818).

Victor's Café Even in its heyday, Havana didn't offer a restaurant as spectacular as this New Cuban eatery, a re-created Cuban plantation house courtyard beneath a three-story-high glass dome. Begin with a *mojitos* (a delightful house rum drink with crushed mint) or the white sangria. In season, choose the fresh jumbo stone crabs. Year-round specialties include *maravilla de catibia* quesadillas (yucca flour quesadillas filled with creole spiced shrimp) and yucca French fries served with an out-of-this-world cilantro sauce. Also delicious are the sirloin prepared with adobo (a flavorful herb sauce), oak-grilled *churrasco* (skirt steak), fresh mahimahi filets marinated in *mojo* (a dark, spicy sauce), and shellfish casseroles. Strolling guitarists serenade the guests, and a Latin band entertains nightly in the *Rumba* lounge, with its popular happy hour and late night *tapas* bar. The same people own New York City's *Victor's Café*. Open daily. Reservations necessary. Major credit cards accepted. 2340 SW 32nd Avenue, Coral Gables (phone: 445-1313).

MODERATE

Biltmore The gastronomic choices are legend at this restaurant's Sunday all-you-can-eat brunch. To begin with, there are such delicacies as raw oysters, jumbo shrimp, belly lox, caviar, pâté, and fresh baked breads and pastries. But what makes this brunch unique are some unusual extras—grilled Maine lobsters, a sushi and sashimi bar, sliced prime ribs, rack of lamb, a Häagen-Dazs ice-cream sundae station, and a lavishly hedonistic pastry table. Everything is perfect, from the champagne and freshly squeezed orange juice mimosas to the courtyard setting, complete with a jazz trio. Open Sundays from 11 AM to 4 PM. Last seating at 2:30 PM. Reservations necessary. Major credit cards accepted. At the *Biltmore Hotel,* 1200 Anastasia Ave., Coral Gables (phone: 445-1926; 800-727-1926).

Centro Vasco The present owner's father started this restaurant in Havana, then moved it to Miami when Castro came into power, replicating the traditional Spanish decor, huge portions, and authentic menu. Specialties include a classic black bean soup that's arguably the best this side of Cuba, seafood paella, *rabo encendido* (braised oxtail simmered in a rich red wine sauce), and sea bass served broiled, grilled, baked, or fried. A great sangria is made right at your table. Save room for the *leche frita* (a flan-like fried milk dessert). On weekends there's entertainment in three different rooms, ranging from live Latin-jazz bands to flamenco shows to comedians. Open daily for lunch, dinner, and late night *tapas.* Reservations advised for dinner. Major credit cards accepted. 2235 Calle Ocho (SW Eighth St.), Miami (phone: 643-9606).

Kaleidoscope Fine dining in a romantic enclosed atrium, on a balcony, or in an air conditioned dining room. Favorites include Bahamian grilled seafood cakes, grilled swordfish, and fresh fruit tarts with almond pastry made on the premises. All dinner entrées come with a Caesar salad and vegetables. Open daily. Reservations advised. Major credit cards accepted. 3112 Commodore Plaza, Second Floor, Coconut Grove (phone: 446-5010).

Monty's Stone Crab Casual and known for serving stone crabs year-round (they're brought in from Virginia during the local off-season), this place also offers a wide array of fresh seafood, steaks, and pasta. Guests can eat dockside at picnic tables, or indoors in a cavernous and often noisy setting overlooking the bay. Open daily. Reservations advised. Major credit cards accepted. 2550 S. Bayshore Dr., Coconut Grove (phone: 858-1431).

Purple Dolphin Dine in front of a large mural of frolicking dolphins or on the atrium terrace, which features live jazz. Hummus and *tapenade* (an addictive black olive, garlic, and anchovy dip) are placed on every table along with freshly baked rolls. Try the macadamia nut–crusted yellowtail snapper, served with pancakes made of calabasa (a type of pumpkin) and carrots; meat lovers can choose veal chops, rack of lamb, or grilled steaks. Reserve early for Friday's fabulous, reasonably priced, all-you-can-eat seafood buffet. The desserts are to die for. Open for breakfast, lunch, and dinner daily. Reservations necessary for weekend dinners. Major credit cards accepted. In the *Sonesta Beach Key Biscayne Hotel*, 350 Ocean Dr., Key Biscayne (phone: 361-2021).

South Pointe Seafood House Seafood lovers will find no disappointments at this casual wood-beamed, wharf-styled, Old Florida eatery with 10 dining rooms, each decked out with Tiffany lamps, Victorian curtains, and rustic appointments. There's jumbo shrimp wrapped in bacon; whitewater clams steamed with garlic, shallots, and vermouth; fresh stone crab claws; and champagne-poached salmon. For those that want to try it all, there are five different seafood combination platters. Sweets include homemade Key lime pie and "chocolate decadence" cake. Open daily; brunch served on Sundays. Reservations advised. Major credit cards accepted. 1 Washington Ave., Miami Beach (phone: 673-1708).

I Tre Merli An offshoot of a Manhattan eatery, it recalls its New York ancestry with a 20-foot ceiling, black slate floor, and exposed brick walls stacked with thousands of wine bottles. The Genoese fare includes *trenette* (a linguine-like pasta) with pesto, *vongole al salto* (clams in tomato sauce), and *scottata di salmone* (sliced salmon baked with lemon butter sauce and served with caviar). Open daily. Reservations advised on weekends. Major credit cards accepted. 1437 Washington Ave., Miami Beach (phone: 672-6702).

INEXPENSIVE

Café Tu Tu Tango In the *CocoWalk* complex, this jumping eatery decked out as an artist's loft touts its Italian and Spanish specialties as "food for the starving artist." It offers light, multiethnic dishes such as frittatas (Italian omelettes), pizza, smoked-chicken quesadillas, and kebabs. Entrées are appetizer-sized, so most people order two. Open daily for lunch, dinner, and late snacks. No reservations. Major credit cards accepted. 3015 Grand Ave., Coconut Grove (phone: 529-2222).

11th Street Diner This 1948 diner traveled from its home in Wilkes-Barre, Pennsylvania, to trendy South Beach. Old-fashioned favorites such as meat loaf with mashed potatoes and gravy, and black cows (root beer floats), along with such modern dishes as Cobb salad and marinated dolphin are served. Open daily 24 hours. No reservations. Major credit cards accepted. 1065 Washington Ave., Miami (phone: 534-6373).

Lazy Lizard On Lincoln Road Mall, this place serves some of the best Southwestern fare in town—from chicken or beef *fajitas* to Mexican-style "Aztec" pizza. Closed Mondays and Saturday and Sunday lunch. No reservations. Major credit cards accepted. 646 Lincoln Rd., Miami Beach (phone: 532-2809).

News Café An international newsstand-cum-bookstore-cum–sidewalk café that's an ideal spot for people watching or a pre-beach breakfast. The menu is light, with sandwiches, salads, and cheeses, and emphasizes Middle Eastern fare. Open daily 24 hours. Reservations unnecessary. Major credit cards accepted. Located across from the ocean in the heart of South Beach. 800 Ocean Dr., Miami Beach (phone: 538-6397).

Rascal House One of only two Florida restaurants to make food guru Mimi Sheraton's list of the 50 best US restaurants (the other being *Mark's Place*). Long lines snaking into the parking lot attest to the restaurant's popularity for almost 40 years. Try the pastrami on rye or the *rugelach*. Open daily for breakfast, lunch, dinner, and late snacks. No reservations. No credit cards accepted. 17190 Collins Ave., Miami Beach. (phone: 947-4581).

Unicorn Village An outstanding natural-food restaurant and marketplace, it's on a marina with dockage for diners arriving by boat. Dining is either inside or out. Creative salads, low-fat and low-sodium dishes, vegetarian lasagna and other pasta, plus fish and stir-fry dishes are featured. A large selection of by-the-glass wines includes seven organically produced choices (with no added sulfites). Note: This is a totally nonsmoking place. Open daily; brunch is served Sundays. Reservations advised in winter. Major credit cards accepted. At *The Shops at the Waterways,* 3595 NE 207th St., North Miami Beach (phone: 933-8829).

Wolfie's A Miami Beach institution since 1947, it might be described as an overgrown deli whose eclectic, 500-item menu carries everything from knishes to chicken parmesan and mountainous desserts. Open daily 24 hours. No reservations. Major credit cards accepted. 2038 Collins Ave., Miami Beach (phone: 538-6626).

Milwaukee

At-a-Glance

SEEING THE CITY

Good overviews of the city can be seen from the revolving *Polaris* restaurant atop the *Hyatt Regency* and from the *La Playa* lounge at the *Pfister* hotel (see *Checking In* for details on both hotels).

SPECIAL PLACES

The Milwaukee River divides the downtown area into east and west segments of unequal size (walking east you soon run into the beautiful Lake Michigan shoreline).

DOWNTOWN WEST

WISCONSIN AVENUE WEST Walking west from the river along Wisconsin Avenue, Milwaukee's principal shopping street, you pass *Marshall Field* on the same site that John Plankinton, a pioneer butcher, started his career with one cow and boundless ambition. He became a millionaire, and gave a start to packing tycoons Philip Armour and Patrick Cudahy. The blocks between *Marshall Field* and the *Boston Store* have been converted into the *Grand Avenue* shopping mall.

GRAND AVENUE The center of downtown shopping is the stretch of renovated buildings between Plankinton Avenue and North Fourth Street. The project brought the neighborhood back to life with its airy feel, a hub of fast-food restaurants, and lots of shops. Jugglers, mimes, pianists, choral groups, and other entertainers often perform at various locales (phone: 224-9720).

JOAN OF ARC CHAPEL On the campus of *Marquette University* is the medieval chapel where Joan of Arc prayed before being burned at the stake—not here in Milwaukee but in the French village of Chasse, whence the chapel was transported stone by stone. One of those stones reputedly was kissed by Joan before she went to her death, and is said to be discernibly colder than the others. Open daily except major holidays. Regular Roman Catholic church services are still conducted. 601 N. 14th St. (phone: 288-6873).

MILWAUKEE PUBLIC MUSEUM The basic theme here is how humans and other living creatures adapt to the environment, but there are a lot of variations, and exhibits relate not only to history, geology, and world cultures of the distant past, but also to Native Americans and aspects of American society. It has the fourth-largest collection of natural history displays in the country. This sprawling institution really shines when it comes to its dioramas. At a Northwest Coast Indian exhibition, for instance, smells and sounds envelop visitors from all sides. In the Great Plains area, a rattlesnake rattles a warning, and when the buffalo charge, you can hear the thundering of their hooves getting louder and louder. Particularly interesting is the *Streets of Old Milwaukee* section, where

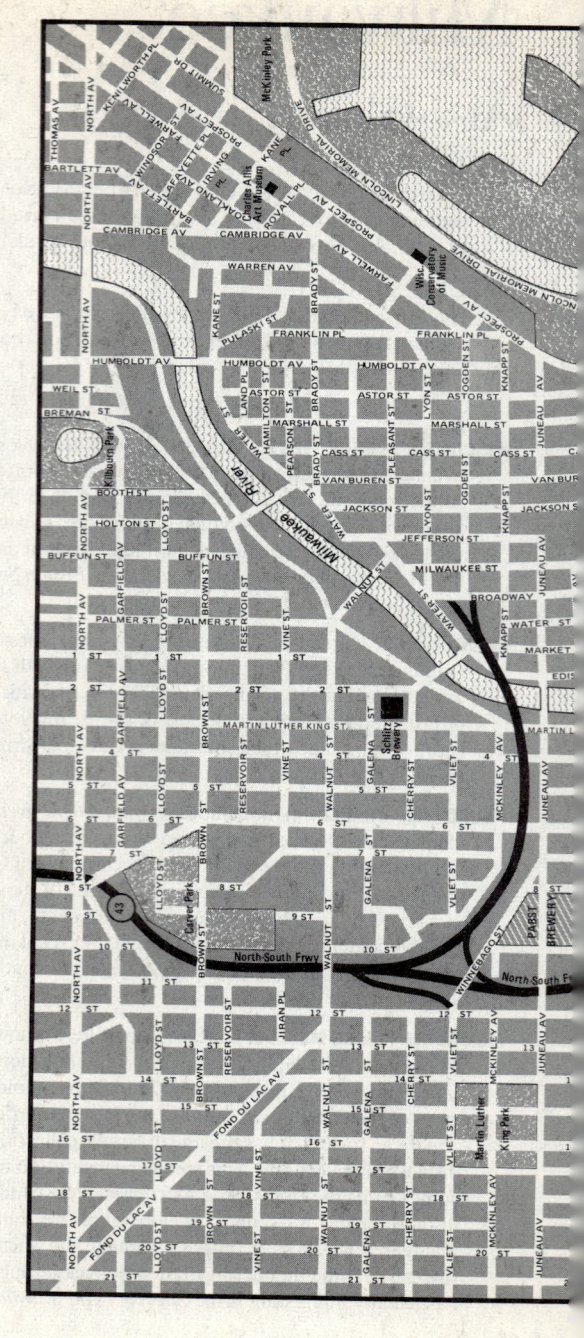

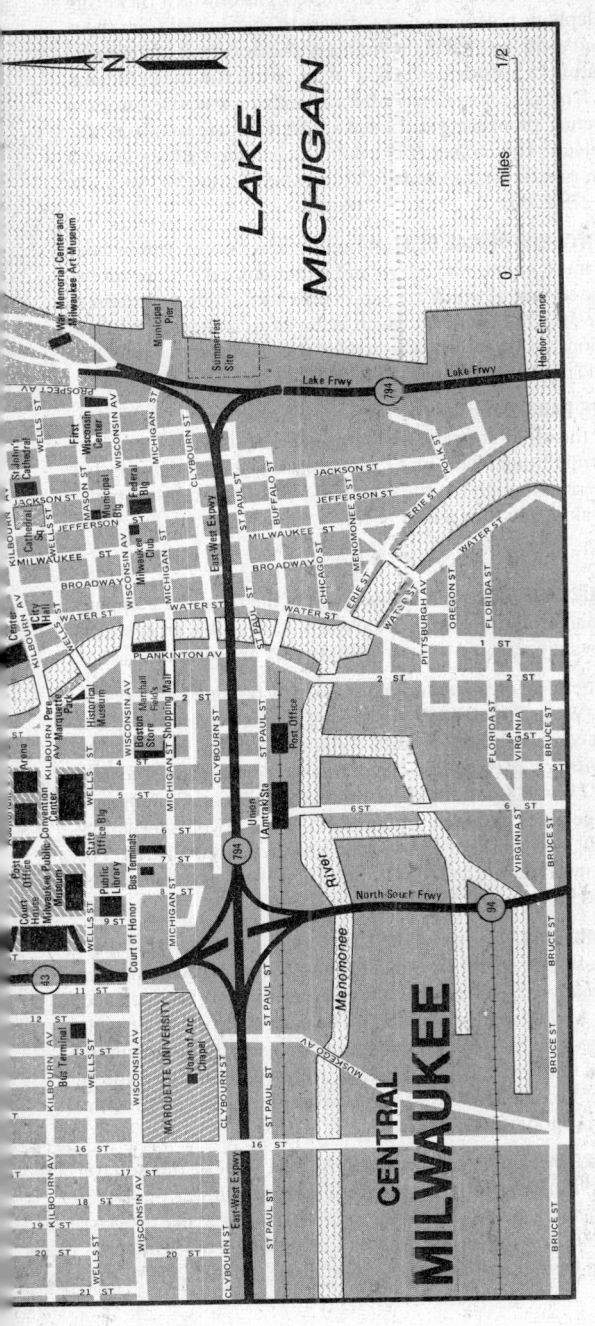

the 19th-century city has been re-created, right down to flickering gaslights, telephone poles wrapped with wire to keep horses from chewing them, and a kite tangled in the treetops. A new exhibit, *A Tribute to Survival,* features a historical overview of the North American Indians. The *Wizard Wing Discovery Center* offers a hands-on way to learn about water, collecting, pioneering skills, and a variety of natural history and cultural subjects. The *Biology Hall* exhibition is a life-size replica of a Costa Rican rain forest. Open daily. Admission charge. 800 W. Wells St. (phone: 278-2700).

MILWAUKEE COUNTY HISTORICAL CENTER Built in a bank once run by beer barons, the museum has an archive and numerous exhibitions on the city's history, several of which are especially entertaining for children. It is near the *MECCA Complex,* which includes an arena and facilities for conventions and meetings. Open daily. No admission charge. 910 N. Old World Third St. (phone: 273-8288).

PÈRE MARQUETTE PARK Between the museum and the river, this park is named after the explorer-priest who stopped briefly in Milwaukee during a canoe trip through the Great Lakes area. Local legend insists that he landed here, although the site was then part of an extensive tamarack swamp along the Milwaukee River.

DOWNTOWN EAST

WISCONSIN AVENUE EAST Wisconsin Avenue, east of the river, is a shopper's haven, with numerous fine stores. Shops on several nearby cross streets have been lovingly restored to their 19th-century appearance.

THIRD WARD Formerly an old warehouse district, now bounded by I-794 on the north, N. Water Street, and Lake Michigan, this neighborhood has made a great comeback. Artists' lofts, restaurants, shops, galleries, the *Milwaukee Institute of Art and Design, Milwaukee* magazine, *Skylight Theater,* and *Theatre X* call the place home. Workers on Commission Row haul vegetables and fruit around BMWs and Toyotas owned by the advertising and marketing execs who now live in the district. For walking tour information, call the *Historic Third Ward Association,* 219 N. Milwaukee St. (phone: 273-1173).

MILWAUKEE ART MUSEUM Located on the lakefront, where Lincoln Memorial Drive crosses Wisconsin Avenue, the museum is housed in the *War Memorial Building,* which was originally designed by Eero Saarinen and built in 1957. A wing was added in 1975. The museum's permanent collection includes Old Masters, contemporary art, and primitive painting and sculpture. Outside, Lake Michigan provides a powerful backdrop for sculpture. Closed Mondays. Admission charge. 750 N. Lincoln Memorial Dr. (phone: 224-3200).

CATHEDRAL SQUARE Between Jackson and Jefferson Streets, this square dates to Wisconsin's territorial days. Except for the belltower, *St. John's Cathedral* was nearly destroyed by fire in 1935. If you feel like a snack, turn left on Jefferson to No. 761, where *George Watts & Son*'s interesting silver shop has a tearoom on the second floor (phone: 291-5120).

CITY HALL Milwaukee's best-known landmark, this building with its 393-foot tower was designed in 1895 in such a way that taxpayers could drive their buggies up in the rain to pay real estate taxes without getting wet. In the tower above the arched entry, Old Sol, a 20-ton bell, gathers dust. In 1922, citizens complained about the noise of Old Sol's tolling, and the city ordered it stilled. Closed weekends. N. Water St. at Wells St. (phone: 286-3200).

ELSEWHERE

ANNUNCIATION GREEK ORTHODOX CHURCH The last major building designed by Wisconsin-born architect Frank Lloyd Wright. Tours of the saucer-shaped structure are offered for groups of 15 or more on weekdays by appointment only. Admission charge. 9400 W. Congress St. (phone: 461-9400).

WHITNALL PARK At 689 acres, this is one of the larger municipal parks in the country. It includes the 40-acre *Boerner Botanical Gardens* (5879 S. 92nd St., Hales Corners; phone: 425-1130) and the 40-acre *Todd Wehr Nature Center* (9701 W. College Ave., Franklin; phone: 425-8550), a nature preserve with a variety of species. Open daily.

MILWAUKEE COUNTY ZOO Among the most famous zoos in the country, it allows the animals to roam free in their natural habitats. Kids adore the miniature railroad and children's zoo. Open daily. Admission charge. 10001 W. Blue Mound Rd. (phone: 771-5500).

SCHLITZ AUDUBON CENTER The 220 acres of undisturbed forest preserve once provided pasture to brewery horses weary from pulling beer wagons. Its 6 miles of trails through different ecological areas provide a good place to wander and wonder. A 60-foot wooden tower built on a 100-foot bluff offers a bird's-eye view of the city and the Lake Michigan countryside. Be warned—there's no elevator. There is a natural history bookstore. Closed Mondays. Admission charge. 1111 E. Brown Deer Rd. (phone: 352-2880).

EXTRA SPECIAL

For an interesting day trip, take I-94 west 78 miles to Madison, the state capital and home of the *University of Wisconsin*. Drop in at the information center at *Memorial Union* (on Park and Langdon Sts.) to pick up a map and find out what's happening on campus. The university is sure to offer more than enough to keep you busy, with its art center, geology museum, planetarium, observatory, and arboretum. The four lakes in Madison—Mendota, Monona, Waubesa, and Wingra—as well as Kegonsa in nearby Edgerton—are great for fishing and swimming. If you continue driving west (toward the Iowa border), or due south toward Illinois, you'll find yourself in Wisconsin cheese country.

Sources and Resources

TOURIST INFORMATION

For information, maps, and brochures, contact the *Greater Milwaukee Convention and Visitors Bureau* (510 W. Kilbourn Ave., Milwaukee, WI 53203; phone: 273-3950). It's open daily during the summer; Mondays through Fridays the rest of the year. Also helpful is the *Public Service Bureau* (phone: 224-2120) in the lobby of the Journal Building (Fourth and State Sts.), which is open Mondays through Fridays. Contact the Wisconsin state tourism hotline (800-432-TRIP) for maps, calendars of events, health updates, and travel advisories.

LOCAL COVERAGE The *Milwaukee Sentinel,* morning daily; *Milwaukee Journal,* afternoon daily; *Shepherd Express Downtown Edition,* weekly; and *Milwaukee* magazine and the *Irish American Post,* monthlies.

TELEVISION STATIONS WTMJ Channel 4–NBC; WITI Channel 6–CBS; WMVS Channel 10–PBS; and WISN Channel 12–ABC.

RADIO STATIONS AM: WTMJ 620 (news, Top 40); WBKV 1470 (adult contemporary); and WAUK 1510 (country music). FM: WUWM 89.8 (jazz/news); WLUM 102.1 (Top 40); WKLH 96.5 (classic rock); and WMYX 99 (mix of 1960s, 1970s, and 1980s pop music).

TELEPHONE The area code for Milwaukee is 414.

SALES TAX There is a 5% state sales tax.

CLIMATE Summer and fall, with average temperatures of 68F and 50F, are generally pleasant, but expect sudden change when the wind shifts to the east. In winter, be prepared for bitter winds. The sub-zero cold is formidable.

GETTING AROUND

AIRPORT *General Mitchell International Airport* handles the city's domestic and international air traffic and is a 15-minute drive from downtown. An economical share-a-ride program is available to those heading to the same destination; make arrangements through the Ground Transportation Coordinator, directly outside the baggage claim area. *Milwaukee County Transit* buses also provide service downtown for $1.25 (exact change required). *A-1 Transportation Airport Shuttle* (phone: 272-1955) leaves every half hour for downtown hotels as well as hotels in the western and northern metro areas.

BUS During major lakefront festivals in the summer, a shuttle bus runs from the lake along Wisconsin Avenue to 10th and Wisconsin. The fare is 50¢. Regular bus service costs $1.25 (exact change required). For information on bus schedules, contact *Milwaukee County Transit System* (1942 N. 17th St.; phone: 344-6711).

CAR RENTAL Most major car rental firms are represented. For a reliable local agency, contact *Heiser Chevrolet* (10200 W. Arthur Ave., West Allis; phone: 327-2300).

HARBOR CRUISES *Iroquois Boat Line* (Clybourn St. Bridge dock; phone: 332-4194) offers two-hour trips along the Milwaukee River daily from *Memorial Day* through *Labor Day*. Dinner cruises and private charters on the *Celebration* (502 N. Harbor Dr.; phone: 278-1113) are offered from April through December, and brunch, lunch, and dinner cruises are available on the *Edelweiss* (1110 Old World Third St.; phone: 272-DOCK) from April through October.

TAXI There are taxi stands at most major hotels, but we recommend calling *City Veterans Taxi* (phone: 291-8080) or *Yellow Cab* (phone: 271-1800).

TOURS The *Department of City Development* runs *MKE Neighborhood Tours Ltd.,* a program intended to get visitors out of downtown and into the communities to sample the diversity of restaurants, shops, and cultures of Milwaukee. Its itineraries include "The Mitchell Street Express," "Neighborhoods 94 West," "Neighborhood North," and "Riverwest," with others scheduled to be added. Discover the *Balkan Trading Company* (938 W. Lapham Blvd., phone: 643-7372) for homemade *burek* pastries and Serbian smoked sausage; the *Woodland Pattern Bookstore* (720 E. Locust St., phone: 263-4001), which offers readings and lectures; the *Comic Stop* (224 N. 35th St., phone: 933-0500) for comic books; and *Suzy's Cream Cheesecakes* (5901 W. Vliet St., phone: 453-2255); as well as other fascinating hideaways. For details, contact the *Department of City Development* (809 N. Broadway; phone: 223-5796).

LOCAL SERVICES

AUDIOVISUAL EQUIPMENT *Midwest Visual Equipment Co.* (phone: 784-5880).

BABY-SITTING *Patty Care Services* (9730 W. Blue Mound Rd.; phone: 774-7272).

BUSINESS SERVICES *Business Offices and Secretarial Services* (*B.O.S.S.;* 5900 N. Port Washington Rd., Glendale; phone: 963-1992); *National Bookkeeping Service* (759 N. Milwaukee St.; phone: 276-6655); *National Business Offices* (1033 N. Mayfair Rd.; phone: 259-9110).

DRY CLEANER/TAILOR *One-Hour Valet Cleaners* (12th and Wells Sts.; phone: 272-5808).

LIMOUSINE *Andrus Limousine Service* (phone: 445-5060); *Sharp Limousine Service* (phone: 769-9985).

MECHANICS *Bodden's Service* (136 N. Water St.; phone: 272-3777); *Tosa Imports* (6102 W. North Ave.; phone: 771-2340), for foreign cars.

MEDICAL EMERGENCY *Mt. Sinai Hospital* (950 N. 12th St.; phone: 283-6666).

MESSENGER SERVICES *Action Express* (phone: 549-3300); *Bonded Messenger Service* (phone: 933-4500).

MONEY TRANSFERS *American Express MoneyGram* (phone: 800-926-9400 for information; 800-866-8800 for money transfers); *Western Union Financial Services* (phone: 800-325-6000 or 800-325-4176).

NATIONAL/INTERNATIONAL COURIER *DHL Worldwide Express* (phone: 800-225-5345); *FedEx* (phone: 800-238-5355).

PHARMACY *Phillips' Juneau Village Pharmacy* (1125 N. Van Buren St.; phone: 272-0922), open weekdays 9 AM to 9 PM, Saturdays 9 AM to 6 PM, Sundays 9 AM to 5 PM.

PHOTOCOPIES *Anderson Graphics* (254 N. Ember La.; phone: 276-4445); *Minuteman Press* (710 N. Milwaukee St.; phone: 278-7997).

POST OFFICE Central office (345 W. St. Paul Ave.; phone: 291-2530).

PROFESSIONAL PHOTOGRAPHER *John Nienhuis* (phone: 442-0927); *Pat Goetzinger Photographic Enterprises* (phone: 645-4567).

TELECONFERENCE FACILITIES *Hyatt Regency, Marc Plaza, Pfister* (see *Checking In,* below).

TRANSLATOR *Berlitz* (phone: 276-4121); *Flagg & Associates* (phone: 278-8322); *Iverson Language Associates* (phone: 271-1144).

WESTERN UNION/TELEX Many offices are located around the city (phone: 800-325-6000 to find the location nearest you).

SPECIAL EVENTS

From mid-December though the end of January, *Winterfest,* Milwaukee's annual winter festival, takes place on weekends with snow sculptures, sporting events, and more. Rock and jazz concerts are part of *Summerfest,* held every June and July on the lakefront. Several ethnic festivals featuring food and entertainment take place at the *Henry W. Maier Festival Park* grounds throughout the summer. *Lakefront Festival of the Arts* is held outdoors near the *Milwaukee Art Museum* in the middle of June with music, food, and arts and crafts exhibits. The *Great Circus Parade* is an annual July event. The *Wisconsin State Fair* takes place for two weeks in mid-August on the fairgrounds adjoining I-94, west of downtown. The weekend before *Thanksgiving,* the *Holiday Folk Fair* features ethnic food, music, and entertainment at the *MECCA Complex* (Kilbourn Ave.).

MUSEUMS

In addition to those described in *Special Places,* Milwaukee has several other museums of note.

BROOKS STEVENS AUTO MUSEUM More than 60 antique cars are on display. Open daily. Admission charge. 10325 N. Port Washington Rd. (phone: 241-4185).

CHARLES ALLIS ART MUSEUM This beautifully preserved mansion is listed on the *National Register of Historic Places.* Closed Mondays and Tuesdays. Admission charge. 1801 N. Prospect Ave. (phone: 278-8295).

CAPTAIN FREDERICK PABST MANSION A Flemish-style mansion built by the famous Milwaukee brewery king, it is listed on the *National Register of Historic Places.* Open daily. Admission charge. 2000 W. Wisconsin Ave. (phone: 931-0808).

DISCOVERY WORLD Visitors can explore science, economics, and technology with hands-on exhibits. Closed weekdays. No admission charge. 818 W. Wisconsin Ave. (phone: 765-9966).

SPORTS AND FITNESS

Tickets to the city's professional sports events, as well as to *Marquette University* basketball games, are available through *Ticketmaster* (phone: 276-4545).

BASEBALL The *American League Brewers* play at *County Stadium* (201 S. 46th St.; phone: 933-9000).

BASKETBALL Milwaukee's *NBA Bucks* and the *Marquette Warriors* play at *Bradley Center* (Fourth and State Sts.; phone: 227-0400).

BICYCLING Bikes can be rented from *East Side Cycle and Hobby Shop* (2031 N. Farwell Ave.; phone: 276-9848) and *Wilson Park Schwinn Cyclery* (2033 W. Howard Ave.; phone: 281-4720).

FISHING Salmon and trout as big as 30 pounds are caught in Lake Michigan, from the shore and breakwaters. You can use launching ramps at *McKinley Marina* and near the private *South Shore Yacht Club*. Half-day boat charters, including bait and tackle, are offered by numerous firms (see the yellow pages).

FOOTBALL The *NFL*'s Green Bay *Packers* play some of their home games at *County Stadium* (201 S. 46th St.; phone: 342-2717).

GOLF The best public 18-hole golf course is at *Mee-Kwon Park* (6333 W. Bonniwell Rd., Mequon: phone: 242-1310).

HOCKEY The minor-league Milwaukee *Admirals* play at the *Bradley Center* (Fourth and State Sts.; phone: 227-0550).

ICE SKATING In winter, many parks open rinks. For year-round ice skating (indoors), try *Wilson Park Center* (4001 S. 20th St.; phone: 281-4610); *Eble Ice Arena* (19400 W. Blue Mound Rd.; phone: 784-5155); and the ice arena at *State Fair Park* (phone: 257-3883).

JOGGING Run in *Lake Front Park*, near *War Memorial Center*, on the beach, sidewalk, or oval track.

POLO On Sundays in summer Milwaukee's polo teams compete at *Uihlein Field* (Good Hope Rd. and N. 70th St.; no phone).

SKIING *Currie, Dretzka,* and *Whitnall Parks* have ski tows and mostly beginners' trails. Cross-country skiers may use all county parks. The *Whitnall Park* trails are particularly good.

SOCCER The Milwaukee *Wave* professional soccer team plays at the *Bradley Center* (Fourth and State; phone: 962-9283).

SWIMMING Seven public beaches along the lakefront have lifeguards and dressing facilities. The water is usually chilly, even in August.

TENNIS Try *North Shore Racquet Club* (5750 N. Glen Park Rd.; phone: 351-2900) or *Le Club* (2001 W. Good Hope Rd.; phone: 352-4900). In warm weather, numerous county parks have courts available for a nominal fee.

THEATERS

Our favorite Milwaukee theater tops the list below, followed by several other fine venues in the area. For complete listings on theatrical and musical events, see the local publications listed in *Local Coverage*.

CENTER STAGE

Milwaukee Repertory Theater (The Rep) This institution, active since 1954, presents classics and exciting contemporary plays, often with a regional emphasis. The *Rep* presents six main-stage productions in its 720-seat *Powerhouse Theater* during its September through May season, and performances also are held at the 198-seat *Stiemke Theater* and the 116-seat *Stackner Cabaret*, both in the three-theater complex. Nearly 200,000 people attend *Rep* productions annually. 108 E. Wells St. (phone: 224-9490).

The *Pabst Theater* (144 E. Wells St.; phone: 278-3663), which stages a variety of shows including the beloved *A Christmas Carol*, is part of the Theater District complex attached to the *Wyndham Milwaukee Center*. The *Performing Arts Center* (929 N. Water St.; phone: 273-7121) is home to *First Stage Milwaukee*, a children's theater. *Riverside Theater* (116 W. Wisconsin Ave.; phone: 224-3000) features stage shows by top performers. Other theaters include: *Skylight Comic Opera* (813 N. Jefferson St.; phone: 271-8815); *Theatre X* (158 N. Broadway; phone: 278-0555) for experimental drama; and the *Irish Fest Theater Company* (phone: 258-9349), which presents works throughout the community as well as regionally.

MUSIC

The *Milwaukee Symphony, Milwaukee Ballet,* and *Florentine Opera Company* perform at the *Performing Arts Center* (929 N. Water St.; phone: 273-7121). "Music Under the Stars" concerts are held in *Washington* and *Humboldt Parks* on Friday and Saturday nights in July and August.

NIGHTCLUBS AND NIGHTLIFE

For jazz, visit *John Hawk's Pub* (Water and Wisconsin Sts.; phone: 272-3199). *Rumors*, in the *Marriott* hotel (20 minutes from central Milwaukee at 375 S. Moorland Rd., Brookfield; phone: 786-1100), has dancing to Top 40 hits and caters to well-dressed young professionals; *La Playa*, atop the *Pfister* hotel (see *Checking In*), has either dancing, jazz, or a deejay, plus a spectacular view. For dinner with piano music, try *Chip & Py's* (15 minutes north of downtown at 1340 W. Towne Square Rd., Mequon; phone: 241-9589). On Saturday nights, the *Brown Bottle Pub* (221 W. Galena; phone: 271-4444) has a *karaoke* machine. Located in the old taprooms of a Schlitz brewery, it also has a selection of 103 different ales and beers from which to choose. For blues, there's *Boobie's Place* (502 W. Garfield Ave.; phone: 263-3399).

Best in Town

CHECKING IN

Milwaukee's hotels range from traditional older properties to the modern and the functional. Expect to pay between $80 and $105 per night for a double room at places listed as expensive and between $55 and $80 at those in the moderate category; there are no exceptional inexpensive hotels in the city. Several offer weekend bargain rates. Unless otherwise noted, hotel rooms have air conditioning, private baths, TV sets, and telephones. All hotels are in the 414 area code unless otherwise indicated.

EXPENSIVE

Hyatt Regency This $28-million, 18-story property helped to end what was a chronic shortage of rooms for conventions. And, by no coincidence, it is next to the downtown *Convention Center.* Topping the 485-room structure, with its atrium lobby, is the *Polaris,* a revolving restaurant. Room service continues until 2 AM. Other amenities include 19 meeting rooms, a concierge, A/V equipment, photocopiers, and express checkout. Fourth and Kilbourn (phone: 276-1234; 800-233-1234 or 800-228-9000; fax: 276-6338).

Marc Plaza The largest hotel in Milwaukee—its 540 rooms have gone through extensive renovation during their almost 70-year career. Facilities include a heated indoor pool and sauna, and the main restaurant is *Benson's, A Place for Steaks.* There is 24-hour room service, as well as 16 meeting rooms, a concierge, secretarial services, A/V equipment, photocopiers, computers, and express checkout. 509 W. Wisconsin Ave. (phone: 271-7250; fax: 271-8091).

Pfister This 330-room establishment has catered to visiting and local elite since the 1890s. A multimillion-dollar restoration completed in time for its centennial celebration in 1993 brought it back to the level that enchanted Enrico Caruso and every president since McKinley. The bronze lions in the lobby are named Dick and Harry, by the way, and the best views of the lake are from rooms 8, 9, or 10, or from high up in the tower in the romantic *La Playa* lounge. There also is the *English Room,* a fine restaurant (see *Eating Out*). Around-the-clock room service, a concierge, 17 meeting rooms, photocopiers, computers, and express checkout are available. 424 E. Wisconsin Ave. (phone: 273-8222; fax: 273-0747).

MODERATE

Grand Milwaukee Near the airport and next to a convention hall, this property has 400 rooms, two restaurants, two heated pools, and handball, tennis, and racquetball courts. Room service is available until 10:30 PM. Business services include 32 meeting rooms, secretarial services, A/V equipment, photocopiers, computers, and express checkout. 4747 S. Howell Ave. (phone: 481-8000; fax: 481-8065).

Hilton Inn Overlooking the Milwaukee River, this 164-room hostelry includes such amenities as king-size beds and an indoor pool. The adjoining

Anchorage restaurant is noted for its seafood. There's room service daily from 7 AM to 10:30 PM, five meeting rooms, and A/V equipment and photocopiers. On the Milwaukee River, near the Hampton Ave. exit of I-43 (phone: 962-6040; 800-HILTONS; fax: 962-6166).

EATING OUT

Visiting Milwaukee without sampling the Wiener schnitzel would be like going to New Orleans's French Quarter and living on Big Macs. It was once said that visitors could get any kind of food in Milwaukee as long as it was German, but these days it's easy to find Polish, Chinese, Italian, Greek, Japanese, Serbian, and American restaurants as well. Expect to pay between $40 and $60 for dinner for two at those places listed as expensive; between $20 and $40 at restaurants in the moderate category; and under $20 at places in the inexpensive bracket. Prices don't include drinks, wine, tax, or tips. Unless otherwise noted, restaurants are open for lunch and dinner. All restaurants are in the 414 area code unless otherwise indicated.

EXPENSIVE

English Room If you suddenly develop an overwhelming craving for rack of lamb or cherries jubilee, this is the place to go. Flaming dishes are prepared tableside with appropriate theatrical flourish. Open daily. Reservations necessary on weekends. Major credit cards accepted. *Pfister Hotel*, 424 E. Wisconsin Ave. (phone: 273-8222).

Karl Ratzsch's Ranked as one of Milwaukee's top dining spots for many years, it has specialized in Teutonic fare since the days when the city called itself the German Athens. Open daily. Reservations advised on weekends. Major credit cards accepted. 320 E. Mason St. (phone: 276-2720).

Mader's A family-run favorite that goes back to shortly after the century's turn. It's decorated in Bavarian style. For years, the late Gus Mader offered a reward to anyone who could finish his 3½-pound pork shank. The prize? Another one, to be eaten at the same sitting. Open daily. Reservations advised on weekends. Major credit cards accepted. 1037 N. Old World Third St. (phone: 271-3377).

Sanford Several years ago, Sandy D'Amato converted this former grocery store (owned first by his grandparents, then his parents) into a real charmer of a restaurant. His wife, Angie, supervises the dining room while chef Sandy produces basil-flecked *Cima Kenovese* (a rolled veal roast) and shrimp cakes with caramelized onions and tamarind sauce. He's also a whiz at the grill, and daily specials attest to his skill. Closed Sundays. Reservations advised. Major credit cards accepted. 1547 N. Jackson St. (phone: 276-9608).

MODERATE

Old Town At this Serbian spot you can dine to the tune of guitar-like tamburitzas. Fine, you say, but what is Serbian food like? Well, as prepared here, it features sizzling lamb dishes that are somewhat spicier than similar Greek and Turkish fare. Closed Mondays. Reservations advised on weekends. Major credit cards accepted. 522 W. Lincoln Ave. (phone: 672-0206).

Toy's Chinatown The family that owns this downtown Chinese spot has been serving residents for three generations; when you eat here, you're not just getting egg rolls, you're getting tradition. Unless you order 100-year-old duck eggs, you can be sure of fresh Cantonese dishes, like sweet-and-sour shrimp, spareribs, and chow mein. Open daily. Reservations advised on weekends. Major credit cards accepted. 830 N Third St. (phone: 271-5166).

INEXPENSIVE

Bavarian Inn Located in a park owned by a consortium of Germanic clubs, this informal dining room serves generally good German food. The Sunday buffet is one of the best bargains in town—you can help yourself to as much as you like, so be sure to bring a big appetite. Soccer fields and a festival area on the grounds mean that there's usually something to see, as well. Closed Mondays. Reservations advised on weekends. Major credit cards accepted. Take the Silver Spring exit from I-43 north, turn south on North Port Washington Rd., then west on Lexington to 700 West Lexington Ave. (phone: 964-0300).

Jake's Delicatessen If corned beef on rye appeals to you, this is the place to go. You can sit at a booth, at a counter, or take your sandwich with you in a paper bag. Try the specials—Jake's has giant ¾-pound hot dogs. Closed Sundays. No reservations. No credit cards accepted. 1634 W. North Ave. (phone: 562-1272).

Leon's Frozen Custard Drive-In Besides their passion for cheese and beer, Milwaukeeans also love frozen custard. This place has been in operation since 1942 and is one of the favored spots for indulging in the creamy, frozen treat. Open daily. 3131 S. 27th St. (phone: 383-1784).

MILWAUKEE BREWERS

If you're wondering where the smell of malt is coming from, follow your nose to one of the big breweries, where you'll be escorted through the facilities and given samples of the wares (unless you're underage, in which case you only get to look). The breweries that offer tours are *Miller* (visitors' center at 4251 W. State St.; phone: 931-2337), *Pabst* (915 Juneau Ave.; phone: 223-3709), and *Sprecher's* (730 W. Oregon St.; phone: 272-BEER). They're all open to visitors daily except holidays, when everyone stays home testing the product.

Minneapolis–St. Paul

At-a-Glance

SEEING THE CITY

Although the *IDS* and *Norwest Tower* buildings are taller, the best view of the area is from the observation deck of the 32-story *Foshay Tower* (Ninth St. and Marquette Ave., Minneapolis). It's closed October through March. Admission charge. St. Paul's *Cherokee Park,* overlooking the Mississippi River, affords a spectacular panorama of both cities. Another good view is that from *Indian Mounds Park,* also in St. Paul.

SPECIAL PLACES

The most extraordinary feature of downtown Minneapolis and St. Paul is their interior skyways, an interconnected belt of pedestrian malls and escalators lacing in and out of shops, banks, and restaurants at the second-story level. When it's below zero, you still can walk around comfortably without a coat. At street level, courtyards, gardens, fountains, and sculpture form attractive plazas.

MINNEAPOLIS

MINNEAPOLIS INSTITUTE OF ARTS The exterior of this highly esteemed institution is architecturally classic, and inside it houses an equally classic variety of Old Masters and other paintings, sculpture, decorative arts, photographs, and Asian, African, Oceanic, and American art. Be sure to check out the interactive videos in the galleries that explain each exhibit in visual detail. The museum also presents films and lectures and arranges tours of the *Purcell-Cutts House,* a masterpiece of Prairie School architecture. Closed Mondays. Admission charge for traveling exhibitions. 2400 Third Ave. S. (phone: 870-3131).

FREDERICK R. WEISMAN ART MUSEUM This aluminum-clad museum, on the *University of Minnesota*'s East Bank campus, is Minneapolis's newest. The focus is on the first half of the 20th century, with works by Georgia O'Keeffe and the world's largest collections of works by Marsden Hartley, Alfred Maurer, and B. J. O. Nordfeldt. Open daily. No admission charge. 331 E. River Rd. (phone: 625-9641).

WALKER ART CENTER Named for T. B. Walker, a local patron of the arts, and housed in a striking contemporary building, this art center offers a vivid overview of major 20th-century art, complementing the classic collections of the *Minneapolis Institute of Arts* (see above). It originates many touring exhibitions, and conducts a lively program of music, dance, film, theater, and educational activities. Closed Mondays. Admission charge. 725 Vineland Pl. (phone: 375-7600; 375-7622 for the box office).

MINNEAPOLIS SCULPTURE GARDENS Located at the *Walker Art Center,* this is one of the country's grandest monumental sculpture gardens. Among the many pieces installed throughout this seven-acre park is the delightfully whimsical *Spoonbridge and Cherry* by Claes Oldenburg and Coosje van Bruggen. Open daily. No admission charge.

MINNEHAHA PARK In his poem "Hiawatha," Longfellow immortalized the "laughing waters" of Minnehaha Falls near the Mississippi. Enjoy the splendor of the falls, or picnic near a statue of Minnehaha and brave Hiawatha. Minnehaha Pkwy. at Hiawatha Ave. S.

MINNEAPOLIS GRAIN EXCHANGE An ornate hall the size of a large school gym, the world's largest grain exchange is a loud, hectic place where futures and grain samples are bought and sold. Tours available. Visitors' balcony open daily. No admission charge. 400 Fourth St. S. (phone: 338-6212).

ORCHESTRA HALL This hall houses the *Minnesota Orchestra,* which has been playing classical and symphonic pop music since 1903. Though spartan in appearance, *Orchestra Hall* is renowned for its superior acoustics. 1111 *Nicollet Mall* (phone: 371-5656).

MINNESOTA ZOO Set in the rolling hills of Apple Valley, this 500-acre, state-funded zoological park (among the nation's best) provides a natural environment for Siberian tigers, musk oxen, moose, and other northern animals. There are many aquatic species in the aquarium, and a five-story indoor tropical environment houses jungle fauna and flora. In winter, cross-country skiers can enjoy 10 kilometers of groomed trails. Closed *Christmas.* Admission charge. 12101 Johnny Cake Ridge Rd., Apple Valley, 25 minutes south of the city on Hwy. 35 (phone: 431-9200).

ST. PAUL

LANDMARK CENTER This castle-like former federal courts building is a cultural center that is host to performing groups, civic events, and the *Minnesota Museum of American Art.* The 1902 building also houses the *Schubert Club Musical Instrument Museum,* with keyboards dating to the 1600s; here, too, are restored courtrooms where mobsters such as Alvin "Creepy" Karpis were convicted in the 1920s and 1930s. Open daily; tours Thursdays and Sundays. No admission charge. 75 W. Fifth St. (phone: 292-3225).

COMO PARK A 70-acre lake, a small zoo, a golf course, a Japanese garden, and children's rides all contribute to the popularity of this, the largest of St. Paul's many parks. In addition, it has special floral gardens, a year-round conservatory, and a lakeside pavilion where summer concerts are held. Open daily. Admission charge to the conservatory. Lexington Ave. at Midway Pkwy. (phone: 488-4041 for the zoo; 489-5378 for the conservatory).

STATE CAPITOL St. Paul is Minnesota's political center, and its Capitol is one of the most important buildings in the state. Its giant dome—similar to one designed by Michelangelo in Rome—is an outstanding state landmark and the largest unsupported marble dome in the world. Free guided tours. Open daily. Cedar and Aurora Sts. (phone: 296-2881).

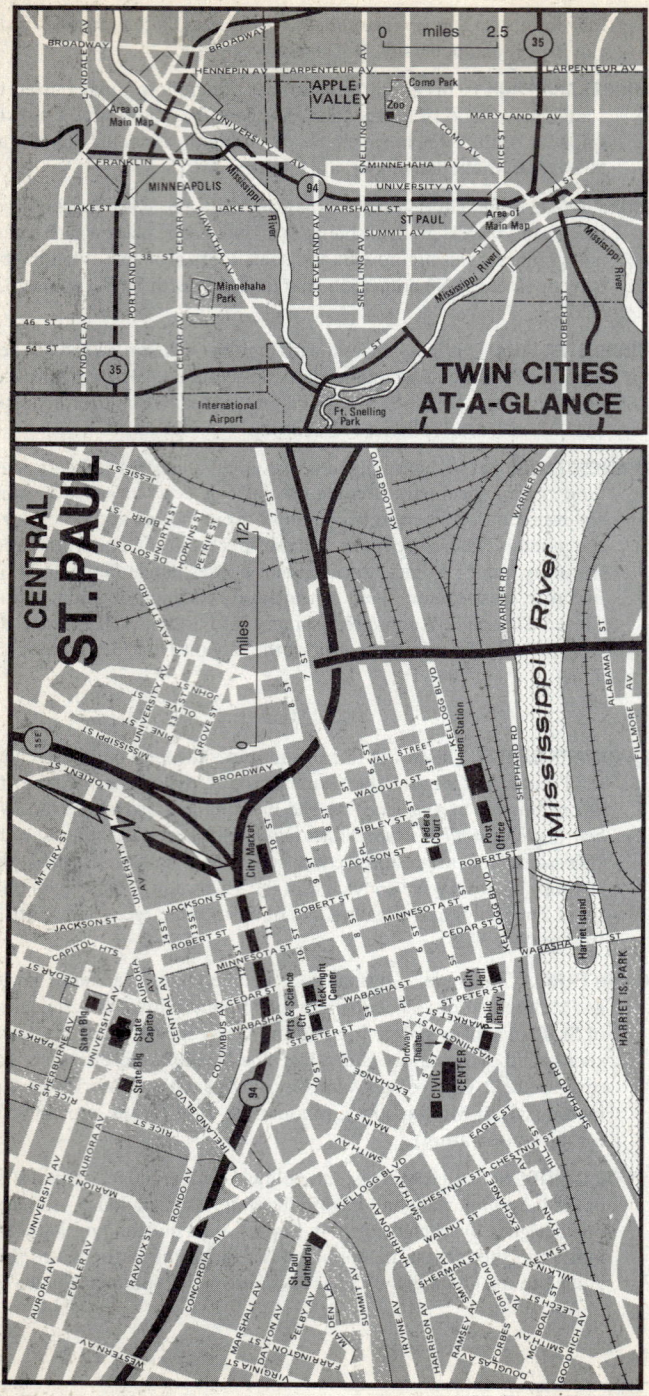

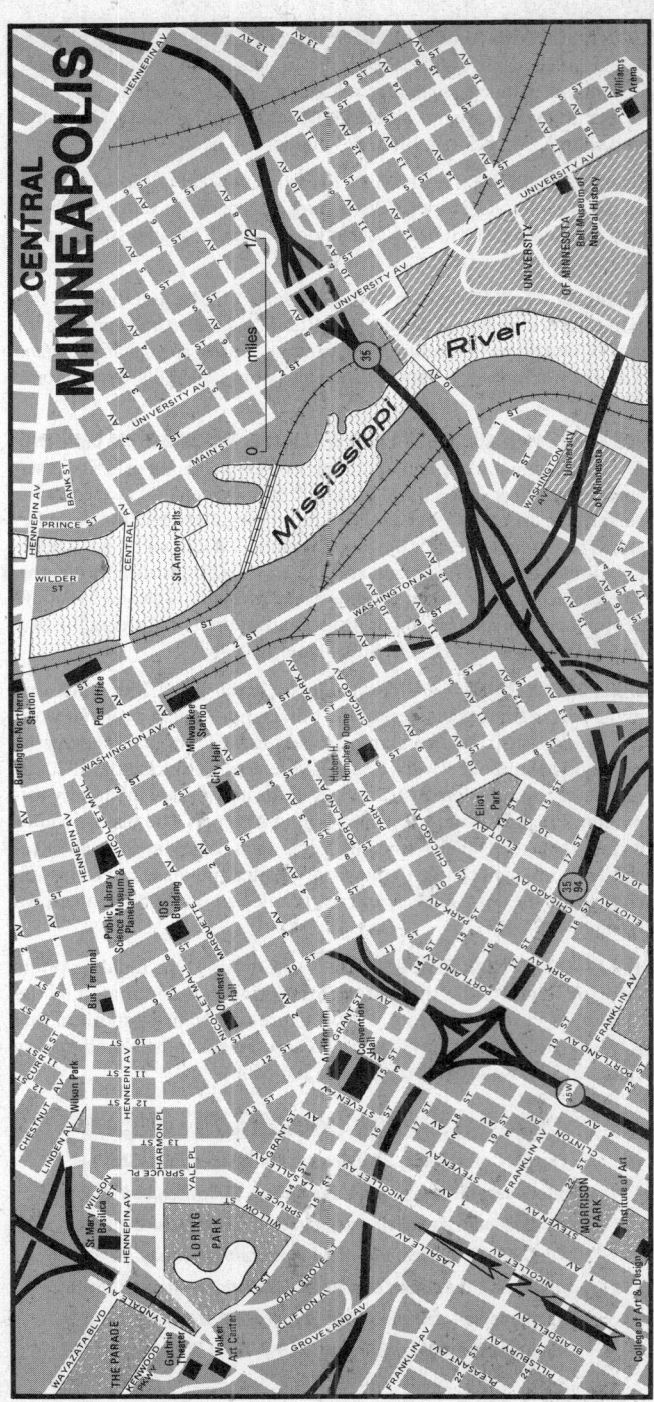

MINNESOTA STATE HISTORICAL SOCIETY Founded in 1849, 10 years before Minnesota became a state, the society houses records of pioneer days. In addition, paintings, sculpture, and other works by contemporary Minnesota artists also are on exhibit. Galleries closed Mondays. No admission charge. 345 Kellogg Blvd. W. (phone: 296-6126).

GOVERNOR'S RESIDENCE This English Tudor residence, built in 1910–11, is on the *National Register of Historic Sites*. It is open for tours on Thursdays, May through October. Reservations required. No admission charge. 1006 Summit Ave. (phone: 297-8177).

CATHEDRAL OF ST. PAUL Center of the Roman Catholic archdiocese, this cathedral is a replica of *St. Peter's* in Rome. Architecturally notable for its 175-foot dome and central rose window, it has a special *Shrine of the Nations,* where visitors can meditate and pray. 239 Selby Ave. (phone: 228-1766).

SCIENCE MUSEUM OF MINNESOTA AND WILLIAM L. MCKNIGHT/3M OMNITHEATER This immensely popular complex offers hands-on exhibits in science, technology, and natural history. It includes a 635-seat theater for performing arts, a 300-seat auditorium, an art gallery, and the omnitheater. The latter, named for the founder of the 3M Company, has a floor-to-ceiling hemispheric screen and the world's largest film projector. The omnitheater is closed Mondays; the museum is closed Mondays September through December. Both charge admission; a combination ticket is available. 30 E. 10th St. (phone: 221-9444).

HISTORIC FORT SNELLING The oldest landmark in the Twin Cities is also one of the first military posts west of the Mississippi—but not very far west: *Fort Snelling* sits high on a bluff overlooking the junction of the Mississippi and Minnesota Rivers. See what life was like during the 1820s as people in costume demonstrate early crafts and parade in military formation. Fife and drum bands perform in summer. The history center is closed weekends year-round; the fort is open daily May through October. No admission charge to the history center and museum; admission charge for the fort. Hwy. 5 and 55, 6 miles southwest of downtown (phone: 725-2413).

CITY HALL—COUNTY COURTHOUSE This 20-story Art Deco building offers exterior reliefs and a three-story Memorial Hall dominated by the "Vision of Peace," a 36-foot, 55-ton figure of a Native American that is the world's largest onyx carving. Closed weekends. No admission charge. 15 W. Kellogg Blvd. (phone: 266-8500).

EXTRA SPECIAL

The St. Croix Valley, 25 miles east of Minneapolis–St. Paul, offers several stops for a day's outing. Stillwater, birthplace of Minnesota, is within easy striking distance of the *Afton Alps, Welch Village,* and *Wild Mountain* ski areas. In Stillwater, visit the *Grand Garage and Gallery* (on Main St.) with its shops and galleries. Two good eating stops are *Brine's Meat Market and Lunchroom* (219 S. Main St.; phone: 439-

1862), which has the *Employees Lunchroom* upstairs, open to anybody employed anywhere, with great bratwurst, pastrami, and chili; and the *Dock Café* (425 E. Nelson St.; phone: 430-3770), offering fresh fish as well as beef and pasta. On the Wisconsin side of the tour is Somerset, where you can go tubing down the Apple River. You get carted about 4 miles upriver, plunked into an inner tube, and sent drifting back to Somerset. The river flows quickly over rapids at the outset, but widens and slows down, and the ride into town is tranquil.

Sources and Resources

TOURIST INFORMATION

Each Twin has its own source: the *Greater Minneapolis Convention and Visitors Association* (1219 Marquette, Minneapolis, MN 55403; phone: 661-4700) and the *St. Paul Convention and Visitors Bureau* (55 E. Fifth St., St. Paul, MN 55101; phone: 297-6985). Both are closed weekends. Contact the Minnesota state tourism hotline (phone: 800-657-3700) for maps, calendars of events, health updates, and travel advisories.

LOCAL COVERAGE There are two daily newspapers: the Minneapolis *Star Tribune* and the *Saint Paul Pioneer Press*. The *Twin Cities Reader*, *Skyway News*, and *City Pages* (distributed free in shopping centers, downtown hotels, and many restaurants) list activities in the Twin Cities. For a complete schedule of musical happenings, see the *Saint Paul Pioneer Press* on Thursdays and the *Star Tribune Variety Weekend* on Fridays. *Mpls.–St. Paul*, a monthly magazine, available at newsstands, gives full details on what's going on. A *Metro Area Visitors Guide* is also available from the convention and visitors bureaus in both St. Paul and Minneapolis, as well as from the *Minnesota Office of Tourism* (375 Jackson St., 250 Skyway Level, St. Paul, MN 55101; phone: 296-5029; 800-657-3700). *Minnesota Explorer*, a guide to events throughout the state, is free from the *Minnesota Office of Tourism*.

TELEVISION STATIONS KTCA Channel 2–PBS; WCCO Channel 4–CBS; KSTP Channel 5–ABC; KMSP Channel 9–Independent; KARE Channel 11–NBC; KLGT Channel 23–Independent; and KTTN Channel 29–Fox.

RADIO STATIONS AM: WCCO 830 (talk/news); KNOW 1330 (public); and KSTP 1500 (talk). FM: KSJN 91.1 (public); KS95 94.5 (top 40); and KTCZ 97.1 (jazz).

TELEPHONE The area code for Minneapolis–St. Paul is 612.

SALES TAX The sales tax in Minneapolis–St. Paul is 7%; in the suburbs, 6½%. There is no tax on clothing or groceries.

CLIMATE In winter, be prepared for anything. The average temperature is 19F, but it can drop to 35F below zero, and snow has fallen as early as October. Summer temperatures are generally in the 70s and 80s.

GETTING AROUND

AIRPORT *Minneapolis–St. Paul International Airport* is a 15- to 20-minute drive from the downtown area of either Twin City. *Airport Taxi* (phone: 721-0000) provides metered transportation to Minneapolis hotels. *Metropolitan Transit Commission* buses run between the airport and downtown Minneapolis; to get to the airport from downtown St. Paul, take bus 54A on Sixth St. and transfer to the 7 at the *Mall of America*. The fare is $1.35 to $1.60, depending on distance and time of day. Limousines travel between the airport and downtown hotels in both cities; one good company is *The Airport Express* (phone: 726-6400).

BUS Minneapolis–St. Paul bus systems are models of efficiency. Express buses make the trip between Minneapolis and St. Paul in 20 minutes. Passengers' queries are handled by an extensive switchboard at the *Metropolitan Transit Commission* (560 Sixth Ave. N., Minneapolis; phone: 349-7000). Fares are $1 during off-peak hours; $1.25 during peak hours.

CAR RENTAL All major firms are represented.

TAXI As in many other cities, taxis are difficult to get when you really need them and plentiful when you don't. Most are radio-dispatched. There are some taxi stands. One of the largest taxi companies in Minneapolis is *Yellow Cab* (500 E. 36th St.; phone: 824-4444), which also has an office in St. Paul (1463 Marshall Ave.; phone: 222-4433). For service from the suburbs to the city, there's *Suburban* (phone: 349-9999) and *Town Taxi* (phone: 331-8294).

LOCAL SERVICES

AUDIOVISUAL EQUIPMENT *AVVA/ProCom* (phone: 339-1876); *Blumberg Communications* (phone: 333-1271).

BABY-SITTING *Eden Prairie Kids Club* (1156 Eden Prairie Center, Mpls.; phone: 941-1007); *Jack and Jill Sitting Service* (1651 Fourth St., at White Bear Lake, St. Paul; phone: 429-2963).

BUSINESS SERVICES *A-1 Secretarial Services* (Pioneer Bldg., Suite 219, 336 N. Robert St., St. Paul; phone: 228-1907); *Executive Business Services*, for word processing and copying (1111 Third Ave. S., Mpls.; phone: 332-5903).

DRY CLEANER/TAILOR *Dunrite Cleaners* (19 N. Sixth St., Mpls.; phone: 332-4033); *Whiteway Cleaners* (286 W. Seventh St., St. Paul; phone: 224-1391).

LIMOUSINE *Glenn Louis Limousines* (phone: 871-8050); *Twin Star Limousine* (phone: 641-1385).

MECHANICS/ROAD SERVICE *Bernie & Jim's Amoco* (phone: 338-5520); *Fisher Tire and Auto* (1022 Hennepin Ave., Mpls.; phone: 338-6953), excellent 24-hour road service at extremely reasonable prices.

MEDICAL EMERGENCY *Hennepin County Medical Center* (701 Park Ave., Mpls.; phone: 347-2121); *St. Paul–Ramsey Medical Center* (640 Jackson St., St. Paul; phone: 221-3456).

MESSENGER SERVICES *Action Messenger* (phone: 881-5100); *Courier Dispatch* (phone: 338-6300).

MONEY TRANSFERS *American Express MoneyGram* (phone: 800-926-9400 for information; 800-866-8800 for money transfers); *Western Union Financial Services* (phone: 800-325-6000 or 800-325-4176).

NATIONAL/INTERNATIONAL COURIER *FedEx* (phone: 340-0887).

PHARMACY *Loop Pharmacy* (Marquette at 10th St., Mpls.; phone: 333-2481); *Metropolitan Pharmacy* (825 S Eighth St., Mpls.; phone: 332-6522); *Moudry Apothecary Shop* (364 St. Peter St., St. Paul; phone: 222-0571), open weekdays 8 AM to 6:30 PM, Saturdays 8 AM to 1 PM.

PHOTOCOPIES *Copies Now* (*American National Bank Building*, Fifth and Minnesota, St. Paul; phone: 291-0800); *Kinko's* (*IDS Center*, Seventh and Nicollet, Mpls.; phone: 338-1541), open 24 hours.

POST OFFICE The central Minneapolis office (100 First St. and Marquette Ave.; phone: 349-4970) has a mailbox in front for pickups and dispatch until midnight. The central office in St. Paul (180 E. Kellogg Blvd.; phone: 293-3130) has a 24-hour, self-service lobby.

PROFESSIONAL PHOTOGRAPHER *David Bank Studios* (607 Marquette Ave., Mpls.; phone: 333-1114); *Dellarson Studios* (480 N. Robert St., St. Paul; phone: 224-2891).

TELECONFERENCE FACILITIES *Marquette Inn, Sofitel* (see *Checking In*, below); *World Trade Center—Conference Center* (phone: 297-1580).

TRANSLATOR *AAA Worldwide Translation Center* (phone: 541-0056); *Berlitz* (phone: 920-4100).

WESTERN UNION/TELEX Many offices are located around the city (phone: 800-325-6000 to find the location nearest you).

OTHER *Greater Minneapolis Convention & Visitors Association* (phone: 661-4700) for meeting and conference planning; *Communications Workshop, Campbell-Mithurn* (phone: 347-1000) for video and audiovisual productions for business training workshops; *Travel Associates* (phone: 291-1222); *Group Travel Directors* (phone: 881-7811).

SPECIAL EVENTS

The *Minneapolis Aquatennial* in July features sailboat races, a torchlight parade, and the "Queen of the Lakes" beauty contest. Throughout July and August, the *Minneapolis Orchestra* presents special concerts in the Marketplatz next to *Orchestra Hall* during *Sommerfest* (phone: 371-5656), with vendors and dance performances. The *Minnesota State Fair* (at Midway Pkwy. and Snelling Aves., St. Paul) runs for 12 days, ending *Labor Day,* and the *St. Paul Winter Carnival,* in early February, is a citywide celebration.

MUSEUMS

In addition to those described in *Special Places,* there are several other noteworthy cultural institutions in the Twin Cities.

AMERICAN SWEDISH INSTITUTE Swedish glass and art, along with immigrant memorabilia, are housed in a 33-room Romanesque mansion. Closed Mondays. Admission charge. 2600 Park Ave., Minneapolis (phone: 871-4907).

BELL MUSEUM OF NATURAL HISTORY The focus is on wildlife, with a *Touch and See Room* where you can feel exhibits ranging from a buffalo hide to a live snake. Closed Mondays. No admission charge Thursdays. 10 Church St. SE, Minneapolis (phone: 624-7083).

MINNEAPOLIS PLANETARIUM Light shows on the stars and planets. Open daily. Admission charge. In the *Minneapolis Public Library,* 300 Nicollet Mall, Minneapolis (phone: 372-6644).

GIBBS FARM MUSEUM Costumed guides show what life was like at a farm and school in 1900. Closed Mondays and November through April. Admission charge. Outside St. Paul at 2097 W. Larpenteur Ave., Falcon Heights (phone: 646-8629).

MINNESOTA CHILDREN'S MUSEUM A hands-on center where kids can run a TV studio and an electromagnetic crane. Open daily. Admission charge. 1217 Bandana Blvd. N., St. Paul (phone: 644-3818).

NATIONAL FIRE FIGHTERS MEMORIAL MUSEUM Kids can climb on old fire trucks, take a ride in a working rig, and try on real firefighting gear. Available for birthday parties. Open Thursdays, Saturdays, the first Sunday of each month, and by arrangement. Admission charge. 1100 Van Buren St. NE, Minneapolis (phone: 623-3817).

PLANES OF FAME More than two dozen World War II–era planes are on display. Closed Mondays. Admission charge. Outside Minneapolis at 14771 Pioneer Trail, Eden Prairie (phone: 941-2633).

SHOPPING

Minneapolis–St. Paul's ethnic diversity is reflected in the interesting variety of shops in its neighborhoods. Several African-American–oriented stores are located along University Avenue between Lexington Avenue and Victoria Street in St. Paul. For African crafts, try *Inside Africa* at *Galtier Plaza* (175 E. Fifth St., St. Paul; phone: 224-3508). Tasty Mexican food items can be purchased at *Boca Chica* (11 Concord St., St. Paul; phone: 222-8499) and *El Burrito Mexican Foods and Bakery* (200 Concord St., St. Paul; phone: 227-2192); several other shops along Concord Street offer Hispanic crafts and clothing. In Minneapolis, Native American artworks are sold at the *Two Rivers Gallery* (1530 E. Franklin Ave.; phone: 871-9421) and the *First Peoples' Gallery* in the Wyman Building (400 First Ave. N.; phone: 672-9630).

Bandana Square Filled with specialty and apparel shops and several restaurants in a renovated railroad repair complex, the square (1021 E. Bandana Blvd., St. Paul; phone: 642-1509) is listed in the *National Register of Historic Places.* Be sure to visit the *Twin City Model Railroad Club,* where models of area railroads as they existed in 1950 are on display. Open daily. Donations requested. Bandana Sq. (phone: 647-9628).

Byerly's Offering a food-shopping experience like no other—with carpeted aisles and chandeliers—this is a place where cantaloupe thumpers and tomato squeezers can browse from the cereal aisle over to the imported crystal and jewelry departments, and even take cooking classes. The food store is open 24 hours a day; some of the other departments close at 10 PM. 3777 Park Center Blvd., *St. Louis Park,* west of Minneapolis (phone: 929-2100).

Galtier Plaza Located in St. Paul's historic Lowertown District, the plaza has a marketplace atmosphere, with shops, four movie theaters, underground parking, and a rooftop garden. Sibley Ave. between Fifth and Sixth Sts., St. Paul (phone: 292-0600).

Mall of America Billed as the world's biggest shopping mall, this behemoth has hundreds of retail stores, including *Bloomingdale's, Macy's,* and *Nordstrom.* There also are 14 movie theaters, dozens of restaurants, and the *Camp Snoopy* theme park for kids. In Bloomington, at the intersection of Hwy. 77 and I-494 (phone: 851-3500).

Vintage Music Co. With more than 25,000 recordings in stock, this is the place for anyone seeking the nostalgic sound of good old vinyl albums. 2931 E. Lake St., Minneapolis (phone: 729-8929).

SPORTS AND FITNESS

BASEBALL The major league Minnesota *Twins* play at the 60,000-seat *Hubert H. Humphrey Metrodome* (500 11th Ave. S., Minneapolis; phone: 375-1116 for ticket information). For outdoor baseball, see the St. Paul *Saints* of the *Northern League* at *Municipal Stadium* (1771 Energy Park Dr., St. Paul; phone: 644-6659).

BASKETBALL The *NBA Timberwolves* play in the *Target Center* (600 First Ave. N., Minneapolis; phone: 337-3865).

BIKING There are bike trails around Lake Harriet, Lake Calhoun, and Lake of the Isles in Minneapolis; Lakes Como and Phalen in St. Paul. Bicycles may be rented from the *Bike Shop* (213 Oak St. SE, Minneapolis; phone: 331-3442).

COLLEGE SPORTS For *University of Minnesota Big 10* athletic tickets, call 624-8080.

FISHING Of the 12 fishing lakes in the Twin Cities metro area, the best is Lake Minnetonka (15 miles west on Hwys. 394 and 12), which has 177 miles of shoreline. Within the city limits, Lake Calhoun has a fishing dock.

FITNESS CENTERS Minneapolis has a modern *YMCA* (30 S. Ninth St.; phone: 371-8750) and *YWCA* (1130 Nicollet Mall; phone: 332-0501), which are open to non-members for a fee. There are many local health clubs and branches of national clubs in the Twin Cities. Consult the yellow pages for phone numbers.

FOOTBALL The *NFL Vikings* take to the field at the *Hubert H. Humphrey Metrodome* (500 11th Ave. S., Minneapolis; phone: 333-8828).

GOLF Minneapolis has five public golf courses (phone: 661-4848 for information); St. Paul has four (phone: 266-6445). Others are in the suburbs.

ICE SKATING The cities clear, test, and maintain outdoor rinks on many of the lakes. Indoor ice arenas offer some free time for public skating. Consult the yellow pages for locations and numbers.

JOGGING An ambitious run leads to Lake of the Isles, 2½ miles from downtown, and from there to Cedar Lake to the west or Lakes Calhoun and Harriet to the south; the perimeter of each lake is about 3 miles. Another route is along the Mississippi on East or West River Road, by the *University of Minnesota*. In St. Paul, joggers take to the trails around Lake Como and Lake Phalen. The most beautiful spot for runners in St. Paul is Summit Avenue and along the Mississippi River.

SKIING The best ski areas in the vicinity are *Afton Alps* in Afton (phone: 436-5245), *Welch Village* in Welch (phone: 258-4567), and *Buck Hill* in Burnsville (phone: 435-7174), all 30 to 45 minutes from town.

SWIMMING There are public beaches at 23 lakes in and around the Twin Cities area that are open during the summer.

TENNIS There are many lighted, outdoor courts as well as indoor courts available throughout the cities. Call for information on public park courts in Minneapolis (phone: 661-4875) and St. Paul (phone: 266-6400).

THEATER

The Twin Cities are filled with great theater companies. Our favorite is listed below, along with several other high-quality choices.

CENTER STAGE

Guthrie Theater After a nationwide search for a hospitable metropolitan environment in which to locate a repertory theater, Sir Tyrone Guthrie selected Minneapolis. His choice has been borne out by the enthusiastic support of audiences and patrons. With 1,309 seats, this is among the largest of the country's regional theaters. It also has one of the longest seasons, and its house, which shares a handsome contemporary building with the *Walker Art Center*, is one of the most unusual; its stage gives audiences access to three sides of the production, and no seat is more than about 50 feet from the stage. The resident acting company performs the classics in rotating repertory. 725 Vineland Pl. (phone: 377-2224).

In addition to the *Guthrie,* the Twin Cities have almost 100 professional and community theaters, with productions ranging from classics or contemporary drama to comedy and experimental theater. The universities and colleges also produce plays and musicals. The options include the *Children's Theatre Company* (phone: 874-0400) and the *Great American History Theatre* (phone: 292-4323) as well as three companies that mount contemporary dramas and the work of new playwrights: *Penumbra Theater* (phone: 224-4601), *Mixed Blood Theatre* (phone: 338-6131), and the *Cricket Theatre* (phone: 337-0747). You also can be a member of the audience at Garrison Keillor's "Prairie Home Companion," broadcast from the *World Theater* (10 E. Exchange St., St. Paul; phone: 290-1221). Since Keillor often takes the show on tour, it's wise to call ahead for tickets; contact either the theater box office or *TicketMaster* (phone: 989-5151). The restored *Historic State* and *Orpheum Theaters* (both at Hennepin Ave. in downtown Minneapolis; phone: 339-7007) offer touring shows.

MUSIC

For a complete schedule of musical happenings, check the newspapers (see *Local Coverage*). *Orchestra Hall* (1111 Nicollet Mall, Minneapolis; phone: 371-5656) is the home of the *Minnesota Orchestra* and presents other concerts as well. The copper-capped, glass-walled *Ordway Music Theatre* (345 Washington St.; phone: 293-5630) presents performances by the *St. Paul Chamber Orchestra,* the *Minnesota Opera,* and the *Schubert Club,* as well as touring Broadway shows and other theater productions. There are outdoor summer concerts at Lake Harriet in Minneapolis and at Lake Como in St. Paul.

NIGHTCLUBS AND NIGHTLIFE

Gallivan's Downtown (354 Wabasha, St. Paul; phone: 227-6688) features professional entertainment. *The Manor* (2550 W. Seventh St., St. Paul; phone: 690-1771) hosts ballroom dancing Thursdays through Saturdays. In the West Bank area near the *University of Minnesota,* there are a number of small clubs and cafés. *America Live!* operates six of the nine bars on the fourth floor of the *Mall of America* (see *Shopping*) in suburban Bloomington, arguably the hottest night scene in the Twin Cities area.

The *Dakota Bar & Grill* (1021 E. Bandana Blvd., St. Paul; phone: 642-1442) hosts the best jazz in the Twin Cities. The former Greyhound Bus Depot in Minneapolis is now the *7th Street Entry* (701 First Ave. N.; phone: 332-1775), a nightclub featured in local rock star Prince's film *Purple Rain. The Fine Line Music Café* (318 First Ave. N., Minneapolis; phone: 338-8100) presents some of the best local talent to a hip audience. One of the hottest places in town for live music is the *Glam Slam* (110 N. Fifth St., Minneapolis; phone: 338-3383). *St. Paul's Hearthrob Café and Nightclub* (30 E. Seventh St.; phone: 224-2783) draws a young, energetic crowd. Comedy-seekers can find laughs at *Scott Hansen's Comedy Gallery* (two locations: Galtier Plaza, St. Paul, and 43 Main St., Minneapolis; phone: 331-5653 for both). The *Gay 90s* (408 Hennepin Ave., Minneapolis; phone: 333-7755) houses eight separate gay bars.

WHEELS OF FORTUNE

Several casinos are only a short drive from the Twin Cities: *Grand Casino Hinckley* (777 Lady Luck Dr., Hinckley; phone: 800-GRAND-21), *Grand Casino Mille Lacs* (Hwy. 169, on the west shore of Mille Lacs Lake, Onamia; phone: 800-626-LUCK), *Jackpot Junction* (in Morton; phone: 800-WIN-CASH), *Mystic Lake Casino* (on the Prior Lake Indian Reservation, 2400 Mystic Lake Blvd., Prior Lake; phone:

800-262-7799), and *Treasure Island Casino* (5734 Sturgeon Lake Rd., Welch; phone: 800-222-7077). All offer slots, bingo, blackjack, and other games of chance; you must be 21 or over to play.

Best in Town

CHECKING IN

There are a number of hotels near the *Minneapolis–St. Paul International Airport*, in the suburb of Bloomington, and downtown. Expect to pay $90 or more per night for a double room at places we've listed as expensive; $70 to $90 at those in the moderate category. *Days Inn, Best Western, Quality Inn,* and other chains provide inexpensive lodging (around $50). Unless otherwise noted, hotels have air conditioning, private baths, TV sets, and telephones. All hotels are in the 612 area code unless otherwise indicated.

We begin with our favorite property in the area, followed by our recommendations of cost and quality choices of hotels, listed alphabetically by price category.

A SPECIAL HAVEN

Lowell Inn Built more than half a century ago, this gracious, colonial-style inn, with its 13 columns and high portico, has been run by the Palmer family since 1930 with an unusual degree of sensitivity to the proper care and feeding of guests. The 21 bedrooms are up-to-date, and each of the three popular dining rooms has a different motif (see *Eating Out*). The inn, a very pricey but rewarding choice, is about 18 miles from St. Paul, and Stillwater is chockablock with antiques shops. 102 N. Second St., Stillwater (phone: 439-1100; fax: 439-4686).

EXPENSIVE

Luxeford Suites This all-suite hotel at the edge of downtown has a European feel. Each of the 230 rooms is equipped with a wet bar, refrigerator, and microwave oven. A complimentary continental breakfast is laid out on the sideboard in the club room off the lobby. Room service is available until midnight. Other amenities include a fitness center, three meeting rooms, photocopiers, complimentary downtown shuttle service, and express checkout. 1101 La Salle Ave., Mpls. (phone: 332-6800; 800-662-3232; fax: 332-8246).

Marquette Inn Connected to the interior skyway in the *IDS Center*, this gracious 281-room inn offers spacious accommodations as well as a bar and restaurant. Among the business amenities are 11 meeting rooms, room service until 2 AM, concierge and secretarial services, A/V equipment, photocopiers, and express checkout. 710 Marquette Ave., Mpls. (phone: 332-2352; 800-328-4782; fax: 376-7419).

Minneapolis Hilton and Towers The city's newest hotel, this 25-story establishment has 814 rooms, including 52 suites. The 71 concierge-level rooms offer private registration and a lounge. Facilities include two restaurants, two lounges, a fitness center, and a pool. Among the business amenities are 20 meeting rooms, room service until 2 AM, A/V equipment and photocopiers, and video checkout (using interactive TV). 1001 Marquette Ave. S., Mpls. (phone: 376-1000; 800-HILTONS; fax: 397-4871).

Minneapolis Marriott City Center Its 583 rooms include 62 with parlors and wet bars, and 20 two-level suites. Guest amenities include a health club, two restaurants, and a lounge. Room service is available until midnight. For business travelers, there are 31 meeting rooms, A/V equipment and photocopiers, and express checkout. 30 S. Seventh St., Mpls. (phone 349-4000; 800-228-9290; fax: 332-7165).

Radisson Plaza Minneapolis Emphasizing personal service to the business traveler, this flagship of the Radisson collection has 357 suites and oversize rooms in the heart of downtown Minneapolis and offers two restaurants, two lounges, a fitness center, and concierge services. Room service is available until 11 PM. Business facilities include eight meeting rooms, A/V equipment and photocopier, secretarial services, and express checkout. 35 S. Seventh St. (phone: 339-4900; 800-333-3333; fax: 337-9766).

Saint Paul At this beautifully restored Victorian hotel, crystal chandeliers sparkle in the lobby, and elegant Biedermeier-style furniture decorates the guestrooms, some of which have lovely views over *Rice Park*. Its restaurants include the *St. Paul Bar & Grill* and *The Café*. The 252-room hotel, across from the *Ordway Music Theatre,* is connected by a skyway to department stores, banks, boutiques, and travel agencies. Room service is on call until 11 PM; there are nine meeting rooms, a concierge desk, A/V equipment, photocopiers, computers, and express checkout. 350 Market St., St. Paul (phone: 292-9292; 800-292-9292; fax: 228-9506).

Sofitel The first North American link in the French hotel chain offers a concierge and authentic croissants for breakfast. Some of the 282 deluxe rooms have bidets. Facilities include three restaurants, a café, an indoor heated pool, a sauna, and a piano bar. Room service delivers until 1 AM. Thirteen meeting rooms, secretarial services, A/V equipment, photocopiers, and express checkout round out the business amenities. I-494 and Hwy. 100, Bloomington (phone: 835-1900; 800-876-6303; fax: 835-2696).

Whitney One of downtown Minneapolis's most deluxe establishments is this renovated turn-of-the-century flour mill overlooking the Mississippi River. Each of its 97 distinctive rooms (some are bi-level suites) is adapted to the old building's unique style. *Whitney's Grill* provides formal dining. 150 Portland Ave., Mpls. (phone: 339-9300; 800-248-1879; fax: 339-1333).

MODERATE

Holiday Inn Airport A five-minute drive from the airport, this six-story, 189-room hotel has a restaurant, pool, exercise room, and sauna. Business amenities include three meeting rooms, A/V equipment, and photocopiers. 2700 Pilot Knob Rd., Eagan (phone: 454-3434; 800-EAGAN64; fax: 454-4904).

Holiday Inn Express Located in St. Paul's historic Bandana Square, this 109-room hotel (formerly the *Sunwood Inn*) occupies a renovated railroad building. Retaining the original structural characteristics, the inn features tracks on the floor, huge entrances, and exposed beams. Photos throughout tell of the "good old days" of Minnesota railroading. Business amenities include five meeting rooms, A/V equipment, and photocopiers. 1010 Bandana Blvd. W., St. Paul (phone: 647-1637; 800-HOLIDAY; fax: 647-0244).

EATING OUT

Almost any kind of food can be found in the Twin Cities, from high-priced, exquisitely prepared continental dishes to Japanese food or a kosher delicatessen. Prices range from $50 or more for dinner for two at places listed as expensive, $30 to $50 at those in the moderate category, and $30 or less at inexpensive places. Prices do not include drinks, wine, tax, or tips. Unless otherwise noted, restaurants serve lunch and dinner. All restaurants are in the 612 area code.

EXPENSIVE

510 Try the pre-theater specials at this elegant place next to the *Guthrie Theater*. The preparation is French, and the results are largely terrific, whether the dish is pork, beef, swordfish, or seafood. Closed Sundays. Reservations necessary. Major credit cards accepted. 510 Groveland Ave., Minneapolis (phone: 874-6440).

Forepaughs French food is served in a gracious 19th-century former home. Free parking and shuttle service to the *Ordway Music Theatre* are provided. Open daily. Reservations advised. Major credit cards accepted. 276 Exchange St., St. Paul (phone: 224-5606).

Goodfellow's Beautiful hardwood floors, a roaring fireplace, and a fine collection of contemporary art are almost peripheral to the creative dishes served here. The menu, which changes every season, lists farm-raised trout, Minnesota-raised duck, beef—and, on occasion, elk, venison, pheasant, and quail. Closed Sundays; dinner only on Saturdays. Reservations advised. Major credit cards accepted. 800 *Nicollet Mall,* Minneapolis (phone: 332-4800).

Lowell Inn The closest thing to a New England inn that you'll find in the Midwest. The *George Washington Room* and the *Garden Room* offer steaks, seafood, and other American fare; the *Matterhorn Room*'s menu features fondues exclusively. Open daily. Reservations necessary. MasterCard and Visa accepted. 102 N. Second St., Stillwater, a northeast suburb of St. Paul (phone: 439-1100).

Murray's Well known for its hickory-smoked shrimp appetizers, award-winning steaks, and homemade rolls, this establishment's decor recalls the 1940s, and there is music in the evening Thursdays through Saturdays. Open daily. Reservations advised. Major credit cards accepted. 26 S. Sixth St., Minneapolis (phone: 339-0909).

MODERATE

D'Amico Cucina This eatery offers the chef's modern interpretation of classic Italian dishes as well as live entertainment. Open daily for dinner only. Reservations advised. Major credit cards accepted. Butler Sq., 100 N. Sixth St., Minneapolis (phone: 338-2401).

Azur Winner of more than 30 culinary awards, this contemporary Art Deco restaurant specializes in the cooking of south and southwestern France. Latin jazz entertainment is provided on weekends. Closed Sundays. Reservations advised. Major credit cards accepted. On the fifth floor of Gaviidae Common, 651 *Nicollet Mall,* Minneapolis (phone: 432-2500).

Black Forest Inn Near the *Minneapolis Institute of Arts,* the inn serves bratwurst-and-sauerkraut dinners, Wiener schnitzel, and other honest, substantial German fare. The restaurant evolved from a tavern that used to serve only beer, and it still offers German brews, which you can enjoy in the outdoor beer garden. Open daily. Reservations advised. Major credit cards accepted. 1 E. 26th St., Minneapolis (phone: 872-0812).

Cairo Café Authentic and tasty Middle Eastern specialties are presented in an informal dining room with Egyptian-style decor. Open daily. Reservations advised. MasterCard and Visa accepted. 704 Hennepin Ave. S., Minneapolis (phone: 338-6810).

Cherokee Sirloin Room Sirloins and tenderloins are the specialties at this steakhouse. Open daily. Reservations advised on weekends. Major credit cards accepted. Two locations: 886 S. Smith, West St. Paul (phone: 457-2729); and outside St. Paul at 4625 Nichols Rd., Eagan (phone: 454-6744).

Dakota Bar & Grill Featuring the Twin Cities' best jazz, this place serves Minnesota-style steaks, lamb with wild rice, and fresh brook trout. Open daily. Reservations advised. Major credit cards accepted. 1021 E. Bandana Blvd., St. Paul (phone: 642-1442).

Figlio The cooking is Italian via California—pizza and pasta topped with unusual combinations, as well as fresh fish and meat from the wood-fired oven and grill in the open kitchen. Open daily. Reservations advised. Major credit cards accepted. 3001 Hennepin Ave. S., Minneapolis (phone: 822-1688).

Lexington This landmark spot has attracted politicians and business leaders for over half a century. The decor is formal and the cooking traditional, with short ribs, lamb shanks, and prime ribs. Open daily. Reservations advised. Major credit cards accepted. 1096 Grand Ave., St. Paul (phone: 222-5878).

Nicollet Island Inn Classic Midwestern cooking with a Mediterranean influence is the staple of this old stone hotel (which also has 24 guestrooms).

It is located on an island in the Mississippi River, only a 10-minute walk from downtown across the Hennepin Suspension Bridge. Open daily. Reservations advised. Major credit cards accepted. 95 Merriam St., Minneapolis (phone: 331-3035).

INEXPENSIVE

Café Brenda The fare at this sunny downtown health food eatery is so tasty and sophisticated you may forget it's also good for you. Try the Wisconsin rainbow trout or meal-size salads. Closed Sundays. Reservations advised. Major credit cards accepted. 300 First Ave. N., Minneapolis (phone: 342-9230).

Ciatti's There's a good selection of Italian dishes here, including a variety of pasta served with different sauces; some non-Italian dishes also are available. Open daily. Reservations advised. Major credit cards accepted. 1346 La Salle Ave. S., Minneapolis (phone: 339-7747); 850 Grand Ave., St. Paul (phone: 292-9942); and several other locations.

Leeann Chin's This cavernous space used to be the *Union Depot*. Now its Oriental decor—stunning vases, jade and ivory carvings, and whimsical modern Chinese paintings—provides a backdrop for buffets that offer everything from cream cheese wontons to lemon chicken and almond cookie ice cream. Open daily. Reservations advised. Major credit cards accepted. Union Depot Pl. at Fourth and Sibley, St. Paul (phone: 224-8814). A branch, closed Sundays, is located at 900 Second Ave., Minneapolis (phone: 338-8488).

Mickey's Diner This St. Paul institution has been serving world class omelettes 24 hours a day since 1939. Near the *Greyhound Bus Depot*, it attracts regulars from all walks of life. Nothing fancy here, just straight, down-to-earth cookin', four booths, and 17 counter stools. Open daily. No reservations. Major credit cards accepted. 36 W. Seventh St. (phone: 222-5633). (The family also operates *Mickey's Restaurant*, with more space but the same ambience at 1950 W. Seventh St.; phone: 698-8387.)

Sidney's Pizza Café Great pasta is served in a North Woods atmosphere. The apple pizza is one of the best desserts in town. Open daily. This popular place doesn't take reservations, but recommends calling 30 minutes before arrival to add your name to the waiting list. Major credit cards accepted. 2120 Hennepin Ave., Minneapolis (phone: 870-7000).

BARBECUE BEAT

What's the best place for barbecue? That question always prompts lively debate here. Current favorites include *Market Bar-Be-Que* (1414 Nicollet Ave. S., Minneapolis; phone: 872-1111), preferred by longtime residents for ribs cooked to dry, smoky perfection over a wood fire. Then there's *Rudolph's Barbecue* (three locations: 1933 Lyndale Ave. S., Minneapolis; phone: 871-8969; 815 E. Hennepin Ave., Minneapolis; phone: 623-3671; and 366 Jackson, St. Paul; phone: 222-2226), with its sloppy, piquant-sauced ribs;

The Pickled Parrot (26 N. Fifth St., Minneapolis; phone: 332-0673), known for its prize-winning hickory-smoked ribs; *The Smoke House* (500 E. Lake St., Minneapolis, phone: 824-0558), with its popular rib tips; and *Ted Cook's 19th Hole Barbeque* (2814 E. 38th St., Minneapolis, phone 721-2023), where pork ribs are the specialty of the house.

Nashville

At-a-Glance

SEEING THE CITY

The *Pinnacle* restaurant atop the *Holiday Inn Crowne Plaza* downtown (Seventh and Union; phone: 742-6015) makes a complete rotation every half hour, providing an excellent view of the city, well worth the cost of lunch, dinner, or a drink.

SPECIAL PLACES

Most of the outstanding attractions are within a couple of miles of the downtown area or are along the southern and eastern outskirts of the city.

DOWNTOWN

DOWNTOWN PRESBYTERIAN CHURCH Designed by renowned architect William Strickland and completed in 1848 after a fire destroyed the original (ca. 1808), this church is a rare example of the Egyptian Revival style popular in the mid-1800s. The highly stylized interior, complete with desert clouds painted on the ceiling, was renovated in the 1880s. Closed weekends except for church services. No admission charge. 154 Fifth Ave. N. (phone: 254-7584).

FORT NASHBORO This partially reconstructed pioneer fort is where Nashville began back in 1779. Open daily. No admission charge. 170 First Ave. N. For information, contact the *Metro Department of Parks and Recreation* (phone: 862-8400).

RYMAN AUDITORIUM Home of the *Grand Ole Opry* between 1943 and 1974, the *Ryman* has recently undergone renovations, expanding its museum displays, restoring the old dressing rooms used by *Opry* performers, and adding modern heating and air conditioning—luxuries that were conspicuously absent during the *Opry*'s heyday. Built in 1891 as a revival temple by Tom Ryman, a riverboat captain who found religion, the auditorium has been a tourist attraction and museum since the *Opry* moved to its present home. Now, it once again hosts live country and bluegrass concerts as well as television tapings. Tours daily; shows Tuesdays through Saturdays. Separate admission charge for each. 116 Opry Pl. (phone: 254-1445).

TENNESSEE STATE CAPITOL Completed in 1859, this picturesque hilltop building was a favorite of its designer, architect William Strickland, who is entombed here. Open daily; tours available weekdays. No admission charge. 505 Deaderick (phone: 741-0830).

MUSIC ROW

COUNTRY MUSIC HALL OF FAME AND MUSEUM Memorabilia of country music stars—such as Elvis Presley's solid gold Cadillac, comedienne Minnie Pearl's straw hat with dangling price tag, Chet Atkins's first guitar, and rare film footage of Patsy Cline—celebrate 60-plus years of the *Grand*

Ole Opry. Special exhibitions or current country stars or country music history are shown. Open daily. Admission charge. Music Row at 4 Music Sq. E. (phone: 256-1639). Included in *Hall of Fame* tours is *Studio B,* where Elvis Presley, Charley Pride, Eddy Arnold, and a score of other greats recorded for RCA in the 1950s and 1960s. Guides discuss its history and the Nashville recording industry. Open daily. Admission to *Studio B* is included in the *Hall of Fame* charge. 17th Ave. at Roy Acuff St. (phone: 256-1639).

EAST

GRAND OLE OPRY This star-studded country-music spectacular is well worth the planning it takes to get tickets. More than a third of the 60-odd acts under contract to the *Opry* will perform on a given night, and you're bound to like some if not all of them. There are shows Fridays and Saturdays year-round. Between *Memorial Day* and *Labor Day,* there also are matinees four days a week. The first show on Saturday night is aired live on radio. All seats are reserved, and if you don't have tickets, call the *Opry*'s *Information Center* to see if any are available. *Information Center,* 2808 Opryland Dr. (phone: 889-3060).

OPRYLAND USA Full of trees and flowers, this 120-acre site on the banks of the Cumberland River at the edge of the city is a treat to behold. But *Opryland* really shines when it comes to music—not just country and bluegrass, as you might expect, but also rock 'n' roll, gospel, Broadway show tunes, and more; up to a dozen stage shows each day, with more than 400 performers. The complex includes the *Grand Ole Opry* and the *General Jackson* showboat, an entertainment palace that cruises the Cumberland River (also see *Eating Out*). There are thrill rides, too: *Chaos,* an eight-story-high ride that incorporates lasers (riders wear 3-D glasses to make images come alive); the *Wabash Cannonball,* a twisting corkscrew roller coaster; the wild *Grizzly River Rampage,* a huge and satisfyingly long whitewater rafting adventure; the *Screamin' Delta Demon* bobsled adventure; and more. Every *Memorial Day* weekend, the big *Opryland Gospel Jubilee* attracts some of the country's top-name gospel groups to the park; throughout the year, television specials are taped here (tickets are free to park guests), and top country stars perform from spring to autumn. Closed weekdays in the spring and fall and from November through March. Separate admission charges for *Opryland,* the *Grand Ole Opry,* and the showboat. 2802 Opryland Dr. (phone: 889-6611 or 889-6700).

HERMITAGE Once the home of President Andrew Jackson, this magnificent old plantation home is now a museum devoted to the Jackson family. *Tulip Grove,* a Greek Revival house completed in 1836, is also on the grounds. The museum features artifacts from the time the Jacksons lived in the mansion, details about its restoration, and a 20-minute film on the Jacksons. Tours are available. Open daily. Admission charge. About a 30-minute drive from downtown in Hermitage (phone: 889-2941).

SOUTH

TRAVELLERS' REST The home of John Overton, one of Nashville's first settlers, has been restored, expanded, and filled with furniture, letters, and

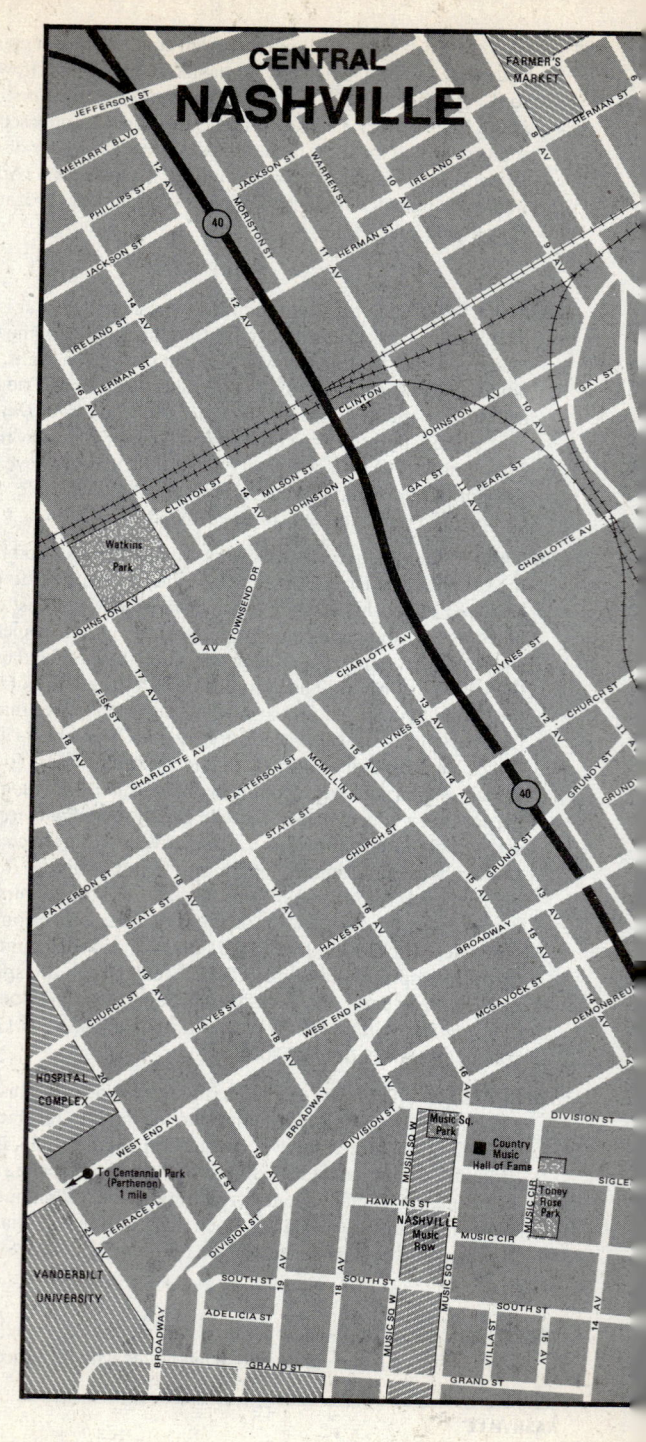

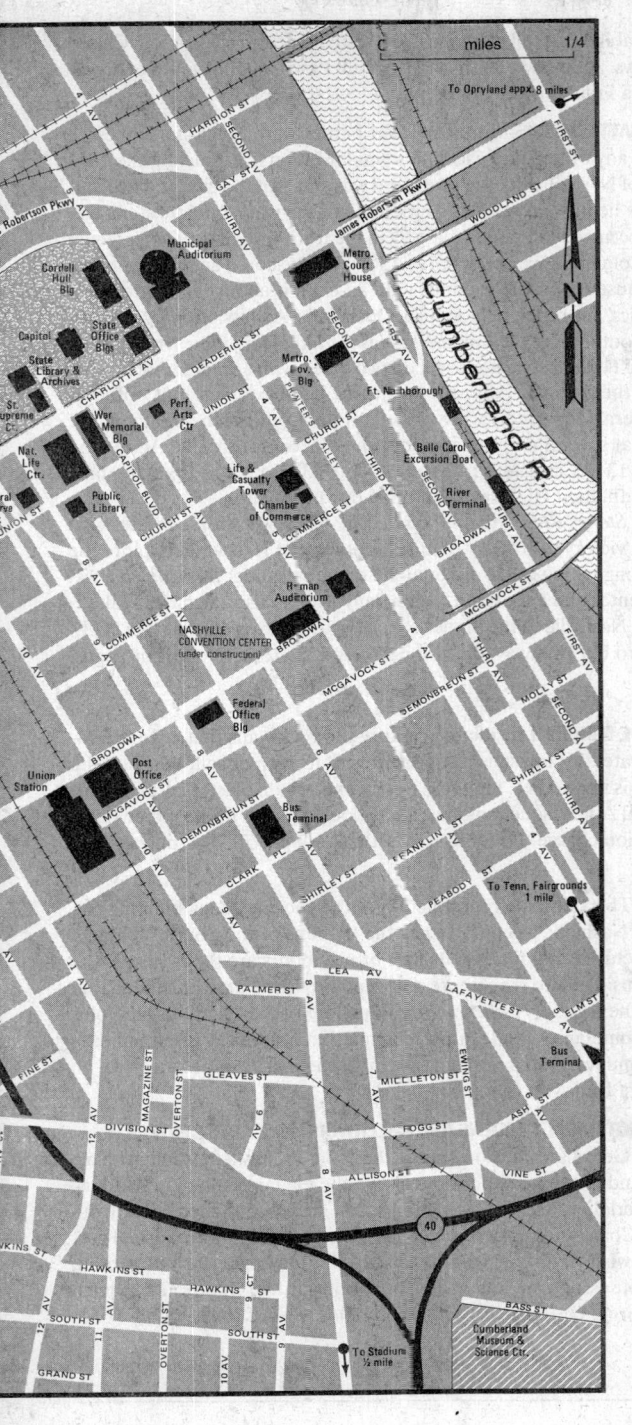

memorabilia that tell of Tennessee's settlement and civilization. Closed Mondays. Admission charge. 636 Farrell Pkwy., 6 miles south of downtown via Franklin Rd./US 31 (phone: 832-2962).

CIVIL WAR BATTLEFIELDS More Civil War battles were fought in Tennessee than in any other state except Virginia. Markers chronicling the 1864 Battle of Nashville dot the south and west sides of the city, and two battlefields lie just a few miles south. One of the war's bloodiest engagements occurred in Franklin, largely in the front yard of the *Carter House* (1140 Columbia Ave.; phone: 791-1861). This restored antebellum home has a museum on the grounds with an exhibit about the battle, Civil War relics, and other memorabilia. Open daily. Admission charge. About 1 mile southeast of the *Carter House* is *Carnton Plantation,* a beautifully restored Federal-style house set on two acres, with a Confederate cemetery on the grounds. After the battle, the bodies of six slain Confederate generals reportedly were placed on the front porch, and there are tales that several ghosts still haunt the place. Open daily. Admission charge. 1345 Carnton La. (phone: 794-0903). To get to Franklin, take I-65 south, then Highway 96 into the downtown area.

The *Stones River National Battlefield,* where the Confederates won a major victory in 1862, is 20 miles southeast of Nashville. Explore the park along hiking trails, either alone or with a guide; there's also a visitors' center and a museum. Open daily. No admission charge. Take I-24 from Nashville to the Stones River/Highway 96 exit, go east on Highway 96 to US Highway 41. Turn north on US 41, then follow the signs.

WEST

BELLE MEADE MANSION Inside the century-old rock walls that edge the 24-acre estate, this house is just a shadow of its former self, but even the shadow is impressive: immense pillars and ornate plaster cornices outside, and Adamesque moldings and a double parlor inside. Open daily. Admission charge. Harding Rd. at Leake Ave., US 70S (phone: 356-0501).

PARTHENON This full-scale reproduction of the ancient Greek building celebrates Nashville's reputation as the "Athens of the South." Though the structure is not marble, its four bronze doors are the largest in the world. Inside there is an impressive replica of the statue of Athena that graced the original *Parthenon,* reproductions of the Elgin Marbles, plus pre-Columbian art and various changing exhibitions. Closed Sundays and Mondays. Admission charge. In *Centennial Park* at 25th Ave. N. and West End Ave. (phone: 862-8431).

TENNESSEE BOTANICAL GARDENS AND CHEEKWOOD FINE ARTS CENTER *Cheekwood,* a Georgian mansion built in the 1930s, is now a museum with art shows and traveling exhibitions. Note the elegant Palladian window, the chandelier, and the swooping spiral staircase (which came from Queen Charlotte's palace at Kew, England). Outdoors are formal gardens, a wisteria arbor, wildflower gardens, a Japanese sand garden, greenhouses, and an outstanding boxwood garden. Open daily. Admission charge. On Forrest Park Dr., 7 miles west of town (phone: 353-2140).

> **EXTRA SPECIAL**
>
> You'll see the announcements for tours of the homes of the stars on big billboards on the way into town, and even if you ordinarily hate group excursions, you may like these for a glimpse into what makes Nashville tick. Each of the following offers several all-day, half-day, evening, or nightlife tours: *Country Western/Gray Line* (2416 Music Valley Dr.; phone: 883-5555; 800-251-1864); *Grand Ole Opry Tours* (2808 Opryland Dr.; phone: 889-9490); and *Nashville Tours* (2626 Music Valley Dr.; phone: 889-4646).

Sources and Resources

TOURIST INFORMATION

For brochures, maps and general tourist information, write the *Nashville Area Chamber of Commerce* (161 Fourth Ave. N., Nashville, TN 37219; phone: 259-4755); or contact the *Convention and Visitors Bureau* (161 Fourth Ave. N.; phone: 259-4700), both closed weekends. The tourist information center at exit 85 on I-65N, just east of downtown (phone: 259-4747), is open daily. Contact the Tennessee state tourism hotline (615-741-2158) for maps, calendars of events, health updates, and travel advisories.

LOCAL COVERAGE *The Tennessean*, morning daily; the *Nashville Banner*, afternoon daily. The former publishes a complete events listing on Fridays and Sundays; the latter on Thursdays. Both available at newsstands. The *Nashville Scene*, a free weekly paper available at many stores and restaurants, publishes a comprehensive listing of area happenings, including a list of every nightspot in town. The *Nashville Visitor's Guide*, on sale at most newsstands, is as comprehensive a city guide as you'll see anywhere.

TELEVISION STATIONS WKRN Channel 2–ABC; WSMV Channel 4–NBC; WTVF Channel 5–CBS; WDCN Channel 8–PBS; and WZTV Channel 17–Fox.

RADIO STATIONS AM: WSIX 980 (country music); WAMB 1160 (big band); WKDA 1240 (contemporary rock); and WLAC 1510 (news/talk). FM: WPLN 90 (classical/public radio); WZEZ 93 (easy listening); WRLT 100 (alternative jazz/rock); and WGFX 104.5 (oldies rock).

TELEPHONE The area code for Nashville is 615.

SALES TAX The city sales tax for most goods is 7¾%; the hotel tax is 11¼%.

CLIMATE Nashville's temperatures hover around the 80s and 90s F in summer, dropping into the 40s and 30s (occasionally into the 20s or lower) between November and February. It gets humid in the summer; expect thunderstorms from March through late summer and rain in the spring and in October and November.

GETTING AROUND

AIRPORT The *Nashville Metropolitan Airport* is a 15- to 20-minute drive from downtown (30 minutes or more during rush hours). Many hotels provide free transportation from the airport; check with your hotel when making reservations.

BUS They are inconvenient at best, but buses are available (phone: 242-4433 for route information). The fare is 90¢.

CAR RENTAL The major national agencies are represented.

TAXI Nashville's principal cab companies are *Yellow* (phone: 256-0101) and *Checker* (phone: 254-5031).

LOCAL SERVICES

AUDIOVISUAL EQUIPMENT *Allied Audio-Visual Services* (phone: 883-4000); *Consolidated Media Systems* (phone: 244-3933); *Nashville's Media Services* (phone: 255-7959), specializing in computer projection.

BABY-SITTING If you think you might need a sitter, ask your hotel or motel to make the arrangements when you book your room. *Duck Duck Goose* (5133 Harding Rd.; phone: 352-4343) offers drop-in child care.

CONVENTION FACILITIES The *Nashville Convention Center* (601 Commerce St.; phone: 742-2000) offers 118,675 square feet of exhibit space and 30,232 square feet of meeting room space. The *Opryland* hotel (phone: 871-5800) also is a popular convention facility.

COMPUTER RENTAL The *MacFactory* (phone: 327-1758).

DRY CLEANER/TAILOR *Dodge Cleaners* (21st and Church Sts.; phone: 327-3144) and nine other locations; many hotels and office buildings offer dry-cleaning services with pickup and delivery.

LIMOUSINE *Capitol Limousines* (phone: 361-3055); *Limousine Connection of Nashville* (phone: 360-8700).

MECHANICS People come from all the way across town to have their foreign and domestic cars fixed at *Garrett Service Center* (2600 Lebanon Rd., Donelson, near *Opryland;* phone: 883-1386). Also good for both foreign and domestic cars is *Wood's Garage* (108 28th Ave. N., by *Centennial Park;* phone: 327-3861).

MEDICAL EMERGENCY *Vanderbilt University Hospital* (22nd and Garland Aves.; phone: 322-3391).

MESSENGER SERVICES *Courier Systems* (phone: 360-8090).

MONEY TRANSFERS *American Express MoneyGram* (phone: 800-926-9400 for information; 800-866-8800 for money transfers); *Western Union Financial Services* (phone: 800-325-6000 or 800-325-4176).

NATIONAL/INTERNATIONAL COURIER *FedEx* (phone: 800-238-5355).

PHARMACY *Farmers Market Pharmacy* (715 Jefferson St.; phone: 242-5561), open daily.

PHOTOCOPIES *Kinko's* has several locations (including 400 21st Ave. S.; phone: 327-4224); *PIP Printing* also has several locations (including 162 Fourth Ave. N.; phone: 254-7514).

POST OFFICE Main office (Royal Pkwy.; phone: 885-1005).

PROFESSIONAL PHOTOGRAPHER *Greg Kinney Photography* (phone: 297-8084); *Bob Schatz Studio* (phone: 254-7197).

TELECONFERENCE FACILITIES *Opryland* (see *Checking In,* below).

TRANSLATOR *Language Services* (phone: 292-7916).

WESTERN UNION/TELEX Many offices are located around the city (phone: 800-325-6000 to find the location nearest you).

OTHER *Events Unlimited* (phone: 329-3091), meeting and convention planning.

SPECIAL EVENTS

The annual *Tennessee Crafts Fair* (PO Box 12006, Nashville, TN 37212; phone: 665-0502), one of the largest shows of its kind in the South, is held in *Centennial Park* on the first full weekend in May. On the second Saturday in May is the *Iroquois Steeplechase,* the day-long series of eight races that's the oldest amateur steeplechase meet in the US (Old Hickory Blvd. in *Percy Warner Park,* 11 miles south of Nashville; for information: PO Box 22711, Nashville, TN 37202; or call 373-2130, beginning in February). The *Opryland Gospel Jubilee* brings gospel bands, choruses, and lots of extra music to the theme park every year over *Memorial Day* weekend (see *Special Places*). *Summer Lights,* a downtown festival produced by the *Metro Nashville Arts Commission* (phone: 726-1875) and held the first weekend after *Memorial Day,* lights up 12 city blocks from the historic Second Avenue "Market Street" area to Legislative Plaza. Local musicians are showcased along with street performers, visual arts exhibits, and other entertainment. Many notable restaurants offer specialties from street booths, and area shops have special outdoor stands. The *International Country Music Fan Fair* (2804 Opryland Dr., Nashville, TN 37214; phone: 889-7503), usually scheduled for the first week of June, brings thousands for five days of spectacular shows, autograph sessions, concerts, and a *Grand Masters Fiddling Contest. Independence Day* celebrations include fireworks displays, performances ranging from the *Nashville Symphony* to country and rock bands, and other entertainment in a huge street party in *Riverfront Park.* In late September or October, there's the *National Quartet Convention* (Dept. N, 54 Music Sq. W., Nashville, TN 37203; phone: 800-333-4849), five days of top-name gospel singing at the *Nashville Municipal Auditorium.* The annual *Fall Crafts Fair* (PO Box 120066, Nashville, TN 37212; phone: 665-0502), organized by the *Tennessee Association of Craft Artists,* is held on a September weekend in *Centennial Park.*

MUSEUMS

In addition to those described above in *Special Places,* Nashville has several other museums worth noting.

CUMBERLAND MUSEUM AND SCIENCE CENTER This children's museum offers live animal shows, science demonstrations, and experiments to try. Closed Mondays except in summer. Admission charge. 800 Ridley Blvd. (phone: 862-5160).

TENNESSEE STATE MUSEUM Located in the *Tennessee Performing Arts Center*, with a branch devoted to military history in the *War Memorial Building*, this museum mounts frequent exhibitions of local arts and crafts. Open daily. No admission charge. Seventh and Union Sts. (phone: 741-2692).

VAN VECHTEN GALLERY Housed here is the *Stieglitz Collection*, more than 100 works of 20th-century art donated to *Fisk University* by artist Georgia O'Keeffe after the death of her husband, photographer Alfred Stieglitz. Closed Mondays. Admission charge. *Fisk University*, 18th Ave. N. and Jackson St. (phone: 329-8543).

SHOPPING

There's something for all tastes, from small, exclusive shops to large, encompassing malls. The region's largest shopping malls are *Hickory Hollow* (near I-24 at Bell Rd.), *Rivergate* (I-65 at Two Mile Pike), *Bellevue Center* (I-40, Bellevue exit), and *Cool Springs Galleria* (I-65 near Franklin). Brave these on weekends only if you enjoy fighting crowds. The *Mall at Green Hills* (entrances off Hillsboro and Abbott-Martin Rds.) offers upscale shops and two major department stores, and is usually less crowded. Antiques shops are all over the city, but several good ones are clustered on Eighth Avenue near the intersection with Wedgewood. For a fun afternoon of browsing, try *White Way Antique Mall* (1200 Villa Place, behind the *White Way Cleaners* on Edgehill).

Davis-Kidd Booksellers The best bookstore in town has a pleasant café built into its upper level where you can sip wine or herb tea and read your purchase. 4007 Hillsboro Rd. (phone: 385-2645).

McClure's The city's best department store has clothes you won't find anywhere else in town. 6000 Highway 100, Belle Meade (phone: 356-8822) or 257 Franklin Rd. in Brentwood (phone: 377-3769).

Stanford Square This collection of exclusive stores features clothing shops and *American Artisan* (phone: 298-4691), which sells interesting objets d'art and jewelry by local and national craftsmen. 4231 Harding Rd.

SPORTS AND FITNESS

BASEBALL The Nashville *Sounds,* a Triple-A farm team for the Chicago *White Sox,* play in *Greer Stadium* (Chestnut, between Fourth and Eighth Aves. S.; phone: 242-4371).

FISHING AND BOATING Two manmade lakes—Old Hickory (phone: 822-4846) and Percy Priest (phone: 889-1975)—are a 20-minute drive from downtown, and several others are within an hour or so. Call the Resource Management office at each lake for boat and equipment rental details. The *Tennessee Wildlife Resources Agency* (phone: 781-6500) can provide details about other area lakes.

FITNESS CENTERS The *Centennial Sportsplex* (25th Ave. N.; phone: 862-8480), which is open to the public for a fee, offers a fitness center with a pool, weight rooms, aerobics programs, and an ice rink.

GOLF There are 10 public courses in Nashville. The best 18-holers are at *Harpeth Hills* (Old Hickory Blvd.. off Rte. 431 S.; phone: 862-8493) and *Nashville Golf and Athletic Club* (Moore's Lane in Franklin; phone: 370-3346). The only 27-hole course is at *McCabe Park* (46th Ave. N. at Murphy Rd.; phone: 269-6951).

JOGGING Follow Church Street (which turns into Elliston Place) to *Centennial Park*, about 1½ miles from downtown and near *Vanderbilt University;* or drive or take the West End–Belle Meade bus (from Sixth and Church, or Deaderick at Fourth or Sixth) to *Percy Warner Park*, 11 miles south of Nashville. Jogging in either area after dark is not recommended.

STOCK CAR RACING Every Saturday night from April through mid-September, there's local racing at the *Tennessee State Fairgrounds* (Wedgewood Ave. between Fourth and Eighth Aves. S.; phone: 726-1818).

SWIMMING Open throughout the summer, *Wave Country* (on Two Rivers Pkwy. near *Opryland*; phone: 883-1092) is the Southeast's largest surf-producing pool. Indoor swimming is available year-round at the *Centennial Sportsplex* (25th Ave. N ; phone: 862-8480).

TENNIS The major public facility is at the *Centennial Sportsplex* (25th Ave. N.; phone: 862-8490), where 17 courts are open from March through October and four indoor courts are open year-round. There's indoor tennis year-round at *Nashboro Athletic Club* (2250 Murfreesboro Rd.; phone: 361-3242), which also has outdoor clay courts available in summer.

THEATER

The *Tennessee Performing Arts Center* (505 Deaderick St.; phone: 741-2787) is home to touring Broadway shows and regional companies. Lively children's theater and classics for adults are presented by the *Nashville Academy Theatre* (724 Second Ave. S.; phone: 254-9103), the city's resident professional company. The *Tennessee Repertory Theatre* performs five plays or musicals each year in the *Polk Theater* of the *Tennessee Performing Arts Center.* Two small companies that perform recent works are *Actors Playhouse* (2318 West End; phone: 327-0049), with productions from September through May; and *The Circle Players* (phone: 383-7469), who present several plays each year, either at the *Johnson Theatre* of the *Tennessee Performing Arts Center* or at the *Alternate Circle Theater* (1703 Church St.). For dinner-theater, try *Chaffin's Barn Dinner Theater* (8204 Hwy. 100; phone: 646-9977).

TV SHOW TAPINGS

The Nashville Network (TNN), a cable TV network originating in *Opryland*, tapes a number of programs before live audiences. For information, contact The Nashville Network, Information Services (2806 Opryland Dr., Nashville, TN 37214; phone: 883-7000).

MUSIC

In addition to the omnipresent *Opry,* the *Nashville Symphony* gives concerts from September through May in the *Tennessee Performing Arts Center* (the symphony box office is at 208 23rd Ave. N.; phone: 329-3033). On Friday and Sunday nights from June through August, there are musical programs at *Centennial Park.* For information, call the *Parks and Recreation Department*'s activities number (phone: 862-8400). Chamber music is offered (often at no charge) at *Fisk University,* at the *Blair School of Music* on the *Vanderbilt* campus, and at *Cheekwood Fine Arts Center* on weekends (phone: 356-8000).

NIGHTCLUBS AND NIGHTLIFE

Nashville isn't called "Music City, USA" for nothing. Even motels sometimes turn up good entertainers. Check newspapers and the *Nashville Visitor's Guide* for a rundown of places to hear country music.

Gaylord Entertainment, which runs *Opryland* and the *Ryman Auditorium,* recently opened the *Wildhorse Saloon* (phone: 889-6600) on historic Second Avenue. The saloon, which is connected to *Opryland* by two 100-passenger river taxis, is a contemporary country-music dance and performance hall used as a set for TNN (The Nashville Network) tapings. There's a limited-menu restaurant and dance instruction. Up the street is *Club Mere Bulles* (phone: 256-2582), which features modern rock and jazz in the club section and a full-service restaurant. From Second Avenue, it's a four-block walk or a short trolley ride to Printer's Alley, where, along with some striptease joints and seedy-looking bars, there are standouts like the *Captain's Table* (phone: 256-3353), a silver and linen tablecloth sort of place, and *Boots Randolph's* (phone: 256-5500), which features Boots (when he's in town), comedy acts, and a house band. For bluegrass, try *Station Inn* (402 12th Ave. S.; phone: 255-3307). Hear jazz, rock, country, and folk music at the nationally renowned *Bluebird Café* (4104 Hillsboro Rd.; phone: 383-1461), which frequently hosts Writers' Nights to give local songwriters a chance to try out their compositions; *Boardwalk Café* (4114 Nolensville Rd.; phone: 832-5104); the *Bullpen Lounge* at the *Stock Yard* restaurant (901 Second Ave. N.; phone: 255-6464); and *328 Performance Hall* (328 Fourth Ave. S.; phone: 259-3288). The city's most active dance club is the *Ace of Clubs* (114 Second Ave. S.; phone: 254-2237), with good music (live bands Mondays through Thursdays) and a big dance floor. Most major hotels have entertainment in their lounges; the *Opryland* hotel has three lounges that offer good live country music. The *General Jackson* showboat (phone: 889-6611 for reservations) offers dinner and an excellent musical show as well as entertainment in the lounge before dinner. *Zanies Comedy Showplace* (2025 Eighth Ave.; phone: 269-0221) features stand-up comedians nightly.

Best in Town

CHECKING IN

Along with dozens of motels, there are some venerable (though refurbished) "Southern Belles" in Nashville. Expect to pay $80 or more per night for a double room at hotels listed as expensive; $45 to $80 at hostelries classified as moderate. Unless noted, hotels have air conditioning, private baths, TV sets, and telephones. All hotels are in the 615 area code unless otherwise indicated.

EXPENSIVE

Hermitage Built in 1910, this luxurious Beaux Arts showpiece has 112 suites, an oak-paneled bar, a fine dining room, and an outrageous Art Deco men's room (a few local ladies have sneaked in for a peek). There's also meeting space for 250 and express checkout. 231 Sixth Ave. N., downtown (phone: 244-3121; 800-251-1908; fax: 254-6909).

Loews Vanderbilt Plaza This modern tower hotel has 338 luxurious rooms, including 10 parlor suites and three executive suites. There's also a restaurant, café, gameroom, and lounge, plus meeting facilities for up to 1,100. Amenities include health club facilities, 24-hour room service, a concierge, secretarial services, A/V equipment, photocopiers, and express checkout. 2100 West End Ave. (phone: 320-1700; 800-336-3335; fax: 320-5019).

Opryland This sprawling hotel has 1,891 rooms and 120 suites near the *Opry* and *Opryland* (but 20 minutes from downtown). The complex includes five lounges, four restaurants, and dozens of specialty shops. The *Old Hickory Room* is a good restaurant, serving continental and traditional Southern fare. The hotel also has a beautiful indoor conservatory with suspended walkways. Other amenities include 24-hour room service, concierge services, 53 meeting rooms, A/V equipment, photocopiers, and express checkout. 2800 Opryland Dr. (phone: 889-1000; fax: 871-7741).

Stouffer's Nashville Next to the *Convention Center* and *Church Street Center*, a mall with shopping and restaurants, this 673-room downtown highrise has location, location, location. There is casual dining at its *Commerce Street Bar and Grill*, and the *Bridge Deli* offers sandwiches. Business amenities include 18 meeting rooms, 24-hour room service, concierge and secretarial services, A/V equipment, photocopiers, computers, and express checkout. 611 Commerce St. (phone: 255-8400; 800-468-3571; fax: 255-8202).

Union Station Located in the National Historic Landmark building that originally was the city's train station, this property now offers 124 uniquely styled rooms along with 13 suites. There are two restaurants: *Arthur's*, which serves fine continental food (see *Eating Out*), and the *Broadway Bistro* café. Sports facilities are available at a nearby fitness center. Other conveniences include five meeting rooms, A/V equipment, and photocopiers. 1001 Broadway (phone: 726-1001; 800-331-2123; fax: 248-3554).

MODERATE

Hampton Inn Vanderbilt Among the extras at this comfortable 171-room hostelry are hearty complimentary continental breakfasts, an exercise facility, and an outdoor pool. Photocopiers and A/V equipment also are available. 1919 West End Ave. and three other area locations (phone: 329-1144; 800-HAMPTON; fax: 320-7112).

Holiday Inn Vanderbilt Though a fairly standard link in the Holiday Inn chain, this 300-room high-rise is a good value. It's conveniently close to *Vanderbilt University*, a horde of good restaurants, the *Parthenon*, *Centennial Park*, and some good nightspots. Business amenities include eight meeting rooms, a fitness center, secretarial services, A/V equipment, and express checkout. 2613 West End Ave. (phone: 327-4707; 800-465-4329; fax: 327-8034).

EATING OUT

Nashville is, as they say, a good eating town, with lots of small, unpretentious restaurants where you'll find fried chicken and shrimp, steaks, home-style vegetables, and the like. Dinner for two (without drinks, wine, tax, or tips) at places listed as expensive will cost $40 or more. Expect to pay $20 to $40 at those categorized as moderate, and less than $20 at inexpensive places. Unless otherwise noted, restaurants serve lunch and dinner. All restaurants are in the 615 area code unless otherwise indicated.

EXPENSIVE

Arthur's Seven-course continental dining (the menu changes daily) and plush decor characterize this chic eating place. Open daily. Reservations necessary. Major credit cards accepted. *Union Station Hotel*, 1001 Broadway (phone: 255-1494).

Mario's Owner Mario Ferrari serves a variety of Italian veal dishes—try the veal saltimbocca—as well as inventive pasta entrées and seasonal specials. Open for dinner only; closed Sundays. Reservations necessary. Major credit cards accepted. 2005 Broadway (phone: 327-3232).

Wild Boar This is not the place to eat light, but it's a good choice if you want to indulge in nicely cooked game or fish after warming up with one of the many appetizers, accompanied by a fine wine and finished off with a rich dessert. Open daily; dinner only on weekends. Reservations advised. Major credit cards accepted. 2014 Broadway (phone: 329-1313).

MODERATE

Cakewalk This small, pleasant café serves excellent and inventive meals—fish and shrimp dishes, salads, quiche, and an attractive weekend brunch. Try any of the daily specials and soups. Open daily. Reservations advised for dinner. Major credit cards accepted. 3001 West End Ave. (phone: 320-7778).

General Jackson Based at *Opryland USA*, this showboat offers brunch and dinner cruises on the Cumberland River. Entertainment is topnotch, and the food—particularly brunch—is good. Open daily, but the cruise schedule depends on the time of year. Reservations necessary well in advance. Major credit cards accepted. *Opryland USA* (phone: 889-6611).

La Paz This upscale Mexican restaurant offers an active bar, fireplaces in winter, and frozen margaritas in the summer. The menu is full of interesting variations on traditional Mexican dishes, with a Southwestern influence. Open daily; dinner only on Saturdays. No reservations. Major credit cards accepted. 3803 Cleghorn Ave. (phone: 383-5200).

Siam Café The place in town for excellent Thai food. If you're in a hurry, go through the cafeteria line and eat in the front section of the restaurant, but we recommend that you take the time to sit in the quiet back section, order one of the day's specials, and try an appetizer or two. Open daily; dinner only on Sundays. No reservations. Major credit cards accepted. Directly off Nolensville Rd. at 316 McCall (phone: 834-3181).

Sunset Grill "Do lunch" or dinner with Music Row moguls and Nashville professionals at this pleasant place, which offers an eclectic range of pasta, vegetarian dishes, and grilled fish and meat. Don't ignore the extensive dessert menu and wine list. Open daily. Reservations advised for dinner. Major credit cards accepted. 2001 Belcourt Ave. (phone: 386-3663).

INEXPENSIVE

Cooker This chain offers some of the best Southern cooking in town—nothing fancy, but plenty of big salads and stick-to-your-ribs main courses in a pleasant atmosphere. Open daily. No reservations, and expect a wait at peak hours. Major credit cards accepted. Three locations: 2609 West End Ave. (phone: 327-2925); 4770 Lebanon Rd., Hermitage (phone: 883-9700); and 1211 Murfreesboro Rd. (phone: 361-4747).

Elliston Place Soda Shop Here good lunches and dinners are served by waitresses who look as if they're about to tell you to eat all your vegetables. The tile and chrome decor from the 1940s is beautifully intact. Closed Sundays. Reservations unnecessary. No credit cards accepted. 211 Elliston Pl. (phone: 327-1090).

Loveless Motel The walls are lined with autographed photos of country music stars who have eaten here. The fried chicken, homemade biscuits, peach and blackberry preserves, and country ham (salty, the way it's supposed to be) with gravy are famous. Have breakfast anytime. Closed Mondays. Reservations advised. No credit cards accepted. Rte. 5, Hwy. 100 (phone: 646-9700).

Rotier's A real Nashville tradition, it serves typical bar food in a "Cheers"-like setting. Locals are slavishly loyal to Mrs. Rotier's cheeseburgers, and the milk shakes get rave reviews. Closed Sundays. No reservations or credit cards accepted. 2413 Elliston Pl. near Vanderbilt (phone: 327-9892).

Swett's The excellent Southern cooking here includes home-cooked pork chops, barbecued chicken and ribs, meat loaf, and side dishes that range from traditional Southern green beans to stewed apples. Open daily. Reservations unnecessary. Major credit cards accepted. 28th and Clifton (phone: 329-4418).

New Haven

At-a-Glance

SEEING THE CITY

Once used by the Quinnipiac Indians for smoke signals, the 359-foot summit of New Haven's eastern cliff in *East Rock Park* commands a panoramic view of the city, the *Yale* campus, the harbor, and on clear days, 18 miles down Long Island Sound to Bridgeport.

SPECIAL PLACES

New Haven, the first architecturally planned city in the US, was designed for walking. Laid out in nine squares, New Haven radiates from the *Green;* the 30-block area surrounding it has a cultural and historic scope that belies its geographic limits.

THE GREEN This 16-acre square of tree-lined lawns dominates the center of town south of the university. It is as much the city's focal point today as it was in the 1600s, when all public buildings were assembled here, along with the cows and pigs. The only buildings left are three churches—one Georgian, one Federal, and one Gothic Revival in style—all built between 1812 and 1815.

NEW HAVEN COLONY HISTORICAL SOCIETY A large model offers a look at New Haven of 1640, and other collections span the city's historical development over the past three centuries. Closed Mondays. No admission charge on Tuesdays. 114 Whitney Ave. (phone: 562-4183).

YALE CAMPUS AND FACILITIES Named for Elihu Yale, East India trader and donor, the university was founded in 1701 in nearby Old Saybrook. In 1716, it moved to New Haven where it flourished, becoming one of the world's most distinguished educational institutions. The lovely campus, with its ivy-covered Gothic buildings, green courtyards, and contemporary architecture, is best seen by taking a free tour led by student guides well versed in college lore. Tours are given daily, starting at the University Information Office, Phelps Gateway, 344 College St. (phone: 432-2300).

PEABODY MUSEUM OF NATURAL HISTORY Exhibits on evolutionary history include a huge skeleton of a brontosaurus, the famous *Age of Reptiles* mural by Rudolph Zallinger, and the *Hall of Mammals.* Open daily. No admission charge weekdays 3 to 5 PM. 170 Whitney Ave. (phone: 432-5050).

YALE CENTER FOR BRITISH ART AND BRITISH STUDIES Designed by Louis I. Kahn, it features works by Hogarth, Constable, Turner, Stubbs, and Blake. There are more British works here than anywhere outside Great Britain. From September through May, the museum sponsors weekly concerts. Closed Mondays. No admission charge. 1080 Chapel St. (phone: 432-2800).

YALE UNIVERSITY ART GALLERY The oldest university art museum in the country, it houses masterpieces from ancient Egypt and Greece, as well as those of artists such as Monet, Picasso, and van Gogh. Of particular interest is the collection of American paintings and decorative arts. Closed Mondays. No admission charge. 1111 Chapel St. (phone: 432-0600).

LIGHTHOUSE POINT PARK Located on Long Island Sound on the east end of town, the 1840 lighthouse overlooks 82 acres containing New Haven's best beach, *Fort Nathan Hale,* a bird sanctuary with nature trails, areas for fishing, and a beautifully restored antique carousel. Special programs include bird/nature walks and concerts during the summer. Open year-round. Lighthouse Rd. (phone: 787-8005).

> **EXTRA SPECIAL**
>
> Some 60 miles east of New Haven on I-95 is the town of Mystic, where the fastest clipper ships and the first ironclad vessels were built in the 19th century. The town has been restored as a 19th-century seaport. You can stroll along the waterfront of the Mystic River or down the cobblestone streets lined with quaint seaport homes.

Sources and Resources

TOURIST INFORMATION

For general information, contact the *Greater New Haven Convention and Visitors Bureau,* One Long Wharf Dr. (phone: 777-8550; 800-332-7829), the *Greater New Haven Chamber of Commerce* (195 Church St.; phone: 787-6735), or the *Cultural Affairs Department* of the *Mayor's Office* (phone: 787-8956), all of which are closed weekends. You also can visit the *Long Wharf Information Office* (at Exit 46 off I-95; phone: 776-0203), run by the visitors' bureau and open daily from mid-April through mid-October. *Yale* has its own information center at Phelps Gateway (344 College St.; phone: 432-2300), open daily except major holidays. Contact the Connecticut state tourism hotline (phone: 258-4290) for maps, calendars of events, health updates, and travel advisories.

LOCAL COVERAGE The *New Haven Register,* mornings and Sundays; and the *New Haven Advocate* (published Thursdays). The Friday *Register* and the *Advocate* list the coming week's attractions. The *Register* is available only at newsstands; the *Advocate* is distributed throughout the city. Recommended reading includes *Enjoying New Haven, A Guide to the Area* by Elizabeth Fledge and Eugenia Fayen (East Rock Press, Ltd.; $8.95) and *Connecticut's Best Dining* by Patricia Brooks (De Gustibus Press; $8.95), which has many New Haven food listings.

TELEVISION STATIONS WFSB Channel 3–CBS; WTNH Channel 8–ABC; WVIT Channel 30–NBC; and WEDH Channel 65–PBS.

RADIO STATIONS AM: WELI 960 (oldies, rock, talk); WAVZ 1300 (oldies); and WNHC 1340 (urban contemporary). FM: WPLR 99.1 (rock).

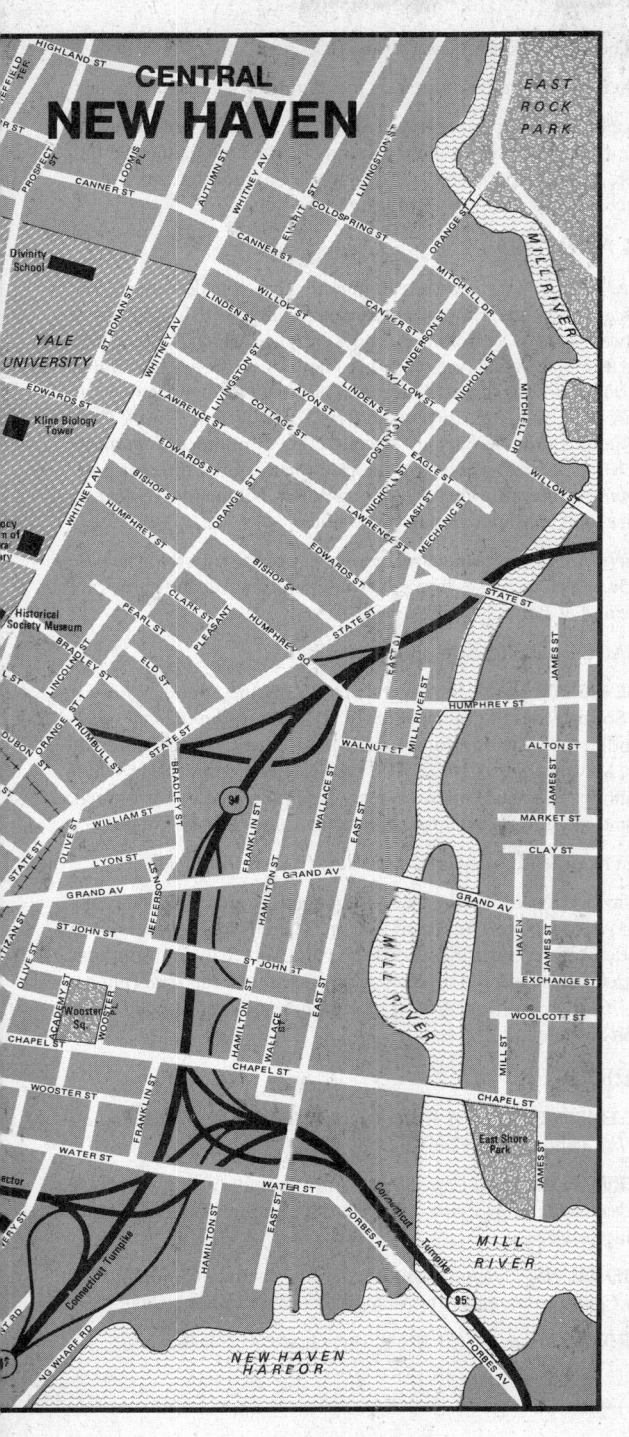

TELEPHONE The area code for New Haven is 203.

SALES TAX There is a 6% state sales tax on meals and most consumer goods.

CLIMATE Since the city is on Long Island Sound, it gets a sea breeze, which gives some relief during the humid summers, the spring, and the fall. However, New Haven usually gets a lot of rain; and that sea breeze often becomes raw during the cold, snowy winters.

GETTING AROUND

AIRPORT *Tweed–New Haven Airport* is a 15-minute drive from downtown. The *Connecticut Transit* bus is not recommended for those with luggage, since it stops two blocks away from the airport entrance, which is a long hike from the terminal. A taxi (see below) is a better bet. *Tweed–New Haven* handles only domestic flights. Those with international connections can get to *JFK* and *La Guardia* airports in New York City and *Newark International* in northern New Jersey by contacting *Connecticut Limousine* (phone: 878-2222; 800-472-5466); the ride to any of the three airports from its terminal (on Brewery St. at Long Wharf, behind the *New Haven Post Office*) will take approximately two hours.

BUS *Connecticut Transit* serves the downtown area and the suburbs. The base fare is 95¢, which increases by zone. Route information and guides are available at 470 James St. (phone: 624-0151).

CAR RENTAL All the national firms are represented.

CRUISING THE HARBOR In season, several vessels ply the Sound. *Schooner Inc.* (60 South Water St.; phone: 865-1737) sails the *Quinnipiack*, a 91-foot wooden tall ship, on windjamming nature trips, Wednesdays and Sundays, May through early October. *Liberty Belle Cruises* (Long Wharf Dock; phone: 562-4163) operates ferry-type power boats for brunch, sunset, and moonlight dancing cruises daily, June through August.

TAXI Cabs can be ordered by calling *Metro Taxi* (phone: 777-7777).

TRAIN New Haven is located on the main *Amtrak* line (phone: 777-4002; 800-872-7245) between New York and Boston. There is frequent service to those cities and to Hartford. Service to New York City and southern Connecticut is also offered by *Metro North Commuter Railroad* (phone: 800-638-7646). Trains leave from the beautifully restored *Union Station* on Union Avenue.

LOCAL SERVICES

AUDIOVISUAL EQUIPMENT *Action Media* (phone: 468-0087); *HB Communications, Inc.* (phone: 234-9246).

BUSINESS SERVICES *Audubon Copy Shoppe* (48 Whitney Ave.; phone: 865-3115); *Tyco Xerox Copy Center* (262 Elm St.; phone: 562-9723), word processing services.

COMPUTER RENTAL *USPC Rental* (360 W. 31st St.; phone: 865-4017); *PCR Personal Computer Rentals* (314 Main St., Yalesville; phone: 265-9887).

DRY CLEANER/TAILOR *Blue Jay* (51 Broadway; phone: 777-2546).

LIMOUSINE *Hy's Livery Service* (phone: 934-6331).

MECHANIC *Libby's Sales and Service* (60 Printer's La.; phone: 772-1112).

MEDICAL EMERGENCY *Yale New Haven Hospital* (20 York St.; phone: 785-2222).

MESSENGER SERVICES *Royal Messenger Service* (phone: 488-6318).

MONEY TRANSFERS *American Express MoneyGram* (phone: 800-926-9400 for information; 800-866-8800 for money transfers); *Western Union Financial Services* (phone: 800-325-6000 or 800-325-4176).

NATIONAL/INTERNATIONAL COURIER *DHL Worldwide Express* (phone: 800-972-2187); *FedEx* (phone: 800-238-5355).

PHARMACY *Medical Center Pharmacy* (50 York St.; phone: 776-7064), open weekdays 7 AM to 11 PM, weekends 9 AM to 6 PM.

PHOTOCOPIES *Audubon Copy Shoppe* (see *Business Services*, above); *Kinko's* (1060 Chapel; phone: 782-6055), open 24 hours daily.

POST OFFICE Main office (50 Brewery St.; phone: 782-7209); Federal Station (170 Orange St.; phone: 782-7110).

SECRETARY *Diversified Employment* (phone: 397-2500); *Olsten Services* (phone: 777-4477).

TRANSLATOR *Berlitz* (phone: 787-4245); *Interpreters and Translators, Inc.* (Manchester; phone: 647-0686).

WESTERN UNION/TELEX Many offices are located around the city (phone: 800-325-6000 to find the location nearest you).

SPECIAL EVENTS

Special indeed this year are the *Special Olympics World Summer Games* in July (phone: 498-7773). The *New Haven Jazz Festival*, a series of concerts featuring well-known artists, runs from early July through mid-August. In August, the *Volvo International Tennis Tournament* is held at *Yale University*'s *Connecticut Tennis Center* (phone: 776-7331 for information; 772-3838 or 800-548-6586 for tickets). The 20-kilometer *Road Race* takes place annually on *Labor Day*. The weekend before *Thanksgiving* in odd-numbered years, the *Yale-Harvard* football game is played at the *Yale Bowl*, with all the fanfare of a traditional rivalry.

MUSEUMS

With *Yale*'s fine collections and New Haven's *Historical Society* (see *Special Places*), the city touches all cultural bases.

BEINECKE RARE BOOK AND MANUSCRIPT LIBRARY Home of a 1455 Gutenberg Bible, hailed as the first printed volume. There's also an abundant collection of first editions and original letters and manuscripts from William Shakespeare, Charles Dickens, Gertrude Stein, and Eugene O'Neill. Closed Sundays. No admission charge. 121 Wall St. (phone: 432-2977).

YALE COLLECTION OF MUSICAL INSTRUMENTS One of the world's finest collections of historical keyboard instruments, as well as a representative selection of Western European wind and string instruments. Closed

Fridays through Mondays, August, and during all *Yale* recesses. There are frequent concerts. No admission charge. 15 Hillhouse Ave. (phone: 432-0822).

SPORTS AND FITNESS

BASEBALL The New Haven *Ravens,* a Double-A expansion team, plays at the smartly refurbished *Yale Field* (252 Derby Ave., West Haven; phone: 782-1666 for information and tickets).

FITNESS CENTERS The *Downtown Health and Racquet Club* (230 George St.; phone: 787-6501) has racquetball, squash, and basketball courts, a sauna, and Nautilus equipment. Open to non-members for a fee and to guests of some local hotels.

FOOTBALL The *Bulldogs, Yale*'s popular football team, play at the *Yale Bowl* (Rte. 34, between Derby Ave. and Chapel St.; phone: 432-1400).

GOLF *Alling Memorial Golf Course* (Eastern St.; phone: 787-8063) is open to the public.

JAI ALAI Just 20 minutes away in Milford (take Rte. I-95 west), the world's fastest off-the-wall (and the ceiling) ball game is played June through November at *Milford Jai-Alai* (311 Old Gate Ln., Milford; phone: 877-4242).

JOGGING Local joggers prefer the run along Whitney Avenue, which borders the university, between Canner and Temple Streets. Also popular is the beach in Westhaven off Captain Thomas Boulevard, just five minutes from the city center.

SKIING The best facilities nearby are at *Powder Ridge* (phone: 349-3454) in Middlefield, 21 miles north of New Haven.

TENNIS There are several good outdoor public courts. Municipal courts at *Wilbur Cross High School* (Orange St. and Mitchell Dr.) are free, while the *College Wood Courts* (Orange and Cold Spring Sts.) charge a small fee. Yalies get preference at the university courts (Derby and Central Aves.), but the public is welcome.

THEATER

The city has an embarrassment of theatrical riches. For up-to-date offerings and performance times, check the publications listed in *Local Coverage* above.

CENTER STAGE

Long Wharf Theatre This prestigious regional theater brings fine ensemble performances by some of America's best actors to "plays of character," produced in two intimate theaters. Numerous *Long Wharf* productions, including *The Gin Game, The Crucible,* and *The Glass Menagerie,* have gone on to New York stages. Closed July through September. 222 Sargent Dr. (phone: 787-4282).

Yale Repertory Theatre The company produces first-rate experimental and classic plays (it earned the 1991 Tony Award for outstanding regional theater). Its productions have received great acclaim in recent years, and many have moved to Broadway, including August Wilson's two Pulitzer Prize winners, *Fences* and *The Piano Lesson*. 222 York St. (phone: 432-1234).

Other New Haven theaters include the *Shubert Performing Arts Center* (247 College St.; phone: 562-5666), which showcases Broadway touring companies; and the *Palace Performing Arts Center* (248 College St.; phone: 789-2120), which features everything from jazz shows to wrestling.

MUSIC

The *New Haven Symphony Orchestra* gives concerts from October through April at *Woolsey Hall* on the *Yale* campus (phone: 776-1444 for ticket information). For information about the *Yale Chorus*, student groups, and visiting artists, call the *Yale School of Music* (phone: 432-4157). Opera buffs should check out the *Shubert* (247 College St.; phone: 562-5666), which features opera performances when a Broadway touring company is not in residence.

NIGHTCLUBS AND NIGHTLIFE

Nightspots come and go in New Haven. For 1950s and 1960s rock 'n' roll, *Bopper's* (239 Crown St.; phone: 562-1957) offers a lively disc jockey. Adding a touch of class to New Haven's nightlife is the *Great Gatsby*, the renovated ballroom of the old *Taft* hotel (261 College St.; phone: 776-3316). *Toad's Place* (300 York St.; phone: 777-7431) features national and local rock acts.

Best in Town

CHECKING IN

The grand old traditional hotel simply doesn't exist here. What you'll find are primarily branches of the familiar chains, which offer rooms in all price ranges. A double room costs $125 to $175 per night at hotels in the expensive category; $80 to $125 at those listed as moderate; and $55 to $80 at inexpensive places. For bed and breakfast accommodations, contact *Bed & Breakfast Ltd.* (PO Box 216, New Haven, CT 06513; phone: 469-3260). Unless otherwise noted, hotels have air conditioning, private baths, TV sets, and telephones. All hotels are in the 203 area code unless otherwise indicated.

EXPENSIVE

Inn at Chapel West A welcome relief to travelers tired of hotel chains, it offers 10 tastefully decorated rooms in the heart of downtown. Rates include continental breakfast and parking. There are meeting rooms for up to 30 and photocopiers. A two-day minimum stay is required on fall foliage weekends. 1201 Chapel St. (phone: 777-1201; fax: 776-7363).

Marriott Resident Inn A favorite of businesspeople, this all-suite hotel provides spacious, airy accommodations with fully equipped kitchens and fireplaces in most rooms. There also is a pool, a whirlpool, use of a health club, and complimentary breakfast. 3 Long Wharf Drive (phone: 777-5337; 800-331-3131).

MODERATE

Holiday Inn Also downtown, but farther away from *Yale,* this 160-room hotel features live entertainment in its lounge, a restaurant, an outdoor pool, and a small weight room. Meeting rooms accommodate up to 110, and A/V equipment, photocopiers, computers, and express checkout are all available. 30 Whalley Ave. (phone: 777-6221; 800-HOLIDAY; fax: 772-1089).

INEXPENSIVE

Colony Steps away from *Yale,* in the heart of Chapel Street's restaurants and shopping, this hostelry offers an optimal combination of location and value. Its 86 rooms have sitting areas and are decorated with reproduction antiques and prints. There is a restaurant, access to a health club, indoor parking, and meeting space for up to 400. 1157 Chapel St. (phone: 776-1234; 800-458-8810; fax: 772-3929).

Duncan Hotel Small, old, and near *Yale* (so near, in fact, that students sometimes live here), it has 90 rooms (no air conditioning) available for visitors and students-at-heart. 1151 Chapel St. (phone: 787-1273).

Quality Inn On the northern edge of town, this 125-room hotel offers an indoor pool, whirlpool, sauna, and exercise room; continental breakfast is included. There are meeting facilities for up to 300. Free downtown shuttle service available. 100 Pond Lily Ave. (phone: 387-6651; 800-228-5151).

EATING OUT

Worthwhile eateries—many of them ethnic—are everywhere, and prices tend to be reasonable. Lining Wooster Street is a variety of Italian places catering to all pocketbooks. On Chapel Street, and around the corner on Howe Street, is a cluster of Middle and Far Eastern restaurants. Many offer lunchtime specials. Expect to pay $50 or more for dinner for two at restaurants we've listed as expensive, $30 to $50 at those categorized as moderate, and $30 or less at inexpensive places. Prices do not include drinks, wine, tax, or tip. Unless otherwise noted, restaurants are open for lunch and dinner. All restaurants are in the 203 area code unless otherwise indicated.

EXPENSIVE

Bagdon's New American cooking is served courtesy of owner Jon Bagdon in an uncluttered, all-white dining room (the low ceiling makes for a high noise level) or at tables in front by the bar. There are great appetizers for grazing, and innovative pasta, seafood, and meat entrées. Open daily; dinner only on weekends. Reservations advised. Major credit cards accepted. 9 Elm St. (phone: 777-1962).

Chart House Considered the city's best steakhouse, this place also offers exotic seafood. Surrounded by water and decorated in a nautical motif, it sits on a pier built over an old oyster bed. Open for dinner only and Sunday brunch. Reservations advised. Major credit cards accepted. 100 S. Water St. (phone: 787-3466).

Delmonico's The decor is strictly Valentino—Rudolph, that is—from the posters on the wall to an occasional screening of an old silent film starring the sheik. Southern Italian dishes complement the passion on the screen. Closed Sundays; dinner only on Saturdays. Reservations advised. Major credit cards accepted. 232 Wooster St. (phone: 865-1109).

Union League Café This has become a gathering place for both social and professional occasions, the latter especially at lunch. Its stunning, airy dining room is enhanced by turn-of-the-century woodwork, marble, and arched, Tiffany-style windows. Chef/owner Jean-Pierre Vuillermet produces a seasonally changing menu of the sturdy provincial flavors of his native Savoie. Open daily; dinner only on weekends. Reservations advised. Major credit cards accepted. 1032 Chapel St. (phone: 789-1010).

MODERATE

Azteca's A welcome addition to yet another reawakening New Haven neighborhood (the Upper State Street District), it offers the finest Mexican and Southwestern food in the area, served in a cheerful setting. Open for dinner only; closed Sundays. Reservations advised. MasterCard and Visa accepted. 14 Mechanic St. (phone: 624-2454).

Bruxelles A favorite with theatergoers, this café also has strong family appeal (thanks to its affordable fare and butcher paper and crayons for coloring). Baked goat cheese and fried potato chips are among the appetizers, and apple harvest chicken and Atlantic swordfish round out the menu. Save room for dessert. There's a great Sunday brunch, too. Open daily. Reservations advised. Major credit cards accepted. 220 College St. (phone: 777-7752).

Hunan Wok The best Chinese eatery in the city—perhaps the best in Connecticut—serves Hunan, Szechuan, and Mandarin fare in a friendly atmosphere. Open daily. Reservations advised on Fridays and Saturdays. Major credit cards accepted. 142 York St. (phone: 776-9475).

Miya's A fine Japanese restaurant with the best sushi in town, it also offers fresh fish specials, tempura, and teriyaki. One tatami room can be reserved for four or more. Open daily for dinner only. Reservations advised. Major credit cards accepted. 68 Howe St. (phone: 777-9760).

The Place This casual steak and barbecue place in a town 20 minutes east of the city is a summer favorite. Diners sit at picnic tables and feast on mussels, clams, steaks, lobster, and corn in the husk, which are cooked on outdoor grills. Open daily from late April through October. Reservations unnecessary. Major credit cards accepted. On Rte. 1, Guilford (phone: 453-9276).

Scoozies New Haven's hottest Italian place, it offers generous portions of pasta and a fine wine list in a bright, contemporary atmosphere. You'll find it two flights below street level, next to the *Yale Repertory Theatre*.

Open daily; dinner only on Sundays. Reservations advised. Major credit cards accepted. 1104 Chapel St. (phone: 776-8268).

INEXPENSIVE

Café Adulis The exotic, slightly spicy flavors of Ethiopia are presented on a communal serve-yourself plate of *injera*—traditional soft bread. Open daily; dinner only on Sundays. Reservations unnecessary. Major credit cards accepted. 228 College St. (phone-777-5081).

Claire's CornerCopia A self-proclaimed "gourmet vegetarian" restaurant, this casual place serves pasta, burritos, and veggie burgers, but best are the daily specials. Perfect for relaxing with a book. Open daily. No reservations. No credit cards accepted. 1000 Chapel St. (phone: 562-3888).

Libbey's At this post-pasta stopover, you can choose from among what seem to be millions of flavors of Italian ices and lots of gooey pastries. Get a cappuccino as well and enjoy it all in a bright room with wrought-iron furniture. Closed Mondays. No reservations. No credit cards accepted. 137-141 Wooster St. (phone: 772-0380).

Louis' Lunch This tiny place, which looks like an English pub, claims to be the birthplace of the hamburger. True or not, the burgers are great—big, juicy, and charcoal grilled. Don't ask for ketchup—they don't have it, and to ask is considered an affront to the quality of the product. Open for lunch only; closed weekends. No reservations. No credit cards accepted. 261 Crown St. (phone: 562-5507).

Mamoun's Falafel Middle Eastern delicacies are served in this friendly, noisy, family-run storefront. Open daily—till 3 AM. No reservations. No credit cards accepted. 85 Howe St. (phone: 562-8444).

Pepe's Pepe claims to have invented pizza. You might not believe him, but in an area where pizza making is a fine art, the long lines attest to the quality of his pies. Closed Tuesdays. No reservations. No credit cards accepted. 157 Wooster St. (phone: 865-5762).

Saigon City Great Vietnamese food and discreet service are offered at this dark, quiet dining room. Closed Mondays; dinner only on Sundays. Reservations advised. Major credit cards accepted. 1180 Chapel St. (phone: 865-5033).

Sally's The battle rages on over whose pizza is better—*Sally's* or *Pepe's* (see above). The answer is to try both. Closed Mondays. No reservations. No credit cards accepted. 237 Wooster St. (phone: 624-5271).

Tandoor Fiery food from the subcontinent is served in this old diner. Open daily. Reservations advised. Major credit cards accepted. 1226 Chapel St. (phone: 776-6620).

Tony and Lucille's Plastic grapes, pictures of the old country, celeb photos—this place has it all, including fresh and imported pasta, seafood, chicken, veal, and great calzones. Open daily. Reservations necessary. Major credit cards accepted. 150 Wooster St. (phone: 787-1621).

New Orleans

At-a-Glance

SEEING THE CITY
The best bird's-eye view of New Orleans is from the *Top of the Mart*, a revolving bar on the 33rd floor of the World Trade Center, where Canal Street meets the Mississippi River (phone: 522-9795). An observation deck is on the same floor (open daily; admission charge). There is a grand view of the French Quarter and the river from the 11th floor of the *Westin–Canal Place* hotel (see *Checking In*).

SPECIAL PLACES
Nestled between the Mississippi River and Lake Pontchartrain, New Orleans's natural crescent shape can be confusing. North, south, east, and west mean very little here. Residents keep life simple by using terms such as "lakeside" or "riverside" and "uptown" or "downtown" for directions.

FRENCH QUARTER (VIEUX CARRÉ)
Many have wondered why French explorer Jean Baptiste le Moyne, Sieur de Bienville, chose this muggy, low-lying spot to establish a colony in 1718. But back then it was the obvious choice—the nearest habitable spot north of the mouth of the Mississippi River and one of the few places for miles around that lay above sea level. The terrain to the south was, at the time, little more than muck, subject to frequent flooding. To this day, when New Orleans and its environs are hit by one of its monsoon-like rains, the French Quarter sits high and dry, while several inches or more cover the lower sections of the area. The street plan of the Vieux Carré (a term that translates roughly from the French as "old squared area") has not changed since it was first laid out in the 1720s. Most of the streets retain their original names, too.

BOURBON STREET Though named for the illustrious French royal family, some say this street now has more in common with the alcoholic beverage that also shares its name. The atmosphere here has been likened to one long, unbroken college spring break. It's legal to drink on the streets throughout New Orleans, as long you are not drinking from metal or glass containers; the legal vessel is the plastic "to-go" cup, offered everywhere. And New Orleans establishments have added many drinks to the bartender's list, with such wicked liquids as the Hurricane and the Absinthe Frappé. Round-the-clock honky-tonks offer live jazz, which can get wild in the wee hours, and late-night booze, which often leads to morning-after regrets. The seven blocks of Bourbon Street extending from Iberville to Dumaine Streets are filled with a hodgepodge of creole restaurants of varying quality, T-shirt stores galore, tacky corn-dog stands and fast food joints, elegant hotels, sleazy strip joints, jazz clubs, porno shops, and every sort of carny attraction. Often rowdy and raunchy, Bourbon Street has been a hot strip since the post-

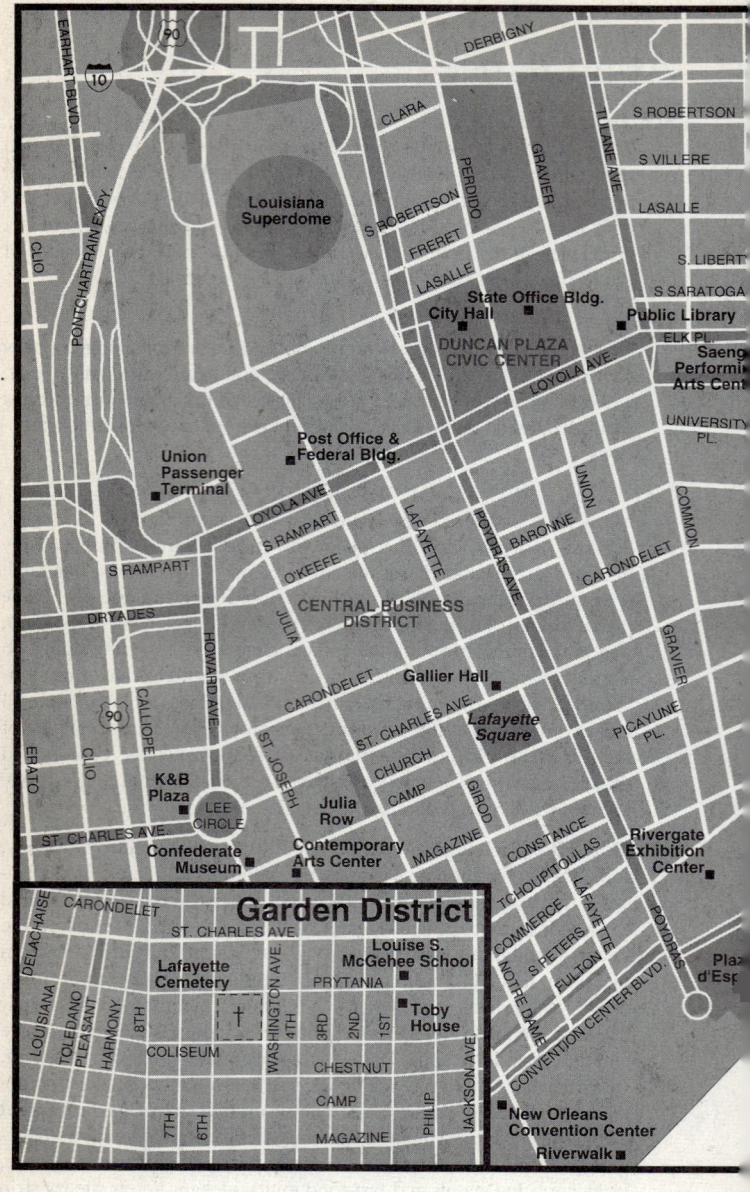

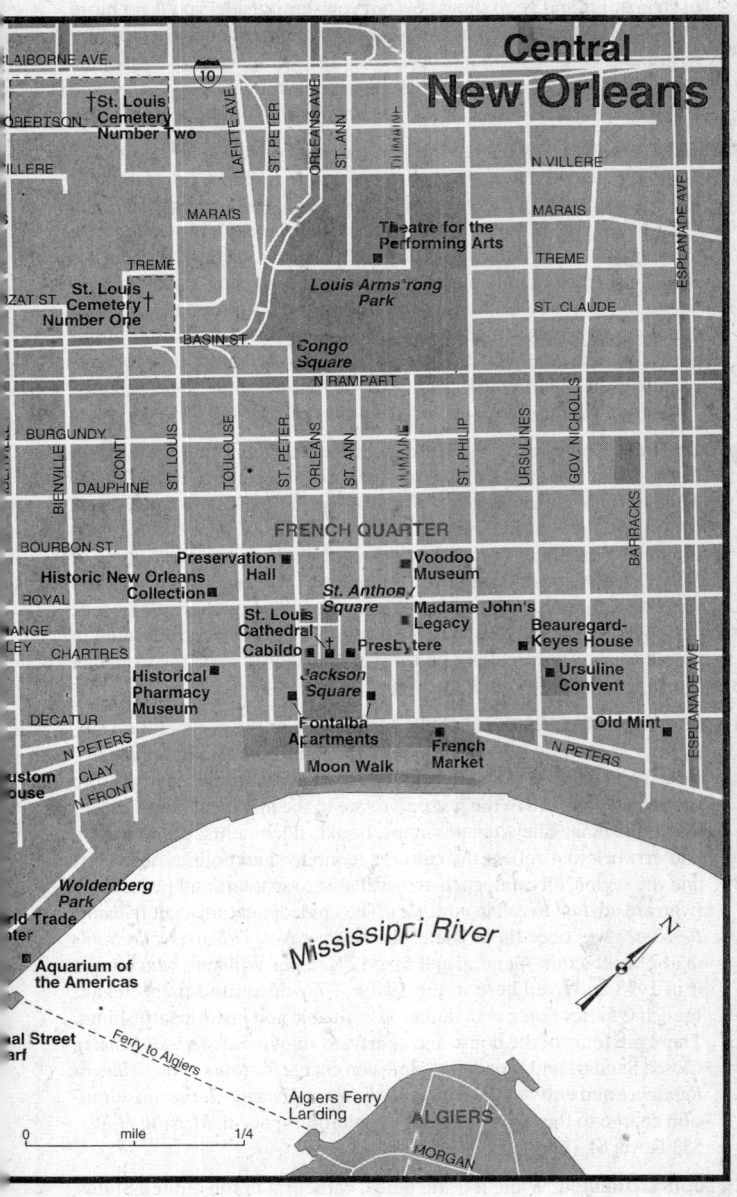

war years; this is where everybody heads to let it all hang out during the *Carnival* season or after a game in the *Superdome*. The area has a lot of strip joints and peep shows; even if you stay outside, you'll get more of an eyeful than a peep as the hawkers swing the doors open to lure customers. Among the hot spots are Al Hirt's club *Jelly Roll's*—the one place left on Bourbon with any really good music, but just once a week— and the *Famous Door* (see *Nightclubs and Nightlife* for details on both).

PRESERVATION HALL What's recorded in the jazz collection at the *Old US Mint* (see below) still happens live before an audience every night at *Preservation Hall*. In this ramshackle old creole building at the French Quarter's heart, 60- and 70-year veterans of the city's jazz scene perform nightly for an audience sitting hip-to-haunch on backless benches in a ramshackle double parlor. The New Orleans jazz renaissance— begun in the 1960s—continues to this day here as the small Dixieland bands perform classic renditions of "St. James Infirmary Blues," "Rampart Street Parade," and "When the Saints Go Marchin' In." The surroundings are spartan at best, but this is the real thing. Open nightly. Admission charge. 726 St. Peter St. (phone: 522-2841).

ROYAL STREET There really was a streetcar named *Desire* that used to run along Royal Street to Canal from the late 19th century to the 1950s. Though the streetcar is gone, along this street the desire for the past continues, and a stroll down here will yield views of some of the Quarter's finest examples of cast- and wrought-iron balconies and some of New Orleans's most distinctive architecture. The city's finest antiques shops still dominate the blocks between Bienville and St. Peter Streets, although T-shirt and inexpensive souvenir outlets have proliferated in recent years. The street is a pedestrian mall closed to traffic from late morning to late afternoon every day.

HISTORIC NEW ORLEANS COLLECTION Maintained at the aristocratic 18th-century *Merieult House*, this is one of the South's most impressive historical and cultural research centers. All of the materials, dating from the pre-colonial era to the present, relate to the history of New Orleans and Louisiana. They include maps, books, documents, photographs, and artwork that reflect the culture, economy, and politics of the city and the region, all catalogued and available to scholars and researchers (who are advised to call in advance). The immediately adjacent *Williams Residence* was once the home of the *Historic New Orleans Collection*'s major benefactors, General and Mrs. L. Kemper Williams, who bought it in 1938 and lived here in the 1940s. They decorated their elegant French Quarter home with numerous valuable and historic furnishings. There are tours of the house and courtyard (inquire at *Merieult House*). Closed Sundays and Mondays. Admission charge for tours of the *Williams Residence* and entry to the *History Galleries* in *Merieult House;* no admission charge to the *Williams Gallery* exhibition space in *Merieult House*. 533 Royal St. (phone: 523-4662).

ST. LOUIS CATHEDRAL While it is the oldest cathedral in the United States, the present-day building is actually the third to occupy the site. The first was the parish church erected by Jean-Baptiste Le Moyne Bienville soon after he founded the colony in 1718. Demolished five years later by a hurricane, the church was rebuilt in 1727, only to be destroyed in the great fire of 1788. In 1793 the parish church was proclaimed a cathedral and the seat of a diocese; a year later, the basic structure existing today was erected, with rounded Spanish-style steeples at the front. The present façade, with its columned entablature and three conical steeples (which took the place of the older ones, which were dismantled) was constructed between 1849 and 1851. This beautiful Spanish-style building also boasts painted ceilings, an altar imported from Belgium, and a bell and clock in the central spire that has marked the hours for the city's inhabitants for more than two centuries. Today it is the seat of the Roman Catholic Archdiocese of New Orleans, and masses, weddings, and other rites are still held here regularly. The interior was completely refurbished in the early 1980s. Tours given daily except Sundays. Donations requested. 700 Chartres St., on Jackson Square (phone: 525-9585).

THE CABILDO AND PRESBYTÈRE Together, the *Cabildo* and the *Presbytère*, the twin Spanish colonial buildings flanking *St. Louis Cathedral* on Jackson Square, form the hub of the *Louisiana State Museum* network. They are filled with exhibits—documents, artifacts, portraits, costumes, and furniture—pertaining to the culture and history of the region. The successor to earlier governmental headquarters on the same site, the *Cabildo* (the Spanish word for "council") was built by the Spaniards in 1795 and served as the seat of the colonial governments of both Spain and France. In a large room on the second floor, documents were signed in 1803 that transferred the entire Louisiana Territory—stretching from the Gulf of Mexico to the Canadian border—from France to the United States. The *Cabildo*, which suffered a fire in 1988, reopened last year with a fresh new look and extensive changes in its exhibits, which cover subject matter from the arrival of the first Europeans in the 1500s to the Reconstruction era after the war; popular artifacts are Napoleon's death mask and some items believed to have belonged to the pirate Jean Lafitte. The *Presbytère*, once the offices of colonial church officials, is now devoted to temporary exhibitions on the history of New Orleans and Louisiana. Closed Mondays. Admission charge. 751 Chartres St., Jackson Square (phone: 568-6968).

JACKSON SQUARE This stately plaza, originally the Place d'Armes, was the town square of the original French colonial settlement and the scene of most of New Orleans's history—from hangings to the transfer ceremony commemorating the Louisiana Purchase. It is also where early French settlers worshiped, peddled their wares, and conducted governmental and military ceremonies. It was rebuilt, and the equestrian statue of General Andrew Jackson, the hero of the Battle of New Orleans, was placed at its center in the 1850s. Today it's a pleasant place from which to watch the passing scene against a backdrop of charming cast-iron and brick buildings, or to browse through shops. Heads no longer roll here, but occasional open-air jazz concerts do, and the only hangings are on the iron fence bounding the area, where local artists display their work. Since the early 1970s, this area has been a pedestrian mall. 700 Chartres (pronounced *Chart*-ers) St., bordered by St. Ann, St. Peter, and Decatur Sts.

PONTALBA APARTMENTS Extending along the two sides of Jackson Square perpendicular to the Mississippi River are these twin, block-long, red brick buildings, said to be the first true apartment houses constructed in the United States. The buildings, each of which contains eight row houses, were designed by Henry Howard for the Spanish Baroness Micaela Almonester y Pontalba. (Her family names, Almonester and Pontalba, are preserved in the "AP" monogram set into the original cast-iron balcony railings. Today, the buildings' upper floors are still private apartments, while the arcades below are lined with ice-cream parlors, boutiques, and cafés. The building at 523 St. Ann Street houses the *1850 House,* furnished as it would have been in the mid-19th century (see *Museums*). Jackson Square at St. Ann and St. Peter Sts.

MOON WALK The name of this promenade alongside the Mississippi River may be a bit misleading: It is politically rather than celestially motivated, since it was named for former Mayor Moon Landrieu, whose administration in the early 1970s oversaw numerous physical improvements to the French Quarter's public spaces, including this one. The steps along Decatur Street lead to a landscaped terrace that offers superb views of the river and Jackson Square. Go to the grass-lined walkway right near the river—to the left is the first of many bends the river takes on its way to the Gulf of Mexico; to the right are fine views of the New Orleans skyline and river bridges. Across the levee from Decatur St. at St. Ann and St. Peter Sts.

FRENCH MARKET This is the oldest established marketplace in the Mississippi Valley. Although the five main buildings were erected between 1813 and the end of the 19th century, even before the French explorers arrived in 1718, the site was a trading post used by the Choctaw and other local Indians. The *French Market* still has a colorful atmosphere, with stalls beneath large stone colonnades offering a variety of local produce—try the Louisiana oranges, creole tomatoes, mirlitons (the pale-green, pear-shape squash known in Mexico as *chayote*), sugarcane, and sweet midget bananas—as well as meat and seafood, including live crabs, turtles, shrimp, catfish, and trout. There also are boutiques, cafés, and a large flea market. At Jackson Square and St. Ann Street is the *Café du Monde* (813 Decatur; phone: 581-2914), a bustling New Orleans coffeehouse serving authentic café au lait (half coffee with chicory, half hot milk) and beignets (square, fried crullers dusted with powdered sugar). The café closes only on *Christmas Day,* and the market itself is open daily. On Decatur St. extending from St. Ann St. to Barracks St.

OLD US MINT Designed in the Federalist style by William Strickland, this stately building is the oldest federal mint building still standing. Built in 1835, it minted nearly $300 million in silver dollars and other coins (including Confederate currency) between 1838 and 1909. Later, the building was used as a prison and then as offices of the *US Coast Guard.* In 1982, it became the home of the *New Orleans Jazz Collection* and *Mardi Gras Museum,* both part of the *Louisiana State Museum.* Fine exhibits trace the development of jazz from its origins in African-American rhythms and the European brass band tradition. Jazz lovers also will find souvenirs of the patron saints of jazz—Louis Armstrong's first horn, Bix Beiderbecke's cuff links, and instruments played by members of the *Original Dixieland Jazz Band*. In addition, there are resplendent costumes worn in the hundreds of *Carnival* parades and balls that precede New Orleans's world-famous *Mardi Gras* celebration. The building also houses a *Historical Center* (phone: 568-8214) which contains historical documents from the French and Spanish Louisiana periods; it is open to the public Wednesdays through Fridays by appointment only for on-site research. The *New Orleans Jazz Collection* and *Mardi Gras Museum* are closed Mondays. Admission charge. 400 Esplanade Ave. (phone: 568-6968).

URSULINE CONVENT Constructed in 1734 in French Provincial style, this building was one of the few to survive the two devastating fires that swept through New Orleans during the 18th century. Originally the home of the city's Ursuline nuns—who came from France in 1727 to care for the sick and orphaned and to teach the slaves, Indians, and the colonists' children—it later served as a Catholic school for boys, the Louisiana Legislature, and the official residence of the Archbishop of New Orleans. Today the structure, topped by a mansard roof and surrounded by a brick stucco wall, contains archives of the Archdiocese of New Orleans. Open to the public for tours only on Tuesdays through Fridays at 10 and 11 AM and 1, 2, and 3 PM; weekends at 11:15 AM and 1 and 2 PM; closed Mondays. Admission charge. 1100 Chartres St. (phone: 529-3040).

BEAUREGARD-KEYES HOUSE Although George Washington never slept here, almost everyone else lived in this neoclassical residence, including the legendary chess champion Paul Morphy, Confederate General Pierre G. T. Beauregard, and, in the 1940s, novelist Frances Parkinson Keyes, whose will designated it for use as a museum. It was also here that a local wine maker was shot by a member of the Sicilian Black Hand, a secret organization that operated in the Quarter during the 1920s. Its rooms today are handsomely furnished, with a cozy, un-museum-like atmosphere, and Mrs. Keyes's antique-doll collection is on view. The adjoining formal garden, enclosed by a brick wall and lined with boxwoods, jasmine, and tropical flora, is one of the French Quarter's prettiest. Closed Sundays. Admission charge. It's across the street from the *Ursuline Convent*. 1113 Chartres St. (phone: 523-7257).

MADAME JOHN'S LEGACY This ancient frame cottage is believed to be one of the oldest buildings in the Mississippi Valley, constructed in 1726 by Jean Pascal, a sea captain from Provence who received the site from La Compagnie des Indes which controlled the Louisiana colony for the King of France. The structure was one of the few to survive the two major fires that all but destroyed New Orleans during the late 1700s. A brick and stucco building, with a sloping roof and colonnaded gallery, it is an excellent example of the West Indies plantation architectural style. The house's name comes from *Tite Poulette*, a romance novel by 19th-century author George W. Cable that chronicles the lives of New Orleans Creoles in the late 1800s. The book's hero lives in the house and bequeaths it to his mistress, known as

Madame John. Although it is one of the *Louisiana State Museum*'s properties and has major historical value, it is not open to the public. 632 Dumaine St.

ST. LOUIS CEMETERY NUMBER ONE About a block from North Rampart Street at the edge of the Vieux Carré, this old New Orleans cemetery, dating back to the early 18th century, is literally a diminutive necropolis. The tombs (the city's marshy ground dictated aboveground burial) are interesting for their structure, inscriptions, and number of remains inside (to solve overcrowding, they are opened and the remaining bones are moved deeper into the vault to accommodate new arrivals). Among the illustrious occupants here are Marie Laveau, who used her charms and spells as a voodoo queen in the 1900s; the two wives of Louisiana's first governor, W. C. C. Claiborne; Jean Etienne de Boré, father of the Louisiana sugar industry and first Mayor of New Orleans; and Louisiana historian Charles Gayarre. Many of the brick-and-stucco tombs have crumbled to near-ruin. The earliest decipherable epitaph is that of Nannette F. de Bailly, dated September 24, 1800. Because of the cemetery's isolation, visitors are strongly advised to visit only in daytime, and in large groups. Open daily. No admission charge to the cemetery, but there is a small charge for guided tours. 400 Basin St.

RIVERFRONT/WAREHOUSE DISTRICT

It has only been within the last two decades that the Mississippi River has been reunited with the city it spawned. During the rehabilitation of the waterfront area, huge wharves and sheds were torn down to make way for parks, bandstands, walkways, excursion-boat docks, plazas, hotels, a shopping mall, and public spaces. Stretching from the French Quarter to the Warehouse District, the riverfront has become a favorite spot to relax and stroll for locals and tourists alike. *Riverwalk,* a vast, two-level mall of trendy shops and eating spots, with exterior walkways and sweeping views of the Mississippi, is a remnant of the New Orleans *1984 World's Fair.* Another benefit of that otherwise ill-fated event was that it motivated city planners to rehabilitate many sturdy, handsome old warehouses, stores, and office buildings in the port area. Fashioned mostly of iron, brick, and wood beams, these highly practical, well-made—and often beautifully proportioned—buildings are getting a new lease on life. Their restoration revitalized the entire area, luring apartment dwellers, lawyers, architects, shop owners, and restaurateurs. The district is bounded by Canal and Poydras Streets. and Convention Center Boulevard.

AQUARIUM OF THE AMERICAS Opened in August 1990 on the bank of the Mississippi, this aquatic adventure has more than 6,000 specimens of marine life on view, including fish, reptiles, birds, and amphibians. The main attractions are the *Gulf of Mexico* exhibit, a two-story, 400,000-gallon tank holding hundreds of species found in the deep waters of the gulf; the walk-through *Amazon Rain Forest,* which re-creates the hot, humid environment of the subtropics with indigenous birds, butterflies, and flora; the *Caribbean Reef,* visible from a see-through, tunnel-shaped walkway; the *Mississippi River Delta Habitat,* featuring the freshwater reptiles and fish that inhabit inland Southern waters; and the sharks and penguins. There's a large and pleasant cafeteria on the second floor. Open daily. Admission charge. 1 Canal St. (phone: 861-2537).

WOLDENBERG PARK Fourteen acres of walkways and park areas bring an oasis-like serenity to the French Quarter riverfront area. Contemporary works by local sculptors are exhibited throughout the park, which also contains benches and a bandstand that is used primarily during festivals. Off Conti St. near the riverfront.

PLAZA D'ESPAÑA The dramatic fountain and intricately patterned tiles that form this huge pavilion along the Mississippi were a gift from the Spanish government in recognition of New Orleans's strong historical Hispanic ties. The pavilion has become a favorite spot for small festivals and band concerts. The *Plaza* is on the riverfront between the *Aquarium of the Americas* (see above) and the end of Poydras St.

ERNEST N. MORIAL CONVENTION CENTER This is the city's primary convention facility, and with more than 700,000 square feet of meeting and exhibition space, it is one of the largest facilities of its kind in the country. Completed in 1985, it was later enlarged. The center's development has spurred a commercial renaissance in the Warehouse District. 900 Convention Center Blvd. (phone: 582-3000).

CONTEMPORARY ARTS CENTER This colorful, lively complex of exhibition and performance spaces is home to the avant-garde—local and regional artists, playwrights, dance groups, composers, and filmmakers. The strikingly contemporary spaces, refashioned from an early-20th-century drugstore and office building, contain no permanent collections, but the galleries are always filled with interesting new works, many by emerging artists. Closed Mondays and Tuesdays. Admission charge. 900 Camp St. (phone: 523-1216).

JULIA ROW Built in 1830–32 to accommodate newly arrived immigrants, this handsome set of 13 row houses is the Warehouse District's most important architectural setpiece. These elegant red brick buildings—once the homes of some of New Orleans's most well-to-do and socially prominent families—have graceful cast-iron balconies, ornamented entrances, fanlights, and sidelights, which were considered an architectural innovation at the time. After decades of neighborhood deterioration, the row houses were restored by local preservationists in the 1970s. Today, the street-level spaces hold offices and shops. *Julia Row* is along the 600 block of Julia St., west of Poydras and just south of St. Charles Ave. The nonprofit *Preservation Resource Center* (604 Julia St.; phone: 581-7032) offers information and interesting exhibitions concerning the district. The center also provides architectural tours of various neighborhoods; it's closed weekdays.

K&B PLAZA One of New Orleans's first examples of the sleek, modern "international style" of architecture, this creation of the Skidmore Owings Merrill architectural firm is now the headquarters of a regional drugstore chain. On the surrounding terrace are works by such noted late-20th-century sculptors as George Segal, George Rickey, Henry Moore, Jacques Lipschitz, and Isamu Noguchi. The ground-floor lobby also houses one of the South's most important privately owned collections of contemporary paintings and sculpture. Closed weekends. No admission charge. 1055 St. Charles Ave. at Lee Circle (phone: 586-1234).

CANAL STREET AND THE CENTRAL BUSINESS DISTRICT

Today's commercial hub of New Orleans, bounded roughly by Canal Street, the Mississippi River, Poydras Street, and South Claiborne Avenue, was where the city's English-speaking population first established roots in the mid-to-late 19th century. This is where cotton brokers traded, department stores flourished, and movie theaters first took hold. The blocks of Canal Street nearest to the French Quarter formed the city's primary shopping district for generations, and still contain many structures dating back 100 years or more. Poydras Street, about five blocks from Canal Street in the business district, is the densest concentration of financial, governmental, and legal offices in the city. Several major hotels and a dozen or more new office towers—including the city's tallest building, the 50-story One Shell Square—overlook the street's leafy median. At one end of Poydras is the *Louisiana Superdome,* and at the other end, the Mississippi Riverfront area.

CANAL STREET For most of the 19th century, this broad, tree-lined avenue formed the dividing line between the French sector of New Orleans and the newer, Anglo-Saxon part of town. The origin of its name is uncertain, since no canal ever existed here (although there were half-serious plans in the 19th century to dig one). In the 1800s, Canal Street boasted a couple of opera houses and a number of tony residences. Two private men's clubs—the *Pickwick Club* on the corner of St. Charles Avenue and the *Boston Club* at 824 Canal—are among the last vestiges of the street's aristocratic past. From the late-19th to the mid-20th century, Canal Street was New Orleans's shopping hub. While such long-established department stores as *Maison Blanche* and *Krauss* and a few other specialty merchants still operate, other buildings have either been boarded up or turned into office buildings. In recent decades, the river end of Canal has been the site of continuing development, with construction of the *Canal Place* office building and shopping mall, the *Rivergate* exhibition center (slated for possible renovation or demolition this year), major hotels, and the *Aquarium of the Americas.*

CUSTOM HOUSE Canal Street's most historic structure, the old *US Custom House*—which takes up the entire block bounded by Canal, Decatur, Iberville, and North Peters Streets—is the city's handsomest specimen of Federalist architecture. A fine example of Greek Revival style is the majestic *Marble Hall* (in the center of the building on the second floor), with its 14 columns of pure white marble that rise to a ceiling of huge iron and ground-glass plates. Begun in 1849, the building was still under construction in 1862, at the peak of the Civil War, and was never completed according to the original plans. The *Custom House* is still home to various offices of the *US Customs Service.* Closed weekends. No admission charge. 423 Canal St. (phone: 589-4532).

LOUISIANA SUPERDOME Completed in 1975, this awesome piece of architectural engineering has been described as the largest freestanding room in the world. Twenty-seven stories tall, with a seating capacity of 100,000 people, it is large enough to accommodate all of Rome's St. Peter's

Basilica. The *1988 Republican National Convention,* several *Super Bowls,* and many rock concerts have taken place here. Primarily a football stadium, it is home to the *NFL's* New Orleans *Saints* as well as to dozens of local high school and college sports teams. Daily tours, lasting 40 minutes, are offered when it's not in use. Admission charge. One Sugar Bowl Dr. at Poydras St. (phone 587-3810).

GALLIER HALL Considered by many to be the best example of Greek Revival public architecture in New Orleans, the hall was designed by James Gallier Sr. and dedicated in 1853 as *City Hall;* it served in this capacity until the late 1950s. The granite and white-marble building has been restored over the years, and the classically proportioned rooms, separated by a 12-foot-wide central hall, are now used mostly for official receptions. It faces *Lafayette Square,* which contains a touching monument to John McDonogh, the 19th-century philanthropist who was the principal benefactor of the city's public school system. Closed weekends. No admission charge. 543 St. Charles Ave. (phone: 565-7457).

GARDEN DISTRICT

In the early 19th century, part of the 65 square blocks that now compose the Garden District formed a plantation. In the 1850s, the district became a residential community of newly arrived Anglo-Saxon entrepreneurs, and since the turn of the century, its image as an urban expression of Old Southern refinement has remained intact. The houses, in a seemingly riotous conglomeration of architectural styles, and the gardens, lush with tropical greenery and shaded by immense oak trees, blend to create a harmonious and unique neighborhood. Most of the Greek Revival mansions of the Lower Garden District, extending roughly from Lee Circle to Jackson Avenue, have succumbed to the demands of creeping commercialism; they have been converted to shops, restaurants, and galleries, although some are still private homes. Happily, the section beyond Jackson Avenue has retained its timeless air of grace and tranquillity. The best strolling is along and off Prytania Street, between First Street and Washington Avenue.

COLISEUM SQUARE When city planners laid out this rectangular park in the Lower Garden District in the 1830s, they designed it as the campus of a university to be called the Prytaneum. Appropriately, they named the nearby streets for seven of the nine Greek muses—Melpomene, Erato, Terpsichore, Clio, Euterpe, Thalia, and Calliope. The university was never built. Instead, the park became the catalyst for a tony neighborhood of Greek Revival residences, most of which remain today. While the square has lost its aristocratic veneer, many of the old homes have been restored. The Prytaneum survives only in the name of nearby Prytania Street.

TOBY-WESTFELDT HOUSE This imposing residence, a raised-frame cottage with a façade of square, white columns, dates from the 1830s. Typical of the period, it was built by Thomas Toby, a Philadelphian who established a large plantation on the site (it once dominated the area that was eventually to become the Garden District). Enclosed within the white picket fence is a garden filled with such typical New Orleans flora as palm and magnolia. Visible from the street is one of the city's finest oak trees, located at the rear of the house. Not open to the public. 2340 Prytania St.

LOUISE S. McGEHEE SCHOOL "Free Renaissance" was the term used to describe the heavily decorative architectural style of this huge old residence, completed in 1870 and now a private school for girls. Pairs of fluted Corinthian columns define the wide porch at the front of the house. The building contains a fully finished basement, a rarity in New Orleans because of the city's watery substratum. The building is open by arrangement only for groups of 50 or more. 2343 Prytania St. (phone: 561-1224).

1300 BLOCK OF FIRST STREET Many a knowledgeable New Orleanian identifies this as the most beautiful residential block in the city, filled as it is with majestic examples of the Greek Revival style of the mid- to late-19th century. Two especially impressive houses are the residences at No. 1331, with its fancy stucco work, dental molding, and ironwork, and at No. 1315, a stately Greek Revival mansion that has been faithfully preserved in a condition close to the original.

LAFAYETTE CEMETERY Fans of New Orleans novelist Anne Rice will find this an especially interesting spot, since it figures prominently in her *Vampire Chronicles*. Before the Garden District became part of New Orleans, it was a suburban town called Lafayette. The community's cemetery, dating from the mid-1850s, was the first one in the area laid out on a grid of symmetrical lanes and driveways. Most of the aboveground tombs hold the remains of prosperous businessmen and traders who inhabited the fancy residences nearby. The gates are open weekdays from 7:30 AM to 2 PM and on Saturdays from 7:30 AM to noon. Visiting the cemetery alone at any time is not advised. For a fee, guided tours are given by *Save Our Cemeteries*, a preservationist organization, on Mondays, Wednesdays, and Fridays. Washington Ave. between Prytania and Coliseum Sts. (phone: 588-9357).

UPTOWN–UNIVERSITY SECTION

Encompassing some of the most genteel and some of the seediest precincts of the Crescent City, the Uptown–University neighborhoods are, alternatively, leafy, lively, rowdy, and downtrodden. There are high-society denizens and their regal homes near world-famous *Tulane University* and *Audubon Park*, as well as middle- and lower-class neighborhoods; near the river are the dive bars and the loafers. The St. Charles streetcar almost perfectly bisects this sprawling area, which stretches from the western edge of the Garden District at Louisiana Avenue to just beyond the last street traveled on the streetcar's route, South Carrollton Avenue.

AUDUBON ZOOLOGICAL GARDEN Once a neglected, foul-smelling place, the *Audubon Zoo* has been transformed since the mid-1970s into one of the country's best. An exotic white tiger is just one of the 1,500 species housed here in habitats that approximate natural conditions. Some fascinating special exhibits re-create in-the-wild environments: Not to be missed is the *Louisiana Swamp*, with alligators and other indigenous creatures slithering and hopping through marshy terrain. Dozens of tropical and shore birds from Louisiana and around the world flit around the trees and shrubs of the huge, walk-through aviary. The *Asian Domain, Grasslands of the World,* and a large pool of frisky sea lions are other favorites. For children, there is a petting zoo, wildlife theater with live animals, and a hands-on natural history museum. Open daily. Admission charge. 6500 Magazine St. (phone: 861-2538).

AUDUBON PARK Under the leafy umbrella of *Audubon Park*'s immense oaks, joggers now tread ground that was, in the late 18th century, a sugarcane plantation. Occupying the 340 acres extending from St. Charles Avenue to the Mississippi River, the park was named for naturalist John James Audubon, who had lived briefly in New Orleans. In 1884-85, it was the site of the *World's Industrial and Cotton Exposition,* commemorating the 100th anniversary of the first shipment of Louisiana cotton to a foreign port. Today it's a haven, not only for joggers, but for picnickers, golfers, tennis players, and bicyclists. While the park's tranquil lagoons are no longer stocked with fish, they form, along with the graceful oaks, a pleasant backdrop for a morning stroll. Main entrances on the 6400 block of St. Charles Ave. and the 6500 block of Magazine St.

AUDUBON PLACE If New Orleans has a millionaire's row, it is this short, private parkway lined with 28 understated but sumptuous residences, which you can only glimpse from the arched gate on St. Charles Avenue; a security guard admits only residents and their visitors through the gate. It was developed early in the 20th century by a Texas real estate speculator, and all but a few of the homes flanking the elaborately landscaped median date from that period. The immense, white-columned manse to the left of the entry gate is the *Zemurray House,* the traditional residence of the President of *Tulane University.* 6900 St. Charles Ave.

ACADEMY OF THE SACRED HEART In 1889 the nuns of the Order of the Sacred Heart opened this school to educate the daughters of prominent Creole families, and French conversation and grammar remain a major part of its curriculum to this day. Elementary and secondary students attend classes in the three buildings that overlook a large, pleasant garden near St. Charles Avenue. The red brick façade, with tiers of arched, shuttered windows, columns, and balconies, is one of the most graceful architectural spaces in the city's Uptown section. 4521 St. Charles Ave.

ORLEANS CLUB One of the few buildings on St. Charles Avenue inspired by the creole architecture of the French Quarter, the *Orleans Club* was built in 1868 as a private residence. Since 1925 it's been the headquarters of a local social-cultural women's group, which has carefully preserved the structure's elegant stucco façade, handsome iron lace balconies, and pleasantly manicured gardens. Not open to the public. 5005 St. Charles Ave.

MILTON H. LATTER MEMORIAL LIBRARY None of St. Charles Avenue's mansions exceeds this one for lavishness. Built in 1907 in the Beaux Arts style and occupying an entire block, it was the home in the 1920s of silent-screen star Marguerite Clarke and her husband, aviator Harry

Williams; their Jazz Age parties were the talk of the town. In 1948, the house was acquired by a couple who donated it to the *New Orleans Public Library* in memory of their son, a casualty of World War II. Many of the original mantels, murals, and ceiling paintings remain, making this branch of the city's library the most beautiful of all. Open daily. 5120 St. Charles Ave. (phone: 596-2625).

"TARA" As far as we know, Vivien Leigh and Clark Gable never set foot in this plantation-style residence, but Scarlett and Rhett would have felt right at home here. The house was constructed during the 1940s according to the antebellum descriptions of *Tara* in *Gone with the Wind*. Everything is here, from the lofty columns of partially exposed, whitewashed brick to the elegant arched doorway inset with a fan-shaped window. Not open to the public. 5705 St. Charles Ave.

THE LAKEFRONT

City Park extends almost to Lake Pontchartrain and, along with Bayou St. John, serves as a kind of gateway to the northern section of the city known as The Lakefront. Technically, Lake Pontchartrain, the body of water forming New Orleans's northern boundary, is a bay rather than a lake. In any case, this comparatively shallow, brackish basin has served the city in countless ways: In winter, the chill of a north wind is warmed considerably as it skims southward; in fair weather, it becomes an ideal playground for picnickers and boaters (although pollution from sewage and industrial sources has made swimming a serious health hazard on the southern, New Orleans side). The northern area of the lake has always been a prime source of trout, crab, and shrimp almost any time of year. Named for Louis XIV's naval minister, Lake Pontchartrain connects with the Gulf of Mexico via narrow straits that have been fertile fishing grounds since before the Europeans arrived.

CITY PARK Dozens of graceful ancient oaks and quiet lagoons make *City Park*'s 1,500 or so acres an ideal environment for jogging, tennis, fishing, biking and any number of participatory sports and games. Its occasional sculptures and formal gardens, especially the *Botanical Garden* and *Conservatory,* offer a pleasant respite from the city. From late November to early January each year, a large section near City Park Avenue is transformed into a magical place, with hundreds of thousands of lights and holiday decorations strung along the gigantic oaks. For children, there are all sorts of amusements, including pony and buggy rides, a puppet show, a vintage carousel, a miniature train, paddleboats, and the *Storyland* theme park. In the late 18th and early 19th centuries, when the park was part of the Allard Plantation, Creole gentlemen defended their honor here, dueling with swords or pistols under the lacy Spanish moss. Main entrance at Esplanade Ave. and Bayou St. John (phone: 482-4888).

NEW ORLEANS MUSEUM OF ART Built in 1912 by local philanthropist Isaac Delgado, *NOMA* has since become an important American museum. Set in pastoral *City Park,* its permanent exhibits include examples of the major European and American art movements as well as specialized collections, including Oriental porcelains and painting, late Gothic and early Renaissance painting from the *Samuel H. Kress Collection,* fine examples of French Impressionism and 20th-century European painting, a wide array of European and American decorative arts (including jewelry, ornamental pieces, exquisite *Easter* eggs, cigarette cases, and boxes created by Peter Carl Fabergé), contemporary photography, and pre-Columbian and African sculpture. Among the more unusual possessions is a portrait by French Impressionist Edgar Degas of his cousin, Estelle Musson; it was painted during the artist's extended 1873 visit to New Orleans, where his relatives were then residing. A major expansion in 1993 added two floors spotlighting African, Asian, Oceanic, and contemporary art. Lectures and other educational programs are presented frequently in the comfortable auditorium. A gift shop and a restaurant are on site. Closed Mondays. Admission charge. *City Park* (phone: 488-2631).

BAYOU ST. JOHN This gently flowing stream extending from *City Park* to Lake Pontchartrain once connected the heart of the Old City with the lake via canals that have long since been filled in or covered over. The local Indians and early settlers used the bayou to transport their wares into town. The bayou's banks have long been a favorite place for outings. A number of family-style resort hotels once dotted the area near the lake known as Old Spanish Fort; it is now the site of seafood restaurants, apartment buildings, and the city's largest marina. Along much of the bayou's length are some of the city's oldest residences, including the Caribbean-style Pitot House (see below), home of New Orleans's first mayor.

PITOT HOUSE Designed in the traditional West Indies style, featuring two stories topped by a high-pitched, gently tapering roof, this small plantation house was originally a country home for the aristocratic Ducayet family, who retreated to the cool edge of Bayou St. John on weekend getaways from their French Quarter cottage. Later, it was the home of the family of James Pitot, who served from 1804 to 1805 as the mayor of the newly incorporated city. The outer wall construction is of *briquets-entre-poteaux* ("bricks between posts") covered with stucco; the interior has been furnished by the *Louisiana Landmarks Society* with Louisiana and American antique furniture, and fabrics and bibelots in the style of the early 1800s. Closed Sundays through Tuesdays. Admission charge. 1440 Moss St. (phone: 482-0312).

TAVERN ON THE PARK This handsome two-story structure—dating from 1860—faces two massive trees, known as the Dueling Oaks, across the avenue. Designed as a restaurant from the start, it was built 10 years after New Orleans's city government acquired the *City Park* tract for public use. The place gained considerable notoriety early in the century as a boxing arena, a speakeasy, and, at one point in its history, a bordello. In the late 1980s, the building was extensively restored to its present state. Currently, it is home to a steak and seafood restaurant, with an interesting but unpredictable menu. 900 City Park Ave. (phone: 486-3333).

LAKESHORE DRIVE The parkway that extends along much of Lake Pontchartrain's southern shore begins in the west with the Orleans Marina, where dozens of sailboats and pleasure craft are berthed when they're not plying the lake's gentle waters. Farther along the breezy landscaped roadway are the old *Southern Yacht Club,* and, just past Marconi Drive, the *Mardi Gras* Fountains (memorializing the *krewes* who make the tradition of the pre-Lenten *Carnival* possible), the campus of the *University of New Orleans,* and the *New Orleans Municipal Airport,* now used mostly for private aircraft. On holiday weekends, the miles of grassy strips between Lakeshore Drive and the lake seawall are often filled with picnickers.

LAKE PONTCHARTRAIN CAUSEWAY Stretching more than 24 miles from the Jefferson Parish shoreline to Mandeville, the roadbed—sitting just a few yards above the lake—is advertised as the world's longest bridge. At midpoint, neither shore is visible, but the occasional spectacular sunset or thunderstorm offers respite from the rather monotonous drive. Entrance at the north end of Causeway Blvd. in Metairie. There's a $1 toll each way for passenger cars.

OTHER SPECIAL PLACES

JEAN LAFITTE NATIONAL HISTORICAL PARK, BARATARIA UNIT If a trip to the Cajun country of southwest Louisiana is not practical, this beautiful slice of Louisiana wetlands, maintained by the *National Park Service,* is an excellent alternative. Less than an hour's drive from the French Quarter via the Crescent City Connection bridge, the park contains most of the marshy flora that flourish on the Louisiana coastline. There are a couple of pretty bayous surrounded by moss-draped cypress; one of the bayous is carpeted with beautiful water lilies. Wooden walkways lead from the parking area through rows of palmetto, oak, and cypress. Guided walking tours conducted by park rangers are available daily. No admission charge. 7400 La. Hwy. 45, in Marrero (phone: 589-2330).

METAIRIE CEMETERY This aboveground necropolis of towering tombs and memorials pays tribute to some of New Orleans's most illustrious dead, mostly successful business and professional figures of the late 19th and early 20th centuries. The architectural styles of the elaborate stone tombs range from Egyptian to rococo; much of the statuary is monumental. Some bizarre examples of funerary art await at almost every turn along the alleys and walkways through the manicured grounds. A free tape-recorded tour is available at the *Lake Lawn Metairie Funeral Home* (5100 Pontchartrain Blvd.; phone: 486-6331).

LONGUE VUE HOUSE AND GARDENS Although built in the mid-20th century, this handsome estate in the elegant, old suburb of Metairie evokes the grandeur of Edwardian England. It was the residence of the late philanthropists Edith and Edgar B. Stern Jr. Beyond the imposing neoclassical entrance, exquisitely decorated rooms contain a trove of treasures—from rare English furniture and porcelain to paintings by major contemporary artists. Inspiration for the design of the fountains and eight acres of gardens came from Mrs. Stern's frequent trips to Europe. Each of the meticulously maintained flower beds, shrubs, and trees is labeled. Closed Sunday mornings. Admission charge. The house is across from *Metairie Cemetery* at the intersection of Bamboo and Metairie Roads and can be most easily reached by tour bus. 7 Bamboo Rd., near Metairie Rd. (phone: 488-5488).

FREEPORT-MCMORAN AUDUBON SPECIES SURVIVAL CENTER Opened last year, this institute is dedicated to the breeding and preservation of such endangered species as the Louisiana black bear and the milky stork. Although the center itself is not open to the public, there is a 130-acre *Wilderness Park* with nature trails, an education center, and a picnic site at English Turn, Algiers (Algiers is the section of New Orleans that lies across the Mississippi River). Open daily until dark. No admission charge. The center can be reached in 20 minutes by car from downtown; cross the river via the Crescent City Connection bridge (enter from the Warehouse District), then turn north toward Algiers Point, where Patterson Road begins. Call the center for precise directions. 10004 Patterson Rd., English Turn (phone: 861-2537).

> ### EXTRA SPECIAL
>
> Somewhere out there in Louisiana country, the heart of the Old South still beats faintly along the banks of the Mississippi. As late as the end of the 19th century, sugarcane was king in Louisiana, and large plantations established commercial empires, as well as an entire social system, around it. A few of these plantations have been restored and are open to visitors, and the life that the Southern gentry created for themselves really is something to see. Just a short drive north of New Orleans, these elegant relics have survived not only the Civil War but countless hurricanes, humidity, and other perils. Among the most impressive are *Oak Alley* (on the west bank of the river at Vacherie) fronted by twin rows of 28 gnarled oaks that form a vast majestic umbrella; *San Francisco Plantation* (on the river's east bank, north of LaPlace), a combination of mid-Victorian and Steamboat Gothic ornamentation second to none in the state; *Houmas House* (on the east bank near Burnside), which boasts a magnificent setting and charming auxiliary buildings; and *Destrehan Plantation* (on the east bank in Destrehan), said to be the oldest building left intact in the Mississippi Valley. Detailed maps and brochures are available at hotels and the *New Orleans Tourist Information Center* in the French Quarter (529 St. Ann St.; phone: 568-5661). Most of the city's tour companies also offer bus tours of the plantation houses.

Sources and Resources

TOURIST INFORMATION

The *New Orleans Tourist Information Center,* in the French Quarter (529 St. Ann St., New Orleans, LA 70116; phone: 568-5661), provides a wealth of information on the city's attractions, including maps, brochures, and personal help. It's open daily. The *Greater New Orleans Tourist and Convention Commission* (1520 Sugar Bowl Dr., New Orleans, LA 70112; phone: 566-5011) has information about the outlying areas. It's also open daily. Contact the Louisiana state hotline (phone: 800-33-GUMBO) for maps, calendars of events, health updates, and travel advisories.

LOCAL COVERAGE The city's daily, *The Times-Picayune,* has a special Friday edition that includes "Lagniappe," an arts-and-entertainment section with a comprehensive list of musical, art, theatrical, film, cultural, historical, and recreational activities. The "Eating Out" column covers local restaurants. Other useful local publications include *Gambit,* a free arts-oriented weekly found in local shops and restaurants, and *New Orleans,* a general-interest monthly. Two other monthlies, *Tourist News* and *Where,* distributed free in hotels, list restaurants, shops, and hotels.

Frenchmen, Desire, Goodchildren, by John C. Chase (Robert L. Crager; $12.95), is an entertaining and informative guide to New Orleans's geography and history. Other recommended reading: *The French Quarter,* by Herbert Asbury (Mockingbird Books; $3.50), *Voodoo in New Orleans,* by Robert Tallant (Pelican; $3.95), and *The New Orleans Eat Book* by Tom Fitzmorris (New Orleans Big Band and Pacific Co.; $6.95). We also immodestly suggest you pick up a copy of *Birnbaum's New Orleans 95* (HarperCollins; $12).

TELEVISION STATIONS WWL Channel 4–CBS; WDSU Channel 6–NBC; WVUE Channel 8–ABC; WNOL Channel 38–Fox; and WYES Channel 12 and WLAE Channel 32–both PBS.

RADIO STATIONS AM: WWL 870 (CBS, ABC Information, talk/news); WNOE 1060 (talk, news). FM: WWNO 89.9 (classical, National Public Radio); WWOZ 90.7 (jazz and folk); WRNO 99.5 (rock); and WLTS 106.3 (pop and light rock).

TELEPHONE The area code for New Orleans is 504.

SALES TAX State and city sales taxes total 9.5%.

CLIMATE New Orleans weather is subtropical with high humidity, temperatures, and substantial rainfall. Moderated by the Gulf of Mexico winds, summer temperatures hover around 90F, while winter temperatures rarely drop to freezing. Summers can get unbearably sticky.

GETTING AROUND

AIRPORT *New Orleans International Airport* is a 25- to 35-minute drive from the downtown area. The *Louisiana Transit Co.* (phone: 737-9611) runs an *Airport-Downtown Express* bus on a 10- to 25-minute schedule (more frequent during rush hours) from downtown at the corner of Loyola and Tulane Avenues; the fare is $1.10. *Airport Shuttle, Inc.* (phone: 592-1991) provides service between the airport and downtown. Its passenger vans depart from the airport every 15 minutes, picking up passengers at most downtown hotels, the Central Business District, French Quarter, and Westbank.

BUS TOURS A variety of itineraries is offered by numerous companies operating bus tours of the French Quarter, Garden District, Lakefront, and major points of interest outside the city proper. Among the companies are *American-Acadian* (phone: 467-1734); *Gray Line* (phone: 587-0861); *Machu Picchu Tours* (phone: 392-5118); *New Orleans Tours* (phone: 592-1991); and *Tours by Isabelle* (phone: 367-3963). All tour companies pick people up, by arrangement, from their hotels.

BUSES AND STREETCARS The city's *Regional Transit Authority* operates buses throughout the city. The St. Charles Avenue streetcar offers a scenic ride through the Central Business District and Uptown. Board at Canal and Carondelet Streets, or at St. Charles Avenue and Common Street. Special lines include the *Easy Rider*, which circuits the Central Business District and the riverfront; the *French Quarter Minibus*, operating between Elysian Fields Avenue and Poydras Street; and the *Riverfront Streetcar*, which runs along the Mississippi River from Esplanade Avenue to Julia Street. Detailed information is available from *RideLine* (phone: 569-2700). Carfare ranges from $1 to $1.25 (express routes are $1.25).

CAR RENTAL For *Carnival* or the *Jazz and Heritage Festival*, be sure to reserve wheels well in advance. All of the major national car rental companies have offices in New Orleans.

CARRIAGE RIDES Mule-drawn carriages, most with fringed tops and holding as many as 10 passengers, may be hired by the hour from early morning to nighttime on the Decatur Street side of Jackson Square. The carriages roll around the streets of the French Quarter as drivers comment on points of interest. Be aware that while carriages are supposedly licensed by the city, they are de facto unregulated, and practices—and prices—can vary. Many of the drivers have been known to deliver "historical" commentary that is more fancy than fact. Also, some drivers may attempt to give you a subtle sales pitch for some shops or restaurants along the way. Fact or fancy, sit back and enjoy the ride. Two of the companies offering carriage rides are *Charbonnet Transportation* (1615 St. Philip St.; phone: 581-4411), which rents carriages that hold eight to 10 passengers by the hour; and *Gay Nineties Carriage Tours* (1824 N. Rampart St.; phone: 943-8820), which offers a half-hour tour.

FERRY The Canal Street ferry, operating daily from 6 AM to 9 PM, provides free rides back and forth across the river to Algiers (phone: 362-2981).

RIVER TOURS The very best of the river excursions are those aboard the *Natchez*, one of the five remaining steamboats on the Mississippi. The large sternwheeler departs the Toulouse Street Wharf (behind *Jax Brewery*) twice a day on two-hour runs up and down the river. The scenic tour includes a narrated history of such landmarks as Jackson Square and the Chalmette Battlefield and, for an extra fee, a luncheon buffet of creole specialties. A dinner cruise with live music by the *Crescent City Jazz Band* is also available. For information contact the *New Orleans Steamboat Company* (World Trade Center; phone: 586-8777; 800-233-BOAT for reservations).

In addition, the *Bayou Jean Lafitte* excursion boat departs the Toulouse Street Wharf for the bayou country, to Bayou Barataria, home of the famous pirate; a small paddle wheeler, the *Cotton Blossom,* makes three runs daily from the Canal Street docks to the *Audubon Zoo;* and a high-speed catamaran, the *Audubon Express,* makes six trips daily between the *Aquarium of the Americas* and the *Audubon Zoo* (for information on these excursions, call 586-8777). The motorized, three-decker *Cajun Queen* and the sternwheeler *Creole Queen* offer both daytime and dinner cruises, which depart from behind the *Riverwalk Mall* and the *Aquarium of the Americas* (phone: 524-0814). *Gray Line* (phone: 587-0861) offers river or combined water and land tours of the city aboard the steamboat *Natchez* and coach bus, as well as swamp and bayou cruises and other combination tours.

TAXIS Cabs can be ordered by telephone, hailed in the streets, or picked up at stands in front of hotels, restaurants, and transportation terminals. Major taxi companies are *United* (phone: 522-9771); *White Fleet* (phone: 948-6605); and *Yellow-Checker* (phone: 525-3311).

VOODOO TOURS Voodoo, the ancient African religion once practiced here, first filtered into Louisiana in the early 1700s. When the government refused to recognize it as a religion and suppressed voodoo rites, believers went underground and voodoo became a cult. Although there are no credible signs that voodoo is seriously practiced in present-day New Orleans, several voodoo-oriented tours are available: a voodoo walking tour of the French Quarter, with a stop at the *Voodoo Museum* (see *Museums*), part of the same outfit that runs these tours; a tour that features a voodoo ceremony; a "Voodoo Ritual Swamp Tour"; and other excursions that wind through mysterious bayous, historic plantations, gardens, villages, Indian burial grounds, and fascinating swamp scenery and wildlife. Tours range from two and a half to 10 hours; for information, contact the *Voodoo Museum* (phone: 523-7685).

WALKING TOURS The *Friends of the Cabildo* (phone: 523-3939) lead walking tours of the French Quarter that begin at Jackson Square; the price includes admission to two of the four following sites: the *Cabildo,* the *Presbytère,* the *Old US Mint* (see *Special Places*), and *1850 House* (see *Museums and Historic Houses*). The *National Park Service* (phone: 589-2636) conducts free walking tours of the French Quarter, *St. Louis Cemetery Number One,* and the Garden District, and occasionally offers specialized tours on subjects that range from the story of pirate Jean Lafitte to the history of the Louisiana legal system. *Magic Walking Tours* (phone: 593-9693) offers on-foot explorations of the French Quarter, the port, and other points relating to such special interests as African history, the Civil War, Storyville, and jazz. The walks offered by *Heritage Tours* (phone: 949-9805) focus on the French Quarter's literary history, with commentary on the places where such writers as Tennessee Williams and William Faulkner lived and worked. *Gray Line* (phone: 587-0861), known for its bus tours, also gives walking tours of the French Quarter that begin at the *Old Ursuline Convent.*

LOCAL SERVICES

For additional information about services not listed below, call the *Chamber of Commerce of New Orleans and the River Region* (phone: 527-6900).

AUDIOVISUAL EQUIPMENT *AV Communications* (210 Decatur St.; phone: 522-9769); *Jasper Ewing & Sons Inc.* (1904 Poydras St.; phone: 525-5257).

BUSINESS SERVICES *Headquarters Business Centers* (*HQ;* 1 Canal Pl.; phone: 525-1175) has word processing, telex and fax machines, and conference rooms.

COMPUTER RENTAL *Audubon Computer Rentals* (1036 Annunciation St.; phone: 522-0348); *New Orleans Computer Rental* (58 Westbank Expwy., Gretna; phone: 394-1324).

DRY CLEANERS/TAILORS *Alessi Cleaners* (837 Gravier St.; phone: 586-9632); *Gonzales Tailoring* (1015 Common St.; phone: 524-2802).

LIMOUSINES *A Confidential Limousine* (phone: 833-9999); *London Livery Ltd.* (phone: 944-1984); *A Touch of Class Limousine Service Inc.* (phone: 522-7565).

MECHANICS *MasterCare Car Service* (800 Camp St.; phone: 525-2241); *Western Battery and Electric Co.* (524 S. Claiborne Ave.; phone: 523-8225).

MEDICAL EMERGENCY *Charity Hospital/Medical Center of Louisiana* (1532 Tulane Ave.; phone: 568-2311); *Mercy Hospital* (301 N. Jefferson Davis Pkwy.; phone: 483-5777); *Touro Infirmary* (1401 Foucher St.; phone: 897-8250); *Tulane Medical Center* (1415 Tulane Ave.; phone: 588-5711).

MESSENGER SERVICES *Controlled Business Deliveries* (401 Carondelet St.; phone: 525-9917); *United Cabs* (1627 Polymnia St.; phone: 524-9606), which offers 24-hour service.

PHOTOCOPIES *Kinko's Copies* (762 St. Charles Ave.; phone: 581-2541; and many other locations).

POST OFFICE The main post office is at 701 Loyola Ave. (phone: 589-1111); there's also a downtown branch at 1022 Iberville St. (phone: 524-0072). The *Postal Emporium* (940 Royal St., in the French Quarter; phone: 525-6651) offers mail, UPS, FedEx, and other shipping and delivery services.

PROFESSIONAL PHOTOGRAPHERS *Mitchell L. Osborne Photography* (920 Frenchmen St.; phone: 949-1366); *Commercial and Industrial Photographers* (613 Fielding Ave., Gretna; phone: 368-6089), which is on call 24 hours daily.

SECRETARIES/STENOGRAPHERS *Dictation Inc.* (phone: 895-8637), which offers 24-hour service; *Workload Inc.* (225 Baronne St.; phone: 522-7171).

TELECONFERENCE FACILITIES The *Inter-Continental, Le Meridien, New Orleans Hilton, Omni Royal Orleans,* and *Westin–Canal Place* hotels have teleconferencing facilities (see *Checking In*).

TRANSLATOR *Professional Translators and Interpreters Inc.* (World Trade Center; phone: 581-3122).

TYPEWRITER RENTAL *Office Machine Rental* (605 S. Jefferson Davis Pkwy.; phone: 482-4408).

WESTERN UNION/TELEX *Western Union* (phone: 800-325-6000) has a number of offices, including one downtown (334 Carondelet St.; phone: 529-5971).

SPECIAL EVENTS

The *Sugar Bowl Classic,* one of football's oldest college bowl games, is held *New Year's Day* in the *Louisiana Superdome* (phone: 522-2600). The next celebration of the year is the biggest—New Orleans's famous pre-Lenten *Carnival* during the two weeks or so preceding the final blowout on *Mardi Gras* (Fat Tuesday). Since *Mardi Gras* is 47 days before *Easter,* the date varies from year to year; this year *Mardi Gras* is February 28. A score or more of street parades and dozens of costume balls (mostly private) are held, and the French Quarter, especially Bourbon Street, fills with revelers.

The first of this culturally diverse city's many annual ethnic celebrations is the *Black Heritage Festival* in early March; it features food booths, jazz and church music, and art exhibits (phone: 861-2537). The city's Irish Americans celebrate *St. Patrick's Day* (March 17) with a huge street party Uptown in the old Irish Channel and parades in several parts of the city and suburbs. A tradition that dates back to the turn of the century is the *St. Joseph's Day* parade, held on the weekend night nearest the March 19 feast day of the patron saint of Sicily. Italian-American men of all ages, dressed in tuxedos and carrying canes festooned with red, white, and green carnations, file through the French Quarter's streets amid floats, marching bands, and statues of the saint and the Virgin Mary.

One weekend in early April, the *French Quarter Festival* fills the Vieux Carré with parades, food vendors, artists, musical groups, and other performers (phone: 522-5730). Also in early April is the *Spring Fiesta,* highlighted by tours of private French Quarter patios by daylight or candlelight and a nighttime parade (phone: 581-1367).

The city's other huge annual outdoor event takes place in late April and early May. The two-week *New Orleans Jazz and Heritage Festival* features dozens of bands, vocalists, and gospel groups from nearby and around the world, as well as food and crafts stalls. Performances are held in the mornings to late afternoons on the grassy expanse inside the racetrack at the *New Orleans Fair Grounds;* nighttime concerts take place on riverboats and in nightclubs and concert halls. For festival information call 522-4786.

The Greek residents of the city have their day in late May, when traditional foods, crafts, and music fill the *Hellenic Cultural Center* near Bayou St. John for a *Greek Festival* (phone: 282-0259). Food is the focus of the *Great French Market Tomato Festival,* held inside the colonnades of the *French Market*'s complex of food and gift shops in the French Quarter, usually the first full weekend in June (phone: 522-2621 on weekdays only). In July the city celebrates *Carnaval Latino* (phone: 522-9927) and August brings the *Latino Festival* to Canal Street (phone: 524-0427). A few weeks later, in early September, the *Fiesta Latina* takes place at the *Audubon Zoo* (phone: 861-2537). On an early fall weekend, the *Patio Planters* organization conducts afternoon tours of private French Quarter gardens (phone: 566-5068). Italian-Americans are in the spotlight again in October, when the *Festa d'Italia* takes over the downtown Piazza d'Italia with traditional food, music, and exhibits (phone: 891-1904). The *Gumbo Festival* is another of October's special events; it's held in Bridge City, across the Huey P. Long Bridge from New Orleans (phone: 436-4712).

The *Christmas* season is observed in *City Park* with the *Celebration in the Oaks*. From late November to early January, several acres of the park's shrubbery and huge oaks are festooned with spectacular electrical ornaments. During December, the French Quarter celebrates *Creole Christmas*—the historic homes are decorated in 19th-century creole style and restaurants offer special menus replicating the traditional French-creole *reveillon* holiday meal.

MUSEUMS AND HISTORIC HOUSES

In addition to those described in *Special Places*, other notable New Orleans museums include the following:

CONFEDERATE MUSEUM Louisiana's oldest, this small, red stone museum, just off Lee Circle, dates from 1891. Civil War buffs will find a trove of weapons, uniforms, maps, records, flags, and other memorabilia. Closed Sundays. Admission charge. 929 Camp St. (phone: 523-4522).

1850 HOUSE This townhouse, one of the row houses that comprise the Pontalba Apartments flanking Jackson Square, has been furnished and decorated as a typical home of prosperous Creoles in the mid-19th century, when the Baroness Pontalba had the twin apartment buildings constructed. A lack of ostentation is the principal asset of the furnishings. Closed Mondays and Tuesdays. Admission charge. 523 St. Ann St. (phone: 524-9118).

GALLIER HOUSE MUSEUM Upper class New Orleans in the Victorian era is mirrored in the elaborate appointments of this meticulously restored mansion in a quiet section of the French Quarter. Designed by architect James Gallier Jr as his family's residence, the house now features wall coverings, fabrics, rugs, and fixtures that authentically re-create the lifestyle of 1857. The small, simple garden contains a facsimile of the house's cistern, and a carriage sits ready in the carriageway separating the residence from the gift shop. After each tour, coffee is served on the balcony overlooking an especially picturesque block of Royal Street. Closed Sundays. Admission charge. 1118-1132 Royal St. (phone: 523-6722).

HERMANN-GRIMA HOUSE A small army of historians, botanists, and social scientists took part in the restoration of this aristocratic, red brick residence to its original state. Built in 1831 by a wealthy merchant at the outset of New Orleans's "golden age" (1830 to 1860), the house, with rooms flanking a central hall, was a departure from typical creole design of the era. The details are remarkably authentic, from the cast-iron pots of the creole-style kitchen to the harnesses in the stables and the aromatic plants in the garden. There are creole cooking demonstrations on Thursdays October through May; there's also an annual cooking workshop in the spring. The appointments in the living quarters also are true to the period. Closed Sundays. Admission charge. 820 St. Louis St. (phone: 525-5661).

HISTORICAL PHARMACY MUSEUM In the 1820s, this little shop was the apothecary of Louis J. Dufilho, said to have been the first licensed pharmacist in the US. Its displays of 19th-century jars and equipment may not be as interesting as the quaint old rooms and the charming interior herbal and botanical garden. Closed Mondays. Admission charge. 514 Chartres St. (phone: 524-9077).

LOUISIANA CHILDREN'S MUSEUM More play-school than museum, this cleverly designed spot features all kinds of hands-on fun for kids under 12. It contains a little coffee factory, numerous games and educational exhibits, and miniature versions of a supermarket, TV studio, and hospital. Closed Mondays. Admission charge. 428 Julia St. (phone: 523-1357).

LOUISIANA NATURE AND SCIENCE CENTER Natural sciences are spotlighted at this small museum, which is connected to nature trails on the city's eastern edge. The planetarium offers a number of astronomical programs (usually on weekends) as well as laser rock shows. Raised wooden walkways winding through the surrounding woods afford visitors a short, pleasant hike. Closed Mondays. Admission charge. *Joe Brown Park;* enter at Read Blvd. and Nature Center Dr. (phone: 246-5672; 246-9381 for recorded information).

MUSÉE CONTI WAX MUSEUM Voodoo, *Mardi Gras,* and the pirate Jean Lafitte are represented in the numerous tableaux here, featuring life-size wax mannequins in elaborate stage settings. Major events and personages of New Orleans's colorful history are the focus. There's printed or tape-recorded commentary. Open daily from 10 AM to 5:30 PM. Admission charge. 917 Conti St. (phone: 525-2605).

RIVERTOWN There are several small museums contained in these nostalgically designed buildings situated on the Mississippi River in the New Orleans suburb of Kenner. The *Freeport-McMoRan Daily Living Science Center* has a planetarium and observatory (409 Williams Blvd.; phone: 582-4000). Six working layouts of toy trains, trolleys, and a toy carousel are on display in the *Louisiana Toy Train Museum* (519 Williams Blvd.; phone: 468-7223). The *Louisiana Wildlife and Fisheries Museum* (303 Williams Blvd.; phone: 468-7232) features an aquarium and preserved wildlife specimens and displays. And the *Saints Hall of Fame Museum* (409 Williams Blvd.; phone: 468-6617) contains memorabilia of New Orleans's pro football team. All are closed Sunday mornings and Mondays; admission charge for each, but discount passes also are sold for those intending to visit more than one museum. The *Mardi Gras Museum* (see *Old US Mint,* above, in *Special Places*) is also included in this discount pass.

VOODOO MUSEUM Despite its name, this tiny outfit is really more a tourist shop than a museum. It displays African masks and voodoo dolls, and sells souvenirs inspired by the voodoo practices that once flourished in the city. Open daily. Admission charge. 724 Dumaine St. (phone: 523-7685).

SHOPPING

Although the largest shopping centers are found in the surrounding suburbs, downtown New Orleans also contains several major malls offering an immense variety of merchandise, as well as hundreds of specialty shops. The principal malls are the *New Orleans Centre* (just steps away from the *Louisiana Superdome* on Poydras St.), where *Macy's* and *Lord & Taylor* are the main tenants; *Canal Place* (at 333 Canal St. near the Mississippi River), with a three-level branch of *Saks Fifth Avenue* and a large *Brooks Brothers;* and *Riverwalk* (extending along the riverfront near Canal St.), with two levels of restaurants and shops that include *Banana Republic* (casual clothing), *Abercrombie & Fitch* (sportswear and gifts), and *Sharper Image* (electronic gadgets). Canal Street itself still contains a few department stores harking back to its years as the city's shopping artery; the two major ones are the upscale *Maison Blanche* (901 Canal St.; phone: 566-1000) and *Krauss* (1201 Canal St., phone: 523-3311). Each is a full-scale emporium. Antiques hunters should focus their attention on the French Quarter, especially Royal and Chartres Streets, which contain all sorts of antiques shops and art galleries, and, farther out from the city center, Magazine Street, which contains dozens of stores offering moderate to expensive antique furniture, rugs, bric-a-brac, and artwork, from regional to European. Below is a list of New Orleans's favorite shopping places.

Adler's A large selection of jewelry, porcelain, gifts, and bibelots fills the two floors of this plush establishment, now operated by the third generation of the Adler family. 723 Canal St. (phone: 523-5292).

Alfredo's Cameras Expert advice and a wide range of cameras and photographic equipment. 916 Gravier St. (phone: 523-2421).

Arthur Roger Gallery Top contemporary artists from New Orleans and other parts of the country show their paintings and sculpture in this spacious, elegantly designed gallery in the Warehouse District. 432 Julia St. (phone: 522-1990).

Bep's Antiques Modest treasures like old bottles, homey Victorian washstands, and charming little side tables are sold here. 2051 Magazine St. (phone: 525-7726).

Bergeron's Dozens of styles by top designers are the stock-in-trade at the city's preeminent source of fine-quality women's shoes. Unusual handbags are another specialty. *Canal Place,* 333 Canal St. (phone: 525-2195).

Bookstar Two very large floors filled with every type of publication. A good selection of audiotapes, magazines, and maps, too. 414 N. Peters St. (phone: 523-6411).

Central Grocery Co. Known for its *muffuletta* sandwiches and a huge array of Italian food specialties, this is also a good source for a wide variety of non-perishable groceries from around the world. 923 Decatur St. (phone: 523-1620).

Coghlan Gallery This shop features odds and ends to decorate your garden or terrace, including hand-crafted copper fountains and other ornaments. 710 Toulouse St. (phone: 525-8550).

Cuisine Classique You're likely to leave here with something for your kitchen that you didn't know you needed—an oversize stockpot, an apple corer, or a lemon zester. Along with the vast array of cooking tools offered, there is also a wide selection of local cookbooks. 439 Decatur St. (phone: 524-0068).

DeVille Books & Prints This is the place to check for hard-to-find authors and unusual literary works. The art, architecture, and photography sections are especially well stocked. Three locations: 1 Shell Sq., St. Charles Ave. at Poydras St. (phone: 525-1846); *Jax Brewery,* 620 Decatur (phone: 525-4508); and *Riverwalk Mall,* Poydras St. at the Mississippi River (phone: 595-8916).

Ditto 19th Century Antiques Specializes in clocks, cut-glass, and above-average bric-a-brac. 4838 Magazine St. (phone: 891-4845).

French Market This famous market sells a wide variety of items—souvenirs, sweets (including pralines), toys, candles, spices, and funky clothes, just to name a few. Outdoor vendors' stalls offer a cornucopia of fresh fruits and vegetables, tropical plants, old books and records, and a hodgepodge of cooking spices. Decatur St., between St. Ann and Barracks Sts.

Galerie Simonne Stern Aficionados of abstract expressionism and other 20th-century schools of art should see this prestigious gallery; exhibitions feature emerging local and national artists. 518 Julia St. (phone: 529-1118) and 305 Royal St. (phone: 524-9757).

A Gallery for Fine Photography The work of the world's best-known photographers, from Matthew Brady to Irving Penn, are represented in this vast collection, shown on two floors. Also look for rare and unusual photographs relating to New Orleans, especially its musicians. 322 Royal (phone: 568-1313).

Gasperi Gallery Contemporary folk art and works that have strong ethnic connections. 320 Julia St. (phone: 524-9373).

Henry Stern Antiques A long-established dealer in fine English furniture and paintings from the late 18th and early 19th centuries. 329-331 Royal St. (phone: 522-8687).

Hové Parfumeur Perfumes, colognes, and soaps are produced on the premises of this charming, family-owned boutique, and dried aromatic herbs such as vetiver are also available. 824 Royal St. (phone: 525-7827).

The Idea Factory Hand-crafted wooden creations—whimsical creatures as well as marquetry boxes and other practical items—can be found here; all are made in a workshop out back. 838 Chartres St. (phone: 524-5195).

Jon Antiques Among the better purveyors of 18th- and 19th-century furniture, china, and objets d'art. 4605 Magazine St. (phone: 899-4482).

K&B Camera Center Whether you're a point-and-shooter or a professional, this is a handy source of camera equipment, film, and accessories; it also operates its own custom-processing laboratory. 227 Dauphine St. (phone: 524-2266).

Kaboom Books The number and selection of bookseller John Dillman's used volumes are excellent, and he's unusually knowledgeable about various editions. 901 Barracks St. (phone: 529-5780).

Kite Shop From the whimsical to the artistic, all kinds of kites crowd the ceiling and walls of this colorful and fascinating little store on Jackson Square. 542 St. Peter St. (phone: 524-0028).

Lucullus Crowded with antique French and English dining room furniture, crystal, porcelain, and decorative objects relating to food and wine. 610 Chartres St. (phone: 528-9620).

Maison Blanche This fine regional department store in the heart of downtown carries nationally known brands as well as designer clothing. 901 Canal St. (phone: 566-1000).

Maple Street Book Shop If New Orleans has a literary heart, it is this unpretentious uptown cottage crammed with a very selective collection of novels, anthologies, and biographies, from the latest best sellers to the most obscure Southern writers. A bookworm's paradise. 7523 Maple St. (phone: 866-4916). The branch at 2727 Prytania St. (phone: 895-2266) is interesting, too.

Merrill B. Domas American Indian Art The work of the best weavers, potters, and painters from the Southwest is sold here, as well as jewelry in silver and gemstones by some of Santa Fe's leading artisans. 824 Chartres St. (phone: 586-0479).

Mignon Faget Ltd. New Orleans's premier jewelry designer offers elegant pieces inspired by nature in precious metals and stones. *Canal Place,* 333 Canal St. (phone: 524-2973); 710 Dublin St. (phone: 865-7361); and 8220 Maple St. (phone: 865-1107).

Morton M. Goldberg Auction Galleries A virtual warehouse filled with every sort of antique, it is worth a visit if only for browsing among the wealth of American, European, and Oriental objects. Estate auctions are a specialty, and good values are there for the cognoscenti. 547 Baronne St. (phone: 592-2300).

M. S. Rau Two large floors packed to the rafters with antiques—everything from art glass to music boxes, and more crystal and porcelain than you may have thought existed. 630 Royal St. (phone: 523-5660).

Old Town Praline Shop Charmingly old-fashioned, it turns out pecan-studded sugar patties wrapped in the same little waxed-paper bags they've used for decades. They'll pack and ship, as well. 627 Royal St. (phone: 525-1413).

Perlis Conservative men's clothing with a dash of élan. Fashion headquarters for many of the city's lawyers and stockbrokers, the styles range from Duck's Head khaki pants to Southwick and Ralph Lauren suits. Boy's and women's clothes are sold, too. 6070 Magazine St. (phone: 895-8661).

Le Petit Soldier Shoppe Collector or not, you're apt to be charmed by the hundreds of exquisitely crafted and painted lead soldiers sold in this museum-cum-shop. There are also all sorts of antique military memorabilia. 528 Royal St. (phone: 523-7741).

Progress Grocery Co. It's part delicatessen, part fancy grocery store, with a *muffuletta* sandwich take-out counter and a huge variety of exotic edibles on the shelves, including the proprietor's own herbed olive oils. Imported pasta and unusual dried legumes are also available. 915 Decatur St. (phone: 525-6627).

Rapp's Luggage and Gifts Whether you're looking for a plastic carry-on or a briefcase of fine leather, you'll probably find it here; also all sorts of handy travel gear. Minor luggage repairs, too. 604 Canal St. (phone: 568-1953).

Record Ron's Good & Plenty Records Everything from Bing Crosby to heavy metal to baroque, with a specialty in rarities and the offbeat, fills the seemingly endless bins of LPs. 1129 Decatur St. (phone: 524-9444) and 407 Decatur St. (phone: 522-2239).

Rubenstein Bros. The fashion-conscious man looking for top American and European designers will find them here. So will the follower of the latest trends in casualwear. The choices, from haberdashery to topcoats, are many and varied. 102 St. Charles Ave. (phone: 581-6666).

Serendipitous A wide variety of brightly colored masks can be found here. 831 Decatur St. (phone: 522-9158).

Stan Levy Imports A good source not only of European pieces but also Southern armoires, 19th-century Louisiana furniture, and more recent objects from the region—affordable, too. 1028 Louisiana Ave., near Magazine St. (phone: 899-6384).

Still-Zinsel Contemporary Fine Art New painters and photographers working in a variety of styles are often introduced here. 328 Julia St. (phone: 588-9999).

Victoria's Designer Discount Shoes From simple pumps to glittery evening shoes, much of the footwear is made by the leading names in fashion—and they're priced to sell. 532 Chartres St. (phone: 568-9990).

Waldhorn An antiques dealer for connoisseurs of English and French furniture. 343 Royal St. (phone: 581-6379).

Wehmeier's Belt Shop The large inventory of men's and women's leather goods includes shoes and handbags; emergency repairs are made on the premises. 719 Toulouse (phone: 525-2758).

SPORTS AND FITNESS

BICYCLING Bicycles can be rented at *Bicycle Michael's* (618 Frenchmen St., a few blocks from the French Quarter; phone: 945-9505). *City Park* rents bikes at Dreyfous Avenue (phone: 483-9371).

BOATING At *City Park*, you can rent canoes, paddleboats, and skiffs to cruise on the lagoons (phone: 483-9371).

CANOEING The swamps and marshes within an hour's drive from the center of town, teeming with vegetation and wildlife, provide an exotic backdrop for explorations by canoe. *Canoe and Trail Outings* (802 Chapelle St.; phone: 283-9400) specializes in "sunset paddling" excursions to the Manchac Swamp, west of the city, and the Honey Island Swamp to the east, among other places. The company rents all the necessary equipment.

FISHING New Orleans's location on the central Gulf Coast makes it ideal for freshwater and saltwater sport fishing year-round. Full-day excursions from New Orleans to Venice, near the mouth of the Mississippi River, are easily arranged for groups of two to 20. Lakes, bays, inlets, and marshes, less than an hour's drive from the center of town, are filled with redfish, largemouth bass, catfish, and freshwater drum. In the very heart of town, *City Park*'s lagoons are pleasant places to drop a line on a balmy afternoon. Temporary state licenses are required for non-state residents for all fishing, crabbing, and shrimping—saltwater and freshwater licenses are sold by the *Louisiana Department of Wildlife and Fisheries* office in the French Quarter (400 Chartres St.; phone: 568-5636), which is closed weekends. Be sure to inquire about seasonal regulations, too.

FITNESS CENTERS The *New Orleans Athletic Club* (222 N. Rampart St.; phone: 525-2375) has a 60-foot indoor lap pool, exercise equipment and classes, a boxing ring, racquetball and basketball courts, and indoor and outdoor tracks. *Racquetball One Fitness Centers* (1 Shell Sq., 13th Floor, Poydras St. and St. Charles Ave.; phone: 522-2956; and *Canal Place*, Suite 380, 333 Canal St.; phone: 525-2956) offer five racquetball courts, aerobics programs, free weights, stair climbers, and exercise cycles. Several hotels also allow non-guests to use their centers for a fee. The *Rivercenter Racquet and Health Club* in the *New Orleans Hilton* (Poydras St. at the Mississippi River; phone: 587-7242) has a jogging track, weight training, saunas, and basketball, racquetball, tennis, and squash courts. *Eurovita Spa* at the *Avenue Plaza Suite* hotel (2111 St. Charles Ave.; phone: 566-1212) offers a fitness room with weights, saunas, steamrooms, a whirlpool bath, and tanning rooms, as well as therapeutic massages. *Le Meridien Sports Center* (*Le Meridien Hotel*, 614 Canal St.; phone: 527-6750) has an outdoor heated pool, Nautilus equipment, Lifecycles, an aerobics program, yoga classes, a sauna, and massage therapists.

FOOTBALL The New Orleans *Saints* play in the *Louisiana Superdome* (Poydras St.; phone: 522-2600). The *Sugar Bowl Classic,* one of football's oldest college bowl games, takes place on *New Year's Day* in the *Superdome.*

GOLF Several public 18-hole courses, all open daily, are short distances from the city center. *City Park* has four courses (phone: 483-9396). *Audubon Park* (in the Uptown section; phone: 861-9511) has its own course. Also check out *Brechtel Park* (on the west bank of the Mississippi River; phone: 362-4761); *Joe Bartholomew Golf Course* (in eastern New Orleans's *Pontchartrain Park;* phone: 288-0928); and *Plantation Golf Course* (1001 Behrman Hwy.; phone: 392-3363).

HORSEBACK RIDING The 2-mile trail at *Cascade Stables* is shaded by *Audubon Park*'s huge oaks. Horses and ponies are available for adults and youngsters daily (phone: 891-2246).

HORSE RACING The *Fair Grounds* (1751 Gentilly Blvd.; phone: 944-5515), one of the country's oldest thoroughbred-racing tracks, is a 15-minute taxi ride from the city center. It operates from *Thanksgiving* to mid-April. Although a fire in December 1993 destroyed the historic clubhouse and grandstand, as well as other major buildings, the track's owners resumed the races within weeks. At press time, plans for rebuilding were in the works.

JOGGING Good routes are in *City Park* at the end of Esplanade Avenue, *Audubon Park* in the Uptown section, *Woldenberg Park* on the French Quarter's edge, and along the Mississippi River levee on Leake Avenue in the Carrollton section.

SAILING Lake Pontchartrain's brisk breezes and typically calm waters make it ideal for Sunday sailors. The bayous and lagoons that ring New Orleans also provide for relaxing excursions along the water. Even if you forgot to tow your boat, there are still ways to take advantage of New Orleans's favorite offshore activity. From March through October, recreational craft can be rented on the New Orleans lakefront from *Sailboats South* (300 Sapphire St.; phone: 288-7245). For lake boating, the choices include monohulls, catamarans, sailboats, and powerboats, ranging in size from nine to 36 feet. *Sailboats South* also rents rowing shells and skiffs for coasting along the nearby bayous and inlets.

TENNIS The 39 lighted courts at the *Wisner Tennis Center* in *City Park* are open from 7 AM to past sunset, and the pro shop provides racquet repairs (phone: 483-9383). *Audubon Park*'s 10 courts, near the Mississippi River in the Uptown section, are open at 8 AM (phone: 895-1042). The *Rivercenter Racquet and Health Club* has eight indoor and three outdoor courts; located at the *New Orleans Hilton* (2 Poydras St.; phone: 587-7242), it has river views. All charge court fees; all are open daily.

THEATER

National touring companies of Broadway shows perform regularly in the fall and spring at the *Saenger Performing Arts Center* (143 N. Rampart St. at Canal St.; phone: 524-2490). For those seeking something more daring, contemporary American plays, many of them by local writers and most of them avant-garde, are presented regularly in the arena theater of the *Contemporary Arts Center* (900 Camp St.; phone: 523-1216). In the French Quarter's community theater, the picturesque *Le Petit Théâtre du Vieux Carré* presents modern musical comedies and dramas from Broadway's past, and original plays for children (616 St. Peter St.; phone: 522-2081). The several productions presented each year by the *Southern Repertory Theater* (1437 S. Carrollton Ave.; phone: 861-2254) stages a broad range of productions, but emphasizes works by Southern playwrights such as Tennessee Williams. Respectable amateur productions, from the spirited performances of the *Dashiki Theatre* group to original spoofs of old Hollywood musicals, are put on in the 100-seat *NORD Theater* space on the ground floor of *Gallier Hall* (543 St. Charles Ave.; phone: 565-7860). Original dramas, some experimental, are the forte of the little *Theater Marigny* (616 Frenchmen St.; phone: 944-2653), while campy satires and musical revues are the specialties of the *Toulouse Theatre* in the French Quarter (615 Toulouse

St.; phone: 523-4207). Meatier works, from 19th-century classics to contemporary plays, are presented by *Tulane University* (*Dixon Performing Arts Center* on the *Newcomb College* campus; phone: 865-5106, the Drama Department, for theater productions during the year; phone: 865-5269, the Music Department, for summer stock musicals by the semi-professional *Summer Lyric Theater,* as well as opera and other music concerts); *Loyola University's Lower Depths Theatre* (on the St. Charles Ave. campus; phone: 865-3824); and the *University of New Orleans Performing Arts Center* (near the Lakefront; phone: 834-9774). Lighter fare, in the form of contemporary Broadway comedies and revues, is the stock-in-trade at the city's numerous dinner-theaters. The main one is *Starcastle Dinner Theater* (2400 Belle Chasse Hwy., Gretna; phone: 366-0999).

CINEMA

If you want to see a particular first-run Hollywood production, you may have to head for a multi-screen theater in the suburbs (Metairie or the West Bank). But a couple of in-town cinemas also show current general-interest films. *Canal Place Cinema* (*Canal Place*, Fifth Floor, 333 Canal St.; phone: 581-5400) has four screens and shows top American and foreign films. Uptown near St. Charles Avenue, the *Prytania* (5339 Prytania St.; phone: 895-4513) focuses on more serious fare—art films and occasionally something from the underground.

MUSIC AND DANCE

The demise of the *New Orleans Symphony Orchestra* in early 1990 left the city without a major orchestra of its own for the first time since the 1930s. Later that year, however, a core group of musicians launched a grass-roots movement that resulted in the creation of the *Louisiana Philharmonic Orchestra,* with a limited season in the spring and fall and a roster of guest conductors. The group's concerts are given in the *Orpheum Theater* (129 University Pl., near Canal St.; phone: 523-6530). Aficionados of chamber music should check the schedule of the *Friends of Music* (phone: 895-0690), a group that sponsors several concerts each year by local and nationally known professionals; the performances are usually held at *Tulane University's Dixon Performing Arts Center* on the *Newcomb College* campus. *Loyola University* and *Sophie Newcomb College* at *Tulane University* sponsor occasional recitals and concerts by students, faculty, and visiting performers at *Loyola's Roussel Performance Hall* on the university campus (7214 St. Charles Ave.; phone: 865-2492) and at *Tulane/Newcomb's Dixon Hall* or *Rogers Memorial Chapel* (information from *Tulane's* Music Department; phone: 865-5269). New Orleans was the first American city to build an opera house, in the early 19th century. The musical tradition continues with several productions yearly by the *New Orleans Opera Association,* featuring internationally known performers offering classical European repertories. They're presented at the *Theatre for the Performing Arts* (N. Rampart St. near the corner of Dumaine St.; phone: 529-2278). Also, the music department of *Xavier University* occasionally stages student opera productions (7325 Palmetto St.; phone: 486-7411, university switchboard; phone: 483-7621, program director's office).

In the 1980s *The New Orleans City Ballet* merged with the *Cincinnati Ballet*, but kept its name and locale (phone: 522-0996); it stages several major productions annually in the *Theatre for the Performing Arts* (see above).

The biggest pop and rock stars regularly perform at the *Saenger Performing Arts Center* downtown (143 N. Rampart St.; phone: 524-2490); the *Kiefer UNO Lakefront Arena* (on the *University of New Orleans* campus; phone: 286-7222); the *Louisiana Superdome* (on Poydras St.; phone: 587-3800); and at private halls and clubs around town.

ALL THAT JAZZ

Jazz and Cajun musicians have brought the Big Easy its international reputation as a musical center. New Orleans is a port city, and nowhere is this more apparent than in the flamboyant overlapping of musical influences that have produced the distinctively syncopated swagger and improvisational fire of this city's music. The music is a rich gumbo created from the cross-fertilization of Caribbean music, African rhythms, the blues, zydeco, and traditional Cajun music. New Orleans has exported its music around the globe and has garnered an enthusiastic international following. Some of the current stars of this musical seedbed include the *Neville Brothers*, Dr. John, the *Dirty Dozen Brass Band*, and such zydeco groups as *Buckwheat Zydeco* and *Rockin' Dopsie and the Zydeco Twisters*. At the same time, never forget that Louis Armstrong, Jelly Roll Morton, Sidney Bechet, and other jazz immortals were the New Orleans musicians who brought jazz to a new plateau of improvisational genius, making a major impact on the evolution of this quintessentially American sound.

NIGHTCLUBS AND NIGHTLIFE

No fan of classic New Orleans jazz should miss the authentic music and incomparable atmosphere of *Preservation Hall* (see *Special Places*). More comfortable, and just as much the real thing musically, is the *Palm Court Jazz Café* (1204 Decatur St.; phone: 525-0200), a spacious restaurant in an old French Quarter building where young and old traditionalists play nightly.

Two of the city's most celebrated Dixieland musicians, clarinetist Pete Fountain and trumpeter Al Hirt, have their own clubs, and the seats are always filled when the masters themselves are onstage. Fountain's headquarters is *Pete Fountain's* in the *New Orleans Hilton* (2 Poydras St.; phone: 523-4374), and Hirt holds forth from time to time at *Jelly Roll's* in the French Quarter (501 Bourbon St.; phone: 568-0501). Good-quality local bands perform in their absence; if you're interested only in the stars themselves, call ahead. Bourbon Street is lined with Dixieland clubs; one of the best is the *Famous Door* (339 Bourbon St.;

phone: 522-7626); another is *Fritzel's* (733 Bourbon St.; phone: 561-0432); or, off Bourbon, try *Maxwell's Toulouse Cabaret* (615 Toulouse St.; phone: 523-4207). A cushy spot to enjoy traditional New Orleans music is the *Louis Armstrong Foundation Jazz Club* in *Le Meridien* hotel's vast ground-floor lobby (see *Checking In*), where *Jacques Gauthé's Yerba Buena Creole Rice Jazz Band* regularly performs on weekends. Another especially compatible setting for Dixieland is *LeMoyne's Landing,* near the Plaza d'España and the *Riverwalk Mall* (Canal St. at the Mississippi River; phone: 524-4809).

The music of southwest Louisiana's bayous has an international following and it is certainly not neglected in New Orleans clubs. Authentic Cajun bands, including groups performing in the even earthier and folksier zydeco style, stomp and fiddle every night in the Warehouse District at *Mulate's* (201 Julia St.; phone: 522-1492), which also has a dance floor and a kitchen dispensing spicy Louisiana dishes. Another choice Cajun dance hall–restaurant is *Michaul's,* on the Warehouse District's fringe (701 Magazine St.; phone: 522-5517). Other clubs where Cajun groups often perform are the *Maple Leaf* (8316 Oak St.; phone: 866-9359), with its tiny dance floor, and *Tipitina's* (501 Napoleon Ave.; phone: 895-8477), an earthy spot deep in the heart of the Uptown waterfront. The "New Orleans Sound" and the blues are also featured at *Tipitina's,* where the music is down-and-dirty and the crowd never stops moving—on or off the dance floor.

The New Orleans sound and the blues also are in the spotlight at *Jimmy's* (8200 Willow St.; phone: 861-8200) and at the *New Orleans Entertainment Hall* in the Warehouse District (907 S. Peters St.; phone: 523-4311). Blues great Marva Wright can often be found at *Muddy Water's* in Carrollton (8301 Oak St.; phone: 866-7174). At *Benny's Bar,* a funky club featuring New Orleans rhythm and blues, the real action doesn't get going until after midnight (938 Valence St.; phone: 895-9405). A new but already premier blues spot in the Quarter is *House of Blues* (225 Decatur St.; phone: 529-2583), an immense music space and restaurant opened last year by comedian Dan Aykroyd. The $7 million complex holds a vast collection of folk art in addition to its awesome sound system.

At *Snug Harbor* (626 Frenchmen St.; phone: 949-0696), a couple of blocks from the French Quarter, you can hear both the New Orleans Sound, performed by such masters as singers Charmaine Neville and Germaine Bazzle, and contemporary jazz; pianist Ellis Marsalis often plays here. At another contemporary jazz spot, the *Crescent City Brewhouse* (527 Decatur St.; phone: 522-0571), Marsalis's son, Delfeayo, holds forth with his quintet nightly.

Other nightspots worth visiting include *The Mint* (504 Esplanade Ave.; phone: 525-2000), a large, laid-back gay bar with a floor show in which homegrown talent performs Friday through Sunday nights. The humor usually has lots of local connotations, but out-of-towners seem to catch on quickly. At *Chris Owens* in the French Quarter (502 Bourbon St.; phone: 523-6400), the club's namesake is the sole performer, and if her maraca shaking and fancy footwork aren't the most advanced in town, her showmanship usually fills the place to the rafters. The *Napoleon House Bar* (500 Chartres St.; phone: 524-9752) is an unpolished, bohemian, yet authentically charming spot to sip the house's special Pimm's Cup Cocktail (Pimm's Cup Mix blended with rum) while soaking up the early 19th-century atmosphere; their hearty Italian-style sandwiches are excellent.

Visitors interested in games of chance should note that plans to open a *Harrah's Grand Palais Casino* on the site of the *Rivergate* exhibition center (Canal Street at the Mississippi River) were incomplete as we went to press, due to contractual tangles and continued debate over whether to renovate or demolish *Rivergate;* check with your hotel or any tourist information officer upon your arrival. Meanwhile, the only other options are riverboat-type casinos, including the *Star Casino,* on Lake Pontchartrain (10001 Lake Forest Blvd.; phone: 243-0400) near the *New Orleans Municipal Airport,* and the *Queen of New Orleans* (2 Poydras Pl.; phone: 587-7777) on the Mississippi River, docked at the *New Orleans Hilton* hotel (see *Checking In,* below). Both operate daily.

Best in Town

CHECKING IN

Hotels in New Orleans usually are more than just places to sleep. Many of them reflect French, Spanish, and/or Louisiana colonial influences, and a good number have serious charm. No matter where you stay or what you pay, make reservations well in advance, particularly during *Sugar Bowl Week* (approximately December 30 to January 2) preceding the annual football classic on *New Year's Day, Carnival* season (in February or early March), and the *New Orleans Jazz and Heritage Festival* (in late April or early May); rates increase by about 25% during these periods. Also note that many hotels have three- or four-day minimum stays during *Carnival.* In general, however, the spate of hotel building that coincided with New Orleans's ill-fated *1984 World's Fair* has tended to keep the hotel business very competitive and rather reasonable—especially on weekends, when many large chains offer promotional package prices. Expect to pay more than $160 per night for those hotels listed as very expensive; from $110 to $160 for a double room (more for suites) at hotels in the expensive range; $75 to $95 at places in the moderate category; and $50 to $70 at establishments in the inexpensive category.

For bed and breakfast accommodations, contact *Bed & Breakfast Inc.* (1360 Moss St., Box 52257, New Orleans, LA 70152; phone: 525-4640; 800-228-9711); *Bed & Breakfast of New Orleans* (671 Rosa Ave., Metairie; phone: 838-0071); or the *Greater New Orleans Tourist and Convention Commission* (1520 Sugar Bowl Dr., New Orleans, LA 70112; phone: 566-5011). Unless we note otherwise, rooms in the hotels listed below have air conditioning, private baths, TV sets, and telephones, and all telephone and fax numbers are in the 504 area code.

VERY EXPENSIVE

Maison de Ville This gem of a hotel in the heart of the French Quarter offers a choice of accommodations: In the *maison*—where Tennessee Williams did his final draft of *Streetcar*—are 16 magnificent rooms and suites furnished with antiques and with balconies and street or courtyard views. Out back are the remodeled slave quarters (ca. 1742), and a stroll away on Dauphine Street are the seven delightful *Audubon Cottages,* where John James Audubon lived and worked in 1821. Built in the creole brick-and-post style (resembling European half-timbered buildings), the cottages have perhaps the most elegant rooms of all, and come with stocked refrigerators, private gardens, and patios with access to a small swimming pool. There is an omniscient concierge; shoes left outside your door are shined; and a classic French breakfast is served on a silver tray, with newspapers and a rose. Enjoy casual dining at the *Bistro* (see *Eating Out*). Room service is available for lunch and dinner only. 727 Toulouse St. (phone: 561-5858; 800-634-1600).

Soniat House No hostelry in New Orleans captures the city's romantic charm and Old Southern gentility quite like this one does. Proprietors Rodney and Frances Smith refurbished two balconied, early-19th-century creole townhouses in the tranquil lower French Quarter and furnished them with stunning period antiques and exquisite paintings and objets d'art. Each of the 16 elegant and comfortable rooms and eight suites in the main houses and rear slave quarters is unique, with canopied beds in the larger rooms. A light breakfast is served (for a small additional charge) in the inner courtyard, shaded by aromatic tropical trees and plants. In the downstairs sitting room, a home-style bar operates after hours on the honor system. Reserve as far in advance as possible. 1133 Chartres St. (phone: 522-0570; 800-544-8808).

Windsor Court The handsome, secluded driveway is an indication of the pleasures that lie within. Delicate Oriental figurines rest in glistening antique cases, sprays of cymbidium orchids crown massive marble tables, and four centuries of art decorate the ground-floor lobby and public rooms. Of the 310 rooms, about 250 are suites with separate living rooms, dressing rooms, and kitchenettes or wet bars. All of the guestrooms have private balconies or bay windows, Italian marble bathrooms, and three telephones equipped with two incoming lines. There are 55 two-bedroom suites and two spectacular penthouse suites on the 22nd floor, each of which includes a library and a large terrace overlooking the Mississippi. In *Le Salon,* a string quartet plays during afternoon tea, and the elegant *Grill Room* (see *Eating Out*) features regional and international delicacies. There is 24-hour room service, a multilingual staff, secretarial services, an Olympic-size pool, a fully equipped health club, and a parking garage. The location, near Canal Street and the Mississippi Riverfront, is another plus. 300 Gravier St. (phone: 523-6000; 800-262-2662).

EXPENSIVE

Fairmont Successor to the legendary *Roosevelt,* which once occupied this same site, this hotel is a delightful blending of the best in San Francisco style and New Orleans charm. The 750 rooms are efficiently maintained (but ask for one in the newer wing). Its location, just a half block from Canal Street and a few blocks from the heart of the French Quarter, makes it convenient for shopping and dining. The *Sazerac,* a luxury restaurant, is frilly and romantic (see *Eating Out*); the more casual *Bailey's,* open 24 hours, offers everything from snacks to good creole fare. There's also a heated pool and two tennis courts. Business conveniences include 30 meeting rooms, a concierge desk, A/V equipment, photocopiers, computers, and express checkout. University Pl. (phone: 529-7111; 800-527-4727; fax: 522-2303).

Inter-Continental The lustrous wood-paneled mezzanine lobby is decorated with striking works by contemporary New Orleans artists, and is further brightened by the fresh flowers. *Veranda,* a dramatic dining room with a lofty glass ceiling and lush greenery, serves continental fare (see *Eating Out*). Among the 482 guestrooms are several suites luxuriously decorated in 19th-century Louisiana style. On the top floor are a health club and pool. The hotel, which attracts a large concentration of business travelers, is steps away from both the business district and the Mississippi Riverfront. There is butler service on the executive floor, and 24-hour room service is available, as are a concierge desk, secretarial services, and complete electronic facilities for business conferences. The 20 meeting rooms include a vast ballroom that has an excellent view. 444 St. Charles Ave. (phone: 525-5566; 800-327-0200).

Lafayette After undergoing a complete refurbishment in 1991, this stately hotel, just two blocks from Poydras Street, has reemerged as a handsome choice among the hotels of the Business District. Its 144 guestrooms and 20 suites, all with high ceilings, are elegantly decorated with handsome period-style furniture. Suites contain marble wet bars and refrigerators, and four are equipped with Jacuzzis. Just off the small ground-floor lobby is *Mike's on the Avenue,* a sleekly designed restaurant offering the eclectic cuisine of chef Mike Fennelly (see *Eating Out*). A conference room and secretarial services are available. 600 St. Charles Ave. (phone: 524-4441; 800-733-4754; fax: 523-7327).

LaMothe House Built in the early 1800s by a successful planter named Jean LaMothe, this exquisite early New Orleans townhouse, surrounded by moss-draped oaks, is a delightful place to call home while visiting the Big Easy. With its stately foyer, lushly planted courtyard, and antique furnishings, this elegant establishment transports visitors to the city's earlier, gentler days, without exposing them to the discomforts of the past. Continental breakfast, the only meal served, is always an event: Everyone sits at a long banquet table and lingers over chicory coffee. The inn is in the French Quarter, very close to the jazz, good food, and intriguing shops. Note that prices range a great deal due to the very different accommodations offered. 621 Esplanade Ave. (phone: 947-1161 or 800-367-5858; fax: 943-6536).

Le Meridien This classy, sleek member of the French chain has become a major presence on Canal Street's hotel row. The *Jazz Meridien* bar has traditional jazz bands nightly, adding a sassy energy to the atmosphere. *La Gauloise,* a bistro-style restaurant, borrows the look of turn-of-the-century Paris and serves excellent buffets featuring creole and French dishes. Chic understatement characterizes the 497 guestrooms and five bi-level suites. To soothe travel-weary muscles, guests can order a massage in the fully equipped penthouse health club or take a swim in the pool. Amenities also include 11 meeting rooms, secretarial and concierge services, translators, a full communications setup, 24-hour room service, and express checkout. 614 Canal St. (phone: 525-6500; 800-543-4300).

New Orleans Hilton The Mississippi River is almost at the doorstep of this immense and impressive link in the Hilton chain. The lavish marble and polished wood lobby connects directly to the *Riverwalk* shopping mall. Located here is *Pete Fountain's* nightclub, where some of the city's top musicians perform, including Fountain himself. At *Kabby's* (see *Eating Out*), diners get Mississippi river views and the authentic creole-Cajun cookery of Stanley Jackson. The state-of-the-art *Racquet and Health Club* has 11 tennis courts—eight indoor and three outdoor—as well as two squash courts and a basketball court. All 1,602 guestrooms are soundproofed, and children occupying their parents' room stay free. The 41 meeting rooms contain 127,000 square feet of space for conferences and exhibitions. Business services include a concierge desk, secretarial assistance, and express checkout. Room service delivers around the clock. 2 Poydras St. (phone: 561-0500; 800-HILTONS).

Pontchartrain With 100 tastefully decorated rooms, each furnished with provincial antiques, this is a favorite of celebrities and dignitaries. There are two restaurants, the casual *Coffee Shop* and the lavishly appointed *Caribbean Room* (see *Eating Out*), which offers creole specialties. A jazz pianist performs nightly in the intimate *Bayou Bar*. Around-the-clock room service is offered, as well as secretarial services. A separate wing for business meetings was added in the late 1980s, with two rooms accommodating up to 300 for banquets and conferences. 2031 St. Charles Ave. (phone: 524-0581; fax: 524-1165).

Westin–Canal Place Its entrance is unassuming, but this hotel located near the French Quarter, Canal Street, and the Mississippi River is as modern and plush as they come. The 11th-floor lobby has a panoramic view of the French Quarter and the river as it begins forming its famous crescent, and public areas are richly furnished with armchairs, antiques, and thick rugs. The glistening marble bar off the lobby—known simply as the *Bar*—is a wonderful place to stop for a drink. Beyond the lobby proper is *Le Jardin* restaurant and bar, serving contemporary creole cuisine, as well as morning coffee and croissants. Most of the 438 spacious rooms and suites, decorated in pastels and accented with prints of the French Quarter, have views of the river. Twenty-four-hour room service is available. There are also eight meeting rooms. 100 Iberville St. (phone: 566-7006; 800-228-3000).

MODERATE

Bourbon Orleans On a quiet block of the French Quarter, this 210-room hotel incorporates what was, from 1815 to the late 19th century, a ballroom for Creole ladies and gentlemen. Today it is certainly more luxurious, with its Queen Anne furniture, canopied king-size beds, marble baths, and crystal and brocade accents. An outdoor pool and secretarial services are other pluses. There is a small restaurant. 717 Orleans St. (phone: 523-2222; 800-521-5338; fax: 525-8166).

Dauphine Orleans Almost hidden along one of the French Quarter's more residential streets is this well-run, 109-room establishment that blends modern conveniences with a reasonable amount of creole charm. Across the street is *Dauphine Patios,* a small annex, with pleasant rooms opening onto a courtyard. Amenities include a complimentary newspaper, a fitness room, free parking, continental breakfast, and a lending library; there is no restaurant. A complimentary open-air jitney transports guests around the Quarter and Central Business District. 415 Dauphine St. (phone: 586-1800; 800-521-7111; fax: 586-1409).

Maison Dupuy Off the French Quarter's beaten track is this modern, handsomely turned out four-story hostelry with a spectacular courtyard and meticulously maintained public spaces. The 195 rooms and suites are decorated in pastels and floral motifs; some suites have three bedrooms. *Le Bon Creole,* a colorful, casual restaurant and lounge, offers updated creole standards. 1001 Toulouse St. (phone: 586-8000; 800-535-9177; fax: 525-5334).

Le Pavillon Eighteenth-century France was the obvious inspiration for this refurbished Poydras Street place, whose style is locally referred to as "barbecue Baroque." The lobby is filled with a profusion of crystal chandeliers, marble, and brocades. There are 200 rooms, a rooftop swimming pool, and a restaurant on the premises. Communications equipment for businesspeople is available. 833 Poydras St. (phone: 581-3111; 800-535-9095; fax: 522-5543).

Place d'Armes A few steps from Jackson Square, this functional but tastefully decorated hostelry has a lovely courtyard with a pool, fountains, and outdoor tables. There are 79 rooms and eight suites in five renovated 18th-century buildings. The lobby is diminutive, but the place is comfortable and clean, and some rooms have balconies overlooking the Chartres Street corner of Jackson Square. Room service delivers a complimentary continental breakfast only (there is no restaurant on the premises), and one small meeting room holds 30 people. 625 St. Ann St. (phone: 524-4531).

De la Poste A comprehensive renovation completed in 1993 added sparkle to this sedate hotel on reasonably quiet Chartres Street. Built in 1973 in traditional French Quarter style, the property has 100 rooms and four carriage house suites with private patios; the drive-through, brick-paved carriageway leads to a spacious courtyard with a fountain and a swimming pool. On the ground floor is *Bacco* (see *Eating Out*), a roomy and handsome Italian restaurant. Coffee and fresh fruit in the lobby are complimentary, as is the weekday newspaper delivered to guests' doors. The courtyard can be reserved for receptions; some conference and function rooms open onto the courtyard as well. 316 Chartres St. (phone: 581-1200; 800-448-4927).

Provincial A personal touch is evident throughout this well-designed establishment on lower Chartres Street. A French-country look characterizes the 106 guestrooms, many of which are furnished with canopied beds and old armoires. The small bar and moderately priced *Honfleur* restaurant are especially picturesque, decorated with unpretentious antiques and old prints. There is no charge for children sharing rooms with adults. Convenient to the *French Market,* Jackson Square, and Decatur Street. 1024 Chartres St. (phone: 581-4995; 800-535-7922; fax: 581-1018).

Le Richelieu This 69-room hostelry on the fringes of the French Quarter was the place where former *Beatle* Paul McCartney hung his hat when he came to town. Fans may be surprised at his rather modest taste. Still, the place does have its charms, such as kitchenettes in the 17 suites and, in many of the rooms, such old-fashioned touches as brass ceiling fans and pull-down ironing boards. Other pluses: a pleasant little restaurant overlooking the pool, and cheerful, efficient service. 1234 Chartres St. (phone: 529-2492; 800-535-9653; fax: 524-8179).

INEXPENSIVE

Château Motor Hotel In a relatively quiet part of the French Quarter, this attractive, serviceable hotel is for the traveler seeking comfort and convenience with a minimum of frills. Access from the small lobby to the 37 rooms and five suites is through a carriageway and patio. While the rooms are not luxurious, they're well maintained and pleasantly decorated. There is also a small restaurant and bar. Jackson Square is a short walk away. 1001 Chartres St. (phone: 524-9636).

French Quarter Maisonettes A converted Vieux Carré townhouse in the French Quarter with a flagstone carriageway and spacious patio, this inn is a quaint and friendly place to stay, with no frills (there is no restaurant, for example). While the seven suites and one double room have no phones, all have private baths and TV sets. The two- or three-room suites are neat and comfortable. The neighborhood, almost entirely residential, is always serene. The proprietor is happy to offer touring suggestions. No credit cards accepted. Reservations must be made between 11 AM and 7 PM central time; be persistent, as they are somewhat erratic about answering their phone. 1130 Chartres St. (phone: 524-9918).

Prytania Inns This one's for budget-minded travelers who enjoy a homey atmosphere. Although it's located in the Lower Garden District, away from the urban hubbub, it's easily accessible to downtown. Made up of three former residences, the property is operated much like a bed and breakfast establishment. The 60 tastefully appointed bedrooms and sitting rooms reflect the turn-of-the-century architecture of the handsome old buildings; there are no TV sets. Traditional creole breakfasts are served, but there's no restaurant. Streetcars and buses are a short walk away. 1415 Prytania St. (phone: 566-1515; fax: 566-1518).

EATING OUT

The distinctive regional cuisine—creole cooking—has been shaped through the years by the cultures of France, Spain, America, and the West Indies, and by the influences of Native and African Americans. Seafood is king in creole recipes, and the nearby waters are filled with crab, shrimp, red snapper, flounder, Gulf pompano, and trout. Vegetables in season, fowl, veal, and fresh herbs and seasonings are culinary staples that add to the regional style. Then there's Acadian (known outside the area as Cajun) cooking, the boldly flavored game, pork and fish dishes developed in backwater, southern Louisiana.

Some useful food terms: One traditional Cajun-creole dish is *étouffée* ("smothered" in French), a thick stew made with seafood in a black iron pot. Jambalaya (not unlike Spanish paella) and gumbo (a thick, spicy soup made with myriad ingredients) are two more staples. Remoulade is a peppery vinaigrette; and more humbly, the po-boy is a two-fisted sandwich of thick French bread, slit open and filled with meat, seafood, and vegetables.

There are numerous excellent chefs here, constantly producing new variations on these themes. The result is that you will find find fancy creole food palaces, trendy Cajun bistros, and basic red-beans-and-rice joints. Our selections, below, should help you find the best of them.

Expect to pay $80 or more for two at the places we've noted as expensive; between $50 and $80, moderate; and $50 or under, inexpensive. Prices include tax and tips, but not drinks or wine. Except where noted, restaurants are open for lunch and dinner, and *reservations are advised;* it is best to call well in advance to reserve, and then confirm your reservation on the day of dining. All telephone numbers are in the 504 area code. Jackets for men are advised for the more expensive restaurants.

EXPENSIVE

Alex Patout's Part creole, part Cajun, this upscale eatery on upper Royal Street is a good place to get familiar with south Louisiana's mainstream cuisine. You'll find rich gumbos, buttery seafood dishes, and robust duck and pork dishes on chef Alex Patout's bill of fare; an especially delectable dish is the duck with oyster stuffing. The ambience in the deep, narrow dining room is elegant but very welcoming. Open daily for dinner only. Major credit cards accepted. 221 Royal St. (phone: 525-7788).

Anacapri Italian regional cooking gets a classy continental veneer in this airy and colorful restaurant near the French Quarter riverfront. Ingredients, especially the seafoods and pasta, are first class. Favorites include fresh Gulf fish baked in aromatic vegetables, and the quail, rabbit, and veal dishes, all done with chef Andrea Apuzzo's native Italian flair. Open daily. Major credit cards accepted. 320 Decatur St. (phone: 522-9056).

Antoine's With a menu that reaches back more than 100 years, and a maze of rooms filled with enough memorabilia for two or three small museums, this place defines the classical creole style in New Orleans. The recipe for oysters Rockefeller was invented here, and it is still excellent. Other good bets are the cool and spicy shrimp remoulade, crabmeat *ravigote* (in a cold, spicy mayonnaise), broiled pompano (a Gulf fish similar to flounder) topped with sautéed lump crabmeat, and baked Alaska emblazoned with the date of the restaurant's founding—1840. Frances Parkinson Keyes wrote the best-selling romance novel *Dinner at Antoine's,* published in the 1940s, that used this place as a setting. Closed Mondays. Major credit cards accepted. 713 St. Louis St. (phone: 581-4422).

Bacco Italian cooking was late in coming to New Orleans. This bright, beautifully decorated restaurant, the brainchild of the owners of *Mr. B's Bistro* (see below), fills the bill. The menu is ambitious, with dozens of choices among antipasti, pizza, pasta, and entrées including *pappardelle* with a rabbit ragout, roasted pork loin in a rosemary sauce, and hickory-smoked swordfish in a Mediterranean-style tomato sauce. Decorative accents in the four dining rooms and bar were inspired by several eras, from the Gothic to the contemporary. Open daily. Major credit cards accepted. *Hotel de la Poste,* 310 Chartres St. (phone: 522-2426).

Bayona The setting is an ancient stucco cottage on a quiet French Quarter street, shaded by banana fronds and magnolia in a rear patio. The food, which combines Mediterranean robustness with contemporary American sophistication, is some of the best in town. Chef Susan Spicer calls her cooking "New World" cuisine, as good a term as any for such creations as tiny medallions of lamb tenderloin in a pinot noir sauce with fennel seed, rosemary, and three types of peppercorns; or a gratinéed casserole of polenta and thin crescents of artichoke in an Italian cheese sauce of fontina, *grana padano,* and *crescenza.* The intimate, handsomely decorated dining rooms are similarly eclectic, with murals and photos depicting lush Mediterranean landscapes and gardens. Closed Sundays. Major credit cards accepted. 430 Dauphine St. (phone: 525-4455).

Bella Luna With views of the lively Mississippi River, the dining room of this posh, second-floor establishment is inside the *French Market.* Soothing gray walls define the mood in the main dining room, while the second one, surrounded by French doors and fan windows, takes on the look of a Viennese ballroom. The osso buco is a standout, as are the pasta, creative salads, and luscious desserts. Open Mondays through Saturdays for dinner only, and for brunch on Sundays. Major credit cards accepted. In the *French Market* complex near the corner of Decatur and Dumaine Sts. (phone: 529-1583).

Brigtsen's Chef Frank Brigtsen augments the evolution of south Louisiana cooking with his brilliant improvisations, served at this small, unpretentious restaurant in the Carrollton section. Roasted, boned duck in pecan gravy is a tour de force, and the blackened tuna elevates that cooking process to new heights. The cream of oysters Rockefeller soup is better than the dish that inspired it. And the fresh ice cream and bread pudding are unsurpassed anywhere in the city. The setting is a small frame cottage near the Mississippi River, and the mood is informal and friendly. Open for dinner only; closed Sundays and Mondays. Reserve well ahead for Saturday nights. Major credit cards accepted. 723 Dante St. (phone: 861-7610).

Caribbean Room The *Pontchartrain* hotel's exceptional dining room serves French and creole dishes. The menu is imaginative, and specialties are beautifully presented—red snapper Eugene (in lemon sauce with crab and shrimp), crabmeat Biarritz (lump crabmeat with whipped cream dressing and topped with caviar), and, if you can go the distance, Mile-High Ice Cream Pie for dessert. Open daily; closed at lunch weekends. Major credit cards accepted. 2031 St. Charles Ave. (phone: 524-0581).

Commander's Palace Few restaurants in the city can match this Garden District dining institution for combining mainstream creole cuisine, a festive atmosphere, and first-rate service. The menu ranges from familiar classics to creative innovations. Among the headliners are a definitive turtle soup, a bountiful seafood and fish bouillabaisse, and excellent remoulades, gumbos, and game dishes. The fried soft-shell crab is superb, as are the sautéed trout with pecans and the bread pudding soufflé. There are several dining rooms in this late-19th-century frame mansion. The glass-walled, second-floor Garden Room overlooks the venerable oak trees in the garden below. Open daily. Reservations necessary a week in advance for dinner. Major credit cards accepted. 1403 Washington Ave. (phone: 899-8221).

Emeril's Chef Emeril Lagasse's vibrant and original creole-American restaurant, in the trendy Warehouse District, remains one of the hottest meal tickets in town. Among the main attractions are an excellent version of New Orleans–style barbecue shrimp, an *étouffée* of duck with wild mushrooms, wonderful soups and salads, and belt-busting desserts that on some nights number more than a dozen. The hard surfaces of brick, glass, and wood make this contemporary dining room noisy; don't plan on an intimate dinner here. Closed Sundays. Reservations necessary a week or more in advance. Major credit cards accepted. 800 Tchoupitoulas St. (phone: 528-9393).

Galatoire's It's been around for almost 100 years, but this classic creole bistro has lost none of its glitter and spunk. The narrow dining room is set off by snowy linen tablecloths, bentwood chairs, wraparound mirror panels, and chandeliers. Choice dishes include a cool and spicy shrimp remoulade, soul-warming eggplant stuffed with shrimp and crab, tender and subtle pompano (a flounder-like gulf fish) with a sprinkle of crab lumps, and lamb chops drenched in béarnaise sauce. Tuxedoed waiters dart around the narrow aisles, adding to the conviviality. Ask what's fresh and you'll dine royally. Drop in at off-hours and you may not have to wait outside for a table. Closed Mondays. No reservations. MasterCard and Visa accepted. 209 Bourbon St. (phone: 525-2021).

Gautreau's The creative force behind the menu at this sophisticated Uptown bistro is chef Selman Larkin, who puts a New York spin on such familiar local ingredients as shrimp, crab, and crawfish. The season's menu might contain a terrific reinterpretation of seafood gumbo, along with succulent slices of guinea hen in sage sauce served with a prune-flavored risotto, and Key lime pie spiked with tequila. Crunchy soft-shell crab arrives under a canopy of matchstick potatoes, and salads are as good as they are adventurous. The downstairs dining room, with its oxblood walls and drugstore-tile floors, is favored by locals. But the brighter, quieter room upstairs is recommended for those who prefer more elegant surroundings. Closed Sundays. Major credit cards accepted. 1728 Soniat St. (phone: 899-7397).

Grill Room Everything about this palatial restaurant—from the Lalique crystal table that stands in the entry to the fresh Japanese oysters—bespeaks money freely spent. The three dining rooms here are decorated with expensive English art, dramatic bronzes, rich fabrics, and more plush than you thought possible. But somehow it's not nearly as intimidating as you'd expect, even with the most precise service in town. And the menu, which changes daily at lunch and dinner, challenges the decor for refinement; a simple but excellent salad of lump crabmeat contrasts with seared foie gras, a glorious shrimp bisque, and smoked blue marlin with zucchini ribbons. And desserts are as spectacular in appearance as they are rewarding in taste. Open daily. Major credit cards accepted. *Windsor Court Hotel,* 300 Gravier St. (phone: 522-1992).

K-Paul's Louisiana Kitchen Upstairs tables can be reserved, but chances are you'll have to cool your heels outside the door for an hour or more at dinnertime for a sampling of trailblazer Paul Prudhomme's creative Cajun dishes. Once inside the rather rudimentary first-floor dining room, you also may have to share a table with strangers. Still, legions of out-of-towners keep coming back for the Cajun guru's earthy gumbos, peppery *étouffées,* and fish dishes—the ones that started the blackening craze almost a decade ago. Wiser customers come at lunch, when the line is shorter, the prices are lower, and the food is much the same as it is at dinner. Closed weekends. American Express accepted. 416 Chartres St. (phone: 942-7500).

Louis XVI French classicism reigns in these soft, elegant spaces flanking the exceptionally pleasant courtyard of a French Quarter hotel. Typical creations are shellfish in puff pastry with cream sauce, beefsteak in wine sauce with mushrooms, Caesar salad, and baroque desserts. The cream soups are especially good. Banks of arched windows and a warm color scheme add to the appealing ambience. Open daily. Major credit cards accepted. *St. Louis Hotel,* 730 Bienville St. (phone: 581-7000).

Mike's on the Avenue "Fusion cooking" (dishes influenced by a blend of many different cultures) is taken to new heights by chef/owner Michael Fennelly at his smartly minimal restaurant in a revitalized old hotel on the edge of the Warehouse District. Fennelly draws inspiration from Japan, Thailand, China, the American Southwest, New Orleans, and any other part of the culinary map that strikes his fancy. The results are such concoctions as spring rolls filled with crawfish, a black-bean dip spiked with Cajun seasonings, a casserole of shrimp, mussels, and Cajun sausage, and sautéed cakes of crab and scallops with three sauces zapped with chilies. Somehow, it all works deliciously in the spare, but beautiful, whitewashed dining rooms, bathed with light from wide glass walls and hung with the chef's own abstract-expressionist paintings. Closed Sundays. Reservations necessary a week in advance for dinner. Major credit cards accepted. *Lafayette Hotel,* 628 St. Charles Ave. (phone: 523-1709).

Mr. B's Bistro The pace is quick, but the style is laid-back in this classy contemporary bistro at the corner of Royal and Iberville Streets. Chef Gerard Maras's ceaseless improvising yields terrific versions of gumbo, barbecue shrimp, bread pudding, and other creole standbys, plus grilled fish in extraordinary sauces, imaginative pasta and pizza, hearty quail and rabbit dishes, and unusual salads. The low-ceilinged rooms, divided with wood and glass partitions, are rather dark, but the place has an energy about it. Service is excellently organized and affable. Open daily. Major credit cards accepted. 201 Royal St. (phone: 523-2078).

Nola A spinoff of *Emeril's* in the Warehouse District, this big, modern eatery is chef Emeril Lagasse's tribute to the gutsy, deep-flavored cuisine of Louisiana's bayous. The menu is filled with robust stews, sausages, earthy-tasting sweet potatoes, hogshead cheese, and novel treatments of regional seafoods. Typical are the creole "cassoulet" with blood sausage, beef brisket, and chicken in a ragout of red and white beans; a green salad with fried oysters and anisette dressing; and coconut cream pie. Downstairs is more casual than upstairs, and both are decidedly contemporary in design. Opens daily at 2:30 PM. Reservations advised, at least a week in advance for dinner. Major credit cards accepted. 534 St. Louis St. (phone: 522-6652).

Palace Café Set in a building that once served as New Orleans's biggest music store, this grand café features "clever creole" cuisine: rabbit ravioli in a Louisiana-style sauce piquant, a red-bean dip with the kitchen's own potato chips, a creamy "napoleon" of seafood, and a yummy white-chocolate bread pudding. The mezzanine, brightened with a large mural of the city's legendary musicians, is reached by a central staircase. Both levels are lively during peak hours, when the bar fills up and things start to sizzle in the open kitchen. Open daily. Major credit cards accepted. 605 Canal St. (phone: 523-1661).

Sazerac With a dining room as frilly as a dozen wedding cakes, this very upscale hotel restaurant is just the place for a romantic—if expensive—evening. White lace covers the red tablecloths, and a dramatic burst of flowers crowns a central cluster of red-velvet banquettes. The menu, which seems to undergo a complete overhaul annually, is a combination of French, south Louisiana, and regional American cuisines. Foie gras, turtle soup, and fancied-up creole dishes are the mainstays, however. Open daily. Major credit cards accepted. *Fairmont Hotel,* University Pl. (phone: 529-4733).

Versailles Located on the fringe of the Garden District, this restaurant has a plush main dining room overlooking St. Charles Avenue. Proprietor/chef Gunter Preuss and his wife Evelyn pair European refinement and creole classicism, and the meat and seafood dishes are of impeccable quality. Among the signature dishes are a light but deep-flavored bouillabaisse, veal medallions in a rich brown sauce, a superb fillet of salmon Argenteuil, and a grill of scallops wrapped in filets of pompano; desserts are also exquisite. While the atmosphere has a touch of the Baroque, the mood is usually convivial. Closed Sundays. Major credit cards accepted. 2100 St. Charles Ave. (phone: 524-2535).

MODERATE

Bacchi Somewhat off the beaten track, but worth the 15-minute taxi ride from the city's heart (and the 20-minute wait for a table), this upscale spot is a must for aficionados of "neo-Italian" restaurant fare. Headliners include imaginative pizza and salads and such seductive dishes as polenta stuffed with braised duck and fried leeks, fettuccine in a shrimp butter with mushrooms and scallions, and grilled fish with yellow tomatoes and basil-nut oil. The bar and split-level dining room, always aflutter with locals, are sleekly contemporary, informal, and bright. Open daily. No reservations. Major credit cards accepted. 900 Harrison Ave. (phone: 486-2500).

Bistro at Maison de Ville While the menu at this French Quarter spot changes almost weekly, some things remain predictable—among them the light and herbal seafood soups, beef tournedos with boursin cheese in a subtle wine sauce, unusual pasta dishes, and first-rate *crème brûlée*. The tiny dining room, with lustrous wood paneling and a full-length maroon banquette, holds 40; the charming little courtyard out back is used in pleasant weather, too. Closed Sunday lunch. Major credit cards accepted. *Maison de Ville Hotel*, 733 Toulouse St. (phone: 528-9206).

Bon Ton Café A strong traditional streak runs through the menu in this rather old-fashioned, but always humming, creole-Cajun bistro at the Central Business District's core. Crawfish is perhaps the biggest seller; the crawfish *étouffée* bisque and the jambalaya are well seasoned. Space is at a premium in the brick-lined dining room, with checkered tablecloths and a cadre of energetic waitresses. Closed weekends. Major credit cards accepted. 401 Magazine St. (phone: 524-3386).

Charley G's "Casual and classy" sums up this large, efficiently run restaurant, a few yards from the boundary line between Orleans and Jefferson Parishes. Spicy south Louisiana cooking is the mainstay of the large menu of hearty appetizers and main courses. Among the better choices are the robustly seasoned crab cakes, the duck and *andouille* sausage gumbo, and fish grilled over mesquite. Desserts, such as the Bullwinkle chocolate mousse pie, are huge and delicious. The uncluttered, contemporary dining spaces are lined in stained woods and warm earth tones, with banquettes flanking the wraparound windows. Open daily. Major credit cards accepted. 111 Veterans Blvd., Metairie (phone: 837-6408).

Clancy's If you're tired of the tourist track, consider this likable contemporary bistro deep within an Uptown residential section. It has tuxedoed waiters, very good food, and a decor so simple it's almost nonexistent. The crab bisque and shrimp remoulade are superb. Almost as good are the sautéed fish in cream sauce, sweetbreads with lemon and capers, lamb chops in béarnaise sauce, and home-style lemon icebox pie. Closed Sundays. Major credit cards accepted. 6100 Annunciation St. (phone: 895-1111).

Dooky Chase's The spirited cooking in this beautifully appointed establishment is traditional creole with a dash of Southern-style soul. Chef Leah Chase's okra with tomatoes is definitive, as are her veal grillades, pork chops smothered with onions, crab soup, and bread pudding. The weekday luncheon buffets are justifiably popular. Just minutes from the French Quarter by taxi, the restaurant is handsomely decorated with good-quality paintings and prints, mostly by local black artists. Open daily. Major credit cards accepted. 2301 Orleans Ave. (phone: 821-2294).

Kelsey's Paul Prudhomme's kitchen has spawned any number of ambitious young chefs. One is Randy Barlow, who carves his own niche in this unassuming but attractive second-floor spot in Algiers, just across the Mississippi from central New Orleans. The menu's stars are the gumbos, a superb shrimp stew, and a terrific all-meat jambalaya. The orange-poppyseed cheesecake is addictive, as are the bread pudding and other desserts. Attractive paintings perk up the pleasant dining spaces. Closed Saturday lunch, Sundays, and Mondays. Major credit cards accepted. 3920 Gen. DeGaulle Dr., Algiers (phone: 366-6722).

Little Greek The deftly prepared traditional Greek food here is a real treat: The spreads and dips, especially the *taramasalata* (carp roe dip with olive oil, lemon juice, and garlic) and *skordalia* (a cold, garlicky sauce made either with mashed potatoes or bread crumbs, plus pine nuts or walnuts and olive oil) are deliciously authentic. Original creations include garlic sautéed fish in buttery phyllo dough and shrimp baked with olive oil, sherry, garlic, and lemon in a paprika sauce. The two colorful dining rooms and bar are hung with every sort of eastern Mediterranean artifact. Closed Mondays. Major credit cards accepted. 619 Pink St., Metairie (phone: 831-9470).

La Provence Nestled in the piney woods of Lacombe, Louisiana, across Lake Pontchartrain, is the exceptionally comfortable establishment of Marseilles-born chef Chris Kerageogiu, who turns out exceptional, earthy Provençal dishes using local and regional ingredients. His quail gumbo, *jambalaya des gourmands,* rack of lamb, leg of rabbit, and fish dishes are among the best in the region. The atmosphere is reminiscent of a French country inn. Closed Mondays and Tuesdays. Major credit cards accepted. About 35 miles from central New Orleans, on the north shore of Lake Pontchartrain on US Hwy. 190, Lacombe (phone: 626-7662).

Ralph & Kacoo's Even with several locations in the French Quarter and in the suburbs, this casual and very popular Cajun eatery fills up fast. The Cajun theme is carried out with a full-size fishing boat in the bar and a jumble of nostalgic artifacts strewn everywhere. Highlights include a fine crab gumbo, trout meunière, fried shrimp or oysters, and good renderings of sautéed fish. Open daily. No reservations. Major credit cards accepted. 519 Toulouse St. (phone: 522-5226) and 601 Veterans Blvd., Metairie (phone: 831-3177).

Upperline In an unpretentious frame building in the Uptown section, chef Tom Cowman builds on a solid creole foundation with such novel, yet sensible, variations as crawfish tamales, sautéed Gulf fish with pecans and garlic, a marvelously creamy hors d'oeuvre of trout mousse, and baked oysters topped with heavenly sauces. Salads, especially the endive and orange in ginger vinaigrette, are consistently good, as are the desserts. The latter include a fine Barbados rum trifle, coconut-banana cake, and silky lemon mousse. Closed Sundays and Tuesdays. Major credit cards accepted. 1413 Upperline St. (phone: 891-9822).

INEXPENSIVE

Alberto's Slightly bohemian and full of energetic pizzazz, this upstairs spot, a few blocks from the French Quarter, serves unusually good Italian food at reasonable prices. Any of the several cannelloni, especially the one with crawfish, is a good way to start. Shrimp with Pernod cream and fettuccine is fresh and flavorful, as are the sautéed soft-shell crab and the veal *panée,* a kind of breaded cutlet. Open for dinner only;

closed Sundays. No reservations. No credit cards accepted. 611 Frenchmen St. (phone: 949-5952).

Casamento's Cleanliness is an obsession in this legendary oyster house on upper Magazine Street, its gleaming white tiles giving the two small dining spaces the look of a large bathroom. Oysters are the stars here, either fried and presented without a trace of grease, freshly shucked and served up on the half shell, or cooked in a homey stew with milk and scallions. The shrimp and oyster "loaves," made with scooped-out white bread, are delicious. The rest of the menu is unimpressive. Closed Mondays and June through August. No reservations. No credit cards accepted. 4330 Magazine St. (phone: 895-9761).

China Blossom What may be the best Chinese-American restaurant in town is tucked away in a small shopping mall across the river. Chef Paul Fung does a great job with shrimp and oysters, grilling or sautéing them before adding marvelous piquant sauces. The pan-Chinese menu covers all the bases from egg rolls to fortune cookies, and it's all reliably good. Closed Mondays. Reservations advised on weekends. Major credit cards accepted. 1801 Stumpf Blvd., Gretna (phone: 361-4598).

Mandina's Once upon a time, every New Orleans neighborhood had its own purveyor of po-boys, red beans, and spaghetti, with a room out back for family gatherings. This place carries on the tradition faithfully. After a wait at the stand-up bar, sit at a Formica-topped table and dig into very good po-boys garlicky cracked crab claws, butter-drenched trout meunière, or a creditable gumbo. Open daily. No reservations. No credit cards accepted. 3800 Canal St. (phone: 482-9179).

Taqueria Corona Aficionados of tacos, nachos, and burritos will find exceptionally good renditions here. Try the "tacocado" salad, a fried tortilla filled with guacamole, meat, lettuce, olives, and cheese. Seating is at both the counter and tables. Service is make-do. Open daily. No reservations. No credit cards accepted. 857 Fulton St. and 5932 Magazine St. (phone: 897-3974 for both locations).

New York City

At-a-Glance

SEEING THE CITY

New York is one of the most complex cities in the world. Even people who have lived here all their lives don't know all of it; its size and diversity challenge even the most ambitious. For the visitor who wants to feel the magic of New York and to understand how the city is laid out, the best bet is to take it in from several vantage points.

BROOKLYN HEIGHTS PROMENADE Standing on this walkway at dusk, with the lights of Manhattan shimmering across the East River, you'll get an idea of the magnitude and beauty of the city. In lower Manhattan the towers of the *World Trade Center* rise before you, and the Brooklyn Bridge spans the river to your right. Farther north stand the *Empire State Building* and the *UN Secretariat Building,* landmarks of midtown. The easiest way to get here is via the *IRT* Seventh Avenue subway line (No. 2 or No. 3 train), Clark St. stop.

WORLD TRADE CENTER Note: Although the terrorists' bomb that exploded here in February 1993 led to fatalities (four men were found guilty and sentenced to life in prison in connection with the bombing), the building itself miraculously escaped structural damage. Security in the buildings is, however, stricter than ever. The elevator to the observation deck of *2 World Trade Center* whisks you more than a quarter of a mile above the street. There is an enclosed deck on the 107th floor and a promenade on the roof above the 110th floor. Manhattan spreads out to the north, Brooklyn is to the east, to the west is New Jersey, and to the south lies New York Harbor, leading to the Atlantic Ocean. Open daily from 9:30 AM to 9:30 PM; to 11:30 PM June through September. The roof promenade may be closed during inclement weather and strong winds; check beforehand. Tickets are sold on the mezzanine level of the building. Liberty and West Sts. (phone: 435-7397). See also *Special Places.*

EMPIRE STATE BUILDING Although many visitors prefer the newer and higher *World Trade Center* observation deck, the old queen of New York, which turned 60 in 1991, attracts more than two million people a year. You can feel the breeze from the 86th floor or ascend to the glass-enclosed 102nd floor. Open daily from 9:30 AM to midnight (the last ascending elevator is at 11:30 PM). Admission charge. Fifth Ave. from W. 33rd to W. 34th St. (phone: 736-3100). See also *Special Places.*

VIEWS FROM THE ROAD Some of the most dramatic views of New York are visible when entering the city by car. The three western access routes have special features: The Holland Tunnel access road from the New Jersey Turnpike, leading into lower Manhattan, offers a panorama of the southern tip of the island; the Lincoln Tunnel access road offers a view of Manhattan's West Side; and the George Washington Bridge, linking New Jersey and the Upper West Side, has spectacular views of the Hudson, the city's long shore along the river, and the New Jersey Palisades. The bridge is a work of art itself, best seen from a distance, from the river, or while driving north on the West Side Highway.

BUS, BOAT, AND FLIGHT TOURS Many of the tour companies in the city will help you get your bearings before setting out on your own. *Gray Line* (900 Eighth Ave., between W. 53rd and W. 54th Sts., and 166 W. 46th St., near Seventh Ave.; phone: 397-2600) provides good bus tours. For a higher perspective, *NY Double Decker Tours* operates old-fashioned double-decker buses from the *Empire State Building* at Fifth Avenue and West 34th Street (phone: 967-6008). The *Manhattan Neighborhood Trolley* now includes Ellis Island (in the summer only) among its escorted tours of popular sites (phone: 677-7268). *NYC Downtown Tours!* gives minibus tours of areas not usually covered by mainstream tour operators; these include lower Manhattan districts like Little Italy, SoHo, and the Lower East Side, with specialty tours centered around downtown nightlife, art, restaurants, and theater (phone: 932-2744). *Circle Line Sightseeing Yachts* offers an interesting three-hour guided boat trip around Manhattan and a new two-hour twilight voyage from early March until December 27. Boats leave from Pier 83 at the foot of W. 42nd Street and the Hudson River (phone: 563-3200). Most spectacular is *Island Helicopter*'s ride around Manhattan. Though the price is considerable ($47 to $119 for flights covering from 7 to 34 air miles), you won't soon forget this trip. At E. 34th St. and the East River (phone: 683-4575).

WALKING TOURS Seeing New York on foot is probably the best way to get acquainted with this complex city. You can do it on your own or take a guided tour. A number of excellent walking tours are available, led by guides who are knowledgeable in everything from architecture and ethnic neighborhoods to literary history, the jazz circuit, movie locations, and noshing spots. Try *Adventures on a Shoestring*, which offers 40 or more walking tours and other activities around Manhattan year-round (phone: 265-2663); *Sidewalks of New York*, which conducts theme tours such as "Ghosts After Sunset," "Writers' New York," and "Hollywood on the Hudson" (phone: 517-0201); *Urban Explorations*, whose walks are organized around such themes as "The Art Deco Era" and "Atriums of New York," with the focus on the city's history, architecture, and ethnic neighborhoods as well as its parks and gardens (phone: 718-721-5254); or *Big Onion Walking Tours*, run by two doctoral candidates in New York history who give lively tours reflecting the history of immigration during trips to Harlem, Chinatown, Ellis Island, and Governors Island, to name a few; Irish and Jewish New York tours are also specialties, as are multiethnic eating tours (phone 439-1090). Also try the *Municipal Art Society* (phone: 935-3960), the *Museum of the City of New York* (phone: 534-1672), the *92nd Street YM/YWHA* (phone: 996-1105), or the *Lower East Side Tenement Museum* (phone: 431-0233), which offers a choice of 11 "living history" tours that explore the city's colorful ethnic heritage.

SPECIAL PLACES

Manhattan is a 12½-mile-long island stretching 2½ miles across at its widest point. Avenues run north and south; streets run east and west.

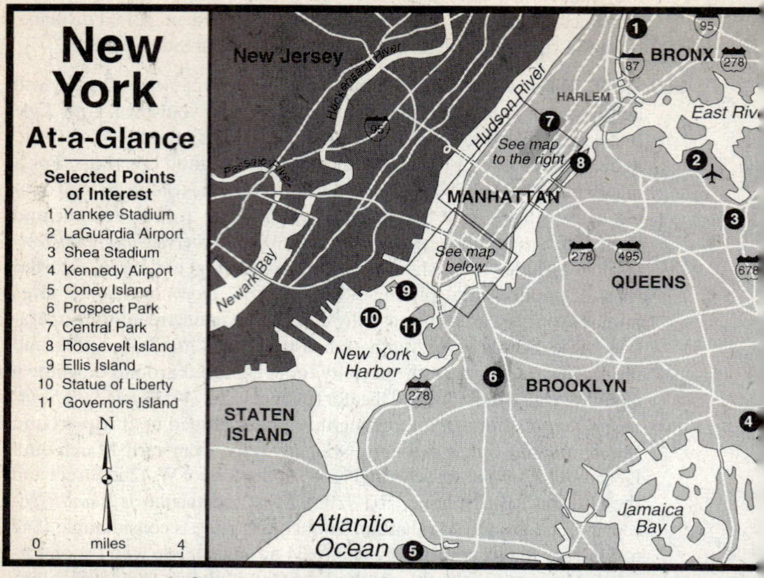

New York
At-a-Glance
Selected Points of Interest
1 Yankee Stadium
2 LaGuardia Airport
3 Shea Stadium
4 Kennedy Airport
5 Coney Island
6 Prospect Park
7 Central Park
8 Roosevelt Island
9 Ellis Island
10 Statue of Liberty
11 Governors Island
N
0 miles 4
New Jersey
Hackensack River
Passaic River
Newark Bay
Hudson River
HARLEM
BRONX
East River
See map to the right
MANHATTAN
See map below
QUEENS
New York Harbor
BROOKLYN
STATEN ISLAND
Atlantic Ocean
Jamaica Bay
95
87
278
495
678

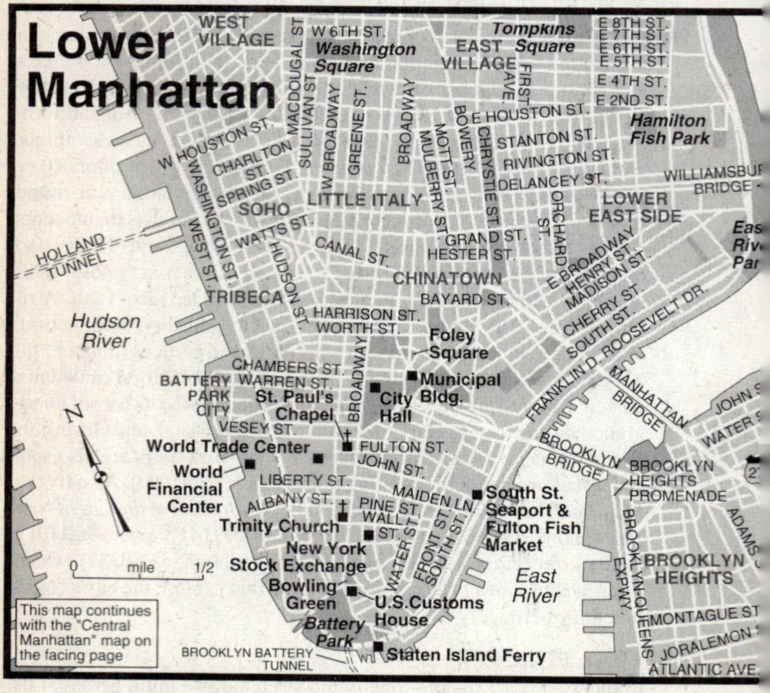

Lower Manhattan
WEST VILLAGE
W 6TH ST.
Washington Square
EAST VILLAGE
Tompkins Square
E 8TH ST.
E 7TH ST.
E 6TH ST.
E 5TH ST.
E 4TH ST.
E 2ND ST.
FIRST AVE.
E HOUSTON ST.
Hamilton Fish Park
STANTON ST.
RIVINGTON ST.
DELANCEY ST.
WILLIAMSBURG BRIDGE
LOWER EAST SIDE
ORCHARD ST.
MACDOUGAL ST
SULLIVAN ST
W BROADWAY
GREENE ST.
BROADWAY
BOWERY
MOTT ST.
MULBERRY ST
CHRYSTIE ST
W HOUSTON ST.
CHARLTON ST.
SPRING ST.
WASHINGTON ST.
WEST ST.
SOHO
LITTLE ITALY
WATTS ST.
HUDSON ST.
CANAL ST.
GRAND ST.
HESTER ST.
HOLLAND TUNNEL
CHINATOWN
E BROADWAY
HENRY ST.
MADISON ST.
BAYARD ST.
CHERRY ST.
SOUTH ST.
FRANKLIN D. ROOSEVELT DR.
TRIBECA
HARRISON ST.
WORTH ST.
Hudson River
Foley Square
CHAMBERS ST.
WARREN ST.
BATTERY PARK CITY
Municipal Bldg.
City Hall
St. Paul's Chapel
VESEY ST.
MANHATTAN BRIDGE
JOHN ST.
WATER ST.
World Trade Center
FULTON ST.
JOHN ST.
BROOKLYN BRIDGE
BROOKLYN HEIGHTS PROMENADE
World Financial Center
LIBERTY ST.
ALBANY ST.
MAIDEN LN.
PINE ST.
WALL ST.
South St. Seaport & Fulton Fish Market
Trinity Church
FRONT ST.
SOUTH ST.
ADAMS
New York Stock Exchange
East River
BROOKLYN-QUEENS EXPWY.
BROOKLYN HEIGHTS
0 mile 1/2
N
Bowling Green
U.S.Customs House
MONTAGUE ST
Battery Park
JORALEMON
This map continues with the "Central Manhattan" map on the facing page
BROOKLYN BATTERY TUNNEL
Staten Island Ferry
ATLANTIC AVE.

Fifth Avenue is the dividing line between addresses designated east and those designated west. For example, 20 E. 57th Street is in the first block of 57th east of Fifth Avenue; 20 W. 57th Street is in the first block west of Fifth Avenue. New York grew from south to north, street by street and neighborhood by neighborhood; the oldest parts of the city are around the docks in lower Manhattan and in the financial district.

You will want to take taxis or public transport between areas—distances can be great—but, in general, the well-populated, active areas of the city offer an interesting environment for walking, so don't hesitate, unless the neighborhood is unfamiliar or it's late at night. The much-touted reputation of New Yorkers as aloof and unfriendly simply isn't true. Just watch what happens when you ask directions on a bus or subway (except during rush hours, when things are, admittedly, a bit primitive). We suggest a copy of *Flashmaps! Instant Guide to New York* (Flashmaps; $5.95), which has the most accessible and best-organized series of maps of New York neighborhoods we've seen. It's available at bookstores and newsstands around the city. The new 36-by-42-inch *New York Identity Map* ($25), a double-sided, highly detailed map of Manhattan south of 65th Street, identifies major buildings by name and provides a color-coded legend for easy identification—yellow for hotel, blue for office, gray for residential, and so on. There are also symbols to pinpoint public sites such as police stations, movie theaters, and law courts. Contact the *Identity Map Co.* (55 Bethune St., Suite 1207; phone: 627-1994; fax: 627-5718).

LOWER MANHATTAN

STATUE OF LIBERTY Given by France as a symbol of friendship with the United States, this great lady has been guarding the entrance to New York Harbor since its dedication in 1886. The *Statue of Liberty Ferry* (phone: 269-5755) from *Battery Park* to Liberty Island runs from 9:30 AM to 3:30 PM, every 45 minutes on weekdays, every half-hour on weekends. The ferry ticket includes admission to the statue and to the *Ellis Island Immigration Museum* on Ellis Island (see below). You can see the statue from a distance as well as the southern tip of the city by riding the *Staten Island Ferry* (phone: 718-390-5253), still one of the world's great transportation bargains at 50¢. The ferry terminal is next to *Battery Park* (the South Ferry stop on the *IRT* Seventh Ave. subway local line, No. 1 or No. 9 train).

ELLIS ISLAND Visible from the *Statue of Liberty* or *Battery Park,* Ellis Island served as a processing center for more than 17 million immigrants from 1892 to 1954. Their dramatic experience is painstakingly portrayed at the *Ellis Island Immigration Museum* (phone: 363-3200), featuring dozens of exhibits of native costumes, instruments, and household implements as well as a film and a series of photographs that eloquently document the tension, terror, and joy of the immigrants' ordeal. The *American Immigrant Wall of Honor* is inscribed with the names of more than 420,000 immigrants to the United States who were commemorated by their descendants through a donation. These donations helped pay for the $160 million, six-year Ellis Island restoration project spearheaded by Lee Iacocca. The *Statue of Liberty Ferry* departs from *Battery Park* at regular intervals every day (see *Statue of Liberty* entry, immediately above) for the statue and then Ellis Island. Admission charge is included in the boat fare.

GOVERNORS ISLAND Now a coast guard base, the island's two pre-1800 structures are the *Governor's House* and *Fort Jay; Castle Williams* was completed in 1811 and has been both a fort and a prison. Here you will also find great oceangoing views, oak, hickory, and chestnut trees, and a Gothic stone chapel hung inside with battle flags from the Mexican War. The island is open to visitors once a month (first or second Saturday) only with *Big Onion Walking Tours* (phone: 439-1090). Off Manhattan's southern tip, it is otherwise accessible only to officials by boat.

BATTERY PARK Twenty-one acres of green overlooking New York Harbor, this is the spot for picnics on hot summer days. There's a statue of Giovanni da Verrazano, who piloted the *Dauphine,* the ship that reached Manhattan in 1524, and there's also a monument to World War II dead. *Castle Clinton,* built as a fort in 1812, has functioned as an opera house, an immigrant landing depot, and an aquarium at various times. Its latest incarnation is as a ticketing center for the *Statue of Liberty Ferry.* Bordered by State St., Battery Pl., and the harbor (phone: 344-7220). Nearby, in Battery Park City, is *South Cove,* a three-acre park directly on the Hudson River.

BATTERY PARK TO WALL STREET This area is a lovely and usually safe place to wander on weekends, when the empty streets emphasize the incongruity of the Merrill Lynch building, the *World Trade Center,* and the *World Financial Center* (where free concerts are held in a magnificent indoor courtyard), surrounded by the 17th- and 18th-century buildings on Pearl Street, *Bowling Green,* and Hanover Square. Two buildings of particular note are *India House,* on the south side of Hanover Square (built in 1837), and the old *US Custom House* (the new *Custom House* is in the *World Trade Center*) on *Bowling Green,* which was erected in 1907 in Beaux Arts style.

NEW YORK STOCK EXCHANGE A tree growing in front of the stock exchange commemorates the one under which the first trading transaction took place in 1792. Today more than 1,600 corporations are listed on the Big Board. You can observe the action from a glass-enclosed gallery reached via the visitors' entrance at 20 Broad Street. Open weekdays; no admission charge, but tickets are required and are distributed at 9 AM on a first-come, first-served basis (phone: 656-5168). Large groups should call in advance for special arrangements. Cameras are prohibited. The *American Stock Exchange* (86 Trinity Pl.) no longer has a visitors' gallery. If you want to see real emotion, head for the *Coffee, Sugar, and Cocoa Exchange,* which makes the *New York Stock Exchange* look like a London tea party. The visitors' gallery is open weekdays; no admission charge. *4 World Trade Center* (phone: 938-2025).

FEDERAL HALL This National Historic Site served as the British headquarters during the Revolution and later was the seat of American government for about a year. George Washington was sworn in as president here in 1789. Open weekdays. No admission charge. At the corner of Wall and Broad Sts. (phone: 264-8711).

TRINITY CHURCH This church was first granted a charter by King William III in 1697. The present rose-colored stone building was completed in 1846 (it got a cleaning in the early 1990s), but the graveyard beside it is even older. For years the *Trinity Church* steeple was the highest point on the New York skyline. On Broadway at the head of Wall St. (phone: 602-0800).

ST. PAUL'S CHAPEL The oldest public building in continuous use in Manhattan, this fine example of colonial architecture was erected in 1766 on what was then a field outside the city. George Washington worshiped here. Classical concerts are held in the chapel on Mondays and Thursdays at noon from September through June. Suggested donation for concerts is $2. On the corner of Broadway and Fulton St. (phone: 602-0874).

BATTERY PARK CITY This $4-billion complex includes apartments, tree-lined streets, public parks and squares, and a sumptuous centerpiece, the *World Financial Center* (not related to the neighboring *World Trade Center*). The *WFC* is the home of the *Winter Garden* (not to be confused with the Broadway theater of the same name), a must-visit while in this part of town, where a variety of free concerts are held and artwork displayed amid towering royal palm trees in the soaring atrium. A true city within a city, this landfill development on the Hudson River is logically designed and decidedly not ostentatious. There is a wealth of other diversions, among them a spa, a 1950s rock 'n' roll club, the *Hudson River Club* restaurant (phone: 786-1500), and numerous shops. The views from the 1.2-mile Esplanade are spectacular. The *Winter Garden* is open from 8 AM to midnight. No admission charge. For general Battery Park City information, call 416-5300; for *Winter Garden* information, call 945-0505.

WORLD TRADE CENTER An unprecedented terrorist bomb attack in the *WTC*'s garage in early 1993 left several dead and all of New York traumatized. Although there was no structural damage, much reconstruction was necessary, and there is now a higher level of security here than in most New York buildings. The "Twin Towers," at 1,350 feet each, are not quite the tallest buildings in the world (the *CN Tower* in Toronto is, at 1,821 feet), but spectacularly set at the southern tip of Manhattan, they are a must-see landmark. In order to build the center, 1.2 million yards of earth and rock were excavated (they're now in the Hudson River). The concourse has a variety of shops and eateries. The *Custom House* is here, as are the *Commodity, Cotton, and Mercantile Exchanges*. Open daily. Admission charge for the *Observation Deck* (see *Seeing the City*, above). Bounded by West, Church, Liberty, and Vesey Sts. (phone: 435-7000).

CITY HALL This is the third *City Hall* in New York; it was built in 1803 and houses the office of the mayor and the City Council chamber. The original construction cost half a million dollars, and in 1956 the restoration cost some $2 million (times change). The building was a site of great importance to New York and US history: Lafayette visited in 1824; Lincoln's body lay in state here in 1865; and in the 1860s *City Hall* and *Tammany Hall* (Park Row and Frankfort St.) were controlled by Boss Tweed, the powerful, corrupt man who dominated New York politics until the 1870s.

Other city government buildings nearby include the *Municipal Building* on the northeast corner of *City Hall Park*, the *United States Court House,* across from Foley Square, the *New York County Courthouse* next door, the *Federal Office Building* on the other side of Lafayette Street, and the *Hall of Records.* In *City Hall Park* is a statue of Nathan Hale, a patriot of the Revolution who was executed here in 1776. Today protestors of every persuasion gather in the park to "fight *City Hall."* Closed weekends. No admission charge. In the triangle formed by Park Row, Broadway, and Chambers St. (phone: 788-7165).

SOUTH STREET SEAPORT AND THE FULTON FISH MARKET Completed in the 1980s, stage one of the *South Street Seaport* redevelopment program enlivened the area with shops and restaurants and additional space for the *South Street Seaport Museum*. The Museum Block is an entire row of rejuvenated buildings (some dating to the 1700s), with room for exhibitions, shops, and offices. The Schermerhorn Row of renovated 19th-century warehouses is also alive with retail outlets and the *South Street Seaport Museum Visitors' Center.* All of these changes have not substantially altered the area's famous old *Fulton Fish Market,* where, from about 2 to 8 AM, trucks still deliver fresh fish to the wholesale outdoor market.

But the old market is now joined by another building called the *Fulton Market,* with restaurants, cafés, and food stalls. Among the many eateries is one of New York's oldest seafood restaurants, *Sloppy Louie's* (92 South St.; phone: 509-9694). Prices are reasonable, but the portions remain hearty and the fish is as fresh as ever. Also of interest are the historic boats docked at Piers 15 and 16, where summertime pop and jazz concerts are staged. The three-story *Pier 17 Pavilion* adds even more shops and restaurants. Fulton St., between South and Water Sts.

BROOKLYN BRIDGE You can stroll from Manhattan to Brooklyn by crossing the Brooklyn Bridge on a pedestrian walk. You'll get a good view of the city and a close look at this engineering feat. The 6,775-foot-long bridge, which spans the East River at a height of 133 feet, was completed in 1883 and cost $25 million; it's considered by many to be one of the most beautiful bridges in the world. Free (unless someone succeeds in selling you title to it). Take the *IRT* Lexington Ave. subway line (No. 4, No. 5, or No. 6 train) to the Worth St.–Brooklyn Bridge–City Hall station.

CHINATOWN The best way to get the feel of New York's Chinese neighborhood is to hit the streets, especially Mott, Bayard, and Pell. The despair of census takers, this crowded, ever-expanding ethnic neighborhood which seeps into Little Italy is loosely estimated to be home to more than 100,000. Some say the Chinese community here is not as large as the one in San Francisco, but it is equally authentic. You'll know when you reach Chinatown by the pagoda-shaped telephone booths and stores that sell shark fins, duck eggs, dried fungi, and squid. Herbs are lined up next to aspirin in the pharmacies. Don't miss the good, inexpensive restaurants, the tea parlors, or the bakeries. At lunchtime try dim sum (steamed or fried dumplings filled with seafood, pork, or beef are just some of the choices). Favorite spots among New Yorkers are the *Golden Unicorn,* whose dim sum are the best in town (see *Eating Out*); *Peking Duck House* (22 Mott St.; phone: 227-1810); *Bo Ky* (80 Bayard St.; phone: 406-2292); and *Sun Hop Kee* (13 Mott St.; phone: 285-9856). Sundays are a good time to visit the area, but if you can, come during the *Chinese New Year* (starting on the first new moon after January 21). The celebration is wild and woolly, with fireworks, dancing dragons, and throngs of people.

LITTLE ITALY Italian music wafting from tenement windows, old men playing *bocce,* old women dressed in black checking the vegetables in the markets, store windows with religious articles, pasta factories, and the ubiquitous aroma of Italian cooking give character to this ever-shrinking neighborhood, which has the reputation of being one of the safest in the city. Mulberry Street is the center of Little Italy (stop for an espresso at *Caffè Roma,* 385 Broome St.; phone: 226-8413), but the area stretches for blocks, surrounding and blending into parts of SoHo and Greenwich Village. Even the section of Bleecker Street near the Avenue of the Americas has a decidedly Italian flavor, with bakeries that sell cannoli and cappuccino sandwiched between Middle Eastern restaurants and stores that sell Chinese window shades. Little Italy is thronged during the festivals of *San Gennaro* and *St. Anthony.* In September *San Gennaro* covers Mulberry Street from Spring Street to Park Row; *St. Anthony* fills Sullivan Street from Houston to Spring in June. The festivals attract people from in and out of the city with game booths, rides, and, most of all, enough food and drink (both Italian and "foreign") for several armies. Bordered by Canal and Houston Sts., the Bowery, and the Ave. of the Americas.

THE BOWERY There is nothing romantic about New York's Skid Row. On this strip are people who are decidedly down on their luck—both old and young. If you drive west on Houston Street, you'll get a look at some of the inhabitants—they'll wipe your windshields whether you like it or not and expect some change for their trouble. The area has a few theaters and music places and some good shopping spots; specialties include lighting and restaurant supplies. The stores have relocated here because of the proximity to one of the most interesting shopping markets in the world: the Lower East Side. Between Cooper Sq. and Chatham Sq.

LOWER EAST SIDE This area is probably the largest melting pot in the city. Eastern European Jews, many of whom are Hasidim (an ultra-religious sect, recognizable by the men's earlocks, called *peyes,* and their broad-brimmed hats and long black coats), sell their wares—everything from designer fashions to bedspreads—at discounted prices; you'll have to bargain if you want the best deal, and these merchants are formidable opponents. Everything is closed on Saturdays, the Jewish sabbath, but it's business as usual on Sundays, the busiest day of the week. The area also is home to Hispanics, African-Americans, Asian-Americans, and various other minority groups; you will hear an assortment of languages spoken, including Yiddish, Spanish, and even some Yiddish-accented Spanish.

The Lower East Side was where the Eastern European Jews, fleeing czarist persecution and deadly pogroms, first settled during their massive migration from 1880 to 1918. Many of the streets, including Rivington, Hester, Essex, and Grand, still look much as they did then. To get a real taste of the area, try the knishes at *Yonah Schimmel's* (137 E. Houston St.; phone: 477-2858); hot dogs at *Katz's* delicatessen (205 E. Houston St.; phone: 254-2246); or the Romanian "broilings" at *Sammy's* (see *Eating Out*).

SOHO The name stands for "*So*uth of *Ho*uston Street" (pronounced *How*-stun). SoHo leads a double life. On weekends uptown New Yorkers and out-of-towners fill the streets to explore its trendy stores, restaurants, and art galleries. During the week SoHo is a very livable combination of 19th-century cast-iron buildings, spillovers from adjacent Little Italy, off-off-Broadway theater groups, and practicing artists. At night the streets are empty, and you can see into the residential lofts of the old buildings; some are simple, open spaces, others are jungles of plants and Corinthian columns. *Fanelli's* (Mercer and Prince Sts.; phone: 226-9412) is one of the oldest bars around and a hangout for residents. Many local artists also have moved to TriBeCa, which is south and west of SoHo. SoHo is between Canal and Houston Sts., and Broadway and Hudson St.

TRIBECA Once neglected, TriBeCa (the name stands for "*Tri*angle *Be*low *Ca*nal Street") has made a flashy comeback. The current artist residents have spawned a plethora of trendy art galleries on White and Franklin Streets and lower Hudson Street. This is where Robert De Niro has his film production studio, and there are also many discount clothing stores, nightclubs, restaurants, and theaters here. Historical oddities worth visiting include the *Bond* hotel (125 Chambers St.), reputedly Manhattan's oldest; Stanford White's "Clocktower" building (346 Broadway); and the Art Deco *Western Union Building* (60 Hudson St.). TriBeCa extends from Canal St. to Chambers St. and from West Broadway to the Hudson River.

EAST VILLAGE Still the center of New York's counterculture, this section has become gentrified, with a growing number of art galleries, restaurants, and nightspots competing for space with poor artists and various ethnic groups (the largest of which is Ukrainian, but there also are Armenians, Czechs, Germans, Russians, Poles, Jews, African-Americans, and Hispanics, many of whom live in low-income housing projects). Famous during the 1960s as the city's psychedelic capital, St. Mark's Place, between Second and Third Avenues, is still a lively block, lined with inexpensive restaurants and shops featuring styles from hippie to punk; it's generally hopping (sometimes with the help of controlled substances) at all hours of the day and night. Two streets south is "India Row," where numerous Indian restaurants line East Sixth Street between First and Second Avenues. Astor Place, on the border of the East and Greenwich Villages, is the site of *Cooper Union,* a liberal arts institute (good for free concerts and lectures); nearby is the *New York Shakespeare Festival* (also called the *Joseph Papp Public Theater;* 425 Lafayette St.; phone: 598-7150), where you'll find both contemporary and classical drama as well as experimental theater. You can have a drink at *McSorley's Old Ale House* (15 E. Seventh St.; phone: 473-9148); established in 1854, it is one of the oldest bars still in operation in New York. A few blocks north is the spiritual home of the Village, *St. Mark's-in-the-Bouwerie* (Second Ave. and E. 10th St.). The church still sponsors community activities, especially poetry readings by some of the best bards in New York. The East Village has housed many writers, from James Fenimore Cooper (6 St. Mark's Pl.; he also lived at 145 Bleecker St. in Greenwich Village) to W. H. Auden (77 St. Mark's Pl.) to Amiri Baraka, born LeRoi Jones (27 Cooper Sq.). Note: Some parts of the East Village, especially east of Avenue A, remain seedy; don't wander here after dark unless you know where you're going—and don't go unaccompanied. Bounded by Lafayette St. and the East River, Houston and 14th Sts.

GREENWICH VILLAGE

You can—and definitely should—stroll around the heart of the Village at night. The area is filled with surprises. You've probably heard of Bleecker Street, the slightly tawdry gathering place of tourists and the high school crowd from the suburbs, or of *Washington Square Park,* with its musicians, mimes, and street people. But you might not have pictured Grove Court, the lovely and secluded row of 19th-century houses near the corner of Grove and Bedford Streets (where O. Henry lived), or the Morton Street pier on the Hudson River, from which you can see the *Statue of Liberty* on a clear day. There are meat-packing factories from the 1920s, old speakeasies turned into restaurants, a miniature Times Square on West Eighth Street, and immaculate (and expensive) brownstones on quiet, tree-lined streets. Get a map (you'll need it—there's nowhere else in Manhattan where West Fourth Street could bisect West 12th) and wander. Or you can ask directions—Villagers love to help, and it's a nice way to meet them. You can eat, go to the theater, sip cappuccino in an outdoor café, hear great jazz, and find your own special places. Bounded by Broadway on the east, the Hudson River on the west, Houston St. on the south, and W. 14th St. on the north.

WASHINGTON SQUARE Actually a park, this is a gathering place for students from *New York University,* Frisbee aficionados, volleyball players, modern bohemians, and people who like to watch them all. The Fifth Avenue entryway, the *Washington Square Arch,* is New York's answer to the *Arc de Triomphe*. Buildings surrounding the square include the *NYU* library, administration buildings, and law school. The north side of the square has some lovely homes, including No. 7, where Edith Wharton lived. Bounded by extensions of W. Fourth St., MacDougal St., Waverly Pl., and University Pl.

BLEECKER STREET Strolling down Bleecker Street (James Fenimore Cooper once made his home at No. 145) from La Guardia Place to Eighth Avenue, you'll pass outdoor cafés, falafel parlors, jazz clubs, Italian specialty stores, and myriad restaurants. Be sure to wander down some of the side streets, like Thompson, MacDougal (Bob Dylan's old stomping ground), and Sullivan. Have a cappuccino at *Caffè Dante* (79 MacDougal St.; phone: 982-5275), then pay homage to Eugene O'Neill at the *Provincetown Playhouse* (133 MacDougal St.; phone: 477-5048; seasonal). Beyond Seventh Avenue, the side streets become more residential; try Charles Street, West 10th Street, and Bank Street for examples of how the upper middle class lives in the Village. You'll also pass Christopher Street, the center of gay life in Manhattan.

LOWER FIFTH AVENUE This is where wealthy Villagers live. The *Salmagundi Club,* built in 1853 (47 Fifth Ave., near 12th St.), is the last of the imposing private mansions that once lined the avenue. On the streets between Fifth and the Avenue of the Americas (which the natives persist in calling Sixth Avenue) are expensive brownstones. The *New School for Social Research* (66 W. 12th St.; phone: 229-5600 or 800-544-1078, ext. 18, for general information) offers courses in everything from fixing a leak to ethnomusicology. From Waverly Pl. to 14th St.

AVENUE OF THE AMERICAS New Yorkers know it as Sixth Avenue. One of the most unusual buildings in the Village is the *Jefferson Market Library* (Sixth Ave. and W. 10th St.), with a small garden alongside. Built in 1874–78 in Italian Gothic style, it served as a courthouse and prison for many years. Across the street is *Balducci's,* an incredible international market (see *Shopping*). *Famous Ray's of Greenwich Village* (465 Sixth Ave. at W. 11th St.; phone: 243-2253)—the place on the corner with the long lines—is considered the source of some of the best pizza in the city. (Note that many pizza places in the city have "Ray's" in their names, but this is the one that gets the raves.) From W. Fourth to W. 14th St.

WEST VILLAGE Farther west (between Seventh Ave. S. and the Hudson River) is a series of small winding streets with some especially interesting places to visit. At 75½ Bedford Street is the house in which Edna St. Vincent Millay and John Barrymore once lived (not at the same time)—it's only nine feet wide. *Chumley's* (86 Bedford St.; phone: 675-4449) used to be a speakeasy during Prohibition and still has no sign on the door—but it does have good food and poetry readings inside. Commerce Street is a small side street lined with lovely old buildings, including the *Cherry Lane Theater* (38 Commerce St.; phone: 989-2020), one of the city's oldest. Two blocks south is Leroy Street with St. Luke's Place, a row of 19th-century houses. No. 6 Leroy was built in 1880 and was once the home of the city's flamboyant Mayor Jimmy Walker. If you walk to the end of the block and north on Hudson, you'll come to the *White Horse Tavern* (567 Hudson St.; phone: 243-9260), Dylan Thomas's hangout on his trips to New York City. Go in and have a drink.

14TH STREET TO 34TH STREET

UNION SQUARE For many years this was a place to avoid—particularly at night, when it was populated by drug pushers and other undesirables. Now, after a major face-lift, it's beginning to resemble itself in the halcyon days of the 19th century, when the square was the core of uppercrust Manhattan life. The open-air produce market on Mondays, Wednesdays, Fridays, and Saturdays and several new cafés, restaurants, discos, and theaters fill the side streets and the lower reaches of Park Avenue South; stop in at the trendy *Coffee Shop* (29 Union Sq. W.; phone: 243-7969) or the more upscale *Union Square Café* (see *Eating Out*). E. 14th to E. 17th St., between University Pl. and Fourth Ave.

GRAMERCY PARK A few blocks northeast of Union Square, *Gramercy Park* is one of the few places where visitors can experience the graciousness of old Manhattan. The park itself is open only to residents on the perimeter streets (they have their own keys), but on a sunny day you can see nannies with their privileged charges sitting on the benches in the shadows of the 19th-century mansions that surround the park. Stop in for a beer on Irving Place, south of the park, at cozy (if frayed), historic *Pete's Tavern* (129 E. 18th St.; phone: 473-7676); one of the oldest bars in New York City and formerly the *Portman* hotel, it is where local resident O. Henry is said to have written some of "The Gift of the Magi." Teddy Roosevelt's birthplace (28 E. 20th St.; phone: 260-1616) is a museum. Closed Mondays and Tuesdays; admission charge. Other well-known park sons and daughters include Herman Melville and Stephen Crane. A few blocks north of *Gramercy Park* on Lexington Avenue are dozens of little Indian shops selling splendid assortments of spices, saris, cotton blouses, jewelry, and food. E. 20th to E. 21st St., between Park Ave. S. and Third Ave.

CHELSEA In this eclectic residential neighborhood in the West 20s, between Seventh and 10th Avenues, you'll find elegant brownstones next door to run-down, four-story, walk-up tenements. The *Chelsea* hotel (222 W. 23rd St., between Seventh and Eighth Aves.; phone: 243-3700) has earned an important place in literary history. Thomas Wolfe, Brendan Behan, Dylan Thomas, and Arthur Miller slept and wrote in its rooms. Andy Warhol made a four-hour movie about its raunchier inhabitants. For a sojourn into tranquillity, step into the inner courtyard of the *General Theological Seminary*, a gift to the city in 1817 by Clement C. Moore, author of "A Visit from Saint Nicholas." The grounds are open daily in the early afternoons (from 2 to 4 PM on Sundays), except during special functions. No admission charge. 175 Ninth Ave. (phone: 243-5150).

MIDTOWN (34TH STREET TO 59TH STREET)

WEST 34TH STREET Still a major shopping street, this is the home of *Macy's* (Broadway from W. 34th to W. 35th St.), the mercantile giant; the nearby multilevel mall known as *A & S Plaza* (Ave. of the Americas from W. 32nd to W. 33rd Sts.; see *Shopping* for both); and scores of boutiques selling inexpensive blue jeans, blouses, shoes, tapes and CDs, and electronic gear. The hub of 34th Street is Herald Square, where Broadway intersects the Avenue of the Americas (Sixth Ave.). The main shopping district runs along 34th Street from Eighth Avenue to Madison Avenue, with a number of smaller shops lining the street as far east as Third Avenue.

MADISON SQUARE GARDEN, THE PARAMOUNT THEATER, AND PENNSYLVANIA STATION This is a huge coliseum-arena, office building, and transportation complex. The *Garden*'s seats (19,800 maximum capacity) usually are fully packed when the New York *Knicks* (*NBA* basketball) or the New

York *Rangers* (*NHL* hockey champions) play home games, when the *Ringling Brothers and Barnum & Bailey Circus* comes to town, or whenever there is a major exhibition, concert, or convention. Formerly the *Felt Forum,* the *Paramount Theater* (not to be confused with the old movie house of the same name), a 5,600-seat subsidiary hall that's part of the *Garden*, is the site of boxing matches, concerts, and smaller exhibitions. The current *Penn Station*, which dates from the mid-1960s, is *Amtrak*'s major New York terminal and also serves the *Long Island Rail Road* (*LIRR*) and *New Jersey Transit* commuter lines; the original *Pennsylvania Station* on the same site, a vaulted and columned neoclassical structure, opened in 1910 and was demolished in 1963. No guided tours. W. 31st to W. 33rd St., from Seventh to Eighth Aves. (phone: 465-6741 for *Garden* and *Paramount Theater* information).

GARMENT DISTRICT Here is the nation's center of the clothing and fashion design industries (Seventh Avenue street signs here actually say "Fashion Avenue"). On any weekday during office hours, racks of the latest apparel are pushed through the teeming streets. From W. 30th to W. 42nd St., between Seventh and Eighth Aves.

EMPIRE STATE BUILDING The first skyscraper in New York to be attacked by King Kong, this 102-story Art Deco edifice was erected in 1931 and was the symbol of the city for decades. There is an open-air observation deck on the 86th floor, to which millions of tourists have ascended over the years to gaze in awe at the surrounding New York skyline; there is another, glass-enclosed viewing area on the 102nd floor. Don't be surprised if the top of the building is bathed in colored lights in the evening (red, white, and blue on *July 4th*, for example, or orange on *Halloween*)— it's the city's way of commemorating holidays and special occasions. Open daily from 9:30 AM to midnight (last elevator up at 11:30 PM). Admission charge. Fifth Ave. from W. 33rd to W. 34th St. (phone: 736-3100).

JACOB K. JAVITS CONVENTION CENTER This glass-and-steel monolith with a 15-story atrium, designed by eminent architect I. M. Pei, hosts the bigger conventions that outgrew the old *New York Coliseum*. The complex covers five square blocks between 11th and 12th Avenues and encompasses 1.8 million square feet of space, making it one of the world's largest buildings. The kitchens can produce banquet meals for up to 10,000, while the cafeteria serves 1,500 people an hour. State-of-the-art facilities include a sophisticated audiovisual system and soundproofing throughout its 131 separate meeting rooms, with simultaneous interpretation in up to eight languages. There's also a VIP lounge, press room, video information center, and cocktail lounge. The only thing missing is a garage. 655 W. 34th St. (phone: 216-2000).

TIMES SQUARE Every *New Year's Eve,* Times Square is where hundreds of thousands of New Yorkers and visitors congregate. Although Times Square is always crowded, the quality of the crowds leaves something to be desired. In spite of its reputation as one of the major crossroads of the world, Times Square is still struggling to shake its attraction for pickpockets, drug pushers, pimps, hookers, junkies, religious fanatics, and assorted street peddlers attempting to fence stolen goods. It is no longer wall-to-wall triple-X cinemas and porn shops, but the sex industry still has a grip on the area. Proposals for rehabilitation have been numerous: Signs of a possibly brighter future for the area included the completion in 1985 of the 50-story *Marriott Marquis* convention hotel (1535 Broadway at W. 45th St.; phone: 398-1900; 800-228-9290; fax: 704-8930). This led to a resurgence of hotels that now include the *New York Renaissance, Macklowe, Paramount,* and *Embassy Suites* (see *Checking In* for all four). Although the overall seediness of Times Square has diminished slightly due to the presence of these upscale hotels, many New Yorkers are skeptical that any of the various cleanup projects their tax money has financed will turn the area completely around. The Times Square area is centered from W. 42nd Street to W. 46th Street, where Broadway and Seventh Avenue converge. The building at 229 W. 43rd Street is the home of the *The New York Times,* after which the district is named (the newspaper formerly had its headquarters on Times Square).

BROADWAY AND THE THEATER DISTRICT On and just north of Times Square are the colorful marquees and billboards for which New York is famous. The lights are still pretty dazzling, twinkling on and off in a glittering electric collage. On most nights the streets are jammed with theater-goers, taxis, and limos; most curtains go up at 8 PM. The main theaters are between West 42nd and West 53rd Streets, east and west of, as well as on, Broadway.

NEW YORK PUBLIC LIBRARY A couple of blocks east of Times Square, this dignified neoclassical building is a good place to relax and catch your breath. Sit on the front steps, between the famous lion statues, or in *Bryant Park,* behind the library. Inside the library is New York's (and one of the world's) largest collection of books and periodicals as well as a gift store; there also are various exhibitions and public programs. Tours are given Tuesdays through Saturdays at 11 AM and 2 PM. Closed Sundays and Mondays. No admission charge. Fifth Ave. from W. 40th to W. 42nd St. (phone: 930-0800).

GRAND CENTRAL STATION This magnificent Beaux Arts relic is worth seeing, and there is a one-hour tour Wednesdays at 12:30 PM (phone: 935-3960); suggested contribution. Otherwise, be sure to check out the illuminated zodiac dotting the immense vaulted ceiling. The *Café at Grand Central,* principally a bar, also offers good food and a great view of the terminal. It is located on the west balcony (phone: 883-0009). The main station entrance is on E. 42nd St., between Vanderbilt and Lexington Aves., although access can be gained from all four sides.

CHRYSLER BUILDING This is the princess of the New York skyline. Its distinctive, graceful spire, decorated with stainless steel, sparkles with more than usual brilliance because of the installation of hand-blown fluorescent lights around its pinnacle. Although it long ago ceded the title of tallest in the city, this Art Deco building completed in 1930 remains, to many New Yorkers, the most beautiful of all. There are no tours, the observatory was closed long ago, but a visit to the small lobby, with its ceiling murals and exquisite inlaid elevator doors, is worth the trip. 405 Lexington Ave. at E. 42nd St.

FORD FOUNDATION BUILDING If you happen to be wandering through New York at sunrise and climb the stairs between First and Second Avenues on 42nd Street, you'll see the bronzed windows of the *Ford Foundation Building* catch the first rays, reflecting copper-colored light into the sky. At other times the building is just as dramatic. Built around a central, glass-enclosed courtyard containing tropical trees and plants, it is the only place in Manhattan where you can feel as if you're in a jungle. It's one of the great New York experiences—especially on snowy afternoons. Open weekdays. No admission charge. 320 E. 43rd St. (phone: 573-5000).

TUDOR CITY A nearly forgotten pocket of Manhattan, this 1920s neo-Tudor apartment complex is one of its most romantic parts. An esplanade overlooks the East River and the nearby *United Nations*. The home of many diplomats and *UN* employees, Tudor City serves as an international campus. (According to local legend, it used to be where executives and industrialists housed their mistresses in the 1930s and 1940s.) The long, curved staircase leading to the sidewalk opposite the *United Nations* is known as the *Isaiah Steps*, because of the biblical quote carved into the wall. Between E. 41st and E. 43rd Sts. at Tudor City Pl. (near First Ave.).

UNITED NATIONS Although the *UN* is open all year, the best time to visit is between September and December, when the General Assembly is in session. Delegates from about 200 nations gather to discuss the world's problems, and there are a limited number of free tickets available to the public. The delegates' dining room also is open to the public for lunch, weekdays throughout the year; overlooking the East River, it offers a lovely international menu and the chance to overhear intriguing conversations. Reservations are essential; pick up a pass in the lobby. The *UN* is open daily. Charge for a guided tour. The visitors' entrance is on First Ave. between E. 45th and E. 46th Sts. (phone: 963-4440).

ROCKEFELLER CENTER A group of skyscrapers built in the 1930s, *Rockefeller Center* is best known for its giant *Christmas* tree in December; for its ice skating rink open October through April; for *Radio City Music Hall*, a theatrical landmark and home of the *Rockettes* (phone: 247-4777); and for the romantic *Rainbow Room*, where dinner for two becomes a Fred Astaire and Ginger Rogers fantasy. After dinner, visit *Rainbow and Stars* for sophisticated cabaret entertainment (see *Nightclubs and Nightlife*). There are tours of the NBC television studios in 30 Rockefeller Plaza daily except Sundays. Admission charge; children under six not permitted. Fifth Ave. from W 49th to W. 51st St. (phone: 664-4000).

ST. PATRICK'S CATHEDRAL A refuge from the crowds of Fifth Avenue, this is the most famous church in the city. Dedicated to Ireland's patron saint, it stands in Gothic splendor across the street from *Rockefeller Center* in the shadow of skyscrapers. Resplendent with gargoyles on the outside, stained glass windows and magnificent appointments on the inside, *St. Patrick's* is a good place for rest, contemplation, and prayer. Catholic services are held daily. Fifth Ave. between E. 50th and E. 51st Sts. (phone: 753-2261).

SIXTH AVENUE It's officially known as the Avenue of the Americas, but no true New Yorker calls it that. The stretch of Sixth Avenue between 42nd and 57th Streets is lined with skyscrapers and is particularly imposing at dusk, when the giant glass and steel buildings light up.

MUSEUM OF MODERN ART Possibly the most complete repository of 20th-century art in the world, its permanent collection includes the work of cubists, abstractionists, expressionists, conceptualists, and others. Among the many great paintings housed here are Wyeth's *Christina's World,* Monet's *Water Lilies* (housed in its own gallery), and van Gogh's *Starry Night.* A four-story glass Garden Hall overlooks the sculpture garden. The museum's permanent collection is installed in chronological order, and by following a suggested route, visitors can see the history of modern painting, photography, and sculpture unfold. The *William S. Paley Collection* (Paley was the founder of CBS) consists of 82 major works by Cézanne, Degas, Matisse, and Picasso, among others. The museum's film department and its leadership in film preservation are internationally renowned. Hollywood classics, award-winning foreign films, and the works of lesser-known directors are screened here regularly. Keep your eye out for the shows in the popular "Projects Series," dedicated to installations by contemporary young artists. Closed Wednesdays. Admission charge; on Thursday and Friday evenings, though, when the museum is open until 8:30 PM, admission is on a pay-as-you-wish basis. 11 W. 53rd St. (phone: 708-9400; 708-9480 for recorded information).

FIFTH AVENUE Although the street runs from Washington Square straight up to Spanish Harlem, when New Yorkers refer to Fifth Avenue, they usually mean the stretch of the world's most opulent shops between *Rockefeller Center* at 49th Street and the *Plaza* hotel opposite the southeastern corner of *Central Park* at Central Park South (59th Street). *Saks Fifth Avenue, Gucci, Tiffany, Cartier, Henri Bendel,* and *Bergdorf Goodman* make walking along the street an incredible test in temptation. Stop in at *Steuben Glass* on the corner of East 56th Street and marvel at its permanent collection of sculpted glass in mythological and contemporary themes. And whether you decide to go in or not, *Trump Tower*'s golden façade across East 56th Street is quite a spectacle, housing luxury apartments and some of the most exclusive (read: expensive) stores in the city.

GRAND ARMY PLAZA This square, with its central fountain just across the street from the southeast corner of *Central Park,* faces *Bergdorf Goodman,* the regal *Plaza* hotel, the *General Motors Building,* and the hansom cabstand where horse-drawn carriages (some with drivers in top hat and tails) wait to carry clients through the park. If you have a lover, be sure to arrange to meet here at least once. Be sure, too, to take at least one ride through the park in a hansom cab, preferably at dusk. In the southern part of the plaza, Pomona, the Roman Goddess of Abundance, stands atop the *Pulitzer Fountain.* Regilded in 1989, the statue of General Sherman shines brightly (to many New Yorkers, too brightly) in the northern part of the plaza. Three times the quantity of gold used on the flame of the *Statue of Liberty* was used to brighten him. Fifth Ave. and Central Park S.

CENTRAL PARK More than 50 blocks in length but only three lengthy blocks wide, this beloved stretch of greenery, designed by Frederick Law Olmsted and Calvert Vaux in the 1860s, is now a *National Historic Landmark*. New Yorkers use it for everything—jogging, biking, walking, ice skating (at *Wollman Rink*), Rollerblading, riding in horse-drawn hansom cabs, listening to concerts (including the *Free Concerts in the Park* series every summer, courtesy of the *New York Philharmonic*) and opera, watching Shakespeare's plays, demonstrating against injustice, flying kites, boating, gazing at sculpture, and playing all kinds of ball games. Although city officials claim that the park is now safer due to increased security efforts, you should definitely avoid it at night; and even when you visit it during the day, be cautious, and don't wander into densely wooded areas, especially on weekdays. In the evenings and on weekends car traffic through the park is reduced or prohibited, leaving the considerable non-vehicular crowd to wend its way around the loop road inside the park much more peacefully. The pretty and very manageably sized *Central Park* zoo, officially known as the *Central Park Wildlife Conservation Center* (entrance on Fifth Ave. between E. 61st and E. 65th Sts., in the southeast corner of the park), is run by the *New York Zoological Society* (phone: 861-6030), which also oversees the Bronx zoo, now called the *International Wildlife Conservation Park*. Despite the renamings, to New Yorkers, their zoos will always—and most affectionately—be zoos. Admission charge. *Central Park* is bounded by Central Park South (W. 59th St.) on the south, W. 110th Street on the north, Fifth Avenue on the east, and Central Park West on the west. Urban rangers offer free walking tours (phone: 427-4040), and there even are guides who describe which items growing in the park are edible. For information on park events, call 360-1333.

UPPER EAST SIDE

For the art lover, upper Fifth Avenue offers "Museum Mile," including the *Metropolitan Museum of Art* and the *Guggenheim* (see below), and the *Cooper-Hewitt,* the *Frick,* the *International Center of Photography,* and the *Jewish Museum* (see *Museums* for all four), plus the *Whitney Museum of American Art,* nearby on Madison Avenue (see below).

METROPOLITAN MUSEUM OF ART Usually considered the finest museum this side of the *Louvre,* it is visited by more than 4.5 million people every year. Here are works by the great masters from the Middle Ages to the present day, a vast assemblage of Greek and Roman sculpture, the most comprehensive collection of Islamic art anywhere, Oriental art, prints and photographs, musical instruments, decorative arts from all ages, and special exhibitions of stunning quality. The *Sackler Wing* contains the *Temple of Dendur;* the *Lila Acheson Wallace Gallery* in the wing of the same name has an extensive Egyptian collection; and an additional 21 more galleries are devoted to 20th-century works. The *American Wing* comprises three centuries of American period rooms, paintings, sculpture, and decorative arts. The *Michael C. Rockefeller Wing* has works from Africa, the Pacific Islands, and pre-Columbian Americas. Asian art galleries include a Buddhist shrine and a Chinese garden court. The *Nineteenth-Century European Paintings and Sculpture Galleries* (formerly the *André Meyer Gallery,* on the second floor) house an unrivaled collection of French Impressionist paintings, including works by Degas and van Gogh. A permanent installation containing 1,300 works created between the third millenium BC and the early 19th century opened last year in 18 of the *Florence and Herbert Irving Galleries for the Arts of South and Southeast Asia.*

A sculpture-filled roof garden offers staggering views. There is also an outdoor sculpture garden overlooking *Central Park* (open May through October). There's a good cafeteria, a restaurant, and two superb, large gift shops. Films and lectures are presented throughout the year, and a distinguished concert series (phone: 570-3949) is held from September through May. The optimum times to visit the museum are Friday and Saturday evenings, when it is open until 9 PM. Closed Mondays and some major holidays. (Note: Some wings occasionally close due to lack of funds.) Suggested donation. The main entrance is at Fifth Ave. and 82nd St. (phone: 535-7710 or 879-5500).

SOLOMON R. GUGGENHEIM MUSEUM Designed in 1959 by Frank Lloyd Wright, this white circular building has an interior quarter-mile-long ramp that spirals upward for seven floors, allowing you to travel through the collections by following the curves of the building. While it is given over primarily to exhibitions of contemporary art (including a large collection of works by Kandinsky, Chagall, and Picasso), some patrons feel that the architecture is more impressive than what it houses. The museum reopened in 1992 after extensive renovations, which included a 10-story tower and a redesign of the interior space to bring it more in line with Wright's original vision. The fourth level of this new addition was recently designated the *Robert Mapplethorpe Gallery;* the museum's primary space for photography, it includes periodic exhibitions drawn from the Mapplethorpe collection and other objects belonging to the late controversial photographer, all donated to the museum by the *Mapplethorpe Foundation.* The on-site *Dean & DeLuca Café* (423-3657) offers a varied menu ranging from full meals to scrumptious desserts. Besides additional gallery space in the annex, the museum also has the *Guggenheim Museum SoHo* gallery (575 Broadway at Prince St.; phone: 423-3500; closed Mondays and Tuesdays; open until 8 PM Saturdays), which features exhibitions from the museum's permanent collection and some traveling shows. The main museum is closed Thursdays; open until 8 PM Fridays and Saturdays. Admission charge for both. 1071 Fifth Ave., between E. 88th and E. 89th Sts. (phone: 423-3500 for both the main museum and the SoHo gallery).

WHITNEY MUSEUM OF AMERICAN ART The permanent collection includes works by Calder, de Kooning, Hopper, Johns, O'Keeffe, Nevelson, Prendergast, Segal, Sheeler, and Warhol, among others. About 15 exhibitions are mounted each year, exclusively featuring 20th-century American art, with the emphasis on the work of living artists. Known locally as the *"Whitney,"* the museum presents an ambitious film and video series focusing on some of the work displayed in the galleries. *Sarabeth's Kitchen* (phone: 570-3670), a branch of the popular Upper East Side eatery, is set in an atrium on the lower level. In addition to the museum's central location in Manhattan (see address below), there are two branches: one in Stamford, CT (1 Champion Plaza; phone: 203-

358-7630) and the *Whitney Museum at Philip Morris* (120 Park Ave. at E. 42nd St.; phone: 878-2550). Closed Mondays and Tuesdays. Admission charge. 945 Madison Ave. at E. 75th St. (phone: 570-3600; 570-3676 for recorded information).

YORKVILLE AND GRACIE MANSION In this interesting ethnic neighborhood of mostly German and Eastern European families, a lot of high-rise apartment towers now are diluting the character somewhat. Nonetheless there are still a number of restaurants and delicatessens selling Wiener schnitzel, sauerbraten, goulash, and kielbasa—plus some splendid bakeries. *Gracie Mansion,* the 1799 official residence of the Mayor of New York, sits in a fenced garden in *Carl Schurz Park,* alongside the East River. The park is popular with joggers and dog walkers and is most attractive at dawn, when the eastern sky comes to life. Yorkville stretches from E. 80th to E. 89th St., between Lexington and York Aves. *Gracie Mansion* and *Carl Schurz Park* are at East End Ave. and E. 88th St. The mansion can be visited by appointment only, on Wednesdays from mid-March to mid-November (phone: 570-4751); suggested donation.

ROOSEVELT ISLAND A self-contained housing development in the middle of the East River, Roosevelt Island is accessible from Manhattan by tramway or subway (the Q train weekdays, the B on weekends), or from Queens by bus and subway. A loop bus encircles the island, which has restricted automobile traffic. Visitors also can stroll the main street from end to end. A landscaped riverside promenade has benches for relaxing while enjoying the unique view of midtown Manhattan. The aerial tramway leaves each side every 15 minutes daily, except during rush hours, when it leaves every seven and a half minutes. The fare at press time was $1.40. The Manhattan terminal is at Second Ave. and E. 60th St. (phone: 832-4543).

UPPER WEST SIDE

LINCOLN CENTER The pulsing water and light of the *Lincoln Center* fountain, the centerpiece of this 14-acre complex, are dramatically framed by the *Metropolitan Opera House,* a contemporary hall with two giant murals by Marc Chagall. The performing arts complex also contains *Avery Fisher Hall,* the *New York State Theater,* the *Vivian Beaumont Theater,* the *Mitzi E. Newhouse Theater, Alice Tully Hall,* the *Juilliard School of Music,* the new *Walter Reade Theatre,* and the *New York Public Library for the Performing Arts* (see *Theater* and *Music and Dance,* below). Guided tours through the major buildings are conducted daily and last about an hour. Admission charge except for children under six. Columbus Ave. from W. 62nd to W. 66th St. (phone: 875-5400 for *Lincoln Center;* 769-7000 for the *Metropolitan Opera Guila*).

AMERICAN MUSEUM OF NATURAL HISTORY With its $45-million face-lift scheduled for completion this year, this museum will be an even greater cornucopia of curiosities. The anthropological and natural history exhibitions in the form of life-size dioramas showing people and animals in realistic settings have made this one of the most famous museums in the world. The new dinosaur and fossil halls, due to open this year, will feature such prehistoric creatures as the baurosaurus (better known as the brontosaurus) and the Tyrannosaurus rex in the largest freestanding dinosaur exhibit in the world. The popular *Naturemax Theater*, with its four-story screen, often shows double features of nature films (phone: 769-5200 or 769-5650). The museum has three cafeterias and three gift shops. Free guided tours leave from the main floor information desk daily at 15 past each hour. Closed *Thanksgiving* and *Christmas*. Donation suggested. Central Park W. and W. 79th St. (phone: 769-5000; 769-5100 for recorded information).

HAYDEN PLANETARIUM Housed here is an amazing collection of astronomical displays on meteorites, comets, space vehicles, and other galactic phenomena. The sky show, in which constellations are projected onto an observatory ceiling, is one of New York's greatest sights. Subjects include lunar expeditions, the formation of the solar system, and UFOs. There are also special children's shows on weekends. Open daily. Admission charge. W. 81st St., between Central Park W. and Columbus Ave. (phone: 769-5920).

CATHEDRAL OF ST. JOHN THE DIVINE The largest Gothic-style cathedral in the world, it has seating capacity for 10,000. A chronic shortage of funds (and skilled stonemasons) has allowed only two-thirds of the impressive church to be completed since work began in 1892. According to current projections, it may be nearly the 22nd century before construction is completed. Nonetheless, religious services (Episcopal), packed-out concerts, and poetry readings continue, as does the community spirit for which this imposing church has become known. There is a stunning Renaissance and Byzantine art collection as well. Free guided tours of the cathedral and the stone yard are conducted every day except Mondays. Open daily. Amsterdam Ave. and W. 112th St. (phone: 316-7540).

COLUMBIA UNIVERSITY This is the Big Apple's member of the Ivy League. Although more than 27,000 students attend classes here, the campus is spacious enough to dispel any sense of crowding. Around it are a number of interesting bookstores, restaurants, and bars, including the *West End Gate Café* (2911 Broadway at W. 113th St.; phone: 662-8830), a student favorite. Guided tours of the campus leave from 201 *Dodge Hall;* call ahead for schedules. No admission charge. The main gate is at Broadway and W. 116th St. (phone: 854-2845).

RIVERSIDE CHURCH Perched on a cliff overlooking the Hudson River, *Riverside* is an interdenominational Christian church with a functioning carillon tower and an amazing statue of the angel Gabriel blowing his trumpet. The tower is open on Sundays only from 12:30 to 3:30 PM; free guided tours of the church also are given on Sundays at 12:30 PM. W. 120th St., between Riverside Dr. and Claremont Ave. (phone: 222-5900).

GRANT'S TOMB Who is buried in Grant's tomb? Suffice it to say, the general and his wife are entombed in a gray building topped with a rotunda, set in *Riverside Park*. The interior was inspired by Napoleon's burial place in the *Invalides* in Paris. A word about the park: Don't wander here after dark. Known officially as the *General Grant National Memorial*, the tomb is closed Mondays and Tuesdays. No admission charge. Riverside Dr. and W. 122nd St. (phone: 666-1640).

THE CLOISTERS AND FORT TRYON PARK One of the most unusual museums in the country, if not the world, the *Cloisters* is a branch of the *Metropolitan Museum* and consists of sections of cloisters originally belonging to monasteries in southern France. It houses an inspiring collection of medieval art from different parts of Europe, of which the *Unicorn Tapestries* are the most famous. Recorded medieval music echoes through the stone corridors and courtyards daily; medieval and Renaissance concerts are held on selected Sundays throughout the year. Set in *Fort Tryon Park* along the Hudson River, the *Cloisters* offers a splendid view of the New Jersey Palisades, the George Washington Bridge, and the Hudson River. Closed Mondays. Suggested admission charge. The closest intersection is Washington Ave. and W. 193rd St. (phone: 923-3700).

HARLEM Some visitors to New York—black or white—are uncomfortable at the thought of entering Harlem, and like any unfamiliar place, it can be intimidating. But there is much to see here, and a visit can dispel the negative image many people have of the neighborhood. Starting at 120th Street and stretching to about 160th Street, it is a community of families who are just as concerned about local problems as are people anywhere else in the city.

The most pleasant part of Harlem is "Strivers Row"—138th Street between Seventh and Eighth Avenues—two blocks of turn-of-the-century brownstones, some designed by Stanford White. Quite a lot of Harlem, however, is undergoing a revival. *Mart 125* (260-262 W. 125th St.; phone: 316-3340) is a shopping center offering handicrafts from developing countries, and there is always a constant flow of activities held on Harlem's 10-block waterfront that includes African-American, Latin, and Caribbean arts, music, entertainment, and food stalls. In August *Harlem Week* is actually 20 days of music, food, and cultural happenings; in the fall the main event is the *Harlem Jazz Festival*; and the famous *Apollo Theater* (253 W. 125th St.; phone: 749-5838) is well worth a visit year-round. The *Harlem Festival Orchestra* performs at the *Church of the Intercession* (550 W. 155th St.; phone: 283-6200) once or twice a year. Condos are going up in the area, and a multi-screen cinema has opened.

In the words of a New York police officer: "The best way to see Harlem is by driving or in a cab. Take a bus rather than a subway if you are using public transportation." Among the reliable tour operators are *Harlem Spirituals* (phone: 757-0425) and *Harlem Your Way* (phone: 690-1687 or 866-6997). Worthwhile sights include the *Morris-Jumel Mansion*, once the home of Aaron Burr and Washington's headquarters (Edgecombe Ave. and W. 160th St.; phone: 923-8008); the *Schomburg Center for Research in Black Culture* (515 Malcolm X Blvd. at W. 135th St.; phone: 491-2200); *Aunt Len's Doll and Toy Museum*, with its collection of more than 5,000 dolls, by appointment only (6 Hamilton Ter. at W. 141 St.; phone: 281-4143); the *Abyssinian Baptist Church* (132 W. 138th St.; phone: 862-7474), where the late Adam Clayton Powell Jr. preached; the *Studio Museum of Harlem* (144 W. 125th St.; phone: 864-4500); and the *Black Fashion Museum*, the country's only museum devoted to black contributions to fashion (155-157 W. 126th St.; phone:

666-1320). For more information on Harlem, call the *Uptown Chamber of Commerce* (phone: 427-7200) or the *New York Convention and Visitors' Bureau* (phone: 397-8222).

BROOKLYN

People who do not know the borough (and that includes many Manhattanites) think purely in terms of the book *A Tree Grows in Brooklyn* or 1930s gangster movies in which Brooklyn-born thugs make snide remarks out of the sides of their mouths while chewing on cigars. Actually, Brooklyn has a lot of trees (more than Manhattan) and some charming neighborhoods that are more European than American in character. Not only is it greener, it is also considerably more rural than Manhattan, even though it has more than four million people and bills itself as the "fourth-largest city in America."

BROOKLYN HEIGHTS The most picturesque streets of classic (and expensive) brownstones and private gardens are found in this historic district. Not only does the Promenade facing the skyline offer a traditional picture-postcard view of Manhattan, but the area behind it retains an aura of dignity that characterized a more gracious past. Montague Street, a narrow thoroughfare lined with restaurants and shops selling ice cream, candles, old prints, flowers, and clothing, runs from the East River to the *Civic Center,* a complex of federal, state, and municipal government buildings. To get to Brooklyn Heights from Manhattan, take the *IRT* Seventh Avenue line (No. 2 or No. 3 train) to Clark Street station; or better yet, walk across the Brooklyn Bridge and bear right. The district extends from the bridge to Atlantic Avenue and from Court Street to the Promenade. For information on events, contact the *Brooklyn Heights Association* (55 Pierrepont St.; phone: 718-858-9193).

ATLANTIC AVENUE Lebanese, Yemeni, Syrian, and Palestinian shops, bakeries, and restaurants line the street, where purveyors of tahini, Syrian bread, baklava, halvah, other assorted foodstuffs, Arabic recordings, and books are to be found. There is even an office of the *Palestinian Red Crescent,* an official branch of the *International Red Cross* that has been helping victims of the wars in Lebanon. Occasionally, women in veils make their way to and from the shops, some incongruously carrying transistor radios. The most active street scene takes place between the waterfront and Court Street.

PARK SLOPE This restored district resembles London's borough of Chelsea, with its many beautiful shade trees and gardens. A large part of Park Slope has been designated a historic district, and there are some truly impressive townhouses here. Grand Army Plaza, with its colossal arch commemorating those who died in the Civil War, stands at the end of the Slope that extends along the western edge of *Prospect Park.* On Sundays you can climb the inside stairway to the top—the view is stupendous. Seventh Avenue, two blocks from the park, is an intriguing shopping street for old furniture, stained glass, ceramics, housewares, flowers, health food, vegetables, and toys. Saturday afternoons get pretty lively. To get to Park Slope from Manhattan, take the *IRT* Seventh Ave. line (No. 2 or No. 3 train) to Grand Army Plaza, or the *IND* line (D or Q train) to the Seventh Ave. station.

PROSPECT PARK AND THE BROOKLYN BOTANIC GARDENS *Prospect Park,* an Olmsted and Vaux creation (as is Manhattan's *Central Park*), is comprised of more than 500 acres of gracefully landscaped greenery with fields, fountains, lakes, a concert band shell, an ice skating rink in winter, a bridle path, and a zoo. The *Botanic Gardens* (1000 Washington Ave.; phone: 718-622-4433) contain 50 acres of serene rose gardens and hothouses with orchids and other tropical plants, as well as an impressive bonsai collection, cherry trees, an herb garden, and hundreds of other flowers and shrubs. Closed Mondays. No admission charge. From Manhattan, take the *IRT* Seventh Ave. line (No. 2 or 3 train) to the Eastern Pkwy. station, or take the *IND* line (D or Q train) to the Prospect Park station.

BROOKLYN MUSEUM In addition to its outstanding anthropological displays devoted to Native Americans of both the Northern and Southern Hemispheres, the museum's 1.5-million-object permanent collection also includes fine exhibits of Oriental arts, American painting and decorative arts, and European painting by the likes of van Gogh, Rodin, Toulouse-Lautrec, Gauguin, Monet, and Chagall. The recently renovated *West Wing* contains the extensive Egyptian and primitive art collections. This museum hosts excellent traveling exhibitions as well. Closed Mondays and Tuesdays. Suggested donation. From Manhattan take the *IRT* Seventh Ave. line (No. 2 or No. 3 train) to the Eastern Pkwy. station. 200 Eastern Pkwy. and Washington Ave. (phone: 718-638-5000).

BAY RIDGE Although Brooklynites have long been fond of this onetime Scandinavian-dominated waterfront community, it took the movie *Saturday Night Fever* to bring it to national attention. Bay Ridge is one of the two anchor points for the world's longest suspension bridge, the Verrazano-Narrows Bridge, which connects Brooklyn with Staten Island. Those moviegoers still suffering from bouts of night fever can revisit the world of the film, although it was in the 1970s that John Travolta tripped down Fourth Avenue. Meanwhile, there is the timeless backdrop of the bridge looming over the tops of houses, shops, restaurants, and discos. A bike path runs along the edge of the Narrows (the body of water that connects New York City's rivers to the Atlantic) from Owl's Head Pier, the pier of the now-defunct Brooklyn–Staten Island ferry, all the way to the bridge. The pier has been renovated and is a great place for fishing, watching the ships come in, and catching a wide-angle view of lower Manhattan. To get to Bay Ridge from Manhattan, take the *BMT* line (R train) to the 95th St. station.

CONEY ISLAND Formerly a summer resort where generations of working class New Yorkers came for a day of sun and fun, Coney Island is now a long strip of garish amusement park rides, penny arcades, food stands, honky-tonk bars along the boardwalk where country-and-western singers compete with the sound of the sea, and low-income housing complexes. It is jam-packed in the summer, eerily deserted in winter. Summer weekends are the worst time to visit; weekday evenings are considerably less frenetic. You can ride the *Cyclone,* one of the most terrifying roller coasters on the East Coast, and the *Wonder Wheel,* a giant Ferris wheel alongside the ocean; the parachute jump, a highly visible Coney Island landmark, is no longer operational. The actual amusement park is called *Astroland Park* (phone: 718-265-2100) and is open mid-April through mid-June on weekends only, and from mid-June through early September seven days a week, noon to midnight. The famous belugas (white whales) are the stars of the *New York Aquarium,* officially called the *Aquarium for Wildlife Conservation* (Surf Ave. and W. Eighth St.; phone: 718-265-3400). If you get a sudden craving for Italian food, head for *Gargiulo's* (2911 W. 15th St.; phone: 718-266-4891) for some good Neapolitan dishes. Another New York treat is to have hot dogs at *Nathan's Famous* (1310 Surf Ave.; phone: 718-946-2202). The area's most recent ethnic flavor is provided by a second wave of Russian immigrants, and nearby Brighton Beach has been affectionately dubbed "Little Odessa." From Manhattan take the *IND* line (F, D, or N train) to the Stillwell Ave. station. For further information, call the *Chamber of Commerce* (phone: 718-266-1234).

SHEEPSHEAD BAY This area operates more at the pace of a New England fishing village than a part of New York City. A few anglers sometimes sell their catch on the dock in the early afternoon; charter boats that take people out for the day leave very early in the morning. For the best view of the scene, cross the wooden footbridge at Ocean Avenue and walk along the mile-long esplanade. A few blocks south of the bay is Manhattan Beach, a neighborhood of tree-lined streets and rather elegant homes. Brighton Beach, a few blocks to the east, joins Manhattan Beach with Coney Island. From Manhattan take the *IND* line (D or Q train) to the Sheepshead Bay station.

THE BRONX

With almost two million inhabitants, the Bronx is smaller than Brooklyn, and it's the only New York borough on the mainland. Although all the points of interest listed here are safe for visitors, some sections of the Bronx are among the most dangerous in the city. The South Bronx has been nicknamed "Fort Apache" by the police, and officers advise staying clear of any place south of Fordham Road.

BRONX ZOO (INTERNATIONAL WILDLIFE CONSERVATION PARK) In 1993 this zoo's name, along with those of all the *New York Zoological Society*'s facilities, was changed to include the word "conservation." Whatever you choose to call it, this is one of the most famous facilities of its kind in the world, with over 265 acres inhabited by more than 4,000 animals. Elephants, tigers, chimps, seals, rhinos, hippos, birds, and buffalos are the favorites. Ride the *Bengali Express* monorail through Wild Asia; visit Jungle World or a children's petting zoo; or survey it all from the *Skyfari* tramway. To get here from Manhattan, take the *IRT* Seventh Ave. line express train (No. 2) to the Pelham Pkwy. station; walk west to the Bronxdale entrance (for other routes, call the zoo). Open daily. Admission charge, except on Wednesdays; parking charge. Fordham Rd. and Bronx River Pkwy. (phone: 718-367-1010).

NEW YORK BOTANICAL GARDENS Adjoining the zoo to the north, these 250 acres of flowering hills, valleys, woods, and gardens are set in an unspoiled natural forest. The site comprises the only surviving remnants of the original woodland that once covered the city. The *Enid A. Haupt Conservatory* (closed Mondays), a crystal palace with 11 pavilions—each with a totally different environment—is a special treat; call to find out its post-renovation reopening date, scheduled for this summer. Other highlights include a rose garden, azalea glen, daffodil hill, botanical museum, and restaurant. It's well worth the trip, especially in the spring. From Manhattan take the *IND* line (D train) to the Bedford Park station and walk eight blocks east (for other routes, call the gardens). Closed Mondays. Suggested donation; parking charge. Southern Blvd. and E. 200th St. (phone: 718-817-8705).

BRONX MUSEUM OF THE ARTS This museum's changing exhibitions have two themes: contemporary art and the artistic expression of the many ethnic groups who live in the borough. Classical music concerts, film programs, poetry readings, and dance performances are held throughout the year. From Manhattan take the *IRT* Lexington Ave. line (No. 4 train) to 161st St., or the *IND* line (C or D train) to 167th St. Closed Mondays and Tuesdays. Donation suggested. 1040 Grand Concourse at E. 165th St. (phone: 718-681-6000).

EDGAR ALLAN POE COTTAGE Adequately cramped to inspire claustrophobia in anyone larger than a raven, this tiny cottage sits incongruously in the middle of the Grand Concourse. Poe lived here during his last years, and the home contains his personal belongings. Open Sunday afternoons and Saturdays. Admission charge. Grand Concourse at E. Kingsbridge Rd. (phone: 718-881-8900).

WAVE HILL This country mansion set on 28 acres has been a home to Mark Twain, Teddy Roosevelt, Arturo Toscanini, William Thackeray, T. H. Huxley, and Social Darwinist Herbert Spencer. It was eventually donated to the city and features a Gothic Armor Hall and beautiful gardens, as well as a considerable mix of dance, jazz, and classical music performances; call for the schedule. Closed Mondays. No admission charge weekdays. In the elegant, residential Riverdale section of the Bronx at 675 W. 252nd St. (phone: 718-549-3200).

YANKEE STADIUM The home of the *"Bronx Bombers,"* this 55,745-seat stadium is where Babe Ruth, Lou Gehrig, Joe DiMaggio, and dozens of other baseball stars played the national sport. From Manhattan take the *IND* line (C or D train) or the *IRT* Lexington Ave. line (No. 4 train) to E. 161st St. Open during baseball season. River Ave. and E. 161st St. (phone: 718-293-5000).

HALL OF FAME OF GREAT AMERICANS About 100 bronze-cast busts of American presidents, poets, and people noted for achievement in the sciences, arts, and humanities are set atop columns outdoors on the *Bronx Community College* campus. From Manhattan take the *IND* line (D train) to W. 183rd St., or the *IRT* Lexington Ave. line (No. 4 train) to Burnside Ave. Open daily. No admission charge. University Ave. and W. 181st St. (phone: 718-220-6450).

QUEENS

Manhattanites used to think of Queens as outer suburbia—until Manhattan's skyrocketing rents prompted many middle class folks to take a second look. Actually, Queens is less than a five-minute subway ride from Manhattan's eastern edge and is the largest of the five boroughs. It boasts 118.6 square miles that include major sports facilities, 196 miles of waterfront, numerous parks, cultural centers, universities, two of the metro area's three airports, and even a growing motion picture industry. Queens also is one of the most ethnically diverse areas in the nation, though nationalities tend to congregate in specific pockets. Greeks have settled in Astoria; Hispanics in Corona and Jackson Heights; Asians in Flushing. The largest Hindu temple in North America is found on Bowne Street in Flushing, and Flushing's Chinatown now rivals Manhattan's. These neighborhoods offer a fascinating assortment of restaurants, groceries, and bakeries—Filipino, Italian, Peruvian, Ecuadoran, Colombian, Argentinian, Greek, German—and also sponsor a number of festivals featuring their own foods, crafts, music, and dancing. For information on these activities, call *Queens Borough Hall* (phone: 718-286-3000).

Queens's architectural ambience can change literally from block to block—from pretty Kew Gardens to elegant Jamaica Estates and Bayside Hills, from the quiet row houses of Flushing to the Victorian homes in Richmond Hill, Old Woodhaven, and College Point. Historical sites abound, including the *Friends Meeting House* (137-16 Northern Blvd., Flushing; phone: 718-358-9636). Built in 1694, it is the oldest house of worship in the US.

Sports buffs flock to Queens to see the *Mets* at *Shea Stadium*, the horse races at *Aqueduct* and *Belmont*, and the *US Open Tennis Championships* at the *USTA National Tennis Center* in *Flushing Meadows Park*. There are abundant facilities for golf, tennis, swimming, ice skating, horseback riding, boating, hiking, and bird watching. Lovers of the great outdoors enjoy the borough's wetlands and woodlands, including the two-mile Pitobik Trail; Turtle Pond; *Alley Pond Environmental Center* (phone: 718-229-4000); *Forest Park* (phone: 718-520-5900); *Jamaica Bay Wildlife Refuge* (phone: 718-318-4340); and the *Queens Botanical Gardens,* in Flushing (phone: 718-886-3800).

BOWNE HOUSE Dating from 1661, this was the home of John Bowne, a Quaker credited with winning religious freedom in the Dutch colony of New Amsterdam from Governor Peter Stuyvesant. The house is now a museum, featuring 17th- and 18th-century furnishings, pewter, and paintings. Officially open 2:30 to 4:30 PM, Tuesdays, Saturdays, and Sundays; call ahead to confirm. Admission charge. 37-01 Bowne St., Flushing (phone: 718-359-0528).

KINGSLAND HOUSE AND THE QUEENS HISTORICAL SOCIETY The sole survivor of what was once the prevalent architectural style in Queens, this Dutch colonial/English house dating to circa 1785 contains antique china and assorted memorabilia. Open 2:30 to 4:30 PM, Tuesdays, Saturdays, and Sundays. Admission charge. 143-35 37th Ave., Flushing (phone: 718-939-0647).

KING MANSION Built in the early 18th century, this home was bought by Rufus King, one of the signers of the Constitution, in 1805. Much of the present structure, a fine example of Georgian-Federal architecture, dates from the 19th century, during which time three generations of King descendants added to it. Tours are available by appointment only. Admission charge. Jamaica Ave. and 153rd St., Jamaica (phone: 718-291-0282).

AMERICAN MUSEUM OF THE MOVING IMAGE A national landmark that pays tribute to New York's revitalized film industry, this museum is located in a building that once housed Paramount Pictures' East Coast facilities and is now home to Kaufmann Astoria Studios. In the 1930s and 1940s the Marx Brothers movies (among others) were produced here; today directors such as Woody Allen, Spike Lee, and Sidney Lumet regularly use this second-largest soundstage in the country. The museum offers lectures and seminars on film and television. An excellent permanent exhibit, "Behind the Screen: Producing, Promoting, and Exhibiting Motion Pictures and Television," displays old movie sets, posters, costumes, and more. Closed Mondays. Admission charge. 35th Ave. and 36th St., Astoria (phone: 718-784-4520).

FLUSHING MEADOW–CORONA PARK The site of the *1939* and *1964 World's Fairs* and the original headquarters of the *UN,* the park is now a center for cultural and outdoor activities (phone: 718-760-6565). The *Queens Museum* hosts a variety of changing exhibitions and includes in its permanent collection a 15,000-square-foot scale model of New York City, updated last year. Closed Mondays; open afternoons only on weekends. Suggested donation (phone: 718-592-2405). The park's *New York Hall of Science* has several permanent exhibits—everything from laser displays to cow's-eye dissections. Closed Mondays and Tuesdays. Admission charge (phone: 718-699-0005). From Manhattan take the *IRT* Flushing line (No. 7 train) to Willets Point/Shea Stadium.

STATEN ISLAND

Much closer to New Jersey than New York, Staten Island is the Big Apple's most remote borough and, with only about 375,000 people, its least populous. This is the borough that keeps threatening to "secede" from the others in New York City's union. In 1993 the island's residents voted two to one in favor of secession, but legislators in Albany, the state capital, have yet to work out what kind of status the borough can be given. Since the Verrazano-Narrows Bridge opened in 1964, Staten Island has been filling up with suburban housing developments and shopping centers, but a few farms remain in the southern reaches. To find them, you can take the bus marked "Richmond Avenue" at the ferry terminal, but getting around by public transportation takes a long time; driving is recommended if at all possible.

STATEN ISLAND ZOO Considerably smaller than the *Bronx Zoo,* this animal house covers eight wooded acres near a lake in *Barret Park.* Its specialty is reptiles of all descriptions. Open daily. Admission charge. 614 Broadway at Clove Rd. (phone: 718-442-3101).

JACQUES MARCHAIS CENTER OF TIBETAN ART One of the more unusual treasures of the city, this is also one of its best-kept secrets. A reconstructed Tibetan prayer hall, featuring an adjoining library and gardens with Oriental sculpture, the center sits on a hill overlooking a pastoral, un–New

York setting of trees. *The Tibetan Book of the Dead,* other esoteric tomes, prayer wheels, statuary, and weavings are on display. Open Wednesday through Friday December through March; Wednesday through Sunday April through November; also open by appointment for group tours. Admission charge. 338 Lighthouse Ave. (phone: 718-987-3478).

CONFERENCE HOUSE Now a national landmark, this manor house was built circa 1680 and hosted such Revolutionary War notables as Benjamin Franklin. Crafts demonstrations are frequently offered; call ahead. Open Wednesday through Sunday afternoons. Admission charge. 7455 Hylan Blvd. (phone: 718-984-6046).

RICHMONDTOWN RESTORATION In this 96-acre park, exhibits and crafts demonstrations depict three centuries of local culture, harking back to the early Dutch settlers. Open Wednesday through Sunday afternoons. Admission charge. 441 Clarke Ave. (phone: 718-351-1617).

Sources and Resources

TOURIST INFORMATION

The *New York Convention and Visitors' Bureau Information Center* (2 Columbus Circle, New York, NY 10019; phone: 397-8222) is an excellent source for hotel and restaurant information, subway and bus maps, descriptive brochures, and current listings of entertainment, special events, and other activities; the office is staffed by multilingual aides. *Big Apple Greeter* (Manhattan Borough President's Office, 1 Centre St., New York, NY 10007; phone: 669-8159) is a program in which New York citizens—from students to seniors—serve as volunteer guides for out-of-towners. Greeters, who are first screened and trained, are matched with a visitor based on the volunteer's expertise and the visitor's interests, needs, and language requirements. During the two- to four-hour neighborhood tours (which usually require at least 24 hours' notice), greeters share their insights and knowledge of their particular slice of the Big Apple. A subscribers-only hotline called *Manhattan Intelligence* provides information on anything from where to pet a lion cub to more mundane data such as cultural events, making restaurant reservations, and finding a parking space for your car (phone: 925-0900 for more information). Call the *New York State Travel Information Center Hotline* (phone: 800-CALL-NYS) for maps, calendars of events, health updates, and travel advisories.

Visitors who require assistance in an emergency—anything from a lost wallet to a lost child—should stop at the *Traveler's Aid Services* office (1481 Broadway; phone: 944-0013); open weekdays from 9 AM to 6 PM (Wednesdays to 1 PM), weekends from 9:30 AM to 3 PM. There is also a branch in the *International Arrivals Building* at *John F. Kennedy International Airport* (phone: 718-656-4870); open weekdays from 10 AM to 8 PM, weekends from 1 to 8 PM.

Numerous excellent guides to the city's architecture and history are available at most good-size bookstores. We immodestly suggest you pick up a copy of *Birnbaum's New York 95* (HarperCollins; $12).

LOCAL COVERAGE *The New York Times,* the *Daily News, New York Newsday,* and the *New York Post* all are morning dailies; the *Village Voice* comes out weekly on Wednesdays. Other publications include the weekly *New Yorker* and *New York* magazines.

TELEVISION STATIONS Channel 2–WCBS; Channel 4–WNBC; Channel 5–WNYW (Fox); Channel 7–WABC; Channel 9–WOR (local); Channel 11–WPIX (local); Channel 13–WNET (PBS).

RADIO STATIONS AM: WFAN 660 (sports/talk); WOR 710 (news/talk); WABC 770 (talk); WCBS 880 (news); WRHD 1570 (oldies). FM: WBGO 88.3 (jazz); WXRK 92.3 (classic rock); WNYC 93.9 (classical); WQXR 96.3 (classical); WNEW 102.7 (rock); WBLS 107.5 (urban contemporary).

TELEPHONE The area code for Manhattan is 212. The area code for the Bronx, Brooklyn, Queens, and Staten Island is 718. The area code for Long Island is 516. Unless otherwise noted, all telephone numbers in this chapter are in Manhattan—area code 212.

SALES TAX New York City's sales tax is 8.25%. The hotel tax is 14.25% plus a $2 per night occupancy tax. Restaurant meals also also are taxed 8.25%.

CLIMATE The best times to visit New York are in the spring—April and May—and in the fall—September through mid-November—when temperatures are comfortable, in the high 50s to low 70s F. Winter and summer are extreme, averaging in the 80s and up in July and August, in the 30s or below during the months of hard winter. However, the weather should not determine your visit, since most of what makes New York great takes place indoors, and air conditioning and central heating are standard. New Yorkers dress informally for many events; anything in good taste goes. Remember, there is no rainy season as such—it can happen any day of the year. Be prepared.

GETTING AROUND

AIRPORTS New York City is served by three major airports: *John F. Kennedy International (JFK)* and *La Guardia* (for domestic flights)—both in the borough of Queens—and *Newark International,* across the Hudson in New Jersey. It takes 50 to 60 minutes to reach *JFK* from midtown Manhattan by cab; *La Guardia* from midtown is a 30- to 45-minute ride. *Newark International* is a 30- to 40-minute drive from midtown.

Quick and relatively inexpensive transportation is available via several bus lines. *Carey Transportation* (phone: 718-632-0500) provides service from *Grand Central Terminal* (arrives at Vanderbilt Ave.; departs from Park Ave., just south of 42nd St.), the *Air Trans Center* at the *Port Authority Bus Terminal,* the *Hilton, Sheraton Manhattan, Marriott Marquis,* and *Holiday Inn Crowne Plaza* hotels in midtown to *JFK* and *La Guardia* airports. Buses leave every 30 minutes (every 20 minutes after 1 PM). *Carey* also runs a shuttle between these two airports. The *Newark Airport Express,* operated by *New Jersey Transit* (phone: 201-762-5100), runs between *Newark Airport* and the *Port Authority Bus Terminal* (Eighth Ave. between W. 40th and W. 42nd Sts.; phone: 212-564-8484).

Olympia Trails (phone: 964-6233 or 718-622-7700 in New York, 908-354-3330 in New Jersey) provides daily coach service every 20 to 30 minutes from all *Newark International* terminals, the *World Trade Center, Grand Central Terminal,* and *Penn Station.* The *Gray Line Air Shuttle* offers a share-ride van service which operates among all New York airports and most midtown hotels. Arrangements can be made by your hotel, at the *Gray Line Air Shuttle* courtesy telephone by the airline baggage claim areas, or by calling 757-6840 or 800-451-0455. For other information about transportation options to and from the New York area airports, call the *New York/New Jersey Port Authority* (phone: 800-247-7433).

BUS New York City buses run frequently. There are more than 220 routes and over 3,800 buses in operation. Although considerably slower than subways, buses often bring you closer to your destination, stopping about every two blocks, except on express routes, which stop only at major crossings. The main routes in Manhattan are north-south on the avenues and east-west (crosstown) on major cross-streets (such as 14th, 34th, 42nd, 57th, and 72nd Streets), as well as some crisscross and circular routes. Check both the sign on the front of the bus and the one at the bus stop to make sure the bus goes where you want and stops where you are waiting. Be sure to have exact change for the fare or a subway token. *Bus drivers do not make change, nor do they accept bills.* The multiple-use *MetroCard* was introduced early last year. Now accepted on buses and in some subway stations, *MetroCards* are intended for use system-wide by the end of this year. The size of a credit card, they are run through a scanner; one fare is deducted each time you use them. They are sold at values of $5 to $80.

At press time the per-trip transit fare was $1.25, no matter what the length of your trip or method of payment; on buses a transfer is necessary for any change of bus on a continuous journey and is free, but there is no free transfer from bus to subway, or vice versa. Most bus routes operate 24 hours a day, seven days a week, but service is less frequent late at night or on Sundays. For information on buses to points outside Manhattan from the *Port Authority Bus Terminal* (Eighth Ave. and W. 42nd St.), call 564-8484 or 564-1114. Free bus maps are available at *Grand Central* and *Penn Stations* or by sending a self-addressed, stamped legal-size (#10) envelope to the *New York Transit Authority,* Room 875, 370 Jay St., Brooklyn, NY 11201, Attn.: Maps.

CAR RENTAL New York is served by all the major car rental companies, as well as a host of small local firms.

SUBWAY The New York subway system has a reputation for being dangerous, dirty, and confusing. The reality is not quite so harrowing as most people fear. The past several years have brought many new trains, tracks, and station improvements to this extensive underground network, as well as an increased transit police presence. The system's convenience and speed can't be duplicated by any other form of transportation. Pick up free subway maps at token booths or at the *New York Convention and Visitors' Bureau Information Center* (see above); system maps are in most cars—but usually not outside on the platforms. Keep in mind that certain interchange stations are large and confusing, so if you don't find a sign that confirms you are on the right platform, double-check with another passenger or any transit worker. Also double-check that you don't board an express if you are better served by a local; the map makes the distinctions relatively clear, but even New Yorkers occasionally whiz 50 or more blocks beyond a desired stop when they don't pay attention to which train they are boarding.

Basically, there are three different subway lines, with express and local routes serving all city boroughs except Staten Island (reached via the *Staten Island Ferry*). The most extensive is the *IRT*, which originates in Brooklyn and travels north through Manhattan en route to the Bronx. The *IRT* has two main divisions: the Seventh Avenue line, which serves the West Side of Manhattan, and the Lexington Avenue line, which covers the East Side. You can go from east to west (crosstown) on the shuttle (S) or IRT No. 7 train (which goes to Flushing, Queens) between *Grand Central Station* and Times Square, and the L train will take you crosstown at 14th Street. The *IND* line serves Brooklyn, Queens, Manhattan, and the Bronx. The *BMT* line serves Brooklyn, Queens, and Manhattan. The subway is the most heavily used means of city transportation (about four million people ride it daily on 722 miles of track) and so is mobbed during rush hours—weekdays from 7:30 to a little after 9 AM and from 4:30 to 7 PM. The fare at press time was $1.25 (no matter how far you travel or how many times you change trains without exiting), but there have been some rumblings about a possible fare hike. Tokens or a *MetroCard* are required to enter. Buy them at booths in the subway stations, and insert them in turnstiles to gain access to the trains. Buy a 10-pack of tokens to save time (but not money); the introduction of the multiple-fare *MetroCard* last year (see *Buses* above) should also streamline subway entry.

The subway system operates 24 hours a day, although most schedules are cut back between midnight and 6 AM. At night the lights outside many stations indicate accessibility: A red light means the station is closed; a yellow light indicates that the station is open but no one is on duty at the token booth; and a green light means both the station and token booth are open. Whenever possible, try to avoid traveling alone late at night when stations and train cars are more deserted and transit police officers are few and far between. For general bus and subway information, call the *New York Transit Authority* (phone: 718-330-1234).

TAXI The handiest—albeit one of the most expensive—way to get around the city is by taxi. Cabs can be identified by their yellow color and are available if the center portion of the roof light is on (if the *entire* roof light is either on or off, this means that the cab is off-duty, or call, or already occupied). They can be hailed almost anywhere and if on-duty, they are required by law to pick you up and deliver you to your specified destination. New Yorkers generally tip cabbies about 20% of the metered fare. There is a 50¢ surcharge on most cab fares between 8 PM and 6 AM and all day Sundays. Passengers must pay any bridge and/or tunnel tolls. The *New York City Taxi and Limousine Commission* (phone: 221-TAXI) publishes a pamphlet called "How to Use a New York City

Taxi." It lists rates, sample fares to common destinations, and other useful information. New York also has dozens of companies that provide conventional sedans with drivers and can be called by phone (known locally as "car services"). Fares run somewhere between those of yellow street cabs and limousines, but are usually cheaper than both for long-distance runs, such as to airports, because a fixed fee is charged. Two such companies are *Dialcar* (phone: 718-743-8383) and *Love* (phone: 718-633-3338).

LOCAL SERVICES

AUDIOVISUAL EQUIPMENT *Ace Sound Rental Co.* (13 E. 31st St.; phone: 685-3344); *Select Audio Visual* (460 W. 34th St.; phone: 290-4800).

BABY-SITTING Ask at your hotel desk for recommendations.

BUSINESS SERVICES *QED Transcription Service* (phone: 563-0740) or *Wordflow* (phone: 725-5111) for taping and immediate transcription of meetings and seminars.

COMPUTER AND TYPEWRITER RENTAL *Cavalier,* two-week minimum (phone: 682-1780); *Business Office Equipment,* from computers to office tables and chairs, weekly rate only (phone: 265-4550).

DRY CLEANER/TAILOR *Newman Cleaners & Dyers* (914 Seventh Ave., between W. 57th and W. 58th Sts.; phone: 247-5207); *S & A Cleaners & Tailors* (134½ E. 62nd St.; phone: 838-0630). There is a high density of dry cleaners in Manhattan, especially in residential areas, and almost all hotels have cleaning and tailoring services.

FORMALWEAR RENTALS *Baldwin Formals* (phone: 245-8190) for classic and designer tuxedos and men's formal accessories, including collapsible top hats; *One Night Stand* (phone: 772-7720) has designer gowns and women's accessories, priced from $120 to $350 per evening. Note: Many rental outlets require appointments.

LIMOUSINE SERVICES *Gotham Limousine* (phone: 868-8860; 800-227-7997); *London Town Cars* (phone: 988-9700; 800-221-4009 outside of New York); *SoHo Car and Limo Service* (phone: 431-9090; 800-441-7646).

MECHANIC *Express Auto* (276 Seventh Ave.; phone: 242-5811) for 24-hour road service and repairs.

MEDICAL EMERGENCY *Bellevue Hospital* (462 First Ave. at 27th St.; phone: 561-4141); *Lenox Hill Hospital* (100 E. 77th St.; phone: 434-3300); *Mount Sinai Hospital* (Fifth Ave. at 100th St.; phone: 241-6500); *New York University Medical Center* (560 First Ave. at 34th St.; phone: 263-7300); *St. Luke's–Roosevelt Hospital Center* (428 W. 59th St. at Ninth Ave.; phone: 523-4000); *St. Vincent's Hospital and Medical Center of New York* (153 W. 11th St. at Seventh Ave.; phone: 790-7000).

MESSENGER SERVICES *Accurate Messenger Service* (phone: 688-5450); *Bullit Messenger Manpower,* 24-hour service (phone: 983-7400).

PHOTOCOPIES *Amal Printing* (630 Fifth Ave., in *Rockefeller Center;* phone: 247-3270); *Commerce Photo-Print,* open late and weekends by appointment (106 Fulton St., in the Wall Street area; phone: 964-2256). *Kinko's* has many sites in the city, some of which are open 24 hours. Check the phone book for exact locations.

POST OFFICE *James A. Farley General Post Office (JAF;* 421 Eighth Ave.; phone: 967-8585), provides 24-hour window service.

PROFESSIONAL PHOTOGRAPHER *Matar Studio* (101 Maiden La.; phone: 809-0080).

SECRETARY/STENOGRAPHER *A Steno Service* (phone: 682-4990); or inquire at your hotel.

TELECONFERENCE FACILITIES The *New York Hilton, Sheraton Manhattan, Sheraton New York,* and the *Waldorf-Astoria* have facilities available to guests (see *Checking In* for all four).

TRANSLATORS *Berlitz* (phone: 777-7878); *Lawyers & Merchants* (phone: 344-2930); *Translation Aces* (phone: 269-4660).

WESTERN UNION/TELEX Many offices around the city (phone: 661-9595 for customer service).

OTHER *ETX Corp.,* simultaneous teleprocessing (phone: 927-8555); *Headquarters Business Centers (HQ),* word processing, telex, fax, and conference rooms (phone: 949-0722); *International Conference Group,* meeting and conference planners (phone: 941-0022); *Miller Associates,* videotaping of meetings (phone: 741-8011); *Manhattan Passport,* a private concierge enterprise providing travel arrangements and customized shopping and sightseeing tours, among other services (phone: 744-0203); *Video Monitoring Service,* for broadcast information, tapes, and transcripts (phone: 736-2010).

SPECIAL EVENTS

In late January or early February (held on the first new moon after January 21), *Chinese New Year Celebration and Dragon Parade,* Chinatown; March 17, *St. Patrick's Day Parade,* Fifth Avenue; *Easter Sunday, Easter Parade,* Fifth Avenue; May, *Ninth Avenue International Food Festival;* May, *Washington Square Outdoor Art Show,* Greenwich Village; first Sunday in June, *Puerto Rican Day Parade,* Fifth Avenue; late June to early July, *JVC Jazz Festival; July 4th, Macy's* fireworks along the East River; July and August, free *Shakespeare Festival, Delacorte Theater, Central Park,* and free performances of the *New York Philharmonic* and *Metropolitan Opera,* all boroughs; August, *Harlem Week;* late August and September, *US Open Tennis Championships, USTA National Tennis Center, Flushing Meadows Park,* Queens; September, *African-American Day Parade;* September, the 10-day *Festival of San Gennaro,* patron saint of Neapolitans, Mulberry Street, Little Italy; September and October, *New York Film Festival, Lincoln Center;* October, *Columbus Day Parade,* Fifth Avenue; October 31, *Halloween Parade,* Greenwich Village; November, *NYC Marathon, Central Park* (finish line); November, *Veterans Day Parade,* Fifth Avenue; November, *Macy's Thanksgiving Day Parade,* Broadway; December, *Christmas Tree Lighting,* Rockefeller Plaza; November through January the *Great Christmas Show, Radio City Music Hall.*

For borough-by-borough information on parades, festivals, exhibits, and free events, call 360-1333 (Manhattan); 718-625-0080 (Brooklyn); 718-590-3500 (Bronx); 718-447-4485 (Staten Island); and 718-291-ARTS (Queens).

MUSEUMS

The city boasts more than 150 museums. In addition to those described in *Special Places,* other notable New York museums include the following:

AMERICAN CRAFT MUSEUM Jewelry, rugs, textiles, metal crafts, and other exhibits. Closed Mondays. Admission charge; under 12, free. 40 W. 53rd St. (phone: 956-6047).

ASIA SOCIETY Changing exhibits of ancient and contemporary Asian art. Closed Mondays. Admission charge except Thursday evenings; under 12, free. 725 Park Ave. at E. 70th St. (phone: 288-6400).

CHILDREN'S MUSEUM OF THE ARTS Hands-on, interactive exhibits with arts-related themes. Children are encouraged to design and make their own collages, clay models, and paintings. Closed Mondays. Admission charge except for children 18 months or younger. 72-78 Spring St. (phone: 941-9198).

COOPER-HEWITT MUSEUM The *National Museum of Design* branch of the *Smithsonian Institution,* featuring a full range of decorative arts. Closed Mondays. Admission charge except for children under 12. 2 E. 91st St. at Fifth Ave. (phone: 860-6868).

FORBES MAGAZINE GALLERIES World's largest collection of Fabergé Imperial Russian *Easter* eggs plus model boats and soldiers. Closed Sundays and Mondays; Thursdays are reserved for guided tours. No admission charge. 62 Fifth Ave. at 12th St. (phone: 206-5548).

FRAUNCES TAVERN MUSEUM This landmark building, the site of Washington's farewell to his officers in 1783, contains memorabilia of the American Revolution (including Washington's hat). Open weekdays and Saturday afternoons. Admission charge. The *Fraunces Tavern* restaurant (269-0144) occupies the ground floor. 54 Pearl St. at Broad St. (phone: 425-1776).

FRICK COLLECTION This magnificent mansion, the former home of Pittsburgh industrialist Henry Clay Frick, houses his staggering collection of sculpture, porcelain, furniture, antiques, and Old Master paintings—among them Renoir's *Mother and Children,* Fragonard's *The Progress of Love,* Rembrandt's *Polish Rider* and a self-portrait, Giovanni Bellini's *St. Francis in Ecstasy,* three canvases by Vermeer, Holbein's portraits of Sir Thomas More and Thomas Cromwell, and works by El Greco, David, Gainsborough, Goya, Lawrence, Reynolds, and Turner. Closed Mondays. Admission charge; children under 10 not permitted. 1 E. 70th St. at Fifth Ave. (phone: 288-0700).

GUINNESS WORLD OF RECORDS Displays featuring feats and strange facts from the *Guinness Book of Records.* The exhibits include life-size models of the tallest, fattest, and shortest men in the world, videos of records being reached, and computer-generated displays. Open daily. Admission charge except for children under three. In the *Empire State Building,* 350 Fifth Ave., from W. 33rd to W. 34th St. (phone: 947-2335).

INTERNATIONAL CENTER OF PHOTOGRAPHY Rotating exhibits of the latest works by internationally renowned photographers; occasionally, these are arranged around particular themes, such as the Holocaust. Closed Mondays. Admission charge. 1130 Fifth Ave. at 94th St. (phone: 860-1777) and 1133 Sixth Ave. at W. 43rd St. (phone: 768-4683).

INTREPID SEA-AIR-SPACE MUSEUM This World War II aircraft carrier has exhibits on the navy, pioneers in aviation, and technology. A lightship (a seagoing lighthouse) and a MiG-21 fighter jet are part of the "fleet," which also includes a submarine and a battleship. Open daily from *Memorial Day* through *Labor Day;* closed Mondays and Tuesdays the rest of the year. Admission charge except for children under six. Permanently moored at Pier 86 in the Hudson River, 12th Ave. and W. 46th St. (phone: 245-0072 or 245-2533).

JEWISH MUSEUM Reopened in 1993 after a $50-million expansion and renovation, this museum houses a permanent collection of more than 27,000 works of art, artifacts, ceremonial objects, and more spanning 4,000 years of Jewish history. Closed Fridays, Saturdays, and major Jewish holidays. Admission charge except for children under 12. 1109 Fifth Ave. at 92nd St. (phone: 423-3200).

LOWER EAST SIDE TENEMENT MUSEUM Reopened last year, America's first urban "living history" museum features a restored replica of a 19th-century tenement building, as well as photographs, drawings, and documents recounting the lives of immigrants. Walking tours and a Wednesday slide show are also offered. Closed Mondays and Saturdays. Donation suggested; admission charge for the slide show. 97 Orchard St. (phone: 431-0233).

MUSEO DEL BARRIO Dedicated to the arts and culture of Puerto Rico, including painting, sculpture, concerts, photography, and films. Closed Mondays and Tuesdays. Donation suggested. 1230 Fifth Ave. at 104th St. (phone: 831-7272).

MUSEUM FOR AFRICAN ART A recently enlarged facility featuring sculpture, paintings, and crafts in both contemporary and traditional styles. The emphasis is on artisans from Zaire, Cameroon, Ghana, and the Ivory Coast. There are also art-history seminars. Closed Mondays. Admission charge. 593 Broadway, between Houston and Prince Sts. (phone: 966-1313).

MUSEUM OF AMERICAN FOLK ART Educational programs, exhibits, and publications devoted to American folk art from the 18th century to the present. Closed Mondays. Donation suggested. Columbus Ave. and W. 66th St. (phone: 595-9533).

MUSEUM OF TELEVISION AND RADIO Formerly the *Museum of Broadcasting,* this repository of over 40,000 radio and television programs and commercials hosts frequent seminars and has excellent research facilities.

Closed Sundays and Mondays. Suggested admission charge. 25 W. 52nd St. (phone: 621-6600).

MUSEUM OF THE CITY OF NEW YORK A free video show, "The Big Apple," is a permanent attraction here; there are also temporary exhibits focusing on the city. Closed Mondays and Tuesdays. Donation suggested. Fifth Ave. and 103rd St. (phone: 534-1672).

NATIONAL MUSEUM OF THE AMERICAN INDIAN A comprehensive collection of artifacts linked to the indigenous peoples of all the Americas, this museum, part of Washington, DC's *Smithsonian Institution,* also is known as the *George Gustav Heye Center,* named after a major collector. Last year it relocated from West 155th Street to the *Alexander Hamilton US Custom House* at the southern tip of the island. The new facility, which features changing displays of its one million objects, also stages educational workshops, film and video festivals, and performances of Native American dance, music, and theater. Although the focus is on North, Central, and South American peoples, there are ethnological materials from as far away as Siberia. Open daily year-round except *Christmas Day.* No admission charge. 1 *Bowling Green* (phone: 668-NMAI).

NEW-YORK HISTORICAL SOCIETY Established in the early 19th century, this institution is a repository of paintings by the Hudson River School, and more; it houses a library of some 700,000 volumes on the history of New York City and New York State. At press time, exhibition spaces were closed pending major renovations; they are scheduled to reopen May 1995. Closed weekends. No admission charge. 170 Central Park W. at W. 76th St. (phone: 873-3400).

NEW YORK TRANSIT MUSEUM Old subway cars and other nostalgic and informative metropolitan memorabilia plus changing exhibitions (including some very imaginative ones geared to children), a lecture series, and tours. Closed Mondays. Admission charge except for children under two. Boerum Pl. and Schermerhorn St., Brooklyn (phone: 718-330-3060).

NOGUCHI MUSEUM This garden museum features more than 300 of Isamu Noguchi's works, including sculptures in stone, clay, and wood; paper lamps; and plans for fountains and playgrounds. Open Wednesdays and Saturdays from April through November. Donation suggested. 32-37 Vernon Blvd., Long Island City, Queens (phone: 718-204-7088).

PIERPONT MORGAN LIBRARY AND ANNEX These elegant buildings house Old Master drawings, early printed books, music manuscripts, plus a private research library. A superb collection of medieval and Renaissance illuminated manuscripts is also on display. The facility includes the adjacent *Morgan House;* the two buildings are linked by the beautifully designed, glass-enclosed Garden Court—a pleasant place to take a breather from viewing exhibits. Closed Mondays. Donation suggested. 29 E. 36th St. at Madison Ave. (phone: 685-0610).

STUDIO MUSEUM OF HARLEM An impressive collection of works by African-American artists. Closed Mondays and Tuesdays. Admission charge. 144 W. 125th St. (phone: 864-4500).

SHOPPING

This city is like no other for acquiring material possessions. It is the commercial center and the fashion capital of the country, and styles that originate here set the trends for fashionable folk from Portland, Maine, to Portland, Oregon. The scope of merchandise available approaches the infinite, and the best part of all is that there are goodies for every budget.

ANTIQUES "Antiques Row" is a district extending from E. 10th Street to E. 14th Street, from Broadway to University Place, with many former wholesalers now open to the public. Elsewhere, there is the *Chelsea Antiques Building* (110 W. 25th St.; phone: 929-0909); the year-round, weekends-only *Indoor Antiques Fair* (122 W. 26th St.; phone: 627-4700), with two floors and 65 vendors; and the nearby *Annex Flea Market*, which spreads from W. 24th to W. 26th Street along the Avenue of the Americas (Sixth Avenue), with more than 150 vendors (this is not for ultra-serious museum collectors, but a discerning eye can ferret out some exquisite pieces from an extensive collection that includes jewelry, decorative objects, and furniture). Much farther west is *John Koch Antiques* (514 W. 24th St., between 10th and 11th Aves., Third Floor; phone: 243-8625), which sells estate objects from the everyday to the elegant. A down-market, downtown source is the *Soho Antiques Fair and Collectibles* (Broadway and Grand St.; phone: 682-2000); this weekend outdoor flea market sells an enormous variety of trinkets, clothes, photographic and electronic equipment, furniture, art, housewares, and oddities.

BED AND TABLE LINEN For good buys on top-quality and designer sheets and pillowcases, New York is definitely the place. At *H & G Cohen Bedding* (306 Grand St.; phone: 226-0818), all the major brands are available at a 25 to 30% discount. (This, like most Lower East Side shops, is closed Saturdays but open Sundays.) *D. Porthault* (18 E. 69th St.; phone: 688-1660) is the French master of extraordinary table and bed linen, many in magnificent floral prints; *Léron* (750 Madison Ave.; phone: 753-6700) imports exquisite bed and table linen and lingerie. *Pratesi* (829 Madison Ave.; phone: 288-2315) and *Frette* (799 Madison Ave.; phone: 988-5221) offer a wide selection of the finest bed, bath, and table linen manufactured at the companies' factories in Italy. The third floor at *ABC Carpet & Home* (888 Broadway; phone: 473-3000) is stocked with hundreds of down comforters, blankets, pillows, tablecloths and napkins, and sheets and pillowcases from the most prestigious domestic and European houses; the nine-floor emporium, which underwent expansion last year, also sells a large selection of furniture and home textiles and accessories. In the Wall Street vicinity, *Century 21* (22 Cortland St., between Broadway and Church St.; phone: 227-9092), which is better known for clothing, has a large collection of discounted linens.

BOOKSTORES The publishing capital of the world, New York is a bibliophile's delight. *Barnes & Noble* (105 Fifth Ave. at W. 18th St.; phone: 807-0099; 675 Ave. of the Americas at 21st St.; phone: 727-1227; 600 Fifth Ave. at W. 48th St.; phone: 765-0590; 2289 Broadway at W. 82nd St.; phone: 362-8835; and 1280 Lexington Ave., between 86th and 87th Sts.; phone: 423-9900) carries wide selections, some at discounted prices. *B. Dalton* (666

Fifth Ave. at W. 53rd St.; phone: 247-1740; and 396 Ave. of the Americas at W. Eighth St.; phone: 674-8780) and *Doubleday* (724 Fifth Ave., between W. 56th and W. 57th Sts.; phone: 397-0550) carry a broad variety of new titles and trade books, as does *Coliseum Books* (1771 Broadway at W. 57th St.; phone: 757-8381). The *Strand* (828 Broadway at E. 12th St.; phone: 473-1452) has eight miles of old and used books and even some rare manuscripts. *Rizzoli* (31 W. 57th St.; phone: 759-2424; 454 West Broadway; phone: 674-1616; and in the *Winter Garden* of the *World Financial Center* at 200 Vesey St.; phone: 385-1400) is best known for its collection of art, music, and photography books. *Kitchen Arts & Letters* (1435 Lexington Ave. at E. 93rd St.; phone: 876-5550) is a bookstore and gallery devoted exclusively to food and wine. *Forbidden Planet* (821 Broadway at E. 12th St.; phone: 473-1576) has the wackiest bunch of comics, science fiction books, masks, and monsters you're liable to find this side of Mars. The *New York Astrology Center* (545 Eighth Ave.; phone: 947-3609) claims to have the country's largest selection of books on astrology. The *Complete Traveller Bookstore* (199 Madison Ave. at E. 35th St.; phone: 685-9007) and the *Traveller's Bookstore* (22 W. 52nd St., in *Rockefeller Center*; phone: 664-0995) have enviable troves of travel guides and books. Architecture buffs should head to *Perimeter* (146 Sullivan St.; phone: 529-2275), and bookish toddlers will be delighted by *Books of Wonder* (132 Seventh Ave.; phone: 989-3270).

BOUTIQUES AND SPECIALTY SHOPS Fifth Avenue in the 50s, the adjacent blocks east (especially East 57th Street), and Madison Avenue in the East 60s and 70s are lined with boutiques that carry haute couture at haute prices, but looking is free. The names are an encyclopedia of style: *Armani, Chanel, Daniel Hechter, Emanuel Ungaro, Gucci, Max Mara, Saint Laurent, Sonia Rykiel, Valentino, Versace,* and the like. Also on the cutting edge of fashion are the styles at *Charivari* (441 Columbus Ave. at W. 81st St.; phone: 496-8700; and five other locations around town). For the finest in rainwear and traditional British tailoring, there's *Burberrys* (9 E. 57th St.; phone: 371-5010) and *Aquascutum of London* (680 Fifth Ave. at W. 54th St.; phone: 975-0250). *Ashanti* (872 Lexington Ave. at E. 65th St.; phone: 535-0740) specializes in stylish clothes for fuller-figured women. *Polo/Ralph Lauren* (867 Madison Ave. at E. 72nd St.; phone: 606-2100), in the 19th-century *Rhinelander Mansion,* is a showcase for the designer's men's, women's, and boys' collections; across the street is *Polo Sport* (888 Madison Ave.; phone: 434-8000). *Fendi* (720 Fifth Ave. at W. 56th St.; phone: 767-0100) features exclusive leather goods and clothes.

CDS, TAPES, AND RECORDS There are a number of places where you can get good prices. *Tower Records* (692 Broadway at E. Fourth St.; phone: 505-1500; 215 E. 86th St.; phone: 369-2500; and 1965 Broadway at W. 66th St.; phone: 799-2500) has enormous music stores open until midnight every day of the year. *J&R Music World* (33 Park Row, near *City Hall;* phone: 349-0062) has the best selection of new and hard-to-find jazz records at good prices. The *House of Oldies* (35 Carmine St.; phone: 243-0500) specializes in records from the past; the *Gryphon Record Shop* (251 W. 72nd St., between Broadway and West End Ave.; phone: 874-1588) has 60,000 out of print recordings. *HMV* (1280 Lexington Ave.

at E. 86th St.; phone: 348-0800; and 2081 Broadway at W. 72nd St.; phone: 721-5900), another gigantic music retailer, has an extensive selection of jazz, blues, gospel, rock, pop, New Age, and new and vintage Broadway show music. For sheet music try the *Music Exchange* (151 W. 46th St.; phone: 354-5858) or the *Joseph Patelson Music House* (160 W. 56th St.; phone: 582-5840).

CHINA, CRYSTAL, AND PORCELAIN The retail branch of *Villeroy & Boch* (974 Madison Ave. at E. 76th St.; phone: 535-2500) carries a full line of elegant tableware. *Royal Copenhagen* (683 Madison Ave. at E. 61st St.; phone: 759-6457) has all that's best in contemporary Danish crystal and porcelain. *Michael C. Fina* (3 W. 47th St.; phone: 869-5050), suitably located in the diamond district, carries a wide selection of the top names in china, crystal, and silver at reasonable prices. For splendid glass sculpture, bowls, and goblets, head for *Steuben Glass* (717 Fifth Ave. at E. 56th St.; phone: 752-1441).

DEPARTMENT STORES *Bloomingdale's* (Lexington Ave. from E. 59th to E. 60th St.; phone: 355-5900 or 705-2073), a world unto itself known affectionately to New Yorkers as *"Bloomie's,"* is considered by many to be the ultimate in Upper East Side chic. *Macy's* (Broadway from W. 34th to W. 35th St.; phone: 695-4400) is the largest New York department store, where you can choose from a huge assortment of high-quality goods. *Macy's* basement emporium, *The Cellar*, is designed as a street of shops carrying everything from fruits and vegetables to housewares, plus restaurants, including the *Cellar Grill*, which serves pizza, pasta, and grilled meat. *Lord & Taylor* (Fifth Ave. from W. 38th to W. 39th St.; phone: 391-3344) has stylish, if conservative, clothing and a bright, airy atmosphere that makes browsing enjoyable. *Saks Fifth Avenue* (Fifth Ave. from E. 49th to E. 50th St.; phone: 753-4000) is where you can be sure to get whatever is fashionable this season. *Bergdorf Goodman* (Fifth Ave. and W. 58th St.) is the epitome of elegant shopping for women; *Bergdorf Goodman Men* is directly across the street (phone: 753-7300 for both). *Henri Bendel* (Fifth Ave. and W. 56th St.; phone: 247-1100) carries an impressively stylish yet often whimsical selection of women's clothes, accessories, and miscellany.

Forward-looking *Barneys New York* is a major fashion player, and the flagship Seventh Avenue store's arty *Christmas* windows are a big draw. The oh-so-posh uptown and *Financial Center* branches carry the same upscale goods (106 Seventh Ave., from W. 16th to W. 17th St.; phone: 929-9000; 225 Liberty St. in the *World Financial Center;* phone: 945-1600; and 660 Madison Ave. at E. 61st St.; phone: 826-8900). *Abraham & Straus (A & S;* Sixth Ave. and W. 33rd St.; phone: 594-8500; and 420 Fulton St. in downtown Brooklyn; phone: 718-875-7200) carries a complete stock of moderately priced goods.

FABRICS AND TRIMMINGS Fabulous silks, imported woolens, and dazzling cotton prints for home decorating or homemade haute couture are available, often at greatly discounted prices, at a number of fascinating and abundant fabric emporiums. *Silk Surplus* (235 E. 58th St.; phone: 753-6511); its nearby annex (223 E. 58th St.; phone: 759-1294); and a third location on the Upper East Side (1147 Madison Ave., between E. 85th and E. 86th Sts.; phone: 794-9373) carry closeouts from their parent company, Scalamandre. While discounts generally are only about 15%, better bargains can be had during June and October sales. A small branch of *Liberty of London* (630 Fifth Ave.; phone: 391-2150) offers a sampling of popular textiles and notions from one of Britain's leading stores. *Paron* (60 W. 57th St.) specializes in discounted designer woolens, cottons, silks, and linen. Even better prices—up to 50% off—can be found on the second floor next door at *Paron's* super-discount store (56 W. 57th St.; phone: 247-6451 for both). On the Lower East Side, *Interiors by Royale* (289 Grand St.; phone: 431-0170) features fine English linen, tapestries, and cotton prints imported from Italy, Spain, and France at discounts of up to 50%. And to add just the right finishing touch, visit *Tender Buttons* (143 E. 62nd St.; phone: 758-7004). The selection of antique and contemporary buttons here is extraordinary, if pricey. For less costly trim, there are dazzling displays at *G & P Buttons and Novelties* (247 W. 37th St.; phone: 719-5333).

FOOD In a city where one can dine out every night of the year at a different ethnic restaurant, it isn't surprising that delicacies and exotic foodstuffs are staples in a host of upscale grocery shops. Whether you're looking for a little something for a picnic, a snack for back at the hotel, a gift for your host, hostess, or the folks back home, or you merely want to take in a dazzling display of way-beyond-average comestibles, a visit to one of the following shops can be a most memorable part of your trip to New York. *Zabar's* (2245 Broadway at W. 80th St.; phone: 787-2000) is a Manhattan institution—a huge, noisy emporium with a mock-Tudor exterior where thousands of New Yorkers and suburbanites stock up each day on pastrami, lox, fresh-roasted coffee beans, bread, pungent cheeses, luscious dried fruit, unusual condiments, and the very latest imported delicacies. *Balducci's* (424 Ave. of the Americas at W. Ninth St.; phone: 673-2600) and the flagship of *Dean & Deluca* (560 Broadway at Prince St.; phone: 431-1691; as well as six other locations) offer pricier fresh fruits and vegetables, plus wonderful imported foods and spices, fresh pasta, and great bread. Worth a visit on the Upper East Side are *Grace's Marketplace* (1237 Third Ave. at E. 71st St.; phone: 737-0600), for phenomenally fresh produce, imported coffees, spices, jams, and preserves, and *Fraser Morris Fine Foods* (1264 Third Ave. at E. 73rd St.; phone: 288-2727), which features items such as fresh caviar, salmon, and imported chocolates and pastries. For an intoxicating sampling of herbs, condiments, spices, and packaged goods from around the world, go to *Adriana's Bazaar* (2152 Broadway, between W. 75th and W. 76th Sts.; phone: 877-5757).

JEWELRY AND GEMS Diamonds are a girl's best friend, but so as not to limit ourselves, we'll include emeralds, rubies, sapphires, pearls, gold, silver, and other precious stones and metals. And so as not to discriminate, we'll include men too. Without a doubt, the most famous of all luxury emporiums is *Tiffany & Co.* (727 Fifth Ave. at E. 57th St.; phone: 755-8000). If you must have something from *Tiffany's* but can't afford a necklace or ring, purchase a novelty like a sterling silver key ring, bookmark, or toothpaste roller. Across the street, *Bulgari* dazzles in its prestigious corner boutique (730 Fifth Ave.; phone: 315-9000). *Cartier* (653 Fifth Ave. at E. 52nd St.; phone: 753-0111; and in *Trump Tower,* 725 Fifth Ave. at E. 56th St.; phone: 308-0840) is renowned for some of the world's finest jewelry and accessories. *Fortunoff* (681 Fifth Ave., between E. 53rd and E. 54th Sts.; phone: 758-6660) has a more moderately priced selection of fine gems, sterling, and gold. *Fred Leighton* (773 Madison Ave. at E. 66th St.; phone: 288-1872; and in *Trump Tower,* 725 Fifth Ave. at E. 56th St.; phone: 751-2330) is known for its exquisite antique and Art Deco designs. For pearls of quality in quantity, try *Mikimoto* (608 Fifth Ave., between W. 48th and W. 49th Sts.; phone: 586-7153). For watches, go to *Tourneau Corner* (500 Madison Ave. at E. 52nd St.; phone: 758-6098; and Madison Ave. and E. 59th St.; phone: 758-6688).

If your budget is limited, do your gem shopping along West 47th Street (the street sign here reads: "Diamond and Jewelry Way") between Fifth and Sixth Avenues. This is the heart of New York's wholesale jewelry district, whose vendors are largely Hasidic Jews of European background, and the best place to find sparkling stuff at mortal prices. If you're planning to get married (or even reaffirm your vows), *1873 Unusual Wedding Bands* (Booth 86 at the *National Jewelery Exchange,* 4 W. 47th St.; phone: 221-1873) is a good place to stop; it has the largest selection of wedding rings in the city.

KITCHEN EQUIPMENT At the *Bridge Co.* (214 E. 52nd St. at Third Ave.; phone: 688-4220), you'll find every possible domestic and imported item, from cherry pitters to copper fish poachers, on display on four floors. The *Broadway Panhandler* (520 Broadway at Spring St.; phone: 966-3434) has an enormous selection of cookware at affordable prices. *Williams-Sonoma* (110 Seventh Ave.; phone: 633-2203; 20 E. 60th St.; phone: 980-5155; and 1175 Madison Ave. at E. 86th St.; phone: 289-6832), of catalogue fame, carries first-rate cookware, and master chefs often do demonstrations on the premises. *Zabar's* (see *Food,* above) has a second floor stocked with a huge selection of kitchenware at competitive prices. In the Bowery, New York's kitchenware and lamp district, you'll find stores selling commercial products at reasonable prices.

LEATHER GOODS AND LUGGAGE You'll have no trouble finding a wide selection of both high- and low-priced leather goods and luggage in New York. *Hermès* (11 E. 57th St.; phone: 751-3181) is headquartered in Paris but known the world over for spectacular silk scarves and ties, as well as saddles and other fine leather goods in a variety of exotic skins, all at heart-stopping prices. *Prada Milan* (45 E. 57th St.; phone: 308-2332) has perhaps the best-quality leather goods and shoes from Italy. *Louis Vuitton* (51 E. 57th St.; phone: 371-6111) has a large selection of leather goods, many sporting the famous "LV" logo. If you prefer interlocking "G"s, visit *Gucci* (685 Fifth Ave. at E. 54th St.; phone: 826-2600). For elegant, high-quality merchandise that's only slightly less costly, try *Crouch & Fitzgerald* (400 Madison Ave. at E. 48th St.; phone: 755-5888) or *Mark Cross* (645 Fifth Ave., between E. 51st and E. 52nd Sts.; phone: 421-3000). Along less expensive lines, you will run into several leather goods and luggage stores during your strolls around the West Side, such as the *Westside Luggage Shop* (955 Eighth Ave.; phone: 757-3880) and *Rio Trading* (10 W. 46th St.; phone: 819-0304). The Lower

East Side has countless stores offering suitcases at substantial savings, including *Altman Luggage* (135 Orchard St.; phone: 254-7275).

MALLS Indoor urban malls are a relatively recent phenomenon in New York City; they arrived a decade ago with the glitzy *Trump Tower* (725 Fifth Ave. at E. 56th St.). The vendors in the tower's six-story marble and mirrored atrium are among the world's most opulent (and most expensive): *Abercrombie & Fitch* (men's and women's sportswear and sporting goods); *Kenneth Jay Lane* (high-end costume jewelry); *Ferragamo* (top-quality Italian footwear; also see *Shoes*, below); *Asprey* (one of London's premier jewelers and silversmiths); *Buccellati* (silversmith); *Charles Jourdan* (men's and women's shoes); and *Harry Winston* (diamond jewelry; the main shop is at Fifth Ave. and W. 56th St.).

Close to *Macy's* is *A & S Plaza* (Ave. of the Americas from W. 32nd to W. 33rd St.; phone: 465-0500), a multilevel complex of shops and stores including *Ann Taylor, Oak Tree* (for menswear), and, of course, *A & S* (see *Department Stores*, above). In lower Manhattan, *Pier 17* at the *South Street Seaport* is another shopper's magnet.

MENSWEAR Manhattan has fashions to fit every man's taste, from the astronomically glitzy at *Bijan* (by appointment only; 699 Fifth Ave., between E. 54th and E. 55th Sts.; phone: 758-7500) to westernwear at *Billy Martin*'s (812 Madison Ave. at E. 68th St.; phone: 861-3100). *Brooks Brothers* (346 Madison Ave. at E. 44th St.; phone: 682-8800; and 1 Liberty Plaza, downtown; phone: 267-2400); *Paul Stuart* (Madison Ave. and 45th St.; phone: 682-0320); and *F. R. Tripler* (366 Madison Ave. at E. 46th St.; phone: 922-1090) all offer expensive, high-quality, conservative business suits and classic furnishings. *St. Laurie* (895 Broadway at E. 20th St.; phone: 473-0100) carries similar merchandise with slightly lower price tags. *Barneys New York* (106 Seventh Ave., from W. 16th to W. 17th St.; phone: 929-9000; 225 Liberty St., in the *World Financial Center;* phone: 945-1600; and 660 Madison Ave. at 61st St.; phone: 826-8900) has an eclectic array of goods but includes top-drawer suits from the world's foremost designers. For Italian *alta moda* in SoHo, try *Di Mitri* (110 Greene St.; phone: 431-1090). *Beau Brummel* (four locations, including 1113 Madison Ave., between E. 83rd and E. 84th Sts.; phone: 737-4200) has everything for the fashion-conscious man. *Syms* (42 Trinity Pl.; phone: 797-1199) stocks fine discounted menswear on five floors. *Bergdorf Goodman Men* is a bastion of male chic (Fifth Ave. and E. 58th St.; phone: 753-7300). To top it all off, visit *Worth & Worth* (331 Madison Ave.; phone: 867-6058) for a large selection of hats.

MUSEUM GIFT SHOPS New York's outstanding art and cultural institutions often have equally fine shops stocked with items related to their collections. Among the best are those at the *Fraunces Tavern Museum*, with books, reproductions of historic documents, and postcards; the *American Museum of Natural History*, with crafts and jewelry from North America, South America, and Asia, model dinosaurs, and prints of pre-Columbian art; and the *Solomon R. Guggenheim Museum*, with textiles, jewelry, posters, and toys. The *Metropolitan Museum of Art* has huge shops that sell fine-arts prints, jewelry, calendars, stationery, toys, and books, and there is also a more central branch in *Rockefeller Center* (15 W. 49th St.; phone: 332-1360). In addition to the bookstore (with posters, stationery, and other smaller gift items) in the *Museum of Modern Art*, there is the *MOMA Design Store* across the street (44 W. 53rd St.; phone: 767-1050), stocked with a large selection of contemporary home and office furnishings and jewelry. The gift shop next door to the *Whitney Museum of American Art* (943 Madison Ave. at E. 75th St.; phone: 606-0200) purveys toys, jewelry, crafts, and furniture. The *Cooper-Hewitt Museum,* part of the *Smithsonian Institution,* has a new shop in the museum's Louis XVI music room which sells books, tabletop items, and jewelry. (See *Special Places* and *Museums* for all addresses and phone numbers not listed above.)

POSTER AND PRINT SHOPS *The Old Print Shop* (150 Lexington Ave. at E. 29th St.; phone: 683-3950) has a huge collection of early American prints, watercolors, and paintings ranging in price from $10 to $20,000. For contemporary theater posters and some collector's items, try the *Triton Gallery* (323 W. 45th St., between Eighth and Ninth Aves.; phone: 765-2472). Rare movie posters are available at *Poster America* (138 W. 18th St.; phone: 206-0499). The *Gallery at Lincoln Center* (136 W. 65th St.; phone: 580-4673) has the largest collection of limited-edition paintings and photographs celebrating the performing arts—dance, theater, and opera—plus original silk-screen posters.

SHOES All of the top Italian designers of both men's and women's footwear are represented: *Gucci* (685 Fifth Ave.; phone: 826-2600); *Fratelli Rossetti* (601 Madison Ave.; phone: 888-5107); *Tanino Crisci* (660 Madison Ave.; phone: 535-1014); *Ferragamo* (for men, 730 Fifth Ave.; phone: 246-6211; for women, 717 Fifth Ave.; phone: 759-3822); and *Bruno Magli* (for men only 677 Fifth Ave.; phone: 752-7900). Fine European shoes also are found at *Bally of Switzerland* (for men, 711 Fifth Ave.; phone: 751-9082; for women, 689 Madison Ave.; phone: 751-2163). For well-made men's boots and shoes, stop at *McCreedy & Schreiber* (37 W. 46th St.; phone: 719-1552; and 213 E. 59th St.; phone: 759-9241). *Susan Bennis/Warren Edwards* (22 W. 57th St.; phone: 755-4197) designs outré American shoes.

SPECIAL SHOPPING DISTRICTS—FOR LESS The ultimate shopping experience is on the Lower East Side of Manhattan along Orchard Street, Delancey Street, and all the side streets. If you're up to it, you'll find incredible bargains in all manner of clothing and housewares; but finding them is only half the battle. Then you have to fight for them, and the haggling begins. The merchant says something along the lines of, "I couldn't give you this for a penny less than $12," to which you respond that it's not worth more than 50¢, and usually you come to terms— apparently unsatisfactory to both of you. A lot of the selling is done in a mixture of Yiddish, English, Russian, and Spanish—particularly the counting—and if you know any or all four, you'll do better than wholesale. Most stores are closed Saturdays, open Sundays; they also close early on Fridays and Jewish holidays.

Quintessential basics and classic clothes made of sumptuous fabrics frequently find their way down to Orchard Street. Unpretentious and impossibly noisy, the little shops that line this street proffer fine items of clothing that in other spots are staggeringly expensive. Casual fashion and a wide range of evening wear are available at *Forman's,* which has three separate shops, for petite, regular, and larger women's sizes (78, 82, and 94 Orchard St., respectively; phone: 228-2500 for all three locations). *Shulie's* (175 Orchard St.; phone: 473-2480) sells Tahari designs at impressive discounts, and *Fine and Klein* (119 Orchard St.; phone: 674-6720) carries an immense selection of handbags by top designers. See *Special Places* for more on the Lower East Side.

SPORTING GOODS The most elegant sporting goods store is *Abercrombie & Fitch* (*South Street Seaport;* phone: 809-9000; and *Trump Tower,* 725 Fifth Ave. at E. 56th St.; phone: 832-1001). *Herman's* (39 W. 34th St.; phone: 279-8900; and six other locations), New York's best-known sporting goods chain, has everything, but *Paragon* (867 Broadway at E. 18th St.; phone: 255-8036) says it has more—and at better prices. Serious joggers should stop in at the *Super Runners Shop* (416 Third Ave. at E. 29th St.; phone: 213-4560; and three other locations); tennis players will find good buys at *Mason's Tennis Mart* (911 Seventh Ave.; phone: 757-5374). *Gerry Cosby's* (3 Penn Plaza, above *Penn Station;* phone: 563-6464) outfits professional teams and offers top-of-the-line sporting goods and souvenirs. *Orvis* (355 Madison Ave.; phone: 697-3133) has fishing and hunting gear.

THRIFT SHOPS AND RETRO FASHION Most thrift shops carry a variety of merchandise, from men's and women's clothing to household items and appliances to battered furniture. And unfortunately, many of the secondhand clothes stores in New York carry the price tags of fine antiques stores. The best area for thrifting in New York is the East 80s along First, Second, and Third Avenues. Two interesting places to try are the *Stuyvesant Square Thrift Shop* (1704 Second Ave. at E. 96th St.; phone: 831-1830) and *Spence-Chapin Thrift Shop* (1430 Third Ave. at E. 81st St.; phone: 737-8448). Downtown the clothes get wilder and the prices lower. Go to *Screaming Mimi's* (382 Lafayette St. at E. Fourth St.; phone: 677-6464), *B-Flat* (125 E. Fourth St.; phone: 260-5220), or the *Antique Boutique* (712-714 Broadway; phone: 460-8830) for secondhand clothing from the 1920s through the 1960s. *Alice Underground*'s two shops (380 Columbus Ave. at W. 78th St.; phone: 724-6682; and 481 Broadway; phone: 431-9067) are other highly affordable havens for a changing collection of casual and dressier clothes. Hats and linen goods are sold as well in the uptown branch.

TOYS Once immersed in the enchanting world of toys and stuffed animals at *FAO Schwarz* (GM Bldg., Fifth Ave. at E. 58th St.; phone: 644-9400), adults have as difficult a time as children leaving empty-handed. It has every kind of plaything—from precious antiques and mechanical spaceships to simple construction sets and building blocks—but some items are very expensive. *Penny Whistle Toys* (448 Columbus Ave.; phone: 873-9090; and 1283 Madison Ave.; phone: 369-3868) offers everything from puppets and bubble machines to wooden blocks and educational toys. The *Enchanted Forest* (85 Mercer St.; phone: 925-6677) stocks fine toys and craft kits.

UNIQUELY NEW YORK Probably nowhere else on earth can you find everything from earplugs to fine silver under one roof. *Hammacher Schlemmer* (147 E. 57th St., between Third and Lexington Aves.; phone: 421-9000), the first store to offer the pop-up toaster and microwave oven, has it all. And what it doesn't have, it will try to order.

Century 21 (22 Cortlandt St., between Broadway and Church St.; phone: 227-9092) is the ultimate discount experience; it's a vast, crowded emporium of designer clothing and accessories, including Bally shoes, Gianni Versace tuxedos, and Carolina Herrera dresses at as much as 50% below retail price. It also stocks discounted linens.

47th St. Photo (67 W. 47th St., Second Floor) is a center for cameras, computers, and other electronic gear with excellent discounts and a huge selection (some 5,000 items in stock). The tiny headquarters and its branch (115 W. 45th St.; phone: 921-1287 for both locations) tend to be packed with customers and consequently chaotic. Know what you want before you go, because the brusque manner of the salesmen doesn't lend itself to extended dialogue; however, when they do answer a question, they know what they're talking about. Closed Friday afternoons and Saturdays.

Finally, travel 'round the world in a unique way via a trip to the *United Nations Gift Shop* (*UN Bldg.*, First Ave. and E. 46th St.; phone: 963-7702), featuring handicrafts, ethnic clothing, native jewelry, indigenous toys—lots of beautiful things from the member countries.

SPORTS AND FITNESS

New York is a sports-minded city, offering a great variety of spectator and participatory activities. It is the home of the *Yankees, Mets, Knicks,* and *Rangers* The *Jets, Giants, Nets,* and *Devils* play about six miles from Manhattan in New Jersey, and the *Islanders* in suburban Nassau County on Long Island. There are racetracks, tennis and basketball courts, bridle and bike paths, pool halls, bowling alleys, skating rinks, running tracks, and swimming pools, to name but a few sporting spots.

BASEBALL The season, April through early October, features the *Mets (National League)* at *Shea Stadium* (Flushing, Queens; phone: 718-507-8499), and the *Yankees (American League)* at *Yankee Stadium* (the Bronx; phone: 718-293-6000). Take the *IRT* Flushing line (No. 7 train) to the Willets Point/Shea Stadium stop to the *Mets;* the *IRT* Lexington Ave. line (No. 4 train) or the *IND* line (C or D train) to the 161st St. stop for the *Yankees.* Tickets can be ordered through *Ticketmaster* for *Yankees* games only (phone: 307-7171).

BASKETBALL The 1994 *NBA* Eastern Conference champion *Knicks* play at *Madison Square Garden* (Seventh Ave. and W. 32rd St.; phone: 465-6741); and the *Nets* at the *Brendan Byrne Arena* in the *Meadowlands Sports Complex* in East Rutherford, New Jersey (phone: 201-935-8888), during the regular season from early November to late April. You can order *Nets* tickets through *Ticketmaster* (phone 307-7171). Buses to the *Meadowlands* leave from the *Port Authority Bus Terminal* (Eighth Ave. and W. 42nd St.; phone: 564-8434 or 564-1114 for ticket and schedule information).

BICYCLING There are over 50 miles of bike paths in the city, with *Central Park* in Manhattan and *Prospect Park* in Brooklyn the two most popular areas. Most roadways within the parks are closed to auto traffic from April through October, except during rush hours on weekdays; they are closed on weekends and holidays year-round. Bikes can be rented in the parks or on nearby side streets, although it's usually less expensive to rent a two-wheeler at one of the many cycling shops around the city. Check the yellow pages for the names of dealers convenient to you. More serious bikers should contact *Transportation Alternatives* (phone: 475-4600) for information on noncompetitive charity events such as bike-a-thons and weekend bicycling tours. For information on competitive cycling events and road races, call Len Preheim at the *Toga Bike Shop* (110 West End Ave.; phone: 799-9625).

BILLIARDS Increasingly popular with New Yorkers, pool halls are plentiful throughout the city. Consult the yellow pages (look under "Billiards") for the nearest location.

BOXING Major bouts are still fought at *Madison Square Garden* (see *Basketball,* above), and the *Daily News* continues to sponsor the *Golden Gloves* competition every winter (phone: 210-1952).

FITNESS CENTERS The *Poly Gym* (428 E. 75th St.; phone: 628-6969) offers one-on-one personal training 24 hours a day, seven days a week. The *Works* (29 W. 17th St.; phone: 627-3309) sponsors ongoing exercise classes for all ages. Open daily; hours vary. Newer and open 24 hours except on Sundays (when it's open from 8 AM to 10 PM) is the *World Gym*'s main location at *Lincoln Center* (1926 Broadway; phone: 874-0942). For information on the various Ys around the city, call 308-2899; 755-2410 after 5 PM.

FOOTBALL During the September–December season, the *Jets* and the *Giants* play at *Giants Stadium* in the *Meadowlands Sports Complex* (see *Basketball,* above). Tickets to *NFL* games are hard to get due to the great number of season subscribers. For *Giants* ticket information, call 201-935-8222; for *Jets* tickets, call 516-538-6600. *Columbia University* leads the local collegiate football scene; games are played at *Baker Field* (Broadway and W. 218th St.; phone: 567-0404).

GOLF While there are no public courses in Manhattan, golf enthusiasts can visit the city's outlying boroughs for an invigorating round—there are 13 courses in municipal parks operated by private concessionaires. Tee times and course information can be obtained by calling 718-225-GOLF. The *Department of Parks* public information office (phone: 800-834-3832) also can provide a complete list of public courses and how to get on them. For up-to-date information on tournaments, call the *Metropolitan Golf Association* (phone: 914-698-0390).

HOCKEY Tickets are expensive and scarce during the early October to early April season, with the *Islanders* at the *Nassau Coliseum* on Long Island (phone: 516-794-4100), the 1994 *NHL Stanley Cup* champion *Rangers* at *Madison Square Garden,* and the *Devils* at the *Brendan Byrne Arena* (see *Basketball,* above, for the latter two).

HORSEBACK RIDING Horses can be rented and boarded at the *Claremont Riding Academy* (175 W. 89th St.; phone: 724-5100), close to *Central Park*, where there are about 6 miles of bridle paths.

ICE SKATING You can show off your figure eights from October through April at the famous *Rockefeller Center* rink (phone: 757-5730); from November through March at the *Wollman Rink* in *Central Park* (phone: 517-4800); and from early November through February at the *Lasker Rink*, also in *Central Park* (phone: 988-1184). The small rink in front of the Rivergate Apartments (401 E. 34th St. at First Ave.; phone: 689-0035) is open from November through March. For information about skating conditions, call 397-3098 or 517-4800. Indoor skating year-round is possible at the Olympic-size *SkyRink* (450 W. 33rd St.; phone: 695-6556).

JOGGING This is undoubtedly the most popular sport in New York, with enthusiastic runners in all the city parks: on the paths at *Riverside Park* (near W. 97th St.); around the *Central Park* reservoir (from 86th to 95th St.); and along the East River promenade (from E. 84th to E. 90th St.). It is unsafe to run in *any* of these places after dark. The *New York Road Runners Club* (9 E. 89th St.; phone: 860-4455) offers guided runs on weekdays at 6:30 and 7:15 PM from their office and on Saturdays at 10 AM from Fifth Avenue and E. 90th Street; they take scenic routes, including a lap around the *Central Park* reservoir.

ROLLER-SKATING AND ROLLER-BLADING *Central Park* on spring and summer weekends is one huge skating rink, with rentals available from *Peck & Goodie* (917 Eighth Ave., between W. 54th and W. 55th Sts.; phone: 246-6123). Don't skate in the park after dark.

SWIMMING Several dozen indoor and outdoor pools are operated throughout the five boroughs by the *Parks Department*. Indoor pools are open most of the year, except Sundays and holidays, usually until 10 PM on weekdays. Call the *Parks Department*'s public information office (phone: 360-8141) for particulars. For information on the pools at the Ys, call 308-2899; 755-2410 after 5 PM.

Ocean swimming is a subway or bus ride away. Beaches within the city and maintained by it are Orchard Beach in the Bronx; Coney Island Beach and Manhattan Beach in Brooklyn; and *Riis Park* and Far Rockaway in Queens. *Jones Beach State Park* (Wantagh, Long Island, 30 miles east of the city) is Long Island's most popular public beach. It is a well-maintained, enormous stretch of sand offering surf bathing, swimming and wading pools, lockers, fishing, outdoor skating rinks, paddleball, swimming instruction, restaurants, and day and evening entertainment. It can be reached via the *Long Island Rail Road* from *Penn Station* (Seventh Ave. and W. 32nd St.; phone: 718-217-5477) and a connecting bus (the JB62 during the week and the JB24 on weekends; both run from *Memorial Day* through *Labor Day*). A note of advice: On summer weekends, despite its large size, Jones Beach can be crowded as early as 10 AM.

TENNIS Courts maintained by the *Parks Department* require a season permit. Municipal facilities include 26 clay courts in *Central Park* (phone: 280-0205), 10 red-clay courts in *Riverside Park* (no phone), and seven clay and four hard-surface courts on Randall's Island (phone: 534-4845). In the Bronx there are 10 hard-surface courts at *Rice Stadium* in *Pelham Bay Park,* and eight clay and four all-weather courts in *Van Cortlandt Park* (no phone for either). In Queens the *USTA National Tennis Center* in *Flushing Meadows Park* (phone: 718-592-8000), home of the *US Open,* has 26 outdoor and nine indoor courts. One of the larger privately owned clubs that will rent by the hour is the *Midtown Tennis Club* (341 Eighth Ave. at W. 27th St.; phone: 989-8572). Check the yellow pages for other locations.

THEATER

New York attracts the best and most accomplished talents in the world. However, there are devoted New York theatergoers who wouldn't dream of stepping inside a Broadway theater. They prefer instead the city's prolific off-Broadway and off-off-Broadway circuit, whose productions are less high-powered but no less professional than the splashiest shows on Broadway. On the other hand, there are theater mavens who've never seen a performance more than a few blocks from Times Square, and who can remember every detail of the opening night of *A Chorus Line* (the final curtain came down after 6,137 performances).

Broadway signifies an area—between West 42nd and West 53rd Streets both east and west and on Broadway—and a kind of production that strives to be the smash hit of the season and run forever. The glitter of the area has tarnished a bit since the halcyon days of the Great White Way, but hopes are that a general reconstruction and renovation of West 42nd Street will turn things around. In any case, the productions are getting more stellar (and pricier) than ever.

Off-Broadway and off-off-Broadway signify types of theater, in playhouses strewn from Greenwich Village to the Upper West Side. Off-Broadway productions are usually smaller in scale, with newer, lesser-known talent, than those on Broadway, and are likely to feature revivals of classics or more daring works. Off-off-Broadway is more experimental still: truly avant-garde productions in coffeehouses, lofts, or any appropriate makeshift arena. Off-Broadway tickets often cost nearly as much as those for a Broadway show, but the cost of a seat for an off-off-Broadway production is usually much less.

Take advantage of all three during a visit. The excitement of a Broadway show is incomparable, but the thrill of finding a tiny theater in SoHo or the West Village in which you are almost nose to nose with the actors is unforgettable. Planning your theater schedule is as easy as consulting any of the daily papers (they all list theaters and current offerings daily, with comprehensive listings on Fridays or Saturdays), the "Goings On About Town" section in *The New Yorker,* or "Theater Listings" in *New York* magazine, which lists current theater fare under headings of "Broadway," "Off-Broadway," and "Off-Off-Broadway."

Broadway tickets can be quite expensive (they average $30 to $65, with an occasional musical costing as much as $100, depending on seat and performance), but with a little patience, you can find cheaper tickets. The *TKTS* booths (Broadway and W. 47th St. in Times Square and in *2 World Trade Center* in lower Manhattan; phone: 768-1818) sell orchestra seats at half price, plus a service charge of $2.50 per ticket, for a wide range of Broadway and off-Broadway productions; tickets are sold only for the same day's performance. You must line up—there are no reservations—and payment must be made in cash or traveler's checks. *TKTS* booths are open as follows: On Broadway, sales for Monday through Saturday evening performances are from 3 to 8 PM; for Wednesday and Saturday matinees from 10 AM to 2 PM; for Sunday matinees and evening performances from noon to 8 PM. At *2 World Trade Center* the booth is open weekdays from 11 AM to 5:30 PM and Saturdays from 11 AM to 3:30 PM; tickets for Wednesday, Saturday, and Sunday matinees are available the day *before* the performance. The *Broadway Show Line* (phone: 563-BWAY), sponsored by the *League of American Theaters and Producers,* gives recorded synopses and short reviews of Broadway and off-Broadway plays as well as ticket prices and schedules.

To help ease the post-theater cab crush, two taxi stands operate in the Broadway area. Line up on W. 45th Street, west of Broadway (near Shubert Alley), or on W. 44th St., east of Eighth Ave. (near the *St. James Theatre*).

THEATER COMPANIES One of New York's newer repertory companies is the *National Actors Theatre,* founded by actor Tony Randall, which presents revivals of classic plays, often featuring well-known artists, at the *Lyceum Theatre* (149 W. 45th St.; phone: 239-6200 for tickets). Others include the *Classic Stage Company (CSC),* which stages intriguing productions of classics of all centuries (126 E. 13th St., between Third and Fourth Aves.; phone: 677-4210); *Circle Rep* (99 Seventh Ave. S.; phone: 924-7100); *Hudson Guild Theater* (441 W. 26th St.; phone: 760-9810); *INTAR Theater* (420 W. 42nd St.; phone: 695-6134); *Irish Arts Center* (553 W. 51st St.; phone: 757-3318); *Jean Cocteau Repertory* (330 Bowery; phone: 677-0060); *Jewish Repertory Theater* (316 E. 96th St.; phone: 831-2000); *La Mama ETC* (74A E. Fourth St.; phone: 475-7710); *Manhattan Theatre Club* (*City Center,* 131 W. 55th St.; phone: 581-7907); *National Black Theatre* (2033 Fifth Ave., Second Floor; phone: 722-3800); *Pan Asian Repertory* (425 W. 46th St.; phone: 505-5655); *Playwrights Horizons Theater* (416 W. 42nd St.; phone: 279-4200); the *Joseph Papp Public Theater,* home of the *New York Shakespeare Festival* (425 Lafayette St.; phone: 598-7150); *Repertorio Español* (138 E. 27th St.; phone: 889-2850); *Charles Ludlum Theater* (1 Sheridan Sq.; phone: 691-2271); *Roundabout* (1530 Broadway; phone: 869-8400); the *Vivian Beaumont Theater* and the *Mitzi E. Newhouse Theater,* both at *Lincoln Center* (phone: 239-6200); and the *Westside Arts Theater* (407 W. 43rd St.; phone: 307-4100). All can provide a schedule of offerings and performance dates. Alternatively, call the *Theatre Development Fund*'s hotline (phone: 587-1111; 800-STAGE-NY outside of New York State) or *New York* magazine's hotline weekdays from 10:30 AM to 4:30 PM (phone: 880-0755).

TV SHOW TAPINGS

Although Los Angeles is more readily associated with the business of television, a large number of popular network and syndicated programs are headquartered in New York, and the public may attend tapings without charge. Although most tickets must be obtained in advance, many programs offer standby seats. The policy for obtaining advance and standby seats varies, and it is best to contact the show you want to see as far ahead of time as possible. Audience members must be 18 or older. For tickets to "Donahue," "Late Night with Conan O'Brien," and "Saturday Night Live," contact NBC (30 Rockefeller Plaza, New York, NY 10112; phone: 664-3056). Other shows taped in New York include "The Late Show with David Letterman" (Tickets, 1697 Broadway, New York, NY 10019; phone: 975-2476); "Geraldo" (CBS Television, 524 W. 57th St., New York, NY 10019; phone: 265-1283); "Live with Regis and Kathie Lee" (Tickets, PO Box 777, Ansonia Station, New York, NY 10023; phone: 456-3537); "The Rush Limbaugh Show" (Unitel Studios, 515 W. 57th St., New York, NY 10019; phone: 397-7367); and "Sally Jessy Raphael" (Tickets, PO Box 1400, Radio City Station, New York, NY 10101; phone: 582-1722). You also can take a tour of the NBC Studios at 30 Rockefeller Plaza; tours leave every 15 minutes throughout the day. For information, call 664-4000.

MUSIC AND DANCE

New York is a world center for performing artists. It presents the best of classical and nonclassical works from all over the world, in a variety of halls and auditoriums filled with appreciative, knowledgeable audiences.

Lincoln Center for the Performing Arts (Columbus Ave. from W. 62nd to W. 66th St.; phone: 875-5400 for general information) represents the city's devotion to concerts, opera, and ballet. It consists of *Avery Fisher Hall,* home of the *New York Philharmonic* (phone: 875-5030); the *New York State Theater,* featuring the *New York City Ballet* and the *New York City Opera* (phone: 870-5570); the *Metropolitan Opera House* and the *American Ballet Theater* (phone: 362-6000); the *Damrosch Bandshell,* an open-air theater used for free concerts in the summertime; the *Juilliard School* for musicians, actors, and dancers (phone: 799-5000); *Alice Tully Hall,* home of the *Chamber Music Society* (phone: 875-5050); and the *Vivian Beaumont* and *Mitzi E. Newhouse Theaters* (see above). In addition, all the auditoriums in *Lincoln Center* present other musical events and recitals. While visiting the city, don't miss the *New York Public Library for the Performing Arts,* a unique repository and museum (phone: 870-1630). Guided tours of *Lincoln Center* are available daily (phone: 875-5000).

Other major venues are *Carnegie Hall,* which celebrated its centennial in 1991 (Seventh Ave. and W. 57th St.; phone: 247-7800), and its *Weill Recital Hall* (phone: 697-4188); *City Center* (131 W. 55th St.; phone: 581-7909); the *Grace Rainey Rogers Auditorium* (in the *Metropolitan Museum,* Fifth Ave. and E. 82nd St.; phone: 570-3949); the *Kaufmann Auditorium* (at the *92nd St. Y,* Lexington Ave. and E. 92nd St.; phone: 996-1100); *Symphony Space* (2537 Broadway at W. 95th St.; phone: 864-5400); and the *Brooklyn Academy of Music* (30 Lafayette Ave., Brooklyn; phone: 718-636-4100). Also check music and dance listings in the newspapers, *New York* magazine, and *The New Yorker.*

The *TKTS* booth in Times Square, which sells discount theater tickets, has a counterpart on the West 42nd Street side of *Bryant Park* (behind the *New York Public Library*, just east of the Ave. of the Americas; phone: 382-2323) for those interested in buying half-price tickets to music and dance events on the day of the performance (very occasionally, they also have tickets for opera and operetta performed by smaller companies). The booth is open Tuesdays through Sundays from noon to 2 PM and 3 to 7 PM. Full-price tickets for future performances also are available here.

Many pop, rock, rhythm-and-blues, and country artists perform at *Madison Square Garden* (Seventh Ave. and W. 32nd St.; phone: 465-6741) and at several clubs around the city (see below). The *Nassau Coliseum* (Hempstead Tpke., Uniondale; phone: 516-794-9300) holds large concerts on Long Island. The downtown weekly, *The Village Voice*, plus *The New Yorker* and *New York* magazine offer good listings of current and upcoming events.

NIGHTCLUBS AND NIGHTLIFE

The scope of nightlife in New York is as vast as the scope of daily life. Cultural trends strongly affect the kinds of clubs that are "in" at any given time, and their popularity has a tendency to peak, then plunge rather quickly. Old jazz and neighborhood clubs, on the other hand, usually remain intact, catering to a regular clientele. They offer various kinds of entertainment, and many stay open until the wee hours of the morning, serving drinks and food. It's a good idea to call clubs in advance to find out when they are open and what performers or acts are appearing; or, consult the "Nightlife Directory" in *New York* magazine. Many of the city's nightclubs with live entertainment and/or dancing have cover charges of $10 and up; most accept major credit cards.

The current focus of the trendy crowd is on clubs that offer a kind of relaxed gentility. This sophisticated atmosphere may include the coveted (or cursed, as the case may be) velvet rope across the entrance, alluring interiors by top designers, elegant cocktails, and ultrachic denizens of the night. One of the swankiest places in town is *Nell's* (246 W. 14th St., between Seventh and Eighth Aves.; phone: 675-1567), a Victorian-style nightclub immortalized by *People* magazine but less exclusive than in its early days. *Tatou* (151 E. 50th St.; phone: 753-1144), another posh spot, is a cozy supper club with live jazz during dinner; it metamorphoses into a disco later in the evening. Among the city's newer nightspots are *Webster Hall* (125 E. 11th St., between Third and Fourth Aves.; phone: 353-1600), a multitiered dance hall with a lot of Art Deco touches, including antique furniture from local flea markets, and *USA* (218 W. 47th St., between Broadway and Eighth Ave.; phone: 869-6001), a cavernous club with a deliberately debauched and decadent atmosphere, replete with blown-up cartoon characters as part of the decor; it's loud, too, except for the upstairs lounge, which is sometimes used for private parties. Another multilevel club is *Le Bar Bat* (311 W. 57th St.; phone: 307-7228), where you can hear live blues Wednesdays through Saturdays. The quiet nights, Mondays and Tuesdays, have recorded music.

POP AND ROCK The Big Apple's top rock 'n' roll clubs generally feature lavish sound systems, videos, live bands, several bars, and lots of room for dancing. Try *Limelight* (47 W. 20th St. at the Ave. of the Americas; phone: 807-7850), a late-night favorite for denizens of the downtown scene, and that dance palace *extraordinaire,* the *Palladium* (126 E. 14th St.; phone: 473-7171), with a cavernous interior that attracts an MTV-generation crowd. The *Big City Diner* (572 11th Ave. at W. 43rd St.; phone: 244-6033), open 24 hours, is a trendy place serving American fare with a dance club bisecting it. The ultra-funky *CBGB & OMFUG* (315 Bowery at Bleecker St.; phone: 982-4052) continues to give fringe groups their moment in the spotlight.

For the younger set, the ubiquitous *Hard Rock Café* (221 W. 57th St.; phone: 489-6565) is a monument to rock 'n' roll sporting all manner of memorabilia, a 45-foot guitar-shape bar, and a 1959 Cadillac jutting out from the second floor over the entrance. At *Planet Hollywood* (40 W. 57th St.; phone: 333-7827), owned (but not operated) by Arnold Schwarzenegger, Sylvester Stallone, and other Hollywood superstars, you can watch trailers for upcoming movies while you munch on burgers and pizza. And at press time, the young and the restless were heading for the reopened *Tunnel* (220 12th Ave.; phone: 695-7292), in Manhattan's seamy meat-packing district.

BLUES AND JAZZ Among popular nightspots that feature live music are *Honeysuckle West* (170 Amsterdam Ave. at W. 68th St.; phone: 873-4100) and *Dan Lynch* (221 Second Ave., between 13th and 14th Sts.; phone: 677-0911), a bare-bones bar with live bands. The *Bitter End* (149 Bleecker St.; phone: 673-7030) and the *Bottom Line* (15 W. Fourth St.; phone: 228-7880) often feature blues, folk, and jazz groups. The *Village Vanguard* (178 Seventh Ave. S.; phone: 255-4037), the *Village Gate* (160 Bleecker St.; phone: 475-5120), *Sweet Basil* (88 Seventh Ave. S.; phone: 242-1785), and the *Blue Note* (131 W. Third St.; phone: 475-8592) also spotlight top jazz artists.

Casual jazz clubs with reasonable prices and a relaxed atmosphere include *Arthur's Tavern* (57 Grove St.; phone: 675-6879) and *Bradley's* (70 University Place; phone: 228-6440). For nostalgic, traditional jazz try downstairs at *Fat Tuesday's* (190 Third Ave.; phone: 533-7900) or *Michael's Pub* (211 E. 55th St.; phone: 758-2272), where Woody Allen often plays his clarinet on Monday nights.

Birdland (2745 Broadway at 105th St.; phone: 749-2228) serves up dinner and jazz combos nightly. For big band sounds try *Red Blazer Too* (349 W. 36th St.; phone: 262-3112). Order up some gumbo and jambalaya with the Dixieland jazz featured nightly at *Cajun* (129 Eighth Ave. at 16th St.; phone: 691-6174). For down-and-dirty Chicago blues head to *Manny's Car Wash* (1558 Third Ave. near 87th St.; phone: 369-2583).

COUNTRY AND INTERNATIONAL Country and rockabilly sounds headline at the *Lone Star Café Roadhouse* (240 W. 52nd St.; phone: 245-2950). The *Eagle Tavern* (355 W. 14th St., between Eighth and Ninth Aves.; phone: 924-0275) is good for country, bluegrass, and Irish music. For dancing to a Latin beat, try the *Sounds of Brazil (S.O.B.)* supper club (204 Varick St.; phone: 243-4940) or *Boca Chica* (13 First Ave. at First St.; phone: 473-0108), where salsa and other rhythms throb until 4 AM. For avant-garde sounds head for the *Knitting Factory* (47 E. Houston St., near Mulberry St.; phone: 219-3055).

SUPPER CLUBS AND CABARETS For a low-key, elegant evening of dancing to live music, a good show, and dinner, try one of New York's supper clubs. Among the city's small, intimate spots with good food and quality entertainment, the *Café Carlyle,* in the hotel of the same name, leads the pack when pianist Bobby Short, a New York institution himself, plays Cole Porter tunes; Harry Connick Jr. made his New York debut tickling the ivories at the *Oak Room* in the *Algonquin* (see *Checking In* for both). *Au Bar* offers all the lofty but cozy accoutrements of London's Belgravia (41 E. 58th St.; phone: 308-9455). The *Rainbow Room* (30 Rockefeller Plaza; phone: 632-5100), restored to the splendor of its 1930s heyday, has good cheek-to-cheek dance music and dazzling views of the city from the 65th floor of the GE Building. The adjacent *Rainbow Promenade* is a less expensive café for midnight snacks, and *Rainbow and Stars* showcases cabaret acts (phone: 632-5100 for all three).

Although it doubles as a *tapas* bar and restaurant, the *Ballroom* (see *Eating Out*) has a regular program of international cabaret stars, including an occasional drag queen. A supper club presentation of popular musical revues is featured at *Steve McGraw's* (158 W. 72nd St.; phone: 595-7400). For traditional ballroom fun with American and Latin live dance music, trip the light fantastic at the famous *Roseland* (239 W. 52nd St.; phone: 247-0200)—it holds up to 4,000 dancers. *Laura Belle* (120 W. 43rd St.; phone: 819-1000), an intimate eatery with a nostalgic 1940s atmosphere, features fine swing and jazz combos.

SINGLES BARS AND COMEDY CLUBS The largest concentration of singles bars in New York can be found on First, Second, and Third Avenues between East 61st and East 86th Streets. Walk along any one of these thoroughfares to find a place that suits your fancy. The low-key *Beach Café* (1326 Second Ave.; phone: 988-7299), with its handsome wood bar, is a popular hangout for a beer and burger. Oversize margaritas are the draw for the youngish bar crowd at *Juanita's* (1309 Third Ave.; phone: 517-3800). The bar at *Jim McMullen's* (1341 Third Ave.; phone: 861-4700), whose owner is a former fashion model, attracts the beautiful people from the top agencies.

The West Side has its strips of bars and restaurants along Broadway, Amsterdam, and Columbus Avenues between West 50th and West 86th Streets. If you're into the urban cowboy scene, try the *Yellow Rose Café* (450 Amsterdam Ave.; phone: 595-8760), also great for its fried chicken. Check out the upstairs jazz room at *B. Smith's* (771 Eighth Ave. at W. 47th St.; phone: 247-2222) or the ever-crowded *Whiskey* bar in the *Paramount* hotel (see *Checking In*), where waitresses wear gray leotards.

Lively "showcase" clubs, where comedians, singers, and musicians try out their acts, include *Caroline's* (1626 Broadway, between W. 49th and W. 50th Sts.; phone: 757-4100); *Improvisation* (433 W. 34th St.; phone: 279-3446); *Catch a Rising Star* (1487 First Ave.; phone: 794-1906); and *Dangerfield's* (1118 First Ave.; phone: 593-1650).

Best in Town

CHECKING IN

Host to more visitors than any other city in the world, New York can be one of the hardest places to find an empty hotel room from Sunday through Thursday nights, even though a rash of new properties has opened. However, don't expect this increased supply to offset inflation's upward push on room rates in the foreseeable future. Do expect to pay $250 or more—often *lots* more—per night for a very expensive room for two in Manhattan; $175 to $250 for an expensive one; $125 to $175 for a moderately priced room; and less than $125 for an inexpensive one. These prices do not include any meals nor the hefty hotel tax (see "Sales Tax" in the *Sources and Resources* section earlier in this chapter for current rates). *Note:* Many hotels offer relatively low-priced weekend packages which also may include a variety of amenities, such as breakfast and/or dinner, champagne, theater tickets, and parking. Reservations always are necessary, so write or call in advance.

Visitors who yearn to be in the thick of New York's theater district will find a variety of options. Choices include the *Macklowe, Holiday Inn Crowne Plaza, Paramount, Embassy Suites, New York Renaissance, Sheraton Manhattan,* and *Sheraton New York* hotels (see below for all).

An alternative to a standard hotel room is to try bed and breakfast accommodations in private homes or in an apartment. This option includes continental breakfast and costs from $60 to $125 per night for a double room. Unhosted, fully furnished apartments also are available, starting at $75 per night for a small studio. Weekly and monthly rates are offered by both B&Bs and apartments. For information, contact *Urban Ventures* (PO Box 426, New York, NY 10024; phone: 594-5650; fax: 947-9320); *At Home in New York* (PO Box 407, New York, NY 10185; phone: 956-3125; fax: 247-3294); the *Bed and Breakfast Network of New York* (134 W. 32nd St.; phone: 645-8134); *Bed and Breakfast and Books* (35 W. 92nd St., New York, NY 10025; phone: 865-8740; 800-900-8134); *City Lights B&B* (P.O. Box 20355, New York, NY 10028; phone: 737-7049; fax: 535-2755); or *Abode B&B* (P.O. Box 20222, New York, NY 10028; phone: 472-2000; 800-835-8880). Other options: Double rooms at many of the coed *Y*s throughout the city run about $45 a night, and the *New York Student Center* (895 Amsterdam Ave., between W. 103rd and W. 104th Sts.; phone: 666-3619; fax: 666-5012), in cooperation with *American Youth Hostels,* offers students and budget travelers accommodations priced as low as $20 per night.

To reserve a suite in one of nine different all-suite hotels around Manhattan, call the *Manhattan East Suite* hotel (phone: 800-637-8483). These accommodations are located in areas that range from the commercial (the *Southgate Tower* at Seventh Ave. and W. 31st St.) to the posh (the *Surrey* at Madison Ave. and E. 76th St.); this service represents a total of 1,633 suites around the city.

All telephone numbers are in the 212 area code unless otherwise indicated. Twenty-four-hour room service and CNN (Cable News Network) are available in all hotels, unless otherwise noted.

VERY EXPENSIVE

Beekman Tower Small and pleasantly old-fashioned, this 171-suite establishment (convenient to the *United Nations*) has a cocktail lounge boasting splendid skyline views, the *Zephyr* restaurant on the ground floor, and a health club. Concierge and secretarial services are available, as well as photocopiers, A/V equipment, and meeting rooms that have a capacity of 150. 3 Mitchell Pl., at First Ave. and E. 49th St. (phone: 355-7300; 800-ME-SUITE; fax: 753-9366).

Carlyle Long the leader among the most luxurious uptown hotels, it's properly noted for its quiet and serenity—with prices that match the high level of service. Predominantly a residential hotel, it provides a homey environment for the rich and respected. The 180 comfortable and tastefully decorated guestrooms afford expansive views of the Upper East Side and *Central Park;* in addition, there is also a deluxe for-guests-only spa and a skylit fitness center on the third floor, complete with exercise machines, saunas, and personal trainers. Other delights are the *Café Carlyle* (see *Nightclubs and Nightlife*) and the excellent restaurant. Concierge and secretarial services are offered, as well as A/V equipment, photocopiers and computers. Meeting rooms have a capacity of 200, and express checkout is available. 35 E. 76th St. (phone: 744-1600; 800-227-5737; fax: 717-4682).

Drake Swissôtel Thanks to the grand entrance on Park Avenue, the familiar billing, "the only Swiss hotel on Park Avenue," takes on new meaning. The 615 guestrooms feature personal computer and fax hookups, marble bathrooms, and even a working fireplace in the Presidential Suite. The *Drake Bar* has its own entrance on Park Avenue, and the *Café Suisse* is popular for breakfast and lunch. Business pluses include meeting rooms that hold up to 300, photocopiers, A/V equipment, and computers. There's an obliging concierge desk, secretarial services, and express checkout. 440 Park Ave. at E. 56th St. (phone: 421-0900; 800-DRAKE-NY; fax: 371-4190).

Essex House Overlooking *Central Park,* this 40-story landmark (now owned by Nikko Hotels International) recaptured its original 1931 grandeur after a $70 million restoration completed in 1991. Its 595 large guestrooms are tastefully decorated in French and English country styles, although the public areas have a 1920s flavor. In addition to its chi-chi restaurant, *Les Célébrités* (which features primarily French fare with Oriental accents), there is the less formal *Café Botanica,* with a pleasant continental/California menu. Meeting rooms, too, take advantage of the park views. Other business facilities include complete secretarial services, two-line phone and fax hookups in the guestrooms, and fax machines. There's a helpful concierge desk, a business center, and meeting rooms with a capacity of 600. Photocopiers, A/V equipment, and computers are available. There's also express checkout. 160 Central Park S. at Seventh Ave. (phone: 247-0300; 800-NIKKO-US; fax: 315-1839).

Four Seasons New York This executive-oriented property opened in 1993 on one of the city's most sought-after shopping streets; it is just steps from

Fifth Avenue. The 52-story French limestone building was designed in a clean, Art Deco–influenced style by eminent American architect I. M. Pei. The 307 exceptionally spacious rooms and 60 one- and two-bedroom suites feature refrigerators, cable TV and VCRs, modems for personal computer hookup, and large, luxuriously equipped marble bathrooms. There are two restaurants (*5757* and the *Lobby Lounge*), a 24-hour concierge, a spa, and a health club. Business services include meeting rooms for up to 150, a fully equipped business center, and express checkout. 57 E. 57th St., between Madison and Park Aves. (phone: 758-5700; 800-332-3442; fax: 758-5711).

Lowell Little expense has been spared in turning this once undistinguished property into an authentic gem, an Art Deco delight—with 65 mostly one- and two-bedroom suites. The cozy rooms are perfect for a modestly proportioned king or queen, and each suite has a working fireplace. The overall feeling is one of being a guest in a well-bred New York townhouse—on what could very well be the most stylish block in Manhattan. The only member of the prestigious Relais & Châteaux group in New York. The hotel's dining room is elegant and intimate. Room service is available until midnight, and there's a fitness center. A concierge and secretarial services are business pluses, as are meeting rooms that accommodate up to 75, A/V equipment, and photocopiers. 28 E. 63rd St. (phone: 838-1400; 800-221-4444; fax: 319-4230).

Mark Noted for understated elegance, its 120 rooms and 80 suites feature overstuffed chairs, credenzas, and sofas, all in a neoclassical Italian motif; cable TV; two-line phones; pantries with refrigerator, sink, and stove; and luxurious bathrooms with heated towel bars and heating lamps, separate glass shower stalls, tub, bidet, and vanity. Suites are large and offer a library, wet bar, large terrace, and separate living, dining, and bedroom areas. The continental *Mark's* restaurant, with its antiques-filled club decor, is an Upper East Side favorite. Quiet elegance throughout. Other pluses include a concierge, secretarial services, A/V equipment, photocopiers, computers, and meeting rooms that accommodate up to 300. 25 E. 77th St. (phone: 744-4300; 800-THE-MARK; fax: 744-2749).

Mayfair Hotel Baglioni Perfect for those who stay at the *Gritti Palace* in Venice and the *Hôtel du Cap* in the south of France. Formerly the *Mayfair Regent*, it features just 80 rooms and 120 suites (28 with wood-burning fireplaces), plus the nonpareil *Le Cirque* restaurant (see *Eating Out*). Uncompromising elegance and superb service with a focus on detail: Their "Pillow Bank" has a budget of $100,000 merely to amass the finest pillows in the world; and guests can request an in-room putting green, complete with golf balls. A favorite spot for afternoon tea, especially among the social set. A concierge and secretarial services are handy, as well as A/V equipment, photocopiers, computers, and express checkout. Meeting rooms can accommodate up to 80. 610 Park Ave. at 65th St. (phone: 288-0800; 800-223-0542; fax: 737-0538).

Michelangelo The former *Parc Fifty One* provides luxury lodgings in a part of town not traditionally associated with deluxe digs. The 178 large guestrooms come with such amenities as multi-line phones, two TV sets, and computer and fax hookups. There are valets to pack and unpack for you and even an electronic paging service. The hotel's lobby bar is a far more quiet and soothing place to have a drink than the popular *Bellini by Cipriani* restaurant that holds court on the ground floor. The hotel is part of the Italian Star chain, which explains the large number of Italian guests, the stylish Italian ambience, and, of course, the name. Services such as a concierge desk and secretarial assistance, complimentary limousines to Wall Street, plus A/V equipment, photocopiers, and computers, are a boon. Meeting rooms accommodate up to 200. Personal fax machines may be obtained upon request. 152 W. 51st St. at Seventh Ave. (phone: 765-1900; 800-237-0990 outside New York State; fax: 541-6604).

New York Palace This midtown property combines the landmark Henry Villard house with a 51-story high-rise as its backdrop. The historic areas of the building boast elegant public rooms decorated in marble, crystal, and gold. The 963 guestrooms are fine, though not special. There are three entrances one less hectic on East 50th Street, one on East 51st Street, and the third through wrought-iron gates on Madison Avenue. At press time this former Helmsley property was in the process of being bought by the Sultan of Brunei, who owns the *Dorchester* in London. Meeting rooms hold up to 500, and there's a full-service business center on the first floor. Concierge service and express checkout are also available. 455 Madison Ave., from E. 50th to E. 51st St. (phone: 888-7000; 800-697-2522; fax: 303-6000).

Omni Berkshire Place This property will undergo an extensive, $50-million renovation that is not expected to be complete before the autumn. Visitors interested in staying here should call for updated information. 21 E. 52nd St. (phone: 753-5800; 800-THE-OMNI; fax: 355-7646).

Parker Meridien Billing itself as New York's "first French hotel," this establishment offers 648 tasteful rooms, several bars, and the new *Shin's,* serving Japanese-American cuisine. The hotel completed renovations last year with the opening of a new lounge, the *Bar Montparnasse,* in the former formal dining room; the food includes *tapas* and seafood, and there is live music at night. The sports-minded will enjoy *Club Raquette,* for racquetball, handball, and squash, and the rooftop running track that encircles an enclosed pool—from which the views of *Central Park* are lovely. There's a health club too. Business assets include a concierge, secretarial services, A/V equipment, photocopiers, and computers. Personal fax machines are obtainable. Meeting rooms can hold up to 250. There's also express checkout. 118 W. 57th St. (phone: 245-5000; fax: 307-1776).

Peninsula This 242-room property is a grand hotel in the best Asian tradition (its original namesake is in Hong Kong), featuring Art Nouveau decor, a fitness center and spa, a rooftop bar, a lounge, and a swank French restaurant and bistro—*Adrienne* and *Le Bistro d'Adrienne,* respectively. Business pluses are a concierge, secretarial services, meeting rooms, A/V equipment, photocopiers, computers, and express checkout. 700 Fifth Ave. at W. 55th St. (phone: 247-2200; 800-262-9467; fax: 903-3974).

Pierre The most luxurious stopping place in midtown, with the most august clientele, the elegance at this hotel is low-key, but consistent, and the 206 rooms are furnished with Chippendale pieces and fabrics in subdued tones. Operated by the superb Four Seasons group, on one of the most attractive corners of the city. For many, it is the only place to stay in New York. *Café Pierre* retains all the elegance of a French château, with its low marble balconies, tall candelabra, and gray velvet chairs; the fare is first-rate. There's also a new gym for guests only. Good news for animal lovers: This is one of the few hotels in New York City where small pets are allowed. Meeting rooms here accommodate up to 1,500. There's a concierge desk and secretarial services; A/V equipment, photocopiers, and computers all are handy. There's also express checkout. Fifth Ave. and E. 61 St. (phone: 838-8000; 800-PIERRE4; fax: 826-0319).

Plaza The only New York City hotel designated a historic landmark, this erratic, but mostly elegant hostelry, with over 800 rooms, affords most guests lovely views of *Central Park*. Hansom cabs can be hired right outside the entrance. Now a Donald Trump property, the hotel has long been renowned for (pricey) tea in the *Palm Court* and drinks in the *Oak Room*, not to mention dinner in the *Oyster Bar* or *Edwardian Room*. Business services include a concierge, secretarial services, photocopiers, computers, A/V equipment, 20 meeting rooms, and express checkout. Fifth Ave. from W. 58th to W. 59th St. (phone: 546-5493; 800-228-3000; fax: 759-3167).

Plaza Athénée Small and sumptuous, this is the US edition of the celebrated *Plaza Athénée* in Paris. The Forte management strives to make the elegant edifice look as unlike a hotel as possible, and prides itself on personal attention to its guests. There are 117 rooms and 36 suites, all decorated with paisley fabrics and velvet headboards, and including such modern amenities as VCRs and dehumidifiers. There's also *Le Régence* restaurant, which serves French fare in elegant surroundings; and a cozy lounge with nightly piano music. Amenities include a multilingual concierge, secretarial services, meeting rooms that accommodate up to 50, A/V equipment, photocopiers, and computers. 37 E. 64th St. (phone: 734-9100; 800-447-8800; fax: 772-0958).

Regency Where many of the movers and shakers of America stay when they're in New York. The "power breakfast" began here, and more commerce is probably conducted in the dining room at breakfast than in all of the rest of the country during a normal business day. Its modern architecture does not detract at all from its appeal, and the basement-to-roof restoration and refurbishing completed in 1993 has only added to its luster. The 374 guestrooms are decorated in mauve, green, and salmon, with tasteful antique reproductions adding to the sense of coziness. Facilities include a health club and meeting rooms that hold up to 250. There also are photocopiers, A/V equipment, and computers (with modem hookups in all guestrooms). The concierge desk and full business center are sure to oblige. There's also express checkout. 540 Park Ave. at E. 61st St. (phone: 759-4100; 800-23-LOEWS; fax: 688-2898).

Rihga Royal New York's tallest hotel (54 stories high) is also the most luxurious of the all-suite properties, catering to the corporate traveler. Each of the 500 one- and two-bedroom suites is equipped with two TV sets, a VCR, a kitchen, three telephones, and computer hookups. There are 11 meeting rooms accommodating up to 150, full-scale business and fitness centers, and even a complimentary shuttle to the Wall Street area. There also is a concierge, secretarial services, A/V equipment, photocopiers, computers, and express checkout. 151 W. 54th St. (phone: 307-5000; 800-937-5454; fax: 765-6530).

Ritz-Carlton A number of the 174 rooms and 40 suites at this classic property offer wonderful views of *Central Park* and the city skyline. Some of the suites have small terraces. Amenities include twice-daily maid service, terry cloth robes in the rooms, two-line telephones, and personal valet service. Facilities include a fitness center with park views and the *Fantino* restaurant, which came about as part of renovations completed last year; the bar is a popular meeting place for both guests and New Yorkers. Meeting rooms accommodate 200, and there also are photocopiers, A/V equipment, and computers. The concierge desk, secretarial services, complimentary limousines to Wall Street, and express checkout are handy. 112 Central Park S. (phone: 757-1900; 800-241-3333; fax: 757-9620).

Royalton The management of ultra-hip *Morgans* (see below) impressed New York once again, this time with a 167-room property not far from Times Square. The block-long lobby, with areas specifically designed for reading, conversation, and board games, is a popular gathering spot (and the restrooms have to be seen to be believed). Many of the guestrooms, designed by architect André Putman, come with a wood-burning fireplace in the living area, which also includes a VCR and stereo cassette deck. The bar/restaurant *44* fills up with fashionable types from the nearby Condé Nast Building on Madison Avenue. Concierge and secretarial services, as well as two meeting rooms, photocopiers, and express checkout, are among the options offered here. 44 W. 44th St. (phone: 869-4400; 800-635-9013; fax: 869-8965).

St. Regis Built in 1904 by John Jacob Astor and now under the Sheraton banner, this elaborate, 20-story Beaux Arts landmark, with its prestigious Fifth Avenue address, offers all the sophisticated grandeur of turn-of-the-century Manhattan. Elegant Louis XV furnishings, marble bathrooms with double sinks, and Oriental rugs are wonderful additions to the 222 rooms and 91 suites, all of which also are equipped with fax machines and two-line phones that can deliver messages and information in five languages, operate the TV set and radio, and adjust the room temperature. The famous *St. Regis Roof* ballroom offers spectacular views of midtown Manhattan, and the equally renowned *King Cole* bar retains its look of yesteryear. Also on the premises is *Lespinasse*, an elegant dining room that features French fare (see *Eating Out*), and *Astor Court*, a handsome first-floor salon where afternoon tea, drinks, and light snacks are served. There are 11 meeting rooms, a concierge, secretarial services, A/V equipment, photocopiers, computers, and express checkout. Fifth Ave. and E. 55th St. (phone: 753-4500; 800-759-7550; fax: 787-3447).

Sherry-Netherland Though a little less renowned than the *Plaza* and the *Pierre* (its immediate neighbors), it is no less luxurious, especially since a full restoration was completed in 1993. Keep in mind that reservations can sometimes be a problem, because this establishment is largely residential, with only about 60 rooms available for visitors. The *Harry Cipriani* restaurant features a northern Italian menu. 781 Fifth Ave. at E. 59th St. (phone: 355-2800; 800-223-0522 outside New York State; fax: 319-4306).

Stanhope This posh, upper Fifth Avenue place has 141 rooms, most of them one- or two-bedroom suites with views of *Central Park* or Manhattan's spectacular skyline. Guests meet and relax in the opulent public rooms and enjoy a wide range of dining options, including an outdoor café in summer and afternoon tea in the sitting room. There is a fitness club, and complimentary limousine service is provided to midtown weekday mornings and to *Lincoln Center, Carnegie Hall*, and the theater district in the evenings. The concierge desk and secretarial services are useful, as are photocopiers, A/V equipment, and computers. Meeting rooms accommodate up to 150. Across from the *Metropolitan Museum of Art* at 995 Fifth Ave. (phone: 288-5800; 800-828-1123 outside New York City; fax: 517-0088).

UN Plaza Park Hyatt In addition to its beautifully integrated modern design, from the sleek, green-tinted glass exterior through the dark green marble reception area to the top 10 floors, this property also offers 428 rooms with magnificent city views. Managed by Hyatt International, it has both a truly international staff and exceptional facilities—including a tennis court, heated pool, and exercise room. Its restaurant is the aptly named *Ambassador Grill*, for the hotel faces the *UN*. Meeting rooms here can hold up to 200, and there are concierge and secretarial services, complimentary limousine service (to Wall Street and the garment district during the day and to the theater district at night), photocopiers, and express checkout. First Ave. and E. 44th St. (phone: 355-3400; 800-228-9000; fax: 702-5051).

Westbury The tapestries at the entrance are Belgian, the soft pink carpeting in the marble lobby, Irish—as befits this tranquil, European-style hotel (part of the Forte group) with its large international clientele. There are 231 handsome rooms, and the *Polo* restaurant serves fine continental fare. Concierge and secretarial services are easily accessible, as are photocopiers, A/V equipment, and computers. Meeting rooms hold up to 500. 15 E. 69th St. at Madison Ave. (phone: 535-2000; 800-225-5843; fax: 535-5058).

EXPENSIVE

Algonquin Long a favorite among literary types, this 165-room hotel's reputation is most closely connected with the days of the literary "Round Table" in the *Oak Room*, its famous piano bar and cabaret restaurant. Convenient to both midtown and the theater district. Business services include room service until 11:30 PM, meeting rooms that hold up to 150,.

A/V equipment, fax machines, and photocopiers. 59 W. 44th St., between Fifth and Sixth Aves. (phone: 840-6800; 800-548-0345; fax: 944-1419).

Box Tree Eccentric, unusual, and housed in two East Side brownstones, this place is for those who appreciate detail-oriented luxury. Each of the 13 rooms is individually designed with different European furnishings. The restaurant serves very good French fare with an English accent. Photocopiers are available. 250 E. 49th St. (phone: 758-8320; fax: 308-3899).

Doral Tuscany In the middle of attractive Murray Hill (between 34th and 40th Sts. on the East Side), this 121-room hotel is not widely known outside the city, but guests who know it well treasure the high level of service and discreet atmosphere. It has a restaurant, and guests have free access to a fitness center a block away. Meeting rooms accommodate up to 150; A/V equipment, photocopiers, a concierge, and secretarial services round out the list of business amenities. 120 E. 39th St. (phone: 686-1600; 800-22-DORAL; fax: 779-7822).

Embassy Suites This 460-suite property has an elegant lobby, well-appointed rooms, and an instantly attentive staff. All suites, some of which look out over Times Square, come equipped with a wet bar, microwave oven, and refrigerator. Business amenities include room service until 1 AM, a multilingual concierge desk, eight meeting rooms, photocopiers, computers, A/V equipment, and express checkout. 1568 Broadway (phone: 719-1600; 800-EMBASSY; fax: 921-5212).

Grand Hyatt Originally, this was Donald Trump's idea of how a glitzy New York City hotel should look: mirrored exterior glass and lots of shiny chrome. Now managed by Hyatt, one of its prime attractions is the lobby's upper-level *Sungarden,* a glass-enclosed bar, cocktail lounge, and restaurant that overhangs the hotel's entrance and the busy East 42nd Street traffic. There are 1,400 smallish rooms dressed in rich, earthy tones and over 30 meeting rooms. A/V equipment, in-room fax machines, photocopiers, and computers are useful for business needs. The business center, concierge desk, and secretarial services are easily accessible. There's also express checkout. 109 E. 42nd St. at Park Ave. (phone: 883-1234; 800-233-1234; 800-228-9000; fax: 697-3772).

Holiday Inn Crowne Plaza This razzle-dazzle, 46-story glass tower in the Times Square area offers 770 guestrooms, six Crowne Plaza Club floors (VIP floors with special services), the 15th floor *New York Health Club* (which has a 50-foot pool under a domed skylight), and the popular *Broadway Grill,* featuring California-style fare. The business center offers secretarial services, A/V equipment, photocopiers, and computers. There's a helpful concierge desk, 12 meeting rooms, and express checkout. 1605 Broadway at W. 49th St. (phone: 977-4000; 800-HOLIDAY; fax: 333-7393).

Inter-Continental New York Formerly the *Barclay,* this large, distinguished property with 692 smallish guestrooms on a busy East Side corner is one block south of the *Waldorf.* The well-appointed suites have two-line phones with speaker capabilities. Amenities include a health club, the oak-paneled *Barclay* restaurant, a concierge, secretarial services, photocopiers and computers, A/V equipment, 16 meeting rooms, and express checkout. 111 E. 48th St. at Lexington Ave. (phone: 755-5900; 800-327-0200; fax: 644-0079).

Loews New York This 726-room midtowner, convenient for businesspeople and conventioneers with East Side interests, offers a reliably good restaurant, the *Lexington Avenue Grill,* the Club 51 floor with a private lounge and concierge, and a fully staffed fitness center. Business services include secretarial assistance, A/V equipment, photocopiers, and express checkout. There are also 12 meeting rooms. Lexington Ave. at E. 51st St. (phone: 752-7000; 800-23-LOEWS; fax: 758-6311).

Macklowe With 638 starkly chic guestrooms by well-known designer Bill Durham, this 52-story tower in the Times Square area features a fitness center as well as a 100,000-square-foot conference center, all built around an existing theater (the *Hudson*). Other business amenities include 33 meeting rooms, photocopiers, computers, a concierge desk, and express checkout. 145 W. 44th St. (phone: 768-4400; fax: 789-7688).

Marriott East Side Formerly the *Halloran House,* this historic 665-room hotel was built in the 1920s by A. L. Harmon, who designed the *Empire State Building;* it is a mix of Gothic, Byzantine, and Italian architectural styles. The informal *Champions* and more formal *Shelton Grille* are both enjoyable dining options; the 16th-floor *Fountain Room and Terrace* is the hotel's private meeting room. There also are nonsmoking and Concierge Club floors. Room service is available until 11:30 PM. There are nine meeting rooms, as well as A/V equipment, photocopiers, and express checkout. 525 Lexington Ave., between E. 48th and E. 49th Sts. (phone: 755-4000; 800-228-9290; fax: 751-3440).

Morgans Without so much as a sign out front, this 112-room treasure by Ian Shrager, of *Paramount* and *Royalton* fame, is named for the nearby *Pierpont Morgan Library.* Some unusual standards include continental breakfast (at no extra charge) each morning, and, in guestrooms, a stereo cassette player and TV with stereo sound (VCRs and videotapes are available). Bathrooms are pure high-tech, and artwork is by the late avant-garde photographer Robert Mapplethorpe. The suites are reasonably priced. A concierge, secretarial services, A/V equipment, photocopiers, and computers round out the business amenities. 237 Madison Ave. at E. 37th St. (phone: 686-0300; 800-334-3408; fax: 779-8352).

New York Helmsley A shining glass skyscraper on East 42nd Street, this executive-oriented, 788-room facility has special services for the business traveler—secretaries, fax machines, photocopying, a concierge desk, express checkout, and seven meeting rooms among them. For dining there's *Mindy's,* a continental restaurant, and for drinks and piano music try *Harry's New York Bar.* Room service can be called upon until 1 AM. 212 E. 42nd St. (phone: 490-8900; 800-221-4982; fax: 986-4792).

New York Hilton An enormous modern structure near *Rockefeller Center,* this is one of New York's largest properties, and it's about as efficiently run as any hotel with more than 2,000 rooms can be. The well-equipped health club has saunas and even a videocassette player for your own workout tape. Small pets (under 20 pounds) are allowed. Business amenities include 47 meeting rooms, a concierge, secretarial services,

A/V equipment, photocopiers, computers, and express checkout. 1335 Ave. of the Americas, between W. 53rd and W. 54th Sts. (phone: 586-7000; 800-HILTONS; fax: 315-1374).

New York Renaissance Built in 1992 as the *Ramada Renaissance Times Square,* this 25-story black tower overlooking the theater district has 305 rooms and 10 suites furnished in Art Deco style. In addition to sybaritic marble baths, there is a fax machine and three telephones in every guestroom, and an exercise room is on the premises. The public rooms include a restaurant, a bar, and a lounge featuring nightly entertainment. There's a full business center and meeting rooms for up to 78. 714 Seventh Ave. at W. 47th St. (phone: 765-7676; 800-228-9898; fax: 765-1962).

Sheraton Manhattan Formerly the *Sheraton City Squire,* this property underwent an enormous renovation in 1992. The façade now features Art Deco grillwork, tinted windows, and an elegant canopy; the lobby and reception area have been expanded and decorated with contemporary furniture and richly textured carpets and upholstery. In addition, the pool has been refurbished, and there is a fitness club. The 659 comfortable, modern rooms offer such amenities as in-room office supplies, computer and fax connections, coffee makers, cable TV, and express video checkout. Meeting facilities for up to 2,500 and a complete executive business center are also available. 790 Seventh Ave. at W. 51st St. (phone: 581-3300; 800-325-3535; fax: 315-4265).

Sheraton New York Part of the same mega-renovation as its *Sheraton* neighbor (above), this 50-story modern monolith, previously the *Sheraton Centre,* is always busy. The 1,752 rooms are quite comfortable, and it's only a short walk to the theater district or the *Museum of Modern Art.* The top five floors, called the *Sheraton Towers,* are for more exclusive "business class" clients. There is a fitness center, too. Meeting rooms accommodate up to 3,000, and there are photocopiers, A/V equipment, computers, and express checkout. 811 Seventh Ave. at W. 53rd St. (phone: 581-1000; 800-325-3535; fax: 315-4265).

Sheraton Park Avenue Formerly the *Russell,* this is one of those "secret" hotels that regulars love to keep to themselves. The 150-room property is convenient to *Grand Central Station* and the garment center, and the comfortable guestrooms boast high ceilings, walk-in closets, three phones, and separate work areas. *Russell's* is a fine dining restaurant, and the *Judge's Chamber* serves buffet lunch in a book-lined club setting. Concierge and secretarial services can lend a hand, and there are three meeting rooms, A/V equipment, photocopiers, and express checkout. 45 Park Ave. at E. 37th St. (phone: 685-7676; 800-325-3535; fax: 889-3193).

Tudor Located in New York's historic Tudor City district, steps away from the *United Nations* and directly across town from major theaters, this 1931 property, with a unique façade combining Art Deco design with Tudor touches, offers 300 comfortable guestrooms. Each has a minibar, two-line telephones, outlets for computers and fax machines, and a marble bathroom with towel heaters; some of the suites have Jacuzzis and private terraces. An innovative touch is the addition of six Circadian rooms, whose special features, including the lighting, help jet-lagged travelers adjust. *Cecil's* serves fine American/English fare; there's also *The Regency* lounge, where afternoon tea is served. The fitness center is fully equipped with massage rooms. Business services include a concierge, meeting space for up to 100 people, and a business center with A/V and secretarial services, fax machines, and photocopiers. 304 E. 42nd St. (phone: 986-8800; 800-TRY-TUDOR; fax: 986-1758).

Waldorf-Astoria and Waldorf Towers A legend on Park Avenue, divided between the basic hotel (with 1,212 rooms) and the more exclusive and opulent *Waldorf Towers* (with 92 rooms, 106 suites, and a number of residential apartments). The degree of comfort delivered here is consistent with the hotel's reputation; it is also a popular convention property. *Peacock Alley* is a lively cocktail rendezvous and excellent French restaurant, and the clock in the middle of the lobby may be New York's favorite meeting place. The hotel's *Plus One* fitness center features a wide variety of exercise equipment, health treatments, and consultations and escorted jogs with licensed trainers. *Kenneth's,* run by the legendary hairdresser himself, is on site. Business pluses include meeting rooms that accommodate up to 1,600, A/V equipment, photocopiers, computers, and express checkout. There's a helpful concierge desk; butler and secretarial services also are available. 301 Park Ave., from E. 49th to E. 50th St. (phone: 355-3000; 800-HILTONS; fax: 872-6380 for *Waldorf-Astoria;* 758-9209 or 872-4799 for *Waldorf Towers*).

MODERATE

Barbizon This East Side establishment offers 345 rooms and a comfortable café. Guests will find an obliging concierge desk, meeting rooms that hold up to 150, photocopiers, and A/V equipment. 140 E. 63rd St. (phone: 838-5700; 800-223-1020; fax: 223-3287).

Gorham The variety of room-and-bed combinations possible in this recently restored hotel, and the fact that all 120 units have a kitchenette, dining table, and color TV set, make this a great boon to families traveling with children. There's also a meeting room that accommodates up to 15 people. 136 W. 55th St. (phone: 245-1800; 800-735-0710; fax: 582-8332).

Holiday Inn Downtown Chinatown's first hotel, this 223-room property (formerly the *Maria*) is reminiscent of Hong Kong: Exotic flowers fill the lobby, and Chinese screens and marble and rosewood furnishings grace the public areas. Although the rooms are not large, many offer fine views of Chinatown and the Hudson River. The *Pacifica Lounge* serves afternoon tea, and the *Pacifica* restaurant features authentic Cantonese cooking as well as continental fare. Additional amenities include a concierge, valet parking, meeting rooms for up to 50, and hookups for computers and fax machines. 138 Lafayette St. (phone: 966-8898; 800-HOLIDAY; fax: 966-3933).

Journey's End This 29-story property is noteworthy for its excellent location (just east of Fifth Avenue, across from the *New York Public Library*) and reasonable rates—well below the city's standard. All 187 guestrooms are equipped with a work area and cable TV set, and guests receive complimentary morning coffee (plus complimentary pastries on weekends) and a copy of *USA Today*. There's a concierge desk, and fax machines and photocopiers are available. 3 E. 40th St. (phone: 447-1500; 800-221-2222; fax: 685-5214 for reservations, 213-0972 for guests).

Mayflower This establishment is a favorite with ballet, opera, and concert buffs (it's close to *Lincoln Center*), as well as celebrities from the art world. Guests enjoy a relaxed atmosphere and 377 large, comfortable rooms with pantries. Room service delivers until midnight. The meeting rooms accommodate up to 100, and there are A/V equipment, photocopiers, computers, and express checkout. 15 Central Park W., between W. 61st and W. 62nd Sts. (phone: 265-0060; 800-223-4164; fax: 265-5098).

New York Hotel Pennsylvania Once the *Statler*, more recently the *Ramada Madison Square Garden*, this 1,700-room Stanford White landmark building across from *Penn Station* offers both comfort and class. It is now part of the Best Western chain. Business services include executive meeting facilities, 35 other meeting rooms, fax machines, photocopiers, and express checkout. 401 Seventh Ave. at W. 33rd St. (phone: 736-5000; 800-223-8585; fax: 212-502-8798).

Paramount Another Ian Schrager dazzler, designed by Philippe Starck, this trendy hotel in the middle of the theater district has 610 tiny guestrooms filled with oddly shaped furniture. There's a theatrical, dual-level lobby for socializing, the *Whiskey* bar, and even a playroom for kids. There also is a concierge, secretarial services, a meeting room that holds up to 30, photocopiers, and express checkout. 235 W. 46th St. (phone: 764-5500; 800-225-7474; fax: 354-5237).

Radisson Empire The 375 rooms in this Metromedia property all offer compact disc players, VCRs, and heated towel racks. The *Empire Grill* is the hotel's restaurant. There's a fax machine and photocopiers, as well as express checkout. 44 W. 63rd St. (phone: 265-7400; 800-333-3333; fax: 315-0349).

Salisbury Owned by the *Calvary Baptist Church* (thus, no alcohol is permitted on the premises), it has a small, welcoming lobby and 320 nice-size, pastel-decorated rooms (all with refrigerators and pantries but no stoves). It's a favorite with musicians who like the location near *Carnegie Hall*. Meeting rooms seat up to 80, and A/V equipment and fax machines are available. 123 W. 57th St. (phone: 246-1300; 800-223-0680; fax: 977-7752).

Shoreham On a fashionable block off Fifth Avenue and fresh from a stylish restoration, this place has 47 contemporary-, good-size rooms and 37 suites, all with modern bathrooms and cable TV. The hotel has a new lounge (for guests only) where breakfast and specialty coffees are served; another addition is the glassed-in roof deck. Each guestroom has a small refrigerator. 33 W. 55th St. (phone: 247-6700 or 800-553-3347; fax: 765-9741).

Wales Comfortable, recently restored, and reasonably priced, this hotel is in a very appealing residential neighborhood, close to *Central Park* and the *Metropolitan* and *Guggenheim Museums*. It offers more than 90 individually decorated rooms and suites, some with kitchenettes or four-poster beds, all with cable TV. One of the city's best breakfasts can be had in the lobby's *Sarabeth's* restaurant. 1295 Madison Ave. at E. 92nd St. (phone: 876-6000; 800-428-5252; fax: 860-7000).

Wyndham This extremely well-located, 125-room property has been fondly described as being like a posh country inn; a fine, small London hotel; and a private club. It takes a certain self-sufficiency to enjoy its special appeal; there's no room service, and the hotel restaurant is closed on weekends. 42 W. 58th St., between Fifth and Sixth Aves. (phone: 753-3500; 800-257-1111; fax: 754-5638).

INEXPENSIVE

Broadway American This Upper West Side establishment is a good bet for the budget-minded. Only 10% of its 430 rooms have private bathrooms; other baths are shared. Each room has a refrigerator, and there are kitchenettes on every other floor in lieu of room service. Broadway and W. 77th St. (phone: 362-1100; fax: 787-9521).

Chelsea At this architectural and historic landmark, Dylan Thomas, Arthur Miller, Lenny Bruce, Diego Rivera, Martha Graham, and others once found their New York home. The down-at-the-heels atmosphere in the 19th-century structure is distinctly unmodern, unhomogenized, and unsterilized. There is a large permanent occupancy in about 200 of the rooms, with 100 rooms available for shorter-term guests. Some rooms have a kitchen, a fireplace, and a bathroom; others have none of the above. Service is quirky, and the management is not overly generous with amenities like washcloths and bath mats. For the adventurous only; make reservations well in advance. 222 W. 23rd St. (phone: 243-3700; fax: 243-3700).

Herald Square With no frills (no room service or restaurant) but neat, clean, and well located, this budget hotel is in a century-old building that served as the original home of *Life* magazine. The 120 rooms are modestly decorated, and a few of the bathrooms have only showers, not tubs. The lobby is purely functional. 19 W. 31st St. (phone: 279-4017; 800-727-1888; fax: 643-4208).

Olcott Comfortable and adequate, this typical New York residential hotel offers some 100 rooms as transient accommodations. Spacious facilities and a homey atmosphere are its advantages. Most rooms are suites, with a living room, bedroom, kitchen, and bathroom. Reservations should be made several weeks in advance. 27 W. 72nd St., only a block from *Central Park* (phone: 877-4200; fax: 580-0511).

Roosevelt Long established, this traditional favorite with 1,008 rooms is quaint, clean—and a little tattered looking these days. For some guests, however, the low price may make up for the worn carpets and wallpaper, and the location is still prime, as evidenced by the hotel's busy meetings schedule. Room service is on call until 11 PM. There are 23 meeting rooms; secretarial services, A/V equipment, and photocopiers are available. There's also express checkout. Madison Ave. at E. 45th St. (phone: 661-9600; 800-223-1870 outside New York State; fax: 687-5064).

EATING OUT

New York City is, plain and simply, the culinary capital of the world. There may be more good French restaurants in Paris or more fine Chinese eating places in Hong Kong, but no other city can offer the gastronomic diversity available in New York; it is not unusual for dedicated eaters to make several pilgrimages to New York each year simply to satisfy their sophisticated palates.

Regrettably, the city's tastiest dishes do not come cheap, though there are places to dine around the city where you need not pay the check in 30-, 60-, or 90-day notes. Currently, a new breed of American bistros is cropping up and challenging the reputation of New York restaurants for being uniformly overpriced and intimidating. Their simple approach toward both food and atmosphere is helping to redefine the way New Yorkers dine out. Although prices have leveled off and even dropped in recent years in response to the recession, you can expect to pay top dollar for top establishments here. For the restaurants we list as very expensive, the tab for two for a three-course dinner will come to $135 or more; at restaurants in the expensive category, $90 to $135; at a moderate restaurant, $60 and $90; and in an inexpensive establishment, $30 to $60. These price ranges do *not* include drinks, wine, tip, or tax. All telephone numbers are in the 212 area code unless otherwise indicated.

RESERVATIONS PLEASE

Unless otherwise mentioned, reservations are *always necessary;* for the higher priced and more popular places, reservations may be necessary several weeks in advance. In addition, men are required to wear a jacket and tie at many of the more expensive restaurants.

VERY EXPENSIVE

Aquavit In a landmark Rockefeller townhouse, this Scandinavian dining place is actually two dining spots: a formal dining room set around an atrium and waterfall, with prix fixe and pre-theater menus, and a more casual, less expensive room upstairs featuring simpler fare from a choice of menus. There are many varieties of salmon and game, such as Arctic venison (reindeer) and snow grouse. Try the smorgasbord, caviar bank, and "aquavit chiller," consisting of eight flavored vodkas. Jacket required in the dining room; the upstairs café calls for casual but neat attire. Closed Saturdays for lunch and Sundays. Major credit cards accepted. 13 W. 54th St. (phone: 307-7311).

Le Bernardin Gilbert and Maguy Le Coze moved their headquarters from Paris to the Big Apple, where they occupy subtly elegant premises. The menu is fiercely seafood-oriented, and no one prepares the products of the world's oceans more imaginatively or deliciously. Since the doors opened here in 1986, such unusual specialties as tuna tartare and sea urchin soup have become staples of the New York restaurant scene, and it's worth a visit just to see what new wonders are swimming out of the kitchen. A prix fixe menu is available at dinner. Closed Saturdays for lunch and Sundays. Major credit cards accepted. 155 W. 51st St. (phone: 489-1515).

Bouley Like going to *grand-mère*'s house in the French countryside—if she happened to be the best cook in the *ville*. In an out-of-the-way area, but well worth the effort, this spot is considered by many food critics to be among New York's best restaurants. The spectacular French (and American) fare—based on what's freshest at the market—is served without fuss. Closed Saturdays for lunch and Sundays. Reservations are necessary at least three to four weeks in advance for Friday and Saturday nights. Major credit cards accepted. 165 Duane St. (phone: 608-3852).

Chanterelle This SoHo eatery, seriously committed to elegant dining, features an excellent prix fixe meal and a tasting menu, plus a relatively reasonably priced lunch. Begin with seafood sausage, then choose from such entrées as salmon *en papillote,* rack of lamb, duck in sherry vinegar, or sautéed soft-shell crabs. A cheese board is offered, and dessert might be chocolate pavé, a dense, rich, mousse-like cake. Jacket and tie required. Closed Sundays and Mondays. Make reservations about one month in advance. Major credit cards accepted. 2 Harrison St. at Hudson St. (phone: 966-6960).

Le Cirque The tables are too close together, the noise level can be deafening, and reservations must be made many weeks and sometimes months in advance. Still, the remarkable continental fare is enough to make legions of dedicated diners put up with the less-than-ideal atmosphere. Everything on the menu is special and prepared perfectly, but the main reason for dining here is to taste the sublime *crème brûlée* for dessert; nowhere in the world is it better. Jacket and tie required. Closed Sundays. Major credit cards accepted. 58 E. 65th St. (phone: 794-9292).

Four Seasons The Pool Room is perhaps the most beautiful dining room in the city, with a proprietorship that is not only creative but extremely able. This is arguably the best restaurant in the US, not just because of its accomplishments, but because of its innovation and boldness. Although the menu is interesting from top to bottom, desserts deserve special mention, and there's one called Chocolate Velvet that is simply ecstasy. Special "spa cuisine" provides careful calorie and sodium monitoring for the health-conscious. The Grill Room continues to be the luncheon favorite of New York's power elite, and is a good choice for dinner as well. Closed Sundays. Major credit cards accepted. 99 E. 52nd St., between Park and Lexington Aves. (phone: 754-9494).

La Grenouille Soft green walls and glorious floral arrangements provide a romantic setting in which to sample such house masterpieces as frogs' legs, thin, sautéed calf's liver, and roast duck. Be prepared, however, for a very haughty, condescending attitude if you're not known to the staff. Closed Sundays and Mondays. Major credit cards accepted. 3 E. 52nd St. (phone: 752-1495).

Lutèce Maintaining its mystique for over three decades as one of the world's finest restaurants, it remains what *The New York Times* dubbed a "culinary cathedral." Chef-proprietor André Soltner personally prepares the classic French fare in a simple East Side townhouse. Of all the premier restaurants in New York, this is the one most hospitable to strangers willing to pay the high price for deluxe French food. If you have the option, dine in the comfortable upstairs room, though the garden room downstairs is a treat in New York City. To sample the combination of classic dishes, innovative nouvelle creations, and Alsatian specialties, order the *menu de dégustation,* a tasting of six or seven small courses, or the reasonably priced prix fixe menu. Closed Sundays. Make reservations a month in advance. Major credit cards accepted. 249 E. 50th St. (phone: 752-2225).

"21" Club The legendary atmosphere and lingering cachet are what lure most visitors, but longtime favorites from the menu, such as the *"21"* burger and chicken hash, are a treat as well. If you're not a regular or a celebrity, the welcome sometimes isn't quite so warm, but to some, just being here is a true New York experience. The elegant upstairs dining room is open on weekdays for lunch only. Closed Sundays. Major credit cards accepted. 21 W. 52nd St. (phone: 582-7200).

EXPENSIVE

Alison on Dominick Street This romantic spot on the western fringe of SoHo serves wonderful French-Mediterranean peasant fare. Try the rabbit stew with white-bean ravioli or chef Tom Valenti's signature dish—crusty braised lamb shank. Jacket suggested. Open daily for dinner only. Reservations advised. Major credit cards accepted. 38 Dominick St. (phone: 727-1188).

An American Place Celebrated chef-owner Larry Forgione is regarded as one of the spearheads of the New American food preparation movement; sample his American/continental specialties and you'll discover why. Gastronomic delights include grilled free-range chicken with Jerusalem artichokes in a cream sauce, and pan-roasted lamb with black pepper and cumin. Closed Sundays. Major credit cards accepted. 2 Park Ave. at E. 32nd St. (phone: 684-2122).

Café des Artistes Under the direction of restaurateur and raconteur George Lang, this West Side favorite is one of New York's most romantic restaurants. (Be sure to note—not that you could help it—the wonderful Howard Chandler Christy murals.) Appetizers and main dishes (French country-style) are all first-rate, but the real lures are the desserts. Save room for their unusual, special offerings such as Ilona torte, a flourless chocolate cake that contains 10 (ah, cholesterol!) eggs. For those with a sweet tooth, it's like visiting paradise. The most beautiful weekend brunch in town (reservations always necessary). Open daily. Major credit cards accepted. 1 W. 67th St. (phone: 877-3500).

Il Cantinori A beamed ceiling, terra cotta floor, and chairs of wood and straw create the charming ambience at this Tuscan eatery, located on one of the city's loveliest blocks. Begin with *risotto nero* (a rice delicacy in squid ink) or *ravioli alla fiorentina* (dumplings filled with spinach and ricotta cheese) before an entrée of excellent fish or game. For dessert try the chef's version of the popular Italian confection *tiramisù,* espresso-soaked ladyfingers and sweet mascarpone cheese. Closed for lunch on weekends. Major credit cards accepted. 32 E. 10th St. (phone: 673-6044).

La Caravelle A traditional bastion of classic French cuisine with all of the attendant hauteur, this is often the choice of New York's smartest set. Menus are consistently interesting, and the kitchen is not merely competent but innovative. The pre-theater menu is a relative bargain. Jacket and tie required. Closed Sundays. Major credit cards accepted. 33 W. 55th St. (phone: 586-4252).

Cesarina Pricey but the good northern Italian fare, including risotto, pasta, and regional specialties prepared with fresh seafood, and pleasant service are the lures here. If osso buco is on the winter menu, go for it. Very popular at lunch with the elite executive crowd and a nice choice for pre-theater dinner, it is owned by Italy's renowned and elegant *Villa d'Este* hotel. Closed weekends. Reservations advised for lunch. Major credit cards accepted. 36 W. 52nd St. (phone: 582-6900).

Gotham Bar & Grill The space here is cavernous (it was originally a warehouse), but an award-winning bi-level design and lofty decor bring the space down to *grand café* scale. Chef Alfred Portale's creations continue to amaze. Sample such dazzlers as grilled Muscovy duck breast with Szechuan peppercorns, apricots, and turnips; grilled salmon; and artichokes *à la grecque*. Open daily. Major credit cards accepted. 12 E. 12 St., between Fifth Ave. and University Pl. (phone: 620-4020).

Grotta Azzurra Neapolitan specialties are served in a basement in the heart of Little Italy. Lobster *fra diavolo* exacts a high price, but it's worth the tariff. The garlic bread (not available on Saturdays) is like none other in this world, and it guarantees that you won't be bothered by vampires for years. Closed Mondays. No reservations, so be prepared to wait in line. No credit cards accepted. 387 Broome St. (phone: 925-8775).

Jo Jo This East Side bistro is another feather in the toque of former *Lafayette* chef Jean-Georges Vongerichten. Currently a New York hot spot, low fat is the rule here, but don't be fooled: Flavor and innovation are at the top of the list. There might be shrimp with a Thai-accented carrot broth; goat cheese and potato terrine with arugula juice; or rabbit, Swiss chard, and tomato oil enveloped in thin pasta. The desserts are the stuff of dreams. Ask to have coffee served around the fireplace upstairs. Closed Sundays. Major credit cards accepted. 160 E. 64th St. (phone: 223-5656).

Lespinasse This serene, formal dining salon in the *St. Regis* hotel gleams with polished marble and goldleaf trim. Gray Kunz, formerly the chef at *Adrienne* in the *Peninsula,* uses his Hong Kong–influenced artistry to produce such dishes as black bass poached in a delicate broth flavored with Asian spices, and gingered chicken with a soy vinegar dressing. The wine list is surprisingly affordable. Closed Sundays. Major credit cards accepted. 2 E. 55th St. (phone: 339-6719).

Manhattan Ocean Club Both the lower-level and upstairs dining rooms of this fine seafood house have original Picasso ceramic plates and prints displayed behind glass on their white walls, set off by a few Greek columns. Although you may find it crowded, this restaurant's appeal is its fresh, delicious fish and shellfish—the Hawaiian wahoo and melt-in-your-mouth *kumomoto* oysters are particularly good. The *pâtissier* is winning awards with such sumptuous treats as calvados ice cream on apple tarts, and the service is attentive. Open daily. Major credit cards accepted. 57 W. 58th St. (phone: 371-7777).

Montrachet The cooking is best described as nouvelle French, with an emphasis on traditional flavors. Favorite dishes include duck in red wine sauce with mission figs or fresh ginger, and roast chicken with garlic and potato purée. In addition to an extensive à la carte menu, there are three excellent prix fixe menus. Jackets requested. Closed Sundays. American Express accepted. 239 West Broadway, between Walker and White Sts. (phone: 219-2777).

Il Nido A superb menu of northern Italian specialties and the highest standards of service are the hallmarks of Adi Giovannetti's attractive, if somewhat cramped, East Side establishment, which is popular for business lunches. *Crostini di polenta* with a mushroom and chicken liver sauce is the perfect starter, to be followed by mixed fried fish, shellfish in marinara sauce, or any of a host of other specialties. Closed Sundays. Major credit cards accepted. 251 E. 53rd St. (phone: 753-8450).

Oyster Bar *The* place for oysters: On any given day, there will be 10 varieties from which to choose. There's also Maine lobster, North Atlantic salmon, Dover sole, mako shark steaks, pompano, pink snapper, swordfish, Florida stone crabs in season, a host of clams, and Mediterranean seafood. The huge volume assures fresh product. (Note, however, that this is *not* the place for nonsmokers; there is an ever-present cloud of cigar smoke in the air.) Closed weekends. Reservations unnecessary. Major credit cards accepted. *Grand Central Station* (lower level), E. 42nd St., between Vanderbilt and Lexington Aves. (phone: 490-6650).

Palio Here is an elegant entry in New York's abundant inventory of fine Italian eateries. The street-level bar is surrounded by artist Sandro Chia's mural of Siena's exciting medieval horse race that gives this place its name; the upstairs dining room is spacious, elegant, and perfect for a pre-theater meal. Closed Saturday lunch and Sundays. Major credit cards accepted. 151 W. 51st St., in the *Equitable Center* (phone: 245-4850).

Palm Good sirloin steaks are served in an atmosphere so unassuming that the draw has got to be the food. Sawdust covers the floor, tables and chairs are refugees from a thrift shop, but the beef is first-rate. The largest (and most expensive) lobsters in New York also are served here. *Palm, Too,* directly across the street at 840 Second Ave. (phone: 697-5198), offers identical food and is open for Sunday lunch. Reservations advised for lunch; for dinner, they are accepted only for parties of four or more. Closed Sunday lunch. Major credit cards accepted. 837 Second Ave., between E. 44th and E. 45th Sts. (phone: 687-2953).

Parioli Romanissimo This classy restaurant in an attractive East Side townhouse is especially popular with executive diners who come to feast on the pricey but delicious Italian specialties. Opt for a meaty main course like veal chop *giardiniera*, then splurge on the chocolate torte for dessert. Service is notoriously chilly, and even when reservations are in hand, expect a wait. Closed Sundays. Major credit cards accepted. 24 E. 81st St. (phone: 288-2391).

Peter Luger The best porterhouse and T-bone steaks in the country, lurking in the shadows under the Brooklyn side of the Williamsburg Bridge. The neighborhood is hardly fashionable, but the food is just great. No menu, but try the thick-sliced onions and tomatoes under the special barbecue sauce, and be sure to taste the best home-fried potatoes the city has to offer (served only in the evenings). Open daily. Reservations for weekends should be made six weeks in advance; only on Mondays or Tuesdays can you get seated without a reservation. No credit cards accepted. 178 Broadway, Brooklyn (phone: 718-387-7400).

Raphael Situated on the ground floor of a townhouse, this classic French dining spot is a series of interconnecting rooms that range from rustic (brick walls and rough plaster) to princely (trompe l'oeil gardens). There's also a real trellised garden where meals are served in summer. The menu offers very good peasant food: Try the loin of rabbit, lentils with garlic sausage, or onion tart. Closed Saturday lunch and Sundays. Major credit cards accepted. 33 W. 54th St. (phone: 582-8993).

Remi Beneath a wraparound mural of Venice, diners indulge in such northern Italian fantasies as cuttlefish in its own ink over polenta, smoked prosciutto with greens and truffled olive oil, and ravioli Marco Polo with fresh tuna and ginger. A dessert favorite is the three-nut tart (pine, pecan, and walnut) with homemade ice cream. And if you've still got the heart and room, there are 45 different kinds of grappa to follow the meal. Open daily. Major credit cards accepted. 145 W. 53rd St., between Sixth and Seventh Aves. (phone: 581-4242).

River Café Set on a barge on the Brooklyn shore of the East River, with spectacular views of the lower Manhattan skyline, this is one of the top American restaurants, with an especially good weekend brunch menu featuring lobster baked in horseradish oil with oyster risotto, poached eggs on smoked salmon waffles, and duck *confit* with roasted garlic and white beans. Jackets required; ties optional. Open daily. Reservations necessary two weeks ahead. Major credit cards accepted. 1 Water St., Brooklyn (phone: 718-522-5200).

Russian Tea Room With enough *blinis* to float diners down the Volga, this festive place (always decked out with *Christmas* ornaments) is an almost obligatory stop for any visitor who plans to attend a concert at adjacent *Carnegie Hall*. Try the borscht or chicken Kiev, abide by the waiter's suggestions, or let your Slavic instincts have free rein. There is now a cabaret on an eclectic schedule some Sunday nights. Jacket and tie requested. Open daily. Major credit cards accepted. 150 W. 57th St. (phone: 265-0947).

Tavern on the Green The food is less famous than the decor and location (just inside *Central Park*) at this, one of New York's most beautiful dining establishments. In winter the snow-covered trees trimmed with tiny white lights outside the Crystal Room make a dazzling display (and reservations are a must a month in advance). Summer is only slightly less spectacular, when diners can sit in the outdoor garden. The *Tavern*

Store (phone: 873-7720) offers souvenirs with the restaurant's logo plus a variety of ornaments, toys, and china. Open daily. Major credit cards accepted. Central Park W. and W. 67th St. (phone: 873-3200).

Tribeca Grill Stargazers come here in hopes of seeing one of the co-owners: Robert De Niro, Sean Penn, Mikhail Baryshnikov, or Bill Murray. Serious diners flock to sample such temptations as duck *confit* with crisp greens, and *cavatelli* with plum tomatoes, basil, and pecorino cheese. Open daily. Reservations necessary three weeks in advance for weekends. Major credit cards accepted. 375 Greenwich St. at Franklin St. (phone: 941-3900).

Union Square Café The menu at this informal, perenially popular eatery changes with the seasons, but classic American dishes prepared with a hint of old Italy are always featured. Appetizers may include *bruschetta* (grilled garlic bread with tomatoes), polenta, or a dish of creamed turnips; filet of tuna, fine hamburgers, and calamari often appear as options for the main course. The atmosphere is airy and pleasant, with Italian-style furnishings and oil paintings. Closed Sunday lunch. Major credit cards accepted. 21 E. 16th St. (phone: 243-4020).

Water Club The decor at this restaurant/barge in the East River is nautical, but with restraint, since the view is decorative enough: river traffic and the twinkling lights of the Manhattan and Queens skylines. The menu, too, is nautical, with similar restraint. Appetizers range from oysters and smoked salmon to beluga caviar, entrées from Maryland crab cakes to Dover sole and lobster—but diners also can order pâté or filet mignon. Jacket requested. Open daily. Major credit cards accepted. It's tricky to get here, so take a cab. East River at E. 30th St., on the northbound service road of the FDR Dr. (phone: 683-3333).

MODERATE

American Festival Café This place is cheery, very American, and right on the famous ice skating rink in *Rockefeller Center*. The reasonably priced and varied menu includes prime ribs, steaks, roast chicken, and warm and cold seafood. It's also noted for its desserts, including Mississippi mud pie, New York cheesecake, and Key lime pie. The atmosphere is best from November to April, when the rink is open. Open daily. Major credit cards accepted. 20 W. 50th St. (phone: 246-6699).

Arqua This stylish Tribeca spot specializes in the food of the Veneto, but chef-owner Leo Pulito (from the town of Arqua, near Venice) has as fine a touch with grilled salmon and rack of lamb as with artichoke lasagna and game prepared Italian-style. Look into the reasonable prix fixe menu for either lunch or dinner. Closed for lunch on weekends. American Express accepted. 281 Church St. at White St. (phone: 334-1888).

Azzurro This Upper East Side bastion of Sicilian specialties attracts hordes of fans with its grilled fish, fine pasta specials, and delectable *vino santo*. Most members of the staff are related, and Mama Sindoni is in the kitchen. Open daily. Major credit cards accepted. 245 E. 84th St. (phone: 517-7068).

Ballroom When it opened in 1983, this very pretty bistro introduced a new twist to Manhattan dining—the *tapas* bar. A changing, varied menu of *tapas* (Spanish for "appetizers") is spread along a lengthy bar, and patrons either nibble their way through dinner there or head for the dining room, where waiters circulate with trays of the same. There's also a less tempting menu of main courses, a reasonable and tasty buffet lunch, and a dessert table that's as much a feast for the eyes as for the taste buds. Cabaret-type entertainment on Tuesdays through Saturdays is another reason to go there. Closed Mondays. Major credit cards accepted. 253 W. 28th St. (phone: 244-3005).

Bice Excellent northern Italian dishes and a warm, informal atmosphere have made this bistro one of the most popular dining places in the city. Homemade pasta is the mainstay of the ever-changing menu; chef Giacomo Galena's specialties on any given day might include *tagliolini* (thin noodles) with white truffles or grilled tuna with black peppercorns. Open daily. Major credit cards accepted. 7 E. 54th St. (phone: 688-1999).

Black Sheep The place has an utterly romantic country French atmosphere, enhanced by a fireplace. The regional farmhouse specialties, primarily from Provence and Burgundy, include duckling braised over an open fire with armagnac, prunes, and apricots; loin rack of lamb Tuscan-style; and subtly flavored seafood. Vegetarian dishes are imaginative and tasty (try the artichokes with potatoes). There is an extensive wine list. Open daily. American Express accepted. 344 W. 11th St. (phone: 242-1010).

Il Bocconcino The celebrity photographs in the window date back to *La Dolce Vita* days, when Gilberto was a paparazzo in Rome. Now he and co-owner Giorgio run this modest but congenial Greenwich Village spot, with lace curtains, white tablecloths, and some murals of Italianate architecture to remind them of home. Sample the *bruschetta* (grilled garlic bread with tomatoes), then follow with pasta, chicken, veal, seafood, or pizza. Sidewalk tables are set outside in summer. Open daily. Major credit cards accepted. 168 Sullivan St. (phone: 982-0329).

Café Luxembourg The interior here is Art Deco in style, brightly lit, and noisy, with everyone appearing to be looking around for someone famous. Not far from *Lincoln Center*, it is especially popular with concertgoers. The fare is nouvelle, though the specials tend to be uneven. For the best look at the chic crowd, come after 8 PM. There's also a Sunday brunch featuring *boudin blanc*, a white pork sausage. Open daily. Reservations advised. Major credit cards accepted. 200 W. 70th St. (phone: 873-7411).

Café Un Deux Trois In this very lively theater district bistro, whose name is its address, patrons draw on the paper tablecloths with crayons while waiting to sample carefully prepared daily specialties that include fresh sea trout, steaks with *pommes frites,* and couscous with chicken, lamb, and chick-peas. Theatergoers should plan to dine very early to be sure to make curtain time. Open daily from noon to midnight (to 11 PM on Sundays). Reservations accepted for parties of five or more. Major credit cards accepted. 123 W. 44th St. (phone: 354-4148).

Cent' Anni A Little Italy gem, it serves down-to-earth northern Italian fare in an unpretentious storefront setting. There are only 60 seats, so evenings tend to be both crowded and convivial as diners enjoy classic pasta. The name comes from the traditional toast "May you live 100 years!" Open daily. American Express accepted. 50 Carmine St., between Bleecker and Bedford Sts. (phone: 989-9494).

Chin Chin This stylish Chinese eatery is somewhat formal at lunchtime, but the atmosphere relaxes in the evening. The three dining rooms are paneled with maple wood, and skylights lend a cheerful brightness. Excellent dishes include Peking duck, Grand Marnier prawns, and cold noodles with sesame sauce. Closed for lunch on weekends. Major credit cards accepted. 216 E. 49th St. (phone: 888-4555).

Jean Lafitte As accurate an evocation of a cozy and unpretentious Parisian neighborhood bistro as exists in New York. Go for the excellent tripe, the authentic *choucroute* (on specials only), or steak *au poivre*. Superb soups, which change daily, are a special treat during a cold New York winter. Convenient to *Carnegie Hall*. Closed for lunch on weekends. Major credit cards accepted. 68 W. 58th St. (phone: 751-2323).

Le Madri Delicacies such as fresh prawns stuffed with wild mushrooms and ricotta cheese, antipasto with caramelized onions, and osso buco are fabulous at this stylish Italian dining spot. The menu changes seasonally, and there is a weekend brunch menu. For dessert try the apple tart with cinnamon ice cream. Open daily. Major credit cards accepted. 168 W. 18th St. (phone: 727-8022).

Mesa Grill The sassy Southwestern fare here, served up by young up-and-coming chef Bobby Flay, surpasses anything of its kind in New York. And the sizzling, noisy social scene adds nearly as much heat as the chilies he uses so liberally. Try the *posole* (a Mexican fish stew made with hominy), the moist, blue corn-encrusted fried chicken, or the grilled swordfish with cilantro pesto. Open daily. Major credit cards accepted. 102 Fifth Ave. (phone: 807-7400).

Moreno The leafy Gramercy Park neighborhood of Manhattan is the home of this gracious but relaxed Italian restaurant with outdoor tables. Its Milanese owner, Moreno Maltagliati, has created a warm ambience by painting the walls ochre and having waiters serve complimentary hors-d'oeuvres shortly after patrons are seated. Featured dishes include starters of grilled vegetables and a gorgonzola, apple, and walnut salad, and main courses such as fresh ravioli and grilled tuna and salmon. Some desserts are Italian, such as the *tiramisù,* but seasonal fresh fruit also appears on the menu. In addition, delicate lace cookies are offered gratis. Prix fixe meals are served Sundays. Closed Saturday lunch. Reservations advised for groups of four or more. 65 Irving Pl. at E. 18th St. (phone: 673-3939).

Odéon In a gray cast-iron building, this high-style, refurbished cafeteria is in the midst of Tribeca. Look for entrées such as squab with shiitake mushrooms and wild rice, and roast loin of lamb with white peppercorns. A dessert worth trying is crêpes with praline butter and apricot liqueur.

Open daily. Major credit cards accepted. 145 West Broadway (phone: 233-0507).

Park Bistro This fashionable French eatery features classic presentations of seafood, chicken, and meat. The menu changes frequently, but shellfish soup, warm potato salad with goat cheese and herb dressing, roast monkfish, and leg of lamb are among the succulent possibilities. Closed for lunch on weekends. Major credit cards accepted. 414 Park Ave. S. (phone: 689-1360).

Periyali In this cool Aegean oasis, patrons enjoy traditional Greek fare prepared with an exceptionally light touch. Specialties include lima bean salad with *skordalia,* a tangy potato-based purée; baked sea bass with garlic, tomato, and white wine; and moussaka with grilled zucchini. For dessert, don't miss the luscious custard-filled *galaktoboreko.* Closed Sundays. Major credit cards accepted. 35 W. 20th St. (phone: 463-7890).

Pierre au Tunnel Onion soup, mussels, frogs' legs, and grilled steaks typify the French provincial dishes featured in this theater district bistro since 1950. Try the loin of veal sautéed with fresh mushrooms and shallots or tripe cooked with white wine and calvados. Closed Sundays. Reservations necessary for pre-theater dinner. Major credit cards accepted. 250 W. 47th St. (phone: 575-1220).

Provence At this perfect French dining spot in the Village, the spices and tomato-based sauces of southeastern France are nowhere better utilized, and the roast chicken with garlic gives a whole new meaning to the serving of fowl. A huge vat of aging brandy adorns the bar and provides an excellent digestive at the conclusion of a meal. In summer the back patio is an idyllic dining spot. Open daily. American Express accepted. 38 MacDougal St. (phone: 475-7500).

Sammy's Roumanian Steak House At this last survivor of a long Lower East Side tradition of ethnic meat restaurants, Eastern European favorites are featured, as is Old Country music of a sort you're not likely to hear in any other establishment. The makings for egg creams (milk, seltzer, and chocolate syrup) are set right on the table—an experience you don't usually find anymore in New York. Open daily. Major credit cards accepted. 157 Chrystie St. (phone: 673-5526 or 673-0330).

Santa Fe Unlike many other Mexican eateries that have sprung up around the city, there are no hanging plants, no neon signs, no ear-splitting noise levels here. Instead, crisp linen and salmon-colored walls hung with Mexican tapestries provide a serene setting for nicely tart margaritas and well-prepared Southwestern dishes. Closed for lunch on weekends. Major credit cards accepted. 72 W. 69th St., just a few blocks from *Lincoln Center* (phone: 724-0822).

Shun Lee Palace The late T. T. Wang was one of New York City's most talented Chinese cooks, and the menu here still includes some of his most exciting temptations. If you can round up a group of 10 to dine together, you might order Wang's special Chinese feast. Jacket required. Open daily. Major credit cards accepted. 155 E. 55th St. (phone: 371-8844).

Shun Lee West More sophisticated both in palette and palate than its older East Side cousin above, this establishment features flavorful Szechuan and Mandarin dishes. Try the giant prawns with black bean sauce, grilled scallops, and jellyfish (for courageous souls only). Choice entrées include crisp Peking duck marinated in five spices; *chan-do* chicken, which is sautéed in hot pepper, scallions, garlic, and ginger; and salmon with Szechuan sauce. This dining spot's proximity to *Lincoln Center* makes it the perfect place for a pre- or post-performance feast. For those looking for lighter fare, the adjoining *Shun Lee Café* serves dim sum—Chinese hors d'oeuvres. Jacket required. Open daily. Reservations advised for pre-theater or pre-concert meals. Major credit cards accepted. 43 W. 65th St. (phone: 595-8895).

Tropica The setting is an amalgam of just about every island in the Caribbean, and the menu is similarly inspired—saucy and piquant, with an emphasis on freshly caught seafood. Its location on the lobby level of the *Met-Life Building* (formerly the *Pan Am Building*), in the middle of the traffic path to and from *Grand Central Station,* attracts crowds of expense-account types at lunch it can be noisy at dinner too. Closed weekends. Major credit cards accepted. *Met-Life Building,* Vanderbilt Ave. and E. 45th St. (phone: 867-6767).

Zarela Among the city's better Mexican eateries, this festive East Sider flourishes under the direction of its high-profile owner, Zarela Martínez. Menu selections range from the familiar to such eclectic dishes as roast duck with tomato and red chili sauce, and shrimp with tomato *poblano* salsa. There are spice levels for every palate, so the cautious needn't fear, and there are great tangy margaritas to shore up everyone's courage. Closed for lunch on weekends. American Express and Diners Club accepted. 953 Second Ave. near E. 50th St. (phone: 644-6740).

INEXPENSIVE

Carmine's This eatery lures the hungry hordes to its two locations with oversize portions of home-style food at reasonable prices. There's nothing "nouvelle" about the menu of Italian favorites like fried calamari, spaghetti with meatballs, and chicken Contadina (with sausage, peppers, and lots of garlic). Waiters are friendly and forthright—they won't hesitate to tell you that you're ordering too much (portions here are huge and meant to be shared). Open daily. Reservations are accepted only for parties of six or more; otherwise, be prepared to wait in a long line. American Express accepted. 2450 Broadway, between W. 90th and W. 91st Sts. (phone: 362-2200), and 200 W. 44th St. (phone: 221-3800).

Carnegie Delicatessen At this, the quintessential New York deli, the sandwiches are enormous, seemingly too big to put in a normal human mouth, and corned beef and pastrami are king. There are communal tables and no atmosphere, except the frantic Seventh Avenue scene, but waiters provide entertaining banter. Save room for the velvety cheesecake. Open daily from 6:30 AM to 3:30 AM. No reservations or credit cards accepted. 854 Seventh Ave., near, of course, *Carnegie Hall* (phone: 757-2245).

Dock's Oyster Bar There are two of these huge seafood palaces, and each is packed at lunch- and dinnertime. The sprawling raw bar attracts social nibblers, while others head for the crisply nautical dining area to tackle a lengthy menu that often includes seared and gingered tuna, tangy chowders, and a catch-of-the-day selection, which regulars order with a side dish of sweet potato fries. Open daily. Major credit cards accepted. 2427 Broadway, between W. 89th and W. 90th Sts. (phone: 724-5588), and 633 Third Ave. at E. 40th St. (phone: 986-8080).

Florent This classic 1940s diner in the wholesale meat district, converted into a hip French restaurant, is the last word in trendy New York style. With so much to look at, one almost forgets to eat! Open 24 hours daily. No credit cards accepted. 69 Gansevoort St., between Washington and Greenwich Sts. (phone: 989-5779).

Fourteen There are two of these attractive, convivial bistros where diners may eat either at the marble-topped bar or in the dining room with oak floor, white linen-draped tables, and a wall of red velvet banquettes. Try the chicory and bacon salad drenched in a hot vinaigrette dressing, then the grilled salmon in choron sauce (a purée of tomato béarnaise) or the grilled chicken. At press time the majority of the main courses came with an easy-to-remember price tag—$14. Choose the crispy, warm, thin-crusted apple tart for dessert. The short wine list includes some interesting, reasonably priced offerings. Formerly called *Quatorze*. Open daily. Major credit cards accepted. 240 W. 14th St. (phone: 206-7006) and 323 E. 79th St. (phone: 535-1414).

Gage & Tollner Holding forth at this stand since 1879, the renowned seafood house is worth a visit, not only for the food but also for the sight of the gaslight glowing over the canopy in the evening. Renowned Southern chef Edna Lewis's specialties include lobster Newburg, crabmeat Virginia, and 15 different styles of potatoes. Open daily. Major credit cards accepted. 372 Fulton St. at Jay St., Brooklyn (phone: 718-875-5181).

Golden Unicorn The dim sum in this Chinatown eatery (served from 8 AM to 4 PM—but try to get here by 10:30 on a Sunday morning) are arguably the city's best. This stylish spot also specializes in Cantonese dishes such as scallops and bean curd in black bean sauce and shrimp with walnuts served with a mayonnaise dressing. If you're unfamiliar with Chinese food, rely on the advice of the courteous and attentive staff. For a special taste treat, try the shark's fin dumpling in its own soup. Open daily. Major credit cards accepted. 18 E. Broadway (phone: 941-0911).

Hatsuhana Still winning kudos from some of New York's toughest restaurant critics, this Japanese eatery serves some of the best sushi, sashimi, and tempura in town. Closed Sundays. Reservations necessary for dinner only. Major credit cards accepted. 17 E. 48th St. (phone: 355-3345).

Hunan House Among Chinatown's best, this pleasant place specializes in the subtly spiced food of the Hunan province. Start off with fried dumplings or hot and sour soup, then have Hunan lamb with scallions; Changsha beef, done in a hot sauce with broccoli; or Confucius prawns with cashews. Open daily. No reservations. American Express and Diners Club accepted. 45 Mott St. (phone: 962-0010).

Louisiana Community Bar & Grill The city's best Cajun and creole specialties, along with extraordinarily friendly and welcoming service, are the attractions at this informal eatery. Try the blackened prime ribs with mashed potatoes, crawfish *étouffée* with rice, and, whenever available, chocolate mocha cake for dessert. Open daily for dinner only. Major credit cards accepted. 622 Broadway, between Bleecker and Houston Sts. (phone: 460-9633).

Mocca Close your eyes and you're dining in downtown Budapest. Start with the gutsy goulash soup, go on to the stuffed cabbage heaped with sauerkraut, then try *palacsintas* (crêpes with jam) for dessert. A bargain at thrice the price. Open daily. Reservations advised for dinner. No credit cards accepted. 1588 Second Ave. at E. 82nd St. (phone: 734-6470).

Pamir Small and family-run, this spot specializes in Afghan (much like Indian) cooking. The delicately seasoned lamb dishes are very good. Open daily. MasterCard and Visa accepted. 1437 Second Ave. (phone: 734-3791). A larger, more comfortable second location is on the corner of First Ave. and E. 58th St. and accepts major credit cards (phone: 644-9258).

Serendipity 3 Definitely not for kids only, this East Side classic has been packing them in for as long as most of us can remember. The front room resembles an old-fashioned general store (but the merchandise is cutting-edge chic and trendy); the rear dining room is a cozy jumble of antique oak tables, Tiffany-style lamps, and old-time tin signs. Chocoholics delight in the bathtub-size hot fudge sundaes; other favorites are the foot-long hot dogs and frozen hot chocolate. It's a great place to rest up after a *Bloomingdale's* binge. Open daily. Major credit cards accepted. 225 E. 60th St., between Second and Third Aves. (phone: 838-3531).

SUNDAY BRUNCH

Sunday brunch is a cherished tradition among New Yorkers. Some popular spots—some of which have long lines waiting to get in—are *Sarabeth's Kitchen* (423 Amsterdam Ave.; phone: 496-6280; and 1295 Madison Ave.; phone: 410-7335); *Man Ray Bistro* (169 Eighth Ave.; phone: 627-4220); the *Brasserie* (100 E. 53rd St.; phone: 751-4840); and *Florent*, the *River Café*, the *Water Club*, *Odéon*, and *Provence* (see above for all five). One of the few places that takes brunch reservations is *Zoë* (90 Prince St.; phone: 966-6722). Hotel dining rooms with copious—and more costly—brunch buffets are the *Café Pierre* at the *Pierre*; the *Ambassador Grill* at the *UN Plaza Park Hyatt*; *Peacock Alley* at the *Waldorf-Astoria*; and the *Palm Court* at the *Plaza* (see *Checking In* for all four).

On board one of *World Yacht*'s five restaurant/yachts, you can enjoy Sunday brunch ($40 per person at press time) while cruising the Hudson River and New York Harbor past the glittering Manhattan skyline. There are luncheon and dinner cruises as well. Jacket required (no tie). Open daily. Advance reservations and tickets are necessary. Major credit cards accepted. Sailings are from *Pier 81* on the Hudson River at W. 41st St. (phone: 630-8100).

TAKING TEA

New Yorkers have become quite fond of the British tradition of afternoon tea, and a number of the city's most posh hotels have jumped on the bandwagon. The *Carlyle*'s *Gallery*, the *Mayfair Hotel Baglioni*, the *Lowell*, the *Plaza*'s *Palm Court*, the *Rotunda Room* at the *Pierre*, the *New York Palace*, and the *Stanhope* (see *Checking In* for all) offer superlative service and a variety of teas, scones, sandwiches, and condiments. Taking tea is a great way to experience the ambience of these elegant hostelries without having to stay the night. Tea for two usually costs $40 to $50; à la carte service is also available at some hotels. Reservations are usually necessary.

For those who prefer cappuccino to a cup of tea, *Caffè Roma* (385 Broome St.; phone: 226-8413), in the heart of Little Italy, is one of the few remaining old-style coffeehouses still operating. Everything from espresso to egg creams and Italian cookies and pastries are served daily from 8 AM to midnight.

A TASTE OF HISTORY

New York has been around for quite some time—and so have many of its most famous restaurants. If you'd like a taste of America's past with your meal, there are lots of choices. *Fraunces Tavern* (54 Pearl St. at Broad St., near Wall St.; phone: 269-0144), built in 1719, is the oldest structure in Manhattan, and George Washington really did eat here. *Gage & Tollner* (see main entry, above) opened in 1879 and specializes in seafood and Virginian victuals. Lillie Langtry, turn-of-the-century British music-hall star and paramour of England's Edward VII, was wont to flout the men-only policy at *Keen's Chophouse* (72 W. 36th St.; phone: 947-3636). The *Old Homestead* (56 Ninth Ave.; phone: 242-9040) has been serving steaks to famous and not-so-famous New Yorkers since 1868. *Sardi's* (234 W. 44th St.; phone: 221-8440), opened in 1921, is the traditional place for theater folks to go to wait for the reviews of their latest Broadway show. (Check out the almost floor-to-ceiling celebrity caricatures.) And Brooklyn's famed *Peter Luger* steakhouse (see full description, above) is more than a century old and a mecca for beef mavens.

Orlando

At-a-Glance

SEEING THE CITY

For most visitors, the Orlando area's premier panorama is the one from the *Top of the World Lounge* in *Walt Disney World*'s *Contemporary Resort*. It's stunning either at sunset, when a rosy aura surrounds the spires of *Cinderella Castle,* or at night, when the rooflines glitter with tiny white lights.

SPECIAL PLACES

Walt Disney World alone requires a minimum of four to five days—and even twice that time would not do justice to all its shows, sporting facilities, restaurants, and other attractions. And the rest of Orlando has plenty to offer as well.

ORLANDO AND ENVIRONS

CYPRESS GARDENS You'd have to visit 75 countries at different times of the year to see all of the 8,000 varieties of plants that can be viewed at this 208-acre attraction developed back in the mid-1930s. In addition, there are the famous water-ski shows, in which athletes ski barefoot and backward; the *Antique Radio Museum*, with more than 100 radios on display; the *Cypress Roots Museum*, featuring the history of the park; the *Wings of Wonder Butterfly Conservatory*, a 5,500-square-foot Victorian-style glass conservatory featuring more than 1,000 free-flying butterflies; Kodak's revolving *Island in the Sky*, which offers spectacular views from 153 feet up; *Cypress Junction*, an elaborate model railroad; and *Feathered Follies*, a comedy show featuring exotic birds that also teaches about species that are becoming extinct. Open daily. Admission charge. Rte. 540, Winter Haven (phone: 813-324-2111; 800-282-2123 in Florida; 800-237-4826 elsewhere in the US).

GATORLAND In a couple of hours here you can see more than 5,000 alligators. Open daily. Admission charge. 14501 S. Orange Blossom Trail (phone: 855-5496).

SEA WORLD The world's most popular marine park ranks among Orlando's must-sees. Among the fine displays are *Shamu: New Visions*, a show featuring the Shamu family of killer whales and incorporating a video presentation; *Manatees: The Last Generation?*, an in-depth look at the underwater world of the endangered manatee; *Pacific Point Preserve*, a natural habitat where visitors can feed sea lions and seals; *Terrors of the Deep*, an introduction to some dangerous sea creatures, including eels, barracuda, and sharks; and the *Penguin Encounter*, where more than 200 feisty penguins waddle and hop to the delight of onlookers. Another fascinating attraction is *Mission: Bermuda Triangle*, which includes a simulated submarine journey through this notorious region. Open daily. Admission charge. 7007 Sea World Dr. (phone: 351-3600).

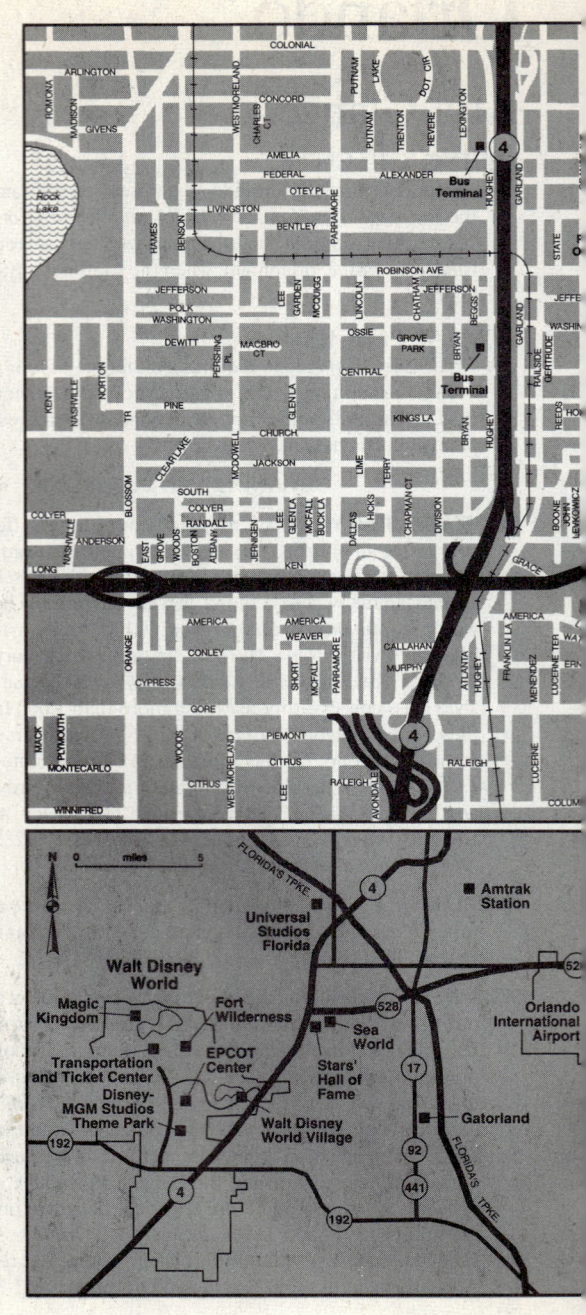

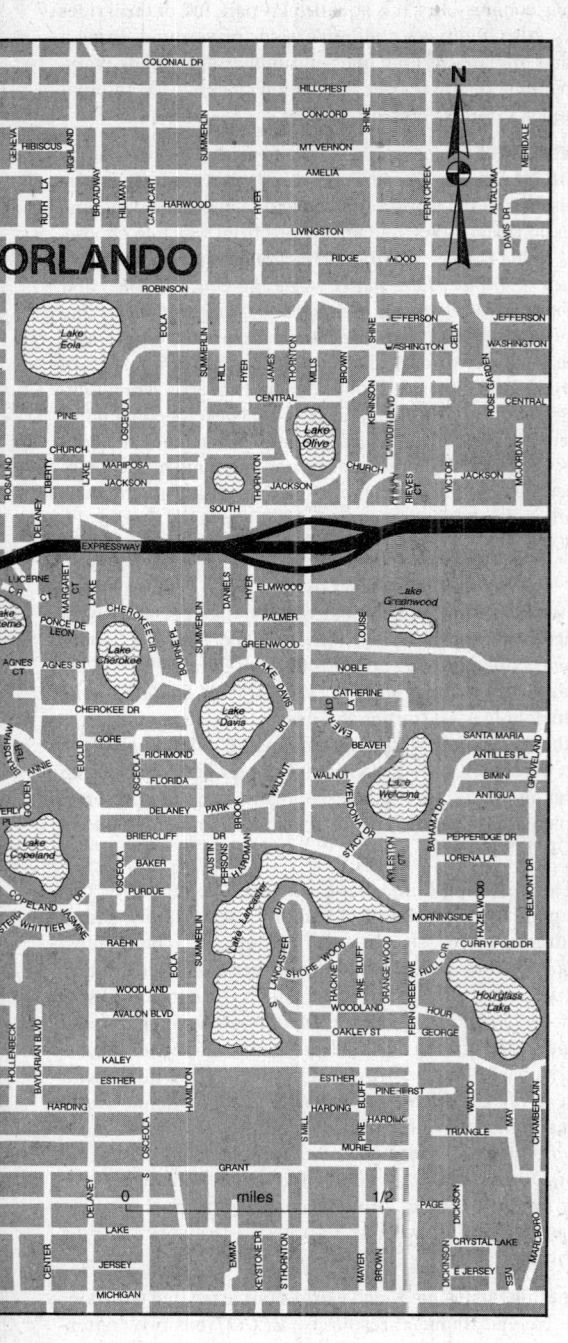

WET 'N' WILD Among connoisseurs, this aquatic play park full of thrill rides gets top marks. Also, there is a children's water playground. Bring a bathing suit, and prepare for long lines on summer afternoons. Varying hours, depending on the season. Admission charge. 6200 International Dr. (phone: 351-1800; 800-992-9453).

UNIVERSAL STUDIOS FLORIDA Moviemaking comes to central Florida. Along with *Disney–MGM Studios Theme Park,* this attraction lets visitors immerse themselves in the world of movie and television production. There are over 40 rides, shows, and attractions from which to choose, including *Back to the Future...The Ride, Kongfrontation, Jaws, The E.T. Adventure, Lucy: A Tribute, Earthquake—The Big One, Jurassic Park: Behind the Scenes, Fievel's Playland, Beetlejuice's Graveyard Revue,* and *The Adventures of Rocky and Bullwinkle.* Guests can take a tram tour or walk at their own pace through the sound stages and famous sets of the world's largest studio outside Hollywood and observe actual filming in progress. Children can watch tapings of the Nickelodeon Studios programs. There are more than 20 themed eateries, including the popular *Hard Rock Café,* and 25 shops featuring one-of-a-kind movie memorabilia, collectibles, clothing, and movie- and television-theme merchandise. Open daily. Admission charge. 1000 Universal Studios Pl. (phone: 363-8000; 800-232-7827).

WALT DISNEY WORLD

Attracting more than 25 million annual visitors, this legendary park plainly shows its lasting appeal; less obvious is its sheer size. The famous *Magic Kingdom* occupies just 98 of the 27,400 acres here; *EPCOT Center* is more than twice as large, and the *Disney–MGM Studios Theme Park* is slated to double in size during this decade. The remaining acres are dotted with villas, hotels, shopping, a nonpareil swimming hole, a state-of-the-art water park, an entertainment complex, six championship golf courses, tennis courts, several lakes, and a huge nature preserve. There is still plenty of land left for future plans. The main telephone number at *WDW* is 824-4321.

MAGIC KINGDOM The glittering *Cinderella Castle* sets the mood for this lushly landscaped fantasy park full of elaborate sets, robots, sound effects, restaurants, shops, shows, and "adventures"—boat rides, roller coasters, and other amusements. Top attractions include *Pirates of the Caribbean* and *Jungle Cruise* in the park's *Adventureland* section; *Splash Mountain* and *Big Thunder Mountain* in *Frontierland;* the beautiful *Haunted Mansion* in *Liberty Square;* the wild *Space Mountain* in-the-dark coaster in *Tomorrowland;* a special celebration with Mickey Mouse at *Mickey's Starland; Fantasyland's It's a Small World,* with mechanical dolls and folk costumes; and the *Hall of Presidents* in *Liberty Square,* where a Disney-manufactured Bill Clinton recently joined the cast. During summer evenings and school holiday periods, be sure to see the brilliantly colored *SpectroMagic* light show, presented twice each evening, with an impressive fireworks display between performances.

EPCOT CENTER Something like a high-tech world's fair, executed with considerable creative and financial resources, *EPCOT* has two "entertainment worlds": *Future World*, which explores the scientific cutting edge; and *World Showcase*, which brings nations of the world to life with ethnic food, entertainment and lively shops stocked with native wares.

As in the *Magic Kingdom*, there are a few attractions here that visitors simply must not miss. In *Future World*, these include the new *InnoVentions* display featuring futuristic household appliances and other gadgets, the entire *Living Seas* pavilion, the ride inside the round ball known as *Spaceship Earth*, the *Journey into Imagination* ride, *Body Wars* and *Cranium Command* in the *Wonders of Life* pavilion, the electronic funhouse known as the *Image Works* (in the *Journey into Imagination* pavilion), and the shows in the *World of Motion* and *Horizons* pavilions. In *World Showcase*, be sure to see the movies in the Canada, China, and France pavilions, which take the travelogue to new heights, and the updated show at the *American Adventure*.

DISNEY–MGM STUDIOS THEME PARK This major Disney attraction has been expanding ever since it opened to rave reviews six years ago. Guests can spend a day at the movies—on both sides of the camera—within a fully operating television and motion picture production facility. There's a backlot and soundstage tour where visitors watch a movie or television show being filmed; *Hollywood Boulevard*, with Art Deco architecture reminiscent of old Hollywood; and a ride through some famous movie set re-creations that come remarkably to life: Gene Kelly in *Singin' in the Rain*, Julie Andrews and Dick Van Dyke in *Mary Poppins*, and Sigourney Weaver in *Aliens*. Also, Robin Williams and Walter Cronkite star in a film about the animation process as guests watch actual animators at work; the late Jim Henson's Muppets are featured in the film *MuppetVision 3-D;* and there's a live *Beauty and the Beast* show. The newest thrill at the *Studios* is *Twilight Zone Tower of Terror*, a 13-story, free-fall ride set in an old hotel. *Star Tours*, the much-acclaimed thrill attraction, is a must-see as well; and a stunt theater, a variety of restaurants, and a sound effects studio round out the offerings. Other attractions include the *Honey, I Shrunk the Kids Adventure* zone, featuring 30-foot-tall stalks of grass and over-size slides and props; and the *Voyage of the Little Mermaid* show. The very colorful *Aladdin's Caravan* parade makes its way down *Hollywood Boulevard* each day.

DISNEY VILLAGE MARKETPLACE The shops here stock everything from vintage wine to toy soldiers and stuffed animals—and then some. You can watch the boats on the lagoon go by—or rent one. Best of all, for R&R, there's the *Baton Rouge Lounge*, aboard the riverboat known as *Empress Lilly*, and *Cap'n Jack's*, across the lagoon, the home of huge strawberry margaritas.

TYPHOON LAGOON A water-fun park set on a 50-acre site that boasts the world's largest manmade watershed mountain, as well as pools for snorkeling, surfing, swimming, and sliding.

RIVER COUNTRY The perfect swimming hole, it's full of curvy water chutes that make even blasé grownups roar with delight.

- **DISCOVERY ISLAND** Crisscrossed by footpaths, this tranquil 11½-acre landfill in Bay Lake is the home of dozens of birds—some in cages or huge aviaries, others running free.

- **HOOP-DEE-DOO REVUE** A lively dinner show with singing, dancing, wisecracking, and country-style vittles. Reservations are required well in advance, as this is one of *WDW*'s most popular live shows. Pioneer Hall, *Ft. Wilderness* (phone: 934-7639).

- **PLEASURE ISLAND** Adjacent to the *Disney Village Marketplace,* this complex features movies, nightclubs, restaurants, and shops that stay open well past midnight.

- **BEHIND THE SCENES** There isn't a *Magic Kingdom* visitor around who wouldn't like to see Disney character costumes being made or talk to a Disney artist in person. The *Wonders of Walt Disney World* program makes this happen for youngsters (ages 10–15), as *Disney Learning Adventures* does for adults. For information, call 828-2405.

Sources and Resources

TOURIST INFORMATION

For details, contact the *Orlando/Orange County Convention and Visitors Bureau* (7208 Sand Lake Rd., Suite 300, Orlando, FL 32819; phone: 363-5800), which is closed weekends; the *Tourist Information Center* (8445 International Dr., *Mercado Shopping Village;* phone: 363-5872), which is open daily; the *Chamber of Commerce* (75 S. Ivanhoe Blvd., Orlando, FL 32802; phone: 425-1234) and *Walt Disney World Co.* (Box 10,000, Lake Buena Vista, FL 32830; phone: 824-4321), both of which are closed weekends. We immodestly believe that the best guides to the area are our own volumes, *Birnbaum's Walt Disney World* and *Birnbaum's Walt Disney World For Kids, By Kids* (Hyperion Books and Hearst Business Publishing, Inc.; $11.95 and $9.95 respectively). Contact the *Florida Office of Tourism* (phone: 904-487-1462) for maps, calendars of events, health updates, and travel advisories.

- **LOCAL COVERAGE** There are what's-doing sections in Friday's *Orlando Sentinel,* a daily, and in *Orlando* magazine.

- **TELEVISION STATIONS** WESH Channel 2–NBC; WCPX Channel 6–CBS; WFTV Channel 9–ABC; WMFE Channel 24–PBS; and WOFL Channel 35–Fox.

- **RADIO STATIONS** AM: WDBO 580 (news/talk/adult contemporary) and WWNZ 740 (news/talk). FM: WDIZ 100.3 (rock); WSTF 101 (Top 40); WTFM 104 (news/talk); WOMX 105.1 (adult contemporary); and WXXL 106.7 (Top 40).

- **TELEPHONE** The area code for Orlando is 407.

- **SALES TAX** The city sales tax is 6%, as is the hotel tax.

- **CLIMATE** Spring and fall temperatures average in the mid-70s F. From November through March, warmer clothing is a must for evening. Summer can be hot and humid. Always pack something for unseasonably warm or cool weather.

GETTING AROUND

AIRPORT *Orlando International Airport* is 12 to 15 miles from downtown and 28 miles from the gates of *Walt Disney World*. *Mear's Motor Shuttle* (phone: 423-5566) provides transportation from the airport to the major downtown hotels. Reserve a seat at the airport. City buses (Route No. 39) run hourly between the airport and Orlando's downtown terminal at Pine and Central; the fare is 75¢ (phone: 841-8240 for information).

BUS *World Transportation* (phone: 826-9999), *Gray Line* (phone: 422-0744), and *Rabbit* (phone: 291-2424) provide transportation from hotels all over the city to the major attractions. For schedule information on *Lynx*, the city bus system, call 841-8240; the fare is 75¢.

CAR RENTAL Most major car rental firms are represented. Orlando has one of the largest fleets of any US city, and the rates (most with unlimited mileage) are relatively modest.

TAXI *Mear's Transportation Group* (phone: 422-4561) has the largest taxi fleet in the city.

LOCAL SERVICES

AUDIOVISUAL EQUIPMENT *Blumberg Communications; Image Resources; Photosound of Orlando* (see *Business Services*, below, for all).

BABY-SITTING There are child-care facilities at the *Beach Club, Contemporary, Grand Floridian, Polynesian Village,* and *Yacht Club*, resorts at *Walt Disney World*. The *Kindercare* children's center at *WDW* (phone: 827-KIDS) is suitable for youngsters ages two through 12. The *Hilton at Walt Disney World Village* offers a "Youth Hotel" where children ages three through 12 can be accommodated. Also at *WDW*, the *Dolphin* and *Swan* hotels offer "Camp Dolphin" and "Camp Swan" for kids ages four through 12. "Camp Hyatt" is a children's program for children ages five to 15 offered at the *Grand Cypress*. The "Lollipop Lounge" at the *Marriott's Orlando World Center* is a baby-sitting service for kids ages five to 12. The *Peabody* has a "Children's Hotel" program for kids over age five, as well as a 24-hour baby-sitting service. The *Sonesta Villa* resort has *"Kids Club,"* a supervised activity program for four- to 12-year-olds.

BUSINESS SERVICES *Blumberg Communications* (7101 Presidents Dr.; Suite 210; phone: 857-4747); *Image Resources* (4545 36th St.; phone: 843-4200); and *Photosound of Orlando* (718 Virginia Dr.; phone: 898-8841).

DRY CLEANER/TAILOR *Acme Cleaners* (600 NW Moreland St.; phone: 841-2301).

LIMOUSINE *Carey Limousine* (phone: 855-0442).

MECHANICS *Car Care Center* (Floridian Way, *Walt Disney World*; phone: 824-4813); *College Park Texaco* (2610 Edgewater Dr.; phone: 841-4846).

MEDICAL EMERGENCY *Buena Vista Medical Center* (12500 Apopka Vineland Rd., immediately north of the *Disney Village Marketplace*; phone: 828-

3434); *Orlando Regional Medical Center* (1414 Kuhl Ave.; phone: 841-5111).

MESSENGER SERVICES *Magic Bee Services* (phone: 339-9667).

MONEY TRANSFERS *American Express MoneyGram* (phone: 800-926-9400 for information; 800-866-8800 for money transfers); *Western Union Financial Services* (phone: 800-325-6000 or 800-325-4176).

NATIONAL/INTERNATIONAL COURIER *DHL Worldwide Express* (phone: 851-1432 or 800-225-5345); *FedEx* (phone: 800-238-5355).

PHARMACY Prescriptions can be filled at the *Buena Vista Medical Center* (see *Medical Emergency,* above); *Central Florida Pharmacy* (1724 S. Orange Ave.; phone: 422-8144), delivery service weekdays 9 AM to 5 PM, Saturdays 9 AM to 2 PM; *Eckerd* (908 Lee Rd., off I-4; phone: 644-6908).

PHOTOCOPIES *Kinko's* (47 E. Robinson St.; phone: 839-5000), open 24 hours; *Sir Speedy* (7400 Southland Blvd., Suite 107; phone: 855-0398); *Superior Quick Print* (5744 International Dr.; phone: 345-8484).

POST OFFICE Main branch (*Orlando International Airport;* phone: 850-6288); downtown branch (46 E. Robinson St. at Magnolia St.; phone: 843-5673).

PROFESSIONAL PHOTOGRAPHER *Bruce Wilson Photography* (phone: 828-8170); *Image Creators—Robert Willmann* (phone: 380-0515).

SECRETARY/STENOGRAPHER *Adia Personnel Services* (phone: 875-1155); *Talent Tree Personnel* (phone: 851-6200).

TELECONFERENCE FACILITIES *Orlando Marriott* (see *Checking In*); *Walt Disney World Conference Center; Walt Disney World Hotel Plaza* (*Buena Vista Palace* and *Hilton Walt Disney World*).

TRANSLATOR *International Planning, Inc.* (phone: 351-0504); *School of Modern Languages* (phone: 898-5555).

WESTERN UNION/TELEX Many offices are located around the city (phone: 800-325-6000 to find the location nearest you).

SPECIAL EVENTS

The *Scottish Highland Games* in January draw huge crowds for Highland dancing and bagpipe competitions. The *Winter Park Sidewalk Art Festival,* the third weekend of March, is one of the Southeast's most prestigious such events. The *Fourth of July* brings a display of pyrotechnics. The *Florida State Air Fair,* held in nearby Kissimmee in October, has performances by the *US Navy*'s *Blue Angels,* the *Army*'s *Golden Knights,* or the *Air Force*'s *Thunder Birds.* At *Walt Disney World,* beautiful decorations are put up at *Christmastime,* and there are parties and extra-large fireworks displays on *New Year's Eve.*

MUSEUMS

Orlando has a few noteworthy institutions:

CHARLES HOSMER MORSE MUSEUM OF AMERICAN ART The highlight of this museum is its collection of Tiffany stained glass. 133 E. Welbourne Ave., Winter Park (phone: 644-3686).

ORLANDO MUSEUM OF ART In addition to permanent displays of paintings and sculpture, this museum offers frequent special exhibits. 2416 N. Mills Ave. (phone: 896-4231).

ORLANDO SCIENCE CENTER In addition to the *John Young Planetarium*, the center offers numerous exhibitions, some of which explore central Florida's ecosystem, the physical sciences, and, for children, the world of water. 810 E. Rollins St. (phone: 896-7151).

SPORTS AND FITNESS

BASEBALL The Orlando *Cubs*, a Chicago *Cubs* farm team, play at *Tinker Field* (287 S. Tampa Ave.; phone: 872-7593) during the spring and summer. The *National League* Houston *Astros* hold their spring training for about six weeks beginning in March at *Osceola County Stadium* in Kissimmee (phone: 933-5500). The *American League* Kansas City *Royals* also prepare for the season during six weeks beginning in March at *Baseball City Stadium*, 28 miles southwest of Orlando (phone: 813-424-2424).

BASKETBALL The *NBA*'s Orlando *Magic* plays home games at the *Orlando Arena* (600 W. Amelia St.; phone: 896-2442).

FISHING Bass anglers flock to Florida's third-largest lake, Tohopekaliga. To find out about nearby fishing camps, contact the *Kissimmee–St. Cloud Convention and Visitors Bureau* (phone: 847-5000).

FITNESS CENTERS The *YMCA* (433 N. Mills Ave.; phone: 896-6901) has an indoor pool, weight room, gymnasium with Nautilus equipment, outdoor track, and racquetball facilities, and is open to non-members for a fee. In addition, many hotels have health clubs for guests.

FOOTBALL The *University of Central Florida Knights* (phone: 823-1000) play at *Orlando Stadium* on campus in the fall.

GOLF Largely due to the presence of *Walt Disney World*, Orlando has a wealth of outstanding public golf courses. If you long for a round or two after (or instead of) taking in Disney's attractions, these are the best places.

TOP TEE-OFF SPOTS

Walt Disney World Veteran golfers seldom consider this resort complex for their vacations, but this ambitious attempt to be all things to all people has 99 holes of golf designed by three of the world's greatest: Pete Dye, Tom Fazio, and Joe Lee. The newer courses are Fazio's *Osprey Ridge* and Dye's *Eagle Pines*. The 7,190-yard *Magnolia* was named for the 1,000 magnolia trees scattered around its lakes, elevated tees, and greens; the 6,957-yard *Palm* course is rated among the nation's most challenging. The 6,829-yard *Lake Buena Vista* course is the third of the original Lee-designed venues. In addition, the par-36, 9-hole *Oak Trail* course offers fun for the entire family. The *Magnolia*, *Palm*, and *Lake Buena Vista* courses host the *PGA Tour's Walt Disney World/Oldsmobile Golf Classic*. Added attractions include the *Golf Studio* instructional program, which uses videotapes and one-on-one attention to hone skills and style. There also are five driving ranges and five practice putting greens, plus three pro shops where clubs and shoes may be rented (phone: 934-7639; 824-2270 for the *Golf Studio*).

Grand Cypress This Jack Nicklaus course at the *Hyatt Regency Grand Cypress* resort transcends its relatively flat terrain by creating dune-like roughs on which high grass grows; the sense of playing in a Scottish environment is inescapable. Perhaps the most notable element of the landscape is the number of two-tiered fairways. Double greens are another unusual aspect. The *New* course added 18 holes to the original 27. These factors make position play all-important and add a new dimension to playing here. Unfortunately, access to the course currently is restricted to resort guests. 1 N. Jacaranda (phone: 239-4700).

JOGGING Run around Lake Eola in downtown Orlando, on a trail at *Ft. Wilderness,* or on the roads of *WDW.*

SWIMMING *Wet 'n' Wild* and *WDW*'s *River Country* and *Typhoon Lagoon* (see *Special Places*) are good bets for a dip, and most hotels have pools. There are especially good-size pools at the *Royal Plaza* (phone: 828-2828) and within the boundaries of *WDW* at the *Contemporary* resort (phone: 824-1000), *Dolphin* resort (phone: 934-4000), and *Buena Vista Palace* hotel (phone: 827-2727).

TENNIS It's possible to play on the many lighted *Walt Disney World* courts (where court reservations, lessons, rental racquets, and even a partner-finding service are available; phone: 824-3578). Or you can play for a small fee on Orlando parks' courts (phone: 246-2161). The *Grosvenor* resort, *Royal Plaza, Buena Vista Palace, Hilton at Walt Disney World Village, Hyatt Orlando, Peabody, Hyatt Regency Grand Cypress, Marriott's Orlando World Center, Orlando Marriott, Stouffer Orlando* resort, and, at *Disney World, Contemporary, Yacht Club, Beach Club, Swan,* and *Dolphin* resorts are among the establishments with courts for guests.

THEATER AND MUSIC

Mark Two (3376 Edgewater Dr.; phone: 422-3191) features a buffet meal followed by a Broadway-style musical with a professional cast. At *King Henry's Feast* (8984 International Dr.; phone: 351-5151), a four-course repast is served in true Elizabethan style, while some of the Bard's characters perform. *Mardi Gras* (8445 International Dr.; phone: 351-5151) offers a cabaret with a New Orleans–style jazz band along with a four-course Louisiana dinner. *Wild Bill's Wild West Dinner Show* (5260 W. US 192; phone: 351-5151) serves up a four-course Southern-style meal, accompanied by country-and-western music and an entertaining show. The *Civic Center of Central Florida* (1001 E. Princeton St.; phone: 896-7365) features musicals, dramas, and mysteries. Programs of dance, music, and theater are often presented at the *Bob Carr Performing Arts Centre* (401 W. Livingston St.; phone: 849-2001). Concerts, ice shows, and the circus are held at the *Orlando Arena* (600 W. Amelia St.; phone: 849-2020).

NIGHTCLUBS AND NIGHTLIFE

Once a pair of decaying hotels in a depressed downtown area, the *Church Street Station* complex of bars, shops, and restaurants (129 W. Church St.; phone: 422-2434), which charges an admission fee in the evening, is now very popular, thanks in part to a one-year admission pass for locals and frequent tourists. Adjoining it is the *Church Street Station Exchange* (124 W. Pine; phone: 422-2434, ext. 291), a complex of specialty shops and informal restaurants, which does not charge admission. There's Dixieland to keep things lively at the vast *Rosie O'Grady's Good Time Emporium,* specialty cocktails at the plant-and-wicker-decked *Apple Annie's Courtyard,* Top 40 at *Phineas Phogg's Balloon Works,* live rock 'n' roll at *Orchid Garden Bellroom,* traditional American and continental food at *Lili Marlene's,* oysters and other seafood at *Crackers Oyster Bar,* and country music plus barbecue and all the fixings at the *Cheyenne Saloon & Opera House.* Be aware that the charge for many specialty drinks at these clubs includes the price of the glass (you can turn it in at the gift shop for a refund).

WDW has a variety of nightspots, from the elegant, intimate *Empress Lilly Lounge* and the comfortable *Village Lounge,* which attracts jazz entertainers, to the mad, merry *Baton Rouge Lounge,* which features Disney's own more than competent musician-comedians. At *Pleasure Island,* try the *Jazz Company,* the *Comedy Warehouse,* the *Neon Armadillo,* or *Mannequins,* or catch a movie at the adjacent *AMC* theaters.

Best in Town

CHECKING IN

Most Orlando-area accommodations cluster along International Drive and nearby Sand Lake Road at the Orlando city limits, a 10- to 15-minute drive from *WDW;* along the east-west US 192, which intersects I-4 in Kissimmee near *WDW;* and within *WDW* itself. Expect to pay $150 to $300 per night for a double room at those places designated as expensive; $80 to $150 at those identified as moderate, and less than $80 at those listed as inexpensive. Rates are occasionally less during quiet periods in winter. Unless otherwise noted, hotel rooms have air conditioning, private baths, TV sets, and telephones. All hotels are in the 407 area code unless otherwise indicated.

WITHIN WALT DISNEY WORLD—WDW-OWNED PROPERTIES

For both facilities and convenience, the hotels and villas owned by the Disney organization can't be beat, and the addition of four inexpensive and moderately priced resorts means that even budget-conscious travelers can enjoy staying right on the *Walt Disney World* property. For details, call *WDW* Central Reservations (phone: 934-7639). There are meeting facilities at many of the resorts and at the *WDW Conference Center.* For details about organizing a *Walt Disney World* meeting or convention, call 828-3200.

VERY EXPENSIVE

Grand Floridian This 900-room, Victorian-style resort, with broad verandahs and gabled roofs, is *WDW*'s first luxury hotel. A turn-of-the-century theme predominates—in everything from the room decor to the staff's Edwardian costumes. Facilities include five restaurants, two lounges, a pool, a health club, a marina, and a meeting space. Near the *Magic Kingdom* (phone: 824-3000).

EXPENSIVE

Beach Club Like its adjacent sister hotel, the *Yacht Club*, this 580-room resort was designed by noted architect Robert A. M. Stern. A beach motif dominates its decor from the spacious rooms to the seafood restaurant. The two hotels share a host of convention and sports facilities, including a marina, tennis courts, and a health club. Near *EPCOT Center* (phone: 934-8000).

Contemporary This bustling 1,050-room hotel offers magical views, a lake's-edge location, three restaurants, two terrific pools, and one of the biggest gamerooms anywhere. And the monorail runs right through its 90-foot-high lobby. There are also meeting facilities. Near the *Magic Kingdom* (phone: 824-1000).

Disney's Village Resort Delightful one-, two-, and three-bedroom treehouse-type villas surrounded by pines and peacocks overlook a lake and a golf course. Other types of villa accommodations are available. All are equipped with kitchens and are especially good values for families. Near the shops at *Disney Village Marketplace* (phone: 827-1100).

Dolphin The 1,510-room *Dolphin* and its sister hotel, the *Swan* (see below), comprise the Southeast's largest hotel and convention complex. Designed by architect Michael Graves, they epitomize what is known as entertainment architecture—you can't miss the two 55-foot dolphins atop the hotel. Several restaurants and bars as well as an enormous pool and state-of-the-art fitness center keep visitors busy. Near *EPCOT Center* (phone: 934-4000).

Polynesian This resort's 853 rooms are set in several lakeside buildings on lushly landscaped grounds; the atmosphere is tranquil, the architecture tropical. The Polynesian motif pervades several eating spots and lounges, and there are two pools, a children's program, and a marina. Near the *Magic Kingdom* (phone: 824-2000).

Swan With its two 55-foot swan statues, this distinctive 760-room hotel faces the *Dolphin*, its sister property, across Crescent Lake. Decorated in coral and turquoise, the Michael Graves–designed hotel offers vast meeting spaces, several restaurants and lounges, eight lighted tennis courts, a large pool, and a fitness center. Near *EPCOT Center* (phone: 934-3000).

Wilderness Lodge The newest hotel in the *Magic Kingdom* area is a comfortably rustic re-creation of US national park lodges. Its 780 rooms and two restaurants evoke the overall American West theme. Bike and boat rentals are available, and there's an innovative playground and swimming area. Between the *Contemporary* resort and *Fort Wilderness* (phone: 824-3200).

Yacht Club Like its sister property, the *Beach Club,* this 635-room property, designed by architect Robert A. M. Stern, is set on a 25-acre lake. Its nautical theme extends to the guestrooms, two restaurants, and two lounges. The resort shares a wide range of sports and convention facilities with the *Beach Club*. Near *EPCOT Center* (phone: 934-7000).

MODERATE

The Caribbean Beach This 2,112-room resort is composed of five brightly colored villages—each named for a Caribbean island—set on a 42-acre lake. Each has its own pool. The island theme continues throughout the rooms and the six counter-service restaurants. Near *EPCOT Center* and the *Disney–MGM Studios Theme Park* (phone: 934-3400).

Dixie Landings This plantation-style resort, divided into "parishes," evokes the upriver South. Its 2,048 rooms are in either the elegant, columned Mansion homes or the more rustic Bayou buildings. The food court and restaurant are designed to resemble a cotton mill. There are several pools, boat and bike rentals, and a fishing hole. Near *EPCOT Center* (phone: 934-6000).

Port Orleans Reminiscent of the architectural style of the French Quarter in New Orleans, this 1,008-room resort offers creole cooking in its restaurant. Bike and boat rentals are available, and there's a pool and water slide shaped like a serpent. Near *EPCOT Center* (phone: 934-5000).

INEXPENSIVE

All-Star Sports Sports are the thing here; there are five separate buildings, each devoted to a different sport—tennis, football, surfing, baseball, and basketball. Even the pool is shaped like a baseball diamond. The rooms are comparatively small, and there is a food court for informal dining. Near the *Disney–MGM Studios Theme Park* (phone: 939-5000).

Fort Wilderness Campground Accommodations at this 780-acre area of cypress and pine range from campsites to luxurious villa-like trailers, complete with bathrooms, TV sets, and full kitchens (the latter are comparable in price to expensive hotel rooms). There's also a marina, a beach, and a number of waterways for fishing and canoeing. Southeast of the *Magic Kingdom* (phone: 824-2900).

WITHIN WALT DISNEY WORLD—HOTEL PLAZA

The following hotels are not Disney-owned, but they are designated as "official" hotels and are in *WDW* within walking distance of the *Disney Village Marketplace* and *Pleasure Island*. Reservations for all of these properties can be made through *WDW* Central Reservations (phone: 934-7639). All are moderate to expensive depending on the season.

Buena Vista Palace Our favorite in the complex, this hotel has 1,028 handsomely decorated rooms embellished with Mickey Mouse telephones and old-fashioned ceiling fans (as well as air conditioning), plus outstanding sporting facilities and several restaurants. The convention facility has more than 90,000 square feet of meeting space, with 40 meeting rooms and 58 suites. 1900 Buena Vista Dr. (phone: 827-2727; 800-327-2990; fax: 827-6034).

Guest Quarters Each of the 229 suites at this resort features a wet bar, refrigerator, microwave, and three TV sets. Other amenities include a restaurant, a pool, lighted tennis courts, and a gameroom. The largest of the four meeting rooms accommodates up to 100 people. 2305 Hotel Plaza Blvd. (phone: 934-1000; 800-424-2900; fax: 934-1011).

Hilton at Walt Disney World Set on 23 acres, this 813-room hotel features nine restaurants and lounges, two lighted tennis courts, two pools, and a "Youth Hotel" for guests with children. Meeting space can accommodate up to 2,350 people. 1751 Hotel Plaza Blvd. (phone: 827-4000; 800-782-4414; fax: 827-6380).

Howard Johnson This handsome 323-room resort consists of a 14-story tower (the elevators have glass walls) and a six-story annex. Facilities include three pools, a restaurant, and a conference center that can accommodate up to 200. 1805 Hotel Plaza Blvd. (phone: 828-8888; 800-223-9930; fax: 827-4623).

Royal Plaza Each of the rooms at this newly renovated, 396-room high-rise hotel has a patio or balcony. In addition to its family-oriented restaurant, facilities include tennis courts, a spa, and a pool. The hotel specializes in meetings for under 300 people. 1905 Hotel Plaza Blvd. (phone: 828-2828; 800-248-7890; fax: 827-6338).

OUTSIDE WDW

EXPENSIVE

Hyatt Regency Grand Cypress This glittering, 750-room luxury hotel is the star of a 1,500-acre complex that has more facilities than most visitors can ever use, including one of the largest free-form pools anywhere. The 45-hole, Jack Nicklaus–designed golf course is surrounded by some 146 luxury villas. There are seven restaurants as well as 24-hour room service, a concierge desk, and express checkout. Secretarial services, photocopying, A/V equipment, and computers can be provided. Meeting space can accommodate up to 2,700 people. At the villas, the *Grand Cypress Executive Meeting Center* offers meeting space for up to 200. 1 Grand Cypress Blvd., Lake Buena Vista (phone: 239-1234; 800-233-1234; fax: 239-3800; for the villas 239-4700; 800-835-7377; fax: 239-7219).

Marriott's Orlando World Center A 1,503-room, 27-story resort hotel set on nearly 200 beautifully landscaped acres, it's just minutes from *EPCOT Center*. Features include an 11-story lobby atrium, four pools, nine lighted tennis courts, an 18-hole Joe Lee golf course, a new miniature golf course, a complete health spa, a gameroom, seven restaurants, three lounges, 24-hour room service, and a concierge desk. The vast meeting facilities offer 150,000 square feet on one level; secretarial services, A/V equipment, photocopying, and computers all are available. World Center Dr. (phone: 239-4200; 800-621-0638; fax: 238-8777).

Peabody Orlando The sister property of the well-known *Peabody* in Memphis, this imposing 27-story, 891-room hotel is International Drive's most luxurious. Facilities include a pool that's twice Olympic size, four lighted tennis courts, a health club, a fitness trail, a gameroom, 24-hour room service, and a concierge desk. The hotel is located directly across from the *Orlando/Orange County Convention Center*, but also has 54,000 square feet of meeting space on site. A/V equipment, secretarial services, photocopiers, and computers are available. The famous Peabody ducks are here, too: every day at 11 AM, they waddle into the enormous lobby, down the red carpet, and into the marble fountain—a spectacle that attracts hotel guests and locals. (They return via the same route at 5 PM.) There's also a good restaurant called *Dux* that serves imaginative American nouvelle cuisine. 9801 International Dr. (phone: 352-4000; 800-732-2639; fax: 351-0073).

Stouffer Orlando This 780-room property overlooking *Sea World* is built around a 10-story atrium replete with free-flying birds and exotic fish. A fitness center, five tennis courts, a pool, four restaurants, 24-hour room service, and a concierge desk round out the offerings. A convention center has 185,000 square feet of meeting space, including a 36,000-square-foot ballroom. 6677 Sea Harbor Dr. (phone: 351-5555; 800-327-6677; fax: 351-9991).

MODERATE

Doubletree Club The 167 rooms, decorated in seafoam green and mauve, come with either two double beds or a queen-size bed and a sleep sofa. Bathrooms are small, however. A restaurant, a pool, an exercise room, a gameroom, and laundry facilities round out the amenities. 8688 Palm Pkwy., Lake Buena Vista (phone: 239-8500; 800-228-2846; fax: 239-8591).

Orlando Marriott Arranged in two-story stucco villas scattered around landscaped grounds, the 1,076 rooms here are popular with business travelers (it's convenient to the *Orlando/Orange County Convention Center*) but fine for any visitor in search of quiet. Facilities include two restaurants, three heated pools, four lighted tennis courts, a jogging trail, a children's playground, and 27,000 square feet of meeting space. 8001 International Dr. (phone: 351-2420; 800-421-8001; fax: 345-5611).

Quality Suites Maingate East This hotel features 225 one- and two-bedroom suites, each with a full kitchen. Spacious bathrooms are a plus. 5876 W. Irlo Bronson Memorial Hwy., Kissimmee (phone: 396-8040; 800-848-4148; fax: 396-6766).

Sonesta Villa Resort This full-service escape set on a tranquil lake is about 10 miles from *Walt Disney World* and 2 miles from *Sea World*. There are 370 one- and two-bedroom villas, all with fully equipped kitchenettes. Located on more than 97 acres, it offers a heated pool, 11 Jacuzzis, two tennis courts, three children's playgrounds, a gameroom, and a small health club. 10000 Turkey Lake Rd. (phone: 352-8051; 800-424-0708; fax: 345-5384).

EATING OUT

Orlando's growth during the last decade has attracted chefs from all over the world, so good dining experiences are easy to find. Expect to pay more than $150 for dinner for two at the restaurant listed as very expensive; between $50 and $75 at those places described as expensive; between $40 and $50 at those categorized as moderate; and less than $40 at those rated inexpensive. Prices do not include drinks, wine, tax, or tips. Unless otherwise noted, restaurants are open for lunch and dinner. All restaurants are in the 407 area code unless otherwise indicated.

VERY EXPENSIVE

Victoria & Albert's In *Walt Disney World*'s *Grand Floridian*, this small but elegant dining room seats only 65 and serves an ever-changing menu on fine china. All the waitresses and waiters are "named" Victoria or Albert. Jackets required for men. No smoking allowed. Open daily. Reservations necessary. Major credit cards accepted. *Grand Floridian Resort, Walt Disney World* (phone: 824-2383).

EXPENSIVE

Chatham's Place Two talented young chefs (who happen to be brothers) present a different menu each season. Specialties created in the open kitchen may include rack of lamb, black grouper in pecan butter, and lobster bisque. No smoking allowed. Open daily. Reservations advised. Major credit cards accepted. 7575 Dr. Phillips Blvd. (phone: 345-2992).

Chefs de France Three of France's finest chefs—Paul Bocuse, Roger Vergé, and Gaston LeNôtre—have created a menu of fine nouvelle cuisine specialties. The turn-of-the-century decor is as appealing as the food. There's also a separate menu "for the little gourmet" (kids under 12) at reduced prices. A first-rate bistro thrives upstairs. No smoking allowed. Open daily. Reservations necessary (they are available to *Walt Disney World* hotel guests by telephone—check with the hotel desk clerks; otherwise, reservations are available only in person at *EPCOT Center*). Major credit cards accepted. *World Showcase, EPCOT Center, Walt Disney World.*

Le Cordon Bleu The unpretentious decor of this popular spot gives no hint of the quality of the food—mushrooms filled with crabmeat and glazed with Mornay sauce, snails in garlic butter, rack of lamb, and fresh fish specialties. Closed Sundays. Reservations advised. Major credit cards accepted. 537 W. Fairbanks, Winter Park (phone: 647-7575).

Empress Room Elegant, cordial service and surroundings replete with crystal and gold leaf make this dining room in the *Empress Lilly* riverboat a favorite among residents out for a big celebration. Jackets required for men. No smoking allowed. Open daily. Reservations necessary well in advance. Major credit cards accepted. *Disney Village Marketplace, Walt Disney World* (phone: 828-3900).

Jordan's Grove Set under a canopy of oak trees, this warm-hearted place serves American regional cuisine with a menu that changes daily. Expect the extraordinary here; it's not the place for a steak-and-potatoes meal.

Closed Mondays. Reservations advised. Major credit cards accepted. 1300 S. Orlando Ave., Maitland (phone: 628-0020).

Maison & Jardin An elegant dining spot with high ceilings and vast windows overlooking formal gardens, nicknamed "Mason Jar" by locals. The menu features fresh game, fish, meat, and fowl. Open daily. Reservations advised. Major credit cards accepted. 430 S. Wymore Rd., Altamonte Springs (phone: 862-4410).

MODERATE

La Cantina The generously portioned steaks and Italian specialties make this one of the most popular dining spots in Orlando. Closed Sundays and Mondays. Reservations advised. MasterCard and Visa accepted. 4721 E. Colonial Dr. (phone: 894-4491).

Pebbles This café is set amid lots of indoor greenery. Interesting appetizers include baked goat cheese served in tomato *concassée* (purée) with garlic bread. There are fresh seafood dishes and steaks daily and a variety of salads, pasta, and soups. Open daily. No reservations. Major credit cards accepted. Crossroad Plaza, State Rd. 535 (phone: 827-1111).

INEXPENSIVE

Bubbalou's Bodacious BBQ This unpretentious spot has 20 picnic tables, red ruffled curtains, and baseball caps hanging from the ceiling. The food is hot, fast, fresh, and smoky. Closed Sundays. No reservations. MasterCard and Visa accepted. 1471 Lee Rd., Winter Park (phone: 628-1212).

Bubble Room This place is pure kitsch—from the yellow-brick path leading to the front door to the waiters and waitresses known as Bubble Scouts. Most of the selections are classic American: burgers, fish platters, and chili for lunch; steaks, chicken, and seafood for dinner. Desserts are obscenely huge. Open daily. No reservations. Major credit cards accepted. 1351 S. Orlando Ave., Maitland (phone: 628-3331).

MORE WALT DISNEY WORLD RESTAURANTS

Most first-time visitors are surprised to discover that *WDW* offers unusual specialties such as amaretto-flavored soufflés along with familiar hot dogs and hamburgers. Even cafeterias and fast-food stops have a bit of atmosphere that makes them a little special. Where you eat at *WDW* will be determined by where you are; below are a few of the more noteworthy spots.

In the *Magic Kingdom, Crystal Palace,* an old-fashioned glass-and-plant-filled cafeteria on Main Street, is very pretty. *Tony's Town Square Café* nearby serves delicious Monte Cristo sandwiches. *King Stefan's Banquet Hall* in *Cinderella Castle* has waitress service (you must reserve in person, first thing in the morning).

EPCOT Center offers even greater variety. In *Future World,* at the *Living Seas* pavilion, try the fresh seafood at the *Coral Reef* restaurant, complete with a panoramic view of a living underwater coral reef. *Stargate* serves unique breakfast pizza. In *World Showcase,* don't miss Canada's *Le Cellier,* a cafeteria that offers a tasty pork and potato pie called *tourtière;* Italy's *Alfredo's,* for good Italian fare; Germany's *Biergarten,* for its hearty food and oompah entertainment; Mexico's *San Angel Inn,* which takes Mexican fare beyond tacos; and China's *Nine Dragons,* where meals are prepared in a variety of provincial cooking styles. Dinner reservations, a must at many restaurants, must be made in person in *Earth Station.* (*WDW* hotel guests can make reservations by telephone; check with the hotel desk clerks.) Otherwise, arrive at the front gate a half hour before the published park opening, decide where to eat, and send the speediest member of your group to book your table when the park opens. (Be aware that most restaurants are usually booked for prime dinner times within an hour of the park's opening.) Lunch reservations can be made at the restaurant in person on the day of the seating or at *Earth Station.* Booking procedures sometimes change, so call on arrival at *WDW* (phone: 824-4321).

The eateries at the *Disney–MGM Studios* offer trendy cuisine in an atmosphere reminiscent of old Hollywood. The *Hollywood Brown Derby* features the famous Cobb Salad created by owner Bob Cobb in the 1930s. Try the Fettuccine Derby, pasta in a parmesan sauce with chicken, red and green peppers, and filet of red snapper—and leave room for dessert! The *50's Prime Time Café* recalls 1950s sitcoms, with decor straight out of a suburban kitchen. The menu offers new versions of old standbys, such as vegetarian chili and Magnificent Meat Loaf, made with fresh veal and shiitake mushrooms and served with mashed potatoes and gravy. Or eat under the stars (indoors) at the *Sci-Fi Dine-In Theater* where diners sit in cut-out 1950s-style cars in a drive-in movie setting. For reservations at all three places, call 828-4000.

The superb banana-stuffed French toast served in *Polynesian Village's Coral Isle Café* is worth a detour. At the *Grand Floridian,* the octagonal *Narcoosee's* offers seafood and steaks in a delightful setting. Try *Ariel's* for seafood at the *Beach Club;* and the *Yacht Club* has the *Yachtsman's Steakhouse,* a prime choice for beef.

At the *Disney Village Marketplace,* the comfortable *Chef Mickey's Village* restaurant has fine lake views. At *Pleasure Island* there's the *Portobello Yacht Club* for imaginative Italian fare and pizza, or the *Fireworks Factory* for barbecued ribs and chicken. Aboard the *Empress Lilly* riverboat, there's the charming *Fisherman's Deck,* with a view of a churning paddle wheel.

Travelers with children should make note of the special breakfasts with Disney characters (phone: 824-4321; 934-7639 for reservations).

Philadelphia

At-a-Glance

SEEING THE CITY

You don't have to *run* up the steps of the *Philadelphia Museum of Art* (26th and Parkway; phone: 763-8100) the way Sylvester Stallone did in *Rocky* to get the same far-reaching view of the city's skyline. Another exhilarating view, encompassing the city, its surrounding rivers, and New Jersey, can be had from the observation deck of *City Hall Tower* (Broad and Market Sts.; phone: 569-3187). Tours of the *Tower* include exhibits and a narrated history of *City Hall*. Some mornings are reserved for school groups; check ahead by calling 686-9074.

SPECIAL PLACES

Philadelphia's tight city blocks and narrow streets make it great for walking, not driving. Streets, laid out in checkerboard fashion, are easy to understand, but they always are choked with traffic. The city's main places of interest are clustered in *Independence Hall National Historical Park* and around *Fairmount Park* in West Philadelphia.

INDEPENDENCE HALL HISTORICAL AREA

VISITORS' CENTER This is a good place to launch a tour of the historical area and pick up maps and brochures. There's also a half-hour film that provides helpful historical background. You can park your car in the Second Street garage (behind the visitors' center between Chestnut and Walnut Sts.) or the underground garage at Fifth and Market Streets. Open daily except some winter holidays that change from year to year. Third and Chestnut Sts. (phone: 597-8974).

INDEPENDENCE NATIONAL HISTORICAL PARK "The most historic square mile in America," it's what everyone comes to see. Within the park are the major colonial and Revolutionary era buildings, which are listed below. No admission charge. The general park area runs from Third to Seventh Street between Market and Walnut Streets (phone: 627-1776 for a 24-hour recording).

INDEPENDENCE HALL The attraction most indelibly associated with the city, its solid tower, massive clock, and graceful spire are unmistakable. Here, the Declaration of Independence was signed and, 11 years later, the Constitution was written. Guided tours are given, beginning in the East Wing. No admission charge. Chestnut St. between Fifth and Sixth (phone: 597-8974).

CONGRESS HALL The first *US Congress* met here, between 1789 and 1800. George Washington delivered his final congressional address in these halls; here, too, the Bill of Rights was adopted. No admission charge. Sixth and Chestnut Sts. (phone: 597-3974).

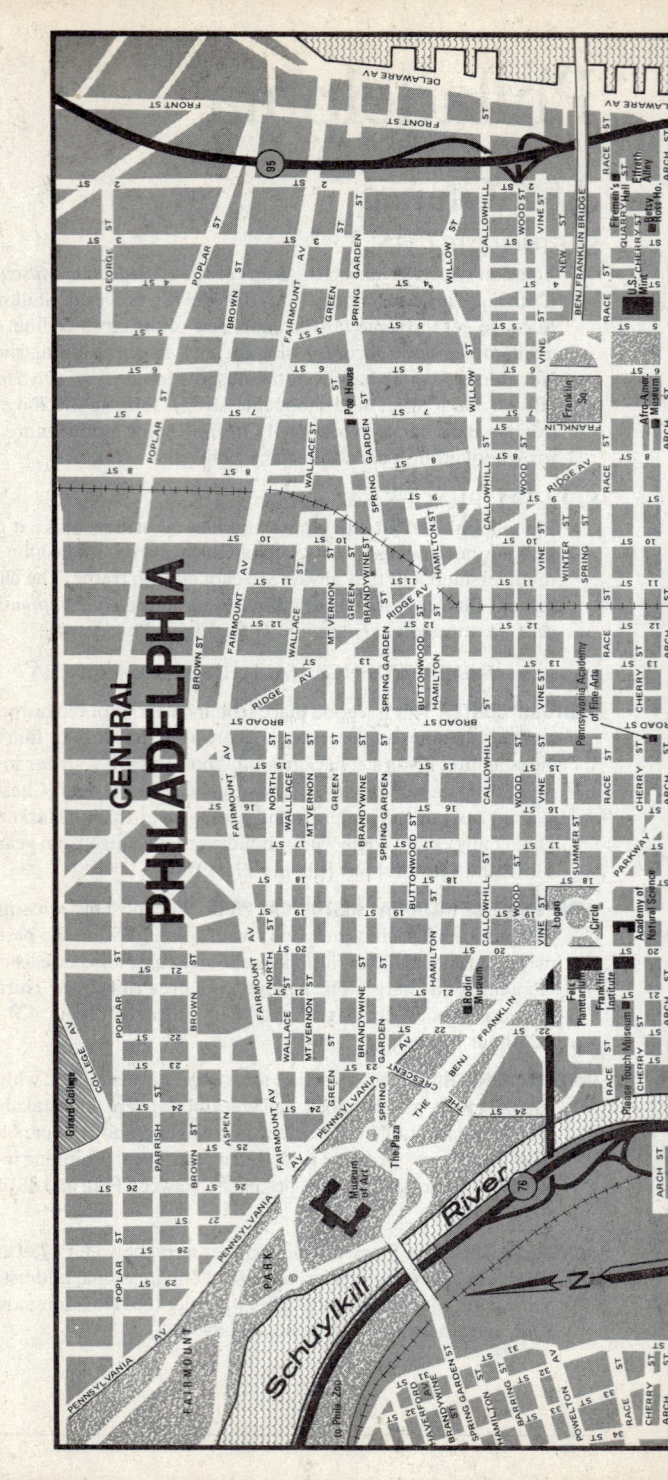

OLD CITY HALL The first *US Supreme Court* issued judgments from the bench inside this building from 1789 until 1800, when it moved with the rest of the federal government to Washington, DC. No admission charge. Sixth and Chestnut Sts. (phone: 597-8974).

INDEPENDENCE MALL Across the street from the various halls, this leafy stretch of grass, fountains, and tree-lined walks contains the glass pavilion housing the Liberty Bell. It was moved from *Independence Hall* so more people could see it. No admission charge. Market and Fifth Sts. (phone: 597-8974).

CARPENTERS' HALL The *Carpenters' Company Guild* was housed here during the colonial era (before unions). The oldest building organization in the US still owns the hall, and early carpentry tools are on display. In 1774, the *First Continental Congress* met here. Closed Mondays; closed Tuesdays in January and February. No admission charge. 320 Chestnut St. (phone: 925-0167).

ARMY-NAVY MUSEUM (PEMBERTON HOUSE) AND MARINE CORPS MEMORIAL MUSEUM (NEW HALL) The exhibitions and collections of these military branches focus on the years 1775 to 1805. The buildings are on Carpenters' Court (leading back to *Carpenters' Hall*). No admission charge. Chestnut, between Third and Fourth Sts. (phone: 597-8974).

SECOND BANK OF THE UNITED STATES One of the earliest buildings designed by noted architect William Strickland, this early-19th-century building is a fine example of Greek Revival architecture. It houses "The Portraits of the Capitol City," which highlights people who were important in government, industry, the arts, and religion during the late 1700s. A brief slide show depicts the life of Charles Willson Peale, who painted most of the portraits. No admission charge. Chestnut, between Fourth and Fifth Sts. (phone: 597-8974).

TODD HOUSE Before she became Dolley Madison—wife of fourth president James, famed First Lady, and society hostess—she was Dolley Payne Todd, whose husband, Quaker lawyer John Todd, died of yellow fever in 1793. Their 1775 home is typical of middle class residences of the period. Free guided tours must be arranged in person at the *Visitors' Center* (Third and Chestnut Sts.) on the day of the tour. Fourth and Walnut Sts. (phone: 597-8974).

BISHOP WHITE HOUSE While the *Todd House* reflects a middle class lifestyle, this home displays the affluence of people such as Bishop William White, a politically active Episcopalian minister (from the 1770s to the 1790s) who served as rector of both *Christ Church* and *St. Peter's*. A tour of this house must be combined with the *Todd House* tour (see above). Third and Walnut Sts. (phone: 597-8974).

CHRIST CHURCH Benjamin Franklin sat in pew 70, George Washington in pew 58. The original church was built in 1695; this larger one was erected in 1745 and is significant both for its architecture and as a National Shrine. This Episcopal church remains an active parish with weekly worship services. Tours available. Closed Mondays and Tuesdays from

January through mid-March. Donations suggested. Second St. above Market (phone: 922-1695).

CHRIST CHURCH BURIAL GROUND Throw a penny on the grave of Benjamin Franklin and his wife, Deborah—it's a Philadelphia custom. Tours by appointment only year-round. Enter between Fourth and Fifth Sts. on Arch St. (phone: 922-1695).

BETSY ROSS HOUSE According to tradition, this is where George Washington directed Elizabeth Ross, an upholsterer's widow, in the stitching of the first American flag. The *Philadelphia Historical Commission*, however, says that Betsy Ross never lived here and had nothing to do with the first US flag. Make up your own mind, after you've seen this tiny cottage filled with household items and memorabilia allegedly pertinent to the famous seamstress. Closed Mondays except holidays. Donations suggested. 239 Arch (phone: 627-5343).

ELFRETH'S ALLEY This is America's oldest continuously occupied residential street, dating to 1690. Only one block long and six feet wide, it is lined with 200-year-old houses. *Elfreth's Alley* usually celebrates its annual *Fête Days* with house tours and crafts shows on the first weekend in June. The homes don't open their doors to the public again until the first Friday in December for a holiday tour. The *Museum House* (126 Elfreth's Alley) puts on special programs daily in April, May, and October through December; closed weekdays January through February, but tours can be arranged by appointment. Off Second St. between Arch and Race Sts. (phone: 574-0560).

HEADHOUSE SQUARE Built in 1775, this sole survivor of the middle-of-the-street markets that once flourished in the city is surrounded by good restaurants and revitalized shops. In summer, it hosts crafts demonstrations and concerts. Be sure to stop in at *Koffmeyer's Cookies* (Second and Lombard Sts.; phone: 922-0717) to taste some wickedly delicious cookies and pastries; an especially good choice is the Headhouse Square, a vanilla brownie peppered with chocolate chips and walnuts. Second and Pine.

FRANKLIN COURT Benjamin Franklin came to Philadelphia in 1723. In his later years he resided in a brick house on this site until his death in 1790. Although the house itself is no longer standing (it was demolished in 1812), three of the surrounding houses designed by Franklin are here, along with an 18th-century garden with a mulberry tree, a print shop, and a post office. An underground museum has Franklin stoves and a phone where you can "dial-an-opinion" from Benjamin Franklin. Open daily. No admission charge. Running from Chestnut to Market between Third and Fourth Sts (phone: 557-8974).

USS OLYMPIA AND USS BECUNA The oldest steel-hulled American warship afloat, the *Olympia* was Commodore George Dewey's flagship at Manila Bay in the Spanish-American War. Also here is the *Becuna,* a submarine used in the Pacific during World War II. Closed *Christmas* and *New Year's Day.* Admission charge. Penn's Landing, near Delaware Ave. and Spruce St. (phone: 922-1898).

PENN'S LANDING TROLLEY After leaving the USS *Olympia* and *Becuna*, take a 20-minute ride on a restored trolley that served the Delaware Valley between 1904 and 1958. The conductor provides commentary as passengers ride along Delaware Avenue between the Society Hill and Queen Village areas and beside the Delaware River, where many tall ships are berthed. Weekends and holidays from April through November; there are also two "Santa Special" weekends in December. Fare charge. Board at Delaware Ave. at Dock or Spruce St. (phone: 627-0807).

WEST PHILADELPHIA

BOATHOUSE ROW A collection of Victorian boathouses used by collegiate and club oarsmen, it's the hub of many national competitions. East River Drive, running along the east bank of the Schuylkill River, north of the *Museum of Art*. If you're driving west of the museum on the Schuylkill Expressway (Route 76), or on the West River Drive after dark, don't miss the view across the river of the historic boathouses outlined in white lights.

FAIRMOUNT PARK This huge park—with approximately 8,000 acres of meadows, gardens, creeks, trails, and bridle paths—begins at the *Philadelphia Museum of Art* and extends northwest on both sides of the Schuylkill River and Wissahickon Creek. For 25¢, you can get a detailed park map at the *Philadelphia Museum of Art*. Then be sure to take in the *Japanese House and Garden* (where, weather permitting, you can witness a tea ceremony), *Glendinning Rock Garden,* and, if children are along, *Smith Memorial Playground*. Open daily. No admission charge.

PHILADELPHIA ZOO Established in 1874, this is the nation's oldest zoo and is considered one of the best-run. More than 1,700 mammals, reptiles, and birds live within its 42 acres. There are several natural habitat displays, a children's zoo, and a safari monorail aerial tram. Don't miss the tree house. Closed *Thanksgiving, Christmas Eve, Christmas, New Year's Eve,* and *New Year's Day.* Admission charge except on Mondays from December through February. 34th St. and Girard Ave. (phone: 243-1100).

PHILADELPHIA MUSEUM OF ART In an imposing Greco-Roman Revival building constructed in 1928, it houses art from the Middle Ages and Renaissance up through the 20th century. On display are outstanding collections of French Impressionist paintings and American furniture, as well as the largest Thomas Eakins collection in the US. Notable holdings include Roger van der Weyden's 15th-century painting of the crucifixion, Peter Paul Rubens's *Prometheus Bound,* van Gogh's *Sunflowers,* Cézanne's *Bathers,* Marcel Duchamp's *Nude Descending a Staircase,* Picasso's *Three Musicians,* and the famous statue of Diana that topped New York City's first *Madison Square Garden.* There's a Japanese tea house, designed to convey the atmosphere as well as the art of Japan, a Chinese scholar's study, a large collection of arms and armor, and distinguished collections of china, porcelain, glass, jade, graphics, sculpture, and decorative arts. Closed Mondays and holidays. No admission charge on Sundays before 1 PM. 26th St. and Parkway (phone: 763-8100).

RODIN MUSEUM Sculpture, sketches, and drawings make up the largest collection of Auguste Rodin's work outside France. An afternoon can easily be spent wandering through the halls and gardens. Closed Mondays and holidays. Donations suggested. 22nd and Parkway (phone: 763-8100).

FRANKLIN INSTITUTE SCIENCE MUSEUM This huge, hands-on science museum has all kinds of new exhibits on subjects from aviation and astronomy to mechanics, light, math, patterns, and electricity. Watch light bend as it passes through concave and convex mirrors, walk through a 15,000-times-life-size heart, board a T-33 Jet Trainer, and take a ride on Philadelphia's beloved 350-ton Baldwin locomotive. Daily demonstrations show how lightning works and what energy is all about. Planetarium shows discuss black holes, satellite technology, and the constellations. The *Institute* also includes the four-story *Tuttleman Omniverse Theater* and the *Mandell Futures Center,* dubbed the "First Museum of the Future." Closed *Thanksgiving, Christmas Eve, Christmas,* and *New Year's Day.* Admission charge. 20th and Parkway (phone: 448-1200; 448-1292 for the planetarium).

OTHER SPECIAL PLACES

CITY HALL Philadelphia's most distinctive landmark has been called "an architectural nightmare," but some people praise its elaborate decor: sculpture, marble pillars, alabaster chandeliers, goldleaf ceilings, and carved mahogany. The *Tower,* at William Penn's feet, looks out on the Delaware and Schuylkill Rivers. Guided tours of the restored *Conversation Hall,* the Mayor's reception room, City Council chambers and caucus room, and the State Supreme Court are available weekdays. No admission charge. Broad and Market Sts. (phone: 568-5534).

RITTENHOUSE SQUARE Named after David and Benjamin Rittenhouse, who designed the first astronomical instruments in the US in the 18th century, Rittenhouse Square is one of the city's loveliest, most elegant residential areas. Handsome brownstones and high-rise apartment houses surround a green park, where people from all over town congregate. Art shows, flower shows, and concerts take place here in spring and summer. 18th and Walnut Sts.

US MINT The largest facility of its kind in the world, this mint can produce 10,000 coins per minute. At each observation post, a button activates a taped commentary on the different stages of the minting process. Historic coins are exhibited, and a special counter sells proof sets and medals. Closed Sundays, September through June; Saturdays, September through April; and federal holidays. Coinage machines not in operation on weekends or federal holidays. No admission charge. Fifth and Arch Sts. (phone: 597-7350).

EDGAR ALLAN POE HOUSE Known for "The Raven" and his chilling story "The Murders in the Rue Morgue," the famed American writer is said to have written "The Black Cat" and "The Gold-Bug" while living here. Closed *Thanksgiving, Christmas,* and *New Year's Day.* No admission charge. 532 N. Seventh (phone: 597-8780).

PENNSYLVANIA HORTICULTURAL SOCIETY The formal gardens of the 18th century are re-created, with flowers, shrubs, and pruned trees typical of the era. This is the oldest horticultural association in the US; it also has a botanical library. Closed weekends. No admission charge. 325 Walnut (phone: 625-8250).

READING TERMINAL MARKET Multitudes of shoppers come to forage for fresh ground horseradish and French brie. Check out the homemade soup and hot-from-the-oven shoofly pie (a molasses and crumb dessert). Ice cream at *Bassett's* is a must. Closed Sundays. 12th and Arch Sts. (phone: 922-2317).

ITALIAN MARKET Also known as *Rocky's* market, it is part of Sylvester Stallone's famous jogging trail. In south Philly, vendors line the sidewalks every day except Monday with their bargain-priced meat, fish, poultry, fruits, and vegetables along Ninth Street between Washington and Passyunk Avenues. Top off the morning's stroll with a Philly cheesesteak at *Pat's* or *Geno's,* the rivals at the south end of the market (see *Say Cheese*). Ninth St. and Washington Ave.

THOMAS H. KEAN NEW JERSEY STATE AQUARIUM This multimillion-dollar aquarium sits across the river in New Jersey. Exhibits include a "petting tank," where visitors can get in touch with skates, rays, starfish, and even small sharks; a 760,000-gallon ocean tank featuring 50 species of North Atlantic fish; a trout stream; and seals in a display that replicates their natural habitat. The auditorium offers changing shows from movies to musicals, and the *Conservation Puppet Theater* teaches children about protecting coral reefs. The *Riverbus* shuttle (phone: 800-634-4027 for schedule) between Philadelphia and the aquarium leaves regularly from Penn's Landing; the fare is $2 each way. Closed *New Year's Day, Thanksgiving,* and *Christmas*. Admission charge. 1 S. Riverside Dr., Camden, NJ (phone: 609-365-3300; 800-922-NJSA to order tickets with a credit card).

EXTRA SPECIAL

During the winter of 1777–78, General George Washington and 11,000 Revolutionary troops retreated to *Valley Forge.* The site is now a state park. The visitors' center shows a film in its museum (open daily), and the park itself has a number of interesting historical buildings, including Washington's original headquarters. There also is a self-guided auto tour; information is available at the visitors' center. Closed *Christmas*. Admission charge to the headquarters building. Take the Schuylkill Expressway (Rte. 76) west to the Valley Forge exit (about 20 miles), then follow Route 363 north to the park (phone: 783-1077).

For another kind of outdoor experience, visit *Longwood Gardens,* a horticultural display in Kennett Square (30 miles west of the city) where more than 11,000 types of plants are carefully tended on 350 acres; some of its trees were planted in the late 1700s. *Longwood Gardens* also hosts more than 300 performing arts events annually, and there is a restaurant. Take Interstate 95 south to Route 322 west, then continue about 8 miles to Route 1 south. From there, proceed another 8 miles to the entrance. Open daily. No admission charge for children under six (phone: 610-388-6741).

Just 5 miles north of the gardens on Route 1 is the *Brandywine River Museum and Conservancy,* which houses paintings by three generations of Wyeths (N. C., Andrew, and Jamie), along with works by several other artists including Maxfield Parrish and Howard Pyle. An impressive display of model trains is shown during the *Christmas* season. Closed *Christmas.* Admission charge. Located at the intersection of Rtes. 1 and 100, Chadds Ford (phone: 610-388-2700).

Sources and Resources

TOURIST INFORMATION

Located only steps from *City Hall* is the *Philadelphia Visitors Center* (16th St. at John F. Kennedy Blvd., or write to 1515 Market St., Suite 2020, Philadelphia, PA 19102.; phone: 636-1666; 800-537-7676), which is open daily. Ask specifically for the vacation packet containing the *Official Visitor's Guide* to restaurants, hotels, and tours; maps; a "Calendar of Events"; and other helpful information. Visitors may also request the *African-American Historical and Cultural Guide* and buy tickets to the *Thomas H. Kean New Jersey State Aquarium* (see *Special Places,* above). For a recording on what to see and where to go, call the Donnelley Directory Events 24-hour hotline (phone: 337-7777, ext. 2540).

LOCAL COVERAGE The *Inquirer,* morning daily; the *Daily News,* afternoon daily; *Philadelphia* magazine, monthly.

TELEVISION STATIONS KYW Channel 3–NBC; WPVI Channel 6–ABC; WCAU Channel 10–CBS; and WHYY Channel 12–PBS.

RADIO STATIONS AM: WIP 610 (sports); KYW 1060 (news); and WCAU 1210 (news/talk). FM: WHYY 90.9 (news/talk/public affairs); WXTU 92.5 (country); WFLN 95.7 (classical music); WUSL 98.9 (black urban); WMGK 102.9 (soft rock); and WEGX 106.1 (jazz).

TELEPHONE The area code for Philadelphia is 215.

SALES TAX There is a 7% sales tax on most purchases, excluding many clothing items.

CLIMATE Winter temperatures in Philadelphia generally hover in the 20s and 30s F. Spring and autumn are the best times to visit—temperatures then are usually in the 50s to 70s. Summer tends to be hot and sticky, with thermometer readings in the 80s and 90s.

GETTING AROUND

AIRPORT *Philadelphia International Airport* is a 30-minute drive to Center City (up to an hour during rush periods). The *SEPTA (Southeastern Pennsylvania Transportation Authority) Airport Express* train (phone: 580-7800) makes the 20-minute trip to the city's main terminal, *30th St. Station,* for $5. Trains stop at most of the airport terminals every half hour.

BUS, RAIL, AND SUBWAY *SEPTA (Southeastern Pennsylvania Transportation Authority)* will take you everywhere, by bus, trolley, train, or subway. The fare is $1.50. A good *SEPTA* map showing routes for all public transportation is available at newsstands and rail stations. The *Ben Franklin* line runs from Penn's Landing to the *Museum of Art* by way of Market Street and costs 50¢. Buses and stops are marked with red kites (phone: 580-7800).

CAR RENTAL Philadelphia is served by all the national firms.

HORSE-DRAWN CARRIAGE TOURS Tours depart from the carriage stand on Chestnut between Fifth and Sixth Streets daily, weather permitting. After 6 PM, carriages depart from New Market Square on Second Street, between Pine and South Streets (phone: 922-6840).

TAXI Cab fare is costly, but worth it for short hops to transport three or four people. Hail taxis in the street or do as Philadelphians do and pick them up in front of the *30th Street* train station, the *Greyhound/Trailways* bus terminal, or the nearest hotel, where most of them wait for customers. Call *Yellow Cab Company* (phone: 922-8400), *Quaker City Cab* (phone: 728-8000), or *United Cab Association* (phone: 238-9500).

TROLLEY TOURS *American Trolley Tours* (phone: 333-2119) offers a two-and-one-half-hour narrated tour from Rittenhouse Square and Antique Row to Penn's Landing and Society Hill, and includes time at *Independence National Historical Park*. The trolley leaves four times daily from the *Philadelphia Visitors Center* (16th and John F. Kennedy Blvd.) and twice daily from the visitors' center at Third and Chestnut Streets, and will stop at hotels upon request.

The *Philadelphia Museum of Art* runs a two-hour narrated trolley tour of three of *Fairmount Park*'s seven restored mansions—*Cedar Grove, Laurel Hill, Lemon Hill, Mt. Pleasant, Strawberry, Sweetbriar,* and *Woodford*. Tours leave from the Third Street visitors' center, the 16th Street visitors' center, and the museum, daily, June through November except Mondays and holidays (phone: 684-7926). It's best to arrange several weeks in advance. Don't miss the *Christmas* tour the first week in December (see *Special Events*).

WALKING TOURS The *Foundation for Architecture* offers a variety of walking and bus tours, organized around a particular theme, such as skyscrapers, Art Deco architecture, taverns, or a specific neighborhood. Another noteworthy option is "Philadelphia Illuminated," a nighttime tour that displays the bright lights of the city. For a walking tour brochure, contact the foundation at 1 Penn Center, Suite 1165,

Philadelphia, PA 19103 (phone: 569-3187; 569-TOUR for recorded information).

LOCAL SERVICES

AUDIOVISUAL EQUIPMENT *Joseph Goins Multimedia Specialists Inc.* (phone: 843-6032), for videotaping, photography, audiovisual equipment rental; *Projection Inc.* (phone: 864-0456), audiovisual supplies.

BUSINESS SERVICES *CPS Services* (1700 Walnut St., Suite 809; phone: 985-9535), typing and notary public weekdays 8 AM to 5 PM.

COMPUTER RENTAL *PCR Personal Computer Rental of Philadelphia* (phone: 727-6666), for computers, printers, and presentation equipment; *USPC Rental* (phone: 963-9699).

DRY CLEANER/TAILOR *Academy Cleaners* (1417 Locust St.; phone: 732-2627); *British Imperial* (several locations including 1322 Locust St. at Juniper St.; phone: 545-6880).

LIMOUSINE *Lazer Limousine Service* (phone: 525-0144); *Premiere Limousine Service* (phone: 586-6008).

MEDICAL EMERGENCY *Hahnemann University Hospital* (Broad and Vine Sts.; phone: 448-7963).

MESSENGER SERVICES *Quick Courier Service* (phone: 592-9933); *Rapid Delivery and Messenger Service* (phone: 496-9600), same-day service.

MONEY TRANSFERS *American Express MoneyGram* (phone: 800-926-9400 for information; 800-866-8800 for money transfers); *Western Union Financial Services* (phone: 800-325-6000 or 800-325-4176).

NATIONAL/INTERNATIONAL COURIER *DHL Worldwide Express* (phone: 461-8111); *FedEx* (phone: 923-3085).

PHARMACY *Penn Towers* (1821 JFK Blvd.; phone: 568-2366), open weekdays 8:30 AM to 6 PM.

PHOTOCOPIES AND PRINTING SERVICES *The Copy Center, Inc.* (two locations: 615 Chestnut, phone: 928-1900; and 1805 JFK Blvd., phone: 448-2100).

POST OFFICE Central office (30th and Market Sts.; phone: 895-8989 during business hours; 895-8981, a 24-hour line for information and parcel pickup arrangements).

PROFESSIONAL PHOTOGRAPHER *Addison Geary* (3810 Lancaster Ave.; phone: 387-3342); *Quaker Photo Service Co.* (1025 Arch St.; phone: 922-4444), photo lab processing only; *Standard Photo Service* (2031 Chestnut St.; phone: 561-0770).

SECRETARY/STENOGRAPHER *Accurate Business Services* (801 Arch St., Suite 603; phone: 592-9280), typing and word processing service only; *Headquarters Business Centers (HQ)* (15th and Market Sts.; phone: 246-3400) provides word processing, dictation via telephone, telex and fax service, photocopying, office suites and conference rooms with full secretarial staff.

TELECONFERENCE FACILITIES *Headquarters Companies* (phone: 246-3400).

TRANSLATOR *Berlitz* (1608 Walnut St., Suite 1701; phone: 735-8500), written translation and oral interpretation, closed weekends; *ICOA Translations* (phone: 875-0975), written translations into English only.

WESTERN UNION/TELEX Many offices are located around the city (phone: 800-325-6000 to find the location nearest you).

OTHER *Meeting Planners* (phone: 494-2323).

SPECIAL EVENTS

The *Mummers Parade,* a Philadelphia tradition on January 1, is eight hours of string bands strutting up Broad Street, their members dressed in elaborate suits. The *Philadelphia Flower and Garden Show* is held at the *Civic Center* (34th and Civic Center Blvd.) the second week in March. During the first two weeks in May, many residents open their homes and gardens for tours as part of *Philadelphia Open House.* Make arrangements through the visitors' center (Third and Chestnut Sts.; phone: 597-8974). Come fall, *Super Sunday,* usually the second Sunday in October, is a day of free culture at institutions along the Benjamin Franklin Parkway, with folk dancing, flea markets, music, and food. The *Philadelphia Craft Show,* held the first or second weekend in November at the Engineers' Armory (33rd and Lancaster Ave.), displays and sells a variety of crafts by artisans from around the country. *Fairmount Park* holds its *Christmas* tour the first week in December, during which the mansions and *Horticultural Society* building are decked out in colonial fashion for the holiday.

MUSEUMS

In addition to those described in *Special Places,* Philadelphia has many other museums of note. All charge admission, unless otherwise indicated.

ACADEMY OF NATURAL SCIENCES Particularly known for its dinosaur exhibits, this museum also offers *Outside In,* a hands-on children's section with live animals. Open daily. 19th St. and Parkway (phone: 299-1000).

AFRO-AMERICAN HISTORICAL AND CULTURAL MUSEUM African-American art in a variety of media is on display, and there are lectures and movies. Closed Mondays. Seventh and Arch Sts. (phone: 574-0380).

ATTWATER KENT MUSEUM This small local history museum offers everything from silver miniatures and sketches to artifacts from nearby digs. Closed Sundays and Mondays. 15 S. Seventh St. (phone: 922-3031).

BARNES FOUNDATION The French Impressionist art from this museum is completing an international tour, with its final stop at the *Philadelphia Museum of Art* (through April); then it will return to the Barnes for rehanging in its remodeled galleries, scheduled to reopen later this year. Call ahead for the schedule. 300 N. Latch's La., Merion Station (phone: 667-0290).

FIREMAN'S HALL MUSEUM The exhibits here are all about fire fighting and include tools, helmets, and an 18th-century hand-drawn pumper. Closed Sundays and Mondays. Second and Quarry Sts. between Race and Arch Sts. (phone: 923-1438).

INSTITUTE OF CONTEMPORARY AWARENESS Contemporary art by established artists as well as emerging talents is the focus here. Closed Mondays and Tuesdays. *University of Pennsylvania,* 36th and Sansom Sts. (phone: 898-7108).

MUMMERS MUSEUM Exhibits of Mummers' memorabilia and history as well as sound recordings showcase a Philadelphia tradition. Tours available. Closed Sundays and Mondays in July and August. Second St. and Washington Ave. (phone: 336-3050).

MUTTER MUSEUM Exhibits explore medical history. Closed Saturdays through Mondays. Donations suggested. *College of Physicians of Philadelphia,* 19 S. 22nd St. (phone: 563-3737).

NORMAN ROCKWELL MUSEUM An extensive collection of *Saturday Evening Post* covers is on display. Open daily. *Curtis Center,* Sixth and Sansom Sts. (phone: 922-4345).

PENNSYLVANIA ACADEMY OF FINE ARTS The country's oldest art school displays a permanent collection of 20th-century paintings. Closed Mondays. Broad and Cherry Sts. (phone: 972-7600).

PLEASE TOUCH MUSEUM Terrific hands-on exhibits are made for young children. Open daily. 210 N. 21st St. (phone: 963-0667).

ROSENBACH MUSEUM AND LIBRARY This 19th-century townhouse contains thousands of rare books, manuscripts, and original illustrations as well as furniture, silver, paintings, and decorative arts of the time. Tours available. Closed Mondays, holidays, and August. 2010 Delancey Pl., between Spruce and Pine Sts. (phone: 732-1600).

UNIVERSITY OF PENNSYLVANIA MUSEUM Anthropology and archaeology exhibitions are featured here. Closed Mondays. 33rd and Spruce Sts. (phone: 898-4000).

WAGNER FREE INSTITUTE OF SCIENCE This national landmark houses natural history exhibits. Closed Mondays; weekends by appointment. 17th St. and Montgomery Ave. (phone: 763-6529).

SHOPPING

For the best in department store shopping, head to the landmark *John Wanamaker* (Chestnut and Market Sts. at 13th St.) or *Strawbridge & Clothier,* an anchor store at the *Gallery,* one of the largest urban malls in the nation with more than 200 stores and eateries. Running along Market Street from Ninth to 12th, it connects with *SEPTA*'s *Market East* rail stop and several subway stations. The *Mellon Independence Center* (on Market St., between Seventh and Eighth) houses upscale shops, as does the *Bourse,* a restored Victorian building (on Fifth between Market and Chestnut Sts.). *The Shops at Liberty Place* (16th and Chestnut Sts.), a two-story circular mall in the heart of the business district, is laid out in a wheel shape. At the hub, a magnificent marble and skylighted central court, a pianist plays at noon. The stores here range from the upscale to the practical, and there's a large food court with fast-food eateries and a more formal Italian restaurant.

To see some of Philadelphia's most exclusive clothing shops and art galleries, such as *Nan Duskin* for female finery (Rittenhouse Sq.; phone: 735-6400), walk along Walnut Street. Philadelphia also is known for its jewelers' row, which dates from the 1850s and is the second-largest diamond center in the country. Its heart lies between Sixth and Eighth, along Sansom Street. Similarly, an antiques row with both colonial and international crafts runs along Pine Street, between Ninth and 12th. For the ultimate funky experience, don't miss a stroll down South Street from 10th to the river. You'll probably enjoy the people watching as much as the many boutiques and small restaurants.

> **SWEET TREATS**
>
> "Tastykakes" are the things about which exiled Philadelphians dream most. The little packages of cakes and pies are available at most grocery stores. But the biggest local food thrill is Bassett's ice cream, available all around the city. (For other gustatory thrills, see *Eating Out*, below.)

SPORTS AND FITNESS

Whether you like to watch or play, there are plenty of sports around.

BASEBALL From April through early October, the 1993 *National League* champions *Phillies* chase the pennant at *Veterans Stadium* (Broad St. and Pattison Ave.; phone: 463-1000).

BASKETBALL Pro basketball's *76ers* pack them in at the *Spectrum* (Broad St. and Pattison Ave.; phone: 339-7676) from November through April.

BICYCLING Some 10.6 miles of *Fairmount Park* are devoted to bike paths. Though not convenient to the park, *Bike Line* (1234 Locust St.; phone: 735-1503) rents bikes—and Rollerblades, too—year-round.

FOOTBALL The *NFL Eagles* play at *Veterans Stadium* (Broad St. and Pattison Ave.; phone: 463-5500).

GOLF Try to get invited to a private country club. If you can't, your next best bet is *Cobbs Creek*, a public course (72nd and Lansdowne Ave.; phone: 877-8707). Nearby, the *Golf Corp. Sports Center* (7900 City Line Ave.; phone: 879-3536) has a driving range and miniature golf as well as batting cages.

HOCKEY The *Flyers* play at the *Spectrum* (Broad St. and Pattison Ave.; phone: 755-9700) from October through April. Tickets are hard to get, but try *Ticket Master* (phone: 336-2000).

HORSE RACING *Philadelphia Park* has thoroughbred and harness racing at Street and Richlieu Roads (phone: 639-9000).

JOGGING In *Fairmount Park*, run alongside the Schuylkill River behind the art museum.

SKIING Everybody goes to the Pocono Mountains, two hours away in northeastern Pennsylvania. Best bets: *Camelback Mountain* (Tannersville; phone: 717-629-1661; 800-233-8100 for ski report), *Big Boulder* (Lake

Harmony; phone: 717-722-0101), and *Jack Frost* (Whitehaven; phone: 717-443-8425).

TENNIS The nation's number one indoor event, the *US Pro Indoor,* is held annually at the *Spectrum* in mid-February. The city runs more than 200 all-weather courts (contact individual recreation centers for availability), and *Fairmount Park* also has that many. Call the *Fairmount Park Commission* (phone: 685-0000).

THEATER

The Philadelphia theater scene has continued its expansion in the 1990s with Broadway productions presented at the larger houses and many new plays debuting in more intimate settings. The leading theaters for the more extravagant productions are the *Forrest Theater* (1114 Walnut St.; phone: 923-1515), the *Merriam Theater* (250 S. Broad St.; phone: 732-5446), and the *Walnut Street Theater* (Ninth and Walnuts Sts.; phone: 574-3550). There also is the *Wilma Theater* (2030 Sansom St.; phone: 963-0249) for contemporary and often controversial offerings; the *Society Hill Playhouse* (507 S. Eighth St.; phone: 923-0210) for musical comedies; and the *Annenberg Center* (3680 Walnut St.; phone: 898-6791), with its three theaters: the *Philadelphia Drama Guild,* which presents a range of traditional plays; the *Dance Celebration Series;* and the *Philadelphia Festival Theater for New Plays.* The *Pennsylvania Ballet* performs at the *Academy of Music* (Broad and Locust Sts.; phone: 893-1999).

MUSIC

The *Philadelphia Orchestra,* under conductor Wolfgang Sawallisch, performs at the stately *Academy of Music* (Broad and Locust Sts.; phone: 893-1999) September through May. In summer, they play under the stars at the *Mann Music Center* (Fairmount Park; phone: 567-0707), where rock concerts are also held. In summer, call 878-7707 for classical as well as rock and pop concert tickets. A limited number of free tickets to orchestra concerts are available at the *Philadelphia Visitors Center* (16th and John F. Kennedy Blvd.) on the day of a performance. The *Opera Company of Philadelphia* and the *Soloists Chamber Orchestra of Philadelphia* also perform at the *Academy of Music* throughout the year.

NIGHTCLUBS AND NIGHTLIFE

The city's waterfront area along Delaware Avenue and Christopher Columbus Boulevard has become the latest nightclub scene. *Egypt* (520 N. Christopher Columbus Blvd.; phone 922-6500), completely decorated in an Egyptian theme, features dancing to 1980s and 1990s music; *Katmando Village* (415 N. Delaware Ave.) combines the *Elizabeth* (phone: 627-5151), a permanently docked ship serving as nightclub and restaurant, with the *Katmando* open-air nightclub (phone 629-7400), open April through September. Other samplings around the city include jazz at the *Blue Moon Jazz Club and Restaurant* (21 S. Fifth St. in the Bourse Building; phone: 413-2273); rock and roll and rhythm and blues at the *Chestnut Cabaret* (3801 Chestnut St.; phone: 382-1201); and nightly deejay dancing with country-and-western music on Wednesdays at the *Main Event* (Eighth and Market Sts.; phone: 413-1776). A variety of entertainers headline at the *Valley Forge Music Fair* in nearby Devon (Rte. 202; phone: 889-9896). You also can take a dinner or moonlight cruise on *The Spirit of Philadelphia* (Pier No. 3, Penn's Landing, on Delaware Ave. at Market St.; phone: 923-1419; 923-4993 for groups of 20 or more). Sail along the Delaware as waiters serve your meal and then perform a Broadway revue. Cruises run March through December; lunchtime cruises are also available.

Best in Town

CHECKING IN

Hotels range from famous, durable places to sleek contemporary spots with loud, lively lobbies. Expect to pay $225 or more (sometimes much more) per night for a double room at places we've listed as very expensive; $150 to $225 at those categorized as expensive; and $75 to $150 at those rated moderate; there are no exceptional inexpensive hotels in the city. Most hotels offer weekend packages at significantly reduced rates. For bed and breakfast accommodations, contact *Bed and Breakfast Connections/Bed & Breakfast of Philadelphia* (PO Box 21, Devon, PA 19333; phone: 610-687-3565; 800-448-3619 outside the 610 area code), whose listings cover the city as well as outlying areas such as the Main Line, Valley Forge, and the Brandywine River region. Hotel rooms have air conditioning, private baths, TV sets, and telephones unless otherwise indicated. All hotels are in the 215 area code unless otherwise indicated.

VERY EXPENSIVE

Four Seasons The height of local elegance, this hostelry has 371 luxurious rooms and suites. Its gracious *Fountain* restaurant (see *Eating Out*) is renowned for fine dining; the *Swan Café* is less formal. The *Swan Lounge* serves afternoon tea and cocktails and features weekend entertainment, and a courtyard café is open during the summer. The hotel offers a health spa with a pool, sauna, and whirlpool, and a beauty salon. Special amenities include 24-hour valet and room service, a concierge, and twice-daily maid service. Among the business features are meeting rooms for up to 600, secretarial services, A/V equipment, photocopiers, computers, and express checkout. 1 Logan Sq. (phone: 963-1500; 800-332-3442; fax: 963-9506).

Hotel Atop the Bellevue One of the nation's grandest properties early in this century, it fell on hard times in the 1970s. After extensive renovations, however, this landmark now features 154 rooms and 18 spacious suites. The room decor is turn-of-the-century, but there are many modern amenities, including an entertainment center with VCR, stereo, and mini-bar; voice mail; and computer hookups. Fine dining and weekend dancing are available in *Founders*. The *Library* lounge, which serves light fare and drinks, and the *Ethel Barrymore Room,* with afternoon tea and weekend entertainment, are perfect for relaxing. The *Conservatory* serves breakfast and lunch. Guests receive a complimentary pass to the adjacent health club. Meeting rooms hold up to 1,200; also available are secretarial services, A/V equipment, photocopiers, computers, a valet, a concierge, and 24-hour room service. 1415 Chancellor Court (phone: 893-1776; 800-221-0833; fax: 721-8518).

Rittenhouse Appointed in classic European style, it has 87 spacious rooms and 11 suites. There also are 30 "apartments" with fully equipped kitchens and laundry facilities for businesspeople who want longer-term accommodations. Amenities include spacious marble bathrooms, two-line phones with computer hookups, VCRs, and daily newspaper delivery. *Restaurant 210* provides elegant dining, and *Treetops* offers attractive pre- and post-theater menus as well as picnic baskets to go. The *Cassatt Room* serves afternoon tea. An in-house spa offers a pool, a sauna, workout equipment, and massages. Business conveniences include 24-hour room service, a valet, a concierge, secretarial services, A/V equipment, photocopiers, and computers. The meeting rooms accommodate up to 400. 210 W. Rittenhouse Sq. (phone: 546-9000; 800-635-1042; fax: 732-3364).

EXPENSIVE

Latham This hotel is a favorite of businesspeople who seek a central location and first-rate service. Its 139 rooms are furnished with marble-topped bureaus and graceful French writing desks. Each room has two phones with computer hookups, and a complimentary *Wall Street Journal* is delivered every business day. Guests may use a health club a block away. The restaurant, *Michel's* (see *Eating Out*), and the lounge are places to see and be seen. Meeting rooms accommodate up to 50. Room service, a concierge, a valet, and secretarial services are available, as well as A/V equipment, photocopiers, computers, and express checkout. 17th and Walnut (phone: 563-7474; 800-LATHAM-1; fax: 563-4034).

Omni Hotel at Independence Park Its grand marble lobby with working fireplace and its marvelous view of *Independence National Historic Park* make this hotel special. Original watercolors of city scenes adorn the 137 rooms and six suites, which have two-line phones with voice mail and computer hookups. Complimentary coffee and the morning paper are provided. The *Azalea* restaurant features a regional menu in an elegant atmosphere; more casual meals are served at the lobby bar in the evening. There's twice-daily maid service, 24-hour room service, a valet, a concierge, and a health club with a pool, saunas, and a Jacuzzi. Meeting rooms accommodate up to 50; secretarial services, A/V equipment, photocopiers, and express checkout are available. Fourth and Chestnut Sts. (phone: 925-0000; 800-THE OMNI; fax: 925-1263).

Penn's View Inn This inn has a touch of European elegance in its 31 rooms, no two of which are decorated or furnished alike. Premium rooms overlook the Delaware and have fireplaces. *Panorama* serves northern Italian food and features the city's largest *cruvinet*, which dispenses more than 120 different wines by the glass. There is valet and room service as well as a concierge. Fitness privileges are available nearby at the *Sheraton* hotel for a modest fee. Business facilities include a conference room for up to 50 and A/V equipment. 14 N. Front St. (phone: 922-7600; 800-331-7634; fax: 922-7642).

Ritz-Carlton Located in Liberty Place (the first two floors are devoted to retail shops and restaurants), this 290-room hotel has been designed and decorated in the style of the city's Federal period, with lots of molding and wainscoting. Rooms have mini-bars and marble bathrooms. Two floors provide a concierge and an all-day buffet. The *Dining Room* serves regional fare with international flair, while *The Grill* offers fine American food; a lounge serves afternoon tea. There is an exercise and fitness center with workout equipment, a massage room, and saunas; guests can arrange to use the pool at a nearby sports club. Meeting rooms accommodate up to 800, and other amenities include A/V equipment, photocopiers, computers, 24-hour room service, a valet, a concierge, and secretarial services. 17th and Chestnut Sts. (phone: 563-1600; 800-241-3333; fax: 564-9559).

Sheraton Society Hill A short walk from Penn's Landing and *Independence Mall*, this inn has a brick and wood decor, which lends colonial overtones to its rooms and lobby. Balconies overlook a verdant lobby atrium, where a pianist plays nightly in the *Courtyard Lounge*. There's casual dining at *Hadley's*, the pub-style *Wooden Nickel* lounge, an indoor pool, and a health club. The 365 guestrooms have computerized snack bars (you select your items from a machine and they are billed to your room). Valet service, a concierge, and 24-hour room service are available; computer hookups can be requested. Meeting rooms accommodate up to 900, and there are photocopiers, A/V equipment, secretarial services, and express checkout. 1 Dock St. (phone: 238-6000; 800-325-3535; fax: 922-2709).

Wyndham Franklin Plaza One of the city's best, it's four blocks from *City Hall* and a few steps from the Parkway. Facilities include 720 modern rooms and 36 suites, racquetball, basketball, and tennis courts, a health club with indoor pool, a sauna, a Jacuzzi, and Nautilus equipment. *Between Friends* offers fine dining; *The Terrace* serves more casual American fare, and there's an atrium lobby bar lounge. Amenities include a valet, room service, and a concierge. Meeting space for up to 2,500 and secretarial services are available, as well as A/V equipment, photocopiers, computers, and express checkout. 17th and Vine Sts. (phone: 448-2000; 800-WYNDHAM; fax: 448-2864).

MODERATE

Doubletree of Philadelphia This first class establishment has replaced its contemporary look with one that is more traditional. In the center of the city, it has 427 rooms; its two tower floors, each with concierge service, offer suites with upgraded amenities. The second-level *Café Academie* overlooks the atrium lobby and bar. The athletically inclined can use the indoor pool, jogging track, racquetball courts, and exercise room or relax in the tanning salon, sauna, or whirlpool. Conveniences include valet and room service, as well as a concierge desk. Meeting facilities accommodate up to 500, and there are secretarial services, A/V equipment, a business center, and express checkout. Broad and Locust Sts. (phone: 893-1600; 800-222-TREE; fax: 893-1663).

Holiday Inn–City Line Convenient to City Line shops and restaurants, this 343-room inn offers an indoor/outdoor pool, an exercise room, a restaurant, a lounge, valet and room service, and limousine service to and from the airport. There's also a casual, family-style restaurant next door. Business amenities include meeting rooms for up to 400, A/V and photocopying equipment, and express checkout. City Line and 4100 Presidential Blvd. (phone: 477-0200; 800-HOLIDAY; fax: 473-2709).

Ramada Inn, Center City In the heart of the museum district and within walking distance of most major attractions, this 279-room hotel offers casual comfort. Amenities include a restaurant, a lounge, an outdoor pool, a valet, and room service. There's meeting space for up to 100. 22nd and Parkway (phone: 568-8300; 800-228-2828; fax: 557-0259).

EATING OUT

The city boasts quite a few outstanding restaurants, some spacious and lively, others intimate and cozy. Expect to pay $75 or more for dinner for two at places we've listed as very expensive; $50 to $75 at those categorized as expensive; $20 to $50 at those rated moderate; and less than $20 at those rated inexpensive. Prices do not include drinks, wine, tax, or tips. Unless otherwise noted, restaurants are open for lunch and dinner. All restaurants are in the 215 area code unless otherwise indicated.

VERY EXPENSIVE

Le Bec Fin This is the best restaurant in town—and one of the finest in the country as well. The setting is intimate yet elegant with crystal chandeliers and damask wall coverings. The menu of imaginative French fare—such as *homard à la presse* (pressed lobster sautéed tableside)—changes frequently, but it always offers lavish desserts. Diners can choose the prix fixe dinner (about $90 per person) or lunch (about $30 per person). Closed Sundays; dinner only on weekends. Reservations necessary. Major credit cards accepted. 1523 Walnut (phone: 567-1000).

Deux Cheminées This elegant dining spot in a 19th-century townhouse features old Philadelphia decor, with Oriental rugs and polished hardwood floors. The menu is classic French; crab soup and rack of lamb are standouts. Private parties of up to 100 can be accommodated. Open for dinner only; closed Mondays and selected Sundays (except for private parties). Reservations advised. Major credit cards accepted. 1221 Locust St. (phone: 790-0200).

Fountain In the *Four Seasons* hotel, this place is one of Philadelphia's finest. Experience truly gracious dining accompanied by attentive service. Rich mahogany walls and picture windows overlooking the stately, flag-draped Benjamin Franklin Parkway add to the elegant setting. A changing menu features fine continental cuisine. An alternate low-sodium, low-cholesterol menu is available, as are prix fixe selections. Enjoy an extensive wine selection and the after-dinner trolley stocked with liqueurs and ports. Sunday brunch includes a combination buffet and à la carte menu selections. Open daily. Reservations necessary (non-hotel guests must call well in advance for Saturday nights). Major credit cards accepted. 1 Logan Sq. (phone: 963-1500).

EXPENSIVE

Bookbinder's Seafood House better of the two restaurants bearing this famous name (see below), this large, bustling eatery offers a casual setting with wood walls and paper placemats. Fresh, well-prepared seafood is the chief attraction—try the baked crab. Open daily. Reservations advised. Major credit cards accepted. 215 S. 15th (phone: 545-1137).

Café Nola A taste of New Orleans in Philadelphia, the selections here are mostly Cajun and creole; the place is known for its seasonal decorations, especially at *Christmas* and during *Mardi Gras*. Roast duck with coffee glaze, banana stuffed chicken, and prime ribs are among the offerings. At *Hurricane Alley*, a Caribbean-style bistro next door under the same ownership, there's a *tapas* menu and tropical drinks. Open daily. Reservations advised. Major credit cards accepted. 328 South St. (phone: 627-2590).

Dickens Inn In the historic *Harper House,* the period pieces imported from England create an inn where Charles Dickens would feel at home. Spend an enjoyable evening sipping a yard of ale and nibbling shepherd's pie in the tavern, or dine in the restaurant on a continental menu that includes traditional English roast beef and Yorkshire pudding, as well as pasta and seafood. Delicious desserts are baked on site, and the inn has three more pubs. Open daily. Reservations necessary. Major credit cards accepted. Second between Pine and Lombard Sts. (phone: 928-9307).

DiLullo Centro Set in a former theater, this large establishment has world class atmosphere and small restaurant quality. Opulence is everywhere, from the glass elevator to the Impressionist murals. The menu features homemade pasta as well as veal and seafood dishes and fresh pastries. Note that an inexpensive assortment of salads, pasta, pizza, and desserts is served in *Café Centro* lounge. Closed Sundays. Reservations advised. Major credit cards accepted. 1407 Locust St. (phone: 546-2000).

Garden Fresh seafood and game in season are served in a stylish old townhouse. Dine outdoors in the courtyard when the weather's good, or sit at the cozy *Oyster Bar.* Scallops Provençale over *capellini* is a signature dish. Two *cruvinets* dispense a variety of French and California wines by the glass. Closed Sundays. Reservations advised. Major credit cards accepted. 1617 Spruce St. (phone: 546-4455).

Michel's Famed chef Michel Richard has created a California bistro-style restaurant made bright with large, light-filled windows. At lunch, try the backfin crab cakes in phyllo dough. The dinner menu offers a variety of fish, chicken, steak, and pasta dishes. Save room for one of the fabulous desserts (such as chocolate hazelnut bars or crunchy napoleons with butterscotch sauce), Michel's specialty. Open daily (for breakfast as well). Reservations advised. Major credit cards accepted. *Latham Hotel,* 17th and Walnut Sts. (phone: 563-9444).

Old Original Bookbinder's Philadelphia's best-known restaurant, with mahogany and gleaming leather. Many love it, many find it overpriced. The seafood is as much of a legend as many of the celebrities who dine here, but the menu offers meat and chicken as well. Open daily. Reservations necessary. Major credit cards accepted. 125 Walnut St. (phone: 925-7027).

Susanna Foo Fine Chinese food in an elegant atmosphere of polished mahogany furniture, fresh flowers, and linen tablecloths. Hunan dishes are prepared with a touch of French flair; the menu changes seasonally but usually features pheasant, quail, and other game in winter and fresh fish and seafood in summer. The luscious desserts include a variety of mousses, tarts, and fresh fruit in season. Open daily; dinner only on weekends. Reservations advised weekdays, necessary for dinner on Fridays and Saturdays. Major credit cards accepted. 1512 Walnut St. (phone: 545-2666).

White Dog Café In a Victorian brownstone near the *University of Pennsylvania,* this place has the charm of a country inn. The menu offers contemporary American fare with influences from Europe, Asia, and Mexico; good entrées include herb-charred leg of lamb with caraway glaze, grilled yellowfin tuna with ginger-basil hot sauce, and stir-fried vegetables served over rice noodles. Don't pass up the restaurant's signature dessert—*crème brûlée* with raspberries. Open daily; brunch on weekends. Reservations advised. Major credit cards accepted. 3420 Sansom St. (phone: 386-9224).

MODERATE

Dock Street Brewery and Restaurant This pub has a thoroughly polished look, with cherry tables, comfortable library chairs, and a long marble bar; the antique billiard tables and dart boards are another part of the attraction. The glass-enclosed brewery is the focal point and can be toured on Saturday afternoons. The menu features pub fare but with a twist: Many dishes are prepared with beer and reflect the foods of the major beer-making countries. Open daily. Reservations necessary only for six or more on Fridays and Saturdays. Major credit cards accepted. 18th and Cherry Sts. in 2 Logan Square Building (phone: 496-0413).

Downey's A local favorite for relaxing and partying, this eatery in Society Hill is noted for its Irish stew and liquored cakes. The continental menu features steaks; and an oyster bar offers seafood and soups. Roast turkey and beef are served at the carving station daily. The wood and brass decor is complemented with Irish artifacts, including a mahogany bar brought over from a bank in Cork. In season, patrons can eat on an outdoor deck. Sunday brunch features live entertainment. Open daily. Reservations unnecessary. Major credit cards accepted. Front and South Sts. (phone: 629-0525).

Marabella's chain of Italian eateries featuring mesquite-grilled seafood, pizza, and Italian delicacies including homemade pasta. Try tortellini with goat cheese, sun-dried tomatoes, and olives; or hot and spicy grilled chicken with mixed vegetables. Follow up (if you still can) with homemade chocolate truffle or ricotta cheesecake, or sample the gelati (Italian ice cream). Open daily. Reservations necessary for lunch only. Major credit cards accepted. Three locations: 1420 Locust St. in *Academy House* (phone: 545-1845); 401 City Ave. (phone: 668-5353); and 1700 Benjamin Franklin Pkwy. (phone: 981-5555).

Sansom Street Oyster House With a large, remarkable collection of oyster plates displayed overhead and highly polished wooden tables, the casual warmth of this place is a Philadelphia tradition. Among the specialties are superb Maryland crab cakes, fresh fish, and oysters (what else?), as well as bread and rice puddings for dessert. Closed Sundays. Dinner reservations advised for groups of five or more. Major credit cards accepted. 1516 Sansom St. (phone: 567-7683).

INEXPENSIVE

Famous Delicatessen Famous for celebrity customers, as its picture-lined walls prove, this Jewish deli features hot pastrami, roast beef, roast turkey, and corned beef sandwiches, followed by the crowning touch: delicious chocolate chip cookies. In traditional style, the food comes on paper plates. Open for breakfast and lunch only. Reservations unnecessary. American Express accepted. 700 S. Fourth St. (phone: 627-9198).

Imperial Inn One of the best-known spots in Chinatown, this eclectic restaurant features Szechuan, Mandarin, and Cantonese dishes. Cantonese-style dim sum also is offered during the more casual lunch hours; lights are dimmed and linen tablecloths are added at dinner. Open daily. Reservations advised. Major credit cards accepted. 146 N. 10th St. (phone: 627-5588).

SAY CHEESE

While in Philadelphia, don't forget to sink your teeth into a famous Philly cheesesteak—a sandwich loaded with steak, onions, cheese, and peppers. Try *Pat's King of Steaks* (1237 E. Passyunk Ave., South Philadelphia; phone: 468-1546) for one of the best cheesesteaks in town. It's open 24 hours, seven days a week. Another favorite is *Jim's Steaks* (400 South St.; phone: 928-1911), which also has great hoagies (also known as heros or sub sandwiches). Open daily. *Olivieri's* is the next best thing if you are in the *Reading Terminal Market* (12th and Arch Sts.; phone: 625-9369).

Phoenix

At-a-Glance

SEEING THE CITY
There is no view more beautiful than the one from South Mountain, especially when the last rays of sun paint the sky in layers of orange, red, and purple. Drive south on Central Avenue into *South Mountain Park* and stop at one of the lookouts.

SPECIAL PLACES
Street numbers start at zero in the center of downtown. Central Avenue, the business and financial district, runs north and south, bisecting the city into east and west. Numbered avenues lie to the west of Central, numbered streets to the east.

STATE CAPITOL The building shows what granite from the Salt River Mountains looks like when put to constructive use. It has now been restored to the way it originally appeared in 1912, the year of statehood. The murals inside depict Arizona's discovery and exploration in the 16th century, and life in the region through the 1930s. There also is an exhibit displaying an array of bola (string) ties, the official state neckwear. Closed weekends and holidays. No admission charge. W. Washington and 17th Ave. (phone: 542-4675).

HEARD MUSEUM Founded in the late 1920s, this museum focuses on the native cultures of the Southwest. Its award-winning "Native Peoples of the Southwest" exhibit serves as a centerpiece and is the largest display of its kind in North America. Tracing the history of the region from 15,000 BC to the present, it includes everything from prehistoric pottery vessels to contemporary Navajo textiles. There's also a hands-on children's exhibit called "Old Ways, New Ways," which focuses on the Southwest Zuni, Northwest Coast Tsimshiam, and the Great Plains Kiowa. A special gallery features a large number of Hopi kachina dolls—perhaps the museum's best-known collection—many of which were donated by Barry Goldwater. These painted and feathered dolls, according to Hopi lore, are given to children by the kachina spirits, who represent ancestors and nature. The museum also exhibits jewelry, baskets, textiles, ceramics, and artifacts of the Hopi. Of two other galleries devoted to changing shows, one focuses on contemporary Native American fine art; the other compares this native culture to others around the world. Closed major holidays. Admission charge. 22 E. Monte Vista (phone: 252-8840; 252-8848, for recorded information).

PHOENIX ART MUSEUM Specializing in contemporary Southwestern art, this institution also has other collections that cover North American art in general (including Mexican) and a small exhibition of Renaissance, 17th-, and 18th-century work. Closed Mondays and major holidays. No admission charge on Wednesdays. 1625 N. Central (phone: 257-1222).

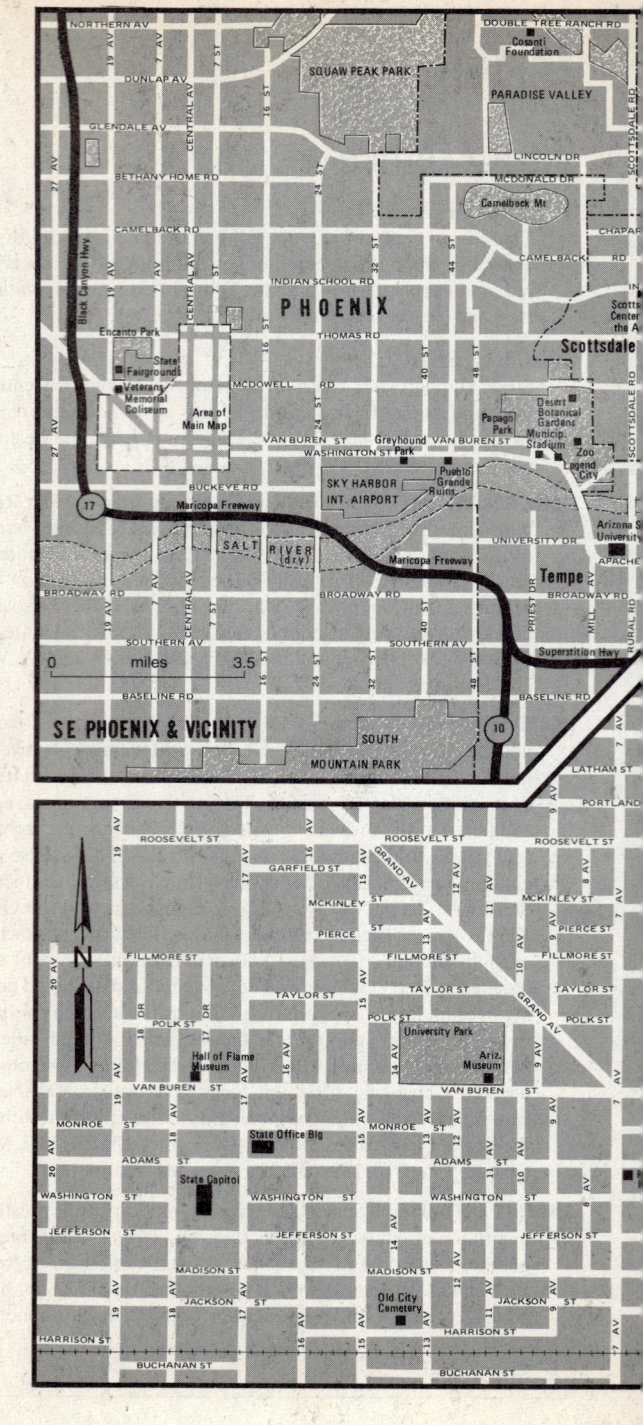

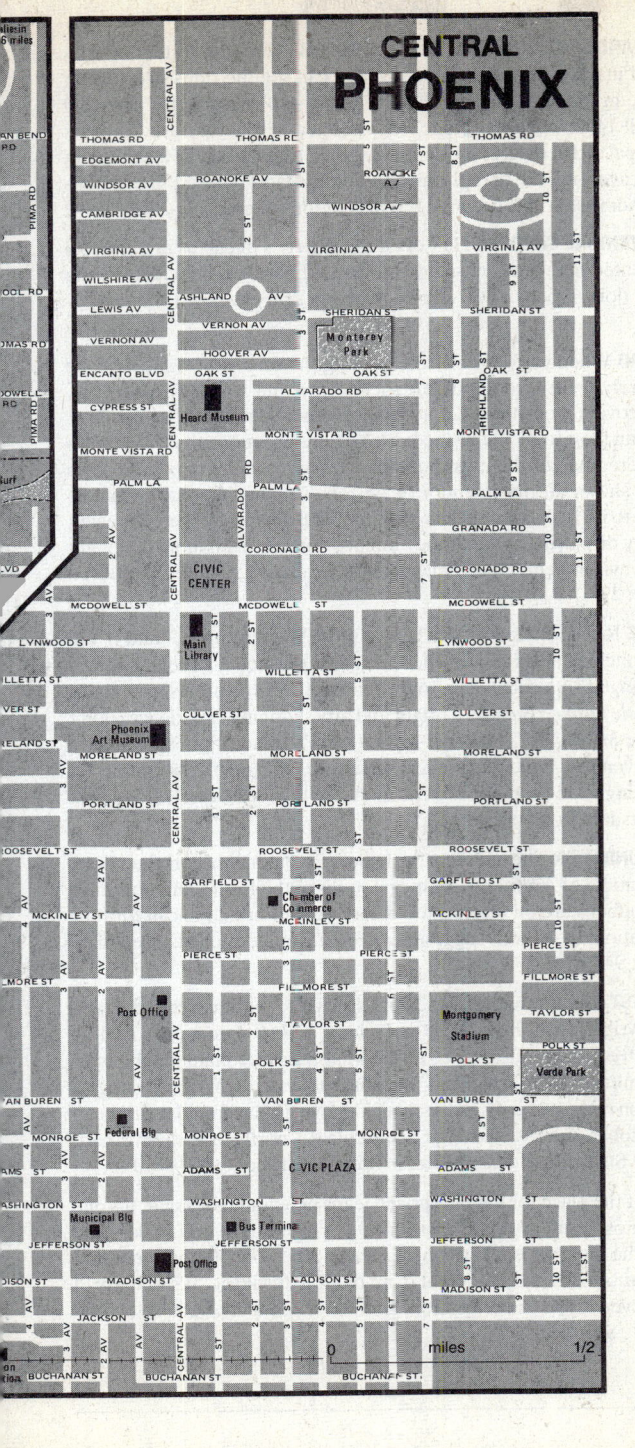

PUEBLO GRANDE MUSEUM AND INDIAN RUINS By climbing to the top of a mound marked into seven stations, you can see the ruins of a former Hohokam Indian settlement, believed to have been occupied from 200 BC until 1400, when the Hohokam vanished without a trace. Phoenix municipal archaeologists are continuing their excavations. In the museum are excavation photographs and Indian artifacts. Closed major holidays. Admission charge. 4619 E. Washington (phone: 275-3452).

DESERT BOTANICAL GARDENS Half of all the varieties of cactus in the world are planted here, and self-guided tours and booklets help identify the prickly flora. Open daily. Admission charge. *Papago Park* (phone: 941-1217).

PHOENIX ZOO When you've finished exploring the *Botanical Gardens,* take a leisurely drive through desert rock formations to the *Phoenix Zoo,* which covers more than 125 acres in another section of *Papago Park.* (You can stop to picnic in the park.) There are more than 1,200 animals here. One of the most popular attractions is the oryx herd. One exhibit shows off the splendor of Arizona's natural habitats, from its deserts to its 10,000-foot peaks; another focuses on endangered species, not only displaying some of the animals, but also explaining the plight of the environment. Open daily. Admission charge. 5810 E. Van Buren (phone: 273-7771).

SCOTTSDALE Residents call it "the West's most Western town," and it still has its hitching posts and touches of cowboy mystique, although its face has changed somewhat. The town boasts one of the area's best malls, *Scottsdale Fashion Square,* a bright and airy shopping experience (don't miss the *Museum of Northern Arizona* shop). In addition, Scottsdale's Fifth Avenue is lined with galleries (see *Art Galleries*). The simple act of walking is an aesthetic adventure here. Take McDowell Road east to Scottsdale Road north.

COSANTI FOUNDATION The architect Paolo Soleri maintains a workshop here, with a model of Arcosanti, his megalopolis of the future. His sculpture and windbells are on display, too. Closed major holidays; call for tour information. Donations suggested. 6433 E. Doubletree Rd., Scottsdale (phone: 948-6145).

TALIESIN WEST The future owes much of its shape to master architect Frank Lloyd Wright. His former office and school, *Taliesin* (pronounced Tal-ly-ess-en) *West,* offers the chance to see what goes into planning the marvelous, ultramodern structures that students base on Wright's designs. Closed on rainy days and holidays; limited, varying hours from June through mid-October. Admission charge. Scottsdale Rd. north, to Shea Blvd. east, to 108th St. north, to *Taliesin West* in Scottsdale (phone: 860-8810).

BORGATA Not the place for bargain-priced jeans or a pound of sugar, it's one of the most opulent retail operations this side of Beverly Hills—and one of the most unusual anywhere. There are about 50 boutiques and restaurants in a setting redolent of an old Italian village. It's well worth a visit, even if you can only afford to look. Open daily. 6166 N. Scottsdale Rd., Scottsdale.

HERITAGE SQUARE This Victorian complex in the heart of downtown is a refreshing change in this relatively young city. Spend an afternoon in the museums, shops, and restaurants. *Rosson House* (1894), an open-air lathe house, is particularly notable. Don't miss the weekly *Farmers' Markets* held here October through February. Closed Mondays and Tuesdays. Admission charge. 127 N. Sixth St. (phone: 262-5071).

ARIZONA CENTER Shops and restaurants line this L-shaped, two-story center, and fountains, shade trees, and wide lawns help deflect the summer's heat. Open daily. 455 N. Third St. (phone: 271-4000).

RAWHIDE'S 1880S WESTERN TOWN Set in the middle of 160 acres of natural desert is a replica of an entire Old West town. Along the rickety main street are shops, a shooting gallery, a blacksmith, and a general store. You can get arrested by a US marshal (though you don't have to commit a crime, just pay $3). Ride on a stagecoach, pan for gold, ride a burro, and wash hearty, old-fashioned meals down with sarsaparilla. A large collection of antiques is on display throughout the town, and the *Rawhide Museum* has more than 5,000 items of historical interest, including Geronimo's moccasins and items owned by the likes of Diamond Jim Brady and Belle Starr. Children will enjoy *Kid's Territory,* which has a petting ranch. Sunset haywagon rides on Saturday nights and a desert cookout with country dancing complete the Western theme. Open daily. Admission charge for attractions. 23023 N. Scottsdale Rd., Scottsdale (phone: 563-1880).

DOLLY'S STEAMBOAT This is a unique way to tour the desert. Board this replica of a historic steamboat to cruise Canyon Lake, in the breathtaking *Superstition Wilderness.* Guides give an informal history and geography lesson. Cruises daily, with sunset charter rides available. Admission charge. 5106 E. Emilita, Mesa (phone: 827-9144).

EXTRA SPECIAL

For a picturesque day trip through open desert, take the Black Canyon Highway north to Cordes Junction, then travel west through the old territorial capital of Prescott to Sedona, famous for its dramatic red cliffs. At Sedona, take a breathtaking drive up Oak Creek Canyon to Flagstaff, or complete the circle by driving back to Verde Valley, returning via the Black Canyon Highway. Be sure to stop in Jerome, the ghost town too ornery to die. A community of artists now lives in the old wooden buildings that cling precariously to the steep mountainside of this former copper mining town. Jerome has great curio and antiques shops specializing in mining paraphernalia and one of the best restaurants in Arizona, the *House of Joy* (Hull St. and US 89A; phone: 634-5339). The food is continental, the prices are reasonable, and it's open only on weekends (so reservations are necessary).

Sources and Resources

TOURIST INFORMATION

For maps, brochures, and information, contact the *Phoenix and Valley of the Sun Convention and Visitors Bureau* (505 N. Second St., Phoenix, AZ 85004; phone: 254-6500) or the *Arizona Office of Tourism* (1100 W. Washington Ave., Phoenix, AZ 85003; phone: 542-8687). Both are closed weekends. Contact the state tourism hotline (phone: 602-542-8687) for maps, calendars of events, health updates, and travel advisories.

LOCAL COVERAGE *Arizona Republic*, morning daily; *Phoenix Gazette*, evening daily except Sundays; *Scottsdale Progress*, afternoon daily; *Mesa, Tempe and Chandler Tribune*, morning daily; *New Times, Business Journal*, and *Arizona Business Gazette*, all weekly; *Phoenix Metro* magazine, *Arizona Trend, Phoenix Home & Garden*, all monthly. The best guide is *Phoenix Metro* magazine's *City Guide* (Phoenix Publishing; $3.95). *100 Best Restaurants in Arizona*, by John and Joan Bogert (ADM; $3.95) is a good food guide.

TELEVISION STATIONS KTVK Channel 3–ABC; KTSP Channel 10–CBS; KPNX Channel 12–NBC; and KAET Channel 8–PBS.

RADIO STATIONS AM: KTAR 620 (news/talk); KAMJ 1230 (contemporary); and KLFF 1360 (big band music). FM: KSLX 100.7 (nostalgia); KVRY 104.7 (adult contemporary); and KNIX 102.5 (country).

TELEPHONE The area code for Phoenix is 602.

SALES TAX The city sales tax is 6.7%.

CLIMATE Try not to visit in summer (though hotel prices go down), when it's more than 100F during the day and in the 90s at night. Fall, winter, and spring are dry, warm, and sunny. Temperatures range from daytime highs of between 60 and 80F to nighttime lows of about 35 to 50F.

GETTING AROUND

Getting around Phoenix is next to impossible without a car.

AIRPORT *Sky Harbor International Airport* is just a 10-minute drive from downtown. (Taxi fares vary widely, so be sure to agree on a price before getting into a cab.) *Supershuttle* (phone: 244-9000) offers transportation from the airport to downtown and to most other Valley locations. For rides to the airport, call 24 hours in advance. *Phoenix Transit* (phone: 253-5000) buses stop at terminals 3 and 4 at *Sky Harbor* every half hour. One goes downtown and one to the east Valley. Fare is $1; transfers are free.

BUS The system is sketchy, with interminable waiting periods, erratic schedules, limited nighttime service, and few buses on Sundays. However, you can call *Phoenix Transit System* (phone: 253-5000) for schedule information. Fare: $1.50 on express routes; $1 on local routes.

CAR RENTAL All major national firms are represented. Of local companies, *Rent A Wreck* (phone: 252-4897) is among the least expensive.

TAXI Call *Yellow Cab* (phone: 252-5071) or *Triple A* (phone: 437-4000).

LOCAL SERVICES

AUDIOVISUAL EQUIPMENT *Arizona Audio Visual Center* (phone: 860-9321); *Photo & Sound Co.* (phone: 437-1560).

BABY-SITTING *Ace Baby-sitting Service* (3737 E. Turney Ave.; phone: 956-2848).

BUSINESS SERVICES *Alison's Secretarial Service* (3270 E. Camelback Rd.; phone: 955-3542).

COMPUTER RENTAL *AccuRent Computer Systems* (phone: 829-6500); *Use 'R Computers* (phone: 263-5599).

DRY CLEANER/TAILOR *Downtown Laundry & Dry Cleaning* (308 N. Second Ave.; phone: 253-7245).

LIMOUSINE *Arizona Limousines* (phone: 267-7097); *Valley Limousines* (phone: 254-1955).

MECHANIC *Western States Tire Co.* (201 W. Van Buren; phone: 254-4131).

MEDICAL EMERGENCY *St. Luke's Hospital* (1800 E. Van Buren; phone: 251-8183; 245-1657 for emergency medics and paramedics).

MESSENGER SERVICES *Dial-a-Messenger* (phone: 240-6060).

MONEY TRANSFERS *American Express MoneyGram* (phone: 800-926-9400 for information; 800-866-8800 for money transfers); *Western Union Financial Services* (phone: 800-325-6000 or 800-325-4176).

NATIONAL/INTERNATIONAL COURIER *DHL Worldwide Express* (phone: 800-225-5345); *FedEx* (phone: 254-4662).

PHARMACY *Lahr Pharmacy* (9220 N. Central Ave.; phone: 944-3326), open daily from 7 AM to midnight.

PHOTOCOPIES *Acme Blueprint* (1425 N. First St.; phone: 254-6171); *Alphagraphics Printshop of the Future* (2918 N. Central Ave.; phone: 274-2345), delivery service.

POST OFFICE Main office (522 N. Central Ave.; phone: 253-4102).

PROFESSIONAL PHOTOGRAPHER *Hassen Photography* (phone: 279-1199); *Rick Mueller Photography* (phone: 446-1633).

SECRETARY/STENOGRAPHER *American Clerical and Secretarial Services* (phone: 957-4741), pickup and delivery.

TRANSLATOR *Berlitz* (phone: 468-9494).

WESTERN UNION/TELEX Many offices are located around the city (phone: 800-325-6000 to find the location nearest you).

SPECIAL EVENTS

The *Phoenix Open Golf Tournament* (phone: 263-0757) takes place in January; other golf tournaments are played throughout the year. In February, the *Arabian Horse Show and Sale* (phone: 264-5691) is a spectacular event. In March, the *Veterans Memorial Coliseum* (1826 W. McDowell; phone: 264-4808) is the site of the *Phoenix Jaycees Rodeo of Rodeos.* In May, one of the city's most vibrant celebrations is the *Cinco de Mayo,* an annual holiday celebrating the Mexican victory over French troops in 1862. In October, the *Arizona State Fair* fills up the *State Fairgrounds* (phone: 252-6711) and the *Cowboy Artists of America* bring their works to town for the nationally recognized sale and exhibition at the *Phoenix Art Museum* (phone: 257-1880). November finds hundreds of colorful balloons dotting the turquoise skies in the annual *Thunderbird Balloon Race* at the *Glendale Municipal Airport* (phone: 978-7208). Watch for the month-long schedule of activities that begin in December for the *Sunkist Fiesta Bowl,* capped by a *New Year's* weekend that brings a parade, a national high school band pageant, and two of the country's top collegiate football teams together in a bowl game.

MUSEUMS

In addition to those described in *Special Places,* Phoenix has two other museums of note.

ARIZONA MINERAL MUSEUM Polished gems and minerals glitter under spotlights in this warehouse-size museum. Closed Sundays. No admission charge. 1826 W. McDowell (phone: 255-3791).

HALL OF FLAME MUSEUM No kidding. This collection of firefighting paraphernalia dates from 1725. Closed weekends. No admission charge. 6101 E. Van Buren (phone: 275-3473).

ART GALLERIES

Although Phoenix does have some interesting galleries, most of the finest are in Scottsdale, within walking distance of one another. They exhibit a rich and vast array of art forms—paintings, sculpture, graphics—and many are devoted to contemporary western and American Indian art.

ARTISTIC GALLERY Among the artists exhibited here is the nationally acclaimed R. C. Gorman. 7077 E. Main St., Scottsdale (phone: 945-6766).

ELAINE HORWITCH GALLERIES The work of a wide variety of contemporary artists—both sculptors and painters—is on view here. 4211 N. Marshall Way, Scottsdale (phone: 945-0791).

GALLERY MCGOFFIN This is the country's only batik gallery. 902 W. Roosevelt, Phoenix (phone: 255-0785).

HAND AND THE SPIRIT Tapestries, ceramics, jewelry, and other crafts can be seen here. 4222 N. Marshall Way, Scottsdale (phone: 946-4529).

LOVENA OHL GALLERY Indian arts and crafts, from primitive to contemporary, are on display here. 4251 N. Marshall Way, Scottsdale (phone: 945-8212).

MARILYN BUTLER FINE ART Fritz Scholder is among the artists exhibited here. 4160 N. Craftsman Court, Scottsdale (phone: 994-9550).

SUZANNE BROWN GALLERY The contemporary western art here ranges from abstract to representational. 7156 E. Main St., Scottsdale (phone: 945-8475).

SPORTS AND FITNESS

The year-round sun makes Phoenix ideal for watching or participating in outdoor athletics.

BASEBALL Phoenix and the surrounding area are major spring training venues. The Oakland *A's* train at *Phoenix Municipal Stadium* (5999 E. Van Buren, Phoenix; phone: 392-0074); the California *Angels* spend the season at *Diablo Stadium* (2200 W. Alameda, Tempe; phone: 678-2222); the Milwaukee *Brewers* play at *Compadre Stadium* (4001 S. Alma School, Chandler; phone: 895-6000); and the Chicago *Cubs* at *HoHoKam Park* (1235 N. Center, Mesa; phone: 800-638-4253). Both the San Diego *Padres* (phone: 878-4337) and the Seattle *Mariners* (phone: 784-4444) train at *Peoria Stadium* (16101 N. 80 Third Ave., Peoria). The San Francisco *Giants* set up camp at the *Scottsdale Stadium* (7408 E. Osborn Rd., Scottsdale; phone: 990-7972).

BASKETBALL The *NBA* Phoenix *Suns* play in the *America West Arena* (Second and Washington Sts.; phone: 258-6711). The *Arizona State University Sun Devils* play at the *University Athletic Center* in Tempe (phone: 965-2381).

BICYCLING Rent bikes from *Airplane and Bicycle Works* (4400 N. Scottsdale Rd., Scottsdale; phone: 949-1978).

DOG RACING Canines compete at *Greyhound Park* (40th and E. Washington Sts.; phone: 273-7181).

FISHING Trout, bass, and crappie can be caught at Apache Lake and in the Salt River.

FOOTBALL The *NFL* Arizona *Cardinals* (phone: 379-0102) and the *Arizona State Sun Devils* (phone: 965-2381) play at *Sun Devil Stadium* (*Arizona State University,* Tempe).

GOLF There are about 90 courses in the Phoenix area, many of them at resorts that welcome transient players.

TOP TEE-OFF SPOTS

Boulders Located in the Sonora Desert, this incredible golfing playground has revamped itself into two 18-hole courses, *Boulders' North* (6,731 yards, par 72) and *Boulders' South* (6,589 yards, par 71). Of the two, *Boulders' South* is the more scenic and challenging; the green of No. 5 is set in an amphitheater of boulders, while the tee at No. 6 is at the very foot of a high, boulder-strewn hill. Each course offers dramatic desert scenery. Members of the *Boulders Golf Club* and hotel guests switch courses every other day. In Carefree, about 30 miles north of Phoenix (phone: 488-9009; 800-553-1717).

Scottsdale Princess A lovely setting for the *Stadium* course (phone: 585-3939) of the *Tournament Players Club* of Scottsdale, adjacent to the impressive *Desert* course (phone: 585-3800). Both were designed by the team of Weiskopf, Morrish, and Twitty and are operated to the high standards of the *PGA Tour*. The 6,992-yard, par 71 PGA-TPC *Stadium* track is the site of the annual *Phoenix Open*, a *PGA Tour* event. The *Desert* course is a challenging 6,525-yard, par 71. There also is a full-service pro shop. 7575 E. Princess Dr. (phone: 585-4848; 800-344-4758).

Troon North Host to the *PGA* tournament *Merrill Lynch "Shootout,"* this 18-hole, par 72 course, designed by Weiskopf and Morrish, was recently listed by *Golf* magazine and *Golf Digest* among the top 50 courses in the US. At 7,008 yards from the back tees, there are no parallel fairways. The elevated tees allow for miles of desert vistas of boulders, cacti, and mountains. According to the pro shop, the best time to play is in the fall, when it's less crowded and the weather is nearly always perfect. 10320 E. Dynamite Blvd. (phone: 585-5300).

Visitors are also welcome at *Papago Park* municipal course (phone: 275-8428).

HORSEBACK RIDING Hourly rentals are available at *Ponderosa Stable* (10215 S. Central; phone: 268-1261), *South Mountain Stable* (10005 S. Central; phone: 276-8131), and *All Western Stables* (10220 S. Central; phone: 276-5862).

HORSE RACING The season runs from October through April at *Turf Paradise* (19th Ave. and Bell Rd.; phone: 942-1101).

JOGGING On scorchingly hot days, the air conditioned *Paradise Valley Mall* (at the intersection of Tatum and Cactus; phone: 996-8840) is an enclosed haven for walkers before it officially opens to shoppers. Run under the sun along the banks of the Arizona Canal (pick it up beside the *Biltmore* hotel) or the Grand Canal, reachable by jogging about a mile north along Central Avenue. *Encanto Park,* about three-quarters of a mile from downtown, also attracts runners.

SPAS Many area hotels feature spa services among their amenities, but one in particular deserves special note.

A SYBARITIC SPA

Spa at Marriott's Camelback Inn This super-indulgent center concentrates on total wellness; its program was designed by Dr. Kenneth Cooper of the *Institute of Aerobic Research*. After a strenuous workout, slip into one of the eight outdoor or 12 indoor massage rooms, and try the Bindi Herbal Body Treatment, a mélange of aromatherapy and massage that uses fragrant herbal formulas. The beauty salon has skincare and beauty experts. 5402 E. Lincoln Dr. (phone: 948-1700; 800-24-CAMEL)

SURFING If you've always wanted to surf but can't quite brave the force of the ocean, the Island of Big Surf in Tempe (1500 N. Hayden Rd.; phone: 947-2478) is a good place to break in. There are artificial beaches and waves, and you can rent the entire facility. Closed October through March; Mondays (except holiday weekends); and weekdays in September. Admission charge.

SWIMMING The Salt River is good for a swim, and there are 23 municipal pools in Phoenix. Every large park has one. Try the pool at *Coronado Park* (N. 12th St. and Coronado Rd.; phone: 256-3220).

TENNIS In all, there are more than 1,000 courts in the Phoenix area, but two places score high with us.

CHOICE COURTS

Arizona Biltmore This ultra-posh, large-scale, superstar resort (also see *Checking In*) has eight Plexipave courts, plus video replay and ball machines; reservations possible; private lessons and clinics are also available. 24th St. and Missouri (phone: 955-6600; 800-950-0086).

John Gardiner's Some people call this place the most complete and professional training establishment in the world—for good reason. Facilities and services include 22 Plexipave outdoor courts and two Omni courts, video replay and ball machines (plus other instructional aids), tennis clinics, private lessons, and complimentary court time for guests. You can lodge in small casitas or in three- or four-bedroom casas, some with their own pool and court. Champagne is on the house when it rains. 5700 E. McDonald Dr., Scottsdale (phone: 948-2100; 800-245-2051; fax: 483-7314).

In addition, the *Phoenix Tennis Center* (6330 N. 21st Ave.; phone: 249-3712) has 22 lighted courts for night play.

TUBING On any given weekend, as many as 20,000 residents strap beer-filled ice chests and their bottoms to old inner tubes and float down 5 or 10 miles of the free-flowing Salt River, below Saguaro Lake, just north of Mesa. The trip is free and you can buy tubes—the bigger the better—at gas stations and stands along the route. This utterly relaxing pastime is called "tubing down the Salt." For tube rental and shuttle service, contact *Salt River Recreation*, Mesa (phone: 984-3305).

THEATER

There's quite a lot of drama in Phoenix and Scottsdale. Many plays take place on campuses, and world-renowned performers have come to play Shakespeare. Check the local publications listed under *Local Coverage* for schedules. The major theaters include: *Phoenix Little Theater* (25 E.

Coronado Rd.; phone: 254-2151); *Herberger Theater Center* (222 E. Monroe St.; phone: 252-8497); *Gammage Auditorium* (a Frank Lloyd Wright building on the campus of *Arizona State University* in Tempe; phone: 965-3434); and *Scottsdale Center for the Arts* (Civic Center Plaza, on the corner of Second St. and Civic Center Blvd., Scottsdale; phone: 994-2787). *Arizona Ballet Theater* performs at *Scottsdale Center for the Arts*. Traveling dance troupes perform at *Gammage Auditorium* and the *Scottsdale Center for the Arts*.

MUSIC

The *Phoenix Symphony* (phone: 264-4754) and *Arizona Opera Company* (phone: 254-1664) play at *Symphony Hall* (225 E. Adams); the *Scottsdale Symphony* performs at *Scottsdale Center for the Arts* (see above). Nationally known rock performers and classical musicians appear at *Gammage Auditorium* (see above). Rock groups also give concerts at *Veterans Memorial Coliseum* (1826 W. McDowell; phone: 258-6711). Good music also is found on college and university campuses.

NIGHTCLUBS AND NIGHTLIFE

After work, professionals belly up to the oyster bar at *Steamers* (*Biltmore Fashion Park;* phone: 956-3631; see *Eating Out*). Another good meeting place is *Timothy's* (6335 N. 16th St.; phone: 277-7634), with live jazz nightly. *Arizona Live!* at the *Arizona Center* (455 N. Third; phone: 271-4000) is a collection of clubs that includes a sports bar, a country-and-western bar, and a comedy club. If you crave a little Mexican food, don your dancing shoes and head to *Acapulco Bay Beach Club* (3837 E. Thomas; phone: 273-6077). And for margaritas and music that will knock your socks off, try *Depot Cantina* (300 S. Ash, Tempe; phone: 966-6677).

Best in Town

CHECKING IN

If you're going to Phoenix on business, you'll probably want to stay downtown. If it's a vacation, you can't beat the resorts, which offer full recreational activities and Valley tours. Meals usually are included in the room rate at a resort, but be sure to check first. Expect to pay between $120 and $300 per night for a double room at hotels and resorts listed under *Grand Hotels and Special Havens;* between $75 and $120 at hotels categorized as expensive; $30 to $75 at those listed as moderate; and around $30 at inexpensive places. For bed and breakfast accommodations, contact *Bed & Breakfast in Arizona* (PO Box 8628, Scottsdale, AZ 85252; phone: 995-2831) or *Mi Casa, Su Casa* (PO Box 950, Tempe, AZ 85280; phone: 990-0682). Unless noted otherwise, hotel rooms have air conditioning, private baths, TV sets, and telephones. All hotels are in the 602 area code unless otherwise indicated.

Here are our favorites in the Phoenix area, followed by our recommendations of cost and quality choices, listed by price category.

GRAND HOTELS AND SPECIAL HAVENS

Arizona Biltmore Frank Lloyd Wright was the consulting architect for this grande dame of desert resorts, designed by Albert Chase McArthur, his admirer. The 502-room place, which recently underwent a multimillion-dollar renovation, sports some very Gatsbyesque features, including the gold leaf ceiling in the dining room and the glass mural in the lobby. The food is good enough to bring diners from all over the Valley, and there is an endless assortment of facilities—tennis courts (see *Tennis,* above), two first-rate 18-hole golf courses, and three pools (one lined with Catalina tile, comparable to the one at William Randolph Hearst's *San Simeon*). Business amenities include a concierge desk, A/V equipment, photocopiers, secretarial services, computers, and express checkout. 24th St. and Missouri (phone: 955-6600; 800-528-3696; fax: 954-2548).

Boulders Opened in 1985 by Rockresorts (although no longer part of that group), this is a "rock resort" in another sense: It is set on 1,300 acres of desert foothills, at the base of towering piles of boulders. The resort's 136 adobe-colored casitas blend remarkably well with the surrounding terrain, and while the landscape has been tamed slightly to allow for the hotel, the proliferation of desert vegetation has actually been enhanced. Walking from any guestroom to the nearby lodge for a meal is to stroll through an entire spectrum of cactus varieties, to say nothing of sage and desert honeysuckle. The interior landscape is equally impressive: Each casita contains a room with a wet bar and a large oval tub; easy chairs face a juniper wood–burning fireplace in the conversation area. For recreation, there are six tennis courts, first-rate golf (see *Golf,* above), exercise facilities, horseback riding on desert trails, desert jeep tours, and hot-air ballooning. Also available is an obliging concierge desk, six meeting rooms, A/V equipment, photocopiers, secretarial services, computers, and express checkout. Carefree, about 30 miles north of Phoenix (phone: 488-9009; 800-553-1717; fax: 488-4118).

Marriott's Camelback Inn This resort at the foot of Mummy Mountain, facing its namesake across the Valley, was built in 1936 of adobe mud dug up for the foundation; and in recent years, the total number of rooms on the 120 acres has expanded to 423. There are three pools, 10 tennis courts, two of the area's fancier 18-holers, as well as a staff big enough to put room service and overall maintenance head and shoulders above that of most far smaller hotels. You also can go biking, hiking, or horseback riding on an Indian reservation a few miles away; play Ping-Pong, basketball, volleyball, shuffleboard—or get a massage at the wonderful spa (see *Spas,* above). 5402 E. Lincoln Dr., Scottsdale (phone: 948-1700; 800-24-CAMEL; fax: 596-7019).

Phoenician An exclusive and secluded retreat on 130 acres at the base of the dramatic Camelback Mountains, its isolation belies its proximity to Scottsdale and Phoenix. The main hotel is marvelously appointed, with geometric fountains, crystal chandeliers, and a ceiling aglitter with gold leaf. The view of the Valley is simply overwhelming. There are 442 rooms, plus 107 luxury casitas, 31 deluxe suites, and two presidential suites. Those with a physical bent can enjoy 11 lighted tennis courts, an 18-hole golf course with a driving range, putting green, seven pools, a whirlpool, two children's pools, and a 165-foot water slide. Other activities include croquet, badminton, volleyball, basketball, biking, lawn bowling, a children's program, and jogging. A fully equipped spa and fitness center offers guests weight training, saunas, Swiss showers, massage therapy, and beauty treatments. Four restaurants offer European and Southwestern cuisine. Among the business amenities are a concierge desk, 30 meeting rooms, A/V equipment, photocopiers, computers, secretarial services, 24-hour room service, and express checkout. 6000 E. Camelback Rd., Scottsdale (phone: 941-8200; 800-888-8234; fax: 947-4311).

Scottsdale Princess This eight-year-old, $90-million property has quickly become one of the premier resort destinations in the Southwest. There are 363 rooms and 37 suites in its main building, plus 125 casitas; all rooms have been designed around the earthy accents of the Southwest, and feature living and working areas, terraces, wet bars, refrigerators, and large bathrooms; casitas offer wood-burning fireplaces. Service is attentive, yet not overbearing, and the facilities are diverse. Activities include two 18-hole championship golf courses (see *Golf,* above), nine world class tennis courts including a 10,000-seat stadium, three heated pools, a spa and fitness center, a nearby polo field, and numerous restaurants. A recreational program offers volleyball, croquet, biking, hiking, fitness walks, and jogging; during the holidays, there are supervised programs for kids ages five through 12. Adjacent to *Westworld,* Scottsdale's 400-acre horse park. Among the other amenities are concierge and secretarial services, 24-hour room service, 23 meeting rooms, A/V equipment, photocopiers, computers, and express checkout. 7575 E. Princess Dr., Scottsdale (phone: 585-4848; 800-223-1818; fax: 585-0086).

EXPENSIVE

Embassy Suites The goal here is to provide a homey atmosphere, and since 95% of the guests return, it appears that the management is successful. Accommodations are in two-room suites with kitchens; breakfasts and late afternoon cocktails are complimentary. Note: Tipping is *not* permitted. Six locations: 5001 N. Scottsdale Rd., Scottsdale; 1515 N. 44th St., 2333 E. Thomas Rd., 2630 E. Camelback Rd., and 3210 NW Grand Ave., Phoenix; and 4400 S. Rural Rd., Tempe (phone: 800-362-2779).

Hermosa Resort Long one of the Valley's most exclusive guest ranches and tennis resorts, it says it is "not just a resort, it's an attitude." That sounds like hype until you see its 35 charming rooms (with gas-fired fireplaces, wet bars, and Jacuzzis) and its recently redone restaurant; the staff treats every guest like a VIP. 5532 N. Palo Cristi Rd., Paradise Valley (phone: 955-8614).

Hyatt Regency Scottsdale Built at Gainey Ranch, a planned community, this $75-million, 497-room luxury resort offers all the basic recreational facilities (pool with swim-up bar, eight tennis courts, 27 holes of championship golf, health club, and Jacuzzi), as well as a few extras (lawn tennis and croquet). Guests can sate hunger and thirst at the two restaurants, entertainment lounge, or lobby bar. Twenty-four-hour room service is available, as well as a concierge desk, 21 meeting rooms, A/V equipment, photocopiers, secretarial services, computers, and express checkout. 7500 E. Doubletree Ranch, Scottsdale (phone: 991-3388; 800-228-9000; fax: 483-5511).

Marriott's Mountain Shadows With a 1,500-seat grand ballroom and 10 meeting rooms, it's no wonder this place is popular with convention groups and business travelers. And after all those meetings, guests can relax by taking advantage of the three pools, two Jacuzzis, eight tennis courts, and three 18-hole golf courses. There are two informal restaurants; business amenities include a concierge, A/V equipment, photocopiers, secretarial services, computers, and express checkout. 5641 E. Lincoln Dr., Scottsdale (phone: 948-7111; 800-228-9290; fax: 948-7111, ext. 1898).

Pointe Hilton at Squaw Peak Lovely Southwestern decor characterizes this 576-room mountainside resort (now a link in the Hilton chain), which manages to remain almost fully booked even during the summer. *Pointe of View* (see *Eating Out*) is one of several good restaurants here. Room service is available around the clock; there's a concierge desk, 28 meeting rooms, A/V equipment, photocopiers, secretarial services, computers, and express checkout. 7677 N. 16th St. (phone: 997-6000; 800-HILTONS; fax: 997-2391).

Pointe Hilton at Tapatio Cliffs Patterned after the successful *Pointe Hilton at Squaw Peak* (above) this mountainside resort has attractive Spanish-Southwestern architecture and luxurious amenities. The dazzling *Etienne's Different Pointe of View* restaurant is a mountaintop facility that serves fine French fare. Around-the-clock room service is available; also concierge and secretarial services, 26 meeting rooms, A/V equipment, photocopiers, computers, and express checkout. 11111 N. Seventh St. (phone: 997-6000; 800-HILTONS; fax: 993-0276).

Radisson Resort A good choice for those who want to go first class, this busy 318-room place (formerly the *Registry Resort*) borders several golf courses and has three pools, a fitness center, and nightly entertainment. Its *La Champagne* (see *Eating Out*) restaurant is considered one of the Valley's best, and Sunday brunch in the *Phoenician Room* combines live music with a remarkable array of food. Business amenities include a concierge desk, 24-hour room service, 12 meeting rooms, A/V equipment, photocopiers, secretarial services, computers, and express checkout. 7171 N. Scottsdale Rd., Scottsdale (phone: 991-3800; 800-247-9810; fax: 948-9843).

Ritz-Carlton This 301-room hotel looks as if it was plucked right off the East Coast and plunked down in the desert. No cactus, no adobe-style architecture or kachina dolls here. Instead, it remains traditional, from the leaded glass chandeliers overhead to the plush Oriental rugs. And just like other members of its group, the emphasis here is on service for well-heeled corporate travelers and affluent vacationers. Pluses include a restaurant, 24-hour room service, a concierge, 14 meeting rooms, secretarial services, A/V equipment, photocopiers, computers, and express checkout. 2401 E. Camelback Rd. (phone: 468-0700; 800-241-3333; fax: 468-9883).

Westcourt Located next to the *Metrocenter*—which is packed with shops and restaurants—this ultramodern hostelry has more original artwork in its 284 luxury rooms and suites than many galleries. It also has a dining room called *Trumps*. Among the business amenities are 12 meeting rooms, concierge and secretarial services, A/V equipment, photocopiers, computers, and express checkout. 10220 N. Metro Pkwy. E. (phone: 997-5900; 800-858-1033; fax: 997-1034).

Wyndham Paradise Valley This 20-acre, $40-million facility offers 380 rooms, including 27 suites, as well as two pools, a health club and spa, racquetball courts, tennis courts, and two restaurants. Computers, 18 meeting rooms, A/V equipment, photocopiers, a concierge, secretarial services, and express checkout are all offered. 5401 N. Scottsdale Rd., Scottsdale (phone: 947-5400; 800-822-4200; fax: 481-0209).

MODERATE

Doubletree Suites Quiet, comfortable, and lushly landscaped, this hotel is only minutes from the airport at *Gateway Center*. Muted Southwestern tones decorate each of its 242 suites. Relax in *Topper's* restaurant, a cozy dining room just off the lobby. Complimentary airport shuttle and health club are included. There are meeting rooms, A/V equipment, photocopiers, and express checkout. 320 N. 44th St. (phone: 225-0500; 800-528-0444; fax: 225-0957).

Fiesta Inn This venerable favorite is a true Southwest delight, with Mexican tiles and room-size fireplaces. In addition to a restaurant, health club, and jogging trails, there's also a concierge desk, seven meeting rooms, A/V equipment, photocopiers, computers, and a complimentary airport shuttle. 2100 S. Prest Dr., Tempe (phone: 967-1441; 800-528-6481; fax: 967-0224).

Lexington This is a good place for an extended visit since all 139 suites come with kitchens, continental breakfast, and hospitality hour. There are discounts for long stays/relocation. 1660 W. Elliot Rd. (phone: 345-8585; 800-53-SUITE; fax: 990-7873).

INEXPENSIVE

Travel Inn 9 Smaller and quieter than others in town, this 68-unit motel (with pool) also is kinder to your budget. 201 N. Seventh Ave. (phone: 254-6521).

EATING OUT

Best bets in Phoenix are Mexican restaurants and steakhouses. Expect to pay $60 or more for a dinner for two at places listed as expensive; between $35 and $60 at those categorized as moderate; less than $35 at inexpensive places. Prices do not include drinks, wine, tax, or tips. Unless otherwise noted, restaurants are open for lunch and dinner. All restaurants are in the 602 area code.

EXPENSIVE

La Champagne Part of the prestigious *Radisson Resort*, this ambitious restaurant offers American nouvelle and French cuisine, black tie service, an extensive wine list, and piano music. Closed Sundays and Mondays. Reservations advised. Major credit cards accepted. 7171 N. Scottsdale Rd., Scottsdale (phone: 991-3800).

Christopher's Chef and owner Christopher Gross has a well-deserved local reputation for his well-prepared French dishes, and glowing writeups in several magazines, including *Gourmet,* have given him a high profile nationally as well. Grilled sea scallops with Provençal vegetables, veal chop with carrot and onion potato purée, and sautéed venison with huckleberries and red wine sauce are just some of the selections offered here. Open daily. Reservations advised. Major credit cards accepted. 2398 E. Camelback Rd. (phone: 957-3214).

Mancuso's The decor at the Scottsdale location will transport you to an Italian Renaissance castle, and the continental dishes and service merit applause. Entrées include soup, salad, and more. Closed major holidays. Reservations advised. Major credit cards accepted. 6166 N. Scottsdale Rd., Scottsdale (phone: 948-9988). Also a branch at 4949 E. Lincoln Dr., Paradise Valley (phone: 840-8670).

Palm Court Tuxedoed waiters prepare much of the food at your table at this dining room in the *Scottsdale Conference Resort.* While gazing out on Camelback Mountain and Lake McCormick, you can select from the brief but tempting à la carte continental menu. Recommended are the Bibb lettuce salad, the lobster bisque, and the rack of lamb. Sunday brunch here is considered among the Valley's finest. Open daily. Reservations advised. Major credit cards accepted. 7700 E. McCormick Pkwy., Scottsdale (phone: 991-3400).

Pointe of View Charcoal-broiled steaks and pasta are house specialties. The view affords an impressive panorama of the Valley. Open daily. Reservations advised. Major credit cards accepted. *Pointe Hilton at Squaw Peak,* 7677 N. 16th St. (phone: 997-5859).

Tomaso's This dining spot and its siblings are known for their northern Italian specialties. Closed *Thanksgiving* and *Christmas*. Reservations advised. Major credit cards accepted. Three locations: 610 E. Bell Rd. (phone: 866-1906); 3225 E. Camelback Rd. (phone: 956-0836); and 1954 S. Dobson Rd., Mesa (phone: 897-0140).

Vincent Guerithault on Camelback Get a real taste of the Southwest in this elegant eatery headed by one of the finest chefs in the Southwest. You can order tacos and tamales anywhere, but never have they been prepared with such unique ingredients—try a duck tamale or a lobster corn pancake. Closed Sundays. Reservations advised. Major credit cards accepted. 3930 E. Camelback Rd. (phone: 224-0225).

MODERATE

Christopher's Bistro Christopher Gross, chef and owner of *Christopher's* (see above), has extended his talents to the adjacent café. Dishes such as grilled mahimahi with honey, cardamom, and couscous; osso buco with white beans and a roasted tomato; and grilled rib eye steaks with peppercorns and roquefort cheese, as well as dessert soufflés made to order, crown the menu. Open daily. Reservations advised. Major credit cards accepted. 2398 E. Camelback Rd. (phone: 957-3214).

Don & Charlie's If your appetite is bigger than your budget, try this place. The menu's American dishes may seem standard, but just wait till they arrive at your table. Steaks are huge and perfectly cooked, and the meaty pork ribs are good, too. It boasts one of the best happy hour spreads in town. Closed *Thanksgiving*. Reservations advised. Major credit cards accepted. 7501 E. Camelback Rd., Scottsdale (phone: 990-0900).

Los Dos Molinos The New Mexican fare here is painstakingly prepared and presented. Owners Vickie and Eddie Chavez roast their own green and red chilies, which they then add to pizza, beef dishes, and the obligatory (but excellent) salsa. Marinated pork ribs are also first-rate. You can cool your palate with an iced raspberry tea, and sopapillas (fried dough) served with honey make a fine dessert. Open daily. Reservations advised. Major credit cards accepted. 8646 S. Central Ave. (phone: 243-9113).

Durant's A fashionable place for everyone from politicians to local celebrities for 30 years. Enjoy the traditional appetizers before dinner, then choose steaks or prime ribs. Closed major holidays. Reservations advised. Major credit cards accepted. 2611 N. Central Ave. (phone: 264-5967).

Golden Palace Cuisine of India One of the city's best Indian restaurants, it serves tandoori chicken and fiery specialties such as lamb *vindaloo*. The pace is leisurely, the atmosphere friendly. Open daily. Reservations unnecessary. Major credit cards accepted. 4320 W. Thomas Rd. (phone: 352-1100).

Monti's La Casa Vieja A Valley landmark, this spot serves some of the best steaks anywhere. It's always crowded, but the service is good and the side dishes are plentiful. Open daily. Reservations advised for lunch only. Major credit cards accepted. 3 W. First, Tempe (phone: 967-7594).

Paniolo Located in a trendy area of Phoenix, this bar and grill combines Southwestern and Hawaiian cooking styles (*paniolo* is the Hawaiian word for cowboy). Try the barbecued pig on an onion roll with shallot soy sauce; the menu also includes barbecued chicken, ribs, grilled shrimp, and fiery Texas Chainsaw Chili. Open daily. Reservations advised. Major credit cards accepted. 2566 E. Camelback Rd. (phone: 381-8772).

Pinnacle Peak Patio No trip to Arizona would be complete without a visit to a real Western cowboy steakhouse. This one's the oldest and most famous, with two-pound porterhouses broiled over mesquite coals and served with sourdough bread and pinto beans. Don't wear a tie! Closed *Thanksgiving, Christmas Eve,* and *Christmas*. Reservations necessary for large groups only. Major credit cards accepted. 10426 E. Jomax Rd., Scottsdale (phone: 967-8082).

Piñon Grill Who said hotel restaurants had to be boring or uncreative? If you hunger for authentic Southwestern fare, head to the grill at the *Inn at McCormick Ranch*. The lakeside setting and the copper and cactus decor only enhance the topnotch fare. Open daily. Reservations unnecessary. Major credit cards accepted. 7401 N. Scottsdale Rd., Scottsdale (phone: 948-5050).

RoxSand One of the most talked-about dining spots to open in the Valley in years, this stylish place features "intercontinental" dishes that vary widely in price, complexity, and origin. There are enticing entrées from Italy, Korea, Mongolia, Morocco, Sweden, and Russia, but nothing beats the desserts. Closed on major holidays. Reservations advised. Major credit cards accepted. 2594 E. Camelback Rd., Scottsdale (phone: 381-0444).

Steamers It may seem impossible to find excellent seafood in the Southwest, but here it is. Try the Maine lobster, the Baltimore crab cakes, or the Boston clam chowder. Open daily. Reservations advised. Major credit cards accepted. 2576 E. Camelback Rd. (phone: 956-3631).

Yamakasa Japanese fare, including a wonderful sushi bar and teriyaki beef and chicken, is presented with great care and style. One section of the restaurant has low tables and legless chairs for diners who want to eat in traditional style. Open daily. Reservations advised. Major credit cards accepted. 9301 Shea Blvd., Scottsdale (phone: 860-5605).

INEXPENSIVE

Coffee Plantation This outdoor café in one of the most eclectic neighborhoods in the area is great for people watching. As you sit sipping your cappuccino or hot chocolate, you can see a fantastic assortment of citizenry strolling by. Soups and salads are also available. Closed *Thanksgiving* and *Christmas*. No reservations. Major credit cards accepted. 680 S. Mill Ave., Tempe (phone: 829-7878).

Ed Debevic's Short Orders Deluxe Step back in time to a 1950s diner, complete with a blue-plate special and wisecracking, gum-snapping waitresses. Order the meat loaf sandwich with a real cherry Coke. It's as much fun as you remember. Closed *Thanksgiving* and *Christmas*. Reservations unnecessary. Major credit cards accepted. 2102 East Highland St. (phone: 956-2760).

Honey Bear's BBQ Tender chicken and pork are doused in a sweet spicy sauce. The eatery's motto, "You don't need teeth to eat our meat," is close to the mark. Open daily. Reservations unnecessary. Major credit cards accepted. 5012 E. Van Buren St. (phone: 273-9148).

Hops Bistro Brewery This pub offers the usual assortment of burgers and sandwiches, but its beer is the area's best. Among the varieties offered are an amber ale, a pilsner, summer-wheat and dark-wheat brews, and seasonal varieties. Closed *Thanksgiving* and *Christmas*. No reservations. Major credit cards accepted. 7000 E. Camelback Rd., Scottsdale (phone: 945-4677).

El Norteño This small take-out place is cramped and far from elegant, but the food more than makes up for the lack of atmosphere. It serves some of the best Mexican fare in Phoenix. Open daily. Reservations unnecessary. Major credit cards accepted. 1002 N. Seventh Ave. (phone: 254-4429).

Los Olivos A family operation for more than three decades, this is the Valley's oldest Mexican eatery. Thoroughly modern decor belies its age, but the food explains its longevity. Try such house specialties as sour cream enchiladas and *carne asada*. Closed major holidays. Reservations accepted. Major credit cards accepted. 7328 E. Second St., Scottsdale (phone: 946-2256).

Pink Pepper A few years ago, the Valley had only one Thai restaurant; now there are about two dozen. This ultramodern spot is the prettiest of the lot, and since it uses moderation when sprinkling on the spices, it's a good place for the uninitiated to try this often-fiery food. The soup with lemongrass and coconut milk is tops, as are the meat dishes with Phonaeng curry. Open daily. Reservations advised. Major credit cards accepted. 2003 N. Scottsdale Rd., Scottsdale (phone: 945-9300). Two other locations: 4967 W. Bell (phone: 843-0070); and 1941 W. Guadalupe, Mesa (phone: 839-9009).

Unique Foods and Services Much of the fare here is nourishing as well as tasty: greens, beans, black-eyed peas, okra gumbo, and other vegetarian dishes, all prepared with fresh produce from the local markets. Diners also can enjoy beef barbecued in a spicy sauce, as well as fried chicken. At lunchtime, there is an all-you-can-eat buffet with a different theme each day; these specialties range from European to African dishes. Listen to live jazz on Tuesday, Wednesday, and Friday nights. Open daily. Reservations unnecessary. Major credit cards accepted. 1153 E. Jefferson St. (phone: 257-0701).

Pittsburgh

At-a-Glance

SEEING THE CITY
Go to the top of Mt. Washington via either of two inclines for a sweeping 17-mile view of the three area rivers. The Duquesne incline (W. Carson St.; phone: 381-1665) and the Monongahela incline (E. Carson St., behind the *Freight House Shops* of *Station Square;* phone: 231-5707), in operation since 1870, cost $1.25 each way (exact change required).

SPECIAL PLACES
Most of Pittsburgh's places of interest are in four main sections of the city: the Golden Triangle downtown area, the North Side, the East End, and the South Side.

GOLDEN TRIANGLE
Though most major attractions are within walking distance, use the subway for quick crosstown transportation.

POINT STATE PARK At the tip of the Golden Triangle, it covers 36 acres of broad walks and spacious gardens on the banks of the river junction. The park contains *Fort Pitt Blockhouse,* a 1764 fortification; and the *Fort Pitt Museum* (phone: 281-9284), with exhibitions on the French and Indian War and early Pennsylvania history. Museum closed Mondays and Tuesdays. Admission charge to the museum.

PPG PLACE The "crown jewel" in the skyline is a plaza surrounded by six modern Gothic buildings with mirrored glass façades, designed by Philip Johnson and John Burgee. On the ground floor of PPG 1 is the *Wintergarden,* open for civic functions. Several international food establishments and retail boutiques are in buildings 2 through 6. Summer concerts are given in the plaza. Stanwix St. between Third and Fourth Aves.

FIFTH AVENUE PLACE This striking office building contains a collection of specialty shops, along with a food court. The building is linked by a skywalk to *Joseph Horne Co.,* a locally owned department store that's been affiliated with Pittsburgh for more than a century. Penn and Liberty Aves.

ONE OXFORD CENTRE This office tower at Grant Street and Fourth Avenue has three lower floors dedicated to designer shops, including *Polo/Ralph Lauren* and *Gucci.* Several restaurants and nightclubs featuring live jazz are here when you've had your fill of shopping.

CIVIC ARENA Recognizable by its stainless steel roof, this is the home of the Pittsburgh *Penguins* hockey team, winners of the *NHL Stanley Cup* in 1991 and 1992. The circus, ice shows, dog show, and top-name concerts also are held here. Bordered by Washington and Crawford Sts., Bedford and Centre Aves.

CENTRAL PITTSBURGH

LANDMARKS

1. Fort Pitt Museum
2. Bank Center
3. David L. Lawrence Convention Center
4. Heinz Hall
5. Monongahela Incline
6. West Park Conservatory—Aviary
7. PPG Place
8. Buhl Planetarium
9. Cathedral of Learning
10. Carnegie Museum and Library
11. Mellon Institute
12. Phipps Conservatory
13. Historical Society of Western Pennsylvania
14. Frick Fine Arts Building
15. Pittsburgh Playhouse Theater Center
16. Penn. Central Station
17. Station Square
18. U.S. Steel Building
19. First Blast Furnace
20. "Mexican War" District
21. Liberty Center
22. Oxford Center

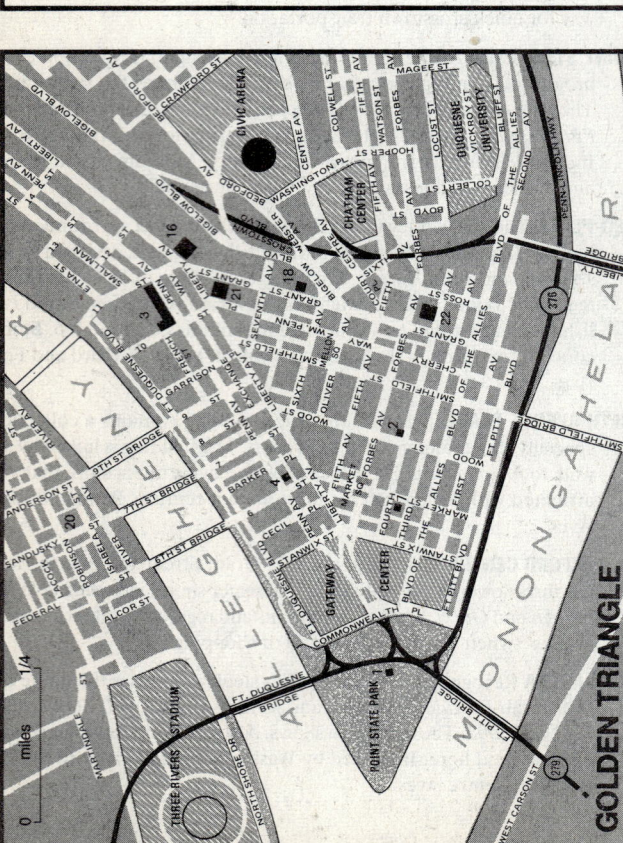

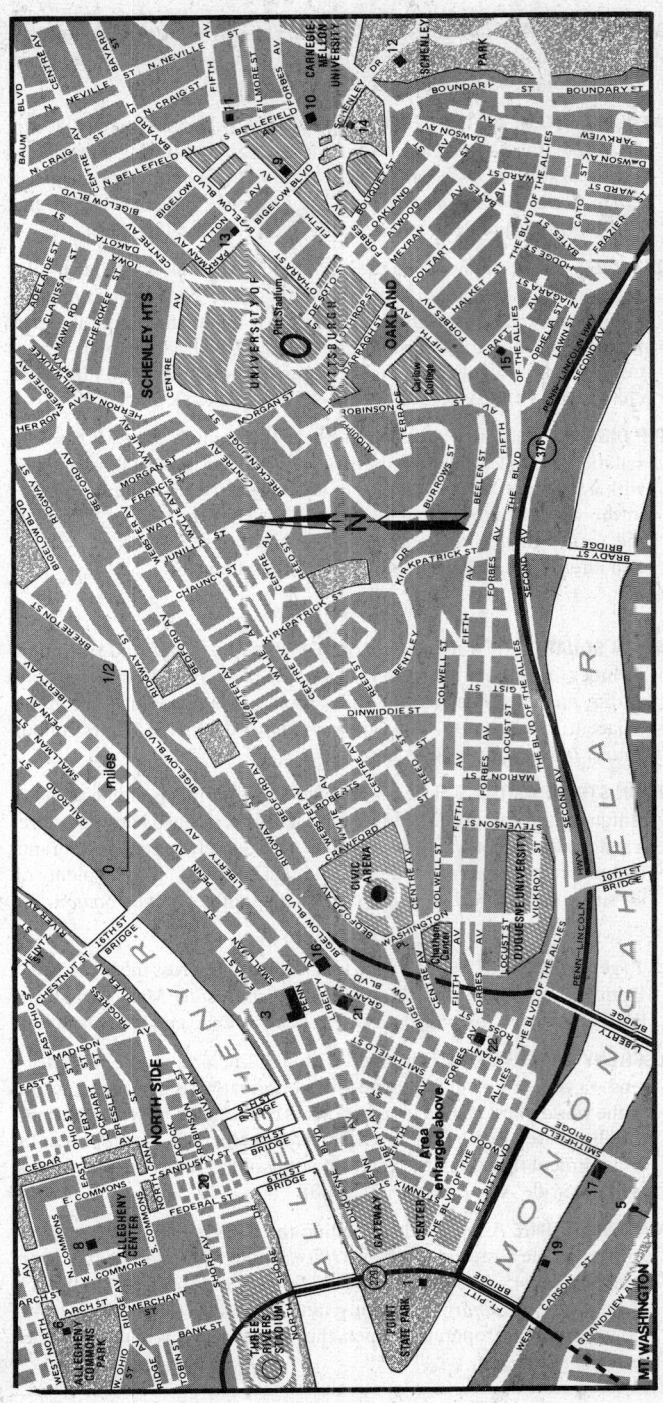

DAVID L. LAWRENCE CONVENTION CENTER The city's exposition hall has 131,000 square feet of space and hosts a variety of trade shows. Penn Ave. (phone: 565-6000 for a schedule of events).

BENEDUM CENTER FOR THE PERFORMING ARTS An elegant movie palace in the 1920s, this theater has been restored into a glittering showplace. The backstage is bigger than New York's *Metropolitan Opera,* and is home to the *Pittsburgh Opera* and the *Pittsburgh Ballet,* as well as the *Civic Light Opera.* Penn and Seventh Aves. (phone: 456-6666).

HEINZ HALL A very classy movie theater in 1926, the hall is now a stately, acoustically balanced auditorium, home of the *Pittsburgh Symphony* (which currently enjoys international favor under the baton of Lorin Maazel), and host to performing arts troupes. Worth a look for its ornate decorations and gold leaf. Guided tours by appointment. Admission charge. 600 Penn Ave. (phone: 392-4900 for tickets).

STRIP DISTRICT This noisy, hectic hub where the region's food wholesalers sell their produce can be somewhat overwhelming, especially compared with a supermarket. In addition to the markets, everything from hole-in-the-wall cafés to an Italian espresso bar lines the streets. Stop in at the *Society for Arts in Crafts,* which displays and sells finely made local and international crafts. Penn Ave. and Smallman St.

SOUTH SIDE

STATION SQUARE A beautifully restored 19th-century railroad station, it includes an outdoor museum with antique rail cars and Bessemer converter, an elegant restaurant and saloon, and a shopping mall in the adjacent freight house. The *Gateway Clipper* dock (see "Tours" under *Tourist Information*) also is here.

CARSON STREET DISTRICT Here is a browser's Elysian Fields, home to many antiques shops, art galleries, bookstores, an old-fashioned hardware store, a restored neighborhood movie theater, and numerous good restaurants and nightclubs, where jazz and blues reign supreme. There's plenty of on-street parking. Cross Smithfield Bridge, south of *Station Square.*

NORTH SIDE

To get to the North Side from the Golden Triangle, cross the Sixth Street Bridge, then proceed north to the *Allegheny Center Mall.* Crosstown buses leave from *Joseph Horne Co.,* at Penn Avenue and Stanwix Street.

ALLEGHENY OBSERVATORY Equipped with a 30-inch-diameter refractory lens—a very powerful telescope—this observatory is acclaimed as one of the world's best. Amateur astronomers can scan the heavens or attend the illustrated lectures. Closed November through March; open by appointment the rest of the year. No admission charge. Riverview Park off Perrysville Ave. (phone: 321-2400).

LANDMARK SQUARE Almost hidden behind the bunker-like *Allegheny Center Mall* is the restored *Old Post Office,* home to the innovative *Pittsburgh Children's Museum* (phone: 322-5059) and the regional branch of the *Carnegie Library.* In the museum, tots and preteens can play with video equipment, operate puppets they know from TV, and participate in a kids' clinic where they are the doctor to an injured dummy. Open daily; seasonal hours. Admission charge. Just steps away is the first *Carnegie Public Library,* opened in 1890. The building also houses the *Pittsburgh Public Theater.*

CARNEGIE SCIENCE CENTER This riverside museum complex is one of the country's most advanced. Its facilities, designed for both children and adults, include an Omnimax theater with a three-story-high movie screen, a computerized planetarium, a one-of-a-kind science workshop featuring a combination theater and hands-on laboratory, projects for children as young as two, and a vintage submarine from World War II. Closed *Christmas.* Admission charge. Near *Three Rivers Stadium* (phone: 237-3400).

THE NATIONAL AVIARY At the former *Pittsburgh Aviary,* which was designated the *National Aviary* by Congress in 1993, 200 species of birds chatter away in walk-through and enclosed exhibits. A series of educational programs is offered as well. This is a good place to escape from urban America for a while. Open daily. Admission charge. In *West Park* near Arch St., *Allegheny Commons* (phone: 323-7324).

WARHOL MUSEUM This new museum pays tribute to Pittsburgh native son Andy Warhol. Mounted in a renovated early 20th-century warehouse, it encompasses seven floors and features a celebrity portrait gallery, an auditorium in which the artist's films will be shown, and a "time capsule" of his personal artifacts. Admission charge. 117 Sandusky St. (phone: 237-8300).

EAST END

CATHEDRAL OF LEARNING Part of the *University of Pittsburgh,* this imposing 42-story Gothic tower is the only skyscraper of classrooms in the country. Of particular interest are the 19 Nationality Rooms on the first floor, devoted to each of the city's major ethnic groups. Open daily. No admission charge. Bigelow Blvd. and Fifth Ave. (phone: 624-6000).

THE CARNEGIE A complex comprising the main branch of the *Carnegie Libraries,* a music hall, a museum with a magnificent collection of French Impressionist art, and the *Carnegie Museum of Natural History,* featuring 10,000 objects from all fields of natural history and anthropology. Closed Sunday mornings and Mondays. Donation suggested. 4400 Forbes Ave. (phone: 622-3131).

PHIPPS CONSERVATORY Rare tropical and domestic blossoms flourish in the greenhouses and gardens of this 2½-acre publicly owned conservatory. Annual flower shows take place in spring, fall, and during *Christmas.* The 13 greenhouses are only a fraction of the greenery of surrounding *Schenley Park,* which covers 422 acres and has tennis courts, baseball fields, a golf course, an ice skating rink, picnic areas, and nature trails. Open daily. Admission charge. *Schenley Park* (phone: 255-2375).

HISTORICAL SOCIETY OF WESTERN PENNSYLVANIA Antique glass bottles, hand-carved furniture, and other memorabilia line the halls, walls, and shelves, and you can peruse old documents on Pennsylvania history in the library. Closed Sundays and Mondays. No admission charge. 4338 Bigelow Blvd. (phone: 681-5533).

PITTSBURGH ZOO Seventy acres feature open habitats for the more than 2,000 animals. A recent addition is the *Primate House,* with species from South America, Africa, and Asia. There's also an *Aquazoo,* which has tanks full of domestic trout and pike, and esoteric species like penguins and piranhas. Open daily. Admission charge. *Highland Park* (phone: 665-3640).

FRICK ART MUSEUM A magnificent Renaissance-style building houses Old Masters from the Renaissance through the 18th century. Marie Antoinette's furniture is on display in an ornate living room. The eclectic collection comprises Russian silver, Flemish tapestries, and Chinese porcelains. Closed Mondays and Tuesdays. No admission charge. 7227 Reynolds St. and S. Homewood Ave., Point Breeze (phone: 371-0600).

CLAYTON Near the *Frick Art Museum* stands the restored home of its namesake, steel tycoon Henry Clay Frick. Tours are given by reservation only. Closed Mondays. Admission charge. 72 Penn Ave. (phone: 371-0606).

> **EXTRA SPECIAL**
>
> For a change of scene, try the Laurel Highlands, just a 90-minute drive from the city. Take the Pennsylvania Turnpike to the Donhal exit. Follow Route 711 to Ligonier; here is the *Compass Inn* (phone: 238-4983), an old coaching inn used by travelers in the 18th century. Lively tours are given on Sundays from late May through late October, with special candlelight tours in November and December. Admission charge. Also nearby is *Fort Ligonier* (phone: 238-9701), a restored fort from the French and Indian War. Closed mid-November through mid-April. Admission charge. The *Mountain Playhouse* (phone: 814-629-9201 for reservations and information), one of the oldest summer theaters in the country, is a half-mile north of Jennerstown on Route 985 off Route 30. Hungry theatergoers can dine next door at the excellent *Green Gables* restaurant.

Sources and Resources

TOURIST INFORMATION

For information on places of interest and events, contact the visitor information center (phone: 281-9222), open daily in *Gateway Center,* the Golden Triangle. The information center is run by the *Greater Pittsburgh Convention and Visitors Bureau* (4 Gateway Center, Pittsburgh, PA 15222; phone: 281-7711), which offers a variety of city guides and is closed weekends. For recorded information on daily events, call 800-255-0855 in Pennsylvania; 800-821-1888 elsewhere. Contact the Pennsylvania state tourism hotline (phone: 800-VISIT-PA) for maps, calendars of events, health updates, and travel advisories.

LOCAL COVERAGE *Post-Gazette,* morning daily; *Business Times-Journal,* weekly; *Pittsburgh* magazine, monthly.

TELEVISION STATIONS KDKA Channel 2–CBS; WTAE Channel 4–ABC; WPXI Channel 11–NBC; WQED Channel 13–PBS; and WPGH Channel 53–Fox.

RADIO STATIONS AM: KDKA 1020 (contemporary/oldies); WTAE 1250 (talk); and KQV 1410 (news/talk). FM: WQED 89.3 (classical); WDUQ 90.5 (jazz); WBZZ 94.6 (Top 40); and WYDD 104.7 (Top 40/jazz weekends).

TELEPHONE The area code for Pittsburgh is 412.

SALES TAX There is a 7% sales tax on everything except clothing, shoes, and groceries.

CLIMATE Pittsburgh has a moderate climate with frequent precipitation. Summer temperatures climb into the 80s F; winters drop into the 20s F. About 200 days of the year are cloudy, and winters are wet.

GETTING AROUND

AIRPORT The *Pittsburgh International Airport* is about 20 minutes from downtown, but in heavy traffic, the ride will take longer. *Airline Transportation Service* (phone: 471-7887) offers frequent connections between the airport and major hotels.

BUS *Port Authority Transit (PAT)* provides efficient bus service (phone: 442-2000 for information). The fare starts at $1.25.

CAR RENTAL All major national firms are represented.

LRT (LIGHT RAPID TRANSIT) SUBWAY PAT underground service (phone: 442-2000 for information) operates from downtown to South Hills, through *Station Square,* across the Monongahela River. Ultramodern trains run frequently during the day and every 15 to 30 minutes at night. They are free in the downtown Golden Triangle until 7 PM; all other route fares range from $1.25 to $2, depending on time of day.

TAXIS Call *People's Cab* (phone: 441-5334) or *Yellow Cab of Pittsburgh* (phone: 665-8100).

TOURS Cruises on ships of the *Gateway Clipper* fleet (phone: 355-7979) leave from the dock at *Station Square.* The captain aboard the two-hour sightseeing cruise will highlight points of interest. The *Good Ship Lollipop* has clowns to amuse children while parents enjoy the sights on its one-hour cruise. Reservations are required for the daily dinner cruise. Specialty cruises include a tour of the river lock system. Some cruises are seasonal.

VAN SERVICE Contact *People's Cab* (phone: 441-5334).

LOCAL SERVICES

AUDIOVISUAL EQUIPMENT *Chujko Brothers Audio Visual Connection* (phone: 331-3308); *KVL Audio Visual, Inc.* (at the *Vista International* hotel; phone: 281-1722).

BABY-SITTING Most major hotels have baby-sitting services. Another option is *Child Care Connection* (in the *Westin William Penn* hotel; phone: 471-2730).

BUSINESS SERVICES *Allegheny Personnel Services* (2 Oliver Plaza; phone: 391-2044).

DRY CLEANER/TAILOR *Galardi's* (119 Forbes Ave.; phone: 471-7686), pickup and delivery.

LIMOUSINE *Allegheny Limousines* (phone: 731-8671); *Limo Center* (phone: 931-1800); *Royal Limousine* (phone: 884-8306).

MECHANIC *Goodyear Auto Center* (phone: 281-9318).

MEDICAL EMERGENCY *Allegheny General Hospital* (320 E. North Ave.; phone: 359-3252); *Mercy Hospital* (1400 Locust; phone: 232-8222).

MESSENGER SERVICES *Mercury Messenger Service* (phone: 391-2600).

MONEY TRANSFERS *American Express MoneyGram* (phone: 800-926-9400 for information; 800-866-8800 for money transfers); *Western Union Financial Services* (phone: 800-325-6000 or 800-325-4176).

NATIONAL/INTERNATIONAL COURIER *DHL Worldwide Express* (phone: 262-2764); *FedEx* (phone: 800-238-5355).

PHARMACY *Brooks* (429 Smithfield St.; phone: 261-4846).

PHOTOCOPIES *Kinko's* (210 Grant St.; phone: 471-8004).

POST OFFICE (Grant and Seventh Sts.; phone: 644-4500).

PROFESSIONAL PHOTOGRAPHER *Associated Photographers* (phone: 642-2728).

SECRETARY/STENOGRAPHER *Executive Secretarial Service* (phone: 561-2360).

TELECONFERENCE FACILITIES *Pittsburgh Hilton & Towers* (see *Checking In*, below).

TRANSLATOR *Berlitz* (phone: 471-0900); *Language Center, Inc.* (phone: 261-1101).

WESTERN UNION/TELEX Many offices are located around the city (phone: 800-325-6000 to find the location nearest you).

OTHER *David L. Lawrence Convention Center* (phone: 565-6000); *Stetson Convention Service* (phone: 366-3103), rentals include booths, furniture, and equipment.

SPECIAL EVENTS

The *Pittsburgh Marathon,* which draws an international field of runners, is held in early May, as is the *Children's Festival,* a five-day event featuring international performers. From the end of May through mid-August, the *Three Rivers Shakespeare Festival* stages two productions at the *Stephen Foster Memorial*. The *Three Rivers Arts Festival,* displaying the work of over 600 artists, spans 17 days in June. Performing arts and a film festival are a small part of the Carnegie-sponsored festivities. Allegheny County presents a summer-long schedule of free dance and music events at *Hartwood Acres,* a former country estate. The *Shady-*

side *Arts Festival* takes place in the nearby town of Shadyside in early August. The festive *Three Rivers Regatta,* the first weekend in August, features the *Grand Prix of Formula I Boat Racing, Steamboat Races for the Mayors Cup,* the *Race of the River Belles,* and the not-to-be-missed *Anything That Floats* race. A hot-air balloon race, live music, and water-ski shows enliven the event. *Schenley Park* becomes a racetrack of yesteryear during the *Pittsburgh Vintage Grand Prix* the third weekend in August. The *Great Race,* a 10-kilometer footrace with over 10,000 participants, is held in September; in October, school teams compete in the *Head of the Ohio* crew races.

MUSEUMS

In addition to those described in *Special Places,* there are two other museums of note.

OLD ECONOMY MUSEUM AND VILLAGE Several restored buildings recall a 19th-century experiment in communal living. Closed Mondays. Admission charge. 14th and Church Sts., Ambridge (phone: 266-4500).

PITTSBURGH CENTER FOR THE ARTS On display are contemporary paintings, sculpture, photography, and crafts, mostly by local artists. Closed Mondays. Donation suggested. Fifth and Shady Aves. (phone: 361-0873).

SPORTS AND FITNESS

BASEBALL The major league *Pirates* play at *Three Rivers Stadium* (Stadium Circle, North Side; phone: 323-5000).

BICYCLING There are no bike rental shops in town, but the county parks (like *North* and *South Parks*) have rental facilities.

CANOEING, KAYAKING You can canoe and kayak through exciting whitewater rapids in the Laurel Highlands. *Canoe, Kayak and Sailing Craft* (712 Rebecca Ave., Wilkinsburg; phone: 371-4802) offers lessons and guided tours. *Canoe Pittsburgh* (74 S. 20th St., South Side; phone: 481-0700) is another source for lessons and information.

FITNESS CENTER The *YMCA* (330 Blvd. of the Allies; phone: 227-3800) has a pool, racquetball courts, a track, and exercise classes. Facilities are open to non-members for a fee.

FOOTBALL The pro *Steelers'* home grid is at *Three Rivers Stadium* (Stadium Circle, North Side; phone: 323-1200).

GOLF *Schenley Park,* a municipal course in Oakland (phone: 521-1224), has 18 holes, but the *North Park* course (off Rte. 19; phone: 935-1967) and the 27-hole *South Park* course (off Rte. 88; phone: 835-3545) are more challenging. For championship caliber, try the *Quicksilver* course (about 20 miles west of Pittsburgh on Route 980; phone: 796-1594). There are approximately 75 other public courses to choose from within a 90-minute drive of downtown; contact the *Greater Pittsburgh Convention and Visitors Bureau* (phone: 281-7711) for specific information.

HIKING There are quite a few hiking programs. For information on *Parks Department* nature tours and programs for the disabled, contact *Schenley Nature Center* (*Schenley Park;* phone: 681-2272). For information on hiking, backpacking, canoeing, and camping in the area, contact the *Sierra Club* (phone: 561-0203).

HOCKEY The *NHL* 1991 and 1992 *Stanley Cup* champion *Penguins* play at *Civic Arena* (Washington Pl., Center and Bedford Aves.; phone: 642-1985).

HORSE RACING Fans have a choice of the *Meadows* (in Washington County; phone: 563-1224) or *Waterford Park* (Chester, WV; phone: 304-387-2400).

HORSEBACK RIDING Hit the trail in *South Park*. You can rent a horse or sign on for a hayride at *Valleybrook Stables* (phone: 835-9687).

ICE SKATING There are three outdoor rinks in the area: at *North Park* (phone: 935-1780); at *South Park* (phone: 833-1199), about 10 miles outside of Pittsburgh; and at *Schenley Park* (phone: 422-6547).

JOGGING *Point State Park,* where the Allegheny and Monongahela meet; *Schenley Park,* east of downtown in Oakland; and *North Park,* 10 miles north of the city, all offer good jogging.

SCUBA DIVING In Pittsburgh? Check it out. *Sub-Aquatics* (1593 Banksville Rd.; phone: 531-5577) gives a 36-hour course in essentials with tips on local lakes and water-filled quarries.

TENNIS The best municipal courts are at *Mellon Park,* east of downtown, and there are excellent suburban courts at *North* and *South Parks,* both about 10 miles outside the city.

THEATER

The city has plenty of professional theater performances all year. The *Public Theater* presents traditional plays in its handsome *Hazlett Theater* (1 Allegheny Sq.; phone: 321-9800), and the *City Theater* offers more avant-garde productions at the corner of 13th and Bingham Streets on the South Side (phone: 431-4900). Smaller companies include the *Upstairs Theater* (phone: 361-5443); listings of scheduled productions can be found in the city's daily newspaper (see *Local Coverage*). The *Benedum Center for the Performing Arts* (207 Seventh St.; phone: 456-6666) and *Heinz Hall* (600 Penn Ave.; phone: 392-4900) present touring musicals and plays. There are also several top-flight professional dance companies; standouts are the internationally renowned *Pittsburgh Ballet Theatre* (2900 Liberty Ave.; phone: 281-0360), *Dance Alloy* (phone: 621-6670) for modern dance, and the *Pittsburgh Dance Council* (phone: 355-0330), which brings in touring companies.

High-quality collegiate productions are presented by the *Carnegie Mellon Theater Company* at *Kresge Theater* (Carnegie-Mellon University, Schenley Park; phone: 268-2407), and *Point Park College*'s *Pittsburgh Playhouse* (phone: 621-4445), which stages modern plays and musicals for both adults and children. In the summer, the *University of Pittsburgh*'s *Three Rivers Shakespeare Festival* (phone: 624-7529) pays homage to the Bard, while the *Civic Light Opera* re-creates the great Broadway musicals of the past at the *Benedum Center for the Performing Arts* (207 Seventh St.; phone: 456-6666). Also in summer,

Allegheny County offers its *Theater at Hartwood* (phone: 767-4738), dramas performed under a tent.

MUSIC

The world-famous *Pittsburgh Symphony Orchestra* performs from September through May at *Heinz Hall* (600 Penn Ave.; phone: 392-4900). In the *Benedum Center for the Performing Arts,* the *Pittsburgh Opera,* in its 52nd year, performs the classics and the not-so-classic in lavish productions. Also try the *River City Brass Band* (phone: 322-7222), based at the *Carnegie Music Hall,* which performs in several locations throughout the city and surrounding area. For fans of pop and rock, the city is a regular stop on the road-show circuit. The *Civic Arena* and *Pa'umbo Center* at *Duquesne University* (phone: 434-6058) are venues for popular performing artists. The *Star Lake Amphitheater* (phone: 947-4700) is an outdoor performance area about 45 minutes from downtown where rock groups appear regularly during the summer.

NIGHTCLUBS AND NIGHTLIFE

Long a jazz haven, the city continues that tradition at numerous clubs such as *The Balcony* (phone: 681-0110), *Cardillo's* (phone: 381-3777), and *James Street Tavern* (phone: 323-2222), as well as several spots along Carson Street on the South Side. The top dance places in town are in the vibrant Strip District. Try *Metropol* (phone: 261-2221) for hard rock and *Donzi's* (phone: 281-1600) for riverside dancing. The center for contemporary folk and rock music is *Grafitti* (phone: 682-4210) while the *Decade* (phone: 682-1211) is a local band hangout. *Rosebud* (phone: 261-2221), next door to *Metropol* in the Strip District, presents a European-style coffeehouse atmosphere. And for a quieter evening, the lobby of the *Westin William Penn* hotel (Mellon Sq.; phone: 553-5100) offers piano music in an elegant setting.

Best in Town

CHECKING IN

With the city's second renaissance has come an influx of much-needed hotel space, mostly in the nearby suburbs of Green Tree, Coraopolis, and Monroeville. All hotels listed below are downtown. Expect to pay $95 or more per night for a double room at those listed in the expensive category and $50 to $95 at those described as moderate; there are no exceptional inexpensive hotels in the city. Unless otherwise noted, hotels have air conditioning, private baths, TV sets, and telephones. All hotels are in the 412 area code.

EXPENSIVE

Hyatt Pittsburgh Near the *Civic Arena,* this property has 400 rooms, all of which have been redecorated. The improvement is very apparent, and the top two Regency floors offer excellent accommodations. *Hugo's Rotisserie* serves a moderately priced lunch and buffet dinner, with roast duckling the house specialty; *QQ's Café* is even less expensive. There's also a concierge, 14 meeting rooms, A/V equipment, computers, limited secretarial services, and express checkout. Chatham Center (phone: 471-1234; 800-233-1234 or 800-228-9000; fax: 355-0315).

Pittsburgh Hilton & Towers Standing at the edge of *Point State Park,* this hostelry overlooks the Monongahela and Allegheny Rivers, and some of its 700 rooms have park views. Its lobby is contemporary, and it offers two restaurants, parlor suites with wet bars, and concierge service. There is business seating for 2,800 in the ballroom, and the executive center has five conference rooms, with secretarial services, A/V equipment, computers, and express checkout. *Gateway Center* (phone: 391-4600; 800-HILTONS; fax: 391-0927).

Ramada Downtown's only all-suite property has 200 studios as well as one-, two-, and three-bedroom units. The quiet *Ruddy Duck* restaurant serves complimentary breakfast on weekdays. Business amenities include 21 meeting rooms, A/V equipment, limited secretarial services, a concierge floor, and express checkout. Bigelow Square Plaza (phone: 281-5800; 800-225-5858; fax: 261-2932).

Vista International Pittsburgh's newest hotel has a contemporary design, with a four-story atrium lobby, 616 rooms, and a fitness center. Guests can dine informally at the *Orchard Café* or more sedately at the *Liberty Grille.* Indoor parking, 24-hour room service, 20 meeting rooms, and secretarial services are just some of the amenities. At Liberty Center on Grant St. (phone: 281-3700; 800-367-8478; fax: 281-2652).

Westin William Penn After a recent renovation, this hostelry has 595 enlarged and modernized rooms and a stunning lobby. Because the building was declared a National Historic Landmark, the exterior remains unchanged. The *Terrace Room* offers dinner daily, as well as Sunday brunch. Other conveniences include an on-site day-care center, a concierge, 24-hour room service, a fitness center, 35 meeting rooms, and express checkout. Mellon Sq. (phone: 553-5100; 800-228-3000; fax: 281-3498).

MODERATE

Priory Built in the 1880s as a residence for priests, this 24-room property has been lovingly restored and converted into an elegant Victorian bed and breakfast inn. There are 12-foot ceilings and a cozy courtyard, and shuttle service to downtown is provided. 614 Pressley Ave. (phone: 231-3338).

EATING OUT

The city offers a wide choice of dining, with a variety of ethnic eateries. These are, for the most part, highly rated, for they offer quality and diversity far greater than those found at anonymous "continental" restaurants. Many places are dressier in the evening. Expect to pay $75 or more for dinner for two at establishments we've described as expensive; and between $40 and $75 at those listed as moderate. Prices don't include drinks, wine, tax, or tips. Unless otherwise noted, restaurants are open for lunch and dinner. All restaurants are in the 412 area code unless otherwise indicated.

EXPENSIVE

Christopher's Ride the exterior glass elevator up to this unusual place, which has a fantastic view, then dine luxuriously on steak Diane, chateaubriand, seafood, and specialties cooked tableside. It tends to be very dressy and offers live entertainment on Friday and Saturday evenings. Closed Sundays. Reservations necessary. Major credit cards accepted. 1411 Grandview Ave., Mt. Washington (phone: 381-4500).

Common Plea This is one of the best downtown eateries, popular with city officials and lawyers and known for its appetizers. The atmosphere is relaxed; the array of fresh seafood, splendid. Closed Sundays; dinner only on Saturdays. Reservations advised for lunch. Major credit cards accepted. 308 Ross St. (phone: 281-5140).

Grand Concourse This elegant remake of the old *Pittsburgh and Lake Erie Railroad Terminal,* adorned with beautiful wood, stained glass, and gleaming brass, offers excellent seafood—oysters, shrimp, clams, crab, and especially a tangy seafood chowder. Open daily; brunch on Sundays. Reservations advised for dinner only. Major credit cards accepted. 1 Station Sq. (phone: 261-1717).

Hyeholde Just a short drive from the Pittsburgh airport is the essence of a medieval castle, with wooden beams, slate floors, European tapestries, and spacious grounds. The dinner menu changes daily but usually consists of classic dishes—filet mignon, trout, breast of fowl—prepared with the freshest ingredients. Bread and desserts are homemade, and don't pass up its acclaimed trifle. The wine list is the most extensive in the area. Closed Sundays. Reservations advised. Major credit cards accepted. 190 Hyeholde Dr., Coraopolis (phone: 264-3116).

Le Mont Classic and contemporary, this restaurant offers French and Italian dishes and a spectacular view of the Golden Triangle. House specialties include prime ribs and veal. Jackets required. Open daily for dinner only. Reservations advised. Major credit cards accepted. 1114 Grandview Ave., Mt. Washington (phone: 431-3100).

Le Pommier Classic French country cooking is beautifully presented in this understated spot on the South Side. The bread is fresh-baked on the premises. Closed Sundays. Reservations necessary. Major credit cards accepted. 2104 E. Carson St. (phone: 431-1901).

MODERATE

Abruzzi's The atmosphere of this popular restaurant, just across the 10th Street Bridge on the city's historic South Side, is that of an Old World country inn in the heart of the city. Its menu reflects the Abruzzi region of Italy, and its sauces have garnered excellent reviews. Open daily; dinner only on Sundays. Reservations necessary on weekends. Major credit cards accepted. 52 S. 10th St. (phone: 431-4511).

Allegheny Brewery and Pub Housed in a renovated 19th-century building, this dining spot with a German accent is the city's only micro-brewery. It offers four different beers on tap, including lagers made only with water, malt, hops, and yeast. Goulash, sauerbraten, and Wiener schnitzel are among the menu items. Closed Sundays. No reservations. Major credit cards accepted. On the North Side at Troy Hill and Vinial (phone: 237-9402).

Juno Trattoria This casual place specializes in regional Italian cooking and homemade pasta. Sample the wide variety of breads and pastries baked daily. Closed Sundays; open until midnight on Fridays and Saturdays. Reservations advised on weekend nights and for parties of five or more. Major credit cards accepted. *One Oxford Centre,* downtown (phone: 392-0225).

Mandarin Gourmet Among the best of the city's Oriental restaurants, this place has an expansive menu, and the service is polite. Closed Sundays. Reservations necessary for groups of four or more. Major credit cards accepted. 305 Wood St. (phone: 261-6151).

Portland, Oregon

At-a-Glance

SEEING THE CITY

Portland offers several exceptional vantage points from which to see the city, the valley in which it lies, and the mountains beyond. *Pittock Acres Park,* the grounds of the former *Pittock Mansion* (see *Special Places*), sits 1,000 feet above the city. At your feet are the port, business section, Willamette River, and southeast residential areas. In the distance are the Cascade Mountains—Mt. Hood in Oregon, and Mt. Rainier, Mt. Adams, and Mt. St Helens in Washington. One of Portland's highest points at 1,073 feet is *Council Crest Park,* which offers panoramic views of the whole city and the nearby mountains. And visit *Washington Park* (400 SW Kingston); the best view is from the *International Rose Test Gardens,* looking east toward the mountains in the background.

SPECIAL PLACES

Portland was made for walking. Her founders frequently built homes in the west hills and walked to work along the waterfront. Especially on the west side, major points of interest are within walking distance of one another. Brochures describing self-guided walking tours are available from the *Portland, Oregon Visitors Association* (see *Tourist Information* below).

WEST SIDE

WASHINGTON PARK One of Portland's oldest parks, it spreads over 145 acres, all part of the city's 40-square-mile park system. There are six points of special interest on the grounds: the *International Rose Test Gardens,* the *Japanese Gardens,* the *Metro Washington Park Zoo,* the *World Forestry Center,* the *Vietnam War Memorial,* and the *Hoyt Arboretum,* as well as some magnificent views of the city and mountains. To experience the park setting, take the zoo train from the *Rose Gardens*—it runs from *Memorial Day* weekend through September. The park grounds are perfect for a picnic (*Elephant's Delicatessen—Uptown Shopping Center,* 13 NW 23rd Pl., phone: 224-3955—will prepare one for you); or you can eat at the zoo's café.

The *International Rose Test Gardens,* one of Portland's greatest attractions, boast hundreds of varieties of roses. June through October is the best time to see them. The *Japanese Gardens* above the *Rose Gardens* are considered some of the most authentic outside of Japan. Portlanders enjoy sneaking an hour or so to come stroll and meditate in the tranquil and meticulously groomed landscape. Bring a camera: It's impos-

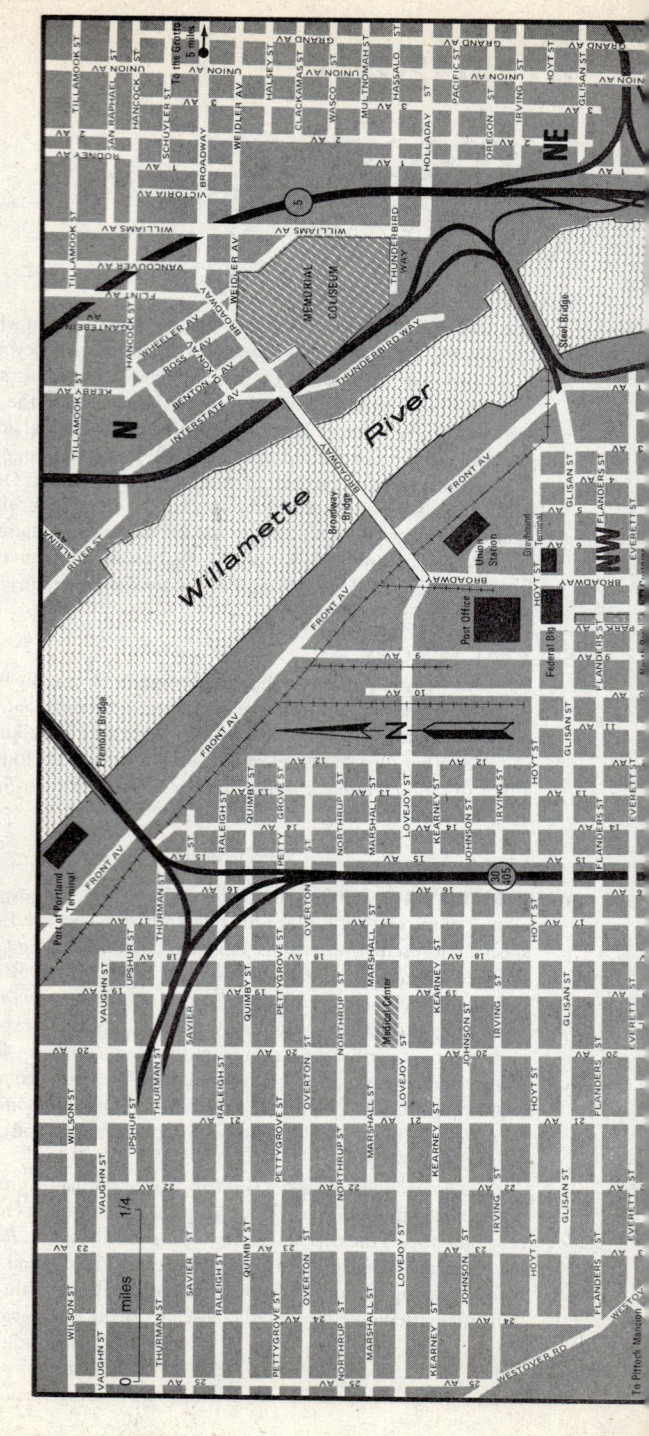

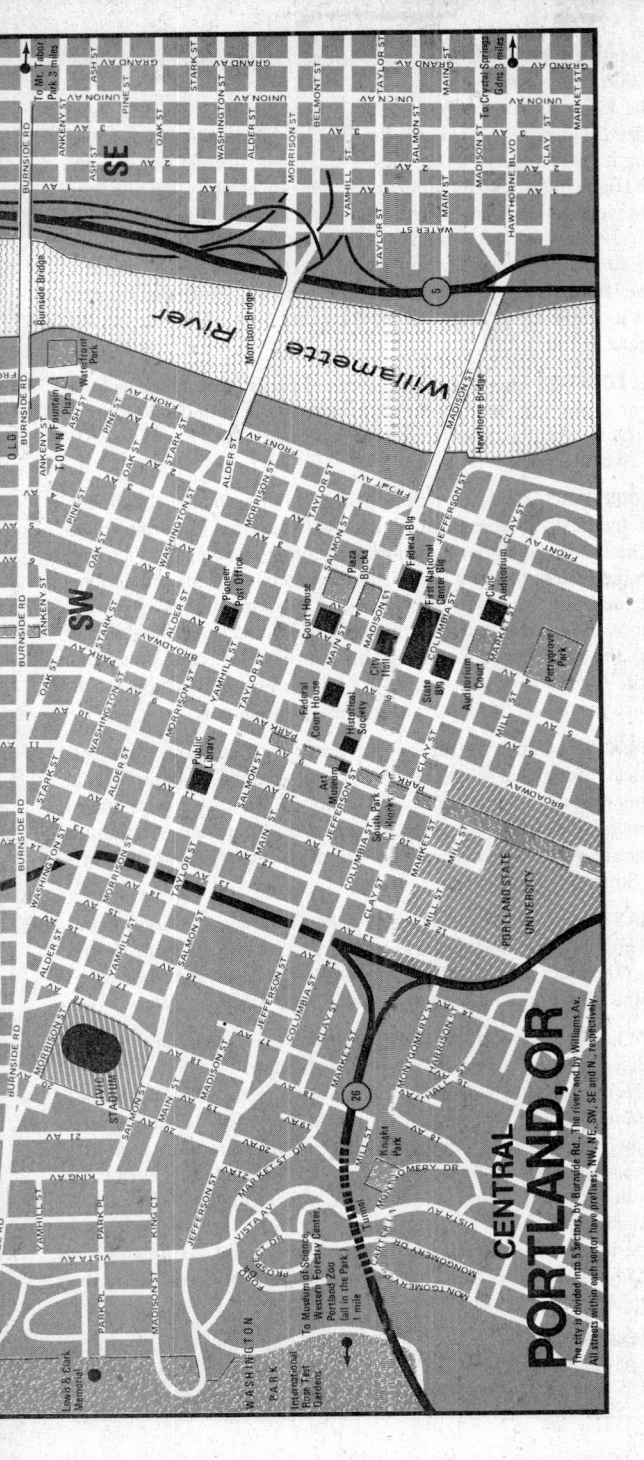

sible to take a poor picture here, rain or shine. Admission charge. (phone: 223-9233).

The *Metro Washington Park Zoo* is easily accessible, varied, and well organized. The zoo is best known for the 25 Asian elephants born here, making its breeding herd the largest and most successful in the zoo world. Highlights are the polar bear and penguin exhibits that allow visitors to view the frolicking above and below water. Simulated African rainforest and savannah displays were added recently. No admission charge for children under two. SW Canyon Rd. (phone: 226-1561).

The *World Forestry Center* has displays and exhibitions on Oregon's largest industry. Open daily. Admission charge. 4033 SW Canyon Rd. (phone: 228-1367).

IRA KELLER FOUNTAIN This block-wide series of pools and waterfalls faces the *Civic Auditorium*. In hot weather, people splash around in its swirling water. Designed by Lawrence Halprin, it is called "Ira's Fountain." SW Third Ave. at Clay.

PIONEER COURTHOUSE The first federal building in the Pacific Northwest, completed in 1875, it has been restored to its original Victorian splendor. The interior includes a working post office, an elegant Victorian courtroom (where the *US Court of Appeals* meets), and adjoining rooms for the judges. The courtroom can be seen by asking the security guard to unlock the door. Closed weekends. Enter at 555 SW Yamhill (no phone). Pioneer Courthouse Square, an open city block across the street from the *Pioneer Courthouse,* has become the hub of downtown. This is a place for music, flowers, food, espresso, and fanfare.

WEATHER MACHINE Check out the forecast every day at noon, when this whimsical mechanical sculpture predicts the weather for the following 24 hours with a trumpet fanfare and a spray of water. Up pops one of three metal sculptures: a gold sun for fair skies; a blue heron for clouds and drizzle; or a copper dragon for stormy weather. Pioneer Courthouse Square.

PORTLANDIA This sculpture by Raymond Kaskey is the second-largest hammered copper figure in the world (the largest is the *Statue of Liberty*). It's over the main portico of the Portland Building, which was designed by postmodern architect Michael Graves. 1120 SW Fifth Ave.

OLD TOWN When the *Pioneer Courthouse* was brand new, some folks thought it much too far from the downtown business section—a whole six blocks away. Now "downtown" is called Old Town, a restored shopping and restaurant area. From the North Park Blocks west to NW Flanders, bordered by Burnside, is the Pearl District, a working warehouse area. Art galleries, nightclubs, bistros, and brew pubs have made this Portland's newest hot spot. Next door is Chinatown, which formally begins at the ceremonial gate at NW Fourth and Burnside, and where wonderful eating experiences are close at hand. At the northern end of Chinatown is *Union Station*. Built in 1894, this train and bus depot is listed on the *National Registry of Historic Places*.

PITTOCK MANSION The imposing French Renaissance home was built by Henry Pittock, a poor boy who made good as publisher of the *Oregon-*

ian at the turn of the century. The grounds, which command one of the city's finest views, are open daily; the house is open every afternoon. Admission charge to the house. *The Gate Lodge* restaurant serves lunch and tea. 3229 NW Pittock Dr. (phone: 823-3624, mansion; 221-1730, restaurant).

TRYON CREEK STATE PARK This is Oregon's only metropolitan state park, with 643 acres of wilderness for biking, hiking, and naturalists (horses are welcome, but there are none for rent). Adjoining Lake Oswego, 2 miles south of central Portland at 11321 SW Terwilliger Blvd. (phone: 653-3166).

POWELL'S BOOKS Owner Michael Powell says visitors sometimes stop here before they go to their hotel. The reason? About 500,000 new and used books (travel tomes are especially noted). One of the largest bookstores in the country at more than a block long, this funky, cavernous store thoughtfully provides maps so you can find your way around. You'll find espresso, pastries, and readings by local authors at the *Anne Hughes Coffee Shop*, which is part of the store. Open daily. 1005 W. Burnside (phone: 228-4651).

EAST SIDE

OREGON MUSEUM OF SCIENCE AND INDUSTRY (OMSI) Opened in 1992, this $40-million complex covers more than two and a half city blocks and includes six large halls with exhibits focusing on the earth, space, communications, and the life and physical sciences. There's an Omnimax theater, a planetarium, and a riverfront cafeteria. Among the displays is the *Transparent Woman*, a see-through model whose organs light up; a simulated earthquake; and an exhibit examining the ethical issues surrounding organ transplants, genetic engineering, and the use of life-support systems. A special *Toddler Zone* allows little ones to explore the physical worlds of air, sand, and water. Open daily. Admission charge. 1945 SE Water St. (phone: 797-4000; 800-955-6674 for tickets).

THE GROTTO At this shrine, an outdoor chapel has been built in a grotto on one level; on a cliff 10 stories above, there is another level with a monastery and gardens. The 64 acres of grounds are open for contemplation, quiet walks, and solitude. Sunday mass is celebrated in the chapel. 8840 NE Skidmore (phone: 254-7371).

CRYSTAL SPRINGS RHODODENDRON GARDENS More than 2,000 rhododendron plants are maintained by the Portland chapter of the *American Rhododendron Society*. During April and May the azaleas reach their peak, followed by the rhododendrons. No admission charge. SE 28th Ave. near SE Woodstock.

MT. TABOR PARK Believed to be the only extinct volcano within a mainland US city's limits, the park offers some of the best views of the city. Between Yamhill and Division, east of SE 60th Ave.

EXTRA SPECIAL

Sauvie Island, the largest island in the Columbia River, is just north of Portland on US 30. Devoted primarily to farmland, it is ideal for biking, bird watching, picnicking, fishing, swimming, fruit and berry picking, and boating. Required parking permits can be purchased at any general store on the island. Here, the *Oregon Historical Society* maintains the *Bybee-Howell House,* a restored pre–Civil War farmhouse on the channel, open from June to *Labor Day* (donations accepted).

The Columbia River Highway runs east and west of Portland. Drive northeast along the breathtaking Columbia River Gorge, with its 2,000-foot cliffs and 11 waterfalls.

Sources and Resources

TOURIST INFORMATION

The visitors' information center at the *Portland, Oregon Visitors Association* (26 SW Salmon St.; phone: 222-2223; 800-962-3700 outside Oregon) is best for brochures, maps, general tourist information, and personal help; if you arrive after hours or on Sunday when it is closed, outdoor map dispensers and kiosks provide a basic orientation. The *Oregon State Welcome Center* (open daily at 12348 N. Center Ave.; phone: 285-1631) offers travel information. Another visitors' center, located at the *Oregon Convention Center* (777 NE Martin Luther King Jr. Blvd.; phone: 731-7858), offers self-service information available daily. Contact the Oregon state tourism hotline (phone: 800-547-7842) for maps, calendars of events, health updates, and travel advisories.

LOCAL COVERAGE *Oregonian,* morning and afternoon daily; *Willamette Week* offers a liberally opinionated study of the city. *The Portland Guidebook* by Linda Lampman and Julie Sterling (The Writing Works; $9.95) and *Portland's Best Places* by Kim Carlson and Stephanie Irving (Sasquatch Books; $11.95) are comprehensive guides to Portland and its environs.

TELEVISION STATIONS KATU Channel 2–ABC; KOIN Channel 6–CBS; KGW Channel 8–NBC; KOAP Channel 10–PBS; and KPDX Channel 49–Fox.

RADIO STATIONS AM: KXL 750 (news/talk). FM: KGON 92.3 (classic rock); KUPL 98.5 (country); KWJJ 99.5 (country); and KINK 101.9 (adult contemporary).

TELEPHONE The area code for Portland is 503.

SALES TAX At this writing, there is no sales tax in Oregon. But buyer beware— a sales tax measure is on the ballot in almost every election.

CLIMATE The good news: It doesn't get too cold (snow is pretty rare) or too hot (summer temperatures above 90F last only two or three days). However, it certainly does rain. November through May are the wettest months. June through September are fairly clear, and the average temperature is in the 70s; Indian summers are not uncommon. That's prime tourist time, so book ahead.

GETTING AROUND

AIRPORT *Portland International Airport* is a 15- to 20-minute drive from downtown. The *Raz Tranz Portland Airporter* bus (phone: 246-4676) provides transportation to major hotels downtown. The trip takes about 35 minutes, 60 minutes during rush hour. *Tri-Met* city bus No. 12 also stops in front of the airport and goes downtown; the fare is 95¢ to $1.25.

BUS Portland's *Tri-Met* system covers three counties; exact-change-only fare (95¢ to $1.25) is zoned except within the 340-block downtown shopping area (including Old Town, major shopping complexes, *Portland Art Museum*, riverfront), which is free and called Fareless Square. Complete route and tourist information is available from the downtown *Customer Assistance Office* (1 Pioneer Courthouse Sq.; phone: 238-7433); enter under the waterfall.

CAR RENTAL All national firms are represented. *Bee Rent-A-Car* (84 NE Weidler St.; phone: 233-7368) is a good local firm; for others, check the yellow pages.

LIGHT RAIL The bus system is complemented by *MAX*, the light rail network of streetcars serving downtown and the eastern suburbs. Schedules are available at light rail stops along the streets as well as at the Pioneer Courthouse Square transit office. Fare is 95¢ to $1.25.

TAXI Cabs must be called or picked up at taxi stations in front of the major hotels; they *cannot* be hailed. Most hotels have direct phone connections to the two largest companies, *Broadway Cab* (phone: 227-1234) and *Radio Cab* (phone: 227-1212).

TROLLEY Replicas of Portland's grand old "Council Crest" trolleys from the 1890s run on weekends and holidays on the *MAX* light rail tracks. The trolleys feature hand-finished wood paneling and clanging bells. The fare is $1.

LOCAL SERVICES

AUDIOVISUAL EQUIPMENT *Peter Corvallis Productions, Inc.* (79 SW Oak; phone: 222-1664).

BABY-SITTING *Wee-Ba-Bee Child Care* (1301 SE Rusk Rd., Milwaukie; phone: 786-3837).

BUSINESS SERVICES *Business Service Bureau* (1208 SW 13th Ave.; phone: 228-4107); *HQ Business Centers* (1001 SW Fifth Ave.; phone: 220-1600).

COMPUTER RENTAL *Bit by Bit* (10222 SW Nimbus, Tigard; phone: 639-5467), delivery available.

DRY CLEANER/TAILOR *Bee Tailors & Cleaners* (939 SW 10th St.; phone: 227-1144); *Levines* (2086 W. Burnside; phone: 223-7221).

LIMOUSINE *Classic Chauffeur* (phone: 238-8880); *Oregon Limousine Service* (phone: 252-5882).

MECHANICS *Firestone* (815 W. Burnside; phone: 228-9268); *Tune Up Specialties* (8060 NE Glisan; phone: 252-8096).

- **MEDICAL EMERGENCY** *Good Samaritan Hospital* (1015 NW 22nd St.; phone: 229-7260); *Providence Medical Center* (4805 NE Glisan St.; phone: 230-6000).

- **MESSENGER SERVICES** *On-Time Delivery* (phone: 255-5825); *Pronto Messenger Co.* (phone: 239-7666).

- **MONEY TRANSFERS** *American Express MoneyGram* (phone: 800-926-9400 for information; 800-866-8800 for money transfers); *Western Union Financial Services* (phone: 800-325-6000 or 800-325-4176).

- **NATIONAL/INTERNATIONAL COURIER** *DHL Worldwide Express* (phone: 800-225-5345); *FedEx* (phone: 800-238-5355).

- **PHARMACY** *Stadium Fred Meyer Pharmacy* (100 NW 20th Pl. and Burnside; phone: 226-7179), open Mondays through Saturdays 9 AM to 10 PM, Sundays 10 AM to 7 PM.

- **PHOTOCOPIES** *Copies Now* (*World Trade Center,* 903 SW First Ave.; phone: 243-2234); *Kinko's* (1605 NE Seventh St.; phone: 284-2129), open 24 hours.

- **POST OFFICE** Main office (715 NW Hoyt St.; phone: 294-2300).

- **PROFESSIONAL PHOTOGRAPHER** *Leonard Conkling Photography* (phone: 252-1257); *Photo Art Commercial Studios, Inc.* (phone: 224-5665).

- **SECRETARY/STENOGRAPHER** *Affordable Typing Service* (phone: 235-5054); *Bays Secretarial Service* (phone: 223-3201); also see *Business Services,* above.

- **TRANSLATOR** *International Language Bank* (phone: 234-0168).

- **WESTERN UNION/TELEX** Many offices are located around the city (phone: 800-325-6000 to find the location nearest you).

SPECIAL EVENTS

Something is always happening in Portland, so it pays to check with the visitors' association and read the local paper (see *Local Coverage* above). Among the myriad events that enliven the city are the *Portland Rose Festival,* which features everything from beauty queens to bicycle races and takes place during the first half of June, and the *Mt. Hood Festival of Jazz,* which brings the best jazz musicians to town every August.

MUSEUMS

In addition to those listed in *Special Places,* Portland has several museums of note.

- **AMERICAN ADVERTISING MUSEUM** One of the nation's best collections of persuasive media, from sandwich boards to videos, is here in the country's only museum dedicated to advertising in all media. Closed Mondays and Tuesdays. Admission charge. 9 NW Second Ave. (phone: 226-0000).

- **CHILDREN'S MUSEUM** Kids can amuse themselves with a children's grocery store, switchboard, clay workshop, bistro, water exhibit, tunnel, and more. Open daily. Admission charge. 3037 SW Second Ave. (phone: 823-2227).

CONTEMPORARY CRAFTS GALLERY A not-for-profit institution that seeks to support and promote crafts as a fine art. Changing exhibits of work in glass, fiber, wood, metal, and clay by artists worldwide as well as lectures and demonstrations are presented here. The sales gallery concentrates primarily on the works of local Northwest artists. Closed Mondays. No admission charge. 3934 SW Corbett (phone: 223-2654).

COWBOYS THEN AND NOW MUSEUM Here's the beef on the Wild West, focusing on the history of cattle and cowpokes. You can see a 100-year-old chuck wagon, a tack room with authentic cowboy gear, a 600-volume library, and videos on the cattle industry. Closed Mondays and Tuesdays. No admission charge. 729 NE Oregon St. (phone: 731-3333).

OREGON HISTORICAL SOCIETY MUSEUM The exhibitions concentrate on Oregon history, before and after the arrival of European settlers. There's also a fine series of dioramas on Indian life, a research library with open stacks, and changing exhibitions. Closed Mondays. Admission charge. 1200 SW Park Ave. (phone: 222-1741).

PORTLAND ART MUSEUM With an outstanding permanent collection of Northwest Indian art, the museum also features a representative group of Oregon's prolific contemporary artists and a wide variety of traveling shows. Also part of the *Institute* is the outdoor *Sculpture Mall,* the *Pacific Northwest College of Art,* and the *Northwest Film and Video Center.* Closed Mondays. Admission charge. 1219 SW Park Ave. (phone: 226-2811).

PARKS AND GARDENS

Even the freeways into Portland are divided by banks of wild roses and iris; the city is surrounded by green mountains and garlanded with 7,608 acres of parkland. In addition to those described in *Special Places,* other notable Portland parks include *Council Crest Park,* above Portland Heights (SW Fairmount Blvd.) and *Westmoreland Park* (SE 22nd Ave. at Bybee). The city even holds the distinction of having the world's smallest park: *Mill Ends Park,* on Front Street at Taylor Avenue, measures only 24 square inches. Planted with a suitably small evergreen tree surrounded by flowers, it was created to honor the late Dick Fagen, a well-known journalist in Portland during the 1940s.

SHOPPING

The absence of any sales tax makes Portland especially attractive to shoppers. The downtown shopping district is adjacent to Pioneer Courthouse Square. *Pioneer Place* (SW Fifth Ave.; phone: 228-5800) includes *Saks Fifth Avenue* among its 80 specialty stores nestled in a glass-enclosed, four-level pavilion. The *Galleria* (921 SW Morrison; phone: 228-2748), one of the city's first historic renovations, offers some 50 stores and restaurants within its three stories. *Lloyd Center* (phone: 282-2511), east of downtown near the *Oregon Convention Center,* features more than 150 stores. Also, see "Old Town" under *Special Places.*

Made in Oregon These shops carry products made, caught, or grown in the state, including filberts, cranberry candy, smoked salmon, Pendleton woolen goods, and Oregon wines. They can be found at several locations: *Portland International Airport* (phone: 282-7827); *Washington*

Square Mall (Tigard; phone: 620-4670); *Galleria* (921 SW Morrison; phone: 241-3630); *Clackamas Town Center* (12000 SE 82nd Ave.; phone: 659-3155); *Lloyd Center* (phone: 282-7636); and Old Town (10 NW First; phone: 273-8354).

Norm Thompson This shop stocks British duffel coats and other luxurious outdoorwear from around the world. 1805 NW Thurman (phone: 221-0764).

Oregon Trail Store The products featured here—blankets, dolls, bonnets, and food—are connected with the history of the Oregon Trail. *Galleria,* 921 SW Morrison (phone: 273-5666).

Powell's Travel Store A huge selection of books shares space here with all sorts of travel paraphernalia: money belts, journals, maps, and canteens. Owner Michael Powell also operates *Powell's Books* (see *Special Places*). At Pioneer Courthouse Sq., 701 SW Sixth Ave. (phone: 228-1108).

The Real Mother Goose A virtual woodland, this place sells finely crafted pieces that range from wooden kaleidoscopes and carved canes to furniture made from exotic woods. There's also hand-crafted jewelry and garments that have been carefully woven, dyed, painted, and/or beaded by hand. 901 SW Yamhill (phone: 223-9510).

Saturday Market Plan to spend the greater part of the morning here. Artists from all over the state come to sell their work under the Burnside Bridge between SW First and Front every weekend, March through December 24 (phone: 222-6072).

TAKE SOME PORTLAND HOME WITH YOU

Fresh chinook and silver salmon are two of Portland's best-known exports, and airlines are accustomed to seeing passengers board an outbound flight with a cold fin under one arm. *Newman's Fish Market* (*Holladay's Market,* 1200 NE Broadway; phone: 284-4537) will supply fresh salmon and crab, specially packed to travel.

SPORTS AND FITNESS

Portlanders are dedicated athletes—there are running and bike paths all over town—and avid basketball fans.

BASKETBALL The *NBA Trail Blazers* play their home games at *Memorial Coliseum* (phone: 235-8771) from November through April.

BICYCLING Rent from *Agape Cycle & Fitness* (2314 SE Division; phone: 230-0317). Mountain bikes can be rented from *Fat Tire Farm* (2714 NW Thurman; phone: 222-3276). Numerous city and country rides are described in *The Portland Guidebook.*

FISHING For chinook salmon, try the lower Willamette or Willamette Slough from March through early May. Steelhead are found in the Clackamas and Sandy Rivers from December through February; sturgeon at Sauvie

Island (see *Extra Special*). For fishing information in the area call the Sport Fishing Info Line at 800-ASK-FISH.

FITNESS CENTERS The *YMCA* has a number of branches: 6036 SE Foster Rd. (phone: 294-3311); 1630 NE 38th St. (phone: 294-3377); and 2831 SW Barbur Blvd. (phone: 294-3366). All are open to non-members for a fee.

GOLF The metropolitan area has 35 public courses, one of which, an 18-hole championship course, is located at the *Pumpkin Ridge Golf Club* (12930 Old Pumpkin Ridge Rd., Cornelius; phone: 647-4747), 20 minutes west of the city. For information on golfing in the area, call the *Oregon Golf Association* (phone: 643-2610).

HORSE AND DOG RACING There's racing and pari-mutuel betting at *The New Portland Meadows* (1001 N. Schmeer Rd.; phone: 285-9144), with a season from October through April; and *Multnomah Greyhound Park*, 12 miles from the city (NE 223 and Glisan, Fairview; phone: 667-7700), from May through September.

ICE SKATING An enduring Portland tradition is the indoor *Ice Pavilion* at *Lloyd Center* (phone: 288-6073). Skates available for rent.

JOGGING A popular and picturesque run is along the Willamette River at *Waterfront Park*. Most of the city's parks offer trails or tracks. Contact the *Oregon Roadrunners* (phone: 646-7867) for suggestions or information on local running events.

SKIING The closest areas, on Mt. Hood, are *Timberline* (phone: 231-7979), *Ski-Bowl* (phone: 272-3206), and *Mt. Hood Meadows* (phone: 337-2222); better is *Mt. Bachelor* (phone: 382-7888), 180 miles from Portland at Bend.

SWIMMING Call the *City of Portland Park Department* (phone: 823-2223) for public pool information. Also see *Fitness Centers*.

TENNIS The *Park Bureau* runs seven indoor and dozens of outdoor courts. The indoor courts may be reserved by the *Portland Tennis Center* (324 NE 12th Ave.; phone: 823-3189 or 823-3190).

THEATER

Portland has more than a dozen theaters offering musical and dramatic performances, some locally produced, others from out of town. One of the best bets for information and ticket sales is the *Portland Center for the Performing Arts* (1111 SW Broadway; phone: 248-4496), an umbrella organization for many of the city's theaters and companies: *Arlene Schnitzer Concert Hall* (home of the *Oregon Symphony*, phone: 228-1353); *Intermediate Theater; Dolores Winningstad Theatre;* and the *Portland Civic Auditorium*, home of the *Oregon Ballet Theatre* (phone: 222-5538) and the *Portland Opera* (phone: 241-1802). Other theatrical venues include: *Tygres Heart Shakespeare Company* (phone: 222-9220), *Portland Center Stage* (phone: 274-6588), which mounts a range of productions from classical to contemporary, and *Portland Repertory* (phone: 224-4491), where you'll see contemporary dramas and comedies. For children's theater: *Oregon Children's Theatre Company* (phone: 248-4496) and the *Carousel Company* (phone: 238-0012).

MUSIC

Portland's opera, ballet, and symphony are well respected and their programs ambitious (see *Theater* above for musical offerings at the *Portland Center for the Performing Arts*). There are also free summer concerts in *Washington Park* between mid-July and mid-August; free concerts at *Waterfront Park* from July to mid-September; and the always-happening Pioneer Courthouse Square's free concerts that run from June through August (phone: 223-1613).

NIGHTCLUBS AND NIGHTLIFE

Portland has become renowned as a blues town, with jazz not far behind. Homegrown groups like the *Tom Grant Band* and the *Mel Brown Quintet* have gained national attention. Current favorites: *Brasserie Montmartre* (626 SW Park; phone: 224-5552), where the jazz is mellow weeknights and heats up on weekends; *Bojangles* (2229 SE Hawthorne; phone: 233-1201), serving up blues and Hawaiian food; and *Dandelion Pub* (31 NW 23rd Pl.; phone: 223-0099), with good blues, pop music, Dixieland, folk, and rock. Try the *Roseland Theatre* (8 NW Sixth Ave.; phone: 224-7469) for shows like B. B. King; *Key Largo* (31 NW First Ave.; phone: 223-9919) for blues and rock; and the *Buffalo Gap Saloon and Eatery* (6835 SW Macadam; phone: 244-7111) for acoustic guitar music. The *Goose Hollow Inn* (1927 SW Jefferson; phone: 228-7010) is a singularly Oregonian pub whose owner, the former mayor of Portland, frequently can be seen in the crowd. It offers blues during the summer on Sundays.

BREW PUBS

Portland boasts the most breweries of any US city, so it's not surprising that the marriage of microbreweries and public houses has created a mini-industry here. In downtown Portland, there's the *B. Moloch/Heathman Bakery and Pub* (901 SW Salmon; phone: 227-5700), and farther out of town are the *Hillsdale Brewery and Public House* (1505 SW Sunset Blvd.; phone: 246-3938) and *Fulton Pub and Brewery* (0618 SW Nebraska St.; phone: 246-9530). On the waterfront downtown, the *Pilsner Room* (0309 SW Montgomery; phone: 220-1865) offers 20 microbrews on tap. The McMenamin brothers operate the *Baghdad Theatre & Pub* (3702 SE Hawthorne Blvd.; phone: 230-0895) and the *Mission Theatre & Pub* (1624 NW Glisan St.; phone: 223-4031), where customers can view films while they quaff a brew and munch on burgers. The brothers' most ambitious addition is *McMenamin's Edgefield*, located in the eastern suburb of Troutdale (2126 SW Halsey St.; phone: 492-4686); the complex includes a brew pub, a winery, a theater, bed and breakfast accommodations, and a restaurant.

Best in Town

CHECKING IN

Portland's choice hotels have made it possible to slumber in splendor as well as in comfort and convenience—although the privilege carries a rather high price tag. Expect to pay $125 or more per night for a double room at hotels we've categorized as expensive; $70 to $125 at lodgings listed as moderate; and less than $70 at inexpensive places. For bed and breakfast accommodations, contact the *Oregon Bed and Breakfast Guild* (PO Box 3187, Ashland, OR 97520; phone: 482-8707; 800-944-6196) or *Northwest Bed & Breakfast* (610 SW Broadway, Suite 606, Portland, OR 97205; phone: 243-7616). Unless otherwise noted, hotel rooms have air conditioning, private baths, TV sets, and telephones. All hotels are in the 503 area code unless otherwise indicated.

EXPENSIVE

Benson Built in 1913 by wealthy logger Simon Benson, this premier hotel has been restored to its original grandeur. The lobby maintains a feeling of Old World luxury, with its white Italian marble floor, Oriental carpets, walnut paneling, and high transom windows. There are 290 rooms and suites, two with gas fireplaces. The *London Grill* restaurant is quite good, as is *Trader Vic's*. There is also a coffee shop, a concierge, a health club, 24-hour room service, and valet parking. Thirteen meeting rooms are available, as well as photocopiers, secretarial services, A/V equipment, and express checkout. 309 SW Broadway (phone: 228-2000; 800-426-0670; fax: 226-4603).

Governor Listed on the *National Register of Historic Places,* it is actually two buildings: a 1909 mission-style edifice and an Italian Renaissance-style structure built in 1923. In the mahogany-paneled lobby, massive murals depict the adventures of Lewis and Clark. While the 100 rooms are not as grand as the public areas, they are well appointed and comfortable. The dining room, *Celio,* serves fine local fare (see *Eating Out*). Business amenities include a business center with fax and computer hookups and several ballrooms that can double as meeting space. SW 10th St. at Alder St. (phone: 224-3400; 800-554-3456; fax: 224-2122).

Heathman Adjoining the *Performing Arts Center* are 151 of the most luxurious rooms and suites in town. Listed in the *National Register of Historic Places* and included in the *National Trust for Historic Preservation*'s list of Historic Hotels of America, it has emerged as an authentic first class property. Rooms are decorated in floral chintz, and facilities include a complimentary video movie library, a mezzanine bar, a library with signed editions from authors who have stayed here, a concierge, valet parking, complimentary taxi passes to entertainment events, and access to a nearby health club as well as a new on-site fitness suite. Its main restaurant is noted for its fresh Pacific Northwest seafood and game. Additional amenities include around-the-clock room service, a concierge, limited secretarial services, eight meeting rooms, A/V equipment, and photocopiers. SW Broadway at Salmon (phone: 241-4100; 800-551-0011; fax: 790-7110).

River Place One of the city's smallest inns: only 84 rooms and suites clustered on the waterfront (as well as 10 condos available for rent in the complex next door). Six suites have wood-burning fireplaces and wet bars. Guests awaken to views of the marina and to continental breakfast. The *Esplanade* restaurant prepares Northwest regional dishes. A concierge, 24-hour room service, and access to an adjacent health club are also available. Other conveniences include five meeting rooms, photocopiers, A/V equipment, limited secretarial services, and express checkout. 1510 SW Harbor Way (phone: 228-3233; 800-227-1333; fax: 295-6161).

Vintage Plaza Just two blocks from Pioneer Courthouse Square downtown, this charming European-style hotel dates back to 1894. It was designed around a winery theme, complete with an extensive wine cellar and a tasting area. The cozy lobby has a fireplace and a baby grand piano. All of the 107 rooms and suites are stylishly decorated and have direct-dial phones and computer hookups; the two-level suites on the seventh floor have a magnificent view of the city. There also is a fitness center. *Pazzo*, the adjacent restaurant, serves innovative Italian food (see *Eating Out*). Business amenities include eight conference rooms accommodating up to 200, A/V equipment, two boardrooms, and a business center with a fax machine, a computer, a photocopier, and secretarial services. 422 SW Broadway (phone: 228-1212; 800-243-0555; fax: 228-3598).

MODERATE

Red Lion Hotels and Inns One giant complex on the Columbia River, between Portland and Vancouver (Washington) and 10 minutes from the airport, contains three inns with a total of 830 rooms: the *Red Lion/Columbia River* (1401 N. Hayden Island Dr.; phone: 283-2111); the *Red Lion/Jantzen Beach* (909 N. Hayden Island Dr.; phone: 283-4466); and the *Red Lion Inn at the Quay* (on the Washington side at 100 Columbia St., Vancouver; phone: 206-285-0636). The *Red Lion/Lloyd Center* (1000 NE Multnomah St.; phone: 281-6111) and the *Red Lion/Coliseum* (1225 N. Thunderbird Wy.; phone: 235-8311) are in Portland itself. All the properties have fine restaurants, live entertainment, convention facilities, grand ballrooms, and room service. There is a pool, tennis, and mini-golf at the *Red Lion/Jantzen Beach*. Other conveniences are a concierge and limited secretarial services, meeting rooms, A/V equipment and photocopiers, and express checkout. (Fax: 206-694-2023 for the *Red Lion Inn at the Quay;* 283-4743 for all other locations.)

INEXPENSIVE

Mallory A step down from the Jacuzzis and decorator suites, but a comfortable, clean, and quiet 1950s-style hostelry that offers 144 rooms and adequate restaurant facilities at a reasonable price. 729 SW 15th Ave. (phone: 223-6311; 800-228-8657; fax: 223-0522).

EATING OUT

Portland shines brightly as an international dining town. Restaurants put to use the abundant local seafood, farm fresh vegetables, and excellent regional wines in unique and satisfying variations. Our restaurant selections range in price from $60 or more for dinner for two in the expensive category, $30 to $60 in the moderate, and $30 or less in the inexpensive category. Prices do not include drinks, wine, tax, or tips. Unless otherwise noted, restaurants are open for lunch and dinner. All restaurants are in the 503 area code unless otherwise indicated.

EXPENSIVE

Atwater's Occupying the entire 30th floor of the *US Bancorp Tower*, it offers a 360-degree view over all downtown. The kitchen does justice to the striking panorama, with a seasonal Northwest menu that relies on only the freshest local products, such as seafood and game. Open daily for dinner only. Reservations advised. Major credit cards accepted. 111 SW Fifth Ave. (phone: 275-3600).

L'Auberge Admirers of grilled swordfish with cilantro pesto or spearfish in raspberry beurre blanc will find true contentment at this unstuffy French eatery that uses fresh Northwest ingredients. In summer, patrons can dine on a deck overlooking a lovely garden. Open daily for dinner only. Reservations advised. Major credit cards accepted. 2601 NW Vaughn St. (phone: 223-3302).

Celio The dining room of the *Governor* hotel serves contemporary dishes in a turn-of-the-century atmosphere. The decor features mahogany paneling and pillars, ceiling fans, plants, and curtained booths for privacy; the menu offers sumptuous entrées, such as roast duck, Asian stir-fry with Manila clams, and all manner and style of fresh fish. Also featured is an extensive list of Oregon wines and specialty teas. Open daily. Reservations advised. Major credit cards accepted. SW 10th St. at Alder St. (phone: 241-2100).

Jake's Famous Crawfish Restaurant *The* dining spot Portlanders recommend to visitors, it has been around since 1892. Especially delectable are oysters on the half shell, grilled chinook salmon with béarnaise sauce, and bouillabaisse. Save room for Jake's famous chocolate truffle cake or hot three-berry cobbler. Open daily; dinner only on weekends. Reservations advised. Major credit cards accepted. 401 SW 12th (phone: 226-1419).

Zafiro With its chic, minimalist decor and inventive continental menu, this has quickly become the city's most popular dining spot. Entrées often involve presenting native Northwest ingredients in Old World and Mediterranean dishes, such as lamb ragout served on mashed potatoes. Open daily. Reservations advised. Major credit cards accepted. 500 NW 21st Ave. (phone: 226-3394).

MODERATE

Bangkok Kitchen This is Portland's reward for being an international port: Thai food at its best. Among the addictive dishes are hot and sour shrimp soup with coconut milk, *phad Thai* (a noodle dish with peanuts and preserved radishes), vegetarian spring rolls, curried peanut sauce, and on occasion, whole red snapper with chili sauce. Closed Sundays and Mondays. No credit cards accepted. 2534 SE Belmont St. (phone: 236-7349).

Café des Amis Lace curtains, candlelight, and delightfully personable waiters set the welcoming tone. The menu is Pacific Northwest with French touches. Stuffed quail, duck with blackberry sauce, and fettuccine with mussels are done distinctively. Open for dinner only; closed Sundays. Reservations advised. Major credit cards accepted. 1987 NW Kearny (phone: 295-6487).

Chen's Dynasty For Chinese specialties such as stir-fried pork with pickled mustard greens and peanuts or cracked crab with Hunan black beans, this is the place. The menu seems to go on forever. Open daily. Reservations advised. Major credit cards accepted. 622 SW Washington (phone: 248-9491).

Huber's Café Tucked away in the Oregon Pioneer Building, Portland's oldest operating restaurant (1879) has booths, polished mahogany, stained glass, and an atmosphere as appealing as the food. A traditional turkey dinner with all the trimmings is served six days a week. The excellent Spanish coffee is a favorite with the after-theater crowd. Closed Sundays. Major credit cards accepted. 411 SW Third (phone: 228-5686).

Pazzo Next door to the *Vintage Plaza* hotel, this spot serves northern Italian and Tuscan seafood and pasta specialties, but there are chicken, lamb, and veal dishes as well. Particularly good are the ravioli filled with smoked salmon served with an asparagus and lemon cream sauce, and *penne* with lamb sausage. The decor features dark wood paneling and red and white checkered tablecloths. Open daily. Reservations advised. Major credit cards accepted. SW Broadway and SW Washington St. (phone: 228-1515).

Plainfield's Mayur East Indian dishes are prepared in full dramatic view at the tandoor, a deep clay oven with a 1,000-degree fire at the bottom. Tandoori chicken, lamb, breads, and other Indian specialties are served in the pleasant surroundings of an elegant old Portland home with bone china and good-quality silver. Open for dinner only. Reservations advised. Major credit cards accepted. 852 SW 21st Ave. (phone: 223-2995).

INEXPENSIVE

Berbati More than a Greek restaurant, it's a scene, as lively and crowded as its menu. Especially noteworthy are the fried calamari, stuffed grape leaves, vegetarian moussaka, lamb chops, homemade sweet cookies, and if you are lucky, *crema,* a sybaritic custard. Closed Mondays. Reservations for six or more. Major credit cards accepted. 19 SW Second (phone: 226-2122).

Dan and Louis Oyster Bar A Portland institution with a nautical theme. It opened at a time when restaurants didn't worry about "ambience," and it still doesn't. Clams, crabs, and oysters can be grilled, fried, or steamed, and desserts are fresh baked. Open daily. Reservations advised for five or more. Major credit cards accepted. 208 SW Ankeny (phone: 227-5906).

Papa Haydn Select dessert first, then order a light meal that won't spoil it. There's almost always a crowd gathered around the pastry case, where delights ranging from "autumn meringue" to *boccone dolce* (a mélange of meringue, cream, strawberries, and chocolate) are on display. Dinners feature light, continental dishes emphasizing seafood and chicken. Closed Mondays; open for Sunday brunch. Reservations only for brunch. Major credit cards accepted. 5829 SE Milwaukee Ave. (phone: 232-9440) and 801 NW 23rd Ave. (phone: 228-7317).

St. Louis

At-a-Glance

SEEING THE CITY

A tour of St. Louis must begin along the Mississippi River, where the city began, and the riverfront offers an irresistible focal point: the *Gateway Arch* (in *Jefferson National Expansion Memorial Park*), which soars 630 feet above the levee. Ride to the observation room at the top of the *Arch* in one of two trams; from that vantage, there's a spectacular 30-mile view of both sides of the river. While waiting for the tram, visit the *Museum of Westward Expansion* (11 N. Fourth St.; phone: 425-4465), browse in the *Museum Shop,* on the plaza beneath the *Arch,* or see a film on the construction of the *Arch* in the *Tucker Theater.* Built in 1966 by architect Eero Saarinen, the *Arch* is so delicately engineered that its last segment—the apex where the two columns are connected—couldn't be installed until the weather was perfect, so that the steel would neither contract nor expand even a fraction until it was in place.

SPECIAL PLACES

Though it's convenient to get around St. Louis by car, most areas lend themselves to walking. You can park along the riverfront, for example, and explore the levee, *Laclede's Landing,* and downtown.

RIVERFRONT AND DOWNTOWN

THE LEVEE Moored on the river side of the cobblestone levee are St. Louis's most famous riverboats: the *Huck Finn, Becky Thatcher,* and *Tom Sawyer* (phone: 621-4040 for all three), offering day and night trips along the Mississippi. You'll also find the New Orleans–based *Delta Queen* (phone: 800-543-1949) and the *Robert E. Lee* (phone: 241-1282), luxurious sternwheelers from the golden era of steamboats, as well as the world's only floating *McDonald's* and the *Belle of St. Louis,* an excursion dining boat (phone: 342-7200 or 621-4040).

On the city side of the levee is *Jefferson National Expansion Memorial Park,* with the *Arch* at its center, and on one side, the *Old Cathedral,* the oldest cathedral west (just west) of the Mississippi. It started as a log cabin in 1764 when the city was founded and took its present form in 1834. Second and Walnut Sts. (phone: 231-3250).

LACLEDE'S LANDING In the 50 years after the Civil War, St. Louis became rich as well as famous, and *Laclede's Landing,* a 10-block area just north of the levee on the far side of massive Eads Bridge, was part of that early boom; it contains some fine examples of cast-iron-fronted buildings (*Raeder Place,* formerly the *Old Missouri* hotel, at 806 N. First is best of all). It's now the home of a new generation of restaurants and galleries, and one of the few areas in the city where liquor can be served until 3 AM. Some suggestions while wandering the area are *Kennedy's 2nd Street Company* (612 N. Second St.; phone: 421-3655), for a lunch of chili, burgers, and sandwiches, and a great place to hear local bands;

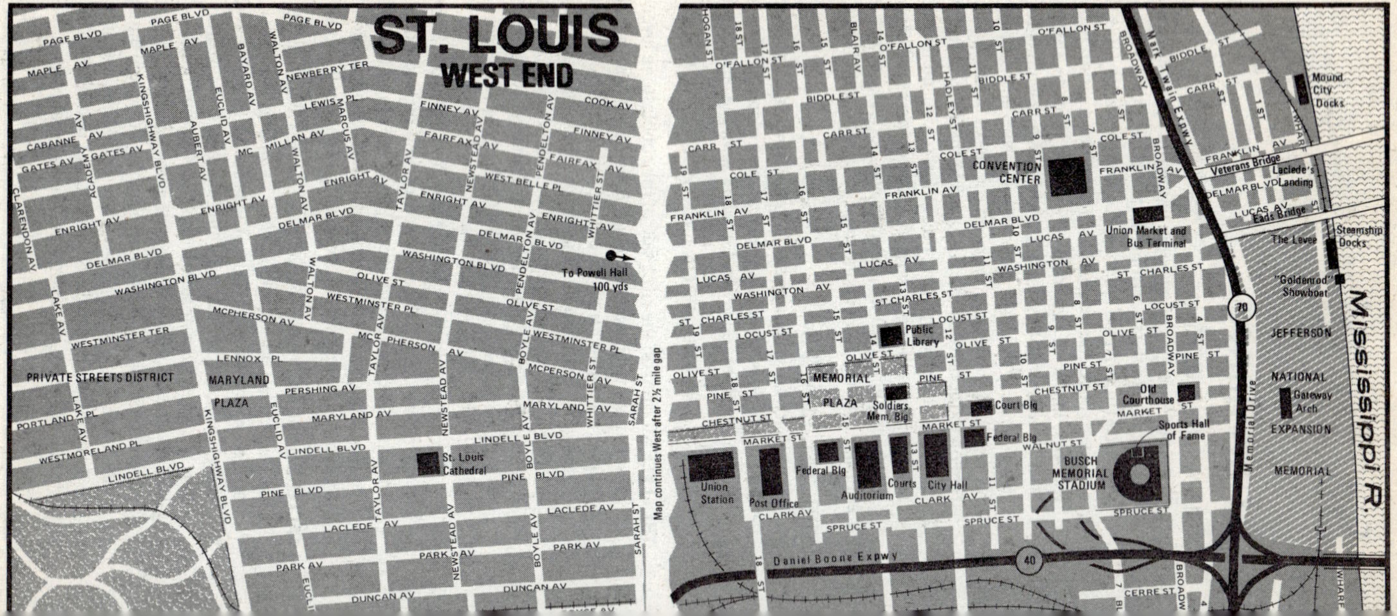
ST. LOUIS
WEST END
To Powell Hall 100 yds
St. Louis Cathedral
PRIVATE STREETS DISTRICT
MARYLAND PLAZA
Map continues West after 2½ mile gap
Mississippi R.
Mound City Docks
Veterans Bridge
Laclede's Landing
Eads Bridge
The Levee
Steamship Docks
"Goldenrod" Showboat
JEFFERSON NATIONAL EXPANSION MEMORIAL
Gateway Arch
Memorial Drive
Mark Twain Expwy
Daniel Boone Expwy
CONVENTION CENTER
Union Market and Bus Terminal
Public Library
MEMORIAL PLAZA
Soldiers Mem. Blg
Court Blg
Old Courthouse
Sports Hall of Fame
Federal Blg
BUSCH MEMORIAL STADIUM
Union Station
Post Office
Federal Blg
Auditorium
Courts
City Hall
70
40

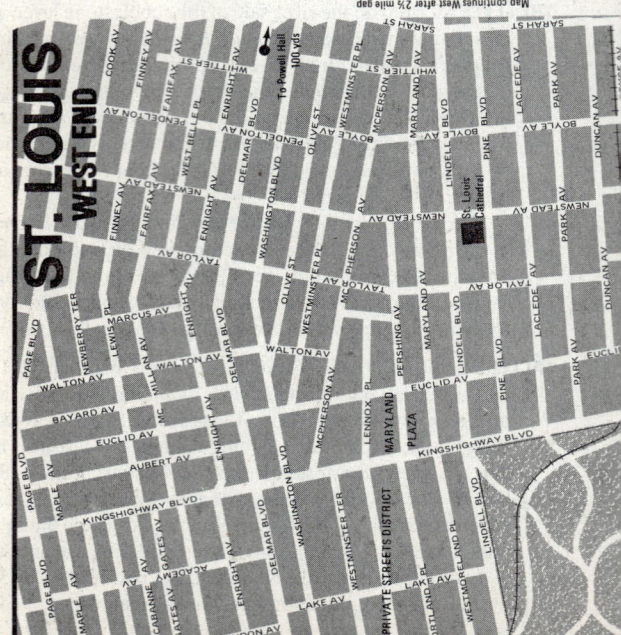

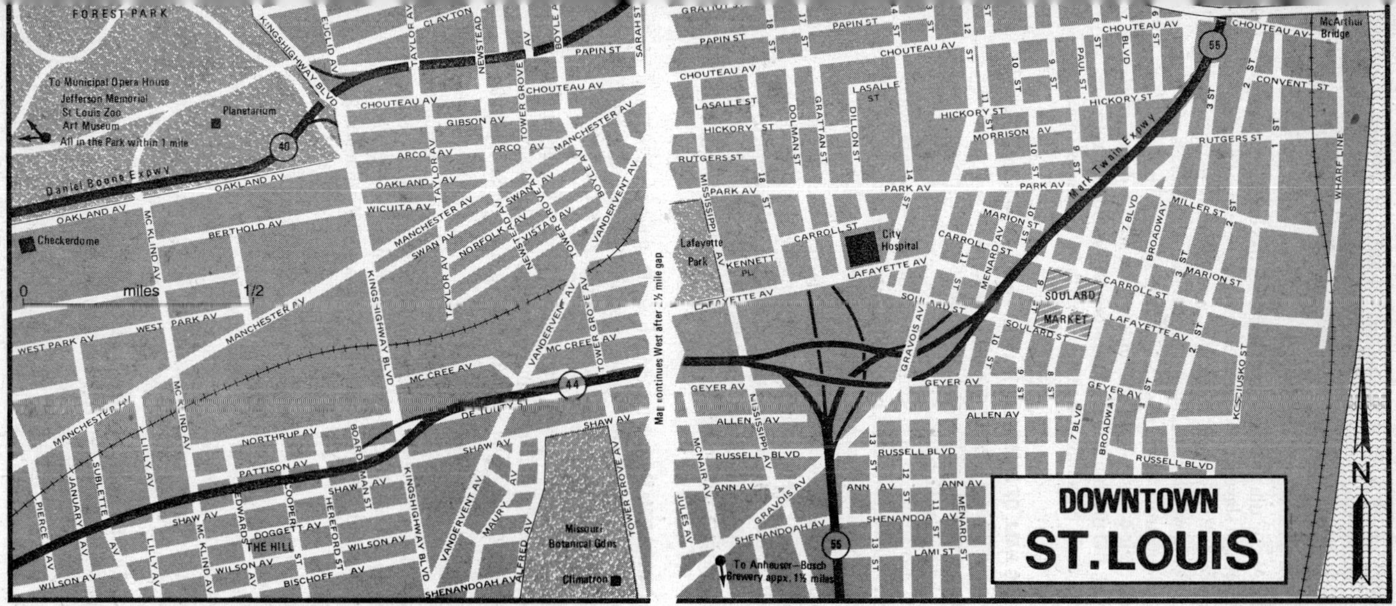
DOWNTOWN
ST. LOUIS
N
Map continues West after ½ mile gap
0 miles 1/2
FOREST PARK
To Municipal Opera House
Jefferson Memorial
St Louis Zoo
Art Museum
All in the Park within 1 mile
Planetarium
Checkerdome
Daniel Boone Expwy
Mark Twain Expwy
McArthur Bridge
WHARF LINE
City Hospital
Lafayette Park
SOULARD MARKET
Missouri Botanical Gdns
Climatron
THE HILL
To Anheuser-Busch Brewery appx. 1½ miles
40
44
55
KINGSHIGHWAY BLVD
CHOUTEAU AV
MANCHESTER AV
GRAVOIS AV
LAFAYETTE AV
SHENANDOAH AV
TOWER GROVE AV
VANDERVENT AV
RUSSELL BLVD
BROADWAY
PARK AV
MISSISSIPPI AV

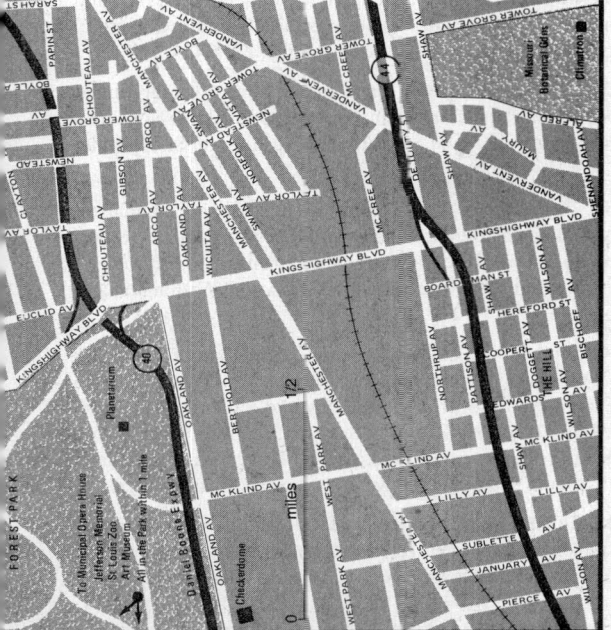

Mississippi Nights (914 N. First St.; phone: 421-3853), which features local as well as national bands; and the *Old Spaghetti Factory* (727 N. First St.; phone: 621-0276), for inexpensive Italian dishes and old European decor.

OLD COURTHOUSE At one time a site of slave auctions, this building was also where an American slave named Dred Scott tested the legality of slavery by suing for his freedom in 1846; the case eventually reached the *US Supreme Court,* which ruled against him. Inside are displays of Old St. Louis and courtrooms where great lawyers such as Thomas Hart Benton tried their cases. Notice the building's cast-iron dome, completed in 1859, and the mural that adorns its interior. Guided tours are offered. Open daily. No admission charge. Fourth St. at Market (phone: 425-4465).

NATIONAL BOWLING HALL OF FAME Headquarters of the *American Bowling Congress* and the *Women's International Bowling Congress,* it traces the history and development of bowling from 5200 BC to the present. Two interactive children's exhibits use bowling scores to make math more fun. There's also an old-time bowling alley, videodisc program, widescreen theater, and restaurant. Open daily. Admission charge. Eighth and Walnut, across from *Busch Stadium* (phone: 231-6340).

EUGENE FIELD HOUSE Primarily an antique toy collection, the exhibit also has some artifacts of the famous St. Louis author Eugene Field, who wrote *Little Boy Blue.* In December, the house prepares a complete Victorian *Christmas* display. Closed Mondays, Tuesdays, and January through February. Admission charge. 634 S. Broadway (phone: 421-4689).

CHRIST CHURCH CATHEDRAL Though the church was built between 1867 and 1911, it beautifully re-creates 14th-century English Gothic architecture. Tours are given on Sundays. 1210 Locust (phone: 231-3454).

MERCANTILE MONEY MUSEUM Here you can learn everything you ever wanted to know about money, including counterfeiting. Open daily. No admission charge. *Mercantile Tower,* Seventh and Washington Sts. (phone: 421-1819).

ST. LOUIS CENTRE One of the country's largest urban shopping complexes, the four-level, glass-enclosed mall consists of 150 shops and 20 restaurants and connects two of the city's largest department stores, *Dillard's* and *Famous-Barr.* Between Sixth and Seventh Sts., and Washington and Olive Blvds.

UNION STATION Old and new St. Louis meet here. Originally built during the glory days of railroads 100 years ago, this was once the busiest train station in the country. Today, the main lobby and lounge of the *Hyatt Regency St. Louis* (see *Checking In*) occupy the station's Grand Hall. Exclusive shops, deluxe restaurants, and a 10-screen movie theater occupy the far south end of the renovated station. 18th and Market Sts.

DENTAL HEALTH THEATRE The props are three-foot-high fiberglass teeth and a carpeted pink tongue, the characters are marionettes, and the show's all about teeth and dental health. A good place to take the kids. Open weekdays. No admission charge. 727 N. First St., Suite 103, on *Laclede Landing* (phone: 241-7391).

ST. LOUIS PUBLIC LIBRARY This 1912 Italianate building contains an art gallery, the *Steedman Architectural Library,* and extensive reference collections. Tours available. Closed Sundays. 1301 Olive St. (phone: 241-2288).

ST. LOUIS MERCANTILE LIBRARY ASSOCIATION Founded in 1846, this is the oldest circulating library west of the Mississippi River. Among its significant photo/print collections are works by George Caleb Bingham and George Catlin, painters who meticulously documented the westward expansion. Also contained here are the old archives of the city newspaper. Closed Sundays. 510 Locust St. (phone: 621-0670).

ST. LOUIS SPORTS HALL OF FAME A century of St. Louis sports is celebrated here, including photographs of yesterday's *Browns* and today's *Cardinals,* as well as football, soccer, and hockey displays. First baseman Stan Musial's glove is here, as well as other artifacts. In the *Hall of Fame Theater,* a film of the *Cardinals'* achievements is continuously played. Open daily. Admission charge. 100 Stadium Plaza (phone: 421-3263).

SOLDIERS' MEMORIAL MILITARY MUSEUM In addition to a variety of military memorabilia, this museum, dedicated to St. Louis's veterans, recently acquired a replica of Washington, DC's *Vietnam War Memorial.* Closed *Thanksgiving, Christmas,* and *New Year's Day.* 1315 Chestnut St. (phone: 622-4550).

SOUTH ST. LOUIS

South St. Louis is primarily German, Italian, and Eastern European. The most determinedly ethnic neighborhood in the area is the Hill (between South Kingshighway and Shaw). From its *bocce* courts and front yard shrines to its green, white, and red hydrants, the Hill is 20 blocks of solid Italian consciousness—great for walking and snacking. Two suggestions: *John Volpi & Co.* (5256 Daggett; phone: 772-8550) for salami, prosciutto, and Italian sausage; and *Amighetti Bakery* (5141 Wilson; phone: 776-2855) for fresh bread and carry-out po-boys. This area is particularly noted for its fine Italian restaurants.

ANHEUSER-BUSCH BREWERY The makers of Michelob and Budweiser offer free one-hour tours of the world's largest brewery and grounds, featuring, naturally, a healthy sampling of the King of Beers. Best on the tour: the stables, a registered landmark building and home of the mighty Clydesdale horses. Closed weekends and holidays. No admission charge. 610 Pestalozzi St. (phone: 577-2626).

CHEROKEE STREET ANTIQUE ROW This six-block historic district is filled with charming mid-19th–century row houses and more than 56 antiques shops offering furniture and collectibles from the Victorian to the Art Deco periods. Cherokee St., between Jefferson and Lemp Aves.

MISSOURI BOTANICAL GARDEN (SHAW'S GARDEN) After Henry Shaw got very rich operating a hardware store in downtown St. Louis, he repaid the city by opening his southside garden estate to the public. Since 1860 its reputation and its collection have grown apace. Highlights of the 79-

acre park: the *Climatron,* a tropical geodesic-dome greenhouse; *Seiwa-En,* a beautiful Japanese garden; the *Scented Garden,* a collection of scented plants with descriptions in braille for the blind; and the *William T. Kemper Center for Home Gardening,* an educational resource. Henry Shaw's home is open for tours. Other features include the *Boehm Porcelain Gallery,* a gift shop, and the *Garden View* restaurant. Open daily. Admission charge. 2101 Tower Grove (phone: 577-5100).

SOULARD MARKET Open for business since 1847, when the ground was given to the city to be used as a public farmers' market. Busiest on Saturday mornings, when everything from live rabbits to homemade apple butter is for sale. The outside stalls around the main building open whenever fresh goods—meat or poultry, vegetables, fruit, homemade specialties—come into the city. Closed Sundays and Mondays; most active Fridays and Saturdays. Seventh St. and Lafayette (phone: 622-4180).

CENTRAL WEST END

Named for its location near famous *Forest Park* at the western edge of the city limits, the Central West End (CWE) is St. Louis's most cosmopolitan and elegant section. A collection of small specialty shops, restaurants, and ornate mansions dot this historic neighborhood. Private "places" such as Portland and Westmoreland, beautifully maintained by residents, are worth exploring. Mississippi-born Thomas "Tennessee" Williams set *The Glass Menagerie* in a CWE Westminster Place apartment, where his family lived during the 1920s.

MARYLAND PLAZA Abutting Euclid Avenue, this is a stroller's delight, with the best people watching in town. A potpourri of shops and restaurants makes for good food and great buys. Try *Duff's* (392 N. Euclid; phone: 361-0522), for sandwiches and imported beer; or the *Saint Louis Bread Company* (4651 Maryland Ave.; phone: 367-7636), which serves delicious sandwiches, fresh bread, pastries, and a variety of piping hot coffees. Sample *Dressel's* (392 N. Euclid; phone: 361-1060), for hearty Welsh pub fare (and the city's best selection of beer and ale). The Central West End also offers restaurants like *Balaban's* (405 N. Euclid; phone: 381-8085), for seafood, French cuisine, or their unusual dinner crêpes; the *Sunshine Inn* (8½ N. Euclid; phone: 367-1413), with an assortment of health food dishes; and *Culpeppers* (300 N. Euclid; phone: 361-2828), well known for its spicy chicken wings, club sandwiches, and soups.

SCOTT JOPLIN HOUSE Scott Joplin (1868–1917) was considered one of the masters of ragtime music; his "Maple Leaf Rag" was among the first important examples of the genre. The 1973 film *The Sting* brought his music to the attention of a worldwide audience. In 1976, the composer's home was listed on the *National Register of Historic Places,* and it is now a museum with exhibits about Joplin's life and work, including a replica of his piano and a re-creation of his seven-room apartment on the second floor. Open daily. Admission charge. 2658 Delmar Ave. (phone: 533-1003).

ST. LOUIS CATHEDRAL It is not only the immense size of the cathedral that is awesome; it is also the mosaics that adorn almost the whole interior space—millions of pieces of stone and glass in thousands of shades depicting saints, apostles, and religious scenes. Considered one of the finest examples of mosaicwork in this hemisphere, it's not to be missed. Tours are conducted on Sundays (except *Easter*). Lindell at Newstead (phone: 533-2824).

FABULOUS FOX THEATER This restored 1929 movie palace now has all the gilt and glitz of its yesteryears. At night the house lights come on, and the *Fox* presents some of the biggest entertainment names in the country—Las Vegas–style shows and pop concerts at Midwestern prices. Tours of the theater are offered. 527 N. Grand Blvd. (phone: 534-1678 for entertainment information).

UNIVERSITY CITY AREA This historic district on Delmar Avenue just west of the Central West End, known as the U. City Loop (where the streetcars turned around), houses a "strip" containing resale shops, modern boutiques, art galleries, and bookstores. Walkers should check out the pavement with stars honoring famous St. Louisans. *Blueberry Hill* (6504 Delmar; phone: 727-0880), a bar/restaurant where Chuck Berry, Elvis Presley, and Bo Diddley are held in esteem, serves Rock 'n' Roll beer. The *Tivoli Theatre* (6350 Delmar; phone: 725-5222) features a repertory of foreign, classical, and modern films, as does the nearby *High Pointe Cinema* (1001 McCausland; phone: 781-0800).

EXTRA SPECIAL

An hour south of St. Louis just off Route 55 is Ste. Genevieve, one of the oldest permanent settlements west of the Mississippi (established in 1735) and a town that has maintained its old homes with admirable care. A number of the oldest are open daily, as is an excellent old inn, *St. Gemme Beauvais* (78 N. Main St.; phone: 883-5744). If you are in the area during the second weekend of August, don't miss *Ste. Genevieve's Jour de Fête*, when all the old homes are open for a festive two days.

Take a day trip to *Six Flags Over Mid-America* (I-44 and Allenton Rd. in Eureka; phone: 938-4800 or 938-5300), a 200-acre theme park with rides, unique shows, and interesting shops. It's about a 20-minute drive from downtown. Call for schedule information. Or visit the stomping grounds of Huck Finn and Tom Sawyer—Hannibal, Missouri (phone: 221-1101). Described as the "World's Most Famous Small Town," it was the home of Samuel Clemens, better known as Mark Twain. Another unusual attraction is Silver Dollar City. Tucked away in the heart of 2,000 acres overlooking Table Rock Lake, it is a community of good-time shows, old-time crafts, fun-time rides, and farm-fresh food in a variety of good restaurants.

Other nearby attractions: *Meramec Caverns* (take I-44 west to the Stanton exit; phone: 468-3166), one of the largest cave formations in the world and former hideout of Jesse James (closed January and February). Camping and canoeing on the Meramec River are available from April through October. *Cahokia Mounds State Historic Site and Museum* (7850 Collinsville Rd., Collinsville, IL; phone: 618-346-5160) displays artifacts dating from AD 700 to 1450, when Indians inhabited the area, and conducts tours, craft classes, and a variety of seasonal events. Open daily. Donations accepted.

Missouri has about 25 wineries, many of which offer tasting tours. Internationally renowned *Mount Pleasant Winery* (5634 High St., Augusta; phone: 228-4419) is open daily.

Sources and Resources

TOURIST INFORMATION

The *St. Louis Convention and Visitors Commission* (10 S. Broadway, Suite 1000, St. Louis, MO 63102; phone: 421-1023; 800-888-3861) publishes a free visitors' guide that lists special events (festivals, street fairs, house tours); it also has maps and other tourist information. It's closed weekends. Contact the Missouri state tourism hotline (phone: 800-877-1234) for maps, calendars of events, health updates, and travel advisories.

The *American Institute of Architects* (phone: 621-3484) provides architectural maps of the city, pinpointing interesting buildings. The *Landmarks Association* (phone: 421-6474) has information on neighborhoods and restoration projects .

LOCAL COVERAGE *St. Louis Post-Dispatch,* daily (Thursday's edition carries a calendar of coming events); the *St. Louis American,* the city's most informative black community newspaper, is published each Thursday; *St. Louis* magazine, monthly. The *St. Louis Business Journal* is a weekly update on the business scene, and the weekly *Riverfront Times* focuses on city happenings.

TELEVISION STATIONS KTVI Channel 2–ABC; KMOV Channel 4–CBS; KSDK Channel 5–NBC; KETC Channel 9–PBS; KPLR Channel 11–Independent; and KDNL Channel 30–UHF-Fox.

RADIO STATIONS AM: KUSA 550 (classic country); KEZK 590 (soft rock/Top 40); KMOX 1120 (news/sports); and KGLD 1380 (oldies). FM: KWMU 90.7 (national news/music); KSD 93.7 (classic rock); KATZ 100.3 (jazz); KEZK 102.5 (easy listening); and KMJM 107.7 (urban contemporary).

TELEPHONE The area code for St. Louis is 314.

SALES TAX There is a 6% sales tax on general merchandise. In addition, restaurants charge a 1.5% tax, and hotels charge a 3.75% tax, plus $2 extra per night in the city; the hotel tax is 3.5% in the rest of the county.

CLIMATE St. Louis weather is unpredictable, with temperatures ranging from -10F to 103F. From mid-June through September, the heat and humidity are high, particularly in August. Dress coolly, but be aware that most places are air conditioned. Autumn is crisp, cool, and beautiful. Winters are very cold, with snow and ice. Spring is wonderful, but be prepared for occasional rain and very strong winds from April to June.

GETTING AROUND

AIRPORT *Lambert–St. Louis International Airport* usually is a 30-minute drive from downtown (up to an hour during rush periods). The airport limo service to downtown leaves the airport every 15 minutes. The city's *Natural Bridge Airport* bus leaves for downtown from the air terminal's main entrance every 45 minutes to an hour and costs 85¢.

BUS The *Bi-State* bus system (707 N. First St.; phone: 231-2345) serves most of the metropolitan area. The fare is 85¢, with a 15¢ charge for transfers. Call for route information and maps. From mid-May through December, free *Levee Line* buses run every few minutes between *Union Station* and the riverfront. Also, for $1 you can take the *Gus Bus,* which runs Mondays through Fridays from *Union Station* to the *Galleria Mall* in West County.

CAR RENTAL St. Louis is served by all the major national companies. A reliable local service is *Enterprise Leasing* (phone: 231-4440), with a dozen locations around the city.

LIGHT RAIL The *MetroLink* aboveground rail system provides transportation throughout the St. Louis metropolitan area and suburban Illinois. The fare is $1, with a 10¢ charge for transfers. For more information, call 231-2345.

TAXI Cabs can be picked up at the major department stores and hotels, hailed in the streets, or ordered by phone. Major companies are *Laclede Cab* (phone: 652-3456); *Yellow Cab* (phone: 361-2345); *County Cab* (phone: 991-5300); *Allen Cab* (phone: 531-4545).

TOURS Neighborhood organizations offer various walking tours, such as the *Central West End House Tour* (phone: 367-2220), which takes a look at the city's mansions, and the *Lafayette Square Home Tour* (phone: 772-5724), which visits restored Victorian homes. For the less energetic, *Tram Tour* (516 Cerre St.; phone: 241-1400) offers a two-hour narrated tram tour of the downtown area. The *St. Louis Symphony Society* (712 N. Grand Blvd.; phone: 533-2500) arranges special group (20 or more) tours of any part of the city, with proceeds going to the society's treasury.

LOCAL SERVICES

AUDIOVISUAL EQUIPMENT *Bradley Business Services* (7777 Bonhomme; phone: 854-9111); *Creve Coeur Camera and Video Center* (phone: 576-9000).

BABY-SITTING A number of agencies are listed in the yellow pages; *Missouri Baptist Hospital* (phone: 569-5193) supplies nursing students with good references and their own transportation.

BUSINESS SERVICES *Bradley Business Services* (see *Audiovisual Equipment*, above).

DRY CLEANER/TAILOR *Erlich's Cleaners* (1400 Washington; phone: 241-8935), shoe repair also.

LIMOUSINE *Jed Limousine Service* (phone: 991-0767).

MECHANIC *Automobile Club of Missouri* (phone: 523-7300).

MEDICAL EMERGENCY *Barnes Hospital* (4949 Barnes Hospital Plaza; phone: 362-5000); *St. Louis University Hospital* (1221 S. Grand; phone: 771-6400).

MESSENGER SERVICES *National Courier Systems* (phone: 423-8484).

MONEY TRANSFERS *American Express MoneyGram* (phone: 800-926-9400 for information; 800-866-8800 for money transfers); *Western Union Financial Services* (phone: 800-325-6000 or 800-325-4176).

NATIONAL/INTERNATIONAL COURIER *DHL Worldwide Express* (phone: 800-227-6177); *FedEx* (phone: 367-8278).

PHARMACY *Walgreens* (6733 Clayton Rd.; phone: 721-2033), open 24 hours.

PHOTOCOPIES *Brady Drake* (1113 Olive; phone: 421-1311); *Kinko's* (8809 Ladue Rd.; phone: 725-8704); *PIP* (616 Olive St.; phone: 621-0991).

POST OFFICE Main office (1720 Market St.; phone: 436-4461); airport mail facility (9855 Air Cargo Rd.; phone: 436-4550), open 24 hours.

PROFESSIONAL PHOTOGRAPHER *DayPhoto* (phone: 231-3381); *Mind's Eye Commercial Photography* (phone: 426-6773).

SECRETARY/STENOGRAPHER *Kelly Services* (phone: 421-4111); *Professional Business Center* (phone: 436-7335).

TELECONFERENCE FACILITIES *Airport Marriott; Marriott Pavilion* (see *Checking In*, below).

TRANSLATOR *Berlitz* (phone: 721-1070); *Calvin Communication Service* (phone: 725-9466).

WESTERN UNION/TELEX Many offices are located around the city (phone: 800-325-6000 to find the location nearest you).

SPECIAL EVENTS

The *Huck Finn* and the *Tom Sawyer* riverboats compete in the *Memorial Day Riverboat Race*. On the *Goldenrod Showboat*, St. Louis ragtimers host the *National Ragtime and Jazz Festival* (phone: 621-3311) in June. The *VP Fair* (phone: 367-FAIR) on the *Arch* grounds is a four-day entertainment extravaganza, featuring a parade of 20 or more lavishly outfitted floats, fireworks, marathons, music, and air and water events, that takes place during the *Independence Day* holiday. German food and culture are celebrated during the *Strassenfest*, a weekend celebration usually held the end of July. The *Japanese Festival* (phone: 577-5100) at *Missouri Botanical Gardens* is an annual *Labor Day* weekend celebration of Japanese culture through music, dance, food, and crafts. In mid-October, the two-day *International Folkfest* (phone: 773-9090), held at *Queeny Park* in West St. Louis County, features ethnic dance, music, food, and crafts from more than 80 cultures. The *Great Forest Park Balloon Race* (phone: 726-5896), an annual St. Louis tradition since 1904, begins in *Forest Park* and ends wherever the wind carries it. Contact the visitors' bureau (phone: 421-1023) for exact dates.

MUSEUMS

In addition to those listed in *Special Places,* there are a number of other museums of interest in St. Louis.

DOG MUSEUM Canines throughout history are depicted in 19th-century English art, photography, and literature. Closed holidays. Admission charge. 1721 S. Mason Rd., in *Queeny Park* in West County (phone: 821-DOGS).

THE MAGIC HOUSE This is a place that dares children to have a good time and learn something, too. Closed Mondays. Admission charge. 516 S. Kirkwood (phone: 822-8900).

MCDONNELL DOUGLAS PROLOGUE ROOM At the world headquarters of the aerospace giant, the room displays some of McDonnell Douglas's achievements, including the first *Gemini* and *Mercury* space capsules. Closed September through May and Sundays. No admission charge. McDonnell Blvd. and Airport Rd., on the northeast side of the airport (phone: 232-5421).

MISSOURI HISTORICAL SOCIETY AND HISTORY MUSEUM Colorful displays show the history of St. Louis, of Missouri, and of the American West. Of particular interest are the exhibits depicting 100 years of St. Louis advertising and the *1904 World's Fair;* Charles Lindbergh memorabilia; and the extensive collections of firearms and period costumes. There's also a public library (225 S. Skinker Blvd., west of the museum). The museum is closed Mondays; the library is open daily. Guided tours by appointment on weekdays. No admission charge. *Forest Park,* Lindell Blvd., and DeBaliviere (phone: 746-4599).

NATIONAL MUSEUM OF TRANSPORT Vehicles, from horse-drawn buggies to '50s singer Bobby Darin's dream car, are on display. The train collection is heralded as one of the greatest in the nation. Closed holidays. Admission charge. 3015 Barrett Station Rd., in West County (phone: 965-7998).

ST. LOUIS ART MUSEUM This turn-of-the-century building is one of a few extant from the *1904 World's Fair.* Note the 47-foot statue of King Louis, the Crusader. Closed Mondays. Admission charge for special exhibits. *Forest Park* (phone: 721-0067).

ST. LOUIS SCIENCE CENTER (MCDONNELL PLANETARIUM) The *McDonnell Planetarium* and the *Museum of Science and Natural History* are part of the same entertainment and educational complex. The planetarium features a *Star Theater* and hands-on science and natural history exhibitions. A second building houses the 330-seat *OMNIMAX Theater,* galleries devoted to ecological and technological themes, and a unique structure that shows the physics of highway construction and then plunges downward for a look at a Missouri mine and a city sewer. Open daily. Admission charge for special exhibits. 5100 Clayton Ave., *Forest Park* (phone: 289-4400).

ST. LOUIS WAX MUSEUM Over 130 lifelike wax figures of movie stars, presidents, sports celebrities, and other public figures are on display. Open daily. Admission charge. Second and Morgan Sts. (phone: 241-1155).

NATIONAL VIDEO GAME AND COIN-OP MUSEUM This institution will appeal to those pinball wizards and Nintendo fans who wonder where it all started. Here is the first video game, the first pinball machine to use flippers, and other landmarks in the evolution of the video game fad. Visitors are encouraged to try their skills. Open daily. Admission charge (part of which goes for tokens to play the machines). 801 N. Second St. (phone: 621-2900).

VAUGHN CULTURAL CENTER Site of many traveling African-American art and photography shows, it is also a resource for research into local and national African-American history. Closed weekends. Admission charge for specific exhibits. 527 North Grand Blvd. (phone: 535-9227).

PARKS AND GARDENS

For information on the *Missouri Botanical Garden,* see *Special Places. Forest Park,* one of America's largest city parks, offers far too much to see in even a long day. Highlights are the zoo, whose exhibits include *"Big Cat Country,"* the famous *Monkey House,* the walk-through *Bird Cage,* and the grand *Jungle of the Apes House,* as well as a state-of-the-art educational center. Admission charge. The *Children's Zoo* also has a modest admission charge. There is a café on the premises (phone: 781-0900). The *Jewel Box,* an immense greenhouse with dozens of species of flowers from all over the world, is open daily in *Forest Park.* Admission charge (phone: 531-0800). *Laumeier International Sculpture Park* (12580 Rott Rd.; phone: 821-1209) features huge outdoor sculptures in a woodsy setting.

SPORTS AND FITNESS

St. Louisans love their professional teams, and sports events are well attended.

BASEBALL *Busch Memorial Stadium* (Broadway at Walnut St., downtown; phone: 421-3060) is the home of the *National League Cardinals.* Tickets are available at the stadium and from *Famous-Barr* and *Dillard's* department stores.

BICYCLING The largest biking event in St. Louis is the *Moonlight Ramble,* a 17-mile bike ride that starts at 2 AM on the last Sunday of every August and lasts until dawn. Call 644-4660 for information. For recreational biking, pick one of the many trails in the city's *Forest Park;* bikes can be rented at *Touring Cyclist* (1101 S. Big Bend Blvd.; phone: 781-9951). *Katy Trail State Park* (phone: 800-334-6946) stretches more than 200 miles across the state from St. Charles (just west of St. Louis on I-70) to Sedalia. The compacted limestone surface is ideal for bikers.

FITNESS CENTERS The revamped *Downtown YMCA* (1528 Locust St.; phone: 436-4100) has a pool, racquetball courts, a track, and exercise equipment. The *Marquette YMCA* (314 N. Broadway; phone: 436-7070), also downtown, offers a high-tech exercise environment but no pool. Both are open to non-members for a fee.

GOLF *Forest Park* (phone: 367-6868) has two public courses, nine and 18 holes respectively. The 18-hole course has a reputation for being tough, but the greens and tees are not in the best condition, though work is being done to improve them. There also is a nine-hole course in *Ruth Park* (8211 Groby Rd., in St. Louis County; phone: 727-4800). Modest fees are charged.

HOCKEY The *Blues* play NHL hockey at the *Arena* (5700 Oakland; phone: 644-0900).

HORSE RACING There's thoroughbred racing at *Cahokia Downs* (Rte. 460, about 20 minutes from St. Louis; phone: 618-332-8481); and harness racing at *Fairmount Park* (Rte 40 East, Collinsville, IL; phone: 618-436-1517).

JOGGING Start at Wharf Street below the *Gateway Arch* and run the 2-mile stretch along the river; jog the 6-mile perimeter of *Forest Park*, or follow Wydown Road by the *Washington University* campus for about a 2-mile run.

SOCCER The St. Louis *Ambush* play major league soccer at the *Arena* (5700 Oakland; phone: 647-1001).

TENNIS Best for the visitor are the courts at *Dwight F. Davis Tennis Center* in *Forest Park* (phone: 367-0220), open during daylight hours; obtain permits for daily play at the center.

THEATER

St. Louis's Grand Center Arts and Entertainment district is home to several theaters and art galleries. For information about events, contact the main office (634 N. Grand Ave.; phone: 533-1884). There's also the fine *Repertory Theatre of St. Louis* (136 Edgar Rd.; phone: 968-4925), offering a range of contemporary drama; the *Fabulous Fox* (527 N. Grand Blvd.; phone: 534-1111), home of traveling Broadway shows and name entertainers, and the *Westport Playhouse* (600 Westport Plaza; phone: 275-8787), one of St. Louis's newest and most attractive venues, for productions ranging from plays to well-known entertainers. The *Muny Opera* (*Forest Park*; phone: 361-1900) offers a summer stock program of musicals. At every performance, about 1,400 seats are free; line up outside the *Muny* about 6:30 PM for tickets. *St. Louis Black Repertory* (*Grandel Square Theatre*, 3601 Grandel Sq.; phone: 534-3807) is entering its 17th season.

MUSIC

Concerts and opera are performed by the *St. Louis Symphony* at *Powell Hall* (phone: 533-2500); by the *Opera Theater of St. Louis* at *Loretto-Hilton Theater* (phone: 961-0171); and at *Sheldon Concert Hall* (3648 Washington; phone: 533-9900), one of the country's most accustically perfect auditoriums. *American Theater* (416 N. Ninth; phone: 231-7000) is a cabaret setting that hosts topnotch entertainment acts and musical groups.

NIGHTCLUBS AND NIGHTLIFE

After dark, from *Laclede's Landing* to the suburbs, night crawlers can enjoy a variety of activities. Hear live jazz at *Just Jazz* in the *Majestic* hotel (1019 Pine St.; phone: 436-2355). Dance at *Evolution* (1227 Washington; phone: 621-9493) or *Mississippi Nights* (914 N. First St.; phone: 421-3853), the only "nightclub" on *Laclede's Landing,* with a large dance floor and live blues and rock bands. Popular happy-hour venues include *Café Balaban* (405 N. Euclid in the Central West End; phone: 361-8085), where St. Louis's old money rubs elbows with the nouveau riche; the *Links Club* (408 N. Euclid Ave.; phone: 367-1900), just down the street, with a DJ playing Top 40 music and with reggae on Wednesdays; and *Cardwell's* (8100 Maryland, in the suburb of Clayton; phone: 726-5055), for both business and cocktail chatter. More live music and displays of the work of local artists liven up the *Hi-Pointe Café/Bar* (1001 McCausland Ave.; phone: 781-4716). *Moose Lounge* (4571 Pope St.; phone: 385-5700) is an excellent jazz/blues club, but take note that it's in a rougher part of the city.

Gaming is establishing a foothold in the St. Louis area. Just last summer the *President Casino* on the *Admiral* riverboat (phone: 800-772-3647) debuted as the first dockside casino in Missouri. Docked just north of *Gateway Arch,* it offers skill-based games including blackjack and poker. On the Illinois side of the Mississippi, the *Casino Queen* (phone: 618-874-5000) offers several cruises a day, with slots, craps, roulette, blackjack, and other casino games, as does the *Alton Belle Riverboat Casino* (219 Piasa St., Alton; phone: 800-336-SLOT). For information on area casinos, call 800-916-0040.

Best in Town

CHECKING IN

High-quality hotels are available throughout the city. Expect to pay $80 or more per night for a double room at places in the expensive category; from $55 to $80 at those rated moderate; there are no exceptional inexpensive hotels in the city. Unless otherwise noted, hotels have air conditioning, private baths, TV sets, and telephones. All hotels are in the 314 area code unless otherwise indicated.

EXPENSIVE

Adam's Mark In the shadow of the *Gateway Arch,* this is one of the city's best. It features 17th-century Flemish tapestries, French crystal chandeliers, Russian lithographs, and an Italian marble lobby, reflecting the grand tradition of Europe's finest hotels. In addition to several restaurants, there is a business center that provides secretarial services, A/V equipment, and computers. Meeting rooms can accommodate up to 1,000. There is also a concierge, 24-hour room service, and express checkout. Fourth and Chestnut (phone: 241-7400; 800-444-ADAM; fax: 241-6618).

Airport Marriott At *Lambert Field Airport,* half an hour from downtown, this 433-room hotel features extensive sports facilities—two pools, tennis courts, putting greens, a sauna and exercise rooms—and is good both for businesspeople and for families who'd like to relax after a busy day. There is a restaurant, as well as meeting rooms that hold up to 1,500, secretarial services and A/V equipment, a concierge, around-the-clock room service, free parking and parking lot shuttle service, and express checkout. I-70 at the airport (phone: 423-9700; 800-228-9290; fax: 423-0213).

Doubletree Mayfair Suites Listed on the *National Register of Historic Places,* this 1925 structure has been restored to its original glamour. The 184 suites are elegant and comfortable; the three penthouse suites have fireplaces and Jacuzzis. Amenities include 24-hour room service, an on-site fitness center, a rooftop pool, and a fine restaurant. 806 St. Charles St. (phone: 421-2500; 800-222-TREE; fax: 421-0770).

Hyatt Regency More than just a hotel, it's an event—part of the complex that includes the beautifully restored *Union Station.* Of its 546 rooms, 68 are in *Head House,* which actually was part of the station; the rest are located under the original roof of the train shed. There are two restaurants, the elegant *Aldo's* and the less formal *Station Grille,* as well as the *Grand Hall* bar. Surrounded by more than 11 acres of fine shops and marketplaces, it is truly an experience. Business amenities include meeting rooms that hold up to 1,500, secretarial assistance, computers, photocopiers, and A/V equipment. Other pluses are 24-hour room service, a concierge, and express checkout. 1820 Market St. (phone: 231-1234; 800-233-1234; fax: 923-3970).

Majestic Distinctively European, this 74-year-old National Historic Landmark sets the standard for fine service and the most luxurious accommodations in downtown St. Louis. Each of the 91 guestrooms or mini-suites is unique in design and appointments. Jazz is played nightly in the hotel dining room. There also are meeting rooms that can accommodate up to 50, as well as a concierge and 24-hour room service. 1019 Pine St. (phone: 436-2355; 800-451-2355; fax: 436-2355, ext. 493).

Marriott Pavilion "Pavilion" refers to the *Spanish Pavilion,* jewel of the *1964 New York World's Fair,* dismantled and moved to downtown St. Louis by former Mayor Alfonso Cervantes amid great controversy. The *Pavilion* is now the two-story lobby of this 671-room property. Among the facilities are a coffee shop, two restaurants, a bar, a pool, and a sauna. A business center provides photocopiers, A/V equipment, and computers; secretarial services are also on call. Meeting rooms accommodate up to 1,000, and there's a concierge, 24-hour room service, and express checkout. 1 Broadway (phone: 421-1776; 800-228-9290; fax: 331-9029).

Ritz-Carlton Halfway between downtown and the airport, this world class establishment has 302 rooms, including 30 executive suites and one Ritz-Carlton Suite. Private concierge service is available, as is a fitness and exercise center with an indoor climate-controlled pool. *The Restaurant* and *The Grill* are both full-service dining rooms. There is a complete range of business services available, including secretarial assistance, A/V equipment, photocopiers, and computers. The 24-hour room service and express checkout are other bonuses. Located in the suburb of Clayton at Forsyth and Hanley Sts. (phone: 863-6300; 800-241-3333; fax: 863-3525).

Seven Gables Inn With 32 charming European-style guestrooms and suites in the heart of Clayton's business district, this Tudor-style, vintage 1916 inn, originally modeled after the house in Nathaniel Hawthorne's *House of the Seven Gables,* is listed in the *National Register of Historic Places.* There are two restaurants, *Chez Louis* and turn-of-the-century *Bernard's* bistro, as well as three meeting rooms, secretarial services, and a concierge desk. 26 N. Meramec (phone: 863-8400; 800-433-6590; fax: 863-8846).

MODERATE

Cheshire Inn Located one block west of *Forest Park,* this 110-room hotel has the feel of an English country inn, complete with reproductions of English antiques—beware: Beds are set very high off the floor. Amenities include a pool and a good restaurant. Secretarial services and A/V equipment are available upon request, and there are double-decker airport shuttle buses. Clayton Rd. at Skinker (phone: 647-7300; 800-325-7378; fax: 647-0442).

Drury Inn Retaining the elegance of the 1907 railroad *YMCA* building adjacent to *Union Station,* this downtown hostelry with above-average service is a favorite of vacationers as well as businesspeople. There are 180 guestrooms and mini-suites as well as an indoor pool and a Jacuzzi; guests receive breakfast. Amenities include four meeting rooms, A/V equipment, and express checkout. 201 S. 20th St., southwest of *Union Station* (phone: 231-3900; 800-325-8300; fax: 231-3900).

Regal Riverfront Directly across from the *Gateway Arch, Busch Stadium,* and the Old Courthouse, what was formerly the *Clarion* hotel has been renovated and renamed. In its new incarnation, the hotel offers 800 rooms and 54 executive suites, three restaurants, and the largest hotel ballroom in the state. There's also a health club, a gameroom, and both indoor and outdoor pools. Business amenities include 13 meeting rooms and computers. 200 S. Fourth St. (phone: 241-9500; 800-242-8333; fax: 241-6171).

EATING OUT

St. Louis has a host of good restaurants offering wide variety at reasonable prices. Expect to pay about $60 for dinner for two at places listed as expensive; $30 to $60 at those categorized as moderate; and less than $30 at inexpensive places. Drinks, wine, tax, and tip are not included. Unless otherwise noted, restaurants serve lunch and dinner. All restaurants are in the 314 area code unless otherwise indicated.

EXPENSIVE

Busch's Grove This county landmark offers a club-like atmosphere and excellent barbecue. Open daily. Reservations necessary. Major credit cards accepted. 9160 Clayton at Price Rd. (phone: 993-9070).

Nantucket Cove Housed in a fashionable Central West End apartment building, this eatery has a cozy, New England fisherman's decor. Fresh Maine lobster, swordfish, red snapper, and oysters for a dime apiece are the lively specialties. Open daily. Reservations advised. Major credit cards accepted. 40 N. Kingshighway (phone: 361-0625).

Premio This eatery offers Italian dining and seafood specialties along with a great street-level view of downtown and service with flair. Closed Sundays; dinner only on Saturdays. Reservations necessary. Major credit cards accepted. One *Gateway Mall* (phone: 231-0911).

Tony's According to the *Wall Street Journal,* owner Vince Bommarito is the Vince Lombardi of the restaurant world—a stickler for detail and a perfectionist. What began as a spaghetti house has grown into a first-rate Italian eatery. Open for dinner only; closed Sundays and Mondays. No reservations (the wait on Saturday nights can last more than three hours). Major credit cards accepted. 410 Market St. (phone: 231-7007).

MODERATE

Café Zoe The decor at this informal and trendy spot suggests Southern California, and the menu lists contemporary versions of classic American seafood and pasta dishes. Risotto, prepared a different way every day, is the specialty. Closed Sundays. Reservations advised. Major credit cards accepted. 12 N. Meramec (phone: 725-5554).

Cardwell's Here, seasonal dishes are served in an atmosphere of relaxed elegance. Specialties include meat grilled over pecan wood, and mouthwatering pasta. There is a daily happy hour with complimentary hors d'oeuvres. Open daily; brunch on Sundays. Reservations advised. Major credit cards accepted. 8100 Maryland, in the suburb of Clayton (phone: 726-5055).

Cunetto's House of Pasta Located on The Hill, where everything Italian prospers, and where the heart and soul of good food is pasta, this place serves it hot, fresh, and in a variety of styles. The menu also lists veal, steaks, and other Italian specialties. Closed Sundays; dinner only on Saturdays. No reservations (long waits at dinnertime). Major credit cards accepted. 5453 Magnolia (phone: 781-1135).

La Patisserie The quiche and house coffee cake are the most sought-after treats at this European café. There may be a wait on weekends, but it's worth it. Open daily; dinner only on weekends. Reservations accepted on weekdays. Major credit cards accepted. 6269 Delmar (phone: 725-4902).

Riddles Penultimate Café Modern American cooking with a dash of Cajun makes this a favorite among the business set and college students. The wine bar ranks high, and there are daily "chalkboard specials." Closed Mondays; dinner only on weekends. Reservations advised on weekends. Major credit cards accepted. 6307 Delmar, in University City (phone: 725-6985).

St. Louis Brewery, Inc. Taproom The production of beer and ale is the backdrop at this brew pub, where the menu offers British and German food as well as burgers. Depending on the time of day, diners can view, through a window, a variety of brews being churned out of huge stainless steel vats. In the evenings, there's likely to be poetry readings or jazz. Open daily. Reservations unnecessary. MasterCard accepted. 2100 Locust (phone: 241-2337).

INEXPENSIVE

Murphys In downtown Clayton, this cozy restaurant/bar features grilled food (burgers, hot dogs, chicken wings), salads, and soup. Closed Sundays. Reservations unnecessary. Major credit cards accepted. 20 N. Central Ave. (phone: 862-8666).

Salad Bowl Cafeteria American home cooking, served cafeteria-style, is the focus at this family-oriented eatery. Closed Saturdays. No reservations. Major credit cards accepted. 3949 Lindell Blvd. (phone: 535-4274).

Salt Lake City

At-a-Glance

SEEING THE CITY
For a panoramic view, go to the top of Capitol Hill, where you can look out over the entire city.

SPECIAL PLACES
Salt Lake City's grid pattern is simplicity itself. Everything radiates from Temple Square. For example: 18 blocks south is 18th South, five blocks west is Fifth West. Most of the city's attractions are within walking distance of the square, except for the lake and the university.

CENTRAL CITY

TEMPLE SQUARE The logical place to start a tour of the city is the heart of the worldwide Mormon church. The 10-acre grounds draw about four million visitors a year. Enclosed behind a 15-foot wall are the granite *Salt Lake Temple*, which took 40 years to build; the dome-shaped, acoustically perfect *Tabernacle*, home of the *Mormon Tabernacle Choir;* and an information center, where you can join any one of many free, daily guided tours.

FAMILY HISTORY LIBRARY It houses the world's largest genealogical collection, parish registers, and biographies; the friendly staff will be glad to help you search for your ancestors. Closed Sundays. 35 N. West Temple (phone: 240-2331).

MUSEUM OF CHURCH HISTORY AND ART This building houses art exhibits and Mormon memorabilia. Open daily. No admission charge. 45 N. West Temple (phone: 240-3310).

JOSEPH SMITH MEMORIAL BUILDING Formerly the *Hotel Utah*, now renovated at a cost of more than $42 million into a public meeting place, this busy landmark is ornately beautiful in the grand pre–World War I style. Outstanding features are free showings of *Legacy*, a film telling the pioneer story (call 240-3893 for reservations), rooftop dining overlooking Temple Square, and computer-assisted searches of genealogical records. Corner of South Temple and Main Sts.

BEEHIVE HOUSE Built by Brigham Young as his official residence in 1854, it is now a museum run by the church. Closed *Thanksgiving, Christmas,* and *New Year's Day*. The patriarch himself is buried half a block northeast in a quiet park. No admission charge. 67 E. South Temple (phone: 240-2671).

CAPITOL HILL The Corinthian-style *Capitol Building* of granite and marble, the *Pioneers Museum,* and the *Council Hall* are all within easy reach. Exhibitions of Utah products and art are on display in the *Capitol Building;* the *Council Hall,* across the street to the south, now houses the *Utah Travel Council,* where you can pick up brochures and maps (see

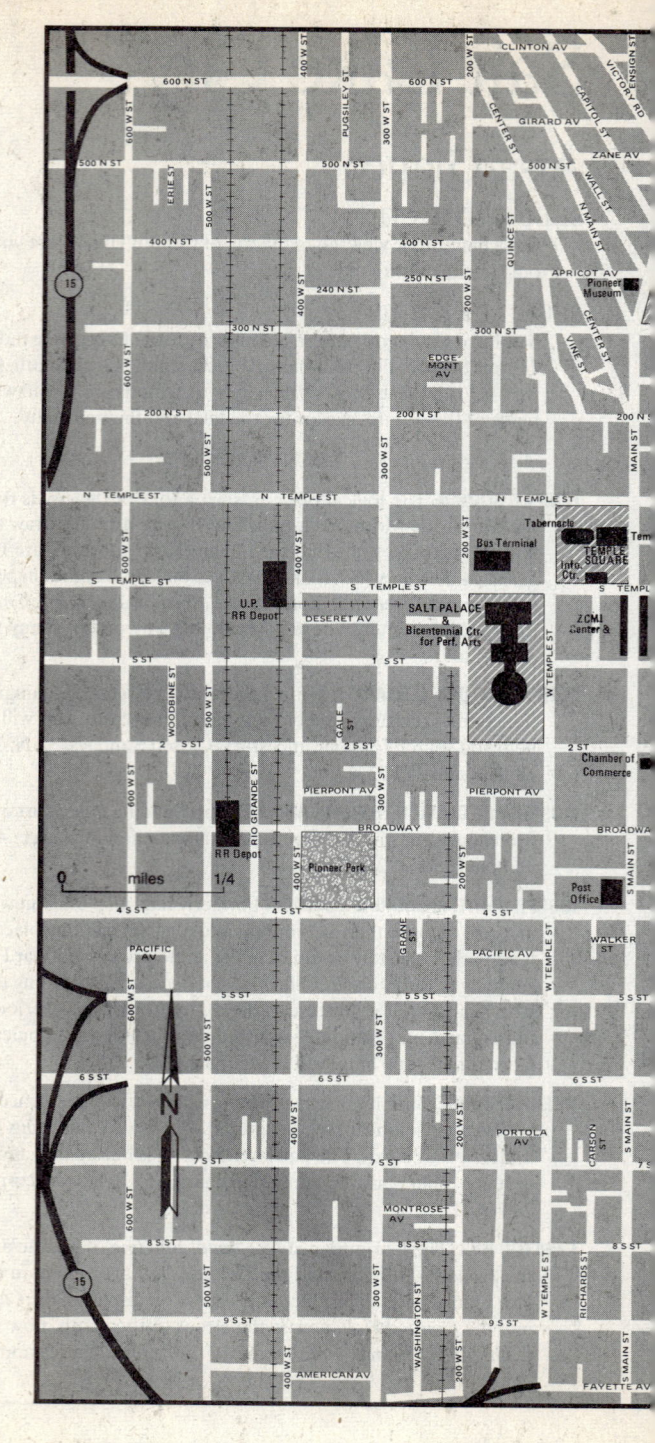

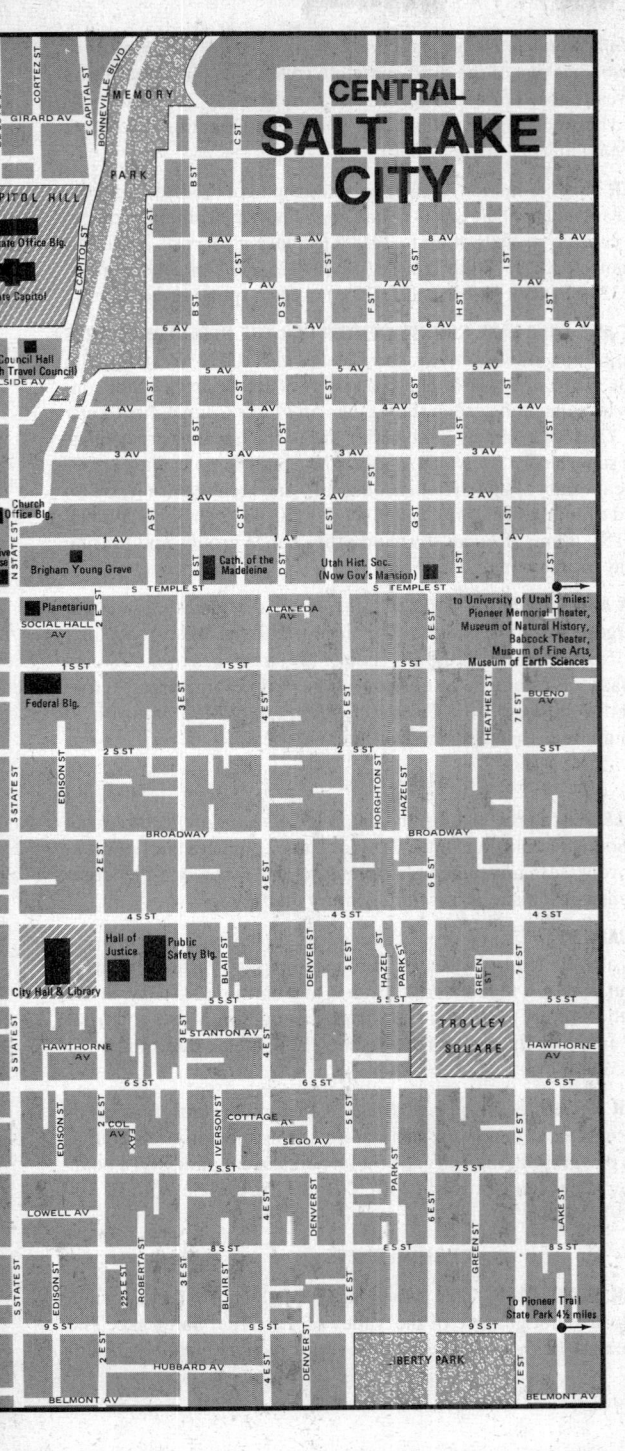

Tourist Information). *Daughters of the Utah Pioneers Museum,* west of the *Capitol,* has one of the most complete collections of pioneer relics in the West. Closed Sundays September through May, on major holidays, and between *Christmas* and *New Year's Day.* Donations accepted. 300 N. Main St. (phone: 538-1050).

DELTA CENTER This $90-million arena is the playground of the Utah *Jazz* basketball team and the Salt Lake *Golden Eagles* hockey team. In addition, it treats capacity crowds of up to 20,000 to touring concerts and other performances. 301 W. South Temple (phone: 325-2000 for general information; 325-SEAT or 800-358-SEAT for tickets to sports and concerts).

SALT PALACE AND SALT LAKE COUNTY CENTER FOR THE PERFORMING ARTS The hub of downtown activity, the *Salt Palace* (100 S. West Temple; phone: 363-7681 or 534-6370) hosts a variety of events, from major conventions to home and garden shows. The *Salt Lake County Arts Center* (phone: 328-4201), a triangular building displaying traveling art exhibits, is on the same block. *Symphony Hall* (123 W. South Temple; phone: 533-6683), beautifully designed both acoustically and architecturally, is also here, and a block away is the *Capitol Theater* (50 W. 200th South; phone: 355-ARTS), home of *Ballet West* and other dance groups and touring Broadway productions.

ZCMI CENTER AND CROSSROADS PLAZA Off tree-lined Main Street are two of the largest downtown covered shopping malls in the West. The *ZCMI Center* (15 S. Main St.), on the east side of the street, has over 60 stores and 20 fast-food stands clustered around a main dining area. Across the street to the west is the *Crossroads Plaza* (18 S. Main St.) with 70 stores, numerous theaters, and fast-food eateries.

MID-CITY

SOUTH TEMPLE Start at the beautifully restored *Cathedral of the Madeleine* (331 E. South Temple), a Roman Gothic church completed in 1909, featuring lovely German stained glass windows. Farther along the street are dozens of exquisite turn-of-the-century mansions.

TROLLEY SQUARE In 1972, in a project that garnered national acclaim, several old, abandoned trolley barns were ingeniously transformed into a collection of shops, theaters, restaurants, and boutiques. Today, in the turn-of-the-century entries and courtyards, wandering artists and troubadours entertain the mall's many visitors. Fifth S. and Seventh E. Sts. (phone: 521-9877).

LIBERTY PARK Three blocks south of *Trolley Square* on Seventh East is 80-acre *Liberty Park,* with bowers, picnic areas, tennis and horseshoe courts, a pool, a playground, the *Tracy Aviary,* an amusement park, and a boating center. Between Ninth and 13th S., and Fifth and Seventh E. Sts. (phone: 972-6714).

ELSEWHERE

PIONEER TRAIL STATE PARK "This is the place," Brigham Young said when he caught his first glimpse of the Valley of the Great Salt Lake. The park contains *Old Deseret Village,* 12 renovated pioneer buildings including the *Brigham Young Farm Home* and the *Social Hall,* as well as *This Is The Place Monument* and a visitors' center with an audiovisual exhibit showing the Mormon trek from Illinois to Utah. Grounds open daily; attractions closed Mondays. Tours of *Old Deseret Village* are given during the summer. No admission charge for children under six; group rates available for families. Sleigh and wagon rides are included. Emigration Canyon, 2601 Sunnyside Ave. (phone: 584-8391)

HOGLE ZOOLOGICAL GARDENS Across from *Pioneer Trail State Park,* this 50-acre zoo draws about 790,000 visitors a year. About half of the 1,300 animals are housed outdoors in simulated natural surroundings. Other exhibits include *Discovery Land,* with a nursery for young animals, hands-on displays, and animals from various climates. Closed *Christmas* and *New Year's.* No admission charge for children under three. 2600 Sunnyside Ave. (phone: 582-1631).

GREAT SALT LAKE A popular tourist attraction, this marshy, salty, 73-mile-long lake is the most important natural feature of the region. Although the rising waters have diluted the salt concentration over the years, floating on these briny waters is still a unique experience. Showers, food, and sailboat and paddleboat rentals are available. 17 miles west on US 40, I-80.

EXTRA SPECIAL

One of the busiest forests in the country, the 848,000-acre *Wasatch National Forest* contains the *High Uintas Primitive Area,* full of mountain lakes, rugged spruce, dramatic canyons, and mountain peaks as high as 13,400 feet; a winter elk feeding ground at *Hardware Ranch* in Logan (phone: 245-3131); and camping and picnic grounds at Little Cottonwood and Big Cottonwood Canyons (picnicking only at Mill Creek). Call the *Salt Lake Ranger District* for information (phone: 943-1794). Trout fishing is excellent, and deer, elk, and moose can be hunted in the fall; for details, call the *Utah Division of Wildlife Resources* (phone: 538-4700 for general information; 596-8660 for recorded fishing, wildlife viewing, and hunting information). In winter, skiers flock to *Alta,* 25 miles southeast of the city on Route 210; *Brighton,* 27 miles southeast on Route 152; and *Snowbird,* in Gad Valley, 2 miles from *Alta* (see *Sports*). To get to the eastern section of *Wasatch,* take US 40 and Routes 152 and 210; to reach the northern part, follow US 89 and 91. For further information, contact the Supervisor's Office, *Wasatch-Cache National Forests* (125 S. State St. Salt Lake City, UT 84138; phone: 524-5030 for campground information; 364-1581 for avalanche information).

Sources and Resources

TOURIST INFORMATION

Brochures and maps are available through the *Salt Lake County Convention and Visitors Bureau* (180 S. West Temple, Salt Lake City, UT 84101; phone: 521-2822), which is closed Sundays except during the summer. Information centers also are at *Salt Lake City International Airport* and *Great Salt Lake State Park*. Contact the *Utah Travel Council* (*Council Hall*, Capitol Hill, Salt Lake City, UT 84114; phone: 538-1030) for city and state information. For information on winter skiing and summer recreation, call 521-8102. For current road conditions, call 964-6000. Contact the Utah state tourism hotline (801-538-1030) for maps, calendars of events, and travel packets.

LOCAL COVERAGE *Salt Lake Tribune,* morning daily; *Deseret News,* evening daily; *Salt Lake City,* bimonthly magazine. The *Salt Lake Visitor's Guide,* a free magazine available from the convention and visitors bureau, is the best city reference guide.

TELEVISION STATIONS KUTV Channel 2–NBC; KTVX Channel 4–ABC; KSL Channel 5–CBS; KUED Channel 7–PBS; KBYU Channel 11–PBS; KSTU Channel 13–Fox; KJZZ Channel 14–Independent; and KOOG Channel 30–Independent.

RADIO STATIONS AM: KALL 910 (adult contemporary); KSL 1160 (CBS news/talk); KSOP 1370 (country); and KSUN 1490 (news/talk). FM: KUER 90.1 (NPR, classical); KISN 97.1 (adult contemporary); KCPX 98.7 (Top 40); and KSOP 104.3 (country).

TELEPHONE The area code for all of Utah is 801.

SALES TAX The sales tax is 6.25%; hotel room tax is 3%.

CLIMATE Wintertime is for skiing. Spring is beautiful but fickle, with apricot blossoms sometimes covered in snow. Summer is hot and dry, with temperatures in the 90s F and above. Fall is gorgeous, especially in the nearby canyons.

GETTING AROUND

AIRPORT *Salt Lake City International Airport* is a 15- to 20-minute ride from downtown. *Utah Transit Authority* buses run hourly from airport terminals into the city center for 65¢. Special *Downtowner* buses run from the airport to downtown hotels on a regular basis.

BUS For information on schedules in and around Salt Lake, call *Utah Transit Authority* (phone: 287-4636). The fare is 65¢. There is a free fare zone downtown; consult any bus map for details.

CAR RENTAL All major firms are represented. An inexpensive local alternative is *Payless Car Rental* (1974 W. North Temple; phone: 596-2596; 800-327-3631).

HORSE-DRAWN CARRIAGES Carriages will pick up customers anywhere in the downtown area. Contact *Carriage Connection,* 428 W. 200 North (phone: 363-8687).

TAXI The best way to get a cab is to call *Yellow Cab* (phone: 521-2100) or *Ute Cab* (phone: 359-7788).

TROLLEY An old-fashioned trolley circles the downtown area and major hotels, with pick-up points at Trolley Square and Temple Square. Fare is 65¢. Contact the *Utah Transit Authority* (phone: 287-4636).

LOCAL SERVICES

AUDIOVISUAL EQUIPMENT *Audio-Visual Services* (phone: 484-3344); *Inkley's Audio-Visual* (phone: 486-5985).

BUSINESS SERVICES *Aztec Typing Service* (211 E. Third South; phone: 364-6806), typing, faxing, and photocopying services; *Office Works* (phone: 350-9050); *One-Stop Business Centers* (phone: 575-5200).

COMPUTER RENTAL *Kinko's* (19 E. Second South; phone: 533-9444); also offers typing and videoconferencing services.

DRY CLEANER/TAILOR *Henrie's Cleaners* (476 E. South Temple and other downtown locations; phone: 595-1076).

LIMOUSINE *Presidential Limousine* (phone: 571-7737).

MECHANIC *Andy Stevens Automotive* (458 Montague Ave.; phone: 328-9222).

MEDICAL EMERGENCY *LDS Hospital* (Eighth Ave. and C St.; phone: 321-1180).

MESSENGER SERVICES *Pony Express Courier Services* (phone: 486-4906).

MONEY TRANSFERS *American Express MoneyGram* (phone: 800-926-9400 for information; 800-866-8800 for money transfers); *Western Union Financial Services* (phone: 800-325-6000 or 800-325-4176).

NATIONAL/INTERNATIONAL COURIER *DHL Worldwide Express* (phone: 800-225-5345).

PHARMACY *Smith's Food King Pharmacy* (402 Sixth Ave.; phone: 355-4617), open Mondays through Saturdays 9 AM to 10 PM, Sundays 10 AM to 6 PM.

PHOTOCOPIES *Alpha Graphics* (140 S. Main St.; phone: 364-8451); *Aztec Typing Service* (see *Business Services* above); *Kinko's* (see *Computer Rental,* above).

POST OFFICE Main office (230 W. Second South; phone: 530-5902).

PROFESSIONAL PHOTOGRAPHER *Dave Newman Photography* (phone: 272-8221); *Bill Shipler Photo* (phone: 582-3821).

TELECONFERENCE FACILITIES *Kinko's* (see *Computer Rental,* above); *Salt Lake Hilton* and *Salt Lake Marriott* (see *Checking In,* below).

TRANSLATOR *Bilingual Services* (phone: 288-2766); *Foreign Translators & Interpreters* (phone: 487-4861).

WESTERN UNION/TELEX Many offices are located around the city (phone: 800-325-6000 to find the location nearest you).

SPECIAL EVENTS

In January, the 10-day *Sundance Film Festival,* hosted by Robert Redford's *Sundance Institute,* regularly attracts major Hollywood stars and directors. The works of topflight independent film makers are shown in both Park City and Salt Lake City; seminars and discussion groups also are scheduled (phone: 328-3456). In April and October, thousands of Mormons from all over the world converge on Temple Square for the conferences of the LDS Church. On July 24, a huge parade and other events mark *Pioneer Day,* celebrating the arrival of the Mormon pioneers. Also in July, the *Japanese Obon Festival* is held at the Buddhist temple (211 W. First South). In September, the *Greek Festival* takes place at the Hellenic Memorial Building (279 S. 300 West). For information on other special events, call 521-2868.

MUSEUMS

In addition to those described in *Special Places,* Salt Lake City has a number of museums worthy of note.

HANSEN PLANETARIUM Exhibitions on astronomy and natural sciences, along with laser and star shows. Open daily. Admission charge. 15 S. State St. (phone: 538-2104).

MUSEUM OF CHURCH HISTORY AND ART Features exhibits on the heritage of the Mormons, including paintings, artifacts, and rare documents dating from 1820 to the present. Open daily. No admission charge. 45 N. West Temple (phone: 240-3310).

SALT LAKE ARTS CENTER Traveling exhibits of works by regional and national artists in a sculpture court and two bi-level galleries. Closed Mondays. No admission charge. 20 S. West Temple (phone: 328-4201).

UTAH MUSEUM OF FINE ARTS The only public art gallery in the state, featuring American and European art from the 17th century to the present, as well as some ancient Egyptian pieces. Open daily. No admission charge. On the *University of Utah* campus (phone: 581-7332).

UTAH MUSEUM OF NATURAL HISTORY Dinosaur bones, dioramas on the Great Basin area, and displays of minerals and rock paintings. Open daily. Admission charge. On the *University of Utah* campus (phone: 581-6927).

SPORTS AND FITNESS

BASEBALL The new Triple A Salt Lake *Buzz* play from mid-June through *Labor Day* at the new *Franklin Quest Field* (65 W. 1300 South; phone: 485-3800).

BASKETBALL The *NBA* Utah *Jazz* play at the *Delta Center* (301 W. South Temple; phone: 325-SEAT; 800-358-SEAT). Tickets usually sell out quickly, so try to reserve well in advance.

FITNESS CENTERS The *Deseret Gym* (161 N. Main; phone: 359-3911) has a pool, sauna, steamroom, track, Nautilus exercise rooms, plus basketball, racquetball, and squash courts. It is open to the public for a fee.

GOLF There are eight public courses in the Salt Lake Valley. The best is *Mountain Dell* (Parley's Canyon; phone: 582-3812).

HOCKEY The Salt Lake *Golden Eagles* (minor league) play at the *Delta Center* (301 W. South Temple; phone: 325-SEAT; 800-358-SEAT).

ICE SKATING AND SLEIGH RIDING Skate at *Bountiful Recreation Center* (150 W. Sixth North, Bountiful; phone: 298-6120) year-round, or at *Triad Center* outdoor ice rink (350 W. South Temple; phone: 575-5423) or the new *John W. Gallivan Plaza* (Second South and State Sts.) during the winter. Visit *Sugarhouse Park* (21 S. 16th East; phone: 467-1721) for sleigh riding.

JOGGING Run in *Memory Grove Park*, half a mile from downtown, or in *Liberty Park* (1-mile perimeter), about 2 miles from downtown.

SKIING Utah claims to have the "Greatest Snow on Earth," and downhill and cross-country skiers from all over the world enthusiastically attest to the excellence of the ski conditions here. The season runs from mid-November through April or May. For a ski report, call 521-8102. Other local favorites include *Brighton* (at the top of Big Cottonwood Canyon, 27 miles southeast of Salt Lake City on Rte. 152; phone: 943-8309), with an average annual snowfall of 430 inches; *Solitude,* also in Big Cottonwood Canyon (phone: 534-1400); and *Park West,* located 3 miles from *Park City* (east of Salt Lake City on I-80; phone: 649-5400).

SWIMMING Beaches are open at the Great Salt Lake (take I-80 west of town). For freshwater swimming try *Raging Waters* (1200 W. 1700 South; phone: 973-9900), a huge aquatic park with 40 water attractions, picnic areas, arcades, and gift shops. Closed September through May.

TENNIS There are 17 parks in the city with tennis courts. The most popular are the 16 courts (14 lighted) at *Liberty Park*. Lessons are available spring and summer only (phone: 596-5036). The *University of Utah* has quite a few outdoor public courts.

THE CALL OF THE WILD

At *Wasatch-Cache National Forest* (phone: 524-5030), you can fish, hunt, camp, and backpack (see *Extra Special*). For hunting and fishing regulations, contact the *Utah Division of Wildlife Resources* (1596 W. North Temple; phone: 596-8660). For information on backpacking, river running, and primitive wilderness areas in general, call the *Bureau of Land Management Office of Public Affairs* (324 S. State St.; phone: 539-4001).

THEATER

The *Pioneer Theater Company* on the *University of Utah* campus is an important regional theater. The *Babcock Theater,* in the same building, stages more intimate productions (phone: 581-6961 for both). Downtown, the *Salt Lake Acting Company* (168 W. 500 North; phone 363-7522) produces lively drama. *Salt Lake Repertory Theatre* (688 S. State St.; phone: 532-6000) performs musicals. *Ballet West, Ririe-Woodbury Dance Company, Repertory Dance Theater,* and touring Broadway shows appear at the *Capitol Theater* (phone: 355-ARTS for tickets). Check local listings for other groups.

MUSIC

Salt Lake City has many concerts. For information, call 521-2868 or 325-7328. The *Mormon Tabernacle Choir*'s rehearsals on Thursdays at 8 PM are free and open to the public, as are its Sunday morning performances, which are broadcast nationally on radio and television. If you're planning to attend the Sunday program, show up by 9:15 AM. Recitals on the great *Tabernacle* organ are given daily. *The Mormon Youth Symphony* presents free mini-concerts on Tuesdays at 8 PM; the *Mormon Youth Chorus* performs similar programs at the same time on Wednesdays. All of these events take place at Temple Square (phone: 240-4872). The *Utah Symphony Orchestra* performs at *Symphony Hall* (123 W. South Temple; phone 533-6407). Big-name rock and country artists take the stage at the *Delta Center* (301 W. South Temple; phone: 325-SEAT; 800-358-SEAT).

NIGHTCLUBS AND NIGHTLIFE

Room at the Top in the *Salt Lake Hilton* (150 W. Fifth South; phone: 532-3344) has a piano bar and fine food. The *Zephyr* (301 S. West Temple; phone: 355-2582) features blues and rock music. More comfortable but less trendy is Salt Lake City's oldest private club, *D. B. Cooper's* (19 E. 200 South; phone: 532-2948). Utah liquor laws require that you buy a two-week membership ($5) for clubs; you may bring up to five friends.

Best in Town

CHECKING IN

More than 10 million people a year visit Utah, making tourism the state's largest industry. Accommodations are plentiful and varied. Expect to pay between $60 and $110 per night for a double room at those places listed as expensive; and between $45 and $65 at those categorized as moderate; there are no exceptional inexpensive hotels in the city. Unless otherwise noted, hotels have air conditioning, private baths, TV sets, and telephones. All hotels are in the 801 area code.

EXPENSIVE

Inn at Temple Square This place has a posh, old English atmosphere. Meals are served in the *Carriage Court* restaurant (see *Eating Out*), and there is a complimentary breakfast buffet. Its 90 rooms are equipped with refrigerators, and suites come with Jacuzzis in oversize tubs. An ice-cream parlor located downstairs is a perfect spot for a snack. Room service is available until 10 PM. There are four meeting rooms, as well as A/V equipment, photocopiers, and a free airport shuttle. 71 W. South Temple (phone: 531-1000; 800-843-4668; fax: 536-7272).

Little America On the city's main thoroughfare, within walking distance of downtown shopping and the *Convention Center*, this 850-room hotel covers an entire block. Accommodations range from luxury tower suites to garden-view rooms to less expensive motel units. It has year-round swimming in an indoor-outdoor pool, plus an outdoor pool, saunas, a

Jacuzzi, and an exercise center. Children under 12 stay free. Room service is available until midnight. Other amenities include a concierge desk, 14 meeting rooms, A/V equipment, photocopiers, express checkout, and a free bus service to the airport. 500 S. Main St. (phone: 363-6781; 800-453-9450; fax: 596-5911).

Salt Lake Hilton Exuding an aura of contemporary sophistication, this 353-room property has suites with sunken baths; there is an outdoor swimming pool, a therapy pool, a sauna, a masseuse, and two dining rooms, one of which is a private club (guests automatically become members). Pets are welcome. Room service is available until 11 PM. Concierge and secretarial services are available, as well as A/V equipment, photocopiers, computers, and express checkout on the concierge floor. 150 W. Fifth South (phone: 532-3344; 800-421-7602; fax: 532-3344).

Salt Lake Marriott With 515 rooms, it has two restaurants, a lounge, an indoor-outdoor pool, saunas, and direct access to *Crossroads Plaza*. Guests have privileges at an adjoining health spa. Room service is available until midnight. Business amenities include 17 meeting rooms, concierge and secretarial services, photocopiers, computers, A/V equipment, and express checkout. The 16-story structure is opposite the *Salt Palace* on the corner of West Temple and First South (phone: 531-0800; 800-228-9290; fax: 532-4127).

MODERATE

Comfort Inn–Salt Lake Airport/International Center Conveniently located 7 miles from downtown and 2 miles from the airport, it has 152 rooms (some of which are nonsmoking). Other features: a heated pool (open in season), a hot tub, a 24-hour restaurant, and complimentary morning coffee in the lobby. Room service is available until 10 PM. There are two meeting rooms, A/V equipment, photocopiers, and an airport shuttle service. 200 N. Admiral Byrd Rd. (phone: 537-7444; 800-535-8742; fax: 532-4721).

Peery The city's oldest hotel, it is small (just 77 rooms) but elegant, with the charm of the early 1900s. Amenities include an outstanding café, two restaurants, complimentary continental breakfast, newspaper, shoeshine, a Jacuzzi, a tanning salon, and an exercise room. Room service is available until 10:30 PM. There are also four meeting rooms, concierge and secretarial services, A/V equipment, photocopiers, and free airport transportation. 110 W. Third South (phone: 521-4300; 800-331-0073; fax: 575-5014).

EATING OUT

Salt Lake Valley restaurants offer a variety of cuisines. In a major concession to the tourist trade, Utah's liquor laws were revised a few years ago. The old practice of "brown bagging," where customers brought their own alcohol to a restaurant, has been eliminated; twice as many restaurants now have liquor licenses, and drinks are served after 1 PM. Expect to pay $80 or more for dinner for two at the restaurant listed as very expensive; between $40 and $50 at those places listed as expensive; between $20 and $40 at places designated as moderate; and less than $20 at inexpensive places. Prices do not include drinks, wine, tax, or tips. Unless otherwise noted, restaurants serve lunch and dinner. All restaurants are in the 801 area code.

VERY EXPENSIVE

La Caille at Quail Run One of Utah's finest dining spots, it occupies a building that resembles a French country house; the dining room overlooks formal gardens. The French menu is as inspired as the atmosphere. Although the prices are high, the quality of the fare and the ambience make it worthwhile. Open for dinner only Mondays through Saturdays; brunch only on Sundays. Reservations advised. Major credit cards accepted. 9565 Wasatch Blvd. (phone: 942-1751).

EXPENSIVE

Carriage Court Fashionable and popular, this restaurant, built around an entrance court in the *Inn at Temple Square*, looks like an English manor. House specialties are prime ribs, shrimp scampi, and fresh seafood. Valet parking. Open daily; breakfast only on Sunday. Reservations advised. Major credit cards accepted. 71 W. South Temple (phone: 536-7200).

La Fleur de Lys This downtown place features traditional French food in an elegant, unhurried atmosphere. Open for dinner only; closed Sundays. Reservations advised. Major credit cards accepted. 39 W. Market St. (phone: 359-5753).

MODERATE

Lamb's The oldest restaurant in Utah, open since the early 1900s, this downtown institution is where the city's power brokers power lunch. There's an extensive menu with good seafood. Closed Sundays. Reservations unnecessary. Major credit cards accepted. 169 S. Main St. (phone: 364-7166).

Market Street Grill A popular gathering spot, especially at lunchtime, it's in a handsomely renovated old building. The menu features fresh seafood (flown in daily) as well as steaks, prime ribs, and lamb. There's also an oyster bar that serves liquor (but you must buy a membership for $5). Open daily. No reservations. Major credit cards accepted. 60 Post Office Pl. (phone: 322-4668; 531-6044, oyster bar).

INEXPENSIVE

Marianne's Delicatessen The menu features German specialties, from homemade sausages to scrumptious desserts. There are daily specials and a long list of sandwiches as well as a deli that is open all day. Be prepared to wait if you arrive between noon and 1 PM. Open for lunch only; closed Sundays and Mondays. No reservations. Major credit cards accepted. 149 W. Second South (phone: 364-0513).

Old Spaghetti Factory One of the more popular eating places in town, it has lots of friendly ambience. You may find yourself dining on an old brass bed or in a trolley car with turn-of-the-century furnishings. Be sure to try the clam sauce with your spaghetti. Open daily. No reservations. Major credit cards accepted. 189 Trolley Sq. (phone: 521-0424).

San Antonio

At-a-Glance

SEEING THE CITY

The 750-foot *Tower of the Americas,* San Antonio's most visible landmark, offers the best vantage point from which to view the city and the surrounding countryside. From the revolving observation deck, you see flatland stretching south and gently rolling hills northwest, leading to the Texas Hill Country. Directly below are the buildings of *HemisFair Urban Water Park,* the site of the *HemisFair* in 1968, and a tributary of the San Antonio River that cuts a horseshoe path through town and branches into *HemisFair Urban Water Park* and *Rivercenter Mall.*

SPECIAL PLACES

The heart of San Antonio is great for walking, with the lovely *Paseo del Río (River Walk)* tracing the course of the river, and short distances between many of the attractions. Visitors can also take a slow-paced, horse-drawn carriage tour of downtown and the King William District, or catch a 10¢ trolley ride between the *Alamo* and Market Square (see *Getting Around*). Jump on the trolley one block south of the *Alamo* at the corner of Commerce and Alamo Streets. Other sights, including the missions along *Mission Trail* and the zoo, are best reached by car or bus.

CENTRAL CITY

THE ALAMO Established in 1718 by Spanish priests as the *Misión San Antonio de Valero,* this is where Davy Crockett, James Bowie, William B. Travis, and 186 other Texans fought against Mexican general Santa Anna and his force of 5,000 in Texas's 1836 struggle for independence. The original mission has been restored and the site turned into a block-square state park that includes a museum with displays on the *Alamo* and Texas history as well as an excellent weapons collection featuring derringers, swords, and an original bowie knife. Open daily. No admission charge. Alamo Plaza (phone: 225-1391). After visiting the *Alamo,* it's an easy stroll along the *Paseo del Río,* which now reaches the west side of S. Alamo Street, directly across from the park; the steps from street level are bounded by a series of waterfalls that lead to the *Hyatt* hotel.

IMAX THEATER *Alamo: The Price of Freedom,* a first-rate 45-minute docudrama, is shown on a six-foot-high screen with a six-track magnetic sound system. Viewers are drawn into the action, while learning about the history of the *Alamo.* Open daily. Admission charge. *Rivercenter Mall,* 849 E. Commerce St. (phone: 225-4629).

LA VILLITA This little Spanish town in the center of the city looks very much as it did more than 250 years ago, when it was San Antonio's first residential area. Girded by a stone wall and surrounded by banana palms and bougainvillea, the stone patios and adobe dwellings have been

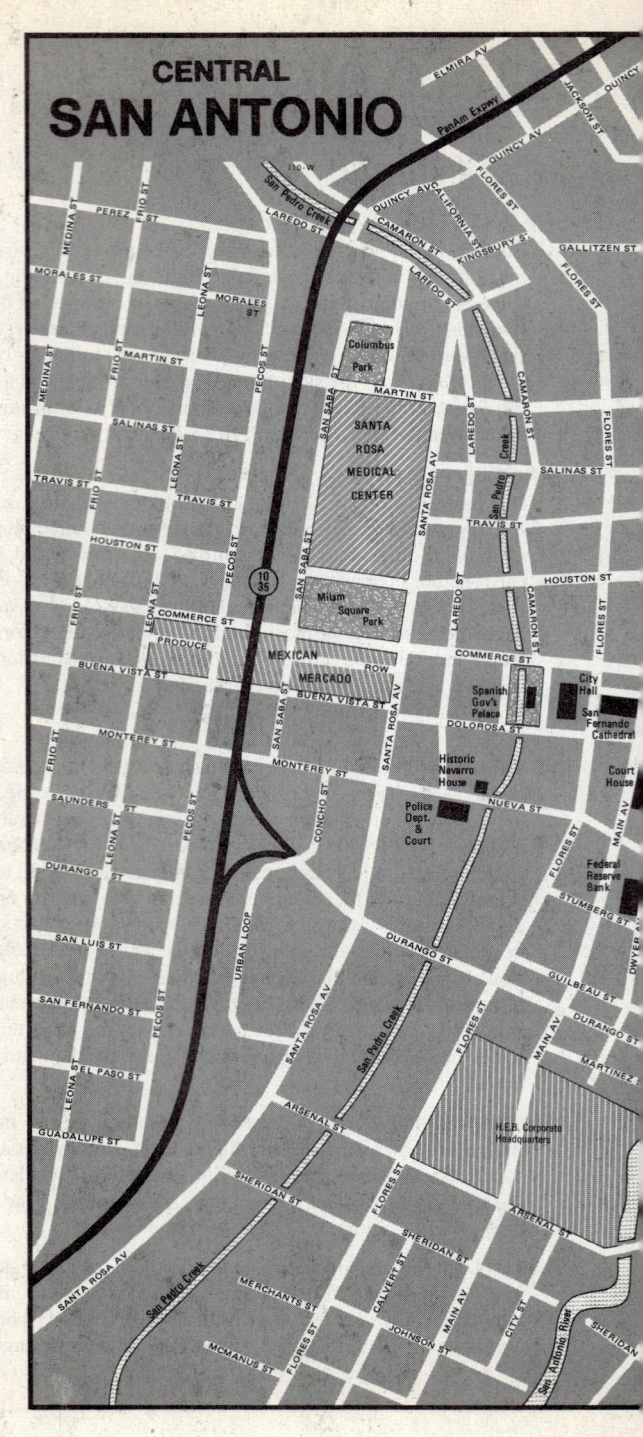

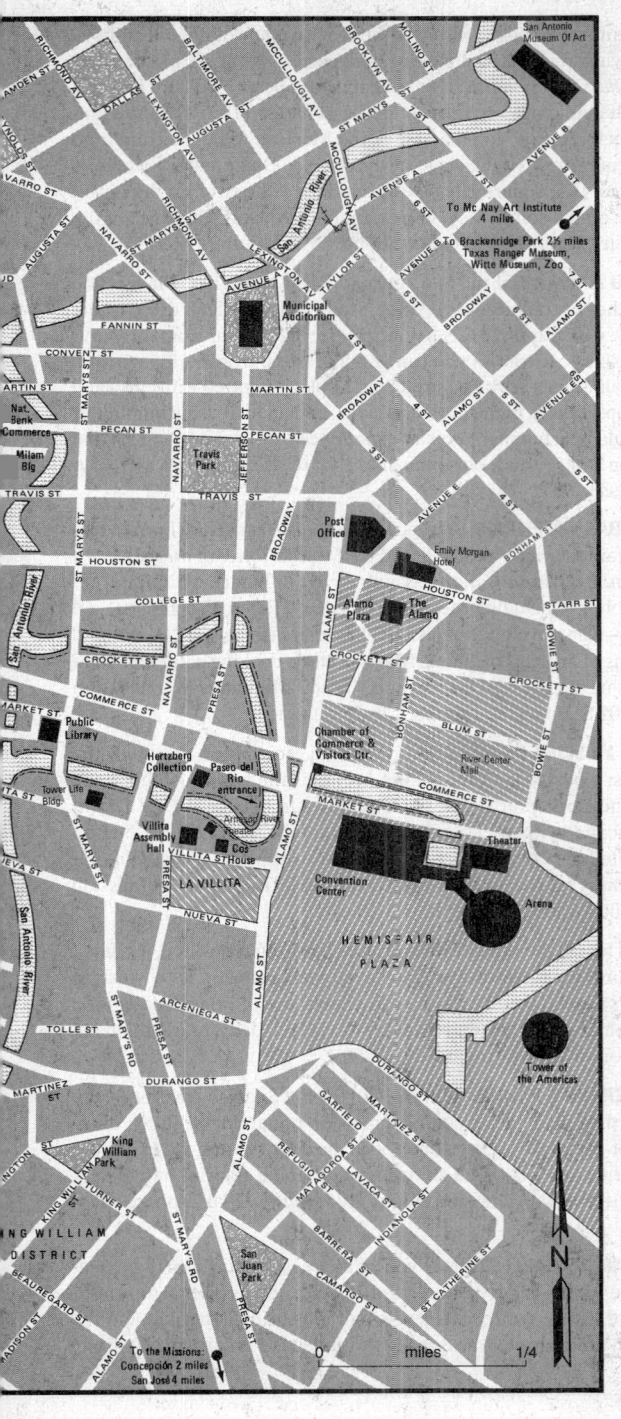

restored and now house artisans' shops where many of the old crafts—glass blowing, weaving, dollmaking, and pottery—still are practiced. *A Night in Old San Antonio* is an annual, four-day fiesta held here in April. Among the buildings are the restored *Cos House* (1835), where General Perfecto de Cos, commander of the Mexican forces, surrendered to the Texans prior to the siege of the *Alamo*. Open daily. No admission charge. One square city block bounded by the river on the north, Nueva St. on the south, S. Alamo St. on the east, and Villita St. on the west. Main office, 418 Villita St. (phone: 299-8610 or 224-INFO).

PASEO DEL RÍO A branch of the San Antonio River winds like a horseshoe through the central business district. Stone stairways lead down to the *River Walk* which, only 20 feet below street level, is as far from the world of the business district as you can get. Tall trees, tropical foliage, and banana palms line the walks, stretching 21 blocks, dotted with curio and crafts shops, hotels, nightspots, and cafés, and an increasing number of fashionable apartments. You can experience the 1½-mile-long section of river on a barge and, on some, dine aboard by candlelight (see *Getting Around*).

HEMISFAIR URBAN WATER PARK A legacy of the *1968 HemisFair*, the area features a dramatic water design at the base of the *Tower of the Americas*. The *Institute of Texan Cultures* examines the influence of 26 different ethnic groups—including Mexicans, Germans, Poles, Hungarians, and the Irish—who developed the state. There are films, slide shows, and exhibitions of artifacts including Mexican stone cooking equipment and examples of the dress of each group. Closed Mondays. No admission charge. 801 S. Bowie St. (phone: 226-7651).

SAN ANTONIO MUSEUM OF ART Rapidly gaining recognition as one of the Southwest's best museums, *SAMA* occupies the buildings that once housed the Lone Star Brewery Company. On display is *Con Cariño* (which means "with affection"), a Mexican folk art collection. Nelson A. Rockefeller's extensive private collection comprises the bulk of *Con Cariño* and is said to be the largest in the US. Open daily. Admission charge. 200 W. Jones Ave. (phone: 978-8100).

EL MERCADO Though the original marketplace has been renovated, it is lined with Spanish buildings and retains its old market flavor, with Mexican merchants who do their best to lure you into shops offering hand-crafted baskets, piñatas, pottery, and silver jewelry. Open daily. Market Square, 514 W. Commerce St. (phone: 299-8600).

SPANISH GOVERNOR'S PALACE Built in 1749 for the Spanish governors, the palace is the only Spanish colonial mansion remaining in Texas. It has three-foot-thick walls, a keystone above the door bearing the Hapsburg coat of arms, original Spanish furnishings, and a floor of native flagstone. Open daily. Admission charge. 105 Military Plaza (phone: 224-0601).

HERTZBERG CIRCUS COLLECTION If you're a circus fanatic, you'll go ring-crazy here with displays of more than 20,000 artifacts tracing the development of the circus from its English origins to P. T. Barnum and the American three-ring extravaganza. The collection is particularly strong in miniatures, including the original carriage of Tom Thumb and an entire circus in one room. Closed Sundays. Admission charge. 210 W. Market St. in *Library Annex* (phone: 299-7810).

KING WILLIAM HISTORIC DISTRICT On the southern edge of downtown, this elegant area was established in the late 1800s by successful German merchants whose graceful and sometimes colorful mansions have been meticulously restored. Among the finest is the *Steves Homestead*, a Gothic Revival masterpiece with fascinating appointments. Open daily for tours. Admission charge. 509 King William St. (phone: 225-5924).

VIETNAM VETERANS MEMORIAL This outdoor sculpture portrays a moment from a Vietnam War battle: a soldier radioing for help for a wounded comrade. Local residents often leave flowers, letters, poems, drawings, and photos in memory of loved ones who died in the war. In front of the *Municipal Auditorium*, at the corner of E. Martin and Jefferson Sts.

SOUTH SIDE

MISSIONS The *Alamo* was the first of five missions established under Spanish rule. All except the *Alamo* are still active parish churches and are located along the well-marked *Mission Trail*, starting at the southern tip of the city. *VIA Metropolitan Transit*, the city's public transportation system, runs shuttles along the trail every half hour starting at Alamo Plaza. The most notable missions are the following:

Misión Concepción Established in 1731, the oldest unrestored church in the country is nonetheless remarkably well preserved, with original frescoes painted by the padres and Indians using a mixture of vegetable and mineral dyes. Open daily. 807 Mission Rd. (phone: 229-5732).

Misión San José Established in 1720 and called the Queen of the Missions, it's the finest and largest example of early mission life. The original parish church, built of limestone and tufa, features Rosa's Window, an impressive stone carving, and is surrounded by a six-acre compound including a restored mill, former Indian quarters, and a granary. Check out the colorful mariachi mass on Sundays at noon. Open daily. 6539 San José Dr., 6 miles south on US 281 (phone: 229-4770).

BUCKHORN HALL OF HORNS AND TEXAS HISTORY WAX MUSEUM Once an old shoot-'em-up saloon, *Buckhorn Hall* was transported to tamer grounds. The collection is as wild as ever—some of the fastest guns in the West, and hunting trophies of everything from horns and antlers of elk, buffalo, and antelope to whole polar and grizzly bears. The *Texas History Wax Museum*, in an adjacent building, features 14 dioramas of Wild West history. Open daily. Admission charge. At the Lone Star Brewing Company, 600 Lone Star Blvd. (phone: 270-9467).

NORTH SIDE

BRACKENRIDGE PARK This 433-acre park includes the Southwest's largest zoo (3903 N. St. Mary's; phone: 734-7183) with about 700 species. Cliffs provide a backdrop for fine displays of animals in their natural settings. The best attractions are *Monkey Island,* an outdoor hippo pool, open bear pits, and a $3-million children's zoo. Open daily. Admission charge.

There's also the *Brackenridge Eagle*, a mini-railway that makes a 3½-mile tour, and *Skyride* cable cars, which give a panoramic view of the city (additional charge for both; phone: 736-9534). A good place to relax and meditate is the Japanese tea garden (no admission charge; 3800 N. St. Mary's; phone: 299-8480).

SAN ANTONIO BOTANICAL CENTER A living museum of diverse plant life, ranging from desert to tropical, is presented in lovely formal gardens on this 38-acre site near downtown. The centerpiece is the *Lucile Halsell Conservatory*, a 90,000-square-foot below-ground courtyard surrounded by greenhouses. Closed Mondays. Admission charge. 555 Funston (phone: 821-5115).

MCNAY ART MUSEUM Set in a lovely Spanish-Mediterranean building, this small but fine collection includes works by Picasso and Chagall. The museum also mounts shows of international scope and exhibitions of regional artists. Closed Mondays. No admission charge. 6000 N. New Braunfels (phone: 824-5368).

WEST SIDE

SEA WORLD OF TEXAS The world's largest marine entertainment showplace, on 250 acres of rolling hills 20 miles west of San Antonio, features spectacular performances of killer whales, sea lions, and dolphins, as well as professional water skiing and speed boat shows, concerts, and other events. Closed in winter and on weekdays in spring and fall; open daily *Memorial Day* through *Labor Day*. Admission charge. 10500 Sea World Dr., reached by city bus service (phone: 523-3611).

FIESTA TEXAS A 200-acre, uniquely Texan theme park, 15 miles northwest of downtown, it focuses on the state's history and culture, including the contribution of ethnic groups that have lived in the region. Musical productions, rides, food stands, and shops are set in four different areas of the park, labeled Rockville, Spassburg, Los Festivales, and Crackaxle Canyon. Among the attractions are the *Rattler*, billed as the world's fastest, highest, and steepest wooden roller coaster; the *Gully Washer*, a rapid river ride; *Power Surge*, a combination roller coaster and water slide; and *Motorama*, which allows you to drive replicas of classic 1950s cars. Closed in winter and on weekdays in spring and fall; open daily *Memorial Day* through *Labor Day*. Admission charge. 17000 I-10 at Loop 1604 (phone: 697-5050).

EXTRA SPECIAL

Two day trips from the city can introduce you to the state's European heritage. Gruene (pronounced *green*) is a 150-year-old German settlement about 45 minutes north of San Antonio on I-35. The meticulously restored area includes art galleries, shops, a winery, rafting on the Guadalupe River, and several good cafés. For more information, call the town's visitors' center (phone: 210-625-0684). Castroville, a village 20 minutes west of the city via US 90,

boasts 19th-century homes, antiques shops, walking tours, and several Alsatian restaurants. For details, contact the *Castroville Chamber of Commerce* (PO Box 572, Castroville, TX 78009; phone: 538-3142).

Sources and Resources

TOURIST INFORMATION

General tourist information, brochures, maps, and events calendars are available at the *San Antonio Convention and Visitors Bureau* (121 Alamo Plaza, San Antonio, TX 78205; phone: 270-8700; 800-447-3372; or write: PO Box 2277, San Antonio, TX 78298), which is closed weekends. More convenient is the *San Antonio Visitor Information Center* (317 Alamo Plaza, San Antonio, TX 78205; phone: 270-8700), which is directly across from the *Alamo* and open daily. Contact the Texas state tourism hotline (phone: 880-8888-TEX) for maps, calendars of events, health updates, and travel advisories.

LOCAL COVERAGE The *San Antonio Express-News,* morning and afternoon daily; the *San Antonio Current,* weekly. *Paseo del Río Association*'s *Feflexiónes* lists upcoming events and is available at the convention and visitors' bureau and in hotel lobbies. The free *San Antonio Convention & Visitor's Guide* is a good area source.

TELEVISION STATIONS KMOL Channel 4–NBC; KENS Channel 5–CBS; KLRN Channel 9–PBS; and KSAT Channel 12–ABC.

RADIO STATIONS AM: KTSA 550 (news); KKYX 680 (country); and WOAI 1200 (news/talk). FM: KCYY 100.3 (country); KQXT 102.7 (adult contemporary); and KMIX 106.7 (soft rock).

TELEPHONE The area code for San Antonio is 210.

SALES TAX The sales tax is 8%; hotel room tax is 15%.

CLIMATE San Antonio winters are sunny and mild with temperatures averaging above 50F; summers are blistering and humid, with temperatures over 90F and lots of sunshine except for an occasional tropical storm from the Gulf of Mexico.

GETTING AROUND

AIRPORT *San Antonio International Airport* is about a 20-minute drive from downtown. Public buses run between the airport and downtown during certain hours in the morning and afternoon for 75¢; call *VIA Metropolitan Transit* (phone: 227-2020) for schedules. Another option is the *Star Shuttle* (phone: 366-3183), which travels to the downtown area. Limousine service is provided by most major hotels.

BUS *VIA Metropolitan Transit System* serves all sections of the city. The basic fare is 40¢; second-zone (outside I-410) is an additional 10¢; and express buses are 75¢. Complete route and tourist information is available from the transit office, 800 W. Myrtle St. (phone: 227-2020).

CAR RENTAL All national firms are represented.

HORSE-DRAWN CARRIAGE Old World and romantic, these open carriages are most abundant at the *Alamo*. The companies running them include *H.R.H.* (phone: 225-6490); *Lone Star* (phone: 656-7527); and *Yellow Rose* (phone: 225-6490).

RIVER TAXI The *Paseo del Río* boat company operates a river taxi from hotels and various points along the river to the commercial center. They also offer a 45-minute boat tour, during which a commentator describes the historical points of interest along the way. Information: 430 E. Commerce, San Antonio, TX 78205 (phone: 222-1701).

STREETCAR Attractive reproductions of antique trolleys (on rubber wheels) follow four distinct tourist and traffic loops to and through major points of interest around the city. The fare is 10¢. Free maps are available from any visitors' center.

TAXI Cabs may be ordered by phone or picked up at taxi stations in front of major hotels. Some will answer a hail in the street, most will not. Two of the largest firms are *Checker* (phone: 222-2151) and *Yellow* (phone: 226-4242).

TOURS *Gray Line* (phone: 226-1706 or 240-2826) offers a selection of guided tours.

LOCAL SERVICES

AUDIOVISUAL EQUIPMENT *Audio Visual Concepts Inc.* (phone: 737-1262); *AVW Audio Visual* (phone: 226-1376).

BABY-SITTING *Northside Sitters Club* (8610 McCullough, No. 701E; phone: 341-9313).

BUSINESS SERVICES *ADIA Personnel Service* (7330 San Pedro, No. 150; phone: 349-4499).

DRY CLEANER/TAILOR *Famous Cleaners* (1409 E. Commerce St.; phone: 227-1636), tuxedo rental, too.

LIMOUSINE *River City Limo Inc.* (2401 Boardwalk; phone: 824-2275).

MECHANIC *Goodyear* (816 S. St. Mary's; phone: 590-1331).

MEDICAL EMERGENCY *Baptist Medical Center* (111 Dallas St.; phone: 222-8431).

MESSENGER SERVICES *Consolidated Parcel Service* (phone: 654-4547); *Couriers of San Antonio* (phone: 225-8605).

MONEY TRANSFERS *American Express MoneyGram* (phone: 800-926-9400 for information; 800-866-8800 for money transfers); *Western Union Financial Services* (phone: 800-325-6000 or 800-325-4176).

NATIONAL/INTERNATIONAL COURIER *DHL Worldwide Express* (phone: 800-225-5345); *FedEx* (phone: 800-238-5355).

PHARMACY *Eckerd* (6900 San Pedro Ave.; phone: 824-3237), 24-hour prescription service.

PHOTOCOPIES *Kwik Kopy* (111 Soledad, No. 150; phone: 224-9405); *Minuteman Press* (110 Broadway; phone: 222-0002).

POST OFFICE Main office (605 E. Houston St.; phone: 657-8300).

PROFESSIONAL PHOTOGRAPHER *Alamo Photographic* (phone: 662-7146); *Frost & Associates* (phone: 734-2887); *Professional Images* (phone: 490-3314).

SECRETARY/STENOGRAPHER *Headquarters Business Centers* (*HQ;* phone: 558-2807), word processing, telex, fax machines, conference rooms.

TELECONFERENCE FACILITIES *Hilton Palacio del Río, Hyatt Hill Country Resort, Hyatt Regency, Plaza San Antonio, San Antonio Marriott Rivercenter,* and *Sheraton Gunter* (see *Checking In,* below).

TRANSLATOR *Associated Translators and Interpreters* (phone: 691-1076); *Berlitz* (phone: 681-7050).

WESTERN UNION/TELEX Many offices are located around the city (phone: 800-325-6000 to find the location nearest you).

SPECIAL EVENTS

In early February at *Freeman Coliseum* is the city's popular *Livestock Show and Rodeo*. The most elaborate blowout in this city of fiestas is the 10-day *Fiesta San Antonio* in mid-April, celebrating Sam Houston's victory over Santa Anna with parades, the *Battle of the Flowers,* the *Fiesta Flambeau* in the streets, and the *Fiesta River Parade* with lighted floats on the river, a king and queen, and lots of food and drink. The *Starving Artists Show* in early April has works of art by hungry local artists, with nothing priced much higher than $20. San Antonio celebrates the Mexican defeat of the French in the Battle of Puebla in true Mexican form during the *Cinco de Mayo* festival, at Market Square during the first weekend in May. The *Texas Folklife Festival,* staged the first weekend in August at the *Institute of Texan Cultures,* showcases ethnic customs and foods, crafts and games, and 30 cultures that helped shape Texas. Also in August is the *Carver Jazz Festival,* held at the *Carver Cultural Center*. In early December, *Las Posadas* is a Hispanic folklore drama re-enacting the Holy Family's search for shelter in Bethlehem. It is set against a dazzling *River Walk* backdrop of 60,000 red, blue, and green *Christmas* lights; mariachis herald the arrival of the pilgrims and a choir sings the traditional *posada* songs. *Fiesta de las Luminarias* takes place on the first three weekends of December. Nearly 2,000 candles placed in sand-filled paper bags line the *River Walk,* symbolizing the lighting of the Holy Family's way to Bethlehem.

MUSEUMS

In addition to those described in *Special Places,* there are several other museums of note in San Antonio.

COWBOY MUSEUM AND GALLERY A collection of artifacts and memorabilia illustrate life in an Old West town. Open daily. Admission charge. 209 Alamo Plaza (phone: 229-1257).

ECHOES FROM THE PAST This collection of Elvis Presley memorabilia, including photos, records, and other souvenirs, belongs to a local woman who is related to the King's former drummer. Adjacent to the museum is a vintage musical instrument and machine exhibit. Open daily. Admission charge. 517 E. Houston St. (phone: 225-3714).

FORT SAM HOUSTON MUSEUM Exhibits display the history of the *US Army* in San Antonio since 1845 and the fort's role in national military activities. Closed Mondays and Tuesdays. No admission charge. *Fort Sam Houston,* Bldg. 123 (phone: 221-1886).

INSTITUTE OF TEXAN CULTURES The artifacts here represent various ethnic groups that helped establish Texas culture; exhibits describe Indian, French, Spanish, German, Jewish, and African-American influences. Closed Mondays. No admission charge. 801 S. Bowie (phone: 226-7651).

PIONEER MUSEUM The history of the Texas Rangers since their inception in 1823 is explained. Closed Mondays. Admission charge. 3805 Broadway (phone: 824-2537).

WITTE MEMORIAL MUSEUM Shown here are award-winning special exhibits about Texas history. Open daily. Admission charge. 3801 Broadway (phone: 978-8100; 829-7262 for recorded information).

ZOOLOGICAL GARDENS AND AQUARIUM Located in a rock quarry by the river, the zoo has a wonderful exhibit of koalas, as well as an African antelope collection and a variety of exotic birds. Elephant and camel rides are offered for children, and the zoo has the only whooping crane in captivity in the US. Open daily. Admission charge. 3903 N. St. Mary's St. (phone: 734-7183).

ART GALLERIES

Artists and craftspeople from all over the world have found that San Antonio is an accommodating place to live and work. The artistic community has grown rapidly, and galleries are numerous. Try the *Raul Gutierrez Gallery of Fine Arts* (8940 Wurzbach; phone: 614-3897) for Western oils, acrylics, and bronze sculptures; *Blue Star Art Space* (116 Blue Star; phone: 227-6960) for paintings and photographs; and *Rattlesnake and Star* (209 N. Presa; phone: 225-5977). At the *Southwest Craft Center* (300 Augusta; phone: 224-1848), you can watch art objects being created.

SPORTS AND FITNESS

BASEBALL The LA *Dodgers'* minor league team, the San Antonio *Missions,* plays at *V. J. Keefe Field* (*St. Mary's University;* phone: 675-7275).

BASKETBALL The *NBA Spurs* play from November through April at the *Alamodome* (near I-37 at Market; phone: 223-DOME).

FITNESS CENTER The *YMCA* (903 N. St. Mary's and Lexington; phone: 246-9600), which is open to non-members for a fee, has a pool, track, weights, and handball and racquetball courts.

GOLF There are 19 courses in the city, all open year-round. Best for visitors are *Olmos Basin Municipal Course* (7022 McCullough; phone: 826-4041) and *Pecan Valley Golf Club* (4700 Pecan Valley; phone: 333-9018).

JOGGING Run along the *River Walk* early or late in the day; up Broadway to *Brackenridge Park;* or follow the *Mission Trail,* along Mission Road (the marathon route), to the missions.

RIDING *Brackenridge Stables* (840 E. Mulberry; phone: 732-8881) are ideal for urban cowboys wishing to ride along bridle paths in *Brackenridge Park.*

SWIMMING There are 21 municipal pools open from May through *Labor Day* (phone: 821-3000). Best is *Alamo Heights Pool* (229 Greeley St., phone: 824-2595). For serious lap swimmers, two 50-meter pools are open year-round: *Northside Aquatics Center* (7001 Culebra; phone: 681-4026) and *Northeast Aquatics Center* (12002 Jones-Maltsberger; phone: 491-6136).

TENNIS *McFarlin Tennis Center* (1503 San Pedro Ave.; phone: 732-1223) is a municipal facility. Reservations advised.

THEATER

A variety of traveling and locally produced shows is offered by more than a dozen theaters, the most impressive of which is the *Majestic Performing Arts Center* (212 E. Houston St.; phone: 226-3333). This ornate structure has been restored to its 1920s grandeur and hosts everything from traveling national theater companies to rock concerts. The area's colleges and universities also produce plays. For shows: *San Antonio Little Theater* (800 W. Ashby; phone: 733-7258); *Harlequin Dinner Theater* (2652 Harney Rd.; phone: 222-9694); *Carver Cultural Center* (226 N. Hackberry; phone: 225-6516), where musical theater often focuses on African American life; *Alamo City Theater* (339 W. Josephine; phone: 734-4646); and *Arneson River Theater* (Villita St.; phone: 299-8610), where the audience is separated from the stage by the river, and an occasional passing barge upstages the actors.

MUSIC

The *San Antonio Symphony* performs at the *Majestic Performing Arts Center* (212 E. Houston St.; phone: 226-3333) with guest stars from September through May. *Fiesta Noche del Río,* a program of Mexican and Spanish music, dance, and theater, is offered by local professionals from June through August at *Arneson River Theater* (*River Walk* at La Villita; phone: 226-4651). The *Fifth Army Band* stages free gazebo concerts at *Fort Sam Houston* on the third Sunday of each month, May through August (phone: 221-6896).

NIGHTCLUBS AND NIGHTLIFE

Pop music, jazz, Dixieland, folk, rock, and country-western are all offered at San Antonio's many pubs, taverns, and nightclubs. For a little country, try *Bluebonnet Palace* (16842 I-35 North; phone: 651-6702). For jazz, try *Jim Cullum's Landing* (*Hyatt Regency;* phone: 222-1234); and for Dixieland jazz, *Dick's Last Resort* (406 Navarro on the *River Walk;* phone: 224-0026). You may want to try piano sing-alongs at *Durty Nelly's Irish Pub* (*Hilton Palacio del Río;* phone: 222-1400).

Best in Town

CHECKING IN

San Antonio's hotels offer comfortable and convenient accommodations. If you're looking for a good bed and breakfast establishment, *Bed & Breakfast Hosts of San Antonio* (166 Rockhill; phone: 824-8036) will make reservations for you at historic homes and guest cottages in the area. Expect to pay $100 or more per night for a double room at establishments listed as expensive; $65 to $100 at those in the moderate category; and $65 or less at inexpensive places. Unless otherwise noted, hotels have air conditioning, private baths, TV sets, and telephones. All hotels are in the 210 area code unless otherwise indicated.

EXPENSIVE

Bed and Breakfast on the River A small, lovely inn nestled into the historic district near the San Antonio River, it has seven guestrooms with private sun decks. Hot-air balloon rides are available from the innkeeper, a licensed balloonist. A fine continental breakfast is included, and there is a large new conference room. 129 Woodward Pl. (phone: 225-6333; fax: 225-2682).

Crockett Built in 1909, it has emerged as one of the nicest of San Antonio's "old" hotels. Some of the 202 rooms are small, but all are beautifully decorated. The most impressive accommodations are the luxurious seventh-floor suites overlooking the *Alamo*. *The Landmark* serves breakfast and dinner. Three meeting rooms hold up to 125. Secretarial services, photocopiers, A/V equipment, computers, and express checkout complete the business amenities. 320 Bonham (phone: 225-6500; 800-292-1050; fax: 225-7418).

Fairmount This cozy little landmark offers 36 elegantly appointed rooms and a staff whose pampering makes you feel as if you've landed in Europe. Once a derelict building situated in a downtown renewal area, the hotel made moving history when it was rolled—all of its 3.2 million pounds intact—to its present site across the street from La Villita and Hemis-Fair Plaza. *Polo's* is a fine restaurant and bar, and there's another dining room as well. A concierge desk, 24-hour room service, two meeting rooms that can accommodate up to 72, photocopiers, and A/V equipment are available. 401 S. Alamo (phone: 224-8800; 800-642-3363; fax: 224-2767).

Hilton Palacio del Río Right on the riverside, at the liveliest corner of *Paseo del Río,* this attractive Spanish-style place makes the best use of its prime location. The dining room serves alfresco on the *River Walk;* half of the 482 rooms have river views; and there is an elevator that lets you off at river's edge. Also featured is a rooftop pool, free coffee in the rooms, shops, and *Durty Nellie's* pub, where you can let loose. The business center offers secretarial services, photocopiers, computers, and A/V equipment. Nine meeting rooms hold up to 700; other pluses are a concierge, a car rental desk, and express checkout. 200 S. Alamo St. (phone: 222-1400; 800-HILTONS; fax: 270-0761).

Hyatt Hill Country Resort This remarkable new $100-million luxury establishment features 500 guestrooms, two pools with waterfalls, an outdoor spa, tennis courts, exercise and massage facilities, an 18-hole golf course designed by Arthur Hill, and a picnic pavilion. The structure is made of native Texas materials, and there are wide wooden verandahs and deeply gabled windows. The hotel has seven restaurants and lounges, meeting rooms for up to 2,700, and full business services. Located near *Sea World of Texas* and *Fiesta Texas,* off Texas Hwy. 151 (phone: 647-1234; 800-233-1234; fax: 681-9681).

Hyatt Regency Most of the 632 rooms in this 16-story establishment have views of the San Antonio River and Old San Antonio. For dining and drinking, there's the *Riverbend Saloon, Chaps,* and the multilevel *River Terrace* lounge in the atrium. There is also a pool, as well as 23 meeting rooms that hold up to 1,400. Services include secretarial assistance, photocopiers, computers, A/V equipment, a concierge desk, and express checkout. 123 Losoya (phone: 222-1234; 800-233-1234; fax: 277-4925).

La Mansión del Río This hotel combines a Spanish-style building with a restored 1852 building that originally was part of *St. Mary's University.* Its 337 rooms overlook either the river or an inner courtyard and pool. Two restaurants, the *Capistrano Room* and *Las Canarias,* and *El Colegio* bar provide food and drink; room service delivers around-the-clock. Among the business conveniences are a concierge desk, 22 meeting rooms for up to 500, A/V equipment, and photocopiers. 112 College St. (phone: 225-2581; 800-531-7208; fax: 226-1365).

Menger To the right of the *Alamo,* this 19th-century gem is where Teddy Roosevelt is said to have recruited his Rough Riders. The historic 320-room building has been restored and features a pool, a restaurant, meeting rooms, and full business services. An extra special amenity is the excellent spa with sauna, herbal scrubs, and full beauty treatments. 204 Alamo Plaza (phone: 223-4361 or 223-5772; 800-345-9285; fax: 228-0022).

Ogé House An elegant bed and breakfast inn along the river in the King William Historic District. The renovated 1857 mansion offers nine rooms, some with fireplaces, all furnished with period French and English antiques. Amenities include refrigerators in all the rooms, and an expansive continental breakfast. A small amount of space is available for meetings. 209 Washington St. (phone: 223-2353; 800-242-2770; fax: 226-5812).

Plaza San Antonio Locally known as "The Plaza," this is a garden property on nearly five acres, accented by tropical gardens, tall native Texas trees, and sparkling fountains. Its 252 rooms have balconies overlooking La Villita Historic District. The *Anaqua Grill* (see *Eating Out*) has a distinctive international menu, and incorporated into the complex are three restored 19th-century bungalows, which house the hotel's entertainment facilities. Features include a pool, exercise rooms, a sauna, and tennis courts. Among the business amenities are 15 meeting rooms that hold up to 595, 24-hour room service, concierge and secretarial services, plus A/V equipment, photocopiers, computers, and express checkout. 555 S. Alamo (phone: 229-1000; 800-421-1172; fax: 229-1418).

St. Anthony The richness of this thoroughly restored landmark is reflected in the lobby, decorated with Empire chandeliers, Oriental rugs, marble, and hand-painted Mexican tiles, and a rosewood and goldleaf grand piano. The *Café* offers pasta, steaks, and sandwiches; and there is 24-hour room service and a pool. In addition to 21 meeting rooms, which hold up to 350, there are secretarial services, photocopiers, A/V equipment, and computers. 300 E. Travis St. (phone: 227-4392; 800-338-1338; fax: 227-0915).

San Antonio Marriott Rivercenter Directly across the street from the *Convention Center* and nestled in a bend of the San Antonio River, it is one of the city's largest properties with 1,000 rooms. Most striking is its seven-story atrium with an indoor-outdoor heated swimming pool. *Gambits* on the *River Walk,* a two-story nightclub, opens onto the river across the street; the *Garden Café* offers casual fare, the *River Grill* is for more formal dining, and there is also a lobby bar. A business center is equipped with secretarial, computer, and media services. The 20 meeting rooms accommodate up to 5,400. Other pluses are 24-hour room service, a concierge, airline and car rental desks, and express checkout. 101 Bowie (phone: 223-1000; 800-228-9290; fax: 223-6239).

Sheraton Gunter This place originally opened in 1909 and has twice been declared a Texas landmark. A turn-of-the-century atmosphere still pervades the lobby, with its crystal chandeliers, marble floor, and dark mahogany paneling. More modern are the 326 high-ceilinged rooms. Continental and Texas specialties are served in the *Café Suisse; Pâtisserie Suisse* is a European-style bakery; and *Padre Muldoon's* is a Victorian saloon. Amenities include secretarial assistance, photocopiers, computers, and A/V equipment. There's also 24-hour room service, a concierge desk, and 16 meeting rooms that hold up to 470. 205 E. Houston St. (phone: 227-3241; 800-22-CHARM; fax: 227-9305).

Sheraton Fiesta San Antonio In the midst of the business district and near the airport, this hotel has 284 rooms and seven suites. The Spanish colonial architecture and Mexican-style furnishings lend charm and grace. There is a beautifully landscaped courtyard, a restaurant, a lobby lounge with live piano music nightly, a pool, and an exercise room. Business amenities include a concierge, complimentary shuttle service to and from the airport, secretarial services, fax machines, and eight meeting rooms that can accommodate up to 1,000. 37 NE Loop 410 (phone: 366-2424; 800-535-1980 from Texas; 800-325-3535 from elsewhere in the US; fax: 341-0410).

MODERATE

Emily Morgan This establishment's 177 rooms, which include 11 plush suites with Jacuzzis, overlook the *Alamo. The Yellow Rose* is a modern coffee shop–style restaurant that serves good food. In addition, there are health club facilities and a pool. Among the amenities are four meeting rooms accommodating up to 100. Business services include secretarial assistance, computers, photocopiers, and A/V equipment. 705 E. Houston St. (phone: 225-8486; 800-824-6674; fax: 225-7227).

INEXPENSIVE

Bullis House Inn/San Antonio International Hostel Historic surroundings, lovely appointments (oak wainscoting, paneling, and staircases), and a friendly atmosphere make this seven-room inn popular with travelers who want to stay somewhere comfortable without busting their budgets. There's a restaurant and a pool, and functions for up to 150 can be held in the two parlors and two dining rooms, which are connected. Limited business services can be arranged. 621 Pierce St. (phone: 223-9426).

EATING OUT

Some 26 ethnic groups pioneered Texas, and its current military population has brought back a taste for exotic dishes from remote areas of the globe. As a result, San Antonio enjoys a variety of restaurants. The best, however, are Mexican. Non-Texans (outlanders, as they're called down here) generally are pleasantly surprised by the prices. Expect to pay from $50 to $100 for dinner for two at places in the expensive category, $25 to $50 at those listed as moderate, and $25 or less at inexpensive places. Prices do not include drinks, wine, tax, or tips. Unless noted otherwise, restaurants serve lunch and dinner. All restaurants are in the 210 area code unless otherwise indicated.

EXPENSIVE

Anaqua Grill This is the best hotel restaurant in town. Etched glass partitions give the place an elegant ambience, and the culinary influences are Mediterranean, Asian, and Southwestern. *Tapas* are standouts, as are cold shrimp with herbed white beans and honey-drizzled duck on noodles. Diners also may order margaritas made with either fresh lime or kiwi. Open daily. Reservations advised. Major credit cards accepted. *Plaza San Antonio Hotel,* 555 S. Alamo St. (phone: 229-1000).

Biga This fashionable bistro in a restored 100-year-old mansion combines Mediterranean, Southwestern, and California dishes. Warm quail salad, osso buco, and chili-coated salmon on curried rice are among the entreés. The on-site bakery produces heavenly breads. Closed Sundays. Reservations advised. Major credit cards accepted. 206 E. Locust (phone: 225-0722).

Boudro's This popular *River Walk* place magically blends flavors from New Orleans and New Mexico. A smoked shrimp and peppered-bacon club sandwich, black and white bean soup, and crab and shrimp tamales are among the offerings. Open daily. Reservations necessary for riverside tables only. Major credit cards accepted. 421 E. Commerce St. on the River Walk (phone: 224-8484).

Chez Ardid French nouvelle cuisine is highlighted by such delightful choices as shrimp with sun-dried tomatoes and goat cheese; boneless duck breast with raspberry sauce; and turbot with white wine and caviar or champagne cream. The atmosphere reflects the opulence of the mansion that this restaurant used to be. Jacket and tie required. Closed Sundays. Reservations necessary. Major credit cards accepted. 1919 San Pedro (phone: 732-3203).

L'Etoile This lively bistro turns out the kind of solid cooking that has given French continental food a good name—curried shrimp on a bed of couscous, and sweetbreads with mushrooms and olives, for example. Inside, it's light wood and soft colors under a cathedral ceiling. There's also dining outdoors. Open daily. Reservations advised for dinner. Major credit cards accepted. 6106 Broadway, Alamo Heights (phone: 826-4551).

Fairmount The fine dining room of the *Fairmount* hotel presents a largely Southwestern menu. Service is regal, and the wonderful linguine with wild boar sausage and duck breast, and grilled rack of lamb with herbberry sauce make this an excellent dining choice. Open daily. Reservations advised. Major credit cards accepted. 401 S. Alamo (phone: 225-4242).

Grey Moss Inn To get to this historic inn in Texas hill country, you have to drive through some of the loveliest scenery around. Located in a wildlife sanctuary called *Grey Forest*, it offers outdoor dining on a shaded patio. Specialties include mesquite-grilled steaks and fish served with herbed tomato salad or shrimp cocktail. Open daily for dinner only. Reservations—and directions—necessary. Major credit cards accepted. 19010 Scenic Loop Rd., about 15 miles northwest of town (phone: 695-8301).

Little Rhein This is the city's priciest (but most romantic) steakhouse. Texas caviar, a black-eyed pea dish, is complimentary, while pepper steaks and lamb chops are top menu offerings. Its terraced riverside setting in an 1847 limestone house is a big draw. Open daily for dinner only. Reservations advised. Major credit cards accepted. 231 S. Alamo St. (phone: 225-2111).

La Louisiane When it opened in 1935, this French and creole place offered full dinners for 75¢ to $1.25 (and was immediately criticized for its high prices). Today, a couple willing to pay about 100 times that much can feast on snapper in artichokes, chicken with asparagus and wild rice, and steak Diane. The wonderful new *Courtyard* offers casual dining, too. Open daily. Reservations advised. Major credit cards accepted. 2632 Broadway (phone: 225-7987).

Stetson There's a distinctive air here, and the outdoor seating with a river view is hard to beat. What's more, the menu has been overhauled and delivers sensational fare, including chorizo-stuffed ravioli; tequila-sizzled shrimp; and medallions of tender buffalo. Open for dinner only; closed Sundays. Reservations advised. Major credit cards accepted. In the *Hilton Palacio del Río*, 200 S. Alamo St. (phone 222-1400).

MODERATE

Billy Blue's This is *the* trendy local barbecue place. The menu features pork and other meat smoked over pecan wood, fried jalapeños, and smoked chicken salad. Live blues music keeps the joint jumping in the evenings. Open daily. Reservations unnecessary. Major credit cards accepted. 330 Grayson St. (phone: 225-7409).

Cappy's The kind of place where folks head after work on Fridays to let down their hair. It's upscale but comfy, with exposed brick walls and lots of natural wood; the menu includes shrimp and scallops, shellfish, and Italian sausage with pasta. Open daily. No reservations. Major credit cards accepted. 5011 Broadway, Alamo Heights (phone: 828-9669).

County Line A cheery 1940s roadhouse, it serves some of Texas's best barbecued ribs, beef, pork loin, and chicken, smoked throughout the day. Just as sinful are the beans, potato salad, giant loaves of homemade bread, and fruit cobblers à la mode. Open daily. No reservations. Major credit cards accepted. 607 W. Apton Oaks, near Loop 1604 and US 281 (phone: 496-0011).

Crumpets A soothing atmosphere is enhanced by classical music, a quietly elegant decor, and superlative desserts turned out by the restaurant's pastry shop next door. Try the buttercream cake or fresh fruit tart. Preceding dessert is some very good continental fare, including beef Wellington. Open daily. No reservations. Major credit cards accepted. 5800 Broadway, Alamo Heights (phone: 821-5454).

Diva Seafood Bar and Grill Here's a boisterous nightspot with inspired cooking. Most enjoyable are the generous, flavorful smoked salmon appetizer; bouillabaisse; shrimp cloaked in coconut; and fresh, tender salmon entrées. Closed Sundays; dinner only on Saturdays. No reservations. Major credit cards accepted. 720 E. Mistletoe (phone: 735-3482).

Liberty Bar Down-home yet trendy, it is a favorite of locals as well as visitors. No wonder, given such eclectic well-presented menu items as lamb burgers, grilled snapper filet with thick cilantro sauce, and salads topped with edible flowers. Open daily. Reservations unnecessary. Major credit cards accepted. 328 E. Josephine (phone: 227-1187).

Luna Notte Very contemporary and stylish, this place offers great innovations in Italian fare. The sumptuous *bagna cauda,* or melted cheeses on bread with onions and pepper, is sublime, as are crab cakes with sun-dried tomato aioli and lemon-basil sauce. Service can be uneven, but the overall experience is good. Open daily; dinner only on weekends. Reservations advised. Major credit cards accepted. 6402 N. New Braunfels (phone: 822-4242).

INEXPENSIVE

La Fogata Outstanding and authentic Mexican recipes—such as *tacos chiveros* (tacos filled with goat cheese and guacamole) and seafood served with avocados—may sound exotic, but the prices are down to earth. In nice weather, try to sit on the cheery patio. Open daily. No reservations. Major credit cards accepted. 2427 Vance Jackson (phone: 340-1337).

Mi Tierra Café and Bakery When you tire of souvenir hunting at *El Mercado,* head for the heart of the market square for great Mexican food at low prices. The cheese enchiladas are terrific, and the *cabrito* (kid) is good, too. Open 24 hours a day. No reservations. Major credit cards accepted. 218 Produce Row (phone: 225-1262).

El Mirador Locals say the best, most authentic Mexican food in the city is served here. It's a favorite at lunchtime on Saturdays, when the entire citizenry seems to visit. *Caldo Xochitl* (a chicken-cum-vegetable soup served Saturdays only) is special, and *chilaquiles* (eggs, tortillas, and chilies) makes a great breakfast. Open for breakfast and lunch only; closed Sundays. No reservations or credit cards accepted. 722 S. St. Mary's (phone: 225-9444).

Schilo's Delicatessen This downtown favorite has been around since the 1920s, and locals still come for stick-to-your-ribs German fare. Don't miss the potato pancakes or the heavenly cheesecake. Closed Sundays. No reservations. Major credit cards accepted. 424 E. Commerce (phone: 223-6692).

San Diego

At-a-Glance

SEEING THE CITY
The *Cabrillo National Monument*, where Juan Rodríguez Cabrillo first saw the West Coast, still offers the best view of San Diego. It's the second-most visited national monument in the US—right after the *Statue of Liberty*. Museum and visitors' center open daily. Admission charge. Catalina Blvd. on the tip of Point Loma (phone: 557-5450).

SPECIAL PLACES
San Diego stretches from the fashionable northern suburb of Del Mar to the Mexican border, a span of more than 30 miles along the Pacific Coast. It's advisable to concentrate your sightseeing efforts in one area at a time. There's no way you can see everything in just one day. Each of the Big Four (*Balboa Park, Old Town,* the *San Diego Zoo,* and *Sea World of California*) is an all-day proposition.

SAN DIEGO

SHELTER ISLAND This manmade resort island in the middle of San Diego Bay is lined with boatyards, marinas, and picturesque neo-Polynesian restaurants. Between July and November, marlin sport fishers haul their giant catches into port here. Stop at Marlin Club Landing (2445 Shelter Island Dr.; phone: 222-2502), where the marlin and tuna are weighed in. If the sight of these monsters makes you yearn for the tug of a giant fish on the line, sign up for a marlin expedition at any of the sport fishing marinas two blocks away on Fenelon Street. You also can fish for albacore and yellowtail. To get to Shelter Island from downtown, take Harbor Drive north past the airport and turn left on Scott Street, which feeds into Shelter Island Drive.

HARBOR ISLAND This superdeluxe resort island started as a landfill project in 1961, when the *US Navy,* deepening a channel through the bay, offered surplus harbor muck to the Port of San Diego. Port officials used the three-and-a-half-million tons of waste to create Harbor Island. These humble beginnings have yielded fancy beachside promenades, traffic-free malls, restaurants, and hotels. Take Harbor Drive north from downtown, then follow the signs to Harbor Island.

MISSION BAY PARK A 4,600-acre waterfront park, it features manmade tropical islands, channels, and areas where you can water-ski, swim, and sail. There are golf courses, hotels, and restaurants here, too. The 2-mile stretch of *Mission Beach,* along the western edge of the park, is one of San Diego's oldest beach communities. The visitors' information center is open daily. Take Route 5 to the Mission Bay Drive exit. The information center is right off the exit ramp (phone: 276-8200).

SEA WORLD OF CALIFORNIA This 150-acre oceanarium is the highlight of the *Mission Bay* recreation complex. Performing dolphins, Shamu, the three-

OLD TOWN
SAN DIEGO
SAN DIEGO RIVER
0 miles 1/4
HOTEL CIRCLE PL
TAYLOR ST
HOTEL CIRCLE ST
Junipero Serra Museum
PRESIDIO PARK
Historic District
Casa De Estudillo
Old Town Plaza
Heritage Park
Mormon Memorial
ROSECRANS ST
GAINES ST
CALHOUN ST
CONGRESS ST
JUAN ST
SUNSET ST
SUNSET RD
SUNSET BLVD
JEFFERSON ST
CALIFORNIA ST
LINWOOD ST
ALMEDA DR
VALLE VISTA
To El Campo Santo 200 Yds

SAN DIEGO
AT-A-GLANCE
University of California
Scripps Institute of Oceanography
Sea Caves
Seal Rock
Torrey Pines St. Park
Whale Point
LA JOLLA
Sea World
Mission Bay Park
Old Town
Harbor Island
Shelter Island
Balboa Park
Area of the Main Map
MILITARY RESERVE
NORTH ISLAND (US Navy)
CORONADO
Cabrillo Nat. Monument
Pt Loma
0 miles 2

HAWK ST
SPRUCE ST
REDWOOD ST
CALIFORNIA ST
PACIFIC HWY
HARBOR DR
"Star of India"
Maritime Museum
EMBARCADERO

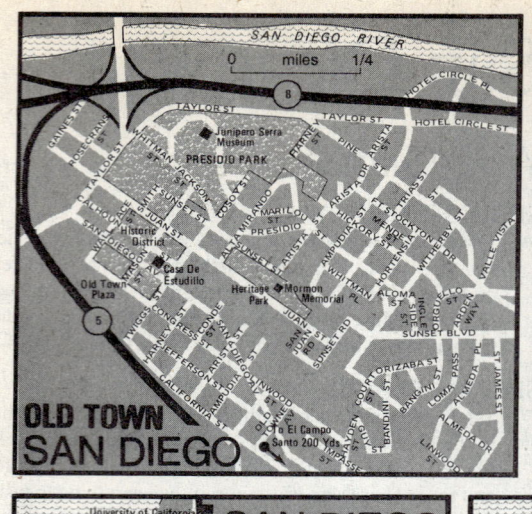

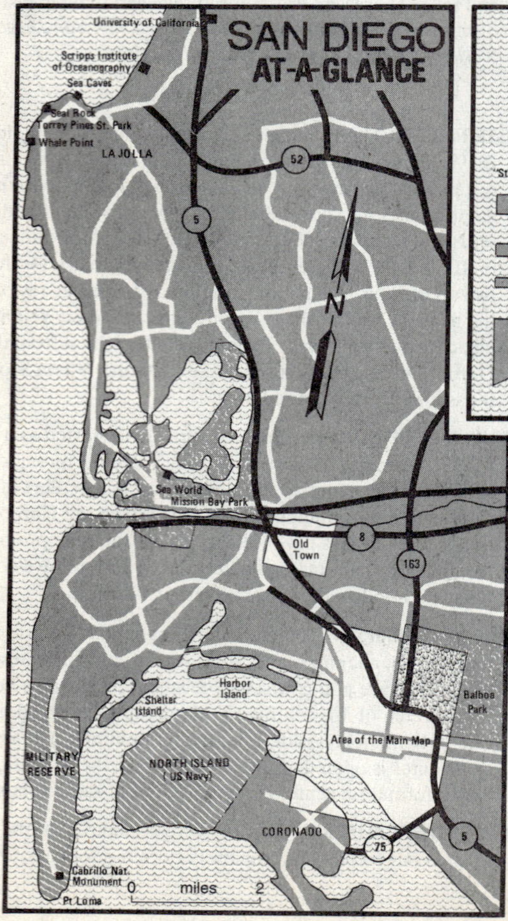

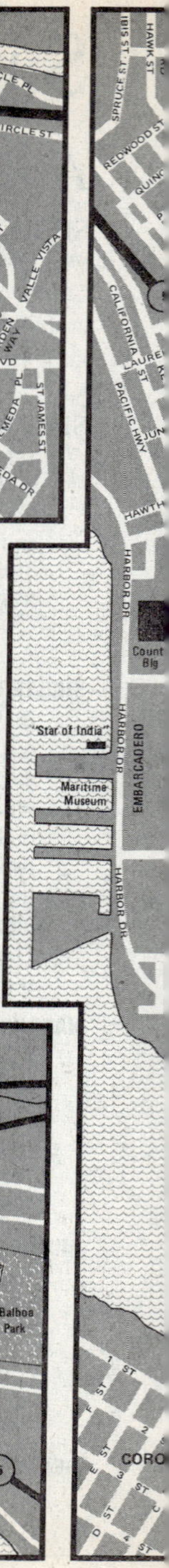

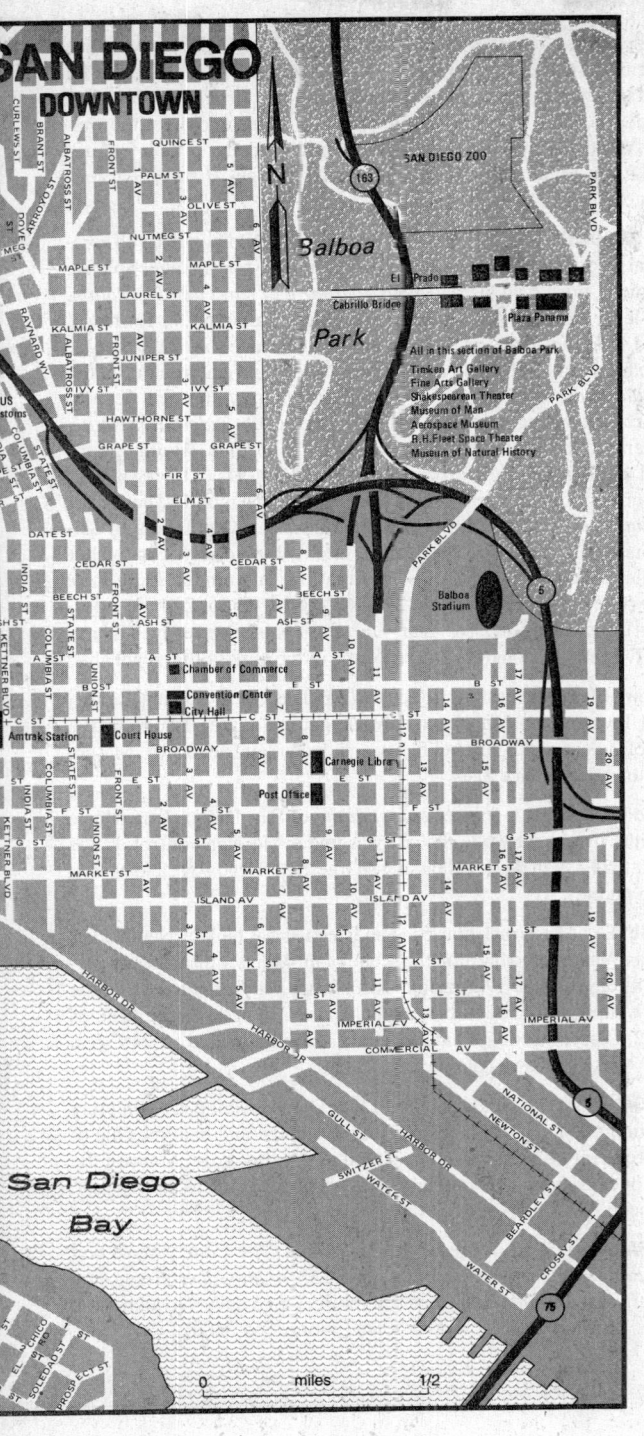

ton killer whale, and Baby Shamu entertain regularly. The shows include performing sea lions and otters. *Penguin Encounter* is a glassed-in bit of Antarctica, where penguins from Emperors to fledglings flourish in zero-degree cold. You also can feed the dolphins and meet the walruses. Yes, there are sharks, too—a multimillion-dollar exhibit features a tankful of them. Open daily. Admission charge. *Mission Bay Park* (phone: 226-3901).

OLD TOWN SAN DIEGO STATE HISTORIC PARK Historic buildings mix with commercial re-creations on the site of California's first permanent Spanish settlement, preserved by the *State Department of Parks and Recreation.* Tours leave from the park headquarters. A diorama of Old Town as it looked 100 years ago is on display. Buildings include the *Seeley Stables,* with exhibits on Californian and western history and children's displays; the *Stuart House,* an early adobe structure where volunteers demonstrate candlemaking, spinning, and weaving; the *Machado-Silvas House,* another adobe structure; and an early dentist's office. (Buildings are closed on *Thanksgiving, Christmas,* and *New Year's Day.*) Living history programs take place on the fourth Saturday of each month. The *Bazaar del Mundo,* an area of shops and restaurants is also here, plus an old-fashioned general store, tobacconist, and confectionery. For further information, contact the visitors' information center in *Robinson-Rose House* (Old Town Plaza; phone: 220-5422; 293-0117 for 24-hour information). *Old Town San Diego State Historic Park* is bounded by Wallace, Juan, Twiggs, and Congress Streets. Some of the park's other highlights:

Old Town Plaza The best way to see Old San Diego is by walking through it. Old Town Plaza (also known as Washington Square) used to be the scene of violent cockfights, bullfights, and duels. San Diego Ave., Mason, Calhoun, and Wallace Sts.

Casa de Estudillo A former *comandante* of San Diego, José María Estudillo, lived here while the city was under Mexican control. It was built in 1829. Open daily. Admission charge. San Diego Ave. and Mason St. (no phone).

WHALEY HOUSE The first brick house in San Diego, it was built by New Yorker Thomas Whaley, and became the scene of many lively high society parties in its day. Ornate 19th-century furnishings still fill the halls, and the house is supposedly haunted by a man who was hanged on the grounds in 1852. Closed Mondays and Tuesdays. Admission charge. 2482 San Diego Ave., Old Town (phone: 298-2482).

EL CAMPO SANTO At the southern end of San Diego Avenue is a cemetery containing the graves of many pioneers, soldiers, and bandits. One of the latter, Antonio Garra, was executed next to his grave. Many of the headstones are missing, but there's enough history here to merit a visit. San Diego Ave. and Noell St., Old Town.

HERITAGE PARK A pocket of preserved Victoriana. The *County Parks and Recreation Department* has its offices in the *Sherman-Gilbert House,* and there are several other mansions to explore. Open daily. No admission charge. Heritage Park Row, Old Town (phone: 565-3600).

MORMON BATTALION MEMORIAL VISITORS CENTER This military museum commemorates the longest infantry march in US history: from 1846 to 1847, when 500 Mormons in a battalion of the *US Army* left Illinois to trek more than 2,000 miles to San Diego. Only 350 made it. It also has exhibits about the Church of Jesus Christ of Latter-Day Saints Open daily. No admission charge. In *Heritage Park* at 2510 Juan St., Old Town (phone: 298-3317).

JUNÍPERO SERRA MUSEUM Built in 1929 and named after Fray Junípero Serra, it contains artifacts from San Diego's early Spanish and Mexican periods. The tower gallery is especially fascinating. The museum is on the site of the first European settlement and mission in California. Closed Mondays. Admission charge. *Presidio Park,* Old Town (phone: 297-3258).

HORTON PLAZA This colorful and confusing multilevel shopping plaza houses major department stores, movie theaters, restaurants, and 150 specialty shops. The legendary *U. S. Grant* hotel is across the street on Broadway (see *Checking In*). Stretching from Broadway to G St. between First and Fourth Aves.

BALBOA PARK A definite must, this is the cultural heart of the city. Within its 1,040 acres of lawns, groves, lakes, and paths are the world-famous *San Diego Zoo,* a complex of fine museums in an area of the park known as El Prado (each is listed separately below), restaurants, and a theater. Open daily. No admission charge to the park. The *Balboa Park Visitors' Center,* located in the *House of Hospitality,* provides a free map to the many museums, shops, restaurants, theaters, and sports facilities in the park. Many *Balboa Park* museums close at 4:30 PM, and some have no admission charge on Tuesdays. Be sure to call ahead. Park Blvd. (phone: 239-0512).

San Diego Zoo One of the world's finest zoos for more than 75 years, it covers over 125 acres, with 3,900 animals ranging from Australian koalas to the only New Zealand kiwis in captivity in the country to Indonesian Komodo dragons. Another exhibit, *Gorilla Tropics,* features the burly beasts in a tropical rain forest. Few of the animals are caged. The *Skyfari Aerial Tramway* offers a bird's-eye view of everything. Guided bus tours leave frequently from the gate. Open daily. Admission charge (except on *Founder's Day,* the first Monday in October). *Balboa Park* (phone: 234-3153 or 231-1515).

Timken Art Gallery Controversial when it was built in 1965 because some people felt its modern bent clashed with its Spanish Baroque architecture, this gallery has French, Spanish, Flemish, and Italian Renaissance art and a world-famous collection of Russian icons. Works by Rembrandt, Brueghel the Elder, and Cézanne adorn the walls. Closed in September and on all major holidays. No admission charge. 1500 El Prado, *Balboa Park* (phone: 239-5548).

San Diego Museum of Art Donated by the Appleton Bridges family in 1926, the gallery was built to resemble the university at Salamanca, Spain; two other wings were added later. Diego Rivera, Rubens, Dalí, and Rembrandt are represented. There's also the *Sculpture Garden Café* for casual dining. Closed Mondays. Admission charge. Plaza de Panama, *Balboa Park* (phone: 232-7931).

San Diego Museum of Man Concerned primarily with anthropology and archaeology, this museum is the only remaining permanent structure from San Diego's 1915 *Panama-California Exposition.* Its Spanish colonial tower is remarkable in itself. Exhibitions focus on the Southwest Indians, pre-Columbian Maya, and Early Man. There's also an ethnic arts shop. Open daily. Admission charge except the third Tuesday of every month. El Prado, *Balboa Park* (phone: 239-2001).

Aerospace Historical Center Containing the *San Diego Aerospace Museum* and the *International Aerospace Hall of Fame,* it has a notable collection of aircraft and spacecraft. Open daily. Admission charge except the fourth Tuesday of every month. Ford Bldg., *Balboa Park* (phone: 234-8291).

Reuben H. Fleet Space Theater and Science Center Simulated space travel is the attraction here. Images projected on the 360° screen give you the impression you're moving in zero-gravity conditions. The *Science Center* also has exhibitions on astronomy and technology, and a free demonstration of lasers. Open daily, and evenings, too. Admission charge. Off Park Blvd., *Balboa Park* (phone: 238-1233).

San Diego Natural History Museum More than a century old, this museum has a collection of birds that nest in the San Diego area, and sharks, whales, and fish who make their home in the surrounding seas. A Sefton seismograph measures tremors and earth movement, and a desert discovery laboratory features live reptiles. Open daily. Admission charge. Across from the *Fleet Space Theater, Balboa Park* (phone: 232-3821).

Japanese Friendship Garden These 11½ acres contain a lake, tea garden, stone garden, meadow, and terrace. Closed Mondays, Wednesdays, and Thursdays. Admission charge. *Balboa Park*, near the *Spreckels Organ Pavilion* (phone: 232-2721).

SEAPORT VILLAGE Built around three main plazas edging San Diego Bay, this 14-acre waterfront complex of restaurants and specialty shops resembles a New England fishing village. A main attraction is the wonderful *Flying Horses Carousel* with its hand-carved wooden animals, constructed at the turn of the century for the amusement park at Coney Island, New York. It's nice to stroll through the village in the evening and have dinner overlooking the water. 849 Harbor Dr. at Pacific Hwy. (phone: 235-4013).

EMBARCADERO This is another interesting place to walk. From the pier you can see the activities on *North Island Naval Air Station* across the bay, and watch cruise ships at anchor and the hundreds of sailboats cruising.

SAN DIEGO MARITIME MUSEUM The oldest square-rigged merchantman afloat, the 125-plus-year-old *Star of India* is berthed here, along with the turn-of-the-century ferryboat *Berkeley* and steam yacht *Medea.* Open daily. Admission charge. Ash St. at Harbor Dr. (phone: 234-9153).

LA JOLLA

MORMON TEMPLE This 190-foot stone-and-glass structure looms over the highway between San Diego and La Jolla. Built to serve the area's 85,000 Mormons, it is used for marriage ceremonies and other sacred rites. Non-Mormons can admire the exterior architecture, which resembles a sparkling Baroque cathedral, but they are not allowed inside. Off Interstate 5, 12 miles north of downtown.

TIDE POOLS Visit the tide pools just beyond Alligator Head at La Jolla Cove at low tide to see a veritable profusion of hermit crabs, sea anemones, and starfish clambering over one another. Wear tennis shoes, since the jagged rocks can cut your feet. From San Diego, take Route 5 to Ardath Road exit. Follow Ardath west until it becomes Torrey Pines Road. Take Torrey Pines west, turn right on Prospect and follow it to Coast Boulevard. Follow signs to La Jolla Cove.

WHALE POINT Every year in late December, January, and February, giant whales migrate south past this point (at least, they have for eight million years or so). Follow the shore south from Alligator Head. Opposite the only large building on the beach is a small cove known as Seal Rock. From Seal Rock, you'll be able to see another cove, marked by a lifeguard stand and a wall. That's Whale Point.

MUSEUM OF CONTEMPORARY ART, SAN DIEGO Situated near the beach between Seal Rock and Whale Point, the gardens and building are well worth a look. You'll find contemporary paintings and sculpture from all over the world. Closed Mondays. Admission charge. Prospect and Silverado (phone: 454-3541).

SEA CAVES North of Seal Rock is a natural formation of seven caves hollowed out by waves. To reach it walk along the cliffs facing the ocean. Take Coast Boulevard to the tunnel leading to Coast Walk.

SCRIPPS INSTITUTION OF OCEANOGRAPHY One of the most highly esteemed marine study research centers and graduate schools in the world, it is part of the *University of California, San Diego*. Stroll through the grounds or relax on the Scripps beach. You can't walk on the pier, but you can enjoy the tide pools nearby. 8602 La Jolla Shores Dr. (phone: 534-3624).

STEPHEN BIRCH AQUARIUM-MUSEUM Overlooking the Pacific Ocean, this facility affiliated with the *Scripps Institution* displays an array of fascinating marine life in 34 tanks (including a 50,000-gallon kelp forest filled with marine specimens indigenous to the waters off La Jolla). There's also an interactive oceanographic museum and an outdoor artificial tide pool. Open daily. Admission and parking charge. 2300 Expedition Way (phone: 534-FISH).

TORREY PINES STATE RESERVE This 2,000-acre park within the city limits is an oasis of wilderness in an urban environment. The pine trees date to the period when Southern California was less arid and forests flourished. On the northern side of the park, Los Penasquitos Lagoon offers a spectacular vantage point for watching blue herons and rare egrets. Mule deer feed in the southern part of the lagoon. The visitors' center is in a 1923 adobe building. Try to arrive early in the day; the number of admissions is limited. Open daily. Admission charge. Torrey Pines Rd. (phone: 755-2063).

EXTRA SPECIAL

No tour of San Diego would be complete without a visit to Mexico. The border city of Tijuana is 17 miles south. Many San Diego visitors and residents drive there, park on the US side of the border, and walk into Tijuana. (The Tijuana taxis are notorious for overcharging. Be sure to agree upon the fare before you start.) If you plan to drive in Mexico, rent a car once you're across the border. Also, purchase insurance at one of the many insurance offices near the border. It can prevent unpleasant detention should you have an accident while in Mexico, as US auto insurance is not valid there.

San Diego's trolley system is a good alternative to driving. The trip to Tijuana takes about 40 minutes and costs $1.75 each way. The trip originates at the *Amtrak* terminal (C St. and Kettner Blvd.) and terminates at San Ysidro (200 feet from the border). *Tijuana City Tour* buses pick up passengers at the trolley stop and, for an additional charge, will tour the Mexican city's main attractions. Trolleys leave the main stations (in either direction) every 15 minutes from 5 to 1 AM daily; tickets are purchased at vending machines at all pick-up points.

Tijuana has many crafts shops selling finely wrought ironwork, pottery, and jewelry at prices that are a fraction of those in the US. You may bring back $400 worth of goods duty-free, once every 30 days. Goods must be declared at retail value at the checkpoint for re-entering the US, but certain items—such as Mexican national treasures—are prohibited. The *Tijuana Cultural Center* (Paseo de los Héroes; phone: 52-66-841111 in Tijuana) has an Omnimax theater which depicts Mexico's cultural heritage, a museum, a performing arts center, shopping, and a restaurant. Tijuana also offers year-round thoroughbred racing at the *Hipódromo Agua Caliente* track, dog racing, jai alai, and bullfighting. *Mexitlan,* a theme park, offers scale models of Mexican archaeological sites and buildings, demonstrations of folk dancing, and restaurants (phone: 52-66-384101 in Tijuana; 531-1112 in San Diego). The *Tijuana Trolley* picks up passengers on the Tijuana side and makes a round-trip journey between the two cities. The $5 ticket allows you to get on and off as often as you like. For more information, call the *Tijuana Tourism and Convention Bureau* (phone: 298-4105 in San Diego; 800-522-1516 from California, Arizona, and Nevada; 800-225-2786 from elsewhere in the US and Canada).

You need a tourist card to travel more than 12½ miles south of the border, or if you plan to stay in Mexico longer than 24 hours. It's a good idea to carry your passport, birth certificate, or voter registration card at all times, as you are in a foreign country; a driver's license alone is not enough. Also, upon re-entering the US, you may be asked for proof of citizenship. Be sure that your documentation is in order *before* crossing the border.

Sources and Resources

TOURIST INFORMATION

The *San Diego Convention and Visitors Bureau* (401 B St., Suite 1400, San Diego, CA 92101; phone: 232-3101), which is closed weekends, distributes maps and brochures. The main *International Visitor Information Center* is at First Avenue and F Street (11 Horton Plaza, San Diego, CA 92101; phone: 236-1212). It is open daily in summer, closed Sundays the rest of the year. Another information center, which is open daily, is on East Mission Drive, off Route 5 (phone: 276-8200). For maps and brochures on walking tours of the historic district, stop at the *State Park Visitor Center* (Old Town Plaza; phone: 220-5422), which is open daily. Contact the California state tourism hotline (phone: 800-TO-CALIF) for maps, calendars of events, health updates, and travel advisories.

LOCAL COVERAGE *Union-Tribune,* daily; *San Diego Reader,* weekly; *San Diego* magazine, monthly. The *San Diego Official Visitors Guide* is available through the visitors' bureau (above). Barry Berndes's *The San Diegan* (San Diego Guide; $1.95) is the most complete guide to the area; write to *The San Diegan,* PO Box 99127, San Diego, CA 92169, or call 453-1633. *K-Lynn Restaurant Guide,* by Lynn Heller and Kathy Glick (AM/PM Publishing; $6.50), has listings of the best eateries in town.

TELEVISION STATIONS KFMB Channel 8–CBS; KGTV Channel 10–ABC; KPBS Channel 12–PBS; and KNSD Channel 7–NBC.

RADIO STATIONS AM: KFMB 760 (adult contemporary); KSDO 1130 (news/talk/sports); and KSON 1240 (country). FM: KFSD 94.1 (classical); KIFM 98.1 (jazz); and KCBQ 105.3 (rock).

TELEPHONE The area code for San Diego is 619.

SALES TAX The city sales tax is 7.75%; the hotel room tax is 9%.

CLIMATE Rainstorms are few and far between, and almost invariably occur in December, January, and February. During these months, the temperature might drop into the high 40s F at night. Daytimes generally are in the 60s. The rest of the year, you can expect bright days and cool evenings with daytime highs in the 70s, lows at night in the 50s (so be sure to pack a sweater or jacket). Bathing suits and tennis shoes are de rigueur year-round.

GETTING AROUND

AIRPORT *San Diego International Airport* at *Lindbergh Field* is within sight of downtown. *San Diego Metropolitan Transit* bus No. 2 leaves from the airport every 20 minutes and runs along Broadway, downtown (phone: 233-3004). *Peerless Shuttle* (phone: 554-1700), *SuperShuttle* (phone: 278-8877), and *Rainbow Ride Shuttle Service* (phone: 695-3830) also operate airport transfer service by mini-van.

BUS The *San Diego Metropolitan Transit System* operates frequent buses connecting downtown with the suburbs. Fares range from $1.50 to $2, depending on distance (phone: 233-3004).

CAR RENTAL The best way to see everything conveniently is by car. Most major national car rental firms are represented. For lower rates, try *Ladki International* (phone: 233-9333; 800-245-2354).

HORSE AND CARRIAGE *Cinderella Carriages* (phone: 239-8080) picks up passengers at *Seaport Village* and takes them on 30-, 45-, or 60-minute drives through different areas of the city.

HOT-AIR BALLOON A unique way to see the city is by hot-air balloon. *Balloon Adventure* (phone: 800-794-7599) can set it up for you—the trip includes champagne in the air and a certificate upon landing. Another choice is *Skysurfer Balloon* (phone: 481-6800).

TAXI Call *Yellow Cab* (phone: 234-6161) or *Radio Cab* (phone: 232-6566).

TROLLEY The *San Diego Trolley* originates at the *Amtrak* terminal (C St. and Kettner Blvd.). The *South Line* runs from the restored Spanish-style depot to the Mexican border, the *East Line* to the town of El Cajón, and the *Bayside Line* to the *Convention Center* and bayside hotels and attractions. Tickets, available from machines at all 27 stops, cost $1 to $1.75, depending on distance (phone: 231-8549). The private *Old Town Trolley Tours* (phone: 298-8687) offers sightseeing loop tours of central San Diego with all-day on-and-off privileges, stops at or near many hotels, and provides additional travel on extension shuttles to Hotel Circle.

WATER TAXI/FERRY The *Harbor Hopper* (phone: 488-2720) makes regular trips between *Sea World of California,* several of the major hotels, El Camino Point, and other places of interest. The 22-foot "water limousines" can carry up to 24 passengers and are equipped with TV sets, VCRs, and stereos. There is a ferry (phone: 435-8895) between the Broadway Pier in San Diego and the Old Ferry Landing on Coronado.

LOCAL SERVICES

AUDIOVISUAL EQUIPMENT *Meeting Services* (phone: 299-6042).

BABY-SITTING *Baby Sitter Service* (phone: 281-7755); *Reliable Babysitter Agency* (phone: 296-0856).

BUSINESS SERVICES *Economic Development Corp. of San Diego* (701-B St.; phone: 234-8484).

DRY CLEANER/TAILOR *Exclusive Cleaners* (3740 Park Blvd.; phone: 295-3156), open daily from 7 AM to 6 PM.

LIMOUSINE *Olde English Livery Service* (phone: 232-6533), sedans also; *VIP Limousine Service* (phone: 299-7000).

MECHANIC *Jimmy on the Spot* (phone: 560-1140), road service only.

MEDICAL EMERGENCY *University of California at San Diego (UCSD) Medical Center* (200 W. Arbor Dr.; phone: 543-6222).

MESSENGER SERVICES *American Messenger Service* (phone: 233-0324).

MONEY TRANSFERS *American Express MoneyGram* (phone: 800-926-9400 for information; 800-866-8800 for money transfers); *Western Union Financial Services* (phone: 800-325-6000 or 800-325-4176).

NATIONAL/INTERNATIONAL COURIER *FedEx* (phone: 295-5545).

PHARMACY *Thrifty Mart* (402 Broadway; phone: 233-1666).

PHOTOCOPIES *We Copy* (5375 Kearny Villa Rd.; phone: 268-2880), open until 9:30 PM.

POST OFFICE Main office (12151 Rancho Carmel Drive; phone: 674-0000); downtown branch (815 "E" St.; phone: 232-5096); Midway branch (2535 Midway Dr.; phone: 574-0477).

PROFESSIONAL PHOTOGRAPHER *Frank Mulligan* (phone: 444-5555).

SECRETARY/STENOGRAPHER *WP Assistance* (phone: 483-4858).

TELECONFERENCE FACILITIES *San Diego Marriott, Sheraton Grande Torrey Pines, Town and Country, Westgate,* and *U. S. Grant* (see *Checking In,* below).

TRANSLATOR *Inlingua* (phone: 453-4534).

WESTERN UNION/TELEX Many offices are located around the city (phone: 800-325-6000 to find the location nearest you).

SPECIAL EVENTS

San Diego holds a summer festival almost all year. The following is only a selection of events. In January (sometimes in December), the *San Diego Marathon* (phone: 929-0909) is run from Quivira Basin loop in Mission Bay. Also in January is the *Mercedes Championships,* a *PGA* golf tournament held at *La Costa Resort and Spa* (Costa del Mar Rd., Carlsbad; phone: 438-9111). Another professional golf tournament, the *Buick Invitational of California* tees off in February at *Torrey Pines* (La Jolla; phone: 452-3226). March sees the *St. Patrick's Day Parade* (phone: 299-7812). April heralds the *San Diego Crew Classic* (West Mission Bay; phone: 488-1039) and the *La Jolla Grand Prix Bicycle Race* (phone: 579-5723). The Mexican-American community hosts the *Cinco de Mayo Fes-*

tival (phone: 296-3161) in early May. In July, the *Festival of the Bells* (phone: 281-8449) celebrates the founding of *San Diego de Alcalá*, and the *Mission San Luis Rey Fiesta* (phone: 757-3651) does the same for *Mission San Luis Rey*. September's *Cabrillo Festival* (phone: 557-5450) marks the discovery of the West Coast, and *Oktoberfest* (phone: 465-7700) is held along La Mesa Boulevard for several days in October. A number of events herald the *Christmas* holiday season: the *Mission Bay Christmas Boat Parade of Lights* (phone: 488-0501), from Quivira Basin to *Sea World of California; San Diego Harbor Parade of Lights* (phone: 222-4081); *Las Posadas* (*Mission San Luis Rey;* phone: 757-3250), a Mexican *Christmas* ceremony; Old Town's *Las Posadas* (phone: 220-5422), a *Christmas* candlelight procession honoring the Holy Family; and *Christmas on the Prado* (*Balboa Park;* phone: 239-0512).

MUSEUMS

In addition to those described in *Special Places,* other museums include the *Museum of San Diego History, Centro Cultural de la Raza, San Diego Museum of Photographic Arts, San Diego Hall of Champions,* and *San Diego Railroad Museum*—all in *Balboa Park.* Hours and days vary; many *Balboa Park* museums close at 4:30 PM, and some have special days when there is no admission charge. Be sure to call ahead (phone: 239-0512) for information. In addition, *Palomar Observatory*'s giant telescope, for many years the most powerful in the world, is still in use. Photographs of the cosmos are on display there. Open daily. Admission charge. County Rd. S6, east of Escondido (phone: 742-2119).

SHOPPING

San Diego has its share of today's marketplaces, huge malls filled with cookie-cutter department stores, chain shops, eateries, and entertainment. Enclaves of commerce with more individuality, however, also are easy to come by—and get to. Museum shops are an excellent source of quality gifts and mementos. Theme "villages" have sprouted near other city attractions, including the following:

Bazaar del Mundo Locals as well as tourists patronize this Old Town shopping center. Be sure to check out *Ariana* (phone: 296-4989) for brightly colored hand-crafted jewelry, and ethnic and hand-painted silk and cotton apparel. 2754 Calhoun St., between Taylor and Mason Sts. (phone: 296-3161).

Horton Plaza This complex is a glittering, multicolored labyrinth with passages and galleries, odd angles and curves, banners, awnings, whimsical sculptures, and plantings, in addition to nearly 150 shops and eateries, seven movie theaters, and two live theaters. *Nordstrom, Robinson's,* the *Broadway,* and *Mervyn's* are the department store anchors; and designer boutiques include *Louis Vuitton* and *Laura Ashley.* Between Broadway and G St., and First and Fourth Aves. (phone: 239-8180).

Ferry Landing Marketplace The counterpart of *Seaport Village* (though on a much smaller scale) on the Coronado side caters to the tourist trade. 1201 First St. at B (phone: 435-8895).

Paladion An upscale mall, it features such tony shops as *Tiffany's, Ferragamo, Cartier,* and *Alfred Dunhill*. There are also two fine restaurants, valet parking, and concierge service. 777 Front St. (phone: 232-1627).

Promenade at Pacific Beach and Belmont Park Located in Mission Beach, these two shopping spots are handy to beach resort hotels. The *Promenade* is at Ventura and Mission Blvds. (phone: 490-9097); *Belmont Park* is at 3146 Mission Blvd. (phone: 488-0668).

Other regions around the city provide a variety of shopping enclaves, with specialty shops as well as national chains. In La Jolla, two streets vie for the title of San Diego's Rodeo Drive. Prospect Street runs on a bluff overlooking the Pacific and is the city's most pleasant street for shopping on foot. Art galleries and restaurants predominate. A fashion parade of boutiques on Girard Avenue, which intersects Prospect, culminates with *Saks Fifth Avenue* to the east. Among the intriguing establishments:

C.J. Felcher This shop features a unique collection of antique and estate jewelry. 1237 Prospect (phone: 459-5166).

Jacques LeLong Stop here for the Southern California–Western look: studs and sequins on leather duds. 1141 Prospect St. (phone: 454-7760).

London Associates Shells The seashells and fossils sold here are polished, and often hand-crafted into jewelry. 1137 Prospect St. (phone: 459-6858).

Ports International This shop is an oasis of classic women's fashions. 7844 Girard Ave. (phone: 454-9151).

SPORTS AND FITNESS

There's something here for just about everybody.

BASEBALL The *National League Padres* play at *Jack Murphy Stadium* (9449 Friars Rd.; phone: 283-4494).

BICYCLING Bikes may be rented at *Hamel's Action Sports Center* (704 Ventura Pl., Mission Beach; phone: 488-5050); *Reid's Bike Rentals* (711 Pacific Beach Dr.; phone: 275-0765); *Rent A Bike Inc.* (1775 E. Mission Bay Dr.; phone: 232-4700); or *Rent-R-Bikes USA* (746 Emerald St.; phone: 581-3665).

FISHING The Oceanside Pier is one of America's longest wooden piers; there also are piers at Mission Bay, San Diego Harbor, and Shelter Island. You need a permit for deep-sea fishing; contact the *California Department of Fish and Game Resources* (1350 Front St., Room 2041, San Diego, CA 92101; phone: 525-4215). Marlin, yellowtail, and sailfish run in the spring. A fishing license is required for those 16 and older. Licenses can be obtained for less than $10 a day at sporting goods stores and at many lakes.

FITNESS CENTERS *Shiley Sports and Health Center of Scripps Clinic* has a comprehensive fitness center (10820 N. Torrey Pines, La Jolla; phone: 554-

FITT); the *YMCA* has a pool and weight room (5505 Friars Rd.; phone: 298-3576). Both are open to visitors for a fee.

FOOTBALL The *NFL Chargers* play home games at *Jack Murphy Stadium* (9449 Friars Rd.; phone 280-2111). The *San Diego State Aztecs* (phone: 283-7378) play at *San Diego State University*'s *Aztec Bowl.*

GOLF San Diego is the golfing capital of Southern California, with nearly six dozen public courses in the area to satisfy local and visiting golfaholics alike. One of these is well above par.

A TOP TEE-OFF SPOT

Torrey Pines Both the *North* and *South* courses at *Torrey Pines* (11480 N. Torrey Pines Rd., La Jolla; phone: 452-3226) are highly acclaimed and worth the attention of serious golfers.

Two other fine courses are the *Mission Bay,* which is lighted for nighttime play (*Mission Bay Park;* phone: 490-3370), and the *Coronado Municipal* (2000 Visalia Row; phone: 435-3121).

HOCKEY The San Diego *Gulls* of the *International Hockey League* play at the *San Diego Sports Arena* (3500 Sports Arena Blvd.; phone: 224-4171).

HORSE RACING Thoroughbreds race at *Del Mar Race Track,* July through September (I-5 to Fairgrounds exit; phone: 481-1207), or contact *Del Mar Thoroughbred Club* (phone: 792-4242). The racetrack at Del Mar is closed on Tuesdays. There's also seasonal racing at *Hipódromo Agua Caliente* racetrack (phone: 52-66-861951 in Tijuana; see *Extra Special*).

ICE SKATING Try the ice at *Ice Capades Chalet* (4545 La Jolla Village Dr.; phone: 452-9110) and *San Diego Ice Arena* (off Hwy. 15, 1001 Black Mountain Rd.; phone: 530-1825).

JAI ALAI This Basque import is played at *Fronton Palacio,* Tijuana (phone: 52-66-852524 in Tijuana), Fridays through Wednesdays.

JOGGING Run along Laurel Street to *Balboa Park,* where there are six different courses, ranging from less than ½ mile to 9 miles. It's possible to jog along Harbor Drive in the direction of the airport, but avoid rush hours because of the fumes. Mileage is marked around Mission Bay. In La Jolla, run along the shore and boardwalk or the La Jolla Cove.

SAILING AND BOATING The *City Lakes Department* rents motorboats and rowboats for use on lakes (phone: 668-2050 for information, 390-0222 for reservations). *Mission Bay Sports Centers* also give sailing courses (phone: 488-1004). *Seaforth Mission Bay Boat Rentals* (1641 Quivira Rd., Mission Bay; phone: 223-1681) and *Coronado Boat Rentals* (1715 Strand Way, Coronado; phone: 437-1514) have sailboats, rowboats, and power boats as well as boats rigged for water skiing; they also rent fishing gear and windsurfing equipment. You can rent sailboats and take sailing lessons at *Harbor Island Sailboats* (2040 Harbor Island Dr., Harbor Island; phone: 291-9568) and at many beach resort hotels.

SKIING The *Torrey Pines Ski Club* (write PO Box 82087, San Diego, CA 92138; phone: 583-8832) organizes trips to nearby mountains.

SOCCER The San Diego *Sockers* of the *Continental Indoor Soccer League (CISL)* kick a few balls around at the *San Diego Sports Arena* (3500 Sports Arena Blvd.; phone: 224-4171).

SCUBA DIVING Diving gear and lessons are available at *Diving Locker* (1020 Grand Ave.; phone: 272-1120), and the San Diego area has one of our very favorite dive spots.

BEST DEPTHS

La Jolla Cove Starting at this 50-yard-deep, 100-yard-wide notch in the Southern California coastline, the *San Diego–La Jolla Underwater Park* takes in about 7 miles of underwater scenery up the coast as far as *Torrey Pines;* within the park there's a look-but-don't-touch area where you can see vast quantities of kelp, abalone, and lobster. One of the best sites is at the edge of a 20-mile-long submarine canyon that borders the underwater park; the drop-off is 11,000 feet. For more information, contact the *Parks and Recreation Department, Coastal Division* (phone: 221-8900).

SURFING *Boomer Beach,* so named because of the rumbling sound of surf crashing to shore, is the body-surfer's first choice. Surfboarders ride the waves at *La Jolla Shores.*

SWIMMING There are 70 miles of public beaches, not to mention *Mission Bay Park*'s manmade lagoons. La Jolla and *Torrey Pines State Park* beaches are especially beautiful (see *Special Places*). There are 10 municipal swimming pools; for information call the *Aquatics Department* of the *City Recreation Office* (phone: 490-0923). Don't miss the *Plunge* water slide at Belmont Shores.

TENNIS San Diego itself has plenty of courts for public use, but just outside the city limits is a *primo* tennis resort.

CHOICE COURTS

Rancho Valencia This resort got its start as a tennis camp, and it's a wonderful place to stay even if you don't like tennis. There are 18 tennis courts, a staff of pros to help you refine your strokes, a pro shop, and a clubhouse; week-long intensive tennis clinics are offered through the well-respected John Gardiner program. Even if you come without a partner, the staff can set up a game for you with someone who matches your level of expertise. The location, just inland from Del Mar and La Jolla, is ideal (5921 Valencia Circle; phone: 756-1123; 800-548-3664).

In the city, there are public courts at *La Jolla Recreation Center* (615 Prospect St.; phone: 522-1658); *Balboa Tennis Club,* Morley Field (2221 Morley Field Dr., *Balboa Park;* phone: 295-9278); *University City Racquet Club, Standley Park* (3585 Governor Dr.; phone: 452-LOVE); and *Peninsula Tennis Club,* Robb Field (2525 Bacon St.; phone: 226-3407).

WHALE WATCHING Watch the migrating sea mammals from *Cabrillo National Monument,* Whale Point in La Jolla, or go on a whale watching excursion from *H & M Landing* (2803 Emerson St.; phone: 222-1144) or *Fisherman's Landing* (2838 Garrison St.; phone: 222-0391), in late December, January, and February. The *Scripps Institution of Oceanography* offers weekend whale watching trips in January and February.

THEATER

The *Old Globe Theatre* stages summer festivals featuring contemporary productions, as well as Shakespeare; the rest of the year, the company performs modern classics, musicals, and dramas at both the *Old Globe* and next-door *Cassius Carter Center Stage* (*Balboa Park;* phone: 239-2255). During the summer, some productions are staged at the outdoor *Lowell Davies Festival Theater. San Diego Repertory Theatre* performs in the *Lyceum Theater*—two stages (*Horton Plaza;* phone: 235-8025). *Gaslamp Quarter Theatre Company* offers cabaret theater at the *Gaslamp Theatre* (547 Fourth St.; phone: 234-9583) and *Hahn Cosmopolitan Theatre* (444 Fourth Ave.; phone: 232-9608). The well-regarded *La Jolla Playhouse,* at the *Mandel Weiss Center* on the *University of California–San Diego* campus, presents a variety of plays from May through November (phone: 534-6760). The *California Ballet* performs the *Nutcracker Suite* at *Christmas* and other classics the rest of the year, at venues around the metro area (phone: 560-6741). Discount tickets for theater and other cultural events are available at the *ARTSTIX* booth (*Horton Plaza;* phone: 238-3810) on the day of the performance (cash only).

MUSIC

Copley Symphony Hall (1245 Seventh Ave.; phone: 699-4200) is the home of the *San Diego Symphony*. The *San Diego Opera Company* performs at the *Civic Theatre* (202 C St.; phone: 232-7636). Free organ concerts are played every Sunday afternoon at the *Spreckels Organ Pavilion* (*Balboa Park;* phone: 226-0819). Most rock concerts take place at the *San Diego Sports Arena* (3500 Sports Arena Blvd.; phone: 224-4176).

NIGHTCLUBS AND NIGHTLIFE

In Cahoots (5373 Mission Center Rd.; phone: 291-8635) features country-and-western music. The *Cannibal Bar* at the *Catamaran* hotel (3999 Mission Blvd.; phone: 488-1081) is a lively, young dance club. *Elario's* in La Jolla features top jazz performances on the top floor of the *Summerhouse Inn* (7955 La Jolla Shores Dr., La Jolla; phone: 459-0541). *Croce's* restaurant (802 Fifth Ave.; phone: 233-4355) features live jazz seven nights a week; jazz is also presented frequently at the *Palace Bar* at the *Horton Grand* hotel (311 Island Ave.; phone: 544-1886). Country-and-western dance lessons accompany the music at *Boots* (1055 Avocado Blvd., El Cajon; phone: 670-3545). *Old Del Mar Café* (273 Via de la Valle, Del Mar; phone: 755-6614) is a popular venue for live jazz, country, and rock. *Dick's Last Resort* (345 Fourth Ave., between J and K Sts.; phone: 231-9100), in the Gaslamp Quarter, is a rowdy restaurant-bar with live Dixieland jazz. For comedy, try *The Comedy Store* (916 Pearl St., La Jolla; phone: 454-9176), the *Improv Comedy Club and Restaurant* (832 Garnet Ave.; phone: 483-4522), or *Comedy Nite, San Diego* in the Gaslamp Quarter (327 Fourth Ave.; phone: 544-7000).

Best in Town

CHECKING IN

The presence of the *Convention Center* and the redevelopment of downtown have caused an increase in the number of fine hotels and resorts in the city. Visitors seeking comfortable, reasonably priced accommodations will find them in all parts of San Diego. Those listed below are special in quality, character, or value. Expect to pay $130 or more per night for a double room at those places categorized as expensive; between $90 and $130 at those rated moderate; and less than $90 at places listed as inexpensive. For accommodations at bed and breakfast establishments, contact *Bed & Breakfast Directory for San Diego* (PO Box 3292, San Diego, CA 92103; phone: 297-3130). One option is to spend the night at sea. The *Dockside Inn* (1450 Harbor Island Dr.; phone: 296-8940) can arrange for you to sleep on board a yacht at one of San Diego's marinas. A continental breakfast is included; catered dinners can be ordered as well. Hotel rooms have air conditioning, private baths, TV sets, and telephones unless otherwise indicated. All hotels are in the 619 area code unless otherwise indicated.

For an unforgettable experience in San Diego, we begin with our favorites, followed by our recommendations of cost and quality choices of accommodations, listed by price category.

SPECIAL HAVENS

Inn at Rancho Santa Fe It was one of those classic corporate bloopers: The *Atchison, Topeka and Santa Fe Railroad* bought up some 10,000 acres of cheap land to plant three million eucalyptus trees to provide—company officials hoped—an endless supply of railroad ties. Nobody had bothered to think, however, that eucalyptus wood is soft and splits easily, and so, though the trees took off, there wasn't a tie to be had. The railroad then went into the citrus business. This inn was first built to house prospective customers, and it just kept on growing until it became what you find here today—a sedate and very restful complex of unpretentious cottages nestled on 20 acres of luxuriant grounds surrounding the original building. There are three tennis courts, a heated swimming pool, an English croquet lawn, and, nearby, two championship golf courses and *Del Mar Beach* (7 miles away). The inn will pack a box lunch for you. There's a wonderful library and a high-ceilinged living room, both with fireplaces, as well as maid service, a fine dining room, and full business services—and all just 25 miles north of San Diego. 5951 Linea del Cielo, Rancho Santa Fe (phone: 756-1131; 800-654-2928; fax: 759-1604).

Rancho Valencia Reminiscent of an early California hacienda, this secluded resort—a popular romantic hideaway among Southern Californians—near Del Mar and La Jolla offers accommodations in 21 Spanish-style casitas, comprising 43 spacious suites with fireplaces, large tiled baths, and terraces; "The Hacienda" suite has its own pool. Although the property is only six years old, the atmosphere is that of a truly well-seasoned place. The decor in both the public areas and the suites combines rustic charm and elegance; the rosebud delivered each morning with your newspaper and fresh-squeezed orange juice is just one extra touch. Known for its extensive tennis facilities and clinics (see *Tennis*), the property also boasts a pool, two Jacuzzis, a croquet lawn, a fitness center, and access to nearby golf courses. Spa treatments and fitness programs round out the on-property diversions, but there's also polo, as well as the *Del Mar Race Track* and some of the most beautiful pink beaches in Southern California nearby; transportation is complimentary. The *Rancho Valencia* dining room (see *Eating Out*) provides fine American fare, and room service is always on call. Meeting rooms can accommodate up to 125, and among the other business services are secretarial assistance, A/V equipment, photocopiers, and computers. There's also a concierge desk and express checkout. 5921 Valencia Circle, Rancho Santa Fe (phone: 756-1123; 800-548-3664; fax: 756-0165).

EXPENSIVE

L'Auberge Del Mar The defunct *Tudor Del Mar* hotel, a favorite pre–World War II seaside hangout of Hollywood stars and *Del Mar Race Track* fans, has been reincarnated as a 123-room luxury resort (now managed by the Bel-Air company) in a cozy, French provincial mode. Located in the heart of Del Mar, it's across the street from *Del Mar Plaza*'s chic boutiques and eateries and only a short stroll from the Pacific. Special treats include award-winning fare at *Tourlas* restaurant, afternoon tea, and weekend dinner dances. Pools, a full health and beauty spa, tennis courts, and chic shops are on the premises. Meeting rooms can hold up to 250, and there's a concierge, secretarial services, A/V equipment, photocopiers, and computers. 1540 Camino Del Mar, Del Mar (phone: 259-1515; 800-553-1336; fax: 755-4940).

Bahia Situated on its own 14-acre peninsula on Mission Bay and great for families, this resort has a tropical feel; it boasts its own beaches, a seal pond, and a plethora of exotic palm trees. Many of its 325 rooms have not only their own kitchens, but also private patios overlooking Mission Bay. Two paddle wheel riverboats ferry guests around the bay on cocktail cruises complete with music and dancing; the boats double as meeting facilities and ballrooms. Amenities include a restaurant/comedy club, a piano bar, an Olympic-size pool, an oversize Jacuzzi, and two lighted tennis courts. There are 10 meeting rooms in addition to the boats, A/V equipment, secretarial services, fax and photocopy machines, and express checkout. 988 West Mission Bay Dr. (phone: 488-0551; 800-288-0770).

Catamaran Resort South Pacific in feeling, this 318-room property features a lobby with a waterfall, ponds filled with *koi*, and a museum-quality collection of Polynesian artifacts. More than 100 varieties of trees, many exotic birds, and a whimsical hippopotamus fountain lend a special ambience to the resort's eight-and-a-half acres. Many rooms have kitchens. The *Cannibal Bar* jumps at night with live entertainment and dancing, while *Moray's Bar* is quieter. One of San Diego's finest restaurants, the *Atoll* (see *Eating Out*) is also here. The *Bahia Belle*, an authentic paddle wheel riverboat, links the *Catamaran* with its sister hotel, the *Bahia*. Business services include meeting rooms for up to 1,000, secretarial services, A/V equipment, and photocopiers. There's also a concierge desk. 3999 Mission Blvd. (phone: 488-1081; 800-288-0770; fax: 488-1081).

Del Coronado When it opened in 1888, it was the largest wooden building in the country and the first hotel in the world to have electric lighting and elevators. Today, the 700-room resort is a National Historic Landmark and one of the world's most picturesque hotels. The first floor oceanview lanai rooms are extraordinary, but other rooms in the historic building are less impressive than the exterior architecture, and there is a modern annex that's downright pedestrian. Then there are those rather noisy early morning flights out of the naval air station. Facilities include a small spa, two pools, tennis courts, three restaurants, and a deli. For businesspeople: 44 meeting rooms, secretarial assistance, A/V equipment, photocopiers, and computers. A concierge desk, 24-hour room service, and express checkout are also available. On the Coronado Peninsula, 1500 Orange Ave. (phone: 435-6611; 800-468-3533 or 800-HOTEL-DEL; fax: 522-8262).

Doubletree at Horton Plaza Adjacent to the *Horton Plaza Shopping Center*, it has 450 rooms, an outdoor pool, and two tennis courts, plus a health club. The interior is done in soft tones, the menu at the *Café San Diego* features regional California cooking, the early bird dinner at the coffee shop is a tasty bargain, and 24-hour room service is available. Business conveniences include meeting rooms that hold up to 240, secretarial services, A/V equipment, photocopiers, computers, and express video checkout. There's also a concierge desk. 910 Broadway Circle (phone: 239-2200; 800-528-0444; fax: 239-0509).

Hyatt Islandia This 423-room property sits on four-and-a-half lush acres overlooking Mission Bay and the Pacific, not far from *Sea World* and other San Diego attractions. A 17-story tower offers 260 spacious rooms with glass-enclosed patios. Upper floors boast terrific nighttime views. The

Regency Club, on the top two floors, provides concierge service and complimentary continental breakfast and hors d'oeuvres. The Marina Suites are in a three-story building overlooking the marina. The resort offers a huge, California-shaped pool, an outdoor Jacuzzi, workout room, whale watching, deep-sea fishing, sailboat rental, and a jogging path; golf and tennis are nearby. There are two restaurants, two lounges, 10 meeting rooms, a concierge, secretarial services, A/V equipment, photocopiers, and express checkout. 1441 Quivira Rd. (phone: 224-1234; 800-233-1234; fax: 224-0348).

Loews Coronado Bay Resort This $80-million, 440-room seaside property sits on a 15-acre private peninsula surrounded by San Diego Bay. Every room offers views of the marina, the bay, or the city skyline. Facilities include a health club, five tennis courts, three pools, and there are sunken tubs in many of the rooms. The hotel has three restaurants (including *Azzura Point;* see *Eating Out*), two lounges, a poolside grill, and an upscale food and gift store. Equipment for bicycling, sailing, and water sports can be rented. Business amenities include a concierge, meeting rooms that accommodate up to 1,400, and a business center. 4000 Coronado Bay Rd., Coronado (phone: 424-4000; 800-81-LOEWS).

Le Meridien San Diego at Coronado It's a fresh, airy, luxury resort in a South Seas island setting, with tropical plants, lagoons, and exotic birds. The 300 rooms are bright, the atmosphere relaxing. An on-site spa soothes the strains of a full range of resort activities, and a spa menu is always available. Food at the elegant *Marius* and the casual brasserie, *L'Escale,* is exquisite (see *Eating Out* for both). Room service is available around the clock. The business center offers secretarial services, A/V equipment, photocopiers, and computers. There's also express checkout and a concierge desk. 2000 Second St., Coronado (phone: 435-3000; 800-543-4300; fax: 435-3032).

San Diego Marriott Two elliptical towers rise 25 floors above San Diego Bay and the hotel's own 19-acre marina. Inside are 1,355 rooms and suites, a shopping arcade, and six restaurants and bars. A fitness center, six lighted tennis courts, and a large outdoor pool provide plenty of workout opportunities, and the marina offers boats for rent. Meeting rooms accommodate up to 3,000, and additional business amenities include secretarial services, A/V equipment, and photocopiers. Other pluses are 24-hour room service, a concierge, and express checkout. 333 W. Harbor Dr. (phone: 234-1500; 800-228-9290; fax: 234-8678).

Sheraton Grande Torrey Pines Next to the two *Torrey Pines* golf courses, this casually elegant, white Mediterranean-style establishment has 400 rooms overlooking the greens and the Pacific beyond. Facilities include a fitness center, a pool with Jacuzzi, privileges at the *Shiley Sports and Health Center of the Scripps Clinic* next door, plus a butler on each floor. The view alone is worth the price of admission. Complimentary transportation within a 6-mile radius. Room service is available around the clock. The business center provides secretarial services, A/V equipment, photocopiers, and computers. Meeting rooms can hold up to 1,500. There's also a concierge desk and express checkout. 10950 N. Torrey Pines Rd. (phone: 558-1500; 800-762-6160; fax: 558-1131).

U. S. Grant Restored to its 1910 ambience, this grand property is listed on the *National Register of Historic Places*. The lobby has pillars and a green and white marble floor, and the public rooms glitter with gold leaf and chandeliers. The 280 rooms are discreetly luxurious and equipped with modern amenities, but vestiges of the past remain, such as windows that open. Light lunch and tea are served in the *Grant Grill Lounge;* meals also are served in the *Grant Grill.* The central downtown location is unbeatable. Complimentary van transportation to and from the airport. There is a health club, a concierge desk, 24-hour room service, secretarial services, A/V equipment, photocopiers, meeting rooms that accommodate up to 1,300, and express checkout. 326 Broadway (phone: 232-3121; 800-334-6957 in California, 800-237-5029 elsewhere in the US; fax: 232-3626).

La Valencia The venerable pink building on La Jolla's browseable Prospect Street is a handsome Spanish *doña* with wrought iron, tiles, and flowers. Both an international 100-room hotel and a local meeting place, it offers three restaurants and the popular *Whaling Bar,* garden dining, a sauna, a fitness room, a Jacuzzi, and a pool. The 10th-floor *Sky Room* provides panoramic views. Around-the-clock room service is available. There are three meeting rooms, as well as A/V equipment and photocopiers, a concierge, and express checkout. 1132 Prospect St., La Jolla (phone: 454-0771; 800-451-0772; fax: 456-3921).

Westgate A 223-room property, it has a convenient downtown location and an excellent reputation. Consistent with the $1 million worth of antiques decorating the premises, the hotel also offers superb service. The *Fontainebleau* is one of the city's most elegant eateries (see *Eating Out*). Additional conveniences are 24-hour room service, a concierge, meeting rooms with a capacity of up to 500, A/V equipment, photocopiers, computers, and express checkout. 1055 Second Ave. (phone: 238-1818; 800-522-1564 in California; 800-221-3802 elsewhere in the US; fax: 557-3737).

MODERATE

Horton Grand Ironically, a former bordello is considered the city's most romantic hostelry. In fact, it is two hotels joined by a sunny courtyard. Gilded mirrors swing open to reveal TV sets, and toilets have pull-chains, but the amenities are modern, the service cheerfully solicitous. The *Ida Bailey* restaurant (named for the original madam) has jazz Thursdays through Sundays. Room service is offered until 11 PM. Meeting rooms hold up to 300; and secretarial services, A/V equipment and photocopiers, and express checkout are available. 311 Island Ave. (phone: 544-1886; 800-542-1886; fax: 239-3823).

Somerset Suites Here are 80 sunny suites with full kitchens, close to *Balboa Park* and the lively restaurant row on Fifth Avenue. A pool, Jacuzzi, complimentary continental breakfast, and cable TV are among the amenities. Each evening, there is a social hour with complimentary beer, wine, and snacks. Another convenience is the shuttle service that transports guests to and from destinations within a 5-mile radius of the hotel, as well as the train and bus stations and the airport. Concierge service is on call, and there are photocopiers. 606 Washington St. (phone: 692-

5200; 800-356-1787 in California; 800-962-9665 elsewhere in the US; fax: 299-6065).

Town and Country One of the best hotels in Mission Valley and among the city's largest, with over 1,000 rooms, this is a popular convention spot. Facilities include pools, saunas, a barber shop, a beauty parlor, and a 24-hour coffee shop. Among the business amenities are meeting rooms that accommodate up to 3,050, concierge and secretarial services, A/V equipment, photocopiers, computers, and express checkout. 500 Hotel Circle (phone: 291-7131; 800-542-6082 in California, 800-854-2608 elsewhere in the US; fax: 291-3584).

INEXPENSIVE

Gaslamp Plaza Suites Another downtown National Historic Landmark, it's a tastefully converted former office building. Previously the *Horton Park Plaza,* its 65 suites are named after famous authors, and there's a sun deck and a two-level restaurant. Meeting rooms can hold up to 40. 520 E St. (phone: 232-9500; 800-443-8012; fax: 238-9945).

Torrey Pines Inn A 74-room property with a spectacular location overlooking the Pacific and right on the two famous *Torrey Pines* golf courses. Surfers and hang gliders can be spotted from the hotel, and La Jolla's beaches are just out the door. A pool and a lounge provide other options. There is a concierge desk, meeting rooms that accommodate up to 300, secretarial services, A/V equipment, photocopiers, computers, and express checkout. 11480 Torrey Pines Rd., La Jolla (phone: 453-4420; 800-448-8355 in California, 800-777-1700 elsewhere in the US; fax: 453-0691).

Travelodge at the Zoo The huge columns at the entrance to this 139-room hotel (formerly the *Lafayette*) near *Balboa Park* resemble those of a Southern plantation; bargain rates that include breakfast and transportation to and from the airport make up for a bit of wear around the edges. Bob Hope was the first registered guest when the hotel was built in 1946, and although the hotel may have seen better days, the pastel rooms are comfortable and many are spacious (room 328 has a long, broad porch and costs $39 a night). There is a whirlpool and a restaurant. Meeting rooms accommodate up to 600. Other business features include A/V equipment, photocopiers, and express checkout. 2223 El Cajón Blvd. (phone: 296-2101; 800-423-1935 in California, 800-843-9988 elsewhere in the US; fax: 296-2101).

EATING OUT

San Diego's range of restaurants has become more innovative and international. Naturally, seafood stars on many menus, and both locals and out-of-towners go for Mexican food here. Expect to pay about $125 for dinner for two at the restaurant in the very expensive category; $60 or more at those places listed as expensive; $30 to $60 at those described as moderate; and less than $30 at those rated inexpensive. Prices do not include drinks, wine, tax, or tips. Unless otherwise noted, restaurants are open for lunch and dinner. All restaurants are in the 619 area code unless otherwise indicated.

VERY EXPENSIVE

Marius The great atmosphere and award-winning cooking evoke Provence. The menu changes three times a year but usually features fine seafood and lamb entrées concocted with a light hand and a touch of whimsy; desserts are sensational. The price is dear, but it costs much less than a trip to France. Closed Sundays and Mondays. Reservations advised. Major credit cards accepted. *Le Meridien San Diego,* 2000 Second St. (phone: 435-3000).

EXPENSIVE

Anthony's Star of the Sea Room One of the best on the West Coast, it overlooks San Diego Harbor and serves fresh-from-the-ocean abalone, as well as other fish dishes. The clams *genovese* often are ordered as an entrée. Jackets and ties required for men. Open for dinner only; closed major holidays. Reservations necessary a day or two in advance. Major credit cards accepted. 1360 N. Harbor Dr. at the foot of Ash St. (phone: 232-7408).

Azzura Point This trendy spot at *Loews Coronado Bay* is a don't-miss dining experience. Since it opened a few years ago, it has been earning raves for its outstanding seafood. The atmosphere is friendly and informal (although that casual attitude sometimes extends to the service). Still, the freshness of the ingredients and the attractiveness of the presentations make eating here more than worthwhile. Open for dinner only. Reservations advised. Major credit cards accepted. 4000 Coronado Bay Rd. (phone: 424-4000).

Delicias This eatery puts everything together perfectly—delicious food, pleasant atmosphere, and great service. Pasta, soups, and pizza baked in a wood-burning oven are among the treats offered in a cheerful room decorated with tapestries, fresh flowers, and French-country fabrics. Diners may also choose to eat outdoors under giant umbrellas. Closed Mondays. Reservations advised. Major credit cards accepted. 6106 Paseo Delicias, Rancho Santa Fe (phone: 756-8000).

Fontainebleau One of San Diego's best restaurants, it offers continental food in palatial surroundings served by waiters wearing white gloves. The dessert cart is fabulous. Closed Sundays. Reservations necessary. Major credit cards accepted. *Westgate Hotel,* 1055 Second Ave. (phone: 238-1818).

Mille Fleur This French restaurant tucked into a charming courtyard has received considerable acclaim over the years. Chef Martin Woesle creates a complex menu of Gallic specialties; the selections change daily, but diners can expect elegant dishes such as grilled Hawaiian swordfish, roast loin of rabbit, sautéed veal sweetbreads, and Norwegian salmon in puff pastry. There's a lounge with live piano music Wednesdays through Saturdays. Open daily; dinner only on weekends. Reservations advised. Major credit cards accepted. 6009 Paseo Delicias, Rancho Santa Fe (phone: 756-3085).

Rancho Valencia Here is award-winning fare served indoors and out. The menu changes frequently, but the food is consistently excellent, and there are always fabulous desserts plus an extensive wine list. On summer evenings, diners can dance under the stars. Open daily. Reservations necessary. Major credit cards accepted. *Rancho Valencia Resort,* 5921 Valencia Circle, Rancho Santa Fe (phone: 756-1123).

Top o' the Cove Looking out onto La Jolla Cove, this restaurant is a favorite with show-biz types from LA, and is consistently voted the area's most romantic. It features squab, venison, and fresh pasta dishes. Open daily. Reservations advised. Major credit cards accepted. 1216 Prospect St., La Jolla (phone: 454-7779).

MODERATE

Atoll Loudly applauded by local restaurant critics, this dining spot offers such dishes as lamb potstickers, and spinach salad with marinated scallops. The outrageously rich desserts, such as the Southwestern lemon citrus tart, are not to be missed. Open daily. Reservations advised. Major credit cards accepted. *Catamaran Resort Hotel,* 3999 Mission Blvd. (phone: 488-1081).

Avanti In an Art Deco setting, this place adds a northern Italian accent to a continental menu, which includes such dishes as braised radicchio served with salmon, and *porcini* mushrooms with beef filet. There's also dancing Wednesday through Saturday evenings. Open daily. Reservations advised. Major credit cards accepted. 875 Prospect St., La Jolla (phone: 454-4288).

Café Pacifica An alternative to Mexican in Old Town, this is among the city's best seafood spots. The fish is fresh, the seasoning sophisticated. The mustard catfish is especially noteworthy; also, save room for dessert. Open daily; dinner only on weekends. Reservations advised. Major credit cards accepted. 2414 San Diego Ave. (phone: 291-6666).

China Camp Not the usual Chinese menu, specialties include "gold miner's chicken" and "beggar's hen," based on the recipes of Chinese immigrants who came to California in 1849 to pan for gold. Open daily; dinner only on weekends. Reservations advised. Major credit cards accepted. Pacific Hwy. at Hawthorne (phone: 232-1367).

Cindy Black's Dynamic, award-winning chef Cindy Black consistently turns out exciting dishes that have attracted a large local following. The huge, grilled portobello mushroom with rosemary oil is an appetizer that could very well be a meal in itself; risotto and Dover sole are other outstanding offerings. Desserts are deliciously sinful. Open daily; lunch Fridays only. Reservations necessary. Major credit cards accepted. 5721 La Jolla Blvd., La Jolla (phone: 456-6299).

Dobson's Downstairs, the pub is crowded and cozy. The dining room above the bar serves delicious seafood and grilled dishes with French flair, and the house specialty—mussel bisque topped with a pastry toque—is a big hit. Closed Sundays; dinner only on Saturdays. Reservations necessary for the dining room. Major credit cards accepted. 956 Broadway Circle (phone: 231-6771).

L'Escale Located in *Le Meridien* hotel, this place offers fabulous outdoor dining under umbrellas overlooking the bay. The emphasis is on fresh seafood and "Fitness Specials" (115 to 282 calories), but you'll have a hard time resisting the cheese twists and fresh bread. There's also a popular Sunday brunch. Open daily. Reservations advised. Major credit cards accepted. 2000 Second St. (phone: 435-3000).

Fio's This northern Italian spot has been packed practically from the instant its doors opened. One of the two dining rooms features stunning murals of Siena's famous *Palio* by local artist Debra Sievers. There's an ever-changing menu, plus homemade pasta and pizza. Don't miss the *tiramisù*. Valet parking is a plus. Open daily; dinner only on weekends. Reservations advised. Major credit cards accepted. 801 Fifth Ave. (phone: 234-FIOS).

Il Fornaio The menu here is as authentically Tuscan as the Carrara marble on the counters, and it includes homemade pasta and pizza from wood-burning ovens. Diners gaze at the Pacific from the terrace or window tables, or at a huge open kitchen with a genuine *girarrosto* spit from the counter seats. Coffee comes in many varieties, and the breads and pastries are delectable. Open daily. Reservations advised. Major credit cards accepted. 1555 Camino Del Mar (phone: 755-8876).

George's at the Cove Pleasant, with big windows overlooking La Jolla cove, this dining spot features regional California cuisine which uses local produce, and an excellent California wine list. Entrées include prawns with *tapenade* (an olive paste), and tuna with *wasabi* (a hot Japanese mustard). Upstairs, *George's Ocean Terrace* offers the same wonderful view and similar food at more moderate prices (no reservations). Open daily. Reservations advised. Major credit cards accepted. 1250 Prospect St., La Jolla (phone: 454-4244)

Pacifica Grill & Rotisserie This downtown sibling of the *Café Pacifica* (see above) overlooks the ground level of a warehouse fetchingly converted into a mini-mall next to the *Amtrak* terminal. There's something for everyone on its regional American menu, including Maryland crab cakes, mustard catfish, pizza, pasta, and ribs. Open daily; dinner only on weekends. Reservations advised. Major credit cards accepted. 1202 Kettner Blvd. (phone: 696-9226).

Rainwater's Next to the historic *Santa Fe Depot*, it reputedly serves the best steaks in town, along with fresh seafood. Open daily. Reservations advised. Major credit cards accepted. 1202 Kettner Blvd. (phone: 233-5757).

Sfuzzi This made-up word (pronounced *foozi*) means "fun food," and that's what is dished up here. Pizza, pasta, grilled meat, and seasonal specialties are presented in an old brick building in the Gaslamp Quarter; its walls are decorated with peeling Pompeii-like frescoes. High ceilings, wood floors, and contemporary lighting complete the picture. There's also a bar and an outdoor patio. Open daily. Reservations advised. Major credit cards accepted. 304 Fifth Ave. (phone: 231-2323).

INEXPENSIVE

Alfonso's of La Jolla The Mexican dishes here are probably the most popular in town. Try *carne asada Alfonso* or one of the burrito or taco combination plates. Ask about Alfonso's Secret—it changes every day, and it's not on the menu. Open daily. Reservations advised. Major credit cards accepted. 1251 Prospect St., La Jolla (phone: 454-2232).

Anthony's Fish Grotto If you're looking for a burger, don't come here, as this casual place serves mostly seafood (the only respite from the sea is a chicken sandwich). This is the flagship link in the popular chain of "grottoes." Others are located in La Mesa, Chula Vista, and Rancho Bernardo. Open daily. No reservations. Major credit cards accepted. 1360 N. Harbor Dr. (phone: 232-5103).

Calliope's A Greek café and take-out place, where both the aromas and the prices are pleasing. Marinated fish, fowl, and meat are roasted or grilled, and there are phyllo specialties and classic Greek appetizers, salads, and daily vegetarian specialties. Open daily; dinner only on weekends. Reservations advised. Major credit cards accepted. 3958 Fifth Ave. (phone: 291-5588).

French Pastry Shop One of our favorite places for breakfast when we're headed for the *Torrey Pines* golf courses. Lunch and dinner are just as good but the freshly baked breads and pastries somehow seem a bit tastier with morning coffee. Open daily. MasterCard and Visa accepted. 5550 La Jolla Blvd., La Jolla (phone: 454-9094).

Hob Nob Hill One of the most delightful places to have breakfast in the entire city. Offerings include "The Three Musketeers," a slice of ham encased in three buttermilk pancakes; eggs Florentine; and delectable pecan waffles. Open daily. Reservations advised. Major credit cards accepted. 2271 First Ave. (phone: 239-8176).

Karinya Pacific Rim cooking worth applauding makes this eatery worth a second visit. Among the more than 80 unique dishes are selections such as *meekrob,* sweet and spicy noodles, and shrimp, beef, and chicken prepared Thai-style with lots of cilantro and curry. Open daily. Reservations advised. Major credit cards accepted. 4475 Mission Blvd. (phone: 270-5050).

Old Town Mexican Café y Cantina A perennial local favorite; *carnitas* are the specialty. The bar stays open to 2 AM. Open daily; Sunday brunch. Reservations advised for parties of 10 or more. Major credit cards accepted. 2489 San Diego Ave. (phone: 297-4330).

Point Loma Seafoods Hickory-smoked fish attracts diners and gulls. Especially popular for takeout. Open daily. Reservations unnecessary. No credit cards accepted. 2805 Emerson St. (phone: 223-6553 or 223-1986).

Taco Auctioneers Bidding isn't necessary, but this hip café warns diners that food fights are not allowed. Despite the place's eccentricities, the food is very, very good. *Enfrijoladas,* three corn tortillas with jack cheese, ranchero beans, and avocados, is a favorite, as is the *sopa mazatleca,* excellent shrimp in tomato broth. Open daily. Reservations unnecessary. MasterCard and Visa accepted. 1951 San Elijo Ave., Cardiff-by-the-Sea (phone: 942-8226).

San Francisco

At-a-Glance

SEEING THE CITY

Coit Tower, on the summit of Telegraph Hill, offers a spectacular panorama of San Francisco and the surrounding area: to the north are the waterfront and San Francisco Bay, the *Golden Gate Bridge,* Alcatraz Island, and on the far shore, Sausalito; downtown San Francisco lies to the south; to the east are Berkeley and the East Bay hills; and Nob Hill and Russian Hill rise to the west. The tower itself, a 212-foot cylindrical column built in 1933 with funds from a bequest by local eccentric and socialite Lillie Coit "to add beauty to the city she loved," is a striking landmark against the skyline. Inside are restored Depression-era frescoes depicting scenes of California in political, economic, and social vignettes. Open daily. Admission charge to view the lobby frescoes and ride the elevator to the top of the tower. (From Lombard St. follow Telegraph Hill Blvd. to the top; phone: 362-0808.) *Twin Peaks,* at nearly 1,000 feet, is the city's highest vantage point. (Follow Twin Peaks Blvd. to the top.) Several cocktail lounges offer fine views, too; among the highest, at 779 feet, is the *Carnelian Room,* the restaurant (don't go for the food) and bar atop the Bank of America building (555 California St.; phone: 433-7500). Another unsurpassed 360° panorama is afforded from the *Top of the Mark Lounge* of the *Mark Hopkins Inter-Continental* (see *Checking In*).

SPECIAL PLACES

San Francisco is a compact city and easy to get around. Most of the attractions are concentrated within a few areas, and the mild weather year-round makes walking pleasant, but you can sightsee by almost anything that rides, flies, or floats, from cable cars and their motorized facsimiles to buses, bicycles, carriages, trains, boats, helicopters, and hot-air balloons to a beautifully preserved DC-3 (see *Tours*).

DOWNTOWN

CIVIC CENTER This 15-square-block area contains the best collection of Beaux Arts–style buildings in America. Among the buildings are *City Hall,* a notable example of Renaissance grandeur with a 300-foot-high dome; the *War Memorial Opera House,* site of the signing of the UN Charter in 1945 and current home of the *San Francisco Opera* and *Ballet;* the *Bill Graham Civic Auditorium,* scene of cultural and political events since 1915; and the modern *Louise M. Davies Symphony Hall.* Wednesdays and Sundays look for the *Heart of the City Farmer's Market* (at the eastern edge of the *Civic Center*), a colorful place rife with exotic fruits and vegetables. Bounded by Franklin, Golden Gate, Leavenworth, and Hayes Streets, the *Civic Center* is a good place to start the *49-Mile Drive,* a well-marked trail that takes in many of the city's highlights. Just follow the blue, white, and orange sea gull signs.

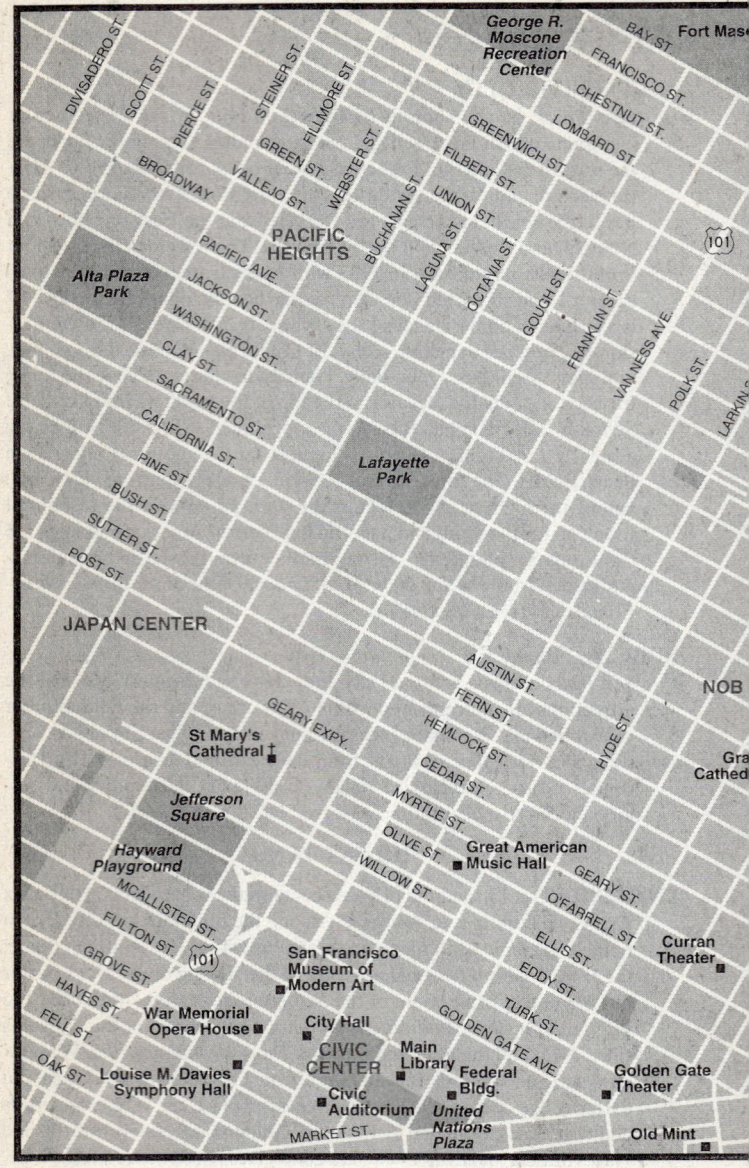

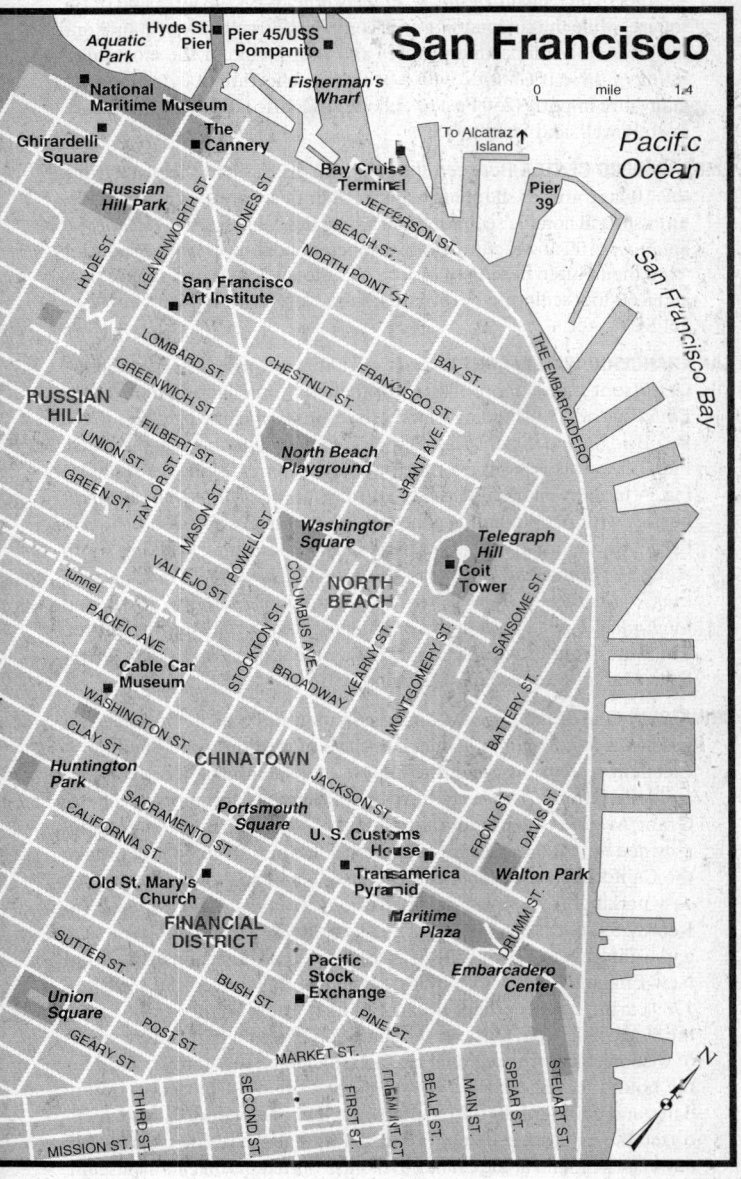

UNION SQUARE Right in the shopping area, Union Square offers a respite from the crowds of people (though not from the hordes of pigeons and panhandlers). You can feed the birds and relax on the benches in good weather. The elegant *Westin St. Francis* hotel is on the west side of the square, while the surrounding area contains sidewalk flower stands and the city's finest department stores and shops. One of the most interesting of these is *Gump's,* with a beautiful collection of jade among its many rare imports (250 Post St.; phone: 982-1616). Bordered by Geary, Post, Powell, and Stockton Sts.

EMBARCADERO CENTER Between the financial district and the waterfront, this 10-acre area of shopping malls, restaurants, hotels, and offices features several notable sculptures, including the controversial *Vaillancourt Fountain* (100 abstractly arranged concrete boxes with water spouting from them, often described by locals as the intestines of a square dog) and a 60-foot sculpture by the late Louise Nevelson. At the foot of Market St.

SAN FRANCISCO WATERFRONT Once a world class working port, the city's waterfront now is more like a world class promenade thanks to *The Embarcadero.* Outstanding views of Treasure Island, the light-festooned Bay Bridge, and distant East Bay Bridge draw an admiring audience. Pier 7 is a walkway out over the bay for strolling, fishing, or sightseeing. A farmers' market held on Saturdays at the foot of Market Street bustles with people and is chockablock with stalls of fresh produce, bread, and ready-to-eat food from local restaurants. Walking south along *The Embarcadero* you pass the *Harbor Court Hotel*'s brick façade, the *Gordon Biersch Brewery* bar and restaurant at Harrison Street, and the *Embarko* restaurant in the Bay Village complex at Brannon Street. The waterfront area runs about half a mile along *The Embarcadero,* from Market Street south to Brannon Street.

CHINATOWN One of the largest Chinese communities outside of Asia, Chinatown is an intriguing 24-block enclave of pagoda-roofed buildings, excellent restaurants, and fine import shops featuring ivory carvings and jade jewelry. There are also several temples and museums here. Grant Avenue is the main thoroughfare—enter through an archway crowned by a dragon (Grant at Bush St.). It's best to go on foot or take the California Street cable car, because the area is too congested for easy parking. If you must drive, try the *Portsmouth Square Garage* (at Kearny St., north of Clay St.). The *Old St. Mary's Church* (Grant Ave. and California St.) built in 1854 of granite from China and bricks from New England, is the city's oldest cathedral. It survived the 1906 and 1989 earthquakes, perhaps because of its warning on the façade above the clock dial: "Son; Observe the Time and Fly from Evil." More words of wisdom, as well as regional artifacts, including tiny slippers used for the bound feet of Oriental ladies, pipes from old Chinatown opium dens, and photographs of some famed telephone operators who memorized the names and numbers of 2,400 Chinatown residents in the old days, can be found at the *Chinese Historical Society of America*'s museum, the largest Chinese-American collection in the US (650 Commercial St., between Kearny and Montgomery; phone: 391-1188). Open Tuesdays through Saturdays, afternoons only. No admission charge. For information on walking tours of Chinatown, contact the *Chinese Cultural Center*, Tuesdays through Saturdays (750 Kearny St., inside the *Holiday Inn*; phone: 986-1822), or *Wok Wiz Chinatown Walking Tours* (750 Kearny St., Suite 800; phone: 355-9657).

NORTH BEACH There is no longer a beach here, but this traditional neighborhood remains colorful and diverse—Italian, Basque, and Chinese. The area's great for strolling and eating—bakeries and bread shops sell cannoli, rum babas, marzipan, and panettone (a sweet bread filled with raisins and candied fruit). Numerous restaurants and cafés serve anything from espresso and cappuccino to complete dinners. One of the best times of year to visit North Beach is in early June, during the street bazaar, when local artists display their wares along Upper Grant Avenue. Other times, numerous galleries and studios exhibit crafts, paintings, jewelry, and unusual clothing. Washington Square is a nice place to sit in the sun or have lunch with the locals under the statue—ironically, not of the square's namesake, but of Benjamin Franklin (Columbus and Union Sts.). North Beach extends north and northwest from Chinatown to Bay Street.

JAPAN CENTER This modern complex, the focal point of culture and trade for San Francisco's substantial Japanese community, is in the area where the Japanese lived before World War II. The five-acre complex contains movie theaters, tea houses, restaurants, sushi and tempura bars, art galleries, shops selling everything from pearls to stereo equipment, and a school that offers classes in Japanese doll making and flower arranging. With its five-tier *Peace Pagoda* in the center of a reflecting pool, the elegantly landscaped Peace Plaza is the scene of the April *Cherry Blossom Festival* and traditional Japanese celebrations, like the *Mochi-Pounding Ceremony* (in which much preparation and even more pounding result in delicious rice cakes). Speaking of pounding, the *Kabuki Hot Springs and Japanese Spa* offers shiatsu massage, traditional Japanese baths, whirlpool baths, saunas, steambaths, and other services; the works will leave you feeling as fresh and crisp as a newly made rice cake (1750 Geary Blvd.; phone: 922-6000). The *Kinokuniya* bookstore, a large, well-appointed place with books and periodicals in English as well as Japanese, offers browsers an unparalleled look at contemporary Japan. The area is bounded by Laguna, Fillmore, Geary, and Post Streets.

FISHERMAN'S WHARF AND VICINITY

FISHERMAN'S WHARF This rambling waterfront section—getting tackier by the year—is both the center of the commercial fishing industry and California's largest tourist attraction after *Disneyland*. On the wharf at Jefferson Street, you walk through an open-air fish market. Locals find it more convenient to shop for fish in their own neighborhoods, but you can create the ultimate urban picnic by buying a loaf of freshly baked sourdough bread at *Boudin's* bakery (156 Jefferson St.; phone: 928-1849) and adding Dungeness crab purchased at one of the numerous sidewalk stalls. The boats return in the afternoon and hoist their crates of fish onto the pier at the foot of Jones and Leavenworth Streets. The wharf restaurants often are crowded and expensive, but try the huge *Alioto's No. 8;* the menu has been upgraded with Sicilian seafood recipes, and the cappuccino is as good as the best in Italy (at the foot of Taylor St.; phone: 673-0183). The area has many outlets stalls selling handcrafted items.

PIER 39 Reconstructed with wood salvaged from other (demolished) piers and looking more like Gloucester, Massachusetts, than the West Coast, *Pier 39* is a popular entertainment complex on the northern waterfront. A pleasant hour or two can be spent moving with the crowds through the plethora of shops—craft, bakery, import, clothing, specialty, toy, jewelry, camera, fine food, crystal and silver, and many others. Meanwhile, mimes, jugglers, and other street performers provide continuous entertainment. For lunch or dinner, there's an international roster of restaurants from which to choose—French, Italian, Chinese, Swiss; grab a bite at one of the numerous stand-up, take-out fresh seafood booths; or simply indulge your sweet tooth at *Breyer's Ice Cream*. The *Eagle Café* (phone: 433-3689) still attracts enough longshoremen to lend a working class aura not otherwise evident in this part of the waterfront. Children can run off excess energy at the pier's playground and park or take a ride on the double-decker Venetian carousel at the end of the pier; weekend sailors and fishermen can charter boats at the marina; and landlubbers can watch the more than 300 sea lions that sun themselves on the docks. *Pier 39* is on *The Embarcadero,* just east of *Fisherman's Wharf*. (There's a parking garage across the way on Beach St.)

SAN FRANCISCO MARITIME NATIONAL HISTORICAL PARK A huge, ship-shape building at the foot of Polk Street, the park's *National Maritime Museum* is a treasure trove of memorabilia documenting shipping development from Gold Rush days to the present: with photographs, figureheads, massive anchors, shipwreck relics, and beautiful model ships. Open daily. No admission charge (*Aquatic Park;* phone: 556-3002). Berthed off nearby Hyde Street Pier, three old ships welcome the public aboard. The *Balclutha* was a British cargo ship that rounded Cape Horn 17 times carrying rice and wine to San Francisco, worked as an Alaskan salmon trader, and even did a stint in Hollywood as a rather oversize prop in films. The *Eureka* used to shuttle passengers and cars across the bay during the early decades of this century. The antique automobiles displayed on deck are sure to delight car buffs. Aboard the schooner *CA Thayer,* old salts sing chanteys some evenings. All open daily. Admission charge (phone: 556-1871). Also here—though unavailable for boarding—are the *Alma,* a scow schooner built in 1891; the *Eppleton Hall,* a 1914 British tugboat; and the *Hercules,* a 1907 oceangoing steam tug that hauled logs to mills down the coast. *The Maritime Store* is full of books about the sea, plus maps and posters (phone: 775-BOOK).

PIER 45/USS PAMPANITO A project of the *National Maritime Museum Association*. On display are historical photographs of this World War II submarine, including its role in the sinking of two Japanese ships with 2,000 British and Australian POWs aboard and the rescue of 73 survivors two days later. On board a narrated tape guides visitors through the operations of a submersible, where every inch of space had to be put to life-and-death use. Open daily. Admission charge. Pier 45 (phone: 929-0202).

BAY CRUISES AND ATTRACTIONS The *Blue & Gold Fleet* (Pier 39; phone: 705-5444) offers daily cruises, and evenings from April through December passengers can dine and dance across the bay. From the north side of the *Ferry Building* (located at the foot of Market St.), relive the days before the bridge was built by sailing to Oakland and Alameda. The *Red & White Fleet* uses Piers 41 and 43½, near *Fisherman's Wharf*, for its cruises and services to the north bay (phone: 546-2805 or 800-229-2784). Choose among Alcatraz (reserve ahead in summer and on holiday weekends), Sausalito, and Tiburon, with optional tours to the redwoods at *Muir Woods National Monument* and to Vallejo, with bus extension to *Marine World Africa USA* (phone: 707-644-4000; fax 707-644-0241). The latter features an enormous and exotic collection of sea, air, and land creatures and visitor participant activities such as playing tug-of-war with the elephants, giraffe feeding, getting close to prairie dogs and pygmy goats in the petting *kraal,* and learning about newborn animals like Bengal tiger cubs in the *Animal Nursery;* the marine part includes a killer whale and dolphin show, a shark habitat with a see-through tunnel, and a seal cove; and a new section includes a *Jurassic Park*–inspired *Dinosaurs!* exhibit. Admission charge is included in the cruise fee. Or, if you want to go on your own, *Marine World Africa USA* can also be reached from downtown San Francisco via high-speed catamaran in one hour, by car in 30 minutes, or by public transport; call the number above for more information. The *Red & White Fleet* also offers a three-winery cruise visit to the Napa Valley. And *Hornblower Dining Yachts* offers brunch, lunch, and dinner on its sails around the bay (Pier 33; phone: 394-8900).

ALCATRAZ ISLAND This famed escape-proof former federal penitentiary stands out grimly in the bay, 1½ miles from Fisherman's Wharf. Such notorious criminals as Al Capone, "Machine Gun" Kelly, and Doc Barker never returned from their stays here. The prison was closed in 1963 because of exorbitant operating costs and has been open to the public since 1973. The *National Park Service* runs tours of the prison block, where you see the "dark holes" in which rebellious prisoners were confined in solitude, and the tiny steel-barred cells. Two-hour tours depart daily on the *Red & White Fleet* (see *Bay Cruises,* above) on a first-come, first-served basis; tickets may be purchased in advance (strongly recommended for the summer and holiday weekends and over holiday weekends) through *Ticketron* (phone: 510-762-2277). Ferries sail from Pier 41.

GHIRARDELLI SQUARE Pronounced *Gear*-a-*del*-li. Originally a woolen mill that turned out Union Army uniforms during the Civil War, then later a chocolate factory, the stately, landmark, red brick buildings here now house import shops that sell anything from Persian rugs to Chinese kites, plus outdoor cafés, art galleries, and fine restaurants. The *Mandarin* (phone: 673-8812) serves excellent Chinese food; *McCormick & Kuleto's* (phone: 929-1730) serves seafood in a flashy setting with stunning bay views; but perhaps sweetest of all is the *Ghirardelli Chocolate*

Manufactory (phone: 474-3938), where you can watch chocolate being made and then eat the spoils afterward. If you're truly inspired, try the Golden Gate banana split. Open daily, on weekends until midnight. Bounded by Beach, Larkin, North Point, and Polk Sts.

THE CANNERY Inspired by *Ghirardelli Square,* this former Del Monte cannery is now a three-level arcade featuring chic boutiques, restaurants, and the *Museum of the City of San Francisco* (see *Museums*). Street musicians and mimes strut their stuff in the olive tree–shaded central courtyard. Open daily. Bounded by Beach, Leavenworth, and Jefferson Sts.

LOMBARD STREET Take the time to appreciate the residential façades and colorful flowers that line what is often referred to as the most twisting urban street in the world.

GOLDEN GATE—FROM THE PROMENADE TO THE PARK

GOLDEN GATE PROMENADE This 3½-mile shoreline trail is among the most spectacular walks (or jogging paths) in America. You meander from *Aquatic Park* past wind-shaped Monterey cypress, eroding rocky points, a classy yacht harbor in front of the *St. Francis Yacht Club,* a grassy park beside an old cobbled seawall, all the while approaching that ultimate span, the *Golden Gate Bridge.* A number of interesting museums line the way. *Fort Point,* completed in 1861 as the West Coast's only Civil War outpost, is now a *National Historic Site.* Closed Mondays and Tuesdays. No admission charge (at the base of the *Golden Gate Bridge,* Presidio; phone: 556-1693). The *Presidio Army Museum,* established in 1776 as a Spanish garrison and housed in the Old Station Hospital, has artifacts tracing its history. Closed Mondays and Tuesdays. No admission charge (Lincoln Blvd. and Funston Ave.; phone: 556-0856). Most unusual is the *Palace of Fine Arts,* a grand Beaux Arts building constructed for the 1915 *Panama-Pacific International Exposition.* It houses the *Exploratorium,* a collection of 800 displays on science, technology, and the reaches and limits of human perception (see *Museums*).

GOLDEN GATE BRIDGE The loftiest and one of the longest single-span suspension bridges ever constructed, the bright-orange *Golden Gate* marked its golden (50th) anniversary in 1987 with a huge celebration that culminated in the permanent lighting of its twin towers. To enjoy a stunning view, follow the handicapped-accessible walk up to the toll plaza level, where you'll also find gardens landscaped with native flowering plants. From here you have several options: You can catch a bus back downtown; turn around, and walk back with the view of the city skyline accompanying you all the way; or follow in the footsteps of great coast trekkers across the bridge and beyond—north along trails on the ridges and shoreline for 60 miles to Tomales Point. Yes, you can walk across the bridge (and under it); if you are driving, take the very first exit across the bridge, park, and enjoy the terrific view of San Francisco.

SAN FRANCISCO ZOO *Gorilla World* and an ultramodern $7-million *Primate Discovery Center* make a visit here particularly worthwhile. More than a thousand birds and animals can be viewed on foot or from aboard the motorized tour train. Adjacent to the main zoo is the *Children's Zoo,* a seven-acre nursery where children can stroke barnyard animals or watch baby lions being bottle fed. An outstanding *Insect Zoo* brings kids face to face with an impressive collection of creepy crawlers. The spectacular primate center has dozens of exotic and/or endangered species, as well as hands-on experiments and informative, fun-to-do computer/slide programs. Open daily. Admission charge. Sloat Blvd. and 45th Ave. (phone: 753-7080).

GOLDEN GATE PARK Developed from 1,000 acres of rolling sand dunes, *Golden Gate Park* has all the amenities of a large recreation area: bike paths, hiking and equestrian trails, three lakes (where you can sail model boats or practice casting), sports fields, and a 25-acre meadow. The park also features a rose garden, the lovely *John McLaren Rhododendron Dell*, the *Strybing Arboretum and Botanical Gardens*—over 70 acres rich with 5,000 species of plants and trees from all over the world—and the *Conservatory of Flowers,* a greenhouse with lush tropical growth. (Arboretum and conservatory open daily. No admission charge to arboretum. Along Martin Luther King Jr. Dr. and John F. Kennedy Dr., respectively.) The *Japanese Tea Garden* is a masterpiece of Oriental landscaping. Open daily. Admission charge. (At the intersection of Martin Luther King Jr. Dr. and Tea Garden Dr., just west of the *de Young Museum.*) No such lyrical setting could be complete without music, and the Music Concourse offers free open-air *Municipal Band* concerts on Sunday afternoons at 1 when the weather is good (between the *de Young Museum* and the *California Academy of Sciences;* see below for both).

ASIAN ART MUSEUM Created to accommodate the collection of Asian art donated by Avery Brundage, this museum is known for the scope of its works, which span a 6,000-year period. More than 500 masterpieces—including the earliest dated bronze Chinese Buddha (AD 338) from his Chinese collection—are on permanent exhibit, as is a 2,000-year-old bronze rhinoceros wine vessel. Also on display is one of the world's most extensive exhibits of Gandharan sculpture (from northern India). Housed in a specially constructed wing of the *de Young Museum,* the *Asian Art Museum* is operated separately. Open Wednesdays through Sundays from 10 AM to 5 PM; admission charge (also good for admission to the *de Young Museum* on the same day). Across from the Music Concourse, *Golden Gate Park* (phone: 668-7855).

CALIFORNIA ACADEMY OF SCIENCES The state's oldest scientific institution offers a wide variety of exhibitions ranging from the *Steinhart Aquarium,* with dolphins, piranhas, talking fish, penguins, and 14,000 other species, to the farthest reaches of space in the *Morrison Planetarium's* changing shows. Open daily from 10 AM to 5 PM; open to 7 PM from *July 4* through *Labor Day;* admission charge. On the Music Concourse (phone: 221-5100).

M. H. DE YOUNG MEMORIAL MUSEUM An outstanding collection of American art, ranging from the colonial era through the 20th century, and including major contributions by Mr. and Mrs. John D. Rockefeller III, hangs on the walls of the 22 galleries in this fine arts museum. Works by John Singer Sargent, Mary Cassatt, and George Caleb Bingham are among those exhibited. Also featured is art from ancient Egypt, Greece, Oceania, and Africa; plus a large textile collection; docent tours daily. The original building was constructed for the *1894 California Midwinter Exposition,* which was backed and publicized by *San Francisco Chronicle* founder M.H. de Young. Lunch and refreshments are served in the *de Young Café.* Open Wednesdays through Sundays from 10 AM to 5 PM; admission charge (good for admission to the *Asian Art Museum* on the same day). Music Concourse, *Golden Gate Park* (phone: 750-3600; 863-3330 for recorded information).

SOUTH OF MARKET STREET

SOMA Formerly the city's gritty warehouse district (the name stands for "South of Market"), this area has been transformed into a vibrant, lived-in, artistic neighborhood of street markets and performers, shops, galleries, small theaters, gay bars, and nightclubs. Even as housing prices have veered upward, it remains one of San Francisco's most accessible, most colorful districts. Some once-elegant residential buildings still stand on Third Street, and living lofts are slowly being fashioned out of the former warehouses. South Park, at the heart of the district, is flanked by several clubs and restaurants. SoMa also is home to the *Moscone Convention Center* (named in memory of the assassinated San Francisco mayor) and the adjacent *Center for the Arts at Yerba Buena Gardens* (see below). There are also enough discount clothing outlets and boutiques to satiate even the most obsessed shopper (see *Shopping*). *Shopper Stopper* (PO Box 535, Sebastopol, CA 95473; phone: 707-829-1597) offers a 6½-hour shopping tour of the area, stopping at wholesalers not usually open to the public. The area is roughly bounded by Market, Embarcadero, China Basin, and Division Streets.

CENTER FOR THE ARTS AT YERBA BUENA GARDENS A sprawling complex of galleries, theaters, gardens, a walk-behind fountain, plus a café and gift shop, the center showcases the city's culture and traditions. Offerings on this theme run the gamut from painting to electronic music, from ballet to video, from sculpture to CD-ROM. A limited number of discounted tickets go on sale at 11 AM Tuesdays at the *Center for the Arts's Ticket Office* (phone: 978-2787); each person is allowed to purchase two tickets to selected performances the same week. 701 Mission St., between Third and Fourth Sts.

SAN FRANCISCO MUSEUM OF MODERN ART California's first museum devoted to modern art moved last year to a $60-million Mario Botta–designed facility across from the *Center for the Arts at Yerba Buena Gardens;* it will open to the public on January 31, 1995. It has a distinguished permanent collection of photography and American abstract expressionist art, with paintings by Jackson Pollock and Clyfford Still, and contemporary works by Bay Area artists such as Wayne Thiebaud and Richard Diebenkorn. Music, lectures, and film events are frequently scheduled; there's also a small, selective bookshop and a café. Open daily, on Thursdays until 9 PM. Admission charge; the first Tuesday of every month is free; Thursday evenings, half price. 151 Third St. at Howard St. (phone: 357-4000).

EXTRA SPECIAL

Within an hour's drive of San Francisco (north along US 101, east on Rte. 37, then north on Rte. 121) begins the number one wine-producing region in the US, the gently rolling Sonoma County and the Napa Valley. The mild weather encourages not only grape production but outdoor activity. Pick up some bread and cheese along Highway 29 en route to *Bothe–Napa Valley State Park*. Its thousand acres of broad-leaved trees, pines, and redwoods are a lovely backdrop for picnicking, biking, and swimming in summer.

If time permits, try one of the Napa Valley's charming bed and breakfast establishments, such as *La Residence* (4066 St. Helena Hwy. N., Napa; phone: 707-253-0337). *Meadowood* (900 Meadowood La., St. Helena, CA 94574; phone: 707-963-3646) and *Auberge du Soleil* (180 Rutherford Hill Rd., Rutherford, CA 94573; phone: 707-963-1211) are both resorts with beautiful rooms and renowned restaurants. Or you may find you don't want to move from Sonoma County, with its rugged coastline, deep woods, and picturesque farms. Be sure to take a meal at *John Ash & Company* (4330 Barnes Rd., Santa Rosa, CA 95403; phone: 707-527-7687), one of Sonoma's best restaurants. If you want the elegance of a 1920s luxury hotel plus a fitness spa, try the *Sonoma Mission Inn & Spa* (PO Box 1447, Sonoma, CA 95476 or 18140 Sonoma Hwy. 12, Boyes Hot Springs, CA 95416; phone: 707-938-9000 or 800-358-9022).

South of San Francisco and about two hours away (via Rte. 101, then Rte. 156, then Rte. 1, or via the slow, scenic coastal Rte. 1 all the way) lies the Monterey Peninsula, rich in history and natural beauty. The town of Monterey was the military capital of California under three flags, and many of its adobe buildings survive in the *State Historic Park*. On Cannery Row, where gift shops and restaurants have taken over defunct sardine canneries, the *Monterey Bay Aquarium* (886 Cannery Row; phone: 408-648-4888) is a spectacular re-creation of the region's marine environment. The peninsula's pine forests and broad white beaches, bright with flowering succulents, are breathtaking. Famous for golf at *Pebble Beach*, the area also attracts nature lovers who come to see monarch butterflies wintering in Pacific Grove, sea otters, seals, and the wild shore lands of *Point*

Lobos State Preserve, south of Carmel. Accommodations in this area include *La Playa* hotel (Camino Real at Eighth, Carmel-by-the-Sea, CA 93921; phone: 408-624-6476 or 800-582-8900) and the elegant *Stonepine* (150 E. Carmel Valley Rd., Carmel Valley, CA 93924; phone: 408-659-2245).

Sources and Resources

TOURIST INFORMATION

The *San Francisco Convention and Visitors' Bureau* (*Visitor Information Center*, PO Box 429097, San Francisco, CA 94142; phone: 391-2000) is best for brochures, maps, general tourist information, and other assistance. If you write ahead, it will send you (for $2) a valuable package of information, including a three-month calendar of events. Call 391-2001 anytime for the lowdown on what's going on in town. The bureau's downtown *Visitor Information Center* on the lower level of *Hallidie Plaza* (just downstairs from the cable car turntable, at 900 Market St. at Powell St.) provides multilingual services. Contact the California state hotline (phone: 800-TO-CALIF) for maps, calendars of events, health updates, and travel advisories.

LOCAL COVERAGE The *San Francisco Chronicle* is a morning daily; the *San Francisco Examiner*, an evening daily. On Fridays, both list events and places to go on weekends. Sundays the two publish a joint edition, including a comprehensive entertainment section, the "Datebook." We also immodestly suggest you pick up a copy of *Birnbaum's San Francisco 95* (HarperCollins; $12); *San Francisco ACCESS* (HarperCollins, $18) is popular for its clarity and interesting layout.

TELEVISION STATIONS KRON Channel 4–NBC; KPIX Channel 5–CBS; KGO Channel 7–ABC; KQED Channel 9–PBS; KTVU Channel 17–CNN.

RADIO STATIONS AM: KFRC 610 (oldies); KCBS 740 (news); KGO 810 (news/talk); FM: KQED 88.5 (National Public Radio); KJAZ 92.7 (jazz); KKHI 95.7 (classical).

FOOD Consult *Best Restaurants of San Francisco: The San Francisco Chronicle Guide to Fine Dining* (Chronicle Books, $10.95) and *Exploring the Best Ethnic Restaurants of the Bay Area* by Sharon Silva and Frank Viviano (S.F. Focus Books, $9.95).

TELEPHONE The area code for San Francisco, Marin, and south to Los Altos is 415. The area code for Oakland and Berkeley is 510.

SALES TAX Sales tax is 8.25%; hotel tax is 12%.

CLIMATE Daytime temperatures average 60F to 65F in summer and 45F to 57F in winter (downpours are common between November and March). In summer, morning and evening fogs make parts of the day very cool; and while it is 65F in San Francisco, it can be in the 80s in the suburbs.

GETTING AROUND

AIRPORTS *San Francisco International Airport* is about 15 miles south of the city, a 20- to 30-minute drive when it's not rush hour. A number of shuttles operate to and from the airport for a more economical fare. *SFO Airporter* buses run every 20 minutes between the airport and a number of downtown hotels for $8 one way, $14 round trip (phone: 673-2432). *San Francisco Supershuttle* (phone: 558-8500) offers transportation between the airport and anywhere in San Francisco. The one-way fare to a downtown hotel is $10; for the return trip, reservations must be made 24 hours in advance. *SAMTRANS* buses (phone: 800-660-4287 in San Francisco; 800-508-6200 elsewhere in the US) serve both the peninsula and downtown San Francisco (the *Transbay Terminal* at Mission and 1st Sts.). Buses depart from the upper levels in North and South Terminals every half hour during the day, hourly at night; the fare runs from 85¢ to $1.50. For more information on the airport's facilities, consult one of its teleguide terminals.

Oakland International Airport is a 30- to 45-minute drive from San Francisco's financial district during non-commuter hours; cab fare should run about $45. Rail service is available via the *Bay Area Rapid Transit (BART)* system (phone: 788-2278 or 510-464-6000); take an *Air BART* shuttle bus to the *Oakland Coliseum Arena* ($2), and then pick up *BART* to Montgomery Street in downtown San Francisco ($1.90). For airport information, call 510-577-4015.

BART If you really want to move, this ultramodern, high-speed railway will whisk you from San Francisco to Oakland, Berkeley, Richmond, Concord, Daly City, and Fremont at up to 80 miles an hour. The system is easy to use, with large maps and signboards in each station clarifying routes and fares (which vary according to distance traveled). For information, contact *Bay Area Rapid Transit (BART)*, 800 Madison St., Oakland (phone: 788-*BART* in San Francisco).

BUS Efficient buses serve the entire metropolitan area; maps appear at the front of the yellow pages in the telephone book. *MUNI (Municipal Transit)* Passports ($2.25 per day, $9 for five days) are good for rides on *MUNI* buses, streetcars, and cable cars. *MUNI* street and transit maps are available at bookstores for $2. For detailed route information, contact the *Municipal Railway of San Francisco*, 949 Presidio Ave. (phone: 673-*MUNI* daily during business hours).

CABLE CAR The best way to travel up and over the hills of downtown is aboard these famous trademarks, which are pulled along at 9½ miles an hour. There are three lines, the most scenic being the *Powell–Hyde* route, which you can pick up at the turntable at Powell and Market Streets. It will take you over both Nob and Russian Hills to gaslit *Victorian Park*.

CAR RENTAL There are a few things to remember if you plan to drive in San Francisco: Cable cars and pedestrians always have the right-of-way; curb your wheels when parking on a hill to prevent runaway cars. The national firms all serve San Francisco. Least expensive, however, is *Bob Leech Auto Rental* (at 435 S. Airport Blvd., South San Francisco—five minutes from the airport; phone: 583-3844).

FERRY For outstanding views of the city, ride the *Golden Gate Ferry* (phone: 332-6600) from the terminal under the clock tower at the foot of Market Street. The 30-minute ride to Sausalito (slightly longer to Larkspur) takes you right past Alcatraz and almost within reach of the *Golden Gate Bridge*. For other service see "Bay Cruises and Attractions" in *Special Places*.

STREETCAR Five lines of the *MUNI Metro* streetcar system run under Market Street, one level above *BART*, and branch off toward various parts of the city. For route information, call 673-MUNI.

TAXI Cabs can be hailed on downtown streets, especially near hotels, or summoned by phone. Major companies are *Luxor Cab* (phone: 282-4141), *Veterans Cab* (phone: 552-1300), and *Yellow Cab* (phone: 626-2345).

TOURS The best way to see San Francisco is on foot. *City Guides* (phone: 557-4266) offers free neighborhood walking tours (every day except Mondays and Fridays) that highlight the city's historical diversity. For example the "Gold Rush City" trek explores the haunts of the original 49ers, and in Haight-Ashbury remnants of the 1960s are still evident in the psychedelic street attire worn by diehards. (There are schedules at city libraries, or send a self-addressed, stamped envelope to *Friends of the Library, Main Library, Civic Center,* San Francisco, CA 94102.) The history of the gold miners that once flooded this town and their legendary vices—gambling, drinking, and women—is traced by *A. M. Walking Tours* (phone: 928-5965) through Nob Hill, Chinatown, the old Barbary Coast, Union Square, and Maiden Lane. "Cruisin' the Castro" is a walking tour of "the heart of gay America" (Castro Street); contact Trevor Hailey (375 Lexington St.; phone: 550-8110). *Wok Wiz Chinatown Walking Tours* (750 Kearny St., Suite 800; phone: 355-9657) provides an insider's view of this city within the city—with stops at Chinese markets, herbal shops, a pastry shop that makes rice noodles, an art gallery, a tea shop, and along the narrow streets and alleys of Chinatown for a dim sum lunch.

Riders Guide Trips on Tape (484 Lake Park Ave., Suite 255, Oakland, CA 94610; phone: 510-653-2553) has audiocassettes for do-it-yourself touring between Big Sur and the Napa and Sonoma Valleys, including San Francisco.

LOCAL SERVICES

AUDIOVISUAL EQUIPMENT *McCune Audio/Visual/Video* (phone: 641-1111).

BUSINESS SERVICES More and more hotels are offering in-house business services; see *Checking In*.

DRY CLEANER/TAILOR *Cable Car Tailors* (84 Ellis St.; phone: 781-4636); *Larry So* (456 Montgomery St.; phone: 981-6343); *Paragon* (635 Bush St.; phone: 781-2646).

LIMOUSINE *Carey Nob Hill Limousine* (phone: 468-7550); *Opera Plaza Limousines* (phone: 826-9630).

MECHANICS *Foreign Car Repair,* for imports (6027 Geary Blvd. between 24th and 25th Aves.; phone: 752-8305); *Honda Auto Repair,* for American and Japanese autos (2941 Geary Blvd.; phone: 751-7860); *San Francisco Golden Gate Motors*, for German-built cars (1444 Green St.; phone: 931-9076).

MEDICAL EMERGENCY *St. Francis Memorial Hospital* (900 Hyde St.; phone: 415-353-6000); *San Francisco General Hospital* (1001 Potrero Ave.; phone: 415-206-8000).

MESSENGER SERVICES *PDQ* (phone: 346-4229); *Western Messenger Service* (phone: 864-4100).

MONEY TRANSFERS *American Express MoneyGram* (phone: 800-926-9400 for information; 800-866-8800 for money transfers) or *Western Union Financial Services* (phone: 800-325-6000 or 800-325-4176).

PHARMACIES *Walgreens,* open 24 hours (3201 Divisadero St. at Lombard St.; phone: 415-931-6415 for general information; 415-931-9971 for pharmacy; and 498 Castro St.; phone: 415-861-3136).

PHOTOCOPIES *Blue Print Service Co.*, with overnight service available (149 Second St.; phone: 495-8700); *The Print & Copy Factory,* open 24 hours (2136 Palou Ave.; phone: 641-7500).

POST OFFICES The main post office is located at 1300 Evans Ave. (phone: 415-550-6500). Branches include offices at *Gateway Station* (1 Embarcadero Center; phone: 415-550-6500), *Macy's* (170 O'Farrell St. at Union Square; phone: 415-956-3570), and *Rincon Finance* (180 Steuart St.; phone: 415-543-3340). The *Civic Center* office (101 Hyde St.; phone: 415-441-8329) handles General Delivery mail only.

PROFESSIONAL PHOTOGRAPHER *Gabriel Moulin Studios* (526 Second St.; phone: 541-9454); *Romaine Photography* (Russ Bldg., 235 Montgomery St.; phone: 989-3536).

SECRETARY *Ancha Business Center* (2500 Mason St., inside the Sheraton at Fisherman's Wharf hotel; phone: 627-6530); *Headquarters Co.* (phone: 781-5000).

TELECONFERENCE FACILITIES Available in most downtown hotels with business clientele (see *Checking In*).

TRANSLATOR *Berlitz* (180 Montgomery St., 15th Floor; phone: 986-5474); *I.E.C.* (690 Market St.; phone: 781-8555).

WESTERN UNION/TELEX Many offices are located around the city (phone: 800-325-6000 to find the location nearest you).

SPECIAL EVENTS

San Franciscans know how to throw a party, and anyone lucky enough to be in town during one—which is usually every week—is welcome to join in the fun. Some are big, some are unusual, and everyone has a favorite reason for celebrating. To find out what's happening in any given week, call the *Visitor Information Center* (phone: 391-2000) or check the "Datebook" section of the Sunday *San Francisco Examiner and Chronicle.*

For nine days each year, Chinatown is even noisier and more crowded than usual when the *Chinese New Year* is celebrated in January or February (based on the lunar calendar). Fireworks explode day and night; the streets and storefronts are rife with red paper envelopes and other symbols of good luck. Hundreds of thousands of onlookers come to see the parade on the final day, when block-long dragons steered from within by more than a hundred people wind through the narrow streets, leading floats and marching bands to a festival in Portsmouth Square. The final celebration runs from 8 AM to midnight; fireworks are shot off at the end of the parade. For further information contact the *Chinese Chamber of Commerce* (phone: 982-3000).

The *Cherry Blossom Festival,* held on two weekends in April at the *Japan Center* (Post and Buchanan Sts.), features traditional tea ceremonies, flower-arranging and doll-making demonstrations, bonsai displays, and performances by folk dancers from Japan. A crosstown parade highlights the events with over 50 Japanese performing groups and intricate floats of shrines and temples.

Fleet Week celebrates the October birthday of the *US Navy* with a parade of ships under the *Golden Gate Bridge* and several days of open houses on the vessels, plus aerial events, fireworks, and boat rides.

The *Grand National Livestock Exposition, Rodeo and Horse Show,* held in late October and early November at the *Cow Palace* (just south of the city on Geneva Ave., off US 101), is one of the biggest events in the country, with all manner of rodeo events, equestrian competitions, and the best livestock in the West.

MUSEUMS

The city's major museums are all described in *Special Places*. Note: The *Achenback Foundation for Graphic Arts* is at the *de Young Museum* (see *Special Places* above) until later this year, when it returns to the *California Palace of the Legion of Honor* in *Lincoln Park* (34th Ave. and Clement St.). Call 863-3330 for further information. Other institutions worth a visit include the following:

AFRICAN-AMERICAN HISTORICAL AND CULTURAL SOCIETY A museum and library honoring black history and culture. Open Wednesdays through Sundays, afternoons only. Admission charge. *Fort Mason* Bldg. C (phone: 441-0640).

ANSEL ADAMS CENTER Changing exhibitions are devoted to the extraordinary photographs of this San Francisco native and environmentalist and to the works of other great photographers. Closed Mondays. Admission charge. 250 Fourth St. (phone: 495-7000).

CABLE CAR MUSEUM This lovely brick building is the powerhouse for the current system and a repository of cable car history. On display here are the first cable car, invented in 1873 by Andrew Hallidie, and exact scale models of cars servicing all the various lines. Open daily 10 AM to 5 PM. No admission charge. 1201 Mason St., near Chinatown (phone: 474-1887).

CARTOON ART MUSEUM Original cartoon art is exhibited: editorial, newspaper, and magazine cartoons, as well as animation boards, plus five 1789 works from British artist William Hogarth, considered among the first cartoons ever created. Special events include lectures and Saturday conversations with cartoonists (call the hotline at 546-9481 for schedules). Closed Sundays through Tuesdays. Admission charge. 665 3rd St., Fifth Floor (phone: 546-3922).

CRAFT AND FOLK ART MUSEUM Exhibitions of contemporary crafts and folk art; small museum shop. Closed Mondays and Tuesdays. Admission charge. *Fort Mason* Bldg. A (phone: 775-0990).

EXPLORATORIUM Expect to hear such sophisticated reactions as "wow" and "cool" when visiting the *Exploratorium*. Touching is a "must" here—more than 650 exhibits require pushing, pulling, throwing, or some other participation to explore the forces of the physical world. Light, sound, gravity, and perception are just four of the subjects examined. The *Tactile Dome*—a definite favorite among the small set—is a touchy-feely experience; crawl through a series of pitch-black tunnels, using your sense of touch to guide you. (Because of its popularity, advance reservations are required for the *Tactile Dome,* but there is no additional admission charge.) Closed Mondays. Admission charge. 3601 Lyon St. (inside the *Palace of Fine Arts*; phone: 561-0360 for recorded information; 561-0362 for *Tactile Dome* reservations).

JEWISH MUSEUM OF SAN FRANCISCO Devoted to a lively exploration of Jewish traditions and art as they relate to current affairs, the galleries and shop are open Sundays through Thursdays, with a 7 PM closing on Thursday; closed holidays. Admission charge. 121 Steuart St., near the Embarcadero *BART* Station (phone: 543-8880).

MEXICAN MUSEUM Colorful displays of handicrafts and paintings from south-of-the-border artists. Closed Mondays and Tuesdays. Admission charge. *Fort Mason* Bldg. D (phone: 441-0404).

MUSEUM OF THE CITY OF SAN FRANCISCO Rotating art exhibits depict the wide diversity of this city by the bay and the struggles of its people. Closed Mondays and Tuesdays. No admission charge. *The Cannery,* 2801 Leavenworth (phone: 928-0289).

SAN FRANCISCO ART COMMISSION GALLERY Emerging Bay Area artists exhibit paintings, sculpture, and nontraditional art forms. Open Thursdays through Saturdays, afternoons only (Thursdays until 8). No admission charge. 155 Grove St. (phone: 554-9682).

SAN FRANCISCO PERFORMING ARTS LIBRARY AND MUSEUM Displays and an extensive research collection of posters, programs, reviews, and other memorabilia. Closed Sundays and Mondays. No admission charge. 399 Grove St., near the *Civic Center* (phone: 255-4800).

SHOPPING

In the various neighborhoods as well as downtown, shopping is easy in this relatively compact city. For Japanese wares one can go to Japantown; for Chinese, Chinatown. With *Ghirardelli Square, The Cannery,* the *Anchorage* on *Fisherman's Wharf,* and *Pier 39,* San Francisco revived the age-old combination of marketplace and fun fair. *Embarcadero Center,* between the waterfront and the financial district, is filled with shops and restaurants. *San Francisco Centre,* on Market Street near

Powell Street, is a stunning, polished-stone structure with a huge, retractable skylight and spiral escalators; *Nordstrom* is the anchor department store here. The highly decorative *Rincon Center,* on Mission Street between Main and Spear Streets, was once an Art Deco–style post office; it now has a restored lobby, a 90-foot waterfall, 30 shops, and several good restaurants. When serious buying is the object—and money is not—the place to be still is Union Square and the streets that frame it. On the square are four major department stores: *Macy's, Saks Fifth Avenue, I. Magnin,* and *Neiman Marcus.* Nearby specialty shops include firms from Britain, France, Germany, Italy, and Switzerland, plus US competitors. Not to be confused with Union Square is a shopping stretch of Union Street on the old dairy land, Cow Hollow, and another on Fillmore Street. Victorian Union Street has exotic and unusual gift shops and designer boutiques featuring European fashions, while Fillmore's specialty is new and vintage fashion and home furnishings. For bargains in high fashion, explore the factory outlets south of Market Street (SoMa). A number of discount stores have opened up in this area; clothing prices are great, but shop decor is usually threadbare.

Note: Serious book browsers should check out both sides of the bay. In San Francisco, don't miss North Beach's *City Lights* (261 Columbus Ave. phone: 362-8193). Launched by Beat poet Lawrence Ferlinghetti in 1953, the bookstore holds hard-to-find and esoteric titles, an excellent selection of contemporary poetry, and an unusual selection of Third World literature. *A Clean, Well Lighted Place for Books* (601 Van Ness Ave., near the *Civic Center,* phone: 441-6670) borrows its name from an Ernest Hemingway short story; it is San Francisco's largest independent bookstore, with particularly strong fiction, science fiction, mystery, and music sections, and frequent book signings and readings. Countering as "A dirty, poorly lit place for books," *McDonald*'s (48 Turk St.; phone: 673-2235) is the largest used bookstore in town; located in the Union Square district, it also has or can find out of print titles, and a selection of secondhand magazines.

Across the bay in Berkeley, waiters have master's degrees and auto mechanics have PhDs, and the bookstores reflect that. Look for *Cody's Books* (phone: 510-845-7852) and *Moe's* (phone: 510-849-2087), both on Telegraph Avenue, and *Black Oak Books* on Shattuck Avenue (phone: 510-486-0698).

Here's a window shopper's view of the classic and the unusual:

UNION SQUARE

Dorothy Weiss Gallery Ceramic sculptures are the stock in trade at this upscale gallery two blocks east of Union Square. 256 Sutter St. (phone: 397-3611).

Giants Dugout Store Paraphernalia for followers of the orange and black and other sports teams; ticket sales, too. 170 Grant Ave. (phone: 982-9400).

Gump's Famous for its jade, art, jewelry, crystal, china, sculpture, furniture, antiques, stationery, and food. 250 Post St. (phone: 982-1616).

Jean-Marc Big, bold designs and colors in womenswear. 262 Sutter St. (phone: 362-1121).

Jessica McClintock Original beaded, lacy fashions for women and girls. 353 Sutter St. (phone: 397-0987).

Obiko One-of-a-kind women's clothing with an artistic bent by contemporary designers. 794 Sutter St. (phone: 775-2882).

La Parisienne Fine jewelry designed and made in Paris, as well as genuine French lithographs, all well priced. 460 Post St. (phone: 788-2255).

Shreve & Co. One of San Francisco's oldest purveyors of the finest silver, crystal, and jewelry. 200 Post St. (phone: 421-2600).

Sidney Mobell Anything and everything that can possibly be studded with jewels, including yo-yos, Frisbees, and fax machines. 950 Mason St. (in the *Fairmont* hotel; phone: 986-4747 or 800-442-7999)

Smile Truly "tongue-in-chic": arts and crafts with a sense of humor. 500 Sutter St. (phone: 986-4380).

Wilkes Bashford High-priced men's and women's clothing. 375 Sutter St. (phone: 986-4380).

HAYES STREET

Antonio Conti Handmade, one-of-a-kind furniture from Bay Area craftspeople. 416 Hayes St. (phone: 864-8307).

Country Java Teak furniture, including pieces that the owner, Terry Starke, shipped from his own home in Java. 572 Hayes St. (phone: 552-2767).

Evelyn's The best collection of Chinese antiques in the city. Head back to the warehouse to see its floor-to-ceiling collection. 381 Hayes St. (phone: 255-1815).

F. Dorian, Inc. Hand-crafted collectibles of many cultures including Mexican, African, and Asian. 388 Hayes St. (phone: 861-3191).

Richard Hilkert Books Books on art, music, design, and architecture. 3 Hayes St. (phone: 863-3339).

Victorian Interiors Everything necessary from decorative wall moldings to brass bath fixtures to spiff up (or create) your Victorian-era dream home. 575 Hayes St. (phone: 431-7191).

Zonal Metal and other materials are fashioned into unique sculptures and other artworks. 568 Hayes St. (phone: 255-9307).

MID-MARKET

Bell'occhio A unique and whimsical collection of dried flowers, antique and hand-dyed ribbons, unusual soaps, sachets, and eccentric little boxes. 8 Brady St. (phone: 864-4048).

Decorum Art Deco furnishings. 1632 Market St. (phone: 864-3326).

Red Desert A wide range of cacti and succulent plants, which can be shipped throughout the country, and other finds from the desert. 1632 Market St. (phone: 552-2800).

20th Century Furniture American furniture, such as armchairs and highboys, from 1930 to 1960. 1612 Market St. (phone: 626-0542).

UNION STREET

Bauer Antiques Mostly French treasures. 1878 Union St. (phone: 921-7656).

Carnevale An eclectic assortment of dresses and hats by American designers. 2206 Union St. (phone: 931-0669).

Coco's Romantic-looking satin and lace women's clothing. 2254 Union St. (phone: 346-9986).

Dolls and Bears of Charlton Court Antique and collectors' one-of-a-kind dolls and teddy bears. 1957 Union St. (phone: 775-3740).

John Wheatman & Assoc. English- and Japanese-style antique and contemporary furniture. 1933 Union St. (phone: 346-8300).

Oggetti Marbleized Florentine papers sold by the sheet, or used on picture frames, or to cover treasure boxes and photo albums. Other gift items, too. 1846 Union St. (phone: 346-0631).

Paris 1925 Antique watches and Art Deco jewelry. 1954 Union St., Second Floor (phone: 567-1925).

Sy Aal High-style men's fashions from a woman's point of view. 1864 Union St. (phone: 929-1864).

Three Bags Full Fabulous sweaters hand-knit with luxurious yarns. 2181 Union St. (phone: 567-5753).

Uko Japanese fashions for men, women, and children. 2070 Union St. (phone: 563-0330).

Yankee Doodle Dandy Cute country crafts and handmade quilts. 1974 Union St. (phone: 346-0346).

Zuni Pueblo A tribe-owned store featuring contemporary Zuni arts. 1749 Union St. (phone: 567-0941).

FILLMORE STREET

Cedanna Arts and crafts by Northern California artists, as well as pottery, a selection of fine foods, and interesting housewares. 1925 Fillmore St. (phone: 474-7152).

Zoe Far-out, expensive women's clothes. 2400 Fillmore St. (phone: 929-0441).

OUTER SACRAMENTO STREET

Dandelion A browser's paradise filled with books, boxes, glassware, gardening tools, and a little bit of everything else. Perhaps the city's best gift shop. 2877 California St. at Broderick St. (phone: 563-3100).

Forrest Jones Everything you might need for the well-accessorized kitchen and dining table. 3274 Sacramento St. (phone 567-2483).

Jasper Byron French and English antiques, reproductions, and accessories in the classic style. 3364 Sacramento St. (phone: 563-8122).

The Master's Mark Custom-designed, custom-built furniture adapted from traditional Asian styles. 3228 Sacramento St. (phone: 885-6700).

SantaFe Handwoven Mexican blankets and color-faded furniture in the Southwestern style. 3571 Sacramento St. (phone: 346-0180).

Sue Fisher King Elegant linen and accessories for bed and table. 3067 Sacramento St. (phone: 922-7276).

V. Breier Contemporary and traditional crafts, including neon sculpture and colorful ceramics, imaginative furniture, and baskets made of handmade papers, leaves, pine cones, and seed pods. 3091 Sacramento St. (phone: 929-7173).

Walker McIntyre-Antiques Exquisite 18th- and 19th-century English furnishings along with Chinese and Japanese accessories. 3419 Sacramento St. (phone: 563-8024).

SOUTH OF MARKET STREET (SOMA)

Baker Hamilton Square A dozen shops selling antiques, art, and furnishings share space in a historic warehouse. Near the train station at 7th and Townsend Sts. (phone: 861-3500).

Basic Brown Bears At this teddy bear lair you can watch the cuddly creatures being made, then pick out one who's ready to travel. 444 De Haro St. (phone: 626-0781).

Discount Bridal Brides-to-be travel cross-country for wedding dresses at sensational savings. 300 Brannon St. (phone: 495-7922).

LIMN Company Avant-garde art and furniture. 290 Townsend St. (phone: 543-5466).

Six Sixty Center Twenty discount outlets under one roof selling everything from sweaters and jeans to jewelry and cosmetics. 660 Third St. (phone: 227-0464).

SPORTS AND FITNESS

Any successful local professional team plays to a full house, especially the *Giants* (their fans are awarded an icicle-draped "Croix de Candlestick" pin for surviving an extra-inning night game), at windy *Candlestick Park*. However, mild year-round weather and varied terrain lures bikers, boaters, and joggers away from arenas, stadiums, and television sets.

BASEBALL The San Francisco *Giants* play from April to October in *Candlestick Park* (Gilman Ave., on the southern edge of the city east of US 101; phone: 467-8000). The Oakland *A's* play at the *Oakland Coliseum* (7000 Coliseum Way; phone: 510-638-4900).

BASKETBALL The NBA's *Golden State Warriors* play from November to April at the *Oakland Coliseum Arena* (phone: 510-638-6300 for information; 510-762-*BASS* for tickets).

BICYCLING A general tour of San Francisco on a bicycle is not the safest way to see the sights, but there are some fine routes that offer grand views with less risk. Mountain bikes can be rented from *Magic Skates and Bikes* at *Golden Gate Park* (3038 Fulton St. at Sixth Ave.; phone: 668-1117). Pedaling along the city's scenic shoreline is breathtaking, even if you don't attempt the hills. On Sundays, roads through the middle of *Golden Gate Park* are off limits to automobiles, which provides a respite from the treachery of riding side by side with cars. Another favorite route is past the Presidio and over the *Golden Gate Bridge*. More ambitious riders head to Sausalito or through the (very hilly) Marin Headlands to the beaches of Marin County. Bike route maps are available at most bicycle shops.

FISHING There is fine salmon fishing in the sea beyond the bay. The season spans mid-February to mid-October; afternoon trips are available June through October. Charter boats leave daily early in the morning and return in the afternoon. For information contact *New Easy Rider Sport Fishing* (phone: 285-2000). You also can cast off San Francisco's municipal pier at *Aquatic Park*, anytime. No license required.

FITNESS CENTERS *Fitness Break* (30 Hotaling Pl. near Washington and Montgomery Sts.; phone: 788-1681) offers weekday workouts; showers and lockers available. The *YMCA* (169 Steuart St.; phone: 957-9622) has a pool, sauna, and weight room (including Nautilus, Cybex, and cardiovascular exercise equipment), along with racquetball and handball courts and aerobics classes.

FOOTBALL The San Francisco *49ers* play from August to December (and sometimes even in January) at *Candlestick Park* (Gilman Ave., on the southern edge of the city east of US 101; 468-2249).

GOLF There are fine public courses at *Lincoln Park* (34th Ave. and Clement St.; phone: 221-9911) and *Harding Park* (Skyline Blvd. and Harding Rd.; phone: 664-4690).

HOCKEY The *NHL*'s San Jose *Sharks* play at the 18,000-seat *Downtown Arena*, on The Alameda near Guadalupe Pkwy. (phone: 800-BE-SHARK for ticket information).

HORSE RACING *Bay Meadows* is the place, in San Mateo (phone: 574-7223). The racing season begins in August and runs into January. In the East Bay *Golden Gate Fields* features thoroughbred racing from late February through late June (phone: 510-559-7300).

HORSEBACK RIDING Guided trail rides and lessons are available at *Golden Gate Stables* at *Golden Gate Park* (John F. Kennedy Dr. at 36th Ave.; phone: 668-7360). Twelve miles of bridle paths wind through the park. Reservations necessary.

JOGGING Run from the *Ferry Building* along *The Embarcadero* to *Fort Point* beneath the *Golden Gate Bridge* (6 miles one way); jog back and forth across the *Golden Gate Bridge* (1½ miles each way) and enjoy the fore and aft views, as well as the one directly below. From Market Street via the *Civic Center* the 21 Hayes bus goes to *Golden Gate Park,* where there are numerous dirt and concrete trails, not to mention plenty of other joggers. (Do not run alone in secluded areas of the park.)

SKATING Roller-skating is very popular in San Francisco, especially in *Golden Gate Park* on Sundays, when traffic is detoured off the park's main roads. You can rent skates from *Magic Skates* (3038 Fulton St. at 6th Ave.; phone: 668-1117) right across from the park.

SWIMMING Though much of San Francisco's waters are too rough and cold for swimming, Phelan Beach (at Sea Cliff Ave. and El Camino del Mar) is good when the weather permits and the current is safe. The *Sheehan* hotel pool and work-out area (620 Sutter St.; phone: 775-6500) is open to the public daily.

TENNIS The *San Francisco Recreation and Parks Department* (phone: 666-7200) maintains more than a hundred tennis courts around the city. Free to the public, they are available on a first-come, first-served basis. *Golden Gate Park* has 21 courts, which can be reserved in advance on weekends for a nominal fee. *Golden Gate Park* at *McLaren Lodge* (Fell and Stanyan Sts.; phone: 753-7101).

YACHT RACING The *Yacht Racing Association* holds most of its races between April and mid-October, but mid-winter regattas also are held. Races start and end off the Marina Green and turn at Blossom Rock Buoy beyond Pier 39 (phone: 772-9500 for information).

THEATER

San Francisco abounds in great theater; among its treasures is one of the best repertory groups in the country.

CENTER STAGE

American Conservatory Theatre (ACT) A bit of Shakespeare, some Chekhov, some Shaw, works by Lanford Wilson, Sam Shepard, and Terence Rattigan—these, as well as world premieres by a slew of others, have been performed by this company, which started out in Pittsburgh and moved to the West Coast in the mid-1960s. The annual year-end production of *A Christmas Carol* is now a Bay Area tradition. Although a 1989 earthquake severely damaged the *Geary,* ACT's home theater, the company continues to produce a full season of works at various theaters throughout the city. 450 Geary St. (phone: 749-2200).

In addition, the *Curran Theater* is a venue for musicals and often stages traveling Broadway productions (445 Geary St.; phone: 474-3800). The *Orpheum Theater* (1192 Market St.; phone: 474-3800) and the *Golden Gate Theater* (Golden Gate and Taylor Sts.; phone: 474-3800) also feature Broadway shows. At *Club Fugazi,* an old North Beach landmark, the camp cult classic *Beach Blanket Babylon* has been running for 18 years (678 Green St.; phone: 421-4222). If you have an urge to see the world through celluloid, visit the *Castro*, a 1922 landmark theater—complete with an organist—that shows classic films (Castro St. near Market St.; phone: 621-6120). Or try the *Paramount,* which holds four Friday night classic film series, including newsreels, cartoons, vintage trailers, and spin-the-wheel door prizes. The theater itself is a prize; tours are offered on the first and third Saturdays of the month, at 10 AM. Meticulously maintained, this Art Deco building is in the *National Register of Historic Places* (2025 Broadway near the 19th St. *BART* station in Oakland; phone: 510-465-6400). The *San Francisco Ballet,* the country's oldest company and among its finest, moves into the *War Memorial Opera House* in the *Civic Center* with its *Nutcracker* production in December, followed by a repertory season from January through May (phone: 703-9400).

MUSIC

The *San Francisco Opera Association* is a world class opera company. It performs at the *War Memorial Opera House* (*Civic Center,* Van Ness Ave. and Grove St.; phone: 864-3330) from September to early December; the summer season is May and early June. Since tickets are difficult to get, it's best to reserve in advance (*War Memorial Opera House* Box Office, San Francisco, CA 94102). The *San Francisco Symphony* season runs from September through May at *Louise M. Davies Symphony Hall* in the *Civic Center* (phone: 431-5400), but the orchestra can be heard at other times, too, such as during its June *Beethoven Festival* or its July *Pops Concerts* in the *Civic Auditorium.* The *Midsummer Music Festival* is a free Sunday series of symphony, opera, jazz, and ethnic programs from mid-June to mid-August at *Sigmund Stern Grove* (19th Ave. and Sloat Blvd.; phone: 252-6252).

Tickets for most music, dance, and theater events can be obtained through *BASS* ticket centers (phone: 510-762-*BASS*). In addition, half-price as well as full-price tickets to many events can be bought (cash or traveler's checks only) on the day of performance at the *TIX* booth on the Stockton Street side of Union Square, Tuesdays through Saturdays from 11 AM to 7:30 PM (phone: 433-7827; you must go to the booth for information on half-price tickets).

NIGHTCLUBS AND NIGHTLIFE

San Francisco is alive at night and can keep you going whether you're inclined toward jazz, pop, or alternative rock. The nightlife glitters all around the city. Current favorites: the *Great American Music Hall* (859 O'Farrell St.; phone: 885-0750), for major jazz and folk artists, and *Lascaux* (248 Sutter St.; phone: 391-1555), for jazz. For comedy: *Cobb's Comedy Club* (2801 Leavenworth St., in *The Cannery;* phone: 928-4320) and *Punch Line* (444 Battery St.; phone: 397-7573). For cabaret try the *Plush Room* (940 Sutter St.; phone: 885-2800). For a view of San Francisco at night try the *Top of the Mark* in the *Mark Hopkins Inter-Continental* hotel; *Oz,* a nightclub atop the *Westin St. Francis* hotel (see *Checking In* for both); or *Starlite Roof* in the *Sir Francis Drake* hotel (Powell St. at Sutter St.; phone: 392-7755). Dance to the Brazilian beat at *Bahia*

Tropical (1600 Market St. at Franklin St.; phone: 861-8657) or to rhythm and blues at *Harry Denton's* (161 Steuart St.; phone: 882-1333). The younger crowd heads to SoMa—the district south of Market Street. On Fridays the nightclub at 1015 Folsom Street (phone: 431-1200) is dubbed *Martini,* featuring diverse music and hetero clubgoers; Saturday nights its name changes to *Product,* which caters to a lively gay crowd. On lower Haight *Nickies* (460 Haight St.; phone: 621-6508) is popular—one night the music is hip-hop, the next it's salsa. The *Elbo Room* (647 Valencia St.; phone: 552-7788) has a hip crowd, with live music upstairs. *Johnny Love's* (1500 Broadway at Polk; phone 931-6053) appeals to a wide range of tastes with offerings of R&B, jazz, American rock, world beat, and reggae. In addition, the historic *Fillmore* (1805 Geary St., near Japantown; phone: 346-6000 for recorded information) reopened last year as a restaurant, bar, and performance hall. Tickets to performances can be purchased at *BASS* outlets (phone: 510-762-BASS).

Best in Town

CHECKING IN

President Taft called San Francisco "the town that knows how," and though he probably wasn't talking about hotels, his statement nonetheless applies. A pleasant embarrassment of riches confronts visitors, from luxurious mammoths to ritzy mid-size establishments to dozens of intimate "boutique" hotels, which mimic European small hotels in character. Expect to pay more than $200 per night for a double room in the very expensive bracket; $140 to $200, expensive; $80 to $140, moderate; and under $80, inexpensive. For bed and breakfast lodgings contact *American Family Inn/Bed & Breakfast San Francisco* (PO Box 420009, San Francisco, CA 94142; phone: 931-3083); or *Bed & Breakfast International* (PO Box 282910, San Francisco, CA 94128-2910; phone: 696-1690 or 800-272-4500; fax: 696-1699) for special accommodations (in a houseboat, aboard a yacht, or even in a Victorian mansion). For daily, weekly, or monthly rentals of condominiums, townhouses, apartments, and homes, contact *American Property Exchange* (170 Page St., San Francisco, CA 94102; phone: 863-8484). Always ask about special packages and discounts. All telephone numbers are in the 415 area code unless otherwise indicated.

VERY EXPENSIVE

ANA San Francisco This elegant 36-floor, 677-room establishment (formerly the *Meridien*) is the epitome of commercial luxury on the inside (apparently nothing can be done about the concrete box it comes in). Located in a still-being-developed South of Market area, just a block from the *Moscone Convention Center,* all the rooms have floor-to-ceiling windows with city views. It features a fine restaurant, *Café Fifty-Three,* which serves classic California, Italian, and Japanese dishes; calories can be burned off in the hotel's health club. Seventeen meeting rooms, a concierge desk, secretarial services, A/V equipment, photocopiers, computers, and express checkout are among the business amenities. 50 Third St. (phone: 974-6400 or 800-262-4683; fax: 543-8268).

Campton Place Kempinski Half a block north of Union Square, this small property in the European tradition has 126 sumptuously decorated (but smallish) rooms and suites fitted with armoires, writing desks, cable TV, marble and brass baths, and even padded coat hangers. The service is impeccable. The location—close to shopping, the financial district, and Chinatown—can't be beat. There's a roof garden for sunning and small receptions, and two conference rooms. On the lobby level, wonderfully innovative and well-prepared American dishes are served at breakfast, lunch, and dinner in the *Campton Place* restaurant (see *Eating Out*); cocktails and coffee are available in the adjacent bar. Other amenities include a concierge, a valet, 24-hour room service, as well as secretarial services, A/V equipment, photocopiers, computers, and express checkout. 340 Stockton St. (phone: 781-5555; 800-235-4300 in California; 800-647-4000 elsewhere in the US; fax: 955-8536).

Donatello One block west of Union Square, this elegant hotel offers 94 spacious rooms (including nine suites), a serene atmosphere, and special touches such as plants, terry cloth robes, valet parking, and a concierge. On the mezzanine level is a restaurant—also called *Donatello*—which serves northern Italian fare. Room service may be ordered until midnight. There are two meeting rooms and photocopiers; secretarial services and A/V equipment can be arranged. 501 Post St. (phone: 441-7100 or 800-227-3184; fax: 885-8842).

Fairmont Just on the other side of the cable car tracks, but on Nob Hill neither side is the wrong one. Adjoining the distinctive old-fashioned main building is a modern tower topped by the *Crown Room*, which serves lunch, dinner, and Sunday brunch. Take the glass-sided elevator for a great view. For other treats try the *Squire* restaurant for continental dishes and the *Tonga Room* for Polynesian fare and dancing. There are 596 rooms and suites. Amenities include around-the-clock room service, a concierge, secretarial services, A/V equipment, photocopiers, and computers. Express checkout. California and Mason Sts. (phone: 772-5000 or 800-527-4727; fax: 781-3929).

Four Seasons Clift The warmth of rich wood paneling is matched by the warm, personalized service of the staff at this refined, 329-room property. Some of its employees have been on staff long enough to serve return guests for decades. Attention to detail can be seen in every corner—each room is individually decorated, and even at 2 AM room service can deliver a perfect cheeseburger in 20 minutes. The antiques-filled lobby harkens to another, more gracious time, and a Viennese dessert buffet is served in the *French Room* in the late evening until midnight. Built from a single giant sequoia, the *Redwood Room* has an altogether different ambience; its selection of cognacs and ports is one of the city's best. Business amenities include secretarial services as well as computer, cellular phone, and beeper rentals; additionally, all rooms have outlets for modems. Meanwhile, the hotel's "Very Important Kids" program pampers children and teens. Playtime offerings include computer and board games, books, toys, and a VCR and tape library. Located next door to the *Curran Theatre*, the hotel offers theatergoer packages. 495 Geary St. (phone: 775-4700 or 800-332-3442; fax: 441-4621).

Huntington The gold and burgundy antiques-filled lobby exudes elegance in this former apartment building. A sleek, chauffeured Lincoln Town Car provides complimentary transportation within downtown. Each of its 140 spacious rooms is distinctively decorated and comfortable, and many have outstanding views. The *Big Four* restaurant (the name refers to the four Gold Rush millionaires) looks like a turn-of-the-century men's club and serves fish, chops, and steaks. Deliveries from room service arrive until midnight. There are four meeting rooms; and such business amenities as a concierge desk, secretarial services, A/V equipment, photocopiers, computers, and express checkout are available. 1075 California St. (phone: 474-5400; 800-652-1539 inside California; 800-227-4683 outside California; fax: 474-6227).

Hyatt Regency Inside this futuristically designed structure is a 17-story atrium lobby with all the activity of a three-ring circus, including a classical guitarist most afternoons and a jazz trio nightly. Glass elevators whisk you up to the top, where a revolving restaurant looks out on San Francisco. The 803 rooms are attractive and modern; nonsmoking floors are available. Business amenities include convention facilities, secretarial services, photocopiers, A/V equipment, computers, and express checkout. Twenty-four-hour room service and a concierge desk complete the picture. 5 *Embarcadero Center* (phone: 788-1234; 800-233-1234 outside California; fax: 398-2567).

Mandarin Oriental This luxurious hostelry occupies the top 11 floors of the 48-story *First Interstate Center* towers in the heart of the financial district, affording each of the 158 rooms unobstructed views of the city and portions of the bay. Glass "sky bridges" connect the two towers. The rooms are graced with Oriental-motif art and marble bathrooms, each one complete with a choice of terry cloth and lightweight kimono robes, slippers, a digital scale, and a hair dryer. Larger rooms include screened sitting areas and expansive windows. (All offer "On Command Video," a choice of 80 children's and adults' films for a fee). The marble-walled lobby, the reception area, and the Business Center are all on the ground level. An outstanding restaurant, *Silks,* is on the second floor. Room service is on call 24 hours a day. There are three meeting rooms, a concierge desk, secretarial services, A/V equipment, photocopiers, computers, and express checkout. There also are portable fax machines and two phone lines in all the guestrooms. 222 Sansome St. (phone: 885-0999 or 800-622-0404; fax: 433-0289).

Mark Hopkins Inter-Continental At the height of elegance, crowning Nob Hill, this hotel has a guest list that has included everyone from Haile Selassie to Frank Sinatra. The 391 suites and rooms feature either classical or contemporary decor, commodious baths and closets, and possibly a grand piano (the Presidential Suite has one). The tower rooms have especially fine views, and the glass-walled *Top of the Mark* lounge offers the best 360° panorama of the city. The *Nob Hill* restaurant (open daily) serves noteworthy California and international fare, with outstanding lamb and duck dishes and wines from 34 states. Twenty-four-hour room service is available. There are 14 meeting rooms, as well as a concierge desk, secretarial services, photocopiers, computers, A/V equipment, and express checkout. 1 Nob Hill (phone: 392-3434 or 800-327-0200; fax: 421-3302).

Pan Pacific Glowing with rosy marble, brass, chrome, and glass, this 330-room property combines an American look with Asian-style service. Three valets per floor are on call to unpack, press clothes, polish shoes, draw baths, and prop matchsticks against room doors (a toppled match signals that the guests may be out and their rooms should be tidied up). Exercise machines for in-room use are complimentary, and computers with software can be rented. The menu at the elegant *Pacific Grill* emphasizes the California influence. From 7 AM to 11 PM, Rolls-Royces shuttle guests free of charge to the financial district or to dinner and the theater, and limousines can be rented for airport trips. Twenty-four-hour room service, a concierge, secretarial services, A/V equipment, photocopiers, and express checkout are also available. 500 Post St. (phone: 771-8600 or 800-533-6465; fax: 398-0267).

Prescott A long Oriental carpet on an Italian marble floor leads guests into the reception area of this 167-room establishment, one block from Union Square. Though in the heart of the city, the lobby has the ambience of a gracious Southwestern living room, with its country hearth fireplace and displays of Native American artifacts. The *Postrio* restaurant is hot, with the clientele clamoring for chef Wolfgang Puck's interpretations of classic San Francisco fare (see *Eating Out*). Other amenities include complimentary wine and cheese in the lobby, complimentary limousine service to the financial district on weekday mornings, plus cable TV and stocked refrigerators in the rooms. Further advantages are room service until midnight, two meeting rooms, a concierge desk, secretarial services, A/V equipment, photocopiers, computers, and express checkout. 545 Post St. (phone: 563-0303 or 800-283-7322; fax: 563-6831).

Ritz-Carlton Originally built in 1909 as the home of the Metropolitan Life Insurance Company, this historic landmark, with its white Greek columns and Ionic architecture, looks like the *United States Treasury*. And it is indeed a treasure; the entire interior has been restored to create 336 guestrooms, a full fitness center with an indoor pool, two restaurants and two lounges, and over 22,000 square feet of meeting space, including an outdoor courtyard. The decor is traditional with 18th- and 19th-century paintings and other artwork throughout. Tea here is a must. Room service is on call 24 hours. Other amenities include a concierge desk, secretarial services, A/V equipment, photocopiers, and computers. There's also express checkout. California and Stockton Sts. (phone: 296-7465 or 800-241-3333; fax: 291-0288).

Sheraton Palace A San Francisco landmark since 1875 and one of America's first grand hotels, with 550 rooms, it has been restored and renovated. The *Garden Court,* a huge, elegant room with a domed, leaded glass ceiling, crystal chandeliers, marble columns and floors, serves all meals, plus afternoon tea. Guestrooms are distinguished by antique furnishings and fixtures, along with such modern conveniences as robes, hair dryers, hookups for personal computers, and fax machines. The spa features an indoor pool, whirlpool bath, and sauna. Nonsmoking floors and handicapped-accessible rooms are available. There are 45,000 square feet of meeting space, 24-hour room service, a concierge, secretarial services, A/V equipment, photocopiers, computers, and express checkout. 2 New Montgomery St., adjacent to the financial district (phone: 392-8600 or 800-325-3535; fax: 543-06711).

Sherman House Once the private mansion of music store owner Leander Sherman, this 14-room inn is the only San Francisco member of the prestigious international Relais & Châteaux group. Interior designer Billy Gaylord created the decor, featuring French Second Empire and Biedermeier design elements. Guestrooms are furnished with hand-woven Persian carpets, fireplaces, feather beds, and down comforters. Some suites have terraces that afford a view of the *Golden Gate Bridge*. Built in 1876, in the Victorian Italianate style, it has a three-story music room where Sherman used to entertain his famous guests (among them, Lillian Russell and Enrico Caruso). French-inspired food is served in the simply named *Dining Room;* room service is available around the clock. 2160 Green St. (phone: 563-3600 or 800-424-5777; fax: 563-1882).

Westin St. Francis A San Francisco landmark since 1904, this hotel has entertained royalty, presidents, and international celebrities with its Old World charm. The 1,200-room establishment still keeps to its traditional theme of red velvet, glimmering crystal, and polished rosewood. At the top of the 32-story tower are *Victor's* restaurant, featuring nouvelle cuisine, and the chic *Oz* disco; both offer lovely panoramic views of the city. Back in the days when society ladies protested that handling coins soiled their white gloves, the hotel provided a coin-washing service for guests. This tradition continues on; when you receive change anywhere in the hotel, the coins are so shiny that they seem freshly minted. A fitness center is open daily, room service is available 24 hours a day, and among the services geared to businesspeople are convention facilities, cellular telephone rental, secretarial assistance, A/V equipment, photocopiers, and computers. There's also a concierge desk and express checkout. Union Sq. (phone: 397-7000 or 800-228-3000; fax: 774-0124).

EXPENSIVE

Archbishop's Mansion Inn This stately structure built in 1904 once served as the home of San Francisco's Archbishop Riordan. Now a romantic bed and breakfast establishment, each of its 15 rooms (all named for operas) have fireplaces and private baths. Antiques and Oriental carpets grace the rooms; fine embroidered linen dresses the beds. Breakfast is delivered to your door each morning, and complimentary wine is served in the parlor every evening. There are two meeting rooms available for business needs, as well as a concierge desk, secretarial services, and photocopiers. A/V equipment can be arranged. 1000 Fulton St. (phone: 563-7872 or 800-543-5820; fax: 885-3193).

Harbor Court Parallel to the waterfront, this landmark property, built right after the 1906 earthquake, offers Old World charm; 30 of the 131 rooms have bay views (enhanced by the demolition of the Embarcadero Freeway after the 1989 earthquake). The vaulted ceilings and architectural details have been retained throughout the large, club-style lobby and the small, subtly colored guestrooms. Amenities include limousine service to the financial district each morning, coffee, tea, and apples served throughout the day, and complimentary wine served each evening from 5 to 7 PM. All rooms have their own refrigerator. Room service is available for dinner. The business center offers photocopying, secretarial, and fax services; conference space can be arranged. 165 Steuart St. (phone: 882-1300 or 800-346-0555).

Miyako This 218-room establishment in Japantown is the place for a plunge into the Orient—and a Japanese bath—especially during the *Cherry Blossom Festival*. The decor is Japanese, but both Japanese- and Western-style suites with saunas are available. The standout fare at the award-winning *Elka* restaurant is seafood cooked the French way but with Asian seasonings. Among the amenities here are 14 meeting rooms, A/V equipment, and secretarial services. 1625 Post St. (phone: 922-3200 or 800-533-4567; fax: 921-0417).

Petite Auberge Near Union Square but closer to the heart of France, this less pricey Gallic sister of the *White Swan Inn* (see below), complete with an antique carousel horse in the foyer, manages to be both cozy and elegant. A sweeping staircase (and a small elevator for the less athletic) leads to 26 rooms (many with fireplaces) on five floors, furnished in country French style. Full concierge service, a buffet breakfast, afternoon tea, and valet parking are provided. Business amenities include A/V equipment and photocopiers. Reserve a month or more in advance. 863 Bush St. (phone: 928-6000; fax: 775-5717).

Stouffer-Stanford Court Set back from the street, the entryway of this 402-room hostelry includes a Beaux Arts fountain and Tiffany-style glass dome. Built on the site of 19th-century Governor Leland Stanford's mansion, this property is now a link in the Stouffer hotel chain. A stay here can include coffee and the newspaper with your wake-up call, afternoon tea and/or wine in the lobby bar, dinner in the hotel's *Fournou's Oven*—and a Rolls-Royce Phantom VI limousine to whisk you off to the theater. No details are overlooked: Breads are baked fresh, on the premises, each morning; soaps are hand-milled. Elizabeth Taylor makes her San Francisco home-away-from-home in the Presidential Suite, as does Mary Tyler Moore. The hotel is conveniently located, with two cable car lines crossing just steps from the main entrance. 905 California St. (phone: 989-3500 or 800-227-4736; fax: 391-0513).

White Swan Inn Converted from an old hotel, this 26-room English-style inn offers a personal welcome, a lounge and library with fireplaces, plus card rooms and a garden. Rooms are spacious and bright, and the amenities luxurious. Full buffet breakfast and afternoon tea, which also includes wine, sherry, and hors d'oeuvres, are complimentary. Valet parking and a meeting room and photocopiers are available. 845 Bush St. (phone: 775-1755; fax: 775-5717).

MODERATE

Andrews This renovated 1905 Victorian building has retained some original brass fixtures and beveled-glass windows, as well as a sense of old-fashioned hospitality, in its 48 rooms. Continental breakfast is included.

Fino, located off the lobby, serves Italian favorites at dinner. The front desk personnel double as concierges. 624 Post St. (phone: 563-6877 or 800-926-3739; fax: 923-6919).

Diva Italianate meets high-tech on seven floors with 108 stunning guestrooms, all furnished with chrome, glass, and brightly lacquered furniture and fixtures. Traditional down comforters and pillows soften the effect. Complimentary California breakfast (fresh fruit and multigrain breads, muffins, and cereals along with coffee). Each room is equipped with a VCR, and there is an extensive library of classic and current videos. The *California Pizza Kitchen* serves "designer" pizza. Perhaps best of all is the location: right near the theaters and just a couple of blocks from Union Square. Complimentary limousine service runs to the financial district on weekdays. There's a concierge desk, a fitness center, one meeting room, and a business center providing secretarial services, photocopiers, A/V equipment, computers, and express checkout. 440 Geary St. (phone: 885-0200 or 800-553-1900; fax: 346-6613).

Inn at the Opera This small, European-style, 48-room hostelry affords easy access to the culturally rich *Civic Center* area, which has improved since the demolition of the nearby elevated freeway. International luminaries like Mikhail Baryshnikov and Luciano Pavarotti stay here, sleeping in rooms with canopy beds and fresh-cut flowers. Pre- and post-performance dinners and desserts are served in the fireplace-cozy *Act IV* restaurant. Promotional packages to arts performances are sometimes available. Small-scale but luxurious rooms have kitchenettes with microwaves and mini-bars. There's also a concierge on duty 24 hours a day, and free limousine service weekdays to downtown. 333 Fulton St. (phone: 863-8400; 800-423-9610 in California; 800-325-2708 elsewhere in the US; fax: 861-0821).

The Inn at Union Square Elegant, European-style, and half a block from Union Square, this hotel is for visitors looking for a home away from home. Each of the 30 rooms and suites boasts elegant Georgian furniture—some made in Bath, England—that suggests Thomas Jefferson's *Monticello.* The furniture is set off by warm, colorful fabrics. The lobby and fireplace on each floor provide an ideal setting to enjoy the morning-to-evening parade of complimentary services: continental breakfast, afternoon tea, wine and hors d'oeuvres. No smoking anywhere in the hotel. Limited business services only: A hotel fax and photocopier are available for guests' use. 440 Post St. (phone: 397-3510 or 800-288-4346; fax: 989-0529).

Orchard Built in 1907, this restored property near Union Square has an elegant, European look: custom-made Italian rosewood furniture in 96 attractive rooms overlooking a garden. The *Sutter Garden* restaurant serves delicious and reasonably priced breakfast and lunch, with unusually good coffee. A concierge desk, secretarial services, photocopiers, and computer hookups in rooms are all available. 562 Sutter St. (phone: 433-4434 or 800-433-4434; fax: 433-3695).

Richelieu In downtown San Francisco, where old hotels never die, this one has been lovingly restored to the 1906 just-post-earthquake style of its birth. The lobby is rich with antique carpets, settees (the hotel cat may be lounging on its favorite one), mirrors, inverted dome chandeliers, and Tiffany-style stained glass. A piano bar and a small exercise gym are on the premises, and the hotel offers complimentary afternoon tea, though there's no restaurant. Chauffeured limousine service is also complimentary. Other amenities include a concierge desk and photocopiers. 1050 Van Ness (phone: 673-4711 or 800-227-3608; fax: 673-9362).

Triton Definitely hip, this 140-room, pastel-decorated establishment in the heart of the gallery district showcases local San Francisco artists. Sophisticated design shows up everywhere—from the hand-painted wall murals to the custom-designed furniture to the staff uniforms. Amenities include CD players and a music library for guests staying in the hotel's moderate-sized ("junior") suites, limousine service to the SoMa district, complimentary wine each evening, bars that serve up plenty of free snacks, and room service. The hotel has a small conference room; computers, fax machines, photocopiers, and secretarial services are available. 342 Grant Ave. (phone: 394-0500 or 800-433-6611; fax: 394-0555).

Victorian Inn on the Park Known as the *Clunie House,* it was built in 1897 in honor of Queen Victoria's *Diamond Jubilee* and now has guests reserving up to a month in advance for one of its 12 bedrooms. Inlaid oak floors, mahogany woodwork, charming period pieces, a handsome oak-paneled dining room (the complimentary continental breakfast features breads baked on the premises), a lavish parlor (complimentary afternoon wine), a concierge desk, fax machines, off-street parking, and express checkout are only some of the drawing cards of this registered historic landmark. Across from *Panhandle Park* near *Golden Gate Park* at 301 Lyon St. (phone: 931-1830 or 800-435-1967; fax: 931-1830).

Vintage Court Everything is up-to-date in this 106-room boutique property, established in 1913. (A glass etching of the original building is in the mauve lobby with a cheerful fireplace.) A night's lodging for two costs less than dinner next door at the famed *Masa's* French restaurant (see *Eating Out*); note, however, that the hotel's complimentary continental breakfast is served at *Masa's.* Every afternoon in the lobby, the hotel serves complimentary California wine; weekday limousine service twice a morning to the financial district is also free. Outside rooms (named for Napa Valley wineries) have bay-window seats, padded headboards, and bedspreads in floral or wine-grape motifs. The hotel's meeting room seats 15; A/V equipment and photocopiers are available. 650 Bush St. (phone: 392-4666 or 800-654-1100; fax: 433-4065).

Washington Square Inn Within walking distance of *Ghirardelli Square* and Chinatown, the turn-of-the-century apartment house–turned-hotel in North Beach has only 15 rooms (10 with private baths), each individually decorated. Three rooms face Washington Square and are more expensive. Complimentary breakfast and afternoon tea are served; there's also a concierge desk. No smoking is permitted in the hotel. 1660 Stockton St. (phone: 981-4220 or 800-388-0220; fax: 397-7242).

INEXPENSIVE

Beresford Here is British charm at a reasonable price: old-fashioned service, a writing parlor off the Victorian lobby, flower boxes in the street windows, and 114 pleasant rooms. Even the lamppost in front has a blue-and-white Wedgwoodesque frieze. Meals served at the *White Horse* tavern here feature fresh vegetables from the hotel's garden. 635 Sutter St. (phone: 673-9900 or 800-533-6533; fax: 474-0449).

Carlton Just five blocks from Union Square, this 165-room property has all the charm of a large home. The hotel's café serves breakfast and dinner daily; complimentary wine is served each evening in the 1920s-style lobby; and room service may be ordered during meal hours. One meeting room is available; there are photocopiers and a concierge desk. 1075 Sutter St. (phone: 673-0242 or 800-227-4496; fax: 673-4904).

Cornell Everything but the name is French—atmosphere, furnishings, the manager's accent—in this lovingly spruced-up antique, with flower beds behind a picket fence, old reproductions of Cluny tapestries, a cage elevator, and rustic furniture in 55 rooms that have private bathrooms, phones, and cable TV. The *Restaurant Jeanne d'Arc*, filled with memorabilia honoring its namesake, serves dinner six days a week and complimentary breakfast. Ask about the special rate—$565 for a double for seven nights including breakfast and five dinners. A concierge desk and photocopiers are on call. Smoking is prohibited. 715 Bush St. (phone: 421-3154 or 800-232-9698; fax: 399-1442).

Dakota Two blocks from Union Square, this 1920 historic landmark hotel has 41 rooms. Geared for budget travelers, it has spacious claw-foot bathtubs but, otherwise, no frills. 606 Post St. (phone: 931-7475).

Golden Gate This is another renovated relic, owned and run by a very friendly, multilingual couple. Period photographs and the cage elevator hark back to the hotel's 1913 beginnings, but the small, comfortable rooms are fresh and bright, with flowered wallpaper and white wicker furniture or mahogany antiques. Of the 23 rooms, 14 have private baths, and nine share three baths in the halls. Continental breakfast and afternoon tea are served in a cheery lounge with a fireplace. There's a concierge, too. 775 Bush St. (phone: 392-3702 or 800-835-1118; fax: 392-6202).

EATING OUT

San Francisco has about 4,300 eating places, serving a wide variety of food, from haute cuisine to ethnic fare, and taking fine advantage of the wonderful seafood and fresh produce so readily available from the ocean and the surrounding valleys. Along with such longtime favorites as *Ernie's* and *Jack's*, San Franciscans welcome new restaurants that show up on the horizon at an astonishing rate. One notable trend is toward first-rate food in hotels, starting with *Campton Place* and extending to even newer establishments like *Postrio* at the *Prescott* hotel. At the other end of the spectrum are the neighborhood places that specialize in Chinese, Japanese, Vietnamese, Thai, or Mexican food at very affordable prices. Our restaurant selections range in price from $75 or more (sometimes much more) for dinner for two in the expensive category; to $45 to $75, moderate; to less than $45, inexpensive—excluding drinks, wine, and tip. Unless otherwise noted, all telephone numbers are in the 415 area code, and all restaurants are open for both lunch and dinner.

EXPENSIVE

Aqua In the financial district, this dramatic dining place—peach-colored walls, huge floral arrangements—features innovative seafood dishes such as ravioli stuffed with a creamy lobster salad, and medallions of *ahi* tuna. Valet parking. Closed Saturdays for lunch and Sundays. Reservations necessary. Major credit cards accepted. 252 California St. (phone: 956-9662).

Campton Place Although it's in the *Campton Place Kempinski* hotel, this is a legitimate magnet for diners in its own right. The relatively small room is decorated in soft shades of rose and gray, while the menu is an outstanding example of American dishes done to perfection—without excessive fuss or fanfare. Breakfast (arguably the best in the city), lunch, and dinner are served daily, and each is marvelous. Reservations at least a week in advance are necessary. Major credit cards accepted. 340 Stockton St. (phone: 781-5555).

Chez Panisse The oft-called "guru of California cookery," Alice Waters, opened this landmark restaurant in the early 1970s. Set in a house in Berkeley, it has a sparse, redwood-beamed dining room where the limited menu offerings reflect the southern French and northern Italian influences on West Coast dishes. Since only one meal is served in the downstairs dining room each evening, you may want to call ahead to know whether it will be spring lamb, grilled salmon, ravioli stuffed with potatoes, or something even more innovative. Upstairs the more casual and less expensive *Chez Panisse Café* specializes in pizza, calzones, salads, and soups. Closed Sundays. Reservations necessary at least a month in advance. Major credit cards accepted. 1517 Shattuck Ave., Berkeley (phone: 510-548-5525).

Ernie's Ernie Carlesso opened his now-famous establishment in 1934; the sons of his original partner continue the tradition. Champagne silk wall coverings and elaborately carved woodwork set the tone for tuxedoed waiters to serve contemporary French dishes. Offerings include leek salad with *osetra* caviar and lemon cream, Dungeness crab cakes with tomato gelée, roast duck or *confit* of duck, salmon tartare, venison *au poivre*, and roulades of veal or tuna. The wine list is extensive: a 17,000-bottle inventory. Open for dinner only; closed Sundays. Reservations advised. Major credit cards accepted. 847 Montgomery St. (phone: 397-5969).

Fleur de Lys One of the oldest French restaurants in the city, it boasts an incredibly romantic setting, with murals and 700 yards of red and green floral fabric decorating the dining area. The fare is French, with California influences, and excellently presented. The menu features such dishes as coconut soup with lobster, corn pancakes with salmon, and roast loin of lamb with parsnip flan. Open for dinner only; closed Sundays. Valet parking is available. Reservations advised. Major credit cards accepted. 777 Sutter St. (phone: 673-7779).

Geordy's From its 1992 opening, this contemporary dining room has delivered consistently well-prepared seasonal dishes. The menu changes, but monkfish with ricotta gnocchi and brioche-stuffed roast chicken surrounded by mushrooms rate raves. Closed Sundays. Reservations necessary. Major credit cards accepted. 1 Tillman Pl., off Grant Ave. between Sutter and Post Sts. (phone: 362-3175).

Harris' Dark oak paneling and leather banquettes create the aura of an elegant men's club with a meat-and-potatoes menu: thick steaks and prime ribs aged for 21 days in a refrigerator to intensify their flavor. For dessert, the chocolate decadence torte is sinful. Open for dinner daily, for lunch on Wednesdays only. Reservations advised. Major credit cards accepted. 2100 Van Ness Ave. (phone 673-1888).

Lark Creek Inn In the kitchen of a historic Victorian house in Marin County, chef Bradley Ogden combines fresh meat and produce from local farms to create fine regional American fare. A wood-burning oven enhances the flavors of baked and roasted entrées; breads and desserts are made on the premises; and the outstanding wine list offers more than 200 selections. Expansive windows afford panoramic views of redwood trees and gardens; in warm weather, the patio along Lark Creek is open for dining. Closed Saturdays for lunch; Sunday brunch instead of lunch. Reservations advised. Major credit cards accepted. 234 Magnolia Ave., Larkspur (phone: 924-7766).

Masa's Although Masa Kobayshi died in 1985, his namesake restaurant, headed by protégé Julian Serrano, still ranks high. Creative combinations, extravagant sauces, and perfect presentation enhance a menu that changes daily. Highlights might include grilled scallops with saffron sauce, sautéed medallions of fallow deer with caramelized apples and zinfandel sauce, or roast squab with risotto. For dessert order the sublime white and dark chocolate mousse with raspberry sauce or the unique baked apple in phyllo pastry with cinnamon-rosemary ice cream. Open Tuesdays through Saturdays, 6 to 9:30 PM. Reservations necessary; call three weeks ahead. Major credit cards accepted. 648 Bush St. (phone: 989-7154).

Postrio Elegant and airy (and expensive), this dining place in the *Prescott* hotel was dreamed up by chef-restaurateur Wolfgang Puck of *Spago* fame, and Anne and David Gingrass, former chefs at *Spago*. Specials feature California's freshest ingredients, prepared with Asian and Mediterranean influences: grilled baby lamb chops on wilted salad with cilantro honey vinaigrette, and roast salmon with almond–black pepper crust and warm spinach salad. Pizza, salads, and sandwiches are served upstairs at the bar. Lighting fixtures, which incorporate hand-blown glass ribbons, were created by a former jewelry designer. Service is impeccable. Open daily for all three meals. Reservations necessary, as far in advance as possible (reservations unnecessary for bar or for breakfast). Major credit cards accepted. 545 Post St. (phone: 776-7825).

Square One Joyce Goldstein, an alumna of *Chez Panisse* (see above), brings together flavors from around the Mediterranean in this Bay City dining place. The à la carte menu changes regularly, depending on what's fresh. An open cooking area makes it easy for guests to watch chefs at work. Bread, desserts, and ice cream are made on the premises, and the wine list is extensive. Closed for lunch on weekends. Reservations advised. Major credit cards accepted. 190 Pacific Ave. (phone: 788-1110).

Stars Colorful, energetic, and sometimes noisy, this is a gathering place for the city's rich and famous. Jeremiah Tower, another graduate of *Chez Panisse,* prepares American classics with contemporary flair—veal shanks, venison, fish (even hamburgers, hot dogs, and pizza). Though the setting is elegant, the mood is casual, and diners come dressed in everything from black tie to blue jeans. Sit at the long, long bar (48 feet), listen to the piano player, and watch the chefs in the open kitchen prepare your meal. The restaurant is open late and within walking distance of the *Opera House* and *Symphony Hall.* Open daily. Reservations advised. Major credit cards accepted. 150 Redwood Alley, between Polk St. and Van Ness Ave. (phone: 861-7827).

Zuni Café The fare at this casual brick and glass, California-Mediterranean–style dining spot (with sidewalk tables, too) changes daily; it's based on the seasonal ingredients chef Judy Rodgers finds at the market each morning. The eclectic menu features the cuisine of southern France with an emphasis on braised meat and poultry and grilled seafood; pasta is also a favorite, and there is an oyster bar. Closed Mondays; open for all three meals the rest of the week. Reservations advised. Major credit cards accepted. 1658 Market St. (phone: 552-2522).

MODERATE

Angkor Wat Expand your Oriental horizons at this Cambodian dining place where specialties include prawn soup, codfish, and curried chicken. The *Cambodian Classical Ballet* performs here on Friday and Saturday nights. Closed Mondays. Reservations unnecessary. Major credit cards accepted. 4127 Geary Blvd. (phone: 221-7887).

China Moon In a cleverly disguised coffee shop setting, owner/chef Barbara Tropp has succeeded in presenting her singular brand of Chinese food. In what other "Chinese" restaurant would you expect to find such appetizers as chili-spiked spring rolls, spicy lamb, fresh water chestnuts, and Peking antipasto plates side by side with a California wine list and Western-style desserts? Portions are small; no smoking is permitted. Closed Sundays for lunch. Reservations advised. MasterCard and Visa accepted. 639 Post St. (phone: 775-4789).

Fog City Diner Not your usual diner, this 1930s Pullman-style eatery is sleek, unique, and perennially packed. Created by chef Cindy Pawlcyn (who also opened *Mustard's* in Napa and several Carmel Valley restaurants), the food and the ambience—dazzling chrome and neon—are dramatically different from that found in a traditional American diner. Chicly dressed patrons like to order appetizer-size plates of red curry mussel stew and crab cakes and play smorgasbord, but milk shakes and hamburgers are also on offer. Open daily. Reservations advised. Major credit cards accepted. 1300 Battery St. (phone: 982-2000).

Flying Saucer Out of this world in more ways than one, this tiny place (19 tables) decorated with UFO-style memorabilia dishes out huge salads and such heavenly entrées as duck *confit* in coconut-lemongrass lentil sauce and sautéed black sea bass. Open Tuesdays through Saturdays for dinner only. Because of its popularity—and its limited number of tables—reserve ahead and be willing to take the last of three nightly seatings. No credit cards accepted. 1000 Guerrero St. (phone: 641-9955).

Gordon Biersch Brewery The financial district meets South of Market at this classy bar and restaurant on *The Embarcadero*. Featured are pitchers of house ales and a bar menu that's long on pizza; restaurant fare ranges from braised lamb shanks to wild mushroom risotto. Open daily. Reservations advised for dinner. Major credit cards accepted. 2 Harrison St. (phone: 243-8246).

Greens Devotees consider this vegetarian eatery the best in the country. Things are always what they seem here; nothing masquerades as meat. Sandwiches, pizza, pasta, chili, salad, and five-course prix fixe dinners on weekends are enhanced by fine views across the marina to the *Golden Gate Bridge*. Closed Mondays; open for brunch only on Sundays. Reservations advised. Major credit cards accepted. *Fort Mason*, Bldg. A (phone: 771-6222).

Happy Immortal This Chinese eatery in the city's Richmond district serves some of the best Hunan crab around. If you're going with a group, try the whole chicken stuffed with sweet rice; delicious and quite reasonable (about $25 for six people), this dish must be ordered in advance. Closed Wednesdays. Reservations necessary on weekends. MasterCard and Visa accepted. 4401 Cabrillo St. (phone: 386-7538).

Hayes Street Grill In a city famous for its seafood restaurants, this is one of the best—a quintessential San Francisco dining experience. Everything is fresh; nothing is overcooked. There always is a long list of daily specials, along with great sourdough bread and an unusually good *crème brûlée* for dessert. Closed for lunch on weekends. Reservations advised; consider dining here after performances start at nearby venues. Major credit cards accepted. 320 Hayes St. (phone: 863-5545).

Jack's This excellent continental restaurant has been a landmark for nearly as long as San Francisco has been on the map, but because it's in the financial district, it's unknown to many visitors. All the grilled entrées are recommended, and for dessert the banana fritters with brandy sauce are unbeatable. The decor is unpretentious, as are the prices (particularly the dinner special), and the service is good. Open weekdays for lunch only, Saturdays for dinner only; closed Sundays. Reservations necessary. American Express accepted. 615 Sacramento St. (phone: 421-7355).

Kyung Bok Palace For fanciers of Korea's kimchee (spicy pickled cabbage) and grilled meat and seafood, this place is San Francisco's finest. Chicken, pork, shrimp, baby octopus, and thinly sliced beef are presented at a buffet, and you can cook selections at your table's own grill. There is no menu, and the price is fixed for all you can eat. Open daily. Reservations necessary. MasterCard and Visa accepted. 6314 Geary Blvd. (phone: 221-0685).

McCormick & Kuleto's A wall of windows provides breathtaking views of San Francisco Bay from this *Ghirardelli Square* eatery. The emphasis is on seafood, with the list of fresh fish and oysters on the half shell changing daily. There's an extensive wine list, and valet parking is available. Open daily. Reservations advised. Major credit cards accepted. 900 North Point (phone: 929-1730).

Pane e Vino The extension of a Santa Barbara establishment, this authentic-looking trattoria features such northern Italian fare as *vitello tonnato* (sliced veal with a sauce of tuna, mayonnaise, and capers), risotto, and grilled fish. It's close to the Triangle area of singles bars, so parking spots are at a premium. Closed Sundays for lunch. Reservations necessary. MasterCard and Visa accepted. 3011 Steiner St. (phone: 346-2111).

Tadich Grill San Francisco's oldest restaurant (ca. 1849) is still going strong with what folks maintain is the freshest seafood in town. Best bets: baked avocado with shrimp *diablo,* rex sole, salmon, and sea bass. Don't pass up the homemade cheesecake for dessert. Open only until 9 PM; closed Sundays and major holidays. No reservations. MasterCard and Visa accepted. 240 California St. (phone: 391-1849).

Wu Kong Far beyond the fringes of Chinatown, Shanghai-style food is served in a well-appointed dining room with a nice atmosphere. Seafood and vegetable dishes are fresh and well prepared. Open daily. Reservations advised. Major credit cards accepted. 101 Spear St. at *Rincon Center* (phone: 957-9300).

Yoshida-Ya This stunning Japanese spot is known for its excellent yakitori— a selection of meat, fish, and vegetables, all marinated, skewered, and grilled over charcoal. Upstairs is less crowded, as are weekends. Open daily. Reservations necessary. Major credit cards accepted. 2909 Webster St. at Union St. (phone: 346-3431).

INEXPENSIVE

Angkor Borei Adventurous diners might enjoy the unusually prepared seafood at this Cambodian eatery. Open daily. Reservations advised on weekends. Major credit cards accepted. 3471 Mission St. (phone: 550-8417).

Burma's House Among the myriad Chinese dishes listed on the extensive menu, there are some unusual—and delicious—Burmese specialties, such as *pat dok* (a salad of fermented tea leaves, toasted lentils, ground shrimp, green chilies, garlic, and sesame seeds) and *moo hing nga* (a traditional Burmese fish chowder with rice noodles, chilies, tamarind, hard-boiled egg, and kernels of corn). Open daily. Reservations necessary on weekends. MasterCard and Visa accepted. 720 Post St. (phone: 775-1156).

Casa Aguila At this haven of south-of-the-border warmth in the fog-shrouded Sunset district, try seafood prepared tableside on the *parrilla* (small grill); portions are large enough to fill several doggie bags. Open daily.

No reservations; you wait outside on the street. Major credit cards accepted. 1240 Noriega St. between 19th and 20th Aves. (phone: 661-5593).

Far East Café Don't let the neon-lit exterior fool you—inside are ornate Chinese lanterns and private, curtained booths. The extensive Cantonese and Mandarin menu features all the old classics and, if you call in advance, an excellent family banquet. Open daily. Reservations advised. Major credit cards accepted. 631 Grant Ave. (phone: 982-3245)

Fly Trap In the trendy SoMa district, this is a re-creation of a turn-of-the-century restaurant that earned its nickname from the squares of flypaper flapping over each table. The flypaper is gone, but the name has stuck; the menu has Californian flair and the nostalgic flavor of old San Francisco, with hearty original dishes. Valet parking. Closed Saturdays for lunch and Sundays. Reservations advised. Major credit cards accepted. 606 Folsom St. (phone: 243-0580).

Isobune There's only counter service at these two sushi and sashimi spots—but what counter service! Japanese-style wooden boats glide by bearing all sorts of wonders, and patrons take what they want. The tab is figured by counting plates. Open daily. No reservations; expect a wait. MasterCard and Visa accepted. 1737 Post St. (phone: 563-1030) and 1451 Burlingame Ave., Burlingame (phone: 344-8433).

Jackson Fillmore Garlicky, steamy, cozy, and informal, this Pacific Heights trattoria is a favorite among locals for early Sunday evening meals. Specialties include osso buco (braised veal shanks); chicken sautéed with tomatoes, olives, onions, and anchovies; and a wide variety of pasta. Open daily for dinner only. Reservations advised for parties of three or more; let them know if you will take a place at the counter. Major credit cards accepted. 2506 Fillmore St. (phone: 346-5288).

Pacific Vietnamese owner Ninh Nguyen prides himself on his *pho,* a beef noodle soup with shallots, ginger, cinnamon, and *nuoc mam,* the Vietnamese version of soy sauce. Also on this creative menu are a good selection of fish and beef dishes—all at extremely reasonable prices. Open daily for breakfast and lunch only. No reservations or credit cards accepted. 607 Larkin St. (phone: 441-6722).

San Francisco Bar-B-Q The aroma of Thai spices wafts over Potrero Hill when the cooks fire up the grill to barbecue spareribs, chicken, salmon, trout, lamb, or even oysters. The meat can be ordered à la carte or as part of a dinner that includes sticky rice, grated carrot salad, and sourdough bread. A bowl of noodles comes cooked in sesame and soy, with crisp grilled pieces of duck. Just about everything on the menu can be ordered to go. Closed Sundays for lunch and Mondays. No reservations or credit cards accepted. 1328 18th St. (phone: 431-8956).

Sears Fine Food A line forms outside on summer mornings at this San Francisco institution serving old-fashioned breakfasts. The pancakes are Swedish; the French toast is made with sourdough bread. The standard lunch menu includes such nonstandard items as lemon soufflé. Open for breakfast and lunch, Wednesdays through Sundays. No reservations or credit cards accepted (avoid a wait by sitting at the counter). 439 Powell St. (phone: 986-1160).

Straits Café Direct from Singapore come such Oriental delicacies as *achar* (pickled vegetables), *kari lembu* (beef curry), *patong kari ayam* (coconut-curry chicken), as well as *satays* and chili crab. Open daily. Reservations advised on weekends. Major credit cards accepted. 3300 Geary Blvd. (phone: 668-1783).

Santa Fe

At-a-Glance

SEEING THE CITY

Visitors with lots of time and stamina should hike the trail up Lake Peak (12,040 feet) from the *Aspen Vista Picnic Area*. The trailhead is on the paved road to the *Santa Fe Ski Area,* a drive that also provides fine views for those who prefer to stay in the car. Another vantage point, the top of Martyr's Hill, affords spectacular views of the city and the mountains; it's about a 15-minute walk from the Plaza.

SPECIAL PLACES

The downtown area of Santa Fe is compact and can be explored on foot easily. A car is helpful for visiting the museums on Camino Lejo or for taking day trips to Taos, *Bandelier, Pecos,* and other nearby places of interest.

THE PLAZA The Plaza has been the center of Santa Fe life for almost four centuries, ever since the day in 1610 when mounted Spanish soldiers in armor first used it as a parade ground. Throughout the centuries it has been the scene of the most important public events in the city: markets, fiestas, proclamations, parades, and even, at one time, bullfights. An obelisk now marks the center of the lovely, tree-shaded square. Along the footpaths emanating from the obelisk are benches where weary shoppers rest, sightseers fiddle with their cameras, and office workers enjoy picnic lunches. The *Palace of the Governors* dominates the north side of the square; the three other sides are lined with shops, restaurants, and galleries.

PALACE OF THE GOVERNORS Built by Spanish settlers in 1609–10, 11 years before the Pilgrims landed at Plymouth Rock, this is the oldest public building in the US, having served as a seat of government for four nations: Spain, Mexico, the Confederacy, and the US. Originally, the entire palace was made of mud except for the roof beams, or *vigas*. The walls, then as now, were adobe. The dirt floor was mixed with animal blood to pack it down and produce a sheen. Following the Pueblo Revolt of 1680, the Indians enlarged the structure and used it as a large pueblo. It again was occupied and further enlarged by the Spanish following the Reconquest in 1692. The palace became a museum in 1909, housing historical exhibitions for the *Museum of New Mexico*. This makes it a natural starting point for a tour of the city. Closed Mondays in January and February; open daily except major holidays the rest of the year. No admission charge for children under 16. On the Plaza (phone: 827-6483).

MUSEUM OF FINE ARTS Next door, moving west from the palace, this museum houses a permanent collection of more than 8,000 works of art. Changing exhibitions throughout the year feature 20th-century photography, prints, and sculpture, with a strong emphasis on the Southwest. Completed in 1917, some 300 years after the *Palace of the Governors,* the build-

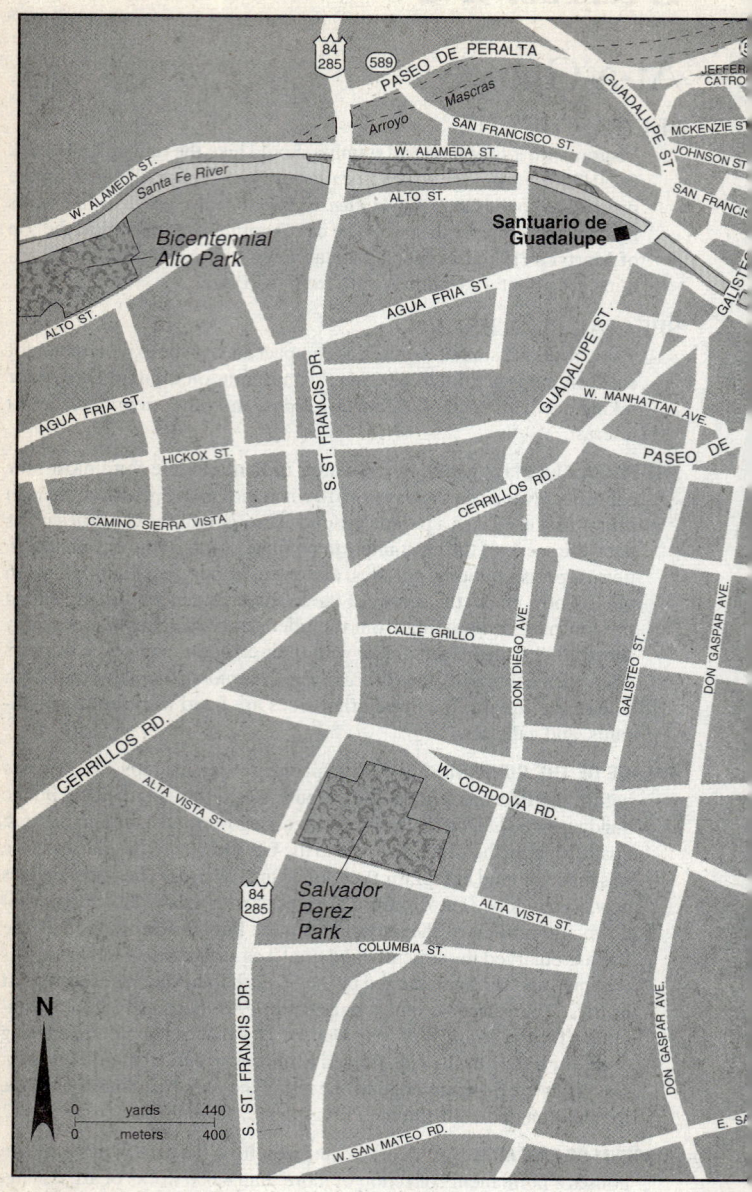

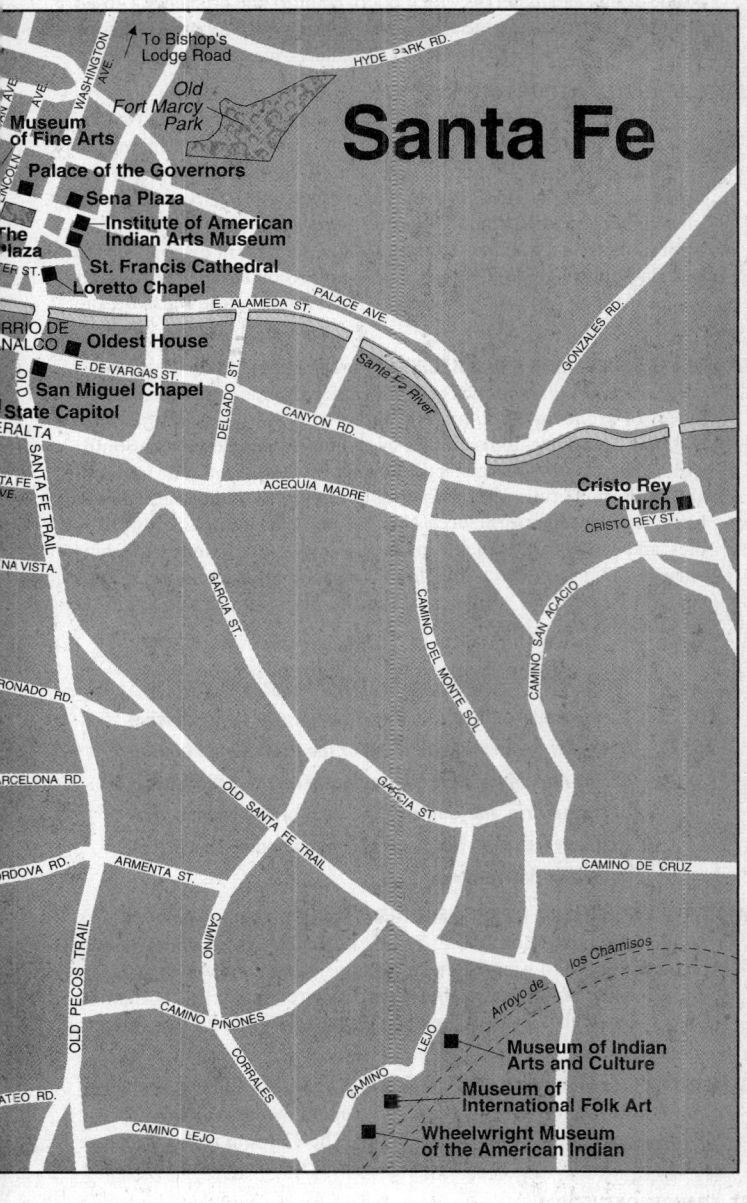

ing is an outstanding example of Pueblo Revival architecture. It became a model for the style that still dominates Santa Fe, combining traditional adobe design and materials with modern comfort and efficiency. Closed Mondays and Tuesdays in January and February. No admission charge for children under 16. On the Plaza, W. Palace Ave. (phone: 827-4455).

MUSEUM OF INTERNATIONAL FOLK ART Housing the world's largest such collection from around the globe, the museum was founded in 1953 by Florence Dibell Bartlett, who believed folk art to be a bond among the peoples of the world. The collection includes traditional costumes and textiles, masks, toys, items of everyday use, and folk art from the Spanish colonial period. The famed *Girard Foundation Collection,* with items from more than a hundred countries, is on permanent exhibit. Closed Mondays in January and February. No admission charge for children under 16. 706 Camino Lejo, about 4 miles south of the Plaza off the Old Santa Fe Trail (phone: 827-6350).

MUSEUM OF INDIAN ARTS AND CULTURE As the exhibition facility for the adjacent *Laboratory of Anthropology,* its collection includes more than 50,000 pieces of prehistoric and historic basketry, pottery, textiles, jewelry, clothing, and other items crafted by the native peoples of the Southwest. Artifacts from this collection are shown in rotation. The museum also offers numerous demonstrations of crafts and traditional arts, lectures, and dance performances. Native American jewelry, pottery, textiles, and baskets are available in the gift shop. Closed Mondays in January and February. No admission charge for children under 16. 710 Camino Lejo, about 4 miles south of the Plaza off the Old Santa Fe Trail (phone: 827-6344).

> **MUSEUM PASSES**
>
> True museum enthusiasts can get a bargain by purchasing three-day passes to the *Palace of the Governors, Museum of Fine Arts, Museum of International Folk Art,* and *Museum of Indian Arts and Culture.* The cost of the pass is substantially less than the combined regular admission prices to the four institutions.

WHEELWRIGHT MUSEUM OF THE AMERICAN INDIAN Indian arts and artifacts are the attractions here. *Note:* The *Case Trading Post* downstairs sells high-quality, award-winning Indian pottery, jewelry, and weavings. Open daily. No admission charge, but donations are accepted. 704 Camino Lejo, about 4 miles south of the Plaza off the Old Santa Fe Trail (phone: 982-4636).

SEÑA PLAZA East of the *Palace of the Governors* is this charming, tree-shaded, and flower-brightened courtyard surrounded by the four wings of the 19th-century home of Major José Seña. The 33-room adobe structure now is divided into shops and offices. E. Palace Ave. (phone: 988-5792).

ST. FRANCIS CATHEDRAL Directly across Palace Avenue, this structure built between 1869 and 1886 is the legacy of the French bishop Jean-Baptiste Lamy, the most influential person in local history. (He was buried in front of the high altar in 1888. The Romanesque style of the building is, like many of Lamy's ideas, a little out of place. Its most interesting feature is the adobe chapel that existed here before the cathedral, most of which was incorporated into the larger structure; it is built of local quarry stone. In continuous use since 1718, the chapel is dedicated to *La Conquistadora* (Our Lady of the Conquest), protector of the early Spanish settlers. In 1992 parishioners renamed her, so that she now is known as *Nuestra Señora de la Paz* (Our Lady of Peace). The carved wooden statue, said to be the oldest representation of the Madonna in North America, was brought here from Mexico by the Spanish in 1625 and is carried in religious processions throughout the year. 131 Cathedral Fl. (phone: 982-5619).

INSTITUTE OF AMERICAN INDIAN ARTS MUSEUM One block east of the Plaza, this museum is housed in a spacious, Pueblo Revival–style, former federal office building facing *St. Francis Cathedral*. Federally funded schooling in the visual arts is offered here free to the most talented Native American students from around the US. (Founded in the 1930s, the institute has been one of the strongest forces in establishing Santa Fe as a major artists' community.) Contemporary paintings and sculptures donated to the school over the years by such renowned alumni as Allan Houser, R. C. Gorman, and Jaune Quick-to-See Smith are on display. Closed Mondays in January and February. No admission charge for children under 6. 108 Cathedral Pl. (phone: 988-6211 or 988-6281).

BARRIO DE ANALCO The Santa Fe River is as slow, irregular, and inexpedient as the town it crosses, yet because it was the main source of water in the early days, almost all the homes were built along it. Many of the old houses on the narrow streets in the Barrio de Analco (as the quarter on the south side of the river was called) have been preserved, particularly on East De Vargas Street.

LORETTO CHAPEL Also known as the *Chapel of Our Lady of Light,* this graceful neo-Gothic stone masterpiece was built in 1873 as a private place of worship for Santa Fe's first nuns. It is famed for its "miraculous staircase," which makes two 360-degree turns with no central support, defying all engineering principles. Open daily. No admission charge for children under 12. 219 Old Santa Fe Trail (phone: 988-5531).

"OLDEST HOUSE" The foundations of this structure are thought to have been laid by the Pueblo people in the 13th century, although the tree rings in the ceiling beams date only to about 1600. However accurate its claim of being the "oldest house in the US," the western portion of this structure is a good example of primitive adobe construction. Most early Santa Fe residents had similar dwellings, with low, log-beamed ceilings, dirt floors, thick mud walls, and a corner fireplace for heating and cooking. Closed Sundays. No admission charge. 215 E. De Vargas St. (no phone).

SAN MIGUEL MISSION Built in 1610, this historic church is as old as the *Palace of the Governors.* Much of the structure was destroyed by the Pueblo Indians in the 1680 Revolt. Rebuilt in 1710, its chapel boasts the massive, 800-pound *San José Bell,* thought by some to have been cast in 1356 in Spain and hauled to its present home via Mexico hundreds of years later. (The

Historic Santa Fe Foundation, however, counters that a local bellcaster did a poor job, and that the date appearing to read 1356 should be 1856.) The most prominent feature of the interior is a fine old reredos, or colonial Spanish altar screen, made in 1798. Most of the paintings on the altar screen were done in Mexico in the 18th century. Closed Sunday mornings, *New Year's Day, Easter, Thanksgiving,* and *Christmas.* 401 Old Santa Fe Trail at E. De Vargas St. (phone: 983-3974).

STATE CAPITOL A bit south of the *San Miguel Mission* is this unusual structure, which residents call the "Round House." With a floor plan in the shape of the Zia sun symbol that graces the state flag, its architects intended to evoke a Pueblo kiva (the ceremonial chamber in which religious rites are performed). No admission charge. Old Santa Fe Trail at Paseo de Peralta.

CANYON ROAD One of the most romantic and picturesque streets in the US, it's also the oldest still in use; it was well established as a Pueblo trail long before the Spanish arrived. By the 18th century residents were building adobe homes and cultivating farms along Canyon Road, which follows the river east from downtown. Sections of some of the current buildings date from that period, and the style of the street's architecture was established in a way that has not changed substantially since. In the early 20th century, Canyon Road became the center of the Santa Fe art colony. Though few struggling artists can afford to live here today, the street still is zoned for residential arts and crafts, limiting its use to galleries, studios, restaurants, and homes. It's an ideal place to see both the residential character of the old city and the latest work of Santa Fe artists.

CRISTO REY CHURCH Built in 1940, this church was designed by architect John Gaw Meem in classic Spanish mission style. Nearly 200,000 adobe bricks were used in its construction, all using soil from the site—the traditional practice. One of the largest adobe structures in existence, it was scaled to house the most famous piece of Spanish colonial art in New Mexico, an ornately carved stone reredos (altar screen), commissioned in 1760. 1107 Cristo Rey (phone: 983-8528).

EL SANTUARIO DE NUESTRA SEÑORA DE GUADALUPE This frontier church, built by Franciscan missionaries in the late 18th century, contains a painting of Our Lady of Guadalupe as well as outstanding woodcarvings and the *Plants of the Holy Land* botanical garden. It is located four blocks west of the Plaza in the Guadalupe historic district, a recently restored area of restaurants and trendy shops. Closed Sundays year-round and Saturdays November through April. 100 Guadalupe St. at Agua Fria St. (phone: 988-2027).

EXTRA SPECIAL

The Sangre de Cristo mountain range, the southernmost part of the Rockies, runs for 300 miles between the Rio Grande Valley to the eastern plains, and from Santa Fe to central Colorado. Santa Fe's own piece of this majestic range is *Pecos Wilderness,* a 167,000-acre expanse of road-

less territory with ancient forests of spruce and fir, broad meadows, alpine lakes, secluded valleys, and exquisite summits such as Santa Fe Baldy (elevation 12,622 feet) and Truchas Peak (13,103 feet). This is New Mexico's ultimate recreation area for hiking, backpacking, pony trekking, and cross-country skiing; there is a network of hundreds of miles of trails suitable for anything from a pleasant summer-morning walk to week-long camping expeditions.

The most popular trailhead into *Pecos* begins at the lower parking lot of the *Santa Fe Ski Area,* located 15 miles east of downtown Santa Fe via the winding, steep Hyde Park/Ski Basin Road. On the way you pass the popular *Hyde Memorial State Park* picnic area and *Aspen Vista* overlook, where another trail leads through a shimmering aspen forest. There are many other places to explore within the *Pecos Wilderness.*

To venture deeper into *Pecos,* take Interstate 25 east for about 25 miles to the old Spanish village of Pecos. From there, a paved road runs up the wonderfully scenic Pecos River Canyon, a popular area for catch-and-release trout fishing during the summer months. After 14 miles, the paved road ends, and a dirt road continues for several more miles into campgrounds and trailheads.

A few miles south of the village of Pecos is *Pecos National Historical Park,* a 300-acre national preserve that includes the ruins of a 12th-century Indian pueblo as well as a 17th-century mission church. This area is now being expanded, thanks to a gift by actress Greer Garson; to protect the region from commercial development, she signed over her 5,500-acre ranch to the *Mellon Foundation,* which is now in the process of turning the land over to the *National Parks Service.* The ranch land contains a beautiful 2-mile stretch of the Pecos River (which was not open to the public at press time, though the rest of the park is). For information, including maps of the *Pecos Wilderness* area, contact *Pecos National Historical Park,* Pecos, NM 87552 (phone: 505-757-6032 or 757-6414).

Sources and Resources

TOURIST INFORMATION

For a free copy of the *Santa Fe Convention and Visitors' Bureau*'s *Visitors' Guide,* call 800-777-CITY, or pick one up at the bureau's office in the *Sweeney Convention Center* (201 W. Marcy St.; phone: 984-6760). A better but more expensive alternative is the newsstand at *La Fonda* hotel (100 E. San Francisco St.), just off the Plaza, which carries all available guides and major works of fiction and nonfiction about the area. For a lively literary introduction to the city and vicinity, pick up Willa Cather's *Death Comes for the Archbishop* and John Nichols's *The Milagro Beanfield War;* the latter was adapted for the screen by Robert Redford and is available on videocassette. Contact the *New Mexico State Information Hotline* (phone: 800-545-2040) for maps, calendars of events, health updates, and travel advisories.

LOCAL COVERAGE The *New Mexican* is published daily; look at Friday's "Pasatiempo" section for information on events of the coming week. Do not, however, rely on the paper for restaurant recommendations. There also are listings in the weekly *Santa Fe Reporter.* And we immodestly recommend our own *Birnbaum's Santa Fe/Taos 95* (HarperCollins; $12), as well as *Santa Fe/Taos/Albuquerque ACCESS* (HarperCollins; $18).

TELEVISION STATIONS KOB Channel 4–NBC; KNME Channel 5–PBS; KOAT Channel 7–ABC; KGGM Channel 13–CBS.

RADIO STATIONS AM: KZSS 610 (rock); KSWV 810 (Spanish); KREO 920 (oldies); KFMG 1080 (rock); KRZY 1450 (country). FM: KUNM 89.9 (public radio); KSFR 90.7 (classical); KNYN 95 (country); KHFM 96.3 (classical); KISS 97 (rock); KBAC 98.1 (contemporary); KIOT 102.3 (progressive adult music); KLSK 104 (jazz); KBOM 107 (rock); KFMG 108 (rock).

TELEPHONE The area code for Santa Fe is 505.

SALES TAX The city sales tax is 6.25%; lodgers' tax is 4%.

CLIMATE Santa Fe's climate is shaped by both the Rocky Mountains and the Southwestern desert. The sun usually is shining, the air is very dry, and the sky is clear and turquoise blue. During the day, the air temperature always feels warm, even when there's snow on the ground, although as soon as the sun sets, the air cools quickly. The average daily temperature is about 80F in summer and about 40F in winter. Note, however, that the high altitude can slow you down a bit until you get used to the thinner air. Take a day or two to acclimate, especially if you're contemplating any serious hiking (and go easy on drinking alcoholic beverages).

GETTING AROUND

Although the downtown area is small enough to see enjoyably by foot, a car or other transportation is needed to visit the farther-flung points of interest.

AIRPORT *Santa Fe Municipal Airport* is serviced by *Mesa Airlines* (phone: 800-MESA-AIR), which flies from Albuquerque and Denver to Santa Fe. Visitors usually fly into *Albuquerque International Airport,* about 65 miles south, and then either rent a car or rely on one of several bus services; one is *Shuttlejack* (phone: 243-3244 or 982-4311), and departures are from *Southwest Airlines*'s baggage claim area approximately every two hours. The trip takes about 80 minutes.

BUS *Santa Fe Trails* (phone: 984-6730), the city's first public bus service, was inaugurated in 1993. Six routes, with both early-morning and late-evening service, link destinations throughout the city limits, including the museums on Camino Lejo, suburban shopping malls, and residential areas. The main transfer area for all routes is located near the intersection of Sheridan Street and Palace Avenue, just off the Plaza.

CAR RENTAL Although cars can be rented in Santa Fe, the rental offices are scattered. All the major car rental agencies are represented at *Albuquerque International Airport*.

TAXI There is no central taxi stand, but you can call *Capital City Cab Co.* (1107 Early Rd.; phone: 989-8888). If you're in a hurry, though, walking may be a better option; it may take anywhere from 20 minutes to an hour for a cab to appear.

WALKING TOURS Daily walking tours of the city depart from *La Fonda* hotel and the *Inn at Loretto;* contact *Santa Fe Walks* (phone: 988-2774), *Afoot in Santa Fe* (phone: 983-3701), or *Fiesta Tours* (phone: 984-8235).

LOCAL SERVICES

AUDIOVISUAL EQUIPMENT *The AV Systems* (535 Cordova Rd.; phone: 982-2499).

BABY-SITTING *Santa Fe Kid Connection* (331 Durango Dr.; phone: 471-3100).

BUSINESS SERVICES *Plaza II Executive Center* (125 Lincoln Ave., Suite 400; phone: 984-8161).

DRY CLEANER/TAILOR *One Hour Martinizing* (200 E. Water St.; phone: 982-8606).

LIMOUSINE *Limotion VIP Limousine Service* (phone: 471-1265).

MECHANIC *Automotive Repair Service* (1212 Calle de Comercio; phone: 473-0031).

MEDICAL EMERGENCY *Lovelace at Alameda* (901 W. Alameda; phone: 986-3656 or 986-3666 for emergency care); *Lovelace Multispecialty Clinic* (440 St. Michael's Dr.; phone: 986-3556 or 986-3566 for emergency care); *St. Vincent Hospital* (455 St. Michael's Dr.; phone: 983-3361 or 820-5247 for emergency care).

MESSENGER SERVICE *Pigeon Express* (phone: 473-3447).

PHOTOCOPIES AND FAX SERVICES *Kinko's* (333 Montezuma Ave.; phone: 982-6311); *Paper Tiger* (120 E. Marcy St.; phone: 983-2839).

POST OFFICE The main office is at 120 S. Federal Pl. (phone: 988-6351); another branch is at 20-71 S. Pacheco (phone: 438-8452).

PROFESSIONAL PHOTOGRAPHER *Arrial Studio* (1422 Second; phone: 983-2410).

SECRETARY/STENOGRAPHER *Bell's Exec* (phone: 988-7374); *Kay Carlson* (phone: 982-3926).

TRANSLATOR *Adelocorp* (phone: 984-2203).

WESTERN UNION For the nearest representative, call 800-325-6000.

SPECIAL EVENTS

Summer is the performing arts season, with cultural events staged most nights of the week in July and August by the *Santa Fe Opera* and the *Santa Fe Chamber Music Festival* (see *Music,* below). The annual *Indian Market* is held the weekend after the third Thursday in August in the Plaza; at this very popular event (the country's oldest and largest Indian arts and crafts fair), Indians from the surrounding pueblos and across the US sell a wide variety of crafts—jewelry, pottery, sand paintings, weavings, kachina figurines, and so on. *Las Fiestas de Santa Fe,* celebrated the weekend after *Labor Day,* originated in 1712. Festivities open with the ritual burning of a 40-foot marionette, called a *Zozobra,* representing Old Man Gloom. After two days of fireworks, parades, dancing, eating, and partying, the fiestas end with mass at *St. Francis Cathedral.* Also part of the festivities are performances by the *Santa Fe Community Theater* (phone: 988-4262), the oldest theater group in New Mexico, founded in the 1920s. The theater's *Fiesta Melodrama,* performed during *Las Fiestas* in the fall, has received national notice for its irreverent satire, poking fun at some of Sante Fe's more prominent citizens. The pueblos near town have very different but equally interesting celebrations; the *Santa Fe Chamber of Commerce* (510 N. Guadalupe St.; phone: 983-7317) usually has information about the events visitors are allowed to attend; or contact the *Eight Northern Pueblos Council* (phone: 852-4265).

SHOPPING

Santa Fe is the best place in New Mexico (and perhaps in the entire Southwest) to shop for Indian art: jewelry, pottery, weavings, paintings, beadwork, baskets, and carved kachina figurines representing principally Hopi ancestral spirits who visit the pueblos intermittently and are represented by masked impersonators at agricultural ceremonies. Decorative pottery has been made by the Pueblo Indians and traded between villages for over 1,200 years; today it commands high prices. Each of the pueblos has its own unique style that has developed over many centuries, such as the micaceous pottery (made from clay laced with mica) found at the *Taos Pueblo.* Some artists have created relatively new crafts, such as the popular clay storyteller dolls (which depict a Native American man or woman whose role is to relate tribal stories and myths to the tribe's children) made at the *Cochiti Pueblo,* south of Santa Fe. The handwoven rugs and blankets made by Navajo women on a simple loom constructed of juniper branches usually take up to a year to complete, which explains the huge price tag—often several thousands of dollars. Silver and turquoise jewelry made by both Navajo and Pueblo artisans is also a Santa Fe hallmark.

Traditional Spanish crafts can be found in small villages throughout New Mexico. Decorative wool blankets, less expensive than Navajo rugs, are made using designs and techniques that date to the colonial era. Spanish woodcarvers are famed for their *bultos* (also called *santos*), statues of saints made for household chapels. Other crafts include tinwork and decorative wrought-iron items.

We recommend that you begin your education in native crafts by visiting Santa Fe's museums, as well as the *Millicent Rogers Museum* in Taos (Museum Rd.; phone: 758-2462). They all display the very distinctive works produced by the various tribes, and you'll soon learn to recognize the traditional patterns and techniques each employs. You also will become familiar with the names of certain families or individuals who have become well known for a particular style. The museum shops at the *Palace of the Governors,* the *Museum of Indian Arts and Culture,* and the *Wheelwright Museum* all carry fine Indian art as well as numerous books on the subject. They also are usually attended by salespeople who are willing to part with a few pointers about how to distinguish quality, what's special about the pieces they carry, and how to care for what you buy.

Visitors can purchase pottery and jewelry directly from Native Americans in front of the *Palace of the Governors,* at a market known as *Under the Portal.* The vendors, from nearby pueblos, are licensed by the *Museum of New Mexico,* which sets high standards for the wares they display. It's also possible to buy while visiting any of several pueblos in the area. Two final bits of advice: Buy what you like when you see it; each piece is handmade and unique, so you are unlikely to find it elsewhere. And bring lots of cash if you shop in the pueblos, because many of the people who sell from their homes won't accept credit cards.

But traditional Indian art is only one aspect of Santa Fe's ever-growing gallery and boutique scene. The city's principal shopping districts are the downtown Plaza area, Canyon Road, and Guadalupe and San Francisco Streets. Some establishments exhibit weaving and woodcarving from remote mountain villages; a growing number are starting to sell folk art from other parts of the world as well. More than 250 art galleries show a wide variety of paintings, sculptures, photographs, and objets d'art; much of the work is by local artists. Cowboy art, religious art, imported art, wearable art, even edible art are available in profusion. Traditionally, downtown galleries host openings on Friday afternoons.

In addition, Canyon Road studios and shops sponsor community open houses called *Art Walks,* which are listed weekly in the *Santa Fe Reporter* and the *New Mexican*'s Friday "Pasatiempo" section. Art enthusiasts also should contact longtime Santa Fe resident Linda Morton, who runs *Studio Entrada Tours* (Box 4934, Santa Fe, NM 87502; phone: 983-8786). This outfit takes groups of up to six adults on a two-and-a-half-hour tour around several local studios for a peek behind the gallery glitz; participants can meet the artists, see works in progress, and make purchases on the spot. Morton picks up visitors at their hotels and drives them around the city and its environs. Tours must be arranged by appointment a week in advance.

Any day of the week, big spenders and browsers alike will discover the chic, the exotic, and the highly unusual along the stylish streets of Santa Fe.

PLAZA DISTRICT

Andrew Smith Fine American Photography Offering selections of prints by Edward Curtis, Ansel Adams, Eliot Porter, and others. 76 E. San Francisco St. (phone: 984-1234).

The Chile Shop Stop in here for tasty, albeit mouth-searing, souvenirs and fine dinnerware. 109 E. Water St. (phone: 983-6080).

Cristof's Fine-quality Navajo rugs. 106 W. San Francisco St. (phone: 988-9881).

Davis-Mather Folk Art Gallery For browsing or buying, there's a jungle of traditional animal woodcarvings. 141 Lincoln Ave. (phone: 983-1660).

Elaine Horwitch Galleries Contemporary art, much of it done by Native Americans, selected with a sense of whimsy. 129 W. Palace Ave. (phone: 988-8997).

Fenn Gallery Featured here are classic regional artworks. 1075 Paseo de Peralta (phone: 982-4631).

La Fonda Indian Shop The best traditional Native American arts gallery in town. In *La Fonda Hotel*, 100 E. San Francisco St. (phone: 988-2488).

Glenn Green Galleries Works in stone and bronze by renowned Apache sculptor Allan Houser. 50 E. San Francisco St. (phone: 988-4168).

Móntez Gallery Traditional Spanish woodcarvings, tinwork, weaving, jewelry, and furniture. In Seña Plaza, 125 E. Palace Ave. (phone: 982-1828).

Nambé Foundry Outlet Contemporary housewares crafted of metal alloys. 112 W. San Francisco St. (phone: 988-3574).

Origins No Southwest staples here. Elegant fashions and jewelry, as well as some imported antiques. 135 W. San Francisco St. (phone: 988-2323).

Owings-Dewey Fine Art High-quality 19th- and 20th-century American paintings. 74 E. San Francisco St., upstairs (phone: 982-6244).

Peyton-Wright Gallery Contemporary paintings. 131 Nusbaum St. (phone: 989-9888).

Prairie Edge Lakota (Sioux) Indian artifacts, jewelry, and contemporary art. 102 E. Water St. (phone: 984-1336).

Rainbow Man Stop here for rare Indian artifacts, especially antique trade blankets (which were made specifically for barter). 107 E. Palace Ave. (phone: 982-8706).

Santa Fe East Museum-quality classic and contemporary American art. 200 Old Santa Fe Trail (phone: 988-3103).

Wadle Galleries Ltd. Traditional Western paintings, especially landscapes. 128 W. Palace Ave. (phone: 983-9219).

CANYON ROAD

Bellas Artes An eclectic assortment of paintings, works in clay, and other curiosities makes this shop an adventure in itself. 653 Canyon Rd. (phone: 983-2745).

Canyon Trading Post Handmade belts, handbags, and one-of-a-kind buckles. 670 Canyon Rd. (phone: 988-5012).

Copeland-Rutherford Fine Arts The works of contemporary New Mexico painters, sculptors, and photographers are represented here. 403 Canyon Rd. (phone: 983-1588).

David Ross Studio Wonderful hand-crafted furniture is made on the premises in this working studio. 610 Canyon Rd. (phone: 988-4017).

Gerald Peters Gallery More quality works by New Mexico artists. 439 Camino del Monte Sol (phone: 988-8961).

Gypsy Alley This cluster of small studios/galleries is reminiscent of the way Canyon Road used to be. 708 Canyon Rd. (no phone).

Kania-Ferrin Gallery Traditional souvenirs plus Indian art, weavings, and kachinas. 708 Canyon Rd. (phone: 982-1186).

Laurel Seth Gallery Southwestern contemporary art is exhibited in this historic building. 1121B Paseo de Peralta (phone: 988-7349).

Linda McAdoo Galleries One of Santa Fe's oldest galleries, featuring traditional artwork. 503 Canyon Rd. (phone: 983-7182).

Meyer Gallery Canyon Road's largest sculpture gallery. 25 Canyon Rd. (phone: 983-1434).

Morning Star Gallery This gallery shows antique Native American art and artifacts, including Pueblo pottery, Navajo chief blankets, and basketry. Especially interesting are the bold, unforgettable ledger drawings made by Plains warriors—and this is the only place in the area that displays them. 513 Canyon Rd. (phone: 982-8187).

Project Tibet You probably won't bump into the Dalai Lama, but Santa Fe's sizable Tibetan refugee community offers a good selection of folk art and gift items here. 403 Canyon Rd. (phone: 982-3002).

Running Ridge Gallery Contemporary glassware, ceramics, sculpture, and paintings. 640 Canyon Rd. (phone: 988-2515).

Spider Woman Designs Stylish handwoven fashions are on display here—wearable art at its best. 225 Canyon Rd. (phone: 984-0136).

Zaplin-Lambert Gallery Paintings by early Taos artists and historical prints reflecting 19th-century Indian life. 651 Canyon Rd. (phone: 982-6100).

GUADALUPE DISTRICT

Expressions in Fine Art Stylish Southwestern art and handmade furniture. 501 S. Guadalupe St. (phone: 988-3631).

Hand Graphics Gallery and Atelier Whether you're looking to shop or just looking, stop to see fine printmakers at work in this studio-cum-gallery. 418 Montezuma Ave (phone: 988-1241).

Woodrow Wilson Fine Art This long-established gallery exhibits paintings by Blumenschein, Nordfeldt, Hurd, and other early New Mexico artists. 319 Read St. (phone: 983-2444).

Worldly Possessions To satisfy the hippie in you—imported beads, silk blouses, peacock feathers, plus a folk art gallery. 330 Garfield St. (phone: 983-6090).

ELSEWHERE

Jackalope Folk Art Center A favorite among locals as well as visitors, this giant complex of interconnected buildings covers six and a half acres. Inside, artisans from all over the world—including Europe, Africa, Mexico, Central America, China, the Philippines, and Indonesia—display and sell their wares. Items include pottery, jewelry, clothing, baskets, candles, and furnishings. A café serves Mexican and Southwestern fare. In addition, there is a greenhouse, an aviary, a goldfish pond, and a prairie dog village (a manmade replica of the rodents' natural habitat). 2820 Cerrillos Rd. (phone: 471-8539).

Santa Fe Flea Market Indian and frontier artifacts dealers, importers from all parts of the world, and local farmers make this one of the most intriguing public marketplaces around. Open Fridays through Sundays. Located 6 miles north of the city on Hwy. 84, near the *Santa Fe Opera* amphitheater (no phone).

Shidoni Art Foundry This vast outdoor sculpture garden displays dozens of large pieces, with indoor galleries for smaller works. On Saturdays visitors can observe the bronze-casting process; call ahead for times. Located 5 miles north of the city on Bishop's Lodge Rd. (phone: 988-8001).

SPORTS AND FITNESS

CAMPING AND HIKING For maps and advice about the Santa Fe area, write to the *US Forest Service* (PO Box 1689, Santa Fe, NM 87504; phone: 988-6940). For information about the *Bandelier National Monument*, write to the *Visitors' Center* (*Bandelier National Monument*, HCR 1 Box 1, Suite 15, Los Alamos, NM 87544-9701; phone: 672-3861). Also refer to the book *Day Hikes in the Santa Fe Area*, published by the local chapter of the *Sierra Club*.

FISHING Among other wilderness areas where fishing is allowed by permit are the *Jemez Pueblo* lands, an 88,000-acre parcel with two spring-fed lakes at the *Holy Ghost* and *Dragonfly* recreation areas. Permits are available for fishing on weekends from sunrise to sundown for a small fee. The waters are stocked with trout, catfish, and bass. Cycling and hiking trails also are open to the public (no fee). At press time, *Jemez Pueblo* residents were planning to expand their recreational facilities to other sports, and were considering opening campgrounds for RVs. For more details, call the *Jemez Pueblo Visitors' Center* (northwest of Bernalillo, off State Hwy. 44; phone: 834-7235 or 834-7265).

FITNESS CENTERS *Santa Fe Spa* (786 N. St. Francis Dr.; phone: 984-8727); *Carl and Sandra's Conditioning Center* (560 Montezuma Ave.; phone: 982-6760).

GOLF The *Santa Fe Country Club* (Airport Rd.; phone: 471-2626) is popular, as is the *Cochiti Lake* golf course (5200 Cochiti Hwy., Cochiti Lake; phone: 465-2239).

HORSE RACING The season at the *Downs,* just south of the city on Interstate 25, extends from early June through *Labor Day,* with races on Fridays and weekends (phone: 471-3311).

HORSEBACK RIDING *Pool Wells* (phone: 852-2013 or 800-882-3024), 4 miles north of Española on the way to Taos, offers trail rides and overnight pack trips into the *Pecos Wilderness, Carson National Forest,* and the *Sebastian Martin Land Grant.*

JOGGING The most pleasant run is along the Santa Fe River, on Palace Avenue or Canyon Road. A more strenuous route is up Bishop's Lodge Road, into the Tesuque Valley.

SKIING Northern New Mexico usually has good powder from mid-December until early March and sunny spring skiing for several weeks after that. The *Santa Fe Ski Area* (phone: 982-4429 or 800-776-7669) is close (just 15 miles from town), moderate in size and challenge, and relatively uncrowded. At *Ten Thousand Waves* (Hyde Park Rd.; phone: 988-1047 or 982-9304), a Japanese bathhouse in the mountains, you can enjoy an après-ski soak in one of the outdoor hot tubs, along with a variety of beauty treatments (including herbal wraps, facials, saunas, and massage). The *Southwest Adventure Group* (*Sanbusco Market Center,* 500 Montezuma Ave; phone: 984-2080; 983-0111; or 800-723-9815) offers full- and half-day cross-country and downhill packages for groups of 10 or more; *Southwest Wilderness Adventures* (phone: 471-0589) offers packages to individuals.

TENNIS There are 32 courts at nine locations around town (phone: 473-7236 for information). Non-guests sometimes are allowed to use the courts at the *Rancho Encantado* resort (see *Checking In*) for a fee.

MUSIC

The *Orchestra of Santa Fe* performs at the *Lensic Theater* downtown (phone: 988-4640) from September through May; in February the orchestra stages a *Bach* or *Mozart Festival,* alternating composers every year. The *Santa Fe Symphony* (phone: 983-3530) performs a similar season. In July and August the *Santa Fe Chamber Music Festival,* widely recognized by its posters reproducing the work of Georgia O'Keeffe, takes place at the *St. Francis Auditorium* in the *Museum of Fine Arts* (W. Palace Ave.; phone: 983-2075). The six-week festival features eminent artists from around the world. The internationally acclaimed *Santa Fe Opera* offers lavish, adventuresome performances in a dramatic outdoor theater from late June through late August (phone: 986-5900 or 986-5955). Lectures and backstage tours are available to the public. The theater is on US 285/84, about 6 miles north of town.

NIGHTCLUBS AND NIGHTLIFE

Santa Fe is not known for its throbbing nightlife; the summertime arts festivals can be exciting, but for the most part, it's a pretty quiet town. There are, however, some diversions. María Benítez, one of the world's great flamenco artists, has a dance company performing June through September (phone: 983-8477). At the *Mañana Bar* (Don Gaspar Ave. and Alameda St.; phone: 982-4333), Broadway tunes and cabaret shows are featured at the piano bar. At *El Farol* (808 Canyon Rd.; phone: 983-9912) jazz, blues, and other live entertainment draw in the crowds. *Vanessies* (434 W. San Francisco St.; phone: 982-9966) has a piano bar for those who want to sing along, and at *La Casa Seña* (125 Palace Ave.; phone: 988-9232) singing waiters and waitresses perform Broadway songs. Live country music and dancing can be found at *Rodeo Nights* (2911 Cerrillos Rd.; phone: 473-4138). *Luna,* Santa Fe's largest dance club (519 Cerrillos Rd.; phone: 989-4888), presents live rock on weekday nights; a deejay plays classic rock and is accompanied by caged go-go dancers on weekends. Live salsa music and Latin jazz keep the dance floor lively at *Salsa's* (3347 Cerrillos Rd.; phone: 473-2800, ext. 491). If you're not up for dancing, while away the evening soaking in a hot tub and contemplating the stars at *Ten Thousand Waves* (see *Skiing*).

Best in Town

CHECKING IN

Santa Fe sees a tremendous influx of visitors every summer, so it's best to book well in advance. Expect to pay more than $200 a day for a double room (with private bath, TV set, and phone, unless otherwise indicated) in hotels listed as very expensive, $100 to $195 in expensive places, and $60 to $100 in moderate ones. During the winter rates usually are 10% to 25% lower. A few of the better bed and breakfast establishments are listed here; for other recommendations, call *Bed & Breakfast de Santa Fe* (phone: 982-5942). All telephone numbers are in the 505 area code unless otherwise indicated.

For an unforgettable experience in Santa Fe, we begin with our favorites, followed by our recommendations of cost and quality choices of accommodations, listed by price category.

SPECIAL HAVENS

Inn of the Anasazi Opened in 1991, this Pueblo Revival–style hotel fulfills ideals of classic Santa Fe architecture. It is beautifully appointed, from the wood and stone floors, *vigas,* and kiva fireplaces to the four-poster beds and hand-painted furnishings. Small yet elegant, the 59 rooms have all the comforts and charms of a small inn. There's also a library and a cozy living room. The caring staff members (including masseuses) are at your beck and call. An excellent restaurant, *Anasazi,* is on the premises (see *Eating Out*), and room service is always available. There is a concierge desk, and secretarial services can be arranged. A/V equipment, photocopiers, and computers are available, and meeting rooms accommodate up to 30. There's also express checkout. 113 Washington Ave. (phone: 988-3030; 800-688-8100).

Rancho Encantado Bordered by the *Tesuque Indian Reservation* and the *Santa Fe National Forest,* this topnotch Old Southwest resort hotel came into being in the 1930s as a very ordinary sort of desert lodge. Today it is a luxurious Western guest ranch—more than a hotel, more than an inn, the sort of establishment where you expect to find cowbells, dried peppers, and Indian weavings hanging here and there, the occasional rawhide chair, and lots of red tile. The 26 guestrooms, furnished with antiques and Southwestern Indian art and artifacts have their own patios; most have fireplaces. Across the road are another 60 guestrooms in two-bedroom villas. The tri-level dining room, walled in white adobe, looks out across the desert, nearly 170 acres of which make up the ranch's spread. You can swim in a heated outdoor pool, play tennis, take escorted trail rides, or join in many other indoor or outdoor activities. The food is Mexican, American, and continental. (Be sure to try the sour-cream chicken enchiladas.) There are big feasts for *Thanksgiving* and *Christmas*. Meeting rooms can accommodate up to 80, and photocopiers and A/V equipment are available. Rte. 592 in Tesuque, 8 miles north of Santa Fe (phone: 982-3537; 800-722-9339; fax: 983-8269).

VERY EXPENSIVE

Las Brisas de Santa Fe This quiet, Southwestern-style compound with 11 beautifully furnished one- and two-bedroom rental condominiums is within walking distance of the Plaza. All units have fireplaces. 624 Galisteo (phone: 982-5795).

Inn on the Alameda Located at the base of Canyon Road, just two blocks from the Plaza, this European-style hostelry is known for its intimate atmosphere. There are 47 charming rooms (some with fireplaces), personal service, and elaborate continental breakfasts. Among the business amenities are a concierge desk, meeting rooms for up to 30 people, A/V equipment, and photocopiers. 303 E. Alameda (phone: 984-2121; 800-289-2122; fax: 986-8325).

EXPENSIVE

Bishop's Lodge Originally Bishop Larry's retirement home in the late 19th century, this quiet retreat nestled in the Sangre de Cristo Mountains is surrounded by beautiful gardens and orchards on a thousand acres of privately owned land. This comfortable place has 88 spacious rooms, its own stables, tennis courts, a pool and sauna, trap and skeet shooting, and an all-day program for children during the summer. The Modified American Plan (MAP) rate in the summer includes two meals a day from the excellent kitchen; room service also is available. For those inclined to tie the knot, there's a tiny, but historic, chapel located on the property. Business services include meeting rooms that will accommodate up to 200, A/V equipment, and photocopiers. Open April through December. Bishop's Lodge Rd. (phone: 983-6377; fax: 989-8739).

Don Gaspar Compound Inn Set in a cluster of adobe- and Spanish mission–style buildings, this charming inn is conveniently located in the Don Gaspar Historic District, a short walk from the Plaza and Canyon Road. The six units (including a double room, two suites, and three separate casitas) are decorated in classic Southwestern style with antique furnishings and feature plenty of luxury amenities, including mini-refrigerators, plush robes, and stereos (but no TV sets). The larger suites and casitas also have full kitchens and fireplaces, and one has its own courtyard and garden. The grounds are beautifully landscaped, with extensive gardens and a fountain. Although there's no restaurant, a full breakfast is included in the rate, and there are several good dining spots in the neighborhood. The staff is friendly and helpful. 623 Don Gaspar Ave. (phone: 986-8664; fax: 986-0696).

Eldorado This 218-room property has handsomely furnished rooms with minibars; many suites boast wood-burning fireplaces and porches. There are remarkable mountain and city vistas, and guests can find everything from local art to *The New York Times* to real estate offerings in the extensive shopping gallery. The *Old House* restaurant features American and regional cooking. Other pluses are masseuses, saunas, and the heated rooftop Jacuzzi. For the celebrity-conscious, former President George Bush and King Juan Carlos of Spain have been overnight guests. Meeting rooms can accommodate up to 600. There's also a concierge desk, limited secretarial services, A/V equipment, photocopiers, and express checkout. 309 W. San Francisco St. (phone: 988-4455; 800-955-4455; fax: 988-5376).

El Farolito Bed and Breakfast More like an inn than a bed and breakfast establishment (although an excellent breakfast is included), it has seven charming Southwestern-style casitas with fireplaces; some have private patios and kitchenettes. There's parking as well. 514 Galisteo St. (phone: 988-1631).

La Fonda A Santa Fe landmark on the Plaza, it's less notable for service than for its striking appearance and historical character: Though the present hotel was built in 1920, an inn (with the same name) has existed on this site since the opening of the Santa Fe Trail, almost 200 years ago. The 153 guestrooms have Spanish colonial accents. There's an outdoor pool, two indoor Jacuzzis, and massages by appointment. An outdoor bar, located in a bell tower, is open seasonally and offers sunset views of the city. Meeting rooms can hold up to 600, and there is a 6,500-square-foot ballroom as well. Other business conveniences include a concierge desk, A/V equipment, and photocopiers. 100 E. San Francisco St. (phone: 982-5511; 800-523-5002; fax: 982-6367).

Grant Corner Inn A small bed and breakfast place in an old home in the downtown area, this is one of the nicest of the neighborhood group, with 13 comfortable rooms and a terrific breakfast on the patio, which also is open to non-guests. 122 Grant Ave. (phone: 983-6678).

Inn of the Animal Tracks This homey bed and breakfast establishment just a five-minute walk from the Plaza offers six guestrooms, each individually decorated in a wild-animal motif—wolf, otter, eagle, and other predators. A spacious Southwestern-style living room with fireplace and a peaceful backyard make this a great downtown haven. The inn's superior breakfast (with changing menu) is one of Santa Fe's secret treasures. 707 Paseo de Peralta (phone: 988-1546).

Inn of the Governors Don't let the motelish exterior dissuade you, for this cozy, 100-room property has an extremely attentive staff and thoughtfully appointed accommodations. Classical music plays continuously in the inviting lobby. Rooms are furnished with contemporary yet rustic Southwest furniture and local art; many have balconies and wood-burning fireplaces. *Mañana* serves dinner nightly, and it has a piano bar and intimate outdoor dining around a huge fireplace. There's also an outdoor heated pool and complimentary coffee, newspapers, and parking. A concierge desk attends to guests, and photocopiers and meeting rooms that seat 50 are available. 234 Don Gaspar Ave. (phone: 982-4333; 800-234-4534; fax: 989-9149).

Inn at Loretto The exterior of this modern, 137-room hostelry near the Plaza is distinctively Spanish Pueblo in style, although the rooms are quite standard, with no surprises. It's named for the historic spot it occupies, that of the old *Loretto Academy*, established in the 1850s by Bishop Lamy and the Sisters of Loretto. Business amenities include secretarial services, meeting rooms for up to 300, a concierge, A/V equipment, photocopiers, and computers. 211 Old Santa Fe Trail (phone: 988-5531; 800-727-5531; fax: 984-7988).

Picacho Plaza and Cielo Grande Condominiums This hostelry offers 133 Southwestern-style guestrooms with hand-carved furnishings; many have private terraces. The hotel also manages 38 fully equipped condominiums with fireplaces and outdoor spas. Highlights are a landscaped garden and a pool. The *Petroglyph* restaurant provides stunning views of the mountains. Guests can use the 19,000-square-foot health club, which has racquetball courts, a lap pool, aerobics classes, and weights. Additional amenities include room service until 10 PM, meeting rooms that seat up to 200, A/V equipment, and photocopiers. 750 N. St. Francis Dr. (phone: 982-5591; 800-441-5591; fax: 988-2821).

Plaza Real Located a half block from the Plaza, this intimate establishment has 56 rooms decorated in muted Southwestern tones. Most are demi-suites with fireplaces and sitting areas, and some have balconies. Although there is no restaurant on the premises, the kitchen delivers a continental breakfast to your room. The cozy lobby has a fireplace. Meeting rooms can seat up to 60, and there's a concierge desk and underground parking. 125 Washington Ave. (phone: 988-4900; 800-279-7325; fax: 988-4900).

La Posada A few blocks from the Plaza, this 116-room inn is spread out over six landscaped acres. The center of the complex is the *Staab House*, a Victorian home dating from 1882 that's been tastefully converted into a good restaurant and a popular lounge. Rates depend on the size and charm of the rooms, some of which are fairly conventional and others romantically Southwestern, with adobe fireplaces and Indian rugs. A concierge desk responds to guests' needs, and A/V equipment, photocopiers, and meeting rooms that hold up to 600 are available. 330 E. Palace Ave. (phone: 986-0000; 800-727-5276; fax: 982-6850).

St. Francis Built in the 1920s and restored to its original style, this small downtown place features 83 rooms decorated with period furnishings, the whole reflecting a simple, romantic elegance; afternoon tea is served. Meeting rooms can accommodate up to 150 people, A/V equipment and photocopiers are available, and there's also a concierge desk and express checkout. 210 Don Gaspar Ave. (phone: 983-5700; 800-666-5700; fax: 989-7690).

Santa Fe This hotel, designed in the Pueblo Revival style, is located in the Guadalupe district, less than a 10-minute walk to the Plaza. Run by a partnership between the Picuris tribe of northern New Mexico and the Santa Fe Hospitality Company, it is the first joint venture of its kind off the reservation trust lands. The 131 rooms include 91 suites, each with a separate bedroom and living area, a microwave oven, and a mini-bar. Complimentary shuttle service to the Plaza also is provided. Meeting rooms can accommodate up to 190, and there are photocopiers and A/V equipment available. There's also a concierge desk. Paseo de Peralta at Cerrillos Rd. (phone: 982-1200; 800-825-9876; fax: 984-2211).

MODERATE

El Paradero Bed & Breakfast Inn Most of the 14 rooms in this cozy, two-story adobe structure have private baths. Full breakfasts are served. Just a couple of blocks from the *State Capitol.* 220 W. Manhattan Ave. (phone: 988-1177).

Preston House Another good bed and breakfast option downtown. Five of the 15 rooms have fireplaces; two Queen Anne–style cottages also are available. 106 Faithway (phone: 982-3465).

Pueblo Bonito Bed & Breakfast Inn This downtown compound with 14 rooms and four suites is decorated in Southwest style. All units have kiva fireplaces. Continental breakfast and afternoon tea are included in the room rate. 138 W. Manhattan Ave. (phone: 984-8001).

El Rey Inn This is the best bargain in town for Santa Fe charm; if it were located downtown (rather than on "motel row"), prices would be at least double. Many of the individually decorated rooms have adobe fireplaces, *vigas* (decorated ceiling beams), and tile murals; some are solar heated and overlook a garden. A continental breakfast is included. There's also a playground, an outdoor pool, a coin-operated laundry, and a hot tub, which is open year-round. 1862 Cerrillos Rd. (phone: 982-1931).

EATING OUT

Northern New Mexico's distinctive regional fare is a variation on Mexican and Spanish dishes such as enchiladas and tamales, with less familiar local favorites like *chiles rellenos* (breaded whole green chili peppers stuffed with cheese) and *carne adovada* (beef or pork strips grilled with red chili marinade). The special ingredients include blue corn, which the Indians of the nearby pueblos believe to be the sacred corn of the gods, and green chili peppers, which are roasted, peeled, and served in a stew or sauce. (Avoid the common mistake of assuming that green chilies are milder than red chilies.) Many restaurants serve conventional northern New Mexican fare, as well as "new Southwestern" cuisine, creative dishes prepared with distinctively local ingredients such as green chilies, piñon nuts, blue corn, or *posole* (Mexican hominy).

With more than 200 dining establishments, Santa Fe's restaurant scene is highly competitive. Expect to pay $40 or more for a meal for two (without drinks, wine, or tip) in restaurants listed below as expensive; between $20 and $40 in those listed as moderate; and around $15 in inexpensive places. Restaurants are open daily for lunch and dinner unless otherwise noted. All telephone numbers are in the 505 area code unless otherwise indicated.

EXPENSIVE

Anasazi The menu here, described by the restaurant as "foods of the earth from the Native American, foods of the soul from the northern New Mexican, and foods of substance from the American cowboy," includes unusual dishes such as ginger shrimp dumplings in red chili oil, grilled shrimp *gorditas* (little tortilla pockets), and grilled pork chops on sun-dried tomato–flecked polenta. Open daily. Reservations advised. Major credit cards accepted. In the *Inn of the Anasazi*, 113 Washington Ave. (phone: 988-3030).

Babba Ganzo If you need a break from all the chilies and tortillas, run—don't walk—to this endearing, Tuscany-inspired trattoria opened just two years ago. Airy and rustic, the "Dapper Daddy" (the English translation of the Florentine name) rewards with exceptional rosemary *focaccia;* pizza with goat cheese and garlic; ravioli stuffed with veal and ricotta in sage butter; and charbroiled rack of lamb marinated in wine and herbs. Do save room, somehow, for the chocolate torte, the lemon custard tart sprinkled with pine nuts, or the *tiramisù*. Open daily. Reservations advised. Major credit cards accepted. 130 Lincoln Ave. (phone: 986-3835).

Café Escalera This light, airy café upstairs in Lincoln Place has attracted a local following because of its tasty health-conscious dishes. The culinary offerings include salads, pasta, grilled Moroccan lamb sausages, and even rib-eye steaks with roquefort butter and sinfully caloric desserts (for those with fewer health worries). There's an extensive wine list. Open Mondays through Saturdays for all three meals; for dinner only on Sundays. Reservations advised. Major credit cards accepted. 130 Lincoln Pl. (phone: 989-8188).

La Casa Seña This elegant yet cozy dining spot offers outdoor seating in historic Seña Plaza. Begin with a chilled margarita, then segue into fantastic blue-corn muffins and *trucha en terracotta,* a fresh Rocky Mountain trout wrapped in vine leaves and baked in a clay dish that's cracked open at tableside. Open daily. Reservations advised. Major credit cards accepted. 125 Palace Ave. (phone: 988-9232).

Coyote Café Chef/owner Mark Miller, who established a national reputation in the San Francisco Bay area and helped pioneer Southwestern cuisine, runs this fashionable place that uses regional ingredients in imaginative ways. Signature dishes include buttermilk corn cakes with *chipotle* (roasted jalapeño) shrimp; rib chops with chili onion rings; and sour-lemon bread pudding. Closed for lunch on weekdays, November through April; brunch menu on weekends. Reservations advised. Major credit cards accepted. 132 W. Water St. (phone: 983-1615).

Encore Provence A lovely private home has been remade into the city's only French dining room by a relocated French couple who successfully create such haute cuisine as shrimp beignets with seaweed salad, swordfish with oyster mushrooms, and halibut with niçoise olives. Landlubbers may opt for rabbit with sage stuffing and risotto, or lamb noisettes with eggplant provençale. Open daily. Reservations advised. Major credit cards accepted. 548 Agua Fria St. (phone: 983-7470).

Geronimo Lodge Housed in an adobe-style building built in 1756 by Geronimo Lopez, this popular dining spot serves unusual dishes with spicy flair. The menu changes often, but be sure to try the salmon piñon sticks with sambuca butter sauce and smoked tomato glaze, an appetizer that will linger in your memory. Closed Mondays for lunch. Reservations necessary. Major credit cards accepted. 724 Canyon Rd. (phone: 982-1500).

Pink Adobe One of the city's best for many years, "the Pink" (as it's known) features an unusual menu that includes steaks, creole dishes, and New Mexican specialties. Try the steak Dunnigan, with green chili peppers, or the chicken enchiladas with green chilies and sour cream. For dessert the hot French apple pie with rum sauce is hard to resist. The locals congregate in the *Dragon Room* bar over margaritas and other libations. Closed for lunch on weekends. Reservations advised. Major credit cards accepted. 406 Old Santa Fe Trail (phone: 983-7712).

Santacafé Locally popular for its casual elegance and fine food, it offers a sophisticated, "adaptive Southwestern" menu (which changes daily) drawing on Thai, Japanese, Chinese, Greek, Spanish, and Italian influences. Closed for lunch on weekends. Reservations advised. MasterCard and Visa accepted. 231 Washington Ave. (phone: 984-1788).

Thao Opened in 1991, this Thai place (pronounced *Tay*-oh) has become a favorite, offering a tasty counterpoint to the usual Santa Fe fare. The three small dining rooms are filled with authentic Asian artifacts: wooden crosses from the Philippines, colorful Burmese sashes, and an antique Chinese ceremonial chest. For an appetizer, try *som tom* (juliennes of papaya, greens, and peppers with dried shrimp and lime salad dressing). Entrées include Thai lacquered duck with turmeric and cassava. Coconut milk *crème brûlée* with palm sugar and cashew cookies end the meal with a flourish. Closed Sundays. Reservations advised. Major credit cards accepted. 322 Garfield St. (phone: 988-9562).

MODERATE

El Farol This longtime local favorite serves Spanish and Mediterranean *tapas* (hors d'oeuvres), as well as curried chicken, pasta with *manchego* cheese, grilled cactus, and salmon. The cozy bar is frequently crowded with locals. Nightly entertainment is eclectic: anything from jazz and flamenco to country blues. Open daily. Reservations advised. MasterCard and Visa accepted. 808 Canyon Rd. (phone: 983-9912).

Maria's At this domain of powerful margaritas and mariachi music, not to mention delicious New Mexican food, diners can watch tortillas being patted out in the front room or head to the cozy cantina in back for chicken *fajitas*, *chiles rellenos*, homemade *posole*, green chili stew, and barbecued ribs. An excellent wine list and scrumptious desserts are not easily forgotten. Open daily. Reservations advised. Major credit cards accepted. 555 W. Cordova Rd. (phone: 983-7929).

Old Mexico Grill Tucked into a shopping center, this lively and popular eatery serves up sizzling *fajitas*, spicy paella, and tacos *al carbón* (mesquite-grilled chicken breast or sirloin, sliced and rolled into a taco shell or a flour or corn tortilla) Closed Sundays for lunch. Limited reservations are accepted. Major credit cards accepted. 2434 Cerrillos Rd. (phone: 473-0338).

Paul's A local secret right in the heart of downtown, this neighborhood spot is bright, airy, and filled with folk art. Chef/owner Paul Hunsicker offers some of the city's best cookery. Try the baked salmon with pecan herb crust and sorrel cream sauce. Closed Sundays. Reservations advised. Major credit cards accepted. 72 W. Marcy St. (phone: 982-8738).

Shohko Café One of several Japanese spots that have become popular in Santa Fe, it serves what could be the only green chili tempura in the world. The rest of the menu includes more traditional dishes—sukiyaki, teriyaki, and so on—and there's a large, crowded sushi bar. Closed weekends for dinner. Reservations advised for dinner. Major credit cards accepted. 321 Johnson St. (phone: 983-7288).

La Tertulia Housed in a converted convent and exuding a Spanish colonial atmosphere, the classiest of the city's dining places serves New Mexican fare as well as paella and filet mignon. The native New Mexican dishes (enchiladas, burritos) tend to be mild but tasty, and the homemade sangria is excellent. Closed Mondays. Reservations necessary. Major credit cards accepted. 416 Agua Fria St. near Guadalupe St. (phone: 988-2769).

INEXPENSIVE

Blue Corn Café This cheery downtown place features local art, friendly service, and plentiful food at most reasonable prices. A real taste treat is the lavish burrito drizzled with both red and green chili (just ask for the "*Christmas* version"). The restaurant, voted best in town by *Santa Fe Reporter* readers, stocks more than 25 brands of tequila. Open daily. Reservations unnecessary. Major credit cards accepted. 133 Water St., upstairs (phone: 984-1800).

Cafe Pasqual's Just a block southwest of the Plaza, this bright, bustling room is homey and merry, with frilly Mexican decorations, bold murals, and friendly service. Breakfast is a celebration of chorizos, eggs, tortillas, whole-wheat pancakes, and pastries—and it's served all day. Fill up on a lunch of salmon-and–goat cheese quesadillas, or go for dinner's heavier Mexican plates with Asian touches. Nothing will disappoint. Open daily for all three meals. No reservations. Major credit cards accepted. 121 Don Gaspar Ave. (phone: 983-9340).

La Choza Obscure, yet cozy, this place in a turn-of-the-century adobe ranch house on a side street just northeast of Cerrillos Road and St. Francis Drive is worth searching out. It has been operated by the same family for generations, and New Mexican cooking doesn't come any more authentic than here. Diners can savor the ambience of Old Santa Fe on the lovely open-air patio. Open daily. No reservations. Major credit cards accepted. 905 Alarid St. (phone: 982-0909).

Cloud Cliff A local artists' hangout, this café is located in a complex of working studios on the city's less-than-charming west side, but the walls serve as one of the most interesting exhibition spaces in Santa Fe. Fresh bread and European pastries are the specialties, and there's also a full menu of croissant sandwiches, homemade soups, and elaborate salads. Open daily for breakfast and lunch. Reservations unnecessary. Major credit cards accepted. 1805 Second St. (phone: 983-6254).

Josie's Casa de Comida A rare example of a dying breed—the small, plain, downtown luncheon café. The *chiles rellenos,* enchiladas, and other regional dishes are terrific. This place is so popular that people will line up and wait patiently on the street for a table. Lunch only. Closed weekends. No reservations or credit cards accepted. 225 E. Marcy St. (phone: 983-5311).

Old Santa Fe Trail Books and Coffeehouse Combine a light meal, a cappuccino, and a good read at this bookstore/café in a cozy Victorian house. Soups and sandwiches are the mainstays. Open daily for breakfast and lunch. No reservations. Major credit cards accepted. 613 Old Santa Fe Trail (phone: 988-8878).

Shed At this popular place for lunch, there usually is a line after 11:30 AM, but the wait is pleasant in the front courtyard, originally the central patio of a large hacienda. The red chili served on blue-corn enchiladas, tacos, or burritos is unmatched, the *posole* and beans are very good, and the desserts are fine. Open Mondays through Saturdays for lunch. No reservations or credit cards accepted. 113½ Palace Ave. (phone: 982-9030).

Tia Sophia's A longtime downtown favorite of locals and visitors, this casual eatery showcases some of the best green chili cookery in town. Try the breakfast burrito, a popular Southwest dish that was invented right here. Daily lunch specials include *carne adovada* (beef marinated in red chili sauce) and blue-corn enchiladas. Open Mondays through Saturdays for breakfast and lunch. No reservations. Major credit cards accepted. 210 W. San Francisco St. (phone: 983-9880).

Tomasita's At another local favorite, the menu selection runs from stuffed sopaipillas to *chalupas* and tacos and steaks to vegetarian dishes. Chili—hot and spicy—is emphasized; portions are large. Unless you arrive early, the wait for a table can easily last as long as your meal. Closed

Sundays. No reservations. MasterCard and Visa accepted. 500 S. Guadalupe St. (phone: 983-5721).

Tortilla Flats Don't let the fast-food exterior deceive you; the New Mexican food is delicious, and the service is friendly. Open daily for all three meals. No reservations. MasterCard and Visa accepted. 3139 Cerrillos Rd. (phone: 471-8685).

Zia Diner and Bakery Nestled in a converted warehouse is a version of a 1950s diner decorated with pink and turquoise Southwestern accents. It's a very popular luncheon spot with the locals. Burgers, homemade soups, and daily specials are featured. The affiliated bakery around the corner offers homemade muffins, pies, and cappuccino in the morning and pot pies, meat loaf, and pizza in the evening. Closed Sundays for lunch. No reservations. Major credit cards accepted. 326 Guadalupe St. (phone: 988-7008).

THE JOY OF SOUTHWEST COOKING

For those with an urge to create their own Southwestern and New Mexican culinary masterpieces, the *Santa Fe School of Cooking and Market* (116 W. San Francisco St., Upper Level, in *Plaza Mercado;* phone: 983-4511) conducts two-and-a-half-hour classes where you can learn to make a variety of native dishes such as *posole*, blue-corn enchiladas, and sopaipilla (pillow-like pastry). Happily, you then get to consume the fruits (or in this case, enchiladas) of your labor and take home the recipes. Reservations advised. MasterCard and Visa accepted. A good place to buy the materials for practicing your newfound culinary skills is the *Farmers' Market,* held Tuesday and Saturday mornings at *Sanbusco Market Center.* Everything from fresh chilies to homemade preserves can be found here.

Savannah

At-a-Glance

SEEING THE CITY

Driving into Savannah on a spectacular (but unnamed) bridge 185 feet above the Savannah River offers a fine view of the city. For a bird's-eye view of the busy river traffic, have lunch, dinner, or drinks at *Windows* restaurant (see *Eating Out*) in the *Hyatt Regency* hotel (2 W. Bay St.; phone: 238-1234).

SPECIAL PLACES

Historic Savannah is appealingly negotiable on foot. Count on a minimum of two days to see everything. Here are some of the city's most favored stops and routes.

RIVERFRONT PLAZA Bordering the thriving seaport's 40-foot-deep channel, this nine-block, brick plaza is alive with commercial establishments housed in former 19th-century cotton warehouses. There also may be a rock concert or a chamber music recital by a *Savannah Symphony* ensemble.

BULL STREET If you spend a morning at the plaza, the afternoon can be spent walking down Bull Street (Savannah's principal north-south street) from *City Hall* to *Forsyth Park*, 12 blocks south. The six-story *City Hall*, on River and Bay Streets, stands alongside two brass cannons captured from Cornwallis at Yorktown. The cannons were presented to the Chatham Artillery, a Savannah military unit, by George Washington, in 1791. East of *City Hall*, *Factor's Walk*, once a center for cotton merchants and now an area of restaurants and shops, runs along the city side of the former cotton buildings. After passing *City Hall*, you will come to the *US Customs House*, built in 1852 on the same site where Georgia's founder, James Edward Oglethorpe, lived in 1733 and where evangelist John Wesley first preached in America. Also here are the city's five most beautiful squares:

Johnson Square Here, two fountains flow and decks of dazzling azaleas bloom in spring. *Christ Episcopal Church*, the first church established in the Colony of Georgia (1773), stands here, too. The present building dates back to 1838.

Wright Square The exquisite Ascension window of the *Lutheran Church of the Ascension*, installed in 1878, is internationally known.

Chippewa Square Here you'll find the *First Baptist Church*, the oldest of its denomination in Georgia; the *Barrow Mansion*, which now houses an insurance firm; and the *Savannah Theater* (222 Bull St.; phone: 233-7764), one of the country's oldest theaters in continuous use.

Madison Square The carillons and stained glass windows of *St. John's Episcopal Church*, built in 1852, are well known to church lovers. Here, too, is the *Green-Meldrim House*, which served as Sherman's headquarters after Savannah was captured in the Civil War.

Monterey Square *Temple Mickve Israel*, consecrated in 1878 for Georgia's oldest Jewish congregation (1733), contains a Torah scroll more than 800 years old. The Gordon and Taylor Street houses facing the square are outstanding examples of historic preservation.

FROM ABERCORN TO ST. JULIAN STREET Starting at Calhoun Square, at Abercorn and Gordon Streets, walk north toward *Massie School* (1856), a Greek Revival structure that is the public school system's education museum. Alongside stands *Wesley Monumental United Methodist Church*. Four blocks north, at Lafayette Square, is the *Colonial Dames House* (1849). Two blocks east, beside Troup Square and on parallel Charlton and Macon Streets, are Savannah's two best examples of slum conversion properties, now tony townhouses. A block and a half north of Troup Square, *Colonial Park Cemetery* contains the graves of Georgia colonists. From the cemetery, it's a two-block walk up Abercorn Street to the 1816 *Owens-Thomas House* at the corner of State Street, hailed as America's finest example of English Regency architecture. Now a museum, the house was visited in 1825 by Revolutionary War hero Marquis de Lafayette. One block east, facing Columbia Square, is *Isaiah Davenport House*, also a museum and the first architecturally important structure to have been reclaimed by the *Historic Savannah Foundation*. From here, it's a three-block walk north to St. Julian Street, which splits three squares: Reynolds Square at Abercorn Street, Warren Square at Habersham Street, and Washington Square at Houston Street. This section has one of Savannah's largest clusters of restored 18th- and 19th-century homes. Facing Reynolds Square is the *Olde Pink House* (23 Abercorn St.; phone: 232-4286), ca. 1790, now a restaurant.

FORT PULASKI This national monument was named for the Revolutionary War hero killed in the 1779 Battle of Savannah. Built between 1829 and 1847, the fort was captured by Union forces in 1862. Open daily. Admission charge. US 80 near Tybee Island (phone: 786-5787).

EXTRA SPECIAL

Hilton Head Island, a luxury resort area in South Carolina about 40 miles northeast of Savannah, has 16 golf courses, pretty beaches, deep-sea fishing, tennis courts, a private airstrip, and plenty of nightlife. Reservations are advised if you plan to stay overnight. *Sea Pines Plantation,* a resort community of private villas and a 204-room, oceanfront inn, has beaches, three championship golf courses (including famed *Harbour Town*), tennis courts, bicycle paths with rental facilities, pools, marinas, and a 625-acre forest preserve. For information, contact *Sea Pines Plantation* (Hilton Head Island, SC 29928; phone: 803-785-3333; 800-845-6131). Reservations for villas, condos, and homes island-wide, but not hotel rooms, may be made through the *Hilton*

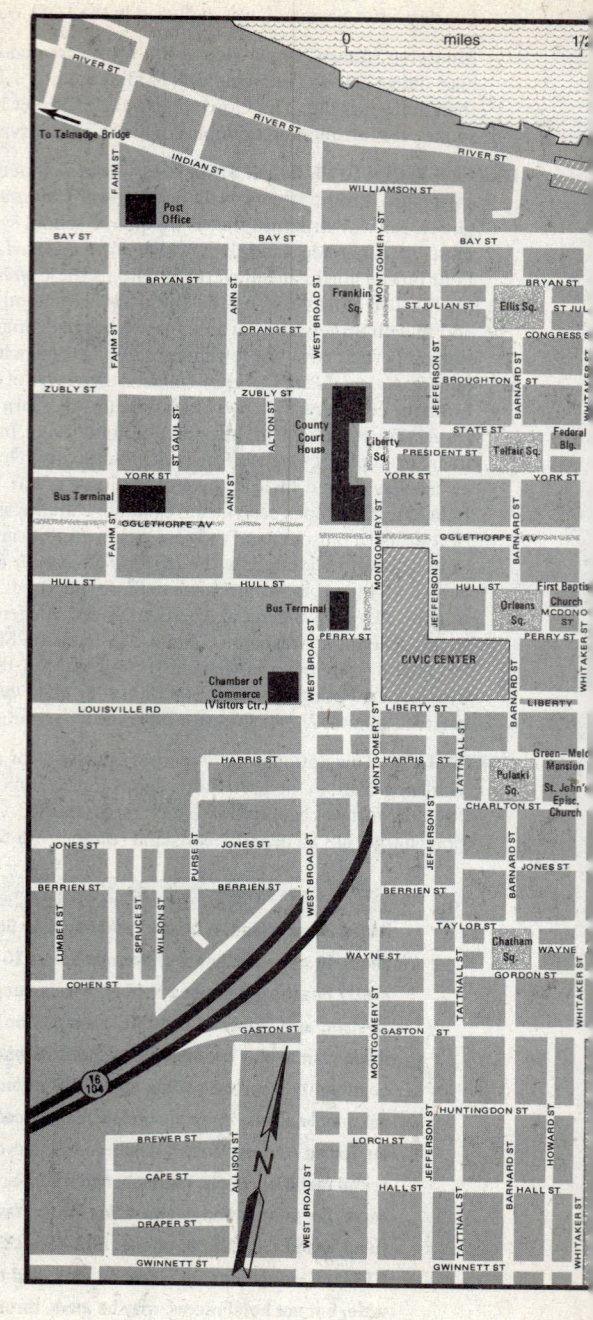

Head Reservation Service (phone: 800-845-7018). For information on Hilton Head activities, call the *Chamber of Commerce* (phone: 803-785-3673).

About 80 miles down the coast lie Georgia's "Golden Isles"—St. Simons Island, Little St. Simons Island, Sea Island, and Jekyll Island. Reached by causeway from Brunswick, Georgia, each has its own personality, and together they lay out an enormous spread of golf, tennis, beaches, lodgings, and dining. St. Simons offers the widest range of accommodations and activities. Little St. Simons (phone: 638-7472 for island information and reservations) is a privately owned, mostly primeval sanctuary, with a comfortably rustic lodge, dense forests, and 6 miles of unspoiled beaches and dunes. Sea Island is the site of the fine *Cloister* hotel (phone: 638-3611; 800-SEA-ISLAND). Jekyll Island's brightest star is the *Jekyll Island Club* (phone: 635-2600; 800-333-3333), a gorgeously restored Victorian clubhouse where the elite once lodged, now operated as a Radisson resort.

Sources and Resources

TOURIST INFORMATION

Your first stop should be the *Savannah Visitors Center* (301 Martin Luther King Jr. Blvd.; phone: 944-0455), which is open daily. Housed in the railway station, which dates to the 1860s, the center has maps, information, tours, and a free slide show and is also the starting point for city tours. Before leaving home, write to the *Savannah Area Convention and Visitors Bureau* (PO Box 1628, Savannah, GA 31402; phone: 944-0456; 800-444-2427). Contact the Georgia state tourism hotline (phone: 404-656-3590) for maps, calendars of events, health updates, and travel advisories.

LOCAL COVERAGE *Savannah Morning News* and *Savannah Evening Press,* dailies. *Sojourn in Savannah* by Betty Rauers and Franklin Traub (*Historic Savannah Foundation;* $5.95) offers detailed information on places of interest.

TELEVISION STATIONS WSAV Channel 3–NBC; WVAN Channel 9–PBS; WTOC Channel 11–CBS; and WJCL Channel 22–ABC.

RADIO STATIONS AM: WBMQ 630 (oldies/talk); WSOK 1230 (gospel music/R&B); WCHY 1290 (country); and WSGA 1400 (nostalgia). FM: WSVH 91 (classical and jazz); WCHY 94.1 (country); WAEZ 97.3 (adult contemporary); and WIXV 95.5 (rock).

TELEPHONE The area code for Savannah is 912.

SALES TAX Combined state and local sales tax is 6%. There is an additional hotel and motel tax of 5%.

CLIMATE Most of the year, temperatures are in the 70s F, but the mercury drops into the 50s and 40s from December through March and climbs to the high 80s or low 90s in summer. Humidity is usually high, except when relief comes from the afternoon thunderstorms that are frequent from June through September.

GETTING AROUND

AIRPORT *Savannah International Airport* is about 11 miles from the downtown Historic District. *McCall's Limousine Service* (phone: 966-5364) operates between the airport and downtown. *Low Country Adventures* (phone: 966-2112) operates between the airport and Hilton Head Island, SC, resort area.

BUS *Chatham Area Transit (CAT)* operates the municipal bus system (900 E. Gwinnett St.; phone: 233-5767). The fare is $1.

CAR RENTAL *Avis, Budget, Enterprise,* and *Hertz* have offices in town.

CRUISES Cocktail and dinner cruises on the Savannah River are offered on the paddle wheel steamboats *Magnolia* (phone: 234-4011) and *Savannah River Queen* (phone: 232-6404).

HORSE-DRAWN CARRIAGES Join *Carriage Tours of Savannah* (phone: 236-6756 for reservations) for a day or night horse-drawn carriage ride around the historic district. As the horses clop gently through the old streets, guides enhance the mood with history, legends, and scandals of old Savannah.

TAXI Cabs can be hailed downtown. There are taxi stands at the main hotels, but you may prefer to call *Adam Cab* (phone: 927-7466).

TOURS To see Savannah from an insider's perspective, contact *At Your Service* (60 E. Broad St.; phone: 232-6866; 800-868-6867), which offers escorted walking tours of gardens, hidden shops, and private homes, spiced with amusing anecdotes. The Low Country Wildlife Tour, run by *Adventure Tours* (210 W. Jones St.; phone: 233-7770), surveys the marshes and waterways around the city.

LOCAL SERVICES

AUDIOVISUAL EQUIPMENT *Audio Visual Resources* (9-B Mall Ter.; phone: 355-2020); *Video Works* (342 Bull St.; phone: 238-2486).

BABY-SITTING *Angels and Imps* (614 Jackson Blvd.; phone: 355-1068).

BUSINESS SERVICES *Norrell Services* (7203 Hodgson Dr.; phone: 354-0044).

DRY CLEANER/TAILOR *Dry Cleaning USA* (4505 Bull St.; phone: 352-2274).

LIMOUSINE *McCall's Limousine Service* (*Savannah International Airport;* phone: 966-5364).

MECHANIC *Jackson Brothers Car Care* (1141 W. Gwinnett St.; phone: 236-0631).

- **MEDICAL EMERGENCY** *Memorial Medical Center* (Waters Ave. and 65th St.; phone: 356-8000).

- **MESSENGER SERVICES** *Colonial Couriers of Savannah* (phone: 234-2161); *Savannah-Chatham Direct Delivery* (1141 W. Gwinnett St.; phone: 236-3434).

- **MONEY TRANSFERS** *American Express MoneyGram* (phone: 800-926-9400 for information; 800-866-8800 for money transfers); *Western Union Financial Services* (phone: 800-325-6000 or 800-325-4176).

- **NATIONAL/INTERNATIONAL COURIER** *DHL Worldwide Express* (phone: 800-225-5345); *FedEx* (phone: 232-0068).

- **PHARMACY** *Revco Medical Arts* (*Medical Arts Shopping Center*, 4725 Waters Ave. at 63rd St.; phone: 355-7111), open 24 hours.

- **PHOTOCOPIES** *Chatham Repro-Graphics* (105 Eisenhower Dr.; phone: 352-2987); *Savannah Blueprint* (11 E. York St.; phone: 232-2162).

- **POST OFFICE** Downtown office (127 Bull St.; phone: 232-2601).

- **PROFESSIONAL PHOTOGRAPHER** *Gerald Pollack & Associates* (111 E. 34th St.; phone: 233-0248).

- **TELECONFERENCE FACILITIES** *Hyatt Regency Savannah* (see *Checking In*, below).

- **TRANSLATOR** *American Red Cross* (phone: 651-5310).

- **WESTERN UNION/TELEX** Many offices are located around the city (phone: 800-325-6000 to find the location nearest you).

- **OTHER** *Convention Consultants of Savannah Delta*, convention planning and services (phone: 234-4088).

SPECIAL EVENTS

Georgia Day, February 12, commemorates the founding of the colony; festivities last for a week. *St. Patrick's Day* (March 17) features the biggest street parade south of New York and traditionally kicks off Savannah's high spring season. Against a Technicolor background of millions of flowering azaleas, dogwood, and forsythia, the annual *Christ Episcopal Church Tour of Homes* (phone: 234-8054), at the end of March and in early April, draws awestruck visitors into more than three dozen private mansions and gardens and to candlelight suppers at historic places around the city. Early April's *Hidden Gardens Tours* (phone: 238-0248) take you behind the walls of some of the city's most historic homes. Also in April, the *Savannah Tour of Homes and Gardens* (phone: 234-8054) sponsors special walking tours, plus a shrimp boil; Sunday dinner at *Mrs. Wilkes' Boarding House* (see *Eating Out*); and a barbecue in the old *City Market*. *Christmas* is a special season, when homes, churches, and public buildings are dressed in colonial finery.

MUSEUMS

In addition to its historic houses, Savannah has several notable museums.

JULIETTE GORDON LOW GIRL SCOUT NATIONAL CENTER The *Wayne-Gordon House*, featuring many original family furnishings, was the birthplace of the Girl Scouts' founder. Closed Wednesdays. Admission charge. 142 Bull St. (phone: 233-4501).

SAVANNAH HISTORY MUSEUM The collection contains a 19th-century steam locomotive, a replica of the cotton gin (invented in Savannah), and many other historic artifacts, as well as films on the city's history. Open daily. Admission charge. 303 Martin Luther King Jr. Blvd. (phone: 238-1779).

SAVANNAH SCIENCE MUSEUM Dedicated to making science fun, it boasts a Foucault pendulum and the skeleton of a giant ground sloth, as well as native reptiles and amphibians and planetarium shows. Closed Mondays. Admission charge. 4405 Paulsen St. (phone: 355-6705).

SHIPS OF THE SEA MARITIME MUSEUM A fine collection of ships' models chronicles maritime history throughout the world. Open daily. Admission charge. 503 E. River St. and 504 E. Bay St. (phone: 232-1511).

TELFAIR ACADEMY OF ARTS AND SCIENCES The oldest public art museum in the South and one of Savannah's most outstanding, it exhibits American and European paintings as well as 19th-century furniture. Closed Mondays. Admission charge. 121 Barnard St. (phone: 232-1177).

TYBEE ISLAND MUSEUM AND LIGHTHOUSE This eclectic collection of Americana emphasizes, but isn't limited to, military history. Closed Tuesdays. Admission charge. Tybee Island (phone: 786-5801).

SPORTS AND FITNESS

Savannah is near many of the country's most popular vacation destinations. Names like Hilton Head, Sea Island, St. Simons, and Jekyll Island are familiar to lovers of the outdoor life, and all are less than a day's drive from Savannah.

BICYCLING Cycling through the historic district can be an unforgettable experience. The *City Market Bicycle Shoppe* (322 W. Broughton St.; phone: 233-9401) rents bikes.

FITNESS CENTER The *YMCA* (6400 Habersham; phone: 354-6223) has an outdoor pool, weight machines, an indoor track, and tennis courts. Facilities are available to non-members for a fee.

GOLF The 18-hole course at the *Sheraton Savannah* resort (Wilmington Island Rd.; phone: 897-1612; 800-533-6706), one of the best known in the South, is open to the public (and will remain open during resort renovations). The best municipal courses are at *Bacon Park* (Skidaway Rd. and Shorty Cooper Dr.; phone: 354-2625) and *Southbridge* golf club (415 Southbridge Blvd.; phone: 651-5455).

JOGGING Run the 1-mile perimeter of *Forsyth Park*, or along the waterfront in the early morning or evening when there is less traffic; Lake Mayer, 15 minutes from town and reachable by car, has an asphalt track. A jogging map is available at the *De Soto Hilton* (see *Checking In*) and the *Savannah Visitors Center*.

SAILING You can rent sailboats and equipment from *Sail Harbor* (618 Wilmington Island Rd.; phone: 897-2896). In 1996, Savannah will host the sailing events of the *Summer Olympic Games*.

SWIMMING AND FISHING Tybee Island (formerly Savannah Beach) is a longtime favorite haunt 18 miles from downtown Savannah. Enjoy swimming, fishing, surfing, crabbing, boating, picnicking, and beachcombing among the dunes; you can even climb the century-old lighthouse.

TENNIS The best public tennis courts are at *Bacon Park,* Lake Mayer, *Forsyth Park,* and *Daffin Park.*

THEATER

For complete performance schedules, check the publications listed under *Local Coverage* above. The *Savannah Civic Center* (Orleans Sq.; phone: 234-6666) is the largest auditorium in the city, presenting touring Broadway productions, ballet, and dance theater performances. *Little Theater* (Chippewa Sq. downtown; phone: 233-7764) is another place for good drama. It occupies the historic *Savannah Theater.*

MUSIC

The *Savannah Civic Center* (Orleans Sq.; phone: 651-6550), home of the *Savannah Symphony Orchestra,* offers the best concerts in the city.

NIGHTCLUBS AND NIGHTLIFE

Riverfront Plaza and the *City Market* area are alive with discos and clubs. Three of the most popular are *The Bottom Line* (206 W. St. Julian St.; phone: 232-0218), *Kevin Barry's Irish Pub* (117 W. River St.; phone: 233-9626), and *Hard-Hearted Hannah's* in the *DeSoto Hilton* (Liberty and Bull Sts.; phone: 232-9000).

Best in Town

CHECKING IN

For reservations at many of Savannah's historic inns, call these central services: *Savannah Historic Inns and Guest Houses* (phone: 233-7666; 800-262-4667); *R.S.V.P. Savannah* (phone: 232-7787; 800-729-7787); and *Historic Savannah Reservation Service* (phone: 444-2427). Expect to pay between $100 and $150 (sometimes more) per night for a double room at those places listed as expensive; and between $60 and $100 at those categorized as moderate; there are no exceptional inexpensive hotels in the city. Unless otherwise noted, hotels have air conditioning, private baths, TV sets, and telephones. All hotels are in the 912 area code unless otherwise indicated.

EXPENSIVE

Ballastone Inn and Townhouse Charming and romantic, this inn has 17 rooms and six suites in either the main mansion or a townhouse four blocks down the street. All are uniquely furnished with 19th-century antiques and reproductions, and have ceiling fans and canopy beds; the suites feature large sitting rooms and kitchens, and some have fireplaces and Jacuzzis. A continental breakfast is served, and although there is no restaurant, the inn is near several fine dining spots. Other amenities include a concierge and nightly turn-down service. 14 E. Oglethorpe Ave. (phone: 236-1484; 800-822-4553).

Comer House This grand Victorian mansion on one of the city's most picturesque squares offers two garden suites with private entrances and kitchenettes and a one-bedroom apartment. Tours of the antiques-filled main rooms are given frequently. 2 E. Taylor St. (phone: 234-2923; 800-262-4667).

DeSoto Hilton In the heart of the historic district, this 264-room property has retained much of the Old World charm that made its 19th-century predecessor—the *DeSoto*—queen of the gaslight era's carriage trade. Amenities include the *Pavilion Room* for fine dining, the *Red Lion* lounge, and recreation facilities. Liberty and Bull Sts. (phone: 232-9000; 800-426-8483).

Eliza Thompson House Some of the 25 rooms in this quaint three-story 1847 restored townhouse in the Historic District are decorated with antiques; a number also feature fireplaces, kitchenettes, or private entrances. Complimentary sherry makes things even cozier. 7 W. Jones St. (phone: 236-3620; 800-348-9378).

Gastonian Inn One of the city's loveliest hostelries, it has 13 rooms rich in antiques and historic Savannah decor, set in a pair of mid-19th-century townhouses. Many rooms have whirlpool baths. A full Southern breakfast, afternoon tea, and late-night cordials are included in the rate. 220 E. Gaston St. (phone: 232-2869; 800-322-6603).

Hyatt Regency Savannah This 346-room property overlooking *Riverfront Plaza* offers views of oceangoing ships in the harbor. *Windows* restaurant, overlooking the river, has become a favorite dining spot (see *Eating Out*), along with the more casual *MD's Lounge* and *Patrick's Porch*. Guests can arrange tours with the concierge. 2 W. Bay St. (phone: 238-1234; 800-233-1234).

Magnolia Place Inn Facing *Forsyth Park* in the heart of Savannah, it offers 13 rooms with antique furnishings and Jacuzzis. Limousine service is available. 503 Whitaker St. (phone: 236-7674; 800-238-7674).

Planters Inn Although built in 1920, this seven-story, 56-room property is a 19th-century-style inn with antiques, Georgian furnishings, and all the modern comforts. The penthouse rooms even have working fireplaces. 29 Abercorn St. (phone: 232-5678; 800-554-1187).

Radisson Plaza Savannah A lighted boardwalk connects this 384-room, eight-story tower to *Riverfront Plaza*'s shops, restaurants, and nightclubs. Among the many amenities are an upscale dining room, a café, two lounges, an indoor pool, and an exercise room. Business conveniences include a concierge, secretarial services, computers, and express checkout. 100 General McIntosh Blvd. (phone: 233-7722; 800-333-3333).

River Street Inn Built in 1817, this intimate hotel is convenient to downtown. Its 44 guestrooms are furnished with Victorian antiques; many also have balconies and lovely river views. Continental breakfast and a daily wine and cheese reception are complimentary. The inn does not have its own restaurant, but *Huey's* (see *Eating Out*) is in the same building. Business amenities include secretarial services, fax machines, photocopiers, and meeting space for up to 40. 115 E. River St. (phone: 234-6400; 800-253-4229).

MODERATE

Bed-and-Breakfast Inn This restored 1853 townhouse offers historic inn charm at reasonable prices. There are 14 rooms, seven with private baths; some have full kitchens as well. 117 W. Gordon St. (phone: 238-0518).

Courtyard by Marriott The 144 attractive, contemporary guestrooms and a good restaurant and bar make this an excellent suburban choice. 6703 Abercorn St. (phone: 354-7878; 800-228-9290).

Days Inn Savannah Across the street from *Riverfront Plaza,* this chain hotel with 253 attractive rooms is a good choice for families. There's a pool, gameroom, and 24-hour restaurant where kids under 12 eat free of charge. 201 W. Bay St. (phone: 236-4440; 800-325-2525).

Hunter House A half-hour's drive from downtown Savannah and a block from the beach at Tybee Island, this three-story 1910 beach house has become a comfortable, casual bed and breakfast. Accommodations range from single rooms to four-room suites with kitchens. Upstairs, overlooking the ocean, there's an excellent seafood restaurant and a lively, locally popular bar. 1701 Butler Ave., Tybee Island (phone: 786-7515).

EATING OUT

With their menus ranging from elegant to home-style, many of the city's chefs do wondrous things with fresh shrimp, oysters, flounder, and blue crabs. Expect to pay $50 or more for dinner for two at restaurants listed as expensive; between $30 and $50 at those categorized as moderate; and less than $30 at inexpensive places. Prices do not include drinks, wine, tax, or tips. Unless otherwise noted, restaurants serve lunch and dinner. All restaurants are in the 912 area code unless otherwise indicated.

EXPENSIVE

Elizabeth on Thirty-Seventh Set in a lovely old Savannah mansion, this restaurant has won acclaim for its innovative Southern fare, featuring fresh ingredients as well as sumptuous desserts. Closed Sundays. Reservations advised. Major credit cards accepted. 105 E. 37th at Drayton (phone: 236-5547).

45 South Located in an 1852 home decorated with Native American art and artifacts, this upscale dining room serves delicious contemporary American fare. Everything is incomparably fresh. Though the menu changes monthly, broiled grouper in burgundy butter sauce and rack of lamb with garlic cream and madeira sauce are satisfying choices. Service is attentive. Closed Sundays. Reservations advised. Major credit cards accepted. 20 E. Broad St. (phone: 233-1881).

17 Hundred 90 This elegant dining room in the inn of the same name serves well-prepared continental fare. The top specialty is rack of lamb Dijon; other good choices are fresh red snapper Parisienne (featuring a lemon butter sauce) and poached Norwegian salmon. The 18th-century fireplaces (now powered by gas), the low lighting, and the crystal chandelier lend romantic touches. Open daily; dinner only on weekends. Reservations advised for dinner. Major credit cards accepted. 307 E. President St. (phone: 236-7122).

Windows This exquisite dining room in the *Hyatt Regency Savannah* offers views of merchant ships on the river as well as a continental menu featuring seafood, duck, and stir-fried Oriental dishes. Open daily; dinner only on Saturdays; brunch only on Sundays. Reservations advised. Major credit cards accepted. 2 W. Bay St. (phone: 238-1234).

MODERATE

Bistro Savannah Located in the *City Market* area, this restaurant presents one of the city's most interesting menus; *vindaloo* chicken (sautéed with curry, fresh tomatoes, brown sugar, and coriander), Louisiana jambalaya, sautéed sweetbreads, and speckled grits crab cakes are featured. Open daily; dinner only on weekends. Reservations advised. Major credit cards accepted. 309 W. Congress St. (phone: 233-6266).

Boar's Head For more than 25 years, this restaurant has served steaks, veal, and seafood in charming brick-walled rooms overlooking *Riverfront Plaza*. Open daily. Reservations advised. Major credit cards accepted. One North Lincoln St. (phone 232-3196).

Chart House Nautical decor, fine seafood and steaks, a cozy bar, and balconies overlooking the Savannah River and *Riverfront Plaza* make this one of the most popular spots in town. Open daily for dinner only. Reservations advised. Major credit cards accepted. 202 W. Bay St. (phone: 234-6686).

Garibaldi's An 1870s firehouse has been refashioned into an Italian café, with marble-top tables, lace curtains, mirrors, and antiques. Excellent pasta, veal, seafood, grilled duck, lamb, and lobster are served. Open daily for dinner only. Reservations advised. Major credit cards accepted. 315 W. Congress St. (phone: 232-7118).

Johnny Harris Specialties here are steaks, prime ribs, barbecue, and chicken, with baking done on the premises. Into its third generation of continuous ownership, this is where the nationally marketed Johnny Harris Barbecue Sauce originated. Closed Sundays. Major credit cards accepted. 1651 E. Victory Dr. (phone: 354-7810).

Sakura The tempura, the teriyaki, and the sushi bar, not to mention the waterfront view, are all excellent reasons to dine at Savannah's only authentic Japanese eatery. Open daily; dinner only on Sundays. Reservations advised. Major credit cards accepted. 21 E. River St. (phone: 233-0203).

Sebastian's This cozy spot, housed in a restored old tavern, offers creative Low Country, American, and European dishes. Closed Sundays. Reservations advised. Major credit cards accepted. 321 Jefferson St., downtown (phone: 234-3211).

INEXPENSIVE

Breakfast Club Transplanted Chicagoan Joseph Sadowsky has turned this humble Tybee Island diner a half-hour from downtown into a culinary landmark. Along with basic breakfast, the morning menu includes a host of innovative omelettes and waffles. It's a great place to meet the laid-back Tybee Islanders. Open daily for breakfast and lunch. No reservations or credit cards accepted. 1500 Butler Ave., Tybee Island (phone: 786-5984).

Clary's Café This cheerful little spot in the historic district is a favorite hangout for locals, who swap news over Southern-style breakfast, salads, soups, pasta, and seafood dishes. Open daily. No reservations or credit cards accepted. At the corner of W. Jones and Abercorn Sts. (phone: 233-0402).

Crystal Beer Parlor For more than half a century, this casual place has been famous for its sandwiches and burgers. Closed Sundays. Reservations unnecessary. Major credit cards accepted. 301 W. Jones St. (phone: 232-1153).

Exchange Tavern This is River Street's oldest restaurant, housed in a riverfront landmark. The Reuben sandwiches and Oompah's famous German potato salad are favorites, as are the fresh local seafood and steaks. There's live entertainment nightly. Open daily. Reservations unnecessary. Major credit cards accepted. 201 E. River St. (phone: 234-9311).

Express Café and Bakery Delicious pastries, croissants, homemade sandwiches, soups, and salads are served in this handsome black-and-white tiled place. Open for breakfast and lunch only; closed Mondays. No reservations or credit cards accepted. 39 Barnard St. (phone: 233-4683).

Huey's A Cajun-style menu is offered at this bright and friendly place, which has a lovely view of the river. On the menu is shrimp creole with *andouille* sausage (a spicy concoction). Excellent breakfasts and a weekend brunch are also offered; try the cinnamon-vanilla French toast. Open daily. No reservations. Major credit cards accepted. 115 E. River St. (phone: 234-7385).

Mrs. Wilkes' Boarding House This is one of Savannah's culinary landmarks and *the* place in town for home cooking. Set out on the tables is enough food to stagger Sherman's army: grits, biscuits, sausages, and eggs for breakfast, or fried chicken, swordfish steaks, potatoes, rice, peas, and corn bread for lunch. Just pull up a chair and help yourself—boardinghouse style. Open for breakfast and lunch; closed weekends. No reservations or credit cards accepted. In the basement of 107 W. Jones St. (phone: 232-5997).

Palmers Seafood House Many consider this casual restaurant, located 15 minutes from downtown on Wilmington Island, to be the best place in the area for fresh seafood. Open daily. No reservations. Major credit cards accepted. 80 Wilmington Island Rd. (phone: 897-2611).

Seattle

At-a-Glance

SEEING THE CITY

The best view of Seattle and the magnificent Washington landscape is from the top of the *Space Needle* (phone: 443-2111) in the *Seattle Center* (see *Special Places*). The observation deck and revolving restaurant offer 360-degree views of the city, Puget Sound, Lake Washington, and the snow-covered peaks of the Cascade and Olympic Mountains. There is an admission charge unless you are dining.

SPECIAL PLACES

Don't be confused by the geographical designations in Seattle street addresses. The directions that follow avenue names and precede street names (Fifth Ave. N. or N. Fifth St.) indicate location in relation to downtown (where only street names and numbers are used).

DOWNTOWN

SEATTLE AQUARIUM Next to the fishing pier at *Waterfront Park*, the aquarium offers a close view of what's swimming in Puget Sound. In the domed viewing room—actually a 400,000-gallon tank—you are surrounded by octopus, starfish, dogfish sharks, rock cod, red snapper, scallops, shrimp, and anemones. There also are tropical fish and a captivating family of sea otters. All along the waterfront, there are seafood bars where you can pick up a good lunch. Open daily. Admission charge. Pier 59 (phone: 386-4320).

PIKE PLACE MARKET Founded in 1907, this public market is now a historic site full of lively vendors selling produce, flowers, and fresh fish. There also are musicians, craftspeople, and specialty restaurants. Closed Sundays except in summer. First Ave. between Pike St. and Virginia St.

SEATTLE ART MUSEUM In the heart of downtown Seattle, the $62-million facility, designed by architect Robert Venturi to great acclaim, houses an extensive array of African, Asian, and Northwest Coast Native American art. Also on display are European and American works, which span the centuries from ancient to contemporary. Besides its beautiful galleries and its imaginative use of videotape, the museum features a large auditorium for films and performances, an art studio, a lecture hall, classrooms, a café, and a shop with one of the best selections of art books anywhere. Closed Mondays. No admission charge on the first Tuesday of each month. 100 University St. between First and Second Aves. (phone: 625-8900; 654-3100 for recorded information).

WESTLAKE CENTER This $110-million retail and office project forms the heart of downtown Seattle. The airy four-level glass and steel retail pavilion features upscale shops, pushcarts, and the *Pacific Picnic* food court, offering ethnic dishes. It is flanked by a 25-story office tower and *Westlake Park*, an urban space with a granite plaza designed in contrasting

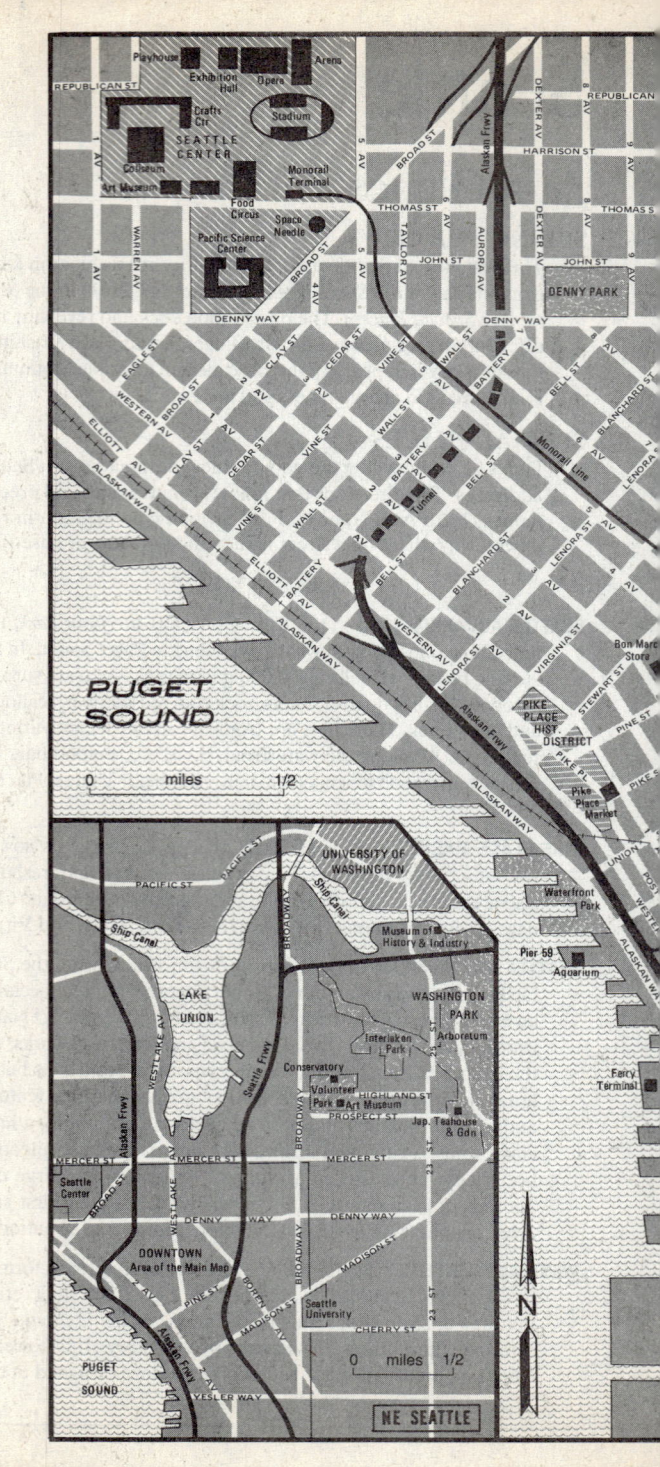

colors to resemble a woven Indian basket. The center, open daily, is connected to the city's main department stores and is served by a monorail terminal. Pine St., between Fourth and Fifth Aves.

PIONEER SQUARE The site where the city was founded in 1852 has become a historic preservation area. The Victorian brick buildings house some of the city's favorite boutiques, galleries, and restaurants. When fire ravaged the district in 1889, the city rebuilt atop the rubble, leaving the remnants of an underground town 10 feet below what is now *Pioneer Square. Bill Speidel's Underground Tours* (610 First Ave.; phone: 682-4646) guides visitors through the subterranean eight-block area, which has some storefronts, interiors, and old waterlines intact. Tours daily. Admission charge. Reservations advised. For Gold Rush nostalgia, visit the *Klondike Gold Rush National Historic Park* (117 S. Main; phone: 553-7220), a museum that traces the history of Klondike gold fever with murals, exhibitions, movies, and a slide show. Open daily. No admission charge.

OTHER SPECIAL PLACES

SEATTLE CENTER A legacy of the *1962 World's Fair,* this 74-acre area contains some of the city's finest facilities. Dominating the 50 buildings and the grassy plazas is the *Space Needle,* a futuristic steel structure that spires 605 feet upward from its tripod base. The *Food Circus* (Center House, 305 Harrison St.) offers inexpensive international delicacies. There are also three playhouses—the *Opera House,* the *Bagley Wright Theatre,* and the newest of them, the *Charlotte Martin Theatre*—as well as the *Fun Forest Amusement Park* (370 Thomas St.). Information about theater tickets and activities is available at a booth in the Center House (Fifth Ave. N. between Denny Way and Mercer St.; phone: 684-7200).

Pacific Science Center In the *Seattle Center,* this museum designed by Minoru Yamasaki features astro-space displays, an operating oceanographic model of Puget Sound that simulates waves, a laserium that uses laser beams to form images, a reconstruction of a Northwest Indian longhouse, and a popular science playground with hands-on exhibitions for children. Open daily. Admission charge. 200 Second Ave. N. (phone: 443-2001).

INTERNATIONAL DISTRICT Seattle has a large Chinese and Japanese community concentrated in this interesting old neighborhood. Among its points of interest are a Buddhist temple, many crafts shops, and Asian restaurants. Shop at *Uwajimaya* (Sixth Ave. S. and S. King; phone: 624-6248), the West Coast's largest Asian retail store, for gifts and specialty foods. The *Wing Luke Memorial Museum* (407 Seventh Ave. S.; phone: 623-5124) features a permanent exhibition tracing the immigration of the Chinese to the Northwest beginning in the 1860s, a folk arts gallery, and a fine arts gallery. It's closed Mondays; there's an admission charge.

MUSEUM OF HISTORY AND INDUSTRY This extensive collection of Pacific Northwest artifacts traces the history of Seattle's first century after European settlement. A mural depicts the fire that leveled the city in 1889, and the displays include almost everything that came afterward—mementos of the Gold Rush, old fire fighting equipment, a maritime display, and a Boeing exhibit that follows the company's development over the past 60-odd years. Open daily. No admission charge on Tuesdays. 2700 24th Ave. E. (phone: 324-1125).

BURKE MUSEUM Here is an extraordinary collection of Northwest Coast Indian art, as well as an Alaskan arctic collection that includes over 6,000 examples of basketry, ivory carvings, and beadwork. There are artifacts from the Western subarctic, the Plains, the Great Lakes, and the Southwest, as well as from Asia, Southeast Asia, and Oceania. The Northwest Coast Indian masks are especially haunting. Open daily. Donation suggested. At the northwest corner of the *University of Washington* campus (phone: 543-5590).

UNIVERSITY OF WASHINGTON ARBORETUM Some 200 lakeside acres contain over 5,000 plant species from all over the world. It also features one of the largest Japanese tea gardens outside Japan. Open daily. Admission charge to *Japanese Garden*. Lake Washington Blvd. between E. Madison and Montlake (phone: 543-8800).

EXTRA SPECIAL

Just an hour and a half south of Seattle is the spectacular *Mt. Rainier National Park*, with over 300 miles of trails; two hours south of the city is Mt. St. Helens, which erupted in May 1980. On Route 161, an hour south of town, is the *Northwest Trek Wildlife Park* (phone: 847-1903), where moose, elk, buffalo, mountain goat, and caribou roam free. The zoo belongs to the animals; visitors tour from a tram and are not allowed off. Admission charge.

Northeast of Seattle, near Sedro Woolley, Washington, is *North Cascades National Park*. Ice falls and waterfalls, hanging valleys and ice caps, some 300 glaciers, plus canyons, granite peaks, and mountain lakes and streams make this a rugged 789 square miles. In addition to the park, there's the 184-square-mile *Ross Lake National Recreation Area* (which lies between the park's north and south units); the 97-square-mile *Lake Chelan National Recreation Area* (adjoining the south unit on its southern border); and surrounding the four units, the *Mt. Baker-Snoqualmie*, *Wenatchee*, and *Okanogan National Forests*. You'll find especially interesting rooms at the rustic *North Cascades Lodge* (phone: 509-682-4711) in Stehekin, at the north end of Lake Chelan. For park information, contact *North Cascades National Park*, 2105 Hwy. 20, Sedro Woolley, WA 98284 (phone: 206-856-5700); for information on backpacking and permits, contact *Wilderness Permits System, Wilderness District Office*, 728 Ranger Station Rd., Marble Mount, WA 98267 (phone: 206-873-4500, ext. 34).

Sources and Resources

TOURIST INFORMATION

The *Seattle/King County Convention and Visitors Bureau* (666 Stewart St.; phone: 461-5840) offers daily events schedules, maps, and information. It is open daily during the summer; closed weekends the rest of the year. Contact the Washington state tourism hotline (phone: 800-544-1800) for maps, calendars of events, health updates, and travel advisories.

LOCAL COVERAGE *Seattle Post-Intelligencer,* morning daily, publishes *What's Happening* on Fridays with coming week's events; *Seattle Times,* afternoon daily, publishes *Tempo* magazine on Fridays. *The Weekly* is an opinionated yuppie-oriented newspaper. All are available at newsstands. The visitors' bureau offers the *Seattle Visitors Guide,* which is also available at hotels, some restaurants, and newsstands. *The Seattle Guidebook* by Archie Satterfield (Globe Pequot; $11.95), available at the *Elliott Bay Book Company* (phone: 624-6600) and elsewhere, is a good guide to Seattle and the surrounding area. *Seattle's Best Places* by David Brewster (Sasquatch Books; $12.95) has restaurant listings. *Seattle ACCESS* (HarperCollins; $18) is a popular and useful guidebook.

TELEVISION STATIONS KOMO Channel 4–ABC; KING Channel 5–NBC; KIRO Channel 7–CBS; and KCTS Channel 9–PBS.

RADIO STATIONS AM: KIXI 880 (music from the 1940s, 1950s, and 1960s); KING 1090 (news/talk); and KLSY 1540 (soft rock). FM: KLSY 92.5 (soft rock); KING 98.1 (classical music); and KMGI 107.7 (adult contemporary).

TELEPHONE The area code for Seattle is 206.

SALES TAX The city sales tax is 8.1%, except on groceries.

CLIMATE Seattle's proximity to Puget Sound keeps the climate mild and moderately moist. Winters are relatively warm, with temperatures averaging around 40F; it seldom snows. The wet season is from October through April. Seattle is best in summer and early fall.

GETTING AROUND

AIRPORT *Seattle-Tacoma International Airport* (known as *Sea-Tac*) is about a 25-minute drive from downtown. *Gray Line Airport Express* (phone: 626-6088) offers service to major hotels. *Shuttle Express* (phone: 622-1424) offers round-trip service between downtown and the airport. *Metro* buses No. 174 and No. 194 leave for *Sea-Tac* from Ninth Avenue and Stewart Street via Second Avenue; the fare ranges from 75¢ to $1.50 depending on distance and time of day. For more information, contact *Metropolitan Transit* (phone: 553-3000).

BUS *Metropolitan Transit* provides extensive service in the metropolitan area with an added attraction: *Metro's* Free Ride Service in the downtown-waterfront area. Bus fare ranges from 75¢ to $1.50 depending on distance and time of day. Route information is available at its office, 821 Second Ave. (phone: 553-3000)

CAR RENTAL Seattle is served by the major national firms.

FERRY RIDE If looking out at Puget Sound isn't enough, you can enjoy the full experience by taking a 30-minute ride to Winslow or a 45-minute ride to Bremerton. *Ferry Terminal* (phone: 464-6400).

MONORAIL The quickest way to get from downtown to the *Seattle Center*, the *World's Fair* monorail leaves every 15 minutes from *Westlake Center*.

TAXI Cabs can be hailed in the street but are best ordered on the phone. Major companies are *Farwest* (phone: 622-1717) and *Yellow Cab* (phone: 622-6500).

TRAIN TOUR Take the *Spirit of Washington* dinner train (phone: 800-876-RAIL) for a scenic excursion. Departing from Renton, southeast of Seattle, the train follows the eastern shore of Lake Washington; passengers feast on fine food and Northwest wines. There's a 45-minute stop at the *Columbia Winery* in Woodinville, where visitors can take a winery tour, visit the tasting room and gift shop, and stroll the lovely grounds. The round-trip journey takes 3½ hours. The train does not run on Mondays. Reservations necessary. Major credit cards accepted.

LOCAL SERVICES

AUDIOVISUAL EQUIPMENT *Photo & Sound* (phone: 632-8461).

BUSINESS SERVICES *Business Service Center* (1001 Fourth Ave. Pl.; phone: 624-9188); *Globe Secretariat* (phone: 448-9441), notary, word processing, 24-hour phone dictation; *Headquarters Business Centers* (*HQ*; phone: 224-8700), word processing, telex, fax services, conference rooms; *Secretarial Assistants* (Columbia Center; phone: 682-6072).

DRY CLEANER/TAILOR *Ange's French Cleaners* (2000 Ninth Ave.; phone: 622-6727); *A-1 Tailors* (1424 Fourth Ave., Suite 822; phone: 625-1455).

LIMOUSINE *Terry Limousine* (phone: 285-5505); *Washington Limousine*, sedans also (phone: 523-8000).

MECHANIC *Salmon Service Center* (25th Ave. and 65th St. NE; phone: 523-9400).

MEDICAL EMERGENCY *Virginia Mason Hospital* (925 Seneca St., phone: 583-6433); *Virginia Mason Fourth Avenue* (1221 Fourth Ave.; phone: 223-6490), a walk-in clinic open 7 AM to 5 PM.

MESSENGER SERVICES *Dependable Messenger Service* (phone: 728-4066); *Fleetfoot* (phone: 728-7700).

MONEY TRANSFERS *American Express MoneyGram* (phone: 800-926-9400 for information; 800-866-8800 for money transfers); *Western Union Financial Services* (phone: 800-325-6000 or 800-325-4176).

NATIONAL/INTERNATIONAL COURIER *DHL Worldwide Express* (phone: 800-225-5345); *FedEx* (phone: 282-9766).

PHARMACY *Jordan Drugs & Grocery Center* (2518 E. Cherry St.; phone: 322-3050), open 7 AM to 2 AM; *Pay Less* (319 Pike St.; phone: 223-0512).

PHOTOCOPIES *Copy Co.* (616 Sixth Ave. S.; phone: 622-4050); *Lazer Quick* (412 Olive Way; phone: 622-4387).

POST OFFICE Downtown (301 Union St.; phone: 442-6340).

PROFESSIONAL PHOTOGRAPHER *Wm. J. Murray* (phone: 441-2154).

TRANSLATOR *Berlitz* (phone: 682-0312).

WESTERN UNION/TELEX Many offices are located around the city (phone: 800-325-6000 to find the location nearest you).

SPECIAL EVENTS

The *Folklife Festival,* featuring folk music and crafts, is held over *Memorial Day* weekend at the *Seattle Center. Seattle Seafair* is a citywide celebration in late July and early August featuring everything from hydroplane races, a torchlight parade, a beauty contest, and a marathon, to a special appearance by ships of the Pacific Fleet. Check newspapers for exact dates. Over *Labor Day* weekend, the *Seattle Center* hosts *Bumbershoot,* a festival featuring a wide variety of live music (the name comes from the British slang term for "umbrella").

MUSEUMS

In addition to those described under *Special Places,* Seattle has a number of notable museums.

BELLEVUE ART MUSEUM This third-floor museum hosts five or six rotating exhibits of contemporary and regional art and crafts each year. Open daily. Admission charge. *Bellevue Sq. Shopping Center* (phone: 454-3322).

FRYE ART MUSEUM Founded by Charles and Emma Frye, this museum contains 19th-century European paintings and sculpture as well as contemporary regional works. Open daily. No admission charge. Terry Ave. and Cherry St. (phone: 622-9250).

MUSEUM OF FLIGHT This aviation museum features a soaring glassed-in gallery with more than 20 full-size planes, including a DC-3 and the first supersonic jet, suspended from the ceiling. Open daily. Admission charge. 9404 E. Marginal Way S., near *Sea-Tac Airport* (phone: 764-5720).

ROSALIE WHYEL MUSEUM OF DOLL ART More than a thousand dolls are on display in a building resembling an oversized Victorian dollhouse. Open daily. Admission charge. 1116 108th Ave. NE, Bellevue (phone: 455-1116).

SEATTLE ASIA ART MUSEUM When the *Seattle Art Museum* moved from *Volunteer Park,* the building underwent a major gallery renovation and reopened as an Asian art center. This branch museum houses more than 7,000 traditional art objects from China, Japan, Korea, and Southeast Asia. Closed Mondays. Admission charge. 14th St. and E. Prospect (phone: 654-3100).

SHOPPING

Westlake Mall encompasses a number of upscale specialty shops, including *Fireworks Gallery* (400 Pine St.; phone: 682-6462), and access to

Seattle's two major department stores, the *Bon* and *Nordstrom*. At the *Pike Place Market* (First Ave. between Pike and Virginia Sts.), shoppers can buy homegrown fresh and dried herbs, locally produced honey, and jams made from mountain berries. Fresh seafood can be packed in ice to be taken on the plane. Craftspeople sell silk-screened T-shirts, hand-painted jackets, and hand-crafted jewelry. *Pioneer Square* is an eight-block area that features a concentration of art galleries. Among its other shops are the following:

Elliott Bay Book Company The staff here is extremely knowledgeable about the store's growing collection of new titles and its recently expanded children's literature section. At the *Elliott Bay Café* downstairs, authors give lectures and readings weekly. 101 S. Main St. (phone: 624-6600).

Fireworks Gallery Browse through one-of-a-kind ceramic pieces, *raku* pottery, and a large selection of unique pins and earrings. 210 First Ave. (phone: 682-8707).

Flying Shuttle Exotic, hand-crafted jewelry, woven jackets, hand-knit sweaters, and whimsical folk art are all on display. 607 First Ave. (phone: 343-9762).

Glass House The city's only working glass studio open to the public, it showcases blown-glass art pieces. 311 Occidental Ave. S. (phone: 682-9939).

SPORTS AND FITNESS

Seattle is in the big leagues, with three professional teams. The best bet is to order tickets by phone and pick them up later at the team's ticket office.

BASEBALL The *Mariners'* season runs from April through early October at the *Kingdome* (201 S. King St.; phone: 628-3555).

BASKETBALL The *NBA SuperSonics* play from November through April at the *Seattle Center Coliseum* (ticket office, at the west entrance; phone: 281-5800).

BICYCLING Rent from *Gregg's Green Lake Cycle* (7007 Woodlawn Ave. NE; phone: 523-1822). *Green Lake Park* and *Burke-Gilman Trail* are good biking areas.

FISHING Seattle provides plenty of sport fishing for the dedicated angler.

WHERE THEY BITE

Puget Sound Stalk the wild king salmon, quill-back rockfish, black cod, and sole, as well as the true cod and Pacific flounder, while you take in the breathtaking Northwest scenery. During the late summer or early fall, you might just be lucky enough to see a pod of killer whales. Contact *Sportfishing of Seattle* (Pier 54 on the waterfront; phone: 623-6364) for information on tackle, boats, and trips.

You also can wet a line from the public pier of *Waterfront Park* or go after the big salmon by renting a boat or taking a charter into the deep sea from *Ballard Salmon Charters* (2620 NW 63rd St.; phone: 789-6202).

FITNESS CENTERS *Fitness Limited* (across from the *Westin* hotel, 2001 Sixth Ave.; phone: 728-1500) has a pool, a Jacuzzi, a sauna, a steamroom, exercise equipment, and weights; athletic clothing is provided. The *YMCA* (909 Fourth Ave. and Madison; phone: 382-5000) has a pool, weight room, and track. Both are open to non-members for a fee. The private *Seattle Club* (2020 Western Ave.; phone: 443-1111) is open to guests of several downtown hotels. Among its many facilities are racquetball courts, a track, a pool, Nautilus equipment, massage, tanning rooms, exercise classes, and a restaurant.

FOOTBALL The *NFL Seahawks* play from August through December at the *Kingdome* (201 S. King St.; phone: 827-9777).

GOLF The city has three good 18-hole public courses: *Jackson Park* (1000 NE 135th St.; phone: 363-4747); *Jefferson Park* (4101 Beacon Ave. S.; phone: 762-4513); and *West Seattle Municipal Course* (4470 35th Ave. SW; phone: 935-5187).

JOGGING Run the 3-mile course at *Myrtle Edwards Park* on the waterfront, at Alaska Way between W. Bay and W. Thomas. Or follow many Seattle residents and run around Green Lake (2.8 miles); to get there, take the No. 6 or No. 16 northbound bus from Third and Pine.

SAILING Seattle has more boats per capita than any other US city. Off Puget Sound, there are hundreds of islands, miles of secluded waterways, marine state parks, and waterside resorts for every type of boat. The season begins in early May and continues until the end of the salmon fishing season in late fall. Many charter outfits rent both bareboats and full crews. For more information, contact *Sportfishing of Seattle* (Pier 54 on the waterfront; phone: 623-6364) or the *Convention and Visitors Bureau* (see *Tourist Information*).

SKIING Popular ski areas include nearby *Alpental* (on the Snoqualmie Pass via I-90; phone: 434-6112) and *Crystal Mountain* (120 miles away near Mt. Rainier; phone: 663-2265).

TENNIS Many of the city parks have outdoor courts. Call the *Seattle Department of Parks and Recreation* (phone: 684-4075) for information.

THEATER

Seattle has the highest ratio of resident equity theater companies per capita in the nation. Listed below is our favorite, along with several other options. For current offerings check the publications listed under *Local Coverage*.

CENTER STAGE

Seattle Repertory Theatre Modern and contemporary comedies and dramas, both classics and premieres, are performed at the 856-seat *Bagley Wright Theatre* at *Seattle Center* (Fifth

Ave. N. between Denny Way and Mercer St.; phone: 684-7200) and in the *PONCHO Forum* (155 Mercer St.; phone: 443-2222), an intimate studio theater seating 133, where controversial plays often are presented.

The *Intiman Theatre Co.* performs works by playwrights as diverse as Noël Coward and Athol Fugard at the *Seattle Center Playhouse* (201 Mercer St.; phone: 626-0782) May through October. *A Contemporary Theater* (100 W. Roy; phone: 285-5110) produces works by up-and-coming playwrights. *Seattle Children's Theater* performs at the new *Charlotte Martin Theater* (Second Ave. N. and Thomas St.: phone: 443-0807) at *Seattle Center*. Productions range from classics to contemporary plays for children of all ages. The *Fifth Avenue Theater* (1308 Fifth Ave.; phone: 625-1900) features top concert artists and touring Broadway plays. The *Empty Space Theatre at First Stage* (3509 Fremont Ave. N.; phone: 547-7500) showcases new plays. The *Bathhouse Theatre* (7312 W. Green Lake Dr. N.; phone: 524-9108) stages experimental productions of classics; the *New City Theatre* (1634 11th Ave.; phone: 323-6800) features works by cutting-edge playwrights, local writers, and visiting artists; and the *Group Theatre* in the *Center House* (305 Harrison Ave.; phone: 441-1299) at *Seattle Center* focuses on ethnic plays.

MUSIC

The *Seattle Symphony* and the *Seattle Opera Association* perform at the *Opera House* from September through April. The *Wagner Ring Festival* is held every four years in August; the next production is this year. The ticket offices for both are in the *Center House* at *Seattle Center*, 305 Harrison Ave. (phone: 443-4747 for symphony; 389-7676 for opera). The restored *Paramount Theater* (907 Pine St.; phone: 682-1414) has pop concerts.

NIGHTCLUBS AND NIGHTLIFE

Seattle is enjoying a national reputation as a leading center of "grunge" music (reminiscent of 1960s and 1970s rock 'n' roll). The city is crawling with clubs where you can while away an evening, and the music has a distinctive sound: aggressive, loud, and moody. In the past few years, several local bands have made it to the big time: *Queensrÿche* is a heavy metal group, and *Nirvana,* the kicky grunge band founded by the late Kurt Cobain, has earned several Grammy nominations. Among the area's hottest nightspots are *Jazz Alley* (Sixth and Lenora; phone: 441-9729) for jazz and *Swannie's* (222 S. Main St.; phone: 622-9353) for headline comedy acts. Good live music—especially alternative rock groups—can be heard at *Crocodile Café* (220 Second Ave.; phone: 441-5611), one of the city's top nightspots; *RKCNDY* (1812 Yale Ave.; phone: 623-0470); and the *Off Ramp Café and Lounge* (109 Eastlake St. E.; phone: 628-0232). Grunge music can be heard live at the *Re-Bar* (1114 Howell St.; phone: 233-9873). The *Virginia Inn Tavern* (1937 First Ave.; phone: 728-1937) entertains its art- and ale-loving patrons with recorded jazz, blues, and rock, and the *Vogue* (2018 First Ave.; phone: 443-0673) re-creates the artsy coffeehouse atmosphere of New York City's Greenwich Village. And if you're in the mood for down-home country music, try the *Timberline* (2015 Boren Ave.; phone: 622-6220).

Best in Town

CHECKING IN

Seattle has an abundance and wide variety of accommodations. Expect to pay $180 or more per night for a double room in hotels listed as expensive; $110 to $180 at those listed as moderate; and between $75 and $110 at places described as inexpensive. For information about bed and breakfast accommodations, contact the *Pacific Bed & Breakfast Agency,* 701 NW 60th St., Seattle, WA 98107 (phone: 784-0539). Unless otherwise noted, hotels have air conditioning, private baths, TV sets, and telephones. All hotels are in the 206 area code unless otherwise indicated.

EXPENSIVE

Alexis For the sophisticated traveler who needs to be pampered, this 51-room hotel may fit the bill. From the optional butler who will do your unpacking to the complimentary shoeshines, the service is attentive and enthusiastic, if not completely polished, *and* there is a no-tipping policy. *The Painted Table* (see *Eating Out*) is a special dining place. Additional amenities include 24-hour room service, a meeting room, a concierge, secretarial assistance, A/V equipment, photocopiers, and computers. First and Madison (phone: 624-4844; 800-426-7033; fax: 621-9009).

Four Seasons Olympic A splendid restoration of an Italian Renaissance–style building, this 450-room hotel seamlessly blends old and new. Highlights include the elegant public rooms; the *Solarium,* a sparkling health spa; and the *Georgian Room* restaurant, a favorite for special occasions. Many of the city's most popular attractions are within walking distance. Room service is always on call. Business amenities include 15 meeting rooms, concierge and secretarial services, A/V equipment, photocopiers, computers, and express checkout. 411 University (phone: 621-1700; 800-821-8106; fax: 682-9633).

Seattle Sheraton With an extensive collection of contemporary Northwestern art, this is the place for those who enjoy culture along with their comfort. Many of the more than 2,000 original works are displayed in public spaces. There are great views as well from many of the 840 rooms. Try out the pool room on the 35th floor, or dine at *Banners, Fullers* (see *Eating Out*), or *Gallery.* Also available is 24-hour room service. The top four floors have their own lobby and concierge. Business services include a concierge, secretarial assistance, A/V equipment, photocopiers, computers, a satellite hookup between the hotel and the *Washington State Convention and Trade Center,* 20 meeting rooms, and express checkout. Sixth and Pike (phone: 621-9000; 800-325-3535; fax: 621-8441).

Vintage Park With 129 rooms, this European-style property is conveniently located downtown, across from the *Seattle Public Library.* The rooms are decorated with cherry furniture, and the lobby resembles an elegant but cozy study, with comfortable furniture and a fireplace. The hotel celebrates the state's excellent local wines with evening tastings and guestrooms named for Washington wineries; guests dine at *Tulio's* Italian restaurant. Amenities include health club access, a concierge, and 24-hour room service; secretarial services, meeting rooms, and adapters for computers are business features. 1100 Fifth Ave. (phone: 624-8000; 800-624-4433; fax: 623-0568).

MODERATE

Inn at the Market A French country–style hostelry with 65 rooms above the *Pike Place Market*. Rooms with a view of Elliott Bay are more expensive but worth it. Guests enjoy complimentary coffee and limousine service around downtown, and the nearby *Campagne* restaurant offers French country cuisine. There is a coffee shop and athletic facilities nearby. Business pluses are a meeting room, secretarial services, A/V equipment, photocopiers, and computers. 86 Pine St. (phone: 443-3600; 800-446-4484; fax: 448-0631).

Mayflower Park In the downtown shopping district, adjacent to *Westlake Center*, it provides 178 guestrooms in a convenient, quiet setting. Children under 17 stay free with their parents. *Clipper's,* a small restaurant, and *Oliver's,* a cocktail lounge, are on the premises. Room service is available around the clock. Business services include secretarial assistance, A/V equipment, photocopiers, and nine meeting rooms. Fourth Ave. and Olive Way (phone: 623-8700 or 382-6990; 800-426-5100; fax: 382-6997).

Sorrento This small (just 76 rooms), first class spot, designed to resemble an Italian Renaissance castle, offers many extras: terry cloth bathrobes, plants and potpourri in every room, a hot water bottle in your bed in winter, and complimentary limousine service. Dine at the *Hunt Club* or enjoy English afternoon tea in the mahogany lobby. Amenities such as a concierge desk, four meeting rooms, limited A/V equipment, and photocopiers are available. Terry Ave. and Madison St. (phone: 622-6400; 800-426-1265; fax: 625-1059).

INEXPENSIVE

Pacific Plaza An older hotel, it appeals to businesspeople and others who want to be in the center of downtown at a reasonable price. It features 168 quiet rooms and complimentary continental breakfast. Secretarial services are available, as well as A/V equipment, computers, and express checkout. 400 Spring St. (phone: 623-3900; 800-426-1165; fax: 623-2059).

EATING OUT

Seattle's restaurant scene is sophisticated and wide-ranging. Several of the top places showcase fresh local ingredients, and Seattle's position as a gateway to the Pacific has encouraged superb Asian culinary influences. Dinner for two costs $70 or more at restaurants listed in the expensive category; $50 to $70 at places classified as moderate; and less than $50 at inexpensive spots. Prices do not include drinks, wine, tax, or tips. Unless otherwise noted, restaurants serve lunch and dinner. All restaurants are in the 206 area code unless otherwise indicated.

EXPENSIVE

Canlis' Along with a sweeping view of Lake Union, this place features charcoal-broiled steaks, poached fresh salmon in hollandaise sauce, and pan-fried Quilcene oysters from nearby Quilcene Bay. Closed Sundays and major holidays. Reservations necessary. Major credit cards accepted. 2576 Aurora Ave. N. (phone: 283-3313).

Elliott's Oyster House As you might expect, the menu here features fresh seafood (although steaks are available). There's whole dungeness crab, mahimahi (in season), salmon, and cioppino (fish stew). The restaurant smokes its own seafood on the premises. The large windows allow a wonderful view of seafaring boats and ferries traveling along Elliott Bay, off Puget Sound. Open daily. Reservations necessary. MasterCard and Visa accepted. 1203 Alaskan Way, Pier 56 (phone: 623-4340).

Fullers In the *Sheraton*, this is one of Seattle's best dining rooms. Elegant booths showcase original artwork by Northwest artists. The menu celebrates Northwest specialties with selections such as *gravlax* (marinated salmon), baby leeks and herb port cream, veal chop with morels, or spinach salad with smoked duck. The wine list showcases the best the state has to offer. Closed Sundays; dinner only on Saturdays. Reservations advised. Major credit cards accepted. Sixth and Pike (phone: 621-9000; 800-325-3535).

Nikko This Japanese dining place in the *Westin Seattle* offers wonderful Asian specialties such as Kasuzuke cod (marinated black cod), sashimi, and a wide variety of sushi. The sushi happy hour features complimentary California rolls. Open daily; dinner only on weekends. Reservations advised. Major credit cards accepted. 1900 Fifth Ave. (phone: 322-4641).

Rover's In a romantic little house with a garden, this delightful restaurant serves seasonal French-Northwest fare, featuring salmon, pheasant, quail, venison, and rabbit. It's an excellent choice for a special occasion or romantic dinner. Closed Sundays and Mondays. Reservations advised. Major credit cards accepted. 2808 E. Madison St. (phone: 325-7442).

MODERATE

Al Boccalino Carefully prepared southern Italian fare—fresh seafood, lamb, beef, and pasta—is served in a cozy *Pioneer Square* setting. Open daily; dinner only on Saturdays. Reservations necessary. MasterCard and Visa accepted. 1 Yesler Way (phone: 622-7688).

Kaspar's Chef Kaspar Donier recently moved his restaurant from First Avenue to this location, which is close to several theaters and convenient for dining either before or after performances. The menu, however, still features fresh, local salmon, mussels, lamb, and duck. Don't miss the popular Northwest shellfish and wild rice chowder in a creamy white sauce. There's also a great Sunday brunch. Open daily. Reservations advised. Major credit cards accepted. 19 W. Harrison St. (phone: 441-4805).

Mikado From its sushi bar to its *shioyaki* seafood dishes, this is a true Japanese dining experience. Tatami rooms are available for six or more. Dinner only; closed Sundays. Reservations advised. Major credit cards accepted. 514 S. Jackson St. (phone: 622-5206).

Metropolitan Grill Aged beef is this upscale steakhouse's specialty, but the salmon's great, too. There's a special *Seahawks* brunch during football season. Closed Saturdays; dinner only on Sundays. Reservations advised. Major credit cards accepted. 820 Second Ave. (phone: 624-3287).

The Painted Table The dining room at the *Alexis* hotel serves elegant continental fare on hand-painted plates; fine art hangs on the walls. Try the crab and corn chowder to whet your appetite, then move on to such well-presented entrees as grilled smoked duck with carmelized pears or chicken breast baked in parchment with a hot and sour broth. The desserts are marvelously sinful, especially the chocolate truffle cake, bittersweet chocolate praline torte, and white chocolate blintzes with berries. Closed Saturdays; dinner only on Sundays. Reservations advised. Major credit cards accepted. 1007 First Ave. (phone: 624-3646).

Ray's Boathouse On the waterfront at Shilshole Bay, this is a great place to have a leisurely dinner while watching the sun go down behind the Olympic Mountains. The seafood offerings are excellent and varied. The more moderate upstairs café is also good. Open daily. Reservations advised. Major credit cards accepted. 6049 Seaview Ave. NW (phone: 789-3770).

Il Terrazzo Carmine With its patio facing a reflecting pool, this is the perfect place for a summer drink or dinner. Choose between Italian and Northwest dishes. Suggestions include ravioli with venison or veal chop with artichokes and sun-dried tomatoes in wine sauce. There's an extensive Italian wine list, plus California and Northwest vintages. Closed Sundays; dinner only on Saturdays. Reservations advised, especially on weekends. Major credit cards accepted. 411 First Ave. S. (phone: 467-7797).

Wild Ginger An eclectic menu of Pacific Rim fare offers Vietnamese, southern Chinese, Korean, and Thai dishes. Try the sweet, succulent duck or fresh *ahi* tuna in an Indonesian candlenut sauce. The *satay* bar is great for sipping local beers and eating exotically seasoned, skewered seafood and meat. Open daily; dinner only on Sundays. Reservations advised. Major credit cards accepted. 1400 Western Ave. (phone: 623-4450).

INEXPENSIVE

Du Jour Salads, soups, and sandwiches are the cornerstone of the menu, but there are also chicken and seafood entrées. The selections change daily; outstanding dishes include chicken pecan salad, chicken breast glazed with saffron, and an unusual version of tortellini salad made of three flavors of pasta (pumpkin, spinach, and egg). Open for breakfast and lunch only; closed Sundays. Reservations advised for large groups only. Major credit cards accepted. 1919 First Ave. (phone: 441-3354).

Ivar's Indian Salmon House With views of Lake Union, this is a favorite stop for out-of-towners. Designed to look like an Indian longhouse, it features heavy timbers, canoes hanging overhead, and totem poles. The menu includes alder-smoked salmon and black cod, prepared in Northwest Indian style, as well as prime ribs. Open daily. Reservations advised. Major credit cards accepted. 401 NE Northlake Way (phone: 632-0767).

Kokeb Seattle's first Ethiopian restaurant serves spicy but simple food to the college crowd that constitutes its loyal clientele. Entrées consist of lamb, chicken, beef, or vegetables surrounded by *injera*, a flat bread that soaks up the sauces. Open daily for dinner only. Reservations advised. Major credit cards accepted. 926 12th Ave. (phone: 322-0485).

JAVA JIVE

To the true coffee connoisseur, Seattle is heaven on earth. Whether your preference is espresso, cappuccino, or *café latte* (coffee mixed generously with steamed milk), you can find it here; feel free to experiment until you've discovered the perfect blend. A few places to begin your search are *Starbucks* (1912 Pike Pl.; phone: 448-8762), whose proprietors started Seattle's coffee craze in the late 1960s; *Uptown Espresso* (525 Queen Anne Ave. N.; phone: 281-8669), quaintly decorated with antique mirrors and furniture; and *M. Coy Books and Espresso* (117 Pine St.; phone: 623-5354), where you can enjoy a good book and a good cup of espresso at the same time.

Washington, DC

At-a-Glance

SEEING THE CITY

The 555-foot *Washington Monument* commands a panorama of the capital in all its glory. To the north stands the *White House,* and below stretches the green *Mall,* with the *Lincoln Memorial* in the west and the *Capitol* perfectly aligned with it to the east. Beyond to the south and west flows the Potomac River, and across the river lies Virginia. (See *Special Places* for details.)

SPECIAL PLACES

In Washington, all roads lead to the *Capitol.* The building marks the center of the District. North–south streets are numbered in relation to it, east–west streets are lettered, and the four quadrants into which Washington is divided (NW, NE, SW, and SE, designated after addresses) meet here. *Note:* A surprising number of remarkable attractions in this city have no admission charge, as they are funded by federal monies.

An easy way to get around the principal sightseeing area, which includes *Arlington National Cemetery* (across the Potomac in Arlington, Virginia), is by *Tourmobile;* for details on this shuttle bus and other tours see "Tours" in *Getting Around.*

CAPITOL HILL AREA

THE CAPITOL The Senate and House of Representatives are housed in the *Capitol,* which is visible from almost every part of the city. The 258-foot cast-iron dome, topped by Thomas Crawford's statue of *Freedom,* was erected during the Civil War; beneath it, the massive *Rotunda* is a veritable art gallery of American history featuring Constantino Brumidi's fresco *The Apotheosis of Washington* in the eye of the dome, John Trumbull's Revolutionary War paintings on the walls, and statues of Washington, Lincoln, Jefferson, and others. The rest of the building also contains much artwork. You must join one of the excellent 40-minute guided tours that leave from the *Rotunda* every quarter hour in order to gain access to the visitors' galleries of Congress (congressional sessions start at noon). You also can ride the monorail subway that joins the House and Senate wings with the congressional office buildings and try the famous bean soup in the Senate dining room. Closed *Christmas, New Year's Day,* and *Thanksgiving.* The last tour is at 3:45 PM; from the first week of May through *Labor Day,* the *Rotunda* is open until 8 PM. No admission charge. First St. between Constitution and Independence Aves. (phone: 224-3121). *Metro: Capitol South* or *Union Station.*

SUPREME COURT BUILDING This neoclassical white marble structure, surrounded by Corinthian columns and with the inscription on its pediment "Equal Justice Under Law," was designed by Cass Gilbert and completed in 1935. The impressive courtroom is flanked by Ionic columns. Court is in session intermittently from the first Monday in

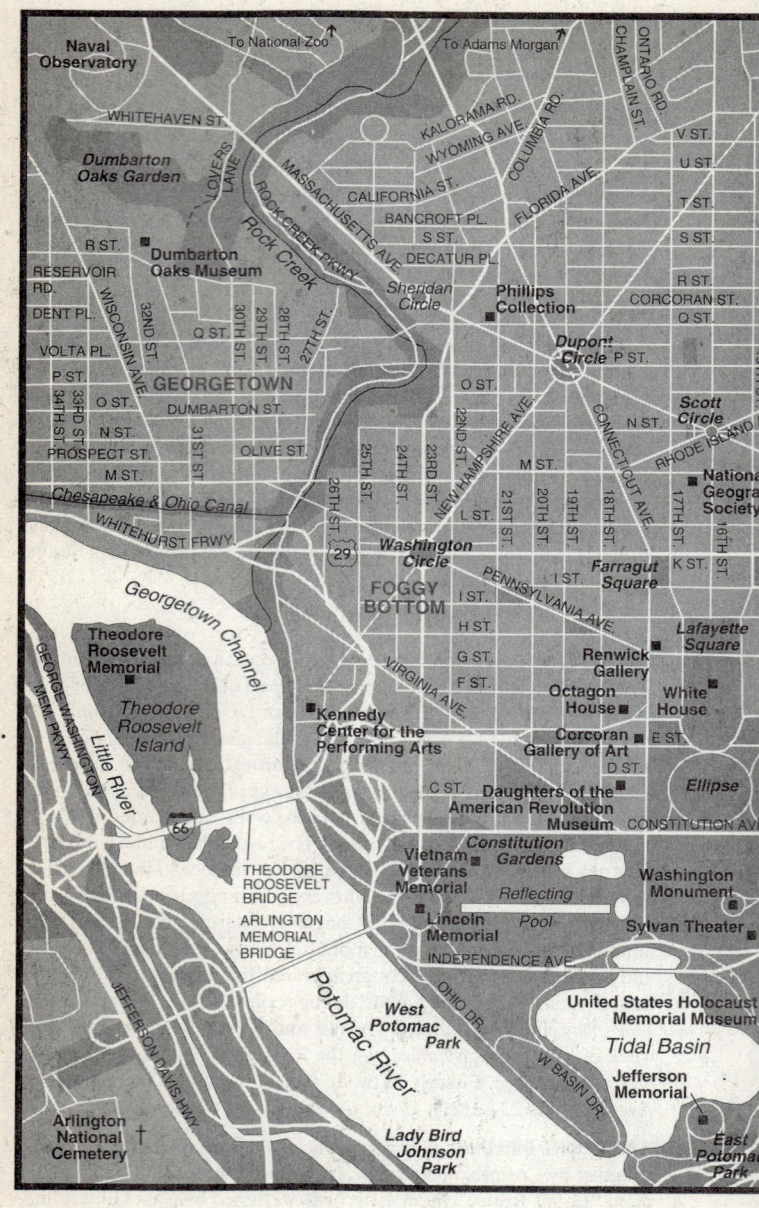

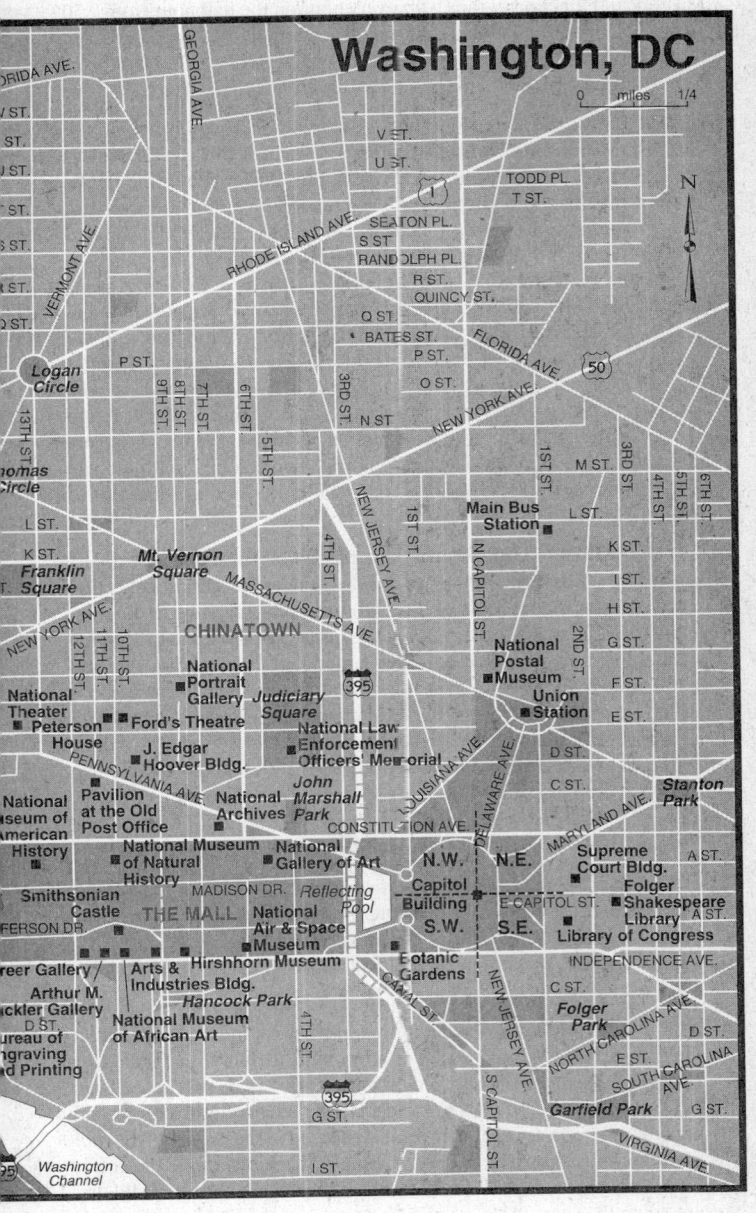

October through June; sessions are open to the public on a first-come, first-served basis. There are 20-minute courtroom presentations on the history and function of the *Court* every hour on the half hour from 9:30 AM to 3:30 PM except when court is in session. Closed weekends. No admission charge. First St. between Maryland Ave. and E. Capitol St. NE (phone: 479-3395). *Metro: Capitol South* or *Union Station.*

LIBRARY OF CONGRESS Three buildings—the *Jefferson*, the *Adams*, and the *Madison*—house the world's largest and richest library. Originally designed as a research aid to Congress, the *Library* serves the public as well with 84 million items in 470 languages, including manuscripts, maps, photographs, motion pictures, and music. The exhibition hall displays include Jefferson's first draft of the *Declaration of Independence* and Lincoln's first two drafts of the *Gettysburg Address.* Among the *Library*'s other holdings are one of three extant copies of the Gutenberg Bible, Pierre L'Enfant's original design for Washington, and the earliest surviving copyrighted film—the 14-second *Sneeze* by Thomas Edison. Forty-five-minute guided tours are offered on weekdays from 10 AM to 4 PM, Saturdays from 10 AM to 3 PM, and Sundays at 1, 2, and 3 PM. Open daily, with evening hours on Mondays, Wednesdays, and Thursdays. No admission charge. First St. between E. Capitol St. and Independence Ave. SE (phone: 707-5458). *Metro: Capitol South* or *Union Station.*

FOLGER SHAKESPEARE LIBRARY The nine bas-reliefs on the façade depict scenes from Shakespeare's plays; inside is the world's finest collection of rare books, manuscripts, and research materials relating to the foremost English-language playwright. The library, an oak-paneled, barrel-vaulted Elizabethan palace, also has a model of the *Globe Theatre* and a full-scale replica of an Elizabethan theater complete with a trapdoor called "the heavens," used for special effects. Visitors can see how productions were mounted in Shakespeare's day and how they are done today. The bookstore features the fine Folger series on the Elizabethan period as well as editions of Shakespeare's plays. Tours are at 11 AM; closed Sundays. No admission charge. 201 E. Capitol St. SE (phone: 546-4600). *Metro: Capitol South* or *Union Station.*

BOTANIC GARDENS If you feel as if you are overdosing on history, the *Botanic Gardens* provide a pleasant antidote of azaleas, orchids, and tropical plants. Closed *Christmas Day.* No admission charge. First St. and Maryland Ave. SW, at the foot of Capitol Hill (phone: 225-8333). *Metro: Federal Center Southwest.*

NATIONAL POSTAL MUSEUM The *Smithsonian*'s newest museum opened in the summer of 1993 and occupies a dramatic atrium area of the *City Post Office Building,* which served as Washington's main post office from 1914 to 1986. It features the world's largest collection of stamps and philatelic materials, which was formerly housed in the *National Museum of American History* (see below). A variety of exhibits traces the colorful history of the ways the mail has been collected, sorted, and delivered over the years. Also included is an extensive, historical stamp collection. Be sure to take a stroll through the old post office's main lobby, with its marble floors and columns restored to their original luster. Also here are an educational *Discovery Center* and the *Library Research Center* (open by appointment from 10 AM to 4 PM on weekdays), specializing in philatelic and postal history. Closed *Christmas*. No admission charge. First St. and Massachusetts Ave. NE (phone: 357-1300). *Metro: Union Station.*

UNION STATION This early 20th-century Beaux Arts landmark was modeled after the *Baths of Diocletian* and the triumphal *Arch of Constantine* in Rome; its marble floors, granite walls, bronze grilles, and classic statuary dazzle visitors. In front of *Amtrak*'s rail terminal is a complex of chic boutiques and dining areas. (*Sfuzzi Washington* is one of our favorites; see *Eating Out.*) The main concourse, once the largest room under a single roof, has been divided into a series of levels and mezzanines for stores and eateries. The lower level houses movie theaters and a score of fast-food outlets. 50 Massachusetts Ave. NE (phone: 371-9441). *Metro: Union Station.*

THE WHITE HOUSE AREA

WHITE HOUSE Probably the most historic house in America; even though George Washington never slept here, every president since has. Designed originally by James Hoban, the *White House* still looks like an Irish country mansion from the outside; inside there are elegant parlors decorated with portraits of the presidents and first ladies, and antique furnishings of many periods. The five state rooms on the first floor are open to the public, and though you actually won't see the business of government going on, you'll be very close to it.

Visitors line up at the East Gate on East Executive Avenue. (Tickets, required during summer months and the week that begins with *Easter Sunday,* are available from the kiosk on the adjacent *Ellipse;* at peak times, for example around *Easter,* the lineup for tickets begins early in the morning.) Congressional tours of seven rooms, instead of the usual five, are available by writing to your congressman in advance. Be sure to specify alternate dates. Tours are conducted Tuesdays through Saturdays from 10 AM to noon. No admission charge. 1600 Pennsylvania Ave. NW (phone: 456-7041). *Metro: McPherson Square.*

LAFAYETTE SQUARE If you do not enter the *White House,* you can get a fine view of it from this square, which was originally proposed by city planner L'Enfant as the mansion's front yard. Statues commemorate Andrew Jackson and the foreign heroes of the American Revolution—Lafayette, de Rochambeau, von Steuben and Kościuszko. Flanking the square are two early 19th-century buildings designed by Benjamin Latrobe, Washington's first public architect. *St. John's Church* (16th and H Sts. NW; phone: 347-8766), constructed along classically simple lines, is better known as the *Church of Presidents* because every president since Madison has attended services here. It's open to the public daily. The *Decatur House* (748 Jackson Pl. NW; phone: 842-0920), built for Commodore Stephen Decatur and occupied after his death by a succession of diplomats, is a Federal-style townhouse featuring handsome woodwork, a spiral staircase, and furniture of the 1820s. It's closed Mondays; admission charge. Near the southwest corner of the square is *Blair House* (1651-1653 Pennsylvania Ave. NW), the president's official guesthouse since 1942; it is not open to the public. *Metro: McPherson Square* or *Farragut West.*

ELLIPSE This grassy 32-acre expanse is the location of the zero milestone from which all distances in Washington are measured. It's the site of everything from demonstrations and ball games to the national *Christmas* tree. 1600 Constitution Ave. NW. *Metro: Farragut West.*

CORCORAN GALLERY OF ART One of the finest collections of 18th-, 19th-, and 20th-century American art anywhere is displayed in this museum's gracious, skylit halls. (It's privately funded, and despite its location is not a *Smithsonian* museum.) Among the distinguished works are paintings by Sargent, Bierstadt, and Copley. You'll also find European paintings and sculpture (some by Corot, some by the animal sculptor Antoine Barye), as well as Renaissance drawings, and a variety of changing exhibitions of contemporary art and photography. Closed Tuesdays; open until 9 PM on Thursdays. No admission charge. One block from the *White House* at 17th and E Sts. NW (phone: 638-3211). *Metro: Farragut West.*

RENWICK GALLERY The nation's first art museum, this beautiful French Second Empire building was designed by *Smithsonian Castle* architect James Renwick in 1859 to house W. W. Corcoran's art collection. Now run by the *Smithsonian Institution,* it is worth a visit for its changing exhibitions of contemporary American crafts and design. The gallery's other noteworthy sights are the entrance foyer, with its impressive staircase, and the 1870 Grand Salon, with overstuffed Louis XV sofas and potted palms. Open daily. No admission charge. Pennsylvania Ave. at 17th St. NW (phone: 357-2531). *Metro: Farragut North* or *West.*

DAUGHTERS OF THE AMERICAN REVOLUTION MUSEUM Though any member of the DAR must prove that she is descended from those who served the cause of American independence with "unfailing loyalty," the museum is open to everyone. Exhibitions feature more than 30 period rooms, including the parlor of a 19th-century Mississippi River steamboat, and the *Oklahoma Room,* with a prairie farm kitchen's utensils. *Continental Hall,* the building that houses the museum, is also one of the world's largest genealogical archives (there's a small charge to do research here). The museum is open and tours are given on a walk-in basis; closed all day Saturday, and Sunday morning. No admission charge. 1776 D St. NW (phone: 628-1776). *Metro: Farragut West.*

OCTAGON HOUSE This stately red brick townhouse, a notable example of Federal architecture, is where President James Madison and his wife Dolley lived for six months after the British burned down the *White House* (and the *Capitol*) in 1814. The British may have spared this structure because the French ambassador had been living here since the outbreak of the War of 1812, and the French tricolor was flying over the house. Today it is maintained as a museum; the American antique furnishings from the Federal period give visitors an idea of the high style of the early 19th century. Tours are available. Closed Mondays. Donations suggested. 1799 New York Ave. NW (phone: 638-3105). *Metro: Farragut West.*

ORGANIZATION OF AMERICAN STATES Architects Paul Cret and Albert Kelsey blended the styles of North and South America in this building of imposing formality and inviting elegance. The *OAS* links the US with the countries of Latin America and the Caribbean, and through its symposiums, lectures, and general precepts tries to promote better political and trade relations. For example, the *OAS* was involved in planning the celebration of the 500th anniversary of Columbus's voyage to the New World. Note the statue of Queen Isabella I as you enter. Also inside are the *Hall of Heroes and Flags;* the *Hall of the Americas;* several Louis Tiffany chandeliers; and the *Aztec Gardens,* a year-round tropical spot that is overgrown with exotic plants sent here from the member nations of the *OAS*. Closed weekends. No admission charge. The *Art Museum of the Americas* is just behind the *Aztec Garden.* Closed Sundays. No admission charge. In the *Pan American Union Building,* 17th St. and Constitution Ave. NW (phone: 458-3000 for *OAS;* 458-6016 for the art museum). *Metro: Farragut West.*

THE MALL AREA

This 2-mile stretch of green from the *Lincoln Memorial* to the *Capitol* forms something of the grand avenue envisioned by Pierre L'Enfant in his original plans for the city.

WORK IN PROGRESS

Due to extensive repairs to the *Lincoln* and *Jefferson* Memorials, visitors might see more scaffolding than monuments for the next year or so. The statues themselves, however, will not be obstructed. Although both will remain open to the public, walking entirely around the colonnades will be prohibited until repairs are completed, sometime next year.

LINCOLN MEMORIAL From the outside, this columned white marble building looks like a Greek temple; inside, the spacious chamber with its colossal seated statue of Lincoln, sculpted by Daniel French, is just as inspiring. Carved on the walls are the words of the *Gettysburg Address* and *Lincoln's Second Inaugural Address. National Park Service* guides present brief talks at regular intervals. Open 24 hours a day, with park rangers on duty until midnight. No admission charge. *Memorial Circle* between Constitution and Independence Aves. (phone: 426-6841 or 426-6895). *Metro: Foggy Bottom.*

WASHINGTON MONUMENT Dominating the *Mall* is the 555-foot marble and granite obelisk designed by Robert Mills (completed in 1888) to commemorate George Washington. The top, reached by elevator, commands an excellent panoramic view of the city. On *National Park Service* tours on weekends, you can walk down the 897 steps, where you see many stones donated by such groups as the "Citizens of the US residing in Foo Chow Foo, China." Open daily, 8 AM to midnight, from the first Sunday in April through *Labor Day;* 9 AM to 5 PM the rest of the year. No admission charge. 15th St. between Independence and Constitution Aves. (phone: 426-6841). *Metro: Smithsonian.*

VIETNAM VETERANS MEMORIAL Maya Ying Lin, while a *Yale* architecture student, designed this simple memorial which evokes complicated feelings about the American soldiers who died or are missing as a result of the Vietnam War. The two arms of the long, V-shaped, polished black granite walls point toward the *Washington Monument* and the *Lincoln Memorial*. On the 492-foot-long wall are inscribed the names of more than 58,000 men and women killed in the war or still missing. A sculpture by Frederick Hart, depicting three soldiers, stands a short distance from the memorial. Also nearby is a memorial honoring the estimated 10,000 women who served in the Vietnam War. The memorial, a bronze sculpture by Gienna Goodacre, depicts two women in uniform attending a wounded male soldier. Many make pilgrimages here to find the names of lost friends and family members, some of them quietly etching an inscribed name onto a piece of paper to take home with them. Constitution Ave. NW and Henry Bacon Dr. (phone: 634-1568). *Metro: Foggy Bottom*.

JEFFERSON MEMORIAL Dominating the south bank of the Tidal Basin, this domed temple-like structure (designed by John Russell Pope) is a tribute to our third president and the drafter of the *Declaration of Independence*. The bronze statue of Jefferson was executed by Rudolph Evans, and inscribed on the walls are quotations from Jefferson's writings. This is the place to be for the most dramatic view of the cherry blossoms in early spring. Open daily. No admission charge. South Basin Dr. SW (phone: 426-6822). *Metro: Smithsonian*.

UNITED STATES HOLOCAUST MEMORIAL MUSEUM Opened in April of 1993, this is a museum dedicated to educating visitors about one of the twentieth century's darkest periods: the persecution and systematic execution by the Nazis of Jews, Gypsies, homosexuals, and other "undesirables" during World War II. Located between the *Washington Monument* and the *Jefferson Memorial*, the red brick and sandstone building was designed by James I. Freed. Upon entering, you are given an ID card bearing the picture and name of an actual victim; as you wend your way through exhibits about book burning, *Kristallnacht*, and the "Final Solution," you discover the eventual fate of "your" victim. There is also a library, archives, and the *Learning Center*, an interactive exhibit that allows visitors access to maps, documents, videos, and music via touch screens. A limited number of (free) same-day tickets is available when the museum opens at 10 AM, but demand has been high and people line up early. Advance tickets (a much better idea), with a fixed date and time of entry, can be ordered through *TicketMaster* (phone: 432-7328); there is a small service charge per ticket when ordering. Closed *Christmas*. No admission charge. 100 Raoul Wallenberg Pl. SW, between 14th and 15th Sts. (phone: 488-0400). *Metro: Smithsonian*.

BUREAU OF ENGRAVING AND PRINTING At the world's largest securities manufacturing establishment, you can watch the making of currency on 25-minute self-guided tours. Open weekdays from 9 AM to 2 PM only. Closed weekends, federal holidays, and from *Christmas* through *New Year's Day*. No admission charge. 14th and C Sts. SW (phone: 874-3019). *Metro: Smithsonian*.

J. EDGAR HOOVER BUILDING If you want to find out a little more about an organization that already knows everything about you, take a tour of the *Federal Bureau of Investigation (FBI)*. In addition to a film on some past investigative activities, you'll get to see the laboratory and a firearms demonstration. One-hour tours start every 20 minutes on weekdays from 8:45 AM to 4:15 PM. Line up early. No admission charge. Pennsylvania Ave. between Ninth and 10th Sts. NW (phone: 324-3447). *Metro: Metro Center* or *Archives/Navy Memorial*.

NATIONAL ARCHIVES The repository for all major American records. The 76 Corinthian columns supporting this handsome building designed by John Russell Pope are nothing compared to the contents. Inside, in special helium-filled glass and bronze cases, reside the very pillars of our democracy—the *Declaration of Independence*, the *Constitution*, and the *Bill of Rights*. Open daily; there are evening hours from April through *Labor Day*. No admission charge. Constitution Ave. between Seventh and Ninth Sts. NW (phone: 501-5205). *Metro: Archives/Navy Memorial*.

US NAVY MEMORIAL PLAZA The plaza has a statue of a lone US sailor overlooking the US portion of a granite world map. The visitors' center includes a gift shop, IMAX theater, and museum. Military bands perform during spring and summer evenings; pick up a brochure at any hotel or call for schedule. Pennsylvania Ave. between Seventh and Ninth Sts. NW (phone: 737-2300; 800-821-8892). *Metro: Archives/Navy Memorial*.

NATIONAL GALLERY OF ART In a John Russell Pope building whose 500,000 square feet make it one of the world's largest marble structures, this museum, built to introduce Americans to the cream of European art, is what one local critic called "the sort of place paintings would aspire to if masterpieces went to heaven." Columns of Tuscan marble, floors of green marble from Vermont and gray marble from Tennessee, and walls of Indiana limestone and Italian travertine produce an unadulturatedly sumptuous effect. Leonardo da Vinci's *Ginevra de' Benci* (America's only da Vinci), Jan Vermeer's *Woman Holding a Balance*, a Rembrandt *Self-Portrait*, Jean-Honoré Fragonard's *A Young Girl Reading*, Pierre-Auguste Renoir's *Girl with a Watering Can*, and Claude Monet's *Rouen Cathedral, West Façade* are among literally thousands of breathtaking canvases and sculptures housed in the original building and the striking *East Building*, designed as a grouping of interlocking triangles by I. M. Pei. It all can be a bit bewildering, so, as an introduction, you might want to join one of the regular tours, rent a taped tour, or pick up the excellent *Brief Guide*. A monthly calendar of events includes free films, lectures, and concerts. Closed *Christmas* and *New Year's Day*. No admission charge. Fourth St. and Constitution Ave. NW (phone: 737-4215). *Metro: Judiciary Square, Federal Center Southwest*, or *Archives/Navy Memorial*.

SMITHSONIAN INSTITUTION Completed in 1855, the red Gothic castle on the *Mall*, built to house the institution's collections, is now the site of the *Smithsonian's Information Center* and the offices of the staff that oversees the *Smithsonian's* scattered museums and galleries. There are nine *Smithsonian* properties on the *Mall*, five (including the *National Zoo*—

see below) in other parts of DC, two in New York City (the *Cooper-Hewitt National Museum of Design* and the *National Museum of the American Indian*), and a half-dozen scientific research facilities around the country. The total collection contains over 137 million items and gains almost one million more every year; only an infinitesimal percentage is displayed at any given time, so there's always something new to see. The *Smithsonian*'s $73-million, three-floor complex just south of the *Castle* on Independence Avenue SW at 10th Street is a bit controversial because it is underground. It houses two museums—the *Arthur M. Sackler Gallery*, featuring Asian art, and the *National Museum of African Art*, which was moved from its former *Capitol Hill* location (see below for details on both). The third floor houses the *International Center* for exhibitions, and atop it all is the *Enid A. Haupt Garden*, a $3-million Victorian delight built around a century-old linden tree. The *Castle* is at 1000 Jefferson Dr. SW (phone: 357-2700).

The following are the *Smithsonian Museums* on the *Mall;* they are listed in clockwise order, starting from the *Smithsonian Castle*. All are closed only on *Christmas Day;* hours are slightly longer in summer. There's no admission charge for any of the *Smithsonian* museums.

National Museum of African Art The most extensive collection of African art in this country, and the only one dedicated exclusively to the arts of sub-Saharan Africa. Exhibitions include figures, masks, and sculptures in ivory, wood, bronze, and clay from 20 African nations; also color panels and audiovisual presentations on the people and environments of Africa. One gallery has an intriguing display concerning the influence of Africa's cultural heritage on modern European and American art. There's also a delightful gift shop. 950 Independence Ave. SW, next to the *Sackler Gallery of Art* (phone: 357-4600). *Metro: Smithsonian.*

Arthur M. Sackler Gallery Donated by Dr. Arthur M. Sackler, a New York medical researcher, the extensive collection of over 1,000 pieces of Eastern art includes Chinese bronzes from the Shang (1523–1028 BC) through Han (206 BC–AD 220) dynasties, Chinese jade that dates from 3000 BC, and Near Eastern works in silver, gold, bronze, and lesser ores. There are also Persian and Indian paintings, Chinese Ming Dynasty furniture, and more. 1050 Independence Ave. SW (phone: 357-4880). *Metro: Smithsonian.*

Freer Gallery An eclectic collection of Asian art, plus late-19th- and early-20th-century American art. Wealthy Detroit businessman Charles Lang Freer donated the works from his personal collection. *The Peacock Room*, painted by Freer's friend, James McNeill Whistler, is a must-see. Jefferson Dr. at 12th St. SW (phone: 357-4880). *Metro: Smithsonian.*

National Museum of American History The wealth of Americana that fills this uniquely austere *Mall* museum includes George Washington's false teeth, the original Star-Spangled Banner that inspired the Francis Scott Key poem (that inspired the national anthem), the desk on which Thomas Jefferson wrote the *Declaration of Independence,* Eli Whitney's cotton gin, Alexander Graham Bell's telephone, and other prized possessions—such as the gowns worn by First Ladies from Martha Washington to Hillary Clinton, modeled by mannequins standing in authentic reproductions of rooms in the *White House*. The museum's ground floor traces the role of machines in our nation's history, from railroad locomotives and a 1913 Model T to atom smashers and computers. The second floor focuses on our nation's people, our home life, our community life, and our relationship to the world beyond. The third floor is packed with exhibits ranging from musical instruments to instruments of war. One of the more interesting exhibits is an entire pre–Civil War post office taken from Headsville, West Virginia, that is still in operation and accepts letters for mail, franking them with a unique *Smithsonian* seal. The various galleries, from the *1776 Gallery* to the *Pain Gallery* (in the *Medical Gallery*), offer a variety of demonstrations—visitors can learn about the workings of the ham radio, methods of type founding and printing, and much more. The *Smithsonian Bookstore* (phone: 357-1784) has the area's best selection of American history books. Constitution Ave. between 12th and 14th Sts. NW (phone: 357-2700). *Metro: Smithsonian* or *Federal Triangle*.

National Museum of Natural History This massive museum on the *Mall* is filled with 118 million items (only a fraction of which are on display) that tell the story of human beings and their environment. The exhibits cover the entire spectrum of the life sciences, from anthropology to marine zoology. Among the more popular exhibits are the *Dinosaur Hall*, exhibits on the evolution of humans, fossils, a collection of beasts bagged by Teddy Roosevelt on his African adventures, the *Insect Zoo*, and displays on birds, plants, rocks, and gems. The gem collection contains the legendary Hope Diamond, smuggled out of India in the 17th century and reputed to bring tragedy to its owners; at 45.5 carats, this blue diamond is the largest in the world. The largest elephant on record, a giant Fenkovi African bush elephant more than 13 feet tall, greets visitors in the museum's octagonal rotunda, where banners point the way to the worlds of fossils, birds, mammals, bones, and the geology of the Earth. Another favorite occupant is "Uncle Beazly," the life-size model of a triceratops dinosaur. The *Sea Life Hall* contains live aquatic specimens and a living coral reef, and the *Discovery Room* is a godsend to parents, with its touchable exhibits of elephant tusks and arrowheads, plus a costume room (in which children can try on costumes from around the world). The museum's gift shops and *Associates Court* cafeteria are excellent. Constitution Ave. at 10th St. NW (phone: 357-2700). *Metro: Smithsonian* or *Federal Triangle*.

National Air & Space Museum This member of the *Smithsonian* complex, housing a fascinating assortment of aerodynamic treasures, draws more visitors annually than any other museum in the world; consequently, a visit here often means braving crowds. But in exchange for a little jostling and waiting, you will learn about the history of flight from people's earliest yearnings and attempts to fly, to World War II rockets, to the modern space probes that now explore the outer reaches of our solar system and beyond. In addition to the mechanics of flying, the 23 galleries in this lofty building explore the politics, physics, and art linked to man's dreams of flight. The entry hall's *Milestones of Flight*

Gallery holds Charles Lindbergh's *Spirit of St. Louis,* the Wright brothers' *Kitty Hawk Flyer,* and the *Gossamer Albatross,* the first human-powered plane to cross the English Channel, but this is just the beginning. In all, there are 240 aircraft and 50 missiles in the collection. The museum's *Albert Einstein Planetarium* is truly a cosmic experience and the *Langley Theater,* which projects films onto a towering five-story-high screen, is the next best thing to having your own wings. Different films are featured periodically but the historic mainstay of the theater is *To Fly,* a hell-for-leather romp through the skies in everything from a hot-air balloon to a fighter jet. Other exhibits allow visitors to design aircraft, observe the history of aerial photography, and inspect a model of Skylab. There's an admission charge for movies. Sixth St. and Independence Ave. SW (phone: 357-2700). *Metro: L'Enfant Plaza.*

Hirshhorn Museum and Sculpture Garden This is the most modern of the city's museums of modern art. The *Hirshhorn* houses the ever-astonishing collection amassed by Joseph H. Hirshhorn (1899–1981), who grew up in such poverty that he never even owned a toy. The collection focuses on American art and includes works by Estes, Golub, Gorky, Henri, Hopper, de Kooning, Noland, and Stella; modern European masters such as Bacon, Balthus, Kiefer, and Magritte also are represented. The extraordinary vitality of the sculpture collection reflects the genius of Calder, Degas, Matisse, Moore, Rodin, Serra, and David Smith—many of whose works are displayed in the sculpture garden—plus the innovations of more recent artists. For this variety alone the museum is fascinating; the building itself—circular and fortress-like—is intriguing as well. Seventh St. and Independence Ave. SW (phone: 357-1300). *Metro: L'Enfant Plaza.*

Arts and Industries Building Just east of the *Castle,* this is the second-oldest *Smithsonian* building on the *Mall.* The *Centennial Exhibition,* displayed in Philadelphia in 1876, has been re-created with marvelous displays of fashions, furnishings, and machinery. Jefferson Dr. and Independence Ave. at Ninth St. SW (phone: 357-1300). *Metro: Smithsonian.*

FOR THE YOUNG AND YOUNG-AT-HEART

The beautiful early 20th-century carousel set in the shadow of the *Smithsonian Castle* operates in the warm weather between 10 AM and 5:30 PM. *Metro: Smithsonian.*

DOWNTOWN

NATIONAL PORTRAIT GALLERY AND NATIONAL MUSEUM OF AMERICAN ART In the *National Portrait Gallery,* an excellent example of Greek Revival architecture, many Americans who have gone down in the history of this country have gone up on the walls (in portrait form, that is). Among those hanging are all the American presidents, Pocahontas, Horace Greeley, and Harriet Beecher Stowe. The *National Museum of American Art* features American painting, sculpture, and graphic arts, including Catlin's paintings of Indians and a choice group of works by the

American Impressionists. Both museums (also administered by the *Smithsonian Institution*) are open daily. No admission charge. Eighth St. at F and G Sts. NW. (phone: 357-2700). *Metro: Gallery Place.*

FORD'S THEATRE The site of Abraham Lincoln's assassination by John Wilkes Booth is a national monument, restored and decorated as it appeared on the fatal night of April 14, 1865. In the basement is a museum of Lincoln memorabilia, including displays showing his life as a lawyer, statesman, husband, father, and president; the clothes he was wearing when he was shot; the flag that covered his casket; the derringer used by the assassin; and Booth's personal diary. Theater performances are held throughout the year. Open daily. Admission charge for shows only. 511 10th St. NW (phone: 426-6924; 347-4833 for theater tickets). *Metro: Metro Center* (11th St. exit).

PETERSON HOUSE Directly across the street from *Ford's Theatre* is the house in which Lincoln died the morning after the shooting. The small, sparsely furnished home appears much the way it did in 1865. Open daily. No admission charge. 516 10th St. NW (phone: 426-6830). *Metro: Metro Center* (11th St. exit).

NATIONAL LAW ENFORCEMENT OFFICERS' MEMORIAL Dedicated in late 1991, this monument honors federal, state, and local law enforcement officers who have died in the line of duty, dating as far back as 1794. The enclosed plaza has walled pathways that encircle a terraced pool, and are guarded on each side by majestic bronze lions. E St. between Fourth and Fifth Sts. NW (phone: 703-827-0518). *Metro: Judiciary Square.*

ADAMS MORGAN

This funky, international neighborhood is now rivaling Georgetown as the area for after-hours fun and frolicking in the nation's capital. Long the bohemian section of town, it has been home to many Salvadoran, Ethiopian, and African immigrants. Surrounding the intersection of Columbia Road and 18th Street NW are foreign-language book and record stores, clothing boutiques with products from Asia and Africa, Ethiopian and Vietnamese restaurants, reggae bars, and hot nightspots. *Adams Morgan Day,* an annual cultural street fair held in early September, is alive with music from all over the world; local restaurants provide a host of international foods to satisfy any palate. *Metro: Dupont Circle.*

GEORGETOWN

Once the Union's major tobacco port, the only tobacco left in Georgetown is in the smoke shops. Still holding fast to its own identity, this neighborhood is particularly nice in the spring when it's pleasant to walk along the Chesapeake and Ohio Canal. The whole area's great for strolling (though too much tourism has produced the occasional tacky stretch). In summer, it's possible to catch a slow barge up the canal. Tickets can be purchased at the *Foundry Mall* (1055 Thomas Jefferson St. NW; phone: 472-4376). Beside the canal (between Jefferson and 31st Sts.), the streets off Wisconsin Avenue house the city's social and political elite in beautifully restored townhouses with prim gardens and lovely magnolia trees. Many of the buildings are on the *National Reg-*

ister of Historic Places and are well worth seeing. The main drags—Wisconsin Avenue and M Street—are where most of the action is. In addition to boasting a shopping mall and some of the hottest nightlife in town (including sports and blues bars), the area is rich with boutiques, movie theaters, and restaurants offering a vast variety of food—from Vietnamese to Indian to French.

At the northern edge of Georgetown (along R St. east of Wisconsin Ave.), large 18th-century country estates mingle with smaller, more modern row houses. The *Dumbarton Oaks Garden* has beautiful formal grounds, and the *Dumbarton Oaks Museum* has a fine collection of early Christian and Byzantine art. The museum is open Tuesdays through Sundays from 2 to 5 PM; no admission charge. The gardens are open daily from 2 to 5 PM; admission charge from April through October (phone: 342-3200 or 338-8278). The entrance to the museum is at 1703 32nd Street NW; the entrance to the gardens is at 31st and R Streets NW.

At 37th and O Streets is the campus of *Georgetown University*. Established in 1789, it is the oldest Jesuit university in the United States and is renowned for its schools of foreign service and languages, as well as one of the best law schools in the country.

ELSEWHERE IN DC

ROCK CREEK PARK New York has its *Central Park*, Chicago its *Grant Park*, and Philadelphia its *Fairmount Park*. Washington's premier city park, where one can escape the traffic, the noise, the concrete, and (mostly) the crowds, is found in a 1,700-acre swath of green in the northwest section of town. From its narrow south tip just outside Georgetown, *Rock Creek Park* (named for the meandering stream that bisects it) widens gradually until it's big enough to contain the *National Zoo* (see below) and, a few miles farther north, a modest 18-hole golf course (see *Golf*). There are bike and jogging trails, picnic tables, even riding stables, but mostly untended greenery, which covers the park's steep hills. A two-lane road meanders down its spine; the northern section of the park is closed to automobiles on Sundays to allow cyclists, Rollerbladers, and strollers free reign. In the northwest quadrant of the city (phone: 426-6829). *Metro: Fort Totten* or *Van Ness* (though it's a bus ride or long walk from either station).

NATIONAL ZOO The *Smithsonian Institution* is best known for its museums on the *Mall*, but its largest facility is located in the midst of verdant *Rock Creek Park* (see above) in the northwest quadrant of the city. Created in 1889 for "the advancement of science and the instruction and recreation of the people," this 163-acre zoological park clings to the side of a gently rolling hill. The *Amazonia* exhibit recreates a tropical river and rain forest, while the *Reptile Discovery Center* allows visitors to meet reptiles and amphibians up close and personal. The *Great Flight Cage* features exotic birds. Sadly, the zoo's female panda Ling-Ling died in late 1992, leaving her male companion Hsing-Hsing the only panda in the zoo; there are no children (although the pair's numerous tries at parenting are documented in a photo display!). There are, however, many infant animals born each year to such species as giraffes, orangutans, and elephants. The *Panda Café* serves refreshments, and souvenir shops are filled with, among other things, panda paraphernalia. Closed *Christmas*. No admission charge. 3301 Connecticut Ave. NW (phone: 673-4800). *Metro: Woodley Park/Zoo* or *Cleveland Park* (the easier walk is from *Cleveland Park*; it's a stiff uphill climb from *Woodley Park/Zoo*).

EXTRA SPECIAL

Just 16 miles south of Washington on George Washington Memorial Parkway is *Mount Vernon,* George Washington's estate from 1754 to 1799 and his final resting place. This lovely 18th-century plantation shows a less familiar aspect of the military-political figure—George Washington as the rich Southern planter. The mansion, overlooking the Potomac, and the outbuildings that housed the shops that made *Mount Vernon* a self-sufficient economic unit have been authentically restored and refurnished. Some 500 of the original 8,000 acres remain; all are well maintained, and the parterre gardens and formal lawns provide a magnificent setting. There's also a museum with Washington memorabilia; the tomb of George and Martha lies at the foot of the hill. During the spring or the summer, start out early to avoid big crowds. Bicycle paths lead from the DC side of Memorial Bridge to *Mount Vernon*—a lovely ride along the Potomac. Open daily. Admission charge (phone: 703-780-2000).

Also overlooking the Potomac is *Arlington National Cemetery,* a solemn reminder of the more turbulent parts of our country's history. Here lie the bodies of many who served their country, both in the military forces and in other ways, among them Admiral Richard Byrd, General George C. Marshall, Robert F. Kennedy, Justice Oliver Wendell Holmes, and John F. Kennedy, whose grave is marked by an *Eternal Flame.* Former first lady Jacqueline Bouvier Kennedy Onassis, who died last year, is interred beside her husband. The *Tomb of the Unknown Soldier,* a 50-ton block of white marble, commemorates the dead of World Wars I and II and the Korean, Vietnam, and Persian Gulf Wars and is always guarded by a solitary soldier. Changing of the guard takes place every hour on the hour (every half hour during summer months). The beautifully landscaped grounds of the cemetery once were part of Robert E. Lee's plantation but were confiscated by the Union after Lee joined the Confederacy. Lee's home, *Arlington House,* has been restored and is open to the public. Cars are not allowed in the cemetery, but you can park at the visitors' center and go on foot or pay and ride the *Tourmobile* (phone: 554-7950). Both *Arlington House* and the cemetery are open daily. Directly west of Memorial Bridge in Arlington, Virginia. *Metro: Arlington Cemetery.*

Sources and Resources

TOURIST INFORMATION

The *Washington, DC, Convention and Visitors Association* (*WCVA;* 1212 New York Ave. NW, Suite 600, Washington, DC 20005; phone: 789-7000; fax: 789-7037) coordinates all Washington tourism information and runs the visitors' center (at 1455 Pennsylvania Ave. NW; phone: 789-7038). The center (closed Sundays) provides free maps and information on where to stay, eat, and shop, and on events.

LOCAL COVERAGE The *Washington Post* and the *Washington Times* are the city's morning daily newspapers; *Washingtonian* magazine is published monthly. All are available at newsstands. *Museum and Arts Washington* lists current museum exhibits. The *City Paper,* a free weekly tabloid published on Thursdays, is an excellent source of cultural and clubs listings; it's available in shops, restaurants, and *Metro* stations. We also immodestly recommend our own *Birnbaum's Washington 95* (Harper-Collins; $12).

TELEVISION STATIONS WRC Channel 4–NBC; WTTG Channel 5–Fox; WJLA Channel 7–ABC; WUSA Channel 9–CBS; Cable Channel 11 or 42–CNN; and WETA Channel 26–PBS.

RADIO STATIONS AM: WTEM 570 (sports); WMAL 630 (news/talk/sports); WWRC 980 (talk); and WTOP 1500 (all news). FM: WPFW 89.3 (jazz/community radio); WETA 90.9 (classical/National Public Radio); WKYS 93.9 (urban contemporary); WMZQ 98.7 (country); WGAY 99.5 (easy listening); WGMS 103.5 (classical); and WCXR 105.9 (classic rock).

FOOD *Best Restaurants and Others* by Phyllis Richman (101 Productions; $8.95) lists fine dining places in Washington, DC, and environs.

TELEPHONE The area code for the District is 202; for Maryland, 301; and for Virginia, 703. The telephone numbers in this chapter are in the 202 area code unless otherwise indicated.

SALES TAX The city sales tax is 6%; there is an 11% tax on hotel rooms.

CLIMATE Washington has four distinct seasons. Summers are Amazonian, falls New Englandish and lovely, winters cold with some snow and lots of slush, and spring—when the cherry blossoms bloom and all is sublime.

GETTING AROUND

AIRPORTS Washington is served by three major airports. *Washington National Airport* is the city's primary facility. The *Washington Flyer* (phone: 703-685-1400) provides express bus and van service from *National* to 1517 K St. NW (at the rear of the *Capital Hilton*). Free shuttle service is available to most downtown and Capitol Hill hotels. The *Metro*'s blue and yellow lines connect downtown with the airport. The blue line leaves from the main terminal at *Metro Center* (11th and G Sts. NW; phone: 637-7000) and the yellow line leaves from Gallery Place (7th and G Sts.).

Dulles International Airport is about 25 miles west of the city, in Virginia. The ride from *Dulles* to downtown DC at 1517 K St. NW usually takes 45 minutes to an hour. The *Washington Flyer* leaves *Dulles* about every half hour and travels to 1517 K St. NW. Free shuttle service to downtown and Capitol Hill hotels is available.

Baltimore/Washington International Airport (*BWI*) also serves the DC area and is a 1-hour drive from downtown. *BWI Airport Connection* (phone: 301-441-2345) also offers bus service. Buses depart every 1½ hours Sundays through Fridays.

BUS The *Metro Bus* system serves the entire District and the surrounding area. Transfers within the District are free; the rates increase when you go into Maryland and Virginia. For complete route information call the *Washington Metropolitan Area Transit Authority* office (phone: 637-7000). *Greyhound/Trailways* runs to and from its main bus station (First St. and L St. NE; phone: 301-565-2662).

CAR RENTAL All the national firms serve Washington.

SUBWAY The fastest way to get around Washington is by *Metrorail*, the subway system. The lines provide a quick and quiet ride, for $1 to $3.15 depending on the route and time of day. (Fare schedules are posted in each station.) You need a farecard to enter and exit platform areas; they are on sale inside the stations. Transfers to the bus system are free. Note: Be sure to pick up a transfer at your boarding station (not the exiting station). Children ages five and under ride free. *Metro* hours are weekdays from 6 AM to midnight; Saturdays and Sundays from 8 AM to midnight. Inquire about discount passes; for example, a two-day *Family/Tourist Pass*, which costs $5, is good for unlimited travel on the *Metro* buses and subway for up to four persons. For complete route and travel information and a map of the system, contact the *Washington Metropolitan Area Transit Authority* office (600 Fifth St. NW; phone: 637-7000).

TAXI Cabs in the District charge by zone. Sharing cabs is common, but ask the driver whether there is a route conflict if you join another passenger. Cabs may be hailed in the street, picked up outside stations and hotels, or ordered on the phone, but there is an extra charge of $1.50 for phone dispatch. By law, basic rates must be posted in all taxis. The major cab companies are *Yellow* (phone: 544-1212) and *Diamond* (phone: 387-6200).

TOURS The *Tourmobile* operates in the downtown sightseeing area between the *Lincoln Memorial* and *Capitol* area (the *Mall*), and also goes to *Arlington National Cemetery*. These 88-passenger shuttle trams make 18 stops, and passengers may get on or off as they wish (*Tourmobiles* pass each stop every 30 minutes). Commentary about the sights also is provided. Tickets can be purchased from the driver or from a booth near the tour sites. For complete information contact the *Tourmobile* office (1000 Ohio Dr. SW; phone: 554-7950).

Old Town Trolley Tours offers two-hour group charter tours or individual tours of the District (phone: 682-0079). *Gray Line* offers guided, narrated bus tours of the District and outlying areas (phone: 289-1995 or 301-386-8300); another bus touring company is *All About Town* (phone: 966-3800). Museum tours as well as special group tours emphasizing historic Washington are run by *National Fine Arts Associates* (4801 Massachusetts Ave. NW; phone: 966-3800). *Spirit Cruises* runs tours such as the "Spirit of Washington" and the "Spirit of Mt. Vernon" (March to mid-October only to *Mount Vernon*) aboard sightseeing boats on the Potomac, from March to December (Pier 4, Sixth and Water Sts. SW; phone: 554-8000 or 554-1542). The *Potomac Riverboat Company* also offers tours from the waterways of the capital area (phone: 703-684-0580).

TRAIN More than 50 *Amtrak* trains daily pull into historic *Union Station* on *Capitol Hill,* including the *Metroliner,* linking the capital to New York and other Northeast Corridor cities. For reservations and information, call 800-872-7245.

LOCAL SERVICES

AUDIOVISUAL EQUIPMENT *Avcom* (1006 Sixth St. NW; phone: 408-0444); *Total Audio-Visual Systems* (303 H St. NW; phone: 737-3900).

BABY-SITTING *Kids First* (15th and K Sts.; phone: 289-5437).

BUSINESS SERVICES *Ecco Temporary Services* (1001 Connecticut Ave. NW; phone: 293-2285). *The Capital Informer* (3240 Prospect St. NW; phone: 965-7420) helps plan conventions and meetings.

DRY CLEANER/TAILOR *Bergmann's* offers pickup and delivery at several locations (2318 Rhode Island Ave. NE; phone: 529-2440; 714 Sixth St. NW; phone: 737-6925; or call 703-247-7600).

LIMOUSINES *Congressional Limousine* (phone: 966-6000) offers 24-hour service. *International Limousine Service* (phone: 388-6800) has multilingual drivers; sedans are also available.

MECHANIC *Call Carl* (5030 Connecticut Ave.; phone: 364-6368) makes repairs from 7:30 PM to 5 PM; gas is available 24 hours a day.

MEDICAL EMERGENCY *Georgetown University Hospital* (3800 Reservoir Rd. NW; phone: 784-2000); *George Washington University Medical Center* (901 23rd St. NW; phone: 994-3884).

MESSENGER SERVICES *U.S. Couriers* (phone: 393-1111).

PHOTOCOPIES *City Duplicating Center* (1615 L St. NW; phone: 296-0700); *Beaver Press* (1333 H St. NW; phone: 347-6400; and 18 Ogelthorpe St. NW; phone: 882-6690) offers pickup and delivery service.

POST OFFICE The main post office is at 900 Brentwood Rd. NE (phone: 636-1532); another branch is at 2 Massachusetts Ave. (phone: 523-2628).

PROFESSIONAL PHOTOGRAPHER *Garrison Studio* (52 O St. NW; phone: 265-5163).

SECRETARIES/STENOGRAPHERS *Courtesy Associates* (655 15th St, NW, Suite 300; phone: 347-5900).

TELECONFERENCE FACILITIES *Four Seasons* (2800 Pennsylvania Ave., NW; phone: 342-0444; 800-332-3442) and at *Loews L'Enfant Plaza* (480 L'Enfant Plaza SW; phone: 484-1000; 800-243-1166).

TRANSLATORS *Berlitz* (1050 Connecticut Ave. NW; phone: 331-1160) for written translations only; *International Translation Center* (1660 L St. NW, Room 613; phone: 296-1344).

WESTERN UNION/TELEX Many offices are located around the city (phone: 624-0100).

SPECIAL EVENTS

A town that knows how to throw presidential inauguration parties is a town that knows how to celebrate. There's plenty to keep the District going between inaugurations, too. The first sighting of white single blossoms and a flood of pink double blossoms means it's *Cherry Blossom* time in Washington. In early April, a big festival celebrates the coming of the blossoms and the spring with concerts, parades, balls, and the lighting of the Japanese Lantern at the Tidal Basin.

Around the same time (give or take a few blossoms) is the *Easter Monday Egg Rolling,* when scads of children descend on the *White House* lawn, usually to be greeted by the First Family; adults are admitted only if accompanied by a child.

House, garden, and embassy tours are given in April and May, allowing entrance to some of Washington's most elegant interiors. For information on the tours, see the "Weekend" section in Friday's *Washington Post.*

During the summer, the *Festival of American Folklife,* sponsored by the *Smithsonian Institution,* sets up its tents on the *Mall* near the *Museum of American History,* and groups from all regions of the country do their stuff; jug band concerts, blues performances, Indian dances, and handicraft demonstrations are just a few of the possibilities. In midsummer the *Twilight Tattoo* features military pageantry. And the *Fourth of July* celebrations in the capital are among the best in the country, with a parade, concerts, fireworks, and other entertainment.

In early September, *Adams Morgan Day* is celebrated in the Adams Morgan neighborhood. The festival, which reflects Spanish, Ethiopian, and African influences, features music, crafts, and food. The city is especially festive at *Christmas.* Special music programs are presented at the *Kennedy Center* and at many other spots around town.

MUSEUMS

In addition to those described in *Special Places,* other notable museums include the following:

HILLWOOD Exquisite 18th- and 19th-century French and Russian icons, portraits, and Fabergé creations are housed in the elegant former home of cereal heiress Marjorie Merriweather Post. Other buildings on the 25-acre site include a dacha, or Russian country house, with a small collection of Russian art; the C. W. Post collection of paintings, sculpture, and furnishings; and a lodge housing Native American artifacts. Be sure to stroll around the *Rose Garden, French Garden,* and *Japanese Garden.* Closed Sundays and Mondays. Open to the public only via tours, which must be arranged by appointment; call well in advance for reservations. Admission charge. 4155 Linnean Ave. NW (phone: 686-5807). *Metro: Van Ness–UDC.*

HISTORICAL SOCIETY OF WASHINGTON, DC A museum devoted to Washington's history, housed in the spectacular Victorian mansion of brewer Christian Heurich. There is also a library and a bookstore. Tours are offered on the hour on Wednesdays through Saturdays starting from noon; the last tour leaves at 3 PM. The museum is closed Mondays. The library is open to the public Wednesdays, Fridays, and Saturdays from 10 AM to 4 PM. Admission charge. 1307 New Hampshire Ave. NW (phone: 785-2068). *Metro: Dupont Circle.*

NATIONAL BUILDING MUSEUM Housed in the old and wonderful *Pension Building,* this museum has permanent and changing exhibits relating to architecture, building, engineering, and design. Presidential inaugural balls are held in its *Great Hall.* Open daily. No admission charge. 401 F St. NW (phone: 272-2448). *Metro: Judiciary Square.*

NATIONAL GEOGRAPHIC SOCIETY EXPLORERS HALL Headquarters for the society; exhibits here document research and discoveries made by its explorers and documentarians. Open daily. No admission charge. 17th and M Sts. NW (phone: 857-7588). *Metro: Farragut North.*

NATIONAL LEARNING CENTER/CAPITAL CHILDREN'S MUSEUM A hands-on museum where children can dress up in period costumes, feed animals, and work on high-tech equipment. Open daily. Admission charge. 800 Third St. NE (phone: 543-8600). *Metro: Union Station.*

NATIONAL MUSEUM OF WOMEN IN THE ARTS In a former Masonic temple, this permanent collection of 500 pieces of pictorial, sculpted, and ceramic art spans 400 years of women's work. Open daily. Admission charge. 1250 New York Ave. at 13th St. NW (phone: 783-5000). *Metro: Metro Center* (13th St. exit).

PHILLIPS COLLECTION Opened in 1918, this is America's oldest museum of "modern art." Set in an elegant Victorian brownstone, the works of such masters as El Greco, Manet, and Chardin are shown together with their artistic progeny: Cézanne, Monet, Klee, O'Keeffe, Rothko, and many others. The pièce de résistance is Renoir's *Luncheon of the Boating Party.* The mahogany-paneled *Music Room* features a long-standing Sunday evening concert series of chamber music from September through May at 5 PM; admission charge). Closed *New Year's Day, July 4, Thanksgiving,* and *Christmas.* Admission charge weekends. 1612 21st St. and Q St. NW (phone: 387-0961). *Metro: Dupont Circle.*

TEXTILE MUSEUM A diverse collection of fabrics from around the world, in a former mansion with a charming garden. Featuring woven goods of both artistic and archaeological significance, it is one of only two museums in the world devoted entirely to woven rugs and fabrics. Even if your interest in the field runs no deeper than getting a good buy on something to cover that stain on the den rug, this may be the place (although goods for sale in the shop are high-priced). Open daily. Admission charge. 2320 S St. NW (phone: 667-0441). *Metro: Dupont Circle.*

WASHINGTON DOLL'S HOUSE AND TOY MUSEUM Featured here is the private collection of dollhouse historian Floragill Jacobs. On display are antique dollhouses and toys, including a section of presidents' games that includes the "Game of Politics or Race for the Presidency," a board game published in 1887, and the "Game of Presidents," a card game dating from the early 20th century. Closed Mondays. Admission charge. 5236 44th St. NW, one block west of Wisconsin Ave., between Jennifer and Harrison Sts. (phone: 244-0024). *Metro: Friendship Heights.*

WOODROW WILSON HOUSE Home to Woodrow Wilson (from 1921 to 1924) and Mrs. Wilson (from 1921 to 1961) this is now a memorial to our 28th president and his wife. Gifts of state, presidential memorabilia, and other items from the 1920s are displayed. Considering Wilson's tireless effort in establishing the *League of Nations* and in expanding America's role in international affairs, it is altogether fitting that he relocated to the Embassy Row district. On display are his library, the dining room, bedrooms, a solarium overlooking a garden, and many personal effects such as the typewriter he used to compose speeches. Only guided tours—which take approximately 45 minutes—are available; the house is closed Mondays. Admission charge. 2340 S St. NW (phone: 387-4062). *Metro: Dupont Circle North.*

SHOPPING

When you've had your fill of monuments, the nation's capital has enough shopping venues to satisfy ever "shop-till-you-drop" appetites. Following the sprucing up of Pennsylvania Avenue some years ago, Washington is now home to a number of excellent shopping malls. For unique gifts, however, the city's impressive museums are the best bet. Most museums, shrines, and churches have their own shops, some offering reproductions of priceless treasures at very affordable prices. Here's a capital shoppers' guide:

SHOPPING MALLS

Connecticut Connection This three-story shopping and dining complex is conveniently located atop the *Farragut North Metro* station. Connecticut Ave. and L St. NW (no main phone number).

Eastern Market An open-air extravaganza on weekends with fresh produce, flowers, and crafts. North Carolina Ave. and Seventh St. SE.

Georgetown Park The centerpiece of Georgetown shopping, this handsome brick complex, with its magnificent Victorian interior, houses more than 100 elegant shops—including *Ann Taylor, FAO Schwarz,* and *Williams-Sonoma*—and restaurants. 3222 M St. NW at Wisconsin Ave. (phone: 298-5577).

International Square In this 12-story atrium with a cascading fountain are 30 retail shops, restaurants, and fast-food eateries. 1850 K St. NW (phone: 223-1850).

Mazza Gallerie On the north end of Wisconsin Avenue, this enclosed mall features high-fashion shops and specialty stores such as *Neiman Marcus.* 5300 Wisconsin Ave. NW (phone: 966-6144).

Pavilion at the Old Post Office The city's oldest Federal building, complete with a bell tower and skylight, has shops, cafés, and restaurants on its lower floors. 12th St. and Pennsylvania Ave. NW (phone: 289-4224).

Shops at National Place A prime shoppers' paradise, it includes such national chains as *Victoria's Secret, Sharper Image,* and *Express.* F St. between 13th and 14th Sts. NW (phone: 783-9090).

2000 Pennsylvania Avenue On the edge of the *George Washington University* campus, this mall, located within a brick townhouse complex, has a variety of specialty shops. Between 20th and 21st Sts. NW (phone: 452-0924).

Union Station The capital's Beaux Arts train station has been restored to its former glory and contains numerous shops as well as unique and entertaining eating spots. 50 Massachusetts Ave. NE (phone: 371-9441).

Washington Harbour This expansive office/retail/residential complex on the Potomac River features unique architectural designs, with fountain-filled courtyards and specialty shops and restaurants. 3000 K St. NW, next to the Whitehurst Freeway in Georgetown (phone: 944-4140).

Watergate A prestigious shopping arcade in the Watergate complex, including *Yves Saint Laurent, Gucci, Valentino,* and *Guy Laroche.* (It also has excellent restaurants and a hotel; see the *Watergate* listing in *Checking In.*) New Hampshire and Virginia Aves. NW (phone: 298-5500).

FOR BUDGET WATCHERS

Thirty minutes south of Washington is *Potomac Mills,* one of the world's largest outlet malls, and a big attraction for Washington shoppers on weekends. Among the almost 200 discount stores are outlets of such well-known retailers as *Eddie Bauer, Laura Ashley, Nordstrom's,* and *Benetton.* Open daily. On I-95S, exit 52, in Prince William, Virginia (phone: 703-643-1770; 800-VA-MILLS).

DOWNTOWN SHOPS

Border's Books and Music One of downtown's new superstores, this print and music emporium has a wide selection, plus a café. 18th and L Sts. NW (phone: 466-4999, books; 466-6999, music).

Britches of Georgetown Casual menswear and womenswear. 1219 Connecticut Ave. NW (phone: 347-8994)

Earl Allen Office clothing for women. *International Sq.,* 1825 I St. NW (phone: 466-3437).

Hecht's One of Washington's top department stores. 12th and G Sts. NW (phone: 628-6661).

Kramer Book Stores A wide selection of classics and new titles. Two locations: *Kramerbooks and Afterwords,* with a café in the rear of the store, open until 1 AM Sundays through Thursdays; all night Fridays and Saturdays (1517 Connecticut Ave. NW; phone: 387-1400); and *Sidney Kramer Books* (1825 I St. NW; phone: 293-2685).

Post Office Exchange Designer and souvenir Washington T-shirts. *Pavilion at the Old Post Office,* 12th St. and Pennsylvania Ave. NW (phone: 842-0504).

Tannery West Leather and suede clothing and bags. *Union Station,* 50 Massachusetts Ave. NE (phone: 371-1705).

Windsor Shirt Company Men's shirts. *International Square,* 1850 K St. NW (phone: 887-0011).

Woodward and Lothrop A popular, traditional department store. 11th and F Sts. NW (phone: 347-5300).

GEORGETOWN

Appalachian Spring Handmade crafts, quilts, and jewelry from all over the US. 1415 Wisconsin Ave. NW (phone: 337-5780).

Britches of Georgetown Casual clothing for men and women. 1247 Wisconsin Ave. NW (phone: 338-3330).

Hats in the Belfry Funny, unusual, elegant, and antique toppers for all occasions. 1237 Wisconsin Ave. NW (phone: 342-2006).

Little Caledonia Unusual furnishings, fabrics, and stationery. 1419 Wisconsin Ave. NW (phone: 333-4700).

The Newsroom In the heart of the embassy district, this newsstand has a wide selection of international newspapers and magazines. 1753 Connecticut Ave. NW (phone 332-1489).

Orpheus Records Specializes in vintage and rare recordings. 3249 M St. NW (phone: 337-7970).

Phoenix Mexican jewelry, crafts, and clothing. 1514 Wisconsin Ave. NW (phone: 338-4404).

Santa Fe Style Crafts and art from the American Southwest. 1525 Wisconsin Ave. NW (phone: 333-3747).

Threepenny Bit Irish items—including hand-knit sweaters, shorts, shirts, ties, and shoes. 3122 M St. NW (phone: 338-1338).

MUSEUM SHOPS

Some fine souvenirs of a visit to the nation's capital await in its museum shops: Lincoln memorabilia, arty T-shirts, posters, and reproductions of historical furnishings and jewelry are just some possibilities.

Arts and Industries Building Stocks items shown in the *Smithsonian* mail-order gift catalogue. Between Jefferson Dr. and Independence Ave. at Ninth St. SW (phone: 357-1367).

Bethune Museum Gift Shop Books on such famous black women as Harriet Tubman and Josephine Baker. 1318 Vermont Ave. NW (phone: 332-1233).

Corcoran Gallery of Art Art reproductions. 17th St. and New York Ave. St. NW (phone: 638-3211).

Dumbarton Oaks The private collection of Byzantine and pre-Columbian jewelry is reproduced for sale. 1703 32nd St. NW (phone: 342-3209).

Ford's Theatre The book and gift store here stocks materials pertaining to President Lincoln, his assassination, and the Civil War. 511 10th St. NW (phone: 426-0179).

Friends of the Kennedy Center Jewelry, tote bags, T-shirts, scarves, cards, cookbooks, and more. New Hampshire Ave. and Rock Creek Pkwy. NW (phone: 416-8343).

Hirshhorn Museum Contemporary jewelry and art reproductions. Independence Ave. and Seventh St. SW (phone: 357-1429).

Mt. Vernon Estate Replicas of George Washington memorabilia, books, and prints. George Washington Memorial Pkwy. (phone: 703-780-2000).

National Air and Space Museum NASA flight jackets, US rocket model kits, and freeze-dried astronauts' dinners. Sixth St. and Independence Ave. SW (phone: 357-1387).

National Geographic Society Its shop offers some of the best bargains around in atlases and maps. 17th and M Sts. NW (phone: 857-7588).

National Museum of African Art Arts and crafts, jewelry, books, graphics, posters, and postcards. 950 Independence Ave. SW (phone: 786-2147).

National Museum of American Art Books, prints, postcards, and jewelry. Eighth St. at F and G Sts. NW (phone: 357-1545).

National Museum of American History Everything from a reproduction of the Hope Diamond to First Lady dolls. Constitution Ave. between 12th and 14th Sts. NW (phone: 357-1527).

National Portrait Gallery Busts of past presidents. Eighth St. at F and G Sts. NW (phone: 357-1447).

National Shrine of the Immaculate Conception Religious items. Fourth and Michigan Sts. NE (phone: 526-4433).

National Trust for Historic Preservation Books, scarves, replicas of antique furniture. *Decatur House,* Lafayette Sq. NW (phone: 842-1856).

Renwick Gallery Pieces by American crafts artists, including ceramics, woodcarvings, clocks, scarves, and quilting. Pennsylvania Ave. at 17th St. NW (phone: 357-1445).

Washington Doll's House and Toy Museum Replicas of dolls and president's games. 5236 44th St. NW (phone: 244-0024).

Washington National Cathedral An extensive gift shop featuring religious items. Massachusetts and Wisconsin Sts. NW (phone: 537-6267).

SPORTS AND FITNESS

BASKETBALL The *NBA's Bullets* hold court from November through April at the *USAir Arena* (1 Harry S. Truman Dr., Landover, Maryland; phone: 301-350-3400). It can be reached via signposted access roads off the Beltway; either take Beltway exit 18 and go east on MD Route 214/Central Avenue for about 100 yards, or take exit 17 and go south about half a mile on MD Route 202. Tickets can be ordered by calling NBA-DUNK.

BICYCLING Rent from *Metropolis Bike & Scooter* (709 Eighth St. SE; phone: 543-8900); *Big Wheel Bikes* (1034 33rd St. NW, Georgetown; phone: 337-0254); or *Thompson's Boat Center* (Virginia Ave. at Rock Creek Pkwy. NW; phone: 333-4861). The latter also has mountain bikes, beach bikes, and tandems available. The towpath of the Chesapeake and Ohio Canal, starting at the barge landing in Georgetown, is a good place to ride.

FITNESS CENTER Most major hotels have health and fitness centers (see *Checking In*).

FOOTBALL The *NFL Redskins* play at *Robert F. Kennedy Stadium* (E. Capitol and 22nd Sts. SE; phone: 547-9077) from September through December. Tickets are hard to come by during the season; it's much easier to get into pre-season games, held in late July and August. Try *Ticketmaster* (phone: 432-7328) or the stadium box office.

GOLF The most convenient public golf courses in the city are at *East Potomac Park* (phone: 554-7660) and *Rock Creek Park* (phone: 882-7332).

HOCKEY The *Capitals,* Washington's pro hockey team, play at the *USAir Arena* (see *Basketball*) from October to April. Tickets are available at *TicketCenter* outlets or by calling the arena.

JOGGING Join plenty of others in making a round trip from the *Lincoln Memorial* to the *Capitol* (4 miles); also run in *Rock Creek Park* and in Georgetown, along the Chesapeake and Ohio Canal.

SKATING From November through March you can ice skate on the rink on the *Mall.* Seventh St. and Constitution Ave. NW (phone: 371-5340).

SWIMMING Year-round facilities are available at the *East Capitol Natatorium* (635 North Carolina Ave. SE; phone: 724-4495). Many of the hotels also have pools (see *Checking In*).

TENNIS Washington has some fine public courts; the best bets are the *Washington Tennis Center* (16th and Kennedy Sts. NW; phone: 722-5949) and the *Hains Point* complex (1090 Ohio Dr.; phone: 554-5962).

THEATER

Washington is America's third city of theater (after New York and Boston), according to *Variety,* the bible of showbiz. The following is Washington's most outstanding stage.

CENTER STAGE

Arena Stage One of the oldest and most consistently admired American theater companies and the first outside New York to receive a Tony for theatrical excellence, the *Arena Stage* is noted for developing American drama and for introducing foreign (particularly Eastern European) plays to the US. The theater's three stages seat 827, 514, and 180; the last is used for small musical revues and experimental works. Sixth St. and Maine Ave. SW (phone: 554-9066; 488-3300, box office; 484-0247, TTY number for hearing-impaired patrons).

The *Kennedy Center for the Performing Arts* is another weighty cultural presence in the District, attracting world-renowned dance, theater, and musical companies to its five theaters and concert halls (off Virginia Ave. on New Hampshire Ave. NW; phone: 467-4600 or 800-444-1324 for all theaters). The center's *Eisenhower Theater* offers musical and dramatic productions, including Broadway previews and road shows; and the *Terrace Theater* offers many different productions—modern dance, ballet, dramas, poetry recitals, and so on. The *National Theatre* (1321 Pennsylvania Ave. NW; phone: 628-6161) presents major productions throughout the year. *Ford's Theatre* (511 10th St. NW; phone: 347-4833) offers American productions. The *Shakespeare Theater Group* offers innovative interpretations of the bard's plays as well as more contemporary works at the *Shakespeare Theater* (450 Seventh St. NW; phone: 547-3230, information; 393-2700, box office). Note: In the summer (usually August), the troupe also performs a free outdoor play at the *Carter Barron Amphitheater,* in *Rock Creek Park* near Kennedy Street NW; call the above number for information. For half-price, same-day performance tickets, try *Ticketplace* (*Lisner Auditorium,* 21st and H Sts. NW; phone: TIC-KETS). If all else fails, a hotel concierge might have some pull. Washington also has what one theater critic calls the "off-off *Kennedy Center* movement"—a network of small avant-garde houses on or near the stretch of 14th Street NW above Thomas Circle: *Studio Theater* (1333 P St. NW; phone: 332-3300); *Woolly Mammoth Theater Company* (1401 Church St. NW; phone: 393-3939); and *Source Theater* (1835 14th St. NW; phone: 462-1073). During the summer the *Olney Theater* (2001 Rte. 108, Olney, Maryland; phone: 301-924-3400), about a half-hour drive from the District, offers summer stock with well-known casts. In winter, the *Barns at Wolf Trap,* a 350-seat theater at *Wolf Trap Farm Park for the Performing Arts* (1624 Trap Rd., off Rte. 7 near Vienna, Virginia;

phone: 703-938-2404), holds performances indoors. To get there, take the *Dulles Airport* toll road Rte. 267, or the *Metro* to West Falls Church, Virginia, where there's a connecting shuttle bus. For a unique dinner-theater experience, see *Mystery on the Menu.* Held only on Saturday evenings, it's a participatory play that takes the form of a Georgetown wedding reception for a senator and his bride. During the reception, a murder occurs and all the audience members/"guests" get a chance to solve the crime. A three-course meal with a glass of champagne is included in the ticket price. Locations vary and reservations are necessary; call for details (phone: 333-6875).

MUSIC

The *National Symphony Orchestra* performs at the *Kennedy Center Concert Hall* (phone: 467-4600) from September through June; in June the concert hall also hosts a *Mostly Mozart Festival.* In addition, concerts are presented at the city's *former* premier venue, *Constitution Hall* (18th and C Sts. NW; phone: 638-2661), which is renowned for its acoustics. The *Washington Opera* (phone: 416-7800) presents seven operas a year, between November and March, at the *Kennedy Center Opera House.* The *Juilliard String Quartet* and other notable ensembles usually perform chamber music concerts on Stradivarius instruments in the *Library of Congress's Coolidge Auditorium* Thursday and Friday evenings in the spring and fall. However, at press time concerts were temporarily being held at the *National Academy of Sciences* (2100 C St. NW), while the *Coolidge* undergoes renovations, scheduled for completion later this year; for tickets, call 707-5502. During the summer, *Wolf Trap Farm Park for the Performing Arts* near Vienna, Virginia (see *Theater,* above), presents musicals, ballet, pop concerts, and symphonic music in a lovely outdoor setting—bring a picnic basket. A shuttle bus runs to the park from downtown (phone: 703-255-1868). There are often free concerts by the service bands on the plaza at the West Front of the *Capitol* or in front of the *Jefferson Memorial.* Consult newspapers for where and when. *Army and Navy Band* concerts are presented at different locations in the winter (phone: 696-3643). The *British Embassy Players* delight audiences with old-fashioned music hall performances; the *British Embassy Rotunda* (3100 Massachusetts Ave. NW) is magically transformed into a cabaret, with some embassy staff and other area Britons providing the entertainment. There are four productions beginning in the fall and ending with three *Music Hall* weekends in June. Tickets are limited and must be reserved well in advance (phone: 703-271-0172).

NIGHTCLUBS AND NIGHTLIFE

For some, Washington is an early-to-bed town, but there's plenty of pub crawling, jazz, bluegrass, soul, rock, and folk music going on after dark—you just have to know where to look for it. Best bets are Georgetown, Adams Morgan, Dupont Circle, and the *Capitol Hill* areas. For up-to-the-minute listings of DC's ever-shifting club scene, consult the weekly *City Paper* (see *Local Coverage*). Some sure favorites: *Blues Alley* (1073 Wisconsin Ave. NW; phone: 337-4141), for mainstream jazz and Dixieland; *Tortilla Coast* (201 Massachusetts Ave. NE; phone: 546-6768), decorated with hot tropical murals and featuring killer margaritas; the

Dubliner Restaurant and Pub (520 N. Capitol St. NW; phone: 737-3773), the place to hear old Irish and Celtic tunes and jigs; *Market Inn* (200 E St. SW; phone: 554-2100), a popular steak and seafood house near *Capitol Hill* where live jazz is featured nightly; and *Cities* (2424 18th St. NW; phone: 328-7194), a watering hole–cum-restaurant-cum-nightclub in what once was a three-story auto dealership. *Cities,* which changes its city theme every six months, is located in the heart of Washington's newest nightlife scene—Adams Morgan, a funky mélange of bars, dance clubs, ethnic restaurants, and shops radiating from the intersection of Columbia Road and 18th Street NW. In recent years Adams Morgan has come to rival Georgetown as "the" place to see and be seen after dark in the capital.

On Saturday nights, the *Bayou* in Georgetown (3135 K St. NW; phone: 783-7212) presents *Clintoons,* a production of *Gross National Product,* a satirical and sometimes ridiculous political revue targeting Washington politicians in the spotlight. Reservations are necessary. Political satirist Mark Russell also performs occasionally in local nightspots (check local newspapers for details). Watch local listings, too, for performances by the *Capitol Steps,* a satirical singing group. The *Comedy Café* (1520 K St. NW; phone: 638-5653) features nationally known comedians in an informal, downtown club. The dining room staff at Georgetown's *La Niçoise* (1721 Wisconsin Ave. NW; phone: 965-9300) not only serves French fare while on roller skates, but the talented crew also presents an amusing after-dinner cabaret. *Déjà Vu* (2119 M St. NW; phone: 452-1966) is a lively dance club with music from the 1960s to today. *West End Café* at the *One Washington Circle* hotel (One Washington Circle; phone: 293-5390) is a popular piano bar where classical and jazz music are featured. Two ever-popular chains have Washington branches: the rock 'n' roll–centered *Hard Rock Café* (999 E St. NW; phone: 737-7625), and the movie world's *Planet Hollywood* (11th St. and Pennsylvania Ave. NW; phone: 783-7827), both brasserie-style bar restaurants.

BAR NONE

Because Washingtonians are serious about their sports teams, especially the *Redskins,* sports bars are scattered around the area and are prime spots for game nights (if you don't have seats at *RFK Stadium*). Try *Champions* (1206 Wisconsin Ave. NW; phone: 965-4005), a Georgetown favorite; *Bottom Line* (1716 I St. NW; phone: 298-8488), a rugby bar popular with local players and their cheering squads; *Poor Robert's* (3419 Connecticut Ave. NW; phone: 363-1839), which offers satellite TV for special sporting events; and *Joe Theismann's* (1800 Diagonal Rd., Alexandria, Virginia; phone: 703-739-0777), a sports bar owned by the former, fabulous *Redskins* quarterback. The capital is also a major saloon town, and some of the best stomping grounds are on the "Hill." *Bullfeathers* (410 First St.

SE; phone: 543-5005), where the Congressional crowd hangs out, has a bar that's always hopping. The *Hawk 'n' Dove* (329 Pennsylvania Ave. SE; phone: 543-3300), a dark, rustic bar, is perfect for after work (or after play), and crowded with both Capitol Hillers and law students. *Clyde's* in Georgetown (3236 M St., NW; phone: 333-9180) is your typical wood and brass fern bar, with cozy pub decor, and *Hamburger Hamlet,* also in Georgetown (3125 M St. NW; phone: 965-6970), offers a casual, warm atmosphere, great summer drinks, and crayons for drawing on the paper tablecloths.

Best in Town

CHECKING IN

Washington enjoys a wealth of good-quality hotel establishments because of a building boom in the late 1930s. Still, accommodations at the best stopping places can dwindle fast, so reservations should be made in advance. Visitors in town for only a few days should stay downtown to make the best use of their limited time; weekends offer the best package deals. Inexpensive taxis, the *Metro* system, and buses facilitate getting around without private cars which can be difficult and expensive to park (although some hotels offer reasonable valet parking). If you're traveling by car, it may make more sense to stay at one of the major motel chains located at the principal entry points to the district—Silver Spring and Bethesda in Maryland, and Arlington, Rosslyn, and Alexandria in Virginia. Expect to pay $175 or more (sometimes much more) per night for a double room at a hotel described as expensive, $100 to $175 at a place in the moderate category, and $70 to $100 at a hotel listed as inexpensive. For information about bed and breakfast accommodations, contact *The Bed and Breakfast League/Sweet Dreams & Toast* (PO Box 9490, Washington, DC 20016; phone: 363-7767). *Washington, DC, Accommodations* (phone: 800-554-2220) provides assistance with hotel reservations at no charge. *Capitol Reservations* (phone: 800-847-4832) offers a free reservation service and discount rates at Washington area hotels. All telephone numbers are in the 202 area code unless otherwise indicated.

EXPENSIVE

ANA This outstanding link in the Westin chain is as elegant inside as it is outside. There is a lovely interior garden, and 415 luxuriously appointed rooms, including 36 Executive Club rooms and 26 suites; three Executive Premier King suites have cable TV, three phones, voice mail, and terry cloth robes. The *Colonnade* is a fine restaurant for formal dining, and there's a more casual brasserie and a lobby lounge in a glass loggia just off the garden. A professionally staffed fitness center—complete with a pool, a Jacuzzi, saunas, squash courts, an aerobics room, weights, state-of-the-art exercise equipment, a beauty salon, and a juice bar—is on the premises. Facilities include 14 meeting rooms, A/V equipment, photocopiers, computers, and secretarial services. Around-the-clock room service, a concierge desk, and express checkout complete the picture. Children under 18 stay free in their parents' rooms. 24th and M Sts. NW (phone: 429-2400; 800-228-3000; fax: 457-5010).

Canterbury Near the downtown business district and not far from the *White House,* this small place has 99 suites with a stocked bar in each, a restaurant, and a bar. Pluses include a complimentary continental breakfast, underground parking, nightly turn-down service, and a complimentary cocktail each evening in the *Union Jack Pub.* Business amenities include six meeting rooms, secretarial services, A/V equipment, photocopiers, and computers. Inquire about weekend package rates. 1733 N St. NW (phone: 393-3000; 800-424-2950; fax: 785-9581).

Capital Hilton One of Washington's most luxurious hostelries is also one of the most conveniently located, just a few minutes from the *White House.* It has 549 expansive rooms, each with a marble foyer, two telephones, a fully stocked mini-bar, and terry cloth robes. The Deluxe Towers' rooms on the top four floors also have VCRs and a separate concierge and check-in area. Restaurants include *Trader Vic's,* which serves Chinese and Polynesian fare, the sophisticated *Twigs Grill,* and the lobby bar. There's also a state-of-the-art fitness center. Business services include 14 meeting rooms, 24-hour room service, a concierge, foreign currency exchange, secretarial services, A/V equipment, photocopiers, foreign language translation, computers, fax machines, and express checkout. 1001 16th at K St. NW (phone: 393-1000; 800-445-8667; fax: 639-5784).

Carlton Host to many presidents and dignitaries, this hotel has an elegant Italian Renaissance lobby, 197 comfortable rooms, and a bar that's good enough to win approval from feisty *New York Newsday* columnist Jimmy Breslin. The *Allegro* dining room is excellent and has a terrific Sunday brunch (see *Eating Out*); there's also a cocktail lounge. Business services include secretarial and concierge assistance, seven meeting rooms, A/V equipment, photocopiers, computers, and express checkout. There's also 24-hour room service. 923 16th St. NW (phone: 638-2626; 800-325-3535; fax: 638-4231).

Four Seasons If the difference between a good and a great hotel is in the details, this is one of the capital city's very best. The property is flanked by the Chesapeake & Ohio Canal (a run along the canal is a Washington ritual) and by *Rock Creek Park,* Washington's premier parkland; in fact, most of the 197 rooms overlook the tranquil green space. The *Seasons* restaurant deserves high praise (see *Eating Out*), as does *Le Petit Champs,* a private nightclub for guests and members. There's also afternoon tea in the sunlit indoor *Garden Terrace.* A traditional concierge offers many personal services including mail delivery. Around-the-clock room service is available, as are six meeting rooms, secretarial services, A/V equipment, photocopiers, computers, express checkout, and complimentary limo service on weekdays. Body-conscious guests can use the fitness club with a skylit lap pool, a whirlpool bath, a sauna, and a steamroom. 2800 Pennsylvania Ave. NW (phone: 342-0444; 800-332-3442; fax: 342-1673).

Grand A distinctive copper dome wedged between walls of brick and granite marks this West End hostelry. In architecture and ambience, it is reminiscent of a small European hotel: A white marble staircase cascades through the lobby, the inner courtyard is meticulously landscaped, and all 263 rooms feature Italian marble baths and three phones; there are working fireplaces in some suites. The elegant *Mayfair* serves *cuisine courante,* a step beyond nouvelle, with a menu that changes daily; the *Promenade Lounge* features breakfast, lunch, dinner, and afternoon tea in a more informal atmosphere. Besides a multilingual concierge and currency conversion service, there is 24-hour room service, valet and dry cleaning, and valet parking. Other pluses include 10 meeting rooms, secretarial services, A/V equipment, photocopiers, and computers. 2350 M St. NW (phone: 429-0100; 800-848-0016; fax: 429-9759).

Grand Hyatt Washington Located in the heart of downtown DC, across from the *Washington Convention Center,* this property has 907 rooms, including 60 suites, and a Regency Club floor with a private lounge and concierge service. The suites, all with living areas, wet bars, and lots of greenery, also feature saunas and marble baths. All rooms have turndown service, free cable television with HBO and ESPN, and full-service honor bars. Dining facilities include the New York–style *Zephyr Deli;* the *Grande Café,* an informal eatery for breakfast, lunch, and dinner; the more formal *Hamilton's; Palladio's,* a three-level lobby bar; and *Grand Slam,* a sports bar with two large-screen TV sets. Business facilities include 13 meeting rooms, the Independence Ballroom and Constitution Ballroom, 24-hour room service, A/V equipment, secretarial services on request, modem hookups in rooms, and express checkout. There's also a health club with an exercise room, a sauna, a Jacuzzi, a lap pool, and aerobics classes. 1000 H St. NW (phone: 582-1234; fax: 637-4781).

Hay-Adams At an incomparable location just off Lafayette Square, within a silver dollar's throw of the *White House.* This 143-room hotel retains its Old World dignity and maintains the standards of the neighborhood with antique furnishings, a paneled lobby, and three fine dining rooms—the formal *Adams Room* for breakfast and lunch, the *John Hay Room* with traditional English decor and original paneling from *Warwick Palace* for afternoon tea and cocktails, and the informal *Eagle Bar & Grill* for soup and salad. Room service is available 24 hours a day. There's also a concierge desk, three meeting rooms, A/V equipment, secretarial service, photocopiers, computers, and express checkout. 16th and H Sts. NW (phone: 638-6600 or 800-424-5054; fax: 638-2716).

Jefferson A clubby place and a favorite of many politicians. Located near the *White House* and the shops on Connecticut Avenue, it has a low-key, traditional atmosphere and outstanding service. The *Hunt Club* serves American and French food, including such dishes as Jefferson macaroni (named after our third president, who, according to the hotel, introduced pasta to the US after his travels through Europe) and vegetable strudel. The 69 rooms and 35 suites offer stereos with CD players, minibars, and at least two phone lines that are fax and computer compatible. There are three meeting rooms, 24-hour concierge and secretarial services, A/V equipment, photocopiers, and computers. Around-the-clock room service and express checkout complete the amenities. 1200 16th St. NW (phone: 347-2200; 800-368-5966; fax: 331-7982).

J. W. Marriott A significant step above other members of the Marriott chain, this property is connected to a mall complex of 160 stores and the *National Theatre.* There are 772 rooms, an indoor pool, and a health spa; the Marquis floors (14 and 15) are especially nice. Concierge Level (14th floor only) extras include breakfast, complimentary hors d'oeuvres, and a private lounge. There also is a *Grand Ballroom* for up to 2,000 people, and the *Capital Ballroom,* which can accommodate up to 800. Room service is available around the clock. Among the business services are concierge and secretarial services, 10 meeting rooms, A/V equipment, photocopiers, computers, and express checkout. 1331 Pennsylvania Ave. NW (phone: 393-2000; 800-228-9290; fax: 626-6991).

Madison With 374 luxurious rooms, this property features gracious Federal decor and excellent service by a well-trained staff. Extras include interpreters, refrigerators, and bathroom phones; there is also a health club. The *Montpelier Room* is quite a good restaurant; it serves a buffet on weekdays and brunch on Sundays. The *Retreat* restaurant is open for afternoon tea on weekdays and for dinner daily; the lobby bar has nightly entertainment. In addition to 24-hour room service, there also are concierge and secretarial services available, as well as 15 meeting rooms, A/V equipment, photocopiers, computers, and express checkout. 15th and M Sts. NW (phone: 862-1600; 800-424-8577; fax: 785-1255).

Ritz-Carlton This is as close to an evocation of a classic European hostelry as exists in Washington. There are 230 rooms, the *Jockey Club* restaurant (see *Eating Out*), and the *Fairfax Bar,* as well as a ballroom and a health club with weights and cardiovascular machines. Standard business amenities include 24-hour room service, a concierge, secretarial assistance, seven meeting rooms, A/V equipment, photocopiers, and computers. 2100 Massachusetts Ave. NW (phone: 293-2100; 800-241-3333; fax: 466-9867).

Sofitel The first North American member of this European chain, it has 145 spacious, elegantly decorated rooms with such extras as fax and computer hookups, mini-bars, safes, and coffee makers. There are two restaurants, plus a fully equipped business center with three meeting rooms, fax machines, computers, photocopiers, and secretarial and translation services. There's also a multilingual concierge, access to a health club, tennis, and golf, and 24-hour room service. Located in the heart of the embassy district. 1914 Connecticut Ave. NW (phone: 797-2000; 800-424-2464; fax: 462-0944).

Stouffer Mayflower This historic property, one of the capital's treasures, has earned laurels over the years for catering to the world's movers and shakers with elegance and style. The yellow brick-and-limestone Beaux Arts building boasts a block-long lobby adorned with Italian marble, glittering chandeliers, and intricately carved, 23-karat gold leaf ceilings. Its central location in the heart of downtown is ideal for sightseers (not far from the *White House* and the *Mall*) and its nearly 700 rooms can accommodate legions of them. The *Grand Ballroom* recalls the splendor of a bygone era, and the *Nicholas* restaurant is a fitting place to feast on mid-Atlantic American fare (a jacket and tie are required for men). Guests also can enjoy a health center, around-the-clock room service, and full concierge service. There are also 17 meeting rooms, as well as a business center equipped with photocopiers and fax machines. 1127 Connecticut Ave. NW (phone: 347-3000; 800-HOTELS-1; fax: 466-9082).

Vista Washington François Mitterrand and Elizabeth Taylor are among those who have stayed at this 399-room hostelry, only six blocks from the *White House*. Its very expensive six one-bedroom suites, designed by Givenchy, sport full-length mirrors, large private balconies, and bathrooms with Jacuzzis, and are completely separate from the rest of the hotel—sharing no walls with any other rooms. Favorite recipes of past presidents are on the menu at the *American Harvest* restaurant; cardiovascular fitness gear is available at the health club along with treadmills and a sauna. Secretarial and concierge assistance are available, and A/V equipment, photocopiers, and computers are on call for guests. Other pluses include 10 meeting rooms, a ballroom, 24-hour room service, and express checkout. 1400 M St. NW (phone: 429-1700; 800-847-8232; fax: 785-0786).

Watergate Though this modern hotel-apartment-office complex doesn't look too historic, appearances can be deceiving (as can small pieces of tape). This property boasts 235 large contemporarily furnished rooms, an indoor swimming pool and health club, the excellent nouvelle French *Jean-Louis* restaurant (see *Eating Out*), and the less pricey, bistro-like *Palladin* (both dining spots are named after chef Jean-Louis Palladin). There is also a cocktail lounge, *The Watergate Shopping Mall* (with even more dining possibilities), all at a location adjacent to the *Kennedy Center*. There's a concierge desk and 24-hour room service, and business amenities include secretarial services, A/V equipment, photocopiers, fax machines, computers, Showtime, and express checkout. 2650 Virginia Ave. NW (phone: 965-2300; 800-424-2736; fax: 337-7915).

Willard Inter-Continental Ten presidents-elect stayed at this Beaux Arts landmark while awaiting their inaugurations, and Charles Dickens and Julia Ward Howe were regulars, too. The carpeting, columns, and much of the furniture are reproductions based on photographs of the original decor; the 365 rooms are decorated in turn-of-the-century style. The hotel dining room, the *Willard Room*, is one of DC's most elegant eateries; the *Occidental Grill*, a popular meeting place for primary powers, is adjacent to the hotel but not under the same ownership (see *Eating Out* for both). Additional amenities include 24-hour room service, a café, two lounges, concierge and secretarial services, 15 meeting rooms, A/V equipment, photocopiers, computers, an exercise room, and express checkout. 1401 Pennsylvania Ave. NW (phone: 628-9100; 800-327-0200; fax: 637-7326).

Wyndham Bristol There are 239 rooms (37 of which are suites) in this English-style hostelry; guests also have access to a health club for a small fee. The *Bristol Grill* offers fine food. Other pluses include 24-hour room service, A/V equipment, photocopiers, fax machines, seven meeting rooms, a concierge desk, and express checkout. 2430 Pennsylvania Ave. NW (phone: 955-6400; 800-822-4200; fax: 955-5765).

MODERATE

Morrison-Clark Inn This popular bed and breakfast–style inn served as the hostel for the *Soldiers, Sailors, Marines, and Airmen Club* from 1923 to 1984. A 1988 addition to the two historic buildings comprises 41 of the 54 tastefully decorated rooms, some furnished with Victorian antiques. The hotel has an excellent restaurant; breakfast is included in the rate. A concierge desk, two meeting rooms, secretarial services, A/V equipment, photocopiers, and computers also are available. Located one block from the *Convention Center* and four blocks from *Metro Center* (*Metrorail* stop) at Massachusetts Ave. and 11th St. NW (phone: 898-1200; 800-332-7898; fax: 289-8576).

Tabard Inn On a charming semi-residential street near the heart of the business district, this establishment offers guests an ambience rare in an American city. The 40 rooms are furnished with antiques and some of them share baths (23 have private baths); there are no in-room TV sets. A restaurant serves breakfast, lunch, and dinner, and brunch on weekends (see *Eating Out*); there's also a library. There is a meeting room, a banquet room, a concierge, photocopiers, and fax machines. 1739 N St. NW (phone: 785-1277; fax: 785-6173).

Washington One of the city's older properties, this comfortable hotel offers an incomparable view from its rooftop restaurant (which makes it a particularly good place to be during an inaugural parade). The 370 rooms feature such luxury amenities as telephones in the bathrooms; downtown shopping is nearby. Room service is available until 11 PM. 15th St. and Pennsylvania Ave. NW (phone: 638-5900; fax: 638-4275).

INEXPENSIVE

Harrington A 310-room, older establishment in the center of Washington's commercial area, it has seen better days but provides clean accommodations and is within walking distance of the *Mall*. Popular with high school and family groups. 11th and E Sts. NW (phone: 628-8140).

Windsor Inn Small and unpretentious, near the trendy Adams Morgan district. A magnet for relocating embassy employees as well as government workers who prefer a modest, homey atmosphere. There are 46 rooms; the staff is personable and attentive. Continental breakfast comes with a newspaper; and for a European touch, afternoon sherry is served. 1842 16th St. NW (phone: 667-0300 or 800-423-9111).

Windsor Park It's modest, but this 40-room property is within walking distance of the *Woodley Park/Zoo Metro* station and near the French diplomats' residence and the *Chinese Embassy*. Continental breakfast is included in the rate. 2116 Kalorama Rd. NW (phone: 483-7700; 800-247-3064; fax: 332-4547).

EATING OUT

Considering the international aspects of Washington—2,000 diplomats and a large number of residents who have lived abroad and brought back a taste for foreign fare—it's not too surprising that the District can provide an international gastronomic tour de force. But though it's always helpful to have an ermine-lined wallet or, better yet, a generous expense account, those who have only a yen for good food needn't go hungry. Expect to pay $100 or more for a dinner for two at places described as very expensive; between $75 and $100 at places listed as expensive; $40 to $75 at restaurants in the moderate category; and less than $40 at dining spots described as inexpensive. Prices do not include drinks, wine, or tips. Reservations are a must at the top-flight restaurants. Unless otherwise noted, restaurants are open for lunch and dinner, and telephone numbers are in the 202 area code.

VERY EXPENSIVE

Galileo *Washingtonian* magazine ranked this as not only the capital's best Italian dining spot, but possibly the best restaurant in town. Try the risotto or the homemade *agnolotti*, a pasta filled with spinach and ricotta. The rack of veal with mushroom and rosemary sauce is also popular. The city's finest breads, fresh-baked, accompany each meal. Closed at lunch on weekends. Reservations advised. Major credit cards accepted. 1110 21st St. NW (phone: 293-7191).

Jean-Louis Named for its chef, this is a small (only 14 tables) and elegant restaurant with gracious service and fine nouvelle cuisine. Fixed-price dinners are available, and the pre-theater seating (5:30 to 6:30 PM) offers a tremendous value. Closed Sundays. Reservations necessary. Major credit cards accepted. In the *Watergate Hotel*, 2650 Virginia Ave. NW (phone: 298-4488).

Le Lion d'Or This establishment is reputed to have the finest French food in town, although some say that the service is unpredictable. Selections from the long and exquisite menu by chef Jean-Pierre Goyenvalle include lobster stew, fillet of lamb, roasted pigeon, and red snapper. Don't leave without tasting one of the spectacular desserts. Closed Saturday lunch and Sundays. Reservations necessary at least two weeks in advance. Major credit cards accepted. 1150 Connecticut Ave. NW, near 18th and M Sts. (phone: 296-7972).

Seasons This handsome dining room in the *Four Seasons* hotel (formerly *Aux Beaux Champs*) is distinguished by stylish service and a highly creative menu that changes daily, specializing in *cuisine courante*—a mixture of French and California food. Specialties include breast of quail stuffed with woodland mushrooms in a zinfandel sauce with wild rice and scallion cake, and stuffed lamb with pistachio crust and risotto fritters in a minted madeira glaze. Open daily. Reservations advised. Major credit cards accepted. 2800 Pennsylvania Ave. NW (phone: 342-0810).

EXPENSIVE

L'Auberge Chez François This Alsatian country inn, 30 minutes west of the District in northern Virginia's hunt country, is a perennial favorite. The service is attentive, and the setting cozy yet refined. There are several working fireplaces, antique grandfather clocks, a mounted elk's head, and a staff dressed in Alsatian garb. The fare blends the hearty proportions of Germanic cooking with French touches like superb sauces, fine cheeses, and artistic presentation. The reasonably priced menu includes a number of Alsatian specialties, among them the famed *choucroute garnie,* a collection of sausages and duck served atop heavily seasoned sauerkraut; gruyère tart; an Alsatian version of cassoulet with sausages and lentils; stuffed rabbit; and chicken stewed in Alsatian riesling. The assortment of pâtés is renowned, and for dessert, we recommend the lime tart. Open daily for dinner only. The reservation book is always filled, so plan far in advance (a well-kept secret among the regulars is that no reservations are necessary for dining in the garden during the warm months). Major credit cards accepted. 332 Springvale Rd., Great Falls, VA (phone: 703-759-3800).

Bice This northern Italian eatery, owned by the proprietors of the New York establishment of the same name, specializes in risotto, fresh pasta, fish dishes, and duck entrées. Only Italian and California wines are served, but the champagne is French. Closed Saturday lunch. Reservations advised. Major credit cards accepted. 601 Pennsylvania Ave. NW, between Sixth and Seventh Sts.; enter on Indiana Ave. (phone: 638-2423).

Jockey Club This *Ritz-Carlton* restaurant is a favorite meeting and eating spot for local movers and shakers. The decor looks like New York's old *"21."* Beyond the soft-shell crabs, the menu is French-influenced; chef Fabrice Canelle was formerly with *Maxim's* in Paris. Open daily. Reservations necessary. Major credit cards accepted. 2100 Massachusetts Ave. NW (phone: 659-8000).

Maison Blanche This elegant French dining room is so close to the *White House* that even a snail could crawl over on its lunch hour. Washington's famous and powerful (such as assorted Kennedys, lobbyists, and Art Buchwald) meet here. Classical French dishes are served, but there are touches of "nouvelle" as well. Chef Christian Gautrois is well known for his exquisite escargots; other favorites are his nouvelle version of Norwegian salmon in a vegetable sauce and shrimp with angel hair pasta. The prix fixe menu (available nightly from 6 to 9:30 PM) is a bargain. The *Kennedy Center* is a short drive or an eight-block walk away. Closed Sundays. Reservations advised. Major credit cards accepted. 1725 F St. NW (phone: 842-0070).

Prime Rib Arguably Washington's premier steakhouse, this first-rate establishment serves a spectacular rib that is perfectly cooked throughout its two-inch thickness. The menu also includes a wide choice of fresh seafood dishes, as well as rack of lamb. Perhaps the city's best lunch value is an on-the-bone cut of prime ribs served with two vegetables for $13. An elegant atmosphere is accompanied by impeccable service. Closed Saturday lunch and Sundays. Reservations advised. Major credit cards accepted. 2020 K St. NW (phone: 466-8811).

Red Sage This dining spot is accented with hand-blown chandeliers, silver and gold decor, and food that is as exquisite as the surroundings. Chef Mark Miller creates dishes with a Southwestern flavor; among the selections is a stew of lobster, scallops, mussels, and clams. Also try plum *ancho* (glazed quail with jalapeño slaw and spoonbread). Open daily. Reservations necessary. Major credit cards accepted. 605 14th St. NW at F St. (phone: 638-4444).

I Ricchi One of the city's hottest eateries, here chef Francesco Ricchi concocts fabulous Florentine fare such as broad noodles tossed with hare sauce, leg of rabbit with rosemary, and quail stuffed with homemade sausage. This trattoria has a warm homey feeling. Closed Saturday lunch and Sundays. Reservations necessary. Major credit cards accepted. 1220 19th St. NW (phone: 835-0459).

Willard Room Bruno Bonnet, formerly of *Le Lion d'Or,* creates delicious, regional American-style dishes all made from local produce. Try the rack of lamb, Dover sole, or Chesapeake Bay fish. Open for all three meals Mondays through Saturdays, brunch and dinner on Sundays. Reservations advised. Major credit cards accepted. In the *Willard Inter-Continental Hotel,* 1401 Pennsylvania Ave. NW (phone: 637-7440).

MODERATE

Allegro This lovely dining room of the *Carlton* hotel is known for its fabulous business buffet lunch featuring jumbo shrimp, salmon, pâté, and carved roast of the day, and is perfect for those under time constraints. Afternoon tea is accompanied by a harpist and Sunday brunch by a pianist. Breakfast might include assorted breads, healthy options such as Bircher muesli and honey yogurt, and international offerings such as miso soup and grilled salmon à la Japanese. Dinner highlights include saffron ravioli with shiitake-morel sauce and asparagus tips, and curry oyster tempura with sake herb sabayon. Open daily for all three meals. Reservations advised, especially for the business lunch and brunch. Major credit cards accepted. 16th and K Sts. NW (phone: 879-6900).

La Colline Charming and reasonably priced, it serves adventurous French food and daily specials as well as wonderful desserts. Try the bouillabaisse and *choucroute alsacienne* (sauerkraut, sausages, pork). Open daily for all three meals. Reservations advised. Major credit cards accepted. 400 N. Capitol St. NW (phone: 737-0400).

Ernie's Original Crab House Across the Potomac in Alexandria, this is an old favorite of crab lovers. Open daily. Reservations advised on weekends. Major credit cards accepted. Two locations: 1623 Fern St. (phone: 703-836-1623) and 7929 Richmond Hwy. (phone: 703-780-0100).

Germaine's The varied Pan-Asian menu includes Japanese, Korean, Vietnamese, and Indonesian fare. Specialties are pine cone fish, scallop salad, *satay,* and squirrelfish. Closed at lunch on weekends. Reservations advised. Major credit cards accepted. 2400 Wisconsin Ave. NW (phone: 965-1185).

I Matti *Galileo* owner Roberto Donna's popular eatery in the Adams Morgan section of town offers both northern Italian dishes and Italian nouvelle cuisine. Aromatic stews, pizza with a paper-thin crust, and meltingly wonderful ricotta cheesecake are the highlights. Open daily. Reservations necessary. Major credit cards accepted. 2436 18th St. NW (phone: 462-8844).

Mr. K's Excellent food from four regions of China, including Peking, Hunan, both spicy and milder Szechuan, and classic Cantonese; favorites include beef mimosa, Peking duck, and any of several lobster dishes. This bustling place has four private dining rooms—very private, for the high-powered lawyers and lobbyists who have lunch or dinner here—decorated with impressive jade statues of dragons and a phoenix. At the end of the meal, a high-tech coffee urn is wheeled out and delivers a delicious brew (they serve tea, too). Open daily. Reservations advised. Major credit cards accepted. 2121 K St. NW (phone: 331-8868).

Occidental Grill Though this historic Washington eatery has shed its stuffy, formal atmosphere, fortunately, its first-rate fare hasn't changed. Specialties of chef Jeff Ruben include a swordfish sandwich, escalope of salmon *au poivre* with black bean purée, crab cakes, and varied meat, fish, and sausage dishes. There is an impressive wine list and a tempting dessert menu. The walls of this clubby brass and leather dining room are covered with more than 3,000 signed photographs of statesmen dating back to the early 1900s. Open daily. Reservations advised. Major credit cards accepted. 1475 Pennsylvania Ave. NW (phone: 783-1475).

Au Pied de Cochon An informal place for a good meal at a decent price 24 hours a day. If *pieds de cochon* (pigs' feet) aren't your style, try asparagus vinaigrette, coq au vin, and other bistro specialties. Open daily. No reservations. Major credit cards accepted. 1335 Wisconsin Ave. NW (phone: 333-5440).

Sfuzzi Washington Northern Italian food with an American touch is served in this *Union Station* dining establishment, founded by the owners of New York City's *Sfuzzi* restaurant. The grilled salmon is recommended, as are the pizza and pasta. Try the chicken *romano tagliatelle* (grilled chicken with gorgonzola cheese and noodles). There's an outdoor café in the summer and a happy hour on weekdays. Open daily. Reservations advised. Major credit cards accepted. 50 Massachusetts Ave. NE (phone: 842-4141).

Tabard Inn The nouvelle-influenced menu at this charmingly quirky inn is strong on fresh seafood such as grilled tuna and swordfish. The vegetables are shipped fresh daily from a nearby farm in Virginia. Sunday brunch is a popular affair, and there's a fire in the hearth in winter. Open daily. Reservations advised. MasterCard and Visa accepted. 1739 N St. NW (phone: 833-2668).

INEXPENSIVE

America The menu at this eatery (whose sister restaurant is in New York City) offers choices from all regions of the United States, from grits to Cajun shrimp to grilled tuna salad. Open daily. Reservations advised.

Major credit cards accepted. In *Union Station,* 50 Massachusetts Ave. NE (phone: 682-9559).

China Inn In Washington's Chinatown, this eatery serves primarily Cantonese fare and some Szechuan dishes. Try the lemon chicken, butterfly shrimp, or sea bass dipped in boiling water and cooked with scallions, ginger and spices. Open daily. Reservations unnecessary. Major credit cards accepted. 631 H St. NW (phone: 842-0909).

Hard Rock Café A relative newcomer to Washington, this outpost of the famous rock-music hangout serves hearty sandwiches, burgers, and salads. Open daily. Reservations advised for large groups. Major credit cards accepted. Corner of 10th and E Sts. NW (phone: 737-7625).

Madurai Vegetarian Indian food is the specialty of this Georgetown establishment. Try the eggplant curry or the vegetable *biryani* (mixed vegetables cooked with rice). Open daily. Reservations advised. Major credit cards accepted. 3318 M St. NW (phone: 333-0997).

Peyote Café This Southwestern bar and grill is located below *Roxanne's* (see below) in the heart of Adams Morgan. Try the chuck wagon beef and pinto bean chili, the mashed potatoes (with skins), and the Texas yardbird (barbecued chicken with melted Monterey jack cheese). Open daily. Reservations advised. Major credit cards accepted. 2319 18th St. NW (phone: 462-8330).

Roma A solid Italian family-style place, best in warm weather when the large outdoor garden is open and musicians and singers add to the relaxed ambience. All the old favorites, from pizza to pasta, are here. Open daily. Reservations advised. Major credit cards accepted. 3419 Connecticut Ave. NW (phone: 363-6611).

Roxanne's Chef Phil DeMott worked with New Orleans's Paul Prudhomme for five years before coming to this Cajun-style eatery in Adams Morgan. Try the barbecued shrimp, the blackened tuna, or the grilled lamb with white bean salad. Open daily. Reservations advised. Major credit cards accepted. 2319 18th St. NW (phone: 462-8330).

Sarinah Satay House A favorite among locals, this place specializes in Indonesian fare. Recommended are the grilled chicken in coconut sauce, the *satay,* and the *gado gado* (salad with peanut sauce). Closed Mondays. Reservations advised. Major credit cards accepted. 1338 Wisconsin Ave. NW (phone: 337-2955).

Star of Siam This is the best Thai restaurant in the district. Try one of the 10 different kinds of curries, the crispy noodles, or the fish cakes. Open daily. Reservations necessary for parties of four or more. Major credit cards accepted. 1136 19th St NW, between L and M Sts. (phone: 785-2838/9). There are two other locations: in Rosslyn, Virginia, across the Key Bridge from Georgetown (1735 N. Lynn St.; phone: 703-524-1208), and in Adams Morgan (2446 18th St. NW; phone: 986-4133).

Vietnam Georgetown Small and intimate, this simple place serves the best Vietnamese food in town. Specialties include deep-fried crispy spring rolls, shrimp with sugarcane, and beef in grape leaves. Open daily. Reservations unnecessary. MasterCard and Visa accepted. 2934 M St. NW (phone: 337-4536).

FOR THE SWEET OF TOOTH

Washington has a homegrown ice cream empire founded by renegade attorney Bob Weiss. *Bob's Famous Ice Cream* has stores on Capitol Hill (236 Massachusetts Ave. NE; phone: 546-3860), near the *Cleveland Park Metro* station (3510 Connecticut Ave. NW; phone: 244-4465), and in Bethesda, Maryland (4706 Bethesda Ave.; phone: 301-657-2963). *Bob's* ice cream also is sold at the *Ice Cream Shop* (2416 Wisconsin Ave. NW; phone: 965-4499).

Index

Index

Abruzzi's, Pittsburgh, 739
Adam's Mark, St. Louis, 770
Adam's Mark Memphis, Memphis, 446
Adam's Rib and Seafood House, Indianapolis, 342
Addis Red Sea, Boston, 87
Admiral Fell Inn, Baltimore, 36
Adolphus, Dallas, 191
Adriano's, Los Angeles, 413
Airport Marriott, St. Louis, 771
Aladdin, Las Vegas, 371
Alana Waikiki, Honolulu, 305
Alberto's, New Orleans, 584–85
Al Boccalino, Seattle, 922
Alcazar, Cleveland, 173
Al Dente, Las Vegas, 376
Alexander, Miami, 472
Alexis, Seattle, 920
Alex Patout's, New Orleans, 578
Alfonso's of La Jolla, San Diego, 829–30
Algonquin, New York City, 646–47
Alison on Dominick Street, New York City, 655
Allegheny Brewery and Pub, Pittsburgh, 739–40
Allegro, Washington, DC, 961

Allen Park Inn, Houston, 328
Allerton, Chicago, 137–38
All-Star Sports, Orlando, 679
A Mano, Miami, 478
Ambria, Chicago, 139
America, Washington, DC, 962–63
American, Kansas City, Missouri, 355
American Festival Café, New York City, 559
American Place, An, New York City, 655
Amerisuites, Dallas, 193
ANA, Washington, DC, 953–54
Anacapri, New Orleans, 578
Anago Bistro, Boston, 79–80
Anaqua Grill, San Antonio, 801
ANA San Francisco, San Francisco, 855
Anasazi, Santa Fe, 891
Andiamo, Las Vegas, 374
André's, Las Vegas, 374
Andrew's, Honolulu, 309
Andrews, San Francisco, 860–61
Angelo's, Ft. Worth, 266
Angkor Borei, San Francisco, 868
Angkor Wat, San Francisco, 866
Ann Sather's, Chicago, 146

Ansley Inn, Atlanta, 18
Anson's, Charleston, 100
Anthony's, Houston, 329
Anthony's Fish Grotto, San Diego, 830
Anthony's Star of the Sea Room, San Diego, 827
Antoine's, New Orleans, 578
Antonio's, Las Vegas, 376
Aqua, San Francisco, 864
Aquavit, New York City, 653
Aragon Café, Miami, 477
Archbishop's Mansion Inn, San Francisco, 859
Arizona Biltmore, Phoenix, 719
Arlington, Texas, 182–83, 259
Armadillo Café, Ft. Lauderdale, 248
Armani Express, Boston, 80
Army & Lou's, Chicago, 146
Arnie Morton's of Chicago, the Steakhouse, Los Angeles, 413
Arqua, New York City, 659
Arthur's, Nashville, 526
Art Institute Restaurant in the Park, Chicago, 142
Art Zone, Boston, 83
Arun's, Chicago, 139
Asiana Garden, Atlanta, 20

Aston Waikiki Beachside, Honolulu, 301
Aston Waikiki Shores, Honolulu, 302
Atheneum, Detroit, 221
Atlanta, Georgia, 3–23
  climate, 11
  getting around, 11–12
  hotels, 16–18
  local services, 12–13
  map, 4–5
  museums, 13
  music, 15
  nightclubs and nightlife, 15–16
  places of special interest, 3, 6–10
    APEX Museum (African-American Panoramic Experience Museum), 3, 6
    Atlanta Heritage Row, 7
    Atlanta History Center, 9
    Carter Presidential Center, 7
    Chattahoochee Nature Center, 8
    CNN Center, Omni Coliseum, Georgia World Congress Center, 6–7
    Cyclorama, 8
    Federal Reserve Bank, 6
    Fernbank Museum of Natural History, 8–9
    Fernbank Science Center, 8
    Fox Theater, 6
    Georgia Capitol, 6
    Herndon Home, 9
    High Museum of Art, 9
    Kennesaw Mountain National Battlefield Park, 10
    Lake Lanier Islands, 10
    Martin Luther King Jr. National Historic District, 6
    Peachtree Center, 3
    Piedmont Park, 8
    Road to Tara Museum, 7
    Robert W. Woodruff Arts Center, 9
    SciTrek Museum, 6
    Six Flags Over Georgia, 9–10
    Stone Mountain Park, 10
    Underground Atlanta, 7
    White Water Park, 10
    Woodruff Park, 3
    World of Coca-Cola Pavilion, 7–8
    Wren's Nest, The, 8
    Zoo Atlanta, 8
  restaurants, 18–23
  sales tax, 11
  shopping, 13–14
  special events, 13
  sports and fitness, 14–15
  telephone, 11
  theater, 15
  tourist information, 10–11
Atoll, San Diego, 828
Atwater's, Portland, 755
L'Auberge, Portland, 755
L'Auberge Chez François, Washington, DC, 959–60
L'Auberge Del Mar, San Diego, 822
Augusta, Denver, 208–9
Aujourd'hui, Boston, 80
Au Pied de Cochon, Washington, DC, 962
Avanti, San Diego, 828
Avenue Diner, Detroit, 225
Avon Old Farms, Hartford, 277
Avon Old Farms Inn, Hartford, 278
Azalea, Atlanta, 20
Azteca's, New Haven, 537
Azur, Minneapolis-St. Paul, 511
Azzura Point, San Diego, 827
Azzurro, New York City, 659

Babba Ganzo, Santa Fe, 891
Babylon, Los Angeles, 413
Baby Routh, Dallas, 193–94
Bacchi, New Orleans, 582–83
Bacco, New Orleans, 579
Bagdon's, New Haven, 536
Bahia, San Diego, 822–23
Bahia Cabana, Ft. Lauderdale, 246–47
Bahia Mar, Ft. Lauderdale, 246
Balaton, Cleveland, 175
Balcony, Ft. Worth, 265
Ba-Le Sandwich Shop, Honolulu, 315
Bali by the Sea, Honolulu, 309
Ballastone Inn and Townhouse, Savannah, 904–5
Ballroom, New York City, 660
Bally's, Las Vegas, 370
Baltimore, Maryland, 24–39
  climate, 30
  getting around, 30–31
  hotels, 35–37
  local services, 31–32
  map, 26–27
  museums, 33–34
  music, 35
  nightclubs and

nightlife, 35
places of special interest, 24–25, 28–29
  Annapolis, Maryland, 29
  Antique Row, 28
  Baltimore Conservatory, 29
  Baltimore Museum of Art, 29
  Baltimore Zoo, 29
  Charles Center, 25
  City Hall, 28
  Edgar Allan Poe Home and Grave, 25, 28
  Fort McHenry National Monument and Historic Shrine, 24–25
  Harborplace, 24
  Lexington Market, 28
  Maryland Historical Society, 28
  Maryland Science Center and Planetarium, 25
  National Aquarium, 24
  Peabody Institute and Conservatory of Music, 28–29
  US Naval Academy, Annapolis, 29
  USS Constellation, 25
  Walters Art Gallery, 28
  Washington Monument, 29
restaurants, 38–39
sales tax, 30
special events, 32
sports and fitness, 34–35
telephone, 30
theater, 35
tourist information, 30
Baltimore Marriott Inner Harbor, Baltimore, 36

Bangkok Cuisine, Hartford, 279
Bangkok Kitchen, Portland, 755
Barbizon, New York City, 650
Barking Crab, The, Boston, 87
Barleycorn's Yacht Club, Cincinnati, 161
Barnabey's, Los Angeles, 411
Battery Carriage House, Charleston, 98
Battista's Hole in the Wall, Las Vegas, 376
Bavarian Inn, Milwaukee, 495
Bayona, New Orleans, 579
Bay Tower Room, Boston, 80
Beach Club, Orlando, 678
Beau Nash, Dallas, 195
Beau Thai, Chicago, 146
Bec Fin, Le, Philadelphia, 703
Bed-and-Breakfast Inn, Savannah, 906
Bed and Breakfast on the River, San Antonio, 798
Beekman Tower, New York City, 641
Bel Age, Los Angeles, 406
Bel-Air, Los Angeles, 405–6
Bella Luna, New Orleans, 579
Bella Vista, Chicago, 142–43
Benihana Village, Las Vegas, 374
Benito's, Ft. Worth, 266
Benson, Portland, 753
Benvenuti, Indianapolis, 342
Benvenuto, Los Angeles, 418–19
Berbati, Portland, 756

Beresford, San Francisco, 863
Berghoff, Chicago, 146
Bernardin, Le, New York City, 653–54
Bertolini's, Las Vegas, 376
Best Western Grant Park, Chicago, 138
Best Western King Charles Inn, Charleston, 99
Beverly Garland Holiday Inn, Los Angeles, 412
Beverly Hilton, Los Angeles, 408
Beverly Prescott, Los Angeles, 411
Biba, Boston, 80
Bice, Chicago, 139
Bice, New York City, 660
Bice, Washington, DC, 960
Biga, San Antonio, 801
Bikini, Los Angeles, 413–14
Billy Blue's, San Antonio, 802
Billy Goat Tavern, Chicago, 146
Biltmore, Los Angeles, 409
Biltmore, Miami, 474, 480
Biltmore Suites, Baltimore, 37
Bimini Boatyard, Ft. Lauderdale, 250
Bishop's Lodge, Santa Fe, 887
Bismarck, Chicago, 138
Bistro 110, Chicago, 143
Bistro at Maison de Ville, New Orleans, 583
Bistro Garden, Los Angeles, 419
Bistro Savannah, Savannah, 907
Black Forest Inn, Minneapolis-St. Paul, 511

Blackhawk Lodge, Chicago, 143
Black Sheep, New York City, 660
Blue Corn Café, Santa Fe, 893
Blue Mesa, Chicago, 143
Blue Room, The, Boston, 83
Boar's Head, Savannah, 907
Bocage, Le, Boston, 80
Boca Grande, Boston, 87
Boca Raton Resort and Club, Boca Raton, 243–44
Bocconcino, Il, New York City, 660
Bon Appetit, Honolulu, 310
Bonaventure, Ft. Lauderdale, 244
Bone's, Atlanta, 18
Bonnie Brae Tavern, Denver, 210
Bon Ton Café, New Orleans, 583
Bookbinder's Seafood House, Philadelphia, 704
Bootlegger, Las Vegas, 376
Boston, Massachusetts, 40–88
  cinema, 72
  climate, 59
  getting around, 59–61
  hotels, 74–79
  local services, 61–63
  map, 42–43
  museums, 64–65
  music, 72–73
  nightclubs and nightlife, 73–74
  places of special interest, 40–41, 44–58
    Arnold Arboretum, 57
    Black Heritage Trail, 46
    Blackstone Block, 48–49
    Boston Athenaeum, 47
    Boston Common, 40
    Boston Tea Party Ship and Museum, 45
    Brattle Street, 55
    Bunker Hill Monument, 53
    Bunker Hill Pavilion, 53
    Charles Street, 47–48
    Children's Museum, 45
    Chinatown, 56
    City Hall, 44
    Commonwealth Avenue, 49
    Commonwealth Museum, 56
    Computer Museum, 46
    Copley Square, 50
    Downtown Crossing, 41
    Esplanade, 49–50
    Faneuil Hall Marketplace, 45
    Fens Park, The, 51
    First Church of Christ, Scientist, in Boston (Christian Science Church World Headquarters), The, 52
    Franklin Park Zoo, 57
    Frederick Law Olmsted National Historic Site, 57
    Freedom Trail, 41
    Globe Corner Bookstore, 44
    Harvard Square, 53–54
    Harvard University Art Museums, 54
    Harvard University Museums, 54
    Harvard Yard, 54
    House of the Seven Gables, Salem, 58
    Institute of Contemporary Art, 51
    Isabella Stewart Gardner Museum, 52
    John F. Kennedy Library, 56
    Kenmore Square, 51
    King's Chapel and Burying Ground, 41
    Massachusetts Institute of Technology, 55
    Mt. Auburn Cemetery, 55–56
    Mt. Vernon Street, 47
    Museum of Fine Arts, 51–52
    Museum of Science and the Charles Hayden Planetarium, 56–57
    Newbury Street, 50
    New England Aquarium, 45
    New England Historic Genealogical Society, 50–51
    Old Burying Ground, 55
    Old Granary Burying Ground, 41
    Old North Church, 48
    Old South Meeting House, 41, 44
    Old State House, 44
    Park Street Church, 41
    Paul Revere House, 48
    Peabody Museum, Salem, 58
    Public Garden, 49
    Radcliffe Yard, 54–55
    Salem, Massachusetts, 58
    Salem Maritime National Historic Site, Salem, 58

Southwest Corridor, 53
State House, 46–47
Union Park, 53
USS Constitution, 53
Weeks Memorial Bridge, 54
Witch Museum, Salem, 58
restaurants, 79–88
sales tax, 59
shopping, 65–69
special events, 63–64
sports and fitness, 69–71
telephone, 59
theater, 71–72
tourist information, 58–59
Boston Harbor, Boston, 75
Bostonian, Boston, 75
Botsford Inn, Detroit, 222–23
Boudro's, San Antonio, 801
Boulders, Phoenix, 719
Bouley, New York City, 654
Bourbon Orleans, New Orleans, 575
Box Tree, New York City, 647
Brasserie Max, Ft. Lauderdale, 250–51
Brazilian Tropicana, Ft. Lauderdale, 251
Breakfast Club, Savannah, 908
Brennan's, Houston, 329
Brigtsen's, New Orleans, 579
Brisas de Santa Fe, La, Santa Fe, 887
Bristol, Louisville, 436
Broad Ripple Brew Pub, Indianapolis, 343
Broadway American, New York City, 652
Broadway Deli, Boston, 83
Brother's, Ft. Lauderdale, 252
Brown, Louisville, 434
Brown Palace, Denver, 207
Brown Thomson & Co., Hartford, 279
Bruxelles, New Haven, 537
Bubbalou's Bodacious BBQ, Orlando, 683
Bubble Room, Orlando, 683
Bub City, Chicago, 143
Buckhead Diner, Atlanta, 20
Buckhorn Exchange, Denver, 209
Buena Vista Palace, Orlando, 679–80
Bukhara, Chicago, 143
Bullis House Inn/San Antonio International Hostel, San Antonio, 801
Burma's House, San Francisco, 868
Burt & Jack's, Ft. Lauderdale, 248
Busch's Grove, St. Louis, 772
By Word of Mouth, Ft. Lauderdale, 249

Dakota, San Francisco, 863
Dakota Bar & Grill, Minneapolis-St. Paul, 511
Dali, Boston, 84
Dallas, Texas, 176–97
 climate, 184
 getting around, 184–85
 hotels, 190–93
 local services, 185
 map, 178–79
 music, 189
 nightclubs and nightlife, 190
 places of special interest, 176–77, 180–83
  Age of Steam Museum, 176
  Ballpark at Arlington, The, 182–83
  Biblical Arts Center, 181
  Dallas Arboretum, 181
  Dallas County Historical Plaza, 180
  Dallas Museum of Art, 177, 180
  Dallas World Aquarium, 180
  Dallas Zoo, 181–82
  Deep Ellum, 180
  Fair Park, 176–77
  Farmers' Market, 180
  Fossil Rim Wildlife Center, 183
  Frontiers of Flight Museum, 181
  Infomart, 181
  John F. Kennedy Memorial, 177
  Meadows Museum, 181
  Memorial Center for Holocaust Studies, 181
  Midway and the Texas Hall of State, 176
  Morton H. Meyerson Symphony Center, 177
  Museum of African-American Life and Culture, 177
  Museum of Natural History, 176
  Neiman Marcus, 180
  Old City Park, 183
  Samuell Farm, 182
  Science Place, 176–77
  Six Flags Over Texas, Arlington, 182
  Southfork Ranch, 182
  Studios at Las Colinas, 182
  Swiss Avenue Historic District, 181

Dallas, Texas (cont.)
  Texas School Book Depository and the Sixth Floor, 177
  Texas Stadium, 182
  Thanks-Giving Square, 180
  Union Station, 177
  Wagon Wheel Ranch, 181
  West End MarketPlace, 180
  Wet 'n' Wild, Arlington, 183
  restaurants, 193–97
  sales tax, 184
  shopping, 186–88
  special events, 185–86
  sports and fitness, 188–89
  telephone, 184
  theater, 189
  tourist information, 183–84
D'Amico Cucina, Minneapolis-St. Paul, 511
Dan and Louis Oyster Bar, Portland, 756
Dante's Down the Hatch, Atlanta, 20–21
Darrel & Oliver's Café Maxx, Ft. Lauderdale, 247–48
Dauphine Orleans, New Orleans, 576
Davide, Boston, 81
David's, Boston, 84
David Slay's La Veranda, Los Angeles, 420
Davio's, Boston, 81
Days Inn, Atlanta, 18
Days Inn Inner Harbor, Baltimore, 37
Days Inn Lake Shore Drive, Chicago, 138–39
Days Inn Meeting St., Charleston, 99
Days Inn Savannah, Savannah, 906

Days Inn South, Indianapolis, 342
Dearborn Inn, Detroit, 223
Deep Ellum Café, Dallas, 195
Del Coronado, San Diego, 823
Del Fresco's, Dallas, 194
Delicias, San Diego, 827
Delmonico's, New Haven, 537
Denver, Colorado, 198–210
  climate, 203
  getting around, 203
  hotels, 207–8
  local services, 203–4
  map, 200–201
  museums, 204
  music, 206
  nightclubs and nightlife, 206
  places of special interest, 198–99, 202
    Capitol, 199
    Children's Museum, 199, 202
    City Park, 199
    Colorado State History Museum, 198–99
    Coors Brewery, 202
    Denver Art Museum, 198
    Denver Public Library, 198
    Elitch Gardens, 202
    Hyland Hills Water World, 199
    Larimer Street, 199
    Molly Brown House, 199
    Rocky Mountain National Park, 202
    US Mint, 198
  restaurants, 208–10
  sales tax, 203
  shopping, 204–5
  special events, 204

  sports and fitness, 205–6
  telephone, 202
  theater, 206
  tourist information, 202–3
Denver Buffalo Company, Denver, 209
DeSoto Hilton, Savannah, 905
Detlef's, Honolulu, 313
Detroit, Michigan, 211–26
  climate, 217
  getting around, 217
  hotels, 221–24
  local services, 217–18
  map, 212–13
  museums, 219
  music, 220
  nightclubs and nightlife, 220–21
  places of special interest, 211, 214–16
    Belle Isle, 214
    Birmingham, 216
    Children's Museum, 214
    Cranbrook, 214–15
    Detroit Historical Museum, 214
    Detroit Institute of Arts, 214
    Detroit Public Library, 214
    Eastern Market, 215
    Fist, The, 211
    Fox Theatre, 215
    Greektown, 215
    Greenfield Village and Henry Ford Museum, 215
    Millender Center, 211
    Motown Museum, 215
    Museum of African-American History, 214
    Philip A. Hart Plaza, 211
    Plant Tours, 215
    Renaissance Center, 211

Royal Oak, 215–16
Washington Boulevard Trolley, 211, 214
Windsor, Ontario, Canada, 216
restaurants, 224–26
sales tax, 217
special events, 218–19
sports and fitness, 219–20
telephone, 217
theaters, 220
tourist information, 216–17
Deux Cheminées, Philadelphia, 703
Diamond Head Beach, Honolulu, 303
Dickens Inn, Philadelphia, 704
Dick's Last Resort, Dallas, 195–96
DiLullo Centro, Philadelphia, 704
Disney's Village Resort, Orlando, 678
For other Disney accommodations, see Walt Disney
Ditto's Food & Drink, Louisville, 436
Diva, San Francisco, 861
Diva Seafood Bar and Grill, San Antonio, 803
DIVE!, Los Angeles, 423
Dixie Landings, Orlando, 679
Dobson's, San Diego, 828
Dock's Oyster Bar, New York City, 664
Dock Street Brewery and Restaurant, Philadelphia, 705
Dolphin, Orlando, 678
Dôme, Le, Los Angeles, 415

Donatello, San Francisco, 856
Don & Charlie's, Phoenix, 724
Don Gaspar Compound Inn, Santa Fe, 888
Dooky Chase's, New Orleans, 583
Doral Ocean Beach, Miami, 472
Doral Resort & Country Club, Miami, 471
Doral Saturnia International Spa, Miami, 472–73
Doral Tuscany, New York City, 647
Los Dos Molinos, Phoenix, 724
Doubletree, Kansas City, Missouri, 354–55
Doubletree Club, Orlando, 681
Doubletree at Horton Plaza, San Diego, 823
Doubletree Mayfair Suites, St. Louis, 771
Doubletree of Philadelphia, Philadelphia, 702
Doubletree Suites, Phoenix, 722
Dover Sea Grille, Boston, 84
Downey's, Philadelphia, 705
Drago, Los Angeles, 415
Drai's, Los Angeles, 415
Drake, Chicago, 135
Drake Swissôtel, New York City, 641
Drury Inn, St. Louis, 772
Du Jour, Seattle, 923
Duncan Hotel, New Haven, 536
Durango Grill, Detroit, 225
Durant's, Phoenix, 724
Durgin-Park, Boston, 85

Dux, Memphis, 446
Dynasty Room, Los Angeles, 415

East Wind, Dallas, 194
Eccentric, The, Chicago, 144
Ed Debevic's, Chicago, 146
Ed Debevic's Short Orders Deluxe, Phoenix, 725–26
Eggs 'n' Things, Honolulu, 316
82 Queen, Charleston, 100
El Charro Avitia, Honolulu, 312–13
Eldorado, Santa Fe, 888
11th Street Diner, Miami, 481
El Farol, Santa Fe, 892–93
El Farolito Bed and Breakfast, Santa Fe, 888
Eliot, Boston, 75–76
Elizabeth on Thirty-Seventh, Savannah, 906
Eliza Thompson House, Savannah, 905
Elliott's Oyster House, Seattle, 922
Elliston Place Soda Shop, Nashville, 527
El Mirador, San Antonio, 803–4
El Norteño, Phoenix, 726
El Paradero Bed & Breakfast Inn, Santa Fe, 890
El Rey Inn, Santa Fe, 890
Embassy Suites, Detroit, 223
Embassy Suites, New York City, 647
Embassy Suites, Phoenix, 720–21
Embassy Suites Northeast, Cincinnati, 158

INDEX 973

Emeril's, New Orleans, 580
Emilio's, Chicago, 144
Emily Morgan, San Antonio, 800
Emporio Armani Express Café and Restaurant, Los Angeles, 423
Empress Room, Orlando, 682
Encore Provence, Santa Fe, 892
Engine Co. No. 28, Los Angeles, 420
English Room, Milwaukee, 494
Epicentre, Los Angeles, 420
Ernie's, San Francisco, 864
Ernie's Bar-B-Que, Ft. Lauderdale, 252
Ernie's Original Crab House, Washington, DC, 961
L'Escale, San Diego, 828–29
L'Escoffier, Los Angeles, 415–16
L'Espalier, Boston, 81
Essential Edibles, Indianapolis, 344
Essex House, New York City, 641
Everest Room, Chicago, 140
Excalibur, Las Vegas, 371
Exchange Tavern, Savannah, 908
Executive House, Chicago, 138
Executive Inn, Louisville, 434–35
Express Café and Bakery, Savannah, 908

Fairmont, Chicago, 135
Fairmont, Dallas, 192
Fairmont, New Orleans, 573–74
Fairmont, San Francisco, 856
Fairmount, San Antonio, 798, 802
Famous Delicatessen, Philadelphia, 706
Far East Café, San Francisco, 869
Farol, El, Santa Fe, 892–93
Farolito Bed and Breakfast, El, Santa Fe, 888
Ferraro's, Las Vegas, 377
Fiesta Inn, Phoenix, 722
Figlio, Minneapolis-St. Paul, 511
Fio's, San Diego, 829
Fishbone's Rhythm Kitchen Café, Detroit, 225
Fish Market, Miami, 477
510, Minneapolis-St. Paul, 510
Flamingo Diner, Ft. Lauderdale, 252
Flamingo Hilton, Las Vegas, 371
Flamingo Room, Las Vegas, 377
Fleur de Lys, La, Salt Lake City, 786
Fleur de Lys, San Francisco, 864
Florent, New York City, 664
Flying Saucer, San Francisco, 867
Fly Trap, San Francisco, 869
Fogata, La, San Antonio, 803
Fog City Diner, San Francisco, 866
Folk's Folly, Memphis, 446–47
Fonda, La, Santa Fe, 888
Fontainebleau, San Diego, 827
Fontainebleau Hilton, Miami, 474
Forbidden City, Indianapolis, 344
Forepaughs, Minneapolis-St. Paul, 510
Forest View Gardens, Cincinnati, 160
Forge, Miami, 477–78
Fornaio, Il, San Diego, 829
Fort, The, Denver, 209
Ft. Lauderdale, Florida, 227–52
  climate, 234
  getting around, 234–35
  hotels, 243–47
  local services, 236–37
  map, 228–29
  museums, 238
  music, 242
  nightclubs and nightlife, 242–43
  places of special interest, 227, 230–33
    Bonnet House, 230–31
    Butterfly World, 232
    Everglades Holiday Park, 231
    Flamingo Gardens, 231
    Goodyear Blimp, 232
    Grand Prix Race-A-Rama, 232
    Hollywood Broadwalk, 230
    Hugh Taylor Birch State Recreation Area, 230
    International Swimming Hall of Fame, 231
    John U. Lloyd Beach State Recreation Area, 232
    Loxahatchee Everglades Tours, 231
    Museum of Discovery and Science, 227, 230
    Ocean World, 230
    Las Olas area, 233
    Port Everglades, 227
    Sawgrass Mills Mall, 231–32
    Seminole Indian Reservation, 232

Stranahan House, 230
Swap Shop, 230
Topeekeegee Yugnee Park, 232
restaurants, 247–52
sales tax, 234
shopping, 238–39
special events, 237
sports and fitness, 239–42
telephone, 234
theaters, 242
tourist information, 233–34
Ft. Lauderdale Marina Marriott, Ft. Lauderdale, 244
Fort Wilderness Campground, Orlando, 679
Ft. Worth, Texas, 253–67
climate, 259
getting around, 259–60
hotels, 263–64
local services, 260–61
map, 254–55
music, 262
nightclubs and nightlife, 263
places of special interest, 253, 256–59
  Amon Carter Museum, 256
  Arlington, Texas, 259
  Botanic and Japanese Gardens, 257
  Caravan of Dreams, 258
  Cattleman's Museum, 257
  Ft. Worth Museum of Science and History, 256–57
  Ft. Worth Stockyards, 253, 256
  Ft. Worth Zoo, 257
  Granbury, Texas, 258–59
  Kimbell Art Museum, 256
  Log Cabin Village, 257
  Modern Art Museum of Ft. Worth, 256
  Old Tyme Postique, 258
  Stockyards Station and the Ft. Worth and Western Railroad, 256
  Sundance Square, 257–58
  Tarrant County Courthouse, 258
  Texas Lil's, 258–59
  Thistle Hill, 257
  Water Gardens, 258
restaurants, 264–67
sales tax, 259
special events, 261
sports and fitness, 261–62
telephone, 259
theater, 262
tourist information, 259
45 South, Savannah, 906
Fountain, Philadelphia, 703
Four Seasons, Boston, 76
Four Seasons, Chicago, 135
Four Seasons, Dallas, 192
Four Seasons, Los Angeles, 406–7
Four Seasons, New York City, 654
Four Seasons, Philadelphia, 700
Four Seasons, Washington, DC, 954
Four Seasons Clift, San Francisco, 856
Four Seasons New York, New York City, 641–42
Four Seasons Olympic, Seattle, 920
Fourteen, New York City, 664
Français, Le, Chicago, 140

French Pastry Shop, San Diego, 830
French Quarter Maisonettes, New Orleans, 577
French Room, Dallas, 194
Fresco, Il, Honolulu, 313
Fresh Fish Company, Denver, 209–10
Frontera Grill and Topolobampo, Chicago, 140
Fullers, Seattle, 922

Gaetano's, Hartford, 279
Gage & Tollner, New York City, 664
Galatoire's, New Orleans, 580
Galileo, Washington, DC, 959
Galt House, Louisville, 435
Garden, Philadelphia, 704
Garibaldi's, Charleston, 101
Garibaldi's, Savannah, 907
Gaslamp Plaza Suites, San Diego, 826
Gastonian Inn, Savannah, 905
Gaulart & Maliclet, Charleston, 101
Gautreau's, New Orleans, 580
Geja's Café, Chicago, 144
Gene and Georgetti, Chicago, 140
General Jackson, Nashville, 526
Geoffrey's, Los Angeles, 413
Geordy's, San Francisco, 865
George's at the Cove, San Diego, 829
Georgia, Los Angeles, 416
Germaine's, Washington, DC, 961

INDEX 975

Geronimo Lodge, Santa Fe, 892
Gibby's, Ft. Lauderdale, 251
Gilliland's, Los Angeles, 420
Giovanni's, Cleveland, 173
Gladstone's Malibu, Los Angeles, 423
Glass Chimney, Indianapolis, 342
Glidden House, Cleveland, 173
Go Fish, Ft. Lauderdale, 249–50
Golden Dragon, Honolulu, 310
Golden Gate, San Francisco, 863
Golden Nugget, Las Vegas, 360–61, 370, 378
Golden Ox, Kansas City, Missouri, 356
Golden Palace Cuisine of India, Phoenix, 724
Golden Unicorn, New York City, 664
Goldstar Chili, Cincinnati, 161
Goode Company Barbecue, Houston, 331
Goode Company Seafood, Houston, 331
Goodfellow's, Minneapolis-St. Paul, 510
Goodwin, Hartford, 277–78
Gordon, Chicago, 140–41
Gordon Biersch Brewery, San Francisco, 867
Gorham, New York City, 650
Gotham Bar & Grill, New York City, 656
Governor, Portland, 753
Grand, Washington, DC, 955

Grand Bay, Miami, 473
Grand Café, Miami, 478
Grand Concourse, Pittsburgh, 739
Grand Floridian, Orlando, 678
Grand Hyatt, New York City, 647
Grand Hyatt Washington, Washington, DC, 955
Grand Kempinski, Dallas, 192
Grand Milwaukee, Milwaukee, 493
Granita, Los Angeles, 416
Grant Corner Inn, Santa Fe, 888
Great Caruso, Houston, 330
Great Lakes Brewing Company, Cleveland, 174
Greek Islands, Chicago, 146–47
Greens, San Francisco, 867
Grenouille, La, New York City, 654
Grey Moss Inn, San Antonio, 802
Grill Room, New Orleans, 580–81
Grisanti's, Memphis, 447
Groceria, La, Boston, 87
Grotta, La, Atlanta, 19
Grotta Azzurra, New York City, 656
Guest Quarters, Ft. Lauderdale, 245
Guest Quarters, Orlando, 680
Guest Quarters Suite, Boston, 76

Hajibaba's, Honolulu, 308
Hala Terrace, Honolulu, 313
Halekulani, Honolulu, 301
Hamayoshi, Los Angeles, 423

Hampshire House, Boston, 81
Hampton Inn Historic District, Charleston, 99
Hampton Inn Vanderbilt, Nashville, 525–26
Hampton's, Baltimore, 38
Happy Immortal, San Francisco, 867
Harbor Court, Baltimore, 36
Harbor Court, San Francisco, 859–60
Harborplace, Baltimore, 39
Hard Rock Café, Atlanta, 22
Hard Rock Café, Chicago, 147
Hard Rock Café, Dallas, 196
Hard Rock Café, Honolulu, 313
Hard Rock Café, Washington, DC, 963
Harlequin's, Honolulu, 310
Harlow's Hollywood Cafe, Houston, 331
Harold's Barbecue, Atlanta, 22
Harrington, Washington, DC, 958
Harris', San Francisco, 865
Hartford, Connecticut, 268–80
  climate, 273
  getting around, 273
  hotels, 277–78
  local services, 274
  map, 270–71
  museums, 275
  music, 276
  nightclubs and nightlife, 276–77
  places of special interest, 268–69, 272
    Bushnell Park, 268
    Butler-McCook Homestead, 268

Center Church, 268
Connecticut State Capitol, 268
Elizabeth Park, 269
Hartford Civic Center, 269
Heublein Tower, 272
Hill-Stead Museum, Farmington, 272
Litchfield, Connecticut, 272
Mark Twain Memorial and Harriet Beecher Stowe House, 269, 272
Old State House, 269
Pratt Street, 269
Raymond E. Baldwin Museum of Connecticut History, 268
Route 44, 272
Science Museum of Connecticut, 272
Simsbury 1820 House, Simsbury, 272
Wadsworth Atheneum, 269
White Flower Farm, 272
restaurants, 278–80
sales tax, 273
special events, 274–75
sports and fitness, 275–76
telephone, 273
theater, 276
tourist information, 273
Hasenour's, Louisville, 436
Hat Dance, Chicago, 144
Hatsuhana, Chicago, 144
Hatsuhana, New York City, 664
Hau Tree Lanai, Honolulu, 311
Hawaiiana, Honolulu, 307

Hawaii Prince, Honolulu, 301–2
Hawthorne Suites at the Market, Charleston, 98
Hay-Adams, Washington, DC, 955
Hayes Street Grill, San Francisco, 867
Heathman, Portland, 753
Hedary's, Ft. Worth, 266
Hedgerose Heights Inn, Atlanta, 19
Helmand, Chicago, 147
Herald Square, New York City, 652
Hermitage, Nashville, 525
Hermosa Resort, Phoenix, 721
Hilton at Walt Disney World, Orlando, 680
Hilton Hawaiian Village, Honolulu, 302
Hilton Inn, Milwaukee, 493–94
Hilton Palacio del Río, San Antonio, 798
Hilton Suites Auburn Hills, Detroit, 223
Hob Nob Hill, San Diego, 830
HoJo Inn, Chicago, 139
Holiday Inn, New Haven, 536
Holiday Inn Airport, Minneapolis-St. Paul, 510
Holiday Inn City Centre, Chicago, 138
Holiday Inn-City Line, Philadelphia, 702–3
Holiday Inn Crowne Plaza, Memphis, 446
Holiday Inn Crowne Plaza, New York City, 647
Holiday Inn Crowne Plaza at Union

Station, Indianapolis, 341
Holiday Inn Downtown, New York City, 650
Holiday Inn Express, Minneapolis-St. Paul, 510
Holiday Inn Hartford Downtown, Hartford, 278
Holiday Inn Inner Harbor, Baltimore, 37
Holiday Inn O'Hare, Chicago, 138
Holiday Inn Vanderbilt, Nashville, 526
Hollyhock Hill, Indianapolis, 343
Honey Bear's BBQ, Phoenix, 726
Honolulu, Hawaii, 281–316
climate, 289–90
getting around, 290–91
hotels, 300–307
local services, 291–92
map, 282–83
museums, 292
music, 299
nightclubs and nightlife, 300
places of special interest, 281, 284–89
Ala Moana Center, 285–86
Aloha Tower/Festival Marketplace, 285
Bishop Museum and Planetarium, 286
Chinatown, 284–85
Contemporary Museum, 288
Diamond Head, 281
Fort DeRussy Army Museum, 284
Foster Botanic Gardens, 286
Hawaii Maritime Museum, 285

INDEX 977

Honolulu, Hawaii (*cont.*)
   Honolulu Academy of Arts, 286
   International Market Place, 284
   Iolani Palace, 285
   island-hopping tours, 288–89
   Kapiolani Park, 281
   Kawaiahao Church, 284
   Maunakea Marketplace, 285
   Mission Houses Museum, 284
   National Memorial Cemetery of the Pacific, 287
   Pacific Aerospace Museum, 286–87
   Polynesian Cultural Center, 287–88
   Queen Emma's Summer Palace, 287
   Royal Mausoleum, 287
   Sea Life Park, 288
   State Capitol, 285
   Tantalus Drive, 284
   USS Arizona Memorial, 286
   Waikiki Beach, 281, 284
   Waimea Falls Park & Valley, 288
   restaurants, 307–16
   sales tax, 289
   shopping, 292–97
   special events, 292
   sports and fitness, 297–99
   telephone, 289
   theater, 299
   tourist information, 289–90
Honto, Atlanta, 21
Hops Bistro Brewery, Phoenix, 726
Horatio's, Honolulu, 313
Horton Grand, San Diego, 825
Hotel Atop the Bellevue, Philadelphia, 700–701
Hot Tomato's, Hartford, 280
Houston, Texas, 317–31
   climate, 323
   getting around, 323
   hotels, 327–29
   local services, 323–24
   map, 318–19
   museums, 325
   music, 327
   nightclubs and nightlife, 327
   places of special interest, 317, 320–22
      Anheuser-Busch Brewery, 321
      Astrodome, 320–21
      Astroworld, 321
      Children's Museum, 317, 320
      Galveston Island, 322
      Houston Zoological Gardens, 317
      International Strip, 320
      Menil Collection, 320
      Museum of Fine Arts, 320
      Museum of Natural Science, 317
      Port of Houston, 321
      River Oaks, 320
      Sam Houston Park, 320
      San Jacinto Battleground, 321
      Space Center Houston at Lyndon B. Johnson Space Center, 321–22
   restaurants, 329–31
   sales tax, 323
   shopping, 325
   special events, 324–25
   sports and fitness, 325–26
   telephone, 323
   theater, 326–27
   tourist information, 322–23
Howard Johnson, Orlando, 680
Howard Johnson's Fenway, Boston, 79
Hubbard's, Hartford, 280
Huber's Café, Portland, 756
Huey's, Atlanta, 22
Huey's, Savannah, 908
Hugo's, Los Angeles, 423–24
Hugo's Cellar, Las Vegas, 375
Hunan House, New York City, 664
Hunan Wok, New Haven, 537
Hunter House, Savannah, 906
Huntington, San Francisco, 857
Huntington's, Dallas, 194
Hyatt Hill Country Resort, San Antonio, 799
Hyatt Islandia, San Diego, 823–24
Hyatt on Printer's Row, Chicago, 135
Hyatt Pittsburgh, Pittsburgh, 737–38
Hyatt Regency, Atlanta, 16
Hyatt Regency, Baltimore, 36
Hyatt Regency, Cambridge, Boston, 76
Hyatt Regency, Cincinnati, 158
Hyatt Regency, Dallas, 192
Hyatt Regency, Kansas City, Missouri, 354
Hyatt Regency, Milwaukee, 493
Hyatt Regency, St. Louis, 771
Hyatt Regency, San Antonio, 799
Hyatt Regency, San Francisco, 857

Hyatt Regency Chicago, Chicago, 135
Hyatt Regency Dearborn, Detroit, 221
Hyatt Regency Denver, Denver, 207
Hyatt Regency D/FW, Ft. Worth, 263
Hyatt Regency Grand Cypress, Orlando, 680
Hyatt Regency Louisville, Louisville, 434
Hyatt Regency O'Hare, Chicago, 135–36
Hyatt Regency Savannah, Savannah, 905
Hyatt Regency Scottsdale, Phoenix, 721
Hyatt Regency Suites, Chicago, 136
Hyatt Regency Waikiki, Honolulu, 303
Hyde Park Grille, Cleveland, 173
Hyeholde, Pittsburgh, 739
Hy's Steak House, Honolulu, 311

Icarus, Boston, 85
Il Bocconcino, New York City, 660
Il Cantinori, New York City, 655
Il Cielo, Los Angeles, 420
L'Ile De France, Ft. Lauderdale, 251
Il Fornaio, San Diego, 829
Il Fresco, Honolulu, 313
Ilikai, Honolulu, 303
Illusions, Indianapolis, 343
Il Nido, New York City, 657
Il Terrazzo Carmine, Seattle, 923
I Matti, Washington, DC, 962
Imperial Inn, Philadelphia, 706
Ina's Kitchen, Chicago, 147
Indianapolis, Indiana, 332–44
 climate, 336
 getting around, 336–37
 hotels, 340–42
 local services, 337–38
 map, 334–35
 music, 340
 nightclubs and nightlife, 340
 places of special interest, 332–33, 336
  Benjamin Harrison Memorial Home, 333
  Children's Museum, 333
  Conner Prairie, 336
  Eiteljorg Museum of American Indians and Western Art, 332
  Garfield Park Conservatory, 336
  Indianapolis Motor Speedway, 333
  Indianapolis Museum of Art, 333
  Indianapolis Zoo, 333
  Indiana State Museum, 332
  James Whitcomb Riley Home, 333
  Lilly Center, 336
  Scottish Rite Cathedral, 332
  Union Station, 332
  Zionsville, 333
 restaurants, 342–44
 sales tax, 336
 special events, 338
 sports and fitness, 333–39
 telephone, 336
 theater, 339–40
 tourist information, 335
Indianapolis Motor Speedway Motel, Indianapolis, 342
Indigo Coastal Grill, Atlanta, 21
Inn at Chapel West, New Haven, 535
Inn at Loretto, Santa Fe, 889
Inn at the Market, Seattle, 921
Inn at the Opera, San Francisco, 861
Inn at Rancho Santa Fe, San Diego, 821–22
Inn at Temple Square, Salt Lake City, 784
Inn at Union Square, The, San Francisco, 861
Inn of the Anasazi, Santa Fe, 886
Inn of the Animal Tracks, Santa Fe, 888–89
Inn of the Governors, Santa Fe, 889
Inn on the Alameda, Santa Fe, 887
Inter-Continental, Chicago, 136
Inter-Continental, New Orleans, 574
Inter-Continental Los Angeles, Los Angeles, 409
Inter-Continental Miami, Miami, 474–75
Inter-Continental New York, New York City, 647–48
I Ricchi, Washington, DC, 961
Island Colony, Honolulu, 306
Isobune, San Francisco, 869
Italian Village, Chicago, 144
I Tre Merli, Miami, 481
Ivar's Indian Salmon House, Seattle, 923–24
Ivy, Los Angeles, 416

Jack Fry's, Louisville, 436
Jackie's, Chicago, 141
Jack's, San Francisco, 867
Jackson Fillmore, San Francisco, 869
Jackson's, Los Angeles, 420
Jae's Café, Boston, 87–88
Jake's Delicatessen, Milwaukee, 495
Jake's Famous Crawfish Restaurant, Portland, 755
Jasper's, Boston, 81
Jasper's, Kansas City, Missouri, 355
Jean Lafitte, New York City, 661
Jean-Louis, Washington, DC, 959
Jefferson, Washington, DC, 955–56
Jimmy's, Los Angeles, 416
Jimmy's Harborside, Boston, 85
Jimmy's Place, Chicago, 141
Jockey Club, Washington, DC, 960
Joe Muer's, Detroit, 224
Joe's Stone Crab, Miami, 478
Joe T. Garcia's, Ft. Worth, 266–67
Joey Tomato's Atlantic City, Dallas, 196
John Dominis, Honolulu, 308
Johnny Harris, Savannah, 907
Johnny's Bar, Cleveland, 173–74
John Rutledge House Inn, Charleston, 98
John W. Faidley Seafood, Baltimore, 39
Jo Jo, New York City, 656
Jonathan's, Indianapolis, 343

Jordan's Grove, Orlando, 682–83
Josie's Casa de Comida, Santa Fe, 894
Joss, Los Angeles, 420–21
Journey's End, New York City, 650–51
Julien, Boston, 81–82
Juno Trattoria, Pittsburgh, 740
Justine's, Memphis, 447
J.W. Marriott, Los Angeles, 407
J.W. Marriott, Washington, DC, 956

Kahala Hilton, Honolulu, 302
Kaleidoscope, Miami, 480
Kansas City, Missouri, 345–56
climate, 349
getting around, 349–50
hotels, 353–55
local services, 350
map, 346–47
museums, 351
music, 352
nightclubs and nightlife, 353
places of special interest, 345, 348
Country Club Plaza, 345
Crown Center, 345
Ft. Osage, Sibley, 348
Harry S. Truman Library and Museum, Independence, 348
Kansas City Stockyards, 348
Missouri River Excursions, 348
NCAA Visitors' Center, 348
Nelson-Atkins Museum of Art, 345, 348
Swope Park, 348
Westport, 345
Worlds of Fun, 348

restaurants, 355–56
sales tax, 349
special events, 350–51
sports and fitness, 351–52
telephone, 349
theater, 352
tourist information, 349
Karinya, San Diego, 830
Karl Ratzsch's, Milwaukee, 494
Kaspar's, Seattle, 922
Kathleen's Art Café, Dallas, 196
Kelsey's, New Orleans, 583–84
Kincaid's, Ft. Worth, 267
King & I, Atlanta, 22
Kings Island Inn, Cincinnati, 158–59
King Tsin, Honolulu, 316
Kirin, Honolulu, 313–14
Kokeb, Seattle, 924
K-Paul's Louisiana Kitchen, New Orleans, 581
KT's, Louisville, 436
Kyung Bok Palace, San Francisco, 867–68

La Caille at Quail Run, Salt Lake City, 786
La Cantina, Orlando, 683
La Caravelle, New York City, 656
La Casa Seña, Santa Fe, 891
La Champagne, Phoenix, 723
La Choza, Santa Fe, 894
La Colline, Washington, DC, 961
La Colombe d'Or, Houston, 327–28, 329–30
La Coquille, Ft. Lauderdale, 249

La Coupole, Denver, 209
La Cuisine, Detroit, 225
Lafayette, Boston, 76–77
Lafayette, New Orleans, 574
La Fleur de Lys, Salt Lake City, 786
La Fogata, San Antonio, 803
La Fonda, Santa Fe, 888
La Grenouille, New York City, 654
La Groceria, Boston, 87
La Grotta, Atlanta, 19
Lakeview, Louisville, 435
La Loma, Denver, 210
La Louisiane, San Antonio, 802
La Mansion del Río, San Antonio, 799
La Mariana, Honolulu, 316
Lamb's, Salt Lake City, 786
La Mer, Honolulu, 308
LaMothe House, New Orleans, 574
La Normandie Grill, Cincinnati, 160
La Paloma, Louisville, 436
La Patisserie, St. Louis, 773
Le Pavillon, New Orleans, 576
La Paz, Nashville, 526–27
La Piazza, Ft. Worth, 265
La Posada, Santa Fe, 889–90
La Provence, New Orleans, 584
La Quinta Motor Inns, Dallas, 193
Lark Creek Inn, San Francisco, 865
Las Brisas de Santa Fe, Santa Fe, 887
Las Vegas, Nevada, 357–78
  climate, 362
  getting around, 362–63
  hotels, 359–73
  local services, 363–64
  map, 358–59
  museums, 364–66
  music, 368
  nightclubs and nightlife, 368–69
  places of special interest, 357, 360–61
    Caesars Palace, 360, 370, 378
    Circus Circus, 360
    Convention Center, 360
    Death Valley, 361
    Excalibur, 360
    Golden Nugget, 360–61, 370, 378
    Hoover Dam and Lake Mead, 361
    MGM Grand Hotel/Casino and Theme Park, 357, 360, 372
    Mirage, The, 360, 370–71, 378
    Mt. Charleston, 361
    Red Rock Canyon Conservation Area, 361
    Wet 'n' Wild, 360
  restaurants, 373–78
  sales tax, 362
  shopping, 366
  special events, 364
  sports and fitness, 366–67
  telephone, 362
  theater, 367–68
  tourist information, 361–62
Las Vegas Hilton, Las Vegas, 370
La Tertulia, Santa Fe, 893
Latham, Baltimore, 37
Latham, Philadelphia, 701
L'Auberge, Portland, 755
L'Auberge Chez François, Washington, DC, 959–60
L'Auberge Del Mar, San Diego, 822
Lazy Lizard, Miami, 482
La Valencia, San Diego, 825
La Vielle Maison, Ft. Lauderdale, 248
Le Bec Fin, Philadelphia, 703
Le Bernardin, New York City, 653–54
Le Bocage, Boston, 80
Le Chardonnay, Ft. Worth, 265
Le Cirque, New York City, 654
Le Cordon Bleu, Orlando, 682
Le Dôme, Los Angeles, 415
Leeann Chin's, Minneapolis-St. Paul, 512
Le Français, Chicago, 140
Legal Sea Foods, Boston, 85
Legend Seafood, Honolulu, 314
Le Lion d'Or, Washington, DC, 959
Le Madri, New York City, 661
Le Meridien, New Orleans, 574–75
Le Meridien Chicago, Chicago, 136
Le Meridien San Diego at Coronado, San Diego, 824
Le Mikado, Chicago, 141
Le Mondrian, Los Angeles, 409
Le Mont, Pittsburgh, 739
Le Montrachet, Las Vegas, 373–74
Lenox, Boston, 77
Leon's Frozen Custard Drive-In, Milwaukee, 495

Le Perroquet, Chicago, 141
Le Pommier, Pittsburgh, 739
Le Relais, Louisville, 435
Le Richelieu, New Orleans, 577
L'Escale, San Diego, 828–29
L'Escoffier, Los Angeles, 415–16
Leslie, Miami, 476
L'Espalier, Boston, 81
Lespinasse, New York City, 656
L'Etoile, San Antonio, 802
Lexington, Minneapolis-St. Paul, 511
Lexington, Phoenix, 722–23
Libbey's, New Haven, 538
Liberty Bar, San Antonio, 803
L'Ile De France, Ft. Lauderdale, 251
Lion d'Or, Le, Washington, DC, 959
Little America, Salt Lake City, 784–85
Little Greek, New Orleans, 584
Little Inn by the Sea, A, Ft. Lauderdale, 247
Little Rhein, San Antonio, 802
Locanda del Lago, Los Angeles, 416
Locanda Veneta, Los Angeles, 416
Locke-Ober Café, Boston, 82
Lodge Alley Inn, Charleston, 98–99
Loews Anatole, Dallas, 192
Loews Coronado Bay Resort, San Diego, 824
Loews Giorgio, Denver, 207
Loews New York, New York City, 648
Loews Santa Monica, Los Angeles, 409
Loews Vanderbilt Plaza, Nashville, 525
Loma, La, Denver, 210
Lombardi's, Atlanta, 21
López y González, Cleveland, 174
L'Orangerie, Los Angeles, 413
Los Angeles, California, 379–424
  climate, 393
  getting around, 393–94
  hotels, 405–12
  local services, 394–95
  map, 380–81
  museums, 396–97
  music, 403–4
  nightclubs and nightlife, 404–5
  places of special interest, 379, 382–92
    Beverly Hills, 384–85
    Catalina Island, 389
    Chinatown, 386
    Disneyland, 390
    El Pueblo de Los Angeles, 385
    Farmers' Market, 387
    Forest Lawn Memorial Park, 389
    Gower Street, 383
    Griffith Park and the Los Angeles Zoo, 388
    Hollywood Studio Museum, 382
    Hollywood Wax Museum, 382
    J. Paul Getty Museum, 389–90
    Knott's Berry Farm, 391
    La Brea Tar Pits, 387
    Little Tokyo, 386
    Los Angeles Civic Center and Mall, 385
    Los Angeles Museum of Art, 387–88
    Mann's Chinese Theatre, 382
    Max Factor Beauty Museum, 383
    Medieval Times, 390
    Movieland Wax Museum, 390
    Museum of Contemporary Art, 387
    Music Center, 386
    Natural History Museum, 386
    Olvera Street, 385
    Pacific Coast Highway (Route 1), 391
    Paramount Pictures, 382–83
    Ports o' Call Village, 389
    Queen Mary Seaport, 389
    Redondo Beach Marina, 389
    Santa Barbara, California, 391–92
    Six Flags Magic Mountain, 388–89
    Third and Broadway, 385–86
    Universal CityWalk, 384
    Universal Studios Hollywood, 383–84
    Warner Brothers, 383
    Warner Brothers Studios, 384
  restaurants, 412–24
  sales tax, 393
  shopping, 397–400
  special events, 395
  sports and fitness, 401–3
  telephone, 393
  theater, 403
  tourist information, 392–93
Louis' Charleston Grill, Charleston, 100

Louisiana Community
    Bar & Grill, New
    York City, 665
Louisiane, La, San
    Antonio, 802
Louis' Lunch, New
    Haven, 538
Louisville, Kentucky,
    425–36
  climate, 430
  getting around, 430
  hotels, 433–35
  local services, 430–31
  map, 426–27
  music, 433
  nightclubs and
      nightlife, 433
  places of special
      interest, 425,
      428–29
    Bardstown,
        Kentucky, 429
    Belle of Louisville,
        428
    Churchill Downs,
        425
    Farmington, 428
    J. B. Speed Art
        Museum, 428
    Kentucky Derby
        Museum, 428
    Kentucky King-
        dom, 429
    Locust Grove, 428
    Louisville Falls
        Fountain, 428
    Louisville Zoologi-
        cal Gardens, 428
    Maker's Mark
        Distillery, 429
    Museum of History
        and Science, 428
    My Old Kentucky
        Home State
        Park, 429
    Star of Louisville,
        428
  restaurants, 435–36
  sales tax, 430
  shopping, 431–32
  special events, 431
  sports and fitness,
      432–33
  telephone, 430
  theater, 433
  tourist information,
      429–30

Louis XVI, New
    Orleans, 581
Lou Mitchell's,
    Chicago, 147
Loveless Motel,
    Nashville, 527
Lowell, New York City,
    642
Lowell Inn, Minneapo-
    lis-St. Paul, 508,
    510
Lucile's, Ft. Worth, 266
Luna Notte, San Anto-
    nio, 803
Lutèce, New York City,
    654–55
Luxeford Suites, Min-
    neapolis-St.
    Paul, 508
Luxor, Las Vegas,
    371–72
Macklowe, New York
    City, 648
Mader's, Milwaukee,
    494
Madison, Washington,
    DC, 956
Madri, Le, New York
    City, 661
Madurai, Washington,
    DC, 963
Maggiano's, Chicago,
    144
Magnolia Place Inn,
    Savannah, 905
Magnolia's, Charleston,
    100
Mai-Kai, Ft.
    Lauderdale, 250
Maile, Honolulu, 308
Maison Blanche, Wash-
    ington, DC, 960
Maison de Ville, New
    Orleans, 572–73
Maison Du Pré,
    Charleston, 99
Maison Dupuy, New
    Orleans, 576
Maisonette, Cincinnati,
    159
Maison & Jardin,
    Orlando, 683
Maison Marconi,
    Baltimore, 38
Maison Robert,
    Boston, 82
Majestic, St. Louis, 771

Mallorca, Cincinnati,
    160
Mallory, Portland, 754
Mamoun's Falafel, New
    Haven, 538
Mancuso's, Phoenix,
    723
Mandarin, Los Ange-
    les, 421
Mandarin Gourmet,
    Pittsburgh, 740
Mandarin Oriental,
    San Francisco,
    857
Mandina's, New
    Orleans, 585
Manfredi's Limelight,
    Las Vegas, 377
Manhattan Ocean
    Club, New York
    City, 656–57
Manoa Valley Inn,
    Honolulu, 303
Mansion, Dallas, 194
Mansion del Río, La,
    San Antonio,
    799
Mansion on Turtle
    Creek, Dallas,
    191
Maple Drive, Los
    Angeles, 417
Maps
  Atlanta, Georgia, 4–5
  Baltimore, Maryland,
      26–27
  Boston, Massachu-
      setts, 42–43
  Charleston, South
      Carolina, 90–91
  Chicago, Illinois,
      104–5
  Cincinnati, Ohio,
      152–53
  Cleveland, Ohio,
      164–65
  Dallas, Texas, 178–79
  Denver, Colorado,
      200–201
  Detroit, Michigan,
      212–13
  Ft. Lauderdale,
      Florida, 228–29
  Ft. Worth, Texas,
      254–55
  Hartford, Connecti-
      cut, 270–71

Maps (*cont.*)
 Honolulu, Hawaii, 282–83
 Houston, Texas, 318–19
 Indianapolis, Indiana, 334–35
 Kansas City, Missouri, 346–47
 Las Vegas, Nevada, 358–59
 Los Angeles, California, 380–81
 Louisville, Kentucky, 426–27
 Memphis, Tennessee, 438–39
 Miami-Miami Beach, Florida, 450–51
 Milwaukee, Wisconsin, 484–85
 Minneapolis-St. Paul, Minnesota, 498–99
 Nashville, Tennessee, 516–17
 New Haven, Connecticut, 530–31
 New Orleans, Louisiana, 540–41
 New York City, New York, 588–89
 Orlando, Florida, 668–69
 Philadelphia, Pennsylvania, 686–87
 Phoenix, Arizona, 708–9
 Pittsburgh, Pennsylvania, 728–29
 Portland, Oregon, 742–43
 St. Louis, Missouri, 758–59
 Salt Lake City, Utah, 776–77
 San Antonio, Texas, 788–89
 San Diego, California, 806–7
 San Francisco, California, 832–33
 Santa Fe, New Mexico, 872–73
 Savannah, Georgia, 898–99
 Seattle, Washington, 910–11
 Washington, DC, 926–27
Marabella's, Philadelphia, 705
Marais, Boston, 82
Marc Plaza, Milwaukee, 493
Mariana, La, Honolulu, 316
Marianne, Charleston, 101
Marianne's Delicatessen, Salt Lake City, 786
Maria's, Santa Fe, 893
Mario's, Nashville, 526
Mario's Chiquita, Dallas, 196
Mario's East, Ft. Lauderdale, 251
Marius, San Diego, 827
Mark, New York City, 642
Market Bar-Be-Que, Minneapolis-St. Paul, 512
Market Street Grill, Salt Lake City, 786
Mark Hopkins InterContinental, San Francisco, 857–58
Mark Pi's China Gate, Indianapolis, 343
Mark's Place, Miami, 479
Marlin, Miami, 475
Marquette Inn, Minneapolis-St. Paul, 508–9
Marrakech, Las Vegas, 377
Marra's Seafood Grill, Atlanta, 21
Marriott, Long Wharf, Boston, 77
Marriott Courtyard, Denver, 208
Marriott Downtown, Chicago, 138
Marriott East Side, New York City, 648
Marriott Harbor Beach Resort, Ft. Lauderdale, 244–45
Marriott Pavilion, St. Louis, 771
Marriott Resident Inn, New Haven, 535–36
Marriott's Camelback Inn, Phoenix, 719–20
Marriott's Mountain Shadows, Phoenix, 721
Marriott Society Center, Cleveland, 172
Marriott Solana, Ft. Worth, 263
Marriott's Orlando World Center, Orlando, 680
Marriott West, Cleveland, 172
Martha Lou's Kitchen, Charleston, 101
Martha's, Ft. Lauderdale, 250
Masa's, San Francisco, 865
Massey's, Ft. Worth, 267
Matsuhisa, Los Angeles, 421
Matteo's, Honolulu, 311
Matt's No Place, Dallas, 196
Max on Main, Hartford, 279
Mayfair Grill, Miami, 479
Mayfair Hotel Baglioni, New York City, 642
Mayfair House, Miami, 473
Mayflower, New York City, 651
Mayflower Bed & Breakfast, Detroit, 223
Mayflower Park, Seattle, 921
McCormick & Kuleto's, San Francisco, 868

MCL Cafeterias, Indianapolis, 344
Melrose, Dallas, 192
Memphis, Tennessee, 437–48
　climate, 442
　getting around, 442
　hotels, 445–46
　local services, 442–43
　map, 438–39
　museums, 443–44
　music, 445
　nightclubs and nightlife, 445
　places of special interest, 437, 440–41
　　Beale Street, 437, 440
　　Chucalissa Archaeological Museum, 440
　　Graceland, 440–41
　　Henning, Tennessee, 441
　　Libertyland, 440
　　Memphis International Motorsports Park, 441
　　Memphis Pink Palace Museum and Planetarium, 440
　　Memphis Zoo and Aquarium, 440
　　Mud Island, 437
　　National Civil Rights Museum, 440
　　Overton Square, 440
　　Pyramid, The, 437
　　Shiloh National Military Park, 441
　　Sun Recording Studio, 441
　　Victorian Village, 440
　restaurants, 446–48
　sales tax, 442
　special events, 443
　sports and fitness, 444
　telephone, 442
　theater, 444
　tourist information, 441–42
Menger, San Antonio, 799
Mer, La, Honolulu, 308
Meridien, Boston, 77
Meridien, Le, New Orleans, 574–75
Meridien Chicago, Le, Chicago, 136
Meridien San Diego at Coronado, Le, San Diego, 824
Merritt House, Denver, 208
Mesa Grill, New York City, 661
Metropolitan Grill, Seattle, 923
Mezzanine, Honolulu, 314
MGM Grand Hotel/Casino and Theme Park, Las Vegas, 357, 360, 372
Miami Airport Hilton, Miami, 475
Miami—Miami Beach, Florida, 449–82
　climate, 457
　dance, 469
　getting around, 457–58
　hotels, 470–76
　local services, 458–60
　map, 450–51
　museums, 461–62
　music, 469
　nightclubs and nightlife, 469–70
　places of special interest, 449, 452–55
　　Art Deco District, 449
　　Bass Museum of Art, 449
　　Bayside Marketplace, 452
　　Bill Baggs Cape Florida Recreation Area, 454
　　Coral Castle, 455
　　Fairchild Tropical Garden, 453
　　Fruit and Spice Park, 455
　　Holocaust Memorial, 449
　　Little Havana, 452
　　Metro-Dade Cultural Center, 452
　　Metrozoo, 454
　　Miami Seaquarium, 454
　　Miccosukee Indian Village, 455
　　Monkey Jungle, 455
　　Museum of Science and Space Transit Planetarium, 453–54
　　Parrot Jungle, 454
　　Port of Miami, 452
　　Venetian Pool, 453
　　Vizcaya Museum, 453
　restaurants, 476–82
　sales tax, 457
　shopping, 462–64
　special events, 460–61
　sports and fitness, 464–68
　telephone, 456
　theater, 469
　tourist information, 456–57
Miami River Inn, Miami, 476
Mia's, Dallas, 196
Michael's, Las Vegas, 375
Michael's, Los Angeles, 417
Michelangelo, New York City, 642–43
Michel's, Honolulu, 309
Michel's, Philadelphia, 704
Mickey's Diner, Minneapolis-St. Paul, 512
Midtown, Boston, 79
Mikado, Le, Chicago, 141
Mikado, Seattle, 923
Mike Fink, Cincinnati, 160
Mike's on the Avenue, New Orleans, 581

Milano Inn, Indianapolis, 343–44
Mille Fleur, San Diego, 827
Mills House, Charleston, 99
Milwaukee, Wisconsin, 483–95
 climate, 488
 getting around, 488–89
 hotels, 493–94
 local services, 489–90
 map, 484–85
 museums, 490
 music, 492
 nightclubs and nightlife, 492
 places of special interest, 483, 486–87
  Annunciation Greek Orthodox Church, 487
  Cathedral Square, 486
  City Hall, 487
  Grand Avenue, 483
  Joan of Arc Chapel, 483
  Madison, Wisconsin, 487
  Milwaukee Art Museum, 486
  Milwaukee County Historical Center, 486
  Milwaukee County Zoo, 487
  Milwaukee Public Museum, 483, 486
  Père Marquette Park, 486
  Schlitz Audubon Center, 487
  Third Ward, 486
  Whitnall Park, 487
  Wisconsin Avenue East, 486
  Wisconsin Avenue West, 483
 restaurants, 494–95
 sales tax, 488
 special events, 490
 sports and fitness, 491
 telephone, 488
 theater, 492
 tourist information, 488
Minneapolis Hilton and Towers, Minneapolis-St. Paul, 509
Minneapolis Marriott City Center, Minneapolis-St. Paul, 509
Minneapolis-St. Paul, Minnesota, 496–513
 climate, 501
 getting around, 502
 hotels, 508–10
 local services, 502–3
 map, 498–99
 museums, 503–4
 music, 507
 nightclubs and nightlife, 507
 places of special interest, 496–97, 500–501
  casinos, 507–8
  Cathedral of St. Paul, 500
  City Hall—County Courthouse, 500
  Como Park, 497
  Frederick R. Weisman Art Museum, 496
  Governor's Residence, 500
  Historic Ft. Snelling, 500
  Landmark Center, 497
  Minneapolis Grain Exchange, 497
  Minneapolis Institute of Arts, 496
  Minneapolis Sculpture Gardens, 496–97
  Minnehaha Park, 497
  Minnesota State Historical Society, 500
  Minnesota Zoo, 497
  Orchestra Hall, 497
  St. Croix Valley, 500–501
  Science Museum of Minnesota and William L. McKnight/3M Omnitheater, 500
  Somerset, Wisconsin, 501
  State Capitol, 497
  Stillwater, Minnesota, 500–501
  Walker Art Center, 496
 restaurants, 510–13
 sales tax, 501
 shopping, 504–5
 special events, 503
 sports and fitness, 505–6
 telephone, 501
 theater, 506–7
 tourist information, 501
Mirabelle, Boston, 85
Mirador, El, San Antonio, 803–4
Mirage, The, Las Vegas, 360, 370–71, 378
Mirror of Korea, Atlanta, 22
Miss Molly's, Ft. Worth, 264
Mister or Missus. *See entries under* Mr. *or* Mrs.
Mistral, Ft. Lauderdale, 252
Mi Tierra Café and Bakery, San Antonio, 803
Miyako, Honolulu, 311
Miyako, San Francisco, 860
Miya's, New Haven, 537
Mocca, New York City, 665
Mondrian, Le, Los Angeles, 409
Mon Kee's, Los Angeles, 421
Mont, Le, Pittsburgh, 739
Monte Carlo Room,

Las Vegas, 375
Monterey Bay Canners, Honolulu, 314
Montgomery Inn at the Boathouse, Cincinnati, 160
Monti's La Casa Vieja, Phoenix, 724
Montrachet, Le, Las Vegas, 373–74
Montrachet, New York City, 657
Monty's Stone Crab, Miami, 480–81
Moreno, New York City, 661
Morgans, New York City, 648
Morrison-Clark Inn, Washington, DC, 958
Morton's, Los Angeles, 417
Morton's of Chicago, Chicago, 141
Morton's of Chicago, Cincinnati, 159
Morton's of Chicago, Las Vegas, 375
Mr. B's Bistro, New Orleans, 581
Mr. K's, Washington, DC, 962
Mr. Leung's, Boston, 82
Mr. Mole Bed and Breakfast, Baltimore, 37
Mrs. Wilkes' Boarding House, Savannah, 908
Murphy's, St. Louis, 774
Murphy's Bar & Grill, Honolulu, 314
Murray's, Minneapolis-St. Paul, 511
Musashi, Honolulu, 311
Museum Café at the Wadsworth Atheneum, Hartford, 280
Musso & Frank Grill, Los Angeles, 421
My Brother's Bar, Denver, 210

Nantucket Cove, St. Louis, 773
Nashville, Tennessee, 514–27
climate, 519
getting around, 520
hotels, 524–26
local services, 520–21
map, 516–17
museums, 521–22
music, 524
nightclubs and nightlife, 524
places of special interest, 514–15, 518–19
Belle Meade Mansion, 518
Civil War battlefields, 518
Country Music Hall of Fame and Museum, 514–15
Downtown Presbyterian Church, 514
Fort Nashboro, 514
Grand Ole Opry, 515
Hermitage, 515
Opryland USA, 515
Parthenon, 518
Ryman Auditorium, 514
Tennessee Botanical Gardens and Cheekwood Fine Arts Center, 518
Tennessee State Capitol, 514
Travellers' Rest, 515, 518
restaurants, 526–27
sales tax, 519
shopping, 522
special events, 521
sports and fitness, 522–23
telephone, 519
theater, 523
tourist information, 519
TV show tapings, 523
Newbury, Boston, 78

New Haven, Connecticut, 528–38
climate, 532
getting around, 532
hotels, 535–36
local services, 532–33
map, 530–31
museums, 533–34
music, 535
nightclubs and nightlife, 535
places of special interest, 528–29
Green, The, 528
Lighthouse Point Park, 529
Mystic, Connecticut, 529
New Haven Colony Historical Society, 528
Peabody Museum of Natural History, 528
Yale Campus and Facilities, 528
Yale Center for British Art and British Studies, 528
Yale University Art Gallery, 529
restaurants, 536–38
sales tax, 532
special events, 533
sports and fitness, 534
telephone, 532
theater, 534–35
tourist information, 529, 532
New Hellas, Detroit, 226
New Orleans, Louisiana, 539–85
cinema, 569
climate, 556
getting around, 556–58
hotels, 572–77
local services, 558–60
map, 540–41
museums and historic houses, 561–62
music and dance, 569–70

INDEX 987

New Orleans, Louisiana (cont.)
- nightclubs and nightlife, 570–72
- places of special interest, 539, 542–55
  - Academy of the Sacred Heart, 551
  - Aquarium of the Americas, 546–47
  - Audubon Park, 551
  - Audubon Place, 551
  - Audubon Zoological Garden, 550–51
  - Bayou St. John, 553
  - Beauregard-Keyes House, 545
  - Bourbon Street, 539, 542
  - Cabildo and Presbytere, The, 543
  - Canal Street, 548
  - City Park, 552
  - Coliseum Square, 549
  - Contemporary Arts Center, 547
  - Custom House, 548
  - Destrehan Plantation, 555
  - Ernest N. Morial Convention Center, 547
  - Freeport-McMoran Audubon Species Survival Center, 555
  - French Market, 544
  - Gallier Hall, 549
  - Historic New Orleans Collection, 542
  - Houmas House, 555
  - Jackson Square, 543
  - Jean Lafitte National Historical Park, Barataria Unit, 554
  - Julia Row, 547
  - K&B Plaza, 547–48
  - Lafayette Cemetery, 550
  - Lake Pontchartrain Causeway, 554
  - Lakeshore Drive, 553–54
  - Longue Vue House and Gardens, 554
  - Louise S. McGehee School, 550
  - Louisiana Superdome, 548–49
  - Madame John's Legacy, 545–46
  - Metairie Cemetery, 554
  - Milton H. Latter Memorial Library, 551–52
  - Moon Walk, 544
  - New Orleans Museum of Art, 552–53
  - Oak Valley plantation, 555
  - Old US Mint, 544–45
  - Orleans Club, 551
  - Pitot House, 553
  - Plaza d'España, 547
  - Pontalba Apartments, 544
  - Preservation Hall, 542
  - Royal Street, 542
  - St. Louis Cathedral, 542–43
  - St. Louis Cemetery Number One, 546
  - San Francisco Plantation, 555
  - "Tara", 552
  - Tavern on the Park, 553
  - 1300 Block of First Street, 550
  - Toby-Westfeldt House, 549–50
  - Ursuline Convent, 545
  - Woldenberg Park, 547
- restaurants, 577–85
- sales tax, 556
- shopping, 562–66
- special events, 560–61
- sports and fitness, 566–68
- telephone, 556
- theater, 568–69
- tourist information, 555–56
New Orleans Hilton, New Orleans, 575
New Orleans House, Indianapolis, 343
New Otani, Los Angeles, 411
New Otani Kaimana Beach, Honolulu, 304
News Café, Miami, 482
New York City, New York, 586–666
- climate, 615
- getting around, 615–18
- hotels, 640–52
- local services, 618–19
- map, 588–89
- museums, 620–22
- music and dance, 636–37
- nightclubs and nightlife, 637–39
- places of special interest, 586–87, 590–614
  - American Museum of the Moving Image, 613
  - American Museum of Natural History, 605–6
  - Atlantic Avenue, 608
  - Avenue of the Americas, 597
  - Battery Park, 591
  - Battery Park City, 592
  - Battery Park to

Wall Street, 591
Bay Ridge, 609
Bleecker Street, 596–97
Bowery, The, 594
Bowne House, 612
Broadway and the Theater District, 600
Bronx Museum of the Arts, 611
Bronx Zoo (International Wildlife Conservation Park), 610
Brooklyn Bridge, 593
Brooklyn Heights, 608
Brooklyn Heights Promenade, 586
Brooklyn Museum, 609
Cathedral of St. John the Divine, 606
Central Park, 603
Chelsea, 598
Chinatown, 593–94
Chrysler Building, 600
City Hall, 592–93
Cloisters and Ft. Tryon Park, The, 607
Columbia University, 606
Coney Island, 609–10
Conference House, 614
East Village, 595–96
Edgar Allan Poe Cottage, 611
Ellis Island, 590–91
Empire State Building, 586, 599
Federal Hall, 591–92
Fifth Avenue, 602
Flushing Meadow-Corona Park, 613
Ford Foundation Building, 601
Garment District, 599
Governors Island, 591
Gramercy Park, 598
Grand Army Plaza, 602
Grand Central Station, 600
Grant's Tomb, 606–7
Hall of Fame of Great Americans, 611
Harlem, 607–8
Hayden Planetarium, 606
Jacob K. Javits Convention Center, 599
Jacques Marchais Center for Tibetan Art, 613–14
King Mansion, 612–13
Kingsland House and the Queens Historical Society, 612
Lincoln Center, 605
Little Italy, 594
Lower East Side, 594–95
Lower Fifth Avenue, 597
Madison Square Garden, the Paramount Theater, and Penn Station, 598–99
Metropolitan Museum of Art, 603–4
Museum of Modern Art, 602
New York Botanical Gardens, 610–11
New York Public Library, 600
New York Stock Exchange, 591
Park Slope, 608
Prospect Park and the Brooklyn Botanic Gardens, 609
Richmondtown Restoration, 614
Riverside Church, 606
Rockefeller Center, 601
Roosevelt Island, 605
St. Patrick's Cathedral, 601
St. Paul's Chapel, 592
Sheepshead Bay, 610
6th Avenue, 602
SoHo, 595
Solomon R. Guggenheim Museum, 604
South Street Seaport and the Fulton Fish Market, 593
Staten Island Zoo, 613
Statue of Liberty, 590
Times Square, 599–600
TriBeCa, 595
Trinity Church, 592
Tudor City, 601
Union Square, 597–98
United Nations, 601
Washington Square, 596
Wave Hill, 611
West 34th Street, 598
West Village, 597
Whitney Museum of American Art, 604–5
World Trade Center, 586, 592
Yankee Stadium, 611
Yorkville and Gracie Mansion, 605
restaurants, 653–66
sales tax, 615

New York City (cont.)
  seeing the city, 586–87
  shopping, 623–31
  special events, 619–20
  sports and fitness, 631–34
  telephone, 615
  theater, 634–35
  tourist information, 614–15
  tours, 587
  TV show tapings, 635–36
New York Helmsley, New York City, 648
New York Hilton, New York City, 648–49
New York Hotel Pennsylvania, New York City, 651
New York Palace, New York City, 643
New York Renaissance, New York City, 649
Nicholas Nickolas, Honolulu, 311
Nick's at the Miami Beach Marina, Miami, 479
Nick's Fishmarket, Chicago, 141
Nick's Fishmarket, Honolulu, 311
Nicollet Island Inn, Minneapolis-St. Paul, 511–12
Nido, Il, New York City, 657
Nikko, Seattle, 922
Nikko Atlanta, Atlanta, 16
Nikko Beverly Hills, Los Angeles, 409–10
Nikko Chicago, Chicago, 136
Nikolai's Roof, Atlanta, 19
Ninfa's, Houston, 330
Nit Nol, Houston, 330–31
Nola, New Orleans, 582
No-Name Restaurant, Boston, 88

Normandie Grill, La, Cincinnati, 160
Norteño, El, Phoenix, 726
Nosh of Beverly Hills, Los Angeles, 424

Oak Room, Louisville, 435
Occidental Grand Hotel Atlanta, Atlanta, 16–17
Occidental Grill, Washington, DC, 962
Odéon, New York City, 661–62
Ogé House, San Antonio, 799
Olcott, New York City, 652
Olde Obrycki's Crab House, Baltimore, 39
Old Louisville Inn, Louisville, 434
Old Mexico Grill, Santa Fe, 893
Old Original Bookbinder's, Philadelphia, 704–5
Old Santa Fe Trail Books and Coffeehouse, Santa Fe, 894
Old Spaghetti Factory, Salt Lake City, 786
Old Town, Milwaukee, 494–95
Old Town Bakery, Los Angeles, 424
Old Town Mexican Café y Cantina, San Diego, 830
Old Warsaw, Dallas, 195
Olives, Boston, 85
Los Olivos, Phoenix, 726
Omni Ambassador East, Chicago, 136
Omni at CNN Center, Atlanta, 17
Omni at Independence Park, Philadelphia, 701
Omni Berkshire Place, New York City, 643
Omni Charleston Place, Charleston, 98
Omni Houston, Houston, 328
Omni International, Cleveland, 172
Omni International, Detroit, 221–22
Omni Mandalay at Las Colinas, Dallas, 192–93
Omni Netherland Plaza, Cincinnati, 158
Omni Parker House, Boston, 77–78
Omni Severin, Indianapolis, 341
103 West, Atlanta, 19
Ono Hawaiian Foods, Honolulu, 316
On the Border, Dallas, 196
Opryland, Nashville, 525
Opus One, Detroit, 224
L'Orangerie, Los Angeles, 413
Orchard, San Francisco, 861
Orchid, Baltimore, 39
Orchids, Honolulu, 312
Orchids at the Palm Court, Cincinnati, 159
Original Pantry, Los Angeles, 424
Orlando, Florida, 667–84
  climate, 672–73
  getting around, 673
  hotels, 677–81
  local services, 673–74
  map, 668–69
  museums, 674–75
  nightclubs and nightlife, 677
  places of special interest, 667, 670–72
  Behind the Scenes, 672

Cypress Gardens, 667
Discovery Island, 672
Disney-MGM Studios Theme Park, 671
Disney Village Marketplace, 671
EPCOT Center, 670–71
Gatorland, 667
Hoop-Dee-Doo-Revue, 672
Magic Kingdom, 670
Pleasure Island, 672
River Country, 671
Sea World, 667
Typhoon Lagoon, 671
Universal Studios Florida, 670
Wet 'n' Wild, 670
restaurants, 682–84
sales tax, 672
special events, 674
sports and fitness, 675–76
telephone, 672
theater and music, 676–77
tourist information, 672–73
Orlando Marriott, Orlando, 681
Orso, Los Angeles, 417
Orson's, Honolulu, 314
Outrigger Edgewater, Honolulu, 306
Outrigger Prince Kuhio, Honolulu, 306
Outrigger Reef, Honolulu, 304
Outrigger Reef Lanais, Honolulu, 306
Outrigger Waikiki Village, Honolulu, 306
Oxford, Denver, 207
Oyster Bar, New York City, 657

Pacific, San Francisco, 869
Pacifica Grill & Rotisserie, San Diego, 829
Pacific Beach, Honolulu, 304
Pacific Dining Car, Los Angeles, 417
Pacific Plaza, Seattle, 921
Painted Table, The, Seattle, 923
Palace, Cincinnati, 159
Palace Café, New Orleans, 582
Palace Court, Las Vegas, 374
Palio, New York City, 657
Palm, Chicago, 141
Palm, Las Vegas, 375
Palm, New York City, 657
Palm-Aire, Ft. Lauderdale, 246
Palm Court, Phoenix, 723
Palmers Seafood House, Savannah, 908
Paloma, La, Louisville, 436
Pamir, New York City, 665
Pamplemousse, Las Vegas, 375
Pane Caldo Bistro, Los Angeles, 421
Pane e Vino, San Francisco, 868
Paniolo, Phoenix, 725
Pano's & Paul's, Atlanta, 19
Pan Pacific, San Francisco, 858
Paolo, Boston, 85
Papa Haydn, Portland, 756
Pappasito's, Houston, 332
Paradero Bed & Breakfast Inn, El, Santa Fe, 890
Paradise Inn, Miami, 476
Paramount, New York City, 651

Paramount Music Palace, Indianapolis, 344
Parc Café, Honolulu, 314
Parioli Romanissimo, New York City, 657–58
Paris Coffee Shop, Ft. Worth, 267
Park Bistro, New York City, 662
Parker Meridien, New York City, 643
Parker's, Cleveland, 174
Park Hyatt, Chicago, 136–37
Park Plaza, Boston, 78
Parthenon, Chicago, 147
Parthenon, Indianapolis, 344
Partners Morningside Café, Atlanta, 22
Pasteur, Chicago, 147
Patina, Los Angeles, 417
Patio by the River, Atlanta, 19
Patisserie, La, St. Louis, 773
Patrizio, Dallas, 196
Paul's, Santa Fe, 893
Pavillon, Le, New Orleans, 576
Paz, La, Nashville, 526–27
Pazzo, Portland, 756
Peabody, Memphis, 445–46
Peabody Orlando, Orlando, 681
Pearl of the Orient, Cleveland, 174
Peasant Group, The, Atlanta, 21
Pebbles, Orlando, 683
Peery, Salt Lake City, 785
Peggy Sue's BBQ, Dallas, 197
Peninsula, New York City, 643
Peninsula Beverly Hills, Los Angeles, 407

INDEX 991

Penn's View Inn, Philadelphia, 701
Pepe's, New Haven, 538
Peppercorn's Grill, Hartford, 279
Periyali, New York City, 662
Perroquet, Le, Chicago, 141
Pete and Sam's, Memphis, 447
Peter Luger, New York City, 658
Peter's, Indianapolis, 343
Petite Auberge, San Francisco, 860
Peyote Café, Washington, DC, 963
Pfister, Milwaukee, 493
Philadelphia, Pennsylvania, 685–706
  climate, 693–94
  getting around, 694–95
  hotels, 700–703
  local services, 695–96
  map, 686–87
  museums, 696–97
  music, 699
  nightclubs and nightlife, 699–700
  places of special interest, 685, 688–93
    Army-Navy (Pemberton House) and Marine Corps Memorial Museum (New Hall), 688
    Betsy Ross House, 689
    Bishop White House, 688
    Boathouse Row, 690
    Brandywine River Museum and Conservancy, 693
    Carpenters' Hall, 688
    Christ Church, 688–89
    Christ Church Burial Ground, 689
    City Hall, 691
    Congress Hall, 685
    Edgar Allan Poe House, 691
    Elfreth's Alley, 689
    Fairmount Park, 690
    Franklin Court, 689
    Franklin Institute Science Museum, 691
    Headhouse Square, 689
    Independence Hall, 685
    Independence Mall, 688
    Independence National Historical Park, 685
    Italian Market, 692
    Longwood Gardens, 692–93
    Old City Hall, 688
    Penn's Landing Trolley, 690
    Pennsylvania Horticultural Society, 692
    Philadelphia Museum of Art, 690
    Philadelphia Zoo, 690
    Reading Terminal Market, 692
    Rittenhouse Square, 691
    Rodin Museum, 691
    Second Bank of the United States, 688
    Thomas H. Kean New Jersey State Aquarium, 692
    Todd House, 688
    US Mint, 691
    USS Olympia and USS Becuna, 689
    Valley Forge, 692
    Visitors' Center, 685
  restaurants, 703–6
  sales tax, 693
  shopping, 697–98
  special events, 696
  sports and fitness, 698–99
  telephone, 693
  theater, 699
  tourist information, 693–94
Phillip Paolo's, Honolulu, 314
Phoenician, Phoenix, 720
Phoenix, Arizona, 707–26
  art galleries, 714–15
  climate, 712
  getting around, 712–13
  hotels, 718–23
  local services, 713
  map, 708–9
  museums, 714
  music, 718
  nightclubs and nightlife, 718
  places of special interest, 707, 710–11
    Arizona Center, 711
    Borgata, 710
    Cosanti Foundation, 710
    Desert Botanical Gardens, 710
    Dolly's Steamboat, 711
    Heard Museum, 707
    Heritage Square, 711
    Jerome, Arizona, 711
    Phoenix Art Museum, 707, 710
    Phoenix Zoo, 710
    Pueblo Grande Museum and Indian Ruins, 710
    Rawhide's 1880s

Western Town, 711
Scottsdale, Arizona, 710
Sedona, Arizona, 711
State Capitol, 707
Taliesin West, 710
restaurants, 723–26
sales tax, 712
special events, 713–14
sports and fitness, 715–17
telephone, 712
theater, 717–18
tourist information, 712
Piazza, La, Ft. Worth, 265
Picacho Plaza and Cielo Grande Condominiums, Santa Fe, 889
Pickled Parrot, The, Minneapolis-St. Paul, 513
Pier 66 Crowne Plaza, Ft. Lauderdale, 245
Piero's, Las Vegas, 374
Pierre, New York City, 644
Pierre au Tunnel, New York City, 662
Pigalls Café, Cincinnati, 161
Pinckney's Café and Espresso, Charleston, 101
Pink Adobe, Santa Fe, 892
Pink Pepper, Phoenix, 726
Pinnacle Peak Patio, Phoenix, 725
Piñon Grill, Phoenix, 725
Pinot, Los Angeles, 418
Pittsburgh, Pennsylvania, 727–40
  climate, 733
  getting around, 733
  hotels, 737–38
  local services, 733–34
  map, 728–29
  museums, 735
  music, 737
  nightclubs and nightlife, 737
  places of special interest, 727, 730–32
    Allegheny Observatory, 730
    Benedum Center for the Performing Arts, 730
    Carnegie, The, 731
    Carnegie Science Center, 731
    Carson Street District, 730
    Cathedral of Learning, 731
    Civic Arena, 727
    Clayton, 732
    David L. Lawrence Convention Center, 730
    Fifth Avenue Place, 727
    Fort Ligonier, 732
    Frick Art Museum, 732
    Heinz Hall, 730
    Historical Society of Western Pennsylvania, 731
    Landmark Square, 730–31
    Laurel Highlands, 732
    National Aviary, The, 731
    One Oxford Centre, 727
    Phipps Conservatory, 731
    Pittsburgh Zoo, 732
    Point State Park, 727
    PPG Place, 727
    Station Square, 730
    Strip District, 730
    Warhol Museum, 731
  restaurants, 738–40
  sales tax, 733
  special events, 734–35
  sports and fitness, 735–36
  telephone, 733
  theater, 736–37
  tourist information, 732–33
Pittsburgh Hilton & Towers, Pittsburgh, 738
Place, The, New Haven, 537
Place d'Armes, New Orleans, 576
Place St. Michel, Miami, 475
Plainfield's Mayur, Portland, 756
Planters Inn, Savannah, 905
Plaza, Boston, 82
Plaza, New York City, 644
Plaza Athénée, New York City, 644
Plaza III-The Steakhouse, Kansas City, Missouri, 355
Plaza of the Americas, Dallas, 195
Plaza Real, Santa Fe, 889
Plaza San Antonio, San Antonio, 799
Plum Room, Ft. Lauderdale, 248
Pointe Hilton at Squaw Peak, Phoenix, 721
Pointe Hilton at Tapatio Cliffs, Phoenix, 721
Pointe of View, Phoenix, 723
Point Loma Seafoods, San Diego, 830
Polynesian, Orlando, 678
Pommier, Le, Pittsburgh, 739
Pontchartrain, New Orleans, 575
Poogan's Porch, Charleston, 101
Portland, Oregon, 741–56
  brew pubs, 752
  climate, 746
  getting around, 747

Portland Oregon, (cont.) hotels, 752–54
local services, 747–48
map, 742–43
museums, 748–49
music, 752
nightclubs and nightlife, 752
parks and gardens, 749
places of special interest, 741, 744–46
   Bybee-Howell House, Sauvie Island, 746
   Columbia River Gorge, 746
   Crystal Springs Rhododendron Gardens, 745
   Grotto, The, 745
   Ira Keller Fountain, 744
   Mt. Tabor Park, 745
   Old Town, 744
   Oregon Museum of Science and Industry (OMSI), 745
   Pioneer Courthouse, 744
   Pittock Mansion, 744–45
   Portlandia, 744
   Powell's Books, 745
   Sauvie Island, 745–46
   Tryon Creek State Park, 745
   Washington Park, 741, 744
   Weather Machine, 744
restaurants, 754–56
sales tax, 746
shopping, 749–50
special events, 748
sports and fitness, 750–51
telephone, 746
theater, 751
tourist information, 746

Port Orleans, Orlando, 679
Posada, La, Santa Fe, 889–90
De la Poste, New Orleans, 576
Postrio, San Francisco, 865
Prairie, Chicago, 142
Precinct, Cincinnati, 161
Premio, St. Louis, 773
Prescott, San Francisco, 858
Preston House, Santa Fe, 890
Pricci, Atlanta, 19–20
Primavista, Cincinnati, 161
Prime Rib, Baltimore, 38
Prime Rib, Washington, DC, 960
Primerose House, Charleston, 101
Prince Court, Honolulu, 309
Princess Garden, Kansas City, Missouri, 356
Printer's Row, Chicago, 144–45
Priory, Pittsburgh, 738
Provence, La, New Orleans, 584
Provence, New York City, 662
Provincial, New Orleans, 576–77
Prytania Inns, New Orleans, 577
Pueblo Bonito Bed & Breakfast Inn, Santa Fe, 890
Pump Room, Chicago, 142
Purple Dolphin, Miami, 481
Pyramid, Dallas, 195

Quality Inn, New Haven, 536
Quality Inn Downtown, Chicago, 139
Quality Suites Maingate East, Orlando, 681
Queen Anne Inn, Denver, 208
Quilted Toque, Houston, 330
Quinta Motor Inns, La, Dallas, 193

Radisson Denver Downtown, Denver, 207
Radisson Empire, New York City, 651
Radisson Hollywood Roosevelt, Los Angeles, 411–12
Radisson Plaza, Cleveland, 173
Radisson Plaza, Detroit, 222
Radisson Plaza, Ft. Worth, 264
Radisson Plaza, Indianapolis, 341–42
Radisson Plaza Ambassador West, Chicago, 137
Radisson Plaza Minneapolis, Minneapolis-St. Paul, 509
Radisson Plaza Savannah, Savannah, 905
Radisson Resort, Phoenix, 721–22
Rafters, Las Vegas, 377
Rainwater's, San Diego, 829
Ralph & Kacoo's, New Orleans, 584
Ralph's Diner, Las Vegas, 378
Ramada, Pittsburgh, 738
Ramada Beach, Ft. Lauderdale, 246
Ramada Dunwoody, Atlanta, 18
Ramada Inn, Capitol Hill, Hartford, 278
Ramada Inn, Center City, Philadelphia, 703
Ranchman's Café, Dallas, 197

Rancho Encantado, Santa Fe, 886–87
Rancho Valencia, San Diego, 822, 827–28
Raphael, Kansas City, Missouri, 354
Raphael, New York City, 658
Rascal House, Miami, 482
Rattlesnake Club, Detroit, 224
Ray's Boathouse, Seattle, 923
Rebecca's, Boston, 86
Red Lion Hotels and Inns, Portland, 754
Red Sage, Washington, DC, 961
Reflections, Ft. Worth, 265
Regal Cincinnatian, Cincinnati, 159
Regal Riverfront, Saint Louis, 772
Regency, New York City, 644
Regent Beverly Wilshire, Los Angeles, 407
Relais, Le, Louisville, 435
Remi, Los Angeles, 418
Remi, New York City, 658
Rendezvous, Memphis, 447
Restaurant at the Phoenix, Cincinnati, 159–60
Restaurant Million, Charleston, 100
Rey Inn, El, Santa Fe, 890
Richelieu, Le, New Orleans, 577
Richelieu, San Francisco, 861–62
Riddles Penultimate Café, St. Louis, 773
Rihga Royal, New York City, 645
Rio Bravo, Atlanta, 22
Rio Ranch, Houston, 331
Rio Suite Hotel & Casino, Las Vegas, 372
Rittenhouse, Philadelphia, 701
Ritz-Carlton, Atlanta, 17, 20
Ritz-Carlton, Boston, 78, 82
Ritz-Carlton, Buckhead, Atlanta, 17, 20
Ritz-Carlton, Chicago, 137
Ritz-Carlton, Cleveland, 172
Ritz-Carlton, Houston, 328
Ritz-Carlton, Huntington, Los Angeles, 410
Ritz-Carlton, Kansas City, Missouri, 354
Ritz-Carlton, New York City, 645
Ritz-Carlton, Philadelphia, 702
Ritz-Carlton, Phoenix, 722
Ritz-Carlton, St. Louis, 771–72
Ritz-Carlton, San Francisco, 858
Ritz-Carlton, Washington DC, 956
Ritz-Carlton Dearborn, Detroit, 222
Ritz-Carlton Marina de Rey, Los Angeles, 407–8
Ritz Plaza, Miami, 476
River Café, New York City, 658
River Place, Portland, 753–54
Riverside, Ft. Lauderdale, 247
River Street Inn, Savannah, 905–6
Riviera, Dallas, 195
Riviera, Las Vegas, 372
Robert's of Charleston, Charleston, 100
Rocco's, Boston, 86
Rockenwagner, Los Angeles, 421–22
Rodeway Inn-Southwest Freeway, Houston, 329
Roma, Washington, DC, 963
Rookwood Pottery, Cincinnati, 161
Roosevelt, New York City, 652
Rotier's, Nashville, 527
Rover's, Seattle, 922
Roxanne's, Washington, DC, 963
RoxSand, Phoenix, 725
Royal Garden at Waikiki, Honolulu, 306
Royal Grove, Honolulu, 307
Royal Hawaiian, Honolulu, 304
Royal Islander, Honolulu, 306–7
Royal Plaza, Orlando, 680
Royalton, New York City, 645
Roy's, Honolulu, 309
Rubin's Kosher Delicatessen, Boston, 88
Rudolph's Barbecue, Minneapolis-St. Paul, 512
Russian Tea Room, New York City, 658
Rustica, Los Angeles, 422
Rusty Pelican, Miami, 479
Ruthie and Moe's, Cleveland, 175
Ruth's Chris Steak House, Houston, 330

Tabard Inn, Washington, DC, 958, 962
Taco Auctioneers, San Diego, 830
Tadich Grill, San Francisco, 868
Tahitian Lanai, Honolulu, 316

Tandoor, New Haven, 538
Tante Louis, Denver, 209
Taqueria Corona, New Orleans, 585
Taste of New Orleans, A, Atlanta, 21
Tatou, Los Angeles, 418
Tavern on the Green, New York City, 658–59
Ted Cook's 19th Hole Barbeque, Minneapolis-St. Paul, 513
Terrace Garden, Cincinnati, 161
Terrazzo Carmine, Il, Seattle, 923
Tertulia, La, Santa Fe, 893
Thao, Santa Fe, 892
That Place on Bellflower, Cleveland, 175
Thousand Cranes, A, Los Angeles, 422
Three Happiness, Chicago, 147–48
311 Lombardi's, Dallas, 195
3660 on the Rise, Honolulu, 312
Thunder Roadhouse, Los Angeles, 424
Tia Sophia's, Santa Fe, 894
Tillerman, Las Vegas, 377
Tio Pepe, Baltimore, 38
Tomasita's, Santa Fe, 894–95
Tomaso's, Phoenix, 724
Tommy's, Cleveland, 175
Tony and Lucille's, New Haven, 538
Tony Roma's, Las Vegas, 378
Tony's, Houston, 330
Tony's, St. Louis, 773
Too Chez, Detroit, 224
Top o' the Cove, San Diego, 828
Torrey Pines Inn, San Diego, 826
Tortilla Flats, Santa Fe, 895
Toscano, Boston, 86
Touch of East, Honolulu, 312
Touch of India, Atlanta, 22–23
Town and Country, San Diego, 826
Townsend, Detroit, 222
Toy's Chinatown, Milwaukee, 495
Traffic Jam and Snug, Detroit, 225
Trattoria, Honolulu, 315
Travel Inn 9, Phoenix, 723
Travelodge at the Zoo, San Diego, 826
Treasure Island, Las Vegas, 373
Tremont, Baltimore, 37
Tremont, Chicago, 137
Très Vite, Detroit, 226
Tribeca Grill, New York City, 659
Triton, San Francisco, 862
Tropica, New York City, 663
Tropicana, Las Vegas, 373
Troy Marriott, Detroit, 222
Truc Orient Express, Hartford, 280
Tucci Milan, Chicago, 145
Tudor, New York City, 649–50
Tulpe, Chicago, 148
Turnberry Isle, Miami, 471
Tuscany, Chicago, 145–46
"21" Club, New York City, 655
267 Commonwealth, Boston, 79
Two Meeting Street Inn, Charleston, 99

Unicorn Village, Miami, 482
Union League Café, New Haven, 537
Union Square Café, New York City, 659
Union Station, Nashville, 525
Unique Foods and Services, Phoenix, 726
UN Plaza Park Hyatt, New York City, 646
Upperline, New Orleans, 584
Upstairs at the Pudding, Boston, 83
Uraku, Honolulu, 312
U. S. Grant, San Diego, 825

Valencia, La, San Diego, 825
Varsity, Atlanta, 23
Venue, Kansas City, Missouri, 355–56
Versailles, New Orleans, 582
Victoria & Albert's, Orlando, 682
Victorian Inn on the Park, San Francisco, 862
Victoria Park, Ft. Lauderdale, 251–52
Victor's Café, Miami, 479–80
Vielle Maison, La, Ft. Lauderdale, 248
Vietnam Georgetown, Washington, DC, 963–64
Vincent Guerithault on Camelback, Phoenix, 724
Vincenzo's, Louisville, 435–36
Vintage Court, San Francisco, 862
Vintage Park, Seattle, 920–21
Vintage Plaza, Portland, 754
Vista International, Pittsburgh, 738
Vista Washington, Washington, DC,

Waikikian, Honolulu, 307
Waikiki Banyan, Honolulu, 305
Waikiki Joy, Honolulu, 305
Waikiki Lanais, Honolulu, 305
Waikiki Surf, Honolulu, 307
Waldorf-Astoria and Waldorf Towers, New York City, 650
Wales, New York City, 651–52
Walt Disney World, Hilton at, Orlando, 680
Walt Disney World-owned Properties, Orlando, 677–79
Walt Disney World Restaurants, Orlando, 683–84
Washington, DC, 925–64
  climate, 940
  getting around, 941–42
  hotels, 953–58
  local services, 942–43
  map, 926–27
  museums, 944–45
  music, 951
  nightclubs and nightlife, 951–53
  places of special interest, 925, 928–40
    Adams, Morgan, 937
    Arlington National Cemetery, 939–40
    Botanic Gardens, 928
    Bureau of Engraving and Printing, 932
    Capitol, The, 925
    Corcoran Gallery of Art, 930
    Daughters of the American Revolution Museum, 930
    Ellipse, 930
    Folger Shakespeare Library, 928
    Ford's Theatre, 937
    Georgetown, 937–38
    J. Edgar Hoover Building, 933
    Jefferson Memorial, 932
    Lafayette Square, 929–30
    Library of Congress, 928
    Lincoln Memorial, 931
    Mount Vernon, 939
    National Archives, 933
    National Gallery of Art, 933
    National Law Enforcement Officers' Memorial, 937
    National Portrait Gallery and National Museum of American Art, 936–37
    National Postal Museum, 928–29
    National Zoo, 938–39
    Octagon House, 930
    Organization of American States, 931
    Peterson House, 937
    Renwick Gallery, 930
    Rock Creek Park, 938
    Smithsonian Institution, 933–36
    Supreme Court Building, 925, 928
    Union Station, 929
    United States Holocaust Memorial Museum, 932
    US Navy Memorial Plaza, 933
    Vietnam Veterans Memorial, 932
    Washington Monument, 931
    White House, 929
  restaurants, 959–64
  sales tax, 940
  shopping, 945–49
  special events, 943
  sports and fitness, 949–50
  telephone, 940
  theater, 950–51
  tourist information, 940
Washington, Washington, DC, 958
Washington Square Inn, San Francisco, 862
Water Club, New York City, 659
Waterfront, Cincinnati, 160
Watergate, Washington, DC, 957
Water Grill, Los Angeles, 418
Westbury, New York City, 646
Westcourt, Phoenix, 722
Westgate, San Diego, 825
Westin, Cincinnati, 158
Westin, Copley Place, Boston, 78
Westin, Indianapolis, 341
Westin, LA Airport, Los Angeles, 411
Westin Bonaventure, Los Angeles, 410
Westin-Canal Place, New Orleans, 575
Westin Crown Center, Kansas City, Missouri, 354
Westin Cypress Creek, Ft. Lauderdale, 245–46

Westin Galleria, Dallas, 193
Westin Oaks and Westin Galleria, Houston, 328
Westin Peachtree Plaza, Atlanta, 17–18
Westin Renaissance Center, Detroit, 222
Westin St. Francis, San Francisco, 859
Westin Tabor Center, Denver, 208
Westin William Penn, Pittsburgh, 738
West Street Grill, Boston, 86
Westwood Marquis, Los Angeles, 408
White Dog Café, Philadelphia, 705
White Swan Inn, San Francisco, 860
Whitney, Detroit, 224–25
Whitney, Minneapolis-St. Paul, 509
Whitney's, Los Angeles, 424
Wild Boar, Nashville, 526
Wilderness Lodge, Orlando, 678–79
Wild Ginger, Seattle, 923
Willard Inter-Continental, Washington, DC, 957
Willard Room, Washington, DC, 961
Windows, Savannah, 907
Windsor Court, New Orleans, 573
Windsor Hilton, Detroit, 223
Windsor Inn, Washington, DC, 958
Windsor Park, Washington, DC, 958
Wishbone, Chicago, 148
Wo Fat, Honolulu, 316
Wolfie's, Miami, 482
Woodlands, Honolulu, 316
Worthington, Ft. Worth, 264
Wu Kong, San Francisco, 868
Wyndham, New York City, 652
Wyndham Bristol, Washington, DC, 957–58
Wyndham Franklin Plaza, Philadelphia, 702
Wyndham Garden, Detroit, 223–24
Wyndham Paradise Valley, Phoenix, 722
Wyndham Warwick, Houston, 328
Wynkoop Brewing Company, Denver, 210

Xochimilco, Detroit, 226

Yacht Club, Orlando, 679
Yamakasa, Phoenix, 725
Yanagi Sushi, Honolulu, 315
Ye Olde Union Oyster House, Boston, 86–87
Yoshida-Ya, San Francisco, 868
Yoshi's Café, Chicago, 142
Yuca, Miami, 478

Zafiro, Portland, 755
Zarela, New York City, 663
Z Contemporary Cuisine, Cleveland, 174
Zia Diner and Bakery, Santa Fe, 895
Zuni Café, San Francisco, 866